The Editors

HERSHEL PARKER, H. Fletcher Brown Professor Emeritus, University of Delaware, is an editor of *The Norton Anthology of American Literature* and author of the two-volume *Herman Melville: A Biography*.

HARRISON HAYFORD was Northwestern University Professor Emeritus, General Editor of the Northwestern University Press–Newberry Library *Writings of Herman Melville*, and author of *Melville's Prisoners*.

A NORTON CRITICAL EDITION

Herman Melville
MOBY-DICK

AN AUTHORITATIVE TEXT
BEFORE *MOBY-DICK:* INTERNATIONAL
CONTROVERSY
REVIEWS AND LETTERS BY MELVILLE
ANALOGUES AND SOURCES
REVIEWS OF *MOBY-DICK*
CRITICISM

SECOND EDITION

Edited by

HERSHEL PARKER
UNIVERSITY OF DELAWARE, EMERITUS

HARRISON HAYFORD
LATE OF NORTHWESTERN UNIVERSITY

PICTORIAL MATERIALS PREPARED BY
JOHN B. PUTNAM

W • W • NORTON & COMPANY • *New York* • *London*

The text of *Moby-Dick* used in this Norton Critical Edition was first published in Volume 6, *Moby-Dick; or, The Whale,* of *The Writings of Herman Melville,* by Northwestern University Press. Copyright © 1988 by Northwestern University Press and The Newberry Library.

The text of this book is composed in Fairfield Medium
with the display set in Bernhard Modern.
Composition by Publishing Synthesis Ltd., New York.
Manufacturing by Courier Westford.
Book design by Antonina Krass.

Library of Congress Cataloging-in-Publication Data

Melville, Herman, 1819–1891.
    Moby-Dick / Herman Melville ; edited by Hershel Parker, Harrison Hayford ; pictorial
material prepared by John B. Putnam. — 2nd ed.
        p. cm. — (A Norton critical edition.)
    "An authoritative text, before Moby Dick, international controversy, reviews and letters
by Melville, analogues and sources, reviews of Moby-Dick, criticism."
Includes bibliographical references.

ISBN 0-393-97283-6 (pbk.)

1. Ahab, Captain (Fictitious character)—Fiction. 2. Melville, Herman, 1819–1891.
Moby Dick. 3. Whaling—Fiction. 4. Whales—Fiction. I. Hayford, Harrison. II. Parker,
Hershel. III. Title.

PS2384.M6 2001
813'.3—dc21

                                                                                    2001042716

W. W. Norton & Company, Inc., 500 Fifth Avenue, New York, N.Y. 10110
www.wwnorton.com

W. W. Norton & Company Ltd., Castle House, 75/76 Wells Street, London W1T 3QT

Contents

Criticism

Preface

Herman Melville (1819–1891), the author of *Moby-Dick*, was a Romantic writer (slightly belated, and American), profoundly influenced from his youth by the lives and writings of international literary celebrities such as Lord Byron, Sir Walter Scott, Goethe, and Washington Irving, and later by Wordsworth, Coleridge, and others, including many now little read, such as the poet laureate of his youth, Robert Southey. Melville was also a child of the American Revolution (grandson of two military heroes who had known George Washington and other notables) and of the War of 1812 (then still vivid in the American consciousness). During his tri umphal return to the United States the old Marquis de Lafayette, revered as the youthful hero of the Revolution, paid honor to Melville's grand mother Gansevoort, widow of the hero of Fort Stanwix, at her home in Al bany in 1825, and in Boston at the dedication of the Bunker Hill Monument he paid tribute to Melville's paternal grandfather (one of the last survivors of the Tea Party of 1773). Even more crucially, Melville was a child of the cataclysmic French Revolution and of Napoleonic Europe. His uncle Thomas Melvill spent years in the Paris of Napoleon as a sort of merchant-banker, and his father, an importer of dry goods, fluent in French, visited Paris repeatedly.

In the post-Napoleonic era of Melville's youth, Americans obsessively followed such remote events as the Greek struggle for independence from the Turks and marveled at the indirect consequences of military action. Everyone knew that one basalt hunk of war booty from Napoleon's invasion of Egypt, the Rosetta Stone, had allowed a heroic French civilian to decipher the hieroglyphics and initiate the study of ancient Egypt (of fervent, if limited, interest to many religious Americans as the home of the Hebrews from Joseph to Moses). Archaeological excavations, at Pompeii and elsewhere, were transforming historical and aesthetic knowledge of the classical world of Greece and Rome as decisively as the deciphering of the hieroglyphics was transforming knowledge of ancient Egypt. *Moby-Dick* is laced with offhand allusions to such recent events, not just military, political, and religious but also scientific, including advances in the study of archaeology, geography, oceanography, and astronomy. Advances in anatomy and geology were already creating pre-Darwinian evolutionary thought and challenging religious chronologies that set the creation of the world around 5000 B.C.E.

More than a third of a century after 1967, when the first edition of the Hayford-Parker Norton Critical Edition was published, the United States is once again in a recurrent phase of thinking globally, as Melville was doing in *Moby-Dick*, even while many Americans were using the Monroe Doctrine to justify isolationism. Early in the twenty-first century Americans are concerned as never before with the effects that human beings have on their environment, from immediate surroundings to the entire planet Earth. Many of the geopolitical themes Melville dealt with from his own experience—Pacific Rim commerce, colonialism, deliberate or careless destruction of indigenous cultures and environments, exploitation of nature, racism, enslavement, immigration—are themes uppermost in the minds of many modern Americans. In recent years Roger Payne, the author of *Among Whales,* and other marine biologists are learning how whales feed, reproduce, communicate, and migrate and how they are being pushed toward extermination. In the new environmental activism, the "Sea Shepherd" movement led by Paul Watson is dedicated to saving whales, now threatened not only by commercial whaling fleets but also by global pollution. Knowing about newly defined dangers (*global warming* was not in the national vocabulary in the 1960s), we think differently about extinction of species and read such chapters in *Moby-Dick* as 105, "—Will he Perish?" differently than earlier generations did.

Such worries, about extinction of species, loss of rain forests, pollution (of land, air, and water), human overpopulation, global warming, the possibility of world famine, all these and other concerns have been accompanied by a new interest in tales of high adventure, escapist outer-space adventure at one extreme, and at another extreme stringent earthly challenges such as climbing the highest mountains and exploring the depths of the oceans. Once again the reading public is fascinated with retellings of dangerous nineteenth-century voyages such as the search for the Northwest Passage and equally hazardous commercial ventures such as whaling voyages. In particular, new readers have been found for retellings of the story of the destruction of the *Essex* by a whale and the price some of the crew paid for survival. (Not since the time of *Moby-Dick* has the dark subject of cannibalism resonated so variously and so perturbingly in the public consciousness as it does now.)

Once written about as if it were on a subject that could be of interest to only some men and to no women, or as if it were a book of philosophy trying to be a work of literature, *Moby-Dick* is now more popular than ever with both sexes and all ages as the greatest sea story ever told, recognized as a national literary treasure arising from the deeply troubled mid-nineteenth century. Turning away from the notion of good literature as something that makes you feel good about yourself just as you are, readers are welcoming *Moby-Dick* as evidence that good literature has power to challenge, exalt, and even transform.

While shared global concerns inform readers who now read or re-read *Moby-Dick,* readers have lost something that previous generations brought to the book, for changes in American education have reduced what once amounted to a common body of national literary readings. Few twenty-first-century readers know as much of the writings of Oliver Goldsmith or Sir Walter Scott, or even Edmund Spenser and John Milton, as Melville and his contemporaries did, or even as high school graduates of the 1960s did. Yet the loss of knowledge once common in classrooms across the country has been offset in astonishing ways. Shakespeare, whose tragedies marked the plot and language of *Moby-Dick,* has disappeared from some high school classes, yet his plays, and not only the great tragedies, are daz-zlingly available in competing movies and videos (even as *Moby-Dick* itself is available in adaptations and recorded readings). Even if a smaller per-centage of religious young Protestants read the King James Bible as the word of God than did a generation ago, that version is now more widely studied, and not only by Protestants, as a literary and historical text. The upshot is that undergraduates and general readers early in the twenty-first century are far more diversely prepared to catch literary allusions in *Moby-Dick* than their counterparts of the 1960s, less knowledgeable in some ways, but far more aware in other ways, and with immeasurably greater ac-cess to information (from worthless to wholly reliable) on the Internet.

This Second Norton Critical Edition of *Moby-Dick* embodies the transformation of knowledge about Melville that has occurred since the original 1967 edition, particularly about his life. Many of the new dis-coveries were stimulated by research for the "Historical Notes" in the successive volumes in the Northwestern-Newberry Edition of *The Writ-ings of Herman Melville*, edited by Harrison Hayford, Hershel Parker, and G. Thomas Tanselle, particularly the "Historical Note" to *Moby-Dick* (1988). Melville biography has also been transformed by strokes of luck unrelated to the NN Edition, notably the salvaging of several hundred letters, a small portion of the previously unknown personal archive of Melville's sister Augusta, most of which was acquired by the New York Public Library in 1983. By the early 1990s these "Augusta Papers" had been transcribed by Parker into his working version of *The New Melville Log*, an expansion of Jay Leyda's 1951 two-volume *The Melville Log*. Other small but important caches of family letters have been discovered in the decades after 1967 and have also been tran-scribed into *The New Melville Log*. So much continues to come to light that passages in the 1988 "Historical Note" to *Moby-Dick* have already been superseded by discoveries reported in several chapters of Hershel Parker's *Herman Melville: A Biography, 1819–1851* (1996) and the sec-ond volume, *Herman Melville: A Biography, 1851–1891*. (In the first volume chapters 33 to 40 are devoted to the composition of *Moby-Dick*; and in the second volume chapters 1, 2, and 4 deal with the American reception of *Moby-Dick* and chapter 5 recounts the British reception of *The Whale*.) Recent discoveries about Melville's life and sources are re-ported in this Norton Critical Edition of *Moby-Dick*, the Parker-Hay-ford edition (names reversed to distinguish the editions). The salting of recently discovered and sometimes previously unpublished biographical information throughout this Norton Critical Edition should make it an essential source for scholars, critics, and even the common readers (who do survive, alive and well, but changed—less like each other, more individualistic).

In this Parker-Hayford edition, our paramount goal has been to help readers grasp the genuine (and occasionally fudged) vastness of Melville's personal experiences and reading that went into the words of *Moby-Dick*. Where the 1967 edition was sparingly footnoted, the Parker-Hayford edi-tion is much more fully annotated. This edition identifies Melville's his-torical allusions (in which category he would include biblical allusions) as well as other allusions, particularly literary and geographical, and identifies his principal whaling sources and passages that reflect episodes in his life. We recognize that footnotes inevitably distract attention from the text and apologize to any reader who looks down to a footnote and finds only what he or she already knew. We hope no one, however learned, will take offence at our giving the birth and death dates for Sir Thomas Browne, or take offence at our giving chapter and verse for biblical allusions and quoting dozens of brief biblical passages.

The Hayford-Parker 1967 Norton Critical Edition holds a permanent place in the history of textual scholarship on *Moby-Dick*. No other edition of *Moby-Dick* included a full list of variants between the English edition (*The Whale,* October 1851) and the American edition (*Moby-Dick*, November 1851). We made some of our editorial decisions on the basis of our then-new discovery that Melville himself was responsible for some of the English variants—corrections he made on the sheets of the book before sending them to England, so that the earlier-published London text contained a few authorial readings that Melville could not get into the later-published American text. The 1967 edition also contained a number of now generally accepted conjectural emendations made for the first time, such as *augured* for *argued,* where we were convinced that neither 1851 edition had printed what Melville had intended. Our editor at Norton, the late John Benedict, altered the design of the Norton Critical Edition textual lists and in other ways facilitated our attempt to use the Norton Critical Edition to help users think about the new textual discoveries, as the first edition of the Norton Critical Edition of *Moby-Dick* was not designed to be "definitive" but to open up the book to textual study. We knew as we worked on it that our textual discoveries would ultimately go into the Northwestern-Newberry (NN) edition, supplemented by whatever textual, bibliographical, biographical, and historical knowledge we and others might bring forth in the intervening years. The Norton Critical Edition became the edition cited in all serious scholarship and criticism for a generation, and the 1988 NN text, as it turned out, remained very close to the Hayford-Parker text.

The existence of that Northwestern-Newberry *Moby-Dick,* which includes a 182-page "Historical Note" and a 46-page "Note on the Text," means that this Parker-Hayford edition does not have to contain an elaborate textual apparatus. In this Parker-Hayford edition we print the NN text, edited by Harrison Hayford, Hershel Parker, and G. Thomas Tanselle, without the formidable apparatus essential in a "standard" edition but inappropriate in a text meant for the classroom and the general reader.

The text of this second Norton Critical Edition (in its now lavishly footnoted form) is followed by a short new section, "Melville's Reading and *Moby-Dick:* An Overview and A Bibliography." The opening essay looks at the sequence in which Melville encountered his written whaling sources for *Moby-Dick* and suggests the range of general reading (including great works of literature) that influenced him. The following list of books makes it easy for a reader to locate full titles, publishers, and dates of Melville's known source books mentioned in the footnotes to the text of *Moby-Dick* and in the later parts of this edition.

The maps and items in "Whaling and Whalecraft" have been retained from the 1967 edition, but we have now added to this section a photograph of the engraved self-portrait of the magnificently tattooed face of the real New Zealander on whom Melville modeled Queequeg—one of two great new discoveries by Geoffrey Sanborn reported in this edition.

A wholly new section, "Before *Moby-Dick*: International Controversy over Melville," contains reviews of Melville's early books that address issues of colonialism, missionary activities, slavery, immigration, and abuses in the navy (principally flogging), for *Moby-Dick* cannot be fully understood without reference to Melville's early historical experiences and the controversies, especially the religious controversies, that dogged him.

The familiar items in the 1967 "Reviews and Letters by Melville" have been retained, but the letter to Nathaniel Hawthorne conventionally dated as about June 1, 1851, has been redated to early May, and the footnotes to "Hawthorne and his *Mosses*" and to the letters have been greatly enriched by recent biographical discoveries, several printed here for the first time. "Analogues and Sources" has been augmented by slight corrections in the transcription of Melville's "Manuscript Notes on Owen Chase" and by two exciting new discoveries (made since the 1988 NN edition), Geoffrey Sanborn's discovery of a source for notes Melville made in his copy of Shakespeare and Steven Olsen-Smith's recovery of significant Melville annotations in Thomas Beale's *The Natural History of the Sperm Whale* (1839).

The section of contemporary reviews has been greatly revised and enlarged to show the impact of the English reviews of *The Whale* on American reviewers of *Moby-Dick*, to show the ongoing attacks on Melville from the American religious press, and to sample reviews discovered by Parker in the Colindale branch of the British Library since the publication of the first volume of his biography (and reprinted here for the first time since 1851). Some items from the 1967 "Interim Appraisals, 1893–1913" have been dropped and some have been incorporated in a new section, "Posthumous Praise and the Melville Revival: 1893–1927." The policy now is to exclude mere hostile grousings, letting some of the contemporary reviews carry the burden of vituperation, slander, and self-complacent ignorance. Everyone now has heard that *Moby-Dick* was a failure for almost three quarters of a century, so space is devoted to celebrating the best that has been said about it rather than recording the long persistence of contemptuous and superficial pronouncements by journalists and professors whose memory has been kept alive only because they did not understand the greatness of *Moby-Dick*.

"A Handful of Critical Challenges" retains from the 1967 edition a classic study, Walter E. Bezanson's "*Moby-Dick*: Work of Art." It represents Harrison Hayford's half-century study of *Moby-Dick* by two highly accessible essays, "Loomings" and "Unnecessary Duplicates." Essays by Paul Brodtkorb Jr. and John Wenke focus on the single most persistent theme in the modern criticism of *Moby-Dick*: Melville's creation of Ishmael as the one who tells (and to some extent admittedly invents) the story of Ahab's quest for the white whale. Camille Paglia offers a very welcome reminder that *Moby-Dick* should be read in the context of European Romanticism. Rather than include any biographical sections from the Northwestern-Newberry "Historical Note" or Parker's *Herman*

Melville: A Biography, we print a previously unpublished talk Parker delivered at the New Bedford Whaling Museum, a rigorous look at the price Melville and his family paid for *Moby-Dick.* A new stringently selective bibliography concludes the volume.

HERSHEL PARKER
HARRISON HAYFORD

Acknowledgments

Our greatest debt is still to the late John Benedict, the editor at W. W. Norton who helped us open up the textual study of *Moby-Dick* more than a third of a century ago. Geoffrey Sanborn and Steven Olsen-Smith generously let us publish some significant new discoveries they had made. Dennis Marnon of Harvard College Library proved himself a forensic librarian, one with infinite access to scholarly resources and the imagination to make best use of them. At the Berkshire Athenaeum, Pittsfield, Massachusetts, Ruth Degenhardt and Kathleen Reilly gave generous help. Mary K. Bercaw, Brian Higgins, Dan Lance, Alma MacDougall, Robert Madison, John B. Putnam, and Mark Wojnar kindly gave advice, mainly nautical. For their hospitality during Parker's review-hunting at the Colindale Branch of the British Library, Parker thanks the actress Lisa Harrow and the whaleman Roger Payne, as well as Cormac McCarthy, who deftly arranged this kindness by proxy so as to get the job done. Maurice Sendak responded with heartening ferocity to titbits (as *Moby-Dick* spells it) of biographical information that ended up in footnotes here. Susan Harris at Northwestern University Press helped us in practical ways. Heddy-Ann Richter helped to verify the footnotes; later with Parker she proofread *Moby-Dick* aloud, all the words and all the punctuation marks. At Norton, Julia Reidhead and Nina Baym gave encouragement. Candace Levy copy-edited expertly and thoughtfully. Editorial assistant Brian Baker expedited the stages of production during which the proofreader Susan Sanfrey, the cover designer Joan Greenfield, and the head of the art department, Debra Morton Hoyt, all made their admirable contributions. Through it all Carol Bemis carried on the tradition established by Benedict, one of the most beloved men in modern American publishing.

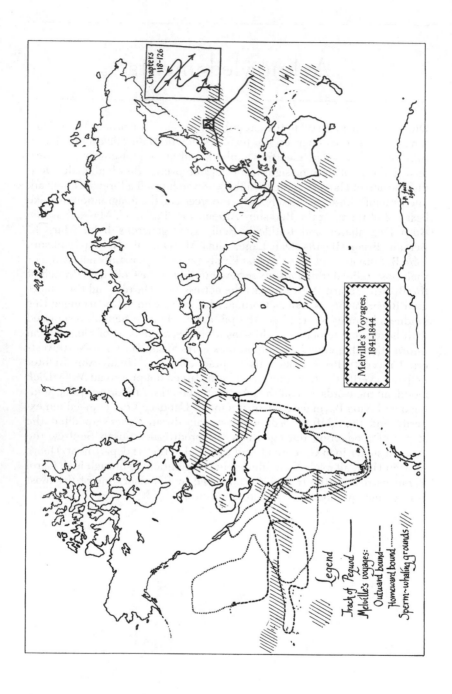

Chapters
118-126

Melville's Voyages,
1841-1844

Legend

Track of Pequod ———
Melville's voyages:
    Outward bound-------
    Homeward bound·········
Sperm-whaling grounds ////

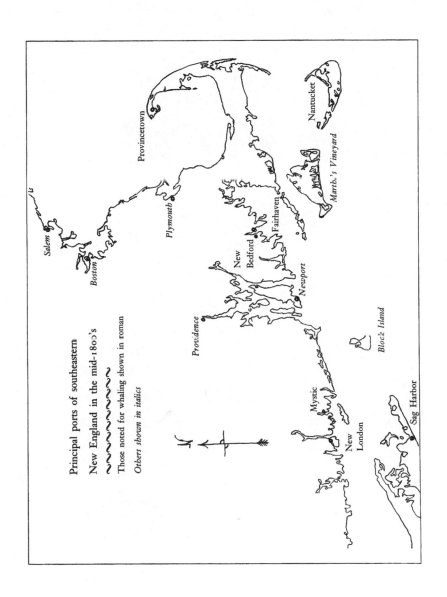

Principal ports of southeastern
New England in the mid-1800's

〜〜〜 Those noted for whaling shown in roman

Others shown in italics

Salem

Boston

Provincetown

Plymouth

New
Bedford

Fairhaven

Marth.'s Vineyard

Nantucket

Providence

Newport

Block Island

Mystic

New
London

Sag Harbor

The Text of
MOBY-DICK; OR,
THE WHALE.

IN TOKEN

OF MY ADMIRATION FOR HIS GENIUS,

𝕿𝖍𝖎𝖘 𝕭𝖔𝖔𝖐 𝖎𝖘 𝕴𝖓𝖘𝖈𝖗𝖎𝖇𝖊𝖉

TO

NATHANIEL HAWTHORNE.

Contents of *Moby-Dick*[1]

1. In the first American edition, as here, a few chapter titles in the Contents vary slightly from those at the chapter heads.

Etymology

(Supplied by a Late Consumptive Usher to a Grammar School.)

[The pale Usher—threadbare in coat, heart, body, and brain; I see him now. He was ever dusting his old lexicons and grammars, with a queer handkerchief, mockingly embellished with all the gay flags of all the known nations of the world. He loved to dust his old grammars; it somehow mildly reminded him of his mortality.]

Etymology

"While you take in hand to school others, and to teach them by what name a whale-fish is to be called in our tongue, leaving out, through ignorance, the letter H, which almost alone maketh up the signification of the word, you deliver that which is not true."

Hackluyt.

"WHALE. * * * Sw. and Dan. *hval.* This animal is named from roundness or rolling; for in Dan. *hvalt* is arched or vaulted."

Webster's Dictionary.

"WHALE. * * * It is more immediately from the Dut. and Ger. *Wallen*; A.S. *Walw-ian*, to roll, to wallow."

Richardson's Dictionary.

ָחן,	*Hebrew.*
κητος,	*Greek.*
CETUS,	*Latin.*
WHÆL,	*Anglo-Saxon.*
HVAL,	*Danish.*
WAL,	*Dutch.*
HWAL,	*Swedish.*
HVALUR,	*Icelandic*
WHALE,	*English.*
BALEINE,	*French.*
BALLENA,	*Spanish.*
PEKEE-NUEE-NUEE,	*Fegee.*
PEHEE-NUEE-NUEE,	*Erromangoan.*

Extracts[1]

(Supplied by a Sub-Sub-Librarian.)

[It will be seen that this mere painstaking burrower and grub-worm of a poor devil[2] of a Sub-Sub appears to have gone through the long Vaticans[3] and street-stalls of the earth, picking up whatever random allusions to whales he could anyways find in any book whatsoever, sacred or profane. Therefore you must not, in every case at least, take the higgledy-piggledy whale statements, however authentic, in these extracts, for veritable gospel cetology. Far from it. As touching the ancient authors generally, as well as the poets here appearing, these extracts are solely valuable or entertaining, as affording a glancing bird's eye view of what has been promiscuously said, thought, fancied, and sung of Leviathan, by many nations and generations, including our own.

So fare thee well, poor devil of a Sub-Sub, whose commentator I am. Thou belongest to that hopeless, sallow tribe which no wine of this world will ever warm; and for whom even Pale Sherry would be too rosy-strong; but with whom one sometimes loves to sit, and feel poor-devilish, too; and grow convivial upon tears; and say to them bluntly, with full eyes and empty glasses, and in not altogether unpleasant sadness—Give it up, Sub-Subs! For by how much the more pains ye take to please the world, by so much the more shall ye for ever go thankless! Would that I could clear out Hampton Court and the Tuileries[4] for ye! But gulp down your tears and hie aloft to the royal-mast with your hearts; for your friends who have gone before are clearing out the seven-storied heavens, and making refugees of long-pampered Gabriel, Michael, and Raphael,[5] against your coming. Here ye strike but splintered hearts together—there, ye shall strike unsplinterable glasses!]

Extracts

"And God created great whales."

Genesis.

"Leviathan maketh a path to shine after him;
One would think the deep to be hoary."

Job.

"Now the Lord had prepared a great fish to swallow up Jonah."

Jonah.

"There go the ships; there is that Leviathan whom thou hast made to play therein."

Psalms.

---

1. Melville's sources for all these quotations and his adaptive rewording and paraphrasing of some of them, as well as editorial corrections to them, are discussed in detail in the "Discussions of Adopted Readings" in the Northwestern-Newberry (NN) edition (1988), 813–30; in this NCE the unfoot-noted "extracts" (short quotations) function as Melville intended, giving the reader a "glancing bird's eye view" of whales and whalers throughout history.
2. Pitiable, wretched fellow.
3. Great libraries (like that in the Vatican in Rome).
4. Royal houses in London and Paris, respectively.
5. Archangels.

"In that day, the Lord with his sore, and great, and strong sword, shall punish Leviathan the piercing serpent, even Leviathan that crooked serpent; and he shall slay the dragon that is in the sea."

Isaiah.

"And what thing soever besides cometh within the chaos of this monster's mouth, be it beast, boat, or stone, down it goes all incontinently that foul great swallow of his, and perisheth in the bottomless gulf of his paunch."

Holland's Plutarch's Morals.

"The Indian Sea breedeth the most and the biggest fishes that are: among which the Whales and Whirlpooles called Balænæ, take up as much in length as four acres or arpens of land.

Holland's Pliny.

"Scarcely had we proceeded two days on the sea, when about sunrise a great many Whales and other monsters of the sea, appeared. Among the former, one was of a most monstrous size. * * * This came towards us, open-mouthed, raising the waves on all sides, and beating the sea before him into a foam."

Tooke's Lucian. "The True History."

"He visited this country also with a view of catching horse-whales, which had bones of very great value for their teeth, of which he brought some to the king. * * * The best whales were catched in his own country, of which some were forty-eight, some fifty yards long. He said that he was one of six who had killed sixty in two days."

Other or Octher's verbal narrative taken down from his mouth by King Alfred. A.D. 890.

"And whereas all the other things, whether beast or vessel, that enter into the dreadful gulf of this monster's (whale's) mouth, are immediately lost and swallowed up, the sea-gudgeon retires into it in great security, and there sleeps."

MONTAIGNE.—Apology for Raimond Sebond.

"Let us fly, let us fly! Old Nick take me if it is not Leviathan described by the noble prophet Moses in the life of patient Job."

Rabelais.

"This whale's liver was two cart-loads."

Stowe's Annals.

"The great Leviathan that maketh the seas to seethe like boiling pan."

Lord Bacon's Version of the Psalms.

"Touching that monstrous bulk of the whale or ork we have received nothing certain. They grow exceeding fat, insomuch that an incredible quantity of oil will be extracted out of one whale."

Ibid. "History of Life and Death."

"The sovereignest thing on earth is parmacetti for an inward bruise."

King Henry.

"Very like a whale."

Hamlet.

"Which to recure, no skill of leach's art
Mote him availle, but to returne againe
To his wound's worker, that with lovely dart,
Dinting his breast, had bred his restless paine,
Like as the wounded whale to shore flies from the maine."

The Fairie Queen.

"Immense as whales, the motion of whose vast bodies can in a peaceful calm trouble the ocean till it boil."

Sir William Davenant. Preface to Gondibert.

"What spermacetti is, men might justly doubt, since the learned Hofmannus in his work of thirty years, saith plainly, *Nescio quid sit.*"

*Sir T. Browne. Of Sperma Ceti and the
Sperma Ceti Whale. Vide his V.E.*

"Like Spencer's Talus with his iron flail
He threatens ruin with his ponderous tail.

      *   *   *   *   *

Their fixed jav'lins in his side he wears,
And on his back a grove of pikes appears."

Waller's Battle of the Summer Islands.

"By art is created that great Leviathan, called a Commonwealth or State—(in Latin, Civitas) which is but an artificial man."

Opening sentence of Hobbes's Leviathan.

"Silly Mansoul swallowed it without chewing, as if it had been a sprat in the mouth of a whale."

Holy War.

"That sea beast
Leviathan, which God of all his works
Created hugest that swim the ocean stream."

Paradise Lost.

————"There Leviathan,
Hugest of living creatures, on the deep
Stretched like a promontory sleeps or swims,
And seems a moving land; and at his gills
Draws in, and at his trunk spouts out a sea."

Ibid.

"The mighty whales which swim in a sea of water, and have a sea of oil swimming in them."

Fuller's Profane and Holy State.

"So close behind some promontory lie
The huge Leviathans to attend their prey,
And give no chace, but swallow in the fry,
Which through their gaping jaws mistake the way."

Dryden's Annus Mirabilis.

"While the whale is floating at the stern of the ship, they cut off his head, and tow it with a boat as near the shore as it will come; but it will be aground in twelve or thirteen foot water."

Thomas Edge's Ten Voyages to Spitzbergen, in Purchass.

"In their way they saw many whales sporting in the ocean, and in wantonness fuzzing up the water through their pipes and vents, which nature has placed on their shoulders."

Sir T. Herbert's Voyages into Asia and Africa. Harris Coll.

"Here they saw such huge troops of whales, that they were forced to proceed with a great deal of caution for fear they should run their ship upon them."

Schouten's Sixth Circumnavigation.

"We set sail from the Elbe, wind N. E. in the ship called The Jonas-in-the-Whale. * * *

Some say the whale can't open his mouth, but that is a fable. * * *

They frequently climb up the masts to see whether they can see a whale, for the first discoverer has a ducat for his pains. * * *

I was told of a whale taken near Hitland, that had above a barrel of herrings in his belly. * * *

One of our harpooneers told me that he caught once a whale in Spitzbergen that was white all over."

A Voyage to Greenland, A.D. 1671. Harris Coll.

"Several whales have come in upon this coast (Fife). Anno 1652, one eighty foot in length of the whale-bone kind came in, which, (as I was informed) beside a vast quantity of oil, did afford 500 weight of baleen. The jaws of it stand for a gate in the garden of Pitfirren."

Sibbald's Fife and Kinross.

"Myself have agreed to try whether I can master and kill this Sperma-ceti whale, for I could never hear of any of that sort that was killed by any man, such is his fierceness and swiftness."

Richard Stafford's Letter from the Bermudas.
Phil. Trans. A.D. 1668.

"Whales in the sea
God's voice obey."

N. E. Primer.

"We saw also abundance of large whales, there being more in these southern seas, as I may say, by a hundred to one; than we have to the northward of us."

Captain Cowley's Voyage round the Globe. A.D. 1729.

* * * * * "and the breath of the whale is frequently attended with such an insupportable smell, as to bring on a disorder of the brain."

Ulloa's South America.

"To fifty chosen sylphs of special note,
We trust the important charge, the petticoat.

Oft have we known that seven-fold fence to fail,
Tho' stiff with hoops and armed with ribs of whale."
                                        Rape of the Lock.

"If we compare land animals in respect to magnitude, with those
that take up their abode in the deep, we shall find they will appear
contemptible in the comparison. The whale is doubtless the largest
animal in creation."
                                        Goldsmith, Nat. His.

"If you should write a fable for little fishes, you would make them
speak like great whales."
                                        Goldsmith to Johnson.

"In the afternoon we saw what was supposed to be a rock, but it
was found to be a dead whale, which some Asiatics had killed, and
were then towing ashore. They seemed to endeavor to conceal themselves behind the whale, in order to avoid being seen by us."
                                        Cook's Voyages.

"The larger whales, they seldom venture to attack. They stand in so
great dread of some of them, that when out at sea they are afraid to
mention even their names, and carry dung, brim-stone, juniper-
wood, and some other articles of the same nature in their boats, in
order to terrify and prevent their too near approach."
                        *Uno Von Troil's Letters on Banks's and
                        Solander's Voyage to Iceland in* 1772.

"The Spermacetti Whale found by the Nantuckois, is an active,
fierce animal, and requires vast address and boldness in the fishermen."
                        *Thomas Jefferson's Whale Memorial to the
                        French minister in* 1788.

"And pray, sir, what in the world is equal to it?"
                        *Edmund Burke's reference in Parliament
                        to the Nantucket Whale-Fishery.*

"Spain——a great whale stranded on the shores of Europe."
                        Edmund Burke. (somewhere.)

"A tenth branch of the king's ordinary revenue, said to be grounded
on the consideration of his guarding and protecting the seas from
pirates and robbers, is the right to *royal* fish, which are whale and
sturgeon. And these, when either thrown ashore or caught near the
coasts, are the property of the king."
                                        Blackstone.

"Soon to the sport of death the crews repair:
Rodmond unerring o'er his head suspends
The barbed steel, and every turn attends."
                                        Falconer's Shipwreck.

"Bright shone the roofs, the domes, the spires,
    And rockets flew self driven,
To hang their momentary fires
    Amid the vault of heaven.

"So fire with water to compare,
    The ocean serves on high,
Up-spouted by a whale in air,
    To express unwieldy joy."
                            Cowper, on the Queen's Visit to London.

"Ten or fifteen gallons of blood are thrown out of the heart at a stroke, with immense velocity."
                            John Hunter's account of the dissection
                            of a whale. (A small sized one.)

"The aorta of a whale is larger in the bore than the main pipe of the water-works at London Bridge, and the water roaring in its passage through that pipe is inferior in impetus and velocity to the blood gushing from the whale's heart."
                            Paley's Theology.

"The whale is a mammiferous animal without hind feet."
                            Baron Cuvier.

"In 40 degrees south, we saw Spermacetti Whales, but did not take any till the first of May, the sea being then covered with them."
                            Colnett's Voyage for the Purpose of
                            Extending the Spermacetti Whale Fishery.

"In the free element beneath me swam,
Floundered and dived, in play, in chace, in battle,
Fishes of every color, form, and kind;
Which language cannot paint, and mariner
Had never seen; from dread Leviathan
To insect millions peopling every wave:
Gather'd in shoals immense, like floating islands,
Led by mysterious instinct through that waste
And trackless region, though on every side
Assaulted by voracious enemies,
Whales, sharks, and monsters, arm'd in front or jaw,
With swords, saws, spiral horns, or hooked fangs."
                            Montgomery's World before the Flood.

"Io! Pæan! Io! sing,
To the finny people's king.
Not a mightier whale than this
In the vast Atlantic is;
Not a fatter fish than he,
Flounders round the Polar Sea."
                            Charles Lamb's Triumph of the Whale.

"In the year 1690 some persons were on a high hill observing the whales spouting and sporting with each other, when one observed;

there—pointing to the sea—is a green pasture where our children's grand-children will go for bread."

Obed Macy's History of Nantucket.

"I built a cottage for Susan and myself and made a gateway in the form of a Gothic Arch, by setting up a whale's jaw bones."

Hawthorne's Twice Told Tales.

"She came to bespeak a monument for her first love, who had been killed by a whale in the Pacific ocean, no less than forty years ago."

Ibid.

"No, Sir, 'tis a Right Whale," answered Tom; "I saw his spout; he threw up a pair of as pretty rainbows as a Christian would wish to look at. He's a raal oil-butt, that fellow!"

Cooper's Pilot.

"The papers were brought in, and we saw in the Berlin Gazette that whales had been introduced on the stage there."

Eckermann's Conversations with Goethe.

"My God! Mr. Chase, what is the matter?" I answered, "we have been stove by a whale."

"Narrative of the Shipwreck of the Whale Ship Essex of Nantucket, which was attacked and finally destroyed by a large Sperm Whale in the Pacific Ocean." By Owen Chase of Nantucket, first mate of said vessel. New York. 1821.

"A mariner sat on the shrouds one night,
  The wind was piping free;
Now bright, now dimmed, was the moonlight pale,
And the phospher gleamed in the wake of the whale,
  As it floundered in the sea."

Elizabeth Oakes Smith.

"The quantity of line withdrawn from the different boats engaged in the capture of this one whale, amounted altogether to 10,440 yards or nearly six English miles." * * *

"Sometimes the whale shakes its tremendous tail in the air, which, cracking like a whip, resounds to the distance of three or four miles."

Scoresby.

"Mad with the agonies he endures from these fresh attacks, the infuriated Sperm Whale rolls over and over; he rears his enormous head, and with wide expanded jaw snaps at everything around him; he rushes at the boats with his head; they are propelled before him with vast swiftness, and sometimes utterly destroyed.

* * * It is a matter of great astonishment that the consideration of the habits of so interesting, and, in a commercial point of view, of so important an animal (as the Sperm Whale) should have been so entirely neglected, or should have excited so little curiosity among the numerous, and many of them competent observers, that of late years must have possessed the most abundant and the most convenient opportunities of witnessing their habitudes."

Thomas Beale's History of the Sperm Whale, 1839.

"The Cachalot" (Sperm Whale) "is not only better armed than the True Whale" (Greenland or Right Whale) "in possessing a formidable weapon at either extremity of its body, but also more frequently displays a disposition to employ those weapons offensively, and in a manner at once so artful, bold, and mischievous, as to lead to its being regarded as the most dangerous to attack of all the known species of the whale tribe."

> *Frederick Debell Bennett's Whaling*
> *Voyage Round the Globe.* 1840.

October 13. "There she blows," was sung out from the mast-head.
"Where away?" demanded the captain.
"Three points off the lee bow, sir."
"Raise up your wheel. Steady!"
"Steady, sir."
"Mast-head ahoy! Do you see that whale now?"
"Ay ay, sir! A shoal of Sperm Whales! There she blows! There she breaches!"
"Sing out! sing out every time!"
"Ay ay, sir! There she blows! there—there—*thar* she blows—bowes—bo-o-o-s!"
"How far off?"
"Two miles and a half."
"Thunder and lightning! so near! Call all hands!"

> *J. Ross Browne's Etchings of a Whaling Cruise.* 1846.

"The Whale-ship Globe, on board of which vessel occurred the horrid transactions we are about to relate, belonged to the island of Nantucket."

> *"Narrative of the Globe Mutiny," by*
> *Lay and Hussey, survivors. A. D.* 1828.

"Being once pursued by a whale which he had wounded, he parried the assault for some time with a lance; but the furious monster at length rushed on the boat; himself and comrades only being preserved by leaping into the water when they saw the onset was inevitable."

> *Missionary Journal of Tyerman and Bennet.*

"Nantucket itself," said Mr. Webster, "is a very striking and peculiar portion of the National interest. There is a population of eight or nine thousand persons, living here in the sea, adding largely every year to the National wealth by the boldest and most persevering industry."

> *Report of Daniel Webster's Speech in the U.S. Senate, on the*
> *application for the Erection of a Breakwater at Nantucket.* 1828.

"The whale fell directly over him, and probably killed him in a moment."

> *"The Whale and his Captors, or The Whaleman's*
> *Adventures and the Whale's Biography, as gathered*
> *on the Homewood Cruise of the Commodore*
> *Preble." By Rev. Henry T. Cheever.*

"If you make the least damn bit of noise," replied Samuel, "I will send you to hell."

> *Life of Samuel Comstock (the mutineer), by his brother, William Comstock. Another Version of the whale-ship Globe narrative.*

"The voyages of the Dutch and English to the Northern Ocean, in order, if possible, to discover a passage through it to India, though they failed of their main object, laid open the haunts of the whale."

> *McCulloch's Commercial Dictionary.*

"These things are reciprocal; the ball rebounds, only to bound forward again; for now in laying open the haunts of the whale, the whalemen seem to have indirectly hit upon new clews to that same mystic North-West Passage."

> *From "Something" unpublished.*

"It is impossible to meet a whale-ship on the ocean without being struck by her mere appearance. The vessel under short sail, with look-outs at the mast-heads, eagerly scanning the wide expanse around them, has a totally different air from those engaged in a regular voyage."

> *Currents and Whaling. U.S. Ex. Ex.*

"Pedestrians in the vicinity of London and elsewhere may recollect having seen large curved bones set upright in the earth, either to form arches over gateways, or entrances to alcoves, and they may perhaps have been told that these were the ribs of whales."

> *Tales of a Whale Voyager to the Arctic Ocean.*

"It was not till the boats returned from the pursuit of these whales, that the whites saw their ship in bloody possession of the savages enrolled among the crew."

> *Newspaper Account of the Taking and Retaking of the Whale-ship Hobomock.*

"It is generally well known that out of the crews of Whaling vessels (American) few ever return in the ships on board of which they departed."

> *Cruise in a Whale Boat.*

"Suddenly a mighty mass emerged from the water, and shot up perpendicularly into the air. It was the whale."

> *Miriam Coffin or the Whale Fishermen.*

"The Whale is harpooned to be sure; but bethink you, how you would manage a powerful unbroken colt, with the mere appliance of a rope tied to the root of his tail."

> *A Chapter on Whaling in Ribs and Trucks.*

"On one occasion I saw two of these monsters (whales) probably male and female, slowly swimming, one after the other, within less than a stone's throw of the shore" (Terra Del Fuego), "over which the beech tree extended its branches."

> *Darwin's Voyage of a Naturalist.*

"'Stern all!' exclaimed the mate, as upon turning his head, he saw the distended jaws of a large Sperm Whale close to the head of the boat, threatening it with instant destruction;— 'Stern all, for your lives!'"

Wharton the Whale Killer.

"So be cheery, my lads, let your hearts never fail,
While the bold harpooneer is striking the whale!"

Nantucket Song.

"Oh, the rare old Whale, mid storm and gale
    In his ocean home will be
A giant in might, where might is right,
    And King of the boundless sea."

Whale Song.

Chapter 1

Loomings[1]

Call me Ishmael.[2] Some years ago—never mind how long precisely—having little or no money in my purse, and nothing particular to interest me on shore, I thought I would sail about a little and see the watery part of the world. It is a way I have of driving off the spleen,[3] and regulating the circulation. Whenever I find myself growing grim about the mouth; whenever it is a damp, drizzly November in my soul; whenever I find myself involuntarily pausing before coffin warehouses, and bringing up the rear of every funeral I meet; and especially whenever my hypos[4] get such an upper hand of me, that it requires a strong moral principle to prevent me from deliberately stepping into the street, and methodically knocking people's hats off—then, I account it high time to get to sea as soon as I can. This is my substitute for pistol and ball. With a philosophical flourish Cato[5] throws himself upon his sword; I quietly take to the ship. There is nothing surprising in this. If they but knew it, almost all men in their degree, some time or other, cherish very nearly the same feelings towards the ocean with me.

There now is your insular city of the Manhattoes, belted round by wharves as Indian isles[6] by coral reefs—commerce surrounds it with her surf. Right and left, the streets take you waterward. Its extreme downtown is the Battery,[7] where that noble mole is washed by waves, and cooled by breezes, which a few hours previous were out of sight of land. Look at the crowds of water-gazers there.

Circumambulate the city of a dreamy Sabbath afternoon. Go from Corlears Hook to Coenties Slip, and from thence, by Whitehall, northward. What do you see?—Posted like silent sentinels all around the town, stand thousands upon thousands of mortal men fixed in ocean reveries. Some leaning against the spiles;[8] some seated upon the pier-heads; some looking over the bulwarks of ships from China; some high aloft in the rig-

1. A nautical sense is land or ships beyond the horizon, dimly seen by reflection in peculiar weather conditions.
2. The name of the first-person narrator implies that he is an outcast from a great family. Ishmael is the oldest son of the patriarch Abraham, by the Egyptian Hagar, servant to his then-barren wife Sarah; Sarah mistreats Hagar, who flees into the desert, where an angel feeds her and reveals that she is pregnant with Ishmael, who will be "a wild man," whose "hand will be against every man, and every man's hand against him" (Genesis 16.12). Years later, after Sarah bears Isaac, she prevails on Abraham to send Hagar and Ishmael away; in the wilderness an angel again protects them. Traditionally Ishmael is identified as the ancestor of the Arabs, whereas his younger half-brother Isaac is the ancestor of the Jews; on the point of shared ancestry, DNA analysis establishes the accuracy of the Bible and Muslim traditions.
3. Violent feelings and displays of irritation or anger, formerly attributed to that organ of the body.
4. Slang for "hypochondrias," more like neuroses (nonorganic phobias and anxieties) than our term for a kindred depressive mental state, the "blues."
5. The suicide of this Roman statesman-soldier (95–46 B.C.E.), after his defeat in battle, exemplified his Stoic philosophy.
6. Islands in the East Indies. *Manhattoes*: inhabitants of Manhattan Island, a term picked up from Washington Irving's *Knickerbocker History of New York* (1809).
7. At the southern tip of Manhattan, formerly the site of a fort. In the next paragraph, the reader is directed to start at Corlears Hook, on the East River below Grand Street, and walk to Coenties Slip, almost to the Battery, then follow Whitehall northwest (across Pearl Street, where Melville was born) on its slanting course to Broadway. In Melville's time, Whitehall was in sight of the wharves, and from Broadway any street to the left (with the walker's back turned to the Battery) led to the Hudson River, and more wharves.
8. Large support posts.

ging, as if striving to get a still better seaward peep. But these are all landsmen; of week days pent up in lath and plaster—tied to counters, nailed to benches, clinched to desks. How then is this? Are the green fields gone? What do they here?

But look! here come more crowds, pacing straight for the water, and seemingly bound for a dive. Strange! Nothing will content them but the extremest limit of the land; loitering under the shady lee of yonder warehouses will not suffice. No. They must get just as nigh the water as they possibly can without falling in. And there they stand—miles of them— leagues. Inlanders all, they come from lanes and alleys, streets and avenues—north, east, south, and west. Yet here they all unite. Tell me, does the magnetic virtue of the needles of the compasses of all those ships attract them thither?[9]

Once more. Say, you are in the country; in some high land of lakes. Take almost any path you please, and ten to one it carries you down in a dale, and leaves you there by a pool in the stream. There is magic in it. Let the most absent-minded of men be plunged in his deepest reveries— stand that man on his legs, set his feet a-going, and he will infallibly lead you to water, if water there be in all that region. Should you ever be athirst in the great American desert, try this experiment, if your caravan happen to be supplied with a metaphysical professor. Yes, as every one knows, meditation and water are wedded for ever.

But here is an artist. He desires to paint you the dreamiest, shadiest, quietest, most enchanting bit of romantic landscape in all the valley of the Saco.[1] What is the chief element he employs? There stand his trees, each with a hollow trunk, as if a hermit and a crucifix were within; and here sleeps his meadow, and there sleep his cattle; and up from yonder cottage goes a sleepy smoke. Deep into distant woodlands winds a mazy way, reaching to overlapping spurs of mountains bathed in their hill-side blue. But though the picture lies thus tranced, and though this pine-tree shakes down its sighs like leaves upon this shepherd's head, yet all were vain, unless the shepherd's eye were fixed upon the magic stream before him. Go visit the Prairies in June,[2] when for scores on scores of miles you wade knee-deep among Tiger-lilies—what is the one charm wanting?—Water—there is not a drop of water there! Were Niagara but a cataract of sand, would you travel your thousand miles to see it? Why did the poor poet of Tennessee,[3] upon suddenly receiving two handfuls of silver, deliberate whether to buy him a coat, which he sadly needed, or invest his money in a pedestrian trip to Rockaway Beach?[4] Why is almost every robust healthy boy with a robust healthy soul in him, at some time or other crazy to go to sea? Why upon your first voyage as a passenger, did you yourself feel such a mystical vibration, when first told

9. Melville seems to have known this passage from William Cobbett's *Life and Adventures of Peter Porcupine* (1796): "From the top of Portsdown, I, for the first time, beheld the sea, and no sooner did I behold it than I wished to be a sailor. I could never account for this sudden impulse, nor can I now. Almost all English boys feel the same inclination: it would seem that, like young ducks, instinct leads them to rush on the bosom of the water."
1. During his honeymoon in 1847 Melville had visited the picturesque valley of the Saco, in southern New Hampshire.
2. Melville had visited then-frontier Illinois in early July 1840.
3. Presumably not a reference to a real poet.
4. A popular beach on the southern coast of Long Island.

that you and your ship were now out of sight of land? Why did the old
Persians hold the sea holy? Why did the Greeks give it a separate deity,[5]
and make him the own brother of Jove? Surely all this is not without
meaning. And still deeper the meaning of that story of Narcissus, who
because he could not grasp the tormenting, mild image he saw in the
fountain, plunged into it and was drowned.[6] But that same image, we
ourselves see in all rivers and oceans. It is the image of the ungraspable
phantom of life; and this is the key to it all.

Now, when I say that I am in the habit of going to sea whenever I begin
to grow hazy about the eyes, and begin to be over conscious of my lungs,
I do not mean to have it inferred that I ever go to sea as a passenger. For
to go as a passenger you must needs have a purse, and a purse is but a rag
unless you have something in it. Besides, passengers get sea-sick—grow
quarrelsome—don't sleep of nights—do not enjoy themselves much, as a
general thing;—no, I never go as a passenger; nor, though I am something
of a salt,[7] do I ever go to sea as a Commodore, or a Captain, or a Cook. I
abandon the glory and distinction of such offices to those who like them.
For my part, I abominate all honorable respectable toils, trials, and tribulations of every kind whatsoever. It is quite as much as I can do to take
care of myself, without taking care of ships, barques, brigs, schooners,
and what not.[8] And as for going as cook,—though I confess there is considerable glory in that, a cook being a sort of officer on ship-board—yet,
somehow, I never fancied broiling fowls;—though once broiled, judiciously buttered, and judgmatically salted and peppered, there is no one
who will speak more respectfully, not to say reverentially, of a broiled fowl
than I will. It is out of the idolatrous dotings of the old Egyptians upon
broiled ibis and roasted river horse,[9] that you see the mummies of those
creatures in their huge bake-houses the pyramids.

No, when I go to sea, I go as a simple sailor, right before the mast,
plumb down into the forecastle, aloft there to the royal mast-head.[1] True,
they rather order me about some, and make me jump from spar to spar,
like a grasshopper in a May meadow. And at first, this sort of thing is
unpleasant enough. It touches one's sense of honor, particularly if you
come of an old established family in the land, the Van Rensselaers, or
Randolphs, or Hardicanutes.[2] And more than all, if just previous to
putting your hand into the tar-pot, you have been lording it as a country
schoolmaster, making the tallest boys stand in awe of you.[3] The transition
is a keen one, I assure you, from a schoolmaster to a sailor, and requires

---

5. That is, Poseidon, in Greek mythology (Neptune, in Roman mythology).
6. In Book 3 of Ovid's *Metamorphoses*, Narcissus falls in love with his own reflection in water and
   wastes away pining for it (but does not plunge into the water and drown).
7. Experienced seaman.
8. The largest vessels were steamers, followed, in descending order of size, by ships, barques, brigs,
   schooners, sloops, and barges.
9. Hippopotamus.
1. Top of the highest mast.
2. Danish rulers of England (11th century). Melville's mother was a descendant of Van Rensselaers,
   the dominant Dutch family in colonial New York and the early republic. The Randolphs included
   many eminent Virginians (among them Thomas Jefferson).
3. Melville had taught in a country school the year before sailing to Liverpool as a green hand in
   1839 and did so again in at least three such schools (as late as September 1840, in an unidentified school near Lansingburgh, New York) before sailing on the whaleship *Acushnet* the first week
   of 1841.

a strong decoction of Seneca[4] and the Stoics to enable you to grin and bear it. But even this wears off in time.

What of it, if some old hunks[5] of a sea-captain orders me to get a broom and sweep down the decks? What does that indignity amount to, weighed, I mean, in the scales of the New Testament? Do you think the archangel Gabriel thinks anything the less of me, because I promptly and respectfully obey that old hunks in that particular instance? Who aint a slave?[6] Tell me that. Well, then, however the old sea-captains may order me about—however they may thump and punch me about, I have the satisfaction of knowing that it is all right; that everybody else is one way or other served in much the same way—either in a physical or metaphysical point of view, that is; and so the universal thump is passed round, and all hands should rub each other's shoulder-blades, and be content.

Again, I always go to sea as a sailor, because they make a point of paying me for my trouble, whereas they never pay passengers a single penny that I ever heard of. On the contrary, passengers themselves must pay. And there is all the difference in the world between paying and being paid. The act of paying is perhaps the most uncomfortable infliction that the two orchard thieves[7] entailed upon us. But *being paid*,— what will compare with it? The urbane activity with which a man receives money is really marvellous, considering that we so earnestly believe money to be the root of all earthly ills, and that on no account can a monied man enter heaven.[8] Ah! how cheerfully we consign ourselves to perdition!

Finally, I always go to sea as a sailor, because of the wholesome exercise and pure air of the forecastle deck. For as in this world, head winds are far more prevalent than winds from astern (that is, if you never violate the Pythagorean[9] maxim), so for the most part the Commodore on the quarter-deck gets his atmosphere at second hand from the sailors on the forecastle. He thinks he breathes it first; but not so. In much the same way do the commonalty lead their leaders in many other things, at the same time that the leaders little suspect it. But wherefore it was that after having repeatedly smelt the sea as a merchant sailor, I should now take it into my head to go on a whaling voyage; this the invisible police officer of the Fates,[1] who has the constant surveillance of me, and secretly dogs me,

---

4. Lucius Annaeus Seneca (ca. 4 B.C.E.–65 C.E.), Roman adherent of Stoicism, the belief that people should uncomplainingly accept all events as the unavoidable results of divine will.
5. Bully, grouch (used only of old men, not women).
6. The American text of *Moby-Dick* reflects not only Melville's own free-and-easy casualness about punctuation and spelling but also common usage at his time. Such punctuation as "aint" without an apostrophe and now odd-looking spellings (like the then-common "Affghanistan," later in this chapter) are retained in this edition.
7. In Jewish and Christian doctrine, after the sin of Adam and Eve, who in Eden ate of the fruit of the tree of knowledge of good and evil (Genesis 3), Adam and all his and Eve's descendants must earn their living by the sweat of their brows. *The Whale* (October 1851) omitted this humorous biblical allusion along with many other jocular or merely disrespectful sallies throughout the book.
8. Not money itself but "the love of money" is said to be "the root of all evil" (1 Timothy 6.10); see Matthew 19.24, Mark 10.25, or Luke 18.25: "It is easier for a camel to go through the eye of a needle, than for a rich man to enter into the kingdom of God."
9. The Greek philosopher Pythagoras (6th century B.C.E.) advised not eating beans because they cause flatulence. Melville jokes about the location of the tiny privies on the sides of whaleships— toward the bow, while the captain's quarters are at the stern.
1. Three Greek goddesses who control human destiny. Clotho spins the thread of life, Lachesis determines its length, and Atropos cuts it off.

and influences me in some unaccountable way—he can better answer than any one else. And, doubtless, my going on this whaling voyage, formed part of the grand programme of Providence[2] that was drawn up a long time ago. It came in as a sort of brief interlude and solo between more extensive performances. I take it that this part of the bill must have run something like this:

> "Grand Contested Election for the Presidency of the United States.
> "WHALING VOYAGE BY ONE ISHMAEL.
> "BLOODY BATTLE IN AFFGHANISTAN."

Though I cannot tell why it was exactly that those stage managers, the Fates, put me down for this shabby part of a whaling voyage, when others were set down for magnificent parts in high tragedies, and short and easy parts in genteel comedies, and jolly parts in farces—though I cannot tell why this was exactly; yet, now that I recall all the circumstances, I think I can see a little into the springs and motives which being cunningly presented to me under various disguises, induced me to set about performing the part I did, besides cajoling me into the delusion that it was a choice resulting from my own unbiased freewill and discriminating judgment.

Chief among these motives was the overwhelming idea of the great whale himself. Such a portentous and mysterious monster roused all my curiosity. Then the wild and distant seas where he rolled his island bulk; the undeliverable, nameless perils of the whale; these, with all the attending marvels of a thousand Patagonian[3] sights and sounds, helped to sway me to my wish. With other men, perhaps, such things would not have been inducements; but as for me, I am tormented with an everlasting itch for things remote. I love to sail forbidden seas, and land on barbarous coasts. Not ignoring what is good, I am quick to perceive a horror, and could still be social with it—would they let me—since it is but well to be on friendly terms with all the inmates of the place one lodges in.[4]

By reason of these things, then, the whaling voyage was welcome; the great flood-gates of the wonder-world swung open, and in the wild conceits that swayed me to my purpose, two and two there floated into my inmost soul, endless processions of the whale, and, midmost of them all, one grand hooded phantom, like a snow hill in the air.[5]

---

2. God as the guiding power over human destiny.
3. Patagonia is the barren southernmost region of Argentina, between the Andes and the Atlantic, to the north of Cape Horn.
4. Melville had read in the second part of *Religio Medici* (*A doctor's religion*, 1642, 1643) the eloquent claim by Sir Thomas Browne (1605–1682) to have "no antipathy" whether "in diet, humor, air, anything," including no national prejudices or repugnances. Browne specifies further: "I cannot start at the presence of a serpent, scorpion, lizard, or salamander; at the sight of a toad or viper I find in me no desire to take up a stone to destroy them."
5. "Two and two" recalls Genesis 7.9 ("There went in two and two unto Noah into the ark, the male and the female, as God had commanded Noah"), but in these anticipatory "loomings" Ishmael multiplies the number of whales infinitely and imagines Moby Dick ("one grand hooded phantom") as midmost of them all.

Chapter 2

The Carpet-Bag

I stuffed a shirt or two into my old carpet-bag,[1] tucked it under my arm, and started for Cape Horn and the Pacific. Quitting the good city of old Manhatto, I duly arrived in New Bedford. It was on a Saturday night in December. Much was I disappointed upon learning that the little packet for Nantucket had already sailed, and that no way of reaching that place would offer, till the following Monday.

As most young candidates for the pains and penalties of whaling stop at this same New Bedford, thence to embark on their voyage, it may as well be related that I, for one, had no idea of so doing. For my mind was made up to sail in no other than a Nantucket craft, because there was a fine, boisterous something about everything connected with that famous old island, which amazingly pleased me. Besides though New Bedford has of late been gradually monopolizing the business of whaling, and though in this matter poor old Nantucket is now much behind her, yet Nantucket was her great original—the Tyre of this Carthage;[2]—the place where the first dead American whale was stranded.[3] Where else but from Nantucket did those aboriginal whalemen, the Red-Men, first sally out in canoes to give chase to the Leviathan? And where but from Nantucket, too, did that first adventurous little sloop put forth, partly laden with imported cobble-stones—so goes the story—to throw at the whales, in order to discover when they were nigh enough to risk a harpoon from the bowsprit?[4]

Now having a night, a day, and still another night following before me in New Bedford, ere I could embark for my destined port, it became a matter of concernment where I was to eat and sleep meanwhile. It was a very dubious-looking, nay, a very dark and dismal night, bitingly cold and cheerless. I knew no one in the place. With anxious grapnels[5] I had sounded my pocket, and only brought up a few pieces of silver,—So, wherever you go, Ishmael, said I to myself, as I stood in the middle of a dreary street shouldering my bag, and comparing the gloom towards the north with the darkness towards the south—wherever in your wisdom you may conclude to lodge for the night, my dear Ishmael, be sure to inquire the price, and don't be too particular.

With halting steps I paced the streets, and passed the sign of "The Crossed Harpoons"—but it looked too expensive and jolly there. Further on, from the bright red windows of the "Sword-Fish Inn," there came such fervent rays, that it seemed to have melted the packed snow and ice from before the house, for everywhere else the congealed frost lay ten inches thick in a hard, asphaltic pavement,—rather weary for me, when I struck my foot against the flinty projections, because from hard, remorse-

---

1. Bag made of carpet fabric, for traveling light; the still-current "carpetbagger" (one who moves fast into strange territory to exploit some situation) was coined a decade and a half later, at the end of the Civil War.
2. Mediterranean maritime cities of antiquity. Phoenicians from Tyre (in modern Syria) founded Carthage (in modern Tunisia), in the 9th century B.C.E.
3. Washed or dragged ashore.
4. The spar projecting from the ship's bow.
5. Small anchors with several hooks for dragging; here, his fingers.

less service the soles of my boots were in a most miserable plight. Too expensive and jolly, again thought I, pausing one moment to watch the broad glare in the street, and hear the sounds of the tinkling glasses within. But go on, Ishmael, said I at last; don't you hear? get away from before the door; your patched boots are stopping the way. So on I went. I now by instinct followed the streets that took me waterward, for there, doubtless, were the cheapest, if not the cheeriest inns.

Such dreary streets! blocks of blackness, not houses, on either hand, and here and there a candle, like a candle moving about in a tomb. At this hour of the night, of the last day of the week, that quarter of the town proved all but deserted. But presently I came to a smoky light proceeding from a low, wide building, the door of which stood invitingly open. It had a careless look, as if it were meant for the uses of the public; so, entering, the first thing I did was to stumble over an ash-box in the porch. Ha! thought I, ha, as the flying particles almost choked me, are these ashes from that destroyed city, Gomorrah?[6] But "The Crossed Harpoons," and "The Sword-Fish?"—this, then, must needs be the sign of "The Trap." However, I picked myself up and hearing a loud voice within, pushed on and opened a second, interior door.

It seemed the great Black Parliament sitting in Tophet. A hundred black faces turned round in their rows to peer; and beyond, a black Angel of Doom was beating a book in a pulpit. It was a negro church; and the preacher's text was about the blackness of darkness, and the weeping and wailing and teeth-gnashing there.[7] Ha, Ishmael, muttered I, backing out, Wretched entertainment at the sign of "The Trap!"

Moving on, I at last came to a dim sort of out-hanging light not far from the docks, and heard a forlorn creaking in the air; and looking up, saw a swinging sign over the door with a white painting upon it, faintly repre-senting a tall straight jet of misty spray, and these words underneath— "The Spouter-Inn:—Peter Coffin."

Coffin?—Spouter?—Rather ominous in that particular connexion, thought I. But it is a common name in Nantucket, they say, and I suppose this Peter here is an emigrant from there. As the light looked so dim, and the place, for the time, looked quiet enough, and the dilapidated little wooden house itself looked as if it might have been carted here from the ruins of some burnt district, and as the swinging sign had a poverty-stricken sort of creak to it, I thought that here was the very spot for cheap lodgings, and the best of pea coffee.[8]

It was a queer sort of place—a gable-ended old house, one side palsied as it were, and leaning over sadly. It stood on a sharp bleak corner, where that tempestuous wind[9] Euroclydon kept up a worse howling than ever it did about poor Paul's tossed craft. Euroclydon, nevertheless, is a mighty

---

6. In Genesis 19 God destroys Sodom and Gomorrah, the wicked cities of the plain, by raining brimstone and fire upon them out of heaven.
7. Matthew 8.12: "But the children of the kingdom shall be cast out into outer darkness: there shall be weeping and gnashing of teeth." Tophet: hell. *Angel of Doom:* not biblical ("doom" does not occur in the King James Bible). *Blackness of darkness:* from Jude verse 13. It was also familiar to Melville from Thomas Carlyle's *Sartor Resartus* (1833–34), book 2, ch. 4.
8. Cheap crushed chick-pea beverage, the "best" of which Ishmael sees as a poor substitute for real coffee.
9. Wind that threatened Paul's ship after the master and owner ignored his warnings; see Acts 27.

pleasant zephyr to any one in-doors, with his feet on the hob quietly toasting for bed. "In judging of that tempestuous wind called Euroclydon," says an old writer—of whose works I possess the only copy extant—"it maketh a marvellous difference, whether thou lookest out at it from a glass window where the frost is all on the outside, or whether thou observest it from that sashless window, where the frost is on both sides, and of which the wight Death is the only glazier." True enough, thought I, as this passage occurred to my mind—old black-letter,[1] thou reasonest well. Yes, these eyes are windows, and this body of mine is the house. What a pity they didn't stop up the chinks and the crannies though, and thrust in a little lint here and there. But it's too late to make any improvements now. The universe is finished; the copestone is on, and the chips were carted off a million years ago. Poor Lazarus[2] there, chattering his teeth against the curbstone for his pillow, and shaking off his tatters with his shiverings, he might plug up both ears with rags, and put a corn-cob into his mouth, and yet that would not keep out the tempestuous Euroclydon Euroclydon! says old Dives, in his red silken wrapper (he had a redder one afterwards)—pooh, pooh! What a fine frosty night; how Orion glitters; what northern lights![3] Let them talk of their oriental summer climes of everlasting conservatories; give me the privilege of making my own summer with my own coals.

But what thinks Lazarus? Can he warm his blue hands by holding them up to the grand northern lights? Would not Lazarus rather be in Sumatra[4] than here? Would he not far rather lay him down lengthwise along the line of the equator; yea, ye gods! go down to the fiery pit itself, in order to keep out this frost?

Now, that Lazarus should lie stranded there on the curbstone before the door of Dives, this is more wonderful than that an iceberg should be moored to one of the Moluccas.[5] Yet Dives himself, he too lives like a Czar in an ice palace made of frozen sighs, and being a president of a temperance society,[6] he only drinks the tepid tears of orphans.

But no more of this blubbering now, we are going a-whaling, and there is plenty of that yet to come. Let us scrape the ice from our frosted feet, and see what sort of a place this "Spouter" may be.

---

1. Book in which the type resembles the script of medieval manuscripts. Having invented the "old writer" and the quotation from him, Ishmael then explicates the passage. *Glazier:* one who makes and installs window glass.
2. In Luke 16.19–31, a beggar whom the angels carry to Abraham's bosom in heaven, while the merciless rich man (Dives) suffers in the fires of hell.
3. The Aurora Borealis; greenish flashes from the northern sky. *Orion:* a major constellation.
4. East Indian island.
5. Equatorial Pacific islands.
6. A 19th-century society for promoting the moderate ("temperate") use of alcoholic beverages or to promote total abstinence. Ishmael imagines a rich man as the president of such a society, while living like a czar at the expense of the poor and orphans. Ice palaces were built annually for the Czar in St. Petersburg, Russia, where Peter the Great (1672–1725) built his Winter Palace. At the time of *Moby-Dick* American alcohol consumption was high and reform movements (like the Washingtonian Society of the 1840s) all soon failed. The Melvilles joked about temperance societies, as when the oldest brother, Gansevoort, solemnly sent the twelve-year-old youngest brother, Tom, some "Temperance songs," professing to have remembered that the boy was "a Tee-totaller" (one who abstains from all alcoholic beverages).

Chapter 3

The Spouter-Inn

Entering that gable-ended Spouter-Inn, you found yourself in a wide, low, straggling entry with old-fashioned wainscots, reminding one of the bulwarks of some condemned[1] old craft. On one side hung a very large oil-painting so thoroughly besmoked, and every way defaced, that in the unequal cross-lights by which you viewed it, it was only by diligent study and a series of systematic visits to it, and careful inquiry of the neighbors, that you could any way arrive at an understanding of its purpose. Such unaccountable masses of shades and shadows, that at first you almost thought some ambitious young artist, in the time of the New England hags,[2] had endeavored to delineate chaos bewitched. But by dint of much and earnest contemplation, and oft repeated ponderings, and especially by throwing open the little window towards the back of the entry, you at last came to the conclusion that such an idea, however wild, might not be altogether unwarranted.

But what most puzzled and confounded you was a long, limber, portentous, black mass of something hovering in the centre of the picture over three blue, dim, perpendicular lines floating in a nameless yeast. A boggy, soggy, squitchy[3] picture truly, enough to drive a nervous man distracted. Yet was there a sort of indefinite, half-attained, unimaginable sublimity about it that fairly froze you to it, till you involuntarily took an oath with yourself to find out what that marvellous painting meant. Ever and anon a bright, but, alas, deceptive idea would dart you through.—It's the Black Sea in a midnight gale.—It's the unnatural combat of the four primal elements.—It's a blasted heath.—It's a Hyperborean winter scene.—It's the breaking-up of the ice-bound stream of Time. But at last all these fancies yielded to that one portentous something in the picture's midst. *That* once found out, and all the rest were plain. But stop; does it not bear a faint resemblance to a gigantic fish? even the great leviathan[4] himself?

In fact, the artist's design seemed this: a final theory of my own, partly based upon the aggregated opinions of many aged persons with whom I conversed upon the subject. The picture represents a Cape-Horner in a great hurricane; the half-foundered ship weltering there with its three dismantled masts alone visible; and an exasperated whale, purposing to spring clean over the craft, is in the enormous act of impaling himself upon the three mast-heads.

---

1. Declared unseaworthy. *Bulwarks:* low plank wall around the top deck.
2. Women accused of witchcraft in 17th-century Salem. During the writing of *Moby-Dick* Melville read with great interest in the *Quarterly Review* a scholarly study of the persecution of witches (see Sanborn p. 582, herein).
3. Sloppy, dirty. Ishmael's conjectures about the subject of the painting include the following. *Chaos;* the state of the universe before the creation (see *Paradise Lost,* 1667, 2.890 ff.). *The Black Sea:* in western Asia. *Primal elements:* earth, air, fire, and water. *Blasted heath:* as in *Macbeth* 1.3.77 or *Paradise Lost* 1.615 (the familiar "blasted heath" in *King Lear* is only an editorial stage direction, not in the text). *Winter scene:* in the imaginary sunny Hyperborean region beyond the North Wind. *The breaking up of the ice-bound stream of Time:* compared to the annual thunderous explosive spring breakup of the Hudson River ice Melville had witnessed near Albany. *Cape-Horner:* a whaleship in a tempest off Cape Horn with a sperm whale impaled on its three mastheads.
4. The first of many uses of this word to mean "whale."

The opposite wall of this entry was hung all over with a heathenish array of monstrous clubs and spears. Some were thickly set with glittering teeth resembling ivory saws; others were tufted with knots of human hair; and one was sickle-shaped, with a vast handle, sweeping round like the segment made in the new-mown grass by a long-armed mower. You shuddered as you gazed, and wondered what monstrous cannibal and savage could ever have gone a death-harvesting with such a hacking, horrifying implement. Mixed with these were rusty old whaling lances and harpoons all broken and deformed. Some were storied weapons. With this once long lance, now wildly elbowed, fifty years ago did Nathan Swain kill fifteen whales between a sunrise and a sunset. And that harpoon—so like a corkscrew now—was flung in Javan seas, and run away with by a whale, years afterwards slain off the Cape of Blanco.[5] The original iron entered nigh the tail, and, like a restless needle sojourning in the body of a man, travelled full forty feet, and at last was found imbedded in the hump.

Crossing this dusky entry, and on through yon low-arched way—cut through what in old times must have been a great central chimney with fire-places all round—you enter the public room. A still duskier place is this, with such low ponderous beams above, and such old wrinkled planks beneath, that you would almost fancy you trod some old craft's cockpits, especially of such a howling night, when this corner-anchored old ark rocked so furiously. On one side stood a long, low, shelf-like table covered with cracked glass cases, filled with dusty rarities gathered from this wide world's remotest nooks. Projecting from the further angle of the room stands a dark-looking den—the bar—a rude attempt at a right whale's head. Be that how it may, there stands the vast arched bone of the whale's jaw, so wide, a coach might almost drive beneath it. Within are shabby shelves, ranged round with old decanters, bottles, flasks; and in those jaws of swift destruction, like another cursed Jonah[6] (by which name indeed they called him), bustles a little withered old man, who, for their money, dearly sells the sailors deliriums and death.

Abominable are the tumblers into which he pours his poison. Though true cylinders without—within, the villanous green goggling glasses[7] deceitfully tapered downwards to a cheating bottom. Parallel meridians rudely pecked into the glass, surround these footpads' goblets. Fill to *this* mark, and your charge is but a penny; to *this* a penny more; and so on to the full glass—the Cape Horn measure,[8] which you may gulph down for a shilling.

Upon entering the place I found a number of young seamen gathered about a table, examining by a dim light divers specimens of *skrimshander*.[9] I sought the landlord, and telling him I desired to be accommodated with a room, received for answer that his house was full—not a bed unoccu-

---

5. That is, the whale carried the harpoon from the East Indies (Java) to this cape off the Peruvian coast of South America.
6. The story of Jonah and the great fish is in Jonah 1–2. *Swift destruction:* see 2 Peter 2.1, where "false prophets" and "false teachers" shall bring "upon themselves swift destruction."
7. The doubly deceitful glasses are tapered rather than being true cylinders and also sit on false bottoms, so they look deeper than they are. These glasses rob drinkers as flagrantly as thieves lurking along roads rob passersby.
8. The full glass, thought (mistakenly) to keep the drinker warm in such a frigid place as Cape Horn.
9. Also "scrimshaw." See ch. 57, second paragraph.

pied. "But avast,"[1] he added, tapping his forehead, "you haint no objections to sharing a harpooneer's blanket, have ye? I s'pose you are goin' a whalin', so you'd better get used to that sort of thing."

I told him that I never liked to sleep two in a bed;[2] that if I should ever do so, it would depend upon who the harpooneer might be, and that if he (the landlord) really had no other place for me, and the harpooneer was not decidedly objectionable, why rather than wander further about a strange town on so bitter a night, I would put up with the half of any decent man's blanket.

"I thought so. All right; take a seat. Supper?—you want supper? Supper 'll be ready directly."

I sat down on an old wooden settle, carved all over like a bench on the Battery. At one end a ruminating tar was still further adorning it with his jack-knife, stooping over and diligently working away at the space between his legs. He was trying his hand at a ship under full sail, but he didn't make much headway, I thought.

At last some four or five of us were summoned to our meal in an adjoining room. It was cold as Iceland—no fire at all—the landlord said he couldn't afford it. Nothing but two dismal tallow candles, each in a winding sheet. We were fain to button up our monkey jackets,[3] and hold to our lips cups of scalding tea with our half frozen fingers. But the fare was of the most substantial kind—not only meat and potatoes, but dumplings; good heavens! dumplings for supper! One young fellow in a green box coat, addressed himself to these dumplings in a most direful manner.

"My boy," said the landlord, "you'll have the nightmare to a dead sartainty."

"Landlord," I whispered, "that aint the harpooneer, is it?"

"Oh, no," said he, looking a sort of diabolically funny, "the harpooneer is a dark complexioned chap. He never eats dumplings, he don't—he eats nothing but steaks, and likes 'em rare."

"The devil he does," says I. "Where is that harpooneer? Is he here?"

"He'll be here afore long," was the answer.

I could not help it, but I began to feel suspicious of this "dark complexioned" harpooneer. At any rate, I made up my mind that if it so turned out that we should sleep together, he must undress and get into bed before I did.

Supper over, the company went back to the bar-room, when, knowing not what else to do with myself, I resolved to spend the rest of the evening as a looker on.

Presently a rioting noise was heard without. Starting up, the landlord cried, "That's the Grampus's crew. I seed her reported in the offing this morning; a four years' voyage, and a full ship. Hurrah, boys; now we'll have the latest news from the Feegees."[4]

---

1. Stop. Ishmael's humor here depends on the contrast of the landlord's dialect with his own rather prissy formality.
2. Two (or more) in a bed or on the floor together was common in crowded inns and homes; all American travelers (from the backwoods and small-town lawyer Abraham Lincoln to the Harvard-educated minister-lecturer Ralph Waldo Emerson) had to make do with such accommodations.
3. Tight fitting and waist length. *Winding sheet:* used to wrap a corpse; here, the shrouds around the base of the candles are formed of melted and congealed tallow grease.
4. The Fiji Islands, in the southwest Pacific.

A tramping of sea boots was heard in the entry; the door was flung open, and in rolled a wild set of mariners enough. Enveloped in their shaggy watch coats, and with their heads muffled in woollen comforters,[5] all bedarned and ragged, and their beards stiff with icicles, they seemed an eruption of bears from Labrador. They had just landed from their boat, and this was the first house they entered. No wonder, then, that they made a straight wake for the whale's mouth—the bar—when the wrinkled little old Jonah, there officiating, soon poured them out brimmers all round. One complained of a bad cold in his head, upon which Jonah mixed him a pitch-like potion of gin and molasses, which he swore was a sovereign cure for all colds and catarrhs whatsoever, never mind of how long standing, or whether caught off the coast of Labrador, or on the weather side of an ice-island.

The liquor soon mounted into their heads, as it generally does even with the arrantest topers newly landed from sea, and they began capering about most obstreperously.

I observed, however, that one of them held somewhat aloof, and though he seemed desirous not to spoil the hilarity of his shipmates by his own sober face, yet upon the whole he refrained from making as much noise as the rest. This man interested me at once; and since the sea-gods had ordained that he should soon become my shipmate (though but a sleeping-partner[6] one, so far as this narrative is concerned), I will here venture upon a little description of him. He stood full six feet in height, with noble shoulders, and a chest like a coffer-dam.[7] I have seldom seen such brawn in a man. His face was deeply brown and burnt, making his white teeth dazzling by the contrast; while in the deep shadows of his eyes floated some reminiscences that did not seem to give him much joy. His voice at once announced that he was a Southerner, and from his fine stature, I thought he must be one of those tall mountaineers from the Alleganian Ridge in Virginia. When the revelry of his companions had mounted to its height, this man slipped away unobserved, and I saw no more of him till he became my comrade[8] on the sea. In a few minutes, however, he was missed by his shipmates, and being, it seems, for some reason a huge favorite with them, they raised a cry of "Bulkington! Bulkington! where's Bulkington?" and darted out of the house in pursuit of him.

It was now about nine o'clock, and the room seeming almost supernaturally quiet after these orgies, I began to congratulate myself upon a little plan that had occurred to me just previous to the entrance of the seamen.

No man prefers to sleep two in a bed. In fact, you would a good deal rather not sleep with your own brother. I don't know how it is, but people like to be private when they are sleeping. And when it comes to sleeping

5. Big knitted scarves. *Watch coats:* long overcoats for standing watch in cold or stormy weather.
6. Not someone who alternates with another in occupying the same narrow bunk ("hot bunking," which would not happen on a whaler but might happen on a warship, one sailor vacating a bunk so an off-duty sailor could sleep in it). Ishmael means a secret partner, one who puts up money for a business but never takes any visible part in managing it. Bulkington's importance to the book, in other words, is greater than would appear from the number of times he takes part in the action; it may well be that Melville initially envisioned a larger role for him then brusquely wrote him out with this passage and with ch. 22.
7. Here, tall watertight box fixed to the side of a ship for making repairs below the waterline.
8. Elsewhere only Queequeg is called Ishmael's comrade.

with an unknown stranger, in a strange inn, in a strange town, and that stranger a harpooneer, then your objections indefinitely multiply. Nor was there any earthly reason why I as a sailor should sleep two in a bed, more than anybody else; for sailors no more sleep two in a bed at sea, than bachelor Kings do ashore. To be sure they all sleep together in one apartment, but you have your own hammock,[9] and cover yourself with your own blanket, and sleep in your own skin.

The more I pondered over this harpooneer, the more I abominated the thought of sleeping with him. It was fair to presume that being a harpooneer, his linen or woollen,[1] as the case might be, would not be of the tidiest, certainly none of the finest. I began to twitch all over. Besides, it was getting late, and any decent harpooneer ought to be home and going bedwards. Suppose now, he should tumble in upon me at midnight—how could I tell from what vile hole he had been coming?

"Landlord! I've changed my mind about that harpooneer.—I shan't sleep with him. I'll try the bench here."

"Just as you please; I'm sorry I cant spare ye a table-cloth for a mattress, and it's a plaguy rough board here"—feeling of the knots and notches. "But wait a bit, Skrimshander; I've got a carpenter's plane there in the bar—wait, I say, and I'll make ye snug enough." So saying he procured the plane; and with his old silk handkerchief first dusting the bench, vigorously set to planing away at my bed, the while grinning like an ape. The shavings flew right and left; till at last the plane-iron came bump against an indestructible knot. The landlord was near spraining his wrist, and I told him for heaven's sake to quit—the bed was soft enough to suit me, and I did not know how all the planing in the world could make eider down of a pine plank. So gathering up the shavings with another grin, and throwing them into the great stove in the middle of the room, he went about his business, and left me in a brown study.[2]

I now took the measure of the bench, and found that it was a foot too short; but that could be mended with a chair. But it was a foot too narrow, and the other bench in the room was about four inches higher than the planed one—so there was no yoking them. I then placed the first bench lengthwise along the only clear space against the wall, leaving a little interval between, for my back to settle down in. But I soon found that there came such a draught of cold air over me from under the sill of the window, that this plan would never do at all, especially as another current from the rickety door met the one from the window, and both together formed a series of small whirlwinds in the immediate vicinity of the spot where I had thought to spend the night.

The devil fetch that harpooneer, thought I, but stop, couldn't I steal a march on him—bolt his door inside, and jump into his bed, not to be wakened by the most violent knockings? It seemed no bad idea; but upon second thoughts I dismissed it. For who could tell but what the next morning, so soon as I popped out of the room, the harpooneer might be standing in the entry, all ready to knock me down!

9. Bed, bunk. Warships, including the one on which Melville had served, had actual hammocks, but whaleships had narrow bunks.
1. Underwear (the lower garment was called "drawers," as in ch. 87).
2. Profound meditative state (idiomatic).

Still, looking round me again, and seeing no possible chance of spending a sufferable night unless in some other person's bed, I began to think that after all I might be cherishing unwarrantable prejudices against this unknown harpooneer. Thinks I, I'll wait a while; he must be dropping in before long. I'll have a good look at him then, and perhaps we may become jolly good bedfellows after all—there's no telling.

But though the other boarders kept coming in by ones, twos, and threes, and going to bed, yet no sign of my harpooneer.

"Landlord!" said I, "what sort of a chap is he—does he always keep such late hours?" It was now hard upon twelve o'clock.

The landlord chuckled again with his lean chuckle, and seemed to be mightily tickled at something beyond my comprehension. "No," he answered, "generally he's an airley bird—airley to bed and airley to rise—yes, he's the bird what catches the worm.[3]—But to-night he went out a peddling, you see, and I don't see what on airth keeps him so late, unless, may be, he can't sell his head."

"Can't sell his head?—What sort of a bamboozling story is this you are telling me?" getting into a towering rage. "Do you pretend to say, landlord, that this harpooneer is actually engaged this blessed Saturday night, or rather Sunday morning, in peddling his head around this town?"

"That's precisely it," said the landlord, "and I told him he couldn't sell it here, the market's overstocked."

"With what?" shouted I.

"With heads to be sure; ain't there too many heads in the world?"

"I tell you what it is, landlord," said I, quite calmly, "you'd better stop spinning that yarn to me—I'm not green."[4]

"May be not," taking out a stick and whittling a toothpick, "but I rayther guess you'll be done _brown_[5] if that ere harpooneer hears you a slanderin' his head."

"I'll break it for him," said I, now flying into a passion again at this unaccountable farrago of the landlord's.

"It's broke a'ready," said he.

"Broke," said I—"_broke_, do you mean?"

"Sartain, and that's the very reason he can't sell it, I guess."

"Landlord," said I, going up to him as cool as Mt. Hecla in a snow storm,[6]—"landlord, stop whittling. You and I must understand one another, and that too without delay. I come to your house and want a bed; you tell me you can only give me half a one; that the other half belongs to a certain harpooneer. And about this harpooneer, whom I have not yet seen, you persist in telling me the most mystifying and exasperating stories, tending to beget in me an uncomfortable feeling towards the man whom you design for my bedfellow—a sort of connexion, landlord, which is an intimate and confidential one in the highest degree. I now demand of you to speak out and tell me who and what this harpooneer is, and whether I shall be in all respects safe to spend the night with him. And in

3. The landlord quotes two proverbs (the first of which is a couplet concluding "Makes a man healthy, wealthy, and wise").
4. Innocent, naive, and therefore gullible.
5. Overcooked, mistreated.
6. Externally cool but inwardly furious. Mount Hecla, in Iceland, had been in the news for spectacular volcanic activity as recently as September 1845.

the first place, you will be so good as to unsay that story about selling his
head, which if true I take to be good evidence that this harpooneer is stark
mad, and I've no idea of sleeping with a madman; and you, sir, *you* I mean,
landlord, *you,* sir, by trying to induce me to do so knowingly, would
thereby render yourself liable to a criminal prosecution."

"Wall," said the landlord, fetching a long breath, "that's a purty long sar-
mon for a chap that rips a little now and then. But be easy, be easy, this
here harpooneer I have been tellin' you of has just arrived from the south
seas, where he bought up a lot of 'balmed New Zealand heads (great
curios, you know), and he's sold all on 'em but one, and that one he's trying to sell to-night, cause to-morrow's Sunday, and it would not do to be
sellin' human heads about the streets when folks is goin' to churches. He
wanted to, last Sunday, but I stopped him just as he was goin' out of the
door with four heads strung on a string, for all the airth like a string of
inions."

This account cleared up the otherwise unaccountable mystery, and
showed that the landlord, after all, had had no idea of fooling me—but at
the same time what could I think of a harpooneer who stayed out of a
Saturday night clean into the holy Sabbath, engaged in such a cannibal
business as selling the heads of dead idolators?

"Depend upon it, landlord, that harpooneer is a dangerous man."

"He pays reg'lar," was the rejoinder. "But come, it's getting dreadful
late, you had better be turning flukes—it's a nice bed: Sal and me slept
in that ere bed the night we were spliced.[7] There's plenty room for two
to kick about in that bed; it's an almighty big bed that. Why, afore we
give it up, Sal used to put our Sam and little Johnny in the foot of it.
But I got a dreaming and sprawling about one night, and somehow, Sam
got pitched on the floor, and came near breaking his arm. Arter that,
Sal said it wouldn't do. Come along here, I'll give ye a glim in a jiffy;"
and so saying he lighted a candle and held it towards me, offering to
lead the way. But I stood irresolute; when looking at a clock in the corner, he exclaimed "I vum[8] it's Sunday—you won't see that harpooneer
to-night; he's come to anchor somewhere—come along then; *do* come;
won't ye come?"

I considered the matter a moment, and then up stairs we went, and I
was ushered into a small room, cold as a clam,[9] and furnished, sure
enough, with a prodigious bed, almost big enough indeed for any four harpooneers to sleep abreast.

"There," said the landlord, placing the candle on a crazy old sea chest
that did double duty as a wash-stand and centre table; "there, make yourself comfortable now, and good night to ye." I turned round from eyeing
the bed, but he had disappeared.

Folding back the counterpane, I stooped over the bed. Though none of
the most elegant, it yet stood the scrutiny tolerably well. I then glanced
round the room; and besides the bedstead and centre table, could see no
other furniture belonging to the place, but a rude shelf, the four walls,

---

7. Married. *Turning flukes:* turn into bed like a whale diving down into the ocean. *Flukes:* the tail,
   "two broad, firm, flat palms" (ch. 86).
8. Vow, swear. *Glim:* light.
9. A proverbial comparison.

and a papered fireboard representing a man striking[1] a whale. Of things not properly belonging to the room, there was a hammock lashed up, and thrown upon the floor in one corner; also a large seaman's bag, containing the harpooneer's wardrobe no doubt, in lieu of a land trunk. Likewise, there was a parcel of outlandish bone fish hooks on the shelf over the fireplace, and a tall harpoon standing at the head of the bed.

But what is this on the chest? I took it up, and held it close to the light, and felt it, and smelt it, and tried every way possible to arrive at some satisfactory conclusion concerning it. I can compare it to nothing but a large door mat, ornamented at the edges with little tinkling tags something like the stained porcupine quills round an Indian moccasin. There was a hole or slit in the middle of this mat, the same as in South American ponchos. But could it be possible that any sober harpooneer would get into a door mat, and parade the streets of any Christian town in that sort of guise? I put it on, to try it, and it weighed me down like a hamper, being uncommonly shaggy and thick, and I thought a little damp, as though this mysterious harpooneer had been wearing it of a rainy day. I went up in it to a bit of glass stuck against the wall, and I never saw such a sight in my life. I tore myself out of it in such a hurry that I gave myself a kink in the neck.

I sat down on the side of the bed, and commenced thinking about this head-peddling harpooneer, and his door mat. After thinking some time on the bed-side, I got up and took off my monkey jacket, and then stood in the middle of the room thinking. I then took off my coat, and thought a little more in my shirt sleeves. But beginning to feel very cold now, half undressed as I was, and remembering what the landlord said about the harpooneer's not coming home at all that night, it being so very late, I made no more ado, but jumped out of my pantaloons and boots, and then blowing out the light tumbled into bed, and commended myself to the care of heaven.

Whether that mattress was stuffed with corn-cobs or broken crockery, there is no telling, but I rolled about a good deal, and could not sleep for a long time. At last I slid off into a light doze, and had pretty nearly made a good offing towards the land of Nod, when I heard a heavy footfall in the passage, and saw a glimmer of light come into the room from under the door.

Lord save me, thinks I, that must be the harpooneer, the infernal head-peddler. But I lay perfectly still, and resolved not to say a word till spoken to. Holding a light in one hand, and that identical New Zealand head in the other, the stranger entered the room, and without looking towards the bed, placed his candle a good way off from me on the floor in one corner, and then began working away at the knotted cords of the large bag I before spoke of as being in the room. I was all eagerness to see his face, but he kept it averted for some time while employed in unlacing the bag's mouth. This accomplished, however, he turned round—when, good heavens! what a sight! Such a face! It was of a dark, purplish, yellow color, here and there stuck over with large, blackish looking squares. Yes, it's just as I thought, he's a terrible bedfellow; he's been in a fight, got dreadfully cut, and here he is, just from the surgeon. But at that moment he chanced to turn his face

---

1. Harpooning. *Fireboard:* a covering for closing a fireplace when not in use.

so towards the light, that I plainly saw they could not be sticking-plasters at all, those black squares on his cheeks. They were stains of some sort or other. At first I knew not what to make of this; but soon an inkling of the truth occurred to me. I remembered a story of a white man—a whaleman too—who, falling among the cannibals, had been tattooed by them. I concluded that this harpooneer, in the course of his distant voyages, must have met with a similar adventure. And what is it, thought I, after all! It's only his outside; a man can be honest in any sort of skin. But then, what to make of his unearthly complexion, that part of it, I mean, lying round about, and completely independent of the squares of tattooing. To be sure, it might be nothing but a good coat of tropical tanning; but I never heard of a hot sun's tanning a white man into a purplish yellow one. However, I had never been in the South Seas; and perhaps the sun there produced these extraordinary effects upon the skin. Now, while all these ideas were passing through me like lightning, this harpooneer never noticed me at all. But, after some difficulty having opened his bag, he commenced fumbling in it, and presently pulled out a sort of tomahawk,[2] and a seal-skin wallet with the hair on. Placing these on the old chest in the middle of the room, he then took the New Zealand head—a ghastly thing enough—and crammed it down into the bag. He now took off his hat—a new beaver hat[3]—when I came nigh singing out with fresh surprise. There was no hair on his head—none to speak of at least—nothing but a small scalp-knot twisted up on his forehead. His bald purplish head now looked for all the world like a mildewed skull. Had not the stranger stood between me and the door, I would have bolted out of it quicker than ever I bolted a dinner.

Even as it was, I thought something of slipping out of the window, but it was the second floor back.[4] I am no coward, but what to make of this head-peddling purple rascal altogether passed my comprehension. Ignorance is the parent of fear, and being completely nonplussed and confounded about the stranger, I confess I was now as much afraid of him as if it was the devil himself who had thus broken into my room at the dead of night. In fact, I was so afraid of him that I was not game enough just then to address him, and demand a satisfactory answer concerning what seemed inexplicable in him.

Meanwhile, he continued the business of undressing, and at last showed his chest and arms. As I live, these covered parts of him were checkered with the same squares as his face; his back, too, was all over the same dark squares; he seemed to have been in a Thirty Years' War, and just escaped from it with a sticking-plaster shirt.[5] Still more, his very legs were marked, as if a parcel of dark green frogs were running up the trunks of young palms. It was now quite plain that he must be some abominable savage or other shipped aboard of a whaleman in the South Seas, and so landed in this Christian country. I quaked to think of it. A peddler of

2. A then-common curio, with a blade on one side of the head and a pipe bowl on the other side, meant to symbolize warfare (killing and scalping) and peace (all parties puffing at the same pipe when ratifying a peace treaty).
3. Stovepipe hat, now familiar from photographs of Abraham Lincoln. Gregory Peck as Captain Ahab wore one in the 1956 Warner Brothers film, though the book puts Ahab in soft "slouched" hats (chs. 30, 31, 130, and 132).
4. Room at the back of the second-floor hallway.
5. One made up of bandages, such as might cover various wounds suffered during the long 17th-century European war.

heads too—perhaps the heads of his own brothers. He might take a fancy to mine—heavens! look at that tomahawk!

But there was no time for shuddering, for now the savage went about something that completely fascinated my attention, and convinced me that he must indeed be a heathen. Going to his heavy grego, or wrapall, or dreadnaught,[6] which he had previously hung on a chair, he fumbled in the pockets, and produced at length a curious little deformed image with a hunch on its back, and exactly the color of a three days' old Congo baby. Remembering the embalmed head, at first I almost thought that this black manikin was a real baby preserved in some similar manner. But seeing that it was not at all limber, and that it glistened a good deal like polished ebony, I concluded that it must be nothing but a wooden idol, which indeed it proved to be. For now the savage goes up to the empty fire-place, and removing the papered fire-board, sets up this little hunchbacked image, like a tenpin, between the andirons. The chimney jambs and all the bricks inside were very sooty, so that I thought this fire-place made a very appropriate little shrine or chapel for his Congo idol.

I now screwed my eyes hard towards the half hidden image, feeling but ill at ease meantime—to see what was next to follow. First he takes about a double handful of shavings out of his grego pocket, and places them carefully before the idol; then laying a bit of ship biscuit on top and applying the flame from the lamp, he kindled the shavings into a sacrificial blaze. Presently, after many hasty snatches into the fire, and still hastier withdrawals of his fingers (whereby he seemed to be scorching them badly), he at last succeeded in drawing out the biscuit; then blowing off the heat and ashes a little, he made a polite offer of it to the little negro. But the little devil did not seem to fancy such dry sort of fare at all; he never moved his lips. All these strange antics were accompanied by still stranger guttural noises from the devotee, who seemed to be praying in a sing-song or else singing some pagan psalmody or other, during which his face twitched about in the most unnatural manner. At last extinguishing the fire, he took the idol up very unceremoniously, and bagged it again in his grego pocket as carelessly as if he were a sportsman bagging a dead woodcock.

All these queer proceedings increased my uncomfortableness, and seeing him now exhibiting strong symptoms of concluding his business operations, and jumping into bed with me, I thought it was high time, now or never, before the light was put out, to break the spell in which I had so long been bound.

But the interval I spent in deliberating what to say, was a fatal one. Taking up his tomahawk from the table, he examined the head of it for an instant, and then holding it to the light, with his mouth at the handle, he puffed out great clouds of tobacco smoke. The next moment the light was extinguished, and this wild cannibal, tomahawk between his teeth, sprang into bed with me. I sang out, I could not help it now; and giving a sudden grunt of astonishment he began feeling me.

Stammering out something, I knew not what, I rolled away from him against the wall, and then conjured him, whoever or whatever he might be,

---

6. Three kinds of heavy overcoats. The humor arises from Ishmael's difficulty in defining Queequeg's garment.

to keep quiet, and let me get up and light the lamp again. But his guttural responses satisfied me at once that he but ill comprehended my meaning.

"Who-e debel[7] you?"—he at last said—"you no speak-e, dam-me, I kill-e." And so saying the lighted tomahawk began flourishing about me in the dark.

"Landlord, for God's sake, Peter Coffin!" shouted I. "Landlord! Watch! Coffin! Angels! save me!"

"Speak-e! tell-ee me who-ee be, or dam-me, I kill-e!" again growled the cannibal, while his horrid flourishings of the tomahawk scattered the hot tobacco ashes about me till I thought my linen would get on fire. But thank heaven, at that moment the landlord came into the room light in hand, and leaping from the bed I ran up to him.

"Don't be afraid now," said he, grinning again. "Queequeg here wouldn't harm a hair of your head."

"Stop your grinning," shouted I, "and why didn't you tell me that that infernal harpooneer was a cannibal?"

"I thought ye know'd it;—didn't I tell ye, he was a peddlin' heads around town?—but turn flukes again and go to sleep. Queequeg, look here—you sabbee me, I sabbee you—this man sleepe you—you sabbee?"—

"Me sabbee plenty"—grunted Queequeg, puffing away at his pipe and sitting up in bed.

"You gettee in," he added, motioning to me with his tomahawk, and throwing the clothes to one side. He really did this in not only a civil but a really kind and charitable way. I stood looking at him a moment. For all his tattooings he was on the whole a clean, comely looking cannibal. What's all this fuss I have been making about, thought I to myself—the man's a human being just as I am: he has just as much reason to fear me, as I have to be afraid of him. Better sleep with a sober cannibal than a drunken Christian.

"Landlord," said I, "tell him to stash his tomahawk there, or pipe, or whatever you call it; tell him to stop smoking, in short, and I will turn in with him. But I don't fancy having a man smoking in bed with me. It's dangerous. Besides, I aint insured."

This being told to Queequeg, he at once complied, and again politely motioned me to get into bed—rolling over to one side as much as to say— I wont touch a leg of ye.

"Good night, landlord," said I, "you may go."

I turned in, and never slept better in my life.

Chapter 4

The Counterpane

Upon waking next morning about daylight, I found Queequeg's arm thrown over me in the most loving and affectionate manner. You had almost thought I had been his wife. The counterpane was of patchwork,

---

7. Devil. Queequeg speaks in the presumably universally understood pidgin English, which the landlord uses just below.

full of odd little parti-colored squares and triangles; and this arm of his tattooed all over with an interminable Cretan labyrinth[1] of a figure, no two parts of which were of one precise shade—owing I suppose to his keeping his arm at sea unmethodically in sun and shade, his shirt sleeves irregularly rolled up at various times—this same arm of his, I say, looked for all the world like a strip of that same patchwork quilt. Indeed, partly lying on it as the arm did when I first awoke, I could hardly tell it from the quilt, they so blended their hues together; and it was only by the sense of weight and pressure that I could tell that Queequeg was hugging me.

My sensations were strange. Let me try to explain them. When I was a child, I well remember a somewhat similar circumstance that befell me; whether it was a reality or a dream, I never could entirely settle. The circumstance was this. I had been cutting up some caper or other—I think it was trying to crawl up the chimney, as I had seen a little sweep do a few days previous; and my stepmother who, somehow or other, was all the time whipping me, or sending me to bed supperless,—my mother dragged me by the legs out of the chimney and packed me off to bed, though it was only two o'clock in the afternoon of the 21st June, the longest day in the year in our hemisphere. I felt dreadfully. But there was no help for it, so up stairs I went to my little room in the third floor, undressed myself as slowly as possible so as to kill time, and with a bitter sigh got between the sheets.

I lay there dismally calculating that sixteen entire hours must elapse before I could hope for a resurrection. Sixteen hours in bed! the small of my back ached to think of it. And it was so light too; the sun shining in at the window, and a great rattling of coaches in the streets, and the sound of gay voices all over the house. I felt worse and worse—at last I got up, dressed, and softly going down in my stockinged feet, sought out my stepmother, and suddenly threw myself at her feet, beseeching her as a particular favor to give me a good slippering for my misbehavior; anything indeed but condemning me to lie abed such an unendurable length of time. But she was the best and most conscientious of stepmothers, and back I had to go to my room. For several hours I lay there broad awake, feeling a great deal worse than I have ever done since, even from the greatest subsequent misfortunes. At last I must have fallen into a troubled nightmare of a doze; and slowly waking from it—half steeped in dreams— I opened my eyes, and the before sun-lit room was now wrapped in outer darkness. Instantly I felt a shock running through all my frame; nothing was to be seen, and nothing was to be heard; but a supernatural hand seemed placed in mine. My arm hung over the counterpane, and the nameless, unimaginable, silent form or phantom, to which the hand belonged, seemed closely seated by my bedside. For what seemed ages piled on ages, I lay there, frozen with the most awful fears, not daring to drag away my hand; yet ever thinking that if I could but stir it one single inch, the horrid spell would be broken. I knew not how this consciousness at last glided away from me; but waking in the morning, I shudderingly remembered it all, and for days and weeks and months afterwards I lost

1. In Greek mythology, the maze that imprisoned the half-human, half-bull Minotaur.

myself in confounding attempts to explain the mystery. Nay, to this very
hour, I often puzzle myself with it.

Now, take away the awful fear, and my sensations at feeling the supernatural hand in mine were very similar, in their strangeness, to those
which I experienced on waking up and seeing Queequeg's pagan arm
thrown round me. But at length all the past night's events soberly
recurred, one by one, in fixed reality, and then I lay only alive to the comical predicament. For though I tried to move his arm—unlock his bridegroom clasp—yet, sleeping as he was, he still hugged me tightly, as though
naught but death should part us twain. I now strove to rouse him—
"Queequeg!"—but his only answer was a snore. I then rolled over, my
neck feeling as if it were in a horse-collar; and suddenly felt a slight
scratch. Throwing aside the counterpane, there lay the tomahawk sleeping by the savage's side, as if it were a hatchet-faced baby. A pretty pickle,
truly, thought I; abed here in a strange house in the broad day, with a cannibal and a tomahawk! "Queequeg!—in the name of goodness, Queequeg,
wake!" At length, by dint of much wriggling, and loud and incessant
expostulations upon the unbecomingness of his hugging a fellow male in
that matrimonial sort of style, I succeeded in extracting a grunt; and
presently, he drew back his arm, shook himself all over like a
Newfoundland dog just from the water, and sat up in bed, stiff as a pike-
staff, looking at me, and rubbing his eyes as if he did not altogether
remember how I came to be there, though a dim consciousness of knowing something about me seemed slowly dawning over him. Meanwhile, I
lay quietly eyeing him, having no serious misgivings now, and bent upon
narrowly observing so curious a creature. When, at last, his mind seemed
made up touching the character of his bedfellow, and he became, as it
were, reconciled to the fact; he jumped out upon the floor, and by certain
signs and sounds gave me to understand that, if it pleased me, he would
dress first and then leave me to dress afterwards, having the whole apartment to myself. Thinks I, Queequeg, under the circumstances, this is a
very civilized overture; but, the truth is, these savages have an innate
sense of delicacy, say what you will; it is marvellous how essentially polite
they are. I pay this particular compliment to Queequeg, because he
treated me with so much civility and consideration, while I was guilty of
great rudeness; staring at him from the bed, and watching all his toilette
motions; for the time my curiosity getting the better of my breeding.
Nevertheless, a man like Queequeg you don't see every day, he and his
ways were well worth unusual regarding.

He commenced dressing at top by donning his beaver hat, a very tall
one, by the by, and then—still minus his trowsers—he hunted up his
boots. What under the heavens he did it for, I cannot tell, but his next
movement was to crush himself—boots in hand, and hat on—under the
bed; when, from sundry violent gaspings and strainings, I inferred he was
hard at work booting himself; though by no law of propriety that I ever
heard of, is any man required to be private when putting on his boots. But
Queequeg, do you see, was a creature in the transition state—neither
caterpillar nor butterfly. He was just enough civilized to show off his out-
landishness in the strangest possible manner. His education was not yet
completed. He was an undergraduate. If he had not been a small degree

civilized, he very probably would not have troubled himself with boots at
all; but then, if he had not been still a savage, he never would have dreamt
of getting under the bed to put them on. At last, he emerged with his hat
very much dented and crushed down over his eyes, and began creaking
and limping about the room, as if, not being much accustomed to boots,
his pair of damp, wrinkled cowhide ones—probably not made to order
either—rather pinched and tormented him at the first go off of a bitter
cold morning.

Seeing, now, that there were no curtains to the window, and that the
street being very narrow, the house opposite commanded a plain view into
the room, and observing more and more the indecorous figure that
Queequeg made, made, staving[2] about with little else but his hat and
boots on; I begged him as well as I could, to accelerate his toilet somewhat, and particularly to get into his pantaloons as soon as possible. He
complied, and then proceeded to wash himself. At that time in the morning any Christian would have washed his face, but Queequeg, to my
amazement, contented himself with restricting his ablutions to his chest,
arms, and hands. He then donned his waistcoat, and taking up a piece of
hard soap on the wash-stand centre-table, dipped it into water and commenced lathering his face. I was watching to see where he kept his razor,
when lo and behold, he takes the harpoon from the bed corner, slips out
the long wooden stock, unsheathes the head, whets it a little on his boot,
and striding up to the bit of mirror against the wall, begins a vigorous
scraping, or rather harpooning of his cheeks. Thinks I, Queequeg, this is
using Rogers's[3] best cutlery with a vengeance. Afterwards I wondered the
less at this operation when I came to know of what fine steel the head of
a harpoon is made, and how exceedingly sharp the long straight edges are
always kept.

The rest of his toilet was soon achieved, and he proudly marched out of
the room, wrapped up in his great pilot monkey jacket, and sporting his
harpoon like a marshal's baton.

Chapter 5

Breakfast

I quickly followed suit, and descending into the bar-room accosted the
grinning landlord very pleasantly. I cherished no malice towards him,
though he had been skylarking with me not a little in the matter of my
bedfellow.

However, a good laugh is a mighty good thing, and rather too scarce a
good thing; the more's the pity. So, if any one man, in his own proper person, afford stuff for a good joke to anybody, let him not be backward, but
let him cheerfully allow himself to spend and be spent in that way. And
the man that has anything bountifully laughable about him, be sure there
is more in that man than you perhaps think for.

2. Stalking about rapidly.
3. American silverware company.

The bar-room was now full of the boarders who had been dropping in the night previous, and whom I had not as yet had a good look at. They were nearly all whalemen; chief mates, and second mates, and third mates, and sea carpenters, and sea coopers, and sea blacksmiths, and harpooneers, and ship keepers;[1] a brown and brawny company, with bosky beards; an unshorn, shaggy set, all wearing monkey jackets for morning gowns.

You could pretty plainly tell how long each one had been ashore. This young fellow's healthy cheek is like a sun-toasted pear in hue, and would seem to smell almost as musky; he cannot have been three days landed from his Indian voyage. That man next him looks a few shades lighter; you might say a touch of satin wood[2] is in him. In the complexion of a third still lingers a tropic tawn, but slightly bleached withal; *he* doubtless has tarried whole weeks ashore. But who could show a cheek like Queequeg? which, barred with various tints, seemed like the Andes' western slope, to show forth in one array, contrasting climates, zone by zone.

"Grub, ho!" now cried the landlord, flinging open a door, and in we went to breakfast.

They say that men who have seen the world, thereby become quite at ease in manner, quite self-possessed in company. Not always, though: Ledyard, the great New England traveller, and Mungo Park, the Scotch one;[3] of all men, they possessed the least assurance in the parlor. But perhaps the mere crossing of Siberia in a sledge drawn by dogs as Ledyard did, or the taking a long solitary walk on an empty stomach, in the negro heart of Africa, which was the sum of poor Mungo's performances—this kind of travel, I say, may not be the very best mode of attaining a high social polish. Still, for the most part, that sort of thing is to be had anywhere.

These reflections just here are occasioned by the circumstance that after we were all seated at the table, and I was preparing to hear some good stories about whaling; to my no small surprise, nearly every man maintained a profound silence. And not only that, but they looked embarrassed. Yes, here were a set of sea-dogs, many of whom without the slightest bashfulness had boarded great whales on the high seas—entire strangers to them—and duelled them dead without winking; and yet, here they sat at a social breakfast table—all of the same calling, all of kindred tastes—looking round as sheepishly at each other as though they had never been out of sight of some sheepfold among the Green Mountains.[4] A curious sight; these bashful bears, these timid warrior whalemen!

But as for Queequeg—why, Queequeg sat there among them—at the head of the table, too, it so chanced; as cool as an icicle. To be sure I cannot say much for his breeding. His greatest admirer could not have cordially justified his bringing his harpoon into breakfast with him, and using it there without ceremony; reaching over the table with it, to the imminent jeopardy of many heads, and grappling the beefsteaks towards him. But *that* was certainly very coolly done by him, and every one knows that in most people's estimation, to do anything coolly is to do it genteelly.

---

1. Crewmen who work on the ship only, and do not man its whaleboats.
2. Pale brown East Indian mahogany.
3. John Ledyard and Mungo Park were late-18th-century explorers.
4. In Vermont, but with a pun on *green,* meaning "unsophisticated."

We will not speak of all Queequeg's peculiarities here; how he eschewed coffee and hot rolls, and applied his undivided attention to beefsteaks, done rare. Enough, that when breakfast was over he withdrew like the rest into the public room, lighted his tomahawk-pipe, and was sitting there quietly digesting and smoking with his inseparable hat on, when I sallied out for a stroll.

Chapter 6

The Street

If I had been astonished at first catching a glimpse of so outlandish an individual as Queequeg circulating among the polite society of a civilized town, that astonishment soon departed upon taking my first daylight stroll through the streets of New Bedford.

In thoroughfares nigh the docks, any considerable seaport will frequently offer to view the queerest looking nondescripts from foreign parts. Even in Broadway and Chestnut streets, Mediterranean mariners will sometimes jostle the affrighted ladies. Regent street is not unknown to Lascars and Malays; and at Bombay, in the Apollo Green, live Yankees have often scared the natives. But New Bedford beats all Water street and Wapping. In these last-mentioned haunts you see only sailors; but in New Bedford, actual cannibals stand chatting at street corners; savages outright; many of whom yet carry on their bones unholy flesh. It makes a stranger stare.[1]

But, besides the Feegeeans, Tongatabooans, Erromanggoans, Pannangians, and Brighggians,[2] and, besides the wild specimens of the whaling-craft which unheeded reel about the streets, you will see other sights still more curious, certainly more comical. There weekly arrive in this town scores of green Vermonters and New Hampshire men, all athirst for gain and glory in the fishery. They are mostly young, of stalwart frames; fellows who have felled forests, and now seek to drop the axe and snatch the whale-lance. Many are as green as the Green Mountains whence they came. In some things you would think them but a few hours old. Look there! that chap strutting round the corner. He wears a beaver hat and swallow-tailed coat, girdled with a sailor-belt and sheath-knife. Here comes another with a sou'-wester and a bombazine cloak.[3]

1. Mediterranean sailors are seen on Broadway (in New York) and on Chestnut Street (in Philadelphia). Lascars from India and Malays from the East Indies show up in Regent Street in London. In Bombay, India, the natives may be frightened by "live Yankees," American sailors; a P. T. Barnum–like joke at our egocentricity (or cultural chauvinism), by which we are normal and everyone else is strange. Water Street is in Liverpool, and Wapping is in London.
2. South Sea islanders, like Queequeg (except for the apparently fictional Brighggians).
3. The greenhorn outfits are comically incongruous. In a letter found in 1998 and now in the Berkshire Athenaeum (Pittsfield, Massachusetts), Melville's brother Gansevoort on January 14, 1841, wrote to their younger brother Allan: "Herman sent to [his friend] Fly as a parting souvenir his vest & pantaloons. The coat was exchanged at New Bedford for duck shirts &c. At sea[,] shore toggery is of no use to a sailor." Having sailed on a merchant ship to Liverpool in 1839, Melville was no greenhorn or hayseed when he went whaling (but see ch. 16 for a whaleman's contempt for the merchant service).

No town-bred dandy will compare with a country-bred one—I mean a downright bumpkin dandy—a fellow that, in the dog-days, will mow his two acres in buckskin gloves for fear of tanning his hands. Now when a country dandy like this takes it into his head to make a distinguished reputation, and joins the great whale-fishery, you should see the comical things he does upon reaching the seaport. In bespeaking his sea-outfit, he orders bell-buttons to his waistcoats; straps to his canvas trowsers. Ah, poor Hay-Seed! how bitterly will burst those straps in the first howling gale, when thou art driven, straps, buttons, and all, down the throat of the tempest.

But think not that this famous town has only harpooneers, cannibals, and bumpkins to show her visitors. Not at all. Still New Bedford is a queer place. Had it not been for us whalemen, that tract of land would this day perhaps have been in as howling condition as the coast of Labrador. As it is, parts of her back country are enough to frighten one, they look so bony. The town itself is perhaps the dearest[4] place to live in, in all New England. It is a land of oil, true enough: but not like Canaan; a land, also, of corn and wine.[5] The streets do not run with milk; nor in the spring-time do they pave them with fresh eggs. Yet, in spite of this, nowhere in all America will you find more patrician-like houses; parks and gardens more opulent, than in New Bedford. Whence came they? how planted upon this once scraggy scoria[6] of a country?

Go and gaze upon the iron emblematical harpoons round yonder lofty mansion, and your question will be answered. Yes; all these brave houses and flowery gardens came from the Atlantic, Pacific, and Indian oceans. One and all, they were harpooned and dragged up hither from the bottom of the sea. Can Herr Alexander[7] perform a feat like that?

In New Bedford, fathers, they say, give whales for dowers to their daughters, and portion off their nieces with a few porpoises a-piece. You must go to New Bedford to see a brilliant wedding; for, they say, they have reservoirs of oil in every house, and every night recklessly burn their lengths in spermaceti candles.[8]

In summer time, the town is sweet to see; full of fine maples—long avenues of green and gold. And in August, high in air, the beautiful and bountiful horse-chestnuts, candelabra-wise, proffer the passer-by their tapering upright cones of congregated blossoms. So omnipotent is art; which in many a district of New Bedford has superinduced bright terraces of flowers upon the barren refuse rocks thrown aside at creation's final day.

And the women of New Bedford, they bloom like their own red roses. But roses only bloom in summer; whereas the fine carnation of their cheeks is perennial as sunlight in the seventh heavens.[9] Elsewhere match

---

4. Most expensive. *Howling*: desolate.
5. The Promised Land into which Moses led the Hebrews. Biblical phrases note its resources of "milk and honey" (Exodus 3.8, 17) and wine, corn, and oil (2 Chronicles 31.5).
6. Rough, cindery lava.
7. German magician who performed in the United States in the 1840s. Melville had a chance to see him in Troy, New York, in 1846.
8. Expensive candles made of oil from the sperm whale's head.
9. The highest of the Islamic heavens, where one feels extreme joy.

that bloom of theirs, ye cannot, save in Salem,[1] where they tell me the young girls breathe such musk, their sailor sweethearts smell them miles off shore, as though they were drawing nigh the odorous Moluccas[2] instead of the Puritanic sands.

Chapter 7

The Chapel

In this same New Bedford there stands a Whaleman's Chapel,[1] and few are the moody fishermen, shortly bound for the Indian Ocean or Pacific, who fail to make a Sunday visit to the spot. I am sure that I did not.

Returning from my first morning stroll, I again sallied out upon this special errand. The sky had changed from clear, sunny cold, to driving sleet and mist. Wrapping myself in my shaggy jacket of the cloth called bearskin,[2] I fought my way against the stubborn storm. Entering, I found a small scattered congregation of sailors, and sailors' wives and widows. A muffled silence reigned, only broken at times by the shrieks of the storm. Each silent worshipper seemed purposely sitting apart from the other, as if each silent grief were insular and incommunicable. The chaplain had not yet arrived; and there these silent islands of men and women sat steadfastly eyeing several marble tablets, with black borders, masoned into the wall on either side the pulpit. Three of them ran something like the following, but I do not pretend to quote:—

SACRED
To the Memory
O F
JOHN TALBOT,
Who, at the age of eighteen, was lost overboard,
Near the Isle of Desolation,[3] off Patagonia,
November 1st, 1836.
THIS TABLET
Is erected to his Memory
BY HIS SISTER.

1. This tall tale about Salem girls is a private joke for Nathaniel and Sophia Hawthorne, both Salemites.
2. The Spice Islands of East Indonesia.
1. The Seaman's Bethel on Johnny-Cake Hill still standing there, opposite the whaling museum, is the one rebuilt after a fire in 1866; some of the marble cenotaphs are original, salvaged and reset.
2. Coarse woolen cloth.
3. Uninhabited Chilean island off the tip of South America.

SACRED
𝕿𝖔 𝖙𝖍𝖊 𝕸𝖊𝖒𝖔𝖗𝖞
O F
ROBERT LONG, WILLIS ELLERY,
NATHAN COLEMAN, WALTER CANNY, SETH MACY,
AND SAMUEL GLEIG,
Forming one of the boats' crews
O F
THE SHIP ELIZA,
Who were towed out of sight by a Whale,
On the Off-shore Ground[4] in the
PACIFIC,
December 31st, 1839.
THIS MARBLE
Is here placed by their surviving
Shipmates.

SACRED
𝕿𝖔 𝖙𝖍𝖊 𝕸𝖊𝖒𝖔𝖗𝖞
O F
The late
CAPTAIN EZEKIEL HARDY,
Who in the bows of his boat was killed by a
Sperm Whale on the coast of Japan,
August 3d, 1833.
THIS TABLET
Is erected to his Memory
B Y
HIS WIDOW.

Shaking off the sleet from my ice-glazed hat and jacket, I seated myself near the door, and turning sideways was surprised to see Queequeg near me. Affected by the solemnity of the scene, there was a wondering gaze of incredulous curiosity in his countenance. This savage was the only person present who seemed to notice my entrance; because he was the only one who could not read, and, therefore, was not reading those frigid inscriptions on the wall. Whether any of the relatives of the seamen whose names appeared there were now among the congregation, I knew not; but so many are the unrecorded accidents in the fishery, and so plainly did several women present wear the countenance if not the trappings of some unceasing grief,[5] that I feel sure that here before me were assembled

---

4. Pacific coastal waters of North America.
5. Submerged echo of *Hamlet* 1.2.86, "the trappings and the suits of woe."

those, in whose unhealing hearts the sight of those bleak tablets sympathetically caused the old wounds to bleed afresh.

Oh! ye whose dead lie buried beneath the green grass; who standing among flowers can say—here, *here* lies my beloved; ye know not the desolation that broods in bosoms like these. What bitter blanks in those black-bordered marbles which cover no ashes! What despair in those immovable inscriptions! What deadly voids and unbidden infidelities in the lines that seem to gnaw upon all Faith, and refuse resurrections to the beings who have placelessly perished without a grave. As well might those tablets stand in the cave of Elephanta[6] as here.

In what census of living creatures, the dead of mankind are included; why it is that a universal proverb says of them, that they tell no tales, though containing more secrets than the Goodwin Sands;[7] how it is that to his name who yesterday departed for the other world, we prefix so significant and infidel a word, and yet do not thus entitle him, if he but embarks for the remotest Indies of this living earth, why the Life Insurance Companies pay death-forfeitures upon immortals; in what eternal, unstirring paralysis, and deadly, hopeless trance, yet lies antique Adam who died sixty round centuries ago;[8] how it is that we still refuse to be comforted for those who we nevertheless maintain are dwelling in unspeakable bliss; why all the living so strive to hush all the dead; wherefore but the rumor of a knocking in a tomb will terrify a whole city. All these things are not without their meanings.

But Faith, like a jackal, feeds among the tombs, and even from these dead doubts she gathers her most vital hope.

It needs scarcely to be told, with what feelings, on the eve of a Nantucket voyage, I regarded those marble tablets, and by the murky light of that darkened, doleful day read the fate of the whalemen who had gone before me. Yes, Ishmael, the same fate may be thine. But somehow I grew merry again. Delightful inducements to embark, fine chance for promotion, it seems—aye, a stove boat will make me an immortal by brevet.[9] Yes, there is death in this business of whaling—a speechlessly quick chaotic bundling of a man into Eternity. But what then? Methinks we have hugely mistaken this matter of Life and Death. Methinks that what they call my shadow here on earth is my true substance. Methinks that in looking at things spiritual, we are too much like oysters observing the sun through the water,[1] and thinking that thick water the thinnest of air. Methinks my body is but the lees[2] of my better being. In fact take my body who will, take it I say, it is not me. And therefore three cheers for Nantucket; and come a stove boat and stove body when they will, for stave my soul, Jove himself cannot.

---

6. Immense cave temple on an island in the Bay of Bombay.
7. Shallows near the mouth of the Thames River where many ships have sunk. *Proverb:* Dead men tell no tales.
8. According to a then-current biblical chronology.
9. A promotion by brevet is made on the spot, during battle. *Stove boat:* one broken up by a whale.
1. A figure reminiscent of the parable of the cave in the *Republic* by Plato (428–348 B.C.E.), Greek philosopher.
2. Dregs, last vestiges.

Chapter 8

The Pulpit

I had not been seated very long ere a man of a certain venerable robustness entered; immediately as the storm-pelted door flew back upon
admitting him, a quick regardful eyeing of him by all the congregation,
sufficiently attested that this fine old man was the chaplain. Yes, it was
the famous Father Mapple,[1] so called by the whalemen, among whom he
was a very great favorite. He had been a sailor and a harpooneer in his
youth, but for many years past had dedicated his life to the ministry. At
the time I now write of, Father Mapple was in the hardy winter of a
healthy old age; that sort of old age which seems merging into a second
flowering youth, for among all the fissures of his wrinkles, there shone
certain mild gleams of a newly developing bloom—the spring verdure
peeping forth even beneath February's snow. No one having previously
heard his history, could for the first time behold Father Mapple without
the utmost interest, because there were certain engrafted clerical peculiarities[2] about him, imputable to that adventurous maritime life he had
led. When he entered I observed that he carried no umbrella, and certainly had not come in his carriage, for his tarpaulin hat ran down with
melting sleet, and his great pilot cloth jacket seemed almost to drag him
to the floor with the weight of the water it had absorbed. However, hat
and coat and overshoes were one by one removed, and hung up in a little space in an adjacent corner; when, arrayed in a decent suit, he quietly approached the pulpit.

Like most old fashioned pulpits, it was a very lofty one, and since a regular stairs to such a height would, by its long angle with the floor, seriously contract the already small area of the chapel, the architect, it
seemed, had acted upon the hint of Father Mapple, and finished the pulpit without a stairs, substituting a perpendicular side ladder, like those
used in mounting a ship from a boat at sea. The wife of a whaling captain
had provided the chapel with a handsome pair of red worsted man-ropes
for this ladder, which, being itself nicely headed, and stained with a
mahogany color, the whole contrivance, considering what manner of
chapel it was, seemed by no means in bad taste. Halting for an instant at
the foot of the ladder, and with both hands grasping the ornamental knobs
of the man-ropes, Father Mapple cast a look upwards, and then with a
truly sailor-like but still reverential dexterity, hand over hand, mounted
the steps as if ascending the main-top of his vessel.

The perpendicular parts of this side ladder, as is usually the case with
swinging ones, were of cloth-covered rope, only the rounds were of
wood, so that at every step there was a joint. At my first glimpse of the
pulpit, it had not escaped me that however convenient for a ship, these
joints in the present instance seemed unnecessary. For I was not prepared to see Father Mapple after gaining the height, slowly turn round,

---

1. Partly modeled on a famous Boston sailor-preacher, Father Edward Taylor (1793–1871), and
   partly on Father Enoch Mudge, minister of the Seaman's Bethel (1832–42). Melville heard
   Mudge preach there on December 27, 1840, before embarking on the *Acushnet* for the Pacific.
2. Mannerism peculiar in a clergyman (not peculiar to clergymen).

and stooping over the pulpit, deliberately drag up the ladder step by step, till the whole was deposited within, leaving him impregnable in his little Quebec.[3]

I pondered some time without fully comprehending the reason for this. Father Mapple enjoyed such a wide reputation for sincerity and sanctity, that I could not suspect him of courting notoriety by any mere tricks of the stage. No, thought I, there must be some sober reason for this thing; furthermore, it must symbolize something unseen. Can it be, then, that by that act of physical isolation, he signifies his spiritual withdrawal for the time, from all outward worldly ties and connexions? Yes, for replenished with the meat and wine of the word,[4] to the faithful man of God, this pulpit, I see, is a self-containing stronghold—a lofty Ehrenbreitstein, with a perennial well of water within the walls.

But the side ladder was not the only strange feature of the place, borrowed from the chaplain's former sea-farings. Between the marble cenotaphs on either hand of the pulpit, the wall which formed its back was adorned with a large painting representing a gallant ship beating against a terrible storm off a lee coast of black rocks and snowy breakers. But high above the flying scud[5] and dark-rolling clouds, there floated a little isle of sunlight, from which beamed forth an angel's face; and this bright face shed a distinct spot of radiance upon the ship's tossed deck, something like that silver plate now inserted into the Victory's plank where Nelson fell.[6] "Ah, noble ship," the angel seemed to say, "beat on, beat on, thou noble ship, and bear a hardy helm; for lo! the sun is breaking through; the clouds are rolling off—serenest azure is at hand."

Nor was the pulpit itself without a trace of the same sea-taste that had achieved the ladder and the picture. Its panelled front was in the likeness of a ship's bluff bows, and the Holy Bible rested on a projecting piece of scroll work, fashioned after a ship's fiddle-headed beak.[7]

What could be more full of meaning?—for the pulpit is ever this earth's foremost part; all the rest comes in its rear; the pulpit leads the world. From thence it is the storm of God's quick wrath is first descried, and the bow must bear the earliest brunt. From thence it is the God of breezes fair or foul is first invoked for favorable winds. Yes, the world's a ship on its passage out, and not a voyage complete; and the pulpit is its prow.

---

3. Like that city's fortress above the St. Lawrence River or (next paragraph) like the Ehrenbreitstein across the Rhine from Coblenz; Melville had seen Quebec in 1847 on his honeymoon, the Ehrenbreitstein in 1849.
4. Unlike the meat and wine of King Nebuchadnezzar, which the young Hebrew captive Daniel wisely refused (Daniel 1.5 and 1.6), the meat and wine of the word [meaning Word of God] replenishes, but the meat and wine of Nebuchadnezzar would have been wrong for young Daniel to accept.
5. Seafoam, blown high and fast. Father Taylor's Boston chapel had a similar painting. Lee coast: land toward which the wind is driving the ship (see ch. 23).
6. After seeing relics of the British national hero Admiral Horatio Nelson at Greenwich in 1849, Melville went aboard the preserved flagship, the Victory (at Portsmouth), in which Nelson died while defeating the French fleet at Trafalgar in 1805.
7. An ornament on the bow curved like the scroll at the head of a violin. Bluff bows: full, square front of a ship.

Chapter 9

The Sermon

Father Mapple rose, and in a mild voice of unassuming authority ordered the scattered people to condense. "Starboard gangway, there! side away to larboard—larboard gangway to starboard! Midships! midships!"[1]

There was a low rumbling of heavy sea-boots among the benches, and a still slighter shuffling of women's shoes, and all was quiet again, and every eye on the preacher.

He paused a little; then kneeling in the pulpit's bows, folded his large brown hands across his chest, uplifted his closed eyes, and offered a prayer so deeply devout that he seemed kneeling and praying at the bottom of the sea.

This ended, in prolonged solemn tones, like the continual tolling of a bell in a ship that is foundering at sea in a fog—in such tones he commenced reading the following hymn;[2] but changing his manner towards the concluding stanzas, burst forth with a pealing exultation and joy—

> "The ribs and terrors in the whale,
>   Arched over me a dismal gloom,
> While all God's sun-lit waves rolled by,
>   And left me deepening down to doom.
>
> "I saw the opening maw of hell,
>   With endless pains and sorrows there;
> Which none but they that feel can tell—
>   Oh, I was plunging to despair.
>
> "In black distress, I called my God,
>   When I could scarce believe him mine,
> He bowed his ear to my complaints—
>   No more the whale did me confine.
>
> "With speed he flew to my relief,
>   As on a radiant dolphin borne;
> Awful, yet bright, as lightning shone
>   The face of my Deliverer God.
>
> "My song for ever shall record
>   That terrible, that joyful hour;
> I give the glory to my God,
>   His all the mercy and the power."[3]

Nearly all joined in singing this hymn, which swelled high above the howling of the storm. A brief pause ensued; the preacher slowly turned over the leaves of the Bible, and at last, folding his hand down upon the

---

1. "Those on the left move right, those on the right move left, into the middle."
2. The preacher began calling out (*reading*) the words line by line to the congregation, who did not hold their own books.
3. See Battenfeld (p. 574, herein) for this hymn, adapted from Psalm 18 in the hymn book of the Dutch Reformed Church, the church of Melville's mother's family, the Gansevoorts, descendants of Dutch immigrants to New Amsterdam (New York).

proper page, said: "Beloved shipmates, clinch the last verse of the first chapter of Jonah—'And God had prepared a great fish to swallow up Jonah.'[4]

"Shipmates, this book, containing only four chapters—four yarns—is one of the smallest strands in the mighty cable of the Scriptures. Yet what depths of the soul does Jonah's deep sea-line sound! what a pregnant lesson to us is this prophet! What a noble thing is that canticle in the fish's belly! How billow-like and boisterously grand! We feel the floods surging over us; we sound with him to the kelpy[5] bottom of the waters; sea-weed and all the slime of the sea is about us! But *what* is this lesson that the book of Jonah teaches? Shipmates, it is a two-stranded lesson; a lesson to us all as sinful men, and a lesson to me as a pilot of the living God. As sinful men, it is a lesson to us all, because it is a story of the sin, hard-heartedness, suddenly awakened fears, the swift punishment, repentance, prayers, and finally the deliverance and joy of Jonah. As with all sinners among men, the sin of this son of Amittai was in his wilful disobedience of the command of God—never mind now what that command was, or how conveyed—which he found a hard command. But all the things that God would have us do are hard for us to do—remember that—and hence, he oftener commands us than endeavors to persuade. And if we obey God, we must disobey ourselves; and it is in this disobeying ourselves, wherein the hardness of obeying God consists.

"With this sin of disobedience in him, Jonah still further flouts at God, by seeking to flee from Him. He thinks that a ship made by men, will carry him into countries where God does not reign, but only the Captains of this earth. He skulks about the wharves of Joppa, and seeks a ship that's bound for Tarshish. There lurks, perhaps, a hitherto unheeded meaning here. By all accounts Tarshish could have been no other city than the modern Cadiz. That's the opinion of learned men. And where is Cadiz, shipmates? Cadiz is in Spain; as far by water, from Joppa, as Jonah could possibly have sailed in those ancient days, when the Atlantic was an almost unknown sea. Because Joppa, the modern Jaffa, shipmates, is on the most easterly coast of the Mediterranean, the Syrian; and Tarshish or Cadiz more than two thousand miles to the westward from that, just outside the Straits of Gibraltar. See ye not then, shipmates, that Jonah sought to flee world-wide from God? Miserable man! Oh! most contemptible and worthy of all scorn; with slouched hat and guilty eye, skulking from his God; prowling among the shipping like a vile burglar hastening to cross the seas. So disordered, self-condemning is his look, that had there been policemen in those days, Jonah, on the mere suspicion of something wrong, had been arrested ere he touched a deck. How plainly he's a fugitive! no baggage, not a hat-box, valise, or carpet-bag,—no friends accompany him to the wharf with their adieux. At last, after much dodging search, he finds the Tarshish ship receiving the last items of her cargo; and as he steps on board to see its Captain in the cabin, all the sailors for the moment desist from hoisting in the goods, to mark the stranger's evil

4. Adapted from Jonah 1.17: "Now the Lord had prepared a great fish to swallow up Jonah. And Jonah was in the belly of the fish three days and three nights."
5. Entangled with seaweed. *Sea-line:* weighted rope dropped overboard to measure the depth to the sea bottom ("soundings").

eye. Jonah sees this; but in vain he tries to look all ease and confidence; in vain essays his wretched smile. Strong intuitions of the man assure the mariners he can be no innocent. In their gamesome but still serious way, one whispers to the other—'Jack, he's robbed a widow;' or, 'Joe, do you mark him; he's a bigamist;' or, 'Harry lad, I guess he's the adulterer that broke jail in old Gomorrah, or belike, one of the missing murderers from Sodom.'[6] Another runs to read the bill that's stuck against the spile upon the wharf to which the ship is moored, offering five hundred gold coins for the apprehension of a parricide, and containing a description of his person. He reads, and looks from Jonah to the bill; while all his sympathetic shipmates now crowd round Jonah, prepared to lay their hands upon him. Frighted Jonah trembles, and summoning all his boldness to his face, only looks so much the more a coward. He will not confess himself suspected; but that itself is strong suspicion. So he makes the best of it; and when the sailors find him not to be the man that is advertised, they let him pass, and he descends into the cabin.

"'Who's there?' cries the Captain at his busy desk, hurriedly making out his papers for the Customs—'Who's there?' Oh! how that harmless question mangles Jonah! For the instant he almost turns to flee again. But he rallies. 'I seek a passage in this ship to Tarshish; how soon sail ye, sir?' Thus far the busy Captain had not looked up to Jonah, though the man now stands before him; but no sooner does he hear that hollow voice, than he darts a scrutinizing glance. 'We sail with the next coming tide,' at last he slowly answered, still intently eyeing him. 'No sooner, sir?'—'Soon enough for any honest man that goes a passenger.' Ha! Jonah, that's another stab. But he swiftly calls away the Captain from that scent. 'I'll sail with ye,'—he says,—'the passage money, how much is that?—I'll pay now.' For it is particularly written, shipmates, as if it were a thing not to be overlooked in this history, 'that he paid the fare thereof' ere the craft did sail. And taken with the context, this is full of meaning.

"Now Jonah's Captain, shipmates, was one whose discernment detects crime in any, but whose cupidity exposes it only in the penniless. In this world, shipmates, sin that pays its way can travel freely, and without a passport; whereas Virtue, if a pauper, is stopped at all frontiers. So Jonah's Captain prepares to test the length of Jonah's purse, ere he judge him openly. He charges him thrice the usual sum; and it's assented to. Then the Captain knows that Jonah is a fugitive; but at the same time resolves to help a flight that paves its rear with gold. Yet when Jonah fairly takes out his purse, prudent suspicions still molest the Captain. He rings every coin to find a counterfeit. Not a forger, any way, he mutters; and Jonah is put down for his passage. 'Point out my state-room,[7] Sir,' says Jonah now, 'I'm travel-weary; I need sleep.' 'Thou look'st like it,' says the Captain, 'there's thy room.' Jonah enters, and would lock the door, but the lock contains no key. Hearing him foolishly fumbling there, the Captain laughs lowly to himself, and mutters something about the doors of convicts' cells being never allowed to be locked within. All dressed and dusty as he is, Jonah throws himself into his berth, and finds the little state-room ceiling

6. See n. 6, p. 24.
7. Mapple makes the story accessible to his auditors by endowing the ancient biblical ship with familiar modern features.

almost resting on his forehead. The air is close, and Jonah gasps. Then, in that contracted hole, sunk, too, beneath the ship's water-line, Jonah feels the heralding presentiment of that stifling hour, when the whale shall hold him in the smallest of his bowel's wards.

"Screwed at its axis against the side, a swinging lamp slightly oscillates in Jonah's room; and the ship, heeling over towards the wharf with the weight of the last bales received, the lamp, flame and all, though in slight motion, still maintains a permanent obliquity with reference to the room; though, in truth, infallibly straight itself, it but made obvious the false, lying levels among which it hung. The lamp alarms and frightens Jonah; as lying in his berth his tormented eyes roll round the place, and this thus far successful fugitive finds no refuge for his restless glance. But that contradiction in the lamp more and more appals him. The floor, the ceiling, and the side, are all awry. 'Oh! so my conscience hangs in me!' he groans, 'straight upward, so it burns; but the chambers of my soul are all in crookedness!'

"Like one who after a night of drunken revelry hies to his bed, still reeling, but with conscience yet pricking him, as the plungings of the Roman race-horse but so much the more strike his steel tags[8] into him; as one who in that miserable plight still turns and turns in giddy anguish, praying God for annihilation until the fit be passed; and at last amid the whirl of woe he feels, a deep stupor steals over him, as over the man who bleeds to death, for conscience is the wound, and there's naught to staunch it; so, after sore wrestlings in his berth, Jonah's prodigy of ponderous misery drags him drowning down to sleep.

"And now the time of tide has come; the ship casts off her cables; and from the deserted wharf the uncheered[9] ship for Tarshish, all careening, glides to sea. That ship, my friends, was the first of recorded smugglers! the contraband was Jonah. But the sea rebels; he will not bear the wicked burden. A dreadful storm comes on, the ship is like to break. But now when the boatswain calls all hands to lighten her; when boxes, bales, and jars are clattering overboard; when the wind is shrieking, and the men are yelling, and every plank thunders with trampling feet right over Jonah's head; in all this raging tumult, Jonah sleeps his hideous sleep. He sees no black sky and raging sea, feels not the reeling timbers, and little hears he or heeds he the far rush of the mighty whale, which even now with open mouth is cleaving the seas after him. Aye, shipmates, Jonah was gone down into the sides of the ship—a berth in the cabin as I have taken it, and was fast asleep. But the frightened master comes to him, and shrieks in his dead ear, 'What meanest thou, O sleeper! arise!' Startled from his lethargy by that direful cry, Jonah staggers to his feet, and stumbling to the deck, grasps a shroud,[1] to look out upon the sea. But at that moment he is sprung upon by a panther billow leaping over the bulwarks. Wave after wave thus leaps into the ship, and finding no speedy vent runs roaring fore and aft, till the mariners come nigh to drowning while yet afloat. And ever, as the white moon shows her affrighted face from the steep gul-

8. Here, metal tips of harness.
9. For ships leaving on a voyage, final ceremonial cheers from shore and from crew were customary.
1. Rope from a mast to the ship's side.

lies in the blackness overhead, aghast Jonah sees the rearing bowsprit[2] pointing high upward, but soon beat downward again towards the tormented deep.

"Terrors upon terrors run shouting through his soul. In all his cringing attitudes, the God-fugitive is now too plainly known. The sailors mark him; more and more certain grow their suspicions of him, and at last, fully to test the truth, by referring the whole matter to high Heaven, they fall to casting lots, to see for whose cause this great tempest was upon them. The lot is Jonah's; that discovered, then how furiously they mob him with their questions. 'What is thine occupation? Whence comest thou? Thy country? What people?' But mark now, my shipmates, the behavior of poor Jonah. The eager mariners but ask him who he is, and where from; whereas, they not only receive an answer to those questions, but likewise another answer to a question not put by them, but the unsolicited answer is forced from Jonah by the hard hand of God that is upon him.

"'I am a Hebrew,' he cries—and then—'I fear the Lord the God of Heaven who hath made the sea and the dry land!' Fear him, O Jonah? Aye, well mightest thou fear the Lord God *then!* Straightway, he now goes on to make a full confession; whereupon the mariners become more and more appalled, but still are pitiful. For when Jonah, not yet supplicating God for mercy, since he but too well knew the darkness of his deserts,— when wretched Jonah cries out to them to take him and cast him forth into the sea, for he knew that for *his* sake this great tempest was upon them; they mercifully turn from him, and seek by other means to save the ship. But all in vain; the indignant gale howls louder; then, with one hand raised invokingly to God, with the other they not unreluctantly lay hold of Jonah.

"And now behold Jonah taken up as an anchor and dropped into the sea; when instantly an oily calmness floats out from the east, and the sea is still, as Jonah carries down the gale with him, leaving smooth water behind. He goes down in the whirling heart of such a masterless commotion that he scarce heeds the moment when he drops seething into the yawning jaws awaiting him; and the whale shoots-to all his ivory teeth, like so many white bolts, upon his prison. Then Jonah prayed unto the Lord out of the fish's belly. But observe his prayer, and learn a weighty lesson. For sinful as he is, Jonah does not weep and wail for direct deliverance. He feels that his dreadful punishment is just. He leaves all his deliverance to God, contenting himself with this, that spite of all his pains and pangs, he will still look towards His holy temple. And here, shipmates, is true and faithful repentance; not clamorous for pardon, but grateful for punishment. And how pleasing to God was this conduct in Jonah, is shown in the eventual deliverance of him from the sea and the whale. Shipmates, I do not place Jonah before you to be copied for his sin but I do place him before you as a model for repentance. Sin not; but if you do, take heed to repent of it like Jonah."

While he was speaking these words, the howling of the shrieking, slanting storm without seemed to add new power to the preacher, who, when describing Jonah's sea-storm, seemed tossed by a storm himself. His deep

---

2. A projection from the ship's bow.

chest heaved as with a ground-swell;[3] his tossed arms seemed the warring elements at work; and the thunders that rolled away from off his swarthy brow, and the light leaping from his eye, made all his simple hearers look on him with a quick fear that was strange to them.

There now came a lull in his look, as he silently turned over the leaves of the Book once more; and, at last, standing motionless, with closed eyes, for the moment, seemed communing with God and himself.

But again he leaned over towards the people, and bowing his head lowly, with an aspect of the deepest yet manliest humility, he spake these words:

"Shipmates, God has laid but one hand upon you; both his hands press upon me. I have read ye by what murky light may be mine the lesson that Jonah teaches to all sinners; and therefore to ye, and still more to me, for I am a greater sinner than ye. And now how gladly would I come down from this mast-head and sit on the hatches[4] there where you sit, and listen as you listen, while some one of you reads me that other and more awful lesson which Jonah teaches to me, as a pilot of the living God. How being an anointed pilot-prophet, or speaker of true things, and bidden by the Lord to sound those unwelcome truths in the ears of a wicked Nineveh, Jonah, appalled at the hostility he should raise, fled from his mission, and sought to escape his duty and his God by taking ship at Joppa. But God is everywhere; Tarshish he never reached. As we have seen, God came upon him in the whale, and swallowed him down to living gulfs of doom, and with swift slantings tore him along 'into the midst of the seas,' where the eddying depths sucked him ten thousand fathoms down, and 'the weeds were wrapped about his head,' and all the watery world of woe bowled over him. Yet even then beyond the reach of any plummet—'out of the belly of hell'—when the whale grounded upon the ocean's utmost bones, even then, God heard the engulphed, repenting prophet when he cried. Then God spake unto the fish; and from the shuddering cold and blackness of the sea, the whale came breeching up towards the warm and pleasant sun, and all the delights of air and earth; and 'vomited out Jonah upon the dry land;' when the word of the Lord came a second time; and Jonah, bruised and beaten—his ears, like two sea-shells, still multitudinously murmuring of the ocean—Jonah did the Almighty's bidding. And what was that, shipmates? To preach the Truth to the face of Falsehood! That was it!

"This, shipmates, this is that other lesson; and woe to that pilot of the living God who slights it. Woe to him whom this world charms from Gospel duty! Woe to him who seeks to pour oil upon the waters when God has brewed them into a gale! Woe to him who seeks to please rather than to appal! Woe to him whose good name is more to him than goodness! Woe to him who, in this world, courts not dishonor! Woe to him who would not be true, even though to be false were salvation! Yea, woe to him who, as the great Pilot Paul has it, while preaching to others is himself a castaway!"[5]

---

3. Strong, wide undulation of the ocean, as from a distant storm or earthquake.
4. Here, lids covering hatches, openings in the deck.
5. In 1 Corinthians 9.27: "lest . . . when I have preached to others, I myself should be a castaway."

He drooped and fell away from himself for a moment; then lifting his face to them again, showed a deep joy in his eyes, as he cried out with a heavenly enthusiasm,—"But oh! shipmates! on the starboard hand of every woe, there is a sure delight; and higher the top of that delight, than the bottom of the woe is deep. Is not the main-truck higher than the kelson is low?[6] Delight is to him—a far, far upward, and inward delight—who against the proud gods and commodores of this earth, ever stands forth his own inexorable self. Delight is to him whose strong arms yet support him, when the ship of this base treacherous world has gone down beneath him. Delight is to him, who gives no quarter in the truth, and kills, burns, and destroys all sin though he pluck it out from under the robes of Senators and Judges. Delight,—top-gallant delight[7] is to him, who acknowledges no law or lord, but the Lord his God, and is only a patriot to heaven. Delight is to him, whom all the waves of the billows of the seas of the boisterous mob can never shake from this sure Keel of the Ages.[8] And eternal delight and deliciousness will be his, who coming to lay him down, can say with his final breath—O Father!—chiefly known to me by Thy rod[9]—mortal or immortal, here I die. I have striven to be Thine, more than to be this world's, or mine own. Yet this is nothing; I leave eternity to Thee; for what is man that he should live out the lifetime of his God?"[1]

He said no more, but slowly waving a benediction, covered his face with his hands, and so remained, kneeling, till all the people had departed, and he was left alone in the place.

Chapter 10

A Bosom Friend

Returning to the Spouter-Inn from the Chapel, I found Queequeg there quite alone; he having left the Chapel before the benediction some time. He was sitting on a bench before the fire, with his feet on the stove hearth, and in one hand was holding close up to his face that little negro idol of his; peering hard into its face, and with a jack-knife gently whittling away at its nose, meanwhile humming to himself in his heathenish way.

But being now interrupted, he put up the image; and pretty soon, going to the table, took up a large book there, and placing it on his lap began counting the pages with deliberate regularity; at every fiftieth page—as I fancied—stopping a moment, looking vacantly around him, and giving

---

6. There is less distance between deck and kelson (timber bolted along the ship's keel, its lowest point) than between deck and main truck (the wooden cap topping the ship's highest mast, from which her pennant is flown).

7. Highest ecstasy. *Top-gallant*: the top (third) section of each mast, or the third sails above the deck.

8. God (compare the Toplady and Hastings hymn where Jesus is the "Rock of Ages").

9. Proverbs 13.24: "He that spareth his rod hateth his son: but he that loveth him chastiseth him betimes." ("Betimes": early, fittingly.)

1. The phrasing recalls Job 7.17: "What is man, that thou shouldest magnify him," or Job 15.14: "What is man that he should be clean?"

utterance to a long-drawn gurgling whistle of astonishment. He would then begin again at the next fifty; seeming to commence at number one each time, as though he could not count more than fifty, and it was only by such a large number of fifties being bound[1] together, that his astonishment at the multitude of pages was excited.

With much interest I sat watching him. Savage though he was, and hideously marred about the face—at least to my taste—his countenance yet had a something in it which was by no means disagreeable. You cannot hide the soul. Through all his unearthly tattooings, I thought I saw the traces of a simple honest heart; and in his large, deep eyes, fiery black and bold, there seemed tokens of a spirit that would dare a thousand devils. And besides all this, there was a certain lofty bearing about the Pagan, which even his uncouthness could not altogether maim. He looked like a man who had never cringed and never had had a creditor. Whether it was, too, that his head being shaved, his forehead was drawn out in freer and brighter relief, and looked more expansive than it otherwise would, this I will not venture to decide; but certain it was his head was phrenologically[2] an excellent one. It may seem ridiculous, but it reminded me of General Washington's head, as seen in the popular busts of him. It had the same long regularly graded retreating slope from above the brows, which were likewise very projecting, like two long promontories thickly wooded on top. Queequeg was George Washington cannibalistically developed.

Whilst I was thus closely scanning him, half-pretending meanwhile to be looking out at the storm from the casement, he never heeded my presence, never troubled himself with so much as a single glance; but appeared wholly occupied with counting the pages of the marvellous book. Considering how sociably we had been sleeping together the night previous, and especially considering the affectionate arm I had found thrown over me upon waking in the morning, I thought this indifference of his very strange. But savages are strange beings; at times you do not know exactly how to take them. At first they are overawing; their calm self-collectedness of simplicity seems a Socratic wisdom.[3] I had noticed also that Queequeg never consorted at all, or but very little, with the other seamen in the inn. He made no advances whatever; appeared to have no desire to enlarge the circle of his acquaintances. All this struck me as mighty singular; yet, upon second thoughts, there was something almost sublime in it. Here was a man some twenty thousand miles from home, by the way of Cape Horn, that is—which was the only way he could get there—thrown among people as strange to him as though he were in the planet Jupiter; and yet he seemed entirely at his ease; preserving the utmost serenity; content with his own companionship; always equal to himself. Surely this was a touch of fine philosophy; though no doubt he had never heard there was such a thing as that. But, perhaps, to be true philosophers, we mortals should not be conscious of so living or so striving. So soon as I hear that such or such a man gives himself out for a philosopher, I conclude that, like the dyspeptic old woman, he must have "broken his digester."

---

1. A new emendation by Parker for this NCE; the NN used the 1851 word, "found."
2. According to charts drawn up by practitioners of the pseudo-science of phrenology, who claimed to be able to read character and ability by the conformation of a person's skull.
3. Like that of the Greek philosopher Socrates (470?–399 B.C.E.).

As I sat there in that now lonely room; the fire burning low, in that mild stage when, after its first intensity has warmed the air, it then only glows to be looked at; the evening shades and phantoms gathering round the casements, and peering in upon us silent, solitary twain; the storm booming without in solemn swells; I began to be sensible of strange feelings. I felt a melting in me. No more my splintered heart and maddened hand were turned against the wolfish world. This soothing savage had redeemed it. There he sat, his very indifference speaking a nature in which there lurked no civilized hypocrisies and bland deceits. Wild he was; a very sight of sights to see; yet I began to feel myself mysteriously drawn towards him. And those same things that would have repelled most others, they were the very magnets that thus drew me. I'll try a pagan friend, thought I, since Christian kindness has proved but hollow courtesy. I drew my bench near him, and made some friendly signs and hints, doing my best to talk with him meanwhile. At first he little noticed these advances; but presently, upon my referring to his last night's hospitalities, he made out to ask me whether we were again to be bedfellows. I told him yes; whereat I thought he looked pleased, perhaps a little complimented.

We then turned over the book together, and I endeavored to explain to him the purpose of the printing, and the meaning of the few pictures that were in it. Thus I soon engaged his interest; and from that we went to jabbering the best we could about the various outer sights to be seen in this famous town. Soon I proposed a social smoke; and, producing his pouch and tomahawk, he quietly offered me a puff. And then we sat exchanging puffs from that wild pipe of his, and keeping it regularly passing between us.

If there yet lurked any ice of indifference towards me in the Pagan's breast, this pleasant, genial smoke we had, soon thawed it out, and left us cronies. He seemed to take to me quite as naturally and unbiddenly as I to him; and when our smoke was over, he pressed his forehead against mine, clasped me round the waist, and said that henceforth we were married; meaning, in his country's phrase, that we were bosom friends; he would gladly die for me, if need should be. In a countryman, this sudden flame of friendship would have seemed far too premature, a thing to be much distrusted; but in this simple savage those old rules would not apply.

After supper, and another social chat and smoke, we went to our room together. He made me a present of his embalmed head; took out his enormous tobacco wallet, and groping under the tobacco, drew out some thirty dollars in silver;[4] then spreading them on the table, and mechanically dividing them into two equal portions, pushed one of them towards me, and said it was mine. I was going to remonstrate; but he silenced me by pouring them into my trowsers' pockets. I let them stay. He then went about his evening prayers, took out his idol, and removed the paper fireboard. By certain signs and symptoms, I thought he seemed anxious for me to join him; but well knowing what was to follow, I deliberated a moment whether, in case he invited me, I would comply or otherwise.

---

4. The money may consist of thirty silver dollars or of a mixture of coins of different values, but the phrasing is formulaic, from the thirty pieces of silver the high priests paid Judas to betray Jesus, coins that he returned and that they then used to purchase land from a potter (hence the term "potter's field") for a cemetery where strangers could be buried (Matthew 26.15, 27.3–10).

I was a good Christian; born and bred in the bosom of the infallible Presbyterian Church.[5] How then could I unite with this wild idolator in worshipping his piece of wood? But what is worship? thought I. Do you suppose now, Ishmael, that the magnanimous God of heaven and earth—pagans and all included—can possibly be jealous of an insignificant bit of black wood? Impossible! But what is worship?—to do the will of God—*that* is worship. And what is the will of God?—to do to my fellow man what I would have my fellow man to do to me—*that* is the will of God. Now, Queequeg is my fellow man. And what do I wish that this Queequeg would do to me? Why, unite with me in my particular Presbyterian form of worship. Consequently, I must then unite with him in his; ergo, I must turn idolator. So I kindled the shavings; helped prop up the innocent little idol; offered him burnt biscuit with Queequeg; salamed before him twice or thrice; kissed his nose; and that done, we undressed and went to bed, at peace with our own consciences and all the world. But we did not go to sleep without some little chat.

How it is I know not; but there is no place like a bed for confidential disclosures between friends. Man and wife, they say, there open the very bottom of their souls to each other; and some old couples often lie and chat over old times till nearly morning. Thus, then, in our hearts' honeymoon, lay I and Queequeg—a cosy, loving pair.

Chapter 11

Nightgown

We had lain thus in bed, chatting and napping at short intervals, and Queequeg now and then affectionately throwing his brown tattooed legs over mine, and then drawing them back; so entirely sociable and free and easy were we; when, at last, by reason of our confabulations, what little nappishness remained in us altogether departed, and we felt like getting up again, though day-break was yet some way down the future.

Yes, we became very wakeful; so much so that our recumbent position began to grow wearisome, and by little and little we found ourselves sitting up; the clothes well tucked around us, leaning against the head-board with our four knees drawn up close together, and our two noses bending over

5. Ishmael's questions are blasphemous, according to Exodus 20.3–5: "Thou shalt have no other gods before me. Thou shalt not make unto thee any graven image, or any likeness of any thing that is in heaven above, or that is in the earth beneath, or that is in the water under the earth: Thou shalt not bow down thyself to them, nor serve them: For I the Lord thy God am a jealous god." With his first book, *Typee* (1846), in which he criticized missionaries in the South Seas for all but enslaving their converts, Melville had stirred up the wrath of Presbyterians and other evangelistic Protestants. One of the harshest attacks on *Typee* appeared in the Presbyterian New York *Evangelist* (see p. 477, herein). As Melville might have foreseen, this passage in *Moby-Dick* infuriated many reviewers: see p. 605 herein for the warning in the Congregationalist New York *Independent* that the "Judgment day" would hold Melville liable "for not turning his talents to better account" and that the Harper brothers would also undergo trial "at the bar of God." As staunch Methodists, the Harpers were stung when the reviewer in the *Methodist Quarterly Review* felt "bound to say" that *Moby-Dick* contained "a number of flings at religion, and even of vulgar immoralities that render it unfit for general circulation" and regretted "that Mr. Melville should allow himself to sink so low." More than any other single factor, Melville's defiance of the religious press cost him his career as a writer.

them, as if our knee-pans were warming-pans.[1] We felt very nice and snug, the more so since it was so chilly out of doors; indeed out of bed-clothes too, seeing that there was no fire in the room. The more so, I say, because truly to enjoy bodily warmth, some small part of you must be cold, for there is no quality in this world that is not what it is merely by contrast. Nothing exists in itself. If you flatter yourself that you are all over comfortable, and have been so a long time, then you cannot be said to be comfortable any more. But if, like Queequeg and me in the bed, the tip of your nose or the crown of your head be slightly chilled, why then, indeed, in the general consciousness you feel most delightfully and unmistakably warm. For this reason a sleeping apartment should never be furnished with a fire, which is one of the luxurious discomforts of the rich. For the height of this sort of deliciousness is to have nothing but the blanket between you and your snugness and the cold of the outer air. Then there you lie like the one warm spark in the heart of an arctic crystal.

We had been sitting in this crouching manner for some time, when all at once I thought I would open my eyes; for when between sheets, whether by day or by night, and whether asleep or awake, I have a way of always keeping my eyes shut, in order the more to concentrate the snugness of being in bed. Because no man can ever feel his own identity aright except his eyes be closed; as if darkness were indeed the proper element of our essences, though light be more congenial to our clayey part. Upon opening my eyes then, and coming out of my own pleasant and self-created darkness into the imposed and coarse outer gloom of the unilluminated twelve-o'clock-at-night, I experienced a disagreeable revulsion. Nor did I at all object to the hint from Queequeg that perhaps it were best to strike a light, seeing that we were so wide awake; and besides he felt a strong desire to have a few quiet puffs from his Tomahawk. Be it said, that though I had felt such a strong repugnance to his smoking in the bed the night before, yet see how elastic our stiff prejudices grow when love once comes to bend them. For now I liked nothing better than to have Queequeg smoking by me, even in bed, because he seemed to be full of such serene household joy then. I no more felt unduly concerned for the landlord's policy of insurance. I was only alive to the condensed confidential comfortableness of sharing a pipe and a blanket with a real friend. With our shaggy jackets drawn about our shoulders, we now passed the Tomahawk from one to the other, till slowly there grew over us a blue hanging tester[2] of smoke, illuminated by the flame of the new-lit lamp.

Whether it was that this undulating tester rolled the savage away to far distant scenes, I know not, but he now spoke of his native island; and, eager to hear his history, I begged him to go on and tell it. He gladly complied. Though at the time I but ill comprehended not a few of his words, yet subsequent disclosures, when I had become more familiar with his broken phraseology, now enable me to present the whole story such as it may prove in the mere skeleton I give.

1. Long-handled lidded pans that could be filled with live coals and shoved between cold sheets to warm a bed.
2. Canopy, like the drapery over a four-poster bed.

Chapter 12

Biographical

Queequeg was a native of Kokovoko,[1] an island far away to the West and South. It is not down in any map; true places never are.

When a new-hatched savage running wild about his native woodlands in a grass clout, followed by the nibbling goats, as if he were a green sapling; even then, in Queequeg's ambitious soul, lurked a strong desire to see something more of Christendom than a specimen whaler or two. His father was a High Chief, a King; his uncle a High Priest; and on the maternal side he boasted aunts who were the wives of unconquerable warriors. There was excellent blood in his veins—royal stuff; though sadly vitiated, I fear, by the cannibal propensity he nourished in his untutored youth.

A Sag Harbor[2] ship visited his father's bay, and Queequeg sought a passage to Christian lands. But the ship, having her full complement of seamen, spurned his suit; and not all the King his father's influence could prevail. But Queequeg vowed a vow. Alone in his canoe, he paddled off to a distant strait, which he knew the ship must pass through when she quitted the island. On one side was a coral reef; on the other a low tongue of land, covered with mangrove thickets that grew out into the water. Hiding his canoe, still afloat, among these thickets, with its prow seaward, he sat down in the stern, paddle low in hand; and when the ship was gliding by, like a flash he darted out; gained her side; with one backward dash of his foot capsized and sank his canoe; climbed up the chains; and throwing himself at full length upon the deck, grappled a ring-bolt there, and swore not to let it go, though hacked in pieces.

In vain the captain threatened to throw him overboard;[3] suspended a cutlass over his naked wrists; Queequeg was the son of a King, and Queequeg budged not. Struck by his desperate dauntlessness, and his wild desire to visit Christendom, the captain at last relented, and told him he might make himself at home. But this fine young savage—this sea Prince of Wales,[4] never saw the captain's cabin. They put him down among the sailors, and made a whaleman of him. But like Czar Peter[5] content to toil in the shipyards of foreign cities, Queequeg disdained no seeming ignominy, if thereby he might haply gain the power of enlightening his untutored countrymen. For at bottom—so he told me—he was actuated by a profound desire to learn among the Christians, the arts

---

1. Imagined by Melville.
2. On Long Island, then a major whaling port. In June 1839 Melville considered going there to sign on a whaleship, but signed instead on a merchant ship bound for Liverpool.
3. Geoffrey Sanborn (in his manuscript "Whence Come You, Queequeg?") relates his discovery that Melville based Queequeg on an account in George Lillie Craik's *The New Zealanders* (1830) of an elaborately tattooed Maori chief named Tupai Cupa, who was so determined to go to Europe and "see King Georgy" (318) that he boarded the merchant-ship *Urania* in Cook's Strait, which "divides the two islands that constitute New Zealand," and refused to leave, even when the sailors tried to throw him overboard: Tupai "perceived what was intended; and instantly throwing himself down on the deck, seized two ring-bolts with so powerful a hold that it was impossible to tear him away without such violence as the humanity of Captain Reynolds would not permit."
4. The English king's or queen's son and successor.
5. Peter the Great of Russia worked incognito in the British royal navy's dockyard near London to learn shipbuilding.

whereby to make his people still happier than they were; and more than that, still better than they were. But, alas! the practices of whalemen soon convinced him that even Christians could be both miserable and wicked; infinitely more so, than all his father's heathens. Arrived at last in old Sag Harbor; and seeing what the sailors did there; and then going on to Nantucket, and seeing how they spent their wages in *that* place also, poor Queequeg gave it up for lost. Thought he, it's a wicked world in all meridians; I'll die a pagan.

And thus an old idolator at heart, he yet lived among these Christians, wore their clothes, and tried to talk their gibberish. Hence the queer ways about him, though now some time from home.

By hints, I asked him whether he did not propose going back, and having a coronation; since he might now consider his father dead and gone, he being very old and feeble at the last accounts. He answered no, not yet; and added that he was fearful Christianity, or rather Christians, had unfitted him for ascending the pure and undefiled throne of thirty pagan Kings before him. But by and by, he said, he would return,—as soon as he felt himself baptized again. For the nonce, however, he proposed to sail about, and sow his wild oats[6] in all four oceans. They had made a harpooneer of him, and that barbed iron was in lieu of a sceptre now.

I asked him what might be his immediate purpose, touching his future movements. He answered, to go to sea again, in his old vocation. Upon this, I told him that whaling was my own design, and informed him of my intention to sail out of Nantucket, as being the most promising port for an adventurous whaleman to embark from. He at once resolved to accompany me to that island, ship aboard the same vessel, get into the same watch, the same boat, the same mess with me, in short to share my every hap; with both my hands in his, boldly dip into the Potluck of both worlds. To all this I joyously assented; for besides the affection I now felt for Queequeg, he was an experienced harpooneer, and as such, could not fail to be of great usefulness to one, who, like me, was wholly ignorant of the mysteries of whaling, though well acquainted with the sea, as known to merchant seamen.

His story being ended with his pipe's last dying puff, Queequeg embraced me, pressed his forehead against mine, and blowing out the light, we rolled over from each other, this way and that, and very soon were sleeping.

Chapter 13

Wheelbarrow

Next morning, Monday, after disposing of the embalmed head to a barber, for a block,[1] I settled my own and comrade's bill; using, however, my comrade's money. The grinning landlord, as well as the boarders, seemed

---

6. Proverbial for committing youthful, specifically sexual, indiscretions. The inappropriate casting of seed (semen) was condemned in the Bible, particularly in the early books of the Old Testament.
1. Head-size form, for keeping a wig in shape.

amazingly tickled at the sudden friendship which had sprung up between me and Queequeg—especially as Peter Coffin's cock and bull stories[2] about him had previously so much alarmed me concerning the very person whom I now companied with.

We borrowed a wheelbarrow, and embarking our things, including my own poor carpet-bag, and Queequeg's canvas sack and hammock, away we went down to "the Moss," the little Nantucket packet schooner moored at the wharf. As we were going along the people stared; not at Queequeg so much—for they were used to seeing cannibals like him in their streets,—but at seeing him and me upon such confidential terms. But we heeded them not, going along wheeling the barrow by turns, and Queequeg now and then stopping to adjust the sheath on his harpoon barbs. I asked him why he carried such a troublesome thing with him ashore, and whether all whaling ships did not find[3] their own harpoons. To this, in substance, he replied, that though what I hinted was true enough, yet he had a particular affection for his own harpoon, because it was of assured stuff, well tried in many a mortal combat, and deeply intimate with the hearts of whales. In short, like many inland reapers and mowers, who go into the farmers' meadows armed with their own scythes—though in no wise obliged to furnish them—even so, Queequeg, for his own private reasons, preferred his own harpoon.

Shifting the barrow from my hands to his, he told me a funny story about the first wheelbarrow he had ever seen. It was in Sag Harbor. The owners of his ship, it seems, had lent him one, in which to carry his heavy chest to his boarding house. Not to seem ignorant about the thing—though in truth he was entirely so, concerning the precise way in which to manage the barrow—Queequeg puts his chest upon it; lashes it fast; and then shoulders the barrow and marches up the wharf. "Why," said I, "Queequeg, you might have known better than that, one would think. Didn't the people laugh?"

Upon this, he told me another story. The people of his island of Kokovoko, it seems, at their wedding feasts express the fragrant water of young cocoanuts into a large stained calabash[4] like a punchbowl; and this punchbowl always forms the great central ornament on the braided mat where the feast is held. Now a certain grand merchant ship once touched at Kokovoko, and its commander—from all accounts, a very stately punctilious gentleman, at least for a sea captain—this commander was invited to the wedding feast of Queequeg's sister, a pretty young princess just turned of ten. Well; when all the wedding guests were assembled at the bride's bamboo cottage, this Captain marches in, and being assigned the post of honor, placed himself over against the punchbowl, and between the High Priest and his majesty the King, Queequeg's father. Grace being said,—for those people have their grace as well as we—though Queequeg told me that unlike us, who at such times look downwards to our platters, they, on the contrary, copying the ducks, glance upwards to the great Giver of all feasts—Grace, I say, being said, the High Priest opens the banquet by the immemorial ceremony of the island; that is, dipping his

2. Fantastic stories told as if true.
3. Supply, furnish.
4. Gourd.

consecrated and consecrating fingers into the bowl before the blessed beverage circulates. Seeing himself placed next the Priest, and noting the ceremony, and thinking himself—being Captain of a ship—as having plain precedence over a mere island King, especially in the King's own house—the Captain coolly proceeds to wash his hands in the punch bowl;—taking it I suppose for a huge finger-glass.[5] "Now," said Queequeg, "what you tink now?—Didn't our people laugh?"

At last, passage paid, and luggage safe, we stood on board the schooner. Hoisting sail, it glided down the Acushnet river.[6] On one side, New Bedford rose in terraces of streets, their ice-covered trees all glittering in the clear, cold air. Huge hills and mountains of casks on casks were piled upon her wharves, and side by side the world-wandering whale ships lay silent and safely moored at last; while from others came a sound of carpenters and coopers, with blended noises of fires and forges to melt the pitch, all betokening that new cruises were on the start; that one most perilous and long voyage ended, only begins a second; and a second ended, only begins a third, and so on, for ever and for aye. Such is the endlessness, yea, the intolerableness of all earthly effort.

Gaining the more open water, the bracing breeze waxed fresh; the little Moss tossed the quick foam from her bows, as a young colt his snortings. How I snuffed that Tartar[7] air!—how I spurned that turnpike earth!—that common highway all over dented with the marks of slavish heels and hoofs; and turned me to admire the magnanimity of the sea which will permit no records.

At the same foam-fountain, Queequeg seemed to drink and reel with me. His dusky nostrils swelled apart; he showed his filed and pointed teeth. On, on we flew; and our offing gained, the Moss did homage to the blast; ducked and dived her bows as a slave before the Sultan. Sideways leaning, we sideways darted; every ropeyarn tingling like a wire; the two tall masts buckling like Indian canes in land tornadoes. So full of this reeling scene were we, as we stood by the plunging bowsprit, that for some time we did not notice the jeering glances of the passengers, a lubber-like[8] assembly, who marvelled that two fellow beings should be so companionable; as though a white man were anything more dignified than a whitewashed negro. But there were some boobies and bumpkins there, who, by

---

5. Like the small finger bowls, set at each place at a formal dinner table for dipping messy fingers. Melville's source, *The New Zealanders*, as Sanborn discovered, contains a description (322) of Tupai Cupa's observation and adoption of European manners:

> When in company his manners were perfectly unembarrassed, and he shewed the natural ease of one accustomed to consideration. Yet, conscious of the propriety of conforming himself to the customs of the country in which he was, he was constantly on the watch to observe the behaviour of those around him, and in general his imitation of them was both quick and surprisingly free from awkwardness. . . . The use of finger-glasses and table-napkins he very soon apprehended; and although at first he drank the water from the former, he never again fell into that error.

In the story Queequeg tells Ishmael, Melville humorously inverts the point to make a European captain the blundering violator of the polite social codes of Kokovoko. That is, Sanborn's discovery shows Melville deliberately altering a source so as to upset the unthinking cultural chauvinism of his American and British readers.

6. River flowing between New Bedford and the less-famous Fairhaven (the port from which Melville himself sailed on the *Acushnet* on January 3, 1841).

7. Wild, barbaric, like the medieval Tartar hordes who invaded the broad area in Asia and eastern Europe once called Tartary.

8. Like a clumsy landsman.

their intense greenness, must have come from the heart and centre of all verdure. Queequeg caught one of these young saplings mimicking him behind his back. I thought the bumpkin's hour of doom was come. Dropping his harpoon, the brawny savage caught him in his arms, and by an almost miraculous dexterity and strength, sent him high up bodily into the air; then slightly tapping his stern in mid-somerset, the fellow landed with bursting lungs upon his feet, while Queequeg, turning his back upon him, lighted his tomahawk pipe and passed it to me for a puff.[9]

"Capting! Capting!" yelled the bumpkin, running towards that officer; "Capting, Capting, here's the devil."

"Hallo, *you* sir," cried the Captain, a gaunt rib of the sea, stalking up to Queequeg, "what in thunder do you mean by that? Don't you know you might have killed that chap?"

"What him say?" said Queequeg, as he mildly turned to me.

"He say," said I, "that you came near kill-e that man there," pointing to the still shivering greenhorn.

"Kill-e," cried Queequeg, twisting his tattooed face into an unearthly expression of disdain, "ah! him bery small-e fish-e; Queequeg no kill-e so small-e fish-e; Queequeg kill-e big whale!"

"Look you," roared the Captain, "I'll kill-e *you*, you cannibal, if you try any more of your tricks aboard here; so mind your eye."

But it so happened just then, that it was high time for the Captain to mind his own eye. The prodigious strain upon the main-sail had parted the weather-sheet,[1] and the tremendous boom was now flying from side to side, completely sweeping the entire after part of the deck. The poor fellow whom Queequeg had handled so roughly, was swept overboard; all hands were in a panic; and to attempt snatching at the boom to stay It, seemed madness. It flew from right to left, and back again, almost in one ticking of a watch, and every instant seemed on the point of snapping into splinters. Nothing was done, and nothing seemed capable of being done; those on deck rushed towards the bows, and stood eyeing the boom as if it were the lower jaw of an exasperated whale. In the midst of this consternation, Queequeg dropped deftly to his knees, and crawling under the path of the boom, whipped hold of a rope, secured one end to the bulwarks, and then flinging the other like a lasso, caught it round the boom as it swept over his head, and at the next jerk, the spar was that way trapped, and all was safe. The schooner was run into the wind, and while the hands were clearing away the stern boat, Queequeg, stripped to the waist, darted from the side with a long living arc of a leap. For three minutes or more he was seen swimming like a dog, throwing his long arms straight out before him, and by turns revealing his brawny shoulders through the freezing foam. I looked at the grand and glorious fellow, but saw no one to be saved. The greenhorn

9. Melville alters his source, *The New Zealanders*, Sanborn found, to suppress a rare display of rage by Tupai (and replace it with Queequeg's display of power controlled by good humor):

> In his general demeanour he was very gentle and tractable, but would at times shew a good deal both of the fickleness and the sudden irritability of the savage. On one occasion, when on board the ship, a stout sailor had intentionally affronted him; on which he rushed upon the man, seized him by the neck and the waistband of the trowsers, and after holding him for some moments above his head, dashed him on the deck with great violence (322).

1. Rope (sheet) holding the sails against the force of the wind.

had gone down. Shooting himself perpendicularly from the water, Queequeg now took an instant's glance around him, and seeming to see just how matters were, dived down and disappeared. A few minutes more, and he rose again, one arm still striking out, and with the other dragging a lifeless form. The boat soon picked them up.[2] The poor bumpkin was restored. All hands voted Queequeg a noble trump; the captain begged his pardon. From that hour I clove to Queequeg like a barnacle; yea, till poor Queequeg took his last long dive.

Was there ever such unconsciousness? He did not seem to think that he at all deserved a medal from the Humane and Magnanimous Societies.[3] He only asked for water—fresh water—something to wipe the brine off; that done, he put on dry clothes, lighted his pipe, and leaning against the bulwarks, and mildly eyeing those around him, seemed to be saying to himself—"It's a mutual, joint-stock world,[4] in all meridians. We cannibals must help these Christians."

Chapter 14

Nantucket[1]

Nothing more happened on the passage worthy the mentioning; so, after a fine run, we safely arrived in Nantucket.

Nantucket! Take out your map and look at it. See what a real corner of the world it occupies; how it stands there, away off shore, more lonely than the Eddystone lighthouse.[2] Look at it—a mere hillock, and elbow of sand; all beach, without a background. There is more sand there than you would use in twenty years as a substitute for blotting paper. Some gamesome wights will tell you that they have to plant weeds there, they don't grow naturally; that they import Canada thistles; that they have to send beyond seas for a spile[3] to stop a leak in an oil cask; that pieces of wood in Nantucket are carried about like bits of the true cross in Rome; that people there plant toadstools before their houses, to get under the shade in summer time; that one blade of grass makes an oasis, three blades in a day's walk a prairie; that they wear quicksand shoes, something like Laplander snow-shoes; that they are so shut up, belted about, every way inclosed, surrounded, and made an utter island of by the ocean, that to their very chairs and tables small clams will sometimes be found adher-

---

2. Sanborn points out in *The New Zealanders* a description of the incident that "knit Tupai and Captain Reynolds in indissoluble friendship":

> The Captain fell overboard, and would have perished but for the intrepidity of Tupai, who plunged after him into the water, and having caught hold of him as he was sinking, supported him with the one hand, while he swam with the other, till they were both again taken on board (320).

3. Part of Melville's recurrent jocular references to real or imagined do-good causes and organizations. *Unconsciousness:* lack of self-consciousness.

4. A world like a company whose stockholders share in its responsibilities and profits.

1. Vincent (1949, 81–87) identifies Melville's major sources for this chapter, notably Macy (1835) and Hart (1834) (see the Bibliography on p. 437, herein). Melville visited Nantucket only in 1852, the year after *Moby-Dick* was published.

2. In the English Channel.

3. A wooden plug.

ing, as to the backs of sea turtles. But these extravaganzas only show that Nantucket is no Illinois.

Look now at the wondrous traditional story[4] of how this island was settled by the red-men. Thus goes the legend. In olden times an eagle swooped down upon the New England coast, and carried off an infant Indian in his talons. With loud lament the parents saw their child borne out of sight over the wide waters. They resolved to follow in the same direction. Setting out in their canoes, after a perilous passage they discovered the island, and there they found an empty ivory casket,—the poor little Indian's skeleton.

What wonder, then, that these Nantucketers, born on a beach, should take to the sea for a livelihood! They first caught crabs and quohogs[5] in the sand; grown bolder, they waded out with nets for mackerel; more experienced, they pushed off in boats and captured cod; and at last, launching a navy of great ships on the sea, explored this watery world; put an incessant belt of circumnavigations round it; peeped in at Bhering's Straits;[6] and in all seasons and all oceans declared everlasting war with the mightiest animated mass that has survived the flood;[7] most monstrous and most mountainous! That Himmalehan, salt-sea Mastodon, clothed with such portentousness of unconscious power, that his very panics are more to be dreaded than his most fearless and malicious assaults!

And thus have these naked Nantucketers, these sea hermits, issuing from their ant-hill in the sea, overrun and conquered the watery world like so many Alexanders; parcelling out among them the Atlantic, Pacific, and Indian oceans, as the three pirate powers did Poland. Let America add Mexico to Texas, and pile Cuba upon Canada; let the English overswarm all India, and hang out their blazing banner from the sun; two thirds of this terraqueous globe are the Nantucketer's.[8] For the sea is his; he owns it, as Emperors own empires; other seamen having but a right of way through it. Merchant ships are but extension bridges; armed ones but floating forts; even pirates and privateers, though following the sea as highwaymen[9] the road, they but plunder other ships, other fragments of the land like themselves, without seeking to draw their living from the bottomless deep itself. The Nantucketer, he alone resides and rests on the sea; he alone, in Bible language, goes down to it in ships;[1] to and fro ploughing it as his own special plantation. *There* is his home; *there* lies his

---

4. Melville could have found this in *Collections of the Massachusetts Historical Society*, 2nd series (1815, 3.34) or in another source.
5. Indian name for a native clam.
6. Or Bering Strait, between Asia and North America (Alaska).
7. The flood in Genesis 6–8, thought by some to have killed off prehistoric land mammals (although Noah was said to have taken all species on board the ark). In this extravagant passage, genuinely ancient extinct animals are not distinguished from those now known to have become extinct only relatively recently, such as the mastadon, still occasionally found preserved in ice.
8. Conquerors of two thirds of the *watery world*, they are declared greater than the following. *Alexanders:* Alexander the Great of Macedonia (356–323 B.C.E.). *Three pirate powers:* Russia, Austria, and Prussia, which divided up Poland in the late 18th century. America: the United States, which had annexed Texas in 1845 and the southwest (New Mexico, Arizona, and California) in 1848, and seemed set to gobble up more of Mexico and perhaps all of Cuba and Canada. *English:* the British Empire, which had already taken over most of India.
9. Robbers (also "footpads") who prey on travelers along roads, familiar from Shakespeare's *I Henry IV* 2.2 and 2.4.
1. Psalm 107.23–24: "They that go down to the sea in ships, that do business in great waters; These see the works of the Lord, and his wonders in the deep."

business, which a Noah's flood would not interrupt, though it overwhelmed all the millions in China. He lives on the sea, as prairie cocks in
the prairie; he hides among the waves, he climbs them as chamois hunters
climb the Alps. For years he knows not the land; so that when he comes
to it at last, it smells like another world, more strangely than the moon
would to an Earthsman. With the landless gull, that at sunset folds her
wings and is rocked to sleep between billows; so at nightfall, the
Nantucketer, out of sight of land, furls his sails, and lays him to his rest,
while under his very pillow rush herds of walruses and whales.

Chapter 15

Chowder

It was quite late in the evening when the little Moss came snugly to
anchor, and Queequeg and I went ashore; so we could attend to no business that day, at least none but a supper and a bed. The landlord of the
Spouter-Inn had recommended us to his cousin Hosea Hussey of the Try
Pots,[1] whom he asserted to be the proprietor of one of the best kept hotels
in all Nantucket, and moreover he had assured us that cousin Hosea, as
he called him, was famous for his chowders. In short, he plainly hinted
that we could not possibly do better than try pot-luck at the Try Pots. But
the directions he had given us about keeping a yellow warehouse on our
starboard hand till we opened a white church to the larboard, and then
keeping that on the larboard hand till we made a corner three points[2] to
the starboard, and that done, then ask the first man we met where the
place was: these crooked directions of his very much puzzled us at first,
especially as, at the outset, Queequeg insisted that the yellow warehouse—our first point of departure—must be left on the larboard hand,
whereas I had understood Peter Coffin to say it was on the starboard.
However, by dint of beating about a little in the dark, and now and then
knocking up a peaceable[3] inhabitant to inquire the way, we at last came
to something which there was no mistaking.

Two enormous wooden pots painted black, and suspended by asses'
ears, swung from the cross-trees[4] of an old top-mast, planted in front of
an old doorway. The horns of the cross-trees were sawed off on the other
side, so that this old top-mast looked not a little like a gallows. Perhaps I
was over sensitive to such impressions at the time, but I could not help
staring at this gallows with a vague misgiving. A sort of crick was in my
neck as I gazed up to the two remaining horns; yes, *two* of them, one for
Queequeg, and one for me. It's ominous, thinks I. A Coffin my Innkeeper
upon landing in my first whaling port; tombstones staring at me in the

---

1. Named for the huge vats on the decks of whale ships in which whale blubber is tried out (fried)
to extract the oil.
2. A point is 11.25 degrees of the 360 degrees of a compass card. *Starboard*: right (to one facing the
bow of a ship). *Opened*: sighted. *Larboard*: left.
3. Perhaps not just law-abiding but specifically Quaker. *Knocking up*: waking up, by knocking.
4. Horizontal timbers that sit crosswise to the mast. From such salvaged crosstrees, the inn-sign
pots hang by ear-shaped handles (*asses' ears*).

whalemen's chapel; and here a gallows! and a pair of prodigious black pots too! Are these last throwing out oblique hints touching Tophet?

I was called from these reflections by the sight of a freckled woman with yellow hair and a yellow gown, standing in the porch of the inn, under a dull red lamp swinging there, that looked much like an injured eye, and carrying on a brisk scolding with a man in a purple woollen shirt.

"Get along with ye," said she to the man, "or I'll be combing ye!"

"Come on, Queequeg," said I, "all right. There's Mrs. Hussey."[5]

And so it turned out; Mr. Hosea Hussey being from home, but leaving Mrs. Hussey entirely competent to attend to all his affairs. Upon making known our desires for a supper and a bed, Mrs. Hussey, postponing further scolding for the present, ushered us into a little room, and seating us at a table spread with the relics of a recently concluded repast, turned round to us and said—"Clam or Cod?"

"What's that about Cods, ma'am?" said I, with much politeness.

"Clam or Cod?" she repeated.

"A clam for supper? a cold clam; is *that* what you mean, Mrs. Hussey?" says I; "but that's a rather cold and clammy reception in the winter time, ain't it, Mrs. Hussey?"

But being in a great hurry to resume scolding the man in the purple shirt, who was waiting for it in the entry, and seeming to hear nothing but the word "clam," Mrs. Hussey hurried towards an open door leading to the kitchen, and bawling out "clam for two," disappeared.

"Queequeg," said I, "do you think that we can make out a supper for us both on one clam?"

However, a warm savory steam from the kitchen served to belie the apparently cheerless prospect before us. But when that smoking chowder came in, the mystery was delightfully explained. Oh, sweet friends! hearken to me. It was made of small juicy clams, scarcely bigger than hazel nuts, mixed with pounded ship biscuit,[6] and salted pork cut up into little flakes; the whole enriched with butter, and plentifully seasoned with pepper and salt. Our appetites being sharpened by the frosty voyage, and in particular, Queequeg seeing his favorite fishy food before him, and the chowder being surpassingly excellent, we despatched it with great expedition: when leaning back a moment and bethinking me of Mrs. Hussey's clam and cod announcement, I thought I would try a little experiment. Stepping to the kitchen door, I uttered the word "cod" with great emphasis, and resumed my seat. In a few moments the savory steam came forth again, but with a different flavor, and in good time a fine cod-chowder was placed before us.

We resumed business; and while plying our spoons in the bowl, thinks I to myself, I wonder now if this here has any effect on the head? What's that stultifying saying about chowder-headed[7] people? "But look, Queequeg, ain't that a live eel in your bowl? Where's your harpoon?"

Fishiest of all fishy places was the Try Pots, which well deserved its name; for the pots there were always boiling chowders. Chowder for

5. A "hussy" is a brazen lower class woman, but *Hussey* is a common New England name.
6. Standard shipboard fare, made of flour and water without salt and baked very hard.
7. People with mixed-up or downright stupid minds. But Ishmael intends disrespect toward such people, not toward chowder.

breakfast, and chowder for dinner, and chowder for supper, till you began to look for fish-bones coming through your clothes. The area before the house was paved with clam-shells. Mrs. Hussey wore a polished necklace of codfish vertebra; and Hosea Hussey had his account books bound in superior old shark-skin. There was a fishy flavor to the milk, too, which I could not at all account for, till one morning happening to take a stroll along the beach among some fishermen's boats, I saw Hosea's brindled cow feeding on fish remnants, and marching along the sand with each foot in a cod's decapitated head, looking very slip-shod,[8] I assure ye.

Supper concluded, we received a lamp, and directions from Mrs. Hussey concerning the nearest way to bed; but, as Queequeg was about to precede me up the stairs, the lady reached forth her arm, and demanded his harpoon; she allowed no harpoon in her chambers. "Why not?" said I; "every true whaleman sleeps with his harpoon—but why not?" "Because it's dangerous," says she. "Ever since young Stiggs coming from that unfort'nt v'y'ge of his, when he was gone four years and a half, with ony three barrels of *ile*, was found dead in my first floor back, with his harpoon in his side; ever since then I allow no boarders to take sich dangerous weepons in their rooms a-night. So, Mr. Queequeg" (for she had learned his name), "I will just take this here iron, and keep it for you till morning. But the chowder; clam or cod to-morrow for breakfast, men?"

"Both," says I; "and let's have a couple of smoked herring by way of variety."

Chapter 16

The Ship

In bed we concocted our plans for the morrow. But to my surprise and no small concern, Queequeg now gave me to understand, that he had been diligently consulting Yojo—the name of his black little god—and Yojo had told him two or three times over, and strongly insisted upon it everyway, that instead of our going together among the whaling-fleet in harbor, and in concert selecting our craft; instead of this, I say, Yojo earnestly enjoined that the selection of the ship should rest wholly with me, inasmuch as Yojo purposed befriending us; and, in order to do so, had already pitched upon a vessel, which, if left to myself, I, Ishmael, should infallibly light upon, for all the world as though it had turned out by chance; and in that vessel I must immediately ship myself, for the present irrespective of Queequeg.

I have forgotten to mention that, in many things, Queequeg placed great confidence in the excellence of Yojo's judgment and surprising fore-cast of things; and cherished Yojo with considerable esteem, as a rather good sort of god, who perhaps meant well enough upon the whole, but in all cases did not succeed in his benevolent designs.

---

8. Wearing loose slippers and, therefore, looking slovenly, as the cow looks with each of its feet stuck in a cut-off cod's head.

Now, this plan of Queequeg's, or rather Yojo's, touching the selection of our craft; I did not like that plan at all. I had not a little relied upon Queequeg's sagacity to point out the whaler best fitted to carry us and our fortunes securely. But as all my remonstrances produced no effect upon Queequeg, I was obliged to acquiesce; and accordingly prepared to set about this business with a determined rushing sort of energy and vigor, that should quickly settle that trifling little affair. Next morning early, leaving Queequeg shut up with Yojo in our little bedroom—for it seemed that it was some sort of Lent or Ramadan, or day of fasting,[1] humiliation, and prayer with Queequeg and Yojo that day; how it was I never could find out, for, though I applied myself to it several times, I never could master his liturgies and XXXIX Articles[2]—leaving Queequeg, then, fasting on his tomahawk pipe, and Yojo warming himself at his sacrificial fire of shavings, I sallied out among the shipping. After much prolonged sauntering and many random inquiries, I learnt that there were three ships up for three-years' voyages— The Devil-dam, the Tit-bit,[3] and the Pequod. Devil Dam, I do not know the origin of; Tit-bit is obvious; Pequod, you will no doubt remember, was the name of a celebrated tribe of Massachusetts Indians, now extinct as the ancient Medes.[4] I peered and pryed about the Devil-Dam; from her, hopped over to the Tit-bit; and, finally, going on board the Pequod, looked around her for a moment, and then decided that this was the very ship for us.

You may have seen many a quaint craft in your day, for aught I know;—square-toed luggers; mountainous Japanese junks; butter-box galliots,[5] and what not; but take my word for it, you never saw such a rare old craft as this same rare old Pequod. She was a ship of the old school, rather small if anything; with an old fashioned claw-footed[6] look about her. Long seasoned and weather stained in the typhoons and calms of all four oceans, her old hull's complexion was darkened like a French grenadier's,[7] who has alike fought in Egypt and Siberia. Her venerable bows looked bearded. Her masts—cut somewhere on the coast of Japan, where her original ones were lost overboard in a gale—her masts stood stiffly up like the spines of the three old kings of Cologne.[8] Her ancient decks were worn and wrinkled, like the pilgrim-worshipped flagstone in Canterbury Cathedral where Becket bled.[9] But to all these her

1. Many Christian sects observe Lent, a period (often forty days) before Easter, as a time of prayer and dietary strictness, if not actual fasting (the Episcopalians in Melville's own family were more observant of Lent than the Dutch Reformed were). Ramadan is the ninth month of the Islamic year, during which observant Muslims fast during daylight hours.
2. The official creed of the Church of England since 1563.
3. Or "tidbit," a choice morsel of food; here, slightly vulgar, because it comes right after The Devil-dam (mother of the devil).
4. The Pequots were not extinct, but had been nearly annihilated in 1637. In his youth Melville read of the war against the Pequot (or Pequod) Indians in Benjamin Trumbull's A Complete History of Connecticut (1797, rev. 1818).
5. Or galiots, usually sleek and long, but here (as in Melville's footnote in ch. 61) they are boxy and clumsy. Lugger: small vessel with a lugsail (square sail). Junk: Asian high-topped ship.
6. Like heavy 18th-century furniture with feet carved to resemble the feet of animals, especially lions.
7. Foot soldiers armed with grenades; here, veterans of Napoleon's campaigns in Egypt and Russia (though not as far as Siberia).
8. Late in 1849, on a brief visit to Germany, Melville glimpsed in the great unfinished cathedral three skulls displayed as those of the wise men who followed a star to Bethlehem and gave gifts to the infant Jesus.
9. Landing at Deal in November 1849, Melville walked much of the way to Canterbury, where he toured the cathedral and scrutinized the "ugly place" where four knights of Henry II assassinated Thomas Becket, the archbishop of Canterbury, in 1170.

old antiquities, were added new and marvellous features, pertaining to the wild business that for more than half a century she had followed. Old Captain Peleg, many years her chief-mate, before he commanded another vessel of his own, and now a retired seaman, and one of the principal owners of the Pequod,—this old Peleg, during the term of his chief-mateship, had built upon her original grotesqueness, and inlaid it, all over, with a quaintness both of material and device, unmatched by anything except it be Thorkill-Hake's carved buckler or bedstead.[1] She was apparelled like any barbaric Ethiopian emperor, his neck heavy with pendants of polished ivory. She was a thing of trophies. A cannibal of a craft, tricking herself forth in the chased bones of her enemies. All round, her unpanelled, open bulwarks were garnished like one continuous jaw, with the long sharp teeth of the sperm whale, inserted there for pins, to fasten her old hempen thews and tendons to. Those thews ran not through base blocks of land wood, but deftly travelled over sheaves of sea-ivory. Scorning a turnstile wheel at her reverend helm, she sported there a tiller; and that tiller was in one mass, curiously carved from the long narrow lower jaw of her hereditary foe.[2] The helmsman who steered by that tiller in a tempest, felt like the Tartar,[3] when he holds back his fiery steed by clutching its jaw. A noble craft, but somehow a most melancholy! All noble things are touched with that.

Now when I looked about the quarter-deck, for some one having authority, in order to propose myself as a candidate for the voyage, at first I saw nobody; but I could not well overlook a strange sort of tent, or rather wigwam, pitched a little behind the main-mast. It seemed only a temporary erection used in port. It was of a conical shape, some ten feet high; consisting of the long, huge slabs of limber black bone taken from the middle and highest part of the jaws of the right-whale. Planted with their broad ends on the deck, a circle of these slabs laced together, mutually sloped towards each other, and at the apex united in a tufted point, where the loose hairy fibres waved to and fro like the top-knot on some old Pottowottamie Sachem's[4] head. A triangular opening faced towards the bows of the ship, so that the insider commanded a complete view forward.

And half concealed in this queer tenement, I at length found one who by his aspect seemed to have authority; and who, it being noon, and the ship's work suspended, was now enjoying respite from the burden of command. He was seated on an old-fashioned oaken chair, wriggling all over with curious carving; and the bottom of which was formed of a stout interlacing of the same elastic stuff of which the wigwam was constructed.

There was nothing so very particular, perhaps, about the appearance of the elderly man I saw; he was brown and brawny, like most old sea-

1. Perhaps from an encyclopedia or a magazine, Melville had picked up information about the Icelandic warrior who had his mighty deeds carved on his bed and other furniture.
2. Here the *Pequod* has open bulwarks, unpaneled walls around the upper deck, but in ch. 51 she has solid ones the crew take refuge behind. For steering, here she has a whalebone tiller (one long lever) but later a turnstile wheel (see chs. 61 and 118). *Pins:* belaying pins (clublike fastening pegs). *Thews and tendons:* muscles and cords of a living thing; here, metaphorical. *Blocks* contain the sheave (wheel) of a pulley through which a rope runs.
3. Tartars, Mongolian horsemen who in the 13th century under Genghis Khan overran much of central and western Asia and eastern Europe.
4. Any Algonquin Indian chief of a New York (later Kansas) tribe. Their topknots were scalp locks interwoven with feathers.

men, and heavily rolled up in blue pilot-cloth,[5] cut in the Quaker style; only there was a fine and almost microscopic net-work of the minutest wrinkles interlacing round his eyes, which must have arisen from his continual sailings in many hard gales, and always looking to wind-ward;—for this causes the muscles about the eyes to become pursed together. Such eye-wrinkles are very effectual in a scowl.

"Is this the Captain of the Pequod?" said I, advancing to the door of the tent.

"Supposing it be the Captain of the Pequod, what dost thou[6] want of him?" he demanded.

"I was thinking of shipping."

"Thou wast, wast thou? I see thou art no Nantucketer—ever been in a stove boat?"

"No, Sir, I never have."

"Dost know nothing at all about whaling, I dare say—eh?"

"Nothing, Sir; but I have no doubt I shall soon learn. I've been several voyages in the merchant service, and I think that——"

"Marchant service be damned. Talk not that lingo to me. Dost see that leg?—I'll take that leg away from thy stern, if ever thou talkest of the marchant service to me again. Marchant service indeed! I suppose now ye feel considerable proud of having served in those marchant ships. But flukes! man, what makes thee want to go a whaling, eh?—it looks a little suspicious, don't it, eh?—Hast not been a pirate, hast thou?—Didst not rob thy last Captain, didst thou?—Dost not think of murdering the officers when thou gettest to sea?"

I protested my innocence of these things. I saw that under the mask of these half humorous innuendoes, this old seaman, as an insulated Quakerish Nantucketer, was full of his insular prejudices, and rather distrustful of all aliens, unless they hailed from Cape Cod or the Vineyard.[7]

"But what takes thee a-whaling? I want to know that before I think of shipping ye."

"Well, sir, I want to see what whaling is. I want to see the world."

"Want to see what whaling is, eh? Have ye clapped eye on Captain Ahab?"[8]

"Who is Captain Ahab, sir?"

"Aye, aye, I thought so. Captain Ahab is the Captain of this ship."

"I am mistaken then. I thought I was speaking to the Captain himself."

"Thou art speaking to Captain Peleg—that's who ye are speaking to, young man. It belongs to me and Captain Bildad to see the Pequod fitted out for the voyage, and supplied with all her needs, including crew. We are part owners and agents. But as I was going to say, if thou wantest to know what whaling is, as thou tellest ye do, I can put ye in a way of find-

5. A long overcoat of plain, square cut, this one made of the indigo blue woolen cloth commonly used for mariners' garments.
6. The dialect is explained below as part of "the stately dramatic thee and thou of the Quaker idiom," learned in childhood. Melville and his Ishmael (the self-defined "tragic dramatist," in ch. 33) associate it with the King James Version of the Bible and church services (hence "stately") and with Shakespeare's tragedies (hence "dramatic").
7. Mainland Cape Cod is some thirty miles north of Nantucket Island. The neighboring island of Martha's Vineyard is a little to the west of Nantucket. All are in Massachusetts.
8. The name Ahab is ominous, because 1 Kings 16.28 to 22.40 traces the wicked reign of the idolatrous King Ahab and his wife Jezebel.

ing it out before ye bind yourself to it, past backing out. Clap eye on Captain Ahab, young man, and thou wilt find that he has only one leg."

"What do you mean, sir? Was the other one lost by a whale?"

"Lost by a whale! Young man, come nearer to me: it was devoured, chewed up, crunched by the monstrousest parmacetty that ever chipped a boat!—ah, ah!"

I was a little alarmed by his energy, perhaps also a little touched at the hearty grief in his concluding exclamation, but said as calmly as I could, "What you say is no doubt true enough, sir; but how could I know there was any peculiar ferocity in that particular whale, though indeed I might have inferred as much from the simple fact of the accident."

"Look ye now, young man, thy lungs are a sort of soft, d'ye see; thou dost not talk shark[9] a bit. *Sure*, ye've been to sea before now; sure of that?"

"Sir," said I, "I thought I told you that I had been four voyages in the merchant——"

"Hard down out of that! Mind what I said about the marchant service— don't aggravate me—I won't have it. But let us understand each other. I have given thee a hint about what whaling is; do ye yet feel inclined for it?"

"I do, sir."

"Very good. Now, art thou the man to pitch a harpoon down a live whale's throat, and then jump after it? Answer, quick!"

"I am, sir, if it should be positively indispensable to do so; not to be got rid of, that is; which I don't take to be the fact."

"Good again. Now then, thou not only wantest to go a-whaling, to find out by experience what whaling is, but ye also want to go in order to see the world? Was not that what ye said? I thought so. Well then, just step forward there, and take a peep over the weather-bow,[1] and then back to me and tell me what ye see there."

For a moment I stood a little puzzled by this curious request, not knowing exactly how to take it, whether humorously or in earnest. But concentrating all his crow's feet into one scowl, Captain Peleg started me on the errand.

Going forward and glancing over the weather bow, I perceived that the ship swinging to her anchor with the flood-tide, was now obliquely pointing towards the open ocean. The prospect was unlimited, but exceedingly monotonous and forbidding; not the slightest variety that I could see.

"Well, what's the report?" said Peleg when I came back; "what did ye see?"

"Not much," I replied—"nothing but water; considerable horizon though, and there's a squall coming up, I think."

"Well, what dost thou think then of seeing the world? Do ye wish to go round Cape Horn to see any more of it, eh? Can't ye see the world where you stand?"

I was a little staggered, but go a-whaling I must, and I would; and the Pequod was as good a ship as any—I thought the best—and all this I now

---

9. Straight, tough. Like the landlord at the Spouter Inn, Peleg calls unfavorable attention to Ishmael's formal (schoolmasterly) diction, here also seeming to mistrust his lung power and general health, although Ishmael (below) considers himself of a "broad-shouldered make."

1. That fore side onto which the wind was blowing.

repeated to Peleg. Seeing me so determined, he expressed his willingness to ship me.

"And thou mayest as well sign the papers right off," he added—"come along with ye." And so saying, he led the way below deck into the cabin.

Seated on the transom[2] was what seemed to me a most uncommon and surprising figure. It turned out to be Captain Bildad, who along with Captain Peleg was one of the largest owners of the vessel; the other shares, as is sometimes the case in these ports, being held by a crowd of old annuitants; widows, fatherless children, and chancery wards; each owning about the value of a timber head, or a foot of plank, or a nail or two in the ship. People in Nantucket invest their money in whaling vessels, the same way that you do yours in approved state stocks[3] bringing in good interest.

Now, Bildad, like Peleg, and indeed many other Nantucketers, was a Quaker, the island having been originally settled by that sect; and to this day its inhabitants in general retain in an uncommon measure the peculiarities of the Quaker, only variously and anomalously modified by things altogether alien and heterogeneous. For some of these same Quakers are the most sanguinary of all sailors and whale-hunters. They are fighting Quakers; they are Quakers with a vengeance.[4]

So that there are instances among them of men, who, named with Scripture names—a singularly common fashion on the island—and in childhood naturally imbibing the stately dramatic thee and thou of the Quaker idiom; still, from the audacious, daring, and boundless adventure of their subsequent lives, strangely blend with these unoutgrown peculiarities, a thousand bold dashes of character, not unworthy a Scandinavian sea-king, or a poetical Pagan Roman.[5] And when these things unite in a man of greatly superior natural force, with a globular brain and a ponderous heart; who has also by the stillness and seclusion of many long night-watches in the remotest waters, and beneath constellations never seen here at the north, been led to think untraditionally and independently; receiving all nature's sweet or savage impressions fresh from her own virgin, voluntary, and confiding breast, and thereby chiefly, but with some help from accidental advantages, to learn a bold and nervous lofty language—that man makes one in a whole nation's census—a mighty pageant creature, formed for noble tragedies. Nor will it at all detract from him, dramatically regarded, if either by birth or other circumstances, he have what seems a half wilful over-rul-

---

2. Crossbeam in the stern, used as a seat.
3. Shares of stock issued by (and guaranteed by) a state of the Union. *Annuitants:* people living on payments given at yearly or other regular intervals. *Chancery wards:* people under the guardianship of courts. *Timber head:* the above-deck part of one of the ship's ribs.
4. Quakers (or Friends) were not the first white settlers but had become a large part of the population of Nantucket. Being a sanguinary (bloodthirsty, murderous) "fighting Quaker" contradicts the basic pacifist tenets of the Society of Friends. "Quakers with a vengeance" plays on the term *with a vengeance* ("to an extreme degree"), the point being that Quakers (even more than other modern Christians) are expected to behave as Jesus commanded (Matthew 5.39): "But I say unto you, That ye resist not evil: but whosoever shall smite thee on thy right cheek, turn to him the other also." (Owing to such beliefs, some Quakers in wartime choose to be conscientious objectors.)
5. Fit to be the hero of a saga about the Vikings or of an epic or drama about ancient Rome. In the paragraph as a whole Melville suggests some of the influences that might work together to create "a mighty pageant creature," the sort that an American writer of his own time might dare to celebrate as a believable American tragic hero.

ing morbidness at the bottom of his nature. For all men tragically great are made so through a certain morbidness. Be sure of this, O young ambition, all mortal greatness is but disease. But, as yet we have not to do with such an one, but with quite another; and still a man, who, if indeed peculiar, it only results again from another phase of the Quaker, modified by individual circumstances.

Like Captain Peleg, Captain Bildad was a well-to-do, retired whaleman. But unlike Captain Peleg—who cared not a rush for what are called serious things, and indeed deemed those self-same serious things the veriest of all trifles—Captain Bildad had not only been originally educated according to the strictest sect of Nantucket Quakerism, but all his subsequent ocean life, and the sight of many unclad, lovely island creatures, round the Horn—all that had not moved this native born Quaker one single jot, had not so much as altered one angle of his vest. Still, for all this immutableness, was there some lack of common consistency about worthy Captain Bildad. Though refusing, from conscientious scruples, to bear arms against land invaders, yet himself had illimitably invaded the Atlantic and Pacific; and though a sworn foe to human bloodshed, yet had he in his straight-bodied coat, spilled tuns[6] upon tuns of leviathan gore. How now in the contemplative evening of his days, the pious Bildad reconciled these things in the reminiscence, I do not know; but it did not seem to concern him much, and very probably he had long since come to the sage and sensible conclusion that a man's religion is one thing, and this practical world quite another. This world pays dividends. Rising from a little cabin-boy in short clothes of the drabbest drab, to a harpooneer in a broad shad-bellied waistcoat;[7] from that becoming boat-header, chief-mate, and captain, and finally a ship-owner; Bildad, as I hinted before, had concluded his adventurous career by wholly retiring from active life at the goodly age of sixty, and dedicating his remaining days to the quiet receiving of his well-earned income.

Now Bildad, I am sorry to say, had the reputation of being an incorrigible old hunks, and in his sea-going days, a bitter, hard task-master. They told me in Nantucket, though it certainly seems a curious story, that when he sailed the old Categut[8] whaleman, his crew, upon arriving home, were mostly all carried ashore to the hospital, sore exhausted and worn out. For a pious man, especially for a Quaker, he was certainly rather hard-hearted, to say the least. He never used to swear, though, at his men, they said; but somehow he got an inordinate quantity of cruel, unmitigated hard work out of them. When Bildad was a chief-mate, to have his drab-colored[9] eye intently looking at you, made you feel completely nervous, till you could clutch something—a hammer or a marling-spike,[1] and go to work like mad, at something or other, never mind what. Indolence and idleness perished from before him. His own person was the exact embodiment of his utilitarian character. On his long, gaunt body, he carried no spare flesh, no superfluous beard, his

6. A tun is an enormous barrel containing 252 gallons.
7. Wide-bodied but tight-waisted vest.
8. Possibly, a whaleship named for the Kattegat Strait between Sweden and Denmark.
9. Dull brown.
1. Pointed steel tool for splicing.

chin having a soft, economical nap to it, like the worn nap of his broad-brimmed hat.[2]

Such, then, was the person that I saw seated on the transom when I followed Captain Peleg down into the cabin. The space between the decks was small; and there, bolt-upright, sat old Bildad, who always sat so, and never leaned, and this to save his coat tails. His broad-brim was placed beside him; his legs were stiffly crossed; his drab vesture was buttoned up to his chin; and spectacles on nose, he seemed absorbed in reading from a ponderous volume.

"Bildad," cried Captain Peleg, "at it again, Bildad, eh? Ye have been studying those Scriptures, now, for the last thirty years, to my certain knowledge. How far ye got, Bildad?"

As if long habituated to such profane talk from his old shipmate, Bildad, without noticing his present irreverence, quietly looked up, and seeing me, glanced again inquiringly towards Peleg.

"He says he's our man, Bildad," said Peleg, "he wants to ship."

"Dost thee?" said Bildad, in a hollow tone, and turning round to me.

"I dost," said I unconsciously, he was so intense a Quaker.

"What do ye think of him, Bildad?" said Peleg.

"He'll do," said Bildad, eyeing me, and then went on spelling away at his book in a mumbling tone quite audible.

I thought him the queerest old Quaker I ever saw, especially as Peleg, his friend and old shipmate, seemed such a blusterer. But I said nothing, only looking round me sharply. Peleg now threw open a chest, and drawing forth the ship's articles,[3] placed pen and ink before him, and seated himself at a little table. I began to think it was high time to settle with myself at what terms I would be willing to engage for the voyage. I was already aware that in the whaling business they paid no wages; but all hands, including the captain, received certain shares of the profits called *lays*, and that these lays were proportioned to the degree of importance pertaining to the respective duties of the ship's company. I was also aware that being a green hand at whaling, my own lay would not be very large; but considering that I was used to the sea, could steer a ship, splice a rope, and all that,[4] I made no doubt that from all I had heard I should be offered at least the 275th lay—that is, the 275th part of the clear nett proceeds of the voyage, whatever that might eventually amount to. And though the 275th lay was what they call a rather *long lay*, yet it was better than nothing; and if we had a lucky voyage, might pretty nearly pay for the clothing I would wear out on it, not to speak of my three years' beef and board, for which I would not have to pay one stiver.[5]

It might be thought that this was a poor way to accumulate a princely fortune—and so it was, a very poor way indeed. But I am one of those that never take on about princely fortunes, and am quite content if the world is ready to board and lodge me, while I am putting up at this grim sign of the Thunder Cloud.[6] Upon the whole, I thought that the 275th lay would

2. So characteristic of the males of the sect that *Broad brim* was colloquial for "Quaker."
3. The legal document by which owners contracted for the services of sailors.
4. Skills an owner would expect of an able seaman.
5. Dutch coin worth about two cents.
6. At the ominous inn we all lodge in while here on earth.

be about the fair thing, but would not have been surprised had I been offered the 200th, considering I was of a broad-shouldered make.

But one thing, nevertheless, that made me a little distrustful about receiving a generous share of the profits was this: Ashore, I had heard something of both Captain Peleg and his unaccountable old crony Bildad; how that they being the principal proprietors of the Pequod, therefore the other and more inconsiderable and scattered owners, left nearly the whole management of the ship's affairs to these two. And I did not know but what the stingy old Bildad might have a mighty deal to say about shipping hands, especially as I now found him on board the Pequod, quite at home there in the cabin, and reading his Bible as if at his own fireside. Now while Peleg was vainly trying to mend a pen[7] with his jack-knife, old Bildad, to my no small surprise, considering that he was such an interested party in these proceedings; Bildad never heeded us, but went on mumbling to himself out of his book, "'Lay not up for yourselves treasures upon earth, where moth—'"[8]

"Well, Captain Bildad," interrupted Peleg, "what d'ye say, what lay shall we give this young man?"

"Thou knowest best," was the sepulchral reply, "the seven hundred and seventy-seventh[9] wouldn't be too much, would it?—'where moth and rust do corrupt, but lay—'"

Lay, indeed, thought I, and such a lay! the seven hundred and seventy-seventh! Well, old Bildad, you are determined that I, for one, shall not lay up many lays here below, where moth and rust do corrupt. It was an exceedingly long lay that, indeed; and though from the magnitude of the figure it might at first deceive a landsman, yet the slightest consideration will show that though seven hundred and seventy-seven is a pretty large number, yet, when you come to make a teenth[1] of it, you will then see, I say, that the seven hundred and seventy-seventh part of a farthing is a good deal less than seven hundred and seventy-seven gold doubloons; and so I thought at the time.

"Why, blast your eyes, Bildad," cried Peleg, "thou dost not want to swindle this young man! he must have more than that."

"Seven hundred and seventy-seventh," again said Bildad, without lifting his eyes; and then went on mumbling—"'for where your treasure is, there will your heart be also.'"

"I am going to put him down for the three hundredth," said Peleg, "do ye hear that, Bildad! The three hundredth lay, I say."

Bildad laid down his book, and turning solemnly towards him said, "Captain Peleg, thou hast a generous heart; but thou must consider the duty thou owest to the other owners of this ship—widows and orphans,[2] many of them—and that if we too abundantly reward the labors of this

---

7. Sharpen a quill pen (made from a goose feather).
8. Jesus' words in Matthew 6.19–21: "Lay not up for yourselves treasures upon earth, where moth and rust doth corrupt, and where thieves break through and steal: But lay up for yourselves treasures in heaven, where neither moth nor rust doth corrupt, and where thieves do not break through nor steal: For where your treasure is, there will your heart be also."
9. Biblical number, from Genesis 5.31: "And all the days of Lamech were seven hundred seventy and seven years: and he died."
1. That is, "-tieth."
2. Exodus 22.22: "Ye shall not afflict any widow, or fatherless child." Psalm 94.6: "They slay the widow and the stranger, and murder the fatherless."

young man, we may be taking the bread from those widows and those orphans. The seven hundred and seventy-seventh lay, Captain Peleg."

"Thou Bildad!" roared Peleg, starting up and clattering about the cabin. "Blast ye, Captain Bildad, if I had followed thy advice in these matters, I would afore now had a conscience to lug about that would be heavy enough to founder the largest ship that ever sailed round Cape Horn."

"Captain Peleg," said Bildad steadily, "thy conscience may be drawing ten inches of water, or ten fathoms,[3] I can't tell; but as thou art still an impenitent man, Captain Peleg, I greatly fear lest thy conscience be but a leaky one; and will in the end sink thee foundering down to the fiery pit, Captain Peleg."

"Fiery pit! fiery pit! ye insult me, man; past all natural bearing, ye insult me. It's an all-fired outrage to tell any human creature that he's bound to hell. Flukes and flames! Bildad, say that again to me, and start my soul-bolts, but I'll—I'll—yes, I'll swallow a live goat with all his hair and horns on. Out of the cabin, ye canting, drab-colored son of a wooden gun—a straight wake with ye!"

As he thundered out this he made a rush at Bildad, but with a marvellous oblique, sliding celerity, Bildad for that time eluded him.

Alarmed at this terrible outburst between the two principal and responsible owners of the ship, and feeling half a mind to give up all idea of sailing in a vessel so questionably owned and temporarily commanded, I stepped aside from the door to give egress to Bildad, who, I made no doubt, was all eagerness to vanish from before the awakened wrath of Peleg. But to my astonishment, he sat down again on the transom very quietly, and seemed to have not the slightest intention of withdrawing. He seemed quite used to impenitent Peleg and his ways. As for Peleg, after letting off his rage as he had, there seemed no more left in him, and he, too, sat down like a lamb, though he twitched a little as if still nervously agitated. "Whew!" he whistled at last—"the squall's gone off to leeward, I think. Bildad, thou used to be good at sharpening a lance, mend that pen, will ye. My jack-knife here needs the grindstone. Thank ye; thank ye, Bildad. Now then, my young man, Ishmael's thy name, didn't ye say? Well then, down ye go here, Ishmael, for the three hundredth lay."

"Captain Peleg," said I, "I have a friend with me who wants to ship too—shall I bring him down to-morrow?"

"To be sure," said Peleg. "Fetch him along, and we'll look at him."

"What lay does *he* want?" groaned Bildad, glancing up from the book in which he had again been burying himself.

"Oh! never thee mind about that, Bildad," said Peleg. "Has he ever whaled it any?" turning to me.

"Killed more whales than I can count, Captain Peleg."

"Well, bring him along then."

And, after signing the papers, off I went; nothing doubting but that I had done a good morning's work, and that the Pequod was the identical ship that Yojo had provided to carry Queequeg and me round the Cape.

But I had not proceeded far, when I began to bethink me that the captain with whom I was to sail yet remained unseen by me; though, indeed,

---

3. Displacing ten inches of water (with a clear conscience) or sixty feet (so guilty as to be foundering).

in many cases, a whale-ship will be completely fitted out, and receive all
her crew on board, ere the captain makes himself visible by arriving to
take command; for sometimes these voyages are so prolonged, and the
shore intervals at home so exceedingly brief, that if the captain have a
family, or any absorbing concernment of that sort, he does not trouble
himself much about his ship in port, but leaves her to the owners till all
is ready for sea. However, it is always as well to have a look at him before
irrevocably committing yourself into his hands. Turning back I accosted
Captain Peleg, inquiring where Captain Ahab was to be found.

"And what dost thou want of Captain Ahab? It's all right enough, thou
art shipped."

"Yes, but I should like to see him."

"But I don't think thou wilt be able to at present. I don't know exactly
what's the matter with him; but he keeps close inside the house; a sort of
sick, and yet he don't look so. In fact, he ain't sick; but no, he isn't well
either. Any how, young man, he won't always see me, so I don't suppose
he will thee. He's a queer man, Captain Ahab—so some think—but a good
one. Oh, thou'lt like him well enough; no fear, no fear. He's a grand,
ungodly, god-like man, Captain Ahab; doesn't speak much; but, when he
does speak, then you may well listen. Mark ye, be forewarned; Ahab's
above the common; Ahab's been in colleges, as well as 'mong the cannibals; been used to deeper wonders than the waves; fixed his fiery lance in
mightier, stranger foes than whales. His lance! aye, the keenest and the
surest that, out of all our isle! Oh! he ain't Captain Bildad; no, and he ain't
Captain Peleg; he's Ahab, boy; and Ahab of old, thou knowest, was a
crowned king!"

"And a very vile one. When that wicked king was slain, the dogs, did
they not lick his blood?"[4]

"Come hither to me—hither, hither," said Peleg, with a significance in
his eye that almost startled me. "Look ye, lad; never say that on board the
Pequod. Never say it anywhere. Captain Ahab did not name himself. 'Twas
a foolish, ignorant whim of his crazy, widowed mother, who died when he
was only a twelvemonth old. And yet the old squaw Tistig; at Gay-head,[5]
said that the name would somehow prove prophetic. And, perhaps, other
fools like her may tell thee the same. I wish to warn thee. It's a lie. I know
Captain Ahab well; I've sailed with him as mate years ago; I know what he
is—a good man—not a pious, good man, like Bildad, but a swearing good
man—something like me—only there's a good deal more of him. Aye, aye,
I know that he was never very jolly; and I know that on the passage home,
he was a little out of his mind for a spell; but it was the sharp shooting
pains in his bleeding stump that brought that about, as any one might see.
I know, too, that ever since he lost his leg last voyage by that accursed
whale, he's been a kind of moody—desperate moody, and savage sometimes; but that will all pass off. And once for all, let me tell thee and
assure thee, young man, it's better to sail with a moody good captain than

4. In 1 Kings 21 Ahab covets Naboth's vineyard; and when Naboth will not part with it Ahab's
queen, Jezebel, sets men to accuse Naboth falsely of blasphemy, so that he is stoned to death.
The prophet Elijah warns Ahab (verse 19): "In the place where dogs licked the blood of Naboth
shall dogs lick thy blood, even thine." The Lord further warns, through Elijah (verse 23), that the
"dogs shall eat Jezebel by the wall of Jezreel."
5. The "most westerly promontory of Martha's Vineyard" (ch. 27).

a laughing bad one. So good-bye to thee—and wrong not Captain Ahab, because he happens to have a wicked name. Besides, my boy, he has a wife—not three voyages wedded—a sweet, resigned girl. Think of that; by that sweet girl that old man has a child: hold ye then there can be any utter, hopeless harm in Ahab? No, no, my lad; stricken, blasted, if he be, Ahab has his humanities!"

As I walked away, I was full of thoughtfulness; what had been incidentally revealed to me of Captain Ahab, filled me with a certain wild vagueness of painfulness concerning him. And somehow, at the time, I felt a sympathy and a sorrow for him, but for I don't know what, unless it was the cruel loss of his leg. And yet I also felt a strange awe of him; but that sort of awe, which I cannot at all describe, was not exactly awe; I do not know what it was. But I felt it; and it did not disincline me towards him; though I felt impatience at what seemed like mystery in him, so imperfectly as he was known to me then. However, my thoughts were at length carried in other directions, so that for the present dark Ahab slipped my mind.

Chapter 17

The Ramadan

As Queequeg's Ramadan, or Fasting and Humiliation, was to continue all day, I did not choose to disturb him till towards night-fall; for I cherish the greatest respect towards everybody's religious obligations, never mind how comical, and could not find it in my heart to undervalue even a congregation of ants worshipping a toad-stool; or those other creatures in certain parts of our earth, who with a degree of footmanism[1] quite unprecedented in other planets, bow down before the torso of a deceased landed proprietor merely on account of the inordinate possessions yet owned and rented in his name.

I say, we good Presbyterian Christians[2] should be charitable in these things, and not fancy ourselves so vastly superior to other mortals, pagans and what not, because of their half-crazy conceits on these subjects. There was Queequeg, now, certainly entertaining the most absurd notions about Yojo and his Ramadan;—but what of that? Queequeg thought he knew what he was about, I suppose; he seemed to be content; and there let him rest. All our arguing with him would not avail; let him be, I say: and Heaven have mercy on us all—Presbyterians and Pagans alike—for we are all somehow dreadfully cracked about the head, and sadly need mending.

Towards evening, when I felt assured that all his performances and rituals must be over, I went up to his room and knocked at the door; but no answer. I tried to open it, but it was fastened inside. "Queequeg," said I softly through the key-hole;—all silent. "I say, Queequeg! why don't you

1. Obsequiousness.
2. See n. 4, p. 57. This mild theological observation masked bravado—defiance that all but invited attack from Melville's enemies in the Presbyterian press who represented an extreme of the "religious right" of his time. (See the essays in "Before *Moby-Dick*," p. 465 herein.)

speak? It's I—Ishmael." But all remained still as before. I began to grow
alarmed. I had allowed him such abundant time; I thought he might have
had an apoplectic fit. I looked through the key-hole; but the door opening
into an odd corner of the room, the key-hole prospect was but a crooked
and sinister one. I could only see part of the foot-board of the bed and a
line of the wall, but nothing more. I was surprised to behold resting
against the wall the wooden shaft of Queequeg's harpoon, which the landlady the evening previous had taken from him, before our mounting to the
chamber. That's strange, thought I; but at any rate, since the harpoon
stands yonder, and he seldom or never goes abroad without it, therefore
he must be inside here, and no possible mistake.

"Queequeg!—Queequeg!"—all still. Something must have happened.
Apoplexy! I tried to burst open the door; but it stubbornly resisted.
Running down stairs, I quickly stated my suspicions to the first person I
met—the chamber-maid. "La! La!" she cried, "I thought something must
be the matter. I went to make the bed after breakfast, and the door was
locked; and not a mouse to be heard; and it's been just so silent ever since.
But I thought, may be, you had both gone off and locked your baggage in
for safe keeping. La! La, ma'am!—Mistress! murder! Mrs. Hussey!
apoplexy!"—and with these cries, she ran towards the kitchen, I following.

Mrs. Hussey soon appeared, with a mustard-pot in one hand and a vinegar-cruet in the other, having just broken away from the occupation of
attending to the castors,[3] and scolding her little black boy meantime.

"Wood-house!" cried I, "which way to it? Run for God's sake, and fetch
something to pry open the door—the axe!—the axe!—he's had a stroke;
depend upon it!"—and so saying I was unmethodically rushing up stairs
again empty-handed, when Mrs. Hussey interposed the mustard-pot and
vinegar-cruet, and the entire castor of her countenance.

"What's the matter with you, young man?"

"Get the axe! For God's sake, run for the doctor, some one, while I pry
it open!"

"Look here," said the landlady, quickly putting down the vinegar-cruet,
so as to have one hand free; "look here; are you talking about prying open
any of my doors?"—and with that she seized my arm. "What's the matter
with you? What's the matter with you, shipmate?"

In as calm, but rapid a manner as possible, I gave her to understand the
whole case. Unconsciously clapping the mustard-pot to one side of her
nose, she ruminated for an instant; then exclaimed—"No! I haven't seen
it since I put it there." Running to a little closet under the landing of the
stairs, she glanced in, and returning, told me that Queequeg's harpoon
was missing. "He's killed himself," she cried. "It's unfort'nate Stiggs done
over again—there goes another counterpane—God pity his poor
mother!—it will be the ruin of my house. Has the poor lad a sister?
Where's that girl?—there, Betty, go to Snarles the Painter, and tell him to
paint me a sign, with—'no suicides permitted here, and no smoking in the
parlor;'—might as well kill both birds at once.[4] Kill? The Lord be merci-
ful to his ghost! What's that noise there? You, young man, avast there!"

3. Small trays (to set on tables), containing condiments (here, mustard and vinegar) in little
vessels.
4. From the proverb about economy of effort, killing two birds with one stone.

And running up after me, she caught me as I was again trying to force open the door.

"I won't allow it; I won't have my premises spoiled. Go for the locksmith, there's one about a mile from here. But avast!" putting her hand in her side-pocket, "here's a key that'll fit, I guess; let's see." And with that, she turned it in the lock; but, alas! Queequeg's supplemental bolt remained unwithdrawn within.

"Have to burst it open," said I, and was running down the entry a little, for a good start, when the landlady caught at me, again vowing I should not break down her premises; but I tore from her, and with a sudden bodily rush dashed myself full against the mark.

With a prodigious noise the door flew open, and the knob slamming against the wall, sent the plaster to the ceiling; and there, good heavens! there sat Queequeg, altogether cool and self-collected; right in the middle of the room; squatting on his hams, and holding Yojo on top of his head. He looked neither one way nor the other way, but sat like a carved image with scarce a sign of active life.

"Queequeg," said I, going up to him, "Queequeg, what's the matter with you?"

"He hain't been a sittin' so all day, has he?" said the landlady.

But all we said, not a word could we drag out of him; I almost felt like pushing him over, so as to change his position, for it was almost intolerable, it seemed so painfully and unnaturally constrained; especially, as in all probability he had been sitting so for upwards of eight or ten hours, going too without his regular meals.

"Mrs. Hussey," said I, "he's *alive* at all events; so leave us, if you please, and I will see to this strange affair myself."

Closing the door upon the landlady, I endeavored to prevail upon Queequeg to take a chair; but in vain. There he sat; and all I could do— for all my polite arts and blandishments—he would not move a peg, nor say a single word, nor even look at me, nor notice my presence in any the slightest way.

I wonder, thought I, if this can possibly be a part of his Ramadan; do they fast on their hams that way in his native island. It must be so; yes, it's part of his creed, I suppose; well, then, let him rest; he'll get up sooner or later, no doubt. It can't last for ever, thank God, and his Ramadan only comes once a year; and I don't believe it's very punctual then.

I went down to supper. After sitting a long time listening to the long stories of some sailors who had just come from a plum-pudding voyage, as they called it (that is, a short whaling-voyage in a schooner or brig, confined to the north of the line,[5] in the Atlantic Ocean only); after listening to these plum-puddingers till nearly eleven o'clock, I went up stairs to go to bed, feeling quite sure by this time Queequeg must certainly have brought his Ramadan to a termination. But no; there he was just where I had left him; he had not stirred an inch. I began to grow vexed with him; it seemed so downright senseless and insane to be sitting there all day and half the night on his hams in a cold room, holding a piece of wood on his head.

5. The equator, the latitudinal line dividing the Northern and Southern Hemispheres.

"For heaven's sake, Queequeg, get up and shake yourself; get up and have some supper. You'll starve; you'll kill yourself, Queequeg." But not a word did he reply.

Despairing of him, therefore, I determined to go to bed and to sleep; and no doubt, before a great while, he would follow me. But previous to turning in, I took my heavy bearskin jacket,[6] and threw it over him, as it promised to be a very cold night; and he had nothing but his ordinary round jacket on. For some time, do all I would, I could not get into the faintest doze. I had blown out the candle; and the mere thought of Queequeg—not four feet off—sitting there in that uneasy position, stark alone in the cold and dark; this made me really wretched. Think of it; sleeping all night in the same room with a wide awake pagan on his hams in this dreary, unaccountable Ramadan!

But somehow I dropped off at last, and knew nothing more till break of day; when, looking over the bedside, there squatted Queequeg, as if he had been screwed down to the floor. But as soon as the first glimpse of sun entered the window, up he got, with stiff and grating joints, but with a cheerful look; limped towards me where I lay; pressed his forehead again against mine; and said his Ramadan was over.

Now, as I before hinted, I have no objection to any person's religion, be it what it may, so long as that person does not kill or insult any other person, because that other person don't believe it also. But when a man's religion becomes really frantic; when it is a positive torment to him; and, in fine, makes this earth of ours an uncomfortable inn to lodge in; then I think it high time to take that individual aside and argue the point with him.

And just so I now did with Queequeg. "Queequeg," said I, "get into bed now, and lie and listen to me." I then went on, beginning with the rise and progress of the primitive religions, and coming down to the various religions of the present time, during which time I labored to show Queequeg that all these Lents, Ramadans, and prolonged ham-squattings in cold, cheerless rooms were stark nonsense; bad for the health; useless for the soul; opposed, in short, to the obvious laws of Hygiene and common sense. I told him, too, that he being in other things such an extremely sensible and sagacious savage, it pained me, very badly pained me, to see him now so deplorably foolish about this ridiculous Ramadan of his. Besides, argued I, fasting makes the body cave in; hence the spirit caves in; and all thoughts born of a fast must necessarily be half-starved. This is the reason why most dyspeptic religionists cherish such melancholy notions about their hereafters. In one word, Queequeg, said I, rather digressively; hell is an idea first born on an undigested apple-dumpling; and since then perpetuated through the hereditary dyspepsias nurtured by Ramadans.

I then asked Queequeg whether he himself was ever troubled with dyspepsia; expressing the idea very plainly, so that he could take it in. He said no; only upon one memorable occasion. It was after a great feast given by his father the king, on the gaining of a great battle wherein fifty of the enemy had been killed by about two o'clock in the afternoon, and all cooked and eaten that very evening.

6. As in ch. 7, jacket of coarse woolen cloth, not of actual skins of bears. (However, furs were commonly used. Melville's older brother had been in the fur business in the mid-1830s, and at the time of *Moby-Dick* the family members wrapped themselves in buffalo hides for winter drives.)

"No more, Queequeg," said I, shuddering; "that will do;" for I knew the inferences without his further hinting them. I had seen a sailor who had visited that very island, and he told me that it was the custom, when a great battle had been gained there, to barbecue all the slain in the yard or garden of the victor; and then, one by one, they were placed in great wooden trenchers, and garnished round like a pilau, with breadfruit and cocoanuts; and with some parsley in their mouths, were sent round with the victor's compliments to all his friends, just as though these presents were so many Christmas turkeys.[7]

After all, I do not think that my remarks about religion made much impression upon Queequeg. Because, in the first place, he somehow seemed dull of hearing on that important subject, unless considered from his own point of view; and, in the second place, he did not more than one third understand me, couch my ideas simply as I would; and, finally, he no doubt thought he knew a good deal more about the true religion than I did. He looked at me with a sort of condescending concern and compassion, as though he thought it a great pity that such a sensible young man should be so hopelessly lost to evangelical pagan piety.[8]

At last we rose and dressed; and Queequeg, taking a prodigiously hearty breakfast of chowders of all sorts, so that the landlady should not make much profit by reason of his Ramadan, we sallied out to board the Pequod, sauntering along, and picking our teeth with halibut bones.

Chapter 18

His Mark

As we were walking down the end of the wharf towards the ship, Queequeg carrying his harpoon, Captain Peleg in his gruff voice loudly hailed us from his wigwam, saying he had not suspected my friend was a cannibal, and furthermore announcing that he let no cannibals on board that craft, unless they previously produced their papers.[1]

"What do you mean by that, Captain Peleg?" said I, now jumping on the bulwarks, and leaving my comrade standing on the wharf.

"I mean," he replied, "he must show his papers."

"Yea," said Captain Bildad in his hollow voice, sticking his head from behind Peleg's, out of the wigwam. "He must show that he's converted. Son of darkness," he added, turning to Queequeg, "art thou at present in communion with any christian church?"

"Why," said I, "he's a member of the First Congregational Church." Here be it said, that many tattooed savages sailing in Nantucket ships at last come to be converted into the churches.

"First Congregational Church," cried Bildad, "what! that worships in

---

7. A facetious travesty on the cannibal custom, which Melville had recounted with horror in *Typee*, ch. 32.
8. That is, to Queequeg's proselytizing efforts to win Ishmael to his own cannibal religious faith. Such joking about cultural relativism and particularly about religious relativism triggered some of the most virulent attacks on *Moby-Dick*.
1. Documents certifying their baptism and church membership.

Deacon Deuteronomy Coleman's meeting-house?"[2] and so saying, taking out his spectacles, he rubbed them with his great yellow bandana handkerchief, and putting them on very carefully, came out of the wigwam, and leaning stiffly over the bulwarks, took a good long look at Queequeg.

"How long hath he been a member?" he then said, turning to me; "not very long, I rather guess, young man."

"No," said Peleg, "and he hasn't been baptized right either, or it would have washed some of that devil's blue off his face."

"Do tell, now," cried Bildad, "is this Philistine a regular member of Deacon Deuteronomy's meeting? I never saw him going there, and I pass it every Lord's day."

"I don't know anything about Deacon Deuteronomy or his meeting," said I, "all I know is, that Queequeg here is a born member of the First Congregational Church. He is a deacon himself, Queequeg is."

"Young man," said Bildad sternly, "thou art skylarking with me—explain thyself, thou young Hittite.[3] What church dost thee mean? answer me."

Finding myself thus hard pushed, I replied, "I mean, sir, the same ancient Catholic Church to which you and I, and Captain Peleg there, and Queequeg here, and all of us, and every mother's son and soul of us belong; the great and everlasting First Congregation of this whole worshipping world; we all belong to that; only some of us cherish some queer crotchets noways touching the grand belief; in *that* we all join hands."

"Splice, thou mean'st *splice* hands," cried Peleg, drawing nearer. "Young man, you'd better ship for a missionary, instead of a fore-mast hand; I never heard a better sermon. Deacon Deuteronomy—why Father Mapple himself couldn't beat it, and he's reckoned something. Come aboard, come aboard; never mind about the papers. I say, tell Quohog[4] there—what's that you call him? tell Quohog to step along. By the great anchor, what a harpoon he's got there! looks like good stuff that; and he handles it about right. I say, Quohog, or whatever your name is, did you ever stand in the head of a whale-boat? did you ever strike a fish?"[5]

Without saying a word, Queequeg, in his wild sort of way, jumped upon the bulwarks, from thence into the bows of one of the whale-boats hanging to the side; and then bracing his left knee, and poising his harpoon, cried out in some such way as this:—

"Cap'ain, you see him small drop tar on water dere? You see him? well, spose him one whale eye, well, den!" and taking sharp aim at it, he darted the iron right over old Bildad's broad brim, clean across the ship's decks, and struck the glistening tar spot out of sight.

"Now," said Queequeg, quietly hauling in the line, "spos-ee him whale-e eye; why, dad whale dead."

2. Ishmael "skylarks" with the old captains by playing on the name of the Congregational church, from Puritan colonial times the most common denomination all over New England, with one congregation (and "meeting-house") or more in each town, the oldest being designated "First." *Deacon:* a layman elected to assist the minister. *Deuteronomy:* the fifth book of the Bible (a comically extreme example of the appropriation of biblical names in New England).
3. Idolatrous tribe hostile to the Jews, as were the Philistines.
4. Peleg avoids the pagan name "Queequeg" by converting it into the familiar words, quohog (or quahog), a local clam, then hedgehog.
5. Harpoon a whale.

"Quick, Bildad," said Peleg, to his partner, who, aghast at the close vicinity of the flying harpoon, had retreated towards the cabin gangway. "Quick, I say, you Bildad, and get the ship's papers. We must have Hedgehog there, I mean Quohog, in one of our boats. Look ye, Quohog, we'll give ye the ninetieth lay, and that's more than ever was given a harpooneer yet out of Nantucket."

So down we went into the cabin, and to my great joy Queequeg was soon enrolled among the same ship's company to which I myself belonged.

When all preliminaries were over and Peleg had got everything ready for signing, he turned to me and said, "I guess, Quohog there don't know how to write, does he? I say, Quohog, blast ye! dost thou sign thy name or make thy mark?"

But at this question, Queequeg, who had twice or thrice before taken part in similar ceremonies, looked no ways abashed; but taking the offered pen, copied upon the paper, in the proper place, an exact counterpart of a queer round figure[6] which was tattooed upon his arm; so that through Captain Peleg's obstinate mistake touching his appellative, it stood something like this:—

Quohog.
his ✠ mark.

Meanwhile Captain Bildad sat earnestly and steadfastly eyeing Queequeg, and at last rising solemnly and fumbling in the huge pockets of his broad-skirted drab coat, took out a bundle of tracts, and selecting one entitled "The Latter Day[7] Coming; or No Time to Lose," placed it in Queequeg's hands, and then grasping them and the book with both his, looked earnestly into his eyes, and said, "Son of darkness, I must do my duty by thee; I am part owner of this ship, and feel concerned for the souls of all its crew; if thou still clingest to thy Pagan ways, which I sadly fear, I beseech thee, remain not for aye a Belial bondsman. Spurn the idol Bel, and the hideous dragon; turn from the wrath to come; mind thine eye, I say; oh! goodness gracious! steer clear of the fiery pit!"[8]

Something of the salt sea yet lingered in old Bildad's language, heterogeneously mixed with Scriptural and domestic phrases.

"Avast there, avast there, Bildad, avast now spoiling our harpooneer," cried Peleg. "Pious harpooneers never make good voyagers—it takes the shark out of 'em; no harpooneer is worth a straw who aint pretty sharkish.

---

6. The cross printed in the English and American editions in 1851 (and imitated here) is not "a queer round figure" and was probably supplied by the original typesetter in place of the figure in the manuscript, the words of which were most likely in Melville's sister Augusta's hand.
7. The last day of earth or the following one, the Day of Judgment. *Tracts:* pamphlets proselytizing for one religious sect or another. Melville and his older sister Helen derived much quiet jocular but tolerant bemusement at their sister Augusta's zeal in passing out just such tracts inculcating teachings of the Dutch Reformed Church.
8. Hell. *Belial bondsman:* a son of the devil (see 2 Corinthians 6.15). *Idol Bel and the hideous dragon:* a reference to the apocryphal book Bel and the Dragon ("Cut off from the end of Daniel," according to the King James translators), which relates Daniel's conquest of the Babylonian god Bel. *Wrath to come:* See 1 Thessalonians 1.10. *Mind thine eye:* watch out. *Steer clear:* keep away. *Goodness gracious* avoids taking the name of God in vain; in the mouth of an old salt, a comically mild expression.

There was young Nat Swaine,[9] once the bravest boat-header out of all Nantucket and the Vineyard; he joined the meeting, and never came to good. He got so frightened about his plaguy soul, that he shrinked and sheered away from whales, for fear of after-claps, in case he got stove and went to Davy Jones."[1]

"Peleg! Peleg!" said Bildad, lifting his eyes and hands, "thou thyself, as I myself, hast seen many a perilous time; thou knowest, Peleg, what it is to have the fear of death; how, then, can'st thou prate in this ungodly guise. Thou beliest thine own heart, Peleg. Tell me, when this same Pequod here had her three masts overboard in that typhoon on Japan, that same voyage when thou went mate with Captain Ahab, did'st thou not think of Death and the Judgment then?"

"Hear him, hear him now," cried Peleg, marching across the cabin, and thrusting his hands far down into his pockets,—"hear him, all of ye. Think of that! When every moment we thought the ship would sink! Death and the Judgment then? What? With all three masts making such an everlasting thundering against the side; and every sea breaking over us, fore and aft. Think of Death and the Judgment then? No! no time to think about Death then. Life was what Captain Ahab and I was thinking of; and how to save all hands—how to rig jury-masts[2]—how to get into the nearest port; that was what I was thinking of."

Bildad said no more, but buttoning up his coat, stalked on deck, where we followed him. There he stood, very quietly overlooking some sail-makers who were mending a top-sail in the waist.[3] Now and then he stooped to pick up a patch, or save an end of the tarred twine, which otherwise might have been wasted.

Chapter 19

The Prophet

"Shipmates, have ye shipped in that ship?"

Queequeg and I had just left the Pequod, and were sauntering away from the water, for the moment each occupied with his own thoughts, when the above words were put to us by a stranger, who, pausing before us, levelled his massive fore-finger at the vessel in question. He was but shabbily apparelled in faded jacket and patched trowsers; a rag of a black handkerchief investing his neck. A confluent small-pox had in all directions flowed over his face, and left it like the complicated ribbed bed of a torrent, when the rushing waters have been dried up.

"Have ye shipped in her?" he repeated.

---

9. Presumably not the Nathan Swaine of ch. 3, the prodigious whale killer of the end of the 18th century.
1. Davy Jones's locker, or the bottom of the ocean. *Boat-header:* the man who lances and kills the harpooned whale, as in ch. 62. *Meeting:* of the Friends Church, whose members come together in a "Quaker meeting," not an organized service with a minister. *After-claps:* hell fire.
2. Temporary replacement masts.
3. Mid-section of the top deck.

"You mean the ship Pequod, I suppose," said I, trying to gain a little more time for an uninterrupted look at him.

"Aye, the Pequod—that ship there," he said, drawing back his whole arm, and then rapidly shoving it straight out from him, with the fixed bayonet of his pointed finger darted full at the object.

"Yes," said I, "we have just signed the articles."

"Anything down there about your souls?"

"About what?"

"Oh, perhaps you hav'n't got any," he said quickly. "No matter though, I know many chaps that hav'n't got any,—good luck to 'em; and they are all the better off for it. A soul's a sort of a fifth wheel to a wagon."

"What are you jabbering about, shipmate?" said I.

"*He's* got enough, though, to make up for all deficiencies of that sort in other chaps," abruptly said the stranger, placing a nervous emphasis upon the word *he*.

"Queequeg," said I, "let's go; this fellow has broken loose from some where; he's talking about something and somebody we don't know."

"Stop!" cried the stranger. "Ye said true—ye hav'n't seen Old Thunder yet, have ye?"

"Who's Old Thunder?" said I, again riveted with the insane earnestness of his manner.

"Captain Ahab."

"What! the captain of our ship, the Pequod?"

"Aye, among some of us old sailor chaps, he goes by that name. Ye hav'n't seen him yet, have ye?"

"No, we hav'n't. He's sick they say, but is getting better, and will be all right again before long."

"All right again before long!" laughed the stranger, with a solemnly derisive sort of laugh. "Look ye; when captain Ahab is all right, then this left arm of mine will be all right; not before."

"What do you know about him?"

"What did they *tell* you about him? Say that!"

"They didn't tell much of anything about him; only I've heard that he's a good whale-hunter, and a good captain to his crew."

"That's true, that's true—yes, both true enough. But you must jump when he gives an order. Step and growl; growl and go—that's the word with Captain Ahab. But nothing about that thing that happened to him off Cape Horn, long ago, when he lay like dead for three days and nights; nothing about that deadly skrimmage with the Spaniard afore the altar in Santa?—heard nothing about that, eh? Nothing about the silver calabash he spat into? And nothing about his losing his leg last voyage, according to the prophecy? Didn't ye hear a word about them matters and something more, eh? No, I don't think ye did; how could ye? Who knows it? Not all Nantucket, I guess. But hows'ever, mayhap, ye've heard tell about the leg, and how he lost it; aye, ye have heard of that, I dare say. Oh yes, *that* every one knows a'most—I mean they know he's only one leg; and that a parmacetti took the other off."

"My friend," said I, "what all this gibberish of yours is about, I don't know, and I don't much care; for it seems to me that you must be a little damaged in the head. But if you are speaking of Captain Ahab, of that

ship there, the Pequod, then let me tell you, that I know all about the loss
of his leg."

"*All* about it, eh—sure you do?—all?"

"Pretty sure."

With finger pointed and eye levelled at the Pequod, the beggar-like
stranger stood a moment, as if in a troubled reverie; then starting a little,
turned and said:—"Ye've shipped, have ye? Names down on the papers?
Well, well, what's signed, is signed; and what's to be, will be; and then
again, perhaps it wont be, after all. Any how, it's all fixed and arranged
a'ready; and some sailors or other must go with him, I suppose; as well
these as any other men, God pity 'em! Morning to ye, shipmates, morning; the ineffable heavens bless ye; I'm sorry I stopped ye."

"Look here, friend," said I, "if you have anything important to tell us,
out with it; but if you are only trying to bamboozle us, you are mistaken
in your game; that's all I have to say."

"And it's said very well, and I like to hear a chap talk up that way; you are
just the man for him—the likes of ye. Morning to ye, shipmates, morning!
Oh! when ye get there, tell 'em I've concluded not to make one of 'em."

"Ah, my dear fellow, you can't fool us that way—you can't fool us. It is
the easiest thing in the world for a man to look as if he had a great secret
in him."

"Morning to ye, shipmates, morning."

"Morning it is," said I. "Come along, Queequeg, let's leave this crazy
man. But stop, tell me your name, will you?"

"Elijah."[1]

Elijah! thought I, and we walked away, both commenting, after each
other's fashion, upon this ragged old sailor; and agreed that he was nothing but a humbug, trying to be a bugbear.[2] But we had not gone perhaps
above a hundred yards, when chancing to turn a corner, and looking back
as I did so, who should be seen but Elijah following us, though at a distance. Somehow, the sight of him struck me so, that I said nothing to
Queequeg of his being behind, but passed on with my comrade, anxious
to see whether the stranger would turn the same corner that we did. He
did; and then it seemed to me that he was dogging us, but with what
intent I could not for the life of me imagine. This circumstance, coupled
with his ambiguous, half-hinting, half-revealing, shrouded sort of talk,
now begat in me all kinds of vague wonderments and half-apprehensions,
and all connected with the Pequod; and Captain Ahab; and the leg he had
lost; and the Cape Horn fit; and the silver calabash; and what Captain
Peleg had said of him, when I left the ship the day previous; and the prediction of the squaw Tistig, and the voyage we had bound ourselves to sail;
and a hundred other shadowy things.

I was resolved to satisfy myself whether this ragged Elijah was really
dogging us or not, and with that intent crossed the way with Queequeg,
and on that side of it retraced our steps. But Elijah passed on, without
seeming to notice us. This relieved me; and once more, and finally as it
seemed to me, I pronounced him in my heart, a humbug.

1. The prophet who denounced Ahab (1 Kings 19–22).
2. An obvious phony acting like a scary bogeyman.

Chapter 20

All Astir

A day or two passed, and there was great activity aboard the Pequod. Not only were the old sails being mended, but new sails were coming on board, and bolts of canvas, and coils of rigging; in short, everything betokened that the ship's preparations were hurrying to a close. Captain Peleg seldom or never went ashore, but sat in his wigwam keeping a sharp lookout upon the hands: Bildad did all the purchasing and providing at the stores; and the men employed in the hold and on the rigging were working till long after night-fall.

On the day following Queequeg's signing the articles, word was given at all the inns where the ship's company were stopping, that their chests must be on board before night, for there was no telling how soon the vessel might be sailing. So Queequeg and I got down our traps,[1] resolving, however, to sleep ashore till the last. But it seems they always give very long notice in these cases, and the ship did not sail for several days. But no wonder; there was a good deal to be done, and there is no telling how many things to be thought of, before the Pequod was fully equipped.

Every one knows what a multitude of things—beds, sauce-pans, knives and forks, shovels and tongs, napkins, nut-crackers, and what not, are indispensable to the business of housekeeping. Just so with whaling, which necessitates a three-years' housekeeping upon the wide ocean, far from all grocers, coster-mongers,[2] doctors, bakers, and bankers. And though this also holds true of merchant vessels, yet not by any means to the same extent as with whalemen. For besides the great length of the whaling voyage, the numerous articles peculiar to the prosecution of the fishery, and the impossibility of replacing them at the remote harbors usually frequented, it must be remembered, that of all ships, whaling vessels are the most exposed to accidents of all kinds, and especially to the destruction and loss of the very things upon which the success of the voyage most depends. Hence, the spare boats, spare spars, and spare lines and harpoons, and spare everythings, almost, but a spare Captain and duplicate ship.

At the period of our arrival at the Island, the heaviest stowage of the Pequod had been almost completed; comprising her beef, bread, water, fuel, and iron hoops and staves. But, as before hinted, for some time there was a continual fetching and carrying on board of divers odds and ends of things, both large and small.

Chief among those who did this fetching and carrying was Captain Bildad's sister, a lean old lady of a most determined and indefatigable spirit, but withal very kindhearted, who seemed resolved that, if *she* could help it, nothing should be found wanting in the Pequod, after once fairly getting to sea. At one time she would come on board with a jar of pickles for the steward's pantry; another time with a bunch of quills[3] for the chief

---

1. Got their belongings into their sailor chests and stowed aboard the *Pequod*.
2. Street peddlers, then still common in New York City and other cities.
3. Goose feathers, the points of which were sharpened for use as pens.

mate's desk, where he kept his log; a third time with a roll of flannel for
the small of some one's rheumatic back. Never did any woman better
deserve her name, which was Charity—Aunt Charity, as everybody called
her. And like a sister of charity[4] did this charitable Aunt Charity bustle
about hither and thither, ready to turn her hand and heart to anything
that promised to yield safety, comfort, and consolation to all on board a
ship in which her beloved brother Bildad was concerned, and in which
she herself owned a score or two of well-saved dollars.

But it was startling to see this excellent hearted Quakeress coming on
board, as she did the last day, with a long oil-ladle in one hand, and a still
longer whaling lance[5] in the other. Nor was Bildad himself nor Captain
Peleg at all backward. As for Bildad, he carried about with him a long list
of the articles needed, and at every fresh arrival, down went his mark
opposite that article upon the paper. Every once and a while Peleg came
running out of his whalebone den, roaring at the men down the hatchways, roaring up to the riggers[6] at the mast-head, and then concluded by
roaring back into his wigwam.

During these days of preparation, Queequeg and I often visited the
craft, and as often I asked about Captain Ahab, and how he was, and
when he was going to come on board his ship. To these questions they
would answer, that he was getting better and better, and was expected
aboard every day; meantime, the two Captains, Peleg and Bildad, could
attend to everything necessary to fit the vessel for the voyage. If I had
been downright honest with myself, I would have seen very plainly in my
heart that I did but half fancy being committed this way to so long a voyage, without once laying my eyes on the man who was to be the absolute
dictator of it, so soon as the ship sailed out upon the open sea. But when
a man suspects any wrong, it sometimes happens that if he be already
involved in the matter, he insensibly strives to cover up his suspicions
even from himself. And much this way it was with me. I said nothing, and
tried to think nothing.

At last it was given out that some time next day the ship would certainly
sail. So next morning, Queequeg and I took a very early start.

Chapter 21

Going Aboard

It was nearly six o'clock, but only grey imperfect misty dawn, when we
drew nigh the wharf.

"There are some sailors running ahead there, if I see right," said I to
Queequeg, "it can't be shadows; she's off by sunrise, I guess; come on!"

---

4. A biblical name, from 1 Corinthians 13, where charity is the greatest of the three graces
   described by Paul. There it means Christian (not erotic) love and right feeling toward others; here
   it is used in its more general sense of benevolence. The Sisters of Charity are communities of
   women organized to help the poor; this old Quakeress is both a (non-Catholic) sister bestowing
   gifts and a sister of uncharitable Captain Bildad.
5. See "Contemporary Engravings" (p. 455, herein).
6. Men who prepare the ship's rigging (ropes).

"Avast!"[1] cried a voice, whose owner at the same time coming close behind us, laid a hand upon both our shoulders, and then insinuating himself between us, stood stooping forward a little, in the uncertain twilight, strangely peering from Queequeg to me. It was Elijah.

"Going aboard?"

"Hands off, will you," said I.

"Lookee here," said Queequeg, shaking himself, "go 'way!"

"Aint going aboard, then?"

"Yes, we are," said I, "but what business is that of yours? Do you know, Mr. Elijah, that I consider you a little impertinent?"

"No, no, no; I wasn't aware of that," said Elijah, slowly and wonderingly looking from me to Queequeg, with the most unaccountable glances.

"Elijah," said I, "you will oblige my friend and me by withdrawing. We are going to the Indian and Pacific Oceans,[2] and would prefer not to be detained."

"Ye be, be ye? Coming back afore breakfast?"

"He's cracked, Queequeg," said I, "come on."

"Holloa!" cried stationary Elijah, hailing us when we had removed a few paces.

"Never mind him," said I, "Queequeg, come on."

But he stole up to us again, and suddenly clapping his hand on my shoulder, said—"Did ye see anything looking like men[3] going towards that ship a while ago?"

Struck by this plain matter-of-fact question, I answered, saying "Yes, I thought I did see four or five men; but it was too dim to be sure."

"Very dim, very dim," said Elijah. "Morning to ye."

Once more we quitted him; but once more he came softly after us; and touching my shoulder again, said, "See if you can find 'em now, will ye?"

"Find who?"

"Morning to ye! morning to ye!" he rejoined, again moving off. "Oh! I was going to warn ye against—but never mind, never mind—it's all one, all in the family too;—sharp frost this morning, ain't it? Good bye to ye. Shan't see ye again very soon, I guess; unless it's before the Grand Jury."[4] And with these cracked words he finally departed, leaving me, for the moment, in no small wonderment at his frantic impudence.

At last, stepping on board the Pequod, we found everything in profound quiet, not a soul moving. The cabin entrance was locked within; the hatches were all on, and lumbered with coils of rigging. Going forward to the forecastle, we found the slide of the scuttle[5] open. Seeing a light, we went down, and found only an old rigger there, wrapped in a tattered peajacket. He was thrown at whole length upon two chests, his face downwards and inclosed in his folded arms. The profoundest slumber slept upon him.

---

1. "Stop!"
2. Now the plan is to sail around the Cape of Good Hope into the Indian Ocean, not around Cape Horn. Melville himself never sailed around the Cape of Good Hope.
3. Elijah's phrase ambiguously suggests that there is something unusual about them, something Ishmael had not seen.
4. The Last Judgment.
5. Opening in the deck.

"Those sailors we saw, Queequeg, where can they have gone to?" said I, looking dubiously at the sleeper. But it seemed that, when on the wharf, Queequeg had not at all noticed what I now alluded to; hence I would have thought myself to have been optically deceived in that matter, were it not for Elijah's otherwise inexplicable question. But I beat the thing down; and again marking the sleeper, jocularly hinted to Queequeg that perhaps we had best sit up with the body;[6] telling him to establish himself accordingly. He put his hand upon the sleeper's rear, as though feeling if it was soft enough; and then, without more ado, sat quietly down there.

"Gracious! Queequeg, don't sit there," said I.

"Oh! perry dood seat," said Queequeg, "my country way; won't hurt him face."

"Face!" said I, "call that his face?[7] very benevolent countenance then; but how hard he breathes, he's heaving himself; get off, Queequeg, you are heavy, it's grinding the face of the poor. Get off, Queequeg! Look, he'll twitch you off soon. I wonder he don't wake."

Queequeg removed himself to just beyond the head of the sleeper, and lighted his tomahawk pipe. I sat at the feet. We kept the pipe passing over the sleeper, from one to the other. Meanwhile, upon questioning him, in his broken fashion Queequeg gave me to understand that, in his land, owing to the absence of settees and sofas of all sorts, the king, chiefs, and great people generally, were in the custom of fattening some of the lower orders for ottomans; and to furnish a house comfortably in that respect, you had only to buy up eight or ten lazy fellows, and lay them round in the piers and alcoves. Besides, it was very convenient on an excursion; much better than those garden-chairs which are convertible into walking-sticks; upon occasion, a chief calling his attendant, and desiring him to make a settee of himself under a spreading tree, perhaps in some damp marshy place.

While narrating these things, every time Queequeg received the tomahawk from me, he flourished the hatchet-side of it over the sleeper's head.

"What's that for, Queequeg?"

"Perry easy, kill-e; oh! perry easy!"

He was going on with some wild reminiscences about his tomahawk-pipe, which, it seemed, had in its two uses both brained his foes and soothed his soul, when we were directly attracted to the sleeping rigger. The strong vapor now completely filling the contracted hole, it began to tell upon him. He breathed with a sort of muffledness; then seemed troubled in the nose; then revolved over once or twice; then sat up and rubbed his eyes.

"Holloa!" he breathed at last, "who be ye smokers?"

"Shipped men," answered I, "when does she sail?"

---

6. Ishmael jokes that the sleeper is dead and that they should follow the old respectful ritual and sit up with the body, awaiting the funeral.

7. When Queequeg calls the sleeper's buttocks his "face" (compare the modern idiom, "cheeks" of the buttocks), Ishmael mockingly accuses him of oppression (Isaiah 3.15: "What mean ye that ye beat my people to pieces, and grind the faces of the poor? saith the Lord God of hosts"). This use of biblical phrases in jocular contexts, which infuriated some reviewers, probably reflects Melville's saturation in biblical language more than any disrespect toward the Bible. Those intrigued by this problematical use of borrowed phraseology might treat themselves to a reading of Melville's exuberant second book, *Omoo* (1847), a South Sea adventure remarkably laced with biblical phrases.

"Aye, aye, ye are going in her, be ye? She sails to-day. The Captain came aboard last night."

"What Captain?—Ahab?"

"Who but him indeed?"

I was going to ask him some further questions concerning Ahab, when we heard a noise on deck.

"Holloa! Starbuck's astir," said the rigger. "He's a lively chief mate, that; good man, and a pious; but all alive now, I must turn to." And so saying he went on deck, and we followed.

It was now clear sunrise. Soon the crew came on board in twos and threes; the riggers bestirred themselves; the mates were actively engaged; and several of the shore people were busy in bringing various last things on board. Meanwhile Captain Ahab remained invisibly enshrined within his cabin.

Chapter 22

Merry Christmas

At length, towards noon, upon the final dismissal of the ship's riggers, and after the Pequod had been hauled out from the wharf, and after the ever-thoughtful Charity had come off in a whaleboat, with her last gifts—a night-cap for Stubb, the second mate, her brother-in-law,[1] and a spare Bible for the steward—after all this, the two captains, Peleg and Bildad, issued from the cabin, and turning to the chief mate, Peleg said:

"Now, Mr. Starbuck, are you sure everything is right? Captain Ahab is all ready—just spoke to him—nothing more to be got from shore, eh? Well, call all hands, then. Muster 'em aft here—blast 'em!"[2]

"No need of profane words, however great the hurry, Peleg," said Bildad, "but away with thee, friend Starbuck, and do our bidding."

How now! Here upon the very point of starting for the voyage, Captain Peleg and Captain Bildad were going it with a high hand on the quarter-deck,[3] just as if they were to be joint-commanders at sea, as well as to all appearances in port. And, as for Captain Ahab, no sign of him was yet to be seen; only, they said he was in the cabin. But then, the idea was, that his presence was by no means necessary in getting the ship under weigh, and steering her well out to sea. Indeed, as that was not at all his proper business, but the pilot's;[4] and as he was not yet completely recovered—so they said—therefore, Captain Ahab stayed below. And all this seemed natural enough; especially as in the merchant service many captains never show themselves on deck for a considerable time after heaving up the

---

1. Because Charity is Bildad's sister, Stubb is married to their sister, despite the apparent age gap, Charity and Bildad being old while Stubb is a vigorous fellow who in his "jolly" way later calls his wife his "juicy little pear" and wonders whether she is weeping for him or partying (ch. 39).
2. Not quite an oath, because Peleg does not say "God blast 'em!" but pious Bildad calls it *profane*, whereupon Peleg substitutes *sons of bachelors*, arguably funnier than the common epithet he avoids using.
3. The main deck behind the main mast, by usage the captain's domain.
4. A temporary pilot, based in the port and wise in the peculiar hazards of the local waters, was entrusted with steering ships out of and into harbor.

anchor, but remain over the cabin table, having a farewell merry-making with their shore friends, before they quit the ship for good with the pilot.

But there was not much chance to think over the matter, for Captain Peleg was now all alive. He seemed to do most of the talking and commanding, and not Bildad.

"Aft here, ye sons of bachelors," he cried, as the sailors lingered at the main-mast. "Mr. Starbuck, drive 'em aft."

"Strike the tent there!"—was the next order. As I hinted before, this whalebone marquee was never pitched except in port; and on board the Pequod, for thirty years, the order to strike the tent was well known to be the next thing to heaving up the anchor.

"Man the capstan! Blood and thunder!—jump!"—was the next command, and the crew sprang for the handspikes.

Now, in getting under weigh, the station generally occupied by the pilot is the forward part of the ship. And here Bildad, who, with Peleg, be it known, in addition to his other offices, was one of the licensed pilots of the port—he being suspected to have got himself made a pilot in order to save the Nantucket pilot-fee to all the ships he was concerned in, for he never piloted any other craft—Bildad, I say, might now be seen actively engaged in looking over the bows for the approaching anchor, and at intervals singing what seemed a dismal stave of psalmody, to cheer the hands at the windlass, who roared forth some sort of a chorus about the girls in Booble Alley,[5] with hearty good will. Nevertheless, not three days previous, Bildad had told them that no profane songs would be allowed on board the Pequod, particularly in getting under weigh; and Charity, his sister, had placed a small choice copy of Watts in each seaman's berth.

Meantime, overseeing the other part of the ship, Captain Peleg ripped and swore astern in the most frightful manner. I almost thought he would sink the ship before the anchor could be got up; involuntarily I paused on my handspike, and told Queequeg to do the same, thinking of the perils we both ran, in starting on the voyage with such a devil for a pilot. I was comforting myself, however, with the thought that in pious Bildad might be found some salvation, spite of his seven hundred and seventy-seventh lay; when I felt a sudden sharp poke in my rear, and turning round, was horrified at the apparition of Captain Peleg in the act of withdrawing his leg from my immediate vicinity. That was my first kick.[6]

"Is that the way they heave in the marchant service?" he roared. "Spring, thou sheep-head; spring, and break thy backbone! Why don't ye spring, I say, all of ye—spring, Quohog! spring, thou chap with the red whiskers; spring there, Scotch-cap;[7] spring, thou green pants. Spring, I

5. Sailors' name for a slum street frequented by prostitutes. Melville describes such a Liverpool street in *Redburn* (1849). This song has not been identified, but it was a "profane" one, not one based on the hymns of Isaac Watts (1674–1748), such as the song Bildad sings below. *Windlass* and *capstan*: names of different barrel-shaped devices for reeling in the chains of the heavy anchor by manpower of many crewmen. The men work at levers (here *handspikes,* used on a windlass) while customarily singing, with leader and "chorus," such lively, nonreligious ("profane") work songs (chanteys) as the one these whalemen "roared forth," to coordinate their rhythmic efforts.
6. After this passage, neither Ishmael nor any other crewman is kicked.
7. Brimless woolen cap with two tails or streamers. Peleg singles out, kicks, and exhorts the men to strain ("heave") and exert all muscles to the utmost ("spring"), while Bildad tries to set their work rhythm by leading them in a dismal hymn.

say, all of ye, and spring your eyes out!" And so saying, he moved along the
windlass, here and there using his leg very freely, while imperturbable
Bildad kept leading off with his psalmody. Thinks I, Captain Peleg must
have been drinking something to-day.

At last the anchor was up, the sails were set, and off we glided. It was
a short, cold Christmas; and as the short northern day merged into night,
we found ourselves almost broad upon the wintry ocean, whose freezing
spray cased us in ice, as in polished armor. The long rows of teeth on the
bulwarks glistened in the moonlight; and like the white ivory tusks of
some huge elephant, vast curving icicles depended from the bows.

Lank Bildad, as pilot, headed the first watch,[8] and ever and anon, as the
old craft deep dived into the green seas, and sent the shivering frost all
over her, and the winds howled, and the cordage rang, his steady notes
were heard,—

> "Sweet fields beyond the swelling flood,
>   Stand dressed in living green.
> So to the Jews old Canaan stood,
>   While Jordan rolled between."[9]

Never did those sweet words sound more sweetly to me than then. They
were full of hope and fruition. Spite of this frigid winter night in the boisterous Atlantic, spite of my wet feet and wetter jacket, there was yet, it
then seemed to me, many a pleasant haven in store; and meads and glades
so eternally vernal, that the grass shot up by the spring, untrodden,
unwilted, remains at midsummer.

At last we gained such an offing, that the two pilots were needed no
longer. The stout sail-boat that had accompanied us began ranging
alongside.

It was curious and not unpleasing, how Peleg and Bildad were affected
at this juncture, especially Captain Bildad. For loath to depart, yet; very
loath to leave, for good, a ship bound on so long and perilous a voyage—
beyond both stormy Capes; a ship in which some thousands of his hard
earned dollars were invested; a ship, in which an old shipmate sailed as
captain; a man almost as old as he, once more starting to encounter all
the terrors of the pitiless jaw; loath to say good-bye to a thing so every way
brimful of every interest to him,—poor old Bildad lingered long; paced the
deck with anxious strides; ran down into the cabin to speak another
farewell word there; again came on deck, and looked to windward; looked
towards the wide and endless waters, only bounded by the far-off unseen
Eastern Continents; looked towards the land; looked aloft; looked right
and left; looked everywhere and nowhere; and at last, mechanically coiling a rope upon its pin, convulsively grasped stout Peleg by the hand, and
holding up a lantern, for a moment stood gazing heroically in his face, as
much as to say, "Nevertheless, friend Peleg, I can stand it; yes, I can."

As for Peleg himself, he took it more like a philosopher; but for all his
philosophy, there was a tear twinkling in his eye, when the lantern came

---

8. On voyages, days were usually divided into parts called "watches" (mostly of four hours); each
   crewman was assigned to a group (also called a "watch") under one of the officers and was on
   and off duty in alternate watches.
9. Third stanza of Watts's "A Prospect of Heaven Makes Death Easy."

too near. And he, too, did not a little run from cabin to deck—now a word below, and now a word with Starbuck, the chief mate.

But, at last, he turned to his comrade, with a final sort of look about him,—"Captain Bildad—come, old shipmate, we must go. Back the main-yard there![1] Boat ahoy! Stand by to come close alongside, now! Careful, careful!—come, Bildad, boy—say your last. Luck to ye, Starbuck—luck to ye, Mr. Stubb—luck to ye, Mr. Flask—good-bye, and good luck to ye all—and this day three years I'll have a hot supper smoking for ye in old Nantucket. Hurrah and away!"

"God bless ye, and have ye in His holy keeping, men," murmured old Bildad, almost incoherently. "I hope ye'll have fine weather now,[2] so that Captain Ahab may soon be moving among ye—a pleasant sun is all he needs, and ye'll have plenty of them in the tropic voyage ye go. Be careful in the hunt, ye mates. Don't stave[3] the boats needlessly, ye harpooneers; good white cedar plank is raised full three per cent. within the year. Don't forget your prayers, either. Mr. Starbuck, mind that cooper don't waste the spare staves. Oh! the sail-needles are in the green locker! Don't whale it too much a' Lord's days,[4] men; but don't miss a fair chance either, that's rejecting Heaven's good gifts. Have an eye to the molasses tierce, Mr. Stubb; it was a little leaky, I thought. If ye touch at the islands, Mr. Flask, beware of fornication. Good-bye, good-bye! Don't keep that cheese too long down in the hold, Mr. Starbuck; it'll spoil. Be careful with the butter—twenty cents the pound it was, and mind ye, if—"

"Come, come, Captain Bildad; stop palavering,—away!" and with that, Peleg hurried him over the side, and both dropt into the boat.

Ship and boat diverged; the cold, damp night breeze blew between; a screaming gull flew overhead; the two hulls wildly rolled; we gave three heavy-hearted cheers, and blindly plunged like fate into the lone Atlantic.

Chapter 23

The Lee Shore

Some chapters back, one Bulkington was spoken of, a tall, new-landed mariner, encountered in New Bedford at the inn.

When on that shivering winter's night, the Pequod thrust her vindictive bows into the cold malicious waves, who should I see standing at her helm but Bulkington! I looked with sympathetic awe and fearfulness upon the man, who in midwinter just landed from a four years' dangerous voyage, could so unrestingly push off again for still another tempestuous term. The land seemed scorching to his feet. Wonderfullest things are ever the unmentionable; deep memories yield no epitaphs; this six-inch chapter is the stoneless grave of Bulkington. Let me only say that it fared with him

1. To slow the ship.
2. Bildad's benediction is from Numbers 6.24 ("The Lord bless thee, and keep thee"), and his pre-diction of "a pleasant sun" from the next verse: "The Lord make his face shine upon thee."
3. Crush, because to get a close fling of a lance an impetuous harpooneer may urge the crew right up on the whale, which then may stave the boat.
4. Exodus 20.8: "Remember the sabbath day, to keep it holy." Quakers avoid (as pagan) the English names of the days of the week and month.

as with the storm-tossed ship, that miserably drives along the leeward land. The port would fain give succor; the port is pitiful; in the port is safety, comfort, hearthstone, supper, warm blankets, friends, all that's kind to our mortalities.[1] But in that gale, the port, the land, is that ship's direst jeopardy; she must fly all hospitality; one touch of land, though it but graze the keel, would make her shudder through and through. With all her might she crowds all sail off shore; in so doing, fights 'gainst the very winds that fain would blow her homeward; seeks all the lashed sea's landlessness again; for refuge's sake forlornly rushing into peril; her only friend her bitterest foe!

Know ye, now, Bulkington? Glimpses do ye seem to see of that mortally[2] intolerable truth; that all deep, earnest thinking is but the intrepid effort of the soul to keep the open independence of her sea; while the wildest winds of heaven and earth conspire to cast her on the treacherous, slavish shore?

But as in landlessness alone resides the highest truth, shoreless, indefinite as God—so, better is it to perish in that howling infinite, than be ingloriously dashed upon the lee, even if that were safety! For worm-like, then, oh! who would craven crawl to land! Terrors of the terrible! is all this agony so vain? Take heart, take heart, O Bulkington! Bear thee grimly, demigod! Up from the spray of thy ocean-perishing—straight up, leaps thy apotheosis!

Chapter 24

The Advocate[1]

As Queequeg and I are now fairly embarked in this business of whaling; and as this business of whaling has somehow come to be regarded among landsmen as a rather unpoetical and disreputable pursuit; therefore, I am all anxiety to convince ye, ye landsmen, of the injustice hereby done to us hunters of whales.

In the first place, it may be deemed almost superfluous to establish the fact, that among people at large, the business of whaling is not accounted on a level with what are called the liberal professions. If a stranger were introduced into any miscellaneous metropolitan society, it would but slightly advance the general opinion of his merits, were he presented to the company as a harpooneer, say; and if in emulation of the naval officers he should append the initials S. W. F. (Sperm Whale Fishery) to his visiting card, such a procedure would be deemed pre-eminently presuming and ridiculous.[2]

---

1. Ordinary human feelings and vulnerabilities.
2. All but intolerable, unbearable, to ordinary human perceptions. *Ye:* addressed to the reader.
1. That is, Ishmael now acts as lawyer, arguing for the business of whaling. Here and in subsequent footnotes we point out some of Melville's heavier debts to his printed sources for information about whales and whaling. Mansfield and Vincent (1952, 659) show that the "bulk of this chapter was derived in spirit and in ideas" from Thomas Beale's *The Natural History of the Sperm Whale* (1839), but that William Scoresby Jr.'s *An Account of the Arctic Regions, with a History and Description of the Northern Whale-Fishery* (1820) and J. Ross Browne's *Etchings of a Whaling Cruise* (1846) "also furnished suggestions." See also Olsen-Smith, p. 585, herein.
2. The initials on the officers' calling cards would have been U.S.N.

Doubtless one leading reason why the world declines honoring us whale-men, is this: they think that, at best, our vocation amounts to a butchering sort of business; and that when actively engaged therein, we are sur-rounded by all manner of defilements. Butchers we are, that is true. But butchers, also, and butchers of the bloodiest badge have been all Martial Commanders whom the world invariably delights to honor. And as for the matter of the alleged uncleanliness of our business, ye shall soon be initi-ated into certain facts hitherto pretty generally unknown, and which, upon the whole, will triumphantly plant the sperm whale-ship at least among the cleanliest things of this tidy earth. But even granting the charge in question to be true; what disordered slippery decks of a whale-ship are comparable to the unspeakable carrion of those battle-fields from which so many sol-diers return to drink in all ladies' plaudits? And if the idea of peril so much enhances the popular conceit[3] of the soldier's profession; let me assure ye that many a veteran who has freely marched up to a battery, would quickly recoil at the apparition of the sperm whale's vast tail, fanning into eddies the air over his head. For what are the comprehensible terrors of man com-pared with the interlinked terrors and wonders of God!

But, though the world scouts at us whale hunters, yet does it unwit-tingly pay us the profoundest homage; yea, an all-abounding adoration! for almost all the tapers,[4] lamps, and candles that burn round the globe, burn, as before so many shrines, to our glory!

But look at this matter in other lights; weigh it in all sorts of scales; see what we whalemen are, and have been.

Why did the Dutch in De Witt's time[5] have admirals of their whaling fleets? Why did Louis XVI. of France, at his own personal expense, fit out whaling ships from Dunkirk, and politely invite to that town some score or two of families from our own island of Nantucket? Why did Britain between the years 1750 and 1788 pay to her whalemen in bounties upwards of £1,000,000? And lastly, how comes it that we whalemen of America now outnumber all the rest of the banded whalemen in the world; sail a navy of upwards of seven hundred vessels; manned by eigh-teen thousand men; yearly consuming 4,000,000 of dollars; the ships worth, at the time of sailing, $20,000,000; and every year importing into our harbors a well reaped harvest of $7,000,000. How comes all this, if there be not something puissant in whaling?

But this is not the half; look again.

I freely assert, that the cosmopolite philosopher cannot, for his life, point out one single peaceful influence, which within the last sixty years has operated more potentially upon the whole broad world, taken in one aggre-gate, than the high and mighty business of whaling. One way and another, it has begotten events so remarkable in themselves, and so continuously momentous in their sequential issues, that whaling may well be regarded as that Egyptian mother, who bore offspring themselves pregnant from her womb.[6] It would be a hopeless, endless task to catalogue all these things.

3. Notion, idea.
4. Long, slender candles.
5. In the mid-17th century, under the Dutch statesman Jan de Witt (1625–1672). The next two sen-tences derive from Beale; the rest of the paragraph, from Browne.
6. Melville slightly misstates: Nut in Egyptian mythology is the mother of Osiris and his twin sister, Isis, whom he impregnated while in Nut's womb.

Let a handful suffice. For many years past the whale-ship has been the pioneer in ferreting out the remotest and least known parts of the earth. She has explored seas and archipelagoes which had no chart, where no Cook or Vancouver had ever sailed. If American and European men-of-war now peacefully ride in once savage harbors, let them fire salutes to the honor and the glory of the whale-ship, which originally showed them the way, and first interpreted between them and the savages. They may celebrate as they will the heroes of Exploring Expeditions, your Cooks, your Krusensterns;[7] but I say that scores of anonymous Captains have sailed out of Nantucket, that were as great, and greater than your Cook and your Krusenstern. For in their succorless empty-handedness, they, in the heathenish sharked waters, and by the beaches of unrecorded, javelin islands, battled with virgin wonders and terrors that Cook with all his marines and muskets would not willingly have dared. All that is made such a flourish of in the old South Sea Voyages, those things were but the life-time commonplaces of our heroic Nantucketers. Often, adventures which Vancouver dedicates three chapters to, these men accounted unworthy of being set down in the ship's common log. Ah, the world! Oh, the world!

Until the whale fishery rounded Cape Horn, no commerce but colonial, scarcely any intercourse but colonial, was carried on between Europe and the long line of the opulent Spanish provinces on the Pacific coast. It was the whaleman who first broke through the jealous policy of the Spanish crown, touching those colonies; and, if space permitted, it might be distinctly shown how from those whalemen at last eventuated the liberation of Peru, Chili, and Bolivia from the yoke of Old Spain, and the establishment of the eternal democracy in those parts.[8]

That great America on the other side of the sphere, Australia, was given to the enlightened world by the whaleman. After its first blunder-born discovery by a Dutchman, all other ships long shunned those shores as pestiferously barbarous; but the whale-ship touched there. The whale-ship is the true mother of that now mighty colony. Moreover, in the infancy of the first Australian settlement, the emigrants were several times saved from starvation by the benevolent biscuit of the whale-ship luckily dropping an anchor in their waters. The uncounted isles of all Polynesia confess the same truth, and do commercial homage to the whale-ship, that cleared the way for the missionary and the merchant, and in many cases carried the primitive missionaries to their first destinations. If that double-bolted land, Japan, is ever to become hospitable, it is the whale-ship alone to whom the credit will be due; for already she is on the threshold.[9]

---

7. Adam Ivan Krustenstern (1770–1846), the first Russian circumnavigator of the globe. James Cook (1728–1779) and George Vancouver (1758?–1798), the most famous British explorers of the Pacific. The *Narrative of the United States Exploring Expedition* (1844) was the five-volume report of the 1838–42 American expedition to the Pacific and Antarctic under the command of Charles Wilkes, U.S.N. (1798–1877); its prose descriptions and its many quite remarkable engravings made it a standard authority on the Pacific. Melville drew on reports of all these navigators, but here he has Ishmael oratorically belittle them, lawyer-fashion, in his role as champion of whalemen's achievements.
8. Melville knew that the independence won by Chile in 1828, Peru in 1824, and Bolivia in 1825 had not brought the untroubled establishment of "eternal democracy," the contemporary catch-phrase that Ishmael vehemently holds to in this passage.
9. Australia, although sighted earlier, was first visited by the Dutch in 1606 and was settled in 1788 by England as a penal colony, to reduce the cost of its prison system. Polynesia (the central Pacific islands) was first visited by English, before American, whaleships, as were Japanese waters from

But if, in the face of all this, you still declare that whaling has no æsthetically noble associations connected with it, then am I ready to shiver fifty lances with you there, and unhorse you with a split helmet every time.

The whale has no famous author, and whaling no famous chronicler, you will say.

The whale no famous author, and whaling no famous chronicler? Who wrote the first account of our Leviathan? Who but mighty Job! And who composed the first narrative of a whaling-voyage? Who, but no less a prince than Alfred the Great, who, with his own royal pen, took down the words from Other, the Norwegian whale-hunter of those times! And who pronounced our glowing eulogy in Parliament? Who, but Edmund Burke![1]

True enough, but then whalemen themselves are poor devils; they have no good blood in their veins.

No good blood in their veins? They have something better than royal blood there. The grandmother of Benjamin Franklin was Mary Morrel; afterwards, by marriage, Mary Folger,[2] one of the old settlers of Nantucket, and the ancestress to a long line of Folgers and harpooneers— all kith and kin to noble Benjamin—this day darting the barbed iron from one side of the world to the other.

Good again; but then all confess that somehow whaling is not respectable.

Whaling not respectable? Whaling is imperial! By old English statutory law, the whale is declared "a royal fish."[3]

Oh, that's only nominal! The whale himself has never figured in any grand imposing way.

The whale never figured in any grand imposing way? In one of the mighty triumphs given to a Roman general upon his entering the world's capital, the bones of a whale, brought all the way from the Syrian coast, were the most conspicuous object in the cymballed procession.[4]

Grant it, since you cite it; but, say what you will, there is no real dignity in whaling.

No dignity in whaling? The dignity of our calling the very heavens attest. Cetus is a constellation in the South![5] No more! Drive down your hat in presence of the Czar, and take it off to Queequeg! No more! I know a man that, in his lifetime, has taken three hundred and fifty whales. I account that man more honorable than that great captain of antiquity[6] who boasted of taking as many walled towns.

And, as for me, if, by any possibility, there be any as yet undiscovered prime thing in me; if I shall ever deserve any real repute in that small but

1778 on. Here Ishmael as advocate pushes the priority of American whalemen. Japan was in fact opened to Western trade in 1856, only five years after the publication of *Moby-Dick*.
1. From Browne (1846), Melville took the reference to the Anglo-Saxon King Alfred (849–899). In Browne or in Beale (1839) he found the passage from Edmund Burke's speech "Conciliation with the American Colonies," which he quoted in "Extracts."
2. Wife of Peter Folger (1617 or 1618–1690). Their daughter Abiah was the second wife of Josiah Franklin of Boston, whose tenth son was Benjamin Franklin (1706–1790).
3. See subsequent chapters for something more on this head [Melville's note]. See ch. 90.
4. Melville marked here the second of two passages keyed to the same footnote (n. 3, just above). (The footnote was printed only once, doing double-duty.) Here the relevant chapter is 82; Melville read of this procession in Kitto (1846).
5. In the Southern Hemisphere, one of the largest constellations, prominent in equinoctial skies in the fall.
6. Possibly Demetrius Poliorcetes (337?–283 B.C.E.), a Macedonian king told of in Plutarch's *Lives*.

high hushed world which I might not be unreasonably ambitious of; if hereafter I shall do anything that, upon the whole, a man might rather have done than to have left undone; if, at my death, my executors, or more properly my creditors, find any precious MSS. in my desk, then here I prospectively ascribe all the honor and the glory to whaling; for a whale-ship was my Yale College and my Harvard.[7]

Chapter 25

Postscript[1]

In behalf of the dignity of whaling, I would fain advance naught but sub-stantiated facts. But after embattling his facts, an advocate who should wholly suppress a not unreasonable surmise, which might tell eloquently upon his cause—such an advocate, would he not be blameworthy?

It is well known that at the coronation of kings and queens, even modern ones, a certain curious process of seasoning them for their functions is gone through. There is a saltcellar of state, so called, and there may be a caster of state. How they use the salt, precisely—who knows? Certain I am, however, that a king's head is solemnly oiled at his coronation, even as a head of salad. Can it be, though, that they anoint it with a view of making its interior run well, as they anoint machinery? Much might be ruminated here, concerning the essential dignity of this regal process, because in com-mon life we esteem but meanly and contemptibly a fellow who anoints his hair, and palpably smells of that anointing. In truth, a mature man who uses hair-oil, unless medicinally, that man has probably got a quoggy[2] spot in him somewhere. As a general rule, he can't amount to much in his totality.

But the only thing to be considered here, is this—what kind of oil is used at coronations? Certainly it cannot be olive oil, nor macassar oil, nor castor oil, nor bear's oil, nor train oil, nor cod-liver oil.[3] What then can it possibly be, but sperm oil in its unmanufactured, unpolluted state, the sweetest of all oils?

Think of that, ye loyal Britons! we whalemen supply your kings and queens with coronation stuff!

Chapter 26

Knights and Squires

The chief mate of the Pequod was Starbuck,[1] a native of Nantucket, and a Quaker by descent. He was a long, earnest man, and though born on an

---

7. Ishmael speaks also for Melville, the earliest of great American writers who never went to college.
1. The first English edition solved the problem of the disrespect toward royalty shown here by omit-ting this little chapter.
2. Mushy, boggy.
3. The first three oils are from plants. Train oil is from right whales. Cod-liver oil is from codfish.
1. An old Nantucket family name. In a triumph of modern marketing, the name of the ascetic Starbuck has become associated with exotic coffees and voluptuous additives, as well as baked goods that shame the nautical "duff" or hardtack of Melville's whale ships.

icy coast, seemed well adapted to endure hot latitudes, his flesh being
hard as twice-baked biscuit. Transported to the Indies, his live blood
would not spoil like bottled ale. He must have been born in some time of
general drought and famine, or upon one of those fast days[2] for which his
state is famous. Only some thirty arid summers had he seen; those summers had dried up all his physical superfluousness. But this, his thinness,
so to speak, seemed no more the token of wasting anxieties and cares,
than it seemed the indication of any bodily blight. It was merely the con-
densation of the man. He was by no means ill-looking; quite the contrary.
His pure tight skin was an excellent fit; and closely wrapped up in it, and
embalmed with inner health and strength, like a revivified Egyptian,[3] this
Starbuck seemed prepared to endure for long ages to come, and to endure
always, as now; for be it Polar snow or torrid sun, like a patent chronometer,[4] his interior vitality was warranted to do well in all climates. Looking
into his eyes, you seemed to see there the yet lingering images of those
thousand-fold perils he had calmly confronted through life. A staid, steadfast man, whose life for the most part was a telling pantomime of action,
and not a tame chapter of words. Yet, for all his hardy sobriety and fortitude, there were certain qualities in him which at times affected, and in
some cases seemed well nigh to overbalance all the rest. Uncommonly
conscientious for a seaman, and endued with a deep natural reverence,
the wild watery loneliness of his life did therefore strongly incline him to
superstition; but to that sort of superstition, which in some organizations
seems rather to spring, somehow, from intelligence than from ignorance.
Outward portents and inward presentiments were his. And if at times
these things bent the welded iron of his soul, much more did his far-away
domestic memories of his young Cape wife and child, tend to bend him
still more from the original ruggedness of his nature, and open him still
further to those latent influences which, in some honest-hearted men,
restrain the gush of dare-devil daring, so often evinced by others in the
more perilous vicissitudes of the fishery. "I will have no man in my boat,"
said Starbuck, "who is not afraid of a whale." By this, he seemed to mean,
not only that the most reliable and useful courage was that which arises
from the fair estimation of the encountered peril, but that an utterly fearless man is a far more dangerous comrade than a coward.

"Aye, aye," said Stubb, the second mate, "Starbuck, there, is as careful
a man as you'll find anywhere in this fishery." But we shall ere long see
what that word "careful" precisely means when used by a man like Stubb,
or almost any other whale hunter.

Starbuck was no crusader after perils; in him courage was not a sentiment; but a thing simply useful to him, and always at hand upon all mortally practical occasions. Besides, he thought, perhaps, that in this business of whaling, courage was one of the great staple outfits of the ship,
like her beef and her bread, and not to be foolishly wasted. Wherefore he

2. In the 19th century Massachusetts still proclaimed an annual Fast Day, as it had done since colonial times.
3. A mummy brought back to life—possibly suggested by Edgar Allan Poe's "Some Words with a
Mummy" (1845), in which a mummy is revivified by electric shock.
4. A very accurate weather-proof clock. A ship's longitudinal position at sea could be determined by
calculations using the difference between the Greenwich time shown on its chronometer and
local time.

had no fancy for lowering for whales after sun-down; nor for persisting in fighting a fish that too much persisted in fighting him. For, thought Starbuck, I am here in this critical ocean to kill whales for my living, and not to be killed by them for theirs; and that hundreds of men had been so killed Starbuck well knew. What doom was his own father's? Where, in the bottomless deeps, could he find the torn limbs of his brother?

With memories like these in him, and, moreover, given to a certain superstitiousness, as has been said; the courage of this Starbuck which could, nevertheless, still flourish, must indeed have been extreme. But it was not in reasonable nature that a man so organized, and with such terrible experiences and remembrances as he had; it was not in nature that these things should fail in latently engendering an element in him, which, under suitable circumstances, would break out from its confinement, and burn all his courage up. And brave as he might be, it was that sort of bravery, chiefly visible in some intrepid men,[5] which, while generally abiding firm in the conflict with seas, or winds, or whales, or any of the ordinary irrational horrors of the world, yet cannot withstand those more terrific, because more spiritual terrors, which sometimes menace you from the concentrating brow of an enraged and mighty man.

But were the coming narrative to reveal, in any instance, the complete abasement of poor Starbuck's fortitude, scarce might I have the heart to write it; for it is a thing most sorrowful, nay shocking, to expose the fall of valor in the soul. Men may seem detestable as joint stock-companies and nations; knaves, fools, and murderers there may be; men may have mean and meagre faces; but man, in the ideal, is so noble and so sparkling, such a grand and glowing creature, that over any ignominious blemish in him all his fellows should run to throw their costliest robes. That immaculate manliness we feel within ourselves, so far within us, that it remains intact though all the outer character seem gone; bleeds with keenest anguish at the undraped spectacle of a valor-ruined man. Nor can piety itself, at such a shameful sight, completely stifle her upbraidings against the permitting stars. But this august dignity I treat of, is not the dignity of kings and robes, but that abounding dignity which has no robed investiture. Thou shalt see it shining in the arm that wields a pick or drives a spike; that democratic dignity which, on all hands, radiates without end from God; Himself! The great God absolute! The centre and circumference of all democracy! His omnipresence, our divine equality!

If, then, to meanest mariners, and renegades and castaways, I shall hereafter ascribe high qualities, though dark; weave round them tragic graces; if even the most mournful, perchance the most abased, among them all, shall at times lift himself to the exalted mounts; if I shall touch that workman's arm with some ethereal light; if I shall spread a rainbow over his disastrous set of sun; then against all mortal critics[6] bear me out

5. The first edition reads: "it was that sort of bravery chiefly, visible in some intrepid men." Here, as in the 1967 NCE, the comma is moved to follow "bravery" so it is clear that "chiefly" modifies visible.

6. Melville, or his narrator Ishmael, claims the privilege of weaving tragic graces around ordinary workingmen, despite whatever objections any earthly "critics" might raise. At this point, the only literary critics of Melville's works were the reviewers. See p. 508, herein, for the specific "mortal" critic Melville was remembering, the reviewer of White-Jacket in the New York Albion (March 30, 1850), which he read very early in his work on Moby-Dick. In White-Jacket, published in 1850, just after he began Moby-Dick, Melville contrasted his status as an ordinary seaman in the

in it, thou just Spirit of Equality, which hast spread one royal mantle of humanity over all my kind! Bear me out in it, thou great democratic God! who didst not refuse to the swart convict, Bunyan, the pale, poetic pearl; Thou who didst clothe with doubly hammered leaves of finest gold, the stumped and paupered arm of old Cervantes; Thou who didst pick up Andrew Jackson[7] from the pebbles; who didst hurl him upon a war-horse; who didst thunder him higher than a throne! Thou who, in all Thy mighty, earthly marchings, ever cullest Thy selectest champions from the kingly commons; bear me out in it, O God!

Chapter 27

Knights and Squires

Stubb[1] was the second mate. He was a native of Cape Cod; and hence, according to local usage, was called a Cape-Cod-man. A happy-go-lucky; neither craven nor valiant; taking perils as they came with an indifferent air; and while engaged in the most imminent crisis of the chase, toiling away, calm and collected as a journeyman joiner[2] engaged for the year. Good-humored, easy, and careless, he presided over his whale-boat as if the most deadly encounter were but a dinner, and his crew all invited guests. He was as particular about the comfortable arrangement of his part of the boat, as an old stage-driver is about the snugness of his box. When close to the whale, in the very death-lock of the fight, he handled his unpitying lance coolly and off-handedly, as a whistling tinker his hammer. He would hum over his old rigadig tunes while flank and flank with the most exasperated monster. Long usage had, for this Stubb, converted

---

navy (compelled to witness dozens of brutal floggings and subject to flogging himself) with, first (ch. 69), his later status at a ball in Washington, when he can speak to the commander man to man and, second (ch. 70), with the freedom of his own brother to call on a president (or at least on three former presidents and a president-to-be). The reviewer in the *Albion* jeered at Melville's celebrating the "essential dignity of man" and American "democratic institutions" in *White-Jacket*. The primary aesthetic question Melville was facing in *Moby-Dick* was how an American, a democrat in a country without arbitrary social ranks (except in the army and navy and, always, the built-in constitutional master-slave division), could write a book as tragic as the greatest dramas of Shakespeare, all of which involved rulers, usually kings, queens, princes, and princesses. Traditional definitions of tragedy, Melville knew, involved a fall from a high social status, normally an inherited status rather than an earned one.

7. Jackson (1767–1845), despite extreme poverty in childhood, rose to become military hero and the first common-man president (1829–37, during Melville's own impoverished childhood). John Bunyan (1628–1688) while a convict because of his Dissenter activities wrote *The Pilgrim's Progress* (1678), still enormously influential among Protestants in Melville's time, particularly beloved by his friend Nathaniel Hawthorne. From *Tristram Shandy* (1760–65) by Laurence Sterne (1713–1768) Melville is recalling the passage in which the spirit of sweetest humor is said to have cast its "mystic mantle" over the "withered stump" of the maimed left hand of Miguel de Cervantes Saavedra (1547–1616), author of *Don Quixote* (1605, 1615); Cervantes was impoverished, but his left arm was merely disabled, not "stumped."

   For Americans of Melville's time Jackson's victory against the British at New Orleans in January 1815 was the battle that defined their national identity. This passage is infused with Melville's memories of his return from the Pacific. On November 1, 1844, four days before the election, he witnessed "mighty, earthly marchings," a massive torchlight procession winding through the streets of lower Manhattan, where one of the parading heroes was his older brother Gansevoort, a Democratic orator; another was Jackson's former aide, Auguste Davezac, who carried an old flag, a sacred relic, as a banner explained: "This flag was at the Battle of New Orleans, 8th January, 1815."

1. The name may have been chosen to fit the physique, but Flask (not Stubb) is given a "short, stout" stature and called "King-Post."

2. Competent worker, in training to become a master carpenter.

the jaws of death into an easy chair. What he thought of death itself, there is no telling. Whether he ever thought of it at all, might be a question; but, if he ever did chance to cast his mind that way after a comfortable dinner, no doubt, like a good sailor, he took it to be a sort of call of the watch to tumble aloft, and bestir themselves there, about something which he would find out when he obeyed the order, and not sooner.

What, perhaps, with other things, made Stubb such an easy-going, unfearing man, so cheerily trudging off with the burden of life in a world full of grave peddlers, all bowed to the ground with their packs; what helped to bring about that almost impious good-humor of his; that thing must have been his pipe. For, like his nose, his short, black little pipe was one of the regular features of his face. You would almost as soon have expected him to turn out of his bunk without his nose as without his pipe. He kept a whole row of pipes there ready loaded, stuck in a rack, within easy reach of his hand; and, whenever he turned in, he smoked them all out in succession, lighting one from the other to the end of the chapter; then loading them again to be in readiness anew. For, when Stubb dressed, instead of first putting his legs into his trowsers, he put his pipe into his mouth.

I say this continual smoking must have been one cause, at least, of his peculiar disposition; for every one knows that this earthly air, whether ashore or afloat, is terribly infected with the nameless miseries of the numberless mortals who have died exhaling it; and as in time of the cholera, some people go about with a camphorated handkerchief to their mouths; so, likewise, against all mortal tribulations, Stubb's tobacco smoke might have operated as a sort of disinfecting agent.

The third mate was Flask, a native of Tisbury, in Martha's Vineyard. A short, stout, ruddy young fellow, very pugnacious concerning whales, who somehow seemed to think that the great Leviathans had personally and hereditarily affronted him; and therefore it was a sort of point of honor with him, to destroy them whenever encountered. So utterly lost was he to all sense of reverence for the many marvels of their majestic bulk and mystic ways; and so dead to anything like an apprehension of any possible danger from encountering them; that in his poor opinion, the wondrous whale was but a species of magnified mouse, or at least water-rat, requiring only a little circumvention and some small application of time and trouble in order to kill and boil. This ignorant, unconscious fearlessness of his made him a little waggish in the matter of whales; he followed these fish for the fun of it; and a three years' voyage round Cape Horn was only a jolly joke that lasted that length of time. As a carpenter's nails are divided into wrought nails and cut nails;[3] so mankind may be similarly divided. Little Flask was one of the wrought ones; made to clinch tight and last long. They called him King-Post on board of the Pequod; because, in form, he could be well likened to the short, square timber known by that name in Arctic whalers; and which by the means of many radiating side timbers inserted into it, serves to brace the ship against the icy concussions of those battering seas.

Now these three mates—Starbuck, Stubb, and Flask, were momentous

3. *Wrought nails:* made by hand of forged iron, not cut from a strip of iron by a machine.

men. They it was who by universal prescription commanded three of the Pequod's boats as headsmen. In that grand order of battle in which Captain Ahab would presently marshal his forces to descend on the whales, these three headsmen were as captains of companies. Or, being armed with their long keen whaling spears, they were as a picked trio of lancers; even as the harpooneers were flingers of javelins.

And since in this famous fishery, each mate or headsman, like a Gothic Knight of old, is always accompanied by his boat-steerer or harpooneer, who in certain conjunctures provides him with a fresh lance, when the former one has been badly twisted, or elbowed in the assault; and moreover, as there generally subsists between the two, a close intimacy and friendliness; it is therefore but meet, that in this place we set down who the Pequod's harpooneers were, and to what headsman each of them belonged.

First of all was Queequeg, whom Starbuck, the chief mate, had selected for his squire. But Queequeg is already known.

Next was Tashtego, an unmixed Indian from Gay Head, the most westerly promontory of Martha's Vineyard, where there still exists the last remnant of a village of red men, which has long supplied the neighboring island of Nantucket with many of her most daring harpooneers. In the fishery, they usually go by the generic name of Gay-Headers. Tashtego's long, lean, sable hair, his high cheek bones, and black rounding eyes—for an Indian, Oriental in their largeness,[4] but Antarctic in their glittering expression—all this sufficiently proclaimed him an inheritor of the unvitiated blood of those proud warrior hunters, who, in quest of the great New England moose, had scoured, bow in hand, the aboriginal forests of the main.[5] But no longer snuffing in the trail of the wild beasts of the woodland, Tashtego now hunted in the wake of the great whales of the sea; the unerring harpoon of the son fitly replacing the infallible arrow of the sires. To look at the tawny brawn of his lithe snaky limbs, you would almost have credited the superstitions of some of the earlier Puritans, and half believed this wild Indian to be a son of the Prince of the Powers of the Air.[6] Tashtego was Stubb the second mate's squire.

Third among the harpooneers was Daggoo, a gigantic, coal-black negro-savage, with a lion-like tread—an Ahasuerus[7] to behold. Suspended from his ears were two golden hoops, so large that the sailors called them ring-bolts,[8] and would talk of securing the top-sail halyards to them. In his youth Daggoo had voluntarily shipped on board of a whaler, lying in a lonely bay on his native coast. And never having been anywhere in the world but in Africa, Nantucket, and the pagan harbors most frequented by whalemen; and having now led for many years the bold life of the fishery in the ships of owners uncommonly heedful of what manner of men they shipped; Daggoo retained all his barbaric virtues, and erect as a giraffe, moved about the decks in all the pomp of six feet five in his socks.

---

4. Eyes large and round, more like those of an Asian from India than of an American Indian.
5. Mainland.
6. The devil, as in Ephesians 2.2 ("the prince of the power of the air, the spirit that now worketh in the children of disobedience").
7. In Esther 1.1, Persian king who marries Esther and, at her insistence, spares the Jews. Melville attributes to him a size commensurate with his kingdom, which stretched from India to Ethiopia.
8. Large iron rings bolted in the deck, to which rope could be fastened.

There was a corporeal humility in looking up at him; and a white man standing before him seemed a white flag come to beg truce of a fortress. Curious to tell, this imperial negro, Ahasuerus Daggoo, was the Squire of little Flask, who looked like a chess-man beside him. As for the residue of the Pequod's company, be it said, that at the present day not one in two of the many thousand men before the mast employed in the American whale fishery, are Americans born, though pretty nearly all the officers are. Herein it is the same with the American whale fishery as with the American army and military and merchant navies, and the engineering forces employed in the construction of the American Canals and Railroads. The same, I say, because in all these cases the native American liberally provides the brains, the rest of the world as generously supplying the muscles. No small number of these whaling seamen belong to the Azores, where the outward bound Nantucket whalers frequently touch to augment their crews from the hardy peasants of those rocky shores. In like manner, the Greenland whalers sailing out of Hull or London, put in at the Shetland Islands,[9] to receive the full complement of their crew. Upon the passage homewards, they drop them there again. How it is, there is no telling, but Islanders seem to make the best whalemen. They were nearly all Islanders in the Pequod, *Isolatoes*[1] too, I call such, not acknowledging the common continent of men, but each *Isolato* living on a separate continent of his own. Yet now, federated along one keel, what a set these Isolatoes were! An Anacharsis Clootz deputation[2] from all the isles of the sea, and all the ends of the earth, accompanying Old Ahab in the Pequod to lay the world's grievances before that bar from which not very many of them ever come back. Black Little Pip—he never did! Poor Alabama boy! On the grim Pequod's forecastle, ye shall ere long see him, beating his tambourine; prelusive of the eternal time, when sent for, to the great quarter-deck on high, he was bid strike in with angels, and beat his tambourine in glory; called a coward here, hailed a hero there!

Chapter 28

Ahab

For several days after leaving Nantucket, nothing above hatches was seen of Captain Ahab. The mates regularly relieved each other at the watches, and for aught that could be seen to the contrary, they seemed to be the only commanders of the ship; only they sometimes issued from the cabin with orders so sudden and peremptory, that after all it was plain they but commanded vicariously. Yes, their supreme lord and dictator was there,

9. A group of islands lying about 130 miles to the north of the Scottish mainland. *Azores:* a group of nine islands in the north Atlantic belonging to Portugal and situated 740 miles west of Cape da Roca in Portugal.

1. Apparently a word invented by Melville to play on "isolated" and "island."

2. Composed of different nations and races, like the motley deputation that the Prussian Baron de Cloots (1755–1794) led into the French National Assembly in 1790 to symbolize worldwide support of the French Revolution. Melville read about him in the *French Revolution* (1837, 2.1.10), by Thomas Carlyle (1795–1881).

though hitherto unseen by any eyes not permitted to penetrate into the now sacred retreat of the cabin.

Every time I ascended to the deck from my watches below, I instantly gazed aft to mark if any strange face were visible; for my first vague disquietude touching the unknown captain, now in the seclusion of the sea, became almost a perturbation. This was strangely heightened at times by the ragged Elijah's diabolical incoherences uninvitedly recurring to me, with a subtle energy I could not have before conceived of. But poorly could I withstand them, much as in other moods I was almost ready to smile at the solemn whimsicalities of that outlandish prophet of the wharves. But whatever it was of apprehensiveness or uneasiness—to call it so—which I felt, yet whenever I came to look about me in the ship, it seemed against all warranty to cherish such emotions. For though the harpooneers, with the great body of the crew, were a far more barbaric, heathenish, and motley set than any of the tame merchant-ship companies which my previous experiences had made me acquainted with, still I ascribed this—and rightly ascribed it—to the fierce uniqueness of the very nature of that wild Scandinavian vocation in which I had so abandonedly embarked. But it was especially the aspect of the three chief officers of the ship, the mates, which was most forcibly calculated to allay these colorless misgivings, and induce confidence and cheerfulness in every presentment of the voyage. Three better, more likely sea-officers and men, each in his own different way, could not readily be found, and they were every one of them Americans; a Nantucketer, a Vineyarder, a Cape man. Now, it being Christmas when the ship shot from out her harbor, for a space we had biting Polar weather, though all the time running away from it to the southward; and by every degree and minute of latitude which we sailed, gradually leaving that merciless winter, and all its intolerable weather behind us. It was one of those less lowering, but still grey and gloomy enough mornings of the transition, when with a fair wind the ship was rushing through the water with a vindictive sort of leaping and melancholy rapidity, that as I mounted to the deck at the call of the forenoon watch, so soon as I levelled my glance towards the taffrail,[1] foreboding shivers ran over me. Reality outran apprehension; Captain Ahab stood upon his quarter-deck.

There seemed no sign of common bodily illness about him, nor of the recovery from any. He looked like a man cut away from the stake, when the fire has overrunningly wasted all the limbs without consuming them, or taking away one particle from their compacted aged robustness. His whole high, broad form, seemed made of solid bronze, and shaped in an unalterable mould, like Cellini's cast Perseus.[2] Threading its way out from among his grey hairs, and continuing right down one side of his tawny scorched face and neck, till it disappeared in his clothing, you saw a slender rod-like mark, lividly whitish. It resembled that perpendicular seam sometimes made in the straight, lofty trunk of a great tree, when the

1. Railing at the ship's stern, at the back end of the quarterdeck (which begins at the main mast).
2. From engravings Melville knew the bronze statue by the Italian sculptor Benevenuto Cellini (1500–1571) in the Loggia of the Signoria in Florence. The triumphant Perseus holds aloft the newly severed head of Medusa, one of the snake-haired Gorgons whose eyes turned into stone anyone who looked into them.

upper lightning tearingly darts down it, and without wrenching a single twig, peels and grooves out the bark from top to bottom, ere running off into the soil, leaving the tree still greenly alive, but branded. Whether that mark was born with him, or whether it was the scar left by some desperate wound, no one could certainly say. By some tacit consent, throughout the voyage little or no allusion was made to it, especially by the mates. But once Tashtego's senior, an old Gay-Head Indian among the crew, superstitiously asserted that not till he was full forty years old did Ahab become that way branded, and then it came upon him, not in the fury of any mortal fray, but in an elemental strife at sea. Yet, this wild hint seemed inferentially negatived, by what a grey Manxman insinuated, an old sepulchral man, who, having never before sailed out of Nantucket, had never ere this laid eye upon wild Ahab. Nevertheless, the old sea-traditions, the immemorial credulities, popularly invested this old Manxman with preternatural powers of discernment. So that no white sailor seriously contradicted him when he said that if ever Captain Ahab should be tranquilly laid out—which might hardly come to pass, so he muttered—then, whoever should do that last office for the dead, would find a birth-mark on him from crown to sole.

So powerfully did the whole grim aspect of Ahab affect me, and the livid brand which streaked it, that for the first few moments I hardly noted that not a little of this overbearing grimness was owing to the barbaric white leg upon which he partly stood. It had previously come to me that this ivory leg had at sea been fashioned from the polished bone of the sperm whale's jaw. "Aye, he was dismasted off Japan," said the old Gay-Head Indian once; "but like his dismasted craft, he shipped another mast without coming home for it. He has a quiver of 'em."

I was struck with the singular posture he maintained. Upon each side of the Pequod's quarter deck, and pretty close to the mizen shrouds,[3] there was an auger hole, bored about half an inch or so, into the plank. His bone leg steadied in that hole; one arm elevated, and holding by a shroud; Captain Ahab stood erect, looking straight out beyond the ship's ever-pitching prow. There was an infinity of firmest fortitude, a determinate, unsurrenderable wilfulness, in the fixed and fearless, forward dedication of that glance. Not a word he spoke; nor did his officers say aught to him; though by all their minutest gestures and expressions, they plainly showed the uneasy, if not painful, consciousness of being under a troubled master-eye. And not only that, but moody stricken Ahab stood before them with a crucifixion in his face; in all the nameless regal overbearing dignity of some mighty woe.

Ere long, from his first visit in the air, he withdrew into his cabin. But after that morning, he was every day visible to the crew; either standing in his pivot-hole, or seated upon an ivory stool he had; or heavily walking the deck. As the sky grew less gloomy; indeed, began to grow a little genial, he became still less and less a recluse; as if, when the ship had sailed from home, nothing but the dead wintry bleakness of the sea had then kept him so secluded. And, by and by, it came to pass, that he was almost continually in the air; but, as yet, for all that he said,

3. Ropes at the bulwarks supporting the mast farthest aft.

or perceptibly did, on the at last sunny deck, he seemed as unnecessary there as another mast. But the Pequod was only making a passage now; not regularly cruising; nearly all whaling preparatives needing supervision the mates were fully competent to, so that there was little or nothing, out of himself, to employ or excite Ahab, now; and thus chase away, for that one interval, the clouds that layer upon layer were piled upon his brow, as ever all clouds choose the loftiest peaks to pile themselves upon.

Nevertheless, ere long, the warm, warbling persuasiveness of the pleasant, holiday weather we came to, seemed gradually to charm him from his mood. For, as when the red-cheeked, dancing girls, April and May, trip home to the wintry, misanthropic woods; even the barest, ruggedest, most thunder-cloven old oak will at least send forth some few green sprouts, to welcome such glad-hearted visitants; so Ahab did, in the end, a little respond to the playful allurings of that girlish air. More than once did he put forth the faint blossom of a look, which, in any other man, would have soon flowered out in a smile.

Chapter 29

Enter Ahab; to him, Stubb[1]

Some days elapsed, and ice and icebergs all astern, the Pequod now went rolling through the bright Quito spring,[2] which, at sea, almost perpetually reigns on the threshold of the eternal August of the Tropic. The warmly cool, clear, ringing, perfumed, overflowing, redundant days, were as crystal goblets of Persian sherbet,[3] heaped up—flaked up, with rose-water snow. The starred and stately nights seemed haughty dames in jewelled velvets, nursing at home in lonely pride, the memory of their absent conquering Earls, the golden helmeted suns! For sleeping man, 'twas hard to choose between such winsome days and such seducing nights. But all the witcheries of that unwaning weather did not merely lend new spells and potencies to the outward world. Inward they turned upon the soul, especially when the still mild hours of eve came on; then, memory shot her crystals as the clear ice most forms of noiseless twilights. And all these subtle agencies, more and more they wrought on Ahab's texture.

Old age is always wakeful; as if, the longer linked with life, the less man has to do with aught that looks like death. Among sea-commanders, the old greybeards will oftenest leave their berths to visit the night-cloaked deck. It was so with Ahab; only that now, of late, he seemed so much to live in the open air, that truly speaking, his visits were more to the cabin, than from the cabin to the planks. "It feels like going down into one's tomb,"—he would mutter to himself,—"for an old captain like me to be descending this narrow scuttle, to go to my grave-dug berth."

1. The first use in the book of a stage direction, signifying Ishmael's strategy of presenting Ahab as a tragic hero whose greatness he as dramatist to some extent discovers and even creates (as he says at the end of ch. 33).
2. Invariable weather associated with Quito, Ecuador (named for being on the equator).
3. In Asian stories, a dessert topped with perfumed mountain snow.

So, almost every twenty-four hours, when the watches of the night were set, and the band on deck sentinelled the slumbers of the band below; and when if a rope was to be hauled upon the forecastle, the sailors flung it not rudely down, as by day, but with some cautiousness dropt it to its place, for fear of disturbing their slumbering shipmates; when this sort of steady quietude would begin to prevail, habitually, the silent steersman would watch the cabin-scuttle; and ere long the old man would emerge, griping[4] at the iron banister, to help his crippled way. Some considerating touch of humanity was in him; for at times like these, he usually abstained from patrolling the quarter-deck; because to his wearied mates, seeking repose within six inches of his ivory heel, such would have been the reverberating crack and din of that bony step, that their dreams would have been of the crunching teeth of sharks. But once, the mood was on him too deep for common regardings; and as with heavy, lumber-like[5] pace he was measuring the ship from taffrail to mainmast, Stubb, the odd second mate, came up from below, and with a certain unassured, deprecating humorousness, hinted that if Captain Ahab was pleased to walk the planks, then, no one could say nay; but there might be some way of muffling the noise; hinting something indistinctly and hesitatingly about a globe of tow,[6] and the insertion into it, of the ivory heel. Ah! Stubb, thou did'st not know Ahab then.

"Am I a cannon-ball, Stubb," said Ahab, "that thou wouldst wad me that fashion? But go thy ways; I had forgot. Below to thy nightly grave; where such as ye sleep between shrouds, to use ye to the filling one at last.— Down, dog, and kennel!"

Starting at the unforeseen concluding exclamation of the so suddenly scornful old man, Stubb was speechless a moment; then said excitedly, "I am not used to be spoken to that way, sir; I do but less than half like it, sir."

"Avast!" gritted Ahab between his set teeth, and violently moving away, as if to avoid some passionate temptation.

"No, sir; not yet," said Stubb, emboldened, "I will not tamely be called a dog, sir."

"Then be called ten times a donkey, and a mule, and an ass, and begone, or I'll clear the world of thee!"

As he said this, Ahab advanced upon him with such overbearing terrors in his aspect, that Stubb involuntarily retreated.

"I was never served so before without giving a hard blow for it," muttered Stubb, as he found himself descending the cabin-scuttle. "It's very queer. Stop, Stubb; somehow, now, I don't well know whether to go back and strike him, or—what's that?—down here on my knees and pray for him? Yes, that was the thought coming up in me; but it would be the first time I ever *did* pray. It's queer; very queer;[7] and he's queer too; aye,

---

4. Grasping.
5. Lumbering, lurching.
6. Tight little ball of rope yarn, which Ahab punningly takes to mean the wadding thrust down the muzzle of a cannon. He then goes on to compare Stubb's bed sheets to the cerements ("shrouds") of a corpse.
7. Puzzling, nearer the root sense of something oblique or athwart and, therefore, baffling (stronger than the modern sense, "odd"). The word recurs in the book, expressing its theme of the mystery of existence, whether the puzzler be the complex Ishmael or the simpler Stubb, as here.

take him fore and aft, he's about the queerest old man Stubb ever sailed
with. How he flashed at me!—his eyes like powder-pans! is he mad?
Anyway there's something on his mind, as sure as there must be something on a deck when it cracks. He aint in his bed now, either, more
than three hours out of the twenty-four; and he don't sleep then. Didn't
that Dough-Boy,[8] the steward, tell me that of a morning he always finds
the old man's hammock clothes all rumpled and tumbled, and the sheets
down at the foot, and the coverlid almost tied into knots, and the pillow a sort of frightful hot, as though a baked brick had been on it? A
hot old man! I guess he's got what some folks ashore call a conscience;
it's a kind of Tic-Dolly-row[9] they say—worse nor a toothache. Well, well;
I don't know what it is, but the Lord keep me from catching it. He's full
of riddles; I wonder what he goes into the after hold for, every night, as
Dough-Boy tells me he suspects; what's that for, I should like to know?
Who's made appointments with him in the hold? Ain't that queer, now?
But there's no telling, it's the old game—Here goes for a snooze. Damn
me, it's worth a fellow's while to be born into the world, if only to fall
right asleep. And now that I think of it, that's about the first thing babies
do, and that's a sort of queer, too. Damn me, but all things are queer,
come to think of 'em. But that's against my principles. Think not, is my
eleventh commandment;[1] and sleep when you can, is my twelfth—So
here goes again. But how's that? didn't he call me a dog? blazes! he
called me ten times a donkey, and piled a lot of jackasses on top of *that!*
He might as well have kicked me, and done with it. Maybe he *did* kick
me, and I didn't observe it, I was so taken all aback with his brow, somehow. It flashed like a bleached bone. What the devil's the matter with
me? I don't stand right on my legs. Coming afoul[2] of that old man has
a sort of turned me wrong side out. By the Lord, I must have been
dreaming, though—How? how? how?—but the only way's to stash it; so
here goes to hammock again; and in the morning, I'll see how this
plaguey juggling[3] thinks over by daylight."

Chapter 30

The Pipe

When Stubb had departed, Ahab stood for a while leaning over the bulwarks; and then, as had been usual with him of late, calling a sailor of the
watch, he sent him below for his ivory stool, and also his pipe. Lighting
the pipe at the binnacle lamp[1] and planting the stool on the weather side
of the deck, he sat and smoked.

---

8. A boiled dumpling, so an appropriate nickname for a food handler with a pale loaf-of-bread face
   such as he is said to possess (ch. 34). For more on Melville's odd imagery involving dough, see
   Omoo, ch. 14.
9. From the French *tic douloureux*, a painful facial twitching.
1. That is, next in solemnity after the biblical ten.
2. Nautical for becoming entangled with something, usually another vessel.
3. Treacherous trickery, like that of the "juggling fiends" of *Macbeth* (5.8.19), a drama fresh in
   Melville's mind.
1. Lighted compass box by the tiller.

In old Norse times, the thrones of the sea-loving Danish kings were fabricated, saith tradition, of the tusks of the narwhale. How could one look at Ahab then, seated on that tripod of bones, without bethinking him of the royalty it symbolized? For a Khan[2] of the plank, and a king of the sea, and a great lord of Leviathans was Ahab.

Some moments passed, during which the thick vapor came from his mouth in quick and constant puffs, which blew back again into his face. "How now," he soliloquized at last, withdrawing the tube, "this smoking no longer soothes. Oh, my pipe! hard must it go with me if thy charm be gone! Here have I been unconsciously toiling, not pleasuring,—aye, and ignorantly smoking to windward all the while; to windward, and with such nervous whiffs, as if, like the dying whale, my final jets were the strongest and fullest of trouble. What business have I with this pipe? This thing that is meant for sereneness, to send up mild white vapors among mild white hairs, not among torn iron-grey locks like mine. I'll smoke no more—"

He tossed the still lighted pipe into the sea. The fire hissed in the waves; the same instant the ship shot by the bubble the sinking pipe made. With slouched hat, Ahab lurchingly paced the planks.

Chapter 31

Queen Mab[1]

Next morning Stubb accosted Flask.

"Such a queer dream, King-Post, I never had. You know the old man's ivory leg, well I dreamed he kicked me with it; and when I tried to kick back, upon my soul, my little man, I kicked my leg right off! And then, presto! Ahab seemed a pyramid, and I, like a blazing fool, kept kicking at it. But what was still more curious, Flask—you know how curious all dreams are—through all this rage that I was in, I somehow seemed to be thinking to myself, that after all, it was not much of an insult, that kick from Ahab. 'Why,' thinks I, 'what's the row? It's not a real leg, only a false leg.' And there's a mighty difference between a living thump and a dead thump. That's what makes a blow from the hand, Flask, fifty times more savage to bear than a blow from a cane. The living member—that makes the living insult, my little man. And thinks I to myself all the while, mind, while I was stubbing my silly toes against that cursed pyramid—so confoundedly contradictory was it all, all the while, I say, I was thinking to myself, 'what's his leg now, but a cane—a whalebone cane. Yes,' thinks I, 'it was only a playful cudgelling—in fact, only a whaleboning that he gave me—not a base kick. Besides,' thinks I, 'look at it once; why, the end of it—the foot part—what a small sort of end it is; whereas, if a broad footed farmer kicked me, *there's* a devilish broad insult. But this insult is whittled down to a point only.' But now

2. Absolute monarch, like a sovereign of Tartary.
1. The fairies' midwife who delivers dreams befitting each human sleeper, as in *Romeo and Juliet* 1.4.54. Queen Mab has been with Stubb.

comes the greatest joke of the dream, Flask. While I was battering away at the pyramid, a sort of badger-haired old merman, with a hump on his back, takes me by the shoulders, and slews me round. 'What are you 'bout?' says he. 'Slid![2] man, but I was frightened. Such a phiz! But, somehow, next moment I was over the fright. 'What am I about?' says I at last. 'And what business is that of yours, I should like to know, Mr. Humpback? Do *you* want a kick?' By the lord, Flask, I had no sooner said that, than he turned round his stern to me, bent over, and dragging up a lot of sea-weed he had for a clout[3]—what do you think, I saw?— why thunder alive, man, his stern was stuck full of marlinspikes, with the points out. Says I, on second thoughts, 'I guess I won't kick you, old fellow.' 'Wise Stubb,' said he, 'wise Stubb;' and kept muttering it all the time, a sort of eating of his own gums like a chimney hag.[4] Seeing he wasn't going to stop saying over his 'wise Stubb, wise Stubb,' I thought I might as well fall to kicking the pyramid again. But I had only just lifted my foot for it, when he roared out, 'Stop that kicking!' 'Halloa,' says I, 'what's the matter now, old fellow?' 'Look ye here,' says he; 'let's argue the insult. Captain Ahab kicked ye, didn't he?' 'Yes, he did,' says I—'right *here* it was.' 'Very good,' says he—'he used his ivory leg, didn't he?' 'Yes, he did,' says I. 'Well then,' says he, 'wise Stubb, what have you to complain of? Didn't he kick with right good will? it wasn't a common pitch pine leg he kicked with, was it? No, you were kicked by a great man, and with a beautiful ivory leg, Stubb. It's an honor; I consider it an honor. Listen, wise Stubb. In old England the greatest lords think it great glory to be slapped by a queen, and made garter-knights[5] of; but, be *your* boast, Stubb, that ye were kicked by old Ahab, and made a wise man of. Remember what I say; *be* kicked by him; account his kicks honors; and on no account kick back; for you can't help yourself, wise Stubb. Don't you see that pyramid?' With that, he all of a sudden seemed somehow, in some queer fashion, to swim off into the air. I snored; rolled over; and there I was in my hammock! Now, what do you think of that dream, Flask?"

"I don't know; it seems a sort of foolish to me, tho'."

"May be; may be. But it's made a wise man of me, Flask. D'ye see Ahab standing there, sideways looking over the stern? Well, the best thing you can do, Flask, is to let that old man alone; never speak quick[6] to him, whatever he says. Halloa! what's that he shouts? Hark!"

"Mast-head, there![7] Look sharp, all of ye! There are whales hereabouts! If ye see a white one, split your lungs for him!"

"What d'ye think of that now, Flask? ain't there a small drop of something queer about that, eh? A white whale—did ye mark that, man? Look ye—there's something special in the wind. Stand by for it, Flask. Ahab has that that's bloody on his mind. But, mum; he comes this way."

---

2. "God's lid" (eyelid), an archaic oath, as in *Twelfth Night* 3.4.391.
3. What he has to cover his rear instead of cloth.
4. Old crone, seeking warmth from the fire. Stubb's dream crosses genders as well as species.
5. The queen admitted a knight to the Order of the Garter by striking him upon the shoulder with the flat side of a swordblade.
6. Never speak back to him, defy him.
7. Ahab calls out to the lookouts high up the mast.

Chapter 32

Cetology[1]

Already we are boldly launched upon the deep; but soon we shall be lost in its unshored, harborless immensities. Ere that come to pass; ere the Pequod's weedy hull rolls side by side with the barnacled hulls of the leviathan; at the outset it is but well to attend to a matter almost indispensable to a thorough appreciative understanding of the more special leviathanic revelations and allusions of all sorts which are to follow.

It is some systematized exhibition of the whale in his broad genera, that I would now fain put before you. Yet is it no easy task. The classification of the constituents of a chaos, nothing less is here essayed. Listen to what the best and latest authorities[2] have laid down.

"No branch of Zoology is so much involved as that which is entitled Cetology," says Captain Scoresby, A. D. 1820.

"It is not my intention, were it in my power, to enter into the inquiry as to the true method of dividing the cetacea into groups and families. * * * Utter confusion exists among the historians of this animal" (sperm whale), says Surgeon Beale, A. D. 1839.

"Unfitness to pursue our research in the unfathomable waters." "Impenetrable veil covering our knowledge of the cetacea." "A field strewn with thorns." "All these incomplete indications but serve to torture us naturalists."

Thus speak of the whale, the great Cuvier, and John Hunter, and Lesson, those lights of zoology and anatomy. Nevertheless, though of real knowledge there be little, yet of books there are a plenty; and so in some small degree, with cetology, or the science of whales. Many are the men, small and great, old and new, landsmen and seamen, who have at large or in little, written of the whale. Run over a few:[3]—The Authors of the Bible; Aristotle; Pliny; Aldrovandi; Sir Thomas Browne; Gesner; Ray; Linnæus; Rondeletius; Willoughby; Green; Artedi; Sibbald; Brisson; Marten; Lacépède; Bonnaterre; Desmarest; Baron Cuvier; Frederick Cuvier; John Hunter; Owen; Scoresby; Beale; Bennett; J. Ross Browne; the Author of Miriam Coffin; Olmsted; and the Rev. Henry T. Cheever. But to what ultimate generalizing purpose all these have written, the above cited extracts will show.

Of the names in this list of whale authors, only those following Owen ever saw living whales; and but one of them was a real professional har-

1. The branch of zoology dealing with whales. The chapter rejects and parodies the claims of science to explain the wonders and mysteries of nature and the universe, which require poetic imagination as well, and which even so elude final understanding.
2. Scoresby's *Account of the Arctic Regions* (1820) and his *Journal of a Voyage to the Northern Whale-Fishery* (1823) and Beale (1839), whose credentials are discussed just below. As Vincent (1949, 139) first pointed out, Melville lifted from Beale's epigraph page the quotation from Scoresby (1823), along with the uncredited three, from the English anatomist John Hunter (1728–1793), and the French zoologists René-Primàvere Lesson (1794–1849) and Baron Georges Cuvier (1769–1832).
3. Melville draws on the twenty-five-page article "Whales" in *The Penny Cyclopædia* (London, 1833–43). He took there his list of names through Linnæus, adding only Sir Thomas Browne. Karl von Linné (1707–1778), Latinized as Linnæus, was a Swedish botanist, the founder of modern systematic botanical classification. Melville knew firsthand only the writers from Scoresby on. Chiefly, he used Beale, Browne (1846), Henry T. Cheever's *The Whale and His Captors* (1850, already available when he returned to New York in February), and Scoresby (1820).

pooneer and whaleman. I mean Captain Scoresby. On the separate subject of the Greenland or right-whale, he is the best existing authority. But
Scoresby knew nothing and says nothing of the great sperm whale, compared with which the Greenland whale is almost unworthy mentioning.
And here be it said, that the Greenland whale is an usurper upon the
throne of the seas. He is not even by any means the largest of the whales.
Yet, owing to the long priority of his claims, and the profound ignorance
which, till some seventy years back, invested the then fabulous or utterly
unknown sperm-whale, and which ignorance to this present day still
reigns in all but some few scientific retreats and whale-ports; this usurpation has been every way complete. Reference to nearly all the leviathanic
allusions in the great poets of past days, will satisfy you that the
Greenland whale, without one rival, was to them the monarch of the seas.
But the time has at last come for a new proclamation. This is Charing
Cross;[4] hear ye! good people all,—the Greenland whale is deposed,—the
great sperm whale now reigneth!

There are only two books in being which at all pretend to put the living
sperm whale before you, and at the same time, in the remotest degree succeed in the attempt. Those books are Beale's and Bennett's;[5] both in their
time surgeons to English South-Sea whale-ships, and both exact and reliable men. The original matter touching the sperm whale to be found in
their volumes is necessarily small; but so far as it goes, it is of excellent
quality, though mostly confined to scientific description. As yet, however,
the sperm whale, scientific or poetic, lives not complete in any literature.
Far above all other hunted whales, his is an unwritten life.

Now the various species of whales need some sort of popular comprehensive classification, if only an easy outline one for the present, hereafter to be filled in all its departments by subsequent laborers. As no better man advances to take this matter in hand, I hereupon offer my own
poor endeavors. I promise nothing complete; because any human thing
supposed to be complete, must for that very reason infallibly be faulty. I
shall not pretend to a minute anatomical description of the various
species,[6] or—in this place at least—to much of any description. My object
here is simply to project the draught[7] of a systematization of cetology. I am
the architect, not the builder.

But it is a ponderous task; no ordinary letter-sorter in the Post-office is
equal to it. To grope down into the bottom of the sea after them; to have
one's hands among the unspeakable foundations, ribs, and very pelvis of
the world; this is a fearful thing. What am I that I should essay to hook
the nose of this leviathan! The awful tauntings in Job[8] might well appal
me. "Will he (the leviathan) make a covenant with thee? Behold the hope
of him is vain!" But I have swam through libraries and sailed through
oceans; I have had to do with whales with these visible hands; I am in
earnest; and I will try. There are some preliminaries to settle.

4. At the center of old London, where new monarchs were proclaimed.
5. Frederick Debell Bennett, *Narrative of a Whaling Voyage Round the Globe* (1840).
6. The *Penny Cyclopædia* article on whales gives just this kind of description. Melville never mentions the article while raiding it for numerous items.
7. Draft, preliminary sketch, as in the often-quoted ending of this chapter.
8. Job 41.4, 9.

First: The uncertain, unsettled condition of this science of Cetology is in the very vestibule attested by the fact, that in some quarters it still remains a moot point whether a whale be a fish.[9] In his System of Nature, A.D. 1766, Linnæus declares, "I hereby separate the whales from the fish." But of my own knowledge, I know that down to the year 1850, sharks and shad, alewives and herring, against Linnæus's express edict, were still found dividing the possession of the same seas with the Leviathan.

The grounds upon which Linnæus would fain have banished the whales from the waters, he states as follows: "On account of their warm bilocular heart, their lungs, their movable eyelids, their hollow ears, penem intrantem feminam mammis lactantem," and finally, "ex lege naturæ jure meritoque." I submitted all this to my friends Simeon Macey and Charley Coffin, of Nantucket, both messmates of mine in a certain voyage, and they united in the opinion that the reasons set forth were altogether insufficient. Charley profanely hinted they were humbug.

Be it known that, waiving all argument, I take the good old fashioned ground that the whale is a fish, and call upon holy Jonah to back me. This fundamental thing settled, the next point is, in what internal respect does the whale differ from other fish. Above, Linnæus has given you those items. But in brief, they are these: lungs and warm blood; whereas, all other fish are lungless and cold blooded.

Next: how shall we define the whale, by his obvious externals, so as conspicuously to label him for all time to come? To be short, then, a whale is *a spouting fish with a horizontal tail*. There you have him. However contracted, that definition is the result of expanded meditation. A walrus spouts much like a whale, but the walrus is not a fish, because he is amphibious. But the last term of the definition is still more cogent, as coupled with the first. Almost any one must have noticed that all the fish familiar to landsmen have not a flat, but a vertical, or up-and-down tail. Whereas, among spouting fish the tail, though it may be similarly shaped, invariably assumes a horizontal position.

By the above definition of what a whale is, I do by no means exclude from the leviathanic brotherhood any sea creature hitherto identified with the whale by the best informed Nantucketers; nor, on the other hand, link with it any fish hitherto authoritatively regarded as alien.[1] Hence, all the smaller, spouting, and horizontal tailed fish must be included in this ground-plan of Cetology. Now, then, come the grand divisions of the entire whale host.

First: According to magnitude I divide the whales into three primary BOOKS (subdivisible into CHAPTERS), and these shall comprehend them all, both small and large.

9. The *Penny Cyclopædia* begins "Whales" with this question, citing the work and the words of Linnæus quoted here and in the next paragraph, where the first Latin phrase means "a penis that enters the female, who gives milk from breasts." The second means "From the law of nature, justly and deservedly."
1. I am aware that down to the present time, the fish styled Lamatins and Dugongs (Pig-fish and Sow-fish of the Coffins of Nantucket) are included by many naturalists among the whales. But as these pig-fish are a nosy, contemptible set, mostly lurking in the mouths of rivers, and feeding on wet hay, and especially as they do not spout, I deny their credentials as whales; and have presented them with their passports to quit the Kingdom of Cetology [Melville's note]. Here Melville follows the *Penny Cyclopædia* in excluding these animals; hereafter, he no longer follows its method and its degree of scientific precision.

I. The FOLIO WHALE; II. the OCTAVO WHALE; III. the DUODECIMO WHALE.[2]

As the type of the FOLIO I present the *Sperm Whale*; of the OCTAVO, the *Grampus*; of the DUODECIMO, the *Porpoise*.

FOLIOS. Among these I here include the following chapters:—I. The *Sperm Whale*; II. the *Right Whale*; III. the *Fin Back Whale*; IV. the *Humpbacked Whale*; V. the *Razor Back Whale*; VI. the *Sulphur Bottom Whale*.

BOOK I. (*Folio*), CHAPTER I. (*Sperm Whale*).—This whale, among the English of old vaguely known as the Trumpa whale, and the Physeter whale, and the Anvil Headed whale, is the present Cachalot of the French, and the Pottfisch of the Germans, and the Macrocephalus of the Long Words.[3] He is, without doubt, the largest inhabitant of the globe; the most formidable of all whales to encounter; the most majestic in aspect; and lastly, by far the most valuable in commerce; he being the only creature from which that valuable substance, spermaceti, is obtained. All his peculiarities will, in many other places, be enlarged upon. It is chiefly with his name that I now have to do. Philologically considered, it is absurd. Some centuries ago, when the Sperm whale was almost wholly unknown in his own proper individuality, and when his oil was only accidentally obtained from the stranded fish; in those days spermaceti, it would seem, was popularly supposed to be derived from a creature identical with the one then known in England as the Greenland or Right Whale. It was the idea also, that this same spermaceti was that quickening humor[4] of the Greenland Whale which the first syllable of the word literally expresses. In those times, also, spermaceti was exceedingly scarce, not being used for light, but only as an ointment and medicament. It was only to be had from the druggists as you nowadays buy an ounce of rhubarb.[5] When, as I opine, in the course of time, the true nature of spermaceti became known, its original name was still retained by the dealers; no doubt to enhance its value by a notion so strangely significant of its scarcity. And so the appellation must at last have come to be bestowed upon the whale from which this spermaceti was really derived.

BOOK I. (*Folio*), CHAPTER II. (*Right Whale*).—In one respect this is the most venerable of the leviathans, being the one first regularly hunted by man. It yields the article commonly known as whalebone or baleen; and the oil specially known as "whale oil,"[6] an inferior article in commerce. Among the fishermen, he is indiscriminately designated by all the following titles: The Whale; the Greenland Whale; the Black Whale; the Great Whale; the

---

2. Folio, octavo, and duodecimo are technical terms by which printers and booksellers classify the size of books and their pages, from large to small. See Melville's note (n. 7, p. 121) about his omission of quarto after octavo. His classifying whales simply by size deliberately defies the elaborately detailed scientific system readily available in the *Penny Cyclopædia* article, and his adopting bibliographical terminology for size—treating whales as if they were books—is an added humorous fling.

3. Melville's jab at the pedants who use them. *Trumpa*: from its trump or spout (French *trompe*). *Pottfisch*: German for "pot fish," *Macrocephalus*: Greek for "large head." Just below, Melville knew that the blue, or sulphur bottom, whale is the largest, but his literary purpose required that he call the more evocative sperm whale the largest.

4. Sperm of whales.

5. A laxative made from the plant's leaves and roots. Melville knew *Macbeth* 5.3.55: "What rhubarb, senna, or what purgative drug, Would scour these English hence?"

6. Not to be confused with spermaceti (see ch. 75). *Baleen*: large slats of limber "whalebone" (actually stiff hair) in the whale's mouth.

True Whale; the Right Whale. There is a deal of obscurity concerning the identity of the species thus multitudinously baptized. What then is the whale, which I include in the second species of my Folios? It is the Great Mysticetus of the English naturalists; the Greenland Whale of the English whalemen; the Baleine Ordinaire of the French whalemen; the Gronlands Walfisk[7] of the Swedes. It is the whale which for more than two centuries past has been hunted by the Dutch and English in the Arctic seas; it is the whale which the American fishermen have long pursued in the Indian ocean, on the Brazil Banks, on the Nor' West Coast,[8] and various other parts of the world, designated by them Right Whale Cruising Grounds.

Some pretend to see a difference between the Greenland whale of the English and the right whale of the Americans. But they precisely agree in all their grand features; nor has there yet been presented a single determinate fact upon which to ground a radical distinction. It is by endless subdivisions based upon the most inconclusive differences, that some departments of natural history become so repellingly intricate. The right whale will be elsewhere treated of at some length, with reference to elucidating the sperm whale.

BOOK I. (Folio), CHAPTER III. (Fin-Back).—Under this head I reckon a monster which, by the various names of Fin-Back, Tall-Spout, and Long-John, has been seen almost in every sea and is commonly the whale whose distant jet is so often descried by passengers crossing the Atlantic, in the New York packet-tracks. In the length he attains, and in his baleen, the Fin-back resembles the right whale, but is of a less portly girth, and a lighter color, approaching to olive. His great lips present a cable-like aspect, formed by the intertwisting, slanting folds of large wrinkles. His grand distinguishing feature, the fin, from which he derives his name, is often a conspicuous object. This fin is some three or four feet long, growing vertically from the hinder part of the back, of an angular shape, and with a very sharp pointed end. Even if not the slightest other part of the creature be visible, this isolated fin will, at times, be seen plainly projecting from the surface. When the sea is moderately calm, and slightly marked with spherical ripples, and this gnomon-like fin stands up and casts shadows upon the wrinkled surface, it may well be supposed that the watery circle surrounding it somewhat resembles a dial, with its style and wavy hour-lines graved on it. On that Ahaz-dial the shadow often goes back.[9] The Fin-Back is not gregarious. He seems a whale-hater, as some men are man-haters. Very shy; always going solitary; unexpectedly rising to the surface in the remotest and most sullen waters; his straight and single lofty jet rising like a tall misanthropic spear upon a barren plain; gifted with such wondrous power and velocity in swimming, as to defy all present pursuit from man; this leviathan seems the banished and unconquerable Cain[1] of his race, bearing for his

---

7. Greenland whale. Mysticetus: the supposed Greek word for this whale. Baleine Ordinaire: common whale.
8. Old name for the northernmost coasts of North America, both east and west.
9. In Isaiah 38.8 time already marked off by the shadow on the sundial of Ahaz is called back by the Lord ("Behold, I will bring again the shadow of the degrees, which is gone down in the sun dial of Ahaz, ten degrees backward"). The fin, like the "gnomon" (vertical pin or plate of a sundial) shifts irregularly with the motion of the whale.
1. The first human being to be born, who killed his brother, Abel, and was punished: "And the Lord set a mark upon Cain, lest any finding him should kill him. And Cain went out from the presence of the Lord, and dwelt in the Land of Nod, on the east of Eden" (Genesis 4.15–16).

mark that style upon his back. From having the baleen in his mouth, the Fin-Back is sometimes included with the right whale, among a theoretic species denominated *Whalebone whales*, that is, whales with baleen. Of these so called Whalebone whales, there would seem to be several varieties, most of which, however, are little known. Broad-nosed whales and beaked whales; pike-headed whales; bunched whales; under-jawed whales and ros-trated[2] whales, are the fishermen's names for a few sorts.

In connexion with this appellative of "Whalebone whales," it is of great importance to mention, that however such a nomenclature may be convenient in facilitating allusions to some kind of whales, yet it is in vain to attempt a clear classification of the Leviathan, founded upon either his baleen, or hump, or fin, or teeth,[3] notwithstanding that those marked parts or features very obviously seem better adapted to afford the basis for a regular system of Cetology than any other detached bod-ily distinctions, which the whale, in his kinds, presents. How then? The baleen, hump, back-fin, and teeth; these are things whose peculiarities are indiscriminately dispersed among all sorts of whales, without any regard to what may be the nature of their structure in other and more essential particulars. Thus, the sperm whale and the humpbacked whale, each has a hump; but there the similitude ceases. Then, this same humpbacked whale and the Greenland whale, each of these has baleen; but there again the similitude ceases. And it is just the same with the other parts above mentioned. In various sorts of whales, they form such irregular combinations; or, in the case of any one of them detached, such an irregular isolation; as utterly to defy all general methodization formed upon such a basis. On this rock every one of the whale-natu-ralists has split.

But it may possibly be concieved that, in the internal parts of the whale, in his anatomy—there, at least, we shall be able to hit the right classifi-cation. Nay; what thing, for example, is there in the Greenland whale's anatomy more striking than his baleen? Yet we have seen that by his baleen it is impossible correctly to classify the Greenland whale. And if you descend into the bowels of the various leviathans, why there you will not find distinctions a fiftieth part as available to the systematizer as those external ones already enumerated. What then remains? nothing but to take hold of the whales bodily, in their entire liberal volume, and boldly sort them that way. And this is the Bibliographical system here adopted; and it is the only one that can possibly succeed, for it alone is practicable. To proceed.

BOOK I. (*Folio*), CHAPTER IV. (*Hump Back*).—This whale is often seen on the northern American coast. He has been frequently captured there, and towed into harbor. He has a great pack on him like a peddler; or you might call him the Elephant and Castle[4] whale. At any rate, the pop-ular name for him does not sufficiently distinguish him, since the sperm whale also has a hump, though a smaller one. His oil is not very valu-

2. With an elongated snout. *Pike-headed*: sharp like a spear. *Bunched*: humped. *Underjawed*: with protruding jaws.
3. Melville follows Beale here and in the next paragraph.
4. Elephants in medieval drawings were often shown with "castles" (howdahs) on their backs to carry soldiers, and many inns took that capacious and hospitable emblem as their sign.

able. He has baleen. He is the most gamesome and light-hearted of all the whales, making more gay foam and white water generally than any other of them.

BOOK I. (*Folio*), CHAPTER V. (*Razor Back*).—Of this whale little is known but his name. I have seen him at a distance off Cape Horn. Of a retiring nature, he eludes both hunters and philosophers. Though no coward, he has never yet shown any part of him but his back, which rises in a long sharp ridge. Let him go. I know little more of him, nor does anybody else.

BOOK I. (*Folio*), CHAPTER VI. (*Sulphur Bottom*).—Another retiring gentleman, with a brimstone belly, doubtless got by scraping along the Tartarian[5] tiles in some of his profounder divings. He is seldom seen; at least I have never seen him except in the remoter southern seas, and then always at too great a distance to study his countenance. He is never chased; he would run away with rope-walks[6] of line. Prodigies are told of him. Adieu, Sulphur Bottom! I can say nothing more that is true of ye, nor can the oldest Nantucketer.

Thus ends BOOK I. (*Folio*), and now begins BOOK II. (*Octavo*).

OCTAVOES.[7] These embrace the whales of middling magnitude, among which at present may be numbered:—I., the *Grampus*; II., the *Black Fish*; III., the *Narwhale*; IV., the *Killer*; V., the *Thrasher*.

BOOK II. (*Octavo*), CHAPTER I. (*Grampus*).—Though this fish, whose loud sonorous breathing, or rather blowing, has furnished a proverb to landsmen,[8] is so well known a denizen of the deep, yet is he not popularly classed among whales. But possessing all the grand distinctive features of the leviathan, most naturalists have recognised him for one. He is of moderate octavo size, varying from fifteen to twenty-five feet in length, and of corresponding dimensions round the waist. He swims in herds; he is never regularly hunted, though his oil is considerable in quantity, and pretty good for light. By some fishermen his approach is regarded as premonitory of the advance of the great sperm whale.

BOOK II. (*Octavo*), CHAPTER II. (*Black Fish*).—I give the popular fishermen's names for all these fish, for generally they are the best. Where any name happens to be vague or inexpressive, I shall say so, and suggest another. I do so now, touching the Black Fish, so called, because blackness is the rule among almost all whales. So, call him the Hyena Whale, if you please. His voracity is well known, and from the circumstance that the inner angles of his lips are curved upwards, he carries an everlasting Mephistophelean grin on his face.[9] This whale averages some sixteen or eighteen feet in length. He is found in almost all latitudes. He has a pecu-

---

5. Hell, in Greek mythology. This whale's "brimstone" (sulfur-colored) belly got yellowed by scraping the roof tiles of hell, at the bottom of the ocean.
6. Ropes (line) as those laid straight out in elongated, covered buildings (rope-walks) during manufacture.
7. Why this book of whales is not denominated the Quarto is very plain. Because, while the whales of this order, though smaller than those of the former order, nevertheless retain a proportionate likeness to them in figure, yet the bookbinder's Quarto volume in its diminished form does not preserve the shape of the Folio volume, but the Octavo volume does [Melville's note].
8. That is, "like a grampus," used of a hard-breathing or snoring person.
9. Vincent (1949) traces Melville's lively passage to the simple description ("the angles of the lips are curved upwards" in "an innocent, smiling expression") and picture in Bennett (1840). The hyena is notorious for grinning widely and laughing screechily (as in the title of ch. 49). In *Faust* (1808, 1832) by Johann Wolfgang von Goethe (1749–1832), Mephistopheles does not grin, but Melville may have seen him or another demonic character pictured so.

liar way of showing his dorsal[1] hooked fin in swimming, which looks
something like a Roman nose. When not more profitably employed, the
sperm whale hunters sometimes capture the Hyena whale, to keep up the
supply of cheap oil for domestic employment—as some frugal house-
keepers, in the absence of company, and quite alone by themselves, burn
unsavory tallow[2] instead of odorous wax. Though their blubber is very
thin, some of these whales will yield you upwards of thirty gallons of oil.

BOOK II. (*Octavo*), CHAPTER III. (*Narwhale*), that is, *Nostril whale.*—
Another instance of a curiously named whale, so named I suppose from
his peculiar horn being originally mistaken for a peaked nose.[3] The creature is some sixteen feet in length, while its horn averages five feet,
though some exceed ten, and even attain to fifteen feet. Strictly speaking,
this horn is but a lengthened tusk, growing out from the jaw in a line a
little depressed from the horizontal. But it is only found on the sinister[4]
side, which has an ill effect, giving its owner something analogous to the
aspect of a clumsy left-handed man. What precise purpose this ivory horn
or lance answers, it would be hard to say. It does not seem to be used like
the blade of the sword-fish and bill-fish;[5] though some sailors tell me that
the Narwhale employs it for a rake in turning over the bottom of the sea
for food. Charley Coffin said it was used for an ice-piercer; for the
Narwhale, rising to the surface of the Polar Sea, and finding it sheeted
with ice, thrusts his horn up, and so breaks through. But you cannot prove
either of these surmises to be correct. My own opinion is, that however
this one-sided horn may really be used by the Narwhale—however that
may be—it would certainly be very convenient to him for a folder[6] in reading pamphlets. The Narwhale I have heard called the Tusked whale, the
Horned whale, and the Unicorn whale. He is certainly a curious example
of the Unicornism to be found in almost every kingdom of animated
nature. From certain cloistered old authors I have gathered that this same
sea-unicorn's horn was in ancient days regarded as the great antidote
against poison, and as such, preparations of it brought immense prices. It
was also distilled to a volatile salts[7] for fainting ladies, the same way that
the horns of the male deer are manufactured into hartshorn. Originally it
was in itself accounted an object of great curiosity. Black Letter[8] tells me
that Sir Martin Frobisher on his return from that voyage, when Queen
Bess did gallantly wave her jewelled hand to him from a window of
Greenwich Palace, as his bold ship sailed down the Thames; "when Sir
Martin returned from that voyage," saith Black Letter, "on bended knees

1. On the back.
2. Smoking and bad-smelling fat of cows or sheep.
3. Vincent (1949) shows that for this account Melville follows Scoresby (1820) then makes fun of
   Scoresby's surmises about the use of its horn by attributing them to "Charley Coffin" and "some
   sailors." "Scoresby will help out Melville several times, and on each occasion Melville will sati-
   rize him under a pseudonym" (Vincent 134).
4. Left.
5. A fish whose jaw is shaped like a "bill," a spear with a hook-bladed end.
6. Usually, the cover used when pamphlets are loose leaved, not stitched; here, a page turner.
7. An ammoniac inhalant (another "volatile salts").
8. Melville invents the old writer and the quotation. The account of the voyages of Sir Martin
   Frobisher (1535–1594) in the *Principal Navigations* (1589, 1598–1600) by Richard Hakluyt
   (1552–1616) does mention the queen's having a "horne," though not a gift from Frobisher, and
   mentions her waving to him. Melville also invents the "Irish author" as source of the indelicate
   story about the queen's favorite, earl of Leicester, himself the unicorn "land beast" who in this
   calumny presents to her "another horn."

he presented to her highness a prodigious long horn of the Narwhale, which for a long period after hung in the castle at Windsor." An Irish author avers that the Earl of Leicester, on bended knees, did likewise present to her highness another horn, pertaining to a land beast of the unicorn nature.

The Narwhale has a very picturesque, leopard-like look, being of a milk-white ground color, dotted with round and oblong spots of black. His oil is very superior, clear and fine; but there is little of it, and he is seldom hunted. He is mostly found in the circumpolar seas.

BOOK II. (*Octavo*), CHAPTER IV. (*Killer*).—Of this whale little is precisely known to the Nantucketer, and nothing at all to the professed naturalist. From what I have seen of him at a distance, I should say that he was about the bigness of a grampus. He is very savage—a sort of Feegee[9] fish. He sometimes takes the great Folio whales by the lip, and hangs there like a leech, till the mighty brute is worried to death. The Killer is never hunted. I never heard what sort of oil he has. Exception might be taken to the name bestowed upon this whale, on the ground of its indistinctness. For we are all killers, on land and on sea; Bonapartes and Sharks included.

BOOK II. (*Octavo*), CHAPTER V. (*Thrasher*).—This gentleman is famous for his tail, which he uses for a ferule in thrashing his foes. He mounts the Folio whale's back, and as he swims, he works his passage by flogging him; as some schoolmasters get along in the world by a similar process. Still less is known of the Thrasher than of the Killer. Both are outlaws, even in the lawless seas.

Thus ends BOOK II. (*Octavo*), and begins BOOK III. (*Duodecimo*).

DUODECIMOES.—These include the smaller whales. I: The Huzza Porpoise. II. The Algerine Porpoise. III. The Mealy-mouthed Porpoise.

To those who have not chanced specially to study the subject, it may possibly seem strange, that fishes not commonly exceeding four or five feet should be marshalled among WHALES—a word, which, in the popular sense, always conveys an idea of hugeness. But the creatures set down above as Duodecimoes are infallibly whales, by the terms of my definition of what a whale is—i.e. a spouting fish, with a horizontal tail.

BOOK III. (*Duodecimo*), CHAPTER I. (*Huzza Porpoise*).—This is the common porpoise found almost all over the globe. The name is of my own bestowal; for there are more than one sort of porpoises, and something must be done to distinguish them. I call him thus, because he always swims in hilarious shoals, which upon the broad sea keep tossing themselves to heaven like caps in a Fourth-of-July crowd. Their appearance is generally hailed with delight by the mariner. Full of fine spirits, they invariably come from the breezy billows to windward. They are the lads that always live before the wind. They are accounted a lucky omen. If you yourself can withstand three cheers at beholding these vivacious fish, then heaven help ye; the spirit of godly gamesomeness is not in ye. A well-fed, plump Huzza Porpoise will yield you one good gallon of good oil. But the fine and delicate fluid extracted from his jaws is exceedingly valuable. It is in request among jewellers and watchmak-

9. Fiji Islanders of the southwest Pacific were accounted "very savage" cannibals.

ers. Sailors put it on their hones. Porpoise meat is good eating, you
know. It may never have occurred to you that a porpoise spouts. Indeed,
his spout is so small that it is not very readily discernible. But the next
time you have a chance, watch him; and you will then see the great
Sperm whale himself in miniature.

BOOK III. (*Duodecimo*), CHAPTER II. (*Algerine Porpoise*).—A pirate.
Very savage. He is only found, I think, in the Pacific. He is somewhat
larger than the Huzza Porpoise, but much of the same general make.
Provoke him, and he will buckle to a shark. I have lowered for him many
times, but never yet saw him captured.

BOOK III. (*Duodecimo*), CHAPTER III. (*Mealy-mouthed Porpoise*).—The
largest kind of Porpoise; and only found in the Pacific, so far as it is
known. The only English name, by which he has hitherto been designated, is that of the fishers—Right-Whale Porpoise, from the circumstance that he is chiefly found in the vicinity of that Folio. In shape, he
differs in some degree from the Huzza Porpoise, being of a less rotund and
jolly girth; indeed, he is of quite a neat and gentlemanlike figure. He has
no fins on his back (most other porpoises have), he has a lovely tail, and
sentimental Indian eyes[1] of a hazel hue. But his mealy-mouth spoils all.
Though his entire back down to his side fins is of a deep sable, yet a
boundary line, distinct as the mark in a ship's hull, called the "bright
waist," that line streaks him from stem to stern, with two separate colors,
black above and white below. The white comprises part of his head, and
the whole of his mouth, which makes him look as if he had just escaped
from a felonious visit to a meal-bag. A most mean and mealy aspect! His
oil is much like that of the common porpoise.

                            *   *   *   *   *

Beyond the DUODECIMO, this system does not proceed, inasmuch as the
Porpoise is the smallest of the whales. Above, you have all the Leviathans
of note. But there are a rabble of uncertain, fugitive, half-fabulous
whales, which, as an American whaleman, I know by reputation, but not
personally. I shall enumerate them by their forecastle appellations; for
possibly such a list may be valuable to future investigators, who may complete what I have here but begun. If any of the following whales, shall
hereafter be caught and marked, then he can readily be incorporated into
this System, according to his Folio, Octavo, or Duodecimo magnitude:—
The Bottle-Nose Whale; the Junk Whale; the Pudding-Headed Whale;
the Cape Whale; the Leading Whale; the Cannon Whale; the Scragg
Whale; the Coppered Whale; the Elephant Whale; the Iceberg Whale; the
Quog Whale; the Blue Whale; &c. From Icelandic, Dutch, and old
English authorities, there might be quoted other lists of uncertain whales,
blessed with all manner of uncouth names. But I omit them as altogether
obsolete; and can hardly help suspecting them for mere sounds, full of
Leviathanism, but signifying nothing.[2]

Finally: It was stated at the outset, that this system would not be here,

---

1. A cliché from romantic poems and stories set in India.
2. *Macbeth* 5.5.27–28: "full of sound and fury, signifying nothing."

and at once, perfected. You cannot but plainly see that I have kept my word. But I now leave my cetological System standing thus unfinished, even as the great Cathedral of Cologne was left, with the crane still standing upon the top of the uncompleted tower.[3] For small erections may be finished by their first architects; grand ones, true ones, ever leave the copestone to posterity. God keep me from ever completing anything. This whole book is but a draught—nay, but the draught of a draught. Oh, Time, Strength, Cash, and Patience!

Chapter 33

The Specksynder[1]

Concerning the officers of the whale-craft, this seems as good a place as any to set down a little domestic peculiarity on ship-board, arising from the existence of the harpooneer class of officers, a class unknown of course in any other marine than the whale-fleet.

The large importance attached to the harpooneer's vocation is evinced by the fact, that originally in the old Dutch Fishery, two centuries and more ago, the command of a whale ship was not wholly lodged in the person now called the captain, but was divided between him and an officer called the Specksynder. Literally this word means Fat-Cutter; usage, however, in time made it equivalent to Chief Harpooneer. In those days, the captain's authority was restricted to the navigation and general management of the vessel: while over the whale-hunting department and all its concerns, the Specksynder or Chief Harpooneer reigned supreme. In the British Greenland Fishery, under the corrupted title of Specksioneer, this old Dutch official is still retained, but his former dignity is sadly abridged. At present he ranks simply as senior Harpooneer; and as such, is but one of the captain's more inferior subalterns. Nevertheless, as upon the good conduct of the harpooneers the success of a whaling voyage largely depends, and since in the American Fishery he is not only an important officer in the boat, but under certain circumstances (night watches on a whaling ground) the command of the ship's deck is also his; therefore the grand political maxim of the sea demands, that he should nominally live apart from the men before the mast, and be in some way distinguished as their professional superior; though always, by them, familiarly regarded as their social equal.

Now, the grand distinction drawn between officer and man at sea, is this—the first lives aft, the last forward. Hence, in whale-ships and mer-

---

3. Melville saw the cathedral in 1849, but here he was influenced by the reprinting in *Harper's New Monthly Magazine* (September 1850) of the London *Examiner's* essay on William Wordsworth's posthumous *The Prelude* as part of an "ambiguous conception" that was "doomed to share the fate of so many other colossal undertakings." The *Examiner* continued: "Of the three parts of his *Recluse*, thus planned, only the second (the *Excursion*, published in 1814), has been completed. Of the other two there exists only the first book of the first, and the plan of the third. The *Recluse* will remain in fragmentary greatness, a poetical Cathedral of Cologne."

1. Melville got from Scoresby (1820) this incorrectly Anglicized form of the Dutch word speksnijder (with "sni" instead of the "syn" sound), and got from Scoresby other facts in the second paragraph.

chantmen alike, the mates have their quarters with the captain; and so, too, in most of the American whalers the harpooneers are lodged in the after part of the ship. That is to say, they take their meals in the captain's cabin, and sleep in a place indirectly communicating with it.[2]

Though the long period of a Southern whaling voyage (by far the longest of all voyages now or ever made by man), the peculiar perils of it, and the community of interest prevailing among a company, all of whom, high or low, depend for their profits, not upon fixed wages, but upon their common luck, together with their common vigilance, intrepidity, and hard work; though all these things do in some cases tend to beget a less rigorous discipline than in merchantmen generally; yet, never mind how much like an old Mesopotamian family[3] these whalemen may, in some primitive instances, live together; for all that, the punctilious externals, at least, of the quarter-deck are seldom materially relaxed, and in no instance done away. Indeed, many are the Nantucket ships in which you will see the skipper parading his quarter-deck with an elated grandeur not surpassed in any military navy; nay, extorting almost as much outward homage as if he wore the imperial purple,[4] and not the shabbiest of pilot-cloth.

And though of all men the moody captain of the Pequod was the least given to that sort of shallowest assumption; and though the only homage he ever exacted, was implicit, instantaneous obedience; though he required no man to remove the shoes from his feet ere stepping upon the quarter-deck; and though there were times when, owing to peculiar circumstances connected with events hereafter to be detailed, he addressed them in unusual terms, whether of condescension or *in terrorem*,[5] or otherwise; yet even Captain Ahab was by no means unobservant of the paramount forms and usages of the sea.

Nor, perhaps, will it fail to be eventually perceived, that behind those forms and usages, as it were, he sometimes masked himself; incidentally making use of them for other and more private ends than they were legitimately intended to subserve. That certain sultanism of his brain, which had otherwise in a good degree remained unmanifested; through those forms that same sultanism became incarnate in an irresistible dictatorship. For be a man's intellectual superiority what it will, it can never assume the practical, available supremacy over other men, without the aid of some sort of external arts and entrenchments,[6] always, in themselves, more or less paltry and base. This it is, that for ever keeps God's true princes of the Empire from the world's hustings;[7] and leaves the highest honors that this air can give, to those men who become famous

---

2. Two of the harpooneers, Tashtego and Queequeg, are later shown as quartered forward in the crew's forecastle (chs. 54 and 100).
3. Mesopotamia was one of the earliest patriarchal civilizations, in southwest Asia, north of the Persian Gulf.
4. The color of the toga of a Roman emperor.
5. Threat (Latin).
6. Fortifications, the forms and usages behind which Ahab sometimes masked himself.
7. Historically, the prince-electors of the Holy Roman Empire; here, metaphorically, those by nature the "true princes" of God's empire, the "Divine Inert" who do not seek outward worldly honors or power by promoting themselves in any way, including electioneering "hustings." During the composition of *Moby-Dick* Melville caused great consternation among his family and friends by refusing to have his daguerreotype taken so a portrait could be engraved and published in a magazine. But his idea of fame, he wrote Hawthorne in early May 1851, had changed; this passage suggests the nature of the change.

more through their infinite inferiority to the choice hidden handful of the Divine Inert, than through their undoubted superiority over the dead level of the mass. Such large virtue lurks in these small things when extreme political superstitions invest them, that in some royal instances even to idiot imbecility they have imparted potency. But when, as in the case of Nicholas the Czar,[8] the ringed crown of geographical empire encircles an imperial brain; then, the plebeian herds crouch abased before the tremendous centralization. Nor, will the tragic dramatist who would depict mortal indomitableness in its fullest sweep and direst swing, ever forget a hint, incidentally so important in his art, as the one now alluded to.

But Ahab, my Captain, still moves before me in all his Nantucket grimness and shagginess; and in this episode touching Emperors and Kings, I must not conceal that I have only to do with a poor old whale-hunter like him; and, therefore, all outward majestical trappings and housings are denied me. Oh, Ahab! what shall be grand in thee, it must needs be plucked at from the skies, and dived for in the deep, and featured in the unbodied air![9]

Chapter 34

The Cabin-Table

It is noon; and Dough-Boy, the steward, thrusting his pale loaf-of-bread face from the cabin-scuttle, announces dinner to his lord and master; who, sitting in the lee quarter-boat, has just been taking an observation of the sun;[1] and is now mutely reckoning the latitude on the smooth, medallion-shaped tablet, reserved for that daily purpose on the upper part of his ivory leg. From his complete inattention to the tidings, you would think that moody Ahab had not heard his menial. But presently, catching hold of the mizen shrouds, he swings himself to the deck, and in an even, unexhilarated voice, saying, "Dinner, Mr. Starbuck," disappears into the cabin.

When the last echo of his sultan's[2] step has died away, and Starbuck, the first Emir, has every reason to suppose that he is seated, then Starbuck rouses from his quietude, takes a few turns along the planks, and, after a grave peep into the binnacle, says, with some touch of pleasantness, "Dinner, Mr. Stubb," and descends the scuttle. The second Emir lounges about the rigging awhile, and then slightly shaking the main brace, to see whether it be all right with that important rope, he likewise takes up the old burden,[3] and with a rapid "Dinner, Mr. Flask," follows after his predecessors.

8. Nicholas I, czar of Russia (1796–1855; r. 1825–55).
9. In defining his task as a tragic dramatist Melville (or his Ishmael) echoes Shakespeare's *1 Henry IV* 1.3.201–05: "To pluck bright honor from the pale-faced moon, Or dive into the bottom of the deep. . . . And pluck up drowned honour by the locks."
1. By custom, on ship or shore, the noon or early afternoon meal ("dinner") was the heaviest of the day. High noon was the time to determine the ship's position from observations of the sun.
2. Ahab is here ennobled as sultan and (below) grand turk of Turkey, the Ottoman Empire, with the three mates made his subordinate "emirs" or chieftains.
3. Refrain, recurrent words ending each stanza of a song or poem.

But the third Emir, now seeing himself all alone on the quarter-deck, seems to feel relieved from some curious restraint; for, tipping all sorts of knowing winks in all sorts of directions, and kicking off his shoes, he strikes into a sharp but noiseless squall of a hornpipe right over the Grand Turk's head; and then, by a dexterous sleight, pitching his cap up into the mizen-top[4] for a shelf, he goes down rollicking, so far at least as he remains visible from the deck, reversing all other processions, by bringing up the rear with music. But ere stepping into the cabin doorway below, he pauses, ships a new face altogether, and, then, independent, hilarious little Flask enters King Ahab's presence, in the character of Abjectus,[5] or the Slave.

It is not the least among the strange things bred by the intense artificialness of sea-usages, that while in the open air of the deck some officers will, upon provocation, bear themselves boldly and defyingly enough towards their commander; yet, ten to one, let those very officers the next moment go down to their customary dinner in that same commander's cabin, and straightway their inoffensive, not to say deprecatory and humble air towards him, as he sits at the head of the table; this is marvellous, sometimes most comical. Wherefore this difference? A problem? Perhaps not. To have been Belshazzar,[6] King of Babylon; and to have been Belshazzar, not haughtily but courteously, therein certainly must have been some touch of mundane grandeur. But he who in the rightly regal and intelligent spirit presides over his own private dinner-table of invited guests, that man's unchallenged power and dominion of individual influence for the time; that man's royalty of state transcends Belshazzar's, for Belshazzar was not the greatest. Who has but once dined his friends, has tasted what it is to be Cæsar.[7] It is a witchery of social czarship which there is no withstanding. Now, if to this consideration you superadd the official supremacy of a ship-master, then, by inference, you will derive the cause of that peculiarity of sea-life just mentioned.

Over his ivory-inlaid table, Ahab presided like a mute, maned sea-lion on the white coral beach, surrounded by his war-like but still deferential cubs. In his own proper turn, each officer waited to be served. They were as little children before Ahab; and yet, in Ahab, there seemed not to lurk the smallest social arrogance. With one mind, their intent eyes all fastened upon the old man's knife, as he carved the chief dish before him. I do not suppose that for the world they would have profaned that moment with the slightest observation, even upon so neutral a topic as the weather. No! And when reaching out his knife and fork, between which the slice of beef was locked, Ahab thereby motioned Starbuck's plate towards him, the mate received his meat as though receiving alms; and cut it tenderly; and a little started if, perchance, the knife grazed against the plate; and chewed it noiselessly; and swallowed it, not without circumspection. For, like the Coronation banquet at Frankfort, where the

---

4. Platform near the top of the lowest section of the mizen mast, the one farthest aft. *Hornpipe:* lively folk dance.
5. An underling, one cast down to the ground.
6. Daniel 5.1: "Belshazzar the king made a great feast to a thousand of his lords, and drank wine before the thousand."
7. Roman emperor.

German Emperor profoundly dines with the seven Imperial Electors,[8] so
these cabin meals were somehow solemn meals, eaten in awful silence;
and yet at table old Ahab forbade not conversation; only he himself was
dumb. What a relief it was to choking Stubb, when a rat made a sudden
racket in the hold below. And poor little Flask, he was the youngest son,
and little boy of this weary family party. His were the shinbones of the
saline beef; his would have been the drumsticks. For Flask to have presumed to help himself, this must have seemed to him tantamount to lar-
ceny in the first degree. Had he helped himself at that table, doubtless,
never more would he have been able to hold his head up in this honest
world; nevertheless, strange to say, Ahab never forbade him. And had
Flask helped himself, the chances were Ahab had never so much as
noticed it. Least of all, did Flask presume to help himself to butter.
Whether he thought the owners of the ship denied it to him, on account
of its clotting his clear, sunny complexion; or whether he deemed that, on
so long a voyage in such marketless waters, butter was at a premium, and
therefore was not for him, a subaltern; however it was, Flask, alas! was a
butterless man!

Another thing. Flask was the last person down at the dinner, and Flask
is the first man up. Consider! For hereby Flask's dinner was badly jammed
in point of time. Starbuck and Stubb both had the start of him; and yet
they also have the privilege of lounging in the rear. If Stubb even, who is
but a peg higher than Flask, happens to have but a small appetite, and
soon shows symptoms of concluding his repast, then Flask must bestir
himself, he will not get more than three mouthfuls that day; for it is
against holy usage for Stubb to precede Flask to the deck. Therefore it
was that Flask once admitted in private, that ever since he had arisen to
the dignity of an officer, from that moment he had never known what it
was to be otherwise than hungry, more or less. For what he ate did not so
much relieve his hunger, as keep it immortal in him. Peace and satisfaction, thought Flask, have for ever departed from my stomach.[9] I am an
officer; but, how I wish I could fist a bit of old-fashioned beef in the forecastle, as I used to when I was before the mast. There's the fruits of promotion now; there's the vanity of glory: there's the insanity of life! Besides,
if it were so that any mere sailor of the Pequod had a grudge against Flask
in Flask's official capacity, all that sailor had to do, in order to obtain
ample vengeance, was to go aft at dinner-time, and get a peep at Flask
through the cabin sky-light,[1] sitting silly and dumfoundered before awful
Ahab.

Now, Ahab and his three mates formed what may be called the first
table in the Pequod's cabin. After their departure, taking place in inverted
order to their arrival, the canvas cloth was cleared, or rather was restored
to some hurried order by the pallid steward. And then the three har-

8. Following his election at Frankfurt-am-Main, each new Holy Roman emperor held a banquet
   with the electors.
9. Hardly an allusion, but an example of how saturated Melville was with biblical phraseology (compare 1 Samuel 4.21, "The glory is departed from Israel"), just as he was with Shakespearean
   phraseology (compare at the end of ch. 33, where the echo is verbal, not particularly thematic).
1. This sentence offers one literal suggestion of how Ishmael, a "mere sailor," could know something of what goes on in the cabin-table scene; but see the whole of ch. 46 for a better explanation of Ishmael's freedom to create as he comprehends.

pooneers were bidden to the feast, they being its residuary legatees.[2] They made a sort of temporary servants' hall of the high and mighty cabin.

In strange contrast to the hardly tolerable constraint and nameless invisible domineerings of the captain's table, was the entire care-free license and ease, the almost frantic democracy of those inferior fellows the harpooneers. While their masters, the mates, seemed afraid of the sound of the hinges of their own jaws, the harpooneers chewed their food with such a relish that there was a report to it. They dined like lords; they filled their bellies like Indian ships[3] all day loading with spices. Such portentous appetites had Queequeg and Tashtego, that to fill out the vacancies made by the previous repast, often the pale Dough-Boy was fain to bring on a great baron of salt-junk,[4] seemingly quarried out of the solid ox. And if he were not lively about it, if he did not go with a nimble hopskip-and-jump, then Tashtego had an ungentlemanly way of accelerating him by darting a fork at his back, harpoon-wise. And once Daggoo, seized with a sudden humor, assisted Dough-Boy's memory by snatching him up bodily, and thrusting his head into a great empty wooden trencher, while Tashtego, knife in hand, began laying out the circle preliminary to scalping him. He was naturally a very nervous, shuddering sort of little fellow, this bread-faced steward; the progeny of a bankrupt baker and a hospital nurse. And what with the standing spectacle of the black terrific Ahab, and the periodical tumultuous visitations of these three savages, Dough-Boy's whole life was one continual lip-quiver. Commonly, after seeing the harpooneers furnished with all things they demanded, he would escape from their clutches into his little pantry adjoining, and fearfully peep out at them through the blinds of its door, till all was over.

It was a sight to see Queequeg seated over against Tashtego, opposing his filed teeth to the Indian's: crosswise to them, Daggoo seated on the floor, for a bench would have brought his hearse-plumed[5] head to the low carlines; at every motion of his colossal limbs, making the low cabin framework to shake, as when an African elephant goes passenger in a ship. But for all this, the great negro was wonderfully abstemious, not to say dainty. It seemed hardly possible that by such comparatively small mouthfuls he could keep up the vitality diffused through so broad, baronial, and superb a person. But, doubtless, this noble savage fed strong and drank deep of the abounding element of air; and through his dilated nostrils snuffed in the sublime life of the worlds. Not by beef or by bread, are giants made or nourished. But Queequeg, he had a mortal, barbaric smack of the lip in eating—an ugly sound enough—so much so, that the trembling Dough-Boy almost looked to see whether any marks of teeth lurked in his own lean arms. And when he would hear Tashtego singing out for him to produce himself, that his bones might be picked, the simple-witted Steward all but shattered the crockery hanging round him in the pantry, by his sudden fits of the palsy. Nor did the whetstones which

2. Those who get what's left after payment of a will's specific bequests.
3. Large European ships, or "Indiamen" (often with high stern decks, or poop decks, forming the roof of the captain's cabin), in the East India trade, such as the three boarded and sacked during the Boston Tea Party (December 1773), in which Melville's paternal grandfather participated.
4. Two rib racks of salted beef.
5. Daggoo's bushy black hair (like plumes then displayed on hearses) would bump the ceiling's lower beams ("carlines").

the harpooneers carried in their pockets, for their lances and other weapons; and with which whetstones, at dinner, they would ostentatiously sharpen their knives; that grating sound did not at all tend to tranquillize poor Dough-Boy. How could he forget that in his Island days, Queequeg, for one, must certainly have been guilty of some murderous, convivial indiscretions. Alas! Dough-Boy! hard fares the white waiter who waits upon cannibals. Not a napkin should he carry on his arm, but a buckler. In good time, though, to his great delight, the three salt-sea warriors would rise and depart; to his credulous, fable-mongering ears, all their martial bones jingling[6] in them at every step, like Moorish scimetars in scabbards.

But, though these barbarians dined in the cabin, and nominally lived there; still, being anything but sedentary in their habits, they were scarcely ever in it except at meal-times, and just before sleeping-time, when they passed through it to their own peculiar[7] quarters.

In this one matter, Ahab seemed no exception to most American whale captains, who, as a set, rather incline to the opinion that by rights the ship's cabin belongs to them; and that it is by courtesy alone that anybody else is, at any time, permitted there. So that, in real truth, the mates and harpooneers of the Pequod might more properly be said to have lived out of the cabin than in it. For when they did enter it, it was something as a street-door enters a house; turning inwards for a moment, only to be turned out the next; and, as a permanent thing, residing in the open air. Nor did they lose much hereby; in the cabin was no companionship; socially, Ahab was inaccessible. Though nominally included in the census of Christendom, he was still an alien to it. He lived in the world, as the last of the Grisly Bears lived in settled Missouri. And as when Spring and Summer had departed, that wild Logan[8] of the woods, burying himself in the hollow of a tree, lived out the winter there, sucking his own paws; so, in his inclement, howling old age, Ahab's soul, shut up in the caved trunk of his body, there fed upon the sullen paws of its gloom!

Chapter 35

The Mast-Head

It was during the more pleasant weather, that in due rotation with the other seamen my first mast-head came round.

In most American whalemen the mast-heads are manned almost simultaneously with the vessel's leaving her port; even though she may have fifteen thousand miles, and more, to sail ere reaching her proper cruising ground. And if, after a three, four, or five years' voyage she is drawing nigh home with anything empty in her—say, an empty vial even—then, her mast-heads are kept manned to the last; and not till her skysail-poles[1] sail

6. Dough-Boy takes literally the old expression about one's bones rattling.
7. Private.
8. An 18th-century Indian chief noted for defiance of peace overtures from the colonists, here likened to a hibernating bear in the desolate ("howling") wilderness.
1. Highest portion of masts.

in among the spires of the port, does she altogether relinquish the hope of capturing one whale more.

Now, as the business of standing mast-heads, ashore or afloat, is a very ancient and interesting one, let us in some measure expatiate here. I take it, that the earliest standers of mast-heads were the old Egyptians;[2] because, in all my researches, I find none prior to them. For though their progenitors, the builders of Babel,[3] must doubtless, by their tower, have intended to rear the loftiest mast-head in all Asia, or Africa either; yet (ere the final truck was put to it) as that great stone mast of theirs may be said to have gone by the board, in the dread gale of God's wrath; therefore, we cannot give these Babel builders priority over the Egyptians. And that the Egyptians were a nation of mast-head standers, is an assertion based upon the general belief among archæologists, that the first pyramids were founded for astronomical purposes: a theory singularly supported by the peculiar stair-like formation of all four sides of those edifices; whereby, with prodigious long upliftings of their legs, those old astronomers were wont to mount to the apex, and sing out for new stars; even as the look-outs of a modern ship sing out for a sail, or a whale just bearing in sight. In Saint Stylites,[4] the famous Christian hermit of old times, who built him a lofty stone pillar in the desert and spent the whole latter portion of his life on its summit, hoisting his food from the ground with a tackle; in him we have a remarkable instance of a dauntless stander-of-mast-heads; who was not to be driven from his place by fogs or frosts, rain, hail, or sleet; but valiantly facing everything out to the last, literally died at his post. Of modern standers-of-mast-heads we have but a lifeless set; mere stone, iron, and bronze men; who, though well capable of facing out a stiff gale, are still entirely incompetent to the business of singing out upon discovering any strange sight. There is Napoleon; who, upon the top of the column of Vendome, stands with arms folded, some one hundred and fifty feet in the air; careless, now, who rules the decks below; whether Louis Philippe, Louis Blanc, or Louis the Devil. Great Washington, too, stands high aloft on his towering main-mast in Baltimore, and like one of Hercules' pillars,[5] his column marks that point of human grandeur beyond which few mortals will go. Admiral Nelson, also, on a capstan of gun-metal, stands his mast-head in Trafalgar Square; and even when most obscured by that London smoke, token is yet given that a hidden hero is there; for where there is smoke, must be fire.[6] But neither great

---

2. Vincent (1949, 146) calls this chapter "a nostalgic-ironic remembrance . . . embellished with pseudo-history and parody." Its sources are Macy (1835), Browne (1846), and Scoresby (1820) as well as personal experience. The jocularly treated pyramids were not built to be "stairlike" and became so only when stripped of their original smooth facing.
3. In Genesis 11.1, "the whole earth was of one language, and of one speech," until men in the plain of Shinar began to build a tower the top of which was intended to "reach unto heaven," whereupon the Lord resolved to "confound their language" and "scatter them abroad" (verses 8–9).
4. St. Simeon Stylites, 5th-century Syrian ascetic hermit ("stylites" because he lived on a stylite, or pillar).
5. Rocks on the Spanish and the African coasts at the entrance to the Mediterranean Sea. Emperor Napoleon I; (1769–1821). Louis Philippe, king of France 1830–48. Louis Blanc (1811–1882), French socialist politician and journalist. Louis the devil refers satirically to Louis Napoleon Bonaparte (1808–1873; the first English edition reads "Louis Napoleon"), president of France (1848–52) during the composition of Moby-Dick, later Emperor Napoleon III (1852–70). Melville had seen the pillar statues of Napoleon in Paris and Nelson in London in 1849; he may have seen the statue of Washington in Baltimore in 1847.
6. One of many proverbs in the book.

Washington, nor Napoleon, nor Nelson, will answer a single hail from below, however madly invoked to befriend by their counsels the distracted decks upon which they gaze; however, it may be surmised, that their spirits penetrate through the thick haze of the future, and descry what shoals and what rocks must be shunned.

It may seem unwarrantable to couple in any respect the mast-head standers of the land with those of the sea; but that in truth it is not so, is plainly evinced by an item for which Obed Macy,[7] the sole historian of Nantucket, stands accountable. The worthy Obed tells us, that in the early times of the whale fishery, ere ships were regularly launched in pursuit of the game, the people of that island erected lofty spars along the sea-coast, to which the look-outs ascended by means of nailed cleats, something as fowls go upstairs in a hen-house.[8] A few years ago this same plan was adopted by the Bay whalemen of New Zealand, who, upon descrying the game, gave notice to the ready-manned boats nigh the beach. But this custom has now become obsolete, turn we then to the one proper mast-head, that of a whale-ship at sea. The three mast-heads are kept manned from sun-rise to sun-set; the seamen taking their regular turns (as at the helm), and relieving each other every two hours. In the serene weather of the tropics it is exceedingly pleasant—the mast-head; nay, to a dreamy meditative man it is delightful. There you stand, a hundred feet above the silent decks, striding along the deep, as if the masts were gigantic stilts, while beneath you and between your legs, as it were, swim the hugest monsters of the sea, even as ships once sailed between the boots of the famous Colossus at old Rhodes.[9] There you stand, lost in the infinite series of the sea, with nothing ruffled but the waves. The tranced ship indolently rolls; the drowsy trade winds blow; everything resolves you into languor. For the most part, in this tropic whaling life, a sublime uneventfulness invests you; you hear no news; read no gazettes; extras with startling accounts of commonplaces never delude you into unnecessary excitements; you hear of no domestic afflictions; bankrupt securities; fall of stocks; are never troubled with the thought of what you shall have for dinner—for all your meals for three years and more are snugly stowed in casks, and your bill of fare is immutable.

In one of those southern whalemen, on a long three or four years' voyage, as often happens, the sum of the various hours you spend at the mast-head would amount to several entire months. And it is much to be deplored that the place to which you devote so considerable a portion of the whole term of your natural life, should be so sadly destitute of anything approaching to a cosy inhabitiveness, or adapted to breed a comfortable localness of feeling, such as pertains to a bed, a hammock, a hearse, a sentry box, a pulpit, a coach, or any other of those small and snug contrivances in which men temporarily isolate themselves. Your most usual point of perch is the head of the t' gallant-mast, where you stand upon two thin parallel sticks (almost peculiar to whalemen) called the t' gallant cross-trees. Here, tossed about by the sea, the beginner feels

7. *History of Nantucket* (1835, 31).
8. The rest of this paragraph draws from Browne (1846).
9. Ancient bronze statue of the sun god Helios, later supposed to have been so large as to have straddled the harbor; famous as one of the Seven Wonders of the World.

about as cosy as he would standing on a bull's horns. To be sure, in coolish weather you may carry your house aloft with you, in the shape of a watch-coat; but properly speaking the thickest watch-coat is no more of a house than the unclad body; for as the soul is glued inside of its fleshly tabernacle,[1] and cannot freely move about in it, nor even move out of it, without running great risk of perishing (like an ignorant pilgrim crossing the snowy Alps in winter); so a watch-coat is not so much of a house as it is a mere envelope, or additional skin encasing you. You cannot put a shelf or chest of drawers in your body, and no more can you make a convenient closet of your watch-coat.

Concerning all this, it is much to be deplored that the mast-heads of a southern whale ship are unprovided with those enviable little tents or pulpits, called *crow's-nests*, in which the look-outs of a Greenland whaler are protected from the inclement weather of the frozen seas. In the fire-side narrative of Captain Sleet,[2] entitled "A Voyage among the Icebergs, in quest of the Greenland Whale, and incidentally for the re-discovery of the Lost Icelandic Colonies of Old Greenland;" in this admirable volume, all standers of mast-heads are furnished with a charmingly circumstantial account of the then recently invented *crow's-nest* of the Glacier, which was the name of Captain Sleet's good craft. He called it the *Sleet's crow's-nest*, in honor of himself; he being the original inventor and patentee, and free from all ridiculous false delicacy, and holding that if we call our own children after our own names (we fathers being the original inventors and patentees), so likewise should we denominate after ourselves any other apparatus we may beget. In shape, the Sleet's crow's-nest is something like a large tierce or pipe;[3] it is open above, however, where it is furnished with a movable side-screen to keep to windward of your head in a hard gale. Being fixed on the summit of the mast, you ascend into it through a little trap-hatch in the bottom. On the after side, or side next the stern of the ship, is a comfortable seat, with a locker underneath for umbrellas, comforters, and coats. In front is a leather rack, in which to keep your speaking trumpet, pipe, telescope, and other nautical conveniences. When Captain Sleet in person stood his mast-head in this crow's nest of his, he tells us that he always had a rifle with him (also fixed in the rack), together with a powder flask and shot, for the purpose of popping off the stray narwhales, or vagrant sea unicorns infesting those waters; for you cannot successfully shoot at them from the deck owing to the resistance of the water, but to shoot down upon them is a very different thing. Now, it was plainly a labor of love for Captain Sleet to describe, as he does, all the little detailed conveniences of his crow's-nest; but though he so enlarges upon many of these, and though he treats us to a very scientific account of his experiments in this crow's-nest, with a small compass he kept there for the purpose of counter-acting the errors resulting from what is called the "local attraction" of all binnacle magnets; an error ascribable to the horizontal vicinity of the iron in the ship's planks, and in the Glacier's case, perhaps, to there having

---

1. For tabernacle in the sense of body, see 2 Peter 1.13–14.
2. Another of Melville's comic names for William Scoresby Jr. in whose *Account of the Arctic Regions* (1820) the inventor of the crow's nest is his father, William Scoresby Sr. Melville's compressed parody attributes the father's invention to the son.
3. A large wine cask (tierce), or one three times larger (a pipe).

been so many broken-down blacksmiths among her crew; I say, that though
the Captain is very discreet and scientific here, yet, for all his learned "binnacle deviations," "azimuth compass observations," and "approximate
errors," he knows very well, Captain Sleet, that he was not so much
immersed in those profound magnetic meditations, as to fail being
attracted occasionally towards that well replenished little case-bottle,[4] so
nicely tucked in on one side of his crow's nest, within easy reach of his
hand. Though, upon the whole, I greatly admire and even love the brave,
the honest, and learned Captain; yet I take it very ill of him that he should
so utterly ignore that case-bottle, seeing what a faithful friend and com-
forter it must have been, while with mittened fingers and hooded head he
was studying the mathematics aloft there in that bird's nest within three or
four perches[5] of the pole.

But if we Southern whale-fishers are not so snugly housed aloft as
Captain Sleet and his Greenland-men were; yet that disadvantage is
greatly counterbalanced by the widely contrasting serenity of those seductive seas in which we Southern fishers mostly float. For one, I used to
lounge up the rigging very leisurely, resting in the top to have a chat with
Queequeg, or any one else off duty whom I might find there; then ascending a little way further, and throwing a lazy leg over the top-sail yard, take
a preliminary view of the watery pastures, and so at last mount to my ultimate destination.

Let me make a clean breast of it here, and frankly admit that I kept but
sorry guard. With the problem of the universe revolving in me, how could
I—being left completely to myself at such a thought-engendering altitude,—how could I but lightly hold my obligations to observe all whale-
ships' standing orders, "Keep your weather eye open, and sing out every
time."

And let me in this place movingly admonish you, ye ship-owners of
Nantucket! Beware of enlisting in your vigilant fisheries any lad with lean
brow and hollow eye; given to unseasonable meditativeness; and who
offers to ship with the Phædon instead of Bowditch[6] in his head. Beware
of such an one, I say: your whales must be seen before they can be killed;
and this sunken-eyed young Platonist will tow you ten wakes round the
world, and never make you one pint of sperm the richer. Nor are these
monitions at all unneeded. For nowadays, the whale-fishery furnishes an
asylum for many romantic, melancholy, and absent-minded young men,
disgusted with the carking cares of earth, and seeking sentiment in tar
and blubber. Childe Harold not unfrequently perches himself upon the
mast-head of some luckless disappointed whale-ship, and in moody
phrase ejaculates:—

> "Roll on, thou deep and dark blue ocean, roll!
> Ten thousand blubber-hunters sweep over thee in vain."[7]

---

4. Small flask, square to fit into a case.
5. Humorously meaning three or four resting places for a bird in flight, but as a unit of measurement, Melville knew, a perch is five and a half yards.
6. Nathaniel Bowditch's *New American Practical Navigator* (1802) was the standard handbook on
   every ship. In Plato's *Phædo* Socrates, facing his own death, argues that the soul is immortal
   because the mind is independent of the physical senses.
7. Lord Byron's *Childe Harold's Pilgrimage* (1812–18), canto 4, stanza 179: "Ten thousand fleets
   sweep over thee in vain." As a youth Melville memorized such passages from Byron.

Very often do the captains of such ships take those absent-minded young philosophers to task, upbraiding them with not feeling sufficient "interest" in the voyage; half-hinting that they are so hopelessly lost to all honorable ambition, as that in their secret souls they would rather not see whales than otherwise. But all in vain; those young Platonists have a notion that their vision is imperfect; they are short-sighted; what use, then, to strain the visual nerve? They have left their opera-glasses at home.

"Why, thou monkey," said a harpooneer to one of these lads, "we've been cruising now hard upon three years, and thou hast not raised a whale yet. Whales are scarce as hen's teeth[8] whenever thou art up here." Perhaps they were; or perhaps there might have been shoals of them in the far horizon; but lulled into such an opium-like listlessness of vacant, unconscious reverie is this absent-minded youth by the blending cadence of waves with thoughts, that at last he loses his identity;[9] takes the mystic ocean at his feet for the visible image of that deep, blue, bottomless soul, pervading mankind and nature; and every strange, half-seen, gliding, beautiful thing that eludes him; every dimly-discovered, uprising fin of some undiscernible form, seems to him the embodiment of those elusive thoughts that only people the soul by continually flitting through it. In this enchanted mood, thy spirit ebbs away to whence it came; becomes diffused through time and space; like Wickliff's sprinkled Pantheistic ashes,[1] forming at last a part of every shore the round globe over.

There is no life in thee, now, except that rocking life imparted by a gently rolling ship; by her, borrowed from the sea; by the sea, from the inscrutable tides of God. But while this sleep, this dream is on ye, move your foot or hand an inch, slip your hold at all; and your identity comes back in horror. Over Descartian vortices[2] you hover. And perhaps, at midday, in the fairest weather, with one half-throttled shriek you drop through that transparent air into the summer sea, no more to rise for ever. Heed it well, ye Pantheists!

Chapter 36

The Quarter-Deck

(Enter Ahab: Then, all.)

It was not a great while after the affair of the pipe, that one morning shortly after breakfast, Ahab, as was his wont, ascended the cabin-gang-

---

8. Proverbial (hens have no teeth).
9. In the "mystic" experience the individual soul seems to blend with the universe; this "Platonic" philosophical theme was being popularized in Melville's time by Emerson's essays, such as "The Oversoul." *Shoal:* or school, a large herd of whales.
1. The body of the 14th-century English religious reformer William Wickliff was exhumed and burned and the ashes cast into a brook. From the later historian Thomas Fuller came the fancy that they floated to the ocean and spread worldwide, like his doctrines. The first American edition read "Cranmer's"—a mistaken reference to another martyr, Thomas Cranmer (1489–1556), whose ashes, however, were not cast into a brook.
2. René Descartes (1596–1650) theorized that the physical universe is made up of innumerable vortices.

way to the deck. There most sea-captains usually walk at that hour, as country gentlemen, after the same meal, take a few turns in the garden.

Soon his steady, ivory stride was heard, as to and fro he paced his old rounds, upon planks so familiar to his tread, that they were all over dented, like geological stones, with the peculiar mark of his walk. Did you fixedly gaze, too, upon that ribbed and dented brow; there also, you would see still stranger foot-prints—the foot-prints of his one unsleeping, ever-pacing thought.

But on the occasion in question, those dents looked deeper, even as his nervous step that morning left a deeper mark. And, so full of his thought was Ahab, that at every uniform turn that he made, now at the main-mast and now at the binnacle, you could almost see that thought turn in him as he turned, and pace in him as he paced; so completely possessing him, indeed, that it all but seemed the inward mould of every outer movement.

"D'ye mark him, Flask?" whispered Stubb; "the chick that's in him pecks the shell. 'T'will soon be out."

The hours wore on;—Ahab now shut up within his cabin; anon, pacing the deck, with the same intense bigotry[1] of purpose in his aspect.

It drew near the close of day. Suddenly he came to a halt by the bulwarks, and inserting his bone leg into the auger-hole there, and with one hand grasping a shroud, he ordered Starbuck to send everybody aft.

"Sir!" said the mate, astonished at an order seldom or never given on ship-board except in some extraordinary case.

"Send everybody aft," repeated Ahab. "Mast-heads, there! come down!"

When the entire ship's company were assembled, and with curious and not wholly unapprehensive faces, were eyeing him, for he looked not unlike the weather horizon[2] when a storm is coming up, Ahab, after rapidly glancing over the bulwarks, and then darting his eyes among the crew, started from his stand-point; and as though not a soul were nigh him resumed his heavy turns upon the deck. With bent head and half-slouched hat he continued to pace, unmindful of the wondering whispering among the men; till Stubb cautiously whispered to Flask, that Ahab must have summoned them there for the purpose of witnessing a pedestrian feat. But this did not last long. Vehemently pausing, he cried:—

"What do ye do when ye see a whale, men?"

"Sing out for him!" was the impulsive rejoinder from a score of clubbed voices.

"Good!" cried Ahab, with a wild approval in his tones; observing the hearty animation into which his unexpected question had so magnetically thrown them.

"And what do ye next, men?"

"Lower away, and after him!"

"And what tune is it ye pull to, men?"

"A dead whale or a stove boat!"[3]

More and more strangely and fiercely glad and approving, grew the countenance of the old man at every shout; while the mariners began to

---

1. Obsessive, unreasoning attachment to one's own beliefs.
2. The one from which the wind is bringing the weather.
3. Pithily stated options for the boat's crew—to kill a whale or be wrecked trying.

gaze curiously at each other, as if marvelling how it was that they themselves became so excited at such seemingly purposeless questions.

But, they were all eagerness again, as Ahab, now half-revolving in his pivot-hole, with one hand reaching high up a shroud, and tightly, almost convulsively grasping it, addressed them thus:—

"All ye mast-headers have before now heard me give orders about a white whale. Look ye! d'ye see this Spanish ounce of gold?"[4]—holding up a broad bright coin to the sun—"it is a sixteen dollar piece, men,—a doubloon. D'ye see it? Mr. Starbuck, hand me yon top-maul."

While the mate was getting the hammer, Ahab, without speaking, was slowly rubbing the gold piece against the skirts of his jacket, as if to heighten its lustre, and without using any words was meanwhile lowly humming to himself, producing a sound so strangely muffled and inarticulate that it seemed the mechanical humming of the wheels of his vitality in him.

Receiving the top-maul from Starbuck, he advanced towards the mainmast with the hammer uplifted in one hand, exhibiting the gold with the other, and with a high raised voice exclaiming: "Whosoever of ye raises me a white-headed whale with a wrinkled brow and a crooked jaw; whosoever of ye raises me that white-headed whale, with three holes punctured in his starboard fluke—look ye, whosoever of ye raises me that same white whale, he shall have this gold ounce, my boys!"

"Huzza! huzza!" cried the seamen, as with swinging tarpaulins[5] they hailed the act of nailing the gold to the mast.

"It's a white whale, I say," resumed Ahab, as he threw down the top-maul; "a white whale. Skin your eyes for him, men; look sharp for white water; if ye see but a bubble, sing out."

All this while Tashtego, Daggoo, and Queequeg had looked on with even more intense interest and surprise than the rest, and at the mention of the wrinkled brow and crooked jaw they had started as if each was separately touched by some specific recollection.

"Captain Ahab," said Tashtego, "that white whale must be the same that some call Moby Dick."

"Moby Dick?" shouted Ahab. "Do ye know the white whale then, Tash?"

"Does he fan-tail[6] a little curious, sir, before he goes down?" said the Gay-Header deliberately.

"And has he a curious spout, too," said Daggoo, "very bushy, even for a parmacetty, and mighty quick, Captain Ahab?"

"And he have one, two, tree—oh! good many iron in him hide, too, Captain," cried Queequeg disjointedly, "all twiske-tee be-twisk, like him—him—" faltering hard for a word, and screwing his hand round and round as though uncorking a bottle—"like him—him—"

"Corkscrew!" cried Ahab, "aye, Queequeg, the harpoons lie all twisted and wrenched in him; aye, Daggoo, his spout is a big one, like a whole shock of wheat, and white as a pile of our Nantucket wool after the great annual sheep-shearing; aye, Tashtego, and he fan-tails like a split jib[7] in a

4. An Ecuadorian gold "onza" (ounce) then worth sixteen Spanish silver dollars.
5. Tarred hats, swung in approval.
6. Wave his broad, fan-shaped tail.
7. Triangular sail that stretches from the foretopmast to the jib boom, torn and flapping.

squall. Death and devils! men, it is Moby Dick ye have seen—Moby Dick—Moby Dick!"

"Captain Ahab," said Starbuck, who, with Stubb and Flask, had thus far been eyeing his superior with increasing surprise, but at last seemed struck with a thought which somewhat explained all the wonder. "Captain Ahab, I have heard of Moby Dick—but it was not Moby Dick that took off thy leg?"

"Who told thee that?"[8] cried Ahab; then pausing, "Aye, Starbuck; aye, my hearties all round; it was Moby Dick that dismasted me; Moby Dick that brought me to this dead stump I stand on now. Aye, aye," he shouted with a terrific, loud, animal sob, like that of a heart-stricken moose; "Aye, aye! it was that accursed white whale that razeed[9] me; made a poor pegging lubber of me for ever and a day!" Then tossing both arms, with measureless imprecations he shouted out: "Aye, aye! and I'll chase him round Good Hope, and round the Horn, and round the Norway Maelstrom, and round perdition's flames before I give him up. And this is what ye have shipped for, men! to chase that white whale on both sides of land,[1] and over all sides of earth, till he spouts black blood and rolls fin out. What say ye, men, will ye splice hands on it, now? I think ye do look brave."

"Aye, aye!" shouted the harpooneers and seamen, running closer to the excited old man: "A sharp eye for the White Whale; a sharp lance for Moby Dick!"

"God bless ye," he seemed to half sob and half shout. "God bless ye, men. Steward! go draw the great measure of grog.[2] But what's this long face about, Mr. Starbuck; wilt thou not chase the white whale? art not game for Moby Dick?"

"I am game for his crooked jaw, and for the jaws of Death too, Captain Ahab, if it fairly comes in the way of the business we follow; but I came here to hunt whales, not my commander's vengeance. How many barrels will thy vengeance yield thee even if thou gettest it, Captain Ahab? it will not fetch thee much in our Nantucket market."

"Nantucket market! Hoot! But come closer, Starbuck; thou requirest a little lower layer.[3] If money's to be the measurer, man, and the accountants have computed their great counting-house the globe, by girdling it with guineas,[4] one to every three parts of an inch; then, let me tell thee, that my vengeance will fetch a great premium *here!*"

"He smites his chest," whispered Stubb, "what's that for? methinks it rings most vast, but hollow."

"Vengeance on a dumb brute!" cried Starbuck, "that simply smote thee from blindest instinct! Madness! To be enraged with a dumb thing, Captain Ahab, seems blasphemous."[5]

8. The self-obsessed Ahab fails to realize that his previous crew had told the story throughout Nantucket, and beyond.
9. Sawed off, cut down in height, making him like a limping lubber (landman).
1. Both the Atlantic and Pacific sides of the Americas. *Norway Maelstrom:* tidal whirlpool off Norway.
2. Large pewter utensil for a measured standard amount, here of watered-down rum.
3. Deeper layer of explanation.
4. English gold coins valued at a pound plus one shilling. Melville images a guinea as being three quarters of an inch in diameter.
5. Blasphemous because Ahab is usurping a privilege of God: "Vengeance is mine; I will repay, saith the Lord" (Romans 12.19).

"Hark ye yet again,—the little lower layer. All visible objects, man, are but as pasteboard masks. But in each event—in the living act, the undoubted deed—there, some unknown but still reasoning thing puts forth the mouldings of its features from behind the unreasoning mask. If man will strike, strike through the mask! How can the prisoner reach outside except by thrusting through the wall? To me, the white whale is that wall, shoved near to me. Sometimes I think there's naught beyond. But 'tis enough. He tasks me; he heaps me; I see in him outrageous strength, with an inscrutable malice sinewing it. That inscrutable thing is chiefly what I hate; and be the white whale agent, or be the white whale principal, I will wreak that hate upon him. Talk not to me of blasphemy, man; I'd strike the sun if it insulted me.[6] For could the sun do that, then could I do the other; since there is ever a sort of fair play herein, jealousy presiding over all creations. But not my master, man, is even that fair play. Who's over me? Truth hath no confines. Take off thine eye! more intolerable than fiends' glarings is a doltish stare! So, so; thou reddenest and palest; my heat has melted thee to anger-glow. But look ye, Starbuck, what is said in heat, that thing unsays itself. There are men from whom warm words are small indignity. I meant not to incense thee. Let it go. Look! see yonder Turkish cheeks of spotted tawn[7]—living, breathing pictures painted by the sun. The Pagan leopards—the unrecking and unworshipping things, that live; and seek, and give no reasons for the torrid life they feel! The crew, man, the crew! Are they not one and all with Ahab, in this matter of the whale? See Stubb! he laughs! See yonder Chilian! he snorts to think of it. Stand up amid the general hurricane, thy one tost sapling cannot, Starbuck! And what is it? Reckon it. 'Tis but to help strike a fin; no wondrous feat for Starbuck. What is it more? From this one poor hunt, then, the best lance out of all Nantucket, surely he will not hang back, when every foremast-hand has clutched a whetstone? Ah! constrainings seize thee; I see! the billow lifts thee! Speak, but speak!—Aye, aye! thy silence, then, *that* voices thee. (*Aside*) Something shot from my dilated nostrils, he has inhaled it in his lungs. Starbuck now is mine; cannot oppose me now, without rebellion."[8]

"God keep me!—keep us all!" murmured Starbuck, lowly.

But in his joy at the enchanted, tacit acquiescence of the mate, Ahab did not hear his foreboding invocation; nor yet the low laugh from the hold; nor yet the presaging vibrations of the winds in the cordage; nor yet the hollow flap of the sails against the masts, as for a moment their hearts sank in. For again Starbuck's downcast eyes lighted up with the stubbornness of life; the subterranean laugh died away; the winds blew

6. Ahab sees the whale not, like Starbuck, as just an animal acting on instinct, but as the embodiment or agent of some power outside the physical world of visible nature while acting in it as from behind a "pasteboard mask" or "wall." In orthodox Christian theology both God and the devil are such powers, in conflict; but here it seems uncertain from his own words which one Ahab (clearly unorthodox) is attacking as evilly responsible for his own sufferings and those of mankind. Ahab's theory is that while man cannot strike that spiritual power itself, he can strike at it by striking "through the mask"—like a prisoner "thrusting through the wall," that wall, to Ahab, being Moby Dick.
7. Tan. *Turkish*: wild, savage (a residue of the portrayal of Turks during the Greek struggle for independence, in Melville's childhood).
8. Something within Starbuck ("constrainings") makes him yield, "enchanted" by Ahab's superior force, the initial "abasement" and "fall of valor in the soul" so sorrowfully anticipated by Ishmael in ch. 26. *Whetstone*: for sharpening lances and other weapons.

on; the sails filled out; the ship heaved and rolled as before. Ah, ye admonitions and warnings! why stay ye not when ye come? But rather are ye predictions than warnings, ye shadows! Yet not so much predictions from without, as verifications of the foregoing things within. For with little external to constrain us, the innermost necessities in our being, these still drive us on.

"The measure! the measure!" cried Ahab.

Receiving the brimming pewter, and turning to the harpooneers, he ordered them to produce their weapons. Then ranging them before him near the capstan, with their harpoons in their hands, while his three mates stood at his side with their lances, and the rest of the ship's company formed a circle round the group; he stood for an instant searchingly eyeing every man of his crew. But those wild eyes met his, as the blood-shot eyes of the prairie wolves meet the eye of their leader, ere he rushes on at their head in the trail of the bison; but, alas! only to fall into the hidden snare of the Indian.

"Drink and pass!" he cried, handing the heavy charged flagon to the nearest seaman. "The crew alone now drink. Round with it, round! Short draughts—long swallows, men; 'tis hot as Satan's hoof. So, so; it goes round excellently. It spiralizes in ye; forks out at the serpent-snapping eye. Well done; almost drained. That way it went, this way it comes. Hand it me—here's a hollow! Men, ye seem the years; so brimming life is gulped and gone. Steward, refill!

"Attend now, my braves. I have mustered ye all round this capstan; and ye mates, flank me with your lances; and ye harpooneers, stand there with your irons; and ye, stout mariners, ring me in, that I may in some sort revive a noble custom[9] of my fisherman fathers before me. O men, you will yet see that——Ha! boy, come back? bad pennies come not sooner.[1] Hand it me. Why, now, this pewter had run brimming again, wert not thou St. Vitus' imp[2]—away, thou ague!

"Advance, ye mates! Cross your lances[3] full before me. Well done! Let me touch the axis." So saying, with extended arm, he grasped the three level, radiating lances at their crossed centre; while so doing, suddenly and nervously twitched them; meanwhile, glancing intently from Starbuck to Stubb; from Stubb to Flask. It seemed as though, by some nameless, interior volition, he would fain have shocked into them the same fiery emotion accumulated within the Leyden jar[4] of his own magnetic life. The three mates quailed before his strong, sustained, and mys-

---

9. Mansfield and Vincent (687–88) show that Melville found the old custom of drinking from harpoon sockets in Robert Pearse Gillies, *Tales of a Voyager to the Arctic Ocean*, 1st series (1826, 1.251–52).
1. When you pay for something with a bad penny, sooner or later it comes back to you in your change (proverbial).
2. St. Vitus's dance is a spasmodic muscular jerking, also called chorea. Ahab blames the steward for spilling some of the rum.
3. Melville knew this ritual from Shakespeare (Hamlet makes Horatio and Marcellus swear on his sword in *Hamlet* 1.5.146), but he could have seen it elsewhere, perhaps in a print of the 1784 painting, *The Oath of the Horatii* by Jacques Louis David (1748–1825).
4. In early experiments with electric circuits, glass jar lined with tinfoil with a conducting rod passing through an insulated stopper. Ahab likens himself to this apparatus; in a popular demonstration of conductivity a scientist would administer a shock from it that ran through a group of people holding hands.

tic aspect. Stubb and Flask looked sideways from him; the honest eye of Starbuck fell downright.

"In vain!" cried Ahab; "but, maybe, 'tis well. For did ye three but once take the full-forced shock, then mine own electric thing, *that* had perhaps expired from out me. Perchance, too, it would have dropped ye dead. Perchance ye need it not. Down lances! And now, ye mates, I do appoint ye three cup-bearers to my three pagan kinsmen there—yon three most honorable gentlemen and noblemen, my valiant harpooneers. Disdain the task? What, when the great Pope washes the feet of beggars, using his tiara for ewer? Oh, my sweet cardinals! your own condescension, *that* shall bend ye to it. I do not order ye; ye will it. Cut your seizings and draw the poles,[5] ye harpooneers!"

Silently obeying the order, the three harpooneers now stood with the detached iron part of their harpoons, some three feet long, held, barbs up, before him.

"Stab me not with that keen steel! Cant them; cant them over! know ye not the goblet end? Turn up the socket! So, so; now, ye cup-bearers, advance. The irons! take them; hold them while I fill!" Forthwith, slowly going from one officer to the other, he brimmed the harpoon sockets with the fiery waters from the pewter.

"Now, three to three, ye stand. Commend the murderous chalices![6] Bestow them, ye who are now made parties to this indissoluble league. Ha! Starbuck! but the deed is done! Yon ratifying sun[7] now waits to sit upon it. Drink, ye harpooneers! drink and swear, ye men that man the deathful whaleboat's bow—Death to Moby Dick! God hunt us all, if we do not hunt Moby Dick to his death!" The long, barbed steel goblets were lifted; and to cries and maledictions against the white whale, the spirits were simultaneously quaffed down with a hiss. Starbuck paled, and turned, and shivered. Once more, and finally, the replenished pewter went the rounds among the frantic crew; when, waving his free hand to them, they all dispersed; and Ahab retired within his cabin.

Chapter 37

Sunset

(The cabin; by the stern windows; Ahab sitting alone, and gazing out.)

I leave a white and turbid wake; pale waters, paler cheeks, where'er I sail. The envious billows sidelong swell to whelm my track; let them; but first I pass.

Yonder, by the ever-brimming goblet's rim, the warm waves blush like wine. The gold brow plumbs the blue. The diver sun—slow dived from

5. Ahab parodies the mass as celebrated by pope and cardinals then orders the harpooneers to cut the ropes ("seizings") that lash the iron and wood parts of their harpoons together.
6. Echo of *Macbeth* 1.7.10–12. ("this even-handed justice / Commends the ingredients of our poison'd chalice / To our own lips").
7. Metaphorically, the setting sun will "sit" as in an official session to ratify the day's deed, so that no one can repudiate the pact.

noon,—goes down; my soul mounts up! she wearies with her endless hill. Is, then, the crown too heavy that I wear? this Iron Crown of Lombardy.[1] Yet is it bright with many a gem; I, the wearer, see not its far flashings; but darkly feel that I wear that, that dazzlingly confounds. 'Tis iron—that I know—not gold. 'Tis split, too—that I feel; the jagged edge galls me so, my brain seems to beat against the solid metal; aye, steel skull, mine; the sort that needs no helmet in the most brain-battering fight!

Dry heat upon my brow? Oh! time was, when as the sunrise nobly spurred me, so the sunset soothed. No more. This lovely light, it lights not me; all loveliness is anguish to me, since I can ne'er enjoy. Gifted with the high perception, I lack the low, enjoying power; damned, most subtly and most malignantly! damned in the midst of Paradise! Good night—good night! (*waving his hand, he moves from the window.*)

'Twas not so hard a task. I thought to find one stubborn, at the least; but my one cogged circle fits into all their various wheels, and they revolve. Or, if you will, like so many ant-hills of powder, they all stand before me; and I their match. Oh, hard! that to fire others, the match itself must needs be wasting! What I've dared, I've willed, and what I've willed, I'll do! They think me mad—Starbuck does; but I'm demoniac, I am madness maddened! That wild madness that's only calm to comprehend itself! The prophecy[2] was that I should be dismembered; and—Aye! I lost this leg. I now prophesy that I will dismember my dismemberer. Now, then, be the prophet and the fulfiller one. That's more than ye, ye great gods,[3] ever were. I laugh and hoot at ye, ye cricket-players, ye pugilists, ye deaf Burkes and blinded Bendigoes![4] I will not say as schoolboys do to bullies,— Take some one of your own size; don't pommel *me!* No, ye've knocked me down, and I am up again; but *ye* have run and hidden. Come forth from behind your cotton bags! I have no long gun[5] to reach ye. Come, Ahab's compliments to ye; come and see if ye can swerve me. Swerve me? ye cannot swerve me, else ye swerve yourselves! man has ye there. Swerve me? The path to my fixed purpose is laid with iron rails, whereon my soul is grooved to run.[6] Over unsounded gorges, through the rifled hearts of mountains, under torrents' beds, unerringly I rush! Naught's an obstacle, naught's an angle to the iron way!

1. Crown used at the coronation of Holy Roman emperors, said to contain a nail from the Cross on which Jesus was crucified.
2. As mentioned by Elijah in ch. 19.
3. Here and elsewhere, Ahab is shown as uncertain just which unjust supernatural power or powers he is opposing.
4. Jem ("Deaf") Burke and Bendigo (William Thompson) were English boxing champions in the 1830s and 1840s.
5. Frontiersman's rifle. Another submerged memory of the crucial importance of the Battle of New Orleans (January 1815) in American national consciousness, though here "maddened" Ahab confuses his imagery, because it was Andrew Jackson's motley army, including frontiersmen with their long guns, who, barricaded behind cotton bales and mud, defeated the British.
6. Ahab says his soul is a locomotive running on railroad tracks, then a new mode of transportation.

Chapter 38

Dusk

(By the Mainmast; Starbuck leaning against it.)

My soul is more than matched; she's overmanned; and by a madman! Insufferable sting, that sanity should ground arms on such a field! But he drilled deep down, and blasted all my reason out of me! I think I see his impious end; but feel that I must help him to it. Will I, nill I, the ineffable thing has tied me to him; tows me with a cable I have no knife to cut. Horrible old man! Who's over him, he cries;—aye, he would be a democrat to all above; look, how he lords it over all below! Oh! I plainly see my miserable office,—to obey, rebelling; and worse yet, to hate with touch of pity! For in his eyes I read some lurid woe would shrivel me up, had I it. Yet is there hope. Time and tide flow wide. The hated whale has the round watery world to swim in, as the small gold-fish has its glassy globe. His heaven-insulting purpose, God may wedge aside. I would up heart, were it not like lead. But my whole clock's run down; my heart the all-controlling weight, I have no key to lift again.[1]

(A burst of revelry from the forecastle.)

Oh, God! to sail with such a heathen crew that have small touch of human mothers in them! Whelped somewhere by the sharkish sea. The white whale is their demogorgon.[2] Hark! the infernal orgies! that revelry is forward! mark the unfaltering silence aft! Methinks it pictures life. Foremost through the sparkling sea shoots on the gay, embattled, bantering bow, but only to drag dark Ahab after it, where he broods within his sternward cabin, builded over the dead water of the wake, and further on, hunted by its wolfish gurglings. The long howl thrills me through! Peace! ye revellers, and set the watch! Oh, life! 'tis in an hour like this, with soul beat down and held to knowledge,—as wild, untutored things are forced to feed—Oh, life! 'tis now that I do feel the latent horror in thee! but 'tis not me! that horror's out of me! and with the soft feeling of the human in me, yet will I try to fight ye, ye grim, phantom futures! Stand by me, hold me, bind me, O ye blessed influences!

---

1. The descending weight that moves the clock has reached the bottom, and Starbuck lacks the key ("heart") to wind it back up.
2. Mythological demonic god (variously treated by Milton, Shelley, and other English poets).

Chapter 39

First Night-Watch

FORE-TOP.

(Stubb solus, and mending a brace.)

Ha! Ha! Ha! Ha! Hem! clear my throat!—I've been thinking over it ever since, and that ha, ha's the final consequence. Why so? Because a laugh's the wisest, easiest answer to all that's queer; and come what will, one comfort's always left—that unfailing comfort is, it's all predestinated. I heard not all his talk with Starbuck; but to my poor eye Starbuck then looked something as I the other evening felt. Be sure the old Mogul[1] has fixed him, too. I twigged it, knew it; had had the gift, might readily have prophesied it—for when I clapped my eye upon his skull I saw it. Well, Stubb, wise Stubb—that's my title—well, Stubb, what of it, Stubb? Here's a carcase. I know not all that may be coming, but be it what it will, I'll go to it laughing. Such a waggish leering as lurks in all your horribles! I feel funny. Fa, la! lirra, skirra![2] What's my juicy little pear at home doing now? Crying its eyes out?—Giving a party to the last arrived harpooneers, I dare say, gay as a frigate's pennant, and so am I—fa, la! lirra, skirra! Oh—

> We'll drink to-night with hearts as light,
>   To loves as gay and fleeting
> As bubbles that swim, on the beaker's brim,
>   And break on the lips while meeting.

A brave stave that—who calls? Mr. Starbuck? Aye, aye, sir—*(Aside)* he's my superior, he has his too, if I'm not mistaken.—Aye, aye, sir, just through with this job—coming.

Chapter 40

Midnight, Forecastle

HARPOONEERS AND SAILORS.

(Foresail rises and discovers the watch standing, lounging, leaning, and lying in various attitudes, all singing in chorus.)

> Farewell and adieu to you, Spanish ladies!
> Farewell and adieu to you, ladies of Spain!
> Our captain's commanded—

---

1. Old ruler of the Mongol tribes (Ahab).
2. These nonsense lyrics provoke Stubb to wonder about his wife's behavior at home. Then he sings lines from "Sparkling and Bright," by Melville's friend Charles Fenno Hoffman (1806–1884), the New York novelist and poet who was already, as Melville wrote this, confined in a Pennsylvania madhouse, where he remained.

1ST NANTUCKET SAILOR.

Oh, boys, don't be sentimental; it's bad for the digestion! Take a tonic, follow me!

(Sings, and all follow.)

Our captain stood upon the deck,
   A spy-glass in his hand,
A viewing of those gallant whales
   That blew at every strand.
Oh, your tubs in your boats, my boys,
   And by your braces stand,
And we'll have one of those fine whales,
   Hand, boys, over hand!
So, be cheery, my lads! may your hearts never fail!
While the bold harpooneer is striking the whale![1]

MATE'S VOICE FROM THE QUARTER-DECK.

Eight bells[2] there, forward!

2D NANTUCKET SAILOR.

Avast the chorus! Eight bells there! d'ye hear, bell-boy? Strike the bell eight, thou Pip! thou blackling! and let me call the watch. I've the sort of mouth for that—the hogshead mouth.[3] So, so, *(thrusts his head down the scuttle,)* Star—bo-l-e-e-n-s, a-h-o-y! Eight bells there below! Tumble up!

DUTCH SAILOR.

Grand snoozing to-night, maty; fat night for that. I mark this in our old Mogul's wine; it's quite as deadening to some as filliping to others. We sing; they sleep—aye, lie down there, like ground-tier butts. At 'em again! There, take this copper-pump, and hail 'em through it. Tell 'em to avast dreaming of their lasses. Tell 'em it's the resurrection; they must kiss their last, and come to judgment. That's the way—*that's* it; thy throat ain't spoiled with eating Amsterdam butter.

FRENCH SAILOR.

Hist, boys! let's have a jig or two before we ride to anchor in Blanket Bay. What say ye? There comes the other watch. Stand by all legs! Pip! little Pip! hurrah with your tambourine!

---

1. This song is a version of a song called "Captain Bunker."
2. Midnight.
3. The sailor with a big barrel ("hogshead") of a mouth summons the "starbowlins" or "starbowlines" (the starboard watch) from their sleep below, where they have been stowed tight together like the bottom layer of oil barrels (butts or casks on the ground layer, not yet stacked to the carlines, or beams). When the starboard watch (here, Starbuck's) goes on duty at midnight, the larboard watch (Stubb's) goes off duty and has a dance.

PIP.

(Sulky and sleepy.)

Don't know where it is.

FRENCH SAILOR.

Beat thy belly, then, and wag thy ears, Jig it, men, I say; merry's the word; hurrah! Damn me, won't you dance? Form, now, Indian-file, and gallop into the double-shuffle?[4] Throw yourselves! Legs! legs!

ICELAND SAILOR.

I don't like your floor, maty; it's too springy to my taste. I'm used to ice-floors. I'm sorry to throw cold water on the subject; but excuse me.

MALTESE SAILOR.

Me too; where's your girls? Who but a fool would take his left hand by his right, and say to himself, how d'ye do? Partners! I must have partners!

SICILIAN SAILOR.

Aye; girls and a green!—then I'll hop with ye; yea, turn grasshopper!

LONG-ISLAND SAILOR.

Well, well, ye sulkies, there's plenty more of us. Hoe corn[5] when you may, say I. All legs go to harvest soon. Ah! here comes the music; now for it!

AZORES SAILOR.

(Ascending, and pitching the tambourine up the scuttle.)

Here you are, Pip; and there's the windlass-bitts; up you mount! Now, boys!

(The half of them dance to the tambourine; some go below; some sleep or lie among the coils of rigging. Oaths a-plenty.)

AZORES SAILOR.

(Dancing.)

Go it, Pip! Bang it, bell-boy! Rig it, dig it, stig it, quig it, bell-boy! Make fire-flies; break the jinglers!

PIP.

Jinglers, you say?—there goes another, dropped off; I pound it so.

---

4. A clog dance.
5. A call to a "hoe down," a square dance. The Long-Island sailor intends to dance whenever he can.

CHINA SAILOR.

Rattle thy teeth, then, and pound away; make a pagoda of thyself.[6]

FRENCH SAILOR.

Merry-mad! Hold up thy hoop, Pip, till I jump through it! Split jibs! tear yourselves![7]

TASHTEGO.

(*Quietly smoking.*)

That's a white man; he calls that fun: humph! I save my sweat.

OLD MANX SAILOR.

I wonder whether those jolly lads bethink them of what they are danc-ing over. I'll dance over your grave, I will—that's the bitterest threat of your night-women, that beat head-winds round corners.[8] O Christ! to think of the green navies and the green-skulled crews! Well, well; belike the whole world's one ball, as your scholars have it; and so 'tis right to make one ball-room of it. Dance on, lads, you're young; I was once.

3D NANTUCKET SAILOR.

Spell oh!—whew! this is worse than pulling after whales in a calm—give us a whiff, Tash.

(*They cease dancing, and gather in clusters. Meantime the sky darkens—the wind rises.*)

LASCAR SAILOR.

By Brahma! boys, it'll be douse sail soon. The sky-born, high-tide Ganges turned to wind! Thou showest thy black brow, Seeva![9]

MALTESE SAILOR.

(*Reclining and shaking his cap.*)

It's the waves'—the snow-caps' turn to jig it now. They'll shake their tas-sels soon. Now would all the waves were women, then I'd go drown, and chassee with them evermore! There's naught so sweet on earth—heaven may not match it!—as those swift glances of warm, wild bosoms in the dance, when the over-arboring arms hide such ripe, bursting grapes.

---

6. Ring like all the bells in a Chinese temple.
7. Shred yourselves like sails in a gale.
8. Proverbial threat, here attributed to witches, who while riding the air can execute impossible right-angle turns around corners. Manxmen were thought to have special knowledge of such occult matters.
9. From India, this sailor swears by Brahma, the creator god of his Hindu religion, that they must soon take in ("douse") sail in the approaching high wind—which he sees as the river Ganges recycled. To him the dark sky manifests the frown ("dark brow") of Seeva (or Siva), the god of destruction.

SICILIAN SAILOR.

(Reclining.)

Tell me not of it! Hark ye, lad—fleet interlacings of the limbs—lithe swayings—coyings—flutterings! lip! heart! hip! all graze: unceasing touch and go! not taste, observe ye, else come satiety. Eh, Pagan? *(Nudging.)*

TAHITIAN SAILOR.

(Reclining on a mat.)

Hail, holy nakedness of our dancing girls!—the Heeva-Heeva![1] Ah! low valed, high palmed Tahiti! I still rest me on thy mat, but the soft soil has slid! I saw thee woven in the wood, my mat! green the first day I brought ye thence; now worn and wilted quite. Ah me!—not thou nor I can bear the change! How then, if so be transplanted to yon sky? Hear I the roaring streams from Pirohitee's peak of spears, when they leap down the crags and drown the villages?—The blast! the blast! Up, spine, and meet it! *(Leaps to his feet.)*

PORTUGUESE SAILOR.

How the sea rolls swashing 'gainst the side! Stand by for reefing, hearties! the winds are just crossing swords, pell-mell they'll go lunging presently.

DANISH SAILOR.

Crack, crack, old ship! so long as thou crackest, thou holdest! Well done! The mate there holds ye to it stiffly. He's no more afraid than the isle fort at Cattegat,[2] put there to fight the Baltic with storm-lashed guns, on which the sea-salt cakes!

4TH NANTUCKET SAILOR.

He has his orders, mind ye that. I heard old Ahab tell him he must always kill a squall, something as they burst a water-spout with a pistol—fire your ship right into it!

ENGLISH SAILOR.

Blood! but that old man's a grand old cove! We are the lads to hunt him up his whale!

ALL.

Aye! aye!

---

1. This ceremonial peace dance seemed lascivious to Western observers such as Melville, who described it in a chapter censored from *Typee* before publication in 1846 but preserved and recycled in ch. 63 of *Omoo* (1847). In *Omoo* Melville also described the Tahitian woven mats and the four-peaked mountain, which he spells Pirohitee.
2. In the strait between Denmark and Sweden.

OLD MANX SAILOR.

How the three pines shake! Pines are the hardest sort of tree to live when shifted to any other soil, and here there's none but the crew's cursed clay. Steady, helmsman! steady. This is the sort of weather when brave hearts snap ashore, and keeled hulls split at sea. Our captain has his birth-mark; look yonder, boys, there's another in the sky—lurid-like, ye see, all else pitch black.

DAGGOO.

What of that? Who's afraid of black's afraid of me! I'm quarried out of it!

SPANISH SAILOR.

(*Aside.*) He wants to bully, ah!—the old grudge makes me touchy. (*Advancing.*) Aye, harpooneer, thy race is the undeniable dark side of mankind—devilish dark at that. No offence.

DAGGOO.

(*Grimly.*)

None.

ST. JAGO'S SAILOR.[3]

That Spaniard's mad or drunk. But that can't be, or else in his one case our old Mogul's fire-waters are somewhat long in working.

5TH NANTUCKET SAILOR.

What's that I saw—lightning? Yes.

SPANISH SAILOR.

No; Daggoo showing his teeth.

DAGGOO.

(*Springing.*)

Swallow thine, mannikin! White skin, white liver![4]

SPANISH SAILOR.

(*Meeting him.*)

Knife thee heartily! big frame, small spirit!

---

3. From San (or Sao) Tiago, largest of the Cape Verde Islands in the Atlantic, owned by Portugal.
4. Cowardice. *Mannikin:* toy-size man.

ALL.

A row! a row! a row!

TASHTEGO.

(With a whiff.)

A row a'low, and a row aloft—Gods and men—both brawlers! Humph!

BELFAST SAILOR.

A row! arrah a row! The Virgin be blessed, a row! Plunge in with ye!

ENGLISH SAILOR.

Fair play! Snatch the Spaniard's knife! A ring, a ring!

OLD MANX SAILOR.

Ready formed. There! the ringed horizon. In that ring Cain struck Abel. Sweet work, right work! No? Why then, God, mad'st thou the ring?[5]

MATE'S VOICE FROM THE QUARTER DECK.

Hands by the halyards! in top-gallant sails! Stand by to reef topsails!

ALL.

The squall! the squall! jump, my jollies! *(They scatter.)*

PIP.

(Shrinking under the windlass.)

Jollies? Lord help such jollies! Crish, crash! there goes the jib-stay! Blang-whang! God! Duck lower, Pip, here comes the royal yard! It's worse than being in the whirled woods, the last day of the year! Who'd go climbing after chestnuts now? But there they go, all cursing, and here I don't. Fine prospects to 'em; they're on the road to heaven. Hold on hard! Jimmini, what a squall! But those chaps there are worse yet—they are your white squalls,[6] they. White squalls? white whale, shirr! shirr! Here have I heard all their chat just now, and the white whale—shirr! shirr!—but spoken of once! and only this evening—it makes me jingle all over like my tambourine—that anaconda of an old man swore 'em in to hunt him! Oh, thou big white God aloft there somewhere in yon darkness, have mercy on this small black boy down here; preserve him from all men that have no bowels to feel fear!

* * * * *

5. The Manxman sees the circular horizon as a combat ring made by God, like the field in which Cain killed his brother Abel (Genesis 4.8). He questions whether that first murder was "right work" and, if not, why God made the ring, the battlefield for man to fight in.
6. Sudden, violent winds bringing rain and oddly accompanied by a white cloud in a dark sky.

Chapter 41

Moby Dick

I, Ishmael, was one of that crew; my shouts had gone up with the rest; my oath had been welded with theirs; and stronger I shouted, and more did I hammer and clinch my oath, because of the dread in my soul. A wild, mystical, sympathetical feeling was in me; Ahab's quenchless feud seemed mine. With greedy ears I learned the history of that murderous monster against whom I and all the others had taken our oaths of violence and revenge.

For some time past, though at intervals only, the unaccompanied, secluded White Whale had haunted those uncivilized seas mostly frequented by the Sperm Whale fishermen.[1] But not all of them knew of his existence; only a few of them, comparatively, had knowingly seen him; while the number who as yet had actually and knowingly given battle to him, was small indeed. For, owing to the large number of whale-cruisers; the disorderly way they were sprinkled over the entire watery circumference, many of them adventurously pushing their quest along solitary latitudes, so as seldom or never for a whole twelvemonth or more on a stretch, to encounter a single news-telling sail of any sort; the inordinate length of each separate voyage; the irregularity of the times of sailing from home; all these, with other circumstances, direct and indirect, long obstructed the spread through the whole world-wide whaling-fleet of the special individualizing tidings concerning Moby Dick. It was hardly to be doubted, that several vessels reported to have encountered, at such or such a time, or on such or such a meridian, a Sperm Whale of uncommon magnitude and malignity, which whale, after doing great mischief to his assailants, had completely escaped them; to some minds it was not an unfair presumption, I say, that the whale in question must have been no other than Moby Dick. Yet as of late the Sperm Whale fishery had been marked by various and not unfrequent instances of great ferocity, cunning, and malice in the monster attacked; therefore it was, that those who by accident ignorantly gave battle to Moby Dick; such hunters, perhaps, for the most part, were content to ascribe the peculiar terror he bred, more, as it were, to the perils of the Sperm Whale fishery at large, than to the individual cause. In that way, mostly, the disastrous encounter between Ahab and the whale had hitherto been popularly regarded.

And as for those who, previously hearing of the White Whale, by chance caught sight of him; in the beginning of the thing they had every one of them, almost, as boldly and fearlessly lowered for him, as for any other whale of that species. But at length, such calamities did ensue in these assaults—not restricted to sprained wrists and ancles, broken limbs, or devouring amputations—but fatal to the last degree of fatality; those repeated disastrous repulses, all accumulating and piling their terrors upon

1. Nineteenth-century whalers hunted three of the eleven species of great whales. The bowhead whale (which Melville calls the Greenland whale) was found in the Arctic region of the Northern Hemisphere. The right whale, now nearly extinct, once inhabited every ocean. Female sperm whales, much smaller and less valuable than the males, are normally found near the equator, but the very large male sperm whales roam all the oceans alone and at will.

Moby Dick; those things had gone far to shake the fortitude of many brave hunters, to whom the story of the White Whale had eventually come.

Nor did wild rumors of all sorts fail to exaggerate, and still the more horrify the true histories of these deadly encounters. For not only do fabulous rumors naturally grow out of the very body of all surprising terrible events,—as the smitten tree gives birth to its fungi; but, in maritime life, far more than in that of terra firma, wild rumors abound, wherever there is any adequate reality for them to cling to. And as the sea surpasses the land in this matter, so the whale fishery surpasses every other sort of maritime life, in the wonderfulness and fearfulness of the rumors which sometimes circulate there. For not only are whalemen as a body unexempt from that ignorance and superstitiousness hereditary to all sailors; but of all sailors, they are by all odds the most directly brought into contact with whatever is appallingly astonishing in the sea; face to face they not only eye its greatest marvels, but, hand to jaw, give battle to them. Alone, in such remotest waters, that though you sailed a thousand miles, and passed a thousand shores, you would not come to any chiselled hearthstone, or aught hospitable beneath that part of the sun; in such latitudes and longitudes, pursuing too such a calling as he does, the whaleman is wrapped by influences all tending to make his fancy pregnant with many a mighty birth.

No wonder, then, that ever gathering volume from the mere transit over the widest watery spaces, the outblown rumors of the White Whale did in the end incorporate with themselves all manner of morbid hints, and half-formed fœtal suggestions of supernatural agencies, which eventually invested Moby Dick with new terrors unborrowed from anything that visibly appears. So that in many cases such a panic did he finally strike, that few who by those rumors, at least, had heard of the White Whale, few of those hunters were willing to encounter the perils of his jaw.

But there were still other and more vital practical influences at work. Not even at the present day has the original prestige of the Sperm Whale, as fearfully distinguished from all other species of the leviathan, died out of the minds of the whalemen as a body. There are those this day among them, who, though intelligent and courageous enough in offering battle to the Greenland or Right whale, would perhaps—either from professional inexperience, or incompetency, or timidity, decline a contest with the Sperm Whale; at any rate, there are plenty of whalemen, especially among those whaling nations not sailing under the American flag, who have never hostilely encountered the Sperm Whale, but whose sole knowledge of the leviathan is restricted to the ignoble monster primitively pursued in the North; seated on their hatches, these men will hearken with a childish fireside interest and awe, to the wild, strange tales of Southern whaling. Nor is the pre-eminent tremendousness of the great Sperm Whale anywhere more feelingly comprehended, than on board of those prows which stem him.

And as if the now tested reality of his might had in former legendary times thrown its shadow before it; we find some book naturalists—Olassen and Povelsen[2]—declaring the Sperm Whale not only to be a con-

---

2. What he knew of Olafsen and Povelsen, the authors of *Travels in Iceland* (1805) (even the misspelling of Olafsen's name as Olassen, retained here), Melville picked up secondhand from his frequent source, Thomas Beale's *Natural History of the Sperm Whale* (1839). Melville's information from Frederick Cuvier's *Natural History of Whales* (below) also came from Beale's book.

sternation to every other creature in the sea, but also to be so incredibly ferocious as continually to be athirst for human blood. Nor even down to so late a time as Cuvier's, were these or almost similar impressions effaced. For in his Natural History, the Baron himself affirms that at sight of the Sperm Whale, all fish (sharks included) are "struck with the most lively terror," and "often in the precipitancy of their flight dash themselves against the rocks with such violence as to cause instantaneous death." And however the general experiences in the fishery may amend such reports as these; yet in their full terribleness, even to the bloodthirsty item of Povelsen, the superstitious belief in them is, in some vicissitudes of their vocation, revived in the minds of the hunters.

So that overawed by the rumors and portents concerning him, not a few of the fishermen recalled, in reference to Moby Dick, the earlier days of the Sperm Whale fishery, when it was oftentimes hard to induce long practised Right whalemen to embark in the perils of this new and daring warfare; such men protesting that although other leviathans might be hopefully pursued, yet to chase and point lance at such an apparition as the Sperm Whale was not for mortal man. That to attempt it, would be inevitably to be torn into a quick eternity. On this head, there are some remarkable documents that may be consulted.

Nevertheless, some there were, who even in the face of these things were ready to give chase to Moby Dick; and a still greater number who, chancing only to hear of him distantly and vaguely, without the specific details of any certain calamity, and without superstitious accompaniments, were sufficiently hardy not to flee from the battle if offered.

One of the wild suggestings referred to, as at last coming to be linked with the White Whale in the minds of the superstitiously inclined, was the unearthly conceit that Moby Dick was ubiquitous; that he had actually been encountered in opposite latitudes at one and the same instant of time.

Nor, credulous as such minds must have been, was this conceit altogether without some faint show of superstitious probability. For as the secrets of the currents in the seas have never yet been divulged, even to the most erudite research; so the hidden ways of the Sperm Whale when beneath the surface remain, in great part, unaccountable to his pursuers; and from time to time have originated the most curious and contradictory speculations regarding them, especially concerning the mystic modes whereby, after sounding to a great depth, he transports himself with such vast swiftness to the most widely distant points.

It is a thing well known to both American and English whale-ships, and as well a thing placed upon authoritative record years ago by Scoresby,[3] that some whales have been captured far north in the Pacific, in whose bodies have been found the barbs of harpoons darted in the Greenland seas. Nor is it to be gainsaid, that in some of these instances it has been declared that the interval of time between the two assaults could not have exceeded very many days. Hence, by inference, it has been believed by some whalemen, that the Nor' West Passage,[4] so long a problem to man,

---

3. Accounts of transpolar passages of whales are in William Scoresby Jr.'s *An Account of the Arctic Regions*, (1820, 1.8–12).
4. The hoped-for navigable connection between the Atlantic and Pacific Oceans in the Arctic.

was never a problem to the whale. So that here, in the real living experience of living men, the prodigies related in old times of the inland Strella
mountain in Portugal (near whose top there was said to be a lake in which
the wrecks of ships floated up to the surface); and that still more wonderful story of the Arethusa fountain near Syracuse (whose waters were
believed to have come from the Holy Land by an underground passage);[5]
these fabulous narrations are almost fully equalled by the realities of the
whaleman.

Forced into familiarity, then, with such prodigies as these; and knowing
that after repeated, intrepid assaults, the White Whale had escaped alive; it
cannot be much matter of surprise that some whalemen should go still further in their superstitions; declaring Moby Dick not only ubiquitous, but
immortal (for immortality is but ubiquity in time); that though groves of
spears should be planted in his flanks, he would still swim away unharmed;
or if indeed he should ever be made to spout thick blood,[6] such a sight
would be but a ghastly deception; for again in unensanguined billows hundreds of leagues away, his unsullied jet would once more be seen.

But even stripped of these supernatural surmisings, there was enough
in the earthly make and incontestable character of the monster to strike
the imagination with unwonted power. For, it was not so much his uncommon bulk that so much distinguished him from other sperm whales, but,
as was elsewhere thrown out[7]—a peculiar snow-white wrinkled forehead,
and a high, pyramidical white hump. These were his prominent features;
the tokens whereby, even in the limitless, uncharted seas, he revealed his
identity, at a long distance, to those who knew him.

The rest of his body was so streaked, and spotted, and marbled with the
same shrouded hue, that, in the end, he had gained his distinctive appellation of the White Whale; a name, indeed, literally justified by his vivid
aspect, when seen gliding at high noon through a dark blue sea, leaving a
milky-way wake of creamy foam, all spangled with golden gleamings.

Nor was it his unwonted magnitude, nor his remarkable hue, nor yet his
deformed lower jaw, that so much invested the whale with natural terror,
as that unexampled, intelligent malignity which, according to specific
accounts, he had over and over again evinced in his assaults. More than
all, his treacherous retreats struck more of dismay than perhaps aught
else. For, when swimming before his exulting pursuers, with every apparent symptom of alarm, he had several times been known to turn round
suddenly, and, bearing down upon them, either stave their boats to splinters, or drive them back in consternation to their ship.

Already several fatalities had attended his chase. But though similar
disasters, however little bruited ashore, were by no means unusual in the
fishery; yet, in most instances, such seemed the White Whale's infernal
aforethought of ferocity, that every dismembering or death that he caused,

---

5. In *Isabel; or Sicily* (Philadelphia: Lea & Blanchard, 1839), Melville's friend Hentry T. Tuckerman
told how Diana saved her nymph Arethusa, who was fleeing the god of the Alpheus River in
Greece, by changing her into a fountain that ran under the Mediterranean Sea and emerged near
Syracuse, in Sicily; Alpheus, pursuing her, rose nearby. A saying held that whatever is thrown into
the Alpheus at Elis, in Greece, rises in the Arethusa at Syracuse. Melville might have known a
Christianized version of the story where the waters come from the Holy Land. *Strella*: Serra da
Estrella.
6. When mortally wounded (as at the end of ch. 62).

was not wholly regarded as having been inflicted by an unintelligent agent.

Judge, then, to what pitches of inflamed, distracted fury the minds of his more desperate hunters were impelled, when amid the chips of chewed boats, and the sinking limbs of torn comrades, they swam out of the white curds of the whale's direful wrath into the serene, exasperating sunlight, that smiled on, as if at a birth or a bridal.

His three boats stove around him, and oars and men both whirling in the eddies; one captain, seizing the line-knife from his broken prow, had dashed at the whale, as an Arkansas duellist at his foe, blindly seeking with a six inch blade to reach the fathom-deep life of the whale. That captain was Ahab. And then it was, that suddenly sweeping his sickle-shaped lower jaw beneath him, Moby Dick had reaped away Ahab's leg, as a mower a blade of grass in the field. No turbaned Turk, no hired Venetian or Malay, could have smote him with more seeming malice.[8] Small reason was there to doubt, then, that ever since that almost fatal encounter, Ahab had cherished a wild vindictiveness against the whale, all the more fell for that in his frantic morbidness he at last came to identify with him, not only all his bodily woes, but all his intellectual and spiritual exasperations. The White Whale swam before him as the monomaniac incarnation of all those malicious agencies which some deep men feel eating in them, till they are left living on with half a heart and half a lung. That intangible malignity which has been from the beginning; to whose dominion even the modern Christians ascribe one-half of the worlds; which the ancient Ophites[9] of the east reverenced in their statue devil;—Ahab did not fall down and worship it like them; but deliriously transferring its idea to the abhorred white whale, he pitted himself, all mutilated, against it. All that most maddens and torments; all that stirs up the lees of things; all truth with malice in it; all that cracks the sinews and cakes the brain; all the subtle demonisms of life and thought; all evil, to crazy Ahab, were visibly personified, and made practically assailable in Moby Dick. He piled upon the whale's white hump the sum of all the general rage and hate felt by his whole race from Adam down; and then, as if his chest had been a mortar, he burst his hot heart's shell upon it.

It is not probable that this monomania in him took its instant rise at the precise time of his bodily dismemberment. Then, in darting at the monster, knife in hand, he had but given loose to a sudden, passionate, corporal animosity; and when he received the stroke that tore him, he probably but felt the agonizing bodily laceration, but nothing more. Yet, when by this collision forced to turn towards home, and for long months of days and weeks, Ahab and anguish lay stretched together in one hammock, rounding in mid winter that dreary, howling Patagonian Cape; then it was, that his torn body and gashed soul bled into one another; and so interfusing, made him mad. That it was only then, on the homeward voyage, after the encounter, that the final monomania seized him, seems all but certain from the fact that, at intervals during the passage, he was a raving

8. An echo of *Othello* 5.2.351–55 ("in Aleppo once / Where a malignant and a turban'd Turk / Beat a Venetian and traduced the state, / I took by the throat the circumcised dog / and smote him, thus").
9. A serpent-worshiping Christian sect of the 2nd century C.E.

lunatic; and, though unlimbed of a leg, yet such vital strength yet lurked in his Egyptian chest, and was moreover intensified by his delirium, that his mates were forced to lace him fast, even there, as he sailed, raving in his hammock. In a strait-jacket, he swung to the mad rockings of the gales. And, when running into more sufferable latitudes, the ship, with mild stun'sails spread, floated across the tranquil tropics, and, to all appearances, the old man's delirium seemed left behind him with the Cape Horn swells, and he came forth from his dark den into the blessed light and air; even then, when he bore that firm, collected front, however pale, and issued his calm orders once again; and his mates thanked God the direful madness was now gone; even then, Ahab, in his hidden self, raved on. Human madness is oftentimes a cunning and most feline thing. When you think it fled, it may have but become transfigured into some still subtler form. Ahab's full lunacy subsided not, but deepeningly contracted; like the unabated Hudson, when that noble Northman flows narrowly, but unfathomably through the Highland gorge,[1] But, as in his nar row-flowing monomania, not one jot of Ahab's broad madness had been left behind; so in that broad madness, not one jot of his great natural intellect had perished. That before living agent, now became the living instrument. If such a furious trope[2] may stand, his special lunacy stormed his general sanity, and carried it, and turned all its concentred cannon upon its own mad mark; so that far from having lost his strength, Ahab, to that one end, did now possess a thousand fold more potency than ever he had sanely brought to bear upon any one reasonable object.

This is much; yet Ahab's larger, darker, deeper part remains unhinted. But vain to popularize profundities, and all truth is profound. Winding far down from within the very heart of this spiked Hotel de Cluny[3] where we here stand—however grand and wonderful, now quit it;—and take your way, ye nobler, sadder souls, to those vast Roman halls of Thermes; where far beneath the fantastic towers of man's upper earth, his root of grandeur, his whole awful essence sits in bearded state; an antique buried beneath antiquities, and throned on torsoes! So with a broken throne, the great gods mock that captive king; so like a Caryatid,[4] he patients sits, upholding on his frozen brow the piled entablatures of ages. Wind ye down there, ye prouder, sadder souls! question that proud, sad king! A family likeness! aye, he did beget ye, ye young exiled royalties; and from your grim sire only will the old State-secret come.

Now, in his heart, Ahab had some glimpse of this, namely: all my means are sane, my motive and my object mad. Yet without power to kill, or change, or shun the fact; he likewise knew that to mankind he did long dissemble; in some sort, did still. But that thing of his dissembling was

---

1. The Hudson River at its narrowest point, flowing through the Catskill Mountains just above the wide Tappan Zee. The Hudson is compared to a Viking hero, a "noble Northman." From the time he was in his mother's womb Melville had gone up and down the Hudson in steamboats many times; later he went up and down the eastern bank in railway cars.
2. Extreme figure of speech.
3. Medieval building in the Paris Latin Quarter, built above two-thousand-year-old Roman ruins. When he examined the excavations below the modern rooms in 1849 Melville apparently mistook the word for baths in his guidebook to be a proper name, "Thermes" (below). Powerfully moved, Melville described the building as just the place he would like to live.
4. Structural column in the form of a female sculpture. Melville more correctly would have used "atlas" or "telamon" to mean a male figure so used.

only subject to his perceptibility, not to his will determinate. Nevertheless, so well did he succeed in that dissembling, that when with ivory leg he stepped ashore at last, no Nantucketer thought him otherwise than but naturally grieved, and that to the quick, with the terrible casualty which had overtaken him.

The report of his undeniable delirium at sea was likewise popularly ascribed to a kindred cause. And so too, all the added moodiness which always afterwards, to the very day of sailing in the Pequod on the present voyage, sat brooding on his brow. Nor is it so very unlikely, that far from distrusting his fitness for another whaling voyage, on account of such dark symptoms, the calculating people of that prudent isle were inclined to harbor the conceit, that for those very reasons he was all the better qualified and set on edge, for a pursuit so full of rage and wildness as the bloody hunt of whales. Gnawed within and scorched without, with the infixed, unrelenting fangs of some incurable idea; such an one, could he be found, would seem the very man to dart his iron and lift his lance against the most appalling of all brutes. Or, if for any reason thought to be corporeally incapacitated for that, yet such an one would seem superlatively competent to cheer and howl on his underlings to the attack. But be all this as it may, certain it is, that with the mad secret of his unabated rage bolted up and keyed in him, Ahab had purposely sailed upon the present voyage with the one only and all-engrossing object of hunting the White Whale. Had any one of his old acquaintances on shore but half dreamed of what was lurking in him then, how soon would their aghast and righteous souls have wrenched the ship from such a fiendish man! They were bent on profitable cruises, the profit to be counted down in dollars from the mint. He was intent on an audacious, immitigable, and supernatural revenge.

Here, then, was this grey-headed, ungodly old man, chasing with curses a Job's whale[5] round the world, at the head of a crew, too, chiefly made up of mongrel renegades, and castaways, and cannibals—morally enfeebled also, by the incompetence of mere unaided virtue or right-mindedness in Starbuck, the invulnerable jollity of indifference and recklessness in Stubb, and the pervading mediocrity in Flask. Such a crew, so officered, seemed specially picked and packed by some infernal fatality to help him to his monomaniac revenge. How it was that they so aboundingly responded to the old man's ire—by what evil magic their souls were possessed, that at times his hate seemed almost theirs; the White Whale as much their insufferable foe as his; how all this came to be—what the White Whale was to them, or how to their unconscious understandings, also, in some dim, unsuspected way, he might have seemed the gliding great demon of the seas of life,—all this to explain, would be to dive deeper than Ishmael can go. The subterranean miner that works in us all, how can one tell whither leads his shaft by the ever shifting, muffled sound of his pick? Who does not feel the irresistible arm drag? What skiff in tow of a seventy-four[6] can stand still? For one, I gave myself up to the abandonment of the time and the place; but while yet all a-rush to encounter the whale, could see naught in that brute but the deadliest ill.

5. See Job 41.1: "Canst thou draw leviathan with an hook? or his tongue with a cord which thou lettest down?"
6. A battleship mounting seventy-four guns.

Chapter 42

The Whiteness of the Whale[1]

What the white whale was to Ahab, has been hinted; what, at times, he was to me, as yet remains unsaid.

Aside from those more obvious considerations touching Moby Dick, which could not but occasionally awaken in any man's soul some alarm, there was another thought, or rather vague, nameless horror concerning him, which at times by its intensity completely overpowered all the rest; and yet so mystical and well nigh ineffable was it, that I almost despair of putting it in a comprehensible form. It was the whiteness of the whale that above all things appalled me. But how can I hope to explain myself here; and yet, in some dim, random way, explain myself I must, else all these chapters might be naught.

Though in many natural objects, whiteness refiningly enhances beauty, as if imparting some special virtue of its own, as in marbles, japonicas,[2] and pearls; and though various nations have in some way recognised a certain royal pre-eminence in this hue; even the barbaric, grand old kings of Pegu placing the title "Lord of the White Elephants" above all their other magniloquent ascriptions of dominion; and the modern kings of Siam unfurling the same snow-white quadruped in the royal standard; and the Hanoverian flag bearing the one figure of a snow-white charger; and the great Austrian Empire,[3] Cæsarian heir to overlording Rome, having for the imperial color the same imperial hue; and though this pre-eminence in it applies to the human race itself, giving the white man ideal mastership over every dusky tribe;[4] and though, besides all this, whiteness has been even made significant of gladness, for among the Romans a white stone marked a joyful day; and though in other mortal sympathies and symbolizings, this same hue is made the emblem of many touching, noble things—the innocence of brides, the benignity of age; though among the Red Men of America the giving of the white belt of wampum[5] was the deepest pledge of honor; though in many climes, whiteness typifies the majesty of Justice in the ermine of the Judge, and contributes to the daily state of kings and queens drawn by milk-white steeds; though even in the higher mysteries of the most august religions it has been made the symbol of the divine spotlessness and power; by the Persian fire worshippers,[6] the white forked flame being held the holiest on the altar; and in the Greek mythologies, Great Jove himself being made incarnate in a snow-white bull;[7] and though to the noble Iroquois, the midwinter sacri-

---

1. Melville may have taken hints from treatments of color in writers listed by Mansfield and Vincent (704ff.), including Rabelais, Sir Thomas Browne, Sir Walter Scott, and Goethe.
2. Melville's meaning, a hard white natural substance, is not explained by the O.E.D. or other dictionaries. Japonic acid is a hard black substance.
3. The Holy Roman Empire, claiming succession from the Roman Cæsars. *Pegu:* Lower Burma. *Hanoverian* refers to the German state of Hanover.
4. A conventional racial formula, at odds with attitudes toward race exemplified elsewhere in the book.
5. Mansfield and Vincent (707–08) cite the New York *Literary World* (December 28, 1850) as the probable source for this and the reference below to the Iroquois sacred White Dog.
6. Zoroastrians, commonly understood to worship fire.
7. The shape in which the king of the Greek gods carried away the Princess Europa.

fice of the sacred White Dog was by far the holiest festival of their theology, that spotless, faithful creature being held the purest envoy they could
send to the Great Spirit with the annual tidings of their own fidelity; and
though directly from the Latin word for white, all Christian priests derive
the name of one part of their sacred vesture, the alb or tunic, worn
beneath the cassock; and though among the holy pomps of the Romish
faith, white is specially employed in the celebration of the Passion of our
Lord; though in the Vision of St. John,[8] white robes are given to the
redeemed, and the four-and-twenty elders stand clothed in white before
the great white throne, and the Holy One that sitteth there white like
wool; yet for all these accumulated associations, with whatever is sweet,
and honorable, and sublime, there yet lurks an elusive something in the
innermost idea of this hue, which strikes more of panic to the soul than
that redness which affrights in blood.

  This elusive quality it is, which causes the thought of whiteness, when
divorced from more kindly associations, and coupled with any object terrible in itself, to heighten that terror to the furthest bounds. Witness the
white bear of the poles, and the white shark of the tropics; what but their
smooth, flaky whiteness makes them the transcendent horrors they are?
That ghastly whiteness it is which imparts such an abhorrent mildness,
even more loathsome than terrific, to the dumb gloating of their aspect.
So that not the fierce-fanged tiger in his heraldic coat can so stagger
courage as the white-shrouded bear or shark.[9]

  Bethink thee of the albatross: whence come those clouds of spiritual
wonderment and pale dread in which that white phantom sails in all imag-
inations? Not Coleridge[1] first threw that spell; but God's great, unflatter-
ing laureate, Nature.[2]

---

8. See Revelation 7.9: "After this I beheld, and, lo, a great multitude, which no man could number,
   of all nations, and kindreds, and people, and tongues, stood before the throne, and before the
   Lamb, clothed with white robes, and palms in their hands." Not a strictly accurate account of the
   use of white in Catholic ceremonies.
9. With reference to the Polar bear, it may possibly be urged by him who would fain go still deeper
   into this matter, that it is not the whiteness, separately regarded, which heightens the intolerable
   hideousness of that brute; for, analysed, that heightened hideousness, it might be said, only arises
   from the circumstance, that the irresponsible ferociousness of the creature stands invested in the
   fleece of celestial innocence and love; and hence, by bringing together two such opposite emotions in our minds, the Polar bear frightens us with so unnatural a contrast. But even assuming
   all this to be true; yet, were it not for the whiteness, you would not have that intensified terror.
     As for the white shark, the white gliding ghostliness of repose in that creature, when beheld
   in his ordinary moods, strangely tallies with the same quality in the Polar quadruped. This peculiarity is most vividly hit by the French in the name they bestow upon that fish. The Romish mass
   for the dead begins with "Requiem eternam" (eternal rest), whence *Requiem* denominating the
   mass itself, and any other funereal music. Now, in allusion to the white, silent stillness of death
   in this shark, and the mild deadliness of his habits, the French call him *Requin* [Melville's note].
1. The albatross plays an eerie role in the 1798 ballad, "The Rime of the Ancient Mariner"—the
   "wild Rhyme" cited in Melville's note (n. 2, just below)—by Samuel Taylor Coleridge
   (1722–1834).
2. I remember the first albatross I ever saw. It was during a prolonged gale, in waters hard upon the
   Antarctic seas. From my forenoon watch below, I ascended to the overclouded deck; and there,
   dashed upon the main hatches, I saw a regal, feathery thing of unspotted whiteness, and with a
   hooked, Roman bill sublime. At intervals, it arched forth its vast archangel wings, as if to embrace
   some holy ark. Wondrous flutterings and throbbings shook it. Though bodily unharmed, it uttered
   cries, as some king's ghost in supernatural distress. Through its inexpressible, strange eyes,
   methought I peeped to secrets which took hold of God. As Abraham before the angels, I bowed
   myself; the thing was so white, its wings so wide, and in those for ever exiled waters, I had lost the
   miserable warping memories of traditions and of towns. Long I gazed at that prodigy of plumage.
   I cannot tell, can only hint, the things that darted through me then. But at last I awoke; and turning, asked a sailor what bird was this. A goney, he replied. Goney! I never had heard that name
   before; is it conceivable that this glorious thing is utterly unknown to men ashore! never! But some

Most famous in our Western annals and Indian traditions is that of the White Steed of the Prairies:[3] a magnificent milk-white charger, large-eyed, small-headed, bluff-chested, and with the dignity of a thousand monarchs in his lofty, overscorning carriage. He was the elected Xerxes of vast herds of wild horses, whose pastures in those days were only fenced by the Rocky Mountains and the Alleghanies. At their flaming head he westward trooped it like that chosen star[4] which every evening leads on the hosts of light. The flashing cascade of his mane, the curving comet of his tail, invested him with housings more resplendent than gold and silver-beaters could have furnished him. A most imperial and archangelical apparition of that unfallen, western world,[5] which to the eyes of the old trappers and hunters revived the glories of those primeval times when Adam walked majestic as a god, bluff-bowed and fearless as this mighty steed. Whether marching amid his aides and marshals in the van of countless cohorts that endlessly streamed it over the plains, like an Ohio;[6] or whether with his circumambient subjects browsing all around at the horizon, the White Steed gallopingly reviewed them with warm nostrils reddening through his cool milkiness; in whatever aspect he presented himself, always to the bravest Indians he was the object of trembling reverence and awe. Nor can it be questioned from what stands on legendary record of this noble horse, that it was his spiritual whiteness chiefly, which so clothed him with divineness; and that this divineness had that in it which, though commanding worship, at the same time enforced a certain nameless terror.

But there are other instances where this whiteness loses all that accessory and strange glory which invests it in the White Steed and Albatross.

What is it that in the Albino man so peculiarly repels and often shocks the eye, as that sometimes he is loathed by his own kith and kin? It is that whiteness which invests him, a thing expressed by the name he bears. The Albino is as well made as other men—has no substantive deformity—and yet this mere aspect of all-pervading whiteness makes him more strangely hideous than the ugliest abortion. Why should this be so?

Nor, in quite other aspects, does Nature in her least palpable but not the less malicious agencies, fail to enlist among her forces this crowning attribute of the terrible. From its snowy aspect, the gauntleted ghost of

---

time after, I learned that goney was some seaman's name for albatross. So that by no possibility could Coleridge's wild Rhyme have had aught to do with those mystical impressions which were mine, when I saw that bird upon our deck. For neither had I then read the Rhyme, nor knew the bird to be an albatross. Yet in saying this, I do but indirectly burnish a little brighter the noble merit of the poem and the poet.

I assert, then, that in the wondrous bodily whiteness of the bird chiefly lurks the secret of the spell; a truth the more evinced in this, that by a solecism of terms there are birds called grey albatrosses; and these I have frequently seen, but never with such emotions as when I beheld the Antarctic fowl.

But how had the mystic thing been caught? Whisper it not, and I will tell; with a treacherous hook and line, as the fowl floated on the sea. At last the Captain made a postman of it; tying a lettered, leathern tally round its neck, with the ship's time and place; and then letting it escape. But I doubt not, that leathern tally, meant for man, was taken off in Heaven, when the white fowl flew to join the wing-folding, the invoking, and adoring cherubim! [Melville's note].

3. Mansfield and Vincent (711–12) quote a possible source in James Hall's *The Wilderness and the War Path* (1846), which Melville knew because it was in the same important Wiley & Putnam series as *Typee*, "The Library of American Books."
4. The planet Venus. Xerxes led large Persian armies against the Greeks in the 5th century B.C.E.
5. The Eden-like condition of the North American continent before Europeans settled there.
6. Like that wide river. *Bluff-bowed*: full and square chests, like a whaleship's bows.

the Southern Seas has been denominated the White Squall. Nor, in some historic instances, has the art of human malice omitted so potent an aux- iliary. How wildly it heightens the effect of that passage in Froissart,[7] when, masked in the snowy symbol of their faction, the desperate White Hoods of Ghent murder their bailiff in the market-place!

Nor, in some things, does the common, hereditary experience of all mankind fail to bear witness to the supernaturalism of this hue. It cannot well be doubted, that the one visible quality in the aspect of the dead which most appals the gazer, is the marble pallor lingering there; as if indeed that pallor were as much the badge of consternation in the other world, as of mortal trepidation here. And from that pallor of the dead, we borrow the expressive hue of the shroud in which we wrap them. Nor even in our superstitions do we fail to throw the same snowy mantle round our phantoms; all ghosts rising in a milk-white fog—Yea, while these terrors seize us, let us add, that even the king of terrors, when personified by the evangelist, rides on his pallid horse.[8]

Therefore, in his other moods, symbolize whatever grand or gracious thing he will by whiteness, no man can deny that in its profoundest ide- alized significance it calls up a peculiar apparition to the soul.

But though without dissent this point be fixed, how is mortal man to account for it? To analyse it, would seem impossible. Can we, then, by the citation of some of those instances wherein this thing of whiteness— though for the time either wholly or in great part stripped of all direct associations calculated to impart to it aught fearful, but, nevertheless, is found to exert over us the same sorcery, however modified;—can we thus hope to light upon some chance clue to conduct us to the hidden cause we seek?

Let us try. But in a matter like this, subtlety appeals to subtlety, and without imagination no man can follow another into these halls. And though, doubtless, some at least of the imaginative impressions about to be presented may have been shared by most men, yet few perhaps were entirely conscious of them at the time, and therefore may not be able to recall them now.

Why to the man of untutored ideality, who happens to be but loosely acquainted with the peculiar character of the day, does the bare mention of Whitsuntide marshal in the fancy such long, dreary, speechless proces- sions of slow-pacing pilgrims, down-cast and hooded with new-fallen snow? Or, to the unread, unsophisticated Protestant of the Middle American States,[9] why does the passing mention of a White Friar or a White Nun, evoke such an eyeless statue in the soul?

Or what is there apart from the traditions of dungeoned warriors and kings (which will not wholly account for it) that makes the White Tower of London tell so much more strongly on the imagination of an untrav-

7. A 1379 murder described in Sir John Froissart (1337–1410), *Chronicles of England, France and Spain* (translated by Lord Berners, 1523–25). Several recent London editions were available in Melville's time.
8. Revelation 6.8: "And I looked, and behold a pale horse: and his name that sat on him was Death, and Hell followed with him." The Book of Revelation was attributed to the apostle John, "evan- gelist" because the author of one of the evangels, or gospels.
9. Mid-Atlantic states (New York, New Jersey, Pennsylvania, Delaware, Maryland). *Whitsuntide*: the week beginning with Whitsunday (Pentecost), the seventh Sunday after Easter, when converts in white robes were baptized.

elled American, than those other storied structures, its neighbors—the Byward Tower, or even the Bloody? And those sublimer towers, the White Mountains of New Hampshire, whence, in peculiar moods, comes that gigantic ghostliness over the soul at the bare mention of that name, while the thought of Virginia's Blue Ridge is full of a soft, dewy, distant dreaminess? Or why, irrespective of all latitudes and longitudes, does the name of the White Sea exert such a spectralness over the fancy, while that of the Yellow Sea lulls us with mortal thoughts of long lacquered mild afternoons on the waves, followed by the gaudiest and yet sleepiest of sunsets? Or, to choose a wholly unsubstantial instance, purely addressed to the fancy, why, in reading the old fairy tales of Central Europe, does "the tall pale man" of the Hartz forests, whose changeless pallor unrustlingly glides through the green of the groves—why is this phantom more terrible than all the whooping imps of the Blocksburg?[1]

Nor is it, altogether, the remembrance of her cathedral-toppling earthquakes; nor the stampedoes of her frantic seas; nor the tearlessness of arid skies that never rain; nor the sight of her wide field of leaning spires, wrenched cope-stones, and crosses all adroop (like canted yards of anchored fleets); and her suburban avenues of house-walls lying over upon each other, as a tossed pack of cards;—it is not these things alone which make tearless Lima,[2] the strangest, saddest city thou can'st see. For Lima has taken the white veil; and there is a higher horror in this whiteness of her woe. Old as Pizarro, this whiteness keeps her ruins for ever new; admits not the cheerful greenness of complete decay; spreads over her broken ramparts the rigid pallor of an apoplexy that fixes its own distortions.

I know that, to the common apprehension, this phenomenon of whiteness is not confessed to be the prime agent in exaggerating the terror of objects otherwise terrible; nor to the unimaginative mind is there aught of terror in those appearances whose awfulness to another mind almost solely consists in this one phenomenon, especially when exhibited under any form at all approaching to muteness or universality. What I mean by these two statements may perhaps be respectively elucidated by the following examples.

First: The mariner, when drawing nigh the coasts of foreign lands, if by night he hear the roar of breakers, starts to vigilance, and feels just enough of trepidation to sharpen all his faculties; but under precisely similar circumstances, let him be called from his hammock to view his ship sailing through a midnight sea of milky whiteness—as if from encircling

1. The Harz forests in central Germany were the haunt of such folklore figures as the "pale man," as was Brocken ("Blocksburg"), its central peak, the scene of the Walpurgis Night Witches' celebrations on May Day, as dramatized in Goethe's *Faust*. *White Tower:* one of the moated cluster of thirteen towers on the Thames, formerly whitewashed inside and out. Melville saw the White Tower in 1849. Geographical references are to the Blue Ridge Mountains of western Virginia, the White Sea on the north coast of Russia; and the Yellow Sea between China and Korea.

2. Founded in 1535 by the Spanish conqueror of Peru, Francisco Pizarro (1470?–1541), Lima has an annual rainfall of less than two inches, limiting vegetation. Still visible to Melville when he visited Lima in 1844 were the effects of the earthquake which destroyed the city a century before, in 1746. Other visitors to Lima recorded it as a colorful city, not as peculiarly white. Associated with Venice as overly sophisticated, supersubtle, culturally decadent, theologically dangerous, and spectacularly beautiful, Lima exerted a strong power over Melville's imagination, as is shown by his having Ishmael choose it as the setting where he tells "The Town-Ho's Story" (ch. 54) between his voyage on the *Pequod* and the time he tells the whole story, *Moby-Dick*.

headlands shoals of combed white bears were swimming round him, then he feels a silent, superstitious dread; the shrouded phantom of the whitened waters is horrible to him as a real ghost; in vain the lead assures him he is still off soundings; heart and helm they both go down; he never rests till blue water is under him again. Yet where is the mariner who will tell thee, "Sir, it was not so much the fear of striking hidden rocks, as the fear of that hideous whiteness that so stirred me?"

Second: To the native Indian of Peru, the continual sight of the snow-howdahed Andes conveys naught of dread, except, perhaps, in the mere fancying of the eternal frosted desolateness reigning at such vast altitudes, and the natural conceit of what a fearfulness it would be to lose oneself in such inhuman solitudes. Much the same is it with the backwoodsman of the West, who with comparative indifference views an unbounded prairie sheeted with driven snow, no shadow of tree or twig to break the fixed trance of whiteness. Not so the sailor, beholding the scenery of the Antarctic seas; where at times, by some infernal trick of legerdemain in the powers of frost and air, he, shivering and half shipwrecked, instead of rainbows speaking hope and solace to his misery, views what seems a boundless church-yard grinning upon him with its lean ice monuments and splintered crosses.

But thou sayest, methinks this white-lead[3] chapter about whiteness is but a white flag hung out from a craven soul; thou surrenderest to a hypo, Ishmael.

Tell me, why this strong young colt, foaled in some peaceful valley of Vermont, far removed from all beasts of prey—why is it that upon the sunniest day, if you but shake a fresh buffalo robe behind him, so that he cannot even see it, but only smells its wild animal muskiness—why will he start, snort, and with bursting eyes paw the ground in phrensies of affright? There is no remembrance in him of any gorings of wild creatures in his green northern home, so that the strange muskiness he smells cannot recall to him anything associated with the experience of former perils; for what knows he, this New England colt, of the black bisons of distant Oregon?

No: but here thou beholdest even in a dumb brute, the instinct of the knowledge of the demonism in the world. Though thousands of miles from Oregon, still when he smells that savage musk, the rending, goring bison herds are as present as to the deserted wild foal of the prairies, which this instant they may be trampling into dust.

Thus, then, the muffled rollings of a milky sea; the bleak rustlings of the festooned frosts of mountains; the desolate shiftings of the windrowed snows of prairies; all these, to Ishmael,[4] are as the shaking of that buffalo robe to the frightened colt!

Though neither knows where lie the nameless things of which the mystic sign gives forth such hints; yet with me, as with the colt, somewhere those things must exist. Though in many of its aspects this visible world seems formed in love, the invisible spheres were formed in fright.

---

3. Powder used in making paint.
4. Ishmael, like the colt, has an instinctive knowledge of demonism in the world; in them, certain sensory stimuli stir an intuitive sense of spiritual evil underlying nature.

But not yet have we solved the incantation[5] of this whiteness, and learned why it appeals with such power to the soul; and more strange and far more portentous—why, as we have seen, it is at once the most meaning symbol of spiritual things, nay, the very veil of the Christian's Deity; and yet should be as it is, the intensifying agent in things the most appalling to mankind.

Is it that by its indefiniteness it shadows forth the heartless voids and immensities of the universe, and thus stabs us from behind with the thought of annihilation, when beholding the white depths of the milky way? Or is it, that as in essence whiteness is not so much a color as the visible absence of color, and at the same time the concrete of all colors; is it for these reasons that there is such a dumb blankness, full of meaning, in a wide landscape of snows—a colorless, all-color of atheism from which we shrink? And when we consider that other theory of the natural philosophers,[6] that all other earthly hues—every stately or lovely emblazoning—the sweet tinges of sunset skies and woods; yea, and the gilded velvets of butterflies, and the butterfly cheeks of young girls; all these are but subtile deceits, not actually inherent in substances, but only laid on from without; so that all deified Nature absolutely paints like the harlot, whose allurements cover nothing but the charnel-house within;[7] and when we proceed further, and consider that the mystical cosmetic which produces every one of her hues, the great principle of light, for ever remains white or colorless in itself, and if operating without medium upon matter, would touch all objects, even tulips and roses, with its own blank tinge—pondering all this, the palsied universe lies before us a leper; and like wilful travellers in Lapland, who refuse to wear colored and coloring glasses upon their eyes, so the wretched infidel gazes himself blind at the monumental white shroud that wraps all the prospect around him. And of all these things the Albino whale was the symbol. Wonder ye then at the fiery hunt?

Chapter 43

Hark!

"Hist! Did you hear that noise, Cabaco?"

It was the middle-watch: a fair moonlight; the seamen were standing in a cordon, extending from one of the fresh-water butts in the waist, to the scuttle-butt near the taffrail. In this manner, they passed the buckets to fill the scuttle-butt. Standing, for the most part, on the hallowed precincts of the quarter-deck, they were careful not to speak or rustle their feet. From hand to hand, the buckets went in the deepest silence, only broken

---

5. Magical spell.
6. Scientists such as John Locke (1632–1704), whose empirical philosophy held that such "secondary qualities" of material objects as color are mental constructs, not "primary qualities" inherent in the objects.
7. Nature's beauty, taken by Pantheistic Romantics in Melville's time as the embodiment of a benevolent God, here is taken as the mere cosmetic of an inwardly dead prostitute or the paint of a godless universe—a whited sepulchre ("charnel house"). Below, this becomes the view of the unbeliever, or atheist ("wretched infidel").

by the occasional flap of a sail, and the steady hum of the unceasingly advancing keel.

It was in the midst of this repose, that Archy, one of the cordon, whose post was near the after-hatches, whispered to his neighbor, a Cholo,[1] the words above.

"Hist! did you hear that noise, Cabaco?"

"Take the bucket, will ye, Archy? what noise d'ye mean?"

"There it is again—under the hatches—don't you hear it—a cough—it sounded like a cough."

"Cough be damned! Pass along that return bucket."

"There again—there it is!—it sounds like two or three sleepers turning over, now!"

"Caramba! have done, shipmate, will ye? It's the three soaked biscuits ye eat for supper turning over inside of ye—nothing else. Look to the bucket!"

"Say what ye will, shipmate; I've sharp ears."

"Aye, you are the chap, ain't ye, that heard the hum of the old Quakeress's knitting-needles fifty miles at sea from Nantucket; you're the chap."

"Grin away; we'll see what turns up. Hark ye, Cabaco, there is somebody down in the after-hold that has not yet been seen on deck; and I suspect our old Mogul knows something of it too. I heard Stubb tell Flask, one morning watch, that there was something of that sort in the wind."

"Tish! the bucket!"

Chapter 44

The Chart[1]

Had you followed Captain Ahab down into his cabin after the squall that took place on the night succeeding that wild ratification of his purpose with his crew, you would have seen him go to a locker in the transom, and bringing out a large wrinkled roll of yellowish sea charts, spread them before him on his screwed-down table. Then seating himself before it, you would have seen him intently study the various lines and shadings which there met his eye; and with slow but steady pencil trace additional courses over spaces that before were blank. At intervals, he would refer to piles of old log-books[2] beside him, wherein were set down the seasons and places in which, on various former voyages of various ships, sperm whales had been captured or seen.

While thus employed, the heavy pewter lamp suspended in chains over his head, continually rocked with the motion of the ship, and for ever threw shifting gleams and shadows of lines upon his wrinkled brow, till it

---

1. A Cholo; a Peruvian of part Indian, part Spanish parentage. *Middle-watch:* from midnight to 4 A.M. *Scuttle-butt:* a small barrel from which the sailors get their fresh water; hence "gossip."
1. Mansfield and Vincent (717) show that most of this chapter derives from Wilkes's *Narrative of the United States Exploring Expedition,* vol. 5 (1844), ch. 12: "Currents and Whaling."
2. Bound ledgers where the first mate (or another officer) kept a daily record of such nautical matters as the ship's speed; progress; location; weather conditions; and whales sighted, pursued, and captured as well as any noteworthy events on board and encounters with other ships.

almost seemed that while he himself was marking out lines and courses on the wrinkled charts, some invisible pencil was also tracing lines and courses upon the deeply marked chart of his forehead.

But it was not this night in particular that, in the solitude of his cabin, Ahab thus pondered over his charts. Almost every night they were brought out; almost every night some pencil marks were effaced, and others were substituted. For with the charts of all four oceans before him, Ahab was threading a maze of currents and eddies, with a view to the more certain accomplishment of that monomaniac thought of his soul.

Now, to any one not fully acquainted with the ways of the leviathans, it might seem an absurdly hopeless task thus to seek out one solitary creature in the unhooped oceans of this planet. But not so did it seem to Ahab, who knew the sets of all tides and currents; and thereby calculating the driftings of the sperm whale's food; and, also, calling to mind the regular, ascertained seasons for hunting him in particular latitudes; could arrive at reasonable surmises, almost approaching to certainties, concerning the timeliest day to be upon this or that ground in search of his prey.

So assured, indeed, is the fact concerning the periodicalness of the sperm whale's resorting to given waters, that many hunters believe that, could he be closely observed and studied throughout the world; were the logs for one voyage of the entire whale fleet carefully collated, then the migrations of the sperm whale would be found to correspond in invariability to those of the herring-shoals or the flights of swallows. On this hint, attempts have been made to construct elaborate migratory charts of the sperm whale.[3]

Besides, when making a passage from one feeding-ground to another, the sperm whales, guided by some infallible instinct—say, rather, secret intelligence from the Deity—mostly swim in *veins*, as they are called; continuing their way along a given ocean-line with such undeviating exactitude, that no ship ever sailed her course, by any chart, with one tithe[4] of such marvellous precision. Though, in these cases, the direction taken by any one whale be straight as a surveyor's parallel, and though the line of advance be strictly confined to its own unavoidable, straight wake, yet the arbitrary *vein* in which at these times he is said to swim, generally embraces some few miles in width (more or less, as the vein is presumed to expand or contract); but never exceeds the visual sweep from the whale-ship's mast-heads, when circumspectly gliding along this magic zone. The sum is, that at particular seasons within that breadth and along that path, migrating whales may with great confidence be looked for.

And hence not only at substantiated times, upon well known separate feeding-grounds, could Ahab hope to encounter his prey; but in crossing the widest expanses of water between those grounds he could, by his art,

3. Since the above was written, the statement is happily borne out by an official circular, issued by Lieutenant Maury, of the National Observatory, Washington, April 16th, 1851. By that circular, it appears that precisely such a chart is in course of completion; and portions of it are presented in the circular. "This chart divides the ocean into districts of five degrees of latitude by five degrees of longitude; perpendicularly through each of which districts are twelve columns for the twelve months; and horizontally through each of which districts are three lines; one to show the number of days that have been spent in each month in every district, and the two others to show the number of days on which whales, sperm or right, have been seen" [Melville's note].
4. One tenth.

so place and time himself on his way, as even then not to be wholly with-out prospect of a meeting.

There was a circumstance which at first sight seemed to entangle his delirious but still methodical scheme. But not so in the reality, perhaps. Though the gregarious sperm whales have their regular seasons for par-ticular grounds, yet in general you cannot conclude that the herds which haunted such and such a latitude or longitude this year, say, will turn out to be identically the same with those that were found there the preceding season; though there are peculiar and unquestionable instances where the contrary of this has proved true. In general, the same remark, only within a less wide limit, applies to the solitaries and hermits among the matured, aged sperm whales. So that though Moby Dick had in a former year been seen, for example, on what is called the Seychelle ground in the Indian ocean, or Volcano Bay on the Japanese Coast; yet it did not follow, that were the Pequod to visit either of those spots at any subsequent cor-responding season, she would infallibly encounter him there. So, too, with some other feeding grounds, where he had at times revealed himself. But all these seemed only his casual stopping-places and ocean-inns, so to speak, not his places of prolonged abode. And where Ahab's chances of accomplishing his object have hitherto been spoken of, allusion has only been made to whatever way-side, antecedent, extra prospects were his, ere a particular set time and place were attained, when all possibilities would become probabilities, and, as Ahab fondly thought, every probability the next thing to a certainty. That particular set time and place were con-joined in the one technical phrase—the Season-on-the-Line.[5] For there and then, for several consecutive years, Moby Dick had been periodically descried, lingering in those waters for awhile, as the sun, in its annual round, loiters for a predicted interval in any one sign of the Zodiac.[6] There it was, too, that most of the deadly encounters with the white whale had taken place; there the waves were storied with his deeds; there also was that tragic spot where the monomaniac old man had found the awful motive to his vengeance. But in the cautious comprehensiveness and unloitering vigilance with which Ahab threw his brooding soul into this unfaltering hunt, he would not permit himself to rest all his hopes upon the one crowning fact above mentioned, however flattering it might be to those hopes; nor in the sleeplessness of his vow could he so tranquillize his unquiet heart as to postpone all intervening quest.

Now, the Pequod had sailed from Nantucket at the very beginning of the Season-on-the-Line. No possible endeavor then could enable her commander to make the great passage southwards, double Cape Horn, and then running down sixty degrees of latitude arrive in the equatorial Pacific in time to cruise there. Therefore, he must wait for the next ensu-ing season. Yet the premature hour of the Pequod's sailing had, perhaps, been covertly selected by Ahab, with a view to this very complexion of things. Because, an interval of three hundred and sixty-five days and

5. The optimal time for whaling in the mid-Pacific region along the equator ("the Line"), indicated below as in January.
6. An imaginary belt in the heavens, usually sixteen degrees wide, that encompasses the apparent paths of the moon and the principal planets, has the ecliptic (the sun's path) as its central line, and is divided into twelve constellations (signs), each taken for astrological purposes to extend thirty degrees of longitude.

nights was before him; an interval which, instead of impatiently enduring ashore, he would spend in a miscellaneous hunt; if by chance the White Whale, spending his vacation in seas far remote from his periodical feeding-grounds, should turn up his wrinkled brow off the Persian Gulf, or in the Bengal Bay, or China Seas, or in any other waters haunted by his race. So that Monsoons, Pampas, Nor-Westers, Harmattans, Trades; any wind but the Levanter and Simoom, might blow Moby Dick into the devious zig-zag world-circle of the Pequod's circumnavigating wake.[7]

But granting all this; yet, regarded discreetly and coolly, seems it not but a mad idea, this; that in the broad boundless ocean, one solitary whale, even if encountered, should be thought capable of individual recognition from his hunter, even as a white-bearded Mufti[8] in the thronged thoroughfares of Constantinople? No. For the peculiar snow-white brow of Moby Dick, and his snow-white hump, could not but be unmistakable. And have I not tallied[9] the whale, Ahab would mutter to himself, as after poring over his charts till long after midnight he would throw himself back in reveries—tallied him, and shall he escape? His broad fins are bored, and scalloped out like a lost sheep's ear! And here, his mad mind would run on in a breathless race; till a weariness and faintness of pondering came over him; and in the open air of the deck he would seek to recover his strength. Ah, God! what trances of torments does that man endure who is consumed with one unachieved revengeful desire. He sleeps with clenched hands; and wakes with his own bloody nails in his palms.[1]

Often, when forced from his hammock by exhausting and intolerably vivid dreams of the night, which, resuming his own intense thoughts through the day, carried them on amid a clashing of phrensies, and whirled them round and round in his blazing brain, till the very throbbing of his life-spot became insufferable anguish; and when, as was sometimes the case, these spiritual throes in him heaved his being up from its base, and a chasm seemed opening in him, from which forked flames and lightnings shot up, and accursed fiends beckoned him to leap down among them; when this hell in himself yawned beneath him, a wild cry would be heard through the ship; and with glaring eyes Ahab would burst from his state room, as though escaping from a bed that was on fire. Yet these, perhaps, instead of being the unsuppressable symptoms of some latent weakness, or fright at his own resolve, were but the plainest tokens of its intensity. For, at such times, crazy Ahab, the scheming, unappeasedly steadfast hunter of the white whale; this Ahab that had gone to his hammock, was not the agent that so caused him to burst from it in horror again. The latter was the eternal, living principle or soul in him; and in sleep, being for the time dissociated from the characterizing mind, which at other times employed it for its outer vehicle or agent, it spontaneously sought escape

---

7. *Monsoon:* a periodic, very rainy wind in the Indian Ocean. *Pampa:* or pampero, a strong cold wind from the west or southwest that sweeps over the Argentine pampas (grassland or prairie). *Harmattan:* a wind blowing dust from Africa into the Atlantic. *Trades:* almost continuous winds from northeast or southeast toward the equator. *Levanter:* a strong Mediterranean east wind, from the Levant (the countries bordering the Mediterranean on the east). *Simoom:* a Near East and Arabian easterly wind.
8. A professional interpreter of Muslim law.
9. Reckoned and recorded.
1. That is, he is self-crucified.

from the scorching contiguity of the frantic thing, of which, for the time, it was no longer an integral. But as the mind does not exist unless leagued with the soul, therefore it must have been that, in Ahab's case, yielding up all his thoughts and fancies to his one supreme purpose; that purpose, by its own sheer inveteracy of will, forced itself against gods and devils into a kind of self-assumed, independent being of its own. Nay, could grimly live and burn, while the common vitality to which it was conjoined, fled horror-stricken from the unbidden and unfathered birth. Therefore, the tormented spirit that glared out of bodily eyes, when what seemed Ahab rushed from his room, was for the time but a vacated thing, a formless somnambulistic being, a ray of living light, to be sure, but without an object to color, and therefore a blankness in itself. God help thee, old man, thy thoughts have created a creature in thee; and he whose intense thinking thus makes him a Prometheus;[2] a vulture feeds upon that heart for ever; that vulture the very creature he creates.

Chapter 45

The Affidavit

So far as what there may be of a narrative in this book; and, indeed, as indirectly touching one or two very interesting and curious particulars in the habits of sperm whales, the foregoing chapter, in its earlier part, is as important a one as will be found in this volume; but the leading matter of it requires to be still further and more familiarly enlarged upon, in order to be adequately understood, and moreover to take away any incredulity which a profound ignorance of the entire subject may induce in some minds, as to the natural verity of the main points of this affair.

I care not to perform this part of my task methodically; but shall be content to produce the desired impression by separate citations of items, practically or reliably known to me as a whaleman; and from these citations, I take it—the conclusion aimed at will naturally follow of itself.

First: I have personally known three instances where a whale, after receiving a harpoon, has effected a complete escape; and, after an interval (in one instance of three years), has been again struck by the same hand, and slain; when the two irons, both marked by the same private cypher, have been taken from the body. In the instance where three years intervened between the flinging of the two harpoons; and I think it may have been something more than that; the man who darted them happening, in the interval, to go in a trading ship on a voyage to Africa, went ashore there, joined a discovery party, and penetrated far into the interior, where he travelled for a period of nearly two years, often endangered by serpents, savages, tigers, poisonous miasmas, with all the other common

---

2. In Greek myth, one of the Titans, who stole fire from heaven and gave it to mankind. Zeus punished him by chaining him to a rock where daily a vulture devoured his liver, which each night was made whole again. Mansfield and Vincent (719) cite parallel allusions in Shelley's *Prometheus Unbound* (1820, 1.34–37) and Lord Byron's *Manfred* (1817, 3.4.127–40). For the passage above on "hell in himself," see Sir Thomas Browne's *Religio Medici* (1643, 1.55) and John Milton's *Paradise Lost* (1667, 4.75).

perils incident to wandering in the heart of unknown regions. Meanwhile, the whale he had struck must also have been on its travels; no doubt it had thrice circumnavigated the globe, brushing with its flanks all the coasts of Africa; but to no purpose. This man and this whale again came together, and the one vanquished the other. I say I, myself, have known three instances similar to this; that is in two of them I saw the whales struck; and, upon the second attack, saw the two irons with the respective marks cut in them, afterwards taken from the dead fish. In the three-year instance, it so fell out that I was in the boat both times, first and last, and the last time distinctly recognized a peculiar sort of huge mole under the whale's eye, which I had observed there three years previous. I say three years, but I am pretty sure it was more than that. Here are three instances, then, which I personally know the truth of; but I have heard of many other instances from persons whose veracity in the matter there is no good ground to impeach.

Secondly: It is well known in the Sperm Whale Fishery, however ignorant the world ashore may be of it, that there have been several memorable historical instances where a particular whale in the ocean has been at distant times and places popularly cognisable. Why such a whale became thus marked was not altogether and originally owing to his bodily peculiarities as distinguished from other whales; for however peculiar in that respect any chance whale may be, they soon put an end to his peculiarities by killing him, and boiling him down into a peculiarly valuable oil. No: the reason was this: that from the fatal experiences of the fishery there hung a terrible prestige of perilousness about such a whale as there did about Rinaldo Rinaldini,[1] insomuch that most fishermen were content to recognise him by merely touching their tarpaulins[2] when he would be discovered lounging by them on the sea, without seeking to cultivate a more intimate acquaintance. Like some poor devils ashore that happen to know an irascible great man, they make distant unobtrusive salutations to him in the street, lest if they pursued the acquaintance further, they might receive a summary thump for their presumption.

But not only did each of these famous whales enjoy great individual celebrity—nay, you may call it an ocean-wide renown; not only was he famous in life and now is immortal in forecastle stories after death, but he was admitted into all the rights, privileges, and distinctions of a name; had as much a name indeed as Cambyses or Cæsar. Was it not so, O Timor Jack! thou famed leviathan, scarred like an iceberg, who so long did'st lurk in the Oriental straits of that name, whose spout was oft seen from the palmy beach of Ombay? Was it not so, O New Zealand Tom! thou terror of all cruisers that crossed their wakes in the vicinity of the Tattoo Land? Was it not so, O Morquan! King of Japan, whose lofty jet they say at times assumed the semblance of a snow-white cross against the sky? Was it not so, O Don Miguel! thou Chilian whale, marked like an old tortoise with mystic hieroglyphics upon the back! In plain prose, here

1. Knight in Italian Renaissance epics *Orlando Furioso* (1532) by Ludovico Ariosto (1474–1535) and *Rinaldo* (1562) by Torquato Tasso (1544–1595).
2. Touching their tarred hats, saluting.

are four whales as well known to the students of Cetacean History as Marius or Sylla[3] to the classic scholar.

But this is not all. New Zealand Tom and Don Miguel, after at various times creating great havoc among the boats of different vessels, were finally gone in quest of, systematically hunted out, chased and killed by valiant whaling captains, who heaved up their anchors with that express object as much in view, as in setting out through the Narragansett Woods, Captain Church[4] of old had it in his mind to capture that notorious murderous savage Annawon, the headmost warrior of the Indian King Philip.

I do not know where I can find a better place than just here, to make mention of one or two other things, which to me seem important, as in printed form establishing in all respects the reasonableness of the whole story of the White Whale, more especially the catastrophe. For this is one of those disheartening instances where truth requires full as much bolstering as error. So ignorant are most landsmen of some of the plainest and most palpable wonders of the world, that without some hints touching the plain facts, historical and otherwise, of the fishery, they might scout at Moby Dick as a monstrous fable, or still worse and more detestable, a hideous and intolerable allegory.[5]

First: Though most men have some vague flitting ideas of the general perils of the grand fishery, yet they have nothing like a fixed, vivid conception of those perils, and the frequency with which they recur. One reason perhaps is, that not one in fifty of the actual disasters and deaths by casualties in the fishery, ever finds a public record at home, however transient and immediately forgotten that record. Do you suppose that that poor fellow there, who this moment perhaps caught by the whale-line off the coast of New Guinea, is being carried down to the bottom of the sea by the sounding leviathan—do you suppose that that poor fellow's name will appear in the newspaper obituary you will read to-morrow at your breakfast? No: because the mails are very irregular between here and New Guinea. In fact, did you ever hear what might be called regular news direct or indirect from New Guinea? Yet I tell you that upon one particular voyage which I made to the Pacific, among many others,[6] we spoke thirty different ships, every one of which had had a death by a whale, some of them more than one, and three that had each lost a boat's crew. For God's sake, be economical with your lamps and candles! not a gallon you burn, but at least one drop of man's blood was spilled for it.

3. Rival Roman generals responsible for the civil war in the 2nd century B.C.E. Cambyses II, warrior king of Persia (d. 522 B.C.E.), was the ranting hero of a play by Thomas Preston, older contemporary of Shakespeare, whose Falstaff makes fun of the Cambyses vein of bombastic rhetoric in *1 Henry IV* 2.4.387. As Vincent (1949) points out, Melville found "Timor Jack" and "New Zealand Tom" in Beale (1839) but may have invented Morquan and Don Miguel. *Oriental straits:* the Timor Sea is between Timor and northern Australia. *Ombay:* an island somewhat farther north. *Tattoo Land:* New Zealand, whose Maori natives practiced extensive tattooing.
4. Annawon was captured in 1676 by Captain Benjamin Church (1639–1718). The 1851 editions gave the name "Butler" here, for Lieutenant Colonel William Butler, who pursued the Mohawk Indian leader Joseph Brandt (1742?–1807) in 1778. Apparently Melville in a lapse of memory wrote down the wrong name, recalling Brandt from stories of his Gansevoort grandfather's Revolutionary exploits.
5. Here, "allegory" means something like the sort of rigid symbol where one thing stands only and always for another thing. Melville is not referring to the book *Moby-Dick*, the working title of which was *The Whale*, but to the white whale.
6. The 1967 NCE first put a comma after *many others*, making it clear that Ishmael has made "many" voyages to the Pacific (as references show in chs. 54 and 102); here, the point is that each of the ships encountered on this particular voyage had lost at least one man to a whale.

Secondly: People ashore have indeed some indefinite idea that a whale is an enormous creature of enormous power; but I have ever found that when narrating to them some specific example of this two-fold enormousness, they have significantly complimented me upon my facetiousness; when, I declare upon my soul, I had no more idea of being facetious than Moses, when he wrote the history of the plagues of Egypt.[7]

But fortunately the special point I here seek can be established upon testimony entirely independent of my own. That point is this: The Sperm Whale is in some cases sufficiently powerful, knowing, and judiciously malicious, as with direct aforethought to stave in, utterly destroy, and sink a large ship; and what is more, the Sperm Whale *has* done it.

First: In the year 1820 the ship Essex, Captain Pollard, of Nantucket, was cruising in the Pacific Ocean. One day she saw spouts, lowered her boats, and gave chase to a shoal of sperm whales. Ere long, several of the whales were wounded; when, suddenly, a very large whale escaping from the boats, issued from the shoal, and bore directly down upon the ship. Dashing his forehead against her hull, he so stove her in, that in less than "ten minutes" she settled down and fell over. Not a surviving plank of her has been seen since. After the severest exposure, part of the crew reached the land in their boats. Being returned home at last, Captain Pollard once more sailed for the Pacific in command of another ship, but the gods shipwrecked him again upon unknown rocks and breakers; for the second time his ship was utterly lost, and forthwith forswearing the sea, he has never tempted it since. At this day Captain Pollard is a resident of Nantucket. I have seen Owen Chase,[8] who was chief mate of the Essex at the time of the tragedy; I have read his plain and faithful narrative; I have conversed with his son; and all this within a few miles of the scene of the catastrophe.[9]

Secondly: The ship Union, also of Nantucket, was in the year 1807 totally lost off the Azores by a similar onset, but the authentic particulars

---

7. Told in Exodus 7–12, then supposed to have been written by Moses.
8. For Chase's narrative and Melville's manuscript notes on him, his son, and Captain Pollard (whom he glimpsed in 1852, after publishing *Moby-Dick*), see "Analogues and Sources" (pp. 565 and 571, herein). Melville conversed with a son of Chase while the *Acushnet* was sailing in company with the whaler he was on, in the Pacific; young Chase loaned him a copy of the *Narrative*, which he read there, near enough the site of the *Essex* disaster to make the reading especially memorable. Other Nantucket Chases were captains, and later Melville was convinced, mistakenly, that he had seen Owen Chase himself in the Pacific.
9. The following are extracts from Chase's narrative: "Every fact seemed to warrant me in concluding that it was anything but chance which directed his operations; he made two several attacks upon the ship, at a short interval between them, both of which, according to their direction, were calculated to do us the most injury, by being made ahead, and thereby combining the speed of the two objects for the shock; to effect which, the exact manœuvres which he made were necessary. His aspect was most horrible, and such as indicated resentment and fury. He came directly from the shoal which we had just before entered, and in which we had struck three of his companions, as if fired with revenge for their sufferings." Again: "At all events, the whole circumstances taken together, all happening before my own eyes, and producing, at the time, impressions in my mind of decided, calculating mischief, on the part of the whale (many of which impressions I cannot now recall) induce me to be satisfied that I am correct in my opinion."
   Here are his reflections some time after quitting the ship, during a black night in an open boat, when almost despairing of reaching any hospitable shore. "The dark ocean and swelling waters were nothing; the fears of being swallowed up by some dreadful tempest, or dashed upon hidden rocks, with all the other ordinary subjects of fearful contemplation, seemed scarcely entitled to a moment's thought; the dismal looking wreck, and *the horrid aspect and revenge of the whale*, wholly engrossed my reflections, until day again made its appearance."
   In another place—p. 45,—he speaks of "*the mysterious and mortal attack of the animal.*" * * * * * [Melville's note].

of this catastrophe I have never chanced to encounter, though from the whale hunters I have now and then heard casual allusions to it.

Thirdly: Some eighteen or twenty years ago Commodore J——[1] then commanding an American sloop-of-war of the first class, happened to be dining with a party of whaling captains, on board a Nantucket ship in the harbor of Oahu, Sandwich Islands. Conversation turning upon whales, the Commodore was pleased to be sceptical touching the amazing strength ascribed to them by the professional gentlemen present. He peremptorily denied for example, that any whale could so smite his stout sloop-of-war as to cause her to leak so much as a thimbleful. Very good; but there is more coming. Some weeks after, the commodore set sail in this impregnable craft for Valparaiso.[2] But he was stopped on the way by a portly sperm whale, that begged a few moments' confidential business with him. That business consisted in fetching the Commodore's craft such a thwack, that with all his pumps going he made straight for the nearest port to heave down and repair. I am not superstitious, but I consider the Commodore's interview with that whale as providential. Was not Saul of Tarsus[3] converted from unbelief by a similar fright? I tell you, the sperm whale will stand no nonsense.

I will now refer you to Langsdorff's Voyages for a little circumstance in point, peculiarly interesting to the writer hereof. Langsdorff, you must know by the way, was attached to the Russian Admiral Krusenstern's[4] famous Discovery Expedition in the beginning of the present century. Captain Langsdorff thus begins his seventeenth chapter.

"By the thirteenth of May our ship was ready to sail, and the next day we were out in the open sea, on our way to Ochotsk.[5] The weather was very clear and fine, but so intolerably cold that we were obliged to keep on our fur clothing. For some days we had very little wind; it was not till the nineteenth that a brisk gale from the northwest sprang up. An uncommon large whale, the body of which was larger than the ship itself, lay almost at the surface of the water, but was not perceived by any one on board till the moment when the ship, which was in full sail, was almost upon him, so that it was impossible to prevent its striking against him. We were thus placed in the most imminent danger, as this gigantic creature, setting up its back, raised the ship three feet at least out of the water. The masts reeled, and the sails fell altogether, while we who were below all sprang instantly upon the deck, concluding that we had struck upon some rock; instead of this we saw the monster sailing off with the utmost gravity and solemnity. Captain D'Wolf applied immediately to the pumps to examine whether or not the vessel had received any damage from the shock, but we found that very happily it had escaped entirely uninjured."

Now, the Captain D'Wolf here alluded to as commanding the ship in question, is a New Englander, who, after a long life of unusual adventures

1. Commodore Thomas ap Catesby Jones (1790–1858). The episode presumably occurred when he commanded the *Peacock* in 1825.
2. Port on the coast of Chile.
3. Acts 9.3–4, 6. While persecuting the new Christians, Saul set out from Jerusalem for Damascus; on the way, a sudden light from heaven made him fall to the ground and the voice of Jesus challenged him. Temporarily blinded, he became the apostle Paul (later called St. Paul).
4. Adam Johann von Krusenstern (1770–1846). George H. von Langsdorff (1774–1852) wrote *Voyages and Travels,* cited in "Melville's Reading and *Moby-Dick*" (p. 437, herein).
5. Town on the Sea of Okhotsk on the northwest Pacific coast.

as a sea-captain, this day resides in the village of Dorchester near Boston. I have the honor of being a nephew of his. I have particularly questioned him concerning this passage in Langsdorff.[6] He substantiates every word. The ship, however, was by no means a large one: a Russian craft built on the Siberian coast, and purchased by my uncle after bartering away the vessel in which he sailed from home.

In that up and down manly book of old-fashioned adventure, so full, too, of honest wonders—the voyage of Lionel Wafer,[7] one of ancient Dampier's old chums—I found a little matter set down so like that just quoted from Langsdorff, that I cannot forbear inserting it here for a corroborative example, if such be needed.

Lionel, it seems, was on his way to "John Ferdinando," as he calls the modern Juan Fernandes. "In our way thither," he says, "about four o'clock in the morning, when we were about one hundred and fifty leagues from the Main[8] of America, our ship felt a terrible shock, which put our men in such consternation that they could hardly tell where they were or what to think; but every one began to prepare for death. And, indeed, the shock was so sudden and violent, that we took it for granted the ship had struck against a rock; but when the amazement was a little over, we cast the lead, and sounded, but found no ground. * * * * * The suddenness of the shock made the guns leap in their carriages, and several of the men were shaken out of their hammocks. Captain Davis, who lay with his head over a gun, was thrown out of his cabin!" Lionel then goes on to impute the shock to an earthquake, and seems to substantiate the imputation by stating that a great earthquake, somewhere about that time, did actually do great mischief along the Spanish land. But I should not much wonder if, in the darkness of that early hour of the morning, the shock was after all caused by an unseen whale vertically bumping the hull from beneath.

I might proceed with several more examples, one way or another known to me, of the great power and malice at times of the sperm whale. In more than one instance, he has been known, not only to chase the assailing boats back to their ships, but to pursue the ship itself, and long withstand all the lances hurled at him from its decks. The English ship Pusie Hall[9] can tell a story on that head; and, as for his strength, let me say, that there have been examples where the lines attached to a running sperm whale have, in a calm, been transferred to the ship, and secured there; the whale towing her great hull through the water, as a horse walks off with a cart. Again, it is very often observed that, if the sperm whale, once struck, is allowed time to rally, he then acts, not so often with blind rage, as with wilful, deliberate designs of destruction to his pursuers; nor is it without conveying some eloquent indication of his character, that upon being attacked he will frequently open his mouth, and retain it in that dread

---

6. John D'Wolf (1779–1872), the adventurous "Nor'west John," was the husband of Melville's father's sister Mary (1778–1859). They named a son Langsdorff D'Wolf.
7. The quotation is from his *A New Voyage and Description of the Isthmus of America* (1699); he had sailed with the buccaneer William Dampier as surgeon.
8. The mainland of South America. *Juan Fernandes:* three Chilean Pacific Islands, famous as the scene of the actual abandonment of Alexander Selkirk (1676–1721) on which Daniel Defoe (1660–1731) based his *Robinson Crusoe* (1719), changing the locale to the Caribbean.
9. Melville found this 1835 story in Bennett's *Narrative* (1840).

expansion for several consecutive minutes. But I must be content with only one more and a concluding illustration; a remarkable and most significant one, by which you will not fail to see, that not only is the most marvellous event in this book corroborated by plain facts of the present day, but that these marvels (like all marvels) are mere repetitions of the ages; so that for the millionth time we say amen with Solomon[1]—Verily there is nothing new under the sun.

In the sixth Christian century lived Procopius,[2] a Christian magistrate of Constantinople, in the days when Justinian was Emperor and Belisarius general. As many know, he wrote the history of his own times, a work every way of uncommon value. By the best authorities, he has always been considered a most trustworthy and unexaggerating historian, except in some one or two particulars, not at all affecting the matter presently to be mentioned.

Now, in this history of his, Procopius mentions that, during the term of his prefecture at Constantinople, a great sea-monster was captured in the neighboring Propontis, or Sea of Marmora, after having destroyed vessels at intervals in those waters for a period of more than fifty years. A fact thus set down in substantial history cannot easily be gainsaid. Nor is there any reason it should be. Of what precise species this sea-monster was, is not mentioned. But as he destroyed ships, as well as for other reasons, he must have been a whale; and I am strongly inclined to think a sperm whale. And I will tell you why. For a long time I fancied that the sperm whale had been always unknown in the Mediterranean and the deep waters connecting with it. Even now I am certain that those seas are not, and perhaps never can be, in the present constitution of things, a place for his habitual gregarious resort. But further investigations have recently proved to me, that in modern times there have been isolated instances of the presence of the sperm whale in the Mediterranean. I am told, on good authority, that on the Barbary coast, a Commander Davies of the British navy found the skeleton of a sperm whale. Now, as a vessel of war readily passes through the Dardanelles, hence a sperm whale could, by the same route, pass out of the Mediterranean into the Propontis.

In the Propontis, as far as I can learn, none of that peculiar substance called *brit*[3] is to be found, the aliment of the right whale. But I have every reason to believe that the food of the sperm whale—squid or cuttle-fish— lurks at the bottom of that sea, because large creatures, but by no means the largest of that sort, have been found at its surface. If, then, you properly put these statements together, and reason upon them a bit, you will clearly perceive that, according to all human reasoning, Procopius's sea-monster, that for half a century stove the ships of a Roman Emperor, must in all probability have been a sperm whale.

---

1. Paraphrased from Ecclesiastes 1.9 (a book commonly attributed to King Solomon, one of Melville's favorite wise men).
2. Vincent (1949, 273) shows that Melville's source for this paragraph was the article "Whales" in *Cyclopædia of Biblical Literature* (1845), edited by John Kitto.
3. Described in ch. 58.

Chapter 46

Surmises

Though, consumed with the hot fire of his purpose, Ahab in all his thoughts and actions ever had in view the ultimate capture of Moby Dick; though he seemed ready to sacrifice all mortal interests to that one passion; nevertheless it may have been that he was by nature and long habituation far too wedded to a fiery whaleman's ways, altogether to abandon the collateral prosecution of the voyage. Or at least if this were otherwise, there were not wanting other motives much more influential with him. It would be refining too much, perhaps, even considering his monomania, to hint that his vindictiveness towards the White Whale might have possibly extended itself in some degree to all sperm whales, and that the more monsters he slew by so much the more he multiplied the chances that each subsequently encountered whale would prove to be the hated one he hunted. But if such an hypothesis be indeed exceptionable, there were still additional considerations which, though not so strictly according with the wildness of his ruling passion, yet were by no means incapable of swaying him.

To accomplish his object Ahab must use tools; and of all tools used in the shadow of the moon, men are most apt to get out of order. He knew, for example, that however magnetic his ascendency in some respects was over Starbuck, yet that ascendency did not cover the complete spiritual man any more than mere corporeal superiority involves intellectual mastership; for to the purely spiritual, the intellectual but stands in a sort of corporeal relation. Starbuck's body and Starbuck's coerced will were Ahab's, so long as Ahab kept his magnet at Starbuck's brain; still he knew that for all this the chief mate, in his soul, abhorred his captain's quest, and could he, would joyfully disintegrate himself from it, or even frustate it. It might be that a long interval would elapse ere the White Whale was seen. During that long interval Starbuck would ever be apt to fall into open relapses of rebellion against his captain's leadership, unless some ordinary, prudential, circumstantial influences were brought to bear upon him. Not only that, but the subtle insanity of Ahab respecting Moby Dick was noways more significantly manifested than in his superlative sense and shrewdness in foreseeing that, for the present, the hunt should in some way be stripped of that strange imaginative impiousness which naturally invested it; that the full terror of the voyage must be kept withdrawn into the obscure background (for few men's courage is proof against protracted meditation unrelieved by action); that when they stood their long night watches, his officers and men must have some nearer things to think of than Moby Dick. For however eagerly and impetuously the savage crew had hailed the announcement of his quest; yet all sailors of all sorts are more or less capricious and unreliable—they live in the varying outer weather, and they inhale its fickleness—and when retained for any object remote and blank in the pursuit, however promissory of life and passion in the end, it is above all things requisite that temporary interests and employments should intervene and hold them healthily suspended for the final dash.

Nor was Ahab unmindful of another thing. In times of strong emotion mankind disdain all base considerations; but such times are evanescent. The permanent constitutional condition of the manufactured man, thought Ahab, is sordidness. Granting that the White Whale fully incites the hearts of this my savage crew, and playing round their savageness even breeds a certain generous knight-errantism[1] in them, still, while for the love of it they give chase to Moby Dick, they must also have food for their more common, daily appetites. For even the high lifted and chivalric Crusaders of old times were not content to traverse two thousand miles of land to fight for their holy sepulchre, without committing burglaries, picking pockets, and gaining other pious perquisites by the way. Had they been strictly held to their one final and romantic object—that final and romantic object, too many would have turned from in disgust. I will not strip these men, thought Ahab, of all hopes of cash—aye, cash. They may scorn cash now; but let some months go by, and no perspective[2] promise of it to them, and then this same quiescent cash all at once mutinying in them, this same cash would soon cashier[3] Ahab.

Nor was there wanting still another precautionary motive more related to Ahab personally. Having impulsively, it is probable, and perhaps somewhat prematurely revealed the prime but private purpose of the Pequod's voyage, Ahab was now entirely conscious that, in so doing, he had indirectly laid himself open to the unanswerable charge of usurpation; and with perfect impunity, both moral and legal, his crew if so disposed, and to that end competent, could refuse all further obedience to him, and even violently wrest from him the command. From even the barely hinted imputation of usurpation, and the possible consequences of such a suppressed impression gaining ground, Ahab must of course have been most anxious to protect himself. That protection could only consist in his own predominating brain and heart and hand, backed by a heedful, closely calculating attention to every minute atmospheric influence[4] which it was possible for his crew to be subjected to.

For all these reasons then, and others perhaps too analytic to be verbally developed here, Ahab plainly saw that he must still in a good degree continue true to the natural, nominal purpose of the Pequod's voyage; observe all customary usages; and not only that, but force himself to evince all his well known passionate interest in the general pursuit of his profession.

Be all this as it may, his voice was now often heard hailing the three mast-heads and admonishing them to keep a bright look-out, and not omit reporting even a porpoise. This vigilance was not long without reward.

---

1. In this complicated passage, Melville has his narrator Ishmael surmise what was in Ahab's mind, and attribute to Ahab a genial view of "knight-errantism" tinged by the lovable idealism of the hero of *Don Quixote*. It is Ahab, also, as Ishmael reads his mind, who thinks ironically of the "high lifted and chivalric Crusaders," who in the 11th through the 13th centuries fought to seize the Holy Land from the Muslims.
2. Prospective.
3. In this punning, to be cashiered is to be fired, by the ship owners.
4. Prescientific ideas Melville knew from *King Lear* and other plays by Shakespeare and elsewhere—particularly *The Anatomy of Melancholy* (1621) by Robert Burton (1577–1640); he found such ideas useful in identifying psychological and physiological states.

Chapter 47

The Mat-Maker

It was a cloudy, sultry afternoon; the seamen were lazily lounging about the decks, or vacantly gazing over into the lead-colored waters. Queequeg and I were mildly employed weaving what is called a sword-mat,[1] for an additional lashing to our boat. So still and subdued and yet somehow preluding was all the scene, and such an incantation of revery lurked in the air, that each silent sailor seemed resolved into his own invisible self.

I was the attendant or page of Queequeg, while busy at the mat. As I kept passing and repassing the filling or woof of marline between the long yarns of the warp, using my own hand for the shuttle, and as Queequeg, standing sideways, ever and anon slid his heavy oaken sword between the threads, and idly looking off upon the water, carelessly and unthinkingly drove home every yarn: I say so strange a dreaminess did there then reign all over the ship and all over the sea, only broken by the intermitting dull sound of the sword, that it seemed as if this were the Loom of Time,[2] and I myself were a shuttle mechanically weaving and weaving away at the Fates. There lay the fixed threads of the warp subject to but one single, ever returning, unchanging vibration, and that vibration merely enough to admit of the crosswise interblending of other threads with its own. This warp seemed necessity; and here, thought I, with my own hand I ply my own shuttle and weave my own destiny into these unalterable threads. Meantime, Queequeg's impulsive, indifferent sword, sometimes hitting the woof slantingly, or crookedly, or strongly, or weakly, as the case might be; and by this difference in the concluding blow producing a corresponding contrast in the final aspect of the completed fabric; this savage's sword, thought I, which thus finally shapes and fashions both warp and woof; this easy, indifferent sword must be chance—aye, chance, free will, and necessity—no wise incompatible—all interweavingly working together. The straight warp of necessity, not to be swerved from its ultimate course—its every alternating vibration, indeed, only tending to that; free will still free to ply her shuttle between given threads; and chance, though restrained in its play within the right lines of necessity, and sideways in its motions modified by free will, though thus prescribed to by both, chance by turns rules either, and has the last featuring blow at events.

* * * * *

Thus we were weaving and weaving away when I started at a sound so strange, long drawn, and musically wild and unearthly, that the ball of free will dropped from my hand, and I stood gazing up at the clouds whence that voice dropped like a wing. High aloft in the cross-trees was that mad Gay-Header, Tashtego. His body was reaching eagerly forward,

1. Mat made of closely woven yarns, for padding, to prevent chafing; the name comes from the sword-shaped wooden (here, oak) slat used in the weaving.
2. A phrase Melville found in Thomas Carlyle's *Sartor Resartus* (1833–34, 1.8), as a translation from Johann Wolfgang von Goethe's *Faust* (1808, 1832). *Marline:* tarred rope.

his hand stretched out like a wand, and at brief sudden intervals he continued his cries. To be sure the same sound was that very moment perhaps being heard all over the seas, from hundreds of whalemen's lookouts perched as high in the air; but from few of those lungs could that accustomed old cry have derived such a marvellous cadence as from Tashtego the Indian's.

As he stood hovering over you half suspended in air, so wildly and eagerly peering towards the horizon, you would have thought him some prophet or seer beholding the shadows of Fate, and by those wild cries announcing their coming.

"There she blows! there! there! there! she blows! she blows!"

"Where-away?"

"On the lee-beam, about two miles off! a school of them!"

Instantly all was commotion.

The Sperm Whale blows as a clock ticks, with the same undeviating and reliable uniformity. And thereby whalemen distinguish this fish from other tribes of his genus.

"There go flukes!" was now the cry from Tashtego; and the whales disappeared.

"Quick, steward!" cried Ahab. "Time! time!"

Dough-Boy hurried below, glanced at the watch, and reported the exact minute to Ahab.

The ship was now kept away from the wind, and she went gently rolling before it. Tashtego reporting that the whales had gone down heading to leeward, we confidently looked to see them again directly in advance of our bows. For that singular craft at times evinced by the Sperm Whale when, sounding with his head in one direction, he nevertheless, while concealed beneath the surface, mills round, and swiftly swims off in the opposite quarter—this deceitfulness of his could not now be in action; for there was no reason to suppose that the fish seen by Tashtego had been in any way alarmed, or indeed knew at all of our vicinity. One of the men selected for shipkeepers—that is, those not appointed to the boats, by this time relieved the Indian at the main-mast head. The sailors at the fore and mizzen had come down; the line tubs were fixed in their places; the cranes were thrust out; the mainyard was backed, and the three boats swung over the sea like three samphire[3] baskets over high cliffs. Outside of the bulwarks their eager crews with one hand clung to the rail, while one foot was expectantly poised on the gunwale. So look the long line of man-of-war's men[4] about to throw themselves on board an enemy's ship.

But at this critical instant a sudden exclamation was heard that took every eye from the whale. With a start all glared at dark Ahab, who was surrounded by five dusky phantoms that seemed fresh formed out of air.

---

3. Seacoast plant that can be pickled. The image is from *King Lear* 4.6.14–15, where "Halfway down" a cliff "Hangs one that gathers samphire, dreadful trade."
4. The crew of a warship. As an ordinary seaman aboard the frigate *United States* in 1843–44, Melville practiced this maneuver.

Chapter 48

The First Lowering

The phantoms, for so they then seemed, were flitting on the other side of the deck, and, with a noiseless celerity, were casting loose the tackles and bands of the boat which swung there. This boat had always been deemed one of the spare boats, though technically called the captain's, on account of its hanging from the starboard quarter. The figure that now stood by its bows was tall and swart, with one white tooth evilly protruding from its steel-like lips. A rumpled Chinese jacket of black cotton funereally invested him, with wide black trowsers of the same dark stuff. But strangely crowning this ebonness was a glistening white plaited turban, the living hair braided and coiled round and round upon his head. Less swart in aspect, the companions of this figure were of that vivid, tiger-yellow complexion peculiar to some of the aboriginal natives of the Manillas;—a race notorious for a certain diabolism of subtilty, and by some honest white mariners supposed to be the paid spies and secret confidential agents on the water of the devil, their lord, whose counting-room they suppose to be elsewhere.

While yet the wondering ship's company were gazing upon these strangers, Ahab cried out to the white-turbaned old man at their head, "All ready there, Fedallah?"

"Ready," was the half-hissed reply.

"Lower away then; d'ye hear?" shouting across the deck. "Lower away there, I say."

Such was the thunder of his voice, that spite of their amazement the men sprang over the rail; the sheaves whirled round in the blocks; with a wallow, the three boats dropped into the sea; while, with a dexterous, off-handed daring, unknown in any other vocation, the sailors, goat-like, leaped down the rolling ship's side into the tossed boats below.

Hardly had they pulled out from under the ship's lee, when a fourth keel, coming from the windward side, pulled round under the stern, and showed the five strangers rowing Ahab, who, standing erect in the stern, loudly hailed Starbuck, Stubb, and Flask, to spread themselves widely, so as to cover a large expanse of water. But with all their eyes again riveted upon the swart Fedallah and his crew, the inmates of the other boats obeyed not the command.

"Captain Ahab?—" said Starbuck.

"Spread yourselves," cried Ahab; "give way, all four boats. Thou, Flask, pull out more to leeward!"

"Aye, aye, sir," cheerily cried little King-Post, sweeping round his great steering oar. "Lay back!" addressing his crew. "There!—there!—there again! There she blows right ahead, boys!—lay back!—Never heed yonder yellow boys, Archy."

"Oh, I don't mind 'em, sir," said Archy; "I knew it all before now. Didn't I hear 'em in the hold? And didn't I tell Cabaco here of it? What say ye, Cabaco? They are stowaways, Mr. Flask."

"Pull, pull, my fine hearts-alive; pull, my children; pull, my little ones," drawlingly and soothingly sighed Stubb to his crew, some of whom still showed signs of uneasiness. "Why don't you break your backbones, my boys? What is it you stare at? Those chaps in yonder boat? Tut! They are only five more hands come to help us—never mind from where—the more the merrier. Pull, then, do pull; never mind the brimstone—devils are good fellows enough. So, so; there you are now; that's the stroke for a thousand pounds; that's the stroke to sweep the stakes! Hurrah for the gold cup of sperm oil, my heroes! Three cheers, men—all hearts alive! Easy, easy; don't be in a hurry—don't be in a hurry. Why don't you snap your oars, you rascals? Bite something, you dogs! So, so, so, then;—softly, softly! That's it—that's it! long and strong. Give way there, give way! The devil fetch ye, ye ragamuffin rapscallions; ye are all asleep. Stop snoring, ye sleepers, and pull. Pull, will ye? pull, can't ye? pull, won't ye? Why in the name of gudgeons and ginger-cakes don't ye pull?—pull and break something! pull, and start your eyes out! Here!" whipping out the sharp knife from his girdle; "every mother's son of ye draw his knife, and pull with the blade between his teeth. That's it—that's it. Now ye do something; that looks like it, my steel-bits. Start her—start her, my silver-spoons! Start her, marling-spikes!"[1]

Stubb's exordium to his crew is given here at large, because he had rather a peculiar way of talking to them in general, and especially in inculcating the religion of rowing. But you must not suppose from this specimen of his sermonizings that he ever flew into downright passions with his congregation. Not at all; and therein consisted his chief peculiarity. He would say the most terrific things to his crew, in a tone so strangely compounded of fun and fury, and the fury seemed so calculated merely as a spice to the fun, that no oarsman could hear such queer invocations without pulling for dear life, and yet pulling for the mere joke of the thing. Besides he all the time looked so easy and indolent himself, so loungingly managed his steering-oar, and so broadly gaped—open-mouthed at times—that the mere sight of such a yawning commander, by sheer force of contrast, acted like a charm upon the crew. Then again, Stubb was one of those odd sort of humorists,[2] whose jollity is sometimes so curiously ambiguous, as to put all inferiors on their guard in the matter of obeying them.

In obedience to a sign from Ahab, Starbuck was now pulling obliquely across Stubb's bow; and when for a minute or so the two boats were pretty near to each other, Stubb hailed the mate.

"Mr. Starbuck! larboard boat there, ahoy! a word with ye, sir, if ye please!"

"Halloa!" returned Starbuck, turning round not a single inch as he spoke; still earnestly but whisperingly urging his crew; his face set like a flint from Stubb's.

1. Stubb's "exordium" (couched as coolly as a pep talk, but functioning as an inspiration to life-and-death battle) is a masterpiece of whaleman's rhetoric, as the next paragraph makes clear. *Give way:* pull for your life (*not* move aside). *Gudgeons:* small fresh water fish. *Steel-bits:* the cutting edges of axes (or perhaps "steel-bitts," as on a horse's bridle, so Stubb can curb the men or release them to row faster). *Silver-spoons* means that the men were born with the knives in their mouths (but also it implies that some of the men may be greenhorns, fresh from the protection of their wealthy families). *Marling-spikes:* seasoned oarsmen, as even the new men will become, if they survive.
2. Not "comedians" but those subject to a peculiarity of character because of the proportions of the four bodily fluids (according to medieval physiology), in Stubb's case his jollity.

"What think ye of those yellow boys, sir!"

"Smuggled on board, somehow, before the ship sailed. (Strong, strong, boys!)" in a whisper to his crew, then speaking out loud again: "A sad business, Mr. Stubb! (seethe her, seethe her, my lads!) but never mind, Mr. Stubb, all for the best. Let all your crew pull strong, come what will. (Spring, my men, spring!) There's hogsheads[3] of sperm ahead, Mr. Stubb, and that's what ye came for. (Pull, my boys!) Sperm, sperm's the play! This at least is duty; duty and profit hand in hand!"

"Aye, aye, I thought as much," soliloquized Stubb, when the boats diverged, "as soon as I clapt eye on 'em, I thought so. Aye, and that's what he went into the after hold for, so often, as Dough-Boy long suspected. They were hidden down there. The White Whale's at the bottom of it. Well, well, so be it! Can't be helped! All right! Give way, men! It ain't the White Whale to-day! Give way!"

Now the advent of these outlandish strangers at such a critical instant as the lowering of the boats from the deck, this had not unreasonably awakened a sort of superstitious amazement in some of the ship's company; but Archy's fancied discovery having some time previous got abroad among them, though indeed not credited then, this had in some small measure prepared them for the event. It took off the extreme edge of their wonder; and so what with all this and Stubb's confident way of accounting for their appearance, they were for the time freed from superstitious surmisings; though the affair still left abundant room for all manner of wild conjectures as to dark Ahab's precise agency in the matter from the beginning. For me, I silently recalled the mysterious shadows I had seen creeping on board the Pequod during the dim Nantucket dawn, as well as the enigmatical hintings of the unaccountable Elijah.

Meantime, Ahab, out of hearing of his officers, having sided the furthest to windward, was still ranging ahead of the other boats; a circumstance bespeaking how potent a crew was pulling him. Those tiger yellow creatures of his seemed all steel and whalebone; like five trip-hammers they rose and fell with regular strokes of strength, which periodically started the boat along the water like a horizontal burst boiler out of a Mississippi steamer. As for Fedallah, who was seen pulling the harpooneer oar,[4] he had thrown aside his black jacket, and displayed his naked chest with the whole part of his body above the gunwale, clearly cut against the alternating depressions of the watery horizon; while at the other end of the boat Ahab, with one arm, like a fencer's, thrown half backward into the air, as if to counterbalance any tendency to trip; Ahab was seen steadily managing his steering oar as in a thousand boat lowerings ere the White Whale had torn him. All at once the outstretched arm gave a peculiar motion and then remained fixed, while the boat's five oars were seen simultaneously peaked. Boat and crew sat motionless on the sea. Instantly the three spread boats in the rear paused on their way. The whales had irregularly settled bodily down into the blue, thus giving no distantly dis-

---

3. A large barrel, containing from 63 to 140 gallons. *Seethe her:* Row so fast that the churning water will seem to boil ("seethe").
4. In a whaleboat each of the five oarsmen pulls a single oar; this one is the oar farthest forward, pulled by the harpooneer. The sixth man, at the stern, the boatsteerer, holds the steering oar.

cernible token of the movement, though from his closer vicinity Ahab had
observed it.

"Every man look out along his oar!" cried Starbuck. "Thou, Queequeg,
stand up!"

Nimbly springing up on the triangular raised box in the bow, the savage
stood erect there, and with intensely eager eyes gazed off towards the spot
where the chase had last been descried. Likewise upon the extreme stern
of the boat where it was also triangularly platformed level with the gunwale, Starbuck himself was seen coolly and adroitly balancing himself to
the jerking tossings of his chip of a craft, and silently eyeing the vast blue
eye of the sea.

Not very far distant Flask's boat was also lying breathlessly still; its commander recklessly standing upon the top of the loggerhead, a stout sort of
post rooted in the keel, and rising some two feet above the level of the
stern platform. It is used for catching turns with the whale line. Its top is
not more spacious than the palm of a man's hand, and standing upon
such a base as that, Flask seemed perched at the mast-head of some ship
which had sunk to all but her trucks. But little King-Post was small and
short, and at the same time little King-Post was full of a large and tall
ambition, so that this loggerhead stand-point of his did by no means satisfy King-Post.

"I can't see three seas off; tip us up an oar there, and let me on to that."

Upon this, Daggoo, with either hand upon the gunwale to steady his
way, swiftly slid aft, and then erecting himself volunteered his lofty shoulders for a pedestal.

"Good a mast-head as any, sir. Will you mount?"

"That I will, and thank ye very much, my fine fellow; only I wish you
fifty feet taller."

Whereupon planting his feet firmly against two opposite planks of the
boat, the gigantic negro, stooping a little, presented his flat palm to Flask's
foot, and then putting Flask's hand on his hearse-plumed head and bidding him spring as he himself should toss, with one dexterous fling landed
the little man high and dry on his shoulders. And here was Flask now
standing, Daggoo with one lifted arm furnishing him with a breast-band
to lean against and steady himself by.

At any time it is a strange sight to the tyro to see with what wondrous
habitude of unconscious skill the whaleman will maintain an erect posture in his boat, even when pitched about by the most riotously perverse
and cross-running seas. Still more strange to see him giddily perched
upon the loggerhead itself, under such circumstances. But the sight of
little Flask mounted upon gigantic Daggoo was yet more curious; for
sustaining himself with a cool, indifferent, easy, unthought of, barbaric
majesty, the noble negro to every roll of the sea harmoniously rolled his
fine form. On his broad back, flaxen-haired Flask seemed a snow-flake.
The bearer looked nobler than the rider. Though, truly, vivacious, tumultuous, ostentatious little Flask would now and then stamp with impatience; but not one added heave did he thereby give to the negro's lordly
chest. So have I seen Passion and Vanity stamping the living magnanimous earth, but the earth did not alter her tides and her seasons for
that.

Meanwhile Stubb, the third mate,[5] betrayed no such far-gazing solici-
tudes. The whales might have made one of their regular soundings, not a
temporary dive from mere fright; and if that were the case, Stubb, as his
wont in such cases, it seems, was resolved to solace the languishing interval with his pipe. He withdrew it from his hatband, where he always wore
it aslant like a feather. He loaded it, and rammed home the loading with
his thumb-end; but hardly had he ignited his match across the rough
sand-paper of his hand, when Tashtego, his harpooneer, whose eyes had
been setting to windward like two fixed stars, suddenly dropped like light
from his erect attitude to his seat, crying out in a quick phrensy of hurry,
"Down, down all, and give way!—there they are!"

To a landsman, no whale, nor any sign of a herring, would have been
visible at that moment; nothing but a troubled bit of greenish white water,
and thin scattered puffs of vapor hovering over it, and suffusingly blowing
off to leeward, like the confused scud from white rolling billows. The air
around suddenly vibrated and tingled, as it were, like the air over intensely
heated plates of iron. Beneath this atmospheric waving and curling, and
partially beneath a thin layer of water, also, the whales were swimming.
Seen in advance of all the other indications, the puffs of vapor they
spouted, seemed their forerunning couriers and detached flying outriders.

All four boats were now in keen pursuit of that one spot of troubled
water and air. But it bade fair to outstrip them; it flew on and on, as a
mass of interblending bubbles borne down a rapid stream from the hills.

"Pull, pull, my good boys," said Starbuck, in the lowest possible but
intensest concentrated whisper to his men; while the sharp fixed glance
from his eyes, darted straight ahead of the bow, almost seemed as two visible needles in two unerring binnacle compasses. He did not say much to
his crew, though, nor did his crew say anything to him. Only the silence
of the boat was at intervals startlingly pierced by one of his peculiar whispers, now harsh with command, now soft with entreaty.

How different the loud little King-Post. "Sing out and say something,
my hearties. Roar and pull, my thunderbolts! Beach me, beach me on
their black backs, boys; only do that for me, and I'll sign over to you my
Martha's Vineyard plantation, boys; including wife and children, boys. Lay
me on—lay me on! O Lord, Lord! but I shall go stark, staring mad: See!
see that white water!" And so shouting, he pulled his hat from his head,
and stamped up and down on it; then picking it up, flirted it far off upon
the sea; and finally fell to rearing and plunging in the boat's stern like a
crazed colt from the prairie.

"Look at that chap now," philosophically drawled Stubb, who, with his
unlighted short pipe, mechanically retained between his teeth, at a short
distance, followed after—"He's got fits, that Flask has. Fits? yes, give him
fits—that's the very word—pitch fits into 'em. Merrily, merrily, hearts-alive.
Pudding for supper, you know;—merry's the word. Pull, babes—pull, suck-
lings—pull, all. But what the devil are you hurrying about? Softly, softly,
and steadily, my men. Only pull, and keep pulling; nothing more. Crack all
your backbones, and bite your knives in two—that's all. Take it easy—why
don't ye take it easy, I say, and burst all your livers and lungs!"

5. That is, the third to be mentioned here (in rank Stubb is the second mate).

But what it was that inscrutable Ahab said to that tiger-yellow crew of his—these were words best omitted here; for you live under the blessed light of the evangelical[6] land. Only the infidel sharks in the audacious seas may give ear to such words, when, with tornado brow, and eyes of red murder, and foam-glued lips, Ahab leaped after his prey.

Meanwhile, all the boats tore on. The repeated specific allusions of Flask to "that whale," as he called the fictitious monster which he declared to be incessantly tantalizing his boat's bow with its tail—these allusions of his were at times so vivid and life-like, that they would cause some one or two of his men to snatch a fearful look over the shoulder. But this was against all rule; for the oarsmen must put out their eyes, and ram a skewer through their necks; usage pronouncing that they must have no organs but ears, and no limbs but arms, in these critical moments.

It was a sight full of quick wonder and awe! The vast swells of the omnipotent sea; the surging, hollow roar they made, as they rolled along the eight gunwales, like gigantic bowls in a boundless bowling-green; the brief suspended agony of the boat, as it would tip for an instant on the knife-like edge of the sharper waves, that almost seemed threatening to cut it in two; the sudden profound dip into the watery glens and hollows; the keen spurrings and goadings to gain the top of the opposite hill; the headlong, sled-like slide down its other side;—all these, with the cries of the headsmen and harpooneers, and the shuddering gasps of the oars-men, with the wondrous sight of the ivory Pequod bearing down upon her boats with outstretched sails, like a wild hen after her screaming brood;—all this was thrilling. Not the raw recruit, marching from the bosom of his wife into the fever heat of his first battle; not the dead man's ghost encountering the first unknown phantom in the other world;—neither of these can feel stranger and stronger emotions than that man does, who for the first time finds himself pulling into the charmed, churned circle of the hunted sperm whale.

The dancing white water made by the chase was now becoming more and more visible, owing to the increasing darkness of the dun cloud-shad-ows flung upon the sea. The jets of vapor no longer blended, but tilted everywhere to right and left; the whales seemed separating their wakes. The boats were pulled more apart; Starbuck giving chase to three whales running dead to leeward. Our sail was now set, and, with the still rising wind, we rushed along; the boat going with such madness through the water, that the lee oars could scarcely be worked rapidly enough to escape being torn from the row-locks.

Soon we were running through a suffusing wide veil of mist; neither ship nor boat to be seen.

"Give way, men," whispered Starbuck, drawing still further aft the sheet of his sail; "there is time to kill a fish yet before the squall comes. There's white water again!—close to! Spring!"

Soon after, two cries in quick succession on each side of us denoted that the other boats had got fast; but hardly were they overheard, when

6. Lands blessed by the teachings of Christianity, specifically the four gospels. In Melville, they are usually associated with the "lower church" Protestant sects (the most missionary minded): Presbyterians, for example, were more evangelical than Episcopalians.

with a lightning-like hurtling whisper Starbuck said: "Stand up!" and Queequeg, harpoon in hand, sprang to his feet.

Though not one of the oarsmen was then facing[7] the life and death peril so close to them ahead, yet with their eyes on the intense countenance of the mate in the stern of the boat, they knew that the imminent instant had come; they heard, too, an enormous wallowing sound as of fifty elephants stirring in their litter. Meanwhile the boat was still booming through the mist, the waves curling and hissing around us like the erected crests of enraged serpents.

"That's his hump. *There, there*, give it to him!" whispered Starbuck.

A short rushing sound leaped out of the boat; it was the darted iron of Queequeg. Then all in one welded commotion came an invisible push from astern, while forward the boat seemed striking on a ledge; the sail collapsed and exploded; a gush of scalding vapor shot up near by; something rolled and tumbled like an earthquake beneath us. The whole crew were half suffocated as they were tossed helter skelter into the white curdling cream of the squall. Squall, whale, and harpoon had all blended together; and the whale, merely grazed by the iron, escaped.

Though completely swamped, the boat was nearly unharmed. Swimming round it we picked up the floating oars, and lashing them across the gunwale, tumbled back to our places. There we sat up to our knees in the sea, the water covering every rib and plank, so that to our downward gazing eyes the suspended craft seemed a coral boat grown up to us from the bottom of the ocean.[8]

The wind increased to a howl; the waves dashed their bucklers[9] together; the whole squall roared, forked, and crackled around us like a white fire upon the prairie, in which, unconsumed, we were burning; immortal in these jaws of death! In vain we hailed the other boats; as well roar to the live coals down the chimney of a flaming furnace as hail those boats in that storm. Meanwhile the driving scud, rack, and mist, grew darker with the shadows of night; no sign of the ship could be seen. The rising sea forbade all attempts to bale out the boat. The oars were useless as propellers, performing now the office of life-preservers. So, cutting the lashing of the waterproof match keg, after many failures Starbuck contrived to ignite the lamp in the lantern; then stretching it on a waif pole,[1] handed it to Queequeg as the standard-bearer of this forlorn hope. There, then, he sat, holding up that imbecile candle in the heart of that almighty forlornness. There, then, he sat, the sign and symbol of a man without faith, hopelessly holding up hope in the midst of despair.

Wet, drenched through, and shivering cold, despairing of ship or boat, we lifted up our eyes as the dawn came on. The mist still spread over the sea, the empty lantern lay crushed in the bottom of the boat. Suddenly Queequeg started to his feet, hollowing his hand to his ear. We all heard a faint creaking, as of ropes and yards hitherto muffled by the storm. The sound came nearer and nearer; the thick mists were dimly parted by a

7. They row facing the boat's stern.
8. Coral polyp colonies build up reefs from the ocean floor.
9. The wave crests clash together like the shields ("bucklers").
1. Marker attached to unsecured dead whales.

huge, vague form. Affrighted, we all sprang into the sea as the ship at last loomed into view, bearing right down upon us within a distance of not much more than its length.

Floating on the waves we saw the abandoned boat, as for one instant it tossed and gaped beneath the ship's bows like a chip at the base of a cataract; and then the vast hull rolled over it, and it was seen no more till it came up weltering astern. Again we swam for it, were dashed against it by the seas, and were at last taken up and safely landed on board. Ere the squall came close to, the other boats had cut loose from their fish and returned to the ship in good time. The ship had given us up, but was still cruising, if haply it might light upon some token of our perishing,—an oar or a lance pole.

Chapter 49

The Hyena[1]

There are certain queer times and occasions in this strange mixed affair we call life when a man takes this whole universe for a vast practical joke, though the wit thereof he but dimly discerns, and more than suspects that the joke is at nobody's expense but his own. However, nothing dispirits, and nothing seems worth while disputing. He bolts down all events, all creeds, and beliefs, and persuasions, all hard things visible and invisible, never mind how knobby; as an ostrich of potent digestion gobbles down bullets and gun flints. And as for small difficulties and worryings, prospects of sudden disaster, peril of life and limb; all these, and death itself, seem to him only sly, good-natured hits, and jolly punches in the side bestowed by the unseen and unaccountable old joker. That odd sort of wayward mood I am speaking of, comes over a man only in some time of extreme tribulation; it comes in the very midst of his earnestness, so that what just before might have seemed to him a thing most momentous, now seems but a part of the general joke. There is nothing like the perils of whaling to breed this free and easy sort of genial, desperado philosophy; and with it I now regarded this whole voyage of the Pequod, and the great White Whale its object.

"Queequeg," said I, when they had dragged me, the last man, to the deck, and I was still shaking myself in my jacket to fling off the water; "Queequeg, my fine friend, does this sort of thing often happen?" Without much emotion, though soaked through just like me, he gave me to understand that such things did often happen.

"Mr. Stubb," said I, turning to that worthy, who, buttoned up in his oil-jacket, was now calmly smoking his pipe in the rain; "Mr. Stubb, I think I have heard you say that of all whalemen you ever met, our chief mate, Mr. Starbuck, is by far the most careful and prudent. I suppose then, that going plump on a flying whale with your sail set in a foggy squall is the height of a whaleman's discretion?"

---

1. The unnerving "laugh" of the vicious African and Asian carnivore sets the mood for Ishmael's view of the universe here, as "a vast practical joke."

"Certain. I've lowered for whales from a leaking ship in a gale off Cape Horn."

"Mr. Flask," said I, turning to little King-Post, who was standing close by; "you are experienced in these things, and I am not. Will you tell me whether it is an unalterable law in this fishery, Mr. Flask, for an oarsman to break his own back pulling himself back-foremost into death's jaws?"

"Can't you twist that smaller?" said Flask. "Yes, that's the law. I should like to see a boat's crew backing water up to a whale face foremost. Ha, ha! the whale would give them squint for squint, mind that!"

Here then, from three impartial witnesses, I had a deliberate statement of the entire case. Considering, therefore, that squalls and capsizings in the water and consequent bivouacks on the deep, were matters of common occurrence in this kind of life; considering that at the superlatively critical instant of going on to the whale I must resign my life into the hands of him who steered the boat—oftentimes a fellow who at that very moment is in his impetuousness upon the point of scuttling the craft with his own frantic stampings; considering that the particular disaster to our own particular boat was chiefly to be imputed to Starbuck's driving on to his whale almost in the teeth of a squall, and considering that Starbuck, notwithstanding, was famous for his great heedfulness in the fishery; considering that I belonged to this uncommonly prudent Starbuck's boat; and finally considering in what a devil's chase I was implicated, touching the White Whale: taking all things together, I say, I thought I might as well go below and make a rough draft of my will. "Queequeg," said I, "come along, you shall be my lawyer, executor, and legatee."

It may seem strange that of all men sailors should be tinkering at their last wills and testaments, but there are no people in the world more fond of that diversion. This was the fourth time in my nautical life that I had done the same thing. After the ceremony was concluded upon the present occasion, I felt all the easier; a stone was rolled away[2] from my heart. Besides, all the days I should now live would be as good as the days that Lazarus lived after his resurrection; a supplementary clean gain of so many months or weeks as the case might be. I survived myself; my death and burial were locked up in my chest. I looked round me tranquilly and contentedly, like a quiet ghost with a clean conscience sitting inside the bars of a snug family vault.

Now then, thought I, unconsciously rolling up the sleeves of my frock, here goes for a cool, collected dive at death and destruction, and the devil fetch the hindmost.[3]

---

2. An example of the biblical language that suffuses the book, heightening the significance of the episode without specifically alluding to Jesus' resurrection of Lazarus (John 11.39–44) or to Matthew 28.2, Jesus' own resurrection from his tomb: "the angel of the Lord descended from heaven, and came and rolled back the stone from the door." For many of Melville's first readers, this sort of echo of the Bible was irreligious, barely to be distinguished from outright "flings" at things holy.
3. Commitment to a risky enterprise, whatever the consequences (proverbial).

Chapter 50

Ahab's Boat and Crew • Fedallah

"Who would have thought it, Flask!" cried Stubb; "if I had but one leg you would not catch me in a boat, unless maybe to stop the plug-hole with my timber toe. Oh! he's a wonderful old man!"

"I don't think it so strange, after all, on that account," said Flask. "If his leg were off at the hip, now, it would be a different thing. That would disable him; but he has one knee, and good part of the other left, you know."

"I don't know that, my little man; I never yet saw him kneel."

* * * * *

Among whale-wise people it has often been argued whether, considering the paramount importance of his life to the success of the voyage, it is right for a whaling captain to jeopardize that life in the active perils of the chase. So Tamerlane's[1] soldiers often argued with tears in their eyes, whether that invaluable life of his ought to be carried into the thickest of the fight.

But with Ahab the question assumed a modified aspect. Considering that with two legs man is but a hobbling wight in all times of danger; considering that the pursuit of whales is always under great and extraordinary difficulties; that every individual moment, indeed, then comprises a peril; under these circumstances is it wise for any maimed man to enter a whale-boat in the hunt? As a general thing, the joint-owners of the Pequod must have plainly thought not.

Ahab well knew that although his friends at home would think little of his entering a boat in certain comparatively harmless vicissitudes of the chase, for the sake of being near the scene of action and giving his orders in person, yet for Captain Ahab to have a boat actually apportioned to him as a regular headsman in the hunt—above all for Captain Ahab to be supplied with five extra men, as that same boat's crew, he well knew that such generous conceits never entered the heads of the owners of the Pequod. Therefore he had not solicited a boat's crew from them, nor had he in any way hinted his desires on that head. Nevertheless he had taken private measures of his own touching all that matter. Until Archy's published discovery, the sailors had little foreseen it, though to be sure when, after being a little while out of port, all hands had concluded the customary business of fitting the whaleboats for service; when some time after this Ahab was now and then found bestirring himself in the matter of making thole-pins[2] with his own hands for what was thought to be one of the spare boats, and even solicitously cutting the small wooden skewers, which when the line is running out are pinned over the groove in the bow: when all this was observed in him, and particularly his solicitude in having an extra coat of sheathing in the bottom of the boat, as if to make it better withstand the pointed pressure of his ivory limb; and also the anx-

---

1. Mongol warrior (1336?–1405?), conqueror of much of central Asia and eastern Europe; ruthless hero of *Tamburlane the Great* (1590) by Christopher Marlowe (1564–1593).
2. Wooden pegs set in pairs to keep oars in place.

iety he evinced in exactly shaping the thigh board, or clumsy cleat, as it is sometimes called, the horizontal piece in the boat's bow for bracing the knee against in darting or stabbing at the whale; when it was observed how often he stood up in that boat with his solitary knee fixed in the semi-circular depression in the cleat, and with the carpenter's chisel gouged out a little here and straightened it a little there; all these things, I say, had awakened much interest and curiosity at the time. But almost every-body supposed that this particular preparative heedfulness in Ahab must only be with a view to the ultimate chase of Moby Dick; for he had already revealed his intention to hunt that mortal monster in person. But such a supposition did by no means involve the remotest suspicion as to any boat's crew being assigned to that boat.

Now, with the subordinate phantoms, what wonder remained soon waned away; for in a whaler wonders soon wane. Besides, now and then such unaccountable odds and ends of strange nations come up from the unknown nooks and ash-holes[3] of the earth to man these floating outlaws of whalers; and the ships themselves often pick up such queer castaway creatures found tossing about the open sea on planks, bits of wreck, oars, whale-boats, canoes, blown-off Japanese junks, and what not; that Beelzebub[4] himself might climb up the side and step down into the cabin to chat with the captain, and it would not create any unsubduable excite-ment in the forecastle.

But be all this as it may, certain it is that while the subordinate phan-toms soon found their place among the crew, though still as it were some-how distinct from them, yet that hair-turbaned Fedallah remained a muf-fled mystery to the last. Whence he came in a mannerly world like this, by what sort of unaccountable tie he soon evinced himself to be linked with Ahab's peculiar fortunes; nay, so far as to have some sort of a half-hinted influence; Heaven knows, but it might have been even authority over him; all this none knew. But one cannot sustain an indifferent air concerning Fedallah. He was such a creature as civilized, domestic peo-ple in the temperate zone only see in their dreams, and that but dimly; but the like of whom now and then glide among the unchanging Asiatic com-munities, especially the Oriental isles to the east of the continent—those insulated, immemorial, unalterable countries, which even in these mod-ern days still preserve much of the ghostly aboriginalness of earth's primal generations, when the memory of the first man was a distinct recollection, and all men his descendants, unknowing whence he came, eyed each other as real phantoms, and asked of the sun and the moon why they were created and to what end; when though, according to Genesis,[5] the angels indeed consorted with the daughters of men, the devils also, add the uncanonical Rabbins, indulged in mundane amours.

---

3. Dumps where rubbish was burned.
4. Satan (in 2 Kings 1.2, the pagan god of Ekron). Literally, the lord of the flies; in John Milton's *Paradise Lost*, Satan's lieutenant.
5. Genesis 6.2: "the sons of God saw the daughters of men that they were fair; and they took them wives of all which they chose" and Genesis 6.4: "There were giants in the earth in those days; and also after that, when the sons of God came in unto the daughters of men, and they bare children to them, the same became mighty men which were of old, men of renown." Uncanonical sources are the Book of Enoch and the Book of Jubilees, which Melville may have read about in an ency-clopedia, but which are not in any Bible or Apocrypha he is known to have owned.

Chapter 51

The Spirit-Spout[1]

Days, weeks passed, and under easy sail, the ivory Pequod had slowly swept across four several cruising-grounds; that off the Azores; off the Cape de Verdes; on the Plate (so called), being off the mouth of the Rio de la Plata; and the Carrol Ground, an unstaked, watery locality, southerly from St. Helena.

It was while gliding through these latter waters that one serene and moonlight night, when all the waves rolled by like scrolls of silver; and, by their soft, suffusing seethings, made what seemed a silvery silence, not a solitude: on such a silent night[2] a silvery jet was seen far in advance of the white bubbles at the bow. Lit up by the moon, it looked celestial; seemed some plumed and glittering god uprising from the sea. Fedallah first descried this jet. For of these moonlight nights, it was his wont to mount to the main-mast head, and stand a look-out there, with the same precision as if it had been day. And yet, though herds of whales were seen by night, not one whaleman in a hundred would venture a lowering for them. You may think with what emotions, then, the seamen beheld this old Oriental perched aloft at such unusual hours; his turban and the moon, companions in one sky. But when, after spending his uniform interval there for several successive nights without uttering a single sound; when, after all this silence, his unearthly voice was heard announcing that silvery, moon-lit jet, every reclining mariner started to his feet as if some winged spirit had lighted in the rigging, and hailed the mortal crew. "There she blows!" Had the trump of judgment blown, they could not have quivered more; yet still they felt no terror; rather pleasure. For though it was a most unwonted hour, yet so impressive was the cry, and so deliriously exciting, that almost every soul on board instinctively desired a lowering.

Walking the deck with quick, side-lunging strides, Ahab commanded the t'gallant sails and royals to be set, and every stunsail spread. The best man in the ship must take the helm. Then, with every mast-head manned, the piled-up craft rolled down before the wind. The strange, upheaving, lifting tendency of the taffrail breeze filling the hollows of so many sails, made the buoyant, hovering deck to feel like air beneath the feet; while still she rushed along, as if two antagonistic influences were struggling in her—one to mount direct to heaven, the other to drive yawingly to some horizontal goal. And had you watched Ahab's face that night, you would have thought that in him also two different things were warring. While his one live leg made lively echoes along the deck, every stroke of his dead limb sounded like a coffin-tap. On life and death this old man walked. But though the ship so swiftly sped, and though from every eye, like arrows, the eager glances shot, yet the silvery jet was no more seen that night. Every sailor swore he saw it once, but not a second time.

---

1. See Melville's comment on this chapter in his letter to Sophia Hawthorne, January 8, 1852 (p. 547, herein).
2. Echo of the repeated phrase in Shakespeare's *Merchant of Venice* 5.1.1–25.

This midnight-spout had almost grown a forgotten thing, when, some days after, lo! at the same silent hour, it was again announced: again it was descried by all; but upon making sail to overtake it, once more it disappeared as if it had never been. And so it served us night after night, till no one heeded it but to wonder at it. Mysteriously jetted into the clear moonlight, or starlight, as the case might be; disappearing again for one whole day, or two days, or three; and somehow seeming at every distinct repetition to be advancing still further and further in our van, this solitary jet seemed for ever alluring us on.

Nor with the immemorial superstition of their race, and in accordance with the preternaturalness, as it seemed, which in many things invested the Pequod, were there wanting some of the seamen who swore that whenever and wherever descried; at however remote times, or in however far apart latitudes and longitudes, that unnearable spout was cast by one self-same whale; and that whale, Moby Dick. For a time, there reigned, too, a sense of peculiar dread at this flitting apparition, as if it were treacherously beckoning us on and on, in order that the monster might turn round upon us, and rend us[3] at last in the remotest and most savage seas.

These temporary apprehensions, so vague but so awful, derived a wondrous potency from the contrasting serenity of the weather, in which, beneath all its blue blandness, some thought there lurked a devilish charm, as for days and days we voyaged along, through seas so wearily, lonesomely mild, that all space, in repugnance to our vengeful errand, seemed vacating itself of life before our urn-like prow.

But, at last, when turning to the eastward, the Cape winds began howling around us, and we rose and fell upon the long, troubled seas that are there; when the ivory-tusked Pequod sharply bowed to the blast, and gored the dark waves in her madness, till, like showers of silver chips, the foam-flakes flew over her bulwarks; then all this desolate vacuity of life went away, but gave place to sights more dismal than before.

Close to our bows, strange forms in the water darted hither and thither before us; while thick in our rear flew the inscrutable sea-ravens. And every morning, perched on our stays, rows of these birds were seen; and spite of our hootings, for a long time obstinately clung to the hemp, as though they deemed our ship some drifting, uninhabited craft; a thing appointed to desolation, and therefore fit roosting-place for their homeless selves. And heaved and heaved, still unrestingly heaved the black sea, as if its vast tides were a conscience; and the great mundane soul[4] were in anguish and remorse for the long sin and suffering it had bred.

Cape of Good Hope, do they call ye? Rather Cape Tormentoso,[5] as called of yore; for long allured by the perfidious silences that before had attended us, we found ourselves launched into this tormented sea, where

---

3. Again, not a full biblical allusion but an emergence of phraseology from Matthew 7.6: "lest they trample them under their feet, and turn again and rend you" (in the warning not to give to dogs what is holy and not to cast pearls before swine).

4. The great (pantheistic?) world soul; here seen by Ishmael as responsible for mankind's sin and suffering, and remorseful for causing it.

5. The first American edition spelled the name "Tormentoto." Tormentoso was the name Bartholomew Diaz (1450–1500) gave to the southern tip of Africa, which his ruler strategically renamed the Cape of Good Hope. Melville seems to have thought the word meant "tormented," not "tempestuous."

guilty beings transformed into those fowls and these fish, seemed condemned[6] to swim on everlastingly without any haven in store, or beat that
black air without any horizon. But calm, snow-white, and unvarying; still
directing its fountain of feathers to the sky; still beckoning us on from
before, the solitary jet would at times be descried.

During all this blackness of the elements, Ahab, though assuming for
the time the almost continual command of the drenched and dangerous
deck, manifested the gloomiest reserve; and more seldom than ever
addressed his mates. In tempestuous times like these, after everything
above and aloft has been secured, nothing more can be done but passively
to await the issue of the gale. Then Captain and crew become practical
fatalists. So, with his ivory leg inserted into its accustomed hole, and with
one hand firmly grasping a shroud, Ahab for hours and hours would stand
gazing dead to windward, while an occasional squall of sleet or snow
would all but congeal his very eyelashes together. Meantime, the crew driven from the forward part of the ship by the perilous seas that burstingly
broke over its bows, stood in a line along the bulwarks in the waist; and
the better to guard against the leaping waves, each man had slipped himself into a sort of bowline secured to the rail, in which he swung as in a
loosened belt. Few or no words were spoken; and the silent ship, as if
manned by painted sailors in wax, day after day tore on through all the
swift madness and gladness of the demoniac waves. By night the same
muteness of humanity before the shrieks of the ocean prevailed; still in
silence the men swung in the bowlines; still wordless Ahab stood up to the
blast. Even when wearied nature seemed demanding repose he would not
seek that repose in his hammock. Never could Starbuck forget the old
man's aspect, when one night going down into the cabin to mark how the
barometer stood, he saw him with closed eyes sitting straight in his floor-
screwed chair; the rain and half-melted sleet of the storm from which he
had some time before emerged, still slowly dripping from the unremoved
hat and coat. On the table beside him lay unrolled one of those charts of
tides and currents which have previously been spoken of. His lantern
swung from his tightly clenched hand. Though the body was erect, the
head was thrown back so that the closed eyes were pointed towards the
needle of the tell-tale that swung from a beam in the ceiling.[7]

Terrible old man! thought Starbuck with a shudder, sleeping in this
gale, still thou steadfastly eyest thy purpose.

Chapter 52

The Albatross

South-eastward from the Cape, off the distant Crozetts,[1] a good cruising
ground for Right Whalemen, a sail loomed ahead, the Goney (Albatross)

---

6. Punishment reminiscent of that imposed on carnal sinners (guilty lovers) in the fifth canto of
   Inferno by Dante Alighieri (1265–1321), first translated into English in 1719.
7. The cabin-compass is called the tell-tale, because without going to the compass at the helm, the
   Captain, while below, can inform himself of the course of the ship [Melville's note].
1. Five small islands in the Indian Ocean, fifteen hundred miles southeast of Cape Horn.

by name. As she slowly drew nigh, from my lofty perch at the fore-mast-head, I had a good view of that sight so remarkable to a tyro in the far ocean fisheries—a whaler at sea, and long absent from home.

As if the waves had been fullers,[2] this craft was bleached like the skeleton of a stranded walrus. All down her sides, this spectral appearance was traced with long channels of reddened rust, while all her spars and her rigging were like the thick branches of trees furred over with hoar-frost. Only her lower sails were set. A wild sight it was to see her long-bearded look-outs at those three mast-heads. They seemed clad in the skins of beasts, so torn and bepatched the raiment that had survived nearly four years of cruising. Standing in iron hoops nailed to the mast, they swayed and swung over a fathomless sea; and though, when the ship slowly glided close under our stern, we six men in the air came so nigh to each other that we might almost have leaped from the mast-heads of one ship to those of the other; yet, those forlorn-looking fishermen, mildly eyeing us as they passed, said not one word to our own look-outs, while the quarter-deck hail was being heard from below.

"Ship ahoy! Have ye seen the White Whale?"

But as the strange captain, leaning over the pallid bulwarks, was in the act of putting his trumpet to his mouth, it somehow fell from his hand into the sea; and the wind now rising amain, he in vain strove to make himself heard without it. Meantime his ship was still increasing the distance between. While in various silent ways the seamen of the Pequod were evincing their observance of this ominous incident at the first mere mention of the White Whale's name to another ship, Ahab for a moment paused; it almost seemed as though he would have lowered a boat to board the stranger, had not the threatening wind forbade. But taking advantage of his windward position, he again seized his trumpet, and knowing by her aspect that the stranger vessel was a Nantucketer and shortly bound home, he loudly hailed—"Ahoy there! This is the Pequod, bound round the world! Tell them to address all future letters to the Pacific ocean! and this time three years, if I am not at home, tell them to address them to————"

At that moment the two wakes were fairly crossed, and instantly, then, in accordance with their singular ways, shoals of small harmless fish, that for some days before had been placidly swimming by our side, darted away with what seemed shuddering fins, and ranged themselves fore and aft with the stranger's flanks. Though in the course of his continual voyagings Ahab must often before have noticed a similar sight, yet, to any monomaniac man, the veriest trifles capriciously carry meanings.

"Swim away from me, do ye?" murmured Ahab, gazing over into the water. There seemed but little in the words, but the tone conveyed more of deep helpless sadness than the insane old man had ever before evinced. But turning to the steersman, who thus far had been holding the ship in the wind to diminish her headway, he cried out in his old lion voice,—"Up helm! Keep her off round the world!"

Round the world! There is much in that sound to inspire proud feelings;

2. Cleansers (workers or machines for fulling, cleansing, cloth during manufacture; hence the occupational surname Fuller).

but whereto does all that circumnavigation conduct? Only through numberless perils to the very point whence we started, where those that we left
behind secure, were all the time before us.

Were this world an endless plain, and by sailing eastward we could for
ever reach new distances, and discover sights more sweet and strange
than any Cyclades or Islands of King Solomon,[3] then there were promise
in the voyage. But in pursuit of those far mysteries we dream of, or in tormented chase of that demon phantom that, some time or other, swims
before all human hearts; while chasing such over this round globe, they
either lead us on in barren mazes or midway leave us whelmed.[4]

Chapter 53

The Gam

The ostensible reason why Ahab did not go on board of the whaler we had
spoken was this: the wind and sea betokened storms. But even had this
not been the case, he would not after all, perhaps, have boarded her—
judging by his subsequent conduct on similar occasions—if so it had been
that, by the process of hailing, he had obtained a negative answer to the
question he put. For, as it eventually turned out, he cared not to consort,
even for five minutes, with any stranger captain, except he could contribute some of that information he so absorbingly sought. But all this
might remain inadequately estimated, were not something said here of
the peculiar usages of whaling-vessels when meeting each other in foreign
seas, and especially on a common cruising-ground.

If two strangers crossing the Pine Barrens in New York State, or the
equally desolate Salisbury Plain in England; if casually encountering each
other in such inhospitable wilds, these twain, for the life of them, cannot
well avoid a mutual salutation; and stopping for a moment to interchange
the news; and, perhaps, sitting down for a while and resting in concert:
then, how much more natural that upon the illimitable Pine Barrens and
Salisbury Plains of the sea, two whaling vessels descrying each other at
the ends of the earth—off lone Fanning's Island, or the far away King's
Mills;[1] how much more natural, I say, that under such circumstances
these ships should not only interchange hails, but come into still closer,
more friendly and sociable contact. And especially would this seem to be
a matter of course, in the case of vessels owned in one seaport, and whose
captains, officers, and not a few of the men are personally known to each
other; and consequently, have all sorts of dear domestic things to talk
about.

For the long absent ship, the outward-bounder, perhaps, has letters on
board; at any rate, she will be sure to let her have some papers of a date
a year or two later than the last one on her blurred and thumb-worn files.

3. Greek islands and the biblical King Solomon's fabled spice islands in the east (whence the name
explorers gave to the Solomon Islands in the South Pacific).
4. Engulfed.
1. Islands in the mid-Pacific near the equator. *Pine Barrens:* in east central Suffolk County, Long
Island. *Salisbury Plain:* In south-central England, the site of the ancient Stonehenge.

And in return for that courtesy, the outward-bound ship would receive the latest whaling intelligence from the cruising-ground to which she may be destined, a thing of the utmost importance to her. And in degree, all this will hold true concerning whaling vessels crossing each other's track on the cruising-ground itself, even though they are equally long absent from home. For one of them may have received a transfer of letters from some third, and now far remote vessel; and some of those letters may be for the people of the ship she now meets. Besides, they would exchange the whaling news, and have an agreeable chat. For not only would they meet with all the sympathies of sailors, but likewise with all the peculiar congenialities arising from a common pursuit and mutually shared privations and perils.

Nor would difference of country make any very essential difference; that is, so long as both parties speak one language, as is the case with Americans and English. Though, to be sure, from the small number of English whalers, such meetings do not very often occur, and when they do occur there is too apt to be a sort of shyness between them; for your Englishman is rather reserved, and your Yankee, he does not fancy that sort of thing in anybody but himself. Besides, the English whalers sometimes affect a kind of metropolitan superiority over the American whalers; regarding the long, lean Nantucketer, with his nondescript provincialisms, as a sort of sea-peasant. But where this superiority in the English whalemen does really consist, it would be hard to say, seeing that the Yankees in one day, collectively, kill more whales than all the English, collectively, in ten years. But this is a harmless little foible in the English whalehunters, which the Nantucketer does not take much to heart; probably, because he knows that he has a few foibles himself.

So, then, we see that of all ships separately sailing the sea, the whalers have most reason to be sociable—and they are so. Whereas, some merchant ships crossing each other's wake in the mid-Atlantic, will oftentimes pass on without so much as a single word of recognition, mutually cutting each other on the high seas, like a brace of dandies in Broadway;[2] and all the time indulging, perhaps, in finical criticism upon each other's rig. As for Men-of-War, when they chance to meet at sea, they first go through such a string of silly bowings and scrapings, such a ducking of ensigns, that there does not seem to be much right-down hearty good-will and brotherly love about it at all. As touching Slave-ships meeting, why, they are in such a prodigious hurry, they run away from each other as soon as possible. And as for Pirates, when they chance to cross each other's crossbones, the first hail is—"How many skulls?"—the same way that whalers hail—"How many barrels?" And that question once answered, pirates straightway steer apart, for they are infernal villains on both sides, and don't like to see overmuch of each other's villanous likenesses.

But look at the godly, honest, unostentatious, hospitable, sociable, free-and-easy whaler! What does the whaler do when she meets another whaler in any sort of decent weather? She has a *"Gam,"* a thing so utterly unknown to all other ships that they never heard of the name even; and if by chance

---

2. The main commercial street in New York City, continued as the major road leading north through Manhattan Island.

they should hear of it, they only grin at it, and repeat gamesome stuff about "spouters" and "blubber-boilers," and such like pretty exclamations. Why it is that all Merchant-seamen, and also all Pirates and Man-of-War's men, and Slave-ship sailors, cherish such a scornful feeling towards Whale-ships; this is a question it would be hard to answer. Because, in the case of pirates, say, I should like to know whether that profession of theirs has any peculiar glory about it. It sometimes ends in uncommon elevation, indeed; but only at the gallows. And besides, when a man is elevated in that odd fashion, he has no proper foundation for his superior altitude. Hence, I conclude, that in boasting himself to be high lifted above a whaleman, in that assertion the pirate has no solid basis to stand on.

But what is a *Gam?* You might wear out your index-finger running up and down the columns of dictionaries, and never find the word. Dr. Johnson never attained to that erudition; Noah Webster's ark[3] does not hold it. Nevertheless, this same expressive word has now for many years been in constant use among some fifteen thousand true born Yankees. Certainly, it needs a definition, and should be incorporated into the Lexicon. With that view, let me learnedly define it.

GAM.[4] NOUN—*A social meeting of two (or more) Whale-ships, generally on a cruising-ground; when, after exchanging hails, they exchange visits by boats' crews: the two captains remaining, for the time, on board of one ship, and the two chief mates on the other.*

There is another little item about Gamming which must not be forgotten here. All professions have their own little peculiarities of detail; so has the whale fishery. In a pirate, man-of-war, or slave ship, when the captain is rowed anywhere in his boat, he always sits in the stern sheets on a comfortable, sometimes cushioned seat there, and often steers himself with a pretty little milliner's tiller decorated with gay cords and ribbons.[5] But the whale-boat has no seat astern, no sofa of that sort whatever, and no tiller at all. High times indeed, if whaling captains were wheeled about the water on castors like gouty old aldermen in patent chairs. And as for a tiller, the whale-boat never admits of any such effeminacy; and therefore as in gamming a complete boat's crew must leave the ship, and hence as the boat steerer or harpooneer is of the number, that subordinate is the steersman upon the occasion, and the captain, having no place to sit in, is pulled off to his visit all standing like a pine tree. And often you will notice that being conscious of the eyes of the whole visible world resting on him from the sides of the two ships, this standing captain is all alive to the importance of sustaining his dignity by maintaining his legs. Nor is this any very easy matter; for in his rear is the immense projecting steering oar hitting him now and then in the small of his back, the after-oar reciprocating by rapping his knees in front. He is thus completely wedged before and behind, and can only expand himself sideways by settling down

3. Learned American (1758–1843) who compiled the 1806 dictionary of the English language in the United States, punningly called "Noah's Ark." The learned Englishman Samuel Johnson (1709–1784) compiled a respected dictionary of the English language (1755).
4. Mansfield and Vincent (739) show that Melville was rewriting the definition of "gam" from Cheever's *The Whale and His Captors* (1850). Most of the encounters the *Pequod* has with other ships do not fit this stringent definition.
5. That is, a pretty little tiller decorated like a lady's hat (made by a professional hatmaker, or milliner). By contrast, the whaleboat is steered by an immense oar.

on his stretched legs; but a sudden, violent pitch of the boat will often go far to topple him, because length of foundation is nothing without corresponding breadth. Merely make a spread angle of two poles, and you cannot stand them up. Then, again, it would never do in plain sight of the world's riveted eyes, it would never do, I say, for this straddling captain to be seen steadying himself the slightest particle by catching hold of anything with his hands; indeed, as token of his entire, buoyant self-command, he generally carries his hands in his trowsers' pockets; but perhaps being generally very large, heavy hands, he carries them there for ballast.[6] Nevertheless there have occurred instances, well authenticated ones too, where the captain has been known for an uncommonly critical moment or two, in a sudden squall say—to seize hold of the nearest oarsman's hair, and hold on there like grim death.

Chapter 54

The Town-Ho's Story[1]

(As told at the Golden Inn.)

The Cape of Good Hope, and all the watery region round about there, is much like some noted four corners of a great highway, where you meet more travellers than in any other part.

It was not very long after speaking[2] the Goney that another homeward-bound whaleman, the Town-Ho,[3] was encountered. She was manned almost wholly by Polynesians. In the short gam that ensued she gave us strong news of Moby Dick. To some the general interest in the White Whale was now wildly heightened by a circumstance of the Town-Ho's story, which seemed obscurely to involve with the whale a certain wondrous, inverted visitation of one of those so called judgments of God which at times are said to overtake some men. This latter circumstance, with its own particular accompaniments, forming what may be called the secret part of the tragedy about to be narrated, never reached the ears of Captain Ahab or his mates. For that secret part of the story was unknown to the captain of the Town-Ho himself. It was the private property of three confederate white seamen of that ship, one of whom, it seems, commu-

---

6. Ships carried heavy weights in the hold to keep balanced. For instance, yellow bricks from Holland were used in constructing some houses in New York and Albany, still standing in Melville's time.
1. This chapter first appeared in *Harper's New Monthly Magazine* for October 1851, six weeks in advance of the book's publication in mid-November. Works such as Cervantes's Don Quixote (1605, 1615) and Tom Jones (1749) by Henry Fielding (1707–1754) provided precedents for the "interpolation" of long stories into the main story; the device allows Melville to show Ishmael interacting ashore in a sophisticated company and to introduce the white whale in action without weakening the climax of Ahab's pursuit. Ishmael, the narrator of a story almost too strange to believe, claims the right to tell a basic story more than one way (here, as he told it in specific circumstances, at the Golden Inn in Lima) and (when challenged) to swear only that it is in "substance and great items true," not necessarily true in every detail.
2. Communicating with by signal or voice (as distinguished from "gamming" with).
3. The ancient whale-cry upon first sighting a whale from the mast-head, still used by whalemen in hunting the famous Gallipagos terrapin [Melville's note]. The Galapagos Islands lie off the west coast of Ecuador; Melville had touched there in 1841 and 1842, and in 1854–55 wrote of them in his "The Encantadas."

nicated it to Tashtego with Romish injunctions of secresy,[4] but the following night Tashtego rambled in his sleep, and revealed so much of it in
that way, that when he was wakened he could not well withhold the rest.
Nevertheless, so potent an influence did this thing have on those seamen
in the Pequod who came to the full knowledge of it, and by such a strange
delicacy, to call it so, were they governed in this matter, that they kept the
secret among themselves so that it never transpired abaft the Pequod's
main-mast. Interweaving in its proper place this darker thread with the
story as publicly narrated on the ship, the whole of this strange affair I
now proceed to put on lasting record.

For my humor's sake, I shall preserve the style in which I once narrated
it at Lima, to a lounging circle of my Spanish friends, one saint's eve,
smoking upon the thick-gilt tiled piazza of the Golden Inn. Of those fine
cavaliers, the young Dons, Pedro and Sebastian, were on the closer terms
with me; and hence the interluding questions they occasionally put, and
which are duly answered at the time.

"Some two years prior to my first learning the events which I am about
rehearsing to you, gentlemen, the Town-Ho, Sperm Whaler of Nantucket,
was cruising in your Pacific here, not very many days' sail westward from
the eaves of this good Golden Inn. She was somewhere to the northward
of the Line. One morning upon handling the pumps, according to daily
usage, it was observed that she made more water in her hold than common. They supposed a sword-fish had stabbed her,[5] gentlemen. But the
captain, having some unusual reason for believing that rare good luck
awaited him in those latitudes; and therefore being very averse to quit
them, and the leak not being then considered at all dangerous, though,
indeed, they could not find it after searching the hold as low down as was
possible in rather heavy weather, the ship still continued her cruisings,
the mariners working at the pumps at wide and easy intervals; but no good
luck came; more days went by, and not only was the leak yet undiscovered,
but it sensibly increased. So much so, that now taking some alarm, the
captain, making all sail, stood away for the nearest harbor among the
islands, there to have his hull hove out and repaired.

"Though no small passage was before her, yet, if the commonest chance
favored, he did not at all fear that his ship would founder by the way,
because his pumps were of the best, and being periodically relieved at
them, those six-and-thirty men of his could easily keep the ship free; never
mind if the leak should double on her. In truth, well nigh the whole of this
passage being attended by very prosperous breezes, the Town-Ho had all
but certainly arrived in perfect safety at her port without the occurrence

4. Ishmael's freedom as narrator is enhanced by his depiction, elsewhere, of Tashtego's limited command of English and the presumed difficulty he might have had in comprehending the "Romish"
(Roman Catholic) and presumably Spanish-speaking sailors of the *Town-Ho*. The true story,
Ishmael asserts, was known below decks on both ships, but never known to the captain of the
Town-Ho or to Captain Ahab and his mates.
5. Ishmael's words sound like (and are meant to sound like) tall talk, but a standard strategy in such
humor is to unsettle the audience by inducing disbelief in the unlikely but true so as later to induce
belief in another extravagance that may or may not be true. In fact, swordfish sometimes stabbed
ships, as Melville knew from a well-publicized example while he was in Liverpool in 1839 (Parker,
1.146) and from a story current when he was in Hawaii in 1843. Ishmael uses the formal term
"Gentlemen" for ironic effect, because it distances his decorous audience at the Golden Inn from
the wild events of his story.

of the least fatality, had it not been for the brutal overbearing of Radney, the mate, a Nantucketer, and the bitterly provoked vengeance of Steelkilt, a Lakeman and desperado from Buffalo."

"Lakeman!—Buffalo! Pray, what is a Lakeman, and where is Buffalo?" said Don Sebastian, rising in his swinging mat of grass.

"On the eastern shore of our Lake Erie, Don; but—I crave your courtesy—may be, you shall soon hear further of all that. Now, gentlemen, in square-sail brigs and three-masted ships, well nigh as large and stout as any that ever sailed out of your old Callao to far Manilla; this Lakeman, in the land-locked heart of our America, had yet been nurtured by all those agrarian[6] freebooting impressions popularly connected with the open ocean. For in their interflowing aggregate, those grand fresh-water seas of ours,—Erie, and Ontario, and Huron, and Superior, and Michigan,—possess an ocean-like expansiveness, with many of the ocean's noblest traits; with many of its rimmed varieties of races and of climes. They contain round archipelagoes of romantic isles, even as the Polynesian waters do, in large part, are shored by two great contrasting nations, as the Atlantic is; they furnish long maritime approaches to our numerous territorial colonies from the East, dotted all round their banks; here and there are frowned upon by batteries, and by the goat-like craggy guns of lofty Mackinaw;[7] they have heard the fleet thunderings of naval victories; at intervals, they yield their beaches to wild barbarians, whose red painted faces flash from out their peltry wigwams; for leagues and leagues are flanked by ancient and unentered forests, where the gaunt pines stand like serried lines of kings in Gothic genealogies; those same woods harboring wild Afric beasts of prey, and silken creatures whose exported furs give robes to Tartar Emperors; they mirror the paved capitals of Buffalo and Cleveland, as well as Winnebago villages; they float alike the full-rigged merchant ship, the armed cruiser of the State, the steamer, and the birch canoe; they are swept by Borean[8] and dismasting blasts as direful as any that lash the salted wave; they know what shipwrecks are, for out of sight of land, however inland, they have drowned full many a midnight ship with all its shrieking crew. Thus, gentlemen, though an inlander, Steelkilt was wild-ocean born, and wild-ocean nurtured; as much of an audacious mariner as any. And for Radney, though in his infancy he may have laid him down on the lone Nantucket beach, to nurse at his maternal sea; though in after life he had long followed our austere Atlantic and your contemplative Pacific; yet was he quite as vengeful and full of social quarrel as the backwoods seaman, fresh from the latitudes of buck-horn handled Bowie-knives.[9] Yet was this Nantucketer a man with

---

6. Not a reference to some activist "agrarian" movement, but merely piratical behavior anomalous when occurring among landsmen (or canalmen or lakemen). Compare the condensed construction, "clerical peculiarities," in ch. 8.
7. The fort on Mackinac Island in the straits between Lake Huron and Lake Michigan. The chief naval victory was Oliver H. Perry's (1785–1819) over the British fleet in Lake Erie in 1813. This was recent matter for national and even personal pride, for Melville's own mother had met the heroic Perry at the victory celebration for him in Albany later in 1813. On his trip to then pioneer Illinois in 1840 (when Chicago was only a few years old), Melville went over the Erie Canal then sailed past Mackinac; one vividly remembered detail was Indian faces looking out from "pelty" wigwams (made of animal pelts).
8. Winds from the north (from Boreas, the Greek god of that wind). *Tartar Emperors*: loosely, Asiatic rulers during medieval times. Winnebago Indians inhabited Wisconsin.
9. Single-edged hunting knives favored in Melville's youth by James Bowie (1796?–1836; rhymes with gooey), commonly carried by frontiersmen and freely used in personal combat.

some good-hearted traits; and this Lakeman, a mariner, who though a sort of devil indeed, might yet by inflexible firmness, only tempered by that common decency of human recognition which is the meanest slave's right; thus treated, this Steelkilt had long been retained harmless and docile. At all events, he had proved so thus far; but Radney was doomed and made mad, and Steelkilt—but, gentlemen, you shall hear.

"It was not more than a day or two at the furthest after pointing her prow for her island haven, that the Town-Ho's leak seemed again increasing, but only so as to require an hour or more at the pumps every day. You must know that in a settled and civilized ocean like our Atlantic, for example, some skippers think little of pumping their whole way across it; though of a still, sleepy night, should the officer of the deck happen to forget his duty in that respect, the probability would be that he and his shipmates would never again remember it, on account of all hands gently subsiding to the bottom. Nor in the solitary and savage seas far from you to the westward, gentlemen, is it altogether unusual for ships to keep clanging at their pump-handles in full chorus even for a voyage of considerable length; that is, if it lie along a tolerably accessible coast, or if any other reasonable retreat is afforded them. It is only when a leaky vessel is in some very out of the way part of those waters, some really landless latitude, that her captain begins to feel a little anxious.

"Much this way had it been with the Town-Ho; so when her leak was found gaining once more, there was in truth some small concern manifested by several of her company; especially by Radney the mate. He commanded the upper sails to be well hoisted, sheeted home anew, and every way expanded to the breeze. Now this Radney, I suppose, was as little of a coward, and as little inclined to any sort of nervous apprehensiveness touching his own person as any fearless, unthinking creature on land or on sea that you can conveniently imagine, gentlemen. Therefore when he betrayed this solicitude about the safety of the ship, some of the seamen declared that it was only on account of his being a part owner in her. So when they were working that evening at the pumps, there was on this head no small gamesomeness slily going on among them, as they stood with their feet continually overflowed by the rippling clear water; clear as any mountain spring, gentlemen—that bubbling from the pumps ran across the deck, and poured itself out in steady spouts at the lee scupperholes.[1]

"Now, as you well know, it is not seldom the case in this conventional world[2] of ours—watery or otherwise; that when a person placed in command over his fellow-men finds one of them to be very significantly his superior in general pride of manhood, straightway against that man he conceives an unconquerable dislike and bitterness; and if he have a chance he will pull down and pulverize that subaltern's tower, and make a little heap of dust of it. Be this conceit of mine as it may, gentlemen, at all events Steelkilt was a tall and noble animal with a head like a Roman, and a flowing golden beard like the tasseled housings of your last viceroy's

---

1. Gutter drainholes on the off-wind side ("lee") toward which the deck is leaning.
2. One ruled by social conventions rather than recognition of individual worth. A biblical precedent is Saul's jealousy of the young David (as in 1 Samuel 18). *Billy Budd*, the story Melville was still working on when he died in 1891, takes up much the same theme.

snorting charger; and a brain, and a heart, and a soul in him, gentlemen, which had made Steelkilt Charlemagne,[3] had he been born son to Charlemagne's father. But Radney, the mate, was ugly as a mule; yet as hardy, as stubborn, as malicious. He did not love Steelkilt, and Steelkilt knew it.

"Espying the mate drawing near as he was toiling at the pump with the rest, the Lakeman affected not to notice him, but unawed, went on with his gay banterings.

"'Aye, aye, my merry lads, it's a lively leak this; hold a cannikin, one of ye, and let's have a taste. By the Lord, it's worth bottling! I tell ye what, men, old Rad's investment must go for it! he had best cut away his part of the hull and tow it home. The fact is, boys, that sword-fish only began the job; he's come back again with a gang of ship-carpenters, saw-fish, and file-fish, and what not; and the whole posse of 'em are now hard at work cutting and slashing at the bottom; making improvements, I suppose. If old Rad were here now, I'd tell him to jump overboard and scatter 'em. They're playing the devil with his estate, I can tell him. But he's a simple old soul,—Rad, and a beauty too. Boys, they say the rest of his property is invested in looking-glasses. I wonder if he'd give a poor devil like me the model of his nose.'

"'Damn your eyes! what's that pump stopping for?' roared Radney, pretending not to have heard the sailor's talk. 'Thunder away at it!'

"'Aye, aye, sir,' said Steelkilt, merry as a cricket. 'Lively, boys, lively, now!' And with that the pump clanged like fifty fire-engines; the men tossed their hats off to it, and ere long that peculiar gasping of the lungs was heard which denotes the fullest tension of life's utmost energies.

"Quitting the pump at last, with the rest of his band, the Lakeman went forward all panting, and sat himself down on the windlass; his face fiery red, his eyes bloodshot, and wiping the profuse sweat from his brow. Now what cozening fiend it was, gentlemen, that possessed Radney to meddle with such a man in that corporeally exasperated state, I know not; but so it happened. Intolerably striding along the deck, the mate commanded him to get a broom and sweep down the planks, and also a shovel, and remove some offensive matters consequent upon allowing a pig to run at large.

"Now, gentlemen, sweeping a ship's deck at sea is a piece of household work which in all times but raging gales is regularly attended to every evening; it has been known to be done in the case of ships actually foundering at the time. Such, gentlemen, is the inflexibility of sea-usages and the instinctive love of neatness in seamen; some of whom would not willingly drown without first washing their faces. But in all vessels this broom business is the prescriptive province of the boys,[4] if boys there be aboard. Besides, it was the stronger men in the Town-Ho that had been divided into gangs, taking turns at the pumps; and being the most athletic seaman of them all, Steelkilt had been regularly assigned captain of one of the gangs; consequently he should have been freed from any trivial business not connected with truly nautical duties, such being the case

---

3. Celebrated medieval king and emperor (742–814), great as warrior and as administrator.
4. Here, literally boys, not green hands who happen to be grown men.

with his comrades. I mention all these particulars so that you may understand exactly how this affair stood between the two men.

"But there was more than this: the order about the shovel was almost
as plainly meant to sting and insult Steelkilt, as though Radney had spat
in his face. Any man who has gone sailor in a whale-ship will understand
this; and all this and doubtless much more, the Lakeman fully comprehended when the mate uttered his command. But as he sat still for a
moment, and as he steadfastly looked into the mate's malignant eye and
perceived the stacks of powder-casks heaped up in him and the slow-
match silently burning along towards them; as he instinctively saw all this,
that strange forbearance and unwillingness to stir up the deeper passion-
ateness in any already ireful being—a repugnance most felt, when felt at
all, by really valiant men even when aggrieved—this nameless phantom
feeling, gentlemen, stole over Steelkilt.

"Therefore, in his ordinary tone, only a little broken by the bodily
exhaustion he was temporarily in, he answered him saying that sweeping
the deck was not his business, and he would not do it. And then, without
at all alluding to the shovel, he pointed to three lads as the customary
sweepers; who, not being billeted at the pumps, had done little or nothing all day. To this, Radney replied with an oath, in a most domineering
and outrageous manner unconditionally reiterating his command; meanwhile advancing upon the still seated Lakeman, with an uplifted cooper's
club hammer[5] which he had snatched from a cask near by.

"Heated and irritated as he was by his spasmodic toil at the pumps, for
all his first nameless feeling of forbearance the sweating Steelkilt could
but ill brook this bearing in the mate; but somehow still smothering the
conflagration within him, without speaking he remained doggedly rooted
to his seat, till at last the incensed Radney shook the hammer within a few
inches of his face, furiously commanding him to do his bidding.

"Steelkilt rose, and slowly retreating round the windlass, steadily followed by the mate with his menacing hammer, deliberately repeated his
intention not to obey. Seeing, however, that his forbearance had not the
slightest effect, by an awful and unspeakable intimation with his twisted
hand he warned off the foolish and infatuated man; but it was to no purpose. And in this way the two went once slowly round the windlass; when
resolved at last no longer to retreat, bethinking him that he had now for-
borne as much as comported with his humor, the Lakeman paused on the
hatches and thus spoke to the officer:

"'Mr. Radney, I will not obey you. Take that hammer away, or look to
yourself.' But the predestinated mate coming still closer to him, where the
Lakeman stood fixed, now shook the heavy hammer within an inch of his
teeth; meanwhile repeating a string of insufferable maledictions.
Retreating not the thousandth part of an inch; stabbing him in the eye
with the unflinching poniard of his glance, Steelkilt, clenching his right
hand behind him and creepingly drawing it back, told his persecutor that
if the hammer but grazed his cheek he (Steelkilt) would murder him. But,
gentlemen, the fool had been branded for the slaughter by the gods.
Immediately the hammer touched the cheek; the next instant the lower

---

5. Doubleheaded barrelmaker's steel tool.

jaw of the mate was stove in his head; he fell on the hatch spouting blood like a whale.

"Ere the cry could go aft Steelkilt was shaking one of the backstays leading far aloft to where two of his comrades were standing their mastheads. They were both Canallers."

"Canallers!" cried Don Pedro. "We have seen many whale-ships in our harbors, but never heard of your Canallers. Pardon: who and what are they?"

"Canallers, Don, are the boatmen belonging to our grand Erie Canal. You must have heard of it."

"Nay, Senor; hereabouts in this dull, warm, most lazy, and hereditary land, we know but little of your vigorous North."

"Aye? Well then, Don, refill my cup. Your chicha's[6] very fine; and ere proceeding further I will tell ye what our Canallers are; for such information may throw side-light upon my story.

"For three hundred and sixty miles, gentlemen, through the entire breadth of the state of New York; through numerous populous cities and most thriving villages; through long, dismal, uninhabited swamps, and affluent, cultivated fields, unrivalled for fertility; by billiard-room and bar-room; through the holy-of-holies of great forests; on Roman arches over Indian rivers; through sun and shade; by happy hearts or broken; through all the wide contrasting scenery of those noble Mohawk counties; and especially, by rows of snow-white chapels, whose spires stand almost like milestones, flows one continual stream of Venetianly corrupt and often lawless life. There's your true Ashantee,[7] gentlemen; there howl your pagans; where you ever find them, next door to you; under the long-flung shadow, and the snug patronizing lee of churches. For by some curious fatality, as it is often noted of your metropolitan freebooters that they ever encamp around the halls of justice, so sinners, gentlemen, most abound in holiest vicinities."

"Is that a friar passing?" said Don Pedro, looking downwards into the crowded plaza, with humorous concern.

"Well for our northern friend, Dame Isabella's Inquisition[8] wanes in Lima," laughed Don Sebastian. "Proceed, Senor."

"A moment! Pardon!" cried another of the company. "In the name of all us Limeese, I but desire to express to you, sir sailor, that we have by no means overlooked your delicacy in not substituting present Lima for distant Venice in your corrupt comparison. Oh! do not bow and look surprised; you know the proverb all along this coast—'Corrupt as Lima.' It but bears out your saying, too; churches more plentiful than billiard-tables, and for ever open—and 'Corrupt as Lima.' So, too, Venice; I have been there; the holy city of the blessed evangelist, St. Mark!—St. Dominic,[9] purge it! Your cup! Thanks: here I refill; now, you pour out again."

---

6. South American beer made from fermented Indian corn or sugar cane.
7. African, in what is now Ghana. *Mohawk counties*: in mid-New York, originally the territory of Mohawk Indians.
8. The Spanish Inquisition—set up in 1478 by King Ferdinand and Queen Isabella—questioned, tortured, and even burned suspected heretics.
9. Founder (1215) of the order of Dominican priests and patron saint of the Cathedral of Lima. *St. Mark*: author of the second gospel and patron saint of Venice. Lima, which Melville had seen, and Venice, which he had not yet visited, were associated in Melville's mind as cities of super-subtle personal psychology, sexual deception, dangerous pushing of religious limits, and haunting, decaying architectural beauty.

"Freely depicted in his own vocation, gentlemen, the Canaller would make a fine dramatic hero, so abundantly and picturesquely wicked is he. Like Mark Antony,[1] for days and days along his green-turfed, flowery Nile, he indolently floats, openly toying with his red-cheeked Cleopatra, ripening his apricot thigh upon the sunny deck. But ashore, all this effeminacy is dashed. The brigandish guise which the Canaller so proudly sports; his slouched and gaily-ribboned hat betoken his grand features. A terror to the smiling innocence of the villages through which he floats; his swart visage and bold swagger are not unshunned in cities. Once a vagabond on his own canal, I have received good turns from one of these Canallers;[2] I thank him heartily; would fain be not ungrateful; but it is often one of the prime redeeming qualities of your man of violence, that at times he has as stiff an arm to back a poor stranger in a strait, as to plunder a wealthy one. In sum, gentlemen, what the wildness of this canal life is, is emphatically evinced by this; that our wild whale-fishery contains so many of its most finished graduates, and that scarce any race of mankind, except Sydney[3] men, are so much distrusted by our whaling captains. Nor does it at all diminish the curiousness of this matter, that to many thousands of our rural boys and young men born along its line, the probationary life of the Grand Canal[4] furnishes the sole transition between quietly reaping in a Christian corn-field, and recklessly ploughing the waters of the most barbaric seas."

"I see! I see!" impetuously exclaimed Don Pedro, spilling his chicha upon his silvery ruffles. "No need to travel! The world's one Lima. I had thought, now, that at your temperate North the generations were cold and holy as the hills.—But the story."

"I left off, gentlemen, where the Lakeman shook the backstay. Hardly had he done so, when he was surrounded by the three junior mates and the four harpooneers, who all crowded him to the deck. But sliding down the ropes like baleful comets, the two Canallers rushed into the uproar, and sought to drag their man out of it towards the forecastle. Others of the sailors joined with them in this attempt, and a twisted turmoil ensued; while standing out of harm's way, the valiant captain danced up and down with a whale-pike, calling upon his officers to manhandle that atrocious scoundrel, and smoke[5] him along to the quarter-deck. At intervals, he ran close up to the revolving border of the confusion, and prying into the heart of it with his pike, sought to prick out the object of his resentment. But Steelkilt and his desperadoes were too much for them all; they succeeded in gaining the forecastle deck, where, hastily slewing about three or four large casks in a line with the windlass, these sea-Parisians[6] entrenched themselves behind the barricade.

"'Come out of that, ye pirates!' roared the captain, now menacing them

---

1. Not the crowd mover of *Julius Caesar* but the older hero, visualized as disporting himself with the Egyptian queen on the deck of her golden "barge" (*Antony and Cleopatra* 2.2).
2. Possibly true of Melville, in 1840.
3. Australian seaport first settled (1788) by convicts freed from prison and exiled to this "penal colony"; hence the residual distrust.
4. Epithet for the Erie Canal, from the great central canal of Venice.
5. Forcibly drag (so fast that he travels like smoke along a floor).
6. Rioting revolutionaries, like those in late-18th- and mid-19th-century Paris. Melville saw Paris the year after the Revolution of 1848.

with a pistol in each hand, just brought to him by the steward. 'Come out of that, ye cut-throats!'

"Steelkilt leaped on the barricade, and striding up and down there, defied the worst the pistols could do; but gave the captain to understand distinctly, that his (Steelkilt's) death would be the signal for a murderous mutiny on the part of all hands. Fearing in his heart lest this might prove but too true, the captain a little desisted, but still commanded the insurgents instantly to return to their duty.

"'Will you promise not to touch us, if we do?' demanded their ringleader.

"'Turn to! turn to!—I make no promise;—to your duty! Do you want to sink the ship, by knocking off at a time like this? Turn to!' and he once more raised a pistol.

"'Sink the ship?' cried Steelkilt. 'Aye, let her sink. Not a man of us turns to, unless you swear not to raise a rope-yarn against us. What say ye, men?' turning to his comrades. A fierce cheer was their response.

"The Lakeman now patrolled the barricade, all the while keeping his eye on the Captain, and jerking out such sentences as these:—'It's not our fault; we didn't want it; I told him to take his hammer away; it was boy's business; he might have known me before this; I told him not to prick the buffalo; I believe I have broken a finger here against his cursed jaw; ain't those mincing knives[7] down in the forecastle there, men? look to those hand-spikes, my hearties. Captain, by God, look to yourself; say the word; don't be a fool; forget it all; we are ready to turn to; treat us decently, and we're your men; but we won't be flogged.'

"'Turn to! I make no promises, turn to, I say!'

"'Look ye, now,' cried the Lakeman, flinging out his arm towards him, 'there are a few of us here (and I am one of them) who have shipped for the cruise,[8] d'ye see; now as you well know, sir, we can claim our discharge as soon as the anchor is down; so we don't want a row; it's not our interest; we want to be peaceable; we are ready to work, but we won't be flogged.'

"'Turn to!' roared the Captain.

"Steelkilt glanced round him a moment, and then said:—'I tell you what it is now, Captain, rather than kill ye, and be hung for such a shabby rascal, we won't lift a hand against ye unless ye attack us; but till you say the word about not flogging us, we don't do a hand's turn.'

"'Down into the forecastle then, down with ye, I'll keep ye there till ye're sick of it. Down ye go.'

"'Shall we?' cried the ringleader to his men. Most of them were against it; but at length, in obedience to Steelkilt, they preceded him down into their dark den, growlingly disappearing, like bears into a cave.

"As the Lakeman's bare head was just level with the planks, the Captain and his posse leaped the barricade, and rapidly drawing over the slide of the scuttle, planted their group of hands upon it, and loudly called for the steward to bring the heavy brass padlock belonging to the companion-

---

7. Sharp two-handled knives for slicing blubber.
8. Enlisted for service only until the ship anchors at the next port (not until her return to her home port).

way.[9] Then opening the slide a little, the Captain whispered something
down the crack, closed it, and turned the key upon them—ten in number—leaving on deck some twenty or more, who thus far had remained
neutral.

"All night a wide-awake watch was kept by all the officers, forward and
aft, especially about the forecastle scuttle and fore hatchway;[1] at which
last place it was feared the insurgents might emerge, after breaking
through the bulkhead below. But the hours of darkness passed in peace;
the men who still remained at their duty toiling hard at the pumps, whose
clinking and clanking at intervals through the dreary night dismally
resounded through the ship.

"At sunrise the Captain went forward, and knocking on the deck, summoned the prisoners to work; but with a yell they refused. Water was then
lowered down to them, and a couple of handfuls of biscuit were tossed
after it; when again turning the key upon them and pocketing it, the
Captain returned to the quarter-deck. Twice every day for three days this
was repeated; but on the fourth morning a confused wrangling, and then
a scuffling was heard, as the customary summons was delivered; and suddenly four men burst up from the forecastle, saying they were ready to
turn to. The fetid closeness of the air, and a famishing diet, united perhaps to some fears of ultimate retribution, had constrained them to surrender at discretion. Emboldened by this, the Captain reiterated his
demand to the rest, but Steelkilt shouted up to him a terrific hint to stop
his babbling and betake himself where he belonged. On the fifth morning
three others of the mutineers bolted up into the air from the desperate
arms below that sought to restrain them. Only three were left.

"'Better turn to, now!' said the Captain with a heartless jeer.

"'Shut us up again, will ye!' cried Steelkilt.

"'Oh! certainly,' said the Captain, and the key clicked.

"It was at this point, gentlemen, that enraged by the defection of seven
of his former associates, and stung by the mocking voice that had last
hailed him, and maddened by his long entombment in a place as black as
the bowels of despair;[2] it was then that Steelkilt proposed to the two
Canallers, thus far apparently of one mind with him, to burst out of their
hole at the next summoning of the garrison; and armed with their keen
mincing knives (long, crescentic, heavy implements with a handle at each
end) run a muck from the bowsprit to the taffrail; and if by any devilish-
ness of desperation possible, seize the ship. For himself, he would do this,
he said, whether they joined him or not. That was the last night he should
spend in that den. But the scheme met with no opposition on the part of
the other two; they swore they were ready for that, or for any other mad
thing, for anything in short but a surrender. And what was more, they
each insisted upon being the first man on deck, when the time to make
the rush should come. But to this their leader as fiercely objected, reserv-
ing that priority for himself; particularly as his two comrades would not
yield, the one to the other, in the matter; and both of them could not be

9. The stairs to the officers' cabin. *Hands:* crewmen.
1. Doorway into a storage space. *Forecastle scuttle:* the deck opening to a ladder down into the
   crew's quarters.
2. Quasi-biblical phraseology, as in the hymn in ch. 9.

first, for the ladder would but admit one man at a time. And here, gentlemen, the foul play of these miscreants must come out.

"Upon hearing the frantic project of their leader, each in his own separate soul had suddenly lighted, it would seem, upon the same piece of treachery, namely: to be foremost in breaking out, in order to be the first of the three, though the last of the ten, to surrender; and thereby secure whatever small chance of pardon such conduct might merit. But when Steelkilt made known his determination still to lead them to the last, they in some way, by some subtle chemistry of villany, mixed their before secret treacheries together; and when their leader fell into a doze, verbally opened their souls to each other in three sentences; and bound the sleeper with cords, and gagged him with cords; and shrieked out for the Captain at midnight.

"Thinking murder at hand, and smelling in the dark for the blood, he and all his armed mates and harpooneers rushed for the forecastle. In a few minutes the scuttle was opened, and, bound hand and foot, the still struggling ringleader was shoved up into the air by his perfidious allies, who at once claimed the honor of securing a man who had been fully ripe for murder. But all three were collared, and dragged along the deck like dead cattle; and, side by side, were seized up[3] into the mizen rigging, like three quarters of meat, and there they hung till morning. 'Damn ye,' cried the Captain, pacing to and fro before them, 'the vultures would not touch ye, ye villains!'

"At sunrise he summoned all hands; and separating those who had rebelled from those who had taken no part in the mutiny, he told the former that he had a good mind to flog them all round—thought, upon the whole, he would do so—he ought to—justice demanded it; but for the present, considering their timely surrender, he would let them go with a reprimand, which he accordingly administered in the vernacular.

"'But as for you, ye carrion rogues,' turning to the three men in the rigging—'for you, I mean to mince ye up for the try-pots;'[4] and, seizing a rope, he applied it with all his might to the backs of the two traitors, till they yelled no more, but lifelessly hung their heads sideways, as the two crucified thieves are drawn.[5]

"'My wrist is sprained with ye!' he cried, at last; 'but there is still rope enough left for you, my fine bantam,[6] that wouldn't give up. Take that gag from his mouth, and let us hear what he can say for himself.'

"For a moment the exhausted mutineer made a tremulous motion of his cramped jaws, and then painfully twisting round his head, said in a sort of hiss, 'What I say is this—and mind it well—if you flog me, I murder you!'

"'Say ye so? then see how ye frighten me'—and the Captain drew off with the rope to strike.

"'Best not,' hissed the Lakeman.

3. Lashed up, tied up.
4. A masonry stove approximately ten feet wide by eight feet deep by five feet high, attached to the main deck of a whaler. In it, blubber is heated and rendered into oil; depicted in chs. 95 and 96.
5. Matthew 27.38: "Then were there two thieves crucified with him, one on the right hand, and another on the left."
6. Fighting cock of a diminutive breed; here, an insult, in view of Steelkilt's stature.

"'But I must,'—and the rope was once more drawn back for the stroke.

"Steelkilt here hissed out something, inaudible to all but the Captain; who, to the amazement of all hands, started back, paced the deck rapidly two or three times, and then suddenly throwing down his rope, said, 'I won't do it—let him go—cut him down: d'ye hear?'

"But as the junior mates were hurrying to execute the order, a pale man, with a bandaged head, arrested them—Radney the chief mate. Ever since the blow, he had lain in his berth; but that morning, hearing the tumult on the deck, he had crept out, and thus far had watched the whole scene. Such was the state of his mouth, that he could hardly speak; but mumbling something about *his* being willing and able to do what the captain dared not attempt, he snatched the rope and advanced to his pinioned foe.

"'You are a coward!' hissed the Lakeman.

"'So I am, but take that.' The mate was in the very act of striking, when another hiss stayed his uplifted arm. He paused: and then pausing no more, made good his word, spite of Steelkilt's threat, whatever that might have been. The three men were then cut down, all hands were turned to, and, sullenly worked by the moody seamen, the iron pumps clanged as before.

"Just after dark that day, when one watch had retired below, a clamor was heard in the forecastle; and the two trembling traitors running up, besieged the cabin door, saying they durst not consort with the crew. Entreaties, cuffs, and kicks could not drive them back, so at their own instance they were put down in the ship's run for salvation. Still, no sign of mutiny reappeared among the rest. On the contrary, it seemed, that mainly at Steelkilt's instigation, they had resolved to maintain the strictest peacefulness, obey all orders to the last, and, when the ship reached port, desert her in a body. But in order to insure the speediest end to the voyage, they all agreed to another thing—namely, not to sing out for whales, in case any should be discovered. For, spite of her leak, and spite of all her other perils, the Town-Ho still maintained her mast-heads, and her captain was just as willing to lower for a fish that moment, as on the day his craft first struck the cruising ground; and Radney the mate was quite as ready to change his berth for a boat, and with his bandaged mouth seek to gag in death the vital jaw of the whale.

"But though the Lakeman had induced the seamen to adopt this sort of passiveness in their conduct, he kept his own counsel (at least till all was over) concerning his own proper and private revenge upon the man who had stung him in the ventricles of his heart. He was in Radney the chief mate's watch; and as if the infatuated man sought to run more than half way to meet his doom, after the scene at the rigging, he insisted, against the express counsel of the captain, upon resuming the head of his watch at night. Upon this, and one or two other circumstances, Steelkilt systematically built the plan of his revenge.

"During the night, Radney had an unseamanlike way of sitting on the bulwarks of the quarter-deck, and leaning his arm upon the gunwale of the boat which was hoisted up there, a little above the ship's side. In this attitude, it was well known, he sometimes dozed. There was a considerable vacancy between the boat and the ship, and down beneath this was the sea. Steelkilt calculated his time, and found that his next trick at the helm would come round at two o'clock, in the morning of the third day from that in which he had been betrayed. At his leisure, he employed the interval in braiding something very carefully in his watches below.

"'What are you making there?' said a shipmate.

"'What do you think? what does it look like?'

"'Like a lanyard[7] for your bag; but it's an odd one, seems to me.'

"'Yes, rather oddish,' said the Lakeman, holding it at arm's length before him; 'but I think it will answer. Shipmate, I haven't enough twine,—have you any?'

"But there was none in the forecastle.

"'Then I must get some from old Rad;' and he rose to go aft.

"'You don't mean to go a begging to *him*!' said a sailor.

"'Why not? Do you think he won't do me a turn, when it's to help himself in the end, shipmate?' and going to the mate, he looked at him quietly, and asked him for some twine to mend his hammock. It was given him—neither twine nor lanyard were seen again; but the next night an iron ball, closely netted, partly rolled from the pocket of the Lakeman's monkey jacket, as he was tucking the coat into his hammock for a pillow. Twenty-four hours after, his trick at the silent helm—nigh to the man who was apt to doze over the grave always ready dug to the seaman's hand—that fatal hour was then to come; and in the fore-ordaining soul of Steelkilt, the mate was already stark and stretched as a corpse, with his forehead crushed in.

"But, gentlemen, a fool saved the would-be murderer from the bloody deed he had planned. Yet complete revenge he had, and without being the avenger. For by a mysterious fatality, Heaven itself seemed to step in to take out of his hands into its own the damning thing he would have done.

"It was just between daybreak and sunrise of the morning of the second day, when they were washing down the decks, that a stupid Teneriffe man,[8] drawing water in the main-chains, all at once shouted out, 'There she rolls! there she rolls! Jesu, what a whale!' It was Moby Dick."

"'Moby Dick'!" cried Don Sebastian; "St. Dominic! Sir sailor, but do whales have christenings? Whom call you Moby Dick?"

"A very white, and famous, and most deadly immortal monster, Don;—but that would be too long a story."[9]

"How? how?" cried all the young Spaniards, crowding.

"Nay, Dons, Dons—nay, nay! I cannot rehearse that now. Let me get more into the air, Sirs."

"The chicha! the chicha!" cried Don Pedro; "our vigorous friend looks faint;—fill up his empty glass!"

"No need, gentlemen; one moment, and I proceed.—Now, gentlemen, so suddenly perceiving the snowy whale within fifty yards of the ship—forgetful of the compact among the crew—in the excitement of the moment, the Teneriffe man had instinctively and involuntarily lifted his voice for the monster, though for some little time past it had been plainly beheld from

---

7. Drawstring.
8. Crewman from the largest of the Canary Islands, off Spain.
9. In this gamesomeness about narration, telling the story would amount to Ishmael's telling the whole story of his cruise on the *Pequod* (the memory of which makes him feel faint, "vigorous" a fellow as he is); it would be too long a story for this one night in Lima, but just long enough to satisfy a reader of *Moby-Dick*, later on.

the three sullen mast-heads. All was now a phrensy. 'The White Whale—the White Whale!' was the cry from captain, mates, and harpooneers, who, undeterred by fearful rumors, were all anxious to capture so famous and precious a fish; while the dogged crew eyed askance, and with curses, the appalling beauty of the vast milky mass, that lit up by a horizontal spangling sun, shifted and glistened like a living opal in the blue morning sea. Gentlemen, a strange fatality pervades the whole career of these events, as if verily mapped out before the world itself was charted. The mutineer was the bowsman[1] of the mate, and when fast to a fish, it was his duty to sit next him, while Radney stood up with his lance in the prow, and haul in or slacken the line, at the word of command. Moreover, when the four boats were lowered, the mate's got the start; and none howled more fiercely with delight than did Steelkilt, as he strained at his oar. After a stiff pull, their harpooneer got fast, and, spear in hand, Radney sprang to the bow. He was always a furious man, it seems, in a boat. And now his bandaged cry was, to beach him on the whale's topmost back. Nothing loath, his bowsman hauled him up and up, through a blinding foam that blent two whitenesses together; till of a sudden the boat struck as against a sunken ledge, and keeling over, spilled out the standing mate. That instant, as he fell on the whale's slippery back, the boat righted, and was dashed aside by the swell, while Radney was tossed over into the sea, on the other flank of the whale. He struck out through the spray, and, for an instant, was dimly seen through that veil, wildly seeking to remove himself from the eye of Moby Dick. But the whale rushed round in a sudden maelstrom;[2] seized the swimmer between his jaws; and rearing high up with him, plunged headlong again, and went down.

"Meantime, at the first tap of the boat's bottom, the Lakeman had slackened the line, so as to drop astern from the whirlpool; calmly looking on, he thought his own thoughts. But a sudden, terrific, downward jerking of the boat, quickly brought his knife to the line. He cut it; and the whale was free. But, at some distance, Moby Dick rose again, with some tatters of Radney's red woollen shirt, caught in the teeth that had destroyed him. All four boats gave chase again; but the whale eluded them, and finally wholly disappeared.

"In good time, the Town-Ho reached her port—a savage, solitary place—where no civilized creature resided. There, headed by the Lakeman, all but five or six of the foremast-men deliberately deserted among the palms; eventually, as it turned out, seizing a large double warcanoe of the savages, and setting sail for some other harbor.

"The ship's company being reduced to but a handful, the captain called upon the Islanders to assist him in the laborious business of heaving down the ship to stop the leak. But to such unresting vigilance over their dangerous allies was this small band of whites necessitated, both by night and by day, and so extreme was the hard work they underwent, that upon the vessel being ready again for sea, they were in such a weakened condition that the captain durst not put off with them in so heavy a vessel. After taking counsel with his officers, he anchored the ship as far off shore as pos-

---

1. Second oarsman from the bow—where Radney had rushed from the stern to lance and kill the harpooned whale.
2. Whirlpool.

sible; loaded and ran out his two cannon from the bows; stacked his muskets on the poop; and warning the Islanders not to approach the ship at their peril, took one man with him, and setting the sail of his best whaleboat, steered straight before the wind for Tahiti, five hundred miles distant, to procure a reinforcement to his crew.

"On the fourth day of the sail, a large canoe was descried, which seemed to have touched at a low isle of corals. He steered away from it; but the savage craft bore down on him; and soon the voice of Steelkilt hailed him to heave to, or he would run him under water. The captain presented a pistol. With one foot on each prow of the yoked war-canoes, the Lakeman laughed him to scorn; assuring him that if the pistol so much as clicked in the lock, he would bury him in bubbles and foam.

"'What do you want of me?' cried the captain.

"'Where are you bound? and for what are you bound?' demanded Steelkilt; 'no lies.'

"'I am bound to Tahiti for more men '

"'Very good. Let me board you a moment—I come in peace.' With that he leaped from the canoe, swam to the boat; and climbing the gunwale, stood face to face with the captain.

"'Cross your arms, sir; throw back your head. Now, repeat after me. "As soon as Steelkilt leaves me, I swear to beach this boat on yonder island, and remain there six days. If I do not, may lightnings strike me!"'

"'A pretty scholar,'[3] laughed the Lakeman. 'Adios, Senor!' and leaping into the sea, he swam back to his comrades.

"Watching the boat till it was fairly beached, and drawn up to the roots of the cocoa-nut trees, Steelkilt made sail again, and in due time arrived at Tahiti, his own place of destination. There, luck befriended him; two ships were about to sail for France, and were providentially in want of precisely that number of men which the sailor headed. They embarked; and so for ever got the start of their former captain, had he been at all minded to work them legal retribution.

"Some ten days after the French ships sailed, the whale-boat arrived, and the captain was forced to enlist some of the more civilized Tahitians, who had been somewhat used to the sea. Chartering a small native schooner, he returned with them to his vessel; and finding all right there, again resumed his cruisings.

"Where Steelkilt now is, gentlemen, none know; but upon the island of Nantucket, the widow of Radney still turns to the sea which refuses to give up its dead; still in dreams sees the awful white whale that destroyed him." * * * *

"Are you through?" said Don Sebastian, quietly.

"I am, Don."

"Then I entreat you, tell me if to the best of your own convictions, this your story is in substance really true? It is so passing wonderful! Did you get it from an unquestionable source? Bear with me if I seem to press."

"Also bear with all of us, sir sailor; for we all join in Don Sebastian's suit," cried the company, with exceeding interest.

---

3. Like a good schoolboy ("scholar") in that day of rote learning, the captain has repeated the words dictated to him,

"Is there a copy of the Holy Evangelists[4] in the Golden Inn, gentlemen?"

"Nay," said Don Sebastian; "but I know a worthy priest near by, who will quickly procure one for me. I go for it; but are you well advised? this may grow too serious."

"Will you be so good as to bring the priest also, Don?"

"Though there are no Auto-da-Fés[5] in Lima now," said one of the company to another; "I fear our sailor friend runs risk of the archiepiscopacy. Let us withdraw more out of the moonlight. I see no need of this."

"Excuse me for running after you, Don Sebastian; but may I also beg that you will be particular in procuring the largest sized Evangelists you can."

*　*　*　*　*

"This is the priest, he brings you the Evangelists," said Don Sebastian, gravely, returning with a tall and solemn figure.

"Let me remove my hat. Now, venerable priest, further into the light, and hold the Holy Book before me that I may touch it.

"So help me Heaven, and on my honor, the story I have told ye, gentlemen, is in substance and its great items, true. I know it to be true; it happened on this ball; I trod the ship; I knew the crew; I have seen and talked with Steelkilt[6] since the death of Radney."

Chapter 55

Of the Monstrous Pictures of Whales[1]

I shall ere long paint to you as well as one can without canvas, something like the true form of the whale as he actually appears to the eye of the

---

4. The gospels of Matthew, Mark, Luke, and John, bound together in one volume, on which Ishmael will swear to tell the gospel truth.
5. Ceremonies in which the Inquisition pronounced judgment on heretics before burning them alive. As someone persecuted by reviewers belonging to American Protestant sects, Melville at this time and later saw himself as suffering at the hands of a speech-suppressing modern American Inquisition. By the time he wrote this, Melville had read the article in the *Quarterly Review* (see Sanborn, p. 582, herein) and identified himself with victims in Auto-da-Fe, to whom he later thought of dedicating his satire of American optimism, *The Confidence-Man* (1857).
6. Steelkilt was partly based on Luther Fox, a young man from Rensselaerville, New York (a village named for Melville's mother's ancestors), who was put ashore at Honolulu in irons in 1843, just after Melville arrived there, and with whom Melville had talked at the "calaboose." A naive young man, later appalled at himself, Fox had committed a hotheaded manslaughter because no one had ever taught him that he would not lose his manhood if he backed down after boldly taking his stand (which was simply a declaration that he was going to finish his breakfast before going on duty). Fox struck one blow against the mate of his ship, the *Nassau*, who then uttered a memorable sentence: "Fox has cut my leg off with a mincing knife" (see Parker, 1.251–53). What had been a simple matter of mismanaged masculine pride had become tragic, and the events resonated in Melville's imagination the rest of his life, emerging in the story he was working on when he died, *Billy Budd*.

　　Here, in the minds of the Spanish dons and in the minds of the readers, Ishmael's claim to have talked with Steelkilt clinches the authenticity of the story, hitherto attributed only to sailors of the *Town-Ho* by way of Tashtego. In this story about story-telling, the greatest mystery is why we, sophisticated 21st-century readers of a work of fiction, need the story to be true, just as much as the young Spanish dons in Lima do.
1. Suggested by a passage in *Pseudodoxia Epidemica* (1646) by Sir Thomas Browne. Stuart Frank (1986) reproduces pictures mentioned in this chapter and the next.

whaleman when in his own absolute body the whale is moored alongside the whale-ship so that he can be fairly stepped upon there. It may be worth while, therefore, previously to advert to those curious imaginary portraits of him which even down to the present day confidently challenge the faith of the landsman. It is time to set the world right in this matter, by proving such pictures of the whale all wrong.

It may be that the primal source of all those pictorial delusions will be found among the oldest Hindoo, Egyptian, and Grecian sculptures. For ever since those inventive but unscrupulous times when on the marble panellings of temples, the pedestals of statues, and on shields, medallions, cups, and coins, the dolphin was drawn in scales of chain-armor like Saladin's, and a helmeted head like St. George's;[2] ever since then has something of the same sort of license prevailed, not only in most popular pictures of the whale, but in many scientific presentations of him.

Now, by all odds, the most ancient extant portrait anyways purporting to be the whale's, is to be found in the famous cavern-pagoda of Elephanta, in India. The Brahmins maintain that in the almost endless sculptures of that immemorial pagoda, all the trades and pursuits, every conceivable avocation of man, were prefigured ages before any of them actually came into being. No wonder then, that in some sort our noble profession of whaling should have been there shadowed forth. The Hindoo whale referred to, occurs in a separate department of the wall, depicting the incarnation of Vishnu in the form of leviathan, learnedly known as the Matse Avatar. But though this sculpture is half man and half whale, so as only to give the tail of the latter, yet that small section of him is all wrong.[3] It looks more like the tapering tail of an anaconda, than the broad palms of the true whale's majestic flukes.

But go to the old Galleries, and look now at a great Christian painter's portrait of this fish; for he succeeds no better than the antediluvian Hindoo. It is Guido's picture of Perseus rescuing Andromeda from the sea-monster or whale. Where did Guido get the model of such a strange creature as that? Nor does Hogarth, in painting the same scene in his own "Perseus Descending," make out one whit better. The huge corpulence of that Hogarthian monster undulates on the surface, scarcely drawing one inch of water. It has a sort of howdah on its back, and its distended tusked mouth into which the billows are rolling, might be taken for the Traitors' Gate leading from the Thames by water into the Tower. Then, there are the Prodromus whales of old Scotch Sibbald,[4] and Jonah's whale, as

2. Patron saint of England, 3rd-century legendary slayer of a dragon. *Saladin*: sultan of Egypt and Syria (1174–1193) who fought the Crusaders, as celebrated in chivalric romances and Sir Walter Scott's *The Talisman* (1825), which Melville knew well, as he did almost all of the novels and poems by Scott (1771–1832).
3. Melville sportively puts the "Matse Avatar" in the wrong cavern and alleges that Vishnu was portrayed as a whale with a tail "all wrong," when he was actually portrayed as a fish. There were ornamented rock temples or grottoes in "one major cave and six smaller ones on the island of Elephanta, near Bombay, India, all devoted to Sivaism, the sect of the Hindu religion which worshiped Siva the Destroyer as supreme power rather than Vishnu the Preserver" (Mansfield and Vincent, 613).
4. The Latin word "Prodromus" (Introduction) is in the title *Scotia illustratavise Prodromus historiæ naturalis* (1684) by Robert Sibbald, but the book has no whale pictures; a 1692 book by Sibbald has two plates showing whales. Guido Reni (1575–1642). Melville saw this picture in London in 1849. The picture by William Hogarth (1697–1764) is an illustration in Lewis Theobold's *Perseus and Andromeda* (1730).

depicted in the prints of old Bibles and the cuts of old primers. What shall be said of these? As for the book-binder's whale winding like a vine-stalk round the stock of a descending anchor—as stamped and gilded on the backs and title-pages of many books both old and new—that is a very picturesque but purely fabulous creature, imitated, I take it, from the like figures on antique vases. Though universally denominated a dolphin, I nevertheless call this book-binder's fish an attempt at a whale; because it was so intended when the device was first introduced. It was introduced by an old Italian publisher[5] somewhere about the 15th century, during the Revival of Learning; and in those days, and even down to a comparatively late period, dolphins were popularly supposed to be a species of the Leviathan.

In the vignettes and other embellishments of some ancient books you will at times meet with very curious touches at the whale, where all manner of spouts, jets d'eau, hot springs and cold, Saratoga and Baden-Baden,[6] come bubbling up from his unexhausted brain. In the title-page of the original edition of the "Advancement of Learning"[7] you will find some curious whales.

But quitting all these unprofessional attempts, let us glance at those pictures of leviathan purporting to be sober, scientific delineations, by those who know. In old Harris's collection of voyages there are some plates of whales[8] extracted from a Dutch book of voyages, A. D. 1671, entitled "A Whaling Voyage to Spitzbergen in the ship Jonas in the Whale, Peter Peterson of Friesland, master." In one of those plates the whales, like great rafts of logs, are represented lying among ice-isles, with white bears running over their living backs. In another plate, the prodigious blunder is made of representing the whale with perpendicular flukes.

Then again, there is an imposing quarto, written by one Captain Colnett,[9] a Post Captain in the English navy, entitled "A Voyage round Cape Horn into the South Seas, for the purpose of extending the Spermaceti Whale Fisheries." In this book is an outline purporting to be a "Picture of a Physeter or Spermaceti whale, drawn by scale from one killed on the coast of Mexico, August, 1793, and hoisted on deck." I doubt not the captain had this veracious picture taken for the benefit of his marines.[1] To mention but one thing about it, let me say that it has an eye which applied, according to the accompanying scale, to a full grown sperm whale, would make the eye of that whale a bow-window some five feet long. Ah, my gallant captain, why did ye not give us Jonah looking out of that eye!

Nor are the most conscientious compilations of Natural History for the benefit of the young and tender, free from the same heinousness of mistake. Look at that popular work "Goldsmith's Animated Nature." In the abridged London edition of 1807, there are plates of an alleged "whale" and a "narwhale." I do not wish to seem inelegant, but this unsightly whale

---

5. Aldus Manutius (1450–1515), who founded his printing house in Venice in 1595.
6. Resorts in upstate New York and Germany, respectively.
7. A 1605 book by Sir Francis Bacon (1561–1626).
8. In John Harris's *Navigantium atque Itinerarium Bibliotheca* (1705), facing I, 617, and 629.
9. James Colnett's *Voyage* (1798).
1. These soldiers, assigned to keep order on shipboard, were treated by resentful sailors as credulous in maritime matters, as in the expression, "tell that to the marines," meaning that they will believe anything.

looks much like an amputated sow; and, as for the narwhale, one glimpse at it is enough to amaze one, that in this nineteenth century such a hippogriff[2] could be palmed for genuine upon any intelligent public of schoolboys.

Then, again, in 1825, Bernard Germain, Count de Lacépède, a great naturalist, published a scientific systemized whale book, wherein are several pictures of the different species of the Leviathan. All these are not only incorrect, but the picture of the Mysticetus or Greenland whale (that is to say, the Right whale), even Scoresby, a long experienced man as touching that species, declares not to have its counterpart in nature.

But the placing of the cap-sheaf to all this blundering business was reserved for the scientific Frederick Cuvier, brother to the famous Baron. In 1836, he published a Natural History of Whales, in which he gives what he calls a picture of the Sperm Whale. Before showing that picture to any Nantucketer, you had best provide for your summary retreat from Nantucket. In a word, Frederick Cuvier's Sperm Whale is not a Sperm Whale, but a squash. Of course, he never had the benefit of a whaling voyage (such men seldom have), but whence he derived that picture, who can tell? Perhaps he got it as his scientific predecessor in the same field, Desmarest,[3] got one of his authentic abortions; that is, from a Chinese drawing. And what sort of lively lads with the pencil those Chinese are, many queer cups and saucers inform us.

As for the sign-painters' whales seen in the streets hanging over the shops of oil-dealers, what shall be said of them? They are generally Richard III. whales, with dromedary humps,[4] and very savage; breakfasting on three or four sailor tarts, that is whaleboats full of mariners: their deformities floundering in seas of blood and blue paint.

But these manifold mistakes in depicting the whale are not so very surprising after all. Consider! Most of the scientific drawings have been taken from the stranded fish; and these are about as correct as a drawing of a wrecked ship, with broken back, would correctly represent the noble animal itself in all its undashed pride of hull and spars. Though elephants have stood for their full-lengths, the living Leviathan has never yet fairly floated himself for his portrait. The living whale, in his full majesty and significance, is only to be seen at sea in unfathomable waters; and afloat the vast bulk of him is out of sight, like a launched line-of-battle ship;[5] and out of that element it is a thing eternally impossible for mortal man to hoist him bodily into the air, so as to preserve all his mighty swells and undulations. And, not to speak of the highly presumable difference of contour between a young sucking whale and a full-grown Platonian[6] Leviathan; yet, even in the case of one of those young sucking whales hoisted to a ship's deck, such is then the outlandish, eel-like, limbered, varying shape of him, that his precise expression the devil himself could not catch.

2. Legendary animal that is half-horse, half-griffin (and a griffin is part eagle, part lion). *History of the Earth and Animated Nature* (1774) was a popular work by the Irish author Oliver Goldsmith (1730–1774).
3. Mansfield and Vincent (748) point out that the references to Lacépède, Frederick Cuvier, and Desmarest are secondhand, mainly from Beale, including the notions of Chinese drawings. Melville took from Scoresby (1820) the citation of Lacépède's 1804 (not 1825) work.
4. Like the wicked king in Shakespeare's *Richard III*.
5. Largest battleships, carrying the most guns, for firing broadsides at enemy ships when drawn up at sea in line with others.
6. Ideal; in terms of Plato's philosophy, an actual whale embodying the Idea of the Whale.

But it may be fancied, that from the naked skeleton of the stranded whale, accurate hints may be derived touching his true form. Not at all. For it is one of the more curious things about this Leviathan, that his skeleton gives very little idea of his general shape. Though Jeremy Bentham's skeleton,[7] which hangs for candelabra in the library of one of his executors, correctly conveys the idea of a burly-browed utilitarian old gentleman, with all Jeremy's other leading personal characteristics; yet nothing of this kind could be inferred from any leviathan's articulated bones. In fact, as the great Hunter[8] says, the mere skeleton of the whale bears the same relation to the fully invested and padded animal as the insect does to the chrysalis that so roundingly envelopes it. This peculiarity is strikingly evinced in the head, as in some part of this book will be incidentally shown. It is also very curiously displayed in the side fin, the bones of which almost exactly answer to the bones of the human hand, minus only the thumb. This fin has four regular bone-fingers, the index, middle, ring, and little finger. But all these are permanently lodged in their fleshy covering, as the human fingers in an artificial covering. "However recklessly the whale may sometimes serve us," said humorous Stubb one day, "he can never be truly said to handle us without mittens."

For all these reasons, then, any way you may look at it, you must needs conclude that the great Leviathan is that one creature in the world which must remain unpainted to the last. True, one portrait may hit the mark much nearer than another, but none can hit it with any very considerable degree of exactness. So there is no earthly way of finding out precisely what the whale really looks like. And the only mode in which you can derive even a tolerable idea of his living contour, is by going a whaling yourself; but by so doing, you run no small risk of being eternally stove and sunk by him. Wherefore, it seems to me you had best not be too fastidious in your curiosity touching this Leviathan.

Chapter 56

Of the Less Erroneous Pictures of Whales, and the True Pictures of Whaling Scenes

In connexion with the monstrous pictures of whales, I am strongly tempted here to enter upon those still more monstrous stories of them which are to be found in certain books, both ancient and modern, especially in Pliny, Purchas, Hackluyt, Harris, Cuvier,[1] &c. But I pass that matter by.

---

7. This Utilitarian English philosopher (1748–1832) left his clothed skeleton (with a wax head) to the University of London, where it was exhibited, but not used as a candle holder.
8. Mansfield and Vincent (748) show that Melville had read the Scottish anatomist John Hunter (1728–1793) only as quoted by Beale. Melville copied into Frederick D. Bennett's *Narrative of a Whaling Voyage* (1840) a remarkable tribute he found in *Table Talk* (1824) by William Hazlitt (1778–1830): "John Hunter was a great man. He would set about cutting up the carcass of a whale, with the same greatness of gusto, that Michael Angelo would have hewn a block of marble."
1. Mansfield and Vincent (748–49) point out that Melville found all this discussion in "the ever-reliable Beale."

I know of only four published outlines of the great Sperm Whale; Colnett's, Huggins's, Frederick Cuvier's, and Beale's. In the previous chapter
Colnett and Cuvier have been referred to. Huggins's is far better than
theirs; but, by great odds, Beale's is the best. All Beale's drawings of this
whale are good, excepting the middle figure in the picture of three whales
in various attitudes, capping his second chapter. His frontispiece, boats
attacking Sperm Whales, though no doubt calculated to excite the civil
scepticism of some parlor men, is admirably correct and life-like in its
general effect. Some of the Sperm Whale drawings in J. Ross Browne[2] are
pretty correct in contour; but they are wretchedly engraved. That is not
his fault though.

Of the Right Whale, the best outline pictures are in Scoresby; but they
are drawn on too small a scale to convey a desirable impression. He has
but one picture of whaling scenes, and this is a sad deficiency, because it
is by such pictures only, when at all well done, that you can derive anything like a truthful idea of the living whale as seen by his living hunters.

But, taken for all in all, by far the finest, though in some details not the
most correct, presentations of whales and whaling scenes to be anywhere
found, are two large French engravings, well executed, and taken from
paintings by one Garnery.[3] Respectively, they represent attacks on the
Sperm and Right Whale. In the first engraving a noble Sperm Whale is
depicted in full majesty of might, just risen beneath the boat from the profundities of the ocean, and bearing high in the air upon his back the terrific wreck of the stoven planks. The prow of the boat is partially unbroken, and is drawn just balancing upon the monster's spine; and standing
in that prow, for that one single incomputable flash of time, you behold
an oarsman, half shrouded by the incensed boiling spout of the whale,
and in the act of leaping, as if from a precipice. The action of the whole
thing is wonderfully good and true. The half-emptied line-tub floats on
the whitened sea; the wooden poles of the spilled harpoons obliquely bob
in it; the heads of the swimming crew are scattered about the whale in
contrasting expressions of affright; while in the black stormy distance the
ship is bearing down upon the scene. Serious fault might be found with
the anatomical details of this whale, but let that pass; since, for the life of
me, I could not draw so good a one.

In the second engraving, the boat is in the act of drawing alongside the
barnacled flank of a large running Right Whale, that rolls his black weedy
bulk in the sea like some mossy rock-slide from the Patagonian cliffs.[4] His
jets are erect, full, and black like soot; so that from so abounding a smoke
in the chimney, you would think there must be a brave supper cooking in
the great bowels below. Sea fowls are pecking at the small crabs, shell-
fish, and other sea candies and maccaroni, which the Right Whale sometimes carries on his pestilent back. And all the while the thick-lipped
leviathan is rushing through the deep, leaving tons of tumultuous white
curds in his wake, and causing the slight boat to rock in the swells like a
skiff caught nigh the paddle-wheels of an ocean steamer. Thus, the fore-

2. See Melville's 1847 review on p. 511, herein.
3. French marine painter, Ambrose Louis Garneray (spelled Garnerey in one of the two engravings
   Melville praises).
4. At the southern tip of South America.

ground is all raging commotion; but behind, in admirable artistic contrast, is the glassy level of a sea becalmed, the drooping unstarched sails of the powerless ship, and the inert mass of a dead whale, a conquered fortress, with the flag of capture[5] lazily hanging from the whale-pole inserted into his spout-hole.

Who Garnery the painter is, or was, I know not. But my life for it he was either practically conversant with his subject, or else marvellously tutored by some experienced whaleman. The French are the lads for painting action. Go and gaze upon all the paintings of Europe, and where will you find such a gallery of living and breathing commotion on canvas, as in that triumphal hall at Versailles;[6] where the beholder fights his way, pell-mell, through the consecutive great battles of France; where every sword seems a flash of the Northern Lights, and the successive armed kings and Emperors dash by, like a charge of crowned centaurs? Not wholly unworthy of a place in that gallery, are these sea battle-pieces of Garnery.

The natural aptitude of the French for seizing the picturesqueness of things seems to be peculiarly evinced in what paintings and engravings they have of their whaling scenes. With not one tenth of England's experience in the fishery, and not the thousandth part of that of the Americans, they have nevertheless furnished both nations with the only finished sketches at all capable of conveying the real spirit of the whale hunt. For the most part, the English and American whale draughtsmen seem entirely content with presenting the mechanical outline of things, such as the vacant profile of the whale; which, so far as picturesqueness of effect is concerned, is about tantamount to sketching the profile of a pyramid. Even Scoresby, the justly renowned Right whaleman, after giving us a stiff full length of the Greenland whale, and three or four delicate miniatures of narwhales and porpoises, treats us to a series of classical engravings of boat hooks, chopping knives, and grapnels; and with the microscopic diligence of a Leuwenhoeck[7] submits to the inspection of a shivering world ninety-six fac-similes of magnified Arctic snow crystals. I mean no disparagement to the excellent voyager (I honor him for a veteran), but in so important a matter it was certainly an oversight not to have procured for every crystal a sworn affidavit taken before a Greenland Justice of the Peace.

In addition to those fine engravings from Garnery, there are two other French engravings worthy of note, by some one who subscribes himself "H. Durand."[8] One of them, though not precisely adapted to our present purpose, nevertheless deserves mention on other accounts. It is a quiet noon-scene among the isles of the Pacific; a French whaler anchored, inshore, in a calm, and lazily taking water on board; the loosened sails of

---

5. Pennon (little banner) atop the waif-pole, to keep the whale visible. *Unstarched*: figurative—not stiffened by force of the wind.

6. In 1849 Melville saw the gigantic paintings in the Hall of Battles at Versailles. One of the enormous paintings, General Cornwallis's surrender at Yorktown, provoked hilarity among American viewers, including Melville's friend Henry T. Tuckerman (1813–1871), because George Washington is depicted as a casually involved bystander while the true victor is the French General Rochambeau. Melville would have looked in vain in the painting for his grandfather, General Peter Gansevoort (1749–1812), who was also present at the surrender.

7. Variant spelling for Anton van Leeuwenhoek (1632–1723), Dutch pioneer maker of microscopes.

8. Stuart Frank (1986, 80–83) identifies this artist as Henri Durand-Brager (1814–1879) and reproduces these "two other French engravings worthy of note."

the ship, and the long leaves of the palms in the background, both drooping together in the breezeless air. The effect is very fine, when considered
with reference to its presenting the hardy fishermen under one of their
few aspects of oriental repose. The other engraving is quite a different
affair: the ship hove-to upon the open sea, and in the very heart of the
Leviathanic life, with a Right Whale alongside; the vessel (in the act of
cutting-in) hove over to the monster as if to a quay; and a boat, hurriedly
pushing off from this scene of activity, is about giving chase to whales in
the distance. The harpoons and lances lie levelled for use; three oarsmen
are just setting the mast in its hole; while from a sudden roll of the sea,
the little craft stands half-erect out of the water, like a rearing horse. From
the ship, the smoke of the torments of the boiling whale is going up like
the smoke over a village of smithies;[9] and to windward, a black cloud, rising up with earnest of squalls and rains, seems to quicken the activity of
the excited seamen.

Chapter 57

Of Whales in Paint; in Teeth; in Wood; in Sheet-Iron; in Stone; in Mountains; in Stars

On Tower-hill, as you go down to the London docks, you may have seen
a crippled beggar (or *kedger*, as the sailors say) holding a painted board
before him, representing the tragic scene in which he lost his leg. There
are three whales and three boats; and one of the boats (presumed to contain the missing leg in all its original integrity) is being crunched by the
jaws of the foremost whale. Any time these ten years, they tell me, has
that man held up that picture, and exhibited that stump to an incredulous
world. But the time of his justification has now come. His three whales
are as good whales as were ever published in Wapping,[1] at any rate; and
his stump as unquestionable a stump as any you will find in the western
clearings. But, though for ever mounted on that stump, never a stump-
speech does the poor whaleman make; but, with downcast eyes, stands
ruefully contemplating his own amputation.

Throughout the Pacific, and also in Nantucket, and New Bedford, and
Sag Harbor, you will come across lively sketches of whales and whaling-
scenes, graven by the fishermen themselves on Sperm Whale-teeth, or
ladies' busks[2] wrought out of the Right Whale-bone, and other like
skrimshander articles, as the whalemen call the numerous little ingenious
contrivances they elaborately carve out of the rough material, in their
hours of ocean leisure. Some of them have little boxes of dentistical-look-
ing implements, specially intended for the skrimshandering business. But,
in general, they toil with their jack-knives alone; and, with that almost
omnipotent tool of the sailor, they will turn you out anything you please,
in the way of a mariner's fancy.

9. A village with many blacksmith shops (instead of the usual one or two for any village).
1. An area of docks and slums, not of publishing, to the east of Tower-hill, near the Tower of
London.
2. Corsets.

Long exile from Christendom and civilization inevitably restores a man
to that condition in which God placed him, *i.e.* what is called savagery.
Your true whale-hunter is as much a savage as an Iroquois. I myself am a
savage, owning no allegiance but to the King of the Cannibals; and ready
at any moment to rebel against him.

Now, one of the peculiar characteristics of the savage in his domestic
hours, is his wonderful patience of industry. An ancient Hawaiian war-
club or spear-paddle, in its full multiplicity and elaboration of carving, is
as great a trophy of human perseverance as a Latin lexicon. For, with but
a bit of broken sea-shell or a shark's tooth, that miraculous intricacy of
wooden net-work has been achieved; and it has cost steady years of steady
application.

As with the Hawaiian savage, so with the white sailor-savage. With the
same marvellous patience, and with the same single shark's tooth, of his
one poor jack-knife, he will carve you a bit of bone sculpture, not quite as
workmanlike, but as close packed in its maziness of design, as the Greek
savage, Achilles's shield; and full of barbaric spirit and suggestiveness, as
the prints of that fine old Dutch savage, Albert Durer.[3]

Wooden whales, or whales cut in profile out of the small dark slabs of the
noble South Sea war-wood, are frequently met with in the forecastles of
American whalers. Some of them are done with much accuracy.

At some old gable-roofed country houses you will see brass whales hung
by the tail for knockers to the road-side door. When the porter is sleepy,
the anvil-headed whale would be best. But these knocking whales are seldom remarkable as faithful essays. On the spires of some old-fashioned
churches you will see sheet-iron whales placed there for weather-cocks;
but they are so elevated, and besides that are to all intents and purposes
so labelled with *"Hands off!"* you cannot examine them closely enough to
decide upon their merit.

In bony, ribby regions of the earth, where at the base of high broken
cliffs masses of rock lie strewn in fantastic groupings upon the plain, you
will often discover images as of the petrified forms of the Leviathan partly
merged in grass, which of a windy day breaks against them in a surf of
green surges.

Then, again, in mountainous countries where the traveller is continually girdled by amphitheatrical heights; here and there from some lucky
point of view you will catch passing glimpses of the profiles of whales
defined along the undulating ridges. But you must be a thorough whaleman, to see these sights; and not only that, but if you wish to return to
such a sight again, you must be sure and take the exact intersecting latitude and longitude of your first stand-point, else—so chance-like are such
observations of the hills—your precise, previous stand-point would
require a laborious re-discovery; like the Solomon islands, which still
remain incognita, though once high-ruffed Mendanna trod them and old
Figueroa[4] chronicled them.

---

3. Albrecht Dürer (1471–1528), painter and wood engraver. *Dutch*: colloquial for German
(Deutsch). Homer's *Iliad*, book 18, describes the Greek hero Achilles' shield.
4. Alvaro de Mendaña (1541–1595) discovered the Solomon Islands in 1568, but they were not
found again for two centuries. Christóbal Suarez de Figueroa chronicled de Mendaña's *Voyage*
(1613).

Nor when expandingly lifted by your subject, can you fail to trace out great whales in the starry heavens, and boats in pursuit of them; as when long filled with thoughts of war the Eastern nations saw armies locked in battle among the clouds. Thus at the North have I chased Leviathan[5] round and round the Pole with the revolutions of the bright points that first defined him to me. And beneath the effulgent Antarctic skies I have boarded the Argo-Navis, and joined the chase against the starry Cetus far beyond the utmost stretch of Hydrus and the Flying Fish.[6]

With a frigate's anchors for my bridle-bitts and fasces of harpoons for spurs, would I could mount that whale and leap the topmost skies, to see whether the fabled heavens with all their countless tents really lie encamped beyond my mortal sight!

Chapter 58

Brit

Steering north-eastward from the Crozetts, we fell in with vast meadows of brit,[1] the minute, yellow substance, upon which the Right Whale largely feeds. For leagues and leagues it undulated round us, so that we seemed to be sailing through boundless fields of ripe and golden wheat.

On the second day, numbers of Right Whales were seen, who, secure from the attack of a Sperm Whaler like the Pequod, with open jaws sluggishly swam through the brit, which, adhering to the fringing fibres of that wondrous Venetian blind in their mouths, was in that manner separated from the water that escaped at the lip.

As morning mowers, who side by side slowly and seethingly advance their scythes through the long wet grass of marshy meads; even so these monsters swam, making a strange, grassy, cutting sound; and leaving behind them endless swaths of blue upon the yellow sea.[2]

But it was only the sound they made as they parted the brit which at all reminded one of mowers. Seen from the mast-heads, especially when they paused and were stationary for a while, their vast black forms looked more like lifeless masses of rock than anything else. And as in the great hunting countries of India, the stranger at a distance will sometimes pass on the plains recumbent elephants without knowing them to be such, taking them for bare, blackened elevations of the soil; even so, often, with him, who for the first time beholds this species of the leviathans of the sea. And even when recognised at last, their immense magnitude renders it very hard really to believe that such bulky masses of overgrowth can possibly be instinct, in all parts, with the same sort of life that lives in a dog or a horse.

5. Ishmael imagines riding in the Big Dipper ("the bright points") as it circles the North Pole, in pursuit of the sperm whale.
6. Southern constellations: Argo (the Ship), Cetus (the Whale), Hydrus (the Water Snake) and Pisces (the Flying Fish).
1. Composed of tiny crustaceans.
2. That part of the sea known among whalemen as the "Brazil Banks" does not bear that name as the Banks of Newfoundland do, because of there being shallows and soundings there, but because of this remarkable meadow-like appearance, caused by the vast drifts of brit continually floating in those latitudes, where the Right Whale is often chased [Melville's note].

Indeed, in other respects, you can hardly regard any creatures of the deep with the same feelings that you do those of the shore. For though some old naturalists have maintained that all creatures of the land are of their kind[3] in the sea; and though taking a broad general view of the thing, this may very well be; yet coming to specialities, where, for example, does the ocean furnish any fish that in disposition answers to the sagacious kindness of the dog? The accursed shark alone can in any generic respect be said to bear comparative analogy to him.

But though, to landsmen in general, the native inhabitants of the seas have ever been regarded with emotions unspeakably unsocial and repelling; though we know the sea to be an everlasting terra incognita,[4] so that Columbus sailed over numberless unknown worlds to discover his one superficial western one; though, by vast odds, the most terrific of all mortal disasters have immemorially and indiscriminately befallen tens and hundreds of thousands of those who have gone upon the waters; though but a moment's consideration will teach, that however baby man may brag of his science and skill, and however much, in a flattering future, that science and skill may augment; yet for ever and for ever, to the crack of doom, the sea will insult and murder him, and pulverize the stateliest, stiffest frigate he can make; nevertheless, by the continual repetition of these very impressions, man has lost that sense of the full awfulness of the sea which aboriginally belongs to it.

The first boat[5] we read of, floated on an ocean, that with Portuguese vengeance had whelmed a whole world without leaving so much as a widow. That same ocean rolls now; that same ocean destroyed the wrecked ships of last year. Yea, foolish mortals, Noah's flood is not yet subsided; two thirds of the fair world it yet covers.

Wherein differ the sea and the land, that a miracle upon one is not a miracle upon the other? Preternatural terrors rested upon the Hebrews, when under the feet of Korah[6] and his company the live ground opened and swallowed them up for ever; yet not a modern sun ever sets, but in precisely the same manner the live sea swallows up ships and crews.

But not only is the sea such a foe to man who is an alien to it, but it is also a fiend to its own offspring; worse than the Persian host[7] who murdered his own guests; sparing not the creatures which itself hath spawned. Like a savage tigress that tossing in the jungle overlays her own cubs, so the sea dashes even the mightiest whales against the rocks, and leaves them there side by side with the split wrecks of ships. No mercy, no power but its own controls it. Panting and snorting like a mad battle steed that has lost its rider, the masterless ocean overruns the globe.

---

3. Have counterparts.

4. Unknown land (Latin).

5. Noah's ark, in the flood that "whelmed a world" (Genesis 6–7), as the great 1755 earthquake destroyed Lisbon, Portugal. In the Protestant English-speaking world, the Spanish and Portuguese were associated with ruthless vengeance.

6. Numbers 16.32–33: "And the earth opened her mouth, and swallowed them up, and their houses, and all the men that appertained unto Korah, and all their goods. They, and all that appertained to them, went down alive into the pit."

7. No such Persian has been identified, but Melville repeatedly referred to this specific act of treachery, attributed (in a complicated ironic narration) to an American Indian, Mocmohoc, and the Italian Cesare Borgia (1476–1507) in *The Confidence-Man* (ch. 26) and to Borgia again (in the poem "At the Hostelry").

Consider the subtleness of the sea; how its most dreaded creatures glide under water, unapparent for the most part, and treacherously hidden beneath the loveliest tints of azure. Consider also the devilish brilliance and beauty of many of its most remorseless tribes, as the dainty embellished shape of many species of sharks. Consider, once more, the universal cannibalism of the sea; all whose creatures prey upon each other, carrying on eternal war since the world began.

Consider all this; and then turn to this green, gentle, and most docile earth; consider them both, the sea and the land; and do you not find a strange analogy to something in yourself? For as this appalling ocean surrounds the verdant land, so in the soul of man there lies one insular Tahiti,[8] full of peace and joy, but encompassed by all the horrors of the half known life. God keep thee! Push not off from that isle, thou canst never return!

Chapter 59

Squid[1]

Slowly wading through the meadows of brit, the Pequod still held on her way north-eastward towards the island of Java; a gentle air impelling her keel, so that in the surrounding serenity her three tall tapering masts mildly waved to that languid breeze, as three mild palms on a plain. And still, at wide intervals in the silvery night, the lonely, alluring jet would be seen.

But one transparent blue morning, when a stillness almost preternatural spread over the sea, however unattended with any stagnant calm; when the long burnished sun-glade on the waters seemed a golden finger laid across them, enjoining some secresy; when the slippered waves whispered together as they softly ran on; in this profound hush of the visible sphere a strange spectre was seen by Daggoo from the main-mast-head.

In the distance, a great white mass lazily rose, and rising higher and higher, and disentangling itself from the azure, at last gleamed before our prow like a snow-slide, new slid from the hills. Thus glistening for a moment, as slowly it subsided,[2] and sank. Then once more arose, and silently gleamed. It seemed not a whale; and yet is this Moby Dick? thought Daggoo. Again the phantom went down, but on re-appearing once more, with a stiletto-like cry that started every man from his nod, the negro yelled out— "There! there again! there she breaches! right ahead! The White Whale, the White Whale!"

Upon this, the seamen rushed to the yard-arms, as in swarming-time the bees rush to the boughs. Bare-headed in the sultry sun, Ahab stood on the bowsprit, and with one hand pushed far behind in readiness to wave his orders to the helmsman, cast his eager glance in the direction indicated aloft by the outstretched motionless arm of Daggoo.

8. South Sea island, still like Paradise when Melville spent weeks there as prisoner and beachcomber in 1842 (see *Omoo*, 1847).
1. Mansfield and Vincent (752–53) point out Melville's use in this chapter of Beale (1839), Bennett (1840), and Francis Allyn Olmsted, *Incidents of a Whaling Voyage* (New York, 1841).
2. That is, it subsided as slowly as it had risen.

Whether the flitting attendance of the one still and solitary jet had gradually worked upon Ahab, so that he was now prepared to connect the ideas of mildness and repose with the first sight of the particular whale he pursued; however this was, or whether his eagerness betrayed him; whichever way it might have been, no sooner did he distinctly perceived the white mass, than with a quick intensity he instantly gave orders for lowering.

The four boats were soon on the water; Ahab's in advance, and all swiftly pulling towards their prey. Soon it went down, and while, with oars suspended, we were awaiting its reappearance, lo! in the same spot where it sank, once more it slowly rose. Almost forgetting for the moment all thoughts of Moby Dick, we now gazed at the most wondrous phenomenon which the secret seas have hitherto revealed to mankind. A vast pulpy mass, furlongs in length and breadth, of a glancing cream-color, lay floating on the water, innumerable long arms radiating from its centre, and curling and twisting like a nest of anacondas,[3] as if blindly to clutch at any hapless object within reach. No perceptible face or front did it have; no conceivable token of either sensation or instinct; but undulated there on the billows, an unearthly, formless, chance-like apparition of life.

As with a low sucking sound it slowly disappeared again, Starbuck still gazing at the agitated waters where it had sunk, with a wild voice exclaimed—"Almost rather had I seen Moby Dick and fought him, than to have seen thee, thou white ghost!"

"What was it, Sir?" said Flask.

"The great live squid, which, they say, few whale-ships ever beheld, and returned to their ports to tell of it."

But Ahab said nothing; turning his boat, he sailed back to the vessel; the rest as silently following.

Whatever superstitions the sperm whalemen in general have connected with the sight of this object, certain it is, that a glimpse of it being so very unusual, that circumstance has gone far to invest it with portentousness. So rarely is it beheld, that though one and all of them declare it to be the largest animated thing in the ocean, yet very few of them have any but the most vague ideas concerning its true nature and form; notwithstanding, they believe it to furnish to the sperm whale his only food. For though other species of whales find their food above water, and may be seen by man in the act of feeding, the spermaceti whale obtains his whole food in unknown zones below the surface; and only by inference is it that any one can tell of what, precisely, that food consists. At times, when closely pursued, he will disgorge what are supposed to be the detached arms of the squid; some of them thus exhibited exceeding twenty and thirty feet in length. They fancy that the monster to which these arms belonged ordinarily clings by them to the bed of the ocean; and that the sperm whale, unlike other species, is supplied with teeth in order to attack and tear it.

There seems some ground to imagine that the great Kraken[4] of Bishop Pontoppidan may ultimately resolve itself into Squid. The manner in which the Bishop describes it, as alternately rising and sinking, with some

---

3. A furlong is 220 yards. Semi-aquatic anacondas may be 10 yards long.
4. Monster described in Erik Pontoppidan's *Natural History of Norway* (1752–1753), quoted in John Knox, *A New Collection of Voyages* (1767).

other particulars he narrates, in all this the two correspond. But much abatement is necessary with respect to the incredible bulk he assigns it.

By some naturalists who have vaguely heard rumors of the mysterious creature, here spoken of, it is included among the class of cuttle-fish, to which, indeed, in certain external respects it would seem to belong, but only as the Anak[5] of the tribe.

Chapter 60

The Line[1]

With reference to the whaling scene shortly to be described, as well as for the better understanding of all similar scenes elsewhere presented, I have here to speak of the magical, sometimes horrible whale-line.

The line originally used in the fishery was of the best hemp, slightly vapored with tar, not impregnated with it, as in the case of ordinary ropes; for while tar, as ordinarily used, makes the hemp more pliable to the rope-maker, and also renders the rope itself more convenient to the sailor for common ship use; yet, not only would the ordinary quantity too much stiffen the whale-line for the close coiling to which it must be subjected; but as most seamen are beginning to learn, tar in general by no means adds to the rope's durability or strength, however much it may give it compactness and gloss.

Of late years the Manilla rope has in the American fishery almost entirely superseded hemp as a material for whale-lines; for, though not so durable as hemp, it is stronger, and far more soft and elastic; and I will add (since there is an æsthetics in all things), is much more handsome and becoming to the boat, than hemp. Hemp is a dusky, dark fellow, a sort of Indian;[2] but Manilla is as a golden-haired Circassian to behold.

The whale line is only two thirds of an inch in thickness. At first sight, you would not think it so strong as it really is. By experiment its one and fifty yarns will each suspend a weight of one hundred and twelve pounds; so that the whole rope will bear a strain nearly equal to three tons. In length, the common sperm whale-line measures something over two hundred fathoms.[3] Towards the stern of the boat it is spirally coiled away in the tub, not like the worm-pipe of a still though, but so as to form one round, cheese-shaped mass of densely bedded "sheaves," or layers of concentric spiralizations, without any hollow but the "heart," or minute vertical tube formed at the axis of the cheese. As the least tangle or kink in the coiling would, in running out, infallibly take somebody's arm, leg, or entire body off, the utmost precaution is used in stowing the line in its tub. Some harpooneers will consume almost an entire morning in this

---

5. Numbers 13.33: "And there we saw the giants, the sons of Anak, which come of the giants: and we were in our own sight as grasshoppers, and so were we in their sight."
1. Vincent (1949, 228), shows that Melville adapted his description of hemp rope from Bennett (1840).
2. Native of India. That is, hemp is black, in contrast to Manilla, which is yellow like the hair of Circassians from the Black Sea area of Russia.
3. One fathom is six feet.

business, carrying the line high aloft and then reeving it downwards through a block[4] towards the tub, so as in the act of coiling to free it from all possible wrinkles and twists.

In the English boats two tubs are used instead of one; the same line being continuously coiled in both tubs. There is some advantage in this; because these twin-tubs being so small they fit more readily into the boat, and do not strain it so much; whereas, the American tub, nearly three feet in diameter and of proportionate depth, makes a rather bulky freight for a craft whose planks are but one half-inch in thickness; for the bottom of the whale-boat is like critical ice, which will bear up a considerable distributed weight, but not very much of a concentrated one. When the painted canvas cover is clapped on the American line-tub, the boat looks as if it were pulling off with a prodigious great wedding-cake to present to the whales.

Both ends of the line are exposed; the lower end terminating in an eye-splice or loop coming up from the bottom against the side of the tub, and hanging over its edge completely disengaged from everything. This arrangement of the lower end is necessary on two accounts. First: In order to facilitate the fastening to it of an additional line from a neighboring boat, in case the stricken whale should sound so deep as to threaten to carry off the entire line originally attached to the harpoon. In these instances, the whale of course is shifted like a mug of ale, as it were, from the one boat to the other; though the first boat always hovers at hand to assist its consort. Second: This arrangement is indispensable for common safety's sake; for were the lower end of the line in any way attached to the boat, and were the whale then to run the line out to the end almost in a single, smoking minute as he sometimes does, he would not stop there, for the doomed boat would infallibly be dragged down after him into the profundity of the sea; and in that case no town-crier[5] would ever find her again.

Before lowering the boat for the chase, the upper end of the line is taken aft from the tub, and passing round the loggerhead there, is again carried forward the entire length of the boat, resting crosswise upon the loom or handle of every man's oar, so that it jogs against his wrist in rowing; and also passing between the men, as they alternately sit at the opposite gunwales, to the leaded chocks or grooves in the extreme pointed prow of the boat, where a wooden pin or skewer the size of a common quill, prevents it from slipping out. From the chocks it hangs in a slight festoon over the bows, and is then passed inside the boat again; and some ten or twenty fathoms (called box-line) being coiled upon the box in the bows, it continues its way to the gunwale still a little further aft, and is then attached to the short-warp—the rope which is immediately connected with the harpoon; but previous to that connexion, the short-warp goes through sundry mystifications too tedious to detail.

Thus the whale-line folds the whole boat in its complicated coils, twisting and writhing around it in almost every direction. All the oars-

---

4. Pulley.
5. Town employee who publicly called news, including notices that children were lost or found.

men are involved in its perilous contortions; so that to the timid eye of
the landsman, they seem as Indian jugglers,[6] with the deadliest snakes
sportively festooning their limbs. Nor can any son of mortal woman, for
the first time, seat himself amid those hempen intricacies, and while
straining his utmost at the oar, bethink him that at any unknown instant
the harpoon may be darted, and all these horrible contortions be put in
play like ringed lightnings; he cannot be thus circumstanced without a
shudder that makes the very marrow in his bones to quiver in him like
a shaken jelly. Yet habit—strange thing! what cannot habit accomplish?—Gayer sallies, more merry mirth, better jokes, and brighter repar-
tees, you never heard over your mahogany,[7] than you will hear over the
half-inch white cedar of the whale-boat, when thus hung in hangman's
nooses; and, like the six burghers of Calais before King Edward,[8] the six
men composing the crew pull into the jaws of death, with a halter
around every neck, as you may say.

Perhaps a very little thought will now enable you to account for those
repeated whaling disasters—some few of which are casually chronicled—
of this man or that man being taken out of the boat by the line, and lost.
For, when the line is darting out, to be seated then in the boat, is like
being seated in the midst of the manifold whizzings of a steam-engine in
full play, when every flying beam, and shaft, and wheel, is grazing you. It
is worse; for you cannot sit motionless in the heart of these perils, because
the boat is rocking like a cradle, and you are pitched one way and the
other, without the slightest warning; and only by a certain self-adjusting
buoyancy and simultaneousness of volition and action, can you escape
being made a Mazeppa[9] of, and run away with where the all-seeing sun
himself could never pierce you out.

Again: as the profound calm which only apparently precedes and
prophesies of the storm, is perhaps more awful than the storm itself; for,
indeed, the calm is but the wrapper and envelope of the storm; and contains it in itself, as the seemingly harmless rifle holds the fatal powder,
and the ball, and the explosion; so the graceful repose of the line, as it
silently serpentines about the oarsmen before being brought into actual
play—this is a thing which carries more of true terror than any other
aspect of this dangerous affair. But why say more? All men live enveloped
in whale-lines. All are born with halters round their necks; but it is only
when caught in the swift, sudden turn of death, that mortals realize the
silent, subtle, ever-present perils of life. And if you be a philosopher,
though seated in the whale-boat, you would not at heart feel one whit
more of terror, than though seated before your evening fire with a poker,
and not a harpoon, by your side.

6. Snake charmers in India.
7. Fine dining-room table.
8. To save their city from destruction in 1347, the leading citizens from the French town of Calais
   offered themselves with ropes around their necks to the conquering English king, Edward III.
9. In Lord Byron's poem *Mazeppa* (1819) about this 17th-century Cossack leader, a jealous Polish
   husband ties him to a wild horse, then goads it across the steppes, an ordeal that Mazeppa
   survives.

Chapter 61

Stubb kills a Whale

If to Starbuck the apparition of the Squid was a thing of portents, to Queequeg it was quite a different object.

"When you see him 'quid," said the savage, honing his harpoon in the bow of his hoisted boat, "then you quick see him 'parm whale."

The next day was exceedingly still and sultry, and with nothing special to engage them, the Pequod's crew could hardly resist the spell of sleep induced by such a vacant sea. For this part of the Indian Ocean through which we then were voyaging is not what whalemen call a lively ground; that is, it affords fewer glimpses of porpoises, dolphins, flying-fish, and other vivacious denizens of more stirring waters, than those off the Rio de la Plata, or the in-shore ground off Peru.

It was my turn to stand at the foremast-head; and with my shoulders leaning against the slackened royal shrouds, to and fro I idly swayed in what seemed an enchanted air. No resolution could withstand it; in that dreamy mood losing all consciousness, at last my soul went out of my body; though my body still continued to sway as a pendulum will, long after the power which first moved it is withdrawn.

Ere forgetfulness altogether came over me, I had noticed that the seamen at the main and mizen mast-heads were already drowsy. So that at last all three of us lifelessly swung from the spars, and for every swing that we made there was a nod from below from the slumbering helmsman. The waves, too, nodded their indolent crests; and across the wide trance of the sea, east nodded to west, and the sun over all.

Suddenly bubbles seemed bursting beneath my closed eyes; like vices my hands grasped the shrouds; some invisible, gracious agency preserved me; with a shock I came back to life. And lo! close under our lee, not forty fathoms off, a gigantic Sperm Whale lay rolling in the water like the capsized hull of a frigate, his broad, glossy back, of an Ethiopian[1] hue, glistening in the sun's rays like a mirror. But lazily undulating in the trough of the sea, and ever and anon tranquilly spouting his vapory jet, the whale looked like a portly burgher smoking his pipe of a warm afternoon. But that pipe, poor whale, was thy last. As if struck by some enchanter's wand, the sleepy ship and every sleeper in it all at once started into wakefulness; and more than a score of voices from all parts of the vessel, simultaneously with the three notes from aloft, shouted forth the accustomed cry, as the great fish slowly and regularly spouted the sparkling brine into the air.

"Clear away the boats! Luff!"[2] cried Ahab. And obeying his own order, he dashed the helm down before the helmsman could handle the spokes.

The sudden exclamations of the crew must have alarmed the whale; and ere the boats were down, majestically turning, he swam away to the leeward, but with such a steady tranquillity, and making so few ripples as he swam, that thinking after all he might not as yet be alarmed, Ahab gave

1. Dark.
2. Head the ship just close enough to the wind to fill the sails without shaking them.

orders that not an oar should be used, and no man must speak but in whispers. So seated like Ontario Indians on the gunwales of the boats, we swiftly but silently paddled along; the calm not admitting of the noiseless sails being set. Presently, as we thus glided in chase, the monster perpendicularly flitted his tail forty feet into the air, and then sank out of sight like a tower swallowed up.

"There go flukes!" was the cry, an announcement immediately followed by Stubb's producing his match and igniting his pipe, for now a respite was granted. After the full interval of his sounding had elapsed, the whale rose again, and being now in advance of the smoker's boat, and much nearer to it than to any of the others, Stubb counted upon the honor of the capture. It was obvious, now, that the whale had at length become aware of his pursuers. All silence of cautiousness was therefore no longer of use. Paddles were dropped, and oars came loudly into play. And still puffing at his pipe, Stubb cheered on his crew to the assault.

Yes, a mighty change had come over the fish. All alive to his jeopardy, he was going "head out;" that part obliquely projecting from the mad yeast which he brewed.[3]

"Start her, start her, my men! Don't hurry yourselves; take plenty of time—but start her; start her like thunder-claps, that's all," cried Stubb, spluttering out the smoke as he spoke. "Start her, now; give 'em the long and strong stroke, Tashtego. Start her, Tash, my boy—start her, all; but keep cool, keep cool—cucumbers is the word—easy, easy—only start her like grim death and grinning devils, and raise the buried dead perpendicular out of their graves, boys—that's all. Start her!"

"Woo-hoo! Wa-hee!" screamed the Gay-Header in reply, raising some old war-whoop to the skies; as every oarsman in the strained boat involuntarily bounced forward with the one tremendous leading stroke which the eager Indian gave.

But his wild screams were answered by others quite as wild. "Kee-hee! Kee-hee!" yelled Daggoo, straining forwards and backwards on his seat, like a pacing tiger in his cage.

"Ka-la! Koo-loo!" howled Queequeg, as if smacking his lips over a mouthful of Grenadier's steak.[4] And thus with oars and yells the keels cut the sea. Meanwhile, Stubb retaining his place in the van, still encouraged his men to the onset, all the while puffing the smoke from his mouth. Like desperadoes they tugged and they strained, till the welcome cry was heard—"Stand up, Tashtego!—give it to him!" The harpoon was hurled. "Stern all!" The oarsmen backed water; the same moment something went hot and hissing along every one of their wrists. It was the magical line. An instant before, Stubb had swiftly caught two additional turns with it round the loggerhead, whence, by reason of its increased rapid circlings, a hempen blue smoke now jetted up and mingled with the steady fumes

3. It will be seen in some other place of what a very light substance the entire interior of the sperm whale's enormous head consists. Though apparently the most massive, it is by far the most buoyant part about him. So that with ease he elevates it in the air, and invariably does so when going at his utmost speed. Besides, such is the breadth of the upper part of the front of his head, and such the tapering cut-water formation of the lower part, that by obliquely elevating his head, he thereby may be said to transform himself from a bluff-bowed sluggish galliot into a sharp-pointed New York pilot-boat [Melville's note].

4. Raw steak fit for a soldier in charge of carrying and setting off grenades. Or else steak from the long, tapering, soft-finned deep-water fish of the same name.

from his pipe. As the line passed round and round the loggerhead; so also, just before reaching that point, it blisteringly passed through and through both of Stubb's hands, from which the hand-cloths, or squares of quilted canvas sometimes worn at these times, had accidentally dropped. It was like holding an enemy's sharp two-edged sword by the blade, and that enemy all the time striving to wrest it out of your clutch.

"Wet the line! wet the line!" cried Stubb to the tub oarsman (him seated by the tub) who, snatching off his hat, dashed the sea-water into it.[5] More turns were taken, so that the line began holding its place. The boat now flew through the boiling water like a shark all fins. Stubb and Tashtego here changed places—stem for stern—a staggering business truly in that rocking commotion.

From the vibrating line extending the entire length of the upper part of the boat, and from its now being more tight than a harpstring, you would have thought the craft had two keels—one cleaving the water, the other the air—as the boat churned on through both opposing elements at once. A continual cascade played at the bows; a ceaseless whirling eddy in her wake; and, at the slightest motion from within, even but of a little finger, the vibrating, cracking craft canted over her spasmodic gunwale into the sea. Thus they rushed; each man with might and main clinging to his seat, to prevent being tossed to the foam; and the tall form of Tashtego at the steering oar crouching almost double, in order to bring down his centre of gravity. Whole Atlantics and Pacifics seemed passed as they shot on their way, till at length the whale somewhat slackened his flight.

"Haul in—haul in!" cried Stubb to the bowsman; and, facing round towards the whale, all hands began pulling the boat up to him, while yet the boat was being towed on. Soon ranging up by his flank, Stubb, firmly planting his knee in the clumsy cleat, darted dart after dart into the flying fish; at the word of command, the boat alternately sterning out of the way of the whale's horrible wallow, and then ranging up for another fling.

The red tide now poured from all sides of the monster like brooks down a hill. His tormented body rolled not in brine but in blood, which bubbled and seethed for furlongs behind in their wake. The slanting sun playing upon this crimson pond in the sea, sent back its reflection into every face, so that they all glowed to each other like red men. And all the while, jet after jet of white smoke was agonizingly shot from the spiracle[6] of the whale, and vehement puff after puff from the mouth of the excited heads-man; as at every dart, hauling in upon his crooked lance (by the line attached to it), Stubb straightened it again and again, by a few rapid blows against the gunwale, then again and again sent it into the whale.

"Pull up—pull up!" he now cried to the bowsman, as the waning whale relaxed in his wrath. "Pull up!—close to!" and the boat ranged along the fish's flank. When reaching far over the bow, Stubb slowly churned his long sharp lance into the fish, and kept it there, carefully churning and churning, as if cautiously seeking to feel after some gold watch that the whale might have swallowed, and which he was fearful of breaking ere he

---

5. Partly to show the indispensableness of this act, it may here be stated, that, in the old Dutch fish-ery, a mop was used to dash the running line with water; in many other ships, a wooden piggin, or bailer, is set apart for that purpose. Your hat, however, is the most convenient [Melville's note].
6. Spout-hole.

could hook it out. But that gold watch he sought was the innermost life of the fish. And now it is struck; for, starting from his trance into that unspeakable thing called his "flurry," the monster horribly wallowed in his blood, over-wrapped himself in impenetrable, mad, boiling spray, so that the imperilled craft, instantly dropping astern, had much ado blindly to struggle out from that phrensied twilight into the clear air of the day.

And now abating in his flurry, the whale once more rolled out into view; surging from side to side; spasmodically dilating and contracting his spout-hole, with sharp, cracking, agonized respirations. At last, gush after gush of clotted red gore, as if it had been the purple lees of red wine, shot into the frighted air; and falling back again, ran dripping down his motionless flanks into the sea. His heart had burst!

"He's dead, Mr. Stubb," said Tashtego.

"Yes; both pipes smoked out!" and withdrawing his own from his mouth, Stubb scattered the dead ashes over the water; and, for a moment, stood thoughtfully eyeing the vast corpse he had made.

Chapter 62

The Dart

A word concerning an incident in the last chapter.

According to the invariable usage of the fishery, the whale-boat pushes off from the ship, with the headsman or whale-killer as temporary steersman, and the harpooneer or whale-fastener pulling the foremost oar, the one known as the harpooneer-oar. Now it needs a strong, nervous arm to strike the first iron into the fish; for often, in what is called a long dart, the heavy implement has to be flung to the distance of twenty or thirty feet. But however prolonged and exhausting the chase, the harpooneer is expected to pull his oar meanwhile to the uttermost; indeed, he is expected to set an example of superhuman activity to the rest, not only by incredible rowing, but by repeated loud and intrepid exclamations; and what it is to keep shouting at the top of one's compass, while all the other muscles are strained and half started—what that is none know but those who have tried it. For one, I cannot bawl very heartily and work very recklessly at one and the same time. In this straining, bawling state, then, with his back to the fish, all at once the exhausted harpooneer hears the exciting cry—"Stand up, and give it to him!" He now has to drop and secure his oar, turn round on his centre half way, seize his harpoon from the crotch, and with what little strength may remain, he essays to pitch it somehow into the whale. No wonder, taking the whole fleet of whalemen in a body, that out of fifty fair chances for a dart, not five are successful; no wonder that so many hapless harpooneers are madly cursed and disrated;[1] no wonder that some of them actually burst their blood-vessels in the boat; no wonder that some sperm whalemen are absent four years with four barrels; no wonder that to many ship owners, whaling is but a losing concern; for it is the harpooneer that makes the voyage, and if you

---

1. Demoted (to oarsman).

take the breath out of his body how can you expect to find it there when most wanted!

Again, if the dart be successful, then at the second critical instant, that is, when the whale starts to run, the boat-header and harpooneer likewise start to running fore and aft, to the imminent jeopardy of themselves and every one else. It is then they change places; and the headsman, the chief officer of the little craft, takes his proper station in the bows of the boat.

Now, I care not who maintains the contrary, but all this is both foolish and unnecessary. The headsman should stay in the bows from first to last; he should both dart the harpoon and the lance, and no rowing whatever should be expected of him, except under circumstances obvious to any fisherman. I know that this would sometimes involve a slight loss of speed in the chase; but long experience in various whalemen[2] of more than one nation has convinced me that in the vast majority of failures in the fishery, it has not by any means been so much the speed of the whale as the before described exhaustion of the harpooneer that has caused them.

To insure the greatest efficiency in the dart, the harpooneers of this world must start to their feet from out of idleness, and not from out of toil.

Chapter 63

The Crotch

Out of the trunk, the branches grow; out of them, the twigs. So, in productive subjects, grow the chapters.

The crotch alluded to on a previous page deserves independent mention. It is a notched stick of a peculiar form, some two feet in length, which is perpendicularly inserted into the starboard gunwale near the bow, for the purpose of furnishing a rest for the wooden extremity of the harpoon, whose other naked, barbed end slopingly projects from the prow. Thereby the weapon is instantly at hand to its hurler, who snatches it up as readily from its rest as a backwoodsman swings his rifle from the wall. It is customary to have two harpoons reposing in the crotch, respectively called the first and second irons.

But these two harpoons, each by its own cord, are both connected with the line; the object being this: to dart them both, if possible, one instantly after the other into the same whale; so that if, in the coming drag, one should draw out, the other may still retain a hold. It is a doubling of the chances. But it very often happens that owing to the instantaneous, violent, convulsive running of the whale upon receiving the first iron, it becomes impossible for the harpooneer, however lightning-like in his movements, to pitch the second iron into him. Nevertheless, as the second iron is already connected with the line, and the line is running, hence that weapon must, at all events, be anticipatingly tossed out of the boat, somehow and somewhere; else the most terrible jeopardy would involve all hands. Tumbled into the water, it accordingly is in such cases; the

---

2. Another reference to Ishmael's later whaling voyages, as in ch. 45.

spare coils of box line (mentioned in a preceding chapter)[1] making this feat, in most instances, prudently practicable. But this critical act is not always unattended with the saddest and most fatal casualties.

Furthermore: you must know that when the second iron is thrown overboard, it thenceforth becomes a dangling, sharp-edged terror, skittishly curvetting about both boat and whale, entangling the lines, or cutting them, and making a prodigious sensation in all directions. Nor, in general, is it possible to secure it again until the whale is fairly captured and a corpse.

Consider, now, how it must be in the case of four boats all engaging one unusually strong, active, and knowing whale; when owing to these qualities in him, as well as to the thousand concurring accidents of such an audacious enterprise, eight or ten loose second irons may be simultaneously dangling about him. For, of course, each boat is supplied with several harpoons to bend on to the line should the first one be ineffectually darted without recovery. All these particulars are faithfully narrated here, as they will not fail to elucidate several most important, however intricate passages, in scenes hereafter to be painted.

Chapter 64

Stubb's Supper

Stubb's whale had been killed some distance from the ship. It was a calm; so, forming a tandem of three boats, we commenced the slow business of towing the trophy to the Pequod. And now, as we eighteen men with our thirty-six arms, and one hundred and eighty thumbs and fingers, slowly toiled hour after hour upon that inert, sluggish corpse in the sea; and it seemed hardly to budge at all, except at long intervals; good evidence was hereby furnished of the enormousness of the mass we moved. For, upon the great canal of Hang-Ho,[1] or whatever they call it, in China, four or five laborers on the foot-path will draw a bulky freighted junk at the rate of a mile an hour; but this grand argosy we towed heavily forged along, as if laden with pig-lead in bulk.

Darkness came on; but three lights up and down in the Pequod's main-rigging dimly guided our way; till drawing nearer we saw Ahab dropping one of several more lanterns over the bulwarks. Vacantly eyeing the heaving whale for a moment, he issued the usual orders for securing it for the night, and then handing his lantern to a seaman, went his way into the cabin, and did not come forward again until morning.

Though, in overseeing the pursuit of this whale, Captain Ahab had evinced his customary activity, to call it so; yet now that the creature was dead, some vague dissatisfaction, or impatience, or despair, seemed working in him; as if the sight of that dead body reminded him that Moby Dick was yet to be slain; and though a thousand other whales were brought to

1. Ch. 60.
1. Yün-Ho is the Grand Canal. "Hang-Ho" or "Huang-ho" is the Yellow River whose old bed it partly followed.

his ship, all that would not one jot advance his grand, monomaniac object. Very soon you would have thought from the sound on the Pequod's decks, that all hands were preparing to cast anchor in the deep; for heavy chains are being dragged along the deck, and thrust rattling out of the port-holes. But by those clanking links, the vast corpse itself, not the ship, is to be moored. Tied by the head to the stern, and by the tail to the bows, the whale now lies with its black hull close to the vessel's, and seen through the darkness of the night, which obscured the spars and rigging aloft, the two—ship and whale, seemed yoked together like colossal bullocks, whereof one reclines while the other remains standing.[2]

If moody Ahab was now all quiescence, at least so far as could be known on deck, Stubb, his second mate, flushed with conquest, betrayed an unusual but still good-natured excitement. Such an unwonted bustle was he in that the staid Starbuck, his official superior, quietly resigned to him for the time the sole management of affairs. One small, helping cause of all this liveliness in Stubb, was soon made strangely manifest. Stubb was a high liver; he was somewhat intemperately fond of the whale as a flavorish thing to his palate.

"A steak, a steak, ere I sleep! You, Daggoo! overboard you go, and cut me one from his small!"

Here be it known, that though these wild fishermen do not, as a general thing, and according to the great military maxim, make the enemy defray the current expenses of the war (at least before realizing the proceeds of the voyage), yet now and then you find some of these Nantucketers who have a genuine relish for that particular part of the Sperm Whale designated by Stubb; comprising the tapering extremity of the body.

About midnight that steak was cut and cooked; and lighted by two lanterns of sperm oil, Stubb stoutly stood up to his spermaceti supper at the capstan-head, as if that capstan[3] were a sideboard. Nor was Stubb the only banqueter on whale's flesh that night. Mingling their mumblings with his own mastications, thousands on thousands of sharks, swarming round the dead leviathan, smackingly feasted on its fatness. The few sleepers below in their bunks were often startled by the sharp slapping of their tails against the hull, within a few inches of the sleepers' hearts. Peering over the side you could just see them (as before you heard them) wallowing in the sullen, black waters, and turning over on their backs as they scooped out huge globular pieces of the whale of the bigness of a human head. This particular feat of the shark seems all but miraculous. How, at such an apparently unassailable surface, they contrive to gouge out such symmetrical mouthfuls, remains a part of the universal problem

---

2. A little item may as well be related here. The strongest and most reliable hold which the ship has upon the whale when moored alongside, is by the flukes or tail; and as from its greater density that part is relatively heavier than any other (excepting the side-fins), its flexibility even in death, causes it to sink low beneath the surface; so that with the hand you cannot get at it from the boat, in order to put the chain round it. But this difficulty is ingeniously overcome; a small, strong line is prepared with a wooden float at its outer end, and a weight in its middle, while the other end is secured to the ship. By adroit management the wooden float is made to rise on the other side of the mass, so that now having girdled the whale, the chain is readily made to follow suit; and being slipped along the body, is at last locked fast round the smallest part of the tail, at the point of junction with its broad flukes or lobes [Melville's note].
3. Barrel revolved by bars used to lift heavy weights; its head is the flat, circular top.

of all things. The mark they thus leave on the whale, may best be likened to the hollow made by a carpenter in countersinking for a screw.

Though amid all the smoking horror and diabolism of a sea-fight, sharks will be seen longingly gazing up to the ship's decks, like hungry dogs round a table where red meat is being carved, ready to bolt down every killed man that is tossed to them; and though, while the valiant butchers over the deck-table are thus cannibally carving each other's live meat with carving-knives all gilded and tasselled, the sharks, also, with their jewel-hilted mouths, are quarrelsomely carving away under the table at the dead meat; and though, were you to turn the whole affair upside down, it would still be pretty much the same thing, that is to say, a shocking sharkish business enough for all parties; and though sharks also are the invariable outriders of all slave ships crossing the Atlantic, systematically trotting alongside, to be handy in case a parcel is to be carried anywhere, or a dead slave to be decently buried; and though one or two other like instances might be set down, touching the set terms, places, and occasions, when sharks do most socially congregate, and most hilariously feast; yet is there no conceivable time or occasion when you will find them in such countless numbers, and in gayer or more jovial spirits, than around a dead sperm whale, moored by night to a whale-ship at sea. If you have never seen that sight, then suspend your decision about the propriety of devil-worship, and the expediency of conciliating the devil.

But, as yet, Stubb heeded not the mumblings of the banquet that was going on so nigh him, no more than the sharks heeded the smacking of his own epicurean lips.

"Cook, cook!—where's that old Fleece?"[4] he cried at length, widening his legs still further, as if to form a more secure base for his supper; and, at the same time, darting his fork into the dish, as if stabbing with his lance; "cook, you cook!—sail this way, cook!"

The old black, not in any very high glee at having been previously roused from his warm hammock at a most unseasonable hour, came shambling along from his galley, for, like many old blacks, there was something the matter with his knee-pans, which he did not keep well scoured like his other pans; this old Fleece, as they called him, came shuffling and limping along, assisting his step with his tongs, which, after a clumsy fashion, were made of straightened iron hoops; this old Ebony floundered along, and in obedience to the word of command, came to a dead stop on the opposite side of Stubb's sideboard; when, with both hands folded before him, and resting on his two-legged cane, he bowed his arched back still further over, at the same time sideways inclining his head, so as to bring his best ear into play.

"Cook," said Stubb, rapidly lifting a rather reddish morsel to his mouth, "don't you think this steak is rather overdone? You've been beating this steak too much, cook; it's too tender. Don't I always say that to be good, a whale-steak must be tough? There are those sharks now over the side, don't you see they prefer it tough and rare? What a shindy they are kicking up! Cook, go and talk to 'em; tell 'em they are welcome to help themselves civilly, and in moderation, but they must keep quiet. Blast me, if I

4. The job of sea cooks, as on the *Pequod*, often went to black men.

can hear my own voice. Away, cook, and deliver my message. Here, take this lantern," snatching one from his sideboard; "now then, go and preach to 'em!"

Sullenly taking the offered lantern, old Fleece limped across the deck to the bulwarks; and then, with one hand dropping his light low over the sea, so as to get a good view of his congregation, with the other hand he solemnly flourished his tongs, and leaning far over the side in a mumbling voice began addressing the sharks, while Stubb, softly crawling behind, overheard all that was said.

"Fellow-critters: I'se ordered here to say dat you must stop dat dam noise dare. You hear? Stop dat dam smackin' ob de lip! Massa Stubb say dat you can fill your dam bellies up to de hatchings, but by Gor! you must stop dat dam racket!"

"Cook," here interposed Stubb, accompanying the word with a sudden slap on the shoulder,—"Cook! why, damn your eyes, you mustn't swear that way when you're preaching. That's no way to convert sinners, Cook!"

"Who dat? Den preach to him yourself," sullenly turning to go.

"No, Cook; go on, go on."

"Well, den, Belubed fellow-critters:"—

"Right!" exclaimed Stubb, approvingly, "coax 'em to it; try that," and Fleece continued.

"Dough you is all sharks, and by natur wery woracious, yet I zay to you, fellow-critters, dat dat woraciousness—'top dat dam slappin' ob de tail! How you tink to hear, 'spose you keep up such a dam slappin' and bitin' dare?"

"Cook," cried Stubb, collaring him, "I wont have that swearing. Talk to 'em gentlemanly."

Once more the sermon proceeded.

"Your woraciousness, fellow-critters, I don't blame ye so much for; dat is natur, and can't be helped; but to gobern dat wicked natur, dat is de pint. You is sharks, sartin; but if you gobern de shark in you, why den you be angel; for all angel is not'ing more dan de shark well goberned. Now, look here, bred'ren, just try wonst to be cibil, a helping yourselbs from dat whale. Don't be tearin' de blubber out your neighbour's mout, I say. Is not one shark good right as toder to dat whale? And, by Gor, none on you has de right to dat whale; dat whale belong to some one else. I know some o' you has berry brig mout, brigger dan oders; but den de brig mouts sometimes has de small bellies; so dat de brigness ob de mout is not to swallar wid, but to bite off de blubber for de small fry ob sharks, dat can't get into de scrouge to help demselves."

"Well done, old Fleece!" cried Stubb, "that's Christianity; go on."

"No use goin' on; de dam willains will keep a scrougin' and slappin' each oder, Massa Stubb; dey don't hear one word; no use a-preachin' to such dam g'uttons as you call 'em, till dare bellies is full, and dare bellies is bottomless; and when dey do get em full, dey wont hear you den; for den dey sink in de sea, go fast to sleep on de coral, and can't hear not'ing at all, no more, for eber and eber."

"Upon my soul, I am about of the same opinion; so give the benediction, Fleece, and I'll away to my supper."

Upon this, Fleece, holding both hands over the fishy mob, raised his shrill voice, and cried—

"Cussed fellow-critters! Kick up de damndest row as ever you can; fill your dam' bellies 'till dey bust—and den die."

"Now, cook," said Stubb, resuming his supper at the capstan; "Stand just where you stood before, there, over against me, and pay particular attention."

"All dention," said Fleece, again stooping over upon his tongs in the desired position.

"Well," said Stubb, helping himself freely meanwhile; "I shall now go back to the subject of this steak. In the first place, how old are you, cook?"

"What dat do wid de 'teak," said the old black, testily.

"Silence! How old are you, cook?"

"'Bout ninety, dey say," he gloomily muttered.

"And have you lived in this world hard upon one hundred years, cook, and don't know yet how to cook a whale steak?" rapidly bolting another mouthful at the last word, so that that morsel seemed a continuation of the question. "Where were you born, cook?"

"'Hind de hatchway, in ferry-boat, goin' ober de Roanoke."[5]

"Born in a ferry-boat! That's queer, too. But I want to know what country you were born in, cook?"

"Didn't I say de Roanoke country?" he cried, sharply.

"No, you didn't, cook; but I'll tell you what I'm coming to, cook. You must go home and be born over again; you don't know how to cook a whale-steak yet."

"Bress my soul, if I cook noder one," he growled, angrily, turning round to depart.

"Come back, cook;   here, hand me those tongs;—now take that bit of steak there, and tell me if you think that steak cooked as it should be? Take it, I say"—holding the tongs towards him—"take it, and taste it."

Faintly smacking his withered lips over it for a moment, the old negro muttered, "Best cooked 'teak I eber taste; joosy, berry joosy."

"Cook," said Stubb, squaring himself once more; "do you belong to the church?"

"Passed one once in Cape-Down,"[6] said the old man sullenly.

"And you have once in your life passed a holy church in Cape-Town, where you doubtless overheard a holy parson addressing his hearers as his beloved fellow-creatures, have you, cook! And yet you come here, and tell me such a dreadful lie as you did just now, eh?" said Stubb. "Where do you expect to go to, cook?"

"Go to bed berry soon," he mumbled, half-turning as he spoke.

"Avast! heave to! I mean when you die, cook. It's an awful question. Now what's your answer?"

"When dis old brack man dies," said the negro slowly, changing his whole air and demeanor, "he hisself won't go nowhere; but some bressed angel will come and fetch him."

---

5. River running southeast from central Virginia into North Carolina.
6. Cape Town, the South African seaport.

"Fetch him? How? In a coach and four, as they fetched Elijah?[7] And fetch him where?"

"Up dere," said Fleece, holding his tongs straight over his head, and keeping it there very solemnly.

"So, then, you expect to go up into our main-top, do you, cook, when you are dead? But don't you know the higher you climb, the colder it gets? Main-top eh?"

"Didn't say dat t'all," said Fleece, again in the sulks.

"You said up there, didn't you? and now look yourself, and see where your tongs are pointing. But, perhaps you expect to get into heaven by crawling through the lubber's hole,[8] cook; but, no, no, cook, you don't get there, except you go the regular way, round by the rigging. It's a ticklish business, but must be done, or else it's no go. But none of us are in heaven yet. Drop your tongs, cook, and hear my orders. Do ye hear? Hold your hat in one hand, and clap t'other a'top of your heart, when I'm giving my orders, cook. What! that your heart, there?—that's your gizzard! Aloft! aloft!— that's it—now you have it. Hold it there now, and pay attention."

"All 'dention," said the old black, with both hands placed as desired, vainly wriggling his grizzled head, as if to get both ears in front at one and the same time.

"Well then, cook, you see this whale-steak of yours was so very bad, that I have put it out of sight as soon as possible; you see that, don't you? Well, for the future, when you cook another whale-steak for my private table here, the capstan, I'll tell you what to do so as not to spoil it by overdoing. Hold the steak in one hand, and show a live coal to it with the other; that done, dish it; d'ye hear? And now to-morrow, cook, when we are cutting in the fish, be sure you stand by to get the tips of his fins; have them put in pickle. As for the ends of the flukes, have them soused,[9] cook. There, now ye may go."

But Fleece had hardly got three paces off, when he was recalled.

"Cook, give me cutlets for supper to-morrow night in the mid-watch. D'ye hear? away you sail, then.—Halloa! stop! make a bow before you go.—Avast heaving again! Whale-balls for breakfast—don't forget."

"Wish, by gor! whale eat him, 'stead of him eat whale. I'm bressed if he ain't more of shark dan Massa Shark hisself," muttered the old man, limping away; with which sage ejaculation he went to his hammock.

Chapter 65

The Whale as a Dish

That mortal man should feed upon the creature that feeds his lamp, and, like Stubb, eat him by his own light, as you may say; this seems so out-

---

7. 2 Kings 2.11: "Behold, there appeared a chariot of fire, and horses of fire, . . . and Elijah went up by a whirlwind into heaven."
8. The hole in the floor of the maintop which only timorous, clumsy sailors (lubbers) crawled through to get to the top, whereas the real sailors boldly climbed over the outside edge.
9. Pickled in salt.

landish a thing that one must needs go a little into the history and philosophy of it.

It is upon record, that three centuries ago the tongue of the Right
Whale was esteemed a great delicacy in France, and commanded large
prices there.[1] Also, that in Henry VIIIth's time, a certain cook of the court
obtained a handsome reward for inventing an admirable sauce to be eaten
with barbacued porpoises, which, you remember, are a species of whale.
Porpoises, indeed, are to this day considered fine eating. The meat is
made into balls about the size of billiard balls, and being well seasoned
and spiced might be taken for turtle-balls or veal balls. The old monks of
Dunfermline were very fond of them. They had a great porpoise grant
from the crown.

The fact is, that among his hunters at least, the whale would by all
hands be considered a noble dish, were there not so much of him; but
when you come to sit down before a meat-pie nearly one hundred feet
long, it takes away your appetite. Only the most unprejudiced of men
like Stubb, nowadays partake of cooked whales; but the Esquimaux are
not so fastidious. We all know how they live upon whales, and have rare
old vintages of prime old train oil. Zogranda,[2] one of their most famous
doctors, recommends strips of blubber for infants, as being exceedingly
juicy and nourishing. And this reminds me that certain Englishmen, who
long ago were accidentally left in Greenland by a whaling vessel—that
these men actually lived for several months on the mouldy scraps of
whales which had been left ashore after trying out the blubber. Among
the Dutch whalemen these scraps are called "fritters;" which, indeed,
they greatly resemble, being brown and crisp, and smelling something
like old Amsterdam housewives' dough-nuts or oly-cooks, when fresh.
They have such an eatable look that the most self-denying stranger can
hardly keep his hands off.

But what further depreciates the whale as a civilized dish, is his exceeding richness. He is the great prize ox of the sea, too fat to be delicately
good. Look at his hump, which would be as fine eating as the buffalo's
(which is esteemed a rare dish), were it not such a solid pyramid of fat.
But the spermaceti itself, how bland and creamy that is; like the transparent, half-jellied, white meat of a cocoanut in the third month of its
growth, yet far too rich to supply a substitute for butter. Nevertheless,
many whalemen have a method of absorbing it into some other substance,
and then partaking of it. In the long try watches of the night it is a common thing for the seamen to dip their ship-biscuit into the huge oil-pots
and let them fry there awhile. Many a good supper have I thus made.

In the case of a small Sperm Whale the brains are accounted a fine
dish. The casket of the skull is broken into with an axe, and the two
plump, whitish lobes being withdrawn (precisely resembling two large
puddings), they are then mixed with flour, and cooked into a most delectable mess, in flavor somewhat resembling calves' head, which is quite
a dish among some epicures; and every one knows that some young

---

1. Mansfield and Vincent (757) show that Melville found this item in Scoresby (1820, 2.14) and
   the one from Henry VIII's time and the Monks of Dunfermline (an abbey near Edinburgh) in
   Robert Sibbald's *History . . . of Fife and Kinross* (1710), cited in "Extracts" (p. 11, herein).
2. Another of Melville's private jokes at Scoresby's expense.

bucks among the epicures, by continually dining upon calves' brains, by and by get to have a little brains of their own, so as to be able to tell a calf's head from their own heads; which, indeed, requires uncommon discrimination. And that is the reason why a young buck with an intelligent looking calf's head before him, is somehow one of the saddest sights you can see. The head looks a sort of reproachfully at him, with an "Et tu Brute!"[3] expression.

It is not, perhaps, entirely because the whale is so excessively unctuous that landsmen seem to regard the eating of him with abhorrence; that appears to result, in some way, from the consideration before mentioned: i.e. that a man should eat a newly murdered thing of the sea, and eat it too by its own light. But no doubt the first man that ever murdered an ox was regarded as a murderer; perhaps he was hung; and if he had been put on his trial by oxen, he certainly would have been; and he certainly deserved it if any murderer does. Go to the meat-market of a Saturday night and see the crowds of live bipeds staring up at the long rows of dead quadrupeds. Does not that sight take a tooth out of the cannibal's jaw? Cannibals? who is not a cannibal? I tell you it will be more tolerable for the Fejee that salted down a lean missionary in his cellar against a coming famine; it will be more tolerable for that provident Fejee, I say, in the day of judgment, than for thee, civilized and enlightened gourmand, who nailest geese to the ground and feastest on their bloated livers in thy paté-de-foie-gras.[4]

But Stubb, he eats the whale by its own light, does he? and that is adding insult to injury, is it? Look at your knife-handle, there, my civilized and enlightened gourmand dining off that roast beef, what is that handle made of?—what but the bones of the brother of the very ox you are eating? And what do you pick your teeth with, after devouring that fat goose? With a feather of the same fowl. And with what quill did the Secretary of the Society for the Suppression of Cruelty to Ganders formerly indite his circulars?[5] It is only within the last month or two that that society passed a resolution to patronize nothing but steel pens.

Chapter 66

The Shark Massacre

When in the Southern Fishery, a captured Sperm Whale, after long and weary toil, is brought alongside late at night, it is not, as a general thing at least, customary to proceed at once to the business of cutting him in. For that business is an exceedingly laborious one; is not very soon completed; and requires all hands to set about it. Therefore, the common

3. "And also you, Brutus." Julius Cæsar's dying reproach to his friend Brutus, one of his assassins (*Julius Caesar*, 3.1.77).
4. Matthew 10.15: "I say unto you, It shall be more tolerable for the land of Sodom and Gomorrah in the day of judgment, than for that city" (any city that refuses to hear Jesus' message). The pâté is a delicacy achieved by cruel torture, made from the liver of a goose fattened in the way described.
5. One of Melville's high-sounding invented do-good societies; the 1967 NCE introduced the emendation "formerly" for "formally" (see the time frame in the next sentence).

usage is to take in all sail; lash the helm a'lee; and then send every one below to his hammock till daylight, with the reservation that, until that time, anchor-watches shall be kept; that is, two and two, for an hour each couple, the crew in rotation shall mount the deck to see that all goes well.

But sometimes, especially upon the Line in the Pacific, this plan will not answer at all; because such incalculable hosts of sharks gather round the moored carcase, that were he left so for six hours, say, on a stretch, little more than the skeleton would be visible by morning. In most other parts of the ocean, however, where these fish do not so largely abound, their wondrous voracity can be at times considerably diminished, by vigorously stirring them up with sharp whaling-spades, a procedure notwithstanding, which, in some instances, only seems to tickle them into still greater activity. But it was not thus in the present case with the Pequod's sharks; though, to be sure, any man unaccustomed to such sights, to have looked over her side that night, would have almost thought the whole round sea was one huge cheese, and those sharks the maggots in it.

Nevertheless, upon Stubb setting the anchor-watch after his supper was concluded; and when, accordingly, Queequeg and a forecastle seaman came on deck, no small excitement was created among the sharks; for immediately suspending the cutting stages[1] over the side, and lowering three lanterns, so that they cast long gleams of light over the turbid sea, these two mariners, darting their long whaling-spades, kept up an incessant murdering of the sharks,[2] by striking the keen steel deep into their skulls, seemingly their only vital part. But in the foamy confusion of their mixed and struggling hosts, the marksmen could not always hit their mark; and this brought about new revelations of the incredible ferocity of the foe. They viciously snapped, not only at each other's disembowelments, but like flexible bows, bent round, and bit their own; till those entrails seemed swallowed over and over again by the same mouth, to be oppositely voided by the gaping wound. Nor was this all. It was unsafe to meddle with the corpses and ghosts of these creatures. A sort of generic or Pantheistic vitality[3] seemed to lurk in their very joints and bones, after what might be called the individual life had departed. Killed and hoisted on deck for the sake of his skin, one of these sharks almost took poor Queequeg's hand off, when he tried to shut down the dead lid of his murderous jaw.

"Queequeg no care what god made him shark," said the savage, agonizingly lifting his hand up and down; "wedder Fejee god or Nantucket god; but de god wat made shark must be one dam Ingin."

---

1. Precarious platform fastened to the side of the ship, from which men loosen strips of blubber from the dead whale. See "Contemporary Engravings" (p. 455, herein).
2. The whaling-spade used for cutting-in is made of the very best steel; is about the bigness of a man's spread hand; and in general shape, corresponds to the garden implement after which it is named; only its sides are perfectly flat, and its upper end considerably narrower than the lower. This weapon is always kept as sharp as possible; and when being used is occasionally honed, just like a razor. In its socket, a stiff pole, from twenty to thirty feet long, is inserted for a handle [Melville's note].
3. Natural life force. Queequeg's speech below attributes the shark's making to some god outside nature who is malignant as an Indian, the god being "one dam Injin," the South Sea "savage" ironically learning from exposure to civilization and echoing an extreme white attitude toward American Indians.

Chapter 67

Cutting In

It was a Saturday night, and such a Sabbath as followed! Ex officio professors of Sabbath breaking are all whalemen. The ivory Pequod was turned into what seemed a shamble; every sailor a butcher. You would have thought we were offering up[1] ten thousand red oxen to the sea gods.

In the first place, the enormous cutting tackles, among other ponderous things comprising a cluster of blocks generally painted green, and which no single man can possibly lift—this vast bunch of grapes was swayed up to the main-top and firmly lashed to the lower mast-head, the strongest point anywhere above a ship's deck. The end of the hawser-like rope winding through these intricacies, was then conducted to the windlass, and the huge lower block of the tackles was swung over the whale; to this block the great blubber hook, weighing some one hundred pounds, was attached. And now suspended in stages over the side, Starbuck and Stubb, the mates, armed with their long spades, began cutting a hole in the body for the insertion of the hook just above the nearest of the two side-fins. This done, a broad, semicircular line is cut round the hole, the hook is inserted, and the main body of the crew striking up a wild chorus, now commence heaving in one dense crowd at the windlass. When instantly, the entire ship careens over on her side; every bolt in her starts like the nail-heads of an old house in frosty weather; she trembles, quivers, and nods her frighted mast-heads to the sky. More and more she leans over to the whale, while every gasping heave of the windlass is answered by a helping heave from the billows; till at last, a swift, startling snap is heard; with a great swash the ship rolls upwards and backwards from the whale, and the triumphant tackle rises into sight dragging after it the disengaged semicircular end of the first strip of blubber. Now as the blubber envelopes the whale precisely as the rind does an orange, so is it stripped off from the body precisely as an orange is sometimes stripped by spiralizing it. For the strain constantly kept up by the windlass continually keeps the whale rolling over and over in the water, and as the blubber in one strip uniformly peels off along the line called the "scarf," simultaneously cut by the spades of Starbuck and Stubb, the mates; and just as fast as it is thus peeled off, and indeed by that very act itself, it is all the time being hoisted higher and higher aloft till its upper end grazes the main-top; the men at the windlass then cease heaving, and for a moment or two the prodigious blood-dripping mass sways to and fro as if let down from the sky, and every one present must take good heed to dodge it when it swings, else it may box his ears and pitch him headlong overboard.

One of the attending harpooneers now advances with a long, keen weapon called a boarding-sword, and watching his chance he dexterously slices out a considerable hole in the lower part of the swaying mass. Into this hole, the end of the second alternating great tackle is then hooked so as to retain a hold upon the blubber, in order to prepare for what follows.

---

1. Sacrificing to some god. *Sabbath breaking:* That is, their occupation requires that they break the commandment against working on the Sabbath (Exodus 21.8). *Shamble:* or shambles, slaughterhouse.

Whereupon, this accomplished swordsman, warning all hands to stand off, once more makes a scientific dash at the mass, and with a few side-long, desperate, lunging slicings, severs it completely in twain; so that while the short lower part is still fast, the long upper strip, called a blan-ket-piece, swings clear, and is all ready for lowering. The heavers forward now resume their song, and while the one tackle is peeling and hoisting a second strip from the whale, the other is slowly slackened away, and down goes the first strip through the main hatchway right beneath, into an unfurnished parlor called the blubber-room. Into this twilight apartment sundry nimble hands keep coiling away the long blanket-piece as if it were a great live mass of plaited serpents. And thus the work proceeds; the two tackles hoisting and lowering simultaneously; both whale and windlass heaving, the heavers singing, the blubber-room gentlemen coiling, the mates scarfing, the ship straining, and all hands swearing occasionally, by way of assuaging the general friction.

Chapter 68

The Blanket

I have given no small attention to that not unvexed subject, the skin of the whale. I have had controversies about it with experienced whalemen afloat, and learned naturalists ashore. My original opinion remains unchanged; but it is only an opinion.

The question is, what and where is the skin of the whale? Already you know what his blubber is. That blubber is something of the consistence of firm, close-grained beef, but tougher, more elastic and compact, and ranges from eight or ten to twelve and fifteen inches in thickness.

Now, however preposterous it may at first seem to talk of any crea-ture's skin as being of that sort of consistence and thickness, yet in point of fact these are no arguments against such a presumption; because you cannot raise any other dense enveloping layer from the whale's body but that same blubber; and the outermost enveloping layer of any animal, if reasonably dense, what can that be but the skin? True, from the unmarred dead body of the whale, you may scrape off with your hand an infinitely thin, transparent substance, somewhat resembling the thinnest shreds of isinglass,[1] only it is almost as flexible and soft as satin; that is, previous to being dried, when it not only contracts and thick-ens, but becomes rather hard and brittle. I have several such dried bits, which I use for marks in my whale-books. It is transparent, as I said before; and being laid upon the printed page, I have sometimes pleased myself with fancying it exerted a magnifying influence. At any rate, it is pleasant to read about whales through their own spectacles, as you may say. But what I am driving at here is this. That same infinitely thin, isin-glass substance, which, I admit, invests the entire body of the whale, is not so much to be regarded as the skin of the creature, as the skin of the skin, so to speak; for it were simply ridiculous to say, that the proper

1. Thin pieces of mica.

skin of the tremendous whale is thinner and more tender than the skin of a new-born child. But no more of this.

Assuming the blubber to be the skin of the whale; then, when this skin, as in the case of a very large Sperm Whale, will yield the bulk of one hundred barrels of oil; and, when it is considered that, in quantity, or rather weight, that oil, in its expressed state, is only three fourths, and not the entire substance of the coat; some idea may hence be had of the enormousness of that animated mass, a mere part of whose mere integument yields such a lake of liquid as that. Reckoning ten barrels to the ton, you have ten tons for the net weight of only three quarters of the stuff of the whale's skin.

In life, the visible surface of the Sperm Whale is not the least among the many marvels he presents. Almost invariably it is all over obliquely crossed and re-crossed with numberless straight marks in thick array, something like those in the finest Italian line engravings. But these marks do not seem to be impressed upon the isinglass substance above mentioned, but seem to be seen through it, as if they were engraved upon the body itself. Nor is this all. In some instances, to the quick, observant eye, those linear marks, as in a veritable engraving, but afford the ground for far other delineations. These are hieroglyphical; that is, if you call those mysterious cyphers on the walls of pyramids hieroglyphics, then that is the proper word to use in the present connexion. By my retentive memory of the hieroglyphics upon one Sperm Whale in particular, I was much struck with a plate representing the old Indian characters chiselled on the famous hieroglyphic palisades[2] on the banks of the Upper Mississippi. Like those mystic rocks, too, the mystic-marked whale remains undecipherable. This allusion to the Indian rocks reminds me of another thing. Besides all the other phenomena which the exterior of the Sperm Whale presents, he not seldom displays the back, and more especially his flanks, effaced in great part of the regular linear appearance, by reason of numerous rude scratches, altogether of an irregular, random aspect. I should say that those New England rocks on the sea-coast, which Agassiz[3] imagines to bear the marks of violent scraping contact with vast floating icebergs— I should say, that those rocks must not a little resemble the Sperm Whale in this particular. It also seems to me that such scratches in the whale are probably made by hostile contact with other whales; for I have most remarked them in the large, full-grown bulls of the species.

A word or two more concerning this matter of the skin or blubber of the whale. It has already been said, that it is stript from him in long pieces, called blanket-pieces. Like most sea-terms, this one is very happy and significant. For the whale is indeed wrapt up in his blubber as in a real blanket or counterpane; or, still better, an Indian poncho slipt over his head, and skirting his extremity. It is by reason of this cosy blanketing of his body, that the whale is enabled to keep himself comfortable in all weathers, in all seas, times, and tides. What would become of a Greenland whale, say, in those shuddering, icy seas of the North, if unsupplied with

2. Hieroglyphics near Alton, Illinois, shaped somewhat like a great bird. Melville may have seen them in 1840, before they were destroyed by quarrying.
3. Louis Agassiz (1807–1873), eminent Swiss-born naturalist and geologist, professor at Harvard 1848–73.

his cosy surtout? True, other fish are found exceedingly brisk in those Hyperborean[4] waters; but these, be it observed, are your cold-blooded, lungless fish, whose very bellies are refrigerators; creatures, that warm themselves under the lee of an iceberg, as a traveller in winter would bask before an inn fire; whereas, like man, the whale has lungs and warm blood. Freeze his blood, and he dies. How wonderful is it then—except after explanation—that this great monster, to whom corporeal warmth is as indispensable as it is to man; how wonderful that he should be found at home, immersed to his lips for life in those Arctic waters! where, when seamen fall overboard, they are sometimes found, months afterwards, perpendicularly frozen into the hearts of fields of ice, as a fly is found glued in amber. But more surprising is it to know, as has been proved by experiment, that the blood of a Polar whale is warmer than that of a Borneo negro[5] in summer.

It does seem to me, that herein we see the rare virtue of a strong individual vitality, and the rare virtue of thick walls, and the rare virtue of interior spaciousness. Oh, man! admire and model thyself after the whale! Do thou, too, remain warm among ice. Do thou, too, live in this world without being of it. Be cool at the equator; keep thy blood fluid at the Pole. Like the great dome of St. Peter's,[6] and like the great whale, retain, O man! in all seasons a temperature of thine own.

But how easy and how hopeless to teach these fine things! Of erections, how few are domed like St. Peter's! of creatures, how few vast as the whale!

Chapter 69

The Funeral

"Haul in the chains! Let the carcase go astern!"

The vast tackles have now done their duty. The peeled white body of the beheaded whale flashes like a marble sepulchre; though changed in hue, it has not perceptibly lost anything in bulk. It is still colossal. Slowly it floats more and more away, the water round it torn and splashed by the insatiate sharks, and the air above vexed with rapacious flights of screaming fowls, whose beaks are like so many insulting poniards in the whale. The vast white headless phantom floats further and further from the ship, and every rod that it so floats, what seem square roods of sharks and cubic roods of fowls, augment the murderous din. For hours and hours from the almost stationary ship that hideous sight is seen. Beneath the unclouded and mild azure sky, upon the fair face of the pleasant sea, wafted by the joyous breezes, that great mass of death floats on and on, till lost in infinite perspectives.

There's a most doleful and most mocking funeral! The sea-vultures all

---

4. Icy, as in the mythological region beyond the home of the North Wind, sometimes (but not here) imagined as warm and sunny.
5. Dark-skinned native of this Malayan island.
6. Melville may have read about the constant temperature of this great cathedral in Rome in *Corine* (1807) by Anne Louise Germaine de Staël-Holstein (1766–1817), which he bought in London in 1849.

in pious mourning, the air-sharks all punctiliously in black or speckled. In
life but few of them would have helped the whale, I ween, if peradventure
he had needed it; but upon the banquet of his funeral they most piously
do pounce. Oh, horrible vulturism of earth! from which not the mightiest
whale is free.

Nor is this the end. Desecrated as the body is, a vengeful ghost survives
and hovers over it to scare. Espied by some timid man-of-war or blundering
discovery-vessel from afar, when the distance obscuring the swarming
fowls, nevertheless still shows the white mass floating in the sun, and the
white spray heaving high against it; straightway the whale's unharming
corpse, with trembling fingers is set down in the log—*shoals, rocks, and
breakers hereabouts: beware!* And for years afterwards, perhaps, ships shun
the place; leaping over it as silly sheep leap over a vacuum, because their
leader originally leaped there when a stick was held. There's your law of
precedents; there's your utility of traditions; there's the story of your obstinate survival of old beliefs never bottomed on the earth, and now not even
hovering in the air! There's orthodoxy!

Thus, while in life the great whale's body may have been a real terror to
his foes, in his death his ghost becomes a powerless panic to a world.

Are you a believer in ghosts, my friend? There are other ghosts than the
Cock-Lane one, and far deeper men than Doctor Johnson[1] who believe in
them.

Chapter 70

The Sphynx

It should not have been omitted that previous to completely stripping the
body of the leviathan, he was beheaded. Now, the beheading of the Sperm
Whale is a scientific anatomical feat, upon which experienced whale surgeons very much pride themselves: and not without reason.

Consider that the whale has nothing that can properly be called a neck;
on the contrary, where his head and body seem to join, there, in that very
place, is the thickest part of him. Remember, also, that the surgeon must
operate from above, some eight or ten feet intervening between him and
his subject, and that subject almost hidden in a discolored, rolling, and
oftentimes tumultuous and bursting sea. Bear in mind, too, that under
these untoward circumstances he has to cut many feet deep in the flesh;
and in that subterraneous manner, without so much as getting one single
peep into the ever-contracting gash thus made, he must skilfully steer
clear of all adjacent, interdicted parts, and exactly divide the spine at a
critical point hard by its insertion into the skull. Do you not marvel, then,
at Stubb's boast, that he demanded but ten minutes to behead a sperm
whale?

When first severed, the head is dropped astern and held there by a cable
till the body is stripped. That done, if it belong to a small whale it is hoisted

---

1. Samuel Johnson in fact exposed the faked ghost in London's Cock-Lane in 1762.

on deck to be deliberately disposed of. But, with a full grown leviathan this is impossible; for the sperm whale's head embraces nearly one third of his entire bulk, and completely to suspend such a burden as that, even by the immense tackles of a whaler, this were as vain a thing as to attempt weighing a Dutch barn in jewellers' scales.

The Pequod's whale being decapitated and the body stripped, the head was hoisted against the ship's side—about half way out of the sea, so that it might yet in great part be buoyed up by its native element. And there with the strained craft steeply leaning over to it, by reason of the enormous downward drag from the lower mast-head, and every yard-arm on that side projecting like a crane over the waves; there, that blood-dripping head hung to the Pequod's waist like the giant Holofernes's from the girdle of Judith.[1]

When this last task was accomplished it was noon, and the seamen went below to their dinner. Silence reigned over the before tumultuous but now deserted deck. An intense copper calm, like a universal yellow lotus, was more and more unfolding its noiseless measureless leaves upon the sea.

A short space elapsed, and up into this noiselessness came Ahab alone from his cabin. Taking a few turns on the quarter-deck, he paused to gaze over the side, then slowly getting into the main-chains he took Stubb's long spade—still remaining there after the whale's decapitation—and striking it into the lower part of the half-suspended mass, placed its other end crutch-wise under one arm, and so stood leaning over with eyes attentively fixed on this head.

It was a black and hooded head; and hanging there in the midst of so intense a calm, it seemed the Sphynx's in the desert. "Speak, thou vast and venerable head," muttered Ahab, "which, though ungarnished with a beard, yet here and there lookest hoary with mosses; speak, mighty head, and tell us the secret thing that is in thee. Of all divers, thou hast dived the deepest. That head upon which the upper sun now gleams, has moved amid this world's foundations. Where unrecorded names and navies rust, and untold hopes and anchors rot; where in her murderous hold this frigate earth is ballasted with bones of millions of the drowned; there, in that awful water-land, there was thy most familiar home. Thou hast been where bell or diver never went; hast slept by many a sailor's side, where sleepless mothers would give their lives to lay them down. Thou saw'st the locked lovers when leaping from their flaming ship; heart to heart they sank beneath the exulting wave; true to each other, when heaven seemed false to them. Thou saw'st the murdered mate when tossed by pirates from the midnight deck; for hours he fell into the deeper midnight of the insatiate maw; and his murderers still sailed on unharmed—while swift lightnings shivered the neighboring ship that would have borne a righteous husband to outstretched, longing arms. O head! thou hast seen enough to split the planets and make an infidel of Abraham,[2] and not one syllable is thine!"

"Sail ho!" cried a triumphant voice from the main-mast-head.

"Aye? Well, now, that's cheering," cried Ahab, suddenly erecting him-

---

1. This Jewish heroine in the apocryphal Book of Judith decapitates the Assyrian general Holofernes with his own sword. Judith's maid carries the head home in her "bag of meat" (13.10), her food bag, not hanging from Judith's own belt-like girdle, as pictured by some Renaissance artists.
2. The horrors the head has seen could make even the father of the Jewish people lose faith in God's ways.

self, while whole thunder-clouds swept aside from his brow. "That lively cry upon this deadly calm might almost convert a better man.—Where away?"

"Three points on the starboard bow, sir, and bringing down her breeze to us!"

"Better and better, man. Would now St. Paul would come along that way, and to my breezelessness bring his breeze![3] O Nature, and O soul of man! how far beyond all utterance are your linked analogies! not the smallest atom stirs or lives in matter, but has its cunning duplicate in mind."

Chapter 71

The Jeroboam's Story

Hand in hand, ship and breeze blew on; but the breeze came faster than the ship, and soon the Pequod began to rock.

By and by, through the glass the stranger's boats and manned mast-heads proved her a whale-ship. But as she was so far to windward, and shooting by, apparently making a passage to some other ground, the Pequod could not hope to reach her. So the signal was set to see what response would be made.

Here be it said, that like the vessels of military marines, the ships of the American Whale Fleet have each a private signal; all which signals being collected in a book with the names of the respective vessels attached, every captain is provided with it. Thereby, the whale commanders are enabled to recognise each other upon the ocean, even at considerable distances, and with no small facility.

The Pequod's signal was at last responded to by the stranger's setting her own; which proved the ship to be the Jeroboam of Nantucket. Squaring her yards, she bore down, ranged abeam under the Pequod's lee, and lowered a boat; it soon drew nigh; but, as the side-ladder was being rigged by Starbuck's order to accommodate the visiting captain, the stranger in question waved his hand from his boat's stern in token of that proceeding being entirely unnecessary. It turned out that the Jeroboam[1] had a malignant epidemic on board, and that Mayhew, her captain, was fearful of infecting the Pequod's company. For, though himself and boat's crew remained untainted, and though his ship was half a rifle-shot off, and an incorruptible sea and air rolling and flowing between; yet conscientiously adhering to the timid quarantine of the land, he peremptorily refused to come into direct contact with the Pequod.

But this did by no means prevent all communication. Preserving an interval of some few yards between itself and the ship, the Jeroboam's boat by the occasional use of its oars contrived to keep parallel to the Pequod, as she heavily forged through the sea (for by this time it blew very

---

3. This story (alluded to in ch. 2) is in Acts 27.
1. The ship from Quaker Nantucket oddly takes its name from Jeroboam, the wicked king of Israel who worshiped golden calves (2 Chronicles 13.8).

fresh), with her main-top-sail aback; though, indeed, at times by the sudden onset of a large rolling wave, the boat would be pushed some way ahead; but would be soon skilfully brought to her proper bearings again. Subject to this, and other the like interruptions now and then, a conversation was sustained between the two parties; but at intervals not without still another interruption of a very different sort.

Pulling an oar in the Jeroboam's boat, was a man of a singular appearance, even in that wild whaling life where individual notabilities make up all totalities. He was a small, short, youngish man, sprinkled all over his face with freckles, and wearing redundant yellow hair. A long-skirted, cabalistically-cut coat of a faded walnut tinge enveloped him;[2] the overlapping sleeves of which were rolled up on his wrists. A deep, settled, fanatic delirium was in his eyes.

So soon as this figure had been first descried, Stubb had exclaimed—"That's he! that's he!—the long-togged scaramouch[3] the Town-Ho's company told us of!" Stubb here alluded to a strange story told of the Jeroboam, and a certain man among her crew, some time previous when the Pequod spoke the Town-Ho. According to this account and what was subsequently learned, it seemed that the scaramouch in question had gained a wonderful ascendency over almost everybody in the Jeroboam. His story was this:

He had been originally nurtured among the crazy society of Neskyeuna Shakers,[4] where he had been a great prophet; in their cracked, secret meetings having several times descended from heaven by the way of a trap-door, announcing the speedy opening of the seventh vial, which he carried in his vest-pocket; but, which, instead of containing gunpowder, was supposed to be charged with laudanum.[5] A strange, apostolic whim having seized him, he had left Neskyeuna for Nantucket, where, with that cunning peculiar to craziness, he assumed a steady, common sense exterior, and offered himself as a green-hand candidate for the Jeroboam's whaling voyage. They engaged him; but straightway upon the ship's getting out of sight of land, his insanity broke out in a freshet. He announced himself as the archangel Gabriel, and commanded the captain to jump overboard. He published his manifesto, whereby he set himself forth as the deliverer of the isles of the sea and vicar-general[6] of all Oceanica. The unflinching earnestness with which he declared these things;—the dark, daring play of his sleepless, excited imagination, and all the preternatural terrors of real delirium, united to invest this Gabriel in the minds of the majority of the ignorant crew, with an atmosphere of sacredness. Moreover, they were afraid of him. As such a man, however, was not of much practical use in the ship, especially as he refused to work except when he pleased, the incredulous cap-

2. The edges of the cloth (and perhaps the body of the cloth also) are not straight but cut in fantastic shapes, like esoteric symbols.
3. Boastful, cowardly buffoon in the Italian commedia dell'arte.
4. A Shaker community near Albany, New York, familiar to Melville. There was another at Hancock, Massachusetts, a few miles from his Pittsfield home, which he (in the custom of the time) visited as a tourist attraction, to see the uncouth dancing, to admire the great Round Barn, and to buy small objects, such as baskets, for gifts. He took some details from *A Summary View of the Millennial Church, or United Society of Believers, Commonly Called Shakers* (1848).
5. A tincture of opium. *Seventh vial:* in Revelation 16.17, the last of the vials of wrath poured out by the angels at the place called Armageddon.
6. Administrative deputy of a bishop. The strange young man is not only called Gabriel, the name of one of the archangels, but identifies himself *as* the archangel, the one who, among other duties, announced the forthcoming births of John the Baptist and Jesus (Luke 1).

tain would fain have been rid of him; but apprised that that individual's intention was to land him in the first convenient port, the archangel forthwith opened all his seals and vials—devoting the ship and all hands to unconditional perdition, in case this intention was carried out. So strongly did he work upon his disciples among the crew, that at last in a body they went to the captain and told him if Gabriel was sent from the ship, not a man of them would remain. He was therefore forced to relinquish his plan. Nor would they permit Gabriel to be any way maltreated, say or do what he would; so that it came to pass[7] that Gabriel had the complete freedom of the ship. The consequence of all this was, that the archangel cared little or nothing for the captain and mates; and since the epidemic had broken out, he carried a higher hand than ever; declaring that the plague, as he called it, was at his sole command; nor should it be stayed but according to his good pleasure. The sailors, mostly poor devils, cringed, and some of them fawned before him; in obedience to his instructions, sometimes rendering him personal homage, as to a god. Such things may seem incredible; but, however wondrous, they are true. Nor is the history of fanatics half so striking in respect to the measureless self-deception of the fanatic himself, as his measureless power of deceiving and bedevilling so many others. But it is time to return to the Pequod.

"I fear not thy epidemic, man," said Ahab from the bulwarks, to Captain Mayhew, who stood in the boat's stern; "come on board."

But now Gabriel started to his feet.

"Think, think of the fevers, yellow and bilious! Beware of the horrible plague!"

"Gabriel, Gabriel!" cried Captain Mayhew; "thou must either—" But that instant a headlong wave shot the boat far ahead, and its seethings drowned all speech.

"Hast thou seen the White Whale?" demanded Ahab, when the boat drifted back.

"Think, think of thy whale-boat, stoven and sunk! Beware of the horrible tail!"

"I tell thee again, Gabriel, that—" But again the boat tore ahead as if dragged by fiends. Nothing was said for some moments, while a succession of riotous waves rolled by, which by one of those occasional caprices of the seas were tumbling, not heaving it. Meantime, the hoisted sperm whale's head jogged about very violently, and Gabriel was seen eyeing it with rather more apprehensiveness than his archangel nature seemed to warrant.

When this interlude was over, Captain Mayhew began a dark story concerning Moby Dick; not, however, without frequent interruptions from Gabriel, whenever his name was mentioned, and the crazy sea that seemed leagued with him.

It seemed that the Jeroboam had not long left home, when upon speaking a whale-ship, her people were reliably apprised of the existence of Moby Dick, and the havoc he had made. Greedily sucking in this intelligence, Gabriel solemnly warned the captain against attacking the White Whale, in case the monster should be seen; in his gibbering insanity, pronouncing the White Whale to be no less a being than the Shaker God incarnated; the

---

7. A biblical phrase, often used to indicate the fulfillment of God's words.

Shakers receiving the Bible.[8] But when, some year or two afterwards, Moby Dick was fairly sighted from the mast-heads, Macey, the chief mate, burned with ardor to encounter him; and the captain himself being not unwilling to let him have the opportunity, despite all the archangel's denunciations and forewarnings, Macey succeeded in persuading five men to man his boat. With them he pushed off; and, after much weary pulling, and many perilous, unsuccessful onsets, he at last succeeded in getting one iron fast. Meantime, Gabriel, ascending to the main-royal mast-head, was tossing one arm in frantic gestures, and hurling forth prophecies of speedy doom to the sacrilegious assailants of his divinity. Now, while Macey, the mate, was standing up in his boat's bow, and with all the reckless energy of his tribe was venting his wild exclamations upon the whale, and essaying to get a fair chance for his poised lance, lo! a broad white shadow rose from the sea; by its quick, fanning motion, temporarily taking the breath out of the bodies of the oarsmen. Next instant, the luckless mate, so full of furious life, was smitten bodily into the air, and making a long arc in his descent, fell into the sea at the distance of about fifty yards. Not a chip of the boat was harmed, nor a hair of any oarsman's head; but the mate for ever sank.

It is well to parenthesize here, that of the fatal accidents in the Sperm-Whale Fishery, this kind is perhaps almost as frequent as any. Sometimes, nothing is injured but the man who is thus annihilated; oftener the boat's bow is knocked off, or the thigh-board, in which the headsman stands, is torn from its place and accompanies the body. But strangest of all is the circumstance, that in more instances than one, when the body has been recovered, not a single mark of violence is discernible; the man being stark dead.

The whole calamity, with the falling form of Macey, was plainly descried from the ship. Raising a piercing shriek—"The vial! the vial!" Gabriel called off the terror-stricken crew from the further hunting of the whale. This terrible event clothed the archangel with added influence; because his credulous disciples believed that he had specifically fore-announced it, instead of only making a general prophecy, which any one might have done, and so have chanced to hit one of many marks in the wide margin allowed. He became a nameless terror to the ship.

Mayhew having concluded his narration, Ahab put such questions to him, that the stranger captain could not forbear inquiring whether he intended to hunt the White Whale, if opportunity should offer. To which Ahab answered—"Aye." Straightway, then, Gabriel once more started to his feet, glaring upon the old man, and vehemently exclaimed, with downward pointed finger—"Think, think of the blasphemer—dead, and down there!—beware of the blasphemer's end!"[9]

Ahab stolidly turned aside; then said to Mayhew, "Captain, I have just

8. A puzzling expression. Shaker belief does not account for Gabriel's notion of Moby Dick. Melville may mean merely that this was the way Gabriel received or interpreted the Bible (that this was this particular Shaker's way of interpreting the Bible).

9. Gabriel warns that Ahab, like Mayhew, will go to hell for the blasphemy of attacking Moby Dick (God). Blasphemy was an extremely sensitive topic in the Melville house, for Mrs. Herman Melville's father, Lemuel Shaw, as chief justice of the Massachusetts Supreme Court, a decade earlier had become the last judge in America to sentence someone to jail for blasphemy. After Moby-Dick was published, Melville was angered, his mother wrote, that the local Pittsfield people were gossiping that the book was worse than blasphemous, and the reviewer in the New York Independent publicly threatened him with hell fire for writing the book.

bethought me of my letter-bag; there is a letter for one of thy officers, if I mistake not. Starbuck, look over the bag."

Every whale-ship takes out a goodly number of letters for various ships, whose delivery to the persons to whom they may be addressed, depends upon the mere chance of encountering them in the four oceans. Thus, most letters never reach their mark; and many are only received after attaining an age of two or three years or more.

Soon Starbuck returned with a letter in his hand. It was sorely tumbled, damp, and covered with a dull, spotted, green mould, in consequence of being kept in a dark locker of the cabin. Of such a letter, Death himself might well have been the post-boy.

"Can'st not read it?" cried Ahab. "Give it me, man. Aye, aye, it's but a dim scrawl;—what's this?" As he was studying it out, Starbuck took a long cutting-spade pole, and with his knife slightly split the end, to insert the letter there, and in that way, hand it to the boat, without its coming any closer to the ship.

Meantime, Ahab holding the letter, muttered, "Mr. Har—yes, Mr. Harry—(a woman's pinny hand,—the man's wife, I'll wager)—Aye—Mr. Harry Macey, Ship Jeroboam;—why it's Macey, and he's dead!"

"Poor fellow! poor fellow! and from his wife," sighed Mayhew; "but let me have it."

"Nay, keep it thyself," cried Gabriel to Ahab; "thou art soon going that way."

"Curses throttle thee!" yelled Ahab. "Captain Mayhew, stand by now to receive it;" and taking the fatal missive from Starbuck's hands, he caught it in the slit of the pole, and reached it over towards the boat. But as he did so, the oarsmen expectantly desisted from rowing; the boat drifted a little towards the ship's stern; so that, as if by magic, the letter suddenly ranged along with Gabriel's eager hand. He clutched it in an instant, seized the boat-knife, and impaling the letter on it, sent it thus loaded back into the ship. It fell at Ahab's feet.[1] Then Gabriel shrieked out to his comrades to give way with their oars, and in that manner the mutinous boat rapidly shot away from the Pequod.

As, after this interlude, the seamen resumed their work upon the jacket of the whale, many strange things were hinted in reference to this wild affair.

Chapter 72

The Monkey-rope[1]

In the tumultuous business of cutting-in and attending to a whale, there is much running backwards and forwards among the crew. Now hands are wanted here, and then again hands are wanted there. There is no staying in any one place; for at one and the same time everything has to be done

---

1. That is, right in front of him (his single foot and his peg leg).
1. Mansfield and Vincent (764) show that this chapter was suggested by Francis Allyn Olmsted's *Incidents of a Whaling Voyage* (1841).

everywhere. It is much the same with him who endeavors the description of the scene. We must now retrace our way a little. It was mentioned that upon first breaking ground in the whale's back, the blubber-hook was inserted into the original hole there cut by the spades of the mates. But how did so clumsy and weighty a mass as that same hook get fixed in that hole? It was inserted there by my particular friend Queequeg, whose duty it was, as harpooneer, to descend upon the monster's back for the special purpose referred to. But in very many cases, circumstances require that the harpooneer shall remain on the whale till the whole flensing or stripping operation is concluded. The whale, be it observed, lies almost entirely submerged, excepting the immediate parts operated upon. So down there, some ten feet below the level of the deck, the poor harpooneer flounders about, half on the whale and half in the water, as the vast mass revolves like a tread-mill beneath him. On the occasion in question, Queequeg figured in the Highland costume—a skirt and socks[2]—in which to my eyes, at least, he appeared to uncommon advantage; and no one had a better chance to observe him, as will presently be seen.

Being the savage's bowsman, that is, the person who pulled the bow-oar in his boat (the second one from forward), it was my cheerful duty to attend upon him while taking that hard-scrabble scramble upon the dead whale's back. You have seen Italian organ-boys holding a dancing-ape by a long cord. Just so, from the ship's steep side, did I hold Queequeg down there in the sea, by what is technically called in the fishery a monkey-rope, attached to a strong strip of canvas belted round his waist.

It was a humorously perilous business for both of us. For, before we proceed further, it must be said that the monkey-rope was fast at both ends; fast to Queequeg's broad canvas belt, and fast to my narrow leather one. So that for better or for worse, we two, for the time, were wedded; and should poor Queequeg sink to rise no more, then both usage and honor demanded, that instead of cutting the cord, it should drag me down in his wake. So, then, an elongated Siamese ligature united us. Queequeg was my own inseparable twin brother; nor could I any way get rid of the dangerous liabilities which the hempen bond entailed.

So strongly and metaphysically did I conceive of my situation then, that while earnestly watching his motions, I seemed distinctly to perceive that my own individuality was now merged in a joint stock company of two: that my free will had received a mortal wound; and that another's mistake or misfortune might plunge innocent me into unmerited disaster and death. Therefore, I saw that here was a sort of interregnum in Providence; for its even-handed equity never could have sanctioned so gross an injustice. And yet still further pondering—while I jerked him now and then from between the whale and the ship, which would threaten to jam him—still further pondering, I say, I saw that this situation of mine was the precise situation of every mortal that breathes; only, in most cases, he, one way or other, has this Siamese connexion with a plurality of other mortals. If your banker

---

2. Not an actual Scottish kilt but a something like a butcher's skirtlike apron, no pants, and (for traction) coarse socks and no shoes. "Skirt" is an NN emendation for "shirt"; Melville was recalling a passage in Sir Walter Scott's *Waverley* (1814) on a kilt's showing off a man's sinewy limbs, with the additional joke that in his rolling and swaying on the whale and in Ishmael's jerking him with the rope Queequeg shows off more than his legs to the appreciative Ishmael.

breaks, you snap; if your apothecary by mistake sends you poison in your pills, you die. True, you may say that, by exceeding caution, you may possibly escape these and the multitudinous other evil chances of life. But handle Queequeg's monkey-rope heedfully as I would, sometimes he jerked it so, that I came very near sliding overboard. Nor could I possibly forget that, do what I would, I only had the management of one end of it.[3]

I have hinted that I would often jerk poor Queequeg from between the whale and the ship—where he would occasionally fall, from the incessant rolling and swaying of both. But this was not the only jamming jeopardy he was exposed to. Unappalled by the massacre made upon them during the night, the sharks now freshly and more keenly allured by the before pent blood which began to flow from the carcase—the rabid creatures swarmed round it like bees in a beehive.

And right in among those sharks was Queequeg; who often pushed them aside with his floundering feet. A thing altogether incredible were it not that attracted by such prey as a dead whale, the otherwise miscellaneously carnivorous shark will seldom touch a man.

Nevertheless, it may well be believed that since they have such a ravenous finger in the pie,[4] it is deemed but wise to look sharp to them. Accordingly, besides the monkey-rope, with which I now and then jerked the poor fellow from too close a vicinity to the maw of what seemed a peculiarly ferocious shark—he was provided with still another protection. Suspended over the side in one of the stages, Tashtego and Daggoo continually flourished over his head a couple of keen whale-spades, wherewith they slaughtered as many sharks as they could reach. This procedure of theirs, to be sure, was very disinterested and benevolent of them. They meant Queequeg's best happiness, I admit; but in their hasty zeal to befriend him, and from the circumstance that both he and the sharks were at times half hidden by the blood-mudded water, those indiscreet spades of theirs would come nearer amputating a leg than a tail. But poor Queequeg, I suppose, straining and gasping there with that great iron hook—poor Queequeg, I suppose, only prayed to his Yojo, and gave up his life into the hands of his gods.

Well, well, my dear comrade and twin-brother, thought I, as I drew in and then slacked off the rope to every swell of the sea—what matters it, after all? Are you not the precious image of each and all of us men in this whaling world? That unsounded ocean you gasp in, is Life; those sharks, your foes; those spades, your friends; and what between sharks and spades you are in a sad pickle[5] and peril, poor lad.

But courage! there is good cheer in store for you, Queequeg. For now, as with blue lips and bloodshot eyes the exhausted savage at last climbs up the chains and stands all dripping and involuntarily trembling over the side; the steward advances, and with a benevolent, consolatory glance hands him—what? Some hot Cogniac? No! hands him, ye gods! hands him a cup of tepid ginger and water!

3. The monkey-rope is found in all whalers; but it was only in the Pequod that the monkey and his holder were ever tied together. This improvement upon the original usage was introduced by no less a man than Stubb, in order to afford to the imperilled harpooneer the strongest possible guarantee for the faithfulness and vigilance of his monkey-rope holder [Melville's note].
4. Piece of the action.
5. In a tough spot (proverbial).

"Ginger? Do I smell ginger?" suspiciously asked Stubb, coming near. "Yes, this must be ginger," peering into the as yet untasted cup. Then standing as if incredulous for a while, he calmly walked towards the astonished steward slowly saying, "Ginger? ginger? and will you have the goodness to tell me, Mr. Dough-Boy, where lies the virtue of ginger? Ginger! is ginger the sort of fuel you use, Dough-Boy, to kindle a fire in this shivering cannibal? Ginger!—what the devil is ginger?—sea-coal?—fire-wood?—lucifer matches?—tinder?—gunpowder?[6]—what the devil is ginger, I say, that you offer this cup to our poor Queequeg here?"

"There is some sneaking Temperance Society movement about this business," he suddenly added, now approaching Starbuck, who had just come from forward. "Will you look at that kannakin, sir: smell of it, if you please." Then watching the mate's countenance, he added: "The steward, Mr. Starbuck, had the face to offer that calomel and jalap[7] to Queequeg, there, this instant off the whale. Is the steward an apothecary, sir? and may I ask whether this is the sort of bellows by which he blows back the breath into a half-drowned man?"

"I trust not," said Starbuck, "it is poor stuff enough."

"Aye, aye, steward," cried Stubb, "we'll teach you to drug a harpooneer; none of your apothecary's medicine here; you want to poison us, do ye? You have got out insurances on our lives and want to murder us all, and pocket the proceeds, do ye?"

"It was not me," cried Dough-Boy, "it was Aunt Charity that brought the ginger on board; and bade me never give the harpooneers any spirits, but only this ginger-jub—so she called it."

"Ginger-jub! you gingerly rascal! take that![8] and run along with ye to the lockers, and get something better. I hope I do no wrong, Mr. Starbuck. It is the captain's orders—grog for the harpooneer on a whale."

"Enough," replied Starbuck, "only don't hit him again, but—"

"Oh, I never hurt when I hit, except when I hit a whale or something of that sort; and this fellow's a weazel. What were you about saying, sir?"

"Only this: go down with him, and get what thou wantest thyself."

When Stubb reappeared, he came with a dark flask in one hand, and a sort of tea-caddy in the other. The first contained strong spirits, and was handed to Queequeg; the second was Aunt Charity's gift, and that was freely given to the waves.

Chapter 73

Stubb and Flask kill a Right Whale; and
Then Have a Talk over Him

It must be borne in mind that all this time we have a Sperm Whale's prodigious head hanging to the Pequod's side. But we must let it continue

---

6. Stubb scorns Aunt Charity's nonalcoholic ginger-jub (ginger and water) as not "hot" enough to warm up poor Queequeg, unlike sea coal, firewood, matches (newly invented striking matches), tinder, and gunpowder.
7. Common laxatives.
8. Stubb's hitting the steward is the only time an officer strikes a man until ch. 124.

hanging there a while till we can get a chance to attend to it. For the present other matters press, and the best we can do now for the head, is to pray heaven the tackles may hold.

Now, during the past night and forenoon, the Pequod had gradually drifted into a sea, which, by its occasional patches of yellow brit, gave unusual tokens of the vicinity of Right Whales, a species of the Leviathan that but few supposed to be at this particular time lurking anywhere near. And though all hands commonly disdained the capture of those inferior creatures; and though the Pequod was not commissioned to cruise for them at all, and though she had passed numbers of them near the Crozetts[1] without lowering a boat; yet now that a Sperm Whale had been brought alongside and beheaded, to the surprise of all, the announcement was made that a Right Whale should be captured that day, if opportunity offered.

Nor was this long wanting. Tall spouts were seen to leeward; and two boats, Stubb's and Flask's, were detached in pursuit. Pulling further and further away, they at last became almost invisible to the men at the masthead. But suddenly in the distance, they saw a great heap of tumultuous white water, and soon after news came from aloft that one or both the boats must be fast. An interval passed and the boats were in plain sight, in the act of being dragged right towards the ship by the towing whale. So close did the monster come to the hull, that at first it seemed as if he meant it malice; but suddenly going down in a maelstrom, within three rods of the planks, he wholly disappeared from view, as if diving under the keel. "Cut, cut!" was the cry from the ship to the boats, which, for one instant, seemed on the point of being brought with a deadly dash against the vessel's side. But having plenty of line yet in the tubs, and the whale not sounding very rapidly, they paid out abundance of rope, and at the same time pulled with all their might so as to get ahead of the ship. For a few minutes the struggle was intensely critical; for while they still slacked out the tightened line in one direction, and still plied their oars in another, the contending strain threatened to take them under. But it was only a few feet advance they sought to gain. And they stuck to it till they did gain it; when instantly, a swift tremor was felt running like lightning along the keel, as the strained line, scraping beneath the ship, suddenly rose to view under her bows, snapping and quivering; and so flinging off its drippings, that the drops fell like bits of broken glass on the water, while the whale beyond also rose to sight, and once more the boats were free to fly. But the fagged whale abated his speed, and blindly altering his course, went round the stern of the ship towing the two boats after him, so that they performed a complete circuit.

Meantime, they hauled more and more upon their lines, till close flanking him on both sides, Stubb answered Flask with lance for lance; and thus round and round the Pequod the battle went, while the multitudes of sharks that had before swum round the Sperm Whale's body, rushed to the fresh blood that was spilled, thirstily drinking at every new gash, as the eager Israelites did at the new bursting fountains that poured from the smitten rock.[2]

---

1. Southeastward from the Cape of Good Hope, in the Indian Ocean.
2. Exodus 17.6, where God says: "Behold, I will stand before thee there upon the rock in Horeb; and thou shalt smite the rock, and there shall come water out of it, that the people may drink. And Moses did so in the sight of the elders of Israel."

At last his spout grew thick, and with a frightful roll and vomit, he turned upon his back a corpse.

While the two headsmen were engaged in making fast cords to his flukes, and in other ways getting the mass in readiness for towing, some conversation ensued between them.

"I wonder what the old man wants with this lump of foul lard," said Stubb, not without some disgust at the thought of having to do with so ignoble a leviathan.

"Wants with it?" said Flask, coiling some spare line in the boat's bow, "did you never hear that the ship which but once has a Sperm Whale's head hoisted on her starboard side, and at the same time a Right Whale's on the larboard; did you never hear, Stubb, that that ship can never afterwards capsize?"

"Why not?"

"I don't know, but I heard that gamboge[3] ghost of a Fedallah saying so, and he seems to know all about ships' charms. But I sometimes think he'll charm the ship to no good at last. I don't half like that chap, Stubb. Did you ever notice how that tusk of his is a sort of carved into a snake's head, Stubb?"

"Sink him! I never look at him at all; but if ever I get a chance of a dark night, and he standing hard by the bulwarks, and no one by; look down there, Flask"—pointing into the sea with a peculiar motion of both hands—"Aye, will I! Flask, I take that Fedallah to be the devil in disguise. Do you believe that cock and bull story about his having been stowed away on board ship? He's the devil, I say. The reason why you don't see his tail, is because he tucks it up out of sight; he carries it coiled away in his pocket, I guess. Blast him! now that I think of it, he's always wanting oakum[4] to stuff into the toes of his boots."

"He sleeps in his boots, don't he? He hasn't got any hammock; but I've seen him lay of nights in a coil of rigging."

"No doubt, and it's because of his cursed tail; he coils it down, do ye see, in the eye of the rigging."

"What's the old man have so much to do with him for?"

"Striking up a swap or a bargain, I suppose."

"Bargain?—about what?"

"Why, do ye see, the old man is hard bent after that White Whale, and the devil there is trying to come round him, and get him to swap away his silver watch, or his soul, or something of that sort, and then he'll surrender Moby Dick."

"Pooh! Stubb, you are skylarking; how can Fedallah do that?"

"I don't know, Flask, but the devil is a curious chap, and a wicked one, I tell ye. Why, they say[5] as how he went a sauntering into the old flag-ship once, switching his tail about devilish easy and gentlemanlike, and inquiring if the old governor was at home. Well, he was at home, and asked the

---

3. Yellowish (the color of a pigment from resin of southeast Asian trees).
4. Tarred hemp used for caulking leaks. *Devil in disguise:* Stubb accepts the folk version of the devil as shape-shifting, but with a tail and cloven hooves, a deceiver who bargains for souls and carries them off to hell. *Cock and bull story:* a fantastic tale, told as true.
5. What follows is a travesty of the biblical story of Job, whom God ("the old governor") allowed Satan to afflict.

devil what he wanted. The devil, switching his hoofs, up and says, 'I want John.' 'What for?' says the old governor. 'What business is that of yours,' says the devil, getting mad,—'I want to use him.' 'Take him,' says the governor—and by the Lord, Flask, if the devil didn't give John the Asiatic cholera before he got through with him, I'll eat this whale in one mouthful. But look sharp—aint you all ready there? Well, then, pull ahead, and let's get the whale alongside."

"I think I remember some such story as you were telling," said Flask, when at last the two boats were slowly advancing with their burden towards the ship, "but I can't remember where."

"Three Spaniards? Adventures of those three bloody-minded soldadoes?[6] Did ye read it there, Flask? I guess ye did?"

"No: never saw such a book; heard of it, though. But now, tell me, Stubb, do you suppose that that devil you was speaking of just now, was the same you say is now on board the Pequod?"

"Am I the same man that helped kill this whale? Doesn't the devil live for ever; who ever heard that the devil was dead? Did you ever see any parson a wearing mourning for the devil? And if the devil has a latch-key to get into the admiral's cabin, don't you suppose he can crawl into a porthole? Tell me that, Mr. Flask?"

"How old do you suppose Fedallah is, Stubb?"

"Do you see that mainmast there?" pointing to the ship; "well, that's the figure one; now take all the hoops in the Pequod's hold, and string 'em along in a row with that mast, for oughts, do you see; well, that wouldn't begin to be Fedallah's age. Nor all the coopers in creation couldn't show hoops enough to make oughts enough."

"But see here, Stubb, I thought you a little boasted just now, that you meant to give Fedallah a sea-toss, if you got a good chance. Now, if he's so old as all those hoops of yours come to, and if he is going to live for ever, what good will it do to pitch him overboard—tell me that?"

"Give him a good ducking, anyhow."

"But he'd crawl back."

"Duck him again; and keep ducking him."

"Suppose he should take it into his head to duck you, though—yes, and drown you—what then?"

"I should like to see him try it; I'd give him such a pair of black eyes that he wouldn't dare to show his face in the admiral's cabin again for a long while, let alone down in the orlop there, where he lives, and hereabouts on the upper decks where he sneaks so much. Damn the devil, Flask; do you suppose I'm afraid of the devil? Who's afraid of him, except the old governor who daresn't catch him and put him in double-darbies, as he deserves, but lets him go about kidnapping people; aye, and signed a bond with him, that all the people the devil kidnapped, he'd roast for him? There's a governor!"

"Do you suppose Fedallah wants to kidnap Captain Ahab?"

"Do I suppose it? You'll know it before long, Flask. But I am going now to keep a sharp look-out on him; and if I see anything very suspicious

---

6. Soldiers. Stubb further flaunts his intellectual superiority in teasingly suggesting that Flask may have found the story in George Walker's melodramatic novel *The Three Spaniards* (1800).

going on, I'll just take him by the nape of his neck, and say—Look here,
Beelzebub, you don't do it; and if he makes any fuss, by the Lord I'll make
a grab into his pocket for his tail, take it to the capstan, and give him such
a wrenching and heaving, that his tail will come short off at the stump—
do you see; and then, I rather guess when he finds himself docked in that
queer fashion, he'll sneak off without the poor satisfaction of feeling his
tail between his legs."

"And what will you do with the tail, Stubb?"

"Do with it? Sell it for an ox whip when we get home;—what else?"

"Now, do you mean what you say, and have been saying all along,
Stubb?"

"Mean or not mean, here we are at the ship."

The boats were here hailed, to tow the whale on the larboard side,
where fluke chains and other necessaries were already prepared for securing him.

"Didn't I tell you so?" said Flask; "yes, you'll soon see this right whale's
head hoisted up opposite that parmacetti's."

In good time, Flask's saying proved true. As before, the Pequod steeply
leaned over towards the sperm whale's head, now, by the counterpoise of
both heads, she regained her even keel; though sorely strained, you may
well believe. So, when on one side you hoist in Locke's head, you go over
that way; but now, on the other side, hoist in Kant's[7] and you come back
again; but in very poor plight. Thus, some minds for ever keep trimming
boat. Oh, ye foolish! throw all these thunder-heads overboard, and then
you will float light and right.

In disposing of the body of a right whale, when brought alongside the
ship, the same preliminary proceedings commonly take place as in the
case of a sperm whale; only, in the latter instance, the head is cut off
whole, but in the former the lips and tongue are separately removed and
hoisted on deck, with all the well known black bone attached to what is
called the crown-piece. But nothing like this, in the present case, had
been done. The carcases of both whales had dropped astern; and the
head-laden ship not a little resembled a mule carrying a pair of overbur-
dening panniers.

Meantime, Fedallah was calmly eyeing the right whale's head, and
ever and anon glancing from the deep wrinkles there to the lines in his
own hand. And Ahab chanced so to stand, that the Parsee occupied his
shadow; while, if the Parsee's shadow was there at all it seemed only to
blend with, and lengthen Ahab's. As the crew toiled on, Laplandish[8]
speculations were bandied among them, concerning all these passing
things.

---

7. John Locke (1632–1704), English empirical philosopher whose commonly accepted doctrines
   were then being challenged by "transcendentalists" who used views of the German idealistic
   philosopher Immanuel Kant (1724–1804). This passage rejects both positions and humorously
   advocates dispensing with them, along with views of all such heavy thinkers ("thunderheads," literally, lightning-charged clouds, but with a pun on "dunderheads," blockheads).
8. Mystical, occult, of the sort attributed to witch-haunted natives of this extreme northern region
   of Europe.

Chapter 74

The Sperm Whale's Head—Contrasted View

Here, now, are two great whales, laying their heads together; let us join them, and lay together our own.

Of the grand order of folio leviathans, the Sperm Whale and the Right Whale are by far the most noteworthy. They are the only whales regularly hunted by man. To the Nantucketer, they present the two extremes of all the known varieties of the whale. As the external difference between them is mainly observable in their heads; and as a head of each is this moment hanging from the Pequod's side; and as we may freely go from one to the other, by merely stepping across the deck:—where, I should like to know, will you obtain a better chance to study practical cetology than here?

In the first place, you are struck by the general contrast between these heads. Both are massive enough in all conscience; but there is a certain mathematical symmetry in the Sperm Whale's which the Right Whale's sadly lacks. There is more character in the Sperm Whale's head. As you behold it, you involuntarily yield the immense superiority to him, in point of pervading dignity. In the present instance, too, this dignity is heightened by the pepper and salt color of his head at the summit, giving token of advanced age and large experience. In short, he is what the fishermen technically call a "greyheaded whale."

Let us now note what is least dissimilar in these heads—namely, the two most important organs, the eye and the ear. Far back on the side of the head, and low down, near the angle of either whale's jaw, if you narrowly search, you will at last see a lashless eye, which you would fancy to be a young colt's eye; so out of all proportion is it to the magnitude of the head.

Now, from this peculiar sideway position of the whale's eyes, it is plain that he can never see an object which is exactly ahead, no more than he can one exactly astern. In a word, the position of the whale's eyes corresponds to that of a man's ears; and you may fancy, for yourself, how it would fare with you, did you sideways survey objects through your ears. You would find that you could only command some thirty degrees of vision in advance of the straight side-line of sight; and about thirty more behind it. If your bitterest foe were walking straight towards you, with dagger uplifted in broad day, you would not be able to see him, any more than if he were stealing upon you from behind. In a word, you would have two backs, so to speak; but, at the same time, also, two fronts (side fronts): for what is it that makes the front of a man—what, indeed, but his eyes?

Moreover, while in most other animals that I can now think of, the eyes are so planted as imperceptibly to blend their visual power, so as to produce one picture and not two to the brain; the peculiar position of the whale's eyes, effectually divided as they are by many cubic feet of solid head, which towers between them like a great mountain separating two lakes in valleys; this, of course, must wholly separate the impressions which each independent organ imparts. The whale, therefore, must see one distinct picture on this side, and another distinct picture on that side;

while all between must be profound darkness and nothingness to him. Man may, in effect, be said to look out on the world from a sentry-box with two joined sashes for his window. But with the whale, these two sashes are separately inserted, making two distinct windows, but sadly impairing the view. This peculiarity of the whale's eyes is a thing always to be borne in mind in the fishery; and to be remembered by the reader in some subsequent scenes.

A curious and most puzzling question might be started concerning this visual matter as touching the Leviathan. But I must be content with a hint. So long as a man's eyes are open in the light, the act of seeing is involuntary; that is, he cannot then help mechanically seeing whatever objects are before him. Nevertheless, any one's experience will teach him, that though he can take in an undiscriminating sweep of things at one glance, it is quite impossible for him, attentively, and completely, to examine any two things—however large or however small—at one and the same instant of time; never mind if they lie side by side and touch each other. But if you now come to separate these two objects, and surround each by a circle of profound darkness; then, in order to see one of them, in such a manner as to bring your mind to bear on it, the other will be utterly excluded from your contemporary consciousness. How is it, then, with the whale? True, both his eyes, in themselves, must simultaneously act; but is his brain so much more comprehensive, combining, and subtle than man's, that he can at the same moment of time attentively examine two distinct prospects, one on one side of him, and the other in an exactly opposite direction? If he can, then is it as marvellous a thing in him, as if a man were able simultaneously to go through the demonstrations of two distinct problems in Euclid. Nor, strictly investigated, is there any incongruity in this comparison.

It may be but an idle whim, but it has always seemed to me, that the extraordinary vacillations of movement displayed by some whales when beset by three or four boats; the timidity and liability to queer frights, so common to such whales; I think that all this indirectly proceeds from the helpless perplexity of volition, in which their divided and diametrically opposite powers of vision must involve them.

But the ear of the whale is full as curious as the eye. If you are an entire stranger to their race, you might hunt over these two heads for hours, and never discover that organ. The ear has no external leaf whatever; and into the hole itself you can hardly insert a quill, so wondrously minute is it. It is lodged a little behind the eye. With respect to their ears, this important difference is to be observed between the sperm whale and the right. While the ear of the former has an external opening, that of the latter is entirely and evenly covered over with a membrane, so as to be quite imperceptible from without.

Is it not curious, that so vast a being as the whale should see the world through so small an eye, and hear the thunder through an ear which is smaller than a hare's? But if his eyes were broad as the lens of Herschel's great telescope;[1] and his ears capacious as the porches of cathedrals;

1. The large instrument with which in 1789 the astronomer Sir William Herschel (1738–1822) made notable discoveries.

would that make him any longer of sight, or sharper of hearing? Not at all.—Why then do you try to "enlarge" your mind? Subtilize it.

Let us now with whatever levers and steam-engines we have at hand, cant over the sperm whale's head, so that it may lie bottom up; then, ascending by a ladder to the summit, have a peep down the mouth; and were it not that the body is now completely separated from it, with a lantern we might descend into the great Kentucky Mammoth Cave[2] of his stomach. But let us hold on here by this tooth, and look about us where we are. What a really beautiful and chaste-looking mouth! from floor to ceiling, lined, or rather papered with a glistening white membrane, glossy as bridal satins.

But come out now, and look at this portentous lower jaw, which seems like the long narrow lid of an immense snuff-box, with the hinge at one end, instead of one side. If you pry it up, so as to get it overhead, and expose its rows of teeth, it seems a terrific portcullis: and such, alas! it proves to many a poor wight in the fishery, upon whom these spikes fall with impaling force. But far more terrible is it to behold, when fathoms down in the sea, you see some sulky whale, floating there suspended, with his prodigious jaw, some fifteen feet long, hanging straight down at right-angles with his body, for all the world like a ship's jib-boom. This whale is not dead; he is only dispirited; out of sorts, perhaps; hypochondriac; and so supine, that the hinges of his jaw have relaxed, leaving him there in that ungainly sort of plight, a reproach to all his tribe, who must, no doubt, imprecate lock-jaws upon him.

In most cases this lower jaw—being easily unhinged by a practised artist—is disengaged and hoisted on deck for the purpose of extracting the ivory teeth, and furnishing a supply of that hard white whalebone with which the fishermen fashion all sorts of curious articles, including canes, umbrella-stocks, and handles to riding-whips.

With a long, weary hoist the jaw is dragged on board, as if it were an anchor; and when the proper time comes—some few days after the other work—Queequeg, Daggoo, and Tashtego, being all accomplished dentists, are set to drawing teeth. With a keen cutting-spade, Queequeg lances the gums; then the jaw is lashed down to ringbolts, and a tackle being rigged from aloft, they drag out these teeth, as Michigan oxen drag stumps of old oaks out of wild wood-lands. There are generally forty-two teeth in all; in old whales, much worn down, but undecayed; nor filled after our artificial fashion. The jaw is afterwards sawn into slabs, and piled away like joists for building houses.

Chapter 75

The Right Whale's Head—Contrasted View

Crossing the deck, let us now have a good long look at the Right Whale's head.

---

2. Extensive caverns in Hart County, Kentucky.

As in general shape the noble Sperm Whale's head may be compared to a Roman war-chariot (especially in front, where it is so broadly rounded); so, at a broad view, the Right Whale's head bears a rather inelegant resemblance to a gigantic galliot-toed shoe. Two hundred years ago an old Dutch voyager likened its shape to that of a shoemaker's last. And in this same last or shoe, that old woman of the nursery tale,[1] with the swarming brood, might very comfortably be lodged, she and all her progeny.

But as you come nearer to this great head it begins to assume different aspects, according to your point of view. If you stand on its summit and look at these two f-shaped spout-holes, you would take the whole head for an enormous bass-viol, and these spiracles, the apertures in its sounding-board. Then, again, if you fix your eye upon this strange, crested, comb-like incrustation on the top of the mass—this green, barnacled thing, which the Greenlanders call the "crown," and the Southern fishers the "bonnet" of the Right Whale; fixing your eyes solely on this, you would take the head for the trunk of some huge oak, with a bird's nest in its crotch. At any rate, when you watch those live crabs that nestle here on this bonnet, such an idea will be almost sure to occur to you; unless, indeed, your fancy has been fixed by the technical term "crown" also bestowed upon it; in which case you will take great interest in thinking how this mighty monster is actually a diademed king of the sea, whose green crown has been put together for him in this marvellous manner. But if this whale be a king, he is a very sulky looking fellow to grace a diadem. Look at that hanging lower lip! what a huge sulk and pout is there! a sulk and pout, by carpenter's measurement, about twenty feet long and five feet deep; a sulk and pout that will yield you some 500 gallons of oil and more.

A great pity, now, that this unfortunate whale should be hare-lipped. The fissure is about a foot across. Probably the mother during an important interval was sailing down the Peruvian coast, when earthquakes caused the beach to gape.[2] Over this lip, as over a slippery threshold, we now slide into the mouth. Upon my word were I at Mackinaw, I should take this to be the inside of an Indian wigwam. Good Lord! is this the road that Jonah went? The roof is about twelve feet high, and runs to a pretty sharp angle, as if there were a regular ridge-pole there; while these ribbed, arched, hairy sides, present us with those wondrous, half vertical, scimetar-shaped slats of whalebone, say three hundred on a side, which depending from the upper part of the head or crown bone, form those Venetian blinds[3] which have elsewhere been cursorily mentioned. The edges of these bones are fringed with hairy fibres, through which the Right Whale strains the water, and in whose intricacies he retains the small fish, when open-mouthed he goes through the seas of brit in feeding time. In the central blinds of bone, as they stand in their natural order, there are certain curious marks, curves, hollows, and ridges, whereby

1. In the Mother Goose nursery rhyme, the old woman who lived in a shoe had so many children she didn't know what to do. *Galliot-toed:* square-toed (see Melville's footnote in ch. 61). *Last:* the foot-shaped form a shoemaker molds shoe leather around. The result here is a wide-toed Dutch shoe, like Dutch wooden shoes.
2. *Yawn,* open up. *Important interval:* pregnancy, during which, it was said, the fetus might come to resemble any shocking sight the mother beheld.
3. Mentioned in ch. 58. *Mackinaw:* or Mackinac; in northern Michigan, as referred to in ch. 54.

some whalemen calculate the creature's age, as the age of an oak by its circular rings. Though the certainty of this criterion is far from demonstrable, yet it has the savor of analogical probability. At any rate, if we yield to it, we must grant a far greater age to the Right Whale than at first glance will seem reasonable.

In old times, there seem to have prevailed the most curious fancies concerning these blinds. One voyager in Purchas calls them the wondrous "whiskers" inside of the whale's mouth;[4] another, "hogs' bristles;" a third old gentleman in Hackluyt uses the following elegant language: "There are about two hundred and fifty fins growing on each side of his upper *chop*, which arch over his tongue on each side of his mouth."

As every one knows, these same "hogs' bristles," "fins," "whiskers," "blinds," or whatever you please, furnish to the ladies their busks and other stiffening contrivances. But in this particular, the demand has long been on the decline. It was in Queen Anne's time that the bone was in its glory, the farthingale[5] being then all the fashion. And as those ancient dames moved about gaily, though in the jaws of the whale, as you may say; even so, in a shower, with the like thoughtlessness, do we nowadays fly under the same jaws for protection; the umbrella being a tent spread over the same bone.

But now forget all about blinds and whiskers for a moment, and, standing in the Right Whale's mouth, look around you afresh. Seeing all these colonnades of bone so methodically ranged about, would you not think you were inside of the great Haarlem organ,[6] and gazing upon its thousand pipes? For a carpet to the organ we have a rug of the softest Turkey— the tongue, which is glued, as it were, to the floor of the mouth. It is very fat and tender, and apt to tear in pieces in hoisting it on deck. This particular tongue now before us; at a passing glance I should say it was a six-barreler; that is, it will yield you about that amount of oil.

Ere this, you must have plainly seen the truth of what I started with— that the Sperm Whale and the Right Whale have almost entirely different heads. To sum up, then: in the Right Whale's there is no great well of sperm; no ivory teeth at all; no long, slender mandible of a lower jaw, like the Sperm Whale's. Nor in the Sperm Whale are there any of those blinds of bone; no huge lower lip; and scarcely anything of a tongue. Again, the Right Whale has two external spout-holes, the Sperm Whale only one.

Look your last, now, on these venerable hooded heads, while they yet lie together; for one will soon sink, unrecorded, in the sea; the other will not be very long in following.

Can you catch the expression of the Sperm Whale's there? It is the same he died with, only some of the longer wrinkles in the forehead seem now faded away. I think his broad brow to be full of a prairie-like placidity, born of a speculative indifference as to death. But mark the other

---

4. This reminds us that the Right Whale really has a sort of whisker, or rather a moustache, consisting of a few scattered white hairs on the upper part of the outer end of the lower jaw. Sometimes these tufts impart a rather brigandish expression to his otherwise solemn countenance [Melville's note].
5. A hooped support for a skirt; here, whalebone hoops. Anne reigned as queen of England from 1702 to 1714.
6. The great organ in Haarlem (the city in the Netherlands) had five thousand pipes and was the largest in the world.

head's expression. See that amazing lower lip, pressed by accident against
the vessel's side, so as firmly to embrace the jaw. Does not this whole head
seem to speak of an enormous practical resolution in facing death? This
Right Whale I take to have been a Stoic; the Sperm Whale, a Platonian,
who might have taken up Spinoza in his latter years.[7]

Chapter 76

The Battering-Ram

Ere quitting, for the nonce, the Sperm Whale's head, I would have you,
as a sensible physiologist, simply—particularly remark its front aspect, in
all its compacted collectedness. I would have you investigate it now with
the sole view of forming to yourself some unexaggerated, intelligent estimate of whatever battering-ram power may be lodged there. Here is a vital
point; for you must either satisfactorily settle this matter with yourself, or
for ever remain an infidel as to one of the most appalling, but not the less
true events,[1] perhaps anywhere to be found in all recorded history.

You observe that in the ordinary swimming position of the Sperm
Whale, the front of his head presents an almost wholly vertical plane to
the water; you observe that the lower part of that front slopes considerably backwards, so as to furnish more of a retreat for the long socket
which receives the boom-like lower jaw; you observe that the mouth is
entirely under the head, much in the same way, indeed, as though your
own mouth were entirely under your chin. Moreover you observe that the
whale has no external nose; and that what nose he has—his spout hole—
is on the top of his head; you observe that his eyes and ears are at the sides
of his head, nearly one third of his entire length from the front. Wherefore, you must now have perceived that the front of the Sperm Whale's
head is a dead, blind wall, without a single organ or tender prominence of
any sort whatsoever. Furthermore, you are now to consider that only in
the extreme, lower, backward sloping part of the front of the head, is there
the slightest vestige of bone; and not till you get near twenty feet from the
forehead do you come to the full cranial development. So that this whole
enormous boneless mass is as one wad. Finally, though, as will soon be
revealed, its contents partly comprise the most delicate oil; yet, you are
now to be apprised of the nature of the substance which so impregnably
invests all that apparent effeminacy. In some previous place I have
described to you how the blubber wraps the body of the whale, as the rind
wraps an orange. Just so with the head; but with this difference: about the
head this envelope, though not so thick, is of a boneless toughness, inestimable by any man who has not handled it. The severest pointed harpoon, the sharpest lance darted by the strongest human arm, impotently

7. The Greek Stoic philosophers accepted divine will and taught rationality, endurance, and practical duty. Followers of Plato sought knowledge of transcendent Being, or God, as did the Dutch
   philosopher Spinoza (1632–1677).
1. Whales that rammed and sank ships; rare but well documented, and always highly newsworthy
   in Melville's time.

rebounds from it. It is as though the forehead of the Sperm Whale were paved with horses' hoofs. I do not think that any sensation lurks in it.

Bethink yourself also of another thing. When two large, loaded Indiamen chance to crowd and crush towards each other in the docks, what do the sailors do? They do not suspend between them, at the point of coming contact, any merely hard substance, like iron or wood. No, they hold there a large, round wad of tow and cork, enveloped in the thickest and toughest of ox-hide. That bravely and uninjured takes the jam which would have snapped all their oaken handspikes and iron crow-bars. By itself this sufficiently illustrates the obvious fact I drive at. But supplementary to this, it has hypothetically occurred to me, that as ordinary fish possess what is called a swimming bladder in them, capable, at will, of distension or contraction; and as the Sperm Whale, as far as I know, has no such provision in him; considering, too, the otherwise inexplicable manner in which he now depresses his head altogether beneath the surface, and anon swims with it high elevated out of the water; considering the unobstructed elasticity of its envelop; considering the unique interior of his head; it has hypothetically occurred to me, I say, that those mystical lung-celled honeycombs there may possibly have some hitherto unknown and unsuspected connexion with the outer air, so as to be susceptible to atmospheric distension and contraction. If this be so, fancy the irresistibleness of that might, to which the most impalpable and destructive of all elements contributes.

Now, mark. Unerringly impelling this dead, impregnable, uninjurable wall, and this most buoyant thing within; there swims behind it all a mass of tremendous life, only to be adequately estimated as piled wood is—by the cord; and all obedient to one volition, as the smallest insect. So that when I shall hereafter detail to you all the specialities and concentrations of potency everywhere lurking in this expansive monster; when I shall show you some of his more inconsiderable braining feats; I trust you will have renounced all ignorant incredulity, and be ready to abide by this; that though the Sperm Whale stove a passage through the Isthmus of Darien, and mixed the Atlantic with the Pacific, you would not elevate one hair of your eye-brow. For unless you own the whale, you are but a provincial and sentimentalist in Truth. But clear Truth is a thing for salamander giants only to encounter; how small the chances for the provincials then? What befel the weakling youth lifting the dread goddess's veil at Sais?[2]

Chapter 77

The Great Heidelburgh Tun[1]

Now comes the Baling of the Case. But to comprehend it aright, you must know something of the curious internal structure of the thing operated upon.

2. The goddess was Isis. A youth who lifted the veil of her statue at Sais, in Egypt, was struck senseless, according to Schiller's poem "The Veiled Statue at Sais" (which Melville knew in Edward Bulwer-Lytton's translation).
1. Wine cask in the castle cellar at Heidelberg, celebrated for its size (thirty feet in diameter and more than twenty feet high). Melville exaggerates the size of the whale's "case."

Regarding the Sperm Whale's head as a solid oblong, you may, on an inclined plane, sideways divide it into two quoins,[2] whereof the lower is the bony structure, forming the cranium and jaws, and the upper an unctuous mass wholly free from bones; its broad forward end forming the expanded vertical apparent forehead of the whale. At the middle of the forehead horizontally subdivide this upper quoin, and then you have two almost equal parts, which before were naturally divided by an internal wall of a thick tendinous substance.

The lower subdivided part, called the junk, is one immense honeycomb of oil, formed by the crossing and re-crossing, into ten thousand infiltrated cells, of tough elastic white fibres throughout its whole extent. The upper part, known as the Case, may be regarded as the great Heidelburgh Tun of the Sperm Whale. And as that famous great tierce is mystically carved in front, so the whale's vast plaited forehead forms innumerable strange devices for the emblematical adornment of his wondrous tun. Moreover, as that of Heidelburgh was always replenished with the most excellent of the wines of the Rhenish valleys,[3] so the tun of the whale contains by far the most precious of all his oily vintages; namely, the highly-prized spermaceti,[4] in its absolutely pure, limpid, and odoriferous state. Nor is this precious substance found unalloyed in any other part of the creature. Though in life it remains perfectly fluid, yet, upon exposure to the air, after death, it soon begins to concrete; sending forth beautiful crystalline shoots, as when the first thin delicate ice is just forming in water. A large whale's case generally yields about five hundred gallons of sperm, though from unavoidable circumstances, considerable of it is spilled, leaks, and dribbles away, or is otherwise irrevocably lost in the ticklish business of securing what you can.

I know not with what fine and costly material the Heidelburgh Tun was coated within, but in superlative richness that coating could not possibly have compared with the silken pearl-colored membrane, like the lining of a fine pelisse,[5] forming the inner surface of the Sperm Whale's case.

It will have been seen that the Heidelburgh Tun of the Sperm Whale embraces the entire length of the entire top of the head; and since—as has been elsewhere set forth—the head embraces one third of the whole length of the creature, then setting that length down at eighty feet for a good sized whale, you have more than twenty-six feet for the depth of the tun, when it is lengthwise hoisted up and down against a ship's side.

As in decapitating the whale, the operator's instrument is brought close to the spot where an entrance is subsequently forced into the spermaceti magazine; he has, therefore, to be uncommonly heedful, lest a careless, untimely stroke should invade the sanctuary and wastingly let out its invaluable contents. It is this decapitated end of the head, also, which is at last elevated out of the water, and retained in that position by the enor-

---

2. Quoin is not a Euclidean term. It belongs to the pure nautical mathematics. I know not that it has been defined before. A quoin is a solid which differs from a wedge in having its sharp end formed by the steep inclination of one side, instead of the mutual tapering of both sides [Melville's note].
3. Valleys of the Rhine River in Germany.
4. White, waxy substance used for making ointments and cosmetics, as well as fine candles.
5. A lightweight furred coat.

mous cutting tackles, whose hempen combinations, on one side, make quite a wilderness of ropes in that quarter.

Thus much being said, attend now, I pray you, to that marvellous and—in this particular instance—almost fatal operation whereby the Sperm Whale's great Heidelburgh Tun is tapped.

Chapter 78

Cistern and Buckets

Nimble as a cat, Tashtego mounts aloft; and without altering his erect posture, runs straight out upon the overhanging main-yard-arm, to the part where it exactly projects over the hoisted Tun. He has carried with him a light tackle called a whip, consisting of only two parts, travelling through a single-sheaved block. Securing this block, so that it hangs down from the yard-arm, he swings one end of the rope, till it is caught and firmly held by a hand on deck. Then, hand-over-hand, down the other part, the Indian drops through the air, till dexterously he lands on the summit of the head. There—still high elevated above the rest of the company, to whom he vivaciously cries—he seems some Turkish Muezzin[1] calling the good people to prayers from the top of a tower. A short-handled sharp spade being sent up to him, he diligently searches for the proper place to begin breaking into the Tun. In this business he proceeds very heedfully, like a treasure-hunter in some old house, sounding the walls to find where the gold is masoned in. By the time this cautious search is over, a stout iron-bound bucket, precisely like a well-bucket, has been attached to one end of the whip; while the other end, being stretched across the deck, is there held by two or three alert hands. These last now hoist the bucket within grasp of the Indian, to whom another person has reached up a very long pole. Inserting this pole into the bucket, Tashtego downward guides the bucket into the Tun, till it entirely disappears; then giving the word to the seamen at the whip, up comes the bucket again, all bubbling like a dairy-maid's pail of new milk. Carefully lowered from its height, the full-freighted vessel is caught by an appointed hand, and quickly emptied into a large tub. Then re-mounting aloft, it again goes through the same round until the deep cistern will yield no more. Towards the end, Tashtego has to ram his long pole harder and harder, and deeper and deeper into the Tun, until some twenty feet of the pole have gone down.

Now, the people of the Pequod had been baling some time in this way; several tubs had been filled with the fragrant sperm; when all at once a queer accident happened. Whether it was that Tashtego, that wild Indian, was so heedless and reckless as to let go for a moment his one-handed hold on the great cabled tackles suspending the head; or whether the place where he stood was so treacherous and oozy; or whether the Evil One himself would have it to fall out so, without stating his particular reasons; how it was exactly, there is no telling now; but, on a sudden, as the

1. Muslim crier to hourly prayers.

eightieth or ninetieth bucket came suckingly up—my God! poor Tashtego—like the twin reciprocating bucket in a veritable well, dropped head-foremost down into this great Tun of Heidelburgh, and with a horrible oily gurgling, went clean out of sight!

"Man overboard!" cried Daggoo, who amid the general consternation first came to his senses. "Swing the bucket this way!" and putting one foot into it, so as the better to secure his slippery hand-hold on the whip itself, the hoisters ran him high up to the top of the head, almost before Tashtego could have reached its interior bottom. Meantime, there was a terrible tumult. Looking over the side, they saw the before lifeless head throbbing and heaving just below the surface of the sea, as if that moment seized with some momentous idea; whereas it was only the poor Indian unconsciously revealing by those struggles the perilous depth to which he had sunk.

At this instant, while Daggoo, on the summit of the head, was clearing the whip—which had somehow got foul of the great cutting tackles—a sharp cracking noise was heard; and to the unspeakable horror of all, one of the two enormous hooks suspending the head tore out, and with a vast vibration the enormous mass sideways swung, till the drunk ship reeled and shook as if smitten by an iceberg. The one remaining hook, upon which the entire strain now depended, seemed every instant to be on the point of giving way; an event still more likely from the violent motions of the head.

"Come down, come down!" yelled the seamen to Daggoo, but with one hand holding on to the heavy tackles, so that if the head should drop, he would still remain suspended; the negro having cleared the foul line, rammed down the bucket into the now collapsed well, meaning that the buried harpooneer should grasp it, and so be hoisted out.

"In heaven's name, man," cried Stubb, "are you ramming home a cartridge there?—Avast! How will that help him; jamming that iron-bound bucket on top of his head? Avast, will ye!"

"Stand clear of the tackle!" cried a voice like the bursting of a rocket.

Almost in the same instant, with a thunder-boom, the enormous mass dropped into the sea, like Niagara's Table-Rock[2] into the whirlpool; the suddenly relieved hull rolled away from it, to far down her glittering copper; and all caught their breath, as half swinging—now over the sailors' heads, and now over the water—Daggoo, through a thick mist of spray, was dimly beheld clinging to the pendulous tackles, while poor, buried-alive Tashtego was sinking utterly down to the bottom of the sea! But hardly had the blinding vapor cleared away, when a naked figure with a boarding-sword in its hand, was for one swift moment seen hovering over the bulwarks. The next, a loud splash announced that my brave Queequeg had dived to the rescue. One packed rush was made to the side, and every eye counted every ripple, as moment followed moment, and no sign of either the sinker or the diver could be seen. Some hands now jumped into a boat alongside, and pushed a little off from the ship.

"Ha! ha!" cried Daggoo, all at once, from his now quiet, swinging perch overhead; and looking further off from the side, we saw an arm thrust

2. A ledge beside the falls that collapsed in June 1850, during the composition of *Moby-Dick*.

upright from the blue waves; a sight strange to see, as an arm thrust forth
from the grass over a grave.

"Both! both!—it is both!"—cried Daggoo again with a joyful shout; and
soon after, Queequeg was seen boldly striking out with one hand, and
with the other clutching the long hair of the Indian. Drawn into the waiting boat, they were quickly brought to the deck; but Tashtego was long in
coming to, and Queequeg did not look very brisk.

Now, how had this noble rescue been accomplished? Why, diving after
the slowly descending head, Queequeg with his keen sword had made side
lunges near its bottom, so as to scuttle a large hole there; then dropping
his sword, had thrust his long arm far inwards and upwards, and so hauled
out our poor Tash by the head. He averred, that upon first thrusting in for
him, a leg was presented; but well knowing that that was not as it ought
to be, and might occasion great trouble;—he had thrust back the leg, and
by a dexterous heave and toss, had wrought a somerset upon the Indian;
so that with the next trial, he came forth in the good old way—head foremost.[3] As for the great head itself, that was doing as well as could be
expected.

And thus, through the courage and great skill in obstetrics of Queequeg, the deliverance, or rather, delivery of Tashtego, was successfully
accomplished, in the teeth, too, of the most untoward and apparently
hopeless impediments; which is a lesson by no means to be forgotten.
Midwifery should be taught in the same course with fencing and boxing,
riding and rowing.

I know that this queer adventure of the Gay-Header's will be sure to
seem incredible to some landsmen, though they themselves may have
either seen or heard of some one's falling into a cistern ashore; an accident which not seldom happens, and with much less reason too than the
Indian's, considering the exceeding slipperiness of the curb of the Sperm
Whale's well.

But, peradventure, it may be sagaciously urged, how is this? We
thought the tissued, infiltrated head of the Sperm Whale, was the lightest and most corky part about him; and yet thou makest it sink in an element of a far greater specific gravity than itself. We have thee there. Not
at all, but I have ye; for at the time poor Tash fell in, the case had been
nearly emptied of its lighter contents, leaving little but the dense tendinous wall of the well—a double welded, hammered substance, as I have
before said, much heavier than the sea water, and a lump of which sinks
in it like lead almost. But the tendency to rapid sinking in this substance
was in the present instance materially counteracted by the other parts of
the head remaining undetached from it, so that it sank very slowly and
deliberately indeed, affording Queequeg a fair chance for performing his
agile obstetrics on the run, as you may say. Yes, it was a running delivery,
so it was.

Now, had Tashtego perished in that head, it had been a very precious
perishing; smothered in the very whitest and daintiest of fragrant sper-

---

3. Normal position for delivery. Sometimes the midwife or doctor (like Queequeg) must turn the
baby in the womb to achieve this position. Here, the whale's head (said to be doing well afterward) is the "mother."

maceti; coffined, hearsed, and tombed in the secret inner chamber and sanctum sanctorum[4] of the whale. Only one sweeter end can readily be recalled—the delicious death of an Ohio honey-hunter, who seeking honey in the crotch of a hollow tree, found such exceeding store of it, that leaning too far over, it sucked him in, so that he died embalmed. How many, think ye, have likewise fallen into Plato's honey head, and sweetly perished there?

Chapter 79

The Prairie

To scan the lines of his face, or feel the bumps on the head of this Leviathan; this is a thing which no Physiognomist or Phrenologist has as yet undertaken. Such an enterprise would seem almost as hopeful as for Lavater to have scrutinized the wrinkles on the Rock of Gibraltar, or for Gall to have mounted a ladder and manipulated the Dome of the Pantheon. Still, in that famous work of his, Lavater[1] not only treats of the various faces of men, but also attentively studies the faces of horses, birds, serpents, and fish; and dwells in detail upon the modifications of expression discernible therein. Nor have Gall and his disciple Spurzheim failed to throw out some hints touching the phrenological characteristics of other beings than man. Therefore, though I am but ill qualified for a pioneer, in the application of these two semi-sciences to the whale, I will do my endeavor. I try all things; I achieve what I can.

Physiognomically regarded, the Sperm Whale is an anomalous creature. He has no proper nose. And since the nose is the central and most conspicuous of the features; and since it perhaps most modifies and finally controls their combined expression; hence it would seem that its entire absence, as an external appendage, must very largely affect the countenance of the whale. For as in landscape gardening, a spire, cupola, monument, or tower of some sort, is deemed almost indispensable to the completion of the scene; so no face can be physiognomically in keeping without the elevated open-work belfry of the nose. Dash the nose from Phidias's marble Jove,[2] and what a sorry remainder! Nevertheless, Leviathan is of so mighty a magnitude, all his proportions are so stately, that the same deficiency which in the sculptured Jove were hideous, in him is no blemish at all. Nay, it is an added grandeur. A nose to the whale would have been impertinent. As on your physiognomical voyage you sail round his vast head in your jolly-boat, your noble conceptions of him are never insulted by the reflection that he has a nose to be pulled. A pesti-

---

4. Holy of Holies, the sacred innermost chamber of a temple.
1. Johann Kasper Lataver (1741–1801), Swiss physiognomist who studied human character as revealed in the contours of the face. The more recent phrenologists Franz Joseph Gall (1758–1828) and Johann Spurzheim Kaspar (1776–1832) read the bumps on the skull. Both pseudosciences were widely practiced and credited in the mid-19th century. *Pantheon*: the great domed temple in Rome, built during the Roman Empire and still standing.
2. The statue of Zeus (Jove) by this Greek sculptor (5th century B.C.E.) no longer survives, but Melville's comments apply to any great classical statue.

lent conceit, which so often will insist upon obtruding even when beholding the mightiest royal beadle[3] on his throne.

In some particulars, perhaps the most imposing physiognomical view to
be had of the Sperm Whale, is that of the full front of his head. This
aspect is sublime.

In thought, a fine human brow is like the East when troubled with the
morning. In the repose of the pasture, the curled brow of the bull has a
touch of the grand in it. Pushing heavy cannon up mountain defiles, the
elephant's brow is majestic. Human or animal, the mystical brow is as that
great golden seal affixed by the German emperors to their decrees. It signifies—"God: done this day by my hand."[4] But in most creatures, nay in man
himself, very often the brow is but a mere strip of alpine land lying along the
snow line. Few are the foreheads which like Shakspeare's or Melancthon's[5]
rise so high, and descend so low, that the eyes themselves seem clear, eternal, tideless mountain lakes; and all above them in the forehead's wrinkles,
you seem to track the antlered thoughts descending there to drink, as the
Highland hunters track the snow prints of the deer. But in the great Sperm
Whale, this high and mighty god-like dignity inherent in the brow is so
immensely amplified, that gazing on it, in that full front view, you feel the
Deity and the dread powers more forcibly than in beholding any other
object in living nature. For you see no one point precisely; not one distinct
feature is revealed; no nose, eyes, ears, or mouth; no face; he has none,
proper; nothing but that one broad firmament of a forehead, pleated with
riddles; dumbly lowering with the doom of boats, and ships, and men. Nor,
in profile, does this wondrous brow diminish; though that way viewed, its
grandeur does not domineer upon you so. In profile, you plainly perceive
that horizontal, semi-crescentic depression in the forehead's middle,
which, in man, is Lavater's mark of genius.

But how? Genius in the Sperm Whale? Has the Sperm Whale ever written a book, spoken a speech? No, his great genius is declared in his doing
nothing particular to prove it. It is moreover declared in his pyramidical
silence. And this reminds me that had the great Sperm Whale been known
to the young Orient World, he would have been deified by their child-
magian thoughts. They deified the crocodile of the Nile, because the crocodile is tongueless; and the Sperm Whale has no tongue, or at least it is
so exceedingly small, as to be incapable of protrusion. If hereafter any
highly cultured, poetical nation shall lure back to their birth-right, the
merry May-day gods of old; and livingly enthrone them again in the now
egotistical sky; in the now unhaunted hill; then be sure, exalted to Jove's
high seat, the great Sperm Whale shall lord it.[6]

Champollion deciphered the wrinkled granite hieroglyphics. But there
is no Champollion to decipher the Egypt of every man's and every being's

---

3. Minor ceremonial official; here, a king, disrespectfully seen as merely a beadle, though the most
   powerful one. This line survived the British censor of *The Whale*, who gave the entire book a
   quick and quite thorough scanning to remove any such disrespect toward royalty. *Nose to be
   pulled:* gesture of disrespect.
4. "God" may be an error for "Good," but Melville may have meant that a noble brow is God's own
   stamp (on human or animal), even as the great golden seal of the German Holy Roman emperors symbolized their claim to rule by divine right.
5. Philipp Melanchthon (1497–1560), German Protestant reformer.
6. The great sperm whale, tongueless as the deified crocodile, will then displace Jove (or the
   monotheistic Christian God).

face. Physiognomy, like every other human science, is but a passing fable. If then, Sir William Jones, who read in thirty languages, could not read the simplest peasant's face in its profounder and more subtle meanings, how may unlettered Ishmael hope to read the awful Chaldee[7] of the Sperm Whale's brow? I but put that brow before you. Read it if you can.

Chapter 80

The Nut

If the Sperm Whale be physiognomically a Sphinx, to the phrenologist his brain seems that geometrical circle which it is impossible to square.

In the full-grown creature the skull will measure at least twenty feet in length. Unhinge the lower jaw, and the side view of this skull is as the side view of a moderately inclined plane resting throughout on a level base. But in life—as we have elsewhere seen—this inclined plane is angularly filled up, and almost squared by the enormous superincumbent mass of the junk and sperm. At the high end the skull forms a crater to bed that part of the mass; while under the long floor of this crater—in another cavity seldom exceeding ten inches in length and as many in depth—reposes the mere handful of this monster's brain. The brain is at least twenty feet from his apparent forehead in life; it is hidden away behind its vast outworks, like the innermost citadel within the amplified fortifications of Quebec. So like a choice casket is it secreted in him, that I have known some whalemen who peremptorily deny that the Sperm Whale has any other brain than that palpable semblance of one formed by the cubic-yards of his sperm magazine. Lying in strange folds, courses, and convolutions, to their apprehensions, it seems more in keeping with the idea of his general might to regard that mystic part of him as the seat of his intelligence.

It is plain, then, that phrenologically the head of this Leviathan, in the creature's living intact state, is an entire delusion. As for his true brain, you can then see no indications of it, nor feel any. The whale, like all things that are mighty, wears a false brow to the common world.

If you unload his skull of its spermy heaps and then take a rear view of its rear end, which is the high end, you will be struck by its resemblance to the human skull, beheld in the same situation, and from the same point of view. Indeed, place this reversed skull (scaled down to the human magnitude) among a plate[1] of men's skulls, and you would involuntarily confound it with them; and remarking the depressions on one part of its summit, in phrenological phrase you would say—This man had no self-esteem, and no veneration. And by those negations, considered along with the affirmative fact of his prodigious bulk and power, you can best form to yourself the truest, though not the most exhilarating conception of what the most exalted potency is.

---

7. The language of ancient Babylonian inscriptions. Jean Françoise Champollion (1790–1832), French Egyptologist who deciphered the Rosetta Stone, allowing him to read the hieroglyphs— in Melville's youth, still celebrated as an astounding historical breakthrough. Sir William Jones (1746–1794), English Orientalist.
1. Picture in a book.

But if from the comparative dimensions of the whale's proper brain, you deem it incapable of being adequately charted, then I have another idea for you. If you attentively regard almost any quadruped's spine, you will be struck with the resemblance of its vertebræ to a strung necklace of dwarfed skulls, all bearing rudimental resemblance to the skull proper. It is a German conceit, that the vertebræ are absolutely undeveloped skulls. But the curious external resemblance, I take it the Germans were not the first men to perceive. A foreign friend[2] once pointed it out to me, in the skeleton of a foe he had slain, and with the vertebræ of which he was inlaying, in a sort of basso-relievo, the beaked prow of his canoe. Now, I consider that the phrenologists have omitted an important thing in not pushing their investigations from the cerebellum through the spinal canal. For I believe that much of a man's character will be found betokened in his backbone. I would rather feel your spine than your skull, whoever you are. A thin joist of a spine never yet upheld a full and noble soul. I rejoice in my spine, as in the firm audacious staff of that flag which I fling half out to the world.[3]

Apply this spinal branch of phrenology to the Sperm Whale. His cranial cavity is continuous with the first neck-vertebra; and in that vertebra the bottom of the spinal canal will measure ten inches across, being eight in height, and of a triangular figure with the base downwards. As it passes through the remaining vertebræ the canal tapers in size, but for a considerable distance remains of large capacity. Now, of course, this canal is filled with much the same strangely fibrous substance—the spinal cord—as the brain; and directly communicates with the brain. And what is still more, for many feet after emerging from the brain's cavity, the spinal cord remains of an undecreasing girth, almost equal to that of the brain. Under all these circumstances, would it be unreasonable to survey and map out the whale's spine phrenologically? For, viewed in this light, the wonderful comparative smallness of his brain proper is more than compensated by the wonderful comparative magnitude of his spinal cord.

But leaving this hint to operate as it may with the phrenologists, I would merely assume the spinal theory for a moment, in reference to the Sperm Whale's hump. This august hump, if I mistake not, rises over one of the larger vertebræ, and is, therefore, in some sort, the outer convex mould of it. From its relative situation then, I should call this high hump the organ of firmness or indomitableness in the Sperm Whale. And that the great monster is indomitable, you will yet have reason to know.

Chapter 81

The Pequod meets the Virgin

The predestinated day arrived, and we duly met the ship Jungfrau, Derick De Deer, master, of Bremen.[1]

---

2. A South-Sea one, such as Queequeg.
3. The Melvilles took good posture seriously, and even in his last years observers commented on Melville's erect strides, but "half out" has not been satisfactorily explicated and may not be just what he wrote.
1. A north German port. *Jungfrau:* virgin (German).

At one time the greatest whaling people in the world, the Dutch and Germans are now among the least; but here and there at very wide intervals of latitude and longitude, you still occasionally meet with their flag in the Pacific.

For some reason, the Jungfrau seemed quite eager to pay her respects. While yet some distance from the Pequod, she rounded to, and dropping a boat, her captain was impelled towards us, impatiently standing in the bows instead of the stern.

"What has he in his hand there?" cried Starbuck, pointing to something wavingly held by the German. "Impossible!—a lamp-feeder!"

"Not that," said Stubb, "no, no, it's a coffee-pot, Mr. Starbuck; he's coming off to make us our coffee, is the Yarman; don't you see that big tin can there alongside of him?—that's his boiling water. Oh! he's all right, is the Yarman."

"Go along with you," cried Flask, "it's a lamp-feeder and an oil-can. He's out of oil, and has come a-begging."

However curious it may seem for an oil-ship to be borrowing oil on the whale-ground, and however much it may invertedly contradict the old proverb about carrying coals to Newcastle,[2] yet sometimes such a thing really happens; and in the present case Captain Derick De Deer did indubitably conduct a lamp-feeder as Flask did declare.

As he mounted the deck, Ahab abruptly accosted him, without at all heeding what he had in his hand; but in his broken lingo, the German soon evinced his complete ignorance of the White Whale; immediately turning the conversation to his lamp-feeder and oil can, with some remarks touching his having to turn into his hammock at night in profound darkness—his last drop of Bremen oil being gone, and not a single flying-fish yet captured to supply the deficiency; concluding by hinting that his ship was indeed what in the Fishery is technically called a *clean* one (that is, an empty one), well deserving the name of Jungfrau or the Virgin.

His necessities supplied, Derick departed; but he had not gained his ship's side, when whales were almost simultaneously raised from the mast-heads of both vessels; and so eager for the chase was Derick, that without pausing to put his oil-can and lamp-feeder aboard, he slewed round his boat and made after the leviathan lamp-feeders.

Now, the game having risen to leeward, he and the other three German boats that soon followed him, had considerably the start of the Pequod's keels. There were eight whales, an average pod. Aware of their danger, they were going all abreast with great speed straight before the wind, rubbing their flanks as closely as so many spans of horses in harness. They left a great, wide wake, as though continually unrolling a great wide parchment upon the sea.

Full in this rapid wake, and many fathoms in the rear, swam a huge, humped old bull, which by his comparatively slow progress, as well as by the unusual yellowish incrustations overgrowing him, seemed afflicted with the jaundice, or some other infirmity. Whether this whale belonged to the pod in advance, seemed questionable; for it is not customary for

2. Redundant (proverbial), because coal is mined near that English city on the North Sea.

such venerable leviathans to be at all social. Nevertheless, he stuck to their wake, though indeed their back water must have retarded him, because the white-bone or swell at his broad muzzle was a dashed one, like the swell formed when two hostile currents meet. His spout was short, slow, and laborious; coming forth with a choking sort of gush, and spending itself in torn shreds, followed by strange subterranean commotions in him, which seemed to have egress at his other buried extremity, causing the waters behind him to upbubble.

"Who's got some paregoric?"[3] said Stubb, "he has the stomach-ache, I'm afraid. Lord, think of having half an acre of stomach-ache! Adverse winds are holding mad Christmas in him, boys. It's the first foul wind I ever knew to blow from astern; but look, did ever whale yaw so before? it must be, he's lost his tiller."

As an overladen Indiaman bearing down the Hindostan coast with a deck load of frightened horses, careens, buries, rolls, and wallows on her way; so did this old whale heave his aged bulk, and now and then partly turning over on his cumbrous rib-ends, expose the cause of his devious wake in the unnatural stump of his starboard fin. Whether he had lost that fin in battle, or had been born without it, it were hard to say.

"Only wait a bit, old chap, and I'll give ye a sling for that wounded arm," cried cruel Flask, pointing to the whale-line near him.

"Mind he don't sling thee with it," cried Starbuck. "Give way, or the German will have him."

With one intent all the combined rival boats were pointed for this one fish, because not only was he the largest, and therefore the most valuable whale, but he was nearest to them, and the other whales were going with such great velocity, moreover, as almost to defy pursuit for the time. At this juncture, the Pequod's keels had shot by the three German boats last lowered; but from the great start he had had, Derick's boat still led the chase, though every moment neared by his foreign rivals. The only thing they feared, was, that from being already so nigh to his mark, he would be enabled to dart his iron before they could completely overtake and pass him. As for Derick, he seemed quite confident that this would be the case, and occasionally with a deriding gesture shook his lamp-feeder at the other boats.

"The ungracious and ungrateful dog!" cried Starbuck; "he mocks and dares me with the very poor-box[4] I filled for him not five minutes ago!"— then in his old intense whisper—"give way, greyhounds! Dog to it!"

"I tell ye what it is, men"—cried Stubb to his crew—"It's against my religion to get mad; but I'd like to eat that villanous Yarman—Pull—wont ye? Are ye going to let that rascal beat ye? Do ye love brandy? A hogshead of brandy, then, to the best man. Come, why don't some of ye burst a blood-vessel? Who's that been dropping an anchor overboard—we don't budge an inch—we're becalmed. Halloo, here's grass growing in the boat's bottom—and by the Lord, the mast there's budding. This won't do, boys. Look at that Yarman! The short and long of it is, men, will ye spit fire or not?"

---

3. A common laxative.
4. Box for alms for the poor, usually near the door of a church.

"Oh! see the suds he makes!" cried Flask, dancing up and down—
"What a hump—Oh, *do* pile on the beef—lays like a log! Oh! my lads, *do*
spring—slap-jacks and quohogs for supper, you know, my lads—baked
clams and muffins—oh, *do, do,* spring—he's a hundred barreler—don't
lose him now—don't, oh, *don't!*—see that Yarman—Oh! won't ye pull for
your duff, my lads—such a sog! such a sogger![5] Don't ye love sperm?
There goes three thousand dollars, men!—a bank!—a whole bank! The
bank of England![6]—Oh, *do, do, do!*—What's that Yarman about now?"

At this moment Derick was in the act of pitching his lamp-feeder at the
advancing boats, and also his oil-can; perhaps with the double view of
retarding his rivals' way, and at the same time economically accelerating
his own by the momentary impetus of the backward toss.

"The unmannerly Dutch dogger!" cried Stubb. "Pull now, men, like fifty
thousand line-of-battle-ship loads of red-haired devils. What d'ye say,
Tashtego; are you the man to snap your spine in two-and-twenty pieces
for the honor of old Gay-head? What d'ye say?"

"I say, pull like god-dam,"—cried the Indian.

Fiercely but evenly, incited by the taunts of the German, the Pequod's
three boats now began ranging almost abreast; and, so disposed, momentarily neared him. In that fine, loose, chivalrous attitude of the headsman
when drawing near to his prey, the three mates stood up proudly, occasionally backing the after oarsman with an exhilarating cry of, "There she
slides, now! Hurrah for the white-ash breeze![7] Down with the Yarman! Sail
over him!"

But so decided an original start had Derick had, that spite of all their
gallantry, he would have proved the victor in this race, had not a righteous
judgment descended upon him in a crab[8] which caught the blade of his
midship oarsman. While this clumsy lubber was striving to free his white-
ash, and while, in consequence, Derick's boat was nigh to capsizing, and
he thundering away at his men in a mighty rage;—that was a good time
for Starbuck, Stubb, and Flask. With a shout, they took a mortal start forwards, and slantingly ranged up on the German's quarter. An instant
more, and all four boats were diagonally in the whale's immediate wake,
while stretching from them, on both sides, was the foaming swell that he
made.

It was a terrific, most pitiable, and maddening sight. The whale was
now going head out, and sending his spout before him in a continual tormented jet; while his one poor fin beat his side in an agony of fright. Now
to this hand, now to that, he yawed[9] in his faltering flight, and still at
every billow that he broke, he spasmodically sank in the sea, or sideways
rolled towards the sky his one beating fin. So have I seen a bird with
clipped wing, making affrighted broken circles in the air, vainly striving to
escape the piratical hawks. But the bird has a voice, and with plaintive
cries will make known her fear; but the fear of this vast dumb brute of the

---

5. Something large and heavy. *Sog*: a large whale.
6. As we would say "Fort Knox."
7. Caused by swiftly moving oars (made of white ash wood).
8. To "catch" a crab in rowing is to manage the oar so clumsily that it gets caught in the water, as
by a wave on the backstroke, as if an unseen crab had caught it.
9. Made a wallowing, erratic motion.

sea, was chained up and enchanted in him; he had no voice, save that choking respiration through his spiracle, and this made the sight of him unspeakably pitiable; while still, in his amazing bulk, portcullis jaw, and omnipotent tail, there was enough to appal the stoutest man who so pitied.

Seeing now that but a very few moments more would give the Pequod's boats the advantage, and rather than be thus foiled of his game, Derick chose to hazard what to him must have seemed a most unusually long dart, ere the last chance would for ever escape.

But no sooner did his harpooneer stand up for the stroke, than all three tigers—Queequeg, Tashtego, Daggoo—instinctively sprang to their feet, and standing in a diagonal row, simultaneously pointed their barbs; and, darted over the head of the German harpooneer, their three Nantucket irons entered the whale. Blinding vapors of foam and white-fire! The three boats, in the first fury of the whale's headlong rush, bumped the German's aside with such force, that both Derick and his baffled harpooneer were spilled out, and sailed over by the three flying keels.

"Don't be afraid, my butter-boxes," cried Stubb, casting a passing glance upon them as he shot by; "ye'll be picked up presently—all right—I saw some sharks astern—St. Bernard's dogs, you know—relieve distressed travellers. Hurrah! this is the way to sail now. Every keel a sunbeam! Hurrah!—Here we go like three tin kettles at the tail of a mad cougar! This puts me in mind of fastening to an elephant in a tilbury on a plain—makes the wheel-spokes fly, boys, when you fasten to him that way; and there's danger of being pitched out too, when you strike a hill. Hurrah! this is the way a fellow feels when he's going to Davy Jones[1]—all a rush down an endless inclined plane! Hurrah! this whale carries the everlasting mail!"

But the monster's run was a brief one. Giving a sudden gasp, he tumultuously sounded. With a grating rush, the three lines flew round the loggerheads with such a force as to gouge deep grooves in them; while so fearful were the harpooneers that this rapid sounding would soon exhaust the lines, that using all their dexterous might, they caught repeated smoking turns with the rope to hold on; till at last—owing to the perpendicular strain from the lead-lined chocks of the boats, whence the three ropes went straight down into the blue—the gunwales of the bows were almost even with the water, while the three sterns tilted high in the air. And the whale soon ceasing to sound, for some time they remained in that attitude, fearful of expending more line, though the position was a little ticklish. But though boats have been taken down and lost in this way, yet it is this "holding on," as it is called; this hooking up by the sharp barbs of his live flesh from the back; this it is that often torments the Leviathan into soon rising again to meet the sharp lance of his foes. Yet not to speak of the peril of the thing, it is to be doubted whether this course is always the best; for it is but reasonable to presume, that the longer the stricken whale stays under water, the more he is exhausted. Because, owing to the enormous surface of him—in a full grown sperm whale something less

---

1. From "Duppy Jonah," the ghost of Jonah. In nautical folklore, spirit devil who collects drowned souls and miscellaneous treasures into his locker at the bottom of the sea.

than 2000 square feet—the pressure of the water is immense. We all know what an astonishing atmospheric weight we ourselves stand up under; even here, above-ground, in the air; how vast, then, the burden of a whale, bearing on his back a column of two hundred fathoms of ocean! It must at least equal the weight of fifty atmospheres. One whaleman has estimated it at the weight of twenty line-of-battle ships, with all their guns, and stores, and men on board.

As the three boats lay there on that gently rolling sea, gazing down into its eternal blue noon; and as not a single groan or cry of any sort, nay, not so much as a ripple or a bubble came up from its depths; what landsman would have thought, that beneath all that silence and placidity, the utmost monster of the seas was writhing and wrenching in agony! Not eight inches of perpendicular rope were visible at the bows. Seems it credible that by three such thin threads the great Leviathan was suspended like the big weight to an eight day clock. Suspended? and to what? To three bits of board. Is this the creature of whom it was once so triumphantly said—"Canst thou fill his skin with barbed irons? or his head with fish-spears? The sword of him that layeth at him cannot hold, the spear, the dart, nor the habergeon: he esteemeth iron as straw; the arrow cannot make him flee; darts are counted as stubble; he laugheth at the shaking of a spear!"[2] This the creature? this he? Oh! that unfulfilments should follow the prophets. For with the strength of a thousand thighs in his tail, Leviathan had run his head under the mountains of the sea, to hide him from the Pequod's fish-spears!

In that sloping afternoon sunlight, the shadows that the three boats sent down beneath the surface, must have been long enough and broad enough to shade half Xerxes' army. Who can tell how appalling to the wounded whale must have been such huge phantoms flitting over his head!

"Stand by, men; he stirs," cried Starbuck, as the three lines suddenly vibrated in the water, distinctly conducting upwards to them, as by magnetic wires, the life and death throbs of the whale, so that every oarsman felt them in his seat. The next moment, relieved in great part from the downward strain at the bows, the boats gave a sudden bounce upwards, as a small ice-field will, when a dense herd of white bears are scared from it into the sea.

"Haul in! Haul in!" cried Starbuck again; "he's rising."

The lines, of which, hardly an instant before, not one hand's breadth could have been gained, were now in long quick coils flung back all dripping into the boats, and soon the whale broke water within two ship's lengths of the hunters.

His motions plainly denoted his extreme exhaustion. In most land animals there are certain valves or flood-gates in many of their veins, whereby when wounded, the blood is in some degree at least instantly shut off in certain directions. Not so with the whale; one of whose peculiarities it is, to have an entire non-valvular structure of the blood-vessels, so that when pierced even by so small a point as a harpoon, a deadly drain is at once begun upon his whole arterial system; and when this is height-

2. Job 41.7, 26–29.

ened by the extraordinary pressure of water at a great distance below the surface, his life may be said to pour from him in incessant streams. Yet so vast is the quantity of blood in him, and so distant and numerous its interior fountains, that he will keep thus bleeding and bleeding for a considerable period; even as in a drought a river will flow, whose source is in the well-springs of far-off and undiscernible hills. Even now, when the boats pulled upon this whale, and perilously drew over his swaying flukes, and the lances were darted into him, they were followed by steady jets from the new made wound, which kept continually playing, while the natural spout-hole in his head was only at intervals, however rapid, sending its affrighted moisture into the air. From this last vent no blood yet came, because no vital part of him had thus far been struck. His life, as they significantly call it, was untouched.

As the boats now more closely surrounded him, the whole upper part of his form, with much of it that is ordinarily submerged, was plainly revealed. His eyes, or rather the places where his eyes had been, were beheld. As strange misgrown masses gather in the knot-holes of the noblest oaks when prostrate, so from the points which the whale's eyes had once occupied, now protruded blind bulbs, horribly pitiable to see. But pity there was none. For all his old age, and his one arm, and his blind eyes, he must die the death and be murdered, in order to light the gay bridals and other merry-makings of men, and also to illuminate the solemn churches that preach unconditional inoffensiveness by all to all. Still rolling in his blood, at last he partially disclosed a strangely discolored bunch or protuberance, the size of a bushel, low down on the flank.

"A nice spot," cried Flask; "just let me prick him there once."

"Avast!" cried Starbuck, "there's no need of that!"

But humane Starbuck was too late. At the instant of the dart an ulcerous jet shot from this cruel wound, and goaded by it into more than sufferable anguish, the whale now spouting thick blood, with swift fury blindly darted at the craft, bespattering them and their glorying crews all over with showers of gore, capsizing Flask's boat and marring the bows. It was his death stroke. For, by this time, so spent was he by loss of blood, that he helplessly rolled away from the wreck he had made; lay panting on his side, impotently flapped with his stumped fin, then over and over slowly revolved like a waning world; turned up the white secrets of his belly; lay like a log, and died. It was most piteous, that last expiring spout. As when by unseen hands the water is gradually drawn off from some mighty fountain, and with half-stifled melancholy gurglings the spray-column lowers and lowers to the ground—so the last long dying spout of the whale.[3]

Soon, while the crews were awaiting the arrival of the ship, the body showed symptoms of sinking with all its treasures unrifled. Immediately, by Starbuck's orders, lines were secured to it at different points, so that ere long every boat was a buoy; the sunken whale being suspended a few inches beneath them by the cords. By very heedful management, when the ship drew nigh, the whale was transferred to her side, and was strongly secured there by the stiffest fluke-chains, for it was plain that unless artificially upheld, the body would at once sink to the bottom.

3. See Olsen-Smith (pp. 586–87 herein) for Melville's draft of this simile.

It so chanced that almost upon first cutting into him with the spade, the entire length of a corroded harpoon was found imbedded in his flesh, on the lower part of the bunch before described. But as the stumps of harpoons are frequently found in the dead bodies of captured whales, with the flesh perfectly healed around them, and no prominence of any kind to denote their place; therefore, there must needs have been some other unknown reason in the present case fully to account for the ulceration alluded to. But still more curious was the fact of a lance-head of stone being found in him, not far from the buried iron, the flesh perfectly firm about it. Who had darted that stone lance? And when? It might have been darted by some Nor' West Indian long before America was discovered.

What other marvels might have been rummaged out of this monstrous cabinet there is no telling. But a sudden stop was put to further discoveries, by the ship's being unprecedentedly dragged over sideways to the sea, owing to the body's immensely increasing tendency to sink. However, Starbuck, who had the ordering of affairs, hung on to it to the last; hung on to it so resolutely, indeed, that when at length the ship would have been capsized, if still persisting in locking arms with the body; then, when the command was given to break clear from it, such was the immovable strain upon the timber-heads to which the fluke-chains and cables were fastened, that it was impossible to cast them off. Meantime everything in the Pequod was aslant. To cross to the other side of the deck was like walking up the steep gabled roof of a house. The ship groaned and gasped. Many of the ivory inlayings of her bulwarks and cabins were started from their places, by the unnatural dislocation. In vain handspikes and crows[4] were brought to bear upon the immovable fluke-chains, to pry them adrift from the timber-heads; and so low had the whale now settled that the submerged ends could not be at all approached, while every moment whole tons of ponderosity seemed added to the sinking bulk, and the ship seemed on the point of going over.

"Hold on, hold on, won't ye?" cried Stubb to the body, "don't be in such a devil of a hurry to sink! By thunder, men, we must do something or go for it. No use prying there; avast, I say with your handspikes, and run one of ye for a prayer book and a pen-knife, and cut the big chains."

"Knife? Aye, aye," cried Queequeg, and seizing the carpenter's heavy hatchet, he leaned out of a porthole, and steel to iron, began slashing at the largest fluke-chains. But a few strokes, full of sparks, were given, when the exceeding strain effected the rest. With a terrific snap, every fastening went adrift; the ship righted, the carcase sank.

Now, this occasional inevitable sinking of the recently killed Sperm Whale is a very curious thing; nor has any fisherman yet adequately accounted for it. Usually the dead Sperm Whale floats with great buoyancy, with its side or belly considerably elevated above the surface. If the only whales that thus sank were old, meagre, and broken-hearted creatures, their pads of lard diminished and all their bones heavy and rheumatic; then you might with some reason assert that this sinking is caused by an uncommon specific gravity in the fish so sinking, consequent upon this absence of buoyant matter in him. But it is not so. For

4. Crowbars, for prying.

young whales, in the highest health, and swelling with noble aspirations, prematurely cut off in the warm flush and May of life, with all their panting lard about them; even these brawny, buoyant heroes do sometimes sink.

Be it said, however, that the Sperm Whale is far less liable to this accident than any other species. Where one of that sort go down, twenty Right Whales do. This difference in the species is no doubt imputable in no small degree to the greater quantity of bone in the Right Whale; his Venetian blinds alone sometimes weighing more than a ton; from this incumbrance the Sperm Whale is wholly free. But there are instances where, after the lapse of many hours or several days, the sunken whale again rises, more buoyant than in life. But the reason of this is obvious. Gases are generated in him; he swells to a prodigious magnitude; becomes a sort of animal balloon. A line-of-battle ship could hardly keep him under then. In the Shore Whaling, on soundings, among the Bays of New Zealand, when a Right Whale gives token of sinking, they fasten buoys to him, with plenty of rope; so that when the body has gone down, they know where to look for it when it shall have ascended again.

It was not long after the sinking of the body that a cry was heard from the Pequod's mast-heads, announcing that the Jungfrau was again lowering her boats; though the only spout in sight was that of a Fin-Back, belonging to the species of uncapturable whales, because of its incredible power of swimming. Nevertheless, the Fin-Back's spout is so similar to the Sperm Whale's, that by unskilful fishermen it is often mistaken for it. And consequently Derick and all his host were now in valiant chase of this unnearable brute. The Virgin crowding all sail, made after her four young keels, and thus they all disappeared far to leeward, still in bold, hopeful chase.

Oh! many are the Fin-Backs, and many are the Dericks, my friend.

Chapter 82

The Honor and Glory of Whaling[1]

There are some enterprises in which a careful disorderliness is the true method.

The more I dive into this matter of whaling, and push my researches up to the very spring-head of it, so much the more am I impressed with its great honorableness and antiquity; and especially when I find so many great demi-gods and heroes, prophets of all sorts, who one way or other have shed distinction upon it, I am transported with the reflection that I myself belong, though but subordinately, to so emblazoned a fraternity.

The gallant Perseus, a son of Jupiter, was the first whaleman; and to the eternal honor of our calling be it said, that the first whale attacked

---

1. For chs. 82 and 83 the main sources are the article "Jonas" (Jonah) in Pierre Bayle, *An Historical and Critical Dictionary* (1697); "Jonah" and "Whale" in *Cyclopedia of Biblical Literature,* edited by John Kitto and from Sir Thomas Browne, with Kitto "freshest in Melville's mind" (Mansfield and Vincent, 778).

by our brotherhood was not killed with any sordid intent. Those were the knightly days of our profession, when we only bore arms to succor the distressed, and not to fill men's lamp-feeders. Every one knows the fine story of Perseus and Andromeda; how the lovely Andromeda, the daughter of a king, was tied to a rock on the sea-coast, and as Leviathan was in the very act of carrying her off, Perseus, the prince of whalemen, intrepidly advancing, harpooned the monster, and delivered and married the maid. It was an admirable artistic exploit, rarely achieved by the best harpooneers of the present day; inasmuch as this Leviathan was slain at the very first dart. And let no man doubt this Arkite[2] story; for in the ancient Joppa, now Jaffa, on the Syrian coast, in one of the Pagan temples, there stood for many ages the vast skeleton of a whale, which the city's legends and all the inhabitants asserted to be the identical bones of the monster that Perseus slew. When the Romans took Joppa, the same skeleton was carried to Italy in triumph. What seems most singular and suggestively important in this story, is this: it was from Joppa that Jonah set sail.

Akin to the adventure of Perseus and Andromeda—indeed, by some supposed to be indirectly derived from it—is that famous story of St. George and the Dragon; which dragon I maintain to have been a whale; for in many old chronicles whales and dragons are strangely jumbled together, and often stand for each other. "Thou art as a lion of the waters, and as a dragon of the sea," saith Ezekiel;[3] hereby, plainly meaning a whale; in truth, some versions of the Bible use that word itself. Besides, it would much subtract from the glory of the exploit had St. George but encountered a crawling reptile of the land, instead of doing battle with the great monster of the deep. Any man may kill a snake, but only a Perseus, a St. George, a Coffin,[4] have the heart in them to march boldly up to a whale.

Let not the modern paintings of this scene mislead us; for though the creature encountered by that valiant whaleman of old is vaguely represented of a griffin-like shape, and though the battle is depicted on land and the saint on horseback, yet considering the great ignorance of those times, when the true form of the whale was unknown to artists; and considering that as in Perseus' case, St. George's whale might have crawled up out of the sea on the beach; and considering that the animal ridden by St. George might have been only a large seal, or sea-horse; bearing all this in mind, it will not appear altogether incompatible with the sacred legend and the ancientest draughts of the scene, to hold this so-called dragon no other than the great Leviathan himself. In fact, placed before the strict and piercing truth, this whole story will fare like that fish, flesh, and fowl idol of the Philistines, Dagon[5] by name; who being planted before the ark of Israel, his horse's head and both the

2. Tribe in ancient Syria, the site of Joppa.
3. Ezekiel 32.2. In the King James Version, the Lord tells Ezekiel: "Son of man, take up a lamentation for Pharaoh king of Egypt, and say unto him, Thou art like a young lion of the nations, and thou art as a whale in the seas: and thou camest forth with thy rivers, and troubledst the waters with thy feet, and fouledst their rivers."
4. A member of the Nantucket family famous for its whalemen.
5. 1 Samuel 5.2–4.

palms of his hands fell off from him, and only the stump or fishy part of him remained. Thus, then, one of our own noble stamp, even a whaleman, is the tutelary guardian of England; and by good rights, we harpooneers of Nantucket should be enrolled in the most noble order of St. George. And therefore, let not the knights of that honorable company[6] (none of whom, I venture to say, have ever had to do with a whale like their great patron), let them never eye a Nantucketer with disdain, since even in our woollen frocks and tarred trowsers we are much better entitled to St. George's decoration than they.

Whether to admit Hercules among us or not, concerning this I long remained dubious: for though according to the Greek mythologies, that antique Crockett and Kit Carson[7]—that brawny doer of rejoicing good deeds, was swallowed down and thrown up by a whale; still, whether that strictly makes a whaleman of him, that might be mooted. It nowhere appears that he ever actually harpooned his fish, unless, indeed, from the inside. Nevertheless, he may be deemed a sort of involuntary whaleman; at any rate the whale caught him, if he did not the whale. I claim him for one of our clan.

But, by the best contradictory authorities, this Grecian story of Hercules and the whale is considered to be derived from the still more ancient Hebrew story of Jonah and the whale; and vice versâ; certainly they are very similar. If I claim the demi-god then, why not the prophet?

Nor do heroes, saints, demigods, and prophets alone comprise the whole roll of our order. Our grand master[8] is still to be named; for like royal kings of old times, we find the head-waters of our fraternity in nothing short of the great gods themselves. That wondrous oriental story is now to be rehearsed from the Shaster,[9] which gives us the dread Vishnoo, one of the three persons in the godhead of the Hindoos; gives us this divine Vishnoo himself for our Lord;—Vishnoo, who, by the first of his ten earthly incarnations, has for ever set apart and sanctified the whale. When Bramha, or the God of Gods, saith the Shaster, resolved to recreate the world after one of its periodical dissolutions, he gave birth to Vishnoo, to preside over the work; but the Vedas, or mystical books, whose perusal would seem to have been indispensable to Vishnoo before beginning the creation, and which therefore must have contained something in the shape of practical hints to young architects, these Vedas were lying at the bottom of the waters; so Vishnoo became incarnate in a whale, and sounding down in him to the uttermost depths, rescued the sacred volumes. Was not this Vishnoo a whaleman, then? even as a man who rides a horse is called a horseman?

Perseus, St. George, Hercules, Jonah, and Vishnoo! there's a member-roll for you! What club but the whaleman's can head off like that?

---

6. The Order of the Garter. *Tutelary Gardian:* St. George, here humorously claimed as a whaleman.
7. David Crockett (1786–1836), frontiersman and politician, and Christopher Carson (1809–1868), mountainman; both legendary folk figures, Crockett especially so after his death at the Alamo (during Melville's youth) and Carson for his role in the taking of California, just two years before Melville started *Moby-Dick* (but later known best as an Indian fighter). *Hercules:* Greek demigod and strongman, performer of twelve seemingly impossible labors.
8. A Masonic rank.
9. The sacred writings of the Hindus, among which the oldest are the Vedas (where appears the story of Vishnu that Melville here travesties).

Chapter 83

Jonah Historically Regarded

Reference was made to the historical story of Jonah and the whale in the preceding chapter. Now some Nantucketers rather distrust this historical story of Jonah and the whale. But then there were some sceptical Greeks and Romans, who, standing out from the orthodox pagans of their times, equally doubted the story of Hercules and the whale, and Arion[1] and the dolphin; and yet their doubting those traditions did not make those traditions one whit the less facts, for all that.

One old Sag-Harbor[2] whaleman's chief reason for questioning the Hebrew story was this:—He had one of those quaint old-fashioned Bibles, embellished with curious, unscientific plates; one of which represented Jonah's whale with two spouts in his head—a peculiarity only true with respect to a species of the Leviathan (the Right Whale, and the varieties of that order), concerning which the fishermen have this saying, "A penny roll would choke him;" his swallow is so very small. But, to this, Bishop Jebb's[3] anticipative answer is ready. It is not necessary, hints the Bishop, that we consider Jonah as tombed in the whale's belly, but as temporarily lodged in some part of his mouth. And this seems reasonable enough in the good Bishop. For truly, the Right Whale's mouth would accommodate a couple of whist-tables, and comfortably seat all the players. Possibly, too, Jonah might have ensconced himself in a hollow tooth; but, on second thoughts, the Right Whale is toothless.

Another reason which Sag-Harbor (he went by that name) urged for his want of faith in this matter of the prophet, was something obscurely in reference to his incarcerated body and the whale's gastric juices. But this objection likewise falls to the ground, because a German exegetist supposes that Jonah must have taken refuge in the floating body of a *dead* whale—even as the French soldiers in the Russian campaign[4] turned their dead horses into tents, and crawled into them. Besides, it has been divined by other continental commentators, that when Jonah was thrown overboard from the Joppa ship, he straightway effected his escape to another vessel near by, some vessel with a whale for a figure-head; and, I would add, possibly called "The Whale," as some craft are nowadays christened the "Shark," the "Gull," the "Eagle." Nor have there been wanting learned exegetists who have opined that the whale mentioned in the book of Jonah merely meant a life-preserver—an inflated bag of wind—which the endangered prophet swam to, and so was saved from a watery doom. Poor Sag-Harbor, therefore, seems worsted all round. But he had still another reason for his want of faith. It was this, if I remember right: Jonah was swallowed by the whale in the Mediterranean Sea, and after three days he was vomited up somewhere within three days' journey of Nineveh, a city on the Tigris, very much more than three days' journey across from the nearest point of the Mediterranean coast. How is that?

1. Greek poet whom a dolphin rescued from drowning.
2. Long Island whaling port.
3. John Jebb (1775–1833), bishop of Limerick, author of an influential biblical commentary.
4. Napoleon's catastrophic invasion of Russia (1812).

But was there no other way for the whale to land the prophet within that short distance of Nineveh? Yes. He might have carried him round by the way of the Cape of Good Hope. But not to speak of the passage through the whole length of the Mediterranean, and another passage up the Persian Gulf and Red Sea, such a supposition would involve the complete circumnavigation of all Africa in three days, not to speak of the Tigris waters, near the site of Nineveh, being too shallow for any whale to swim in. Besides, this idea of Jonah's weathering the Cape of Good Hope at so early a day would wrest the honor of the discovery of that great headland from Bartholomew Diaz,[5] its reputed discoverer, and so make modern history a liar.

But all these foolish arguments of old Sag-Harbor only evinced his foolish pride of reason—a thing still more reprehensible in him, seeing that he had but little learning except what he had picked up from the sun and the sea. I say it only shows his foolish, impious pride, and abominable, devilish rebellion against the reverend clergy. For by a Portuguese Catholic priest, this very idea of Jonah's going to Nineveh viâ the Cape of Good Hope was advanced as a signal magnification of the general miracle. And so it was. Besides, to this day, the highly enlightened Turks devoutly believe in the historical story of Jonah. And some three centuries ago, an English traveller in old Harris's Voyages,[6] speaks of a Turkish Mosque built in honor of Jonah, in which mosque was a miraculous lamp that burnt without any oil.

Chapter 84

Pitchpoling

To make them run easily and swiftly, the axles of carriages are anointed; and for much the same purpose, some whalers perform an analogous operation upon their boat; they grease the bottom. Nor is it to be doubted that as such a procedure can do no harm, it may possibly be of no contemptible advantage; considering that oil and water are hostile; that oil is a sliding thing, and that the object in view is to make the boat slide bravely. Queequeg believed strongly in anointing his boat, and one morning not long after the German ship Jungfrau disappeared, took more than customary pains in that occupation; crawling under its bottom, where it hung over the side, and rubbing in the unctuousness as though diligently seeking to insure a crop of hair from the craft's bald keel. He seemed to be working in obedience to some particular presentiment. Nor did it remain unwarranted by the event.

Towards noon whales were raised; but so soon as the ship sailed down to them, they turned and fled with swift precipitancy; a disordered flight, as of Cleopatra's barges from Actium.[1]

5. Portuguese navigator and explorer (1450?–1500), the first European on record to round the Cape of Good Hope (1486).
6. Melville took this report not from Harris but from Bayle's *Dictionary*, Vincent shows (1949, 285).
1. In the naval battle here (31 B.C.E.), the combined fleets of Cleopatra and Mark Antony were defeated by Octavius Caesar. As in the allusion to Antony in ch. 54, Melville's main source is Shakespeare's *Antony and Cleopatra*.

Nevertheless, the boats pursued, and Stubb's was foremost. By great exertion, Tashtego at last succeeded in planting one iron; but the stricken whale, without at all sounding, still continued his horizontal flight, with added fleetness. Such unintermitted strainings upon the planted iron must sooner or later inevitably extract it. It became imperative to lance the flying whale, or be content to lose him. But to haul the boat up to his flank was impossible, he swam so fast and furious. What then remained?

Of all the wondrous devices and dexterities, the sleights of hand and countless subtleties, to which the veteran whaleman is so often forced, none exceed that fine manœuvre with the lance called pitchpoling. Small sword, or broad sword, in all its exercises boasts nothing like it. It is only indispensable with an inveterate running whale; its grand fact and feature is the wonderful distance to which the long lance is accurately darted from a violently rocking, jerking boat, under extreme headway. Steel and wood included, the entire spear is some ten or twelve feet in length; the staff is much slighter than that of the harpoon, and also of a lighter material—pine. It is furnished with a small rope called a warp, of considerable length, by which it can be hauled back to the hand after darting.

But before going further, it is important to mention here, that though the harpoon may be pitchpoled in the same way with the lance, yet it is seldom done; and when done, is still less frequently successful, on account of the greater weight and inferior length of the harpoon as compared with the lance, which in effect become serious drawbacks. As a general thing, therefore, you must first get fast to a whale, before any pitchpoling comes into play.

Look now at Stubb; a man who from his humorous, deliberate coolness and equanimity in the direst emergencies, was specially qualified to excel in pitchpoling. Look at him; he stands upright in the tossed bow of the flying boat; wrapt in fleecy foam, the towing whale is forty feet ahead. Handling the long lance lightly, glancing twice or thrice along its length to see if it be exactly straight, Stubb whistlingly gathers up the coil of the warp in one hand, so as to secure its free end in his grasp, leaving the rest unobstructed. Then holding the lance full before his waistband's middle, he levels it at the whale; when, covering him with it, he steadily depresses the butt-end in his hand, thereby elevating the point till the weapon stands fairly balanced upon his palm, fifteen feet in the air. He minds you somewhat of a juggler, balancing a long staff on his chin. Next moment with a rapid, nameless impulse, in a superb lofty arch the bright steel spans the foaming distance, and quivers in the life spot of the whale. Instead of sparkling water, he now spouts red blood.

"That drove the spigot out of him!" cries Stubb. "'Tis July's immortal Fourth; all fountains must run wine to-day! Would now, it were old Orleans whiskey, or old Ohio, or unspeakable old Monongahela! Then, Tashtego, lad, I'd have ye hold a canakin to the jet, and we'd drink round it! Yea, verily, hearts alive, we'd brew choice punch in the spread of his spout-hole there, and from that live punch-bowl quaff the living stuff!"

Again and again to such gamesome talk, the dexterous dart is repeated, the spear returning to its master like a greyhound held in skilful leash.

The agonized whale goes into his flurry; the tow-line is slackened, and the pitchpoler dropping astern, folds his hands, and mutely watches the monster die.

Chapter 85

The Fountain

That for six thousand years—and no one knows how many millions of ages before—the great whales should have been spouting all over the sea, and sprinkling and mistifying the gardens of the deep, as with so many sprinkling or mistifying pots; and that for some centuries back, thousands of hunters should have been close by the fountain of the whale, watching these sprinklings and spoutings—that all this should be, and yet, that down to this blessed minute (fifteen and a quarter minutes past one o'clock P.M. of this sixteenth day of December, A.D. 1850),[1] it should still remain a problem, whether these spoutings are, after all, really water, or nothing but vapor—this is surely a noteworthy thing.

Let us, then, look at this matter, along with some interesting items contingent. Every one knows that by the peculiar cunning of their gills, the finny tribes in general breathe the air which at all times is combined with the element in which they swim; hence, a herring or a cod might live a century, and never once raise its head above the surface. But owing to his marked internal structure which gives him regular lungs, like a human being's, the whale can only live by inhaling the disengaged air in the open atmosphere. Wherefore the necessity for his periodical visits to the upper world. But he cannot in any degree breathe through his mouth, for, in his ordinary attitude, the Sperm Whale's mouth is buried at least eight feet beneath the surface; and what is still more, his windpipe has no connexion with his mouth. No, he breathes through his spiracle alone; and this is on the top of his head.

If I say, that in any creature breathing is only a function indispensable to vitality, inasmuch as it withdraws from the air a certain element, which being subsequently brought into contact with the blood imparts to the blood its vivifying principle, I do not think I shall err; though I may possibly use some superfluous scientific words. Assume it, and it follows that if all the blood in a man could be aerated with one breath, he might then seal up his nostrils and not fetch another for a considerable time. That is to say, he would then live without breathing. Anomalous as it may seem, this is precisely the case with the whale, who systematically lives, by intervals, his full hour and more (when at the bottom) without drawing a single breath, or so much as in any way inhaling a particle of air; for, remember, he has no gills. How is this? Between his ribs and on each side of his spine he is supplied with a remarkable involved Cretan labyrinth of vermicelli-like vessels, which vessels, when he quits the surface, are completely distended with oxygenated blood. So that for an hour or more, a thousand fathoms in the sea, he carries a surplus

---

1. The first American edition said 1851, the year of publication, an error Melville or someone else corrected in *The Whale*.

stock of vitality in him, just as the camel crossing the waterless desert carries a surplus supply of drink for future use in its four supplementary stomachs. The anatomical fact of this labyrinth is indisputable; and that the supposition founded upon it is reasonable and true, seems the more cogent to me, when I consider the otherwise inexplicable obstinacy of that leviathan in *having his spoutings out,* as the fishermen phrase it. This is what I mean. If unmolested, upon rising to the surface, the Sperm Whale will continue there for a period of time exactly uniform with all his other unmolested risings. Say he stays eleven minutes, and jets seventy times, that is, respires seventy breaths; then whenever he rises again, he will be sure to have his seventy breaths over again, to a minute. Now, if after he fetches a few breaths you alarm him, so that he sounds, he will be always dodging up again to make good his regular allowance of air. And not till those seventy breaths are told, will he finally go down to stay out his full term below. Remark, however, that in different individuals these rates are different; but in any one they are alike. Now, why should the whale thus insist upon having his spoutings out, unless it be to replenish his reservoir of air, ere descending for good? How obvious is it, too, that this necessity for the whale's rising exposes him to all the fatal hazards of the chase. For not by hook or by net could this vast leviathan be caught, when sailing a thousand fathoms beneath the sunlight. Not so much thy skill, then, O hunter, as the great necessities, that strike the victory to thee!

In man, breathing is incessantly going on—one breath only serving for two or three pulsations; so that whatever other business he has to attend to, waking or sleeping, breathe he must, or die he will. But the Sperm Whale only breathes about one seventh or Sunday of his time.

It has been said that the whale only breathes through his spout-hole; if it could truthfully be added that his spouts are mixed with water, then I opine we should be furnished with the reason why his sense of smell seems obliterated in him; for the only thing about him that at all answers to his nose is that identical spout-hole; and being so clogged with two elements, it could not be expected to have the power of smelling. But owing to the mystery of the spout—whether it be water or whether it be vapor—no absolute certainty can as yet be arrived at on this head. Sure it is, nevertheless, that the Sperm Whale has no proper olfactories. But what does he want of them? No roses, no violets, no Cologne-water in the sea.

Furthermore, as his windpipe solely opens into the tube of his spouting canal, and as that long canal—like the grand Erie Canal—is furnished with a sort of locks (that open and shut) for the downward retention of air or the upward exclusion of water, therefore the whale has no voice;[2] unless you insult him by saying, that when he so strangely rumbles, he talks through his nose. But then again, what has the whale to say? Seldom have I known any profound being that had anything to say to this world, unless forced to stammer out something by way of getting a living. Oh! happy that the world is such an excellent listener!

Now, the spouting canal of the Sperm Whale, chiefly intended as it is for the conveyance of air, and for several feet laid along, horizontally, just

---

2. A supposition since disproved. Whales "sing," according to the great modern whale authority Roger Payne, *Among Whales* (1995).

beneath the upper surface of his head, and a little to one side; this curious canal is very much like a gas-pipe laid down in a city on one side of a
street. But the question returns whether this gas-pipe is also a water-pipe;
in other words, whether the spout of the Sperm Whale is the mere vapor
of the exhaled breath, or whether that exhaled breath is mixed with water
taken in at the mouth, and discharged through the spiracle. It is certain
that the mouth indirectly communicates with the spouting canal; but it
cannot be proved that this is for the purpose of discharging water through
the spiracle. Because the greatest necessity for so doing would seem to be,
when in feeding he accidentally takes in water. But the Sperm Whale's
food is far beneath the surface, and there he cannot spout even if he
would. Besides, if you regard him very closely, and time him with your
watch, you will find that when unmolested, there is an undeviating rhyme
between the periods of his jets and the ordinary periods of respiration.

But why pester one with all this reasoning on the subject? Speak out!
You have seen him spout; then declare what the spout is; can you not tell
water from air? My dear sir, in this world it is not so easy to settle these
plain things. I have ever found your plain things the knottiest of all. And
as for this whale spout, you might almost stand in it, and yet be undecided
as to what it is precisely.

The central body of it is hidden in the snowy sparkling mist enveloping
it; and how can you certainly tell whether any water falls from it, when,
always, when you are close enough to a whale to get a close view of his
spout, he is in a prodigious commotion, the water cascading all around
him. And if at such times you should think that you really perceived drops
of moisture in the spout, how do you know that they are not merely condensed from its vapor; or how do you know that they are not those identical drops superficially lodged in the spout-hole fissure, which is coun-
tersunk into the summit of the whale's head? For even when tranquilly
swimming through the mid-day sea in a calm, with his elevated hump
sun-dried as a dromedary's in the desert; even then, the whale always carries a small basin of water on his head, as under a blazing sun you will
sometimes see a cavity in a rock filled up with rain.

Nor is it at all prudent for the hunter to be over curious touching the
precise nature of the whale spout. It will not do for him to be peering into
it, and putting his face in it. You cannot go with your pitcher to this fountain and fill it, and bring it away. For even when coming into slight contact with the outer, vapory shreds of the jet, which will often happen, your
skin will feverishly smart, from the acridness of the thing so touching it.
And I know one, who coming into still closer contact with the spout,
whether with some scientific object in view, or otherwise, I cannot say, the
skin peeled off from his cheek and arm. Wherefore, among whalemen, the
spout is deemed poisonous; they try to evade it. Another thing; I have
heard it said, and I do not much doubt it, that if the jet is fairly spouted
into your eyes, it will blind you. The wisest thing the investigator can do
then, it seems to me, is to let this deadly spout alone.

Still, we can hypothesize, even if we cannot prove and establish. My
hypothesis is this: that the spout is nothing but mist. And besides other
reasons, to this conclusion I am impelled, by considerations touching the
great inherent dignity and sublimity of the Sperm Whale; I account him

no common, shallow being, inasmuch as it is an undisputed fact that he is never found on soundings, or near shores; all other whales sometimes are. He is both ponderous and profound. And I am convinced that from the heads of all ponderous profound beings, such as Plato, Pyrrho, the Devil, Jupiter, Dante, and so on, there always goes up a certain semi-visible steam, while in the act of thinking deep thoughts. While composing a little treatise on Eternity, I had the curiosity to place a mirror before me; and ere long saw reflected there, a curious involved worming and undulation in the atmosphere over my head. The invariable moisture of my hair, while plunged in deep thought, after six cups of hot tea in my thin shingled attic, of an August noon; this seems an additional argument for the above supposition.

And how nobly it raises our conceit of the mighty, misty monster, to behold him solemnly sailing through a calm tropical sea; his vast, mild head overhung by a canopy of vapor, engendered by his incommunicable contemplations, and that vapor—as you will sometimes see it—glorified by a rainbow, as if Heaven itself had put its seal upon his thoughts. For, d'ye see, rainbows do not visit the clear air; they only irradiate vapor. And so, through all the thick mists of the dim doubts in my mind, divine intuitions now and then shoot, enkindling my fog with a heavenly ray. And for this I thank God; for all have doubts; many deny; but doubts or denials, few along with them, have intuitions. Doubts of all things earthly, and intuitions of some things heavenly; this combination makes neither believer nor infidel, but makes a man who regards them both with equal eye.

Chapter 86

The Tail

Other poets have warbled the praises of the soft eye of the antelope, and the lovely plumage of the bird that never alights; less celestial, I celebrate a tail.

Reckoning the largest sized Sperm Whale's tail to begin at that point of the trunk where it tapers to about the girth of a man, it comprises upon its upper surface alone, an area of at least fifty square feet. The compact round body of its root expands into two broad, firm, flat palms or flukes, gradually shoaling away to less than an inch in thickness. At the crotch or junction, these flukes slightly overlap, then sideways recede from each other like wings, leaving a wide vacancy between. In no living thing are the lines of beauty more exquisitely defined than in the crescentic borders of these flukes. At its utmost expansion in the full grown whale, the tail will considerably exceed twenty feet across.

The entire member seems a dense webbed bed of welded sinews; but cut into it, and you find that three distinct strata compose it:—upper, middle, and lower. The fibres in the upper and lower layers, are long and horizontal; those of the middle one, very short, and running crosswise between the outside layers. This triune structure, as much as anything else, imparts power to the tail. To the student of old Roman walls, the middle layer will furnish a curious parallel to the thin course of tiles always alternating with the stone in those wonderful relics of the antique, and which undoubtedly contribute so much to the great strength of the masonry.

But as if this vast local power in the tendinous tail were not enough, the whole bulk of the leviathan is knit over with a warp and woof of muscular fibres and filaments, which passing on either side the loins and running down into the flukes, insensibly blend with them, and largely contribute to their might; so that in the tail the confluent measureless force of the whole whale seems concentrated to a point. Could annihilation occur to matter, this were the thing to do it.

Nor does this—its amazing strength, at all tend to cripple the graceful flexion of its motions; where infantileness of ease undulates through a Titanism of power. On the contrary, those motions derive their most appalling beauty from it. Real strength never impairs beauty or harmony, but it often bestows it; and in everything imposingly beautiful, strength has much to do with the magic. Take away the tied tendons that all over seem bursting from the marble in the carved Hercules,[1] and its charm would be gone. As devout Eckermann lifted the linen sheet from the naked corpse of Goethe, he was overwhelmed with the massive chest of the man, that seemed as a Roman triumphal arch.[2] When Angelo[3] paints even God the Father in human form, mark what robustness is there. And whatever they may reveal of the divine love in the Son, the soft, curled, hermaphroditical Italian pictures, in which his idea has been most successfully embodied; these pictures, so destitute as they are of all brawniness, hint nothing of any power, but the mere negative, feminine one of submission and endurance, which on all hands it is conceded, form the peculiar practical virtues of his teachings.

Such is the subtle elasticity of the organ I treat of, that whether wielded in sport, or in earnest, or in anger, whatever be the mood it be in, its flexions are invariably marked by exceeding grace. Therein no fairy's arm can transcend it.

Five great motions are peculiar to it. First, when used as a fin for progression; Second, when used as a mace in battle; Third, in sweeping; Fourth, in lobtailing; Fifth, in peaking flukes.

First: Being horizontal in its position, the Leviathan's tail acts in a different manner from the tails of all other sea creatures. It never wriggles. In man or fish, wriggling is a sign of inferiority. To the whale, his tail is the sole means of propulsion. Scroll-wise coiled forwards beneath the body, and then rapidly sprung backwards, it is this which gives that singular darting, leaping motion to the monster when furiously swimming. His side-fins only serve to steer by.

Second: It is a little significant, that while one sperm whale only fights another sperm whale with his head and jaw, nevertheless, in his conflicts with man, he chiefly and contemptuously uses his tail. In striking at a

1. In the famous "Farnese Hercules," excavated from Pompeii, the hero is naked, powerfully muscled, but leaning casually on his great club.
2. Johann Peter Eckermann (1792–1854), literary assistant to Goethe, reports this incident in his *Conversations with Goethe* (1839).
3. Michelangelo, on the ceiling of the Sistine Chapel.

boat, he swiftly curves away his flukes from it, and the blow is only inflicted by the recoil. If it be made in the unobstructed air, especially if it descend to its mark, the stroke is then simply irresistible. No ribs of man or boat can withstand it. Your only salvation lies in eluding it; but if it comes sideways through the opposing water, then partly owing to the light buoyancy of the whale-boat, and the elasticity of its materials, a cracked rib or a dashed plank or two, a sort of stitch in the side, is generally the most serious result. These submerged side blows are so often received in the fishery, that they are accounted mere child's play. Some one strips off a frock, and the hole is stopped.

Third: I cannot demonstrate it, but it seems to me, that in the whale the sense of touch is concentrated in the tail; for in this respect there is a delicacy in it only equalled by the daintiness of the elephant's trunk. This delicacy is chiefly evinced in the action of sweeping, when in maidenly gentleness the whale with a certain soft slowness moves his immense flukes from side to side upon the surface of the sea; and if he feel but a sailor's whisker, woe to that sailor, whiskers and all. What tenderness there is in that preliminary touch! Had this tail any prehensile power, I should straightway bethink me of Darmonodes' elephant that so frequented the flower-market, and with low salutations presented nosegays to damsels, and then caressed their zones.[4] On more accounts than one, a pity it is that the whale does not possess this prehensile virtue in his tail; for I have heard of yet another elephant, that when wounded in the fight, curved round his trunk and extracted the dart.

Fourth: Stealing unawares upon the whale in the fancied security of the middle of solitary seas, you find him unbent from the vast corpulence of his dignity, and kitten-like, he plays on the ocean as if it were a hearth. But still you see his power in his play. The broad palms of his tail are flirted high into the air; then smiting the surface, the thunderous concussion resounds for miles. You would almost think a great gun had been discharged; and if you noticed the light wreath of vapor from the spiracle at his other extremity, you would think that that was the smoke from the touch-hole.

Fifth: As in the ordinary floating posture of the leviathan the flukes lie considerably below the level of his back, they are then completely out of sight beneath the surface; but when he is about to plunge into the deeps, his entire flukes with at least thirty feet of his body are tossed erect in the air, and so remain vibrating a moment, till they downwards shoot out of view. Excepting the sublime *breach*—somewhere else to be described— this peaking of the whale's flukes is perhaps the grandest sight to be seen in all animated nature. Out of the bottomless profundities the gigantic tail seems spasmodically snatching at the highest heaven. So in dreams, have I seen majestic Satan thrusting forth his tormented colossal claw from the flame Baltic of Hell. But in gazing at such scenes, it is all in all what mood you are in; if in the Dantean, the devils will occur to you; if in that of Isaiah,[5] the archangels. Standing at the mast-head of my ship during a

---

4. The waists of the "damsels." Darmonodes remains unidentified, but several sources report such behavior from an elephant.
5. Isaiah in a vision sees six-winged seraphims, each with one pair of wings covering his face, another pair covering his feet, and a third pair used for flying; as they fly (with faces covered) they cry to each other, "Holy, holy, holy, is the Lord of Hosts: the whole earth is full of his glory" (Isaiah 6.2–3). *Dantean*: in the mood of Dante's *Inferno*.

sunrise that crimsoned sky and sea, I once saw a large herd of whales in the east, all heading towards the sun, and for a moment vibrating in concert with peaked flukes. As it seemed to me at the time, such a grand embodiment of adoration of the gods was never beheld, even in Persia, the home of the fire worshippers. As Ptolemy Philopater[6] testified of the African elephant, I then testified of the whale, pronouncing him the most devout of all beings. For according to King Juba, the military elephants of antiquity often hailed the morning with their trunks uplifted in the profoundest silence.

The chance comparison in this chapter, between the whale and the elephant, so far as some aspects of the tail of the one and the trunk of the other are concerned, should not tend to place those two opposite organs on an equality, much less the creatures to which they respectively belong. For as the mightiest elephant is but a terrier to Leviathan, so, compared with Leviathan's tail, his trunk is but the stalk of a lily. The most direful blow from the elephant's trunk were as the playful tap of a fan, compared with the measureless crush and crash of the sperm whale's ponderous flukes, which in repeated instances have one after the other hurled entire boats with all their oars and crews into the air, very much as an Indian juggler tosses his balls.[7]

The more I consider this mighty tail, the more do I deplore my inability to express it. At times there are gestures in it, which, though they would well grace the hand of man, remain wholly inexplicable. In an extensive herd, so remarkable, occasionally, are these mystic gestures, that I have heard hunters who have declared them akin to Free-Mason signs and symbols; that the whale, indeed, by these methods intelligently conversed with the world. Nor are there wanting other motions of the whale in his general body, full of strangeness, and unaccountable to his most experienced assailant. Dissect him how I may, then, I but go skin deep; I know him not, and never will. But if I know not even the tail of this whale, how understand his head? much more, how comprehend his face, when face he has none? Thou shalt see my back parts,[8] my tail, he seems to say, but my face shall not be seen. But I cannot completely make out his back parts; and hint what he will about his face, I say again he has no face.

Chapter 87

The Grand Armada

The long and narrow peninsula of Malacca, extending south-eastward from the territories of Birmah, forms the most southerly point of all Asia.

6. Melville's source for this and for King Juba's report is probably *Morals* by Plutarch (ca. 50–125), Greek biographer.
7. Though all comparison in the way of general bulk between the whale and the elephant is preposterous, inasmuch as in that particular the elephant stands in much the same respect to the whale that a dog does to the elephant; nevertheless, there are not wanting some points of curious similitude; among these is the spout. It is well known that the elephant will often draw up water or dust in his trunk, and then elevating it, jet it forth in a stream [Melville's note].
8. Jeremiah 18.17: "I will scatter them as with an east wind before the enemy; I will shew them the back, and not the face, in the day of their calamity."

In a continuous line from that peninsula stretch the long islands of Sumatra, Java, Bally, and Timor; which, with many others, form a vast mole, or
rampart, lengthwise connecting Asia with Australia, and dividing the long
unbroken Indian ocean from the thickly studded oriental archipelagoes.
This rampart is pierced by several sally-ports for the convenience of ships
and whales; conspicuous among which are the straits of Sunda and
Malacca. By the straits of Sunda, chiefly, vessels bound to China from the
west, emerge into the China seas.

Those narrow straits of Sunda divide Sumatra from Java; and standing
midway in that vast rampart of islands, buttressed by that bold green
promontory, known to seamen as Java Head; they not a little correspond
to the central gateway opening into some vast walled empire: and considering the inexhaustible wealth of spices, and silks, and jewels, and gold,
and ivory, with which the thousand islands of that oriental sea are
enriched, it seems a significant provision of nature, that such treasures,
by the very formation of the land, should at least bear the appearance,
however ineffectual, of being guarded from the all-grasping western
world. The shores of the Straits of Sunda are unsupplied with those domineering fortresses which guard the entrances to the Mediterranean, the
Baltic, and the Propontis. Unlike the Danes, these Orientals do not
demand the obsequious homage of lowered top-sails from the endless procession of ships before the wind, which for centuries past, by night and
by day, have passed between the islands of Sumatra and Java, freighted
with the costliest cargoes of the east. But while they freely waive a ceremonial like this, they do by no means renounce their claim to more solid
tribute.

Time out of mind the piratical proas[1] of the Malays, lurking among the
low shaded coves and islets of Sumatra, have sallied out upon the vessels
sailing through the straits, fiercely demanding tribute at the point of their
spears. Though by the repeated bloody chastisements they have received
at the hands of European cruisers, the audacity of these corsairs has of
late been somewhat repressed; yet, even at the present day, we occasionally hear of English and American vessels, which, in those waters, have
been remorselessly boarded and pillaged.

With a fair, fresh wind, the Pequod was now drawing nigh to these
straits; Ahab purposing to pass through them into the Javan sea, and
thence, cruising northwards, over waters known to be frequented here
and there by the Sperm Whale, sweep inshore by the Philippine Islands,
and gain the far coast of Japan, in time for the great whaling season there.
By these means, the circumnavigating Pequod would sweep almost all the
known Sperm Whale cruising grounds of the world, previous to descending upon the Line in the Pacific; where Ahab, though everywhere else
foiled in his pursuit, firmly counted upon giving battle to Moby Dick, in
the sea he was most known to frequent; and at a season when he might
most reasonably be presumed to be haunting it.

But how now? in this zoned quest, does Ahab touch no land? does his
crew drink air? Surely, he will stop for water. Nay. For a long time, now,
the circus-running sun has raced within his fiery ring, and needs no sus-

1. Large Malay war boat.

tenance but what's in himself. So Ahab. Mark this, too, in the whaler. While other hulls are loaded down with alien stuff, to be transferred to foreign wharves; the world-wandering whale-ship carries no cargo but herself and crew, their weapons and their wants. She has a whole lake's contents bottled in her ample hold. She is ballasted with utilities; not altogether with unusable pig-lead and kentledge.[2] She carries years' water in her. Clear old prime Nantucket water; which, when three years afloat, the Nantucketer, in the Pacific, prefers to drink before the brackish fluid, but yesterday rafted off in casks, from the Peruvian or Indian streams. Hence it is, that, while other ships may have gone to China from New York, and back again, touching at a score of ports, the whale-ship, in all that interval, may not have sighted one grain of soil; her crew having seen no man but floating seamen like themselves. So that did you carry them the news that another flood had come; they would only answer—"Well, boys, here's the ark!"

Now, as many Sperm Whales had been captured off the western coast of Java, in the near vicinity of the Straits of Sunda; indeed, as most of the ground, roundabout, was generally recognised by the fishermen as an excellent spot for cruising; therefore, as the Pequod gained more and more upon Java Head, the look-outs were repeatedly hailed, and admonished to keep wide awake. But though the green palmy cliffs of the land soon loomed on the starboard bow, and with delighted nostrils the fresh cinnamon was snuffed in the air, yet not a single jet was descried. Almost renouncing all thought of falling in with any game hereabouts, the ship had well nigh entered the straits, when the customary cheering cry was heard from aloft, and ere long a spectacle of singular magnificence saluted us.

But here be it premised, that owing to the unwearied activity with which of late they have been hunted over all four oceans, the Sperm Whales, instead of almost invariably sailing in small detached companies, as in former times, are now frequently met with in extensive herds, sometimes embracing so great a multitude, that it would almost seem as if numerous nations of them had sworn solemn league and covenant for mutual assistance and protection. To this aggregation of the Sperm Whale into such immense caravans, may be imputed the circumstance that even in the best cruising grounds, you may now sometimes sail for weeks and months together, without being greeted by a single spout; and then be suddenly saluted by what sometimes seems thousands on thousands.

Broad on both bows, at the distance of some two or three miles, and forming a great semicircle, embracing one half of the level horizon, a continuous chain of whale-jets were up-playing and sparkling in the noon-day air. Unlike the straight perpendicular twin-jets of the Right Whale, which, dividing at top, fall over in two branches, like the cleft drooping boughs of a willow, the single forward-slanting spout of the Sperm Whale presents a thick curled bush of white mist, continually rising and falling away to leeward.

Seen from the Pequod's deck, then, as she would rise on a high hill of the sea, this host of vapory spouts, individually curling up into the air, and

2. Pieces of iron laid over the keelson plates for ballast.

beheld through a blending atmosphere of bluish haze, showed like the thousand cheerful chimneys of some dense metropolis, descried of a balmy autumnal morning, by some horseman on a height.

As marching armies approaching an unfriendly defile in the mountains, accelerate their march, all eagerness to place that perilous passage in their rear, and once more expand in comparative security upon the plain; even so did this vast fleet of whales now seem hurrying forward through the straits; gradually contracting the wings of their semicircle, and swimming on, in one solid, but still crescentic centre.

Crowding all sail the Pequod pressed after them; the harpooneers handling their weapons, and loudly cheering from the heads of their yet suspended boats. If the wind only held, little doubt had they, that chased through these Straits of Sunda, the vast host would only deploy into the Oriental seas to witness the capture of not a few of their number. And who could tell whether, in that congregated caravan, Moby Dick himself might not temporarily be swimming, like the worshipped white-elephant in the coronation procession of the Siamese! So with stun-sail piled on stun-sail, we sailed along, driving these leviathans before us; when, of a sudden, the voice of Tashtego was heard, loudly directing attention to something in our wake.

Corresponding to the crescent in our van, we beheld another in our rear. It seemed formed of detached white vapors, rising and falling something like the spouts of the whales; only they did not so completely come and go; for they constantly hovered, without finally disappearing. Levelling his glass at this sight, Ahab quickly revolved in his pivot-hole, crying, "Aloft there, and rig whips and buckets to wet the sails;—Malays, sir, and after us!"

As if too long lurking behind the headlands, till the Pequod should fairly have entered the straits, these rascally Asiatics were now in hot pursuit, to make up for their over-cautious delay. But when the swift Pequod, with a fresh leading wind, was herself in hot chase; how very kind of these tawny philanthropists to assist in speeding her on to her own chosen pursuit,—mere riding-whips and rowels to her, that they were. As with glass under arm, Ahab to-and-fro paced the deck; in his forward turn beholding the monsters he chased, and in the after one the bloodthirsty pirates chasing *him;* some such fancy as the above seemed his. And when he glanced upon the green walls of the watery defile in which the ship was then sailing, and bethought him that through that gate lay the route to his vengeance, and beheld, how that through that same gate he was now both chasing and being chased to his deadly end; and not only that, but a herd of remorseless wild pirates and inhuman atheistical devils were infernally cheering him on with their curses;—when all these conceits had passed through his brain, Ahab's brow was left gaunt and ribbed, like the black sand beach after some stormy tide has been gnawing it, without being able to drag the firm thing from its place.

But thoughts like these troubled very few of the reckless crew; and when, after steadily dropping and dropping the pirates astern, the Pequod at last shot by the vivid green Cockatoo Point on the Sumatra side, emerging at last upon the broad waters beyond; then, the harpooneers seemed more to grieve that the swift whales had been gaining upon the ship, than to rejoice that the ship had so victoriously gained upon the Malays. But still driving on in the wake of the whales, at length they seemed abating their speed; gradually the ship neared them; and the wind now dying away, word was passed to spring to the boats. But no sooner did the herd, by some presumed wonderful instinct of the Sperm Whale, become notified of the three keels that were after them,—though as yet a mile in their rear,—than they rallied again, and forming in close ranks and battalions, so that their spouts all looked like flashing lines of stacked bayonets, moved on with redoubled velocity.

Stripped to our shirts and drawers, we sprang to the white-ash, and after several hours' pulling were almost disposed to renounce the chase, when a general pausing commotion among the whales gave animating token that they were now at last under the influence of that strange perplexity of inert irresolution, which, when the fishermen perceive it in the whale, they say he is *gallied*.[3] The compact martial columns in which they had been hitherto rapidly and steadily swimming, were now broken up in one measureless rout; and like King Porus'[4] elephants in the Indian battle with Alexander, they seemed going mad with consternation. In all directions expanding in vast irregular circles, and aimlessly swimming hither and thither, by their short thick spoutings, they plainly betrayed their distraction of panic. This was still more strangely evinced by those of their number, who, completely paralysed as it were, helplessly floated like water-logged dismantled ships on the sea. Had these leviathans been but a flock of simple sheep, pursued over the pasture by three fierce wolves, they could not possibly have evinced such excessive dismay. But this occasional timidity is characteristic of almost all herding creatures. Though banding together in tens of thousands, the lion-maned buffaloes of the West have fled before a solitary horseman. Witness, too, all human beings, how when herded together in the sheepfold of a theatre's pit, they will, at the slightest alarm of fire, rush helter-skelter for the outlets, crowding, trampling, jamming, and remorselessly dashing each other to death. Best, therefore, withhold any amazement at the strangely gallied whales before us, for there is no folly of the beasts of the earth which is not infinitely outdone by the madness of men.

Though many of the whales, as has been said, were in violent motion, yet it is to be observed that as a whole the herd neither advanced nor retreated, but collectively remained in one place. As is customary in those cases, the boats at once separated, each making for some one lone whale

---

3. To *gally*, or *gallow*, is to frighten excessively,—to confound with fright. It is an old Saxon word. It occurs once in Shakspere:—

> "The wrathful skies
> *Gallow* the very wanderers of the dark,
> And make them keep their caves."
> *Lear*, Act III. sc. ii.

To common land usages, the word is now completely obsolete. When the polite landsman first hears it from the gaunt Nantucketer, he is apt to set it down as one of the whale-man's self-derived savageries. Much the same is it with many other sinewy Saxonisms of this sort, which emigrated to the New-England rocks with the noble brawn of the old English emigrants in the time of the Commonwealth. Thus, some of the best and furthest-descended English words—the etymological Howards and Percys—are now democratised, nay, plebeianised—so to speak—in the New World [Melville's note, not in the first American edition; he wrote it on the American proofs from which the English edition was set].

4. Indian prince defeated at the river Hydaspes by Alexander the Great in 327 B.C.E.

on the outskirts of the shoal. In about three minutes' time, Queequeg's harpoon was flung; the stricken fish darted blinding spray in our faces, and then running away with us like light, steered straight for the heart of the herd. Though such a movement on the part of the whale struck under such circumstances, is in no wise unprecedented; and indeed is almost always more or less anticipated; yet does it present one of the more perilous vicissitudes of the fishery. For as the swift monster drags you deeper and deeper into the frantic shoal,[5] you bid adieu to circumspect life and only exist in a delirious throb.

As, blind and deaf, the whale plunged forward, as if by sheer power of speed to rid himself of the iron leech that had fastened to him; as we thus tore a white gash in the sea, on all sides menaced as we flew, by the crazed creatures to and fro rushing about us; our beset boat was like a ship mobbed by ice-isles in a tempest, and striving to steer through their complicated channels and straits, knowing not at what moment it may be locked in and crushed.

But not a bit daunted, Queequeg steered us manfully; now sheering off from this monster directly across our route in advance; now edging away from that, whose colossal flukes were suspended overhead, while all the time, Starbuck stood up in the bows, lance in hand, pricking out of our way whatever whales he could reach by short darts, for there was no time to make long ones. Nor were the oarsmen quite idle, though their wonted duty was now altogether dispensed with. They chiefly attended to the shouting part of the business. "Out of the way, Commodore!" cried one, to a great dromedary that of a sudden rose bodily to the surface, and for an instant threatened to swamp us. "Hard down with your tail, there!" cried a second to another, which, close to our gunwale, seemed calmly cooling himself with his own fan-like extremity.

All whaleboats carry certain curious contrivances, originally invented by the Nantucket Indians, called druggs. Two thick squares of wood of equal size are stoutly clenched together, so that they cross each other's grain at right angles; a line of considerable length is then attached to the middle of this block, and the other end of the line being looped, it can in a moment be fastened to a harpoon. It is chiefly among gallied whales that this drugg is used. For then, more whales are close round you than you can possibly chase at one time. But sperm whales are not every day encountered; while you may, then, you must kill all you can. And if you cannot kill them all at once, you must wing them, so that they can be afterwards killed at your leisure. Hence it is, that at times like these the drugg comes into requisition. Our boat was furnished with three of them. The first and second were successfully darted, and we saw the whales staggeringly running off, fettered by the enormous sidelong resistance of the towing drugg. They were cramped like malefactors with the chain and ball. But upon flinging the third, in the act of tossing overboard the clumsy wooden block, it caught under one of the seats of the boat, and in an instant tore it out and carried it away, dropping the oarsman in the boat's bottom as the seat slid from under him. On both sides the sea came in at the wounded planks, but we stuffed

5. Herd of whales.

two or three drawers and shirts in,[6] and so stopped the leaks for the time.

It had been next to impossible to dart these drugged-harpoons, were it not that as we advanced into the herd, our whale's way greatly diminished; moreover, that as we went still further and further from the circumference of commotion, the direful disorders seemed waning. So that when at last the jerking harpoon drew out, and the towing whale sideways vanished; then, with the tapering force of his parting momentum, we glided between two whales into the innermost heart of the shoal, as if from some mountain torrent we had slid into a serene valley lake. Here the storms in the roaring glens between the outermost whales, were heard but not felt. In this central expanse the sea presented that smooth satin-like surface, called a sleek, produced by the subtle moisture thrown off by the whale in his more quiet moods. Yes, we were now in that enchanted calm which they say lurks at the heart of every commotion. And still in the distracted distance we beheld the tumults of the outer concentric circles, and saw successive pods of whales, eight or ten in each, swiftly going round and round, like multiplied spans of horses in a ring; and so closely shoulder to shoulder, that a Titanic circus-rider might easily have overarched the middle ones, and so have gone round on their backs. Owing to the density of the crowd of reposing whales, more immediately surrounding the embayed axis of the herd, no possible chance of escape was at present afforded us. We must watch for a breach in the living wall that hemmed us in; the wall that had only admitted us in order to shut us up. Keeping at the centre of the lake, we were occasionally visited by small tame cows and calves; the women and children of this routed host.

Now, inclusive of the occasional wide intervals between the revolving outer circles, and inclusive of the spaces between the various pods in any one of those circles, the entire area at this juncture, embraced by the whole multitude, must have contained at least two or three square miles. At any rate—though indeed such a test at such a time might be deceptive—spoutings might be discovered from our low boat that seemed playing up almost from the rim of the horizon. I mention this circumstance, because, as if the cows and calves had been purposely locked up in this innermost fold; and as if the wide extent of the herd had hitherto prevented them from learning the precise cause of its stopping; or, possibly, being so young, unsophisticated, and every way innocent and inexperienced; however it may have been, these smaller whales—now and then visiting our becalmed boat from the margin of the lake—evinced a wondrous fearlessness and confidence, or else a still, becharmed panic which it was impossible not to marvel at. Like household dogs they came snuffling round us, right up to our gunwales, and touching them; till it almost seemed that some spell had suddenly domesticated them. Queequeg patted their foreheads; Starbuck scratched their backs with his lance; but fearful of the consequences, for the time refrained from darting it.

But far beneath this wondrous world upon the surface, another and still stranger world met our eyes as we gazed over the side. For, suspended in

---

6. They had already stripped to their shirts and drawers, so this leaves them pretty much exposed to the elements.

those watery vaults, floated the forms of the nursing mothers of the whales, and those that by their enormous girth seemed shortly to become mothers. The lake, as I have hinted, was to a considerable depth exceedingly transparent; and as human infants while suckling will calmly and fixedly gaze away from the breast, as if leading two different lives at the time; and while yet drawing mortal nourishment, be still spiritually feasting upon some unearthly reminiscence;—even so did the young of these whales seem looking up towards us, but not at us, as if we were but a bit of Gulf-weed in their new-born sight. Floating on their sides, the mothers also seemed quietly eyeing us. One of these little infants, that from certain queer tokens seemed hardly a day old, might have measured some fourteen feet in length, and some six feet in girth. He was a little frisky; though as yet his body seemed scarce yet recovered from that irksome position it had so lately occupied in the maternal reticule; where, tail to head, and all ready for the final spring, the unborn whale lies bent like a Tartar's bow. The delicate side fins, and the palms of his flukes, still freshly retained the plaited crumpled appearance of a baby's ears newly arrived from foreign parts.

"Line! line!" cried Queequeg, looking over the gunwale; "him fast! him fast!—Who line him! Who struck?—Two whale; one big, one little!"

"What ails ye, man?" cried Starbuck.

"Look-e here," said Queequeg pointing down.

As when the stricken whale, that from the tub has reeled out hundreds of fathoms of rope; as, after deep sounding, he floats up again, and shows the slackened curling line buoyantly rising and spiralling towards the air; so now, Starbuck saw long coils of the umbilical cord of Madame Leviathan, by which the young cub seemed still tethered to its dam. Not seldom in the rapid vicissitudes of the chase, this natural line, with the maternal end loose, becomes entangled with the hempen one, so that the cub is thereby trapped. Some of the subtlest secrets of the seas seemed divulged to us in this enchanted pond. We saw young Leviathan amours in the deep.[7]

And thus, though surrounded by circle upon circle of consternations and affrights, did these inscrutable creatures at the centre freely and fearlessly indulge in all peaceful concernments; yea, serenely revelled in dalliance and delight. But even so, amid the tornadoed Atlantic of my being, do I myself still for ever centrally disport in mute calm; and while ponderous planets of unwaning woe revolve round me, deep down and deep inland there I still bathe me in eternal mildness of joy.

Meanwhile, as we thus lay entranced, the occasional sudden frantic spectacles in the distance evinced the activity of the other boats, still engaged in drugging the whales on the frontier of the host; or possibly carrying on the war within the first circle, where abundance of room and some convenient retreats were afforded them. But the sight of the

---

7. The sperm whale, as with all other species of the Leviathan, but unlike most other fish, breeds indifferently at all seasons; after a gestation which may probably be set down at nine months, producing but one at a time; though in some few known instances giving birth to an Esau and Jacob:—a contingency provided for in suckling by two teats, curiously situated, one on each side of the anus; but the breasts themselves extend upwards from that. When by chance these precious parts in a nursing whale are cut by the hunter's lance, the mother's pouring milk and blood rivallingly discolor the sea for rods. The milk is very sweet and rich; it has been tasted by men; it might do well with strawberries. When overflowing with mutual esteem, the whales salute *more hominum* [Melville's note]. *More hominum:* in the manner of human beings; that is, they face each other.

enraged drugged whales now and then blindly darting to and fro across the circles, was nothing to what at last met our eyes. It is sometimes the custom when fast to a whale more than commonly powerful and alert, to seek to hamstring him, as it were, by sundering or maiming his gigantic tail-tendon. It is done by darting a short-handled cutting-spade, to which is attached a rope for hauling it back again. A whale wounded (as we afterwards learned) in this part, but not effectually, as it seemed, had broken away from the boat, carrying along with him half of the harpoon line; and in the extraordinary agony of the wound, he was now dashing among the revolving circles like the lone mounted desperado Arnold,[8] at the battle of Saratoga, carrying dismay wherever he went.

But agonizing as was the wound of this whale, and an appalling spectacle enough, any way; yet the peculiar horror with which he seemed to inspire the rest of the herd, was owing to a cause which at first the intervening distance obscured from us. But at length we perceived that by one of the unimaginable accidents of the fishery, this whale had become entangled in the harpoon-line that he towed; he had also run away with the cutting-spade in him; and while the free end of the rope attached to that weapon, had permanently caught in the coils of the harpoon-line round his tail, the cutting-spade itself had worked loose from his flesh. So that tormented to madness, he was now churning through the water, violently flailing with his flexible tail, and tossing the keen spade about him, wounding and murdering his own comrades.

This terrific object seemed to recall the whole herd from their stationary fright. First, the whales forming the margin of our lake began to crowd a little, and tumble against each other, as if lifted by half spent billows from afar; then the lake itself began faintly to heave and swell; the submarine bridal-chambers and nurseries vanished; in more and more contracting orbits the whales in the more central circles began to swim in thickening clusters. Yes, the long calm was departing. A low advancing hum was soon heard; and then like to the tumultuous masses of block-ice when the great river Hudson breaks up in Spring, the entire host of whales came tumbling upon their inner centre, as if to pile themselves up in one common mountain. Instantly Starbuck and Queequeg changed places; Starbuck taking the stern.

"Oars! Oars!" he intensely whispered, seizing the helm—"gripe your oars, and clutch your souls, now! My God, men, stand by! Shove him off, you Queequeg—the whale there!—prick him!—hit him! Stand up—stand up, and stay so! Spring, men—pull, men; never mind their backs—scrape them!—scrape away!"

The boat was now all but jammed between two vast black bulks, leaving a narrow Dardanelles[9] between their long lengths. But by desperate endeavor we at last shot into a temporary opening; then giving way rapidly, and at the same time earnestly watching for another outlet. After many similar hair-breadth escapes, we at last swiftly glided into what had just

---

8. Benedict Arnold (1741–1801), later a traitor, was a victorious American general at the battle of Saratoga, north of Albany, October 7, 1777. In the battle another officer was Melville's grandfather, Peter Gansevoort, who had earlier in the same campaign repulsed the British at Fort Stanwix. This was recent family history; and a quarter century later, in 1877, one of Melville's sisters was kept busy loaning letters and artifacts to historical societies celebrating the centennial of these battles.
9. The narrow strait between Greece (in Europe) and Turkey (in Asia).

been one of the outer circles, but now crossed by random whales, all violently making for one centre. This lucky salvation was cheaply purchased by the loss of Queequeg's hat, who, while standing in the bows to prick the fugitive whales, had his hat taken clean from his head by the air-eddy made by the sudden tossing of a pair of broad flukes close by.

Riotous and disordered as the universal commotion now was, it soon resolved itself into what seemed a systematic movement; for having clumped together at last in one dense body, they then renewed their onward flight with augmented fleetness. Further pursuit was useless; but the boats still lingered in their wake to pick up what drugged whales might be dropped astern, and likewise to secure one which Flask had killed and waifed. The waif is a pennoned pole, two or three of which are carried by every boat; and which, when additional game is at hand, are inserted upright into the floating body of a dead whale, both to mark its place on the sea, and also as token of prior possession, should the boats of any other ship draw near.

The result of this lowering was somewhat illustrative of that sagacious saying in the Fishery,—the more whales the less fish. Of all the drugged whales only one was captured. The rest contrived to escape for the time, but only to be taken, as will hereafter be seen, by some other craft than the Pequod.

Chapter 88

Schools and Schoolmasters

The previous chapter gave account of an immense body or herd of Sperm Whales, and there was also then given the probable cause inducing those vast aggregations.

Now, though such great bodies are at times encountered, yet, as must have been seen, even at the present day, small detached bands are occasionally observed, embracing from twenty to fifty individuals each. Such bands are known as schools. They generally are of two sorts; those composed almost entirely of females, and those mustering none but young vigorous males, or bulls, as they are familiarly designated.

In cavalier attendance upon the school of females, you invariably see a male of full grown magnitude, but not old; who, upon any alarm, evinces his gallantry by falling in the rear and covering the flight of his ladies. In truth, this gentleman is a luxurious Ottoman,[1] swimming about over the watery world, surroundingly accompanied by all the solaces and endearments of the harem. The contrast between this Ottoman and his concubines is striking; because, while he is always of the largest leviathanic proportions, the ladies, even at full growth, are not more than one third of the bulk of an average-sized male. They are comparatively delicate, indeed; I dare say, not to exceed half a dozen yards round the waist. Nevertheless, it cannot be denied, that upon the whole they are hereditarily entitled to *en bon point*.[2]

---

1. A Turk, seen as powerful sensualist, keeper of a harem of women, in the light of Romantic poems and tales.
2. Stoutness, or fatness (French).

It is very curious to watch this harem and its lord in their indolent ramblings. Like fashionables, they are for ever on the move in leisurely search of variety. You meet them on the Line in time for the full flower of the Equatorial feeding season, having just returned, perhaps, from spending the summer in the Northern seas, and so cheating summer of all unpleasant weariness and warmth. By the time they have lounged up and down the promenade of the Equator awhile, they start for the Oriental waters in anticipation of the cool season there, and so evade the other excessive temperature of the year.

When serenely advancing on one of these journeys, if any strange suspicious sights are seen, my lord whale keeps a wary eye on his interesting family. Should any unwarrantably pert young Leviathan coming that way, presume to draw confidentially close to one of the ladies, with what prodigious fury the Bashaw assails him, and chases him away! High times, indeed, if unprincipled young rakes like him are to be permitted to invade the sanctity of domestic bliss; though do what the Bashaw will, he cannot keep the most notorious Lothario out of his bed; for, alas! all fish bed in common. As ashore, the ladies often cause the most terrible duels among their rival admirers; just so with the whales, who sometimes come to deadly battle, and all for love. They fence with their long lower jaws, sometimes locking them together, and so striving for the supremacy like elks that warringly interweave their antlers. Not a few are captured having the deep scars of these encounters,—furrowed heads, broken teeth, scolloped fins; and in some instances, wrenched and dislocated mouths.

But supposing the invader of domestic bliss to betake himself away at the first rush of the harem's lord, then is it very diverting to watch that lord. Gently he insinuates his vast bulk among them again and revels there awhile, still in tantalizing vicinity to young Lothario, like pious Solomon devoutly worshipping among his thousand concubines.[3] Granting other whales to be in sight, the fishermen will seldom give chase to one of these Grand Turks; for these Grand Turks are too lavish of their strength, and hence their unctuousness is small. As for the sons and the daughters they beget, why, those sons and daughters must take care of themselves; at least, with only the maternal help. For like certain other omnivorous roving lovers that might be named, my Lord Whale has no taste for the nursery, however much for the bower; and so, being a great traveller, he leaves his anonymous babies all over the world; every baby an exotic. In good time, nevertheless, as the ardor of youth declines; as years and dumps increase; as reflection lends her solemn pauses; in short, as a general lassitude overtakes the sated Turk; then a love of ease and virtue supplants the love for maidens; our Ottoman enters upon the impotent, repentant, admonitory stage of life, forswears, disbands the harem, and grown to an exemplary, sulky old soul, goes about all alone among the meridians and parallels saying his prayers, and warning each young Leviathan from his amorous errors.

Now, as the harem of whales is called by the fishermen a school, so is the lord and master of that school technically known as the schoolmaster.

3. 1 Kings 11.3 specifies that Solomon had "seven hundred wives, princesses, and three hundred concubines: and his wives turned away his heart" away from God. *Lothario*: a seducer in Nicholas Rowe's *The Fair Penitent* (1703).

It is therefore not in strict character, however admirably satirical, that after going to school himself, he should then go abroad inculcating not what he learned there, but the folly of it. His title, schoolmaster, would very naturally seem derived from the name bestowed upon the harem itself, but some have surmised that the man who first thus entitled this sort of Ottoman whale, must have read the memoirs of Vidocq,[4] and informed himself what sort of a country-schoolmaster that famous Frenchman was in his younger days, and what was the nature of those occult lessons he inculcated into some of his pupils.

The same secludedness and isolation to which the schoolmaster whale betakes himself in his advancing years, is true of all aged Sperm Whales. Almost universally, a lone whale—as a solitary Leviathan is called—proves an ancient one. Like venerable moss-bearded Daniel Boone,[5] he will have no one near him but Nature herself; and her he takes to wife in the wilderness of waters, and the best of wives she is, though she keeps so many moody secrets.

The schools composing none but young and vigorous males, previously mentioned, offer a strong contrast to the harem schools. For while those female whales are characteristically timid, the young males, or forty-bar-rel-bulls, as they call them, are by far the most pugnacious of all Leviathans, and proverbially the most dangerous to encounter; excepting those wondrous greyheaded, grizzled whales, sometimes met, and these will fight you like grim fiends exasperated by a penal gout.

The Forty-barrel-bull schools are larger than the harem schools. Like a mob of young collegians, they are full of fight, fun, and wickedness, tumbling round the world at such a reckless, rollicking rate, that no prudent underwriter would insure them any more than he would a riotous lad at Yale or Harvard. They soon relinquish this turbulence though, and when about three fourths grown, break up, and separately go about in quest of settlements, that is, harems.

Another point of difference between the male and female schools is still more characteristic of the sexes. Say you strike a Forty-barrel-bull—poor devil! all his comrades quit him. But strike a member of the harem school, and her companions swim around her with every token of concern, sometimes lingering so near her and so long, as themselves to fall a prey.

Chapter 89

Fast-Fish and Loose-Fish

The allusion to the waifs and waif-poles in the last chapter but one, necessitates some account of the laws and regulations of the whale fishery, of which the waif may be deemed the grand symbol and badge.

It frequently happens that when several ships are cruising in company, a whale may be struck by one vessel, then escape, and be finally killed and

4. In his *Memoires de Vidocq* (1828), the Parisian detective Eugène Françoise Vidocq (1775–1857) tells of seducing his young female students.
5. American frontiersman (1734–1820), remembered for moving westward, time and again, to be out of sight of smoke from a neighbor's chimney.

captured by another vessel; and herein are indirectly comprised many minor contingencies, all partaking of this one grand feature. For example,—after a weary and perilous chase and capture of a whale, the body may get loose from the ship by reason of a violent storm; and drifting far away to leeward, be retaken by a second whaler, who, in a calm, snugly tows it alongside, without risk of life or line. Thus the most vexatious and violent disputes would often arise between the fishermen, were there not some written or unwritten, universal, undisputed law applicable to all cases.

Perhaps the only formal whaling code authorized by legislative enactment, was that of Holland. It was decreed by the States-General in A.D. 1695. But though no other nation has ever had any written whaling law, yet the American fishermen have been their own legislators and lawyers in this matter. They have provided a system which for terse comprehensiveness surpasses Justinian's Pandects and the By-laws of the Chinese Society[1] for the Suppression of Meddling with other People's Business. Yes; these laws might be engraven on a Queen Anne's farthing,[2] or the barb of a harpoon, and worn round the neck, so small are they.

I. A Fast-Fish belongs to the party fast to it.

II. A Loose-Fish is fair game for anybody who can soonest catch it.

But what plays the mischief with this masterly code is the admirable brevity of it, which necessitates a vast volume of commentaries to expound it.

First: What is a Fast-Fish? Alive or dead a fish is technically fast, when it is connected with an occupied ship or boat, by any medium at all controllable by the occupant or occupants,—a mast, an oar, a nine-inch cable, a telegraph wire, or a strand of cobweb, it is all the same. Likewise a fish is technically fast when it bears a waif, or any other recognised symbol of possession; so long as the party waifing it plainly evince their ability at any time to take it alongside, as well as their intention so to do.

These are scientific commentaries; but the commentaries of the whalemen themselves sometimes consist in hard words and harder knocks—the Coke-upon-Littleton[3] of the fist. True, among the more upright and honorable whalemen allowances are always made for peculiar cases, where it would be an outrageous moral injustice for one party to claim possession of a whale previously chased or killed by another party. But others are by no means so scrupulous.

Some fifty years ago there was a curious case of whale-trover litigated in England, wherein the plaintiffs set forth that after a hard chase of a whale in the Northern seas, they (the plaintiffs) had succeeded in harpooning the fish; but at last, through peril of their lives, were obliged to forsake not only their lines, but their boat itself. Ultimately the defendants (the crew of another ship) came up with the whale, struck, killed, seized, and finally appropriated it before the very eyes of the plaintiffs. And when those defendants were remonstrated with, their captain

---

1. Another of Melville's inventions. *Justinian Pandects:* the code of law propounded by Justinian (483–565), Byzantine emperor (r. 527–65).
2. Some commemorative farthings, though not Queen Anne's farthings, were much smaller than an American dime.
3. Standard legal text, Sir Edward Coke's 17th-century commentary on a 15th-century work on real property by Sir Thomas Littleton.

snapped his fingers in the plaintiffs' teeth, and assured them that by way of doxology to the deed he had done, he would now retain their line, harpoons, and boat, which had remained attached to the whale at the time of the seizure. Wherefore the plaintiffs now sued for the recovery of the value of their whale, line, harpoons, and boat.

Mr. Erskine was counsel for the defendants; Lord Ellenborough was the judge. In the course of the defence, the witty Erskine went on to illustrate his position, by alluding to a recent crim. con. case,[4] wherein a gentleman, after in vain trying to bridle his wife's viciousness, had at last abandoned her upon the seas of life; but in the course of years, repenting of that step, he instituted an action to recover possession of her. Erskine was on the other side; and he then supported it by saying, that though the gentleman had originally harpooned the lady, and had once had her fast, and only by reason of the great stress of her plunging viciousness, had at last abandoned her; yet abandon her he did, so that she became a loose fish; and therefore when a subsequent gentleman re-harpooned her, the lady then became that subsequent gentleman's property, along with whatever harpoon might have been found sticking in her.

Now in the present case Erskine contended that the examples of the whale and the lady were reciprocally illustrative of each other.

These pleadings, and the counter pleadings, being duly heard, the very learned judge in set terms decided, to wit,—That as for the boat, he awarded it to the plaintiffs, because they had merely abandoned it to save their lives; but that with regard to the controverted whale, harpoons, and line, they belonged to the defendants; the whale, because it was a Loose-Fish at the time of the final capture; and the harpoons and line because when the fish made off with them, it (the fish) acquired a property in those articles; and hence anybody who afterwards took the fish had a right to them. Now the defendants afterwards took the fish; ergo, the aforesaid articles were theirs.

A common man looking at this decision of the very learned Judge, might possibly object to it. But ploughed up to the primary rock of the matter, the two great principles laid down in the twin whaling laws previously quoted, and applied and elucidated by Lord Ellenborough in the above cited case; these two laws touching Fast-Fish and Loose-Fish, I say, will, on reflection, be found the fundamentals of all human jurisprudence; for notwithstanding its complicated tracery of sculpture, the Temple of the Law, like the Temple of the Philistines,[5] has but two props to stand on.

Is it not a saying in every one's mouth, Possession is half of the law: that is, regardless of how the thing came into possession? But often possession is the whole of the law. What are the sinews and souls of Russian serfs and Republican slaves but Fast-Fish, whereof possession is the whole of the law? What to the rapacious landlord is the widow's last mite[6] but a

---

4. A case of criminal conversation or adultery (*conversation*: sexual intercourse). Scoresby (1820) is Melville's source for this story of Erskine and Lord Ellenborough.

5. The temple brought down by Samson after he was blinded (Judges 16.29–30).

6. A better gift than the gifts cast into the treasury at the temple by the rich, Jesus said: "For all they did cast in of their abundance; but she of her want did cast in all that she had, even all her living" (Mark 12.44). *Republican Slaves:* slaves in a republic, like the United States (in obvious contradiction of the Declaration of Independence).

Fast-Fish? What is yonder undetected villain's marble mansion with a door-plate for a waif; what is that but a Fast-Fish? What is the ruinous discount which Mordecai, the broker, gets from poor Woebegone, the bankrupt, on a loan to keep Woebegone's family from starvation; what is that ruinous discount but a Fast-Fish? What is the Archbishop of Savesoul's income of £100,000 seized from the scant bread and cheese of hundreds of thousands of broken-backed laborers (all sure of heaven without any of Savesoul's help) what is that globular 100,000 but a Fast-Fish? What are the Duke of Dunder's hereditary towns and hamlets but Fast-Fish? What to that redoubted harpooneer, John Bull, is poor Ireland, but a Fast-Fish? What to that apostolic lancer, Brother Jonathan, is Texas but a Fast-Fish? And concerning all these, is not Possession the whole of the law?

But if the doctrine of Fast-Fish be pretty generally applicable, the kindred doctrine of Loose-Fish is still more widely so. That is internationally and universally applicable.

What was America in 1492 but a Loose-Fish, in which Columbus struck the Spanish standard by way of waifing it for his royal master and mistress? What was Poland to the Czar? What Greece to the Turk? What India to England? What at last will Mexico be to the United States? All Loose-Fish.

What are the Rights of Man and the Liberties of the World but Loose-Fish? What all men's minds and opinions but Loose-Fish? What is the principle of religious belief in them but a Loose-Fish? What to the ostentatious smuggling verbalists are the thoughts of thinkers but Loose-Fish? What is the great globe itself but a Loose-Fish? And what are you, reader, but a Loose-Fish and a Fast-Fish, too?

Chapter 90

Heads or Tails

"De balena vero sufficit, si rex habeat caput, et regina caudam."[1]

Bracton, l.3, c.3.

Latin from the books of the Laws of England, which taken along with the context, means, that of all whales captured by anybody on the coast of that land, the King, as Honorary Grand Harpooneer, must have the head, and the Queen be respectfully presented with the tail. A division which, in the whale, is much like halving an apple; there is no intermediate remainder. Now as this law, under a modified form, is to this day in force in England; and as it offers in various respects a strange anomaly touching the general law of Fast and Loose-Fish, it is here treated of in a separate chapter, on the same courteous principle that prompts the English railways to be at the expense of a separate car, specially reserved for the accommodation of royalty. In the first place, in curious proof of the fact that the above-mentioned law is still in force,

---

1. Concerning the whale, truly it suffices, if the king have the head, and the queen the tail.

I proceed to lay before you a circumstance that happened within the last two years.

It seems that some honest mariners of Dover, or Sandwich, or some one of the Cinque Ports, had after a hard chase succeeded in killing and beaching a fine whale which they had originally descried afar off from the shore. Now the Cinque Ports are partially or somehow under the jurisdiction of a sort of policeman or beadle, called a Lord Warden. Holding the office directly from the crown, I believe, all the royal emoluments incident to the Cinque Port territories become by assignment his. By some writers this office is called a sinecure. But not so. Because the Lord Warden is busily employed at times in fobbing[2] his perquisites; which are his chiefly by virtue of that same fobbing of them.

Now when these poor sun-burnt mariners, bare-footed, and with their trowsers rolled high up on their eely legs, had wearily hauled their fat fish high and dry, promising themselves a good £150 from the precious oil and bone; and in fantasy sipping rare tea with their wives, and good ale with their cronies, upon the strength of their respective shares; up steps a very learned and most Christian and charitable gentleman, with a copy of Blackstone[3] under his arm; and laying it upon the whale's head, he says— "Hands off! this fish, my masters, is a Fast-Fish. I seize it as the Lord Warden's." Upon this the poor mariners in their respectful consternation—so truly English—knowing not what to say, fall to vigorously scratching their heads all round; meanwhile ruefully glancing from the whale to the stranger. But that did in nowise mend the matter, or at all soften the hard heart of the learned gentleman with the copy of Blackstone. At length one of them, after long scratching about for his ideas, made bold to speak.

"Please, sir, who is the Lord Warden?"

"The Duke."

"But the duke had nothing to do with taking this fish?"

"It is his."

"We have been at great trouble, and peril, and some expense, and is all that to go to the Duke's benefit; we getting nothing at all for our pains but our blisters?"

"It is his."

"Is the Duke so very poor as to be forced to this desperate mode of getting a livelihood?"

"It is his."

"I thought to relieve my old bed-ridden mother by part of my share of this whale."

"It is his."

"Won't the Duke be content with a quarter or a half?"

"It is his."

In a word, the whale was seized and sold, and his Grace the Duke of Wellington[4] received the money. Thinking that viewed in some particular lights, the case might by a bare possibility in some small degree be deemed, under the circumstances, a rather hard one, an honest clergy-

2. Pocketing.
3. *Commentaries*, famous legal compendium by Sir William Blackstone (1723–1780).
4. Arthur Wellesley (1769–1852), duke of Wellington, victor over Napoleon at Waterloo (1815) and prime minister of England (1828–30) in Melville's boyhood.

man of the town respectfully addressed a note to his Grace, begging him
to take the case of those unfortunate mariners into full consideration. To
which my Lord Duke in substance replied (both letters were published)
that he had already done so, and received the money, and would be
obliged to the reverend gentleman if for the future he (the reverend gentleman) would decline meddling with other people's business. Is this the
still militant old man, standing at the corners of the three kingdoms, on
all hands coercing alms of beggars?

It will readily be seen that in this case the alleged right of the Duke to
the whale was a delegated one from the Sovereign. We must needs inquire
then on what principle the Sovereign is originally invested with that right.
The law itself has already been set forth. But Plowden gives us the reason
for it. Says Plowden,[5] the whale so caught belongs to the King and Queen,
"because of its superior excellence." And by the soundest commentators
this has ever been held a cogent argument in such matters.

But why should the King have the head, and the Queen the tail? A reason for that, ye lawyers!

In his treatise on "Queen-Gold," or Queen-pinmoney, an old King's
Bench author, one William Prynne,[6] thus discourseth: "Y[e] tail is y[e]
Queen's, that y[e] Queen's wardrobe may be supplied with y[e] whalebone."
Now this was written at a time when the black limber bone of the Greenland or Right whale was largely used in ladies' bodices. But this same bone
is not in the tail; it is in the head, which is a sad mistake for a sagacious
lawyer like Prynne. But is the Queen a mermaid, to be presented with a
tail? An allegorical meaning may lurk here.

There are two royal fish so styled by the English law writers—the whale
and the sturgeon; both royal property under certain limitations, and nominally supplying the tenth branch of the crown's ordinary revenue. I know
not that any other author has hinted of the matter; but by inference it
seems to me that the sturgeon must be divided in the same way as the
whale, the King receiving the highly dense and elastic head peculiar to
that fish, which, symbolically regarded, may possibly be humorously
grounded upon some presumed congeniality. And thus there seems a reason in all things, even in law.

Chapter 91

The Pequod meets the Rose-bud

*"In vain it was to rake for Ambergriese in the paunch of this Leviathan,
insufferable fetor denying that inquiry."*

Sir T. Browne, V.E.[1]

It was a week or two after the last whaling scene recounted, and when we
were slowly sailing over a sleepy, vapory, mid-day sea, that the many noses

---

5. Edmund Plowden (1518–1585), English jurist.
6. English Puritan pamphleteer (1600–1669).
1. Sir Thomas Browne's *Pseudodoxia Epidemica*, often called *Vulgar Errors* (1646).

on the Pequod's deck proved more vigilant discoverers than the three pairs of eyes aloft. A peculiar and not very pleasant smell was smelt in the sea.

"I will bet something now," said Stubb, "that somewhere hereabouts are some of those drugged whales we tickled the other day. I thought they would keel up before long."

Presently, the vapors in advance slid aside; and there in the distance lay a ship, whose furled sails betokened that some sort of whale must be alongside. As we glided nearer, the stranger showed French colors from his peak; and by the eddying cloud of vulture sea-fowl that circled, and hovered, and swooped around him, it was plain that the whale alongside must be what the fishermen call a blasted whale, that is, a whale that has died unmolested on the sea, and so floated an unappropriated corpse. It may well be conceived, what an unsavory odor such a mass must exhale; worse than an Assyrian city in the plague, when the living are incompetent to bury the departed. So intolerable indeed is it regarded by some, that no cupidity could persuade them to moor alongside of it. Yet are there those who will still do it; notwithstanding the fact that the oil obtained from such subjects is of a very inferior quality, and by no means of the nature of attar-of-rose.

Coming still nearer with the expiring breeze, we saw that the Frenchman had a second whale alongside; and this second whale seemed even more of a nosegay than the first. In truth, it turned out to be one of those problematical whales that seem to dry up and die with a sort of prodigious dyspepsia, or indigestion; leaving their defunct bodies almost entirely bankrupt of anything like oil. Nevertheless, in the proper place we shall see that no knowing fisherman will ever turn up his nose at such a whale as this, however much he may shun blasted whales in general.

The Pequod had now swept so nigh to the stranger, that Stubb vowed he recognised his cutting spade-pole entangled in the lines that were knotted round the tail of one of these whales.

"There's a pretty fellow, now," he banteringly laughed, standing in the ship's bows, "there's a jackal for ye! I well know that these Crappoes[2] of Frenchmen are but poor devils in the fishery; sometimes lowering their boats for breakers, mistaking them for Sperm Whale spouts; yes, and sometimes sailing from their port with their hold full of boxes of tallow candles, and cases of snuffers, foreseeing that all the oil they will get won't be enough to dip the Captain's wick into; aye, we all know these things; but look ye, here's a Crappo that is content with our leavings, the drugged whale there, I mean; aye, and is content too with scraping the dry bones of that other precious fish he has there. Poor devil! I say, pass round a hat, some one, and let's make him a present of a little oil for dear charity's sake. For what oil he'll get from that drugged whale there, wouldn't be fit to burn in a jail; no, not in a condemned cell. And as for the other whale, why, I'll agree to get more oil by chopping up and trying out these three masts of ours, than he'll get from that bundle of bones; though, now that I think of it, it may contain something worth a good deal more than oil; yes, ambergris. I wonder now if our old man has thought of that. It's worth trying. Yes, I'm in for it;" and so saying he started for the quarter-deck.

---

2. Frogs, derogative for Frenchmen; from *crapauds*, "toads."

By this time the faint air had become a complete calm; so that whether or no, the Pequod was now fairly entrapped in the smell, with no hope of escaping except by its breezing up again. Issuing from the cabin, Stubb now called his boat's crew, and pulled off for the stranger. Drawing across her bow, he perceived that in accordance with the fanciful French taste, the upper part of her stem-piece was carved in the likeness of a huge drooping stalk, was painted green, and for thorns had copper spikes projecting from it here and there; the whole terminating in a symmetrical folded bulb of a bright red color. Upon her head boards, in large gilt letters, he read "Bouton de Rose,"—Rose-button, or Rose-bud; and this was the romantic name of this aromatic ship.

Though Stubb did not understand the *Bouton* part of the inscription, yet the word *rose*, and the bulbous figure-head put together, sufficiently explained the whole to him.

"A wooden rose-bud, eh?" he cried with his hand to his nose, "that will do very well; but how like all creation it smells!"

Now in order to hold direct communication with the people on deck, he had to pull round the bows to the starboard side, and thus come close to the blasted whale; and so talk over it.

Arrived then at this spot, with one hand still to his nose, he bawled— "Bouton-de-Rose, ahoy! are there any of you Bouton-de-Roses that speak English?"

"Yes," rejoined a Guernsey-man[3] from the bulwarks, who turned out to be the chief-mate.

"Well, then, my Bouton-de-Rose-bud, have you seen the White Whale?"

"*What* whale?"

"The *White* Whale—a Sperm Whale—Moby Dick, have ye seen him?"

"Never heard of such a whale. Cachalot Blanche! White Whale—no."

"Very good, then; good bye now, and I'll call again in a minute."

Then rapidly pulling back towards the Pequod, and seeing Ahab leaning over the quarter-deck rail awaiting his report, he moulded his two hands into a trumpet and shouted—"No, Sir! No!" Upon which Ahab retired, and Stubb returned to the Frenchman.

He now perceived that the Guernsey-man, who had just got into the chains, and was using a cutting-spade, had slung his nose in a sort of bag.

"What's the matter with your nose, there?" said Stubb. "Broke it?"

"I wish it was broken, or that I didn't have any nose at all!" answered the Guernsey-man, who did not seem to relish the job he was at very much. "But what are you holding *yours* for?"

"Oh, nothing! It's a wax nose; I have to hold it on. Fine day, aint it? Air rather gardenny,[4] I should say; throw us a bunch of posies, will ye, Bouton-de-Rose?"

"What in the devil's name do you want here?" roared the Guernsey-man, flying into a sudden passion.

"Oh! keep cool—cool? yes, that's the word; why don't you pack those whales in ice while you're working at 'em? But joking aside, though; do you know, Rose-bud, that it's all nonsense trying to get any oil out of such

3. From the island of Guernsey in the English Channel.
4. That is, smelling like a freshly manured garden.

whales? As for that dried up one, there, he hasn't a gill in his whole carcase."

"I know that well enough; but, d'ye see, the Captain here won't believe
it; this is his first voyage; he was a Cologne manufacturer before. But
come aboard, and mayhap he'll believe you, if he won't me; and so I'll get
out of this dirty scrape."

"Anything to oblige ye, my sweet and pleasant fellow," rejoined Stubb,
and with that he soon mounted to the deck. There a queer scene presented itself. The sailors, in tasselled caps of red worsted, were getting the
heavy tackles in readiness for the whales. But they worked rather slow and
talked very fast, and seemed in anything but a good humor. All their noses
upwardly projected from their faces like so many jib-booms. Now and
then pairs of them would drop their work, and run up to the mast-head to
get some fresh air. Some thinking they would catch the plague, dipped
oakum in coal-tar, and at intervals held it to their nostrils. Others having
broken the stems of their pipes almost short off at the bowl, were vigorously puffing tobacco-smoke, so that it constantly filled their olfactories.

Stubb was struck by a shower of outcries and anathemas proceeding
from the Captain's round-house[5] abaft; and looking in that direction saw
a fiery face thrust from behind the door, which was held ajar from within.
This was the tormented surgeon, who, after in vain remonstrating against
the proceedings of the day, had betaken himself to the Captain's round-
house (cabinet he called it) to avoid the pest; but still, could not help
yelling out his entreaties and indignations at times.

Marking all this, Stubb augured well for his scheme, and turning to the
Guernsey-man had a little chat with him, during which the stranger mate
expressed his detestation of his Captain as a conceited ignoramus, who
had brought them all into so unsavory and unprofitable a pickle. Sounding him carefully, Stubb further perceived that the Guernsey-man had not
the slightest suspicion concerning the ambergris. He therefore held his
peace on that head, but otherwise was quite frank and confidential with
him, so that the two quickly concocted a little plan for both circumvent-
ing and satirizing the Captain, without his at all dreaming of distrusting
their sincerity. According to this little plan of theirs, the Guernsey-man,
under cover of an interpreter's office, was to tell the Captain what he
pleased, but as coming from Stubb; and as for Stubb, he was to utter any
nonsense that should come uppermost in him during the interview.

By this time their destined victim appeared from his cabin. He was a
small and dark, but rather delicate looking man for a sea-captain, with
large whiskers and moustache, however; and wore a red cotton velvet vest
with watch-seals at his side. To this gentleman, Stubb was now politely
introduced by the Guernsey-man, who at once ostentatiously put on the
aspect of interpreting between them.

"What shall I say to him first?" said he.

"Why," said Stubb, eyeing the velvet vest and the watch and seals, "you
may as well begin by telling him that he looks a sort of babyish to me,
though I don't pretend to be a judge."

---

5. The Captain's personal privy, perched on the rail. The surgeon prefers the odor of the "cabinet"
to that of the blasted whale.

"He says, Monsieur," said the Guernsey-man, in French, turning to his captain, "that only yesterday his ship spoke a vessel, whose captain and chief-mate, with six sailors, had all died of a fever caught from a blasted whale they had brought alongside."

Upon this the captain started, and eagerly desired to know more.

"What now?" said the Guernsey-man to Stubb.

"Why, since he takes it so easy, tell him that now I have eyed him carefully, I'm quite certain that he's no more fit to command a whale-ship than a St. Jago monkey.[6] In fact, tell him from me he's a baboon."

"He vows and declares, Monsieur, that the other whale, the dried one, is far more deadly than the blasted one; in fine, Monsieur, he conjures us, as we value our lives, to cut loose from these fish."

Instantly the captain ran forward, and in a loud voice commanded his crew to desist from hoisting the cutting-tackles, and at once cast loose the cables and chains confining the whales to the ship.

"What now?" said the Guernsey-man, when the captain had returned to them.

"Why, let me see; yes, you may as well tell him now that—that—in fact, tell him I've diddled[7] him, and (aside to himself) perhaps somebody else."

"He says, Monsieur, that he's very happy to have been of any service to us."

Hearing this, the captain vowed that they were the grateful parties (meaning himself and mate) and concluded by inviting Stubb down into his cabin to drink a bottle of Bordeaux.

"He wants you to take a glass of wine with him," said the interpreter.

"Thank him heartily; but tell him it's against my principles to drink with the man I've diddled. In fact, tell him I must go."

"He says, Monsieur, that his principles won't admit of his drinking; but that if Monsieur wants to live another day to drink, then Monsieur had best drop all four boats, and pull the ship away from these whales, for it's so calm they won't drift."

By this time Stubb was over the side, and getting into his boat, hailed the Guernsey-man to this effect,—that having a long tow-line in his boat, he would do what he could to help them, by pulling out the lighter whale of the two from the ship's side. While the Frenchman's boats, then, were engaged in towing the ship one way, Stubb benevolently towed away at his whale the other way, ostentatiously slacking out a most unusually long tow-line.

Presently a breeze sprang up; Stubb feigned to cast off from the whale; hoisting his boats, the Frenchman soon increased his distance, while the Pequod slid in between him and Stubb's whale. Whereupon Stubb quickly pulled to the floating body, and hailing the Pequod to give notice of his intentions, at once proceeded to reap the fruit of his unrighteous cunning. Seizing his sharp boat-spade, he commenced an excavation in the body, a little behind the side fin. You would almost have thought he was digging a cellar there in the sea; and when at length his spade struck against the gaunt ribs, it was like turning up old Roman tiles and pottery

6. Monkey from that Portuguese island in the Cape Verdes, in the Atlantic.
7. Cheated, swindled. "Screwed" is the best modern equivalent, because "diddle" also has a sexual meaning.

buried in fat English loam. His boat's crew were all in high excitement,
eagerly helping their chief, and looking as anxious as gold-hunters.

And all the time numberless fowls were diving, and ducking, and
screaming, and yelling, and fighting around them. Stubb was beginning to
look disappointed, especially as the horrible nosegay increased, when suddenly from out the very heart of this plague, there stole a faint stream of
perfume, which flowed through the tide of bad smells without being
absorbed by it, as one river will flow into and then along with another,
without at all blending with it for a time.

"I have it, I have it," cried Stubb, with delight, striking something in the
subterranean regions, "a purse! a purse!"

Dropping his spade, he thrust both hands in, and drew out handfuls of
something that looked like ripe Windsor soap, or rich mottled old cheese;
very unctuous and savory withal. You might easily dent it with your
thumb; it is of a hue between yellow and ash color. And this, good friends,
is ambergris, worth a gold guinea an ounce to any druggist. Some six
handfuls were obtained; but more was unavoidably lost in the sea, and
still more, perhaps, might have been secured were it not for impatient
Ahab's loud command to Stubb to desist, and come on board, else the
ship would bid them good bye.

Chapter 92

Ambergris[1]

Now this ambergris is a very curious substance, and so important as an
article of commerce, that in 1791 a certain Nantucket-born Captain Coffin was examined at the bar of the English House of Commons on that
subject. For at that time, and indeed until a comparatively late day, the
precise origin of ambergris remained, like amber itself, a problem to the
learned. Though the word ambergris is but the French compound for grey
amber, yet the two substances are quite distinct. For amber, though at
times found on the sea-coast, is also dug up in some far inland soils,
whereas ambergris is never found except upon the sea. Besides, amber is
a hard, transparent, brittle, odorless substance, used for mouth-pieces to
pipes, for beads and ornaments; but ambergris is soft, waxy, and so highly
fragrant and spicy, that it is largely used in perfumery, in pastiles, precious
candles, hair-powders, and pomatum. The Turks use it in cooking, and
also carry it to Mecca, for the same purpose that frankincense is carried
to St. Peter's in Rome. Some wine merchants drop a few grains into claret,
to flavor it.

Who would think, then, that such fine ladies and gentlemen should
regale themselves with an essence found in the inglorious bowels of a sick
whale! Yet so it is. By some, ambergris is supposed to be the cause, and by
others the effect, of the dyspepsia in the whale. How to cure such a dyspepsia it were hard to say, unless by administering three or four boat loads

---

1. Mansfield and Vincent (793) cite Beale as Melville's main source in this chapter.

of Brandreth's pills,[2] and then running out of harm's way, as laborers do in blasting rocks.

I have forgotten to say that there were found in this ambergris, certain hard, round, bony plates, which at first Stubb thought might be sailors' trousers buttons; but it afterwards turned out that they were nothing more than pieces of small squid bones embalmed in that manner.

Now that the incorruption of this most fragrant ambergris should be found in the heart of such decay; is this nothing? Bethink thee of that saying of St. Paul in Corinthians,[3] about corruption and incorruption; how that we are sown in dishonor, but raised in glory. And likewise call to mind that saying of Paracelsus about what it is that maketh the best musk.[4] Also forget not the strange fact that of all things of ill-savor, Cologne-water, in its rudimental manufacturing stages, is the worst.

I should like to conclude the chapter with the above appeal, but cannot, owing to my anxiety to repel a charge often made against whalemen, and which, in the estimation of some already biased minds, might be considered as indirectly substantiated by what has been said of the Frenchman's two whales. Elsewhere in this volume the slanderous aspersion has been disproved, that the vocation of whaling is throughout a slatternly, untidy business. But there is another thing to rebut. They hint that all whales always smell bad. Now how did this odious stigma originate?

I opine, that it is plainly traceable to the first arrival of the Greenland whaling ships[5] in London, more than two centuries ago. Because those whalemen did not then, and do not now, try out their oil at sea as the Southern ships have always done; but cutting up the fresh blubber in small bits, thrust it through the bung holes of large casks, and carry it home in that manner; the shortness of the season in those Icy Seas, and the sudden and violent storms to which they are exposed, forbidding any other course. The consequence is, that upon breaking into the hold, and unloading one of these whale cemeteries, in the Greenland dock, a savor is given forth somewhat similar to that arising from excavating an old city grave-yard, for the foundations of a Lying-in Hospital.

I partly surmise also, that this wicked charge against whalers may be likewise imputed to the existence on the coast of Greenland, in former times, of a Dutch village called Schmerenburgh or Smeerenberg, which latter name is the one used by the learned Fogo Von Slack,[6] in his great work on Smells, a text-book on that subject. As its name imports (smeer, fat; berg, to put up), this village was founded in order to afford a place for the blubber of the Dutch whale fleet to be tried out, without being taken home to Holland for that purpose. It was a collection of furnaces, fat-kettles, and oil sheds; and when the works were in full operation certainly gave forth no very pleasant savor. But all this is quite different with a South Sea Sperm Whaler; which in a voyage of four years perhaps, after completely filling her hold with oil, does not, perhaps, consume fifty days

---

2. A widely advertised laxative.
3. 1 Corinthians 15.42–43: "So also is the resurrection of the dead. It is sown in corruption; it is raised in incorruption: It is sown in dishonour; it is raised in glory: it is sown in weakness; it is raised in power."
4. "What it is" is excrement.
5. Ships back from whaling near Greenland.
6. Another of Melville's mocking names for Scoresby.

in the business of boiling out; and in the state that it is casked, the oil is nearly scentless. The truth is, that living or dead, if but decently treated, whales as a species are by no means creatures of ill odor; nor can whale-men be recognised, as the people of the middle ages affected to detect a Jew in the company, by the nose. Nor indeed can the whale possibly be otherwise than fragrant, when, as a general thing, he enjoys such high health; taking abundance of exercise; always out of doors; though, it is true, seldom in the open air. I say, that the motion of a Sperm Whale's flukes above water dispenses a perfume, as when a musk-scented lady rustles her dress in a warm parlor. What then shall I liken the Sperm Whale to for fragrance, considering his magnitude? Must it not be to that famous elephant, with jewelled tusks, and redolent with myrrh, which was led out of an Indian town to do honor to Alexander the Great?

Chapter 93

The Castaway

It was but some few days after encountering the Frenchman, that a most significant event befell the most insignificant of the Pequod's crew; an event most lamentable; and which ended in providing the sometimes madly merry and predestinated craft with a living and ever accompanying prophecy of whatever shattered sequel might prove her own.

Now, in the whale ship, it is not every one that goes in the boats. Some few hands are reserved called ship-keepers, whose province it is to work the vessel while the boats are pursuing the whale. As a general thing, these ship-keepers are as hardy fellows as the men comprising the boats' crews. But if there happen to be an unduly slender, clumsy, or timorous wight in the ship, that wight is certain to be made a ship-keeper. It was so in the Pequod with the little negro Pippin by nick-name, Pip by abbrevia-tion. Poor Pip! ye have heard of him before; ye must remember his tam-bourine on that dramatic midnight, so gloomy-jolly.

In outer aspect, Pip and Dough-Boy made a match, like a black pony and a white one, of equal developments, though of dissimilar color, driven in one eccentric span. But while hapless Dough-Boy was by nature dull and torpid in his intellects, Pip, though over tender-hearted, was at bot-tom very bright, with that pleasant, genial, jolly brightness peculiar to his tribe; a tribe, which ever enjoy all holidays and festivities with finer, freer relish than any other race. For blacks, the year's calendar should show naught but three hundred and sixty-five Fourth of Julys and New Year's Days. Nor smile so, while I write that this little black was brilliant, for even blackness has its brilliancy; behold yon lustrous ebony, panelled in king's cabinets. But Pip loved life, and all life's peaceable securities; so that the panic-striking business in which he had somehow unaccountably become entrapped, had most sadly blurred his brightness; though, as ere long will be seen, what was thus temporarily subdued in him, in the end was destined to be luridly illumined by strange wild fires, that fictitiously showed him off to ten times the natural lustre with which in his native

Tolland County in Connecticut, he had once enlivened many a fiddler's frolic on the green; and at melodious even-tide, with his gay ha-ha! had turned the round horizon into one star-belled tambourine. So, though in the clear air of day, suspended against a blue-veined neck, the pure-watered diamond drop will healthful glow; yet, when the cunning jeweller would show you the diamond in its most impressive lustre, he lays it against a gloomy ground, and then lights it up, not by the sun, but by some unnatural gases. Then come out those fiery effulgences, infernally superb; then the evil-blazing diamond, once the divinest symbol of the crystal skies, looks like some crown-jewel stolen from the King of Hell. But let us to the story.

It came to pass, that in the ambergris affair Stubb's after-oarsman chanced so to sprain his hand, as for a time to become quite maimed; and, temporarily, Pip was put into his place.

The first time Stubb lowered with him, Pip evinced much nervousness; but happily, for that time, escaped close contact with the whale; and therefore came off not altogether discreditably; though Stubb observing him, took care, afterwards, to exhort him to cherish his courageousness to the utmost, for he might often find it needful.

Now upon the second lowering, the boat paddled upon the whale; and as the fish received the darted iron, it gave its customary rap, which happened, in this instance, to be right under poor Pip's seat. The involuntary consternation of the moment caused him to leap, paddle in hand, out of the boat; and in such a way, that part of the slack whale line coming against his chest, he breasted it overboard with him, so as to become entangled in it, when at last plumping into the water. That instant the stricken whale started on a fierce run, the line swiftly straightened; and presto! poor Pip came all foaming up to the chocks of the boat, remorselessly dragged there by the line, which had taken several turns around his chest and neck.

Tashtego stood in the bows. He was full of the fire of the hunt. He hated Pip for a poltroon. Snatching the boat-knife from its sheath, he suspended its sharp edge over the line, and turning towards Stubb, exclaimed interrogatively, "Cut?" Meantime Pip's blue, choked face plainly looked, Do, for God's sake! All passed in a flash. In less than half a minute, this entire thing happened.

"Damn him, cut!" roared Stubb; and so the whale was lost and Pip was saved.

So soon as he recovered himself, the poor little negro was assailed by yells and execrations from the crew. Tranquilly permitting these irregular cursings to evaporate, Stubb then in a plain, business-like, but still half humorous manner, cursed Pip officially; and that done, unofficially gave him much wholesome advice. The substance was, Never jump from a boat, Pip, except—but all the rest was indefinite, as the soundest advice ever is. Now, in general, *Stick to the boat*, is your true motto in whaling; but cases will sometimes happen when *Leap from the boat*, is still better. Moreover, as if perceiving at last that if he should give undiluted conscientious advice to Pip, he would be leaving him too wide a margin to jump in for the future; Stubb suddenly dropped all advice, and concluded with a peremptory command, "Stick to the boat, Pip, or by the Lord, I wont pick you up if you jump; mind that. We can't afford to lose whales by the likes of you; a whale would sell for thirty times what you would, Pip, in Alabama. Bear that in mind, and don't jump any more." Hereby perhaps Stubb indirectly hinted, that though man loves his fellow, yet man is a money-making animal, which propensity too often interferes with his benevolence.

But we are all in the hands of the Gods; and Pip jumped again. It was under very similar circumstances to the first performance; but this time he did not breast out the line; and hence, when the whale started to run, Pip was left behind on the sea, like a hurried traveller's trunk. Alas! Stubb was but too true to his word. It was a beautiful, bounteous, blue day; the spangled sea calm and cool, and flatly stretching away, all round, to the horizon, like gold-beater's skin[1] hammered out to the extremest. Bobbing up and down in that sea, Pip's ebon head showed like a head of cloves. No boat-knife was lifted when he fell so rapidly astern. Stubb's inexorable back was turned upon him; and the whale was winged. In three minutes, a whole mile of shoreless ocean was between Pip and Stubb. Out from the centre of the sea, poor Pip turned his crisp, curling, black head to the sun, another lonely castaway, though the loftiest and the brightest.

Now, in calm weather, to swim in the open ocean is as easy to the practised swimmer as to ride in a spring-carriage ashore. But the awful lonesomeness is intolerable. The intense concentration of self in the middle of such a heartless immensity, my God! who can tell it? Mark, how when sailors in a dead calm bathe in the open sea—mark how closely they hug their ship and only coast along her sides.

But had Stubb really abandoned the poor little negro to his fate? No; he did not mean to, at least. Because there were two boats in his wake, and he supposed, no doubt, that they would of course come up to Pip very quickly, and pick him up; though, indeed, such considerateness towards oarsmen jeopardized through their own timidity, is not always manifested by the hunters in all similar instances; and such instances not unfrequently occur; almost invariably in the fishery, a coward, so called, is marked with the same ruthless detestation peculiar to military navies and armies.

But it so happened, that those boats, without seeing Pip, suddenly spying whales close to them on one side, turned, and gave chase; and Stubb's boat was now so far away, and he and all his crew so intent upon his fish, that Pip's ringed horizon began to expand around him miserably. By the merest chance the ship itself at last rescued him; but from that hour the little negro went about the deck an idiot; such, at least, they said he was. The sea had jeeringly kept his finite body up, but drowned the infinite of his soul. Not drowned entirely, though. Rather carried down alive to wondrous depths, where strange shapes of the unwarped primal world glided to and fro before his passive eyes; and the miser-merman, Wisdom, revealed his hoarded heaps; and among the joyous, heartless, ever-juvenile eternities, Pip saw the multitudinous, God-omnipresent, coral insects, that out of the firmament of waters heaved the colossal orbs. He

---

1. Membrane of the large intestine of an ox, used to separate sheets of gold while they are being beaten into gold leaf.

saw God's foot upon the treadle of the loom, and spoke it; and therefore his shipmates called him mad. So man's insanity is heaven's sense; and wandering from all mortal reason, man comes at last to that celestial thought, which, to reason, is absurd and frantic; and weal or woe, feels then uncompromised, indifferent as his God.

For the rest, blame not Stubb too hardly. The thing is common in that fishery; and in the sequel of the narrative, it will then be seen what like abandonment befell myself.

Chapter 94

A Squeeze of the Hand

That whale of Stubb's, so dearly purchased, was duly brought to the Pequod's side, where all those cutting and hoisting operations previously detailed,[1] were regularly gone through, even to the baling of the Heidel-burgh Tun, or Case.

While some were occupied with this latter duty, others were employed in dragging away the larger tubs, so soon as filled with the sperm; and when the proper time arrived, this same sperm was carefully manipulated ere going to the try-works, of which anon.

It had cooled and crystallized to such a degree, that when, with several others, I sat down before a large Constantine's bath[2] of it, I found it strangely concreted into lumps, here and there rolling about in the liquid part. It was our business to squeeze these lumps back into fluid. A sweet and unctuous duty! No wonder that in old times this sperm was such a favorite cosmetic. Such a clearer! such a sweetener! such a softener! such a delicious mollifier! After having my hands in it for only a few minutes, my fingers felt like eels, and began, as it were, to serpentine and spiralize.

As I sat there at my ease, cross-legged on the deck; after the bitter exertion at the windlass; under a blue tranquil sky; the ship under indolent sail, and gliding so serenely along; as I bathed my hands among those soft, gentle globules of infiltrated tissues, woven almost within the hour; as they richly broke to my fingers, and discharged all their opulence, like fully ripe grapes their wine; as I snuffed up that uncontaminated aroma,—literally and truly, like the smell of spring violets; I declare to you, that for the time I lived as in a musky meadow; I forgot all about our horrible oath; in that inexpressible sperm, I washed my hands and my heart of it; I almost began to credit the old Paracelsan superstition that sperm is of rare virtue in allaying the heat of anger: while bathing in that bath, I felt divinely free from all ill-will, or petulance, or malice, of any sort whatsoever.

Squeeze! squeeze! squeeze! all the morning long; I squeezed that sperm till I myself almost melted into it; I squeezed that sperm till a strange sort of insanity came over me; and I found myself unwittingly squeezing my co-laborers' hands in it, mistaking their hands for the gentle globules.

1. In ch. 77.
2. The Roman emperor Constantine the Great (272–337; r. 324–37) died after an attempt to regain his health at the baths of Helenopolis, in Greece.

Such an abounding, affectionate, friendly, loving feeling did this avocation beget; that at last I was continually squeezing their hands, and looking up into their eyes sentimentally; as much as to say,—Oh! my dear fellow beings, why should we longer cherish any social acerbities, or know the slightest ill-humor or envy! Come; let us squeeze hands all round; nay, let us all squeeze ourselves into each other; let us squeeze ourselves universally into the very milk and sperm of kindness.

Would that I could keep squeezing that sperm for ever! For now, since by many prolonged, repeated experiences, I have perceived that in all cases man must eventually lower, or at least shift, his conceit of attainable felicity; not placing it anywhere in the intellect or the fancy; but in the wife, the heart, the bed, the table, the saddle, the fire-side, the country; now that I have perceived all this, I am ready to squeeze case eternally. In thoughts of the visions of the night,[3] I saw long rows of angels in paradise, each with his hands in a jar of spermaceti.

*   *   *   *   *

Now, while discoursing of sperm, it behooves to speak of other things akin to it, in the business of preparing the sperm whale for the try-works.

First comes white-horse, so called, which is obtained from the tapering part of the fish, and also from the thicker portions of his flukes. It is tough with congealed tendons—a wad of muscle—but still contains some oil. After being severed from the whale, the white-horse is first cut into portable oblongs ere going to the mincer. They look much like blocks of Berkshire marble.

Plum-pudding is the term bestowed upon certain fragmentary parts of the whale's flesh, here and there adhering to the blanket of blubber, and often participating to a considerable degree in its unctuousness. It is a most refreshing, convivial, beautiful object to behold. As its name imports, it is of an exceedingly rich, mottled tint, with a bestreaked snowy and golden ground, dotted with spots of the deepest crimson and purple. It is plums of rubies, in pictures of citron. Spite of reason, it is hard to keep yourself from eating it. I confess, that once I stole behind the foremast to try it. It tasted something as I should conceive a royal cutlet from the thigh of Louis le Gros[4] might have tasted, supposing him to have been killed the first day after the venison season, and that particular venison season contemporary with an unusually fine vintage of the vineyards of Champagne.

There is another substance, and a very singular one, which turns up in the course of this business, but which I feel it to be very puzzling adequately to describe. It is called slobgollion; an appellation original with the whalemen, and even so is the nature of the substance. It is an ineffably oozy, stringy affair, most frequently found in the tubs of sperm, after a prolonged squeezing, and subsequent decanting. I hold it to be the wondrously thin, ruptured membranes of the case, coalescing.

Gurry, so called, is a term properly belonging to right whalemen, but sometimes incidentally used by the sperm fishermen. It designates the

3. See Job 20.8.
4. Louis the Fat; that is, Louis VI (1078–1137), king of France (r. 1108–37).

dark, glutinous substance which is scraped off the back of the Greenland or right whale, and much of which covers the decks of those inferior souls who hunt that ignoble Leviathan.

Nippers. Strictly this word is not indigenous to the whale's vocabulary. But as applied by whalemen, it becomes so. A whaleman's nipper is a short firm strip of tendinous stuff cut from the tapering part of Leviathan's tail: it averages an inch in thickness, and for the rest, is about the size of the iron part of a hoe. Edgewise moved along the oily deck, it operates like a leathern squilgee; and by nameless blandishments, as of magic, allures along with it all impurities.

But to learn all about these recondite matters, your best way is at once to descend into the blubber-room, and have a long talk with its inmates. This place has previously been mentioned[5] as the receptacle for the blanket-pieces, when stript and hoisted from the whale. When the proper time arrives for cutting up its contents, this apartment is a scene of terror to all tyros, especially by night. On one side, lit by a dull lantern, a space has been left clear for the workmen. They generally go in pairs,—a pike-and-gaff-man and a spade-man. The whaling-pike is similar to a frigate's boarding-weapon of the same name. The gaff is something like a boat-hook. With his gaff, the gaffman hooks on to a sheet of blubber, and strives to hold it from slipping, as the ship pitches and lurches about. Meanwhile, the spade-man stands on the sheet itself, perpendicularly chopping it into the portable horse-pieces. This spade is sharp as hone can make it; the spademan's feet are shoeless; the thing he stands on will sometimes irresistibly slide away from him, like a sledge. If he cuts off one of his own toes, or one of his assistant's, would you be very much astonished? Toes are scarce among veteran blubber-room men.

Chapter 95

The Cassock

Had you stepped on board the Pequod at a certain juncture of this post-mortemizing of the whale; and had you strolled forward nigh the windlass, pretty sure am I that you would have scanned with no small curiosity a very strange, enigmatical object,[1] which you would have seen there, lying along lengthwise in the lee scuppers. Not the wondrous cistern in the whale's huge head; not the prodigy of his unhinged lower jaw; not the miracle of his symmetrical tail; none of these would so surprise you, as half a glimpse of that unaccountable cone,—longer than a Kentuckian is tall, nigh a foot in diameter at the base, and jet-black as Yojo, the ebony idol of Queequeg. And an idol, indeed, it is; or, rather, in old times, its likeness was. Such an idol as that found in the secret groves of Queen Maachah in Judea; and for worshipping which, king Asa, her son, did depose her,

---

5. In the last paragraph of ch. 67.
1. The penis of the whale.

and destroyed the idol, and burnt it for an abomination at the brook Kedron,[2] as darkly set forth in the 15th chapter of the first book of Kings.

Look at the sailor, called the mincer, who now comes along, and assisted by two allies, heavily backs the grandissimus, as the mariners call it, and with bowed shoulders, staggers off with it as if he were a grenadier carrying a dead comrade from the field. Extending it upon the forecastle deck, he now proceeds cylindrically to remove its dark pelt, as an African hunter the pelt of a boa. This done he turns the pelt inside out, like a pantaloon leg; gives it a good stretching, so as almost to double its diameter; and at last hangs it, well spread, in the rigging, to dry. Ere long, it is taken down; when removing some three feet of it, towards the pointed extremity, and then cutting two slits for arm-holes at the other end, he lengthwise slips himself bodily into it. The mincer now stands before you invested in the full canonicals of his calling. Immemorial to all his order, this investiture alone will adequately protect him, while employed in the peculiar functions of his office.

That office consists in mincing the horse-pieces of blubber for the pots; an operation which is conducted at a curious wooden horse, planted endwise against the bulwarks, and with a capacious tub beneath it, into which the minced pieces drop, fast as the sheets from a rapt orator's desk. Arrayed in decent black; occupying a conspicuous pulpit; intent on bible leaves; what a candidate for an archbishoprick,[3] what a lad for a Pope were this mincer![4]

Chapter 96

The Try-Works

Besides her hoisted boats, an American whaler is outwardly distinguished by her try-works.[1] She presents the curious anomaly of the most solid masonry joining with oak and hemp in constituting the completed ship. It is as if from the open field a brick-kiln were transported to her planks.

The try-works are planted between the foremast and mainmast, the most roomy part of the deck. The timbers beneath are of a peculiar strength, fitted to sustain the weight of an almost solid mass of brick and mortar, some ten feet by eight square, and five in height. The foundation does not penetrate the deck, but the masonry is firmly secured to the surface by ponderous knees of iron bracing it on all sides, and screwing it down to the timbers. On the flanks it is cased with wood, and at top completely covered by a large, sloping, battened hatchway. Removing this hatch we expose the great try-pots, two in number, and each of several

2. 1 Kings 15.11–13: "And Asa did that which was right in the eyes of the Lord, as did David his father. And he took away the sodomites out of the land, and removed all the idols that his fathers had made. And also Maachah his mother, even her he removed from being queen, because she had made an idol in a grove; and Asa destroyed her idol, and burnt it by the brook Kidron."
3. The archaic spelling with the final k emphasizes the phallic pun.
4. Bible leaves! Bible leaves! This is the invariable cry from the mates to the mincer. It enjoins him to be careful, and cut his work into as thin slices as possible, inasmuch as by so doing the business of boiling out the oil is much accelerated, and its quantity considerably increased, besides perhaps improving it in quality [Melville's note].
1. "Contemporary Engravings." See p. 455, herein.

barrels' capacity. When not in use, they are kept remarkably clean. Some-times they are polished with soapstone and sand, till they shine within like silver punch-bowls. During the night-watches some cynical old sailors will crawl into them and coil themselves away there for a nap. While employed in polishing them—one man in each pot, side by side—many confidential communications are carried on; over the iron lips. It is a place also for profound mathematical meditation. It was in the left hand try-pot of the Pequod, with the soapstone diligently circling round me, that I was first indirectly struck by the remarkable fact, that in geometry all bodies glid-ing along the cycloid, my soapstone for example, will descend from any point in precisely the same time.

Removing the fire-board from the front of the try-works, the bare masonry of that side is exposed, penetrated by the two iron mouths of the furnaces, directly underneath the pots. These mouths are fitted with heavy doors of iron. The intense heat of the fire is prevented from com-municating itself to the deck, by means of a shallow reservoir extending under the entire inclosed surface of the works. By a tunnel inserted at the rear, this reservoir is kept replenished with water as fast as it evaporates. There are no external chimneys; they open direct from the rear wall. And here let us go back for a moment.

It was about nine o'clock at night that the Pequod's try-works were first started on this present voyage. It belonged to Stubb to oversee the business.

"All ready there? Off hatch, then, and start her. You cook, fire the works." This was an easy thing, for the carpenter had been thrusting his shavings into the furnace throughout the passage. Here be it said that in a whaling voyage the first fire in the try-works has to be fed for a time with wood. After that no wood is used, except as a means of quick ignition to the staple fuel. In a word, after being tried out, the crisp, shrivelled blubber, now called scraps or fritters, still contains considerable of its unctuous properties. These fritters feed the flames. Like a plethoric burning martyr, or a self-consuming misanthrope, once ignited, the whale supplies his own fuel and burns by his own body. Would that he consumed his own smoke! for his smoke is horrible to inhale, and inhale it you must, and not only that, but you must live in it for the time. It has an unspeakable, wild, Hindoo odor[2] about it, such as may lurk in the vicinity of funereal pyres. It smells like the left wing of the day of judgment;[3] it is an argument for the pit.

By midnight the works were in full operation. We were clear from the carcase; sail had been made; the wind was freshening; the wild ocean darkness was intense. But that darkness was licked up by the fierce flames, which at intervals forked forth from the sooty flues, and illumi-nated every lofty rope in the rigging, as with the famed Greek fire. The burning ship drove on, as if remorselessly commissioned to some venge-ful deed. So the pitch and sulphur-freighted brigs of the bold Hydriote, Canaris,[4] issuing from their midnight harbors, with broad sheets of

2. As from a Hindu cremation.
3. According to Matthew 25.31–33, on the day Jesus comes in judgment the "goats" (those con-demned to hell) shall be set "on the left," the "sheep" (those who will go to heaven) on his right.
4. The Greek hero who developed this fireship strategy in 1822, during the Greek war for indepen-dence from the Turks, a cause with which the younger English Romantics and most Americans sympathized keenly during Melville's boyhood.

flame for sails, bore down upon the Turkish frigates, and folded them in conflagrations.

The hatch, removed from the top of the works, now afforded a wide hearth in front of them. Standing on this were the Tartarean shapes of the pagan harpooneers, always the whale-ship's stokers. With huge pronged poles they pitched hissing masses of blubber into the scalding pots, or stirred up the fires beneath, till the snaky flames darted, curling, out of the doors to catch them by the feet. The smoke rolled away in sullen heaps. To every pitch of the ship there was a pitch of the boiling oil, which seemed all eagerness to leap into their faces. Opposite the mouth of the works, on the further side of the wide wooden hearth, was the windlass. This served for a sea-sofa. Here lounged the watch, when not otherwise employed, looking into the red heat of the fire, till their eyes felt scorched in their heads. Their tawny features, now all begrimed with smoke and sweat, their matted beards, and the contrasting barbaric brilliancy of their teeth, all these were strangely revealed in the capricious emblazonings of the works. As they narrated to each other their unholy adventures, their tales of terror told in words of mirth; as their uncivilized laughter forked upwards out of them, like the flames from the furnace; as to and fro, in their front, the harpooneers wildly gesticulated with their huge pronged forks and dippers; as the wind howled on, and the sea leaped, and the ship groaned and dived, and yet steadfastly shot her red hell further and further into the blackness of the sea and the night, and scornfully champed the white bone in her mouth, and viciously spat round her on all sides; then the rushing Pequod, freighted with savages, and laden with fire, and burning a corpse, and plunging into that blackness of darkness, seemed the material counterpart of her monomaniac commander's soul.

So seemed it to me, as I stood at her helm, and for long hours silently guided the way of this fire-ship on the sea. Wrapped, for that interval, in darkness myself, I but the better saw the redness, the madness, the ghastliness of others. The continual sight of the fiend shapes before me, capering half in smoke and half in fire, these at last begat kindred visions in my soul, so soon as I began to yield to that unaccountable drowsiness which ever would come over me at a midnight helm.

But that night, in particular, a strange (and ever since inexplicable) thing occurred to me. Starting from a brief standing sleep, I was horribly conscious of something fatally wrong. The jaw-bone tiller smote my side, which leaned against it; in my ears was the low hum of sails, just beginning to shake in the wind; I thought my eyes were open; I was half conscious of putting my fingers to the lids and mechanically stretching them still further apart. But, spite of all this, I could see no compass before me to steer by; though it seemed but a minute since I had been watching the card, by the steady binnacle lamp illuminating it. Nothing seemed before me but a jet gloom, now and then made ghastly by flashes of redness. Uppermost was the impression, that whatever swift, rushing thing I stood on was not so much bound to any haven ahead as rushing from all havens astern. A stark, bewildered feeling, as of death, came over me. Convulsively my hands grasped the tiller, but with the crazy conceit that the tiller was, somehow, in some enchanted way, inverted.

My God! what is the matter with me? thought I. Lo! in my brief sleep I had turned myself about, and was fronting the ship's stern, with my back to her prow and the compass. In an instant I faced back, just in time to prevent the vessel from flying up into the wind, and very probably capsizing her. How glad and how grateful the relief from this unnatural hallucination of the night, and the fatal contingency of being brought by the lee!

Look not too long in the face of the fire, O man! Never dream with thy hand on the helm! Turn not thy back to the compass; accept the first hint of the hitching tiller; believe not the artificial fire, when its redness makes all things look ghastly. To-morrow, in the natural sun, the skies will be bright; those who glared like devils in the forking flames, the morn will show in far other, at least gentler, relief; the glorious, golden, glad sun, the only true lamp—all others but liars!

Nevertheless the sun hides not Virginia's Dismal Swamp, nor Rome's accursed Campagna, nor wide Sahara, nor all the millions of miles of deserts and of griefs beneath the moon. The sun hides not the ocean, which is the dark side of this earth, and which is two thirds of this earth. So, therefore, that mortal man who hath more of joy than sorrow in him, that mortal man cannot be true—not true, or undeveloped. With books the same. The truest of all men was the Man of Sorrows,[5] and the truest of all books is Solomon's, and Ecclesiastes is the fine hammered steel of woe. "All is vanity."[6] ALL. This wilful world hath not got hold of unchristian Solomon's wisdom yet. But he who dodges hospitals and jails, and walks fast crossing grave-yards, and would rather talk of operas than hell; calls Cowper, Young, Pascal, Rousseau,[7] poor devils all of sick men; and throughout a care-free lifetime swears by Rabelais[8] as passing wise, and therefore jolly;—not that man is fitted to sit down on tombstones, and break the green damp mould with unfathomably wondrous Solomon.

But even Solomon, he says, "the man that wandereth out of the way of understanding shall remain" (i.e. even while living) "in the congregation of the dead."[9] Give not thyself up, then, to fire, lest it invert thee, deaden thee; as for the time it did me. There is a wisdom that is woe; but there is a woe that is madness. And there is a Catskill eagle in some souls that can alike dive down into the blackest gorges, and soar out of them again and become invisible in the sunny spaces. And even if he for ever flies within the gorge, that gorge is in the mountains; so that even in his lowest swoop the mountain eagle is still higher than other birds upon the plain, even though they soar.

5. Jesus, from a phrase in Isaiah 53.3: "He is despised and rejected of men; a man of sorrows, and acquainted with grief."
6. Ecclesiastes, the book in which "All is vanity" occurs (1.2), was attributed to Solomon.
7. Jean-Jacques Rousseau (1712–1778), Swiss political philosopher and writer. William Cowper (1731–1800), English poet, author of *Olney Hymns*, *The Task*, and "The Castaway." Edward Young (1683–1765), English poet, author of *Night Thoughts*. Blaise Pascal (1623–1662), French mathematician, physicist, and philosopher.
8. François Rabelais (1494–1553), French satirist and humorist whose views in his *Pantagruel* (1532 or 1533) and *Gargantua* (1534) some readers take as "passing wise, and therefore jolly," the contrary of Solomon's attitude.
9. Proverbs 21.16: "The man that wandereth out of the way of understanding shall remain in the congregation of the dead."

Chapter 97

The Lamp

Had you descended from the Pequod's try-works to the Pequod's forecastle, where the off duty watch were sleeping, for one single moment you would have almost thought you were standing in some illuminated shrine of canonized kings and counsellors. There they lay in their triangular oaken vaults, each mariner a chiselled muteness; a score of lamps flashing upon his hooded eyes.

In merchantmen, oil for the sailor is more scarce than the milk of queens. To dress in the dark, and eat in the dark, and stumble in darkness to his pallet, this is his usual lot. But the whaleman, as he seeks the food of light, so he lives in light. He makes his berth an Aladdin's lamp,[1] and lays him down in it; so that in the pitchiest night the ship's black hull still houses an illumination.

See with what entire freedom the whaleman takes his handful of lamps—often but old bottles and vials, though—to the copper cooler at the try-works, and replenishes them there, as mugs of ale at a vat. He burns, too, the purest of oil, in its unmanufactured, and, therefore, unvitiated state; a fluid unknown to solar, lunar, or astral contrivances ashore. It is sweet as early grass butter in April. He goes and hunts for his oil, so as to be sure of its freshness and genuineness, even as the traveller on the prairie hunts up his own supper of game.

Chapter 98

Stowing Down and Clearing Up

Already has it been related how the great leviathan is afar off descried from the mast-head; how he is chased over the watery moors, and slaughtered in the valleys of the deep; how he is then towed alongside and beheaded; and how (on the principle which entitled the headsman of old to the garments in which the beheaded was killed) his great padded surtout becomes the property of his executioner; how, in due time, he is condemned to the pots, and, like Shadrach, Meshach, and Abednego,[1] his spermaceti, oil, and bone pass unscathed through the fire;—but now it remains to conclude the last chapter of this part of the description by rehearsing—singing, if I may—the romantic proceeding of decanting off his oil into the casks and striking them down into the hold, where once again leviathan returns to his native profundities, sliding along beneath the surface as before; but, alas! never more to rise and blow.

While still warm, the oil, like hot punch, is received into the six-barrel casks; and while, perhaps, the ship is pitching and rolling this way and

---

1. Magical lamp in *Arabian Nights*.
1. In Daniel 3, three Jews whom the Assyrian King Nebuchadnezzar had thrown into the fiery furnace; when the king looks into the furnace, he sees "four men loose, walking in the midst of the fire, and they have no hurt; and the form of the fourth is like the Son of God."

that in the midnight sea, the enormous casks are slewed round and
headed over, end for end, and sometimes perilously scoot across the slippery deck, like so many land slides, till at last man-handled and stayed in
their course; and all round the hoops, rap, rap, go as many hammers as
can play upon them, for now, *ex officio*,[2] every sailor is a cooper.

At length, when the last pint is casked, and all is cool, then the great
hatchways are unsealed, the bowels of the ship are thrown open, and
down go the casks to their final rest in the sea. This done, the hatches are
replaced, and hermetically closed, like a closet walled up.

In the sperm fishery, this is perhaps one of the most remarkable incidents in all the business of whaling. One day the planks stream with
freshets of blood and oil; on the sacred quarter-deck enormous masses of
the whale's head are profanely piled; great rusty casks lie about, as in a
brewery yard; the smoke from the try-works has besooted all the bulwarks;
the mariners go about suffused with unctuousness; the entire ship seems
great leviathan himself; while on all hands the din is deafening.

But a day or two after, you look about you, and prick your ears in this
self-same ship; and were it not for the tell-tale boats and try-works, you
would all but swear you trod some silent merchant vessel, with a most
scrupulously neat commander. The unmanufactured sperm oil possesses
a singularly cleansing virtue. This is the reason why the decks never look
so white as just after what they call an affair of oil. Besides, from the
ashes of the burned scraps of the whale, a potent ley[3] is readily made; and
whenever any adhesiveness from the back of the whale remains clinging
to the side, that ley quickly exterminates it. Hands go diligently along the
bulwarks, and with buckets of water and rags restore them to their full
tidiness. The soot is brushed from the lower rigging. All the numerous
implements which have been in use are likewise faithfully cleansed and
put away. The great hatch is scrubbed and placed upon the try-works,
completely hiding the pots; every cask is out of sight; all tackles are coiled
in unseen nooks; and when by the combined and simultaneous industry
of almost the entire ship's company, the whole of this conscientious duty
is at last concluded, then the crew themselves proceed to their own ablutions; shift themselves from top to toe; and finally issue to the immaculate deck, fresh and all aglow, as bridegrooms new-leaped from out the
daintiest Holland.[4]

Now, with elated step, they pace the planks in twos and threes, and
humorously discourse of parlors, sofas, carpets, and fine cambrics; propose to mat the deck; think of having hangings to the top; object not to
taking tea by moonlight on the piazza of the forecastle. To hint to such
musked mariners of oil, and bone, and blubber, were little short of audacity. They know not the thing you distantly allude to. Away, and bring us
napkins!

But mark: aloft there, at the three mast heads, stand three men intent
on spying out more whales, which, if caught, infallibly will again soil the
old oaken furniture, and drop at least one small grease-spot somewhere.
Yes; and many is the time, when, after the severest uninterrupted labors,

2. By virtue of an office; here, part of a sailor's expected skills (you're a sailor, you're a cooper).
3. Lye.
4. Fine bed sheets made of cotton or linen cloth from that country.

which know no night; continuing straight through for ninety-six hours; when from the boat, where they have swelled their wrists with all day rowing on the Line,—they only step to the deck to carry vast chains, and heave the heavy windlass, and cut and slash, yea, and in their very sweatings to be smoked and burned anew by the combined fires of the equatorial sun and the equatorial try-works; when, on the heel of all this, they have finally bestirred themselves to cleanse the ship, and make a spotless dairy room of it; many is the time the poor fellows, just buttoning the necks of their clean frocks, are startled by the cry of "There she blows!" and away they fly to fight another whale, and go through the whole weary thing again. Oh! my friends, but this is man-killing! Yet this is life. For hardly have we mortals by long toilings extracted from this world's vast bulk its small but valuable sperm; and then, with weary patience, cleansed ourselves from its defilements, and learned to live here in clean tabernacles of the soul; hardly is this done, when—*There she blows!*—the ghost is spouted up, and away we sail to fight some other world, and go through young life's old routine again.

Oh! the metempsychosis![5] Oh! Pythagoras, that in bright Greece, two thousand years ago, did die, so good, so wise, so mild; I sailed with thee along the Peruvian coast last voyage—and, foolish as I am, taught thee, a green simple boy, how to splice a rope!

Chapter 99

The Doubloon[1]

Ere now it has been related how Ahab was wont to pace his quarter-deck, taking regular turns at either limit, the binnacle and mainmast; but in the multiplicity of other things requiring narration it has not been added how that sometimes in these walks, when most plunged in his mood, he was wont to pause in turn at each spot, and stand there strangely eyeing the particular object before him. When he halted before the binnacle, with his glance fastened on the pointed needle in the compass, that glance shot like a javelin with the pointed intensity of his purpose; and when resuming his walk he again paused before the mainmast, then, as the same riveted glance fastened upon the riveted gold coin there, he still wore the same aspect of nailed firmness, only dashed with a certain wild longing, if not hopefulness.

But one morning, turning to pass the doubloon, he seemed to be newly attracted by the strange figures and inscriptions stamped on it, as though now for the first time beginning to interpret for himself in some monomaniac way whatever significance might lurk in them. And some certain significance lurks in all things, else all things are little worth, and the round world itself but an empty cipher, except to sell by the

---

5. The passing of the soul of a dead person into a new body, a teaching attributed to the Greek philosopher Pythagoras (6th century B.C.E.).
1. This gorgeous coin is depicted, in color, on the cover of *"Moby-Dick" as Doubloon* (1970), edited by Hershel Parker and Harrison Hayford, by the courtesy of the American Numismatic Society.

cartload, as they do hills about Boston, to fill up some morass in the Milky Way.

Now this doubloon was of purest, virgin gold, raked somewhere out of the heart of gorgeous hills, whence, east and west, over golden sands, the head-waters of many a Pactolus flow. And though now nailed amidst all the rustiness of iron bolts and the verdigris of copper spikes, yet untouchable and immaculate to any foulness, it still preserved its Quito[2] glow. Nor, though placed amongst a ruthless crew and every hour passed by ruthless hands, and through the livelong nights shrouded with thick darkness which might cover any pilfering approach, nevertheless every sunrise found the doubloon where the sunset left it last. For it was set apart and sanctified to one awe-striking end; and however wanton in their sailor ways, one and all, the mariners revered it as the white whale's talisman. Sometimes they talked it over in the weary watch by night, wondering whose it was to be at last, and whether he would ever live to spend it.

Now those noble golden coins of South America are as medals of the sun and tropic token-pieces. Here palms, alpacas, and volcanoes; sun's disks and stars; ecliptics, horns-of-plenty, and rich banners waving, are in luxuriant profusion stamped; so that the precious gold seems almost to derive an added preciousness and enhancing glories, by passing through those fancy mints, so Spanishly poetic.

It so chanced that the doubloon of the Pequod was a most wealthy example of these things. On its round border it bore the letters, REPUBLICA DEL ECUADOR: QUITO. So this bright coin came from a country planted in the middle of the world, and beneath the great equator, and named after it; and it had been cast midway up the Andes, in the unwaning clime that knows no autumn. Zoned by those letters you saw the likeness of three Andes' summits; from one a flame; a tower on another; on the third a crowing cock; while arching over all was a segment of the partitioned zodiac, the signs all marked with their usual cabalistics, and the keystone sun entering the equinoctial point at Libra.[3]

Before this equatorial coin, Ahab, not unobserved by others, was now pausing.

"There's something ever egotistical in mountain-tops and towers, and all other grand and lofty things; look here,—three peaks as proud as Lucifer.[4] The firm tower, that is Ahab; the volcano, that is Ahab; the courageous, the undaunted, and victorious fowl, that, too, is Ahab; all are Ahab; and this round gold is but the image of the rounder globe, which, like a magician's glass, to each and every man in turn but mirrors back his own mysterious self. Great pains, small gains for those who ask the world to solve them; it cannot solve itself. Methinks now this coined sun wears a ruddy face; but see! aye, he enters the sign of storms, the equinox! and but six months before he wheeled out of a former equinox at Aries![5] From

---

2. Capital of Ecuador. *Pactolus:* gold-bearing river in Asia Minor.
3. Libra: The seventh sign of the twelve in the zodiac, between Virgo and Scorpio, represented by a pair of scales. *Cabalistics:* esoteric symbols.
4. King of Babylon (Isaiah 14.12), applied by Milton to the demon of "Sinful Pride" (*Paradise Lost* 10.425).
5. Among the signs in the zodiac, Aries, the Ram, is the northern of the two equinoxial signs, both denoting periods of storms.

storm to storm! So be it, then. Born in throes, 'tis fit that man should live in pains and die in pangs! So be it, then! Here's stout stuff for woe to work on. So be it, then."

"No fairy fingers can have pressed the gold, but devil's claws must have left their mouldings there since yesterday," murmured Starbuck to himself, leaning against the bulwarks. "The old man seems to read Belshazzar's awful writing.[6] I have never marked the coin inspectingly. He goes below; let me read. A dark valley between three mighty, heaven-abiding peaks, that almost seem the Trinity, in some faint earthly symbol. So in this vale of Death, God girds us round; and over all our gloom, the sun of Righteousness still shines a beacon and a hope. If we bend down our eyes, the dark vale shows her mouldy soil; but if we lift them, the bright sun meets our glance half way, to cheer. Yet, oh, the great sun is no fixture; and if, at midnight, we would fain snatch some sweet solace from him, we gaze for him in vain! This coin speaks wisely, mildly, truly, but still sadly to me. I will quit it, lest Truth shake me falsely."

"There now's the old Mogul," soliloquized Stubb by the try-works, "he's been twigging it; and there goes Starbuck from the same, and both with faces which I should say might be somewhere within nine fathoms long. And all from looking at a piece of gold, which did I have it now on Negro Hill or in Corlaer's Hook,[7] I'd not look at it very long ere spending it. Humph! in my poor, insignificant opinion, I regard this as queer. I have seen doubloons before now in my voyagings; your doubloons of old Spain, your doubloons of Peru, your doubloons of Chili, your doubloons of Bolivia, your doubloons of Popayan; with plenty of gold moidores and pistoles, and joes, and half joes, and quarter joes.[8] What then should there be in this doubloon of the Equator that is so killing wonderful? By Golconda![9] let me read it once. Halloa! here's signs and wonders truly! That, now, is what old Bowditch in his Epitome calls the zodiac, and what my almanack below calls ditto. I'll get the almanack; and as I have heard devils can be raised with Daboll's[1] arithmetic, I'll try my hand at raising a meaning out of these queer curvicues here with the Massachusetts calendar. Here's the book. Let's see now. Signs and wonders;[2] and the sun, he's always among 'em. Hem, hem, hem; here they are—here they go—all alive:—Aries, or the Ram; Taurus, or the Bull;—and Jimini! here's Gemini himself, or the Twins. Well; the sun he wheels among 'em. Aye, here on the coin he's just crossing the threshold between two of twelve sitting-rooms all in a ring. Book! you lie there; the fact is, you books must know your places. You'll do to give us the bare words and facts, but we come in to supply the thoughts. That's my small experience, so far as the Massachusetts calendar, and Bowditch's navigator, and Daboll's arithmetic go.

6. The writing by the disembodied fingers of a man's hand, on King Belshazzar's wall, interpreted in Daniel 5.
7. In Manhattan.
8. Spanish and Portuguese gold coins, respectively. Popayan, in Colombia, had a famous mint for making coins.
9. Ruined city in India once famous for wealth and diamonds.
1. Nathan Daboll's *Complete Schoolmaster's Assistant* (1799) was a widely used arithmetic textbook. Nathaniel Bowditch (1773–1838), in his 1802 navigational treatise usually called by the short title *Epitome*.
2. The apostles are said to have performed miracles as "signs and wonders" (e.g., Acts 2.43 and 5.12). *Massachusetts calendar:* an almanac.

Signs and wonders, eh? Pity if there is nothing wonderful in signs, and
significant in wonders! There's a clue somewhere; wait a bit; hist—hark!
By Jove, I have it! Look you, Doubloon, your zodiac here is the life of man
in one round chapter; and now I'll read it off, straight out of the book.
Come, Almanack! To begin: there's Aries, or the Ram—lecherous dog, he
begets us; then, Taurus, or the Bull—he bumps us the first thing; then
Gemini, or the Twins—that is, Virtue and Vice; we try to reach Virtue,
when lo! comes Cancer the Crab, and drags us back; and here, going from
Virtue, Leo, a roaring Lion, lies in the path—he gives a few fierce bites
and surly dabs with his paw; we escape, and hail Virgo, the Virgin! that's
our first love; we marry and think to be happy for aye, when pop comes
Libra, or the Scales—happiness weighed and found wanting; and while
we are very sad about that, Lord! how we suddenly jump, as Scorpio, or
the Scorpion, stings us in rear; we are curing the wound, when whang
come the arrows all round; Sagittarius, or the Archer, is amusing himself.
As we pluck out the shafts, stand aside! here's the battering-ram, Capri-
cornus, or the Goat; full tilt, he comes rushing, and headlong we are
tossed; when Aquarius, or the Water-bearer, pours out his whole deluge
and drowns us; and, to wind up, with Pisces, or the Fishes, we sleep.
There's a sermon now, writ in high heaven, and the sun goes through it
every year, and yet comes out of it all alive and hearty. Jollily he, aloft
there, wheels through toil and trouble; and so, alow here, does jolly
Stubb. Oh, jolly's the word for aye! Adieu, Doubloon! But stop; here
comes little King-Post; dodge round the try-works, now, and let's hear
what he'll have to say. There; he's before it; he'll out with something
presently. So, so; he's beginning."

"I see nothing here, but a round thing made of gold, and whoever raises
a certain whale, this round thing belongs to him. So, what's all this staring been about? It is worth sixteen dollars, that's true; and at two cents
the cigar, that's nine hundred and sixty cigars.[3] I wont smoke dirty pipes
like Stubb, but I like cigars, and here's nine hundred and sixty of them; so
here goes Flask aloft to spy 'em out."

"Shall I call that wise or foolish, now; if it be really wise it has a foolish
look to it; yet, if it be really foolish, then has it a sort of wiseish look to it.
But, avast; here comes our old Manxman—the old hearse-driver, he must
have been, that is, before he took to the sea. He luffs up[4] before the doubloon; halloa, and goes round on the other side of the mast; why, there's
a horse-shoe nailed on that side; and now he's back again; what does that
mean? Hark! he's muttering—voice like an old worn-out coffee-mill. Prick
ears, and listen!"

"If the White Whale be raised, it must be in a month and a day, when
the sun stands in some one of these signs. I've studied signs, and know
their marks; they were taught me two score years ago, by the old witch in
Copenhagen. Now, in what sign will the sun then be? The horse-shoe
sign; for there it is, right opposite the gold. And what's the horse-shoe
sign?[5] The lion is the horse-shoe sign—the roaring and devouring lion.
Ship, old ship! my old head shakes to think of thee."

3. The arithmetic seems shaky.
4. Stops.
5. Conventional symbol for the zodiacal Lion.

"There's another rendering now; but still one text. All sorts of men in one kind of world, you see. Dodge again! here comes Queequeg—all tattooing—looks like the signs of the Zodiac himself. What says the Cannibal? As I live he's comparing notes; looking at his thigh bone; thinks the sun is in the thigh, or in the calf, or in the bowels, I suppose, as the old women talk Surgeon's Astronomy[6] in the back country. And by Jove, he's found something there in the vicinity of his thigh—I guess it's Sagittarius, or the Archer. No: he don't know what to make of the doubloon; he takes it for an old button off some king's trowsers. But, aside again! here comes that ghost-devil, Fedallah; tail coiled out of sight as usual, oakum in the toes of his pumps as usual. What does he say, with that look of his? Ah, only makes a sign to the sign and bows himself; there is a sun on the coin—fire worshipper, depend upon it. Ho! more and more. This way comes Pip—poor boy! would he had died, or I; he's half horrible to me. He too has been watching all of these interpreters—myself included—and look now, he comes to read, with that unearthly idiot face. Stand away again and hear him. Hark!"

"I look, you look, he looks; we look, ye look, they look."

"Upon my soul, he's been studying Murray's Grammar![7] Improving his mind, poor fellow! But what's that he says now—hist!"

"I look, you look, he looks; we look, ye look, they look."

"Why, he's getting it by heart—hist! again."

"I look, you look, he looks; we look, ye look, they look."

"Well, that's funny."

"And I, you, and he; and we, ye, and they, are all bats; and I'm a crow, especially when I stand a'top of this pine tree here. Caw! caw! caw! caw! caw! caw! Ain't I a crow? And where's the scare-crow? There he stands; two bones stuck into a pair of old trowsers, and two more poked into the sleeves of an old jacket."

"Wonder if he means me?—complimentary!—poor lad!—I could go hang myself. Any way, for the present, I'll quit Pip's vicinity. I can stand the rest, for they have plain wits; but he's too crazy-witty for my sanity. So, so, I leave him muttering."

"Here's the ship's navel, this doubloon here, and they are all on fire to unscrew it. But, unscrew your navel, and what's the consequence?[8] Then again, if it stays here, that is ugly, too, for when aught's nailed to the mast it's a sign that things grow desperate. Ha, ha! old Ahab! the White Whale; he'll nail ye! This is a pine tree. My father, in old Tolland county, cut down a pine tree once, and found a silver ring grown over in it; some old darkey's wedding ring. How did it get there? And so they'll say in the resurrection, when they come to fish up this old mast, and find a doubloon lodged in it, with bedded oysters for the shaggy bark. Oh, the gold! the precious, precious gold!—the green miser[9] 'll hoard ye soon! Hish! hish! God goes 'mong the worlds blackberrying. Cook! ho, cook! and cook us! Jenny! hey, hey, hey, hey, hey, Jenny, Jenny! and get your hoe-cake done!"[1]

6. Stubb slurs old backwoods women, imagining them as confusing anatomy and astronomy.
7. *The English Grammar* (1793) by Lindley Murray (1745–1826) was an elementary school text widely used in the United States.
8. According to folklore, the consequence is that one's rectum falls off.
9. Davy Jones, the keeper of ocean-bottom treasures, as in ch. 81.
1. From the minstrel song "Old King Crow."

Chapter 100

Leg and Arm • *The Pequod, of Nantucket, meets the*
Samuel Enderby, of London

"Ship, ahoy! Hast seen the White Whale?"

So cried Ahab, once more hailing a ship showing English colors, bearing down under the stern. Trumpet to mouth, the old man was standing in his hoisted quarter-boat, his ivory leg plainly revealed to the stranger captain, who was carelessly reclining in his own boat's bow. He was a darkly-tanned, burly, good-natured, fine-looking man, of sixty or thereabouts, dressed in a spacious roundabout, that hung round him in festoons of blue pilot-cloth; and one empty arm of this jacket streamed behind him like the broidered arm of a huzzar's surcoat.

"Hast seen the White Whale?"

"See you this?" and withdrawing it from the folds that had hidden it, he held up a white arm of sperm whale bone, terminating in a wooden head like a mallet.

"Man my boat!" cried Ahab, impetuously, and tossing about the oars near him—"Stand by to lower!"

In less than a minute, without quitting his little craft, he and his crew were dropped to the water, and were soon alongside of the stranger. But here a curious difficulty presented itself. In the excitement of the moment, Ahab had forgotten that since the loss of his leg he had never once stepped on board of any vessel at sea but his own, and then it was always by an ingenious and very handy mechanical contrivance peculiar to the Pequod, and a thing not to be rigged and shipped in any other vessel at a moment's warning. Now, it is no very easy matter for anybody—except those who are almost hourly used to it, like whalemen—to clamber up a ship's side from a boat on the open sea; for the great swells now lift the boat high up towards the bulwarks, and then instantaneously drop it half way down to the kelson. So, deprived of one leg, and the strange ship of course being altogether unsupplied with the kindly invention, Ahab now found himself abjectly reduced to a clumsy landsman again; hopelessly eyeing the uncertain changeful height he could hardly hope to attain.

It has before been hinted, perhaps, that every little untoward circumstance that befel him, and which indirectly sprang from his luckless mishap, almost invariably irritated or exasperated Ahab. And in the present instance, all this was heightened by the sight of the two officers of the strange ship, leaning over the side, by the perpendicular ladder of nailed cleets there, and swinging towards him a pair of tastefully-ornamented man-ropes; for at first they did not seem to bethink them that a one-legged man must be too much of a cripple to use their sea bannisters. But this awkwardness only lasted a minute, because the strange captain, observing at a glance how affairs stood, cried out, "I see, I see!—avast heaving there! Jump, boys, and swing over the cutting-tackle."

As good luck would have it, they had had a whale alongside a day or two previous, and the great tackles were still aloft, and the massive curved blubber-hook, now clean and dry, was still attached to the end. This was quickly lowered to Ahab, who at once comprehending it all, slid his solitary thigh into the curve of the hook (it was like sitting in the fluke of an anchor, or the crotch of an apple tree), and then giving the word, held himself fast, and at the same time also helped to hoist his own weight, by pulling hand-over-hand upon one of the running parts of the tackle. Soon he was carefully swung inside the high bulwarks, and gently landed upon the capstan head. With his ivory arm frankly thrust forth in welcome, the other captain advanced, and Ahab, putting out his ivory leg, and crossing the ivory arm (like two sword-fish blades) cried out in his walrus way, "Aye, aye, hearty! let us shake bones together!—an arm and a leg!—an arm that never can shrink, d'ye see; and a leg that never can run. Where did'st thou see the White Whale?—how long ago?"

"The White Whale," said the Englishman, pointing his ivory arm towards the East, and taking a rueful sight along it, as if it had been a telescope; "There I saw him, on the Line, last season."

"And he took that arm off, did he?" asked Ahab, now sliding down from the capstan, and resting on the Englishman's shoulder, as he did so.

"Aye, he was the cause of it, at least; and that leg, too?"

"Spin me the yarn," said Ahab; "how was it?"

"It was the first time in my life that I ever cruised on the Line," began the Englishman. "I was ignorant of the White Whale at that time. Well, one day we lowered for a pod of four or five whales, and my boat fastened to one of them; a regular circus horse he was, too, that went milling and milling round so, that my boat's crew could only trim dish, by sitting all their sterns on the outer gunwale. Presently up breaches from the bottom of the sea a bouncing great whale, with a milky-white head and hump, all crows' feet and wrinkles."

"It was he, it was he!" cried Ahab, suddenly letting out his suspended breath.

"And harpoons sticking in near his starboard fin."

"Aye, aye—they were mine—*my* irons," cried Ahab, exultingly—"but on!"

"Give me a chance, then," said the Englishman, good-humoredly. "Well, this old great-grandfather, with the white head and hump, runs all afoam into the pod, and goes to snapping furiously at my fast-line."

"Aye, I see!—wanted to part it; free the fast-fish—an old trick—I know him."

"How it was exactly," continued the one-armed commander, "I do not know; but in biting the line, it got foul of his teeth, caught there somehow; but we didn't know it then; so that when we afterwards pulled on the line, bounce we came plump on to his hump! instead of the other whale's that went off to windward, all fluking. Seeing how matters stood, and what a noble great whale it was—the noblest and biggest I ever saw, sir, in my life—I resolved to capture him, spite of the boiling rage he seemed to be in. And thinking the hap-hazard line would get loose, or the tooth it was tangled to might draw (for I have a devil of a boat's crew for a pull on a whale-line); seeing all this, I say, I jumped into my first mate's boat— Mr. Mounttop's here (by the way, Captain—Mounttop; Mounttop—the captain);—as I was saying, I jumped into Mounttop's boat, which, d'ye see, was gunwale and gunwale with mine, then; and snatching the first harpoon, let this old great-grandfather have it. But, Lord, look you, sir—hearts and souls alive, man—the next instant, in a jiff, I was blind as a bat—both eyes out—all befogged and bedeadened with black foam—the whale's tail looming straight up out of it, perpendicular in the air, like a marble steeple. No use sterning all, then; but as I was groping at midday, with a blinding sun, all crown-jewels; as I was groping, I say, after the second iron, to toss it overboard—down comes the tail like a Lima tower, cutting my boat in two, leaving each half in splinters; and, flukes first, the white hump backed through the wreck, as though it was all chips. We all struck out. To escape his terrible flailings, I seized hold of my harpoon-pole sticking in him, and for a moment clung to that like a sucking fish. But a combing sea dashed me off, and at the same instant, the fish, taking one good dart forwards, went down like a flash; and the barb of that cursed second iron towing along near me caught me here" (clapping his hand just below his shoulder); "yes, caught me just here, I say, and bore me down to Hell's flames, I was thinking; when, when, all of a sudden, thank the good God, the barb ript its way along the flesh—clear along the whole length of my arm—came out nigh my wrist, and up I floated;—and that gentleman there will tell you the rest (by the way, captain—Dr. Bunger, ship's surgeon: Bunger, my lad,—the captain). Now, Bunger boy, spin your part of the yarn."

The professional gentleman thus familiarly pointed out, had been all the time standing near them, with nothing specific visible, to denote his gentlemanly rank on board. His face was an exceedingly round but sober one; he was dressed in a faded blue woollen frock or shirt, and patched trowsers; and had thus far been dividing his attention between a marlingspike he held in one hand, and a pill-box held in the other, occasionally casting a critical glance at the ivory limbs of the two crippled captains. But, at his superior's introduction of him to Ahab, he politely bowed, and straightway went on to do his captain's bidding.

"It was a shocking bad wound," began the whale-surgeon; "and, taking my advice, Captain Boomer here, stood our old Sammy—"

"Samuel Enderby is the name of my ship," interrupted the one-armed captain, addressing Ahab; "go on, boy."

"Stood our old Sammy off to the northward, to get out of the blazing hot weather there on the Line. But it was no use—I did all I could; sat up with him nights; was very severe with him in the matter of diet—"

"Oh, very severe!" chimed in the patient himself; then suddenly altering his voice, "Drinking hot rum toddies with me every night, till he couldn't see to put on the bandages; and sending me to bed, half seas over, about three o'clock in the morning. Oh, ye stars! he sat up with me indeed, and was very severe in my diet. Oh! a great watcher, and very dietetically severe, is Dr. Bunger.[1] (Bunger, you dog, laugh out! why don't ye? You know you're a precious jolly rascal.) But, heave ahead, boy, I'd rather be killed by you than kept alive by any other man."

"My captain, you must have ere this perceived, respected sir"—said the imperturbable godly-looking Bunger, slightly bowing to Ahab—"is apt to

---

1. One who puts the bung (plug) into a cask of liquid, or (the case here) who pulls it out. The name signals the unreliability of the surgeon's claim to be a total abstinence man.

be facetious at times; he spins us many clever things of that sort. But I may as well say—en passant, as the French remark—that I myself—that is to say, Jack Bunger, late of the reverend clergy—am a strict total abstinence man; I never drink—"

"Water!" cried the captain; "he never drinks it; it's a sort of fits to him; fresh water throws him into the hydrophobia;[2] but go on—go on with the arm story."

"Yes, I may as well," said the surgeon, coolly. "I was about observing, sir, before Captain Boomer's facetious interruption, that spite of my best and severest endeavors, the wound kept getting worse and worse; the truth was, sir, it was as ugly gaping wound as surgeon ever saw; more than two feet and several inches long. I measured it with the lead line. In short, it grew black; I knew what was threatened, and off it came. But I had no hand in shipping that ivory arm there; that thing is against all rule"— pointing at it with the marlingspike—"that is the captain's work, not mine; he ordered the carpenter to make it; he had that club-hammer there put to the end, to knock some one's brains out with, I suppose, as he tried mine once. He flies into diabolical passions sometimes. Do ye see this dent, sir"—removing his hat, and brushing aside his hair, and exposing a bowl-like cavity in his skull, but which bore not the slightest scarry trace, or any token of ever having been a wound—"Well, the captain there will tell you how that came here; he knows."

"No, I don't," said the captain, "but his mother did; he was born with it. Oh, you solemn rogue, you—you Bunger! was there ever such another Bunger in the watery world? Bunger, when you die, you ought to die in pickle, you dog; you should be preserved to future ages, you rascal."

"What became of the White Whale?" now cried Ahab, who thus far had been impatiently listening to this bye-play between the two Englishmen.

"Oh!" cried the one-armed captain, "Oh, yes! Well; after he sounded, we didn't see him again for some time; in fact, as I before hinted, I didn't then know what whale it was that had served me such a trick, till some time afterwards, when coming back to the Line, we heard about Moby Dick—as some call him—and then I knew it was he."

"Did'st thou cross his wake again?"

"Twice."

"But could not fasten?"

"Didn't want to try to: ain't one limb enough? What should I do without this other arm? And I'm thinking Moby Dick doesn't bite so much as he swallows."

"Well, then," interrupted Bunger, "give him your left arm for bait to get the right. Do you know, gentlemen"—very gravely and mathematically bowing to each Captain in succession—"Do you know, gentlemen, that the digestive organs of the whale are so inscrutably constructed by Divine Providence, that it is quite impossible for him to completely digest even a man's arm? And he knows it too. So that what you take for the White Whale's malice is only his awkwardness. For he never means to swallow a single limb; he only thinks to terrify by feints. But sometimes he is like the

2. A morbid dread of water, as in rabies. The captain's point is that the surgeon is not a water drinker.

old juggling fellow, formerly a patient of mine in Ceylon, that making believe swallow jack-knives, once upon a time let one drop into him in good earnest, and there it stayed for a twelvemonth or more; when I gave him an emetic, and he heaved it up in small tacks,[3] d'ye see. No possible way for him to digest that jack-knife, and fully incorporate it into his general bodily system. Yes, Captain Boomer, if you are quick enough about it, and have a mind to pawn one arm for the sake of the privilege of giving decent burial to the other, why in that case the arm is yours; only let the whale have another chance at you shortly, that's all."

"No, thank ye, Bunger," said the English Captain, "he's welcome to the arm he has, since I can't help it, and didn't know him then; but not to another one. No more White Whales for me; I've lowered for him once, and that has satisfied me. There would be great glory in killing him, I know that; and there is a ship-load of precious sperm in him, but, hark ye, he's best let alone; don't you think so, Captain?"—glancing at the ivory leg.

"He is. But he will still be hunted, for all that. What is best let alone, that accursed thing is not always what least allures. He's all a magnet! How long since thou saw'st him last? Which way heading?"

"Bless my soul, and curse the foul fiend's," cried Bunger, stoopingly walking round Ahab, and like a dog, strangely snuffing; "this man's blood —bring the thermometer!—it's at the boiling point!—his pulse makes these planks beat!—sir!"—taking a lancet from his pocket, and drawing near to Ahab's arm.

"Avast!" roared Ahab, dashing him against the bulwarks—"Man the boat! Which way heading?"

"Good God!" cried the English Captain, to whom the question was put. "What's the matter? He was heading east, I think.—Is your Captain crazy?" whispering Fedallah.[4]

But Fedallah, putting a finger on his lip, slid over the bulwarks to take the boat's steering oar, and Ahab, swinging the cutting-tackle towards him, commanded the ship's sailors to stand by to lower.

In a moment he was standing in the boat's stern, and the Manilla men were springing to their oars. In vain the English Captain hailed him. With back to the stranger ship, and face set like a flint to his own, Ahab stood upright till alongside of the Pequod.

Chapter 101

The Decanter

Ere the English ship fades from sight, be it set down here, that she hailed from London, and was named after the late Samuel Enderby, merchant of that city, the original of the famous whaling house of Enderby & Sons;[1] a house which in my poor whaleman's opinion, comes not far behind the

3. More tall-tale humor, akin to that in ch. 14; here, the intricately timed comedic by-play of the mutually admiring pair of put-on artists enrages Ahab, who conspicuously lacks a sense of humor.
4. That is, whispering to Fedallah—not the likeliest crew member to chat up so casually.
1. Melville learned about the Enderby family in Beale (Mansfield and Vincent, 807).

united royal houses of the Tudors and Bourbons, in point of real historical interest. How long, prior to the year of our Lord 1775, this great whaling house was in existence, my numerous fish-documents do not make plain; but in that year (1775) it fitted out the first English ships that ever regularly hunted the Sperm Whale; though for some score of years previous (ever since 1726) our valiant Coffins and Maceys of Nantucket and the Vineyard had in large fleets pursued that Leviathan, but only in the North and South Atlantic: not elsewhere. Be it distinctly recorded here, that the Nantucketers were the first among mankind to harpoon with civilized steel the great Sperm Whale; and that for half a century they were the only people of the whole globe who so harpooned him.

In 1788, a fine ship, the Amelia, fitted out for the express purpose, and at the sole charge of the vigorous Enderbys, boldly rounded Cape Horn, and was the first among the nations to lower a whale-boat of any sort in the great South Sea. The voyage was a skilful and lucky one; and returning to her berth with her hold full of the precious sperm, the Amelia's example was soon followed by other ships, English and American, and thus the vast Sperm Whale grounds of the Pacific were thrown open. But not content with this good deed, the indefatigable house again bestirred itself: Samuel and all his Sons—how many, their mother only knows[2]— and under their immediate auspices, and partly, I think, at their expense, the British government was induced to send the sloop-of-war Rattler on a whaling voyage of discovery into the South Sea. Commanded by a naval Post-Captain, the Rattler made a rattling voyage of it, and did some service; how much does not appear. But this is not all. In 1819, the same house fitted out a discovery whale ship of their own, to go on a testing cruise to the remote waters of Japan. That ship—well called the "Syren"— made a noble experimental cruise; and it was thus that the great Japanese Whaling Ground first became generally known. The Syren in this famous voyage was commanded by a Captain Coffin, a Nantucketer.

All honor to the Enderbies, therefore, whose house, I think, exists to the present day; though doubtless the original Samuel must long ago have slipped his cable for the great South Sea of the other world.

The ship named after him was worthy of the honor, being a very fast sailer and a noble craft every way. I boarded her once at midnight somewhere off the Patagonian coast,[3] and drank good flip down in the forecastle. It was a fine gam we had, and they were all trumps—every soul on board. A short life to them, and a jolly death. And that fine gam I had— long, very long after old Ahab touched her planks with his ivory heel—it minds me of the noble, solid, Saxon hospitality of that ship; and may my parson forget me, and the devil remember me, if I ever lose sight of it. Flip? Did I say we had flip? Yes, and we flipped it at the rate of ten gallons the hour; and when the squall came (for it's squally off there by Patagonia), and all hands—visitors and all—were called to reef topsails,

2. As example of the book's offhand humor, like the pun just below on Rattler, and the one farther down on "flip," a spicy mixture of beer or other alcoholic beverage beaten together with egg. Even amid the comedy is a submerged verbal echo of Othello 5.2.339, where the Moor recalls having done the state "some service," as the Rattler did.
3. In the extremely dangerous waters at southern tip of South America, a highly unlikely place for such a cheerful gam.

we were so top-heavy that we had to swing each other aloft in bowlines; and we ignorantly furled the skirts of our jackets into the sails, so that we hung there, reefed fast in the howling gale, a warning example to all drunken tars. However, the masts did not go overboard; and by and bye we scrambled down, so sober, that we had to pass the flip again, though the savage salt spray bursting down the forecastle scuttle, rather too much diluted and pickled it to my taste.

The beef was fine—tough, but with body in it. They said it was bull-beef; others, that it was dromedary beef; but I do not know, for certain, how that was. They had dumplings too; small, but substantial, symmetrically globular, and indestructible dumplings. I fancied that you could feel them, and roll them about in you after they were swallowed. If you stooped over too far forward, you risked their pitching out of you like billiard-balls. The bread—but that couldn't be helped; besides, it was an anti-scorbutic; in short, the bread contained the only fresh fare they had. But the forecastle was not very light, and it was very easy to step over into a dark corner when you ate it. But all in all, taking her from truck to helm, considering the dimensions of the cook's boilers, including his own live parchment boilers; fore and aft, I say, the Samuel Enderby was a jolly ship; of good fare and plenty; fine flip and strong; crack fellows all, and capital from boot heels to hat-band.

But why was it, think ye, that the Samuel Enderby, and some other English whalers I know of—not all though—were such famous, hospitable ships; that passed round the beef, and the bread, and the can, and the joke; and were not soon weary of eating, and drinking, and laughing? I will tell you. The abounding good cheer of these English whalers is matter for historical research. Nor have I been at all sparing of historical whale research, when it has seemed needed.

The English were preceded in the whale fishery by the Hollanders, Zealanders, and Danes; from whom they derived many terms still extant in the fishery; and what is yet more, their fat old fashions, touching plenty to eat and drink. For, as a general thing, the English merchant-ship scrimps her crew; but not so the English whaler. Hence, in the English, this thing of whaling good cheer is not normal and natural, but incidental and particular; and, therefore, must have some special origin, which is here pointed out, and will be still further elucidated.

During my researches in the Leviathanic histories, I stumbled upon an ancient Dutch volume,[4] which, by the musty whaling smell of it, I knew must be about whalers. The title was, "Dan Coopman," wherefore I concluded that this must be the invaluable memoirs of some Amsterdam cooper in the fishery, as every whale ship must carry its cooper. I was reinforced in this opinion by seeing that it was the production of one "Fitz Swackhammer." But my friend Dr. Snodhead, a very learned man, professor of Low Dutch and High German in the college of Santa Claus and St. Pott's, to whom I handed the work for translation, giving him a box of sperm candles for his trouble—this same Dr. Snodhead, so soon as he spied the book, assured me that "Dan Coopman" did not mean "The

---

4. "This long passage with all its statistics was Melville's parody of a similar one" in Scoresby (Mansfield and Vincent, 807).

Cooper," but "The Merchant." In short, this ancient and learned Low Dutch book treated of the commerce of Holland; and, among other subjects, contained a very interesting account of its whale fishery. And in this chapter it was, headed "Smeer," or "Fat," that I found a long detailed list of the outfits for the larders and cellars of 180 sail of Dutch whalemen; from which list, as translated by Dr. Snodhead, I transcribe the following:

400,000	lbs. of beef.
60,000	lbs. Friesland pork.
150,000	lbs. of stock fish.
550,000	lbs. of biscuit.
72,000	lbs. of soft bread.
2,800	firkins of butter.
20,000	lbs. Texel & Leyden cheese.
144,000	lbs. cheese (probably an inferior article).
550	ankers of Geneva.
10,800	barrels of beer.

Most statistical tables are parchingly dry in the reading; not so in the present case, however, where the reader is flooded with whole pipes, barrels, quarts, and gills of good gin and good cheer.

At the time, I devoted three days to the studious digesting of all this beer, beef, and bread, during which many profound thoughts were incidentally suggested to me, capable of a transcendental and Platonic application; and, furthermore, I compiled supplementary tables of my own, touching the probable quantity of stock-fish, &c., consumed by every Low Dutch harpooneer in that ancient Greenland and Spitzbergen whale fishery. In the first place, the amount of butter, and Texel and Leyden cheese consumed, seems amazing. I impute it, though, to their naturally unctuous natures, being rendered still more unctuous by the nature of their vocation, and especially by their pursuing their game in those frigid Polar Seas, on the very coasts of that Esquimaux country where the convivial natives pledge each other in bumpers of train oil.

The quantity of beer, too, is very large, 10,800 barrels. Now, as those polar fisheries could only be prosecuted in the short summer of that climate, so that the whole cruise of one of these Dutch whalemen, including the short voyage to and from the Spitzbergen sea, did not much exceed three months, say, and reckoning 30 men to each of their fleet of 180 sail, we have 5,400 Low Dutch seamen in all; therefore, I say, we have precisely two barrels of beer per man, for a twelve weeks' allowance, exclusive of his fair proportion of that 550 ankers of gin. Now, whether these gin and beer harpooneers, so fuddled as one might fancy them to have been, were the right sort of men to stand up in a boat's head, and take good aim at flying whales; this would seem somewhat improbable. Yet they did aim at them, and hit them too. But this was very far North, be it remembered, where beer agrees well with the constitution; upon the Equator, in our southern fishery, beer would be apt to make the harpooneer sleepy at the mast-head and boozy in his boat; and grievous loss might ensue to Nantucket and New Bedford.

But no more; enough has been said to show that the old Dutch whalers of two or three centuries ago were high livers; and that the English whalers have not neglected so excellent an example. For, say they, when cruising in an empty ship, if you can get nothing better out of the world, get a good dinner out of it, at least. And this empties the decanter.

Chapter 102

A Bower in the Arsacides

Hitherto, in descriptively treating of the Sperm Whale, I have chiefly dwelt upon the marvels of his outer aspect; or separately and in detail upon some few interior structural features. But to a large and thorough sweeping comprehension of him, it behoves me now to unbutton him still further, and untagging the points of his hose, unbuckling his garters, and casting loose the hooks and the eyes of the joints of his innermost bones, set him before you in his ultimatum; that is to say, in his unconditional skeleton.

But how now, Ishmael? How is it, that you, a mere oarsman in the fishery, pretend to know aught about the subterranean parts of the whale? Did erudite Stubb, mounted upon your capstan, deliver lectures on the anatomy of the Cetacea; and by help of the windlass, hold up a specimen rib for exhibition? Explain thyself, Ishmael. Can you land a full-grown whale on your deck for examination, as a cook dishes a roast-pig? Surely not. A veritable witness have you hitherto been, Ishmael; but have a care how you seize the privilege of Jonah alone; the privilege of discoursing upon the joists and beams; the rafters, ridge-pole, sleepers, and under-pinnings, making up the frame-work of leviathan; and belike of the tallow-vats, dairy-rooms, butteries, and cheeseries in his bowels.

I confess, that since Jonah, few whalemen have penetrated very far beneath the skin of the adult whale; nevertheless, I have been blessed with an opportunity to dissect him in miniature. In a ship I belonged to, a small cub Sperm Whale was once bodily hoisted to the deck for his poke or bag, to make sheaths for the barbs of the harpoons, and for the heads of the lances. Think you I let that chance go, without using my boat-hatchet and jack-knife, and breaking the seal and reading all the contents of that young cub?

And as for my exact knowledge of the bones of the leviathan in their gigantic, full grown development, for that rare knowledge I am indebted to my late royal friend Tranquo, king of Tranque, one of the Arsacides.[1] For being at Tranque, years ago, when attached to the trading-ship Dey of Algiers, I was invited to spend part of the Arsacidean holidays with the lord of Tranque, at his retired palm villa at Pupella; a sea-side glen not very far distant from what our sailors called Bamboo-Town, his capital.

Among many other fine qualities, my royal friend Tranquo, being gifted with a devout love for all matters of barbaric vertù,[2] had brought together in Pupella whatever rare things the more ingenious of his people could invent; chiefly carved woods of wonderful devices, chiselled shells, inlaid

1. Islands south of the Solomon group in Melanesia, northeast of Australia.
2. Curios and antiques, or any strange and rare objects of art.

spears, costly paddles, aromatic canoes; and all these distributed among whatever natural wonders, the wonder-freighted, tribute-rendering waves had cast upon his shores.

Chief among these latter was a great Sperm Whale, which, after an unusually long raging gale, had been found dead and stranded, with his head against a cocoa-nut tree, whose plumage-like, tufted droopings seemed his verdant jet. When the vast body had at last been stripped of its fathom-deep enfoldings, and the bones become dust dry in the sun, then the skeleton was carefully transported up the Pupella glen, where a grand temple of lordly palms now sheltered it.

The ribs were hung with trophies; the vertebræ were carved with Arsacidean annals, in strange hieroglyphics; in the skull, the priests kept up an unextinguished aromatic flame, so that the mystic head again sent forth its vapory spout; while, suspended from a bough, the terrific lower jaw vibrated over all the devotees, like the hair-hung sword that so affrighted Damocles.[3]

It was a wondrous sight. The wood was green as mosses of the Icy Glen;[4] the trees stood high and haughty, feeling their living sap; the industrious earth beneath was as a weaver's loom, with a gorgeous carpet on it, whereof the ground-vine tendrils formed the warp and woof, and the living flowers the figures. All the trees, with all their laden branches; all the shrubs, and ferns, and grasses; the message-carrying air; all these unceasingly were active. Through the lacings of the leaves, the great sun seemed a flying shuttle weaving the unwearied verdure. Oh, busy weaver! unseen weaver!—pause!—one word!—whither flows the fabric? what palace may it deck? wherefore all these ceaseless toilings? Speak, weaver!—stay thy hand!—but one single word with thee! Nay—the shuttle flies—the figures float from forth the loom; the freshet-rushing carpet for ever slides away. The weaver-god, he weaves; and by that weaving is he deafened, that he hears no mortal voice; and by that humming, we, too, who look on the loom are deafened; and only when we escape it shall we hear the thousand voices that speak through it. For even so it is in all material factories. The spoken words that are inaudible among the flying spindles; those same words are plainly heard without the walls, bursting from the opened casements. Thereby have villanies been detected. Ah, mortal! then, be heedful; for so, in all this din of the great world's loom, thy subtlest thinkings may be overheard afar.

Now, amid the green, life-restless loom of that Arsacidean wood, the great, white, worshipped skeleton lay lounging—a gigantic idler! Yet, as the ever-woven verdant warp and woof intermixed and hummed around him, the mighty idler seemed the cunning weaver; himself all woven over with the vines; every month assuming greener, fresher verdure; but himself a skeleton. Life folded Death; Death trellised Life; the grim god wived with youthful Life, and begat him curly-headed glories.

Now, when with royal Tranquo I visited this wondrous whale, and saw the skull an altar, and the artificial smoke ascending from where the real

---

3. A naked sword was suspended by a single hair over the head of this Syracusian courtier of the 4th century B.C.E.
4. Near Stockbridge, Massachusetts, not far from Melville's farmhouse, Arrowhead, south of Pittsfield, where he wrote much of *Moby-Dick*.

jet had issued, I marvelled that the king should regard a chapel as an object of vertù. He laughed. But more I marvelled that the priests should swear that smoky jet of his was genuine. To and fro I paced before this skeleton—brushed the vines aside—broke through the ribs—and with a ball of Arsacidean twine,[5] wandered, eddied long amid its many winding, shaded colonnades and arbors. But soon my line was out; and following it back, I emerged from the opening where I entered. I saw no living thing within; naught was there but bones.

Cutting me a green measuring-rod, I once more dived within the skeleton. From their arrow-slit in the skull, the priests perceived me taking the altitude of the final rib. "How now!" they shouted; "Dar'st thou measure this our god! That's for us." "Aye, priests—well, how long do ye make him, then?" But hereupon a fierce contest rose among them, concerning feet and inches; they cracked each other's sconces with their yard-sticks—the great skull echoed—and seizing that lucky chance, I quickly concluded my own admeasurements.

These admeasurements I now propose to set before you. But first, be it recorded, that, in this matter, I am not free to utter any fancied measurement I please. Because there are skeleton authorities you can refer to, to test my accuracy. There is a Leviathanic Museum, they tell me, in Hull, England, one of the whaling ports of that country, where they have some fine specimens of fin-backs and other whales. Likewise, I have heard that in the museum of Manchester, in New Hampshire, they have what the proprietors call "the only perfect specimen of a Greenland or River Whale in the United States." Moreover, at a place in Yorkshire, England, Burton Constable[6] by name, a certain Sir Clifford Constable has in his possession the skeleton of a Sperm Whale, but of moderate size, by no means of the full-grown magnitude of my friend King Tranquo's.

In both cases, the stranded whales to which these two skeletons belonged, were originally claimed by their proprietors upon similar grounds. King Tranquo seizing his because he wanted it; and Sir Clifford, because he was lord of the seignories of those parts. Sir Clifford's whale has been articulated throughout; so that, like a great chest of drawers, you can open and shut him, in all his bony cavities—spread out his ribs like a gigantic fan—and swing all day upon his lower jaw. Locks are to be put upon some of his trap-doors and shutters; and a footman will show round future visitors with a bunch of keys at his side. Sir Clifford thinks of charging twopence for a peep at the whispering gallery[7] in the spinal column; threepence to hear the echo in the hollow of his cerebellum; and sixpence for the unrivalled view from his forehead.

The skeleton dimensions I shall now proceed to set down are copied verbatim from my right arm, where I had them tattooed; as in my wild wanderings at that period, there was no other secure way of preserving such valuable statistics. But as I was crowded for space, and wished the other parts of my body to remain a blank page for a poem I was then com-

---

5. A recollection of the Greek hero Theseus, who found his way back out of the Cretan labyrinth (by his trail of twine) after killing the part man, part bull Minotaur.
6. Remnants of this whale are still shown there (near Hull).
7. Melville's invention, based on the acoustic peculiarities of St. Paul's Cathedral in London and other great architectural wonders.

posing—at least, what untattooed parts might remain—I did not trouble myself with the odd inches; nor, indeed, should inches at all enter into a congenial admeasurement of the whale.

Chapter 103

Measurement of the Whale's Skeleton

In the first place, I wish to lay before you a particular, plain statement, touching the living bulk of this leviathan, whose skeleton we are briefly to exhibit. Such a statement may prove useful here.

According to a careful calculation I have made, and which I partly base upon Captain Scoresby's estimate, of seventy tons for the largest sized Greenland whale of sixty feet in length; according to my careful calculation, I say, a Sperm Whale of the largest magnitude, between eighty-five and ninety feet in length, and something less than forty feet in its fullest circumference, such a whale will weigh at least ninety tons; so that, reckoning thirteen men to a ton, he would considerably outweigh the combined population of a whole village of one thousand one hundred inhabitants.

Think you not then that brains, like yoked cattle, should be put to this leviathan, to make him at all budge to any landsman's imagination?

Having already in various ways put before you his skull, spout-hole, jaw, teeth, tail, forehead, fins, and divers other parts, I shall now simply point out what is most interesting in the general bulk of his unobstructed bones. But as the colossal skull embraces so very large a proportion of the entire extent of the skeleton; as it is by far the most complicated part; and as nothing is to be repeated concerning it in this chapter, you must not fail to carry it in your mind, or under your arm, as we proceed, otherwise you will not gain a complete notion of the general structure we are about to view.

In length, the Sperm Whale's skeleton at Tranque measured seventy-two feet; so that when fully invested and extended in life, he must have been ninety feet long; for in the whale, the skeleton loses about one fifth in length compared with the living body. Of this seventy-two feet, his skull and jaw comprised some twenty feet, leaving some fifty feet of plain back-bone. Attached to this back-bone, for something less than a third of its length, was the mighty circular basket of ribs which once enclosed his vitals.

To me this vast ivory-ribbed chest, with the long, unrelieved spine, extending far away from it in a straight line, not a little resembled the embryo hull of a great ship new-laid upon the stocks, when only some twenty of her naked bow-ribs are inserted, and the keel is otherwise, for the time, but a long, disconnected timber.

The ribs were ten on a side. The first, to begin from the neck, was nearly six feet long; the second, third, and fourth were each successively longer, till you came to the climax of the fifth, or one of the middle ribs, which measured eight feet and some inches. From that part, the remaining ribs diminished, till the tenth and last only spanned five feet and some inches. In general thickness, they all bore a seemly correspondence to their length. The middle ribs were the most arched. In some of the Arsacides they are used for beams whereon to lay foot-path bridges over small streams.

In considering these ribs, I could not but be struck anew with the circumstance, so variously repeated in this book, that the skeleton of the whale is by no means the mould of his invested form. The largest of the Tranque ribs, one of the middle ones, occupied that part of the fish which, in life, is greatest in depth. Now, the greatest depth of the invested body of this particular whale must have been at least sixteen feet; whereas, the corresponding rib measured but little more than eight feet. So that this rib only conveyed half of the true notion of the living magnitude of that part. Besides, for some way, where I now saw but a naked spine, all that had been once wrapped round with tons of added bulk in flesh, muscle, blood, and bowels. Still more, for the ample fins, I here saw but a few disordered joints; and in place of the weighty and majestic, but boneless flukes, an utter blank!

How vain and foolish, then, thought I, for timid untravelled man to try to comprehend aright this wondrous whale, by merely poring over his dead attenuated skeleton, stretched in this peaceful wood. No. Only in the heart of quickest perils; only when within the eddyings of his angry flukes; only on the profound unbounded sea, can the fully invested whale be truly and livingly found out.

But the spine. For that, the best way we can consider it is, with a crane, to pile its bones high up on end. No speedy enterprise. But now it's done, it looks much like Pompey's Pillar.

There are forty and odd vertebræ in all, which in the skeleton are not locked together. They mostly lie like the great knobbed blocks on a Gothic spire, forming solid courses of heavy masonry. The largest, a middle one, is in width something less than three feet, and in depth more than four. The smallest, where the spine tapers away into the tail, is only two inches in width, and looks something like a white billiard-ball. I was told that there were still smaller ones, but they had been lost by some little cannibal urchins, the priest's children, who had stolen them to play marbles with. Thus we see how that the spine of even the hugest of living things tapers off at last into simple child's play.

Chapter 104

The Fossil Whale[1]

From his mighty bulk the whale affords a most congenial theme whereon to enlarge, amplify, and generally expatiate. Would you, you could not compress him. By good rights he should only be treated of in imperial

---

1. In this chapter Melville used information from the article "Whales" in the *Penny Cyclopædia*.

folio.[2] Not to tell over again his furlongs from spiracle to tail, and the yards he measures about the waist; only think of the gigantic involutions of his intestines, where they lie in him like great cables and hausers coiled away in the subterranean orlop-deck of a line-of-battle-ship.

Since I have undertaken to manhandle this Leviathan, it behoves me to approve myself omnisciently exhaustive in the enterprise; not overlooking the minutest seminal germs of his blood, and spinning him out to the uttermost coil of his bowels. Having already described him in most of his present habatory and anatomical peculiarities, it now remains to magnify him in an archæological, fossiliferous, and antediluvian point of view. Applied to any other creature than the Leviathan—to an ant or a flea— such portly terms might justly be deemed unwarrantably grandiloquent. But when Leviathan is the text, the case is altered. Fain am I to stagger to this emprise under the weightiest words of the dictionary. And here be it said, that whenever it has been convenient to consult one in the course of these dissertations, I have invariably used a huge quarto[3] edition of Johnson, expressly purchased for that purpose; because that famous lexicographer's uncommon personal bulk more fitted him to compile a lexicon to be used by a whale author like me.

One often hears of writers that rise and swell with their subject, though it may seem but an ordinary one. How, then, with me, writing of this Leviathan? Unconsciously my chirography expands into placard capitals. Give me a condor's quill! Give me Vesuvius' crater for an inkstand! Friends, hold my arms! For in the mere act of penning my thoughts of this Leviathan, they weary me, and make me faint with their outreaching comprehensiveness of sweep, as if to include the whole circle of the sciences, and all the generations of whales, and men, and mastodons, past, present, and to come, with all the revolving panoramas of empire on earth, and throughout the whole universe, not excluding its suburbs. Such, and so magnifying, is the virtue of a large and liberal theme! We expand to its bulk. To produce a mighty book, you must choose a mighty theme. No great and enduring volume can ever be written on the flea, though many there be who have tried it.

Ere entering upon the subject of Fossil Whales, I present my credentials as a geologist, by stating that in my miscellaneous time I have been a stone-mason, and also a great digger of ditches, canals and wells, winevaults, cellars, and cisterns of all sorts. Likewise, by way of preliminary, I desire to remind the reader, that while in the earlier geological strata there are found the fossils of monsters now almost completely extinct; the subsequent relics discovered in what are called the Tertiary formations seem the connecting, or at any rate intercepted links, between the antechronical[4] creatures, and those whose remote posterity are said to have entered the Ark; all the Fossil Whales hitherto discovered belong to the Tertiary period, which is the last preceding the superficial formations. And though

2. A very large volume made from printers' paper folded only once.
3. A volume made from printers' paper folded twice; this may be a slip for "folio," where the paper is folded only once. See "imperial folio," just above, and ch. 32. Melville's reference is to Dr. Samuel Johnson's *Dictionary of the English Language* (1755).
4. From the period before man began measuring time ("for time began with man," as Ishmael says three paragraphs later). Editions before the 1967 NCE read "anti-chronical," which would mean against time.

none of them precisely answer to any known species of the present time, they are yet sufficiently akin to them in general respects, to justify their taking rank as Cetacean fossils.

Detached broken fossils of pre-adamite[5] whales, fragments of their bones and skeletons, have within thirty years past, at various intervals, been found at the base of the Alps, in Lombardy, in France, in England, in Scotland, and in the States of Louisiana, Mississippi, and Alabama. Among the more curious of such remains is part of a skull, which in the year 1779 was disinterred in the Rue Dauphine in Paris, a short street opening almost directly upon the palace of the Tuileries; and bones disinterred in excavating the great docks of Antwerp, in Napoleon's time. Cuvier pronounced these fragments to have belonged to some utterly unknown Leviathanic species.

But by far the most wonderful of all cetacean relics was the almost complete vast skeleton of an extinct monster, found in the year 1842, on the plantation of Judge Creagh, in Alabama. The awe-stricken credulous slaves in the vicinity took it for the bones of one of the fallen angels. The Alabama doctors declared it a huge reptile, and bestowed upon it the name of Basilosaurus. But some specimen bones of it being taken across the sea to Owen, the English Anatomist, it turned out that this alleged reptile was a whale, though of a departed species. A significant illustration of the fact, again and again repeated in this book, that the skeleton of the whale furnishes but little clue to the shape of his fully invested body. So Owen rechristened the monster Zeuglodon; and in his paper read before the London Geological Society, pronounced it, in substance, one of the most extraordinary creatures which the mutations of the globe have blotted out of existence.

When I stand among these mighty Leviathan skeletons, skulls, tusks, jaws, ribs, and vertebrae, all characterized by partial resemblances to the existing breeds of sea-monsters; but at the same time bearing on the other hand similar affinities to the annihilated antechronical Leviathans, their incalculable seniors; I am, by a flood, borne back to that wondrous period, ere time itself can be said to have begun; for time began with man. Here Saturn's[6] grey chaos rolls over me, and I obtain dim, shuddering glimpses into those Polar eternities; when wedged bastions of ice pressed hard upon what are now the Tropics; and in all the 25,000 miles of this world's circumference, not an inhabitable hand's breadth of land was visible. Then the whole world was the whale's; and, king of creation, he left his wake along the present lines of the Andes and the Himmalehs. Who can show a pedigree like Leviathan? Ahab's harpoon had shed older blood than the Pharaohs'. Methuselah seems a schoolboy. I look round to shake hands with Shem.[7] I am horror-struck at this antemosaic, unsourced existence of the unspeakable terrors of the whale, which, having been before all time, must needs exist after all humane ages are over.

But not alone has this Leviathan left his pre-adamite traces in the stereotype plates of nature, and in limestone and marl bequeathed his

5. Existing before man was created (according to Genesis).
6. Saturn was chief of the Titans, the pre-Olympian gods of Greek mythology.
7. Noah's eldest son. Genesis 5.27: "And all the days of Methuselah were nine hundred sixty and nine years: and he died."

ancient bust; but upon Egyptian tablets, whose antiquity seems to claim for them an almost fossiliferous character, we find the unmistakable print of his fin. In an apartment of the great temple of Denderah,[8] some fifty years ago, there was discovered upon the granite ceiling a sculptured and painted planisphere, abounding in centaurs, griffins, and dolphins, similar to the grotesque figures on the celestial globe of the moderns. Gliding among them, old Leviathan swam as of yore; was there swimming in that planisphere, centuries before Solomon was cradled.

Nor must there be omitted another strange attestation of the antiquity of the whale, in his own osseous post-diluvian reality, as set down by the venerable John Leo,[9] the old Barbary traveller.

"Not far from the Sea-side, they have a Temple, the Rafters and Beams of which are made of Whale-Bones; for Whales of a monstrous size are oftentimes cast up dead upon that shore. The Common People imagine, that by a secret Power bestowed by God upon the Temple, no Whale can pass by it without immediate death. But the truth of the Matter is, that on either side of the Temple, there are Rocks that shoot two Miles into the Sea, and wound the Whales when they light upon 'em. They keep a Whale's Rib of an incredible length for a Miracle, which lying upon the Ground with its convex part uppermost, makes an Arch, the Head of which cannot be reached by a Man upon a Camel's Back. This Rib (says John Leo) is said to have layn there a hundred Years before I saw it. Their Historians affirm, that a Prophet who prophesy'd of Mahomet, came from this Temple, and some do not stand to assert, that the Prophet Jonas was cast forth by the Whale at the Base of the Temple."

In this Afric Temple of the Whale I leave you, reader, and if you be a Nantucketer, and a whaleman, you will silently worship there.

Chapter 105

Does the Whale's Magnitude Diminish?—Will He Perish?

Inasmuch, then, as this Leviathan comes floundering down upon us from the head-waters of the Eternities, it may be fitly inquired, whether, in the long course of his generations, he has not degenerated from the original bulk of his sires.

But upon investigation we find, that not only are the whales of the present day superior in magnitude to those whose fossil remains are found in the Tertiary system (embracing a distinct geological period prior to man), but of the whales found in that Tertiary system, those belonging to its latter formations exceed in size those of its earlier ones.

Of all the pre-adamite whales yet exhumed, by far the largest is the Alabama one mentioned in the last chapter, and that was less than seventy feet in length in the skeleton. Whereas, we have already seen, that the tape-measure gives seventy-two feet for the skeleton of a large sized modern

8. In Upper Egypt. The planisphere described is now in the Bibliotèque Nationale in Paris.
9. Johannes Leo, 16th-century Moor (known in Europe as Leo Africanus) in his *Geographical Historie of Africa* (1600). Melville found this quotation in the "Harris Collection" (*Navigantium atque Itinerantium Biblioteca* (1705), which he cited in "Extracts."

whale. And I have heard, on whalemen's authority, that Sperm Whales have
been captured near a hundred feet long at the time of capture.

But may it not be, that while the whales of the present hour are an
advance in magnitude upon those of all previous geological periods; may
it not be, that since Adam's time they have degenerated?

Assuredly, we must conclude so, if we are to credit the accounts of such
gentlemen as Pliny,[1] and the ancient naturalists generally. For Pliny tells
us of whales that embraced acres of living bulk, and Aldrovandus of others which measured eight hundred feet in length—Rope Walks and
Thames Tunnels of Whales! And even in the days of Banks and Solander,
Cook's naturalists, we find a Swedish member of the Academy of Sciences
setting down certain Iceland Whales (reydar-fiskur, or Wrinkled Bellies)
at one hundred and twenty yards; that is, three hundred and sixty feet.
And Lacépède, the French naturalist, in his elaborate history of whales,
in the very beginning of his work (page 3), sets down the Right Whale at
one hundred metres, three hundred and twenty-eight feet. And this work
was published so late as A.D. 1825.

But will any whaleman believe these stories? No. The whale of to-day
is as big as his ancestors in Pliny's time. And if ever I go where Pliny is, I,
a whaleman (more than he was), will make bold to tell him so. Because I
cannot understand how it is, that while the Egyptian mummies that were
buried thousands of years before even Pliny was born, do not measure so
much in their coffins as a modern Kentuckian in his socks; and while the
cattle and other animals sculptured on the oldest Egyptian and Nineveh
tablets, by the relative proportions in which they are drawn, just as plainly
prove that the high-bred, stall-fed, prize cattle of Smithfield, not only
equal, but far exceed in magnitude the fattest of Pharaoh's fat kine;[2] in
the face of all this, I will not admit that of all animals the whale alone
should have degenerated.

But still another inquiry remains; one often agitated by the more recondite Nantucketers. Whether owing to the almost omniscient look-outs at
the mast-heads of the whale-ships, now penetrating even through
Behring's straits, and into the remotest secret drawers and lockers of the
world; and the thousand harpoons and lances darted along all continental coasts; the moot point is, whether Leviathan can long endure so wide
a chase, and so remorseless a havoc; whether he must not at last be
exterminated from the waters, and the last whale, like the last man, smoke
his last pipe, and then himself evaporate in the final puff.

Comparing the humped herds of whales with the humped herds of buffalo, which, not forty years ago, overspread by tens of thousands the
prairies of Illinois and Missouri, and shook their iron manes and scowled
with their thunder-clotted brows upon the sites of populous river-capitals,
where now the polite broker sells you land at a dollar an inch; in such a
comparison an irresistible argument would seem furnished, to show that
the hunted whale cannot now escape speedy extinction.

But you must look at this matter in every light. Though so short a
period ago—not a good life-time—the census of the buffalo in Illinois

---

1. For these exaggerated reports of the size of whales Melville plundered the *Penny Cyclopædia* article "Whales."
2. Cattle; see Genesis 41. *Smithfield:* London livestock market.

exceeded the census of men now in London, and though at the present day not one horn or hoof of them remains in all that region; and though the cause of this wondrous extermination was the spear of man; yet the far different nature of the whale-hunt peremptorily forbids so inglorious an end to the Leviathan. Forty men in one ship hunting the Sperm Whale for forty-eight months think they have done extremely well, and thank God, if at last they carry home the oil of forty fish. Whereas, in the days of the old Canadian and Indian hunters and trappers of the West, when the far west (in whose sunset suns still rise) was a wilderness and a virgin, the same number of moccasined men, for the same number of months, mounted on horse instead of sailing in ships, would have slain not forty, but forty thousand and more buffaloes; a fact that, if need were, could be statistically stated.

Nor, considered aright, does it seem any argument in favor of the gradual extinction of the Sperm Whale, for example, that in former years (the latter part of the last century, say) these Leviathans, in small pods, were encountered much oftener than at present, and, in consequence, the voyages were not so prolonged, and were also much more remunerative. Because, as has been elsewhere[3] noticed, those whales, influenced by some views to safety, now swim the seas in immense caravans, so that to a large degree the scattered solitaries, yokes, and pods, and schools of other days are now aggregated into vast but widely separated, unfrequent armies. That is all. And equally fallacious seems the conceit, that because the so-called whale-bone whales no longer haunt many grounds in former years abounding with them, hence that species also is declining. For they are only being driven from promontory to cape; and if one coast is no longer enlivened with their jets, then, be sure, some other and remoter strand has been very recently startled by the unfamiliar spectacle.

Furthermore: concerning these last mentioned Leviathans, they have two firm fortresses, which, in all human probability, will for ever remain impregnable. And as upon the invasion of their valleys, the frosty Swiss have retreated to their mountains; so, hunted from the savannas and glades of the middle seas, the whale-bone whales can at last resort to their Polar citadels, and diving under the ultimate glassy barriers and walls there, come up among icy fields and floes; and in a charmed circle of everlasting December, bid defiance to all pursuit from man.

But as perhaps fifty of these whale-bone whales are harpooned for one cachalot, some philosophers of the forecastle have concluded that this positive havoc has already very seriously diminished their battalions. But though for some time past a number of these whales, not less than 13,000, have been annually slain on the nor' west coast by the Americans alone; yet there are considerations which render even this circumstance of little or no account as an opposing argument in this matter.

Natural as it is to be somewhat incredulous concerning the populousness of the more enormous creatures of the globe, yet what shall we say to Horto,[4] the historian of Goa, when he tells us that at one hunting the King of Siam took 4000 elephants; that in those regions elephants are

3. Ch. 87.
4. Garcia ab Horton, Portuguese historian of Goa in India, as cited in Sir Thomas Browne's *Pseudodoxia Epidemica* (1646, 6.6).

numerous as droves of cattle in the temperate climes. And there seems no reason to doubt that if these elephants, which have now been hunted for thousands of years, by Semiramis, by Porus, by Hannibal,[5] and by all the successive monarchs of the East—if they still survive there in great numbers, much more may the great whale outlast all hunting, since he has a pasture to expatiate in, which is precisely twice as large as all Asia, both Americas, Europe and Africa, New Holland,[6] and all the Isles of the sea combined.

Moreover: we are to consider, that from the presumed great longevity of whales, their probably attaining the age of a century and more, therefore at any one period of time, several distinct adult generations must be contemporary. And what that is, we may soon gain some idea of, by imagining all the grave-yards, cemeteries, and family vaults of creation yielding up the live bodies of all the men, women, and children who were alive seventy-five years ago; and adding this countless host to the present human population of the globe.

Wherefore, for all these things, we account the whale immortal in his species, however perishable in his individuality. He swam the seas before the continents broke water; he once swam over the site of the Tuileries, and Windsor Castle, and the Kremlin.[7] In Noah's flood he despised Noah's Ark; and if ever the world is to be again flooded, like the Netherlands, to kill off its rats, then the eternal whale will still survive, and rearing upon the top-most crest of the equatorial flood, spout his frothed defiance to the skies.

Chapter 106

Ahab's Leg

The precipitating manner in which Captain Ahab had quitted the Samuel Enderby of London, had not been unattended with some small violence to his own person. He had lighted with such energy upon a thwart[1] of his boat that his ivory leg had received a half-splintering shock. And when after gaining his own deck, and his own pivot-hole there, he so vehemently wheeled round with an urgent command to the steersman (it was, as ever, something about his not steering inflexibly enough); then, the already shaken ivory received such an additional twist and wrench, that though it still remained entire, and to all appearances lusty, yet Ahab did not deem it entirely trustworthy.

And, indeed, it seemed small matter for wonder, that for all his pervading, mad recklessness, Ahab did at times give careful heed to the condition of that dead bone upon which he partly stood. For it had not been very long prior to the Pequod's sailing from Nantucket, that he had been

5. Carthaginian general (247–183 B.C.E.), who crossed the Alps with elephants in an effort to defeat Rome. *Semiramis:* legendary queen of Assyria and builder of Babylon. *Porus:* Indian prince defeated by Alexander the Great in 327 B.C.E. (see ch. 87).
6. Early name for Australia.
7. Palaces in Paris, London, and Moscow, respectively.
1. A rower's seat, across the boat.

found one night lying prone upon the ground, and insensible; by some unknown, and seemingly inexplicable, unimaginable casualty, his ivory limb having been so violently displaced, that it had stake-wise smitten, and all but pierced his groin; nor was it without extreme difficulty that the agonizing wound was entirely cured.

Nor, at the time, had it failed to enter his monomaniac mind, that all the anguish of that then present suffering was but the direct issue of a former woe; and he too plainly seemed to see, that as the most poisonous reptile of the marsh perpetuates his kind as inevitably as the sweetest songster of the grove; so, equally with every felicity, all miserable events do naturally beget their like. Yea, more than equally, thought Ahab; since both the ancestry and posterity of Grief go further than the ancestry and posterity of Joy. For, not to hint of this: that it is an inference from certain canonic teachings, that while some natural enjoyments here shall have no children born to them for the other world, but, on the contrary, shall be followed by the joy childlessness of all hell's despair; whereas, some guilty mortal miseries shall still fertilely beget to themselves an eternally progressive progeny of griefs beyond the grave; not at all to hint of this, there still seems an inequality in the deeper analysis of the thing. For, thought Ahab, while even the highest earthly felicities ever have a certain unsignifying pettiness lurking in them, but, at bottom, all heart-woes, a mystic significance, and, in some men, an archangelic grandeur; so do their diligent tracings-out not belie the obvious deduction. To trail the genealogies of these high mortal miseries, carries us at last among the sourceless primogenitures of the gods; so that, in the face of all the glad, hay-making suns, and soft-cymballing, round harvest-moons, we must needs give in to this: that the gods themselves are not for ever glad. The ineffaceable, sad birth-mark in the brow of man, is but the stamp of sorrow in the signers.

Unwittingly here a secret has been divulged, which perhaps might more properly, in set way, have been disclosed before. With many other particulars concerning Ahab, always had it remained a mystery to some, why it was, that for a certain period, both before and after the sailing of the Pequod, he had hidden himself away with such Grand-Lama-like[2] exclusiveness; and, for that one interval, sought speechless refuge, as it were, among the marble senate of the dead. Captain Peleg's bruited reason for this thing appeared by no means adequate; though, indeed, as touching all Ahab's deeper part, every revelation partook more of significant darkness than of explanatory light. But, in the end, it all came out; this one matter did, at least. That direful mishap was at the bottom of his temporary recluseness. And not only this, but to that ever-contracting, dropping circle ashore, who, for any reason, possessed the privilege of a less banned approach to him; to that timid circle the above hinted casualty—remaining, as it did, moodily unaccounted for by Ahab—invested itself with terrors, not entirely underived from the land of spirits and of wails. So that, through their zeal for him, they had all conspired, so far as in them lay, to muffle up the knowledge of this thing from others; and hence it was, that not till a considerable interval had elapsed, did it transpire upon the Pequod's decks.

2. As reclusive as the Grand Lama of Tibet, cloistered Buddhist ruler of that long-unexplored region of Asia.

But be all this as it may; let the unseen, ambiguous synod in the air, or the vindictive princes and potentates of fire, have to do or not with earthly Ahab, yet, in this present matter of his leg, he took plain practical procedures;—he called the carpenter.

And when that functionary appeared before him, he bade him without delay set about making a new leg, and directed the mates to see him supplied with all the studs and joists of jaw-ivory (Sperm Whale) which had thus far been accumulated on the voyage, in order that a careful selection of the stoutest, clearest-grained stuff might be secured. This done, the carpenter received orders to have the leg completed that night; and to provide all the fittings for it, independent of those pertaining to the distrusted one in use. Moreover, the ship's forge was ordered to be hoisted out of its temporary idleness in the hold; and, to accelerate the affair, the blacksmith was commanded to proceed at once to the forging of whatever iron contrivances might be needed.

Chapter 107

The Carpenter

Seat thyself sultanically among the moons of Saturn, and take high abstracted man alone; and he seems a wonder, a grandeur, and a woe. But from the same point, take mankind in mass, and for the most part, they seem a mob of unnecessary duplicates, both contemporary and hereditary. But most humble though he was, and far from furnishing an example of the high, humane abstraction; the Pequod's carpenter was no duplicate; hence, he now comes in person on this stage.

Like all sea-going ship carpenters, and more especially those belonging to whaling vessels, he was, to a certain off-handed, practical extent, alike experienced in numerous trades and callings collateral to his own; the carpenter's pursuit being the ancient and outbranching trunk of all those numerous handicrafts which more or less have to do with wood as an auxiliary material. But, besides the application to him of the generic remark above, this carpenter of the Pequod was singularly efficient in those thousand nameless mechanical emergencies continually recurring in a large ship, upon a three or four years' voyage, in uncivilized and far-distant seas. For not to speak of his readiness in ordinary duties:—repairing stove boats, sprung spars, reforming the shape of clumsy-bladed oars, inserting bull's eyes in the deck, or new tree-nails in the side planks, and other miscellaneous matters more directly pertaining to his special business; he was moreover unhesitatingly expert in all manner of conflicting aptitudes, both useful and capricious.

The one grand stage where he enacted all his various parts so manifold, was his vice-bench; a long rude ponderous table furnished with several vices, of different sizes, and both of iron and of wood. At all times except when whales were alongside, this bench was securely lashed athwartships against the rear of the Try-works.

A belaying pin is found too large to be easily inserted into its hole: the carpenter claps it into one of his ever-ready vices, and straightway files it smaller. A lost land-bird of strange plumage strays on board, and is made a captive: out of clean shaved rods of right-whale bone, and cross-beams of sperm whale ivory, the carpenter makes a pagoda-looking cage for it. An oarsman sprains his wrist: the carpenter concocts a soothing lotion. Stubb longs for vermillion stars to be painted upon the blade of his every oar: screwing each oar in his big vice of wood, the carpenter symmetrically supplies the constellation. A sailor takes a fancy to wear shark-bone earrings: the carpenter drills his ears. Another has the toothache: the carpenter out pincers, and clapping one hand upon his bench bids him be seated there; but the poor fellow unmanageably winces under the unconcluded operation; whirling round the handle of his wooden vice, the carpenter signs him to clap his jaw in that, if he would have him draw the tooth.

Thus, this carpenter was prepared at all points, and alike indifferent and without respect in all. Teeth he accounted bits of ivory; heads he deemed but top-blocks; men themselves he lightly held for capstans. But while now upon so wide a field thus variously accomplished, and with such liveliness of expertness in him, too; all this would seem to argue some uncommon vivacity of intelligence. But not precisely so. For nothing was this man more remarkable, than for a certain impersonal stolidity as it were; impersonal, I say; for it so shaded off into the surrounding infinite of things, that it seemed one with the general stolidity discernible in the whole visible world; which while pauselessly active in uncounted modes, still eternally holds its peace, and ignores you, though you dig foundations for cathedrals. Yet was this half-horrible stolidity in him, involving, too, as it appeared, an all-ramifying heartlessness;—yet was it oddly dashed at times, with an old, crutch-like, antediluvian, wheezing humorousness, not unstreaked now and then with a certain grizzled wittiness; such as might have served to pass the time during the midnight watch on the bearded forecastle of Noah's ark. Was it that this old carpenter had been a life-long wanderer, whose much rolling, to and fro, not only had gathered no moss;[1] but what is more, had rubbed off whatever small outward clingings might have originally pertained to him? He was a stript abstract; an unfractioned integral; uncompromised as a new-born babe; living without premeditated reference to this world or the next. You might almost say, that this strange uncompromisedness in him involved a sort of unintelligence; for in his numerous trades, he did not seem to work so much by reason or by instinct, or simply because he had been tutored to it, or by any intermixture of all these, even or uneven; but merely by a kind of deaf and dumb, spontaneous literal process. He was a pure manipulator; his brain, if he had ever had one, must have early oozed along into the muscles of his fingers. He was like one of those unreasoning but still highly useful, *multum in parvo*,[2] Sheffield contrivances, assuming the exterior—though a little swelled—of a common pocket knife; but containing, not only blades of various sizes, but also screw-drivers, corkscrews, tweezers, awls, pens, rulers, nail-filers, countersinkers. So, if his

1. Said of a rolling stone (proverbial).
2. Much in little (like our term "all-in-one"); like a modern Swiss Army knife.

superiors wanted to use the carpenter for a screw-driver, all they had to
do was to open that part of him, and the screw was fast: or if for tweezers, take him up by the legs, and there they were.

Yet, as previously hinted, this omnitooled, open-and-shut carpenter,
was, after all, no mere machine of an automaton. If he did not have a
common soul in him, he had a subtle something that somehow anomalously did its duty. What that was, whether essence of quicksilver, or a
few drops of hartshorn, there is no telling. But there it was; and there it
had abided for now some sixty years or more. And this it was, this same
unaccountable, cunning life-principle in him; this it was, that kept him a
great part of the time soliloquizing; but only like an unreasoning wheel,
which also hummingly soliloquizes; or rather, his body was a sentry-box
and this soliloquizer on guard there, and talking all the time to keep himself awake.

Chapter 108

Ahab and the Carpenter

THE DECK—FIRST NIGHT WATCH

(*Carpenter standing before his vice-bench, and by the light of two lanterns
busily filing the ivory joist for the leg, which joist is firmly fixed in the
vice. Slabs of ivory, leather straps, pads, screws, and various tools of all
sorts lying about the bench. Forward, the red flame of the forge is seen,
where the blacksmith is at work.*)

Drat the file, and drat the bone! That is hard which should be soft, and that
is soft which should be hard. So we go, who file old jaws and shinbones.
Let's try another. Aye, now, this works better (*sneezes*). Halloa, this bone
dust is (*sneezes*)—why it's (*sneezes*)—yes it's (*sneezes*)—bless my soul, it
won't let me speak! This is what an old fellow gets now for working in dead
lumber. Saw a live tree, and you don't get this dust; amputate a live bone,
and you don't get it (*sneezes*). Come, come, you old Smut, there, bear a
hand, and let's have that ferule and buckle-screw; I'll be ready for them
presently. Lucky now (*sneezes*) there's no knee-joint to make; that might
puzzle a little; but a mere shinbone—why it's easy as making hop-poles; only
I should like to put a good finish on. Time, time; if I but only had the time,
I could turn him out as neat a leg now as ever (*sneezes*) scraped[1] to a lady
in a parlor. Those buckskin legs and calves of legs I've seen in shop windows
wouldn't compare at all. They soak water, they do; and of course get
rheumatic, and have to be doctored (*sneezes*) with washes and lotions, just
like live legs. There; before I saw it off, now, I must call his old Mogulship,
and see whether the length will be all right; too short, if anything, I guess.
Ha! that's the heel; we are in luck; here he comes, or it's somebody else,
that's certain.

---

1. Bowed low, by scraping one foot backward along the floor. *Smut:* sailors' name for the blacksmith
   (from the soot he works in). *Hop-poles:* tall poles to support hop plants.

AHAB *(advancing).*

(During the ensuing scene, the carpenter continues sneezing at times.)

Well, manmaker!

Just in time, sir. If the captain pleases, I will now mark the length. Let me measure, sir.

Measured for a leg! good. Well, it's not the first time. About it! There; keep thy finger on it. This is a cogent vice thou hast here, carpenter; let me feel its grip once. So, so; it does pinch some.

Oh, sir, it will break bones—beware, beware!

No fear; I like a good grip; I like to feel something in this slippery world that can hold, man. What's Prometheus about there?—the blacksmith, I mean—what's he about?

He must be forging the buckle-screw, sir, now.

Right. It's a partnership; he supplies the muscle part. He makes a fierce red flame there!

Aye, sir; he must have the white heat for this kind of fine work.

Um-m. So he must. I do deem it now a most meaning thing, that that old Greek, Prometheus, who made men, they say, should have been a blacksmith, and animated them with fire; for what's made in fire must properly belong to fire; and so hell's probable. How the soot flies! This must be the remainder the Greek made the Africans of. Carpenter, when he's through with that buckle, tell him to forge a pair of steel shoulder-blades; there's a pedlar[2] aboard with a crushing pack.

Sir?

Hold; while Prometheus is about it, I'll order a complete man after a desirable pattern. Imprimis, fifty feet high in his socks; then, chest modelled after the Thames Tunnel; then, legs with roots to 'em, to stay in one place; then, arms three feet through the wrist; no heart at all, brass forehead, and about a quarter of an acre of fine brains; and let me see—shall I order eyes to see outwards? No, but put a sky-light on top of his head to illuminate inwards. There, take the order, and away.

Now, what's he speaking about, and who's he speaking to, I should like to know? Shall I keep standing here? *(aside.)*

'Tis but indifferent architecture to make a blind dome; here's one. No, no, no; I must have a lantern.

Ho, ho! That's it, hey? Here are two, sir; one will serve my turn.

What art thou thrusting that thief-catcher into my face for, man? Thrusted light is worse than presented pistols.

I thought, sir, that you spoke to carpenter.

Carpenter? why that's—but no;—a very tidy, and, I may say, an extremely gentlemanlike sort of business thou art in here, carpenter;—or would'st thou rather work in clay?

Sir?—Clay? clay, sir? That's mud; we leave clay to ditchers, sir.

The fellow's impious.[3] What art thou sneezing about?

Bone is rather dusty, sir.

---

2. That is, Ahab himself, bearing the woes he feels are piled on him.
3. Blasphemous, because by traditional interpretation of Genesis 2.7 God made Adam of clay ("dust of the earth").

Take the hint, then; and when thou art dead, never bury thyself under living people's noses.

Sir?—oh! ah!—I guess so;—yes—oh, dear!

Look ye, carpenter, I dare say thou callest thyself a right good workman-like workman, eh? Well, then, will it speak thoroughly well for thy work, if, when I come to mount this leg thou makest, I shall nevertheless feel another leg in the same identical place with it; that is, carpenter, my old lost leg; the flesh and blood one, I mean. Canst thou not drive that old Adam away?

Truly, sir, I begin to understand somewhat now. Yes, I have heard something curious on that score, sir; how that a dismasted man never entirely loses the feeling of his old spar, but it will be still pricking him at times. May I humbly ask if it be really so, sir?

It is, man. Look, put thy live leg here in the place where mine once was; so, now, here is only one distinct leg to the eye, yet two to the soul. Where thou feelest tingling life; there, exactly there, there to a hair, do I. Is't a riddle?

I should humbly call it a poser, sir.

Hist, then. How dost thou know that some entire, living, thinking thing may not be invisibly and uninterpenetratingly standing precisely where thou now standest; aye, and standing there in thy spite? In thy most solitary hours, then, dost thou not fear eavesdroppers? Hold, don't speak! And if I still feel the smart of my crushed leg, though it be now so long dissolved; then, why mayst not thou, carpenter, feel the fiery pains of hell for ever, and without a body? Hah!

Good Lord! Truly, sir, if it comes to that, I must calculate over again; I think I didn't carry a small figure,[4] sir.

Look ye, pudding-heads should never grant premises.—How long before the leg is done?

Perhaps an hour, sir.

Bungle away at it then, and bring it to me *(turns to go)*. Oh, Life! Here I am, proud as a Greek god, and yet standing debtor to this blockhead for a bone to stand on! Cursed be that mortal inter-indebtedness which will not do away with ledgers. I would be free as air; and I'm down in the whole world's books. I am so rich, I could have given bid for bid with the wealthiest Prætorians[5] at the auction of the Roman empire (which was the world's); and yet I owe for the flesh in the tongue I brag with. By heavens! I'll get a crucible, and into it, and dissolve myself down to one small, compendious vertebra. So.

CARPENTER.

(Resuming his work.)

Well, well, well! Stubb knows him best of all, and Stubb always says he's queer; says nothing but that one sufficient little word queer; he's queer, says Stubb; he's queer—queer, queer; and keeps dinning it into Mr. Starbuck all the time—queer, sir—queer, queer, very queer. And here's his leg!

---

4. Ahab's propositions didn't add up the first time the carpenter tried to comprehend them.
5. This elite Roman guard often chose the emperor and once auctioned the office.

Yes, now that I think of it, here's his bedfellow! has a stick of whale's jaw-bone for a wife! And this is his leg; he'll stand on this. What was that now about one leg standing in three places, and all three places standing in one hell—how was that? Oh! I don't wonder he looked so scornful at me! I'm a sort of strange-thoughted sometimes, they say; but that's only hap-hazard-like. Then, a short, little old body like me, should never undertake to wade out into deep waters with tall, heron-built captains; the water chucks you under the chin pretty quick, and there's a great cry for life-boats. And here's the heron's leg! long and slim, sure enough! Now, for most folks one pair of legs lasts a lifetime, and that must be because they use them mercifully, as a tender-hearted old lady uses her roly-poly old coach-horses. But Ahab; oh he's a hard driver. Look, driven one leg to death, and spavined the other for life, and now wears out bone legs by the cord. Halloa, there, you Smut! bear a hand there with those screws, and let's finish it before the resurrection fellow[6] comes a-calling with his horn for all legs, true or false, as brewery-men go round collecting old beer bar-rels, to fill 'em up again. What a leg this is! It looks like a real live leg, filed down to nothing but the core; he'll be standing on this to-morrow; he'll be taking altitudes on it. Halloa! I almost forgot the little oval slate, smoothed ivory, where he figures up the latitude. So, so; chisel, file, and sand-paper, now!

Chapter 109

Ahab and Starbuck in the Cabin

According to usage they were pumping the ship next morning; and lo! no inconsiderable oil came up with the water; the casks below must have sprung a bad leak. Much concern was shown; and Starbuck went down into the cabin to report this unfavorable affair.[1]

Now, from the South and West the Pequod was drawing nigh to For-mosa[2] and the Bashee Isles, between which lies one of the tropical out-lets from the China waters into the Pacific. And so Starbuck found Ahab with a general chart of the oriental archipelagoes spread before him; and another separate one representing the long eastern coasts of the Japanese islands—Niphon, Matsmai, and Sikoke. With his snow-white new ivory leg braced against the screwed leg of his table, and with a long pruning-hook of a jack-knife in his hand, the wondrous old man, with his back to the gangway door, was wrinkling his brow, and tracing his old courses again.

"Who's there?" hearing the footstep at the door, but not turning round to it. "On deck! Begone!"

---

6. Angel (often identified as Gabriel) with his trumpet or horn, as in 1 Corinthians 15.52.
1. In Sperm-whalemen with any considerable quantity of oil on board, it is a regular semi-weekly duty to conduct a hose into the hold, and drench the casks with sea-water; which afterwards, at varying intervals, is removed by the ship's pumps. Hereby the casks are sought to be kept damply tight; while by the changed character of the withdrawn water, the mariners readily detect any seri-ous leakage in the precious cargo [Melville's note].
2. Taiwan.

"Captain Ahab mistakes; it is I. The oil in the hold is leaking, sir. We must up Burtons[3] and break out."

"Up Burtons and break out? Now that we are nearing Japan; heave-to here for a week to tinker a parcel of old hoops?"

"Either do that, sir, or waste in one day more oil than we may make good in a year. What we come twenty thousand miles to get is worth saving, sir."

"So it is, so it is; if we get it."

"I was speaking of the oil in the hold, sir."

"And I was not speaking or thinking of that at all. Begone! Let it leak! I'm all aleak myself. Aye! leaks in leaks! not only full of leaky casks, but those leaky casks are in a leaky ship; and that's a far worse plight than the Pequod's, man. Yet I don't stop to plug my leak; for who can find it in the deep-loaded hull; or how hope to plug it, even if found, in this life's howling gale? Starbuck! I'll not have the Burtons hoisted."

"What will the owners say, sir?"

"Let the owners stand on Nantucket beach and outyell the Typhoons. What cares Ahab? Owners, owners? Thou art always prating to me, Starbuck, about those miserly owners, as if the owners were my conscience. But look ye, the only real owner of anything is its commander; and hark ye, my conscience is in this ship's keel.—On deck!"

"Captain Ahab," said the reddening mate, moving further into the cabin, with a daring so strangely respectful and cautious that it almost seemed not only every way seeking to avoid the slightest outward manifestation of itself, but within also seemed more than half distrustful of itself; "A better man than I might well pass over in thee what he would quickly enough resent in a younger man; aye, and in a happier, Captain Ahab."

"Devils! Dost thou then so much as dare to critically think of me?—On deck!"

"Nay, sir, not yet; I do entreat. And I do dare, sir—to be forbearing! Shall we not understand each other better than hitherto, Captain Ahab?"

Ahab seized a loaded musket from the rack (forming part of most South-Sea-men's cabin furniture), and pointing it towards Starbuck, exclaimed: "There is one God that is Lord over the earth, and one Captain that is lord over the Pequod.—On deck!"

For an instant in the flashing eyes of the mate, and his fiery cheeks, you would have almost thought that he had really received the blaze of the levelled tube. But, mastering his emotion, he half calmly rose, and as he quitted the cabin, paused for an instant and said: "Thou hast outraged, not insulted me, sir; but for that I ask thee not to beware of Starbuck; thou wouldst but laugh; but let Ahab beware of Ahab; beware of thyself, old man."

"He waxes brave, but nevertheless obeys; most careful bravery that!" murmured Ahab, as Starbuck disappeared. "What's that he said—Ahab beware of Ahab—there's something there!" Then unconsciously using the musket for a staff, with an iron brow he paced to and fro in the little cabin; but presently the thick plaits of his forehead relaxed, and returning the gun to the rack, he went to the deck.

---

3. Hoist tackle to stop the ship so the oil casks can be brought on deck.

"Thou art but too good a fellow, Starbuck," he said lowly to the mate; then raising his voice to the crew: "Furl the t'gallant-sails, and close-reef the top-sails, fore and aft; back the main-yard; up Burtons, and break out in the main-hold."

It were perhaps vain to surmise exactly why it was, that as respecting Starbuck, Ahab thus acted. It may have been a flash of honesty in him; or mere prudential policy which, under the circumstance, imperiously forbade the slightest symptom of open disaffection, however transient, in the important chief officer of his ship. However it was, his orders were executed; and the Burtons were hoisted.

Chapter 110

Queequeg in his Coffin

Upon searching, it was found that the casks last struck into the hold were perfectly sound, and that the leak must be further off. So, it being calm weather, they broke out deeper and deeper, disturbing the slumbers of the huge ground-tier butts; and from that black midnight sending those gigantic moles into the daylight above. So deep did they go; and so ancient, and corroded, and weedy the aspect of the lowermost puncheons, that you almost looked next for some mouldy corner-stone cask containing coins of Captain Noah, with copies of the posted placards, vainly warning the infatuated old world from the flood. Tierce after tierce, too, of water, and bread, and beef, and shooks of staves, and iron bundles of hoops, were hoisted out, till at last the piled decks were hard to get about; and the hollow hull echoed under foot, as if you were treading over empty catacombs, and reeled and rolled in the sea like an air-freighted demijohn. Top-heavy was the ship as a dinnerless student with all Aristotle in his head. Well was it that the Typhoons did not visit them then.

Now, at this time it was that my poor pagan companion, and fast bosom-friend, Queequeg, was seized with a fever, which brought him nigh to his endless end.

Be it said, that in this vocation of whaling, sinecures are unknown; dignity and danger go hand in hand; till you get to be Captain, the higher you rise the harder you toil. So with poor Queequeg, who, as harpooneer, must not only face all the rage of the living whale, but—as we have elsewhere seen—mount his dead back in a rolling sea; and finally descend into the gloom of the hold, and bitterly sweating all day in that subterraneous confinement, resolutely manhandle the clumsiest casks and see to their stowage. To be short, among whalemen, the harpooneers are the holders, so called.

Poor Queequeg! when the ship was about half disembowelled, you should have stooped over the hatchway, and peered down upon him there; where, stripped to his woollen drawers, the tattooed savage was crawling about amid that dampness and slime, like a green spotted lizard at the bottom of a well. And a well, or an ice-house, it somehow proved to him, poor pagan; where, strange to say, for all the heat of his sweatings, he caught a terrible chill which lapsed into a fever; and at last, after some days' suffering, laid him in his hammock, close to the very sill of the door of death. How he wasted and wasted away in those few long-lingering days, till there seemed but little left of him but his frame and tattooing. But as all else in him thinned, and his cheek-bones grew sharper, his eyes, nevertheless, seemed growing fuller and fuller; they became of a strange softness of lustre; and mildly but deeply looked out at you there from his sickness, a wondrous testimony to that immortal health in him which could not die, or be weakened. And like circles on the water, which, as they grow fainter, expand; so his eyes seemed rounding and rounding, like the rings of Eternity. An awe that cannot be named would steal over you as you sat by the side of this waning savage, and saw as strange things in his face, as any beheld who were bystanders when Zoroaster[1] died. For whatever is truly wondrous and fearful in man, never yet was put into words or books. And the drawing near of Death, which alike levels all, alike impresses all with a last revelation, which only an author from the dead could adequately tell. So that—let us say it again—no dying Chaldee or Greek had higher and holier thoughts than those, whose mysterious shades you saw creeping over the face of poor Queequeg, as he quietly lay in his swaying hammock, and the rolling sea seemed gently rocking him to his final rest, and the ocean's invisible flood-tide lifted him higher and higher towards his destined heaven.

Not a man of the crew but gave him up; and, as for Queequeg himself, what he thought of his case was forcibly shown by a curious favor he asked. He called one[2] to him in the grey morning watch, when the day was just breaking, and taking his hand, said that while in Nantucket he had chanced to see certain little canoes of dark wood, like the rich war-wood of his native isle; and upon inquiry, he had learned that all whalemen who died in Nantucket, were laid in those same dark canoes, and that the fancy of being so laid had much pleased him; for it was not unlike the custom of his own race, who, after embalming a dead warrior, stretched him out in his canoe, and so left him to be floated away to the starry archipelagoes; for not only do they believe that the stars are isles, but that far beyond all visible horizons, their own mild, uncontinented seas, interflow with the blue heavens; and so form the white breakers of the milky way. He added, that he shuddered at the thought of being buried in his hammock, according to the usual sea-custom, tossed like something vile to the death-devouring sharks. No: he desired a canoe like those of Nantucket, all the more congenial to him, being a whaleman, that like a whale-boat these coffin-canoes were without a keel; though that involved but uncertain steering, and much lee-way adown the dim ages.

Now, when this strange circumstance was made known aft, the carpenter was at once commanded to do Queequeg's bidding, whatever it might include. There was some heathenish, coffin-colored old lumber aboard, which, upon a long previous voyage, had been cut from the abo-

---

1. Founder of ancient Persian religion (about 6th century B.C.E.).
2. This "one" should be Ishmael, his "bosom companion." The odd mysteriousness is heightened by the submerged biblical wording (see "called" and "one" in a concordance to the Bible, especially to the New Testament).

riginal groves of the Lackaday islands,[3] and from these dark planks the coffin was recommended to be made. No sooner was the carpenter apprised of the order, than taking his rule, he forthwith with all the indifferent promptitude of his character, proceeded into the forecastle and took Queequeg's measure with great accuracy, regularly chalking Queequeg's person as he shifted the rule.

"Ah! poor fellow! he'll have to die now," ejaculated the Long Island sailor.

Going to his vice-bench, the carpenter for convenience sake and general reference, now transferringly measured on it the exact length the coffin was to be, and then made the transfer permanent by cutting two notches at its extremities. This done, he marshalled the planks and his tools, and to work.

When the last nail was driven, and the lid duly planed and fitted, he lightly shouldered the coffin and went forward with it, inquiring whether they were ready for it yet in that direction.

Overhearing the indignant but half-humorous cries with which the people on deck began to drive the coffin away, Queequeg, to every one's consternation, commanded that the thing should be instantly brought to him, nor was there any denying him; seeing that, of all mortals, some dying men are the most tyrannical; and certainly, since they will shortly trouble us so little for evermore, the poor fellows ought to be indulged.

Leaning over in his hammock, Queequeg long regarded the coffin with an attentive eye. He then called for his harpoon, had the wooden stock drawn from it, and then had the iron part placed in the coffin along with one of the paddles of his boat. All by his own request, also, biscuits were then ranged round the sides within: a flask of fresh water was placed at the head, and a small bag of woody earth scraped up in the hold at the foot; and a piece of sail-cloth being rolled up for a pillow, Queequeg now entreated to be lifted into his final bed, that he might make trial of its comforts, if any it had. He lay without moving a few minutes, then told one to go to his bag and bring out his little god, Yojo. Then crossing his arms on his breast with Yojo between, he called for the coffin lid (hatch he called it) to be placed over him. The head part turned over with a leather hinge, and there lay Queequeg in his coffin with little but his composed countenance in view. "Rarmai" (it will do; it is easy), he murmured at last, and signed to be replaced in his hammock.

But ere this was done, Pip, who had been slily hovering near by all this while, drew nigh to him where he lay, and with soft sobbings, took him by the hand; in the other, holding his tambourine.

"Poor rover! will ye never have done with all this weary roving? where go ye now? But if the currents carry ye to those sweet Antilles where the beaches are only beat with water-lilies, will ye do one little errand for me? Seek out one Pip, who's now been missing long: I think he's in those far Antilles.[4] If ye find him, then comfort him; for he must be very sad; for look! he's left his tambourine behind;—I found it. Rig-a-dig, dig, dig! Now, Queequeg, die; and I'll beat ye your dying march."

3. Laccadive Islands, in the Arabian Sea. *Lackaday:* lackadaisical, languishing, lazy.
4. The West Indies, in the Caribbean.

"I have heard," murmured Starbuck, gazing down the scuttle, "that in violent fevers, men, all ignorance, have talked in ancient tongues; and that when the mystery is probed, it turns out always that in their wholly forgotten childhood those ancient tongues had been really spoken in their hearing by some lofty scholars. So, to my fond faith, poor Pip, in this strange sweetness of his lunacy, brings heavenly vouchers of all our heavenly homes. Where learned he that, but there?—Hark! he speaks again: but more wildly now."

"Form two and two! Let's make a General of him! Ho, where's his harpoon? Lay it across here.—Rig-a-dig, dig, dig! huzza! Oh for a game cock now to sit upon his head and crow! Queequeg dies game!—mind ye that; Queequeg dies game!—take ye good heed of that; Queequeg dies game! I say; game, game, game! but base little Pip, he died a coward; died all a'shiver;—out upon Pip! Hark ye; if ye find Pip, tell all the Antilles he's a runaway; a coward, a coward, a coward! Tell them he jumped from a whaleboat! I'd never beat my tambourine over base Pip, and hail him General, if he were once more dying here. No, no! shame upon all cowards—shame upon them! Let 'em go drown like Pip, that jumped from a whale-boat. Shame! shame!"

During all this, Queequeg lay with closed eyes, as if in a dream. Pip was led away, and the sick man was replaced in his hammock.

But now that he had apparently made every preparation for death; now that his coffin was proved a good fit, Queequeg suddenly rallied; soon there seemed no need of the carpenter's box: and thereupon, when some expressed their delighted surprise, he, in substance, said, that the cause of his sudden convalescence was this;—at a critical moment, he had just recalled a little duty ashore, which he was leaving undone; and therefore had changed his mind about dying: he could not die yet, he averred. They asked him, then, whether to live or die was a matter of his own sovereign will and pleasure. He answered, certainly. In a word, it was Queequeg's conceit, that if a man made up his mind to live, mere sickness could not kill him: nothing but a whale, or a gale, or some violent, ungovernable, unintelligent destroyer of that sort.

Now, there is this noteworthy difference between savage and civilized; that while a sick, civilized man may be six months convalescing, generally speaking, a sick savage is almost half-well again in a day. So, in good time my Queequeg gained strength; and at length after sitting on the windlass for a few indolent days (but eating with a vigorous appetite) he suddenly leaped to his feet, threw out arms and legs, gave himself a good stretching, yawned a little bit, and then springing into the head of his hoisted boat, and poising a harpoon, pronounced himself fit for a fight.

With a wild whimsiness, he now used his coffin for a sea-chest; and emptying into it his canvas bag of clothes, set them in order there. Many spare hours he spent, in carving the lid with all manner of grotesque figures and drawings; and it seemed that hereby he was striving, in his rude way, to copy parts of the twisted tattooing on his body. And this tattooing, had been the work of a departed prophet and seer of his island, who, by those hieroglyphic marks, had written out on his body a complete theory of the heavens and the earth, and a mystical treatise on the art of attaining truth; so that Queequeg in his own proper person was a riddle to unfold; a wondrous work in one volume; but whose mysteries not even himself could read, though his own live heart beat against them; and these mysteries were therefore destined in the end to moulder away with the living parchment whereon they were inscribed, and so be unsolved to the last. And this thought it must have been which suggested to Ahab that wild exclamation of his, when one morning turning away from surveying poor Queequeg—"Oh, devilish tantalization of the gods!"

Chapter 111

The Pacific

When gliding by the Bashee isles we emerged at last upon the great South Sea; were it not for other things, I could have greeted my dear Pacific with uncounted thanks, for now the long supplication of my youth was answered; that serene ocean rolled eastwards from me a thousand leagues of blue.

There is, one knows not what sweet mystery about this sea, whose gently awful stirrings seem to speak of some hidden soul beneath; like those fabled undulations of the Ephesian sod over the buried Evangelist St. John.[1] And meet it is, that over these sea-pastures, wide-rolling watery prairies and Potters' Fields[2] of all four continents, the waves should rise and fall, and ebb and flow unceasingly; for here, millions of mixed shades and shadows, drowned dreams, somnambulisms, reveries; all that we call lives and souls, lie dreaming, dreaming, still; tossing like slumberers in their beds; the ever rolling waves but made so by their restlessness.

To any meditative Magian rover, this serene Pacific, once beheld, must ever after be the sea of his adoption.[3] It rolls the midmost waters of the world, the Indian ocean and Atlantic being but its arms. The same waves wash the moles of the new-built Californian towns, but yesterday planted by the recentest race of men, and lave the faded but still gorgeous skirts of Asiatic lands, older than Abraham; while all between float milky-ways of coral isles, and low-lying, endless, unknown Archipelagoes, and impenetrable Japans.[4] Thus this mysterious, divine Pacific zones the world's whole bulk about; makes all coasts one bay to it; seems the tide-beating heart of earth. Lifted by those eternal swells, you needs must own the seductive god, bowing your head to Pan.

But few thoughts of Pan[5] stirred Ahab's brain, as standing like an iron

---

1. As Melville knew from Bayle's *Dictionary* (1697), St. Augustine reported that the sod above St. John's grave in Asia Minor moved like the bedclothes of a man sleeping.
2. Public burial places for poor criminals and unidentified persons, but always with an allusion to the first potter's field, bought with the money paid for Jesus's betrayal (Matthew 27.5–7). Judas took thirty pieces of silver for betraying Jesus, then after Jesus was crucified returned it to the chief priests, who then used it to purchase a field from an actual potter (a man who made pots), so they would have a place to bury strangers.
3. To a rover meditative like an ancient Mede or Persian priest (magus), the Pacific, once he has found it, is the place most suited to his temperament. In Cologne in 1849 Melville mused on the historical associations of the place during the long Holy Roman Empire (alluded to throughout *Moby-Dick*) and the power of such associations for "a pondering man" like him.
4. Japan was opened to Western commerce in 1854 by Admiral Matthew Perry.
5. Pantheistic thoughts about the benign oneness of nature such as those of the youth at the end of ch. 25.

statue at his accustomed place beside the mizen rigging, with one nostril he unthinkingly snuffed the sugary musk from the Bashee isles (in whose sweet woods mild lovers must be walking), and with the other consciously inhaled the salt breath of the new found sea; that sea in which the hated White Whale must even then be swimming. Launched at length upon these almost final waters, and gliding towards the Japanese cruising-ground, the old man's purpose intensified itself. His firm lips met like the lips of a vice; the Delta[6] of his forehead's veins swelled like overladen brooks; in his very sleep, his ringing cry ran through the vaulted hull, "Stern all! the White Whale spouts thick blood!"

Chapter 112

The Blacksmith

Availing himself of the mild, summer-cool weather that now reigned in these latitudes, and in preparation for the peculiarly active pursuits shortly to be anticipated, Perth, the begrimed, blistered old blacksmith, had not removed his portable forge to the hold again, after concluding his contributory work for Ahab's leg, but still retained it on deck, fast lashed to ringbolts by the foremast; being now almost incessantly invoked by the headsmen, and harpooneers, and bowsmen to do some little job for them; altering, or repairing, or new shaping their various weapons and boat furniture. Often he would be surrounded by an eager circle, all waiting to be served; holding boat-spades, pike-heads, harpoons, and lances, and jealously watching his every sooty movement, as he toiled. Nevertheless, this old man's was a patient hammer wielded by a patient arm. No murmur, no impatience, no petulance did come from him. Silent, slow, and solemn; bowing over still further his chronically broken back, he toiled away, as if toil were life itself, and the heavy beating of his hammer the heavy beating of his heart. And so it was.—Most miserable!

A peculiar walk in this old man, a certain slight but painful appearing yawing in his gait, had at an early period of the voyage excited the curiosity of the mariners. And to the importunity of their persisted questionings he had finally given in; and so it came to pass that every one now knew the shameful story of his wretched fate.

Belated, and not innocently, one bitter winter's midnight, on the road running between two country towns, the blacksmith half-stupidly felt the deadly numbness stealing over him, and sought refuge in a leaning, dilapidated barn. The issue was, the loss of the extremities of both feet. Out of this revelation, part by part, at last came out the four acts of the gladness, and the one long, and as yet uncatastrophied fifth act of the grief of his life's drama.

He was an old man, who, at the age of nearly sixty, had postponedly encountered that thing in sorrow's technicals called ruin. He had been an artisan of famed excellence, and with plenty to do; owned a house and

---

6. The veins of Ahab's forehead are sodden with blood, as the delta of a river is loaded with silt-thick water.

garden; embraced a youthful, daughter-like, loving wife, and three blithe, ruddy children; every Sunday went to a cheerful-looking church, planted in a grove. But one night, under cover of darkness, and further concealed in a most cunning disguisement, a desperate burglar slid into his happy home, and robbed them all of everything. And darker yet to tell, the black-smith himself did ignorantly conduct this burglar into his family's heart. It was the Bottle Conjuror![1] Upon the opening of that fatal cork, forth flew the fiend, and shrivelled up his home. Now, for prudent, most wise, and economic reasons, the blacksmith's shop was in the basement of his dwelling, but with a separate entrance to it; so that always had the young and loving healthy wife listened with no unhappy nervousness, but with vigorous pleasure, to the stout ringing of her young-armed old husband's hammer; whose reverberations, muffled by passing through the floors and walls, came up to her, not unsweetly, in her nursery; and so, to stout Labor's iron lullaby, the blacksmith's infants were rocked to slumber.

Oh, woe on woe! Oh, Death, why canst thou not sometimes be timely? Hadst thou taken this old blacksmith to thyself ere his full ruin came upon him, then had the young widow had a delicious grief, and her orphans a truly venerable, legendary sire to dream of in their after years; and all of them a care-killing competency. But Death plucked down some virtuous elder brother, on whose whistling daily toil solely hung the responsibilities of some other family, and left the worse than useless old man standing, till the hideous rot of life should make him easier to harvest.

Why tell the whole? The blows of the basement hammer every day grew more and more between; and each blow every day grew fainter than the last; the wife sat frozen at the window, with tearless eyes, glitteringly gazing into the weeping faces of her children; the bellows fell; the forge choked up with cinders; the house was sold; the mother dived down into the long church-yard grass; her children twice followed her thither; and the houseless, familyless old man staggered off a vagabond in crape; his every woe unreverenced; his grey head a scorn to flaxen curls!

Death seems the only desirable sequel for a career like this; but Death is only a launching into the region of the strange Untried; it is but the first salutation to the possibilities of the immense Remote, the Wild, the Watery, the Unshored; therefore, to the death-longing eyes of such men, who still have left in them some interior compunctions against suicide, does the all-contributed and all-receptive ocean alluringly spread forth his whole plain of unimaginable, taking terrors, and wonderful, new-life adventures; and from the hearts of infinite Pacifics, the thousand mermaids sing to them—"Come hither, broken-hearted; here is another life without the guilt of intermediate death; here are wonders supernatural, without dying for them. Come hither! bury thyself in a life which, to your now equally abhorred and abhorring, landed world, is more oblivious than death. Come hither! put up *thy* grave-stone, too, within the churchyard, and come hither, till we marry thee!"

1. Perth himself, deceived by alcohol, the "Conjurer" in the bottle that robbed his home of its happiness. Something more complicated may be going on here, but Melville (or Ishmael) is playing with the sentimental, melodramatic language of Temperance literature.

Hearkening to these voices, East and West, by early sun-rise, and by fall of eve, the blacksmith's soul responded, Aye, I come! And so Perth went a-whaling.

Chapter 113

The Forge

With matted beard, and swathed in a bristling shark-skin apron, about mid-day, Perth was standing between his forge and anvil, the latter placed upon an iron-wood log, with one hand holding a pike-head in the coals, and with the other at his forge's lungs, when Captain Ahab came along, carrying in his hand a small rusty-looking leathern bag. While yet a little distance from the forge, moody Ahab paused; till at last, Perth, withdrawing his iron from the fire, began hammering it upon the anvil—the red mass sending off the sparks in thick hovering flights, some of which flew close to Ahab.

"Are these thy Mother Carey's chickens,[1] Perth? they are always flying in thy wake; birds of good omen, too, but not to all;—look here, they burn; but thou—thou liv'st among them without a scorch."

"Because I am scorched all over, Captain Ahab," answered Perth, resting for a moment on his hammer; "I am past scorching; not easily can'st thou scorch a scar."

"Well, well; no more. Thy shrunk voice sounds too calmly, sanely woful to me. In no Paradise myself, I am impatient of all misery in others that is not mad. Thou should'st go mad, blacksmith; say, why dost thou not go mad? How can'st thou endure without being mad? Do the heavens yet hate thee, that thou can'st not go mad?—What wert thou making there?"

"Welding an old pike-head, sir; there were seams and dents in it."

"And can'st thou make it all smooth again, blacksmith, after such hard usage as it had?"

"I think so, sir."

"And I suppose thou can'st smoothe almost any seams and dents; never mind how hard the metal, blacksmith?"

"Aye, sir, I think I can; all seams and dents but one."

"Look ye here, then," cried Ahab, passionately advancing, and leaning with both hands on Perth's shoulders; "look ye here—*here*—can ye smoothe out a seam like this, blacksmith," sweeping one hand across his ribbed brow; "if thou could'st, blacksmith, glad enough would I lay my head upon thy anvil, and feel thy heaviest hammer between my eyes. Answer! Can'st thou smoothe this seam?"

"Oh! that is the one, sir! Said I not all seams and dents but one?"

"Aye, blacksmith, it is the one; aye, man, it is unsmoothable; for though thou only see'st it here in my flesh, it has worked down into the bone of my skull—*that* is all wrinkles! But, away with child's play; no more gaffs and pikes to-day. Look ye here!" jingling the leathern bag, as if it were full of gold coins. "I, too, want a harpoon made; one that a thousand yoke of

1. Seabirds, petrels that follow ships at sea.

fiends could not part, Perth; something that will stick in a whale like his own fin-bone. There's the stuff," flinging the pouch upon the anvil. "Look ye, blacksmith, these are the gathered nail-stubs of the steel shoes of racing horses."

"Horse-shoe stubs, sir? Why, Captain Ahab, thou hast here, then, the best and stubbornest stuff we blacksmiths ever work."

"I know it, old man; these stubs will weld together like glue from the melted bones of murderers. Quick! forge me the harpoon. And forge me first, twelve rods for its shank; then wind, and twist, and hammer these twelve together like the yarns and strands of a tow-line. Quick! I'll blow the fire."

When at last the twelve rods were made, Ahab tried them, one by one, by spiralling them, with his own hand, round a long, heavy iron bolt. "A flaw!" rejecting the last one. "Work that over again, Perth."

This done, Perth was about to begin welding the twelve into one, when Ahab stayed his hand, and said he would weld his own iron. As, then, with regular, gasping hems, he hammered on the anvil, Perth passing to him the glowing rods, one after the other, and the hard pressed forge shooting up its intense straight flame, the Parsee passed silently, and bowing over his head towards the fire, seemed invoking some curse or some blessing on the toil. But, as Ahab looked up, he slid aside.

"What's that bunch of lucifers dodging about there for?" muttered Stubb, looking on from the forecastle. "That Parsee smells fire like a fusee;[2] and smells of it himself, like a hot musket's powder-pan."

At last the shank, in one complete rod, received its final heat; and as Perth, to temper it, plunged it all hissing into the cask of water near by, the scalding steam shot up into Ahab's bent face.

"Would'st thou brand me, Perth?" wincing for a moment with the pain; "have I been but forging my own branding-iron, then?"

"Pray God, not that; yet I fear something, Captain Ahab. Is not this harpoon for the White Whale?"

"For the white fiend! But now for the barbs; thou must make them thyself, man. Here are my razors—the best of steel; here, and make the barbs sharp as the needle-sleet of the Icy Sea."

For a moment, the old blacksmith eyed the razors as though he would fain not use them.

"Take them, man, I have no need for them; for I now neither shave, sup, nor pray till————but here—to work!"

Fashioned at last into an arrowy shape, and welded by Perth to the shank, the steel soon pointed the end of the iron; and as the blacksmith was about giving the barbs their final heat, prior to tempering them, he cried to Ahab to place the water-cask near.

"No, no—no water for that; I want it of the true death-temper. Ahoy, there! Tashtego, Queequeg, Daggoo! What say ye, pagans! Will ye give me as much blood as will cover this barb?" holding it high up. A cluster of dark nods replied, Yes. Three punctures were made in the heathen flesh, and the White Whale's barbs were then tempered.

---

2. Stubb is playing on Lucifer (the devil) and lucifers, friction matches, then recently invented, with fusees (bulbs of powder) attached to little wooden sticks, for striking.

"Ego non baptizo te in nomine patris, sed in nomine diaboli!"[3] deliriously howled Ahab, as the malignant iron scorchingly devoured the baptismal blood.

Now, mustering the spare poles from below, and selecting one of hickory, with the bark still investing it, Ahab fitted the end to the socket of
the iron. A coil of new tow-line was then unwound, and some fathoms
of it taken to the windlass, and stretched to a great tension. Pressing
his foot upon it, till the rope hummed like a harp-string, then eagerly
bending over it, and seeing no strandings, Ahab exclaimed, "Good! and
now for the seizings."

At one extremity the rope was unstranded, and the separate spread
yarns were all braided and woven round the socket of the harpoon; the
pole was then driven hard up into the socket; from the lower end the rope
was traced half way along the pole's length, and firmly secured so, with
intertwistings of twine. This done, pole, iron, and rope—like the Three
Fates—remained inseparable, and Ahab moodily stalked away with the
weapon; the sound of his ivory leg, and the sound of the hickory pole,
both hollowly ringing along every plank. But ere he entered his cabin, a
light, unnatural, half-bantering, yet most piteous sound was heard. Oh,
Pip! thy wretched laugh, thy idle but unresting eye; all thy strange mum-
meries not unmeaningly blended with the black tragedy of the melancholy
ship, and mocked it!

Chapter 114

The Gilder

Penetrating further and further into the heart of the Japanese cruising
ground, the Pequod was soon all astir in the fishery. Often, in mild, pleasant weather, for twelve, fifteen, eighteen, and twenty hours on the stretch,
they were engaged in the boats, steadily pulling, or sailing, or paddling
after the whales, or for an interlude of sixty or seventy minutes calmly
awaiting their uprising; though with but small success for their pains.

At such times, under an abated sun; afloat all day upon smooth, slow
heaving swells; seated in his boat, light as a birch canoe; and so sociably
mixing with the soft waves themselves, that like hearth-stone cats they
purr against the gunwale; these are the times of dreamy quietude, when
beholding the tranquil beauty and brilliancy of the ocean's skin, one for-
gets the tiger heart that pants beneath it; and would not willingly remember, that this velvet paw but conceals a remorseless fang.

These are the times, when in his whale-boat the rover softly feels a certain filial, confident, land-like feeling towards the sea; that he regards it
as so much flowery earth; and the distant ship revealing only the tops of

---

3. "I do not baptize you in the name of the father, but in the name of the devil." See the discovery
   by Geoffrey Sanborn (p. 584, herein): long-debated notes Melville made in his copy of Shakespeare were not notes on Shakespeare at all but simply notes he jotted down there as he read an
   essay on the persecution of witches in the July 1823 *Quarterly Review*, where he found this Latin
   formula. (Sanborn's discovery came after 1988, when the NN edition of *Moby-Dick* reprinted
   Melville's notes with transcription and commentary.)

her masts, seems struggling forward, not through high rolling waves, but through the tall grass of a rolling prairie: as when the western emigrants' horses only show their erected ears, while their hidden bodies widely wade through the amazing verdure.

The long-drawn virgin vales; the mild blue hill-sides; as over these there steals the hush, the hum; you almost swear that play-wearied children lie sleeping in these solitudes, in some glad May-time, when the flowers of the woods are plucked. And all this mixes with your most mystic mood; so that fact and fancy, half-way meeting, interpenetrate, and form one seamless whole.

Nor did such soothing scenes, however temporary, fail of at least as temporary an effect on Ahab. But if these secret golden keys did seem to open in him his own secret golden treasuries, yet did his breath upon them prove but tarnishing.

"Oh, grassy glades! oh, ever vernal endless landscapes in the soul; in ye,— though long purched by the dead drought of the earthy life,—in ye, men yet may roll, like young horses in new morning clover; and for some few fleeting moments, feel the cool dew of the life immortal on them. Would to God these blessed calms would last. But the mingled, mingling threads of life are woven by warp and woof: calms crossed by storms, a storm for every calm. There is no steady unretracing progress in this life; we do not advance through fixed gradations, and at the last one pause:— through infancy's unconscious spell, boyhood's thoughtless faith, adolescence' doubt (the common doom), then scepticism, then disbelief, resting at last in manhood's pondering repose of If. But once gone through, we trace the round again; and are infants, boys, and men, and Ifs eternally. Where lies the final harbor, whence we unmoor no more? In what rapt ether sails the world, of which the weariest will never weary? Where is the foundling's father hidden? Our souls are like those orphans whose unwedded mothers die in bearing them: the secret of our paternity lies in their grave, and we must there to learn it."[1]

And that same day, too, gazing far down from his boat's side into that same golden sea, Starbuck lowly murmured:—

"Loveliness unfathomable, as ever lover saw in his young bride's eye!— Tell me not of thy teeth-tiered sharks, and thy kidnapping cannibal ways. Let faith oust fact; let fancy oust memory; I look deep down and do believe."

And Stubb, fish-like, with sparkling scales, leaped up in that same golden light:—

"I am Stubb, and Stubb has his history; but here Stubb takes oaths that he has always been jolly!"

---

1. For the 1967 NCE the editors first suggested putting quotation marks around this paragraph to make it clear that Ahab is the speaker, in a chapter built on a series of soliloquies. The fact that critics can reasonably take the words as Ishmael's is suggestive in light of Ishmael's explicit claim to be tragic dramatist of the book who hopes to make Ahab grand without "majestical trappings and housings" (ch. 33): "Oh, Ahab! what shall be grand in thee, it must needs be plucked at from the skies, and dived for in the deep, and featured in the unbodied air!" This has implications for any critical argument that takes Ishmael and Ahab as embodying opposing values.

Chapter 115

The Pequod meets the Bachelor

And jolly enough were the sights and the sounds that came bearing down before the wind, some few weeks after Ahab's harpoon had been welded.

It was a Nantucket ship, the Bachelor, which had just wedged in her last cask of oil, and bolted down her bursting hatches; and now, in glad holiday apparel, was joyously, though somewhat vain-gloriously, sailing round among the widely-separated ships on the ground, previous to pointing her prow for home.

The three men at her mast-head wore long streamers of narrow red bunting at their hats; from the stern, a whale-boat was suspended, bottom up; and hanging captive from the bowsprit was seen the long lower jaw of the last whale they had slain. Signals, ensigns, and jacks of all colors were flying from her rigging, on every side. Sideways lashed in each of her three basketed tops were two barrels of sperm; above which, in her top-mast cross-trees, you saw slender breakers of the same precious fluid; and nailed to her main truck was a brazen lamp.

As was afterwards learned, the Bachelor had met with the most surprising success; all the more wonderful, for that while cruising in the same seas numerous other vessels had gone entire months without securing a single fish. Not only had barrels of beef and bread been given away to make room for the far more valuable sperm, but additional supplemental casks had been bartered for, from the ships she had met; and these were stowed along the deck, and in the captain's and officers' state-rooms. Even the cabin table itself had been knocked into kindling-wood; and the cabin mess dined off the broad head of an oil-butt, lashed down to the floor for a centrepiece. In the forecastle, the sailors had actually caulked and pitched their chests, and filled them; it was humorously added, that the cook had clapped a head on his largest boiler, and filled it; that the steward had plugged his spare coffee-pot and filled it; that the harpooneers had headed the sockets of their irons and filled them; that indeed everything was filled with sperm, except the captain's pantaloons pockets, and those he reserved to thrust his hands into, in self-complacent testimony of his entire satisfaction.

As this glad ship of good luck bore down upon the moody Pequod, the barbarian sound of enormous drums came from her forecastle; and drawing still nearer, a crowd of her men were seen standing round her huge try-pots, which, covered with the parchment-like *poke* or stomach skin of the black fish, gave forth a loud roar to every stroke of the clenched hands of the crew. On the quarter-deck, the mates and harpooneers were dancing with the olive-hued girls who had eloped with them from the Polynesian Isles; while suspended in an ornamented boat, firmly secured aloft between the foremast and mainmast, three Long Island negroes, with glittering fiddle-bows of whale ivory, were presiding over the hilarious jig. Meanwhile, others of the ship's company were tumultuously busy at the masonry of the try-works, from which the huge pots had been removed. You would have almost thought they were pulling down the cursed Bastile,[1] such wild cries

1. Parisian prison pulled down by a French mob in 1789.

they raised, as the now useless brick and mortar were being hurled into the sea.

Lord and master over all this scene, the captain stood erect on the ship's elevated quarter-deck, so that the whole rejoicing drama was full before him, and seemed merely contrived for his own individual diversion.

And Ahab, he too was standing on his quarter-deck, shaggy and black, with a stubborn gloom; and as the two ships crossed each other's wakes— one all jubilations for things passed, the other all forebodings as to things to come—their two captains in themselves impersonated the whole striking contrast of the scene.

"Come aboard, come aboard!" cried the gay Bachelor's commander, lifting a glass and a bottle in the air.

"Hast seen the White Whale?" gritted Ahab in reply.

"No; only heard of him; but don't believe in him at all," said the other good-humoredly. "Come aboard!"

"Thou art too damned jolly. Sail on. Hast lost any men?"

"Not enough to speak of—two islanders, that's all;[2]—but come aboard, old hearty, come along. I'll soon take that black from your brow. Come along, will ye (merry's the play); a full ship and homeward-bound."

"How wondrous familiar is a fool!" muttered Ahab; then aloud, "Thou art a full ship and homeward bound, thou sayst; well, then, call me an empty ship, and outward-bound. So go thy ways, and I will mine. Forward there! Set all sail, and keep her to the wind!"

And thus, while the one ship went cheerily before the breeze, the other stubbornly fought against it; and so the two vessels parted; the crew of the Pequod looking with grave, lingering glances towards the receding Bachelor; but the Bachelor's men never heeding their gaze for the lively revelry they were in. And as Ahab, leaning over the taffrail, eyed the homeward-bound craft, he took from his pocket a small vial of sand, and then looking from the ship to the vial, seemed thereby bringing two remote associations together, for that vial was filled with Nantucket soundings.

Chapter 116

The Dying Whale

Not seldom in this life, when, on the right side, fortune's favorites sail close by us, we, though all adroop before, catch somewhat of the rushing breeze, and joyfully feel our bagging sails fill out. So seemed it with the Pequod. For next day after encountering the gay Bachelor, whales were seen and four were slain; and one of them by Ahab.

It was far down the afternoon; and when all the spearings of the crimson fight were done: and floating in the lovely sunset sea and sky, sun and whale both stilly died together; then, such a sweetness and such plaintiveness, such inwreathing orisons curled up in that rosy air, that it almost

---

2. This speech of the captain of the *Bachelor* is analogous to the telling answer Mark Twain has Huck Finn give to a question as to whether anyone was hurt in a steamboat explosion (ch. 32): "'No'm. Killed a nigger.'" Like Twain, Melville knew what ironic point he was making about how human life is valued.

seemed as if far over from the deep green convent valleys of the Manilla isles,[1] the Spanish land-breeze, wantonly turned sailor, had gone to sea, freighted with these vesper hymns.

Soothed again, but only soothed to deeper gloom, Ahab, who had sterned off from the whale, sat intently watching his final wanings from the now tranquil boat. For that strange spectacle observable in all sperm whales dying—the turning sunwards of the head, and so expiring—that strange spectacle, beheld of such a placid evening, somehow to Ahab conveyed a wondrousness unknown before.

"He turns and turns him to it,—how slowly, but how steadfastly, his homage-rendering and invoking brow, with his last dying motions. He too worships fire; most faithful, broad, baronial vassal of the sun!—Oh that these too-favoring eyes should see these too-favoring sights. Look! here, far water-locked; beyond all hum of human weal or woe; in these most candid and impartial seas; where to traditions no rocks furnish tablets; where for long Chinese ages, the billows have still rolled on speechless and unspoken to, as stars that shine upon the Niger's unknown source;[2] here, too, life dies sunwards full of faith; but see! no sooner dead, than death whirls round the corpse, and it heads some other way.—

"Oh, thou dark Hindoo half of nature, who of drowned bones hast builded thy separate throne somewhere in the heart of these unverdured seas; thou art an infidel, thou queen, and too truly speakest to me in the wide-slaughtering Typhoon, and the hushed burial of its after calm. Nor has this thy whale sunwards turned his dying head, and then gone round again, without a lesson to me.

"Oh, trebly hooped and welded hip of power! Oh, high aspiring, rainbowed jet!—that one striveth, this one jetteth all in vain! In vain, oh whale, dost thou seek intercedings with yon all-quickening sun, that only calls forth life, but gives it not again. Yet dost thou, darker half, rock me with a prouder, if a darker faith. All thy unnamable imminglings float beneath me here; I am buoyed by breaths of once living things, exhaled as air, but water now.

"Then hail, for ever hail, O sea, in whose eternal tossings the wild fowl finds his only rest. Born of earth, yet suckled by the sea; though hill and valley mothered me, ye billows are my foster-brothers!"

Chapter 117

The Whale Watch

The four whales slain that evening had died wide apart; one, far to windward; one, less distant, to leeward; one ahead; one astern. These last three were brought alongside ere nightfall; but the windward one could not be reached till morning; and the boat that had killed it lay by its side all night; and that boat was Ahab's.

---

1. The Philippines.
2. The source of this great African river had been discovered in Melville's youth, but much of the continent had not been mapped at the time of *Moby-Dick*.

The waif-pole was thrust upright into the dead whale's spout-hole; and the lantern hanging from its top, cast a troubled flickering glare upon the black, glossy back, and far out upon the midnight waves, which gently chafed the whale's broad flank, like soft surf upon a beach.

Ahab and all his boat's crew seemed asleep but the Parsee; who crouching in the bow, sat watching the sharks, that spectrally played round the whale, and tapped the light cedar planks with their tails. A sound like the moaning in squadrons over Asphaltites of unforgiven ghosts of Gomorrah, ran shuddering through the air.[1]

Started from his slumbers, Ahab, face to face, saw the Parsee; and hooped round by the gloom of the night they seemed the last men in a flooded world. "I have dreamed it again," said he.

"Of the hearses? Have I not said, old man, that neither hearse nor coffin can be thine?"

"And who are hearsed that die on the sea?"

"But I said, old man, that ere thou couldst die on this voyage, two hearses must verily be seen by thee on the sea; the first not made by mortal hands; and the visible wood of the last one must be grown in America."

"Aye, aye! a strange sight that, Parsee:—a hearse and its plumes floating over the ocean with the waves for the pall-bearers. Ha! Such a sight we shall not soon see."

"Believe it or not, thou canst not die till it be seen, old man."

"And what was that saying about thyself?"

"Though it come to the last, I shall still go before thee thy pilot."

"And when thou art so gone before—if that ever befall—then ere I can follow, thou must still appear to me, to pilot me still?—Was it not so? Well, then, did I believe all ye say, oh my pilot! I have here two pledges that I shall yet slay Moby Dick and survive it."

"Take another pledge, old man," said the Parsee, as his eyes lighted up like fire-flies in the gloom—"Hemp only can kill thee."

"The gallows, ye mean.—I am immortal then, on land and on sea," cried Ahab, with a laugh of derision;—"Immortal on land and on sea!"

Both were silent again, as one man. The grey dawn came on, and the slumbering crew arose from the boat's bottom, and ere noon the dead whale was brought to the ship.

Chapter 118

The Quadrant

The season for the Line at length drew near; and every day when Ahab, coming from his cabin, cast his eyes aloft, the vigilant helmsman would ostentatiously handle his spokes, and the eager mariners quickly run to the braces, and would stand there with all their eyes centrally fixed on the nailed doubloon; impatient for the order to point the ship's prow for the

---

1. In *Pseudodoxia Epidemica* 7.15, Sir Thomas Browne's name for the Dead Sea, the sites of Sodom and Gomorrah, destroyed by Jehovah for their wickedness (Genesis 19.24–25); the dark bituminous mineral asphalt is abundant there.

equator. In good time the order came. It was hard upon high noon; and Ahab, seated in the bows of his high-hoisted boat, was about taking his wonted daily observation of the sun to determine his latitude.

Now, sometimes, in that Japanese sea, the days in summer are as freshets of effulgences. That unblinkingly vivid Japanese sun seems the blazing focus of the glassy ocean's immeasurable burning-glass. The sky looks lacquered; clouds there are none; the horizon floats; and this naked-ness of unrelieved radiance is as the insufferable splendors of God's throne. Well that Ahab's quadrant was furnished with colored glasses, through which to take sight of that solar fire. So, swinging his seated form to the roll of the ship, and with his astrological-looking instrument placed to his eye, he remained in that posture for some moments to catch the precise instant when the sun should gain its precise meridian. Meantime while his whole attention was absorbed, the Parsee was kneeling beneath him on the ship's deck, and with face thrown up like Ahab's, was eyeing the same sun with him; only the lids of his eyes half hooded their orbs, and his wild face was subdued to an earthly passionlessness. At length the desired observation was taken; and with his pencil upon his ivory leg, Ahab soon calculated what his latitude must be at that precise instant. Then falling into a moment's revery, he again looked up towards the sun and murmured to himself: "Thou sea-mark! thou high and mighty Pilot! thou tellest me truly where I *am*—but canst thou cast the least hint where I *shall* be? Or canst thou tell where some other thing besides me is this moment living? Where is Moby Dick? This instant thou must be eyeing him. These eyes of mine look into the very eye that is even now behold-ing him; aye, and into the eye that is even now equally beholding the objects on the unknown, thither side of thee, thou sun!"

Then gazing at his quadrant, and handling, one after the other, its numerous cabalistical contrivances, he pondered again, and muttered: "Foolish toy! babies' plaything of haughty Admirals, and Commodores, and Captains; the world brags of thee, of thy cunning and might; but what after all canst thou do, but tell the poor, pitiful point, where thou thyself happenest to be on this wide planet, and the hand that holds thee: no! not one jot more! Thou canst not tell where one drop of water or one grain of sand will be to-morrow noon; and yet with thy impotence thou insultest the sun! Science! Curse thee, thou vain toy; and cursed be all the things that cast man's eyes aloft to that heaven, whose live vividness but scorches him, as these old eyes are even now scorched with thy light, O sun! Level by nature to this earth's horizon are the glances of man's eyes; not shot from the crown of his head, as if God had meant him to gaze on his fir-mament. Curse thee, thou quadrant!" dashing it to the deck, "no longer will I guide my earthly way by thee; the level ship's compass, and the level dead-reckoning, by log and by line; *these* shall conduct me, and show me my place on the sea. Aye," lighting from the boat to the deck, "thus I tram-ple on thee, thou paltry thing that feebly pointest on high; thus I split and destroy thee!"

As the frantic old man thus spoke and thus trampled with his live and dead feet, a sneering triumph that seemed meant for Ahab, and a fatalis-tic despair that seemed meant for himself—these passed over the mute, motionless Parsee's face. Unobserved he rose and glided away; while, awestruck by the aspect of their commander, the seamen clustered together on the forecastle, till Ahab, troubledly pacing the deck, shouted out—"To the braces! Up helm!—square in!"

In an instant the yards swung round; and as the ship half-wheeled upon her heel, her three firm-seated graceful masts erectly poised upon her long, ribbed hull, seemed as the three Horatii[1] pirouetting on one sufficient steed.

Standing between the knight-heads, Starbuck watched the Pequod's tumultuous way, and Ahab's also, as he went lurching along the deck.

"I have sat before the dense coal fire and watched it all aglow, full of its tormented flaming life; and I have seen it wane at last, down, down, to dumbest dust. Old man of oceans! of all this fiery life of thine, what will at length remain but one little heap of ashes!"

"Aye," cried Stubb, "but sea-coal ashes—mind ye that, Mr. Starbuck—sea-coal, not your common charcoal. Well, well; I heard Ahab mutter, 'Here some one thrusts these cards into these old hands of mine; swears that I must play them, and no others.' And damn me, Ahab, but thou actest right; live in the game, and die in it!"

Chapter 119

The Candles

Warmest climes but nurse the cruellest fangs: the tiger of Bengal crouches in spiced groves of ceaseless verdure. Skies the most effulgent but basket the deadliest thunders: gorgeous Cuba knows tornadoes that never swept tame northern lands. So, too, it is, that in these resplendent Japanese seas the mariner encounters the direst of all storms, the Typhoon. It will sometimes burst from out that cloudless sky, like an exploding bomb upon a dazed and sleepy town.

Towards evening of that day, the Pequod was torn of her canvas, and bare-poled was left to fight a Typhoon which had struck her directly ahead. When darkness came on, sky and sea roared and split with the thunder, and blazed with the lightning, that showed the disabled masts fluttering here and there with the rags which the first fury of the tempest had left for its after sport.

Holding by a shroud, Starbuck was standing on the quarter-deck; at every flash of the lightning glancing aloft, to see what additional disaster might have befallen the intricate hamper there; while Stubb and Flask were directing the men in the higher hoisting and firmer lashing of the boats. But all their pains seemed naught. Though lifted to the very top of the cranes, the windward quarter boat (Ahab's) did not escape. A great rolling sea, dashing high up against the reeling ship's high tetering side, stove in the boat's bottom at the stern, and left it again, all dripping through like a sieve.

"Bad work, bad work! Mr. Starbuck," said Stubb, regarding the wreck, "but the sea will have its way. Stubb, for one, can't fight it. You see, Mr.

---

1. Three warriors of early Rome who saved the city by defending a bridge—heroes of the popular poem in the *Lays of Ancient Rome* (1842) by Thomas Macaulay (1800–1859).

Starbuck, a wave has such a great long start before it leaps, all round the world it runs, and then comes the spring! But as for me, all the start I have to meet it, is just across the deck here. But never mind; it's all in fun: so the old song says;"—(sings.)

> Oh! jolly is the gale,
> And a joker is the whale,
> A' flourishin' his tail,—
Such a funny, sporty, gamy, jesty, joky, hoky-poky lad, is the Ocean, oh!

> The scud all a flyin',
> That's his flip only foamin';
> When he stirs in the spicin',—
Such a funny, sporty, gamy, jesty, joky, hoky-poky lad, is the Ocean, oh!

> Thunder splits the ships,
> But he only smacks his lips,
> A tastin' of this flip,—
Such a funny, sporty, gamy, jesty, joky, hoky-poky lad, is the Ocean, oh!

"Avast Stubb," cried Starbuck, "let the Typhoon sing, and strike his harp here in our rigging; but if thou art a brave man thou wilt hold thy peace."

"But I am not a brave man; never said I was a brave man; I am a coward; and I sing to keep up my spirits. And I tell you what it is, Mr. Starbuck, there's no way to stop my singing in this world but to cut my throat. And when that's done, ten to one I sing ye the doxology[1] for a wind-up."

"Madman! look through my eyes if thou hast none of thine own."

"What! how can you see better of a dark night than anybody else, never mind how foolish?"

"Here!" cried Starbuck, seizing Stubb by the shoulder, and pointing his hand towards the weather bow, "markest thou not that the gale comes from the eastward, the very course Ahab is to run for Moby Dick? the very course he swung to this day noon? now mark his boat there; where is that stove? In the stern-sheets, man; where he is wont to stand—his standpoint is stove, man! Now jump overboard, and sing away, if thou must!"

"I don't half understand ye: what's in the wind?"

"Yes, yes, round the Cape of Good Hope is the shortest way to Nantucket," soliloquized Starbuck suddenly, heedless of Stubb's question. "The gale that now hammers at us to stave us, we can turn it into a fair wind that will drive us towards home. Yonder, to windward, all is blackness of doom; but to leeward, homeward—I see it lightens up there; but not with the lightning."

At that moment in one of the intervals of profound darkness, following the flashes, a voice was heard at his side; and almost at the same instant a volley of thunder peals rolled overhead.

"Who's there?"

"Old Thunder!" said Ahab, groping his way along the bulwarks to his pivot-hole; but suddenly finding his path made plain to him by elbowed lances of fire.

---

1. From the Greek for giving praise: hymn of praise to God. In Protestant churches, commonly the hymn "Praise God from whom all blessings flow."

Now, as the lightning rod to a spire on shore is intended to carry off the perilous fluid into the soil; so the kindred rod which at sea some ships carry to each mast, is intended to conduct it into the water. But as this conductor must descend to considerable depth, that its end may avoid all contact with the hull; and as moreover, if kept constantly towing there, it would be liable to many mishaps, besides interfering not a little with some of the rigging, and more or less impeding the vessel's way in the water; because of all this, the lower parts of a ship's lightning-rods are not always overboard; but are generally made in long slender links, so as to be the more readily hauled up into the chains outside, or thrown down into the sea, as occasion may require.

"The rods! the rods!" cried Starbuck to the crew, suddenly admonished to vigilance by the vivid lightning that had just been darting flambeaux, to light Ahab to his post. "Are they overboard? drop them over, fore and aft. Quick!"

"Avast!" cried Ahab; "let's have fair play here, though we be the weaker side. Yet I'll contribute to raise rods on the Himmalehs and Andes, that all the world may be secured; but out on privileges! Let them be, sir."

"Look aloft!" cried Starbuck. "The corpusants! the corpusants!"[2]

All the yard-arms were tipped with a pallid fire; and touched at each tri-pointed lightning-rod-end with three tapering white flames, each of the three tall masts was silently burning in that sulphurous air, like three gigantic wax tapers before an altar.

"Blast the boat! let it go!" cried Stubb at this instant, as a swashing sea heaved up under his own little craft, so that its gunwale violently jammed his hand, as he was passing a lashing. "Blast it!"—but slipping backward on the deck, his uplifted eyes caught the flames; and immediately shifting his tone, he cried—"The corpusants have mercy on us all!"

To sailors, oaths are household words; they will swear in the trance of the calm, and in the teeth of the tempest; they will imprecate curses from the topsail-yard-arms, when most they teter over to a seething sea; but in all my voyagings, seldom have I heard a common oath when God's burning finger has been laid on the ship; when His "Mene, Mene, Tekel, Upharsin"[3] has been woven into the shrouds and the cordage.

While this pallidness was burning aloft, few words were heard from the enchanted crew; who in one thick cluster stood on the forecastle, all their eyes gleaming in that pale phosphorescence, like a far away constellation of stars. Relieved against the ghostly light, the gigantic jet negro, Daggoo, loomed up to thrice his real stature, and seemed the black cloud from which the thunder had come. The parted mouth of Tashtego revealed his shark-white teeth, which strangely gleamed as if they too had been tipped by corpusants; while lit up by the preternatural light, Queequeg's tattooing burned like Satanic blue flames on his body.

The tableau all waned at last with the pallidness aloft; and once more the Pequod and every soul on her decks were wrapped in a pall. A moment or two passed, when Starbuck, going forward, pushed against some one.

2. Balls of electricity in a ship's rigging, sources of superstitious awe in sailors.
3. As in ch. 99, cryptic words written by disembodied "fingers of a man's hand" on the wall of King Belshazzar's banquet hall (Daniel 5.25–28).

It was Stubb. "What thinkest thou now, man; I heard thy cry; it was not the same in the song."

"No, no, it wasn't; I said the corpusants have mercy on us all; and I hope they will, still. But do they only have mercy on long faces?—have they no bowels for a laugh? And look ye, Mr. Starbuck—but it's too dark to look. Hear me, then: I take that mast-head flame we saw for a sign of good luck; for those masts are rooted in a hold that is going to be chock a' block with sperm-oil, d'ye see; and so, all that sperm will work up into the masts, like sap in a tree. Yes, our three masts will yet be as three spermaceti candles—that's the good promise we saw."

At that moment Starbuck caught sight of Stubb's face slowly beginning to glimmer into sight. Glancing upwards, he cried: "See! see!" and once more the high tapering flames were beheld with what seemed redoubled supernaturalness in their pallor.

"The corpusants have mercy on us all," cried Stubb, again.

At the base of the mainmast, full beneath the doubloon and the flame, the Parsee was kneeling in Ahab's front, but with his head bowed away from him; while near by, from the arched and overhanging rigging, where they had just been engaged securing a spar, a number of the seamen, arrested by the glare, now cohered together, and hung pendulous, like a knot of numbed wasps from a drooping, orchard twig. In various enchanted attitudes, like the standing, or stepping, or running skeletons in Herculaneum,[4] others remained rooted to the deck; but all their eyes upcast.

"Aye, aye, men!" cried Ahab. "Look up at it; mark it well; the white flame but lights the way to the White Whale! Hand me those main-mast links there; I would fain feel this pulse, and let mine beat against it; blood against fire! So."

Then turning—the last link held fast in his left hand, he put his foot upon the Parsee; and with fixed upward eye, and high-flung right arm, he stood erect before the lofty tri-pointed trinity of flames.

"Oh! thou clear spirit of clear fire, whom on these seas I as Persian once did worship, till in the sacramental act so burned by thee, that to this hour I bear the scar; I now know thee, thou clear spirit, and I now know that thy right worship is defiance. To neither love nor reverence wilt thou be kind; and e'en for hate thou canst but kill; and all are killed. No fearless fool now fronts thee. I own thy speechless, placeless power; but to the last gasp of my earthquake life will dispute its unconditional, unintegral mastery in me. In the midst of the personified impersonal, a personality stands here. Though but a point at best; whencesoe'er I came; wheresoe'er I go; yet while I earthly live, the queenly personality lives in me, and feels her royal rights. But war is pain, and hate is woe. Come in thy lowest form of love, and I will kneel and kiss thee; but at thy highest, come as mere supernal power; and though thou launchest navies of full-freighted worlds, there's that in here that still remains indifferent. Oh, thou clear spirit, of thy fire thou madest me, and like a true child of fire, I breathe it back to thee."

4. Roman city buried in 79 C.E. along with Pompeii. Melville, like many in the young American republic, was enthralled with news of ongoing excavations in Italy (see the reference in ch. 86) and with historical and fictional accounts of the apocalyptic explosion of Vesuvius, such as *The Last Days of Pompeii* (1834) by Edward George Bulwer-Lytton (1803–1873).

(Sudden, repeated flashes of lightning; the nine flames leap lengthwise to thrice their previous height; Ahab, with the rest, closes his eyes, his right hand pressed hard upon them.)

"I own thy speechless, placeless power; said I not so? Nor was it wrung from me; nor do I now drop these links. Thou canst blind; but I can then grope. Thou canst consume; but I can then be ashes. Take the homage of these poor eyes, and shutter-hands. I would not take it. The lightning flashes through my skull; mine eye-balls ache and ache; my whole beaten brain seems as beheaded, and rolling on some stunning ground. Oh, oh! Yet blindfold, yet will I talk to thee. Light though thou be, thou leapest out of darkness; but I am darkness leaping out of light, leaping out of thee! The javelins cease; open eyes; see, or not? There burn the flames! Oh, thou magnanimous! now I do glory in my genealogy. But thou art but my fiery father; my sweet mother, I know not. Oh, cruel! what hast thou done with her? There lies my puzzle; but thine is greater. Thou knowest not how came ye, hence callest thyself unbegotten; certainly knowest not thy beginning, hence callest thyself unbegun. I know that of me, which thou knowest not of thyself, oh, thou omnipotent. There is some unsuffusing thing beyond thee, thou clear spirit, to whom all thy eternity is but time, all thy creativeness mechanical. Through thee, thy flaming self, my scorched eyes do dimly see it. Oh, thou foundling fire, thou hermit immemorial, thou too hast thy incommunicable riddle, thy unparticipated grief. Here again with haughty agony, I read my sire. Leap! leap up, and lick the sky! I leap with thee; I burn with thee; would fain be welded with thee; defyingly I worship thee!"

"The boat! the boat!" cried Starbuck, "look at thy boat, old man!"

Ahab's harpoon, the one forged at Perth's fire, remained firmly lashed in its conspicuous crotch, so that it projected beyond his whale-boat's bow; but the sea that had stove its bottom had caused the loose leather sheath to drop off; and from the keen steel barb there now came a levelled flame of pale, forked fire. As the silent harpoon burned there like a serpent's tongue, Starbuck grasped Ahab by the arm—"God, God is against thee, old man; forbear! 'tis an ill voyage! ill begun, ill continued; let me square the yards, while we may, old man, and make a fair wind of it homewards, to go on a better voyage than this."

Overhearing Starbuck, the panic-stricken crew instantly ran to the braces—though not a sail was left aloft. For the moment all the aghast mate's thoughts seemed theirs; they raised a half mutinous cry. But dashing the rattling lightning links to the deck, and snatching the burning harpoon, Ahab waved it like a torch among them; swearing to transfix with it the first sailor that but cast loose a rope's end. Petrified by his aspect, and still more shrinking from the fiery dart that he held, the men fell back in dismay, and Ahab again spoke:—

"All your oaths to hunt the White Whale are as binding as mine; and heart, soul, and body, lungs and life, old Ahab is bound. And that ye may know to what tune this heart beats; look ye here; thus I blow out the last fear!" And with one blast of his breath he extinguished the flame.

As in the hurricane that sweeps the plain, men fly the neighborhood of some lone, gigantic elm, whose very height and strength but render it so much the more unsafe, because so much the more a mark for thunder-bolts; so at those last words of Ahab's many of the mariners did run from him in a terror of dismay.

Chapter 120

The Deck towards the End of the First Night Watch

(Ahab standing by the helm. Starbuck approaching him.)

"We must send down the main-top-sail yard, sir. The band is working loose, and the lee lift is half-stranded. Shall I strike it, sir?"

"Strike nothing;[1] lash it. If I had sky-sail poles, I'd sway them up now."

"Sir?—in God's name!—sir?"

"Well."

"The anchors are working, sir. Shall I get them inboard?"

"Strike nothing, and stir nothing, but lash everything. The wind rises, but it has not got up to my table-lands yet. Quick, and see to it.—By masts and keels! he takes me for the hunchbacked skipper of some coasting smack. Send down my main-top-sail yard! Ho, gluepots![2] Loftiest trucks were made for wildest winds, and this brain-truck of mine now sails amid the cloud-scud. Shall I strike that? Oh, none but cowards send down their brain-trucks in tempest time. What a hooroosh aloft there! I would e'en take it for sublime, did I not know that the colic is a noisy malady. Oh, take medicine, take medicine!"

Chapter 121

Midnight—The Forecastle Bulwarks

(Stubb and Flask mounted on them, and passing additional lashings over the anchors there hanging.)

"No, Stubb; you may pound that knot there as much as you please, but you will never pound into me what you were just now saying. And how long ago is it since you said the very contrary? Didn't you once say that whatever ship Ahab sails in, that ship should pay something extra on its insurance policy, just as though it were loaded with powder barrels aft and boxes of lucifers forward? Stop, now; didn't you say so?"

"Well, suppose I did? What then? I've part changed my flesh since that time, why not my mind? Besides, supposing we *are* loaded with powder barrels aft and lucifers forward; how the devil could the lucifers get afire in this drenching spray here? Why, my little man, you have pretty red hair, but you couldn't get afire now. Shake yourself; you're Aquarius,[1] or the water-bearer, Flask; might fill pitchers at your coat collar. Don't you see,

1. Ahab rejects Starbuck's suggestion that they stop and work on securing the rigging.
2. Ahab calls for the yard not to be lowered but to be made more secure (as if glued).
1. Flask is so wet that Stubb calls him Aquarius, the zodiacal water bearer.

then, that for these extra risks the Marine Insurance companies have extra guarantees? Here are hydrants, Flask. But hark, again, and I'll answer ye the other thing. First take your leg off from the crown of the anchor here, though, so I can pass the rope; now listen. What's the mighty difference between holding a mast's lightning-rod in the storm, and standing close by a mast that hasn't got any lightning-rod at all in a storm? Don't you see, you timber-head, that no harm can come to the holder of the rod, unless the mast is first struck? What are you talking about, then? Not one ship in a hundred carries rods, and Ahab,—aye, man, and all of us,—were in no more danger then, in my poor opinion, than all the crews in ten thousand ships now sailing the seas. Why, you King-Post, you, I suppose you would have every man in the world go about with a small lightning-rod running up the corner of his hat, like a militia officer's skewered feather, and trailing behind like his sash. Why don't ye be sensible, Flask? it's easy to be sensible; why don't ye, then? any man with half an eye can be sensible."

"I don't know that, Stubb. You sometimes find it rather hard."

"Yes, when a fellow's soaked through, it's hard to be sensible, that's a fact. And I am about drenched with this spray. Never mind; catch the turn there, and pass it. Seems to me we are lashing down these anchors now as if they were never going to be used again. Tying these two anchors here, Flask, seems like tying a man's hands behind him. And what big generous hands they are, to be sure. These are your iron fists, hey? What a hold they have, too! I wonder, Flask, whether the world is anchored anywhere; if she is, she swings with an uncommon long cable, though. There, hammer that knot down, and we've done. So; next to touching land, lighting on deck is the most satisfactory. I say, just wring out my jacket skirts, will ye? Thank ye. They laugh at long-togs so, Flask; but seems to me, a long tailed coat ought always to be worn in all storms afloat. The tails tapering down that way, serve to carry off the water, d'ye see. Same with cocked hats; the cocks form gable-end eave-troughs, Flask. No more monkey-jackets and tarpaulins for me; I must mount a swallow-tail, and drive down a beaver;[2] so. Halloa! whew! there goes my tarpaulin overboard; Lord, Lord, that the winds that come from heaven should be so unmannerly! This is a nasty night, lad."

Chapter 122

Midnight Aloft—Thunder and Lightning

(The Main-top-sail yard.—Tashtego passing new lashings around it.)

"Um, um, um. Stop that thunder! Plenty too much thunder up here. What's the use of thunder? Um, um, um. We don't want thunder; we want rum; give us a glass of rum. Um, um, um!"

---

2. Flask says he must don formal wear instead of his usual monkey jacket and tarpaulin hat.

Chapter 123

The Musket

During the most violent shocks of the Typhoon, the man at the Pequod's jaw-bone tiller had several times been reelingly hurled to the deck by its spasmodic motions, even though preventer tackles[1] had been attached to it—for they were slack—because some play to the tiller was indispensable.

In a severe gale like this, while the ship is but a tossed shuttle-cock to the blast, it is by no means uncommon to see the needles in the compasses, at intervals, go round and round. It was thus with the Pequod's; at almost every shock the helmsman had not failed to notice the whirling velocity with which they revolved upon the cards; it is a sight that hardly any one can behold without some sort of unwonted emotion.

Some hours after midnight, the Typhoon abated so much, that through the strenuous exertions of Starbuck and Stubb—one engaged forward and the other aft—the shivered remnants of the jib and fore and main-top-sails were cut adrift from the spars, and went eddying away to leeward, like the feathers of an albatross, which sometimes are cast to the winds when that storm-tossed bird is on the wing.

The three corresponding new sails were now bent and reefed, and a storm-trysail was set further aft; so that the ship soon went through the water with some precision again; and the course—for the present, East-south-east—which he was to steer, if practicable, was once more given to the helmsman. For during the violence of the gale, he had only steered according to its vicissitudes. But as he was now bringing the ship as near her course as possible, watching the compass meanwhile, lo! a good sign! the wind seemed coming round astern; aye, the foul breeze became fair!

Instantly the yards were squared, to the lively song of *"Ho! the fair wind! oh-he-yo, cheerly, men!"* the crew singing for joy, that so promising an event should so soon have falsified the evil portents preceding it.

In compliance with the standing order of his commander—to report immediately, and at any one of the twenty-four hours, any decided change in the affairs of the deck,—Starbuck had no sooner trimmed the yards to the breeze—however reluctantly and gloomily,—than he mechanically went below to apprise Captain Ahab of the circumstance.

Ere knocking at his state-room, he involuntarily paused before it a moment. The cabin lamp—taking long swings this way and that—was burning fitfully, and casting fitful shadows upon the old man's bolted door,—a thin one, with fixed blinds inserted, in place of upper panels. The isolated subterraneousness of the cabin made a certain humming silence to reign there, though it was hooped round by all the roar of the elements. The loaded muskets in the rack were shiningly revealed, as they stood upright against the forward bulkhead. Starbuck was an honest, upright man; but out of Starbuck's heart, at that instant when he saw the muskets, there strangely evolved an evil thought; but so blent with its neutral or good accompaniments that for the instant he hardly knew it for itself.

---

1. Supporting ropes and pulleys. The *Pequod* is said to be steered by a wheel at times, a tiller at others, as here.

"He would have shot me once," he murmured, "yes, there's the very musket that he pointed at me;—that one with the studded stock; let me touch it—lift it. Strange, that I, who have handled so many deadly lances, strange, that I should shake so now. Loaded? I must see. Aye, aye; and powder in the pan;—that's not good. Best spill it?—wait. I'll cure myself of this. I'll hold the musket boldly while I think.—I come to report a fair wind to him. But how fair? Fair for death and doom,—*that's* fair for Moby Dick. It's a fair wind that's only fair for that accursed fish.—The very tube he pointed at me!—the very one; *this* one—I hold it here; he would have killed me with the very thing I handle now.—Aye and he would fain kill all his crew. Does he not say he will not strike his spars to any gale? Has he not dashed his heavenly quadrant? and in these same perilous seas, gropes he not his way by mere dead reckoning of the error-abounding log? and in this very Typhoon, did he not swear that he would have no light-ning-rods? But shall this crazed old man be tamely suffered to drag a whole ship's company down to doom with him?—Yes, it would make him the wilful murderer of thirty men and more, if this ship come to any deadly harm; and come to deadly harm, my soul swears this ship will, if Ahab have his way. If, then, he were this instant—put aside, that crime would not be his. Ha! is he muttering in his sleep? Yes, just there,—in there, he's sleeping. Sleeping? aye, but still alive, and soon awake again. I can't withstand thee, then, old man. Not reasoning; not remonstrance; not entreaty wilt thou hearken to; all this thou scornest. Flat obedience to thy own flat commands, this is all thou breathest. Aye, and say'st the men have vow'd thy vow; say'st all of us are Ahabs. Great God forbid!—But is there no other way? no lawful way?—Make him a prisoner to be taken home? What! hope to wrest this old man's living power from his own liv-ing hands? Only a fool would try it. Say he were pinioned even; knotted all over with ropes and hawsers; chained down to ring-bolts on this cabin floor; he would be more hideous than a caged tiger, then. I could not endure the sight; could not possibly fly his howlings; all comfort, sleep itself, inestimable reason would leave me on the long intolerable voyage. What, then, remains? The land is hundreds of leagues away, and locked Japan the nearest. I stand alone here upon an open sea, with two oceans and a whole continent between me and law.—Aye, aye, 'tis so.—Is heaven a murderer when its lightning strikes a would-be murderer in his bed, tin-dering sheets and skin together?—And would I be a murderer, then, if"—
——and slowly, stealthily, and half sideways looking, he placed the loaded musket's end against the door.

"On this level, Ahab's hammock swings within; his head this way. A touch, and Starbuck may survive to hug his wife and child again.—Oh Mary! Mary!—boy! boy! boy!—But if I wake thee not to death, old man, who can tell to what unsounded deeps Starbuck's body this day week may sink, with all the crew! Great God, where art thou? Shall I? shall I?——
—The wind has gone down and shifted, sir; the fore and main topsails are reefed and set; she heads her course."

"Stern all! Oh Moby Dick, I clutch thy heart at last!"

Such were the sounds that now came hurtling from out the old man's tormented sleep, as if Starbuck's voice had caused the long dumb dream to speak.

The yet levelled musket shook like a drunkard's arm against the panel; Starbuck seemed wrestling with an angel;[2] but turning from the door, he placed the death-tube in its rack, and left the place.

"He's too sound asleep, Mr. Stubb; go thou down, and wake him, and tell him. I must see to the deck here. Thou know'st what to say."

Chapter 124

The Needle[1]

Next morning the not-yet-subsided sea rolled in long slow billows of mighty bulk, and striving in the Pequod's gurgling track, pushed her on like giants' palms outspread. The strong, unstaggering breeze abounded so, that sky and air seemed vast outbellying sails; the whole world boomed before the wind. Muffled in the full morning light, the invisible sun was only known by the spread intensity of his place; where his bayonet rays moved on in stacks. Emblazonings, as of crowned Babylonian kings and queens, reigned over everything. The sea was as a crucible of molten gold, that bubblingly leaps with light and heat.

Long maintaining an enchanted silence, Ahab stood apart; and every time the tetering ship loweringly pitched down her bowsprit, he turned to eye the bright sun's rays produced ahead; and when she profoundly settled by the stern, he turned behind, and saw the sun's rearward place, and how the same yellow rays were blending with his undeviating wake.

"Ha, ha, my ship! thou mightest well be taken now for the sea-chariot of the sun. Ho, ho! all ye nations before my prow, I bring the sun to ye! Yoke on the further billows; hallo! a tandem, I drive the sea!"

But suddenly reined back by some counter thought, he hurried towards the helm, huskily demanding how the ship was heading.

"East-sou-east, sir," said the frightened steersman.

"Thou liest!" smiting him with his clenched fist. "Heading East at this hour in the morning, and the sun astern?"

Upon this every soul was confounded; for the phenomenon just then observed by Ahab had unaccountably escaped every one else; but its very blinding palpableness must have been the cause.

Thrusting his head half way into the binnacle, Ahab caught one glimpse of the compasses; his uplifted arm slowly fell; for a moment he almost seemed to stagger. Standing behind him Starbuck looked, and lo! the two compasses pointed East, and the Pequod was as infallibly going West.

But ere the first wild alarm could get out abroad among the crew, the old man with a rigid laugh exclaimed, "I have it! It has happened before. Mr. Starbuck, last night's thunder turned our compasses—that's all. Thou hast before now heard of such a thing, I take it."

"Aye; but never before has it happened to me, sir," said the pale mate, gloomily.

2. Jacob wrestled until daylight with an angel in Genesis 32.24–32. Here, Starbuck resists an apparently evil angel who tempts him to shoot Ahab.
1. Melville "built up" this chapter from Scoresby's *Journal of a Voyage to the Northern Whale-Fishery* (1823), according to Mansfield and Vincent (823).

Here, it must needs be said, that accidents like this have in more than one case occurred to ships in violent storms. The magnetic energy, as developed in the mariner's needle, is, as all know, essentially one with the electricity beheld in heaven; hence it is not to be much marvelled at, that such things should be. In instances where the lightning has actually struck the vessel, so as to smite down some of the spars and rigging, the effect upon the needle has at times been still more fatal; all its loadstone virtue being annihilated, so that the before magnetic steel was of no more use than an old wife's knitting needle. But in either case, the needle never again, of itself, recovers the original virtue thus marred or lost; and if the binnacle compasses be affected, the same fate reaches all the others that may be in the ship; even were the lowermost one inserted into the kelson.

Deliberately standing before the binnacle, and eyeing the transpointed compasses, the old man, with the sharp of his extended hand, now took the precise bearing of the sun, and satisfied that the needles were exactly inverted, shouted out his orders for the ship's course to be changed accordingly. The yards were braced hard up; and once more the Pequod thrust her undaunted bows into the opposing wind, for the supposed fair one had only been juggling[2] her.

Meanwhile, whatever were his own secret thoughts, Starbuck said nothing, but quietly he issued all requisite orders; while Stubb and Flask—who in some small degree seemed then to be sharing his feelings—likewise unmurmuringly acquiesced. As for the men, though some of them lowly rumbled, their fear of Ahab was greater than their fear of Fate. But as ever before, the pagan harpooneers remained almost wholly unimpressed; or if impressed, it was only with a certain magnetism shot into their congenial hearts from inflexible Ahab's.

For a space the old man walked the deck in rolling reveries. But chancing to slip with his ivory heel, he saw the crushed copper sight-tubes of the quadrant he had the day before dashed to the deck.

"Thou poor, proud heaven-gazer and sun's pilot! yesterday I wrecked thee, and to-day the compasses would feign have wrecked me. So, so. But Ahab is lord over the level loadstone[3] yet. Mr. Starbuck—a lance without the pole; a top-maul, and the smallest of the sail-maker's needles. Quick!"

Accessory, perhaps, to the impulse dictating the thing he was now about to do, were certain prudential motives, whose object might have been to revive the spirits of his crew by a stroke of his subtile skill, in a matter so wondrous as that of the inverted compasses. Besides, the old man well knew that to steer by transpointed needles, though clumsily practicable, was not a thing to be passed over by superstitious sailors, without some shudderings and evil portents.

"Men," said he, steadily turning upon the crew, as the mate handed him the things he had demanded, "my men, the thunder turned old Ahab's needles; but out of this bit of steel Ahab can make one of his own, that will point as true as any."

Abashed glances of servile wonder were exchanged by the sailors, as

2. Tricking (as in the juggling fiends who are no more to be believed, *Macbeth* 5.8.19).
3. Ahab boasts that he can make the magnetic compass ("loadstone") obey him. *Above:* "feign": fain.

this was said; and with fascinated eyes they awaited whatever magic might follow. But Starbuck looked away.

With a blow from the top-maul Ahab knocked off the steel head of the lance, and then handing to the mate the long iron rod remaining, bade him hold it upright, without its touching the deck. Then, with the maul, after repeatedly smiting the upper end of this iron rod, he placed the blunted needle endwise on the top of it, and less strongly hammered that, several times, the mate still holding the rod as before. Then going through some small strange motions with it—whether indispensable to the magnetizing of the steel, or merely intended to augment the awe of the crew, is uncertain—he called for linen thread; and moving to the binnacle, slipped out the two reversed needles there, and horizontally suspended the sail-needle by its middle, over one of the compass-cards. At first, the steel went round and round, quivering and vibrating at either end; but at last it settled to its place, when Ahab, who had been intently watching for this result, stepped frankly back from the binnacle, and pointing his stretched arm towards it, exclaimed,—"Look ye, for yourselves, if Ahab be not lord of the level loadstone! The sun is East, and that compass swears it!"

One after another they peered in, for nothing but their own eyes could persuade such ignorance as theirs, and one after another they slunk away.

In his fiery eyes of scorn and triumph, you then saw Ahab in all his fatal pride.

Chapter 125

The Log and Line

While now the fated Pequod had been so long afloat this voyage, the log and line had but very seldom been in use. Owing to a confident reliance upon other means of determining the vessel's place, some merchantmen, and many whalemen, especially when cruising, wholly neglect to heave the log; though at the same time, and frequently more for form's sake than anything else, regularly putting down upon the customary slate the course steered by the ship, as well as the presumed average rate of progression every hour. It had been thus with the Pequod. The wooden reel and angular log attached hung, long untouched, just beneath the railing of the after bulwarks. Rains and spray had damped it; sun and wind had warped it; all the elements had combined to rot a thing that hung so idly. But heedless of all this, his mood seized Ahab, as he happened to glance upon the reel, not many hours after the magnet scene, and he remembered how his quadrant was no more, and recalled his frantic oath about the level log and line. The ship was sailing plungingly; astern the billows rolled in riots.

"Forward, there! Heave the log!"

Two seamen came. The golden-hued Tahitian and the grizzly Manxman. "Take the reel, one of ye, I'll heave."

They went towards the extreme stern, on the ship's lee side, where the deck, with the oblique energy of the wind, was now almost dipping into the creamy, sidelong-rushing sea.

The Manxman took the reel, and holding it high up, by the projecting handle-ends of the spindle, round which the spool of line revolved, so stood with the angular log hanging downwards, till Ahab advanced to him.

Ahab stood before him, and was lightly unwinding some thirty or forty turns to form a preliminary hand-coil to toss overboard, when the old Manxman, who was intently eyeing both him and the line, made bold to speak.

"Sir, I mistrust it; this line looks far gone, long heat and wet have spoiled it."

"'Twill hold, old gentleman. Long heat and wet, have they spoiled thee? Thou seem'st to hold. Or, truer perhaps, life holds thee; not thou it."

"I hold the spool, sir. But just as my captain says. With these grey hairs of mine 'tis not worth while disputing, 'specially with a superior, who'll ne'er confess."

"What's that? There now's a patched professor in Queen Nature's gran ite-founded College; but methinks he's too subservient. Where wert thou born?"

"In the little rocky Isle of Man, sir."

"Excellent! Thou'st hit the world by that."

"I know not, sir, but I was born there."

"In the Isle of Man, hey? Well, the other way, it's good. Here's a man from Man; a man born in once independent Man, and now unmanned of Man; which is sucked in—by what? Up with the reel! The dead, blind wall butts all inquiring heads at last. Up with it! So."

The log was heaved. The loose coils rapidly straightened out in a long dragging line astern, and then, instantly, the reel began to whirl. In turn, jerkingly raised and lowered by the rolling billows, the towing resistance of the log caused the old reelman to stagger strangely.

"Hold hard!"

Snap! the overstrained line sagged down in one long festoon; the tugging log was gone.

"I crush the quadrant, the thunder turns the needles, and now the mad sea parts the log-line. But Ahab can mend all. Haul in here, Tahitian; reel up, Manxman. And look ye, let the carpenter make another log, and mend thou the line. See to it."

"There he goes now; to him nothing's happened; but to me, the skewer seems loosening out of the middle of the world. Haul in, haul in, Tahitian! These lines run whole, and whirling out: come in broken, and dragging slow. Ha, Pip? come to help; eh, Pip?"

"Pip? whom call ye Pip? Pip jumped from the whale-boat. Pip's missing. Let's see now if ye haven't fished him up here, fisherman. It drags hard; I guess he's holding on. Jerk him, Tahiti! Jerk him off; we haul in no cowards here. Ho! there's his arm just breaking water. A hatchet! a hatchet! cut it off—we haul in no cowards here. Captain Ahab! sir, sir! here's Pip, trying to get on board again."

"Peace, thou crazy loon," cried the Manxman, seizing him by the arm. "Away from the quarter-deck!"

"The greater idiot ever scolds the lesser," muttered Ahab, advancing. "Hands off from that holiness! Where sayest thou Pip was, boy?"

"Astern there, sir, astern! Lo, lo!"

"And who art thou, boy? I see not my reflection in the vacant pupils of thy eyes. Oh God! that man should be a thing for immortal souls to sieve through! Who art thou, boy?"

"Bell-boy, sir; ship's-crier;[1] ding, dong, ding! Pip! Pip! Pip! Reward for Pip! One hundred pounds of clay—five feet high—looks cowardly—quickest known by that! Ding, dong, ding! Who's seen Pip the coward?"

"There can be no hearts above the snow-line. Oh, ye frozen heavens! look down here. Ye did beget this luckless child, and have abandoned him, ye creative libertines. Here, boy; Ahab's cabin shall be Pip's home henceforth, while Ahab lives. Thou touchest my inmost centre, boy; thou art tied to me by cords woven of my heart-strings. Come, let's down."

"What's this? here's velvet shark-skin," intently gazing at Ahab's hand, and feeling it. "Ah, now, had poor Pip but felt so kind a thing as this, perhaps he had ne'er been lost! This seems to me, sir, as a man-rope; something that weak souls may hold by. Oh, sir, let old Perth now come and rivet these two hands together; the black one with the white, for I will not let this go."

"Oh, boy, nor will I thee, unless I should thereby drag thee to worse horrors than are here. Come, then, to my cabin. Lo! ye believers in gods all goodness, and in man all ill, lo you! see the omniscient gods oblivious of suffering man; and man, though idiotic, and knowing not what he does, yet full of the sweet things of love and gratitude. Come! I feel prouder leading thee by thy black hand, than though I grasped an Emperor's!"

"There go two daft ones now," muttered the old Manxman. "One daft with strength, the other daft with weakness. But here's the end of the rotten line—all dripping, too. Mend it, eh? I think we had best have a new line altogether. I'll see Mr. Stubb about it."

Chapter 126

The Life-Buoy

Steering now south-eastward by Ahab's levelled steel, and her progress solely determined by Ahab's level log and line; the Pequod held on her path towards the Equator. Making so long a passage through such unfrequented waters, descrying no ships, and ere long, sideways impelled by unvarying trade winds, over waves monotonously mild; all these seemed the strange calm things preluding some riotous and desperate scene.

At last, when the ship drew near to the outskirts, as it were, of the Equatorial fishing-ground, and in the deep darkness that goes before the dawn, was sailing by a cluster of rocky islets; the watch—then headed by Flask—was started by a cry so plaintively wild and unearthly—like half-articulated wailings of the ghosts of all Herod's murdered Innocents[1]—that one and all, they started from their reveries, and for the

1. Like the official hired to "cry" (call out) news in a town.
1. The male children two years old or younger whom King Herod slew "in Bethlehem, and in all coasts thereof" in his attempt to kill the young Jesus (Matthew 2.16). Mansfield and Vincent (824) point out that "the episode of the seal cry" was developed from Colnett's A Voyage to the South Atlantic and Round Cape Horn (1798).

space of some moments stood, or sat, or leaned all transfixedly listening, like the carved Roman slave, while that wild cry remained within hearing. The Christian or civilized part of the crew said it was mermaids, and shuddered; but the pagan harpooneers remained unappalled. Yet the grey Manxman—the oldest mariner of all—declared that the wild thrilling sounds that were heard, were the voices of newly drowned men in the sea.

Below in his hammock, Ahab did not hear of this till grey dawn, when he came to the deck; it was then recounted to him by Flask, not unaccompanied with hinted dark meanings. He hollowly laughed, and thus explained the wonder.

Those rocky islands the ship had passed were the resort of great numbers of seals, and some young seals that had lost their dams, or some dams that had lost their cubs, must have risen nigh the ship and kept company with her, crying and sobbing with their human sort of wail. But this only the more affected some of them, because most mariners cherish a very superstitious feeling about seals, arising not only from their peculiar tones when in distress, but also from the human look of their round heads and semi-intelligent faces, seen peeringly uprising from the water alongside. In the sea, under certain circumstances, seals have more than once been mistaken for men.

But the bodings of the crew were destined to receive a most plausible confirmation in the fate of one of their number that morning. At sun-rise this man went from his hammock to his mast-head at the fore; and whether it was that he was not yet half waked from his sleep (for sailors sometimes go aloft in a transition state), whether it was thus with the man, there is now no telling; but, be that as it may, he had not been long at his perch, when a cry was heard—a cry and a rushing—and looking up, they saw a falling phantom in the air; and looking down, a little tossed heap of white bubbles in the blue of the sea.

The life-buoy—a long slender cask—was dropped from the stern, where it always hung obedient to a cunning spring; but no hand rose to seize it, and the sun having long beat upon this cask it had shrunken, so that it slowly filled, and the parched wood also filled at its every pore; and the studded iron-bound cask followed the sailor to the bottom, as if to yield him his pillow, though in sooth but a hard one.

And thus the first man of the Pequod that mounted the mast to look out for the White Whale, on the White Whale's own peculiar ground; that man was swallowed up in the deep. But few, perhaps, thought of that at the time. Indeed, in some sort, they were not grieved at this event, at least as a portent; for they regarded it, not as a foreshadowing of evil in the future, but as the fulfilment of an evil already presaged. They declared that now they knew the reason of those wild shrieks they had heard the night before. But again the old Manxman said nay.

The lost life-buoy was now to be replaced; Starbuck was directed to see to it; but as no cask of sufficient lightness could be found, and as in the feverish eagerness of what seemed the approaching crisis of the voyage, all hands were impatient of any toil but what was directly connected with its final end, whatever that might prove to be; therefore, they were going to leave the ship's stern unprovided with a buoy, when by certain strange signs and inuendoes Queequeg hinted a hint concerning his coffin.

"A life-buoy of a coffin!" cried Starbuck, starting.

"Rather queer, that, I should say," said Stubb.

"It will make a good enough one," said Flask, "the carpenter here can arrange it easily."

"Bring it up; there's nothing else for it," said Starbuck, after a melancholy pause. "Rig it, carpenter; do not look at me so—the coffin, I mean. Dost thou hear me? Rig it."

"And shall I nail down the lid, sir?" moving his hand as with a hammer.

"Aye."

"And shall I caulk the seams, sir?" moving his hand as with a caulking-iron.

"Aye."

"And shall I then pay over the same with pitch, sir?" moving his hands as with a pitch-pot.

"Away! what possesses thee to this? Make a life-buoy of the coffin, and no more.—Mr. Stubb, Mr. Flask, come forward with me."

"He goes off in a huff. The whole he can endure; at the parts he baulks. Now I don't like this. I make a leg for Captain Ahab, and he wears it like a gentleman; but I make a bandbox for Queequeg, and he wont put his head into it. Are all my pains to go for nothing with that coffin? And now I'm ordered to make a life-buoy of it. It's like turning an old coat; going to bring the flesh on the other side now. I don't like this cobbling sort of business—I don't like it at all; it's undignified; it's not my place. Let tinkers' brats do tinkerings; we are their betters. I like to take in hand none but clean, virgin, fair-and-square mathematical jobs, something that regularly begins at the beginning, and is at the middle when midway, and comes to an end at the conclusion; not a cobbler's job, that's at an end in the middle, and at the beginning at the end. It's the old woman's tricks to be giving cobbling jobs. Lord! what an affection all old women have for tinkers. I know an old woman of sixty-five who ran away with a bald-headed young tinker once. And that's the reason I never would work for lonely widow old women ashore, when I kept my job-shop in the Vineyard; they might have taken it into their lonely old heads to run off with me. But heigh-ho! there are no caps at sea but snow-caps. Let me see. Nail down the lid; caulk the seams; pay over the same with pitch; batten them down tight, and hang it with the snap-spring over the ship's stern. Were ever such things done before with a coffin? Some superstitious old carpenters, now, would be tied up in the rigging, ere they would do the job. But I'm made of knotty Aroostook hemlock; I don't budge. Cruppered[2] with a coffin! Sailing about with a grave-yard tray! But never mind. We workers in woods make bridal-bedsteads and card-tables, as well as coffins and hearses. We work by the month, or by the job, or by the profit; not for us to ask the why and wherefore of our work, unless it be too confounded cobbling, and then we stash it if we can. Hem! I'll do the job, now, tenderly. I'll have

---

2. *Crupper:* rear part of a horse's harness. *Tied up:* punished thus for refusing to make a coffin. *Aroostook:* county in northern Maine.

me—let's see—how many in the ship's company, all told? But I've forgotten. Any way, I'll have me thirty separate, Turk's-headed life-lines,[3] each three feet long hanging all round to the coffin. Then, if the hull go down, there'll be thirty lively fellows all fighting for one coffin, a sight not seen very often beneath the sun! Come hammer, calking-iron, pitchpot, and marling-spike! Let's to it."

Chapter 127

The Deck

(The coffin laid upon two line-tubs, between the vice-bench and the open hatchway; the Carpenter calking its seams; the string of twisted oakum slowly unwinding from a large roll of it placed in the bosom of his frock.—Ahab comes slowly from the cabin-gangway, and hears Pip following him.)

"Back, lad; I will be with ye again presently. He goes! Not this hand complies with my humor more genially than that boy.—Middle aisle of a church![1] What's here?"

"Life-buoy, sir. Mr. Starbuck's orders. Oh, look, sir! Beware the hatchway!"

"Thank ye, man. Thy coffin lies handy to the vault."

"Sir? The hatchway? oh! So it does, sir, so it does."

"Art not thou the leg-maker? Look, did not this stump come from thy shop?"

"I believe it did, sir; does the ferrule stand, sir?"

"Well enough. But art thou not also the undertaker?"

"Aye, sir; I patched up this thing here as a coffin for Queequeg; but they've set me now to turning it into something else."

"Then tell me; art thou not an arrant, all-grasping, intermeddling, monopolizing, heathenish old scamp, to be one day making legs, and the next day coffins to clap them in, and yet again life-buoys out of those same coffins? Thou art as unprincipled as the gods, and as much of a jack-of-all-trades."

"But I do not mean anything, sir. I do as I do."

"The gods again. Hark ye, dost thou not ever sing working about a coffin? The Titans, they say, hummed snatches when chipping out the craters for volcanoes; and the grave-digger in the play[2] sings, spade in hand. Dost thou never?"

"Sing, sir? Do I sing? Oh, I'm indifferent enough, sir, for that; but the reason why the grave-digger made music must have been because there was none in his spade, sir. But the calking mallet is full of it. Hark to it."

"Aye, and that's because the lid there's a sounding-board; and what in all things makes the sounding-board is this—there's naught beneath. And yet, a coffin with a body in it rings pretty much the same, Carpenter. Hast

---

3. Ropes ending in large tight elaborate knots, for good grasping.
1. Ahab sees the deck as the middle aisle of a church, where the coffin is placed at funerals.
2. *Hamlet* 5.1.61 (and later).

thou ever helped carry a bier, and heard the coffin knock against the church-yard gate, going in?"

"Faith, sir, I've————"

"Faith? What's that?"

"Why, faith, sir, it's only a sort of exclamation-like—that's all, sir."

"Um, um; go on."

"I was about to say, sir, that————"

"Art thou a silk-worm? Dost thou spin thy own shroud out of thyself? Look at thy bosom! Despatch! and get these traps out of sight."

"He goes aft. That was sudden, now; but squalls come sudden in hot latitudes. I've heard that the Isle of Albemarle, one of the Gallipagos, is cut by the Equator right in the middle. Seems to me some sort of Equator cuts yon old man, too, right in his middle. He's always under the Line—fiery hot, I tell ye! He's looking this way—come, oakum; quick. Here we go again. This wooden mallet is the cork, and I'm the professor of musical glasses—tap, tap!"

(Ahab to himself.)

"There's a sight! There's a sound! The greyheaded woodpecker tapping the hollow tree! Blind and deaf might well be envied now. See! that thing rests on two line-tubs, full of tow-lines. A most malicious wag, that fellow. Rat-tat! So man's seconds tick! Oh! how immaterial are all materials! What things real are there, but imponderable thoughts? Here now's the very dreaded symbol of grim death, by a mere hap, made the expressive sign of the help and hope of most endangered life. A life-buoy of a coffin! Does it go further? Can it be that in some spiritual sense the coffin is, after all, but an immortality-preserver! I'll think of that. But no. So far gone am I in the dark side of earth, that its other side, the theoretic bright one, seems but uncertain twilight to me. Will ye never have done, Carpenter, with that accursed sound? I go below; let me not see that thing here when I return again. Now, then, Pip, we'll talk this over; I do suck most wondrous philosophies from thee! Some unknown conduits from the unknown worlds must empty into thee!"

Chapter 128

The Pequod meets the Rachel

Next day, a large ship, the Rachel,[1] was descried, bearing directly down upon the Pequod, all her spars thickly clustering with men. At the time the Pequod was making good speed through the water; but as the broad-winged windward stranger shot nigh to her, the boastful sails all fell together as blank bladders that are burst, and all life fled from the smitten hull.

---

1. The ship's name recalls Jeremiah 31.15, where "Rachel" is not used to mean the beautiful wife of Jacob but to mean (symbolically) the mother of the Hebrews: "A voice was heard in Ramah, lamentation, and bitter weeping; Rachel weeping for her children refused to be comforted for her children, because they were not."

"Bad news; she brings bad news," muttered the old Manxman. But ere her commander, who, with trumpet to mouth, stood up in his boat; ere he could hopefully hail, Ahab's voice was heard.

"Hast seen the White Whale?"

"Aye, yesterday. Have ye seen a whale-boat adrift?"

Throttling his joy, Ahab negatively answered this unexpected question; and would then have fain boarded the stranger, when the stranger captain himself, having stopped his vessel's way, was seen descending her side. A few keen pulls, and his boat-hook soon clinched the Pequod's main-chains, and he sprang to the deck. Immediately he was recognised by Ahab for a Nantucketer he knew. But no formal salutation was exchanged.

"Where was he?—not killed!—not killed!" cried Ahab, closely advancing. "How was it?"

It seemed that somewhat late on the afternoon of the day previous, while three of the stranger's boats were engaged with a shoal of whales, which had led them some four or five miles from the ship; and while they were yet in swift chase to windward, the white hump and head of Moby Dick had suddenly loomed up out of the blue water, not very far to leeward; whereupon, the fourth rigged boat—a reserved one—had been instantly lowered in chase. After a keen sail before the wind, this fourth boat—the swiftest keeled of all—seemed to have succeeded in fastening—at least, as well as the man at the mast-head could tell anything about it. In the distance he saw the diminished dotted boat; and then a swift gleam of bubbling white water; and after that nothing more; whence it was concluded that the stricken whale must have indefinitely run away with his pursuers, as often happens. There was some apprehension, but no positive alarm, as yet. The recall signals were placed in the rigging; darkness came on; and forced to pick up her three far to windward boats—ere going in quest of the fourth one in the precisely opposite direction—the ship had not only been necessitated to leave that boat to its fate till near midnight, but, for the time, to increase her distance from it. But the rest of her crew being at last safe aboard, she crowded all sail—stunsail on stunsail—after the missing boat; kindling a fire in her try-pots for a beacon; and every other man aloft on the look-out. But though when she had thus sailed a sufficient distance to gain the presumed place of the absent ones when last seen; though she then paused to lower her spare boats to pull all around her; and not finding anything, had again dashed on; again paused, and lowered her boats; and though she had thus continued doing till day light; yet not the least glimpse of the missing keel had been seen.

The story told, the stranger Captain immediately went on to reveal his object in boarding the Pequod. He desired that ship to unite with his own in the search; by sailing over the sea some four or five miles apart, on parallel lines, and so sweeping a double horizon, as it were.

"I will wager something now," whispered Stubb to Flask, "that some one in that missing boat wore off that Captain's best coat; mayhap, his watch—he's so cursed anxious to get it back. Who ever heard of two pious whale-ships cruising after one missing whale-boat in the height of the whaling season? See, Flask, only see how pale he looks—pale in the very buttons of his eyes—look—it wasn't the coat—it must have been the—"

"My boy, my own boy is among them. For God's sake—I beg, I conjure"—here exclaimed the stranger Captain to Ahab, who thus far had but icily received his petition. "For eight-and-forty hours let me charter your ship—I will gladly pay for it, and roundly pay for it—if there be no other way—for eight-and-forty hours only—only that—you must, oh, you must, and you *shall* do this thing."

"His son!" cried Stubb, "oh, it's his son he's lost! I take back the coat and watch—what says Ahab? We must save that boy."

"He's drowned with the rest on 'em, last night," said the old Manx sailor standing behind them; "I heard; all of ye heard their spirits."

Now, as it shortly turned out, what made this incident of the Rachel's the more melancholy, was the circumstance, that not only was one of the Captain's sons among the number of the missing boat's crew; but among the number of the other boats' crews, at the same time, but on the other hand, separated from the ship during the dark vicissitudes of the chase, there had been still another son; as that for a time, the wretched father was plunged to the bottom of the cruellest perplexity; which was only solved for him by his chief mate's instinctively adopting the ordinary procedure of a whale-ship in such emergencies, that is, when placed between jeopardized but divided boats, always to pick up the majority first. But the captain, for some unknown constitutional reason, had refrained from mentioning all this, and not till forced to it by Ahab's iciness did he allude to his one yet missing boy; a little lad, but twelve years old, whose father with the earnest but unmisgiving hardihood of a Nantucketer's paternal love, had thus early sought to initiate him in the perils and wonders of a vocation almost immemorially the destiny of all his race. Nor does it unfrequently occur, that Nantucket captains will send a son of such tender age away from them, for a protracted three or four years' voyage in some other ship than their own; so that their first knowledge of a whaleman's career shall be unenervated by any chance display of a father's natural but untimely partiality, or undue apprehensiveness and concern.

Meantime, now the stranger was still beseeching his poor boon of Ahab; and Ahab still stood like an anvil, receiving every shock, but without the least quivering of his own.

"I will not go," said the stranger, "till you say *aye* to me. Do to me as you would have me do to you in the like case.[2] For *you* too have a boy, Captain Ahab—though but a child, and nestling safely at home now—a child of your old age too—Yes, yes, you relent; I see it—run, run, men, now, and stand by to square in the yards."

"Avast," cried Ahab—"touch not a rope-yarn;" then in a voice that prolongingly moulded every word—"Captain Gardiner, I will not do it. Even now I lose time. Good bye, good bye. God bless ye, man, and may I forgive myself, but I must go. Mr. Starbuck, look at the binnacle watch, and in three minutes from this present instant warn off all strangers: then brace forward again, and let the ship sail as before."

Hurriedly turning, with averted face, he descended into his cabin, leaving the strange captain transfixed at this unconditional and utter rejection

---

2. As Jesus said (Matthew 7.12): "Therefore all things whatsoever ye would that men should do to you, do ye even so to them: for this is the law and the prophets." Also Luke 6.31: "And as ye would that men should do to you, do ye also to them likewise."

of his so earnest suit. But starting from his enchantment, Gardiner silently hurried to the side; more fell than stepped into his boat, and returned to his ship.

Soon the two ships diverged their wakes; and long as the strange vessel was in view, she was seen to yaw hither and thither at every dark spot, however small, on the sea. This way and that her yards were swung round; starboard and larboard, she continued to tack; now she beat against a head sea; and again it pushed her before it; while all the while, her masts and yards were thickly clustered with men, as three tall cherry trees, when the boys are cherrying among the boughs.

But by her still halting course and winding, woful way, you plainly saw that this ship that so wept with spray, still remained without comfort. She was Rachel, weeping for her children,[3] because they were not.

Chapter 129

The Cabin

(Ahab moving to go on deck; Pip catches him by the hand to follow.)

"Lad, lad, I tell thee thou must not follow Ahab now. The hour is coming when Ahab would not scare thee from him, yet would not have thee by him. There is that in thee, poor lad, which I feel too curing to my malady. Like cures like;[1] and for this hunt, my malady becomes my most desired health. Do thou abide below here, where they shall serve thee, as if thou wert the captain. Aye, lad, thou shalt sit here in my own screwed chair; another screw to it, thou must be."

"No, no, no! ye have not a whole body, sir; do ye but use poor me for your one lost leg; only tread upon me, sir; I ask no more, so I remain a part of ye."

"Oh! spite of million villains, this makes me a bigot[2] in the fadeless fidelity of man!—and a black! and crazy!—but methinks like-cures-like applies to him too; he grows so sane again."

"They tell me, sir, that Stubb did once desert poor little Pip, whose drowned bones now show white, for all the blackness of his living skin. But I will never desert ye, sir, as Stubb did him. Sir, I must go with ye."

"If thou speakest thus to me much more, Ahab's purpose keels up in him. I tell thee no; it cannot be."

"Oh good master, master, master!"

"Weep so, and I will murder thee! have a care, for Ahab too is mad. Listen, and thou wilt often hear my ivory foot upon the deck, and still know that I am there. And now I quit thee. Thy hand!—Met! True art thou, lad, as the circumference to its centre. So: God for ever bless thee; and if it come to that,—God for ever save thee, let what will befall."

---

3. See Matthew 2.18, where Jeremiah's prophesy is quoted as being fulfilled by Herod's slaughter of the male children two years old or younger (as referred to in ch. 126).
1. A reference to homeopathy, the medical system in which like cures like is a basic tenet.
2. A fanatical believer.

(Ahab goes; Pip steps one step forward.)

"Here he this instant stood; I stand in his air,—but I'm alone. Now were even poor Pip here I could endure it, but he's missing. Pip! Pip! Ding, dong, ding! Who's seen Pip? He must be up here; let's try the door. What? neither lock, nor bolt, nor bar; and yet there's no opening it. It must be the spell; he told me to stay here: Aye, and told me this screwed chair was mine. Here, then, I'll seat me, against the transom, in the ship's full middle, all her keel and her three masts before me. Here, our old sailors say, in their black seventy-fours[3] great admirals sometimes sit at table, and lord it over rows of captains and lieutenants. Ha! what's this? epaulets! epaulets! the epaulets all come crowding! Pass round the decanters; glad to see ye; fill up, monsieurs! What an odd feeling, now, when a black boy's host to white men with gold lace upon their coats!—Monsieurs, have ye seen one Pip?—a little negro lad, five feet high, hang-dog look, and cowardly! Jumped from a whale-boat once;—seen him? No! Well then, fill up again, captains, and let's drink shame upon all cowards! I name no names. Shame upon them! Put one foot upon the table. Shame upon all cowards.—Hist! above there, I hear ivory—Oh, master! master! I am indeed down-hearted when you walk over me. But here I'll stay, though this stern strikes rocks; and they bulge through; and oysters come to join me."

Chapter 130

The Hat

And now that at the proper time and place, after so long and wide a preliminary cruise, Ahab,—all other whaling waters swept—seemed to have chased his foe into an ocean-fold, to slay him the more securely there; now, that he found himself hard by the very latitude and longitude where his tormenting wound had been inflicted; now that a vessel had been spoken which on the very day preceding had actually encountered Moby Dick;—and now that all his successive meetings with various ships contrastingly concurred to show the demoniac indifference with which the white whale tore his hunters, whether sinning or sinned against; now it was that there lurked a something in the old man's eyes, which it was hardly sufferable for feeble souls to see. As the unsetting polar star, which through the livelong, arctic, six months' night sustains its piercing, steady, central gaze; so Ahab's purpose now fixedly gleamed down upon the constant midnight of the gloomy crew. It domineered above them so, that all their bodings, doubts, misgivings, fears, were fain to hide beneath their souls, and not sprout forth a single spear or leaf.

In this foreshadowing interval too, all humor, forced or natural, vanished. Stubb no more strove to raise a smile; Starbuck no more strove to check one. Alike, joy and sorrow, hope and fear, seemed ground to finest dust, and powdered, for the time, in the clamped mortar of Ahab's iron

---

3. Great warships mounting seventy-four cannons.

soul. Like machines, they dumbly moved about the deck, ever conscious that the old man's despot eye was on them.

But did you deeply scan him in his more secret confidential hours; when he thought no glance but one was on him; then you would have seen that even as Ahab's eyes so awed the crew's, the inscrutable Parsee's glance awed his; or somehow, at least, in some wild way, at times affected it. Such an added, gliding strangeness began to invest the thin Fedallah now; such ceaseless shudderings shook him; that the men looked dubious at him; half uncertain, as it seemed, whether indeed he were a mortal substance, or else a tremulous shadow cast upon the deck by some unseen being's body. And that shadow was always hovering there. For not by night, even, had Fedallah ever certainly been known to slumber, or go below. He would stand still for hours: but never sat or leaned; his wan but wondrous eyes did plainly say—We two watchmen never rest.

Nor, at any time, by night or day could the mariners now step upon the deck, unless Ahab was before them; either standing in his pivot-hole, or exactly pacing the planks between two undeviating limits,—the mainmast and the mizen; or else they saw him standing in the cabin-scuttle,— his living foot advanced upon the deck, as if to step; his hat slouched heavily over his eyes; so that however motionless he stood, however the days and nights were added on, that he had not swung in his hammock; yet hidden beneath that slouching hat, they could never tell unerringly whether, for all this, his eyes were really closed at times: or whether he was still intently scanning them; no matter, though he stood so in the scuttle for a whole hour on the stretch, and the unheeded night-damp gathered in beads of dew upon that stone-carved coat and hat. The clothes that the night had wet, the next day's sunshine dried upon him; and so, day after day, and night after night; he went no more beneath the planks; whatever he wanted from the cabin that thing he sent for.

He ate in the same open air; that is, his two only meals,—breakfast and dinner: supper he never touched; nor reaped his beard; which darkly grew all gnarled, as unearthed roots of trees blown over, which still grow idly on at naked base, though perished in the upper verdure. But though his whole life was now become one watch on deck; and though the Parsee's mystic watch was without intermission as his own; yet these two never seemed to speak—one man to the other—unless at long intervals some passing unmomentous matter made it necessary. Though such a potent spell seemed secretly to join the twain; openly, and to the awe-struck crew, they seemed pole-like asunder. If by day they chanced to speak one word; by night, dumb men were both, so far as concerned the slightest verbal interchange. At times, for longest hours, without a single hail, they stood far parted in the starlight; Ahab in his scuttle, the Parsee by the mainmast; but still fixedly gazing upon each other; as if in the Parsee Ahab saw his forethrown shadow, in Ahab the Parsee his abandoned substance.

And yet, somehow, did Ahab—in his own proper self, as daily, hourly, and every instant, commandingly revealed to his subordinates,—Ahab seemed an independent lord; the Parsee but his slave. Still again both seemed yoked together, and an unseen tyrant driving them; the lean shade siding the solid rib. For be this Parsee what he may, all rib and keel was solid Ahab.

At the first faintest glimmering of the dawn, his iron voice was heard from aft—"Man the mast-heads!"—and all through the day, till after sunset and after twilight, the same voice every hour, at the striking of the helmsman's bell, was heard—"What d'ye see?—sharp! sharp!"

But when three or four days had slided by, after meeting the children-seeking Rachel; and no spout had yet been seen; the monomaniac old man seemed distrustful of his crew's fidelity; at least, of nearly all except the Pagan harpooneers; he seemed to doubt, even, whether Stubb and Flask might not willingly overlook the sight he sought. But if these suspicions were really his, he sagaciously refrained from verbally expressing them, however his actions might seem to hint them.

"I will have the first sight of the whale myself,"—he said. "Aye! Ahab must have the doubloon!" and with his own hands he rigged a nest of basketed bowlines; and sending a hand aloft, with a single sheaved block, to secure to the mainmast head, he received the two ends of the downward-reeved rope; and attaching one to his basket prepared a pin for the other end, in order to fasten it at the rail. This done, with that end yet in his hand and standing beside the pin, he looked round upon his crew, sweeping from one to the other; pausing his glance long upon Daggoo, Queequeg, Tashtego; but shunning Fedallah; and then settling his firm relying eye upon the chief mate, said,—"Take the rope, sir—I give it into thy hands, Starbuck." Then arranging his person in the basket, he gave the word for them to hoist him to his perch, Starbuck being the one who secured the rope at last; and afterwards stood near it. And thus, with one hand clinging round the royal mast, Ahab gazed abroad upon the sea for miles and miles,—ahead, astern, this side, and that,—within the wide expanded circle commanded at so great a height.

When in working with his hands at some lofty almost isolated place in the rigging, which chances to afford no foothold, the sailor at sea is hoisted up to that spot, and sustained there by the rope; under these circumstances, its fastened end on deck is always given in strict charge to some one man who has the special watch of it. Because in such a wilderness of running rigging, whose various different relations aloft cannot always be infallibly discerned by what is seen of them at the deck; and when the deck-ends of these ropes are being every few minutes cast down from the fastenings, it would be but a natural fatality, if, unprovided with a constant watchman, the hoisted sailor should by some carelessness of the crew be cast adrift and fall all swooping to the sea. So Ahab's proceedings in this matter were not unusual; the only strange thing about them seemed to be, that Starbuck, almost the one only man who had ever ventured to oppose him with anything in the slightest degree approaching to decision—one of those too, whose faithfulness on the look-out he had seemed to doubt somewhat;—it was strange, that this was the very man he should select for his watchman; freely giving his whole life into such an otherwise distrusted person's hands.

Now, the first time Ahab was perched aloft; ere he had been there ten minutes; one of those red-billed savage sea-hawks which so often fly incommodiously close round the manned mast-heads of whalemen in these latitudes; one of these birds came wheeling and screaming round his head in a maze of untrackably swift circlings. Then it darted a thousand feet straight up into the air; then spiralized downwards, and went eddying again round his head.

But with his gaze fixed upon the dim and distant horizon, Ahab seemed not to mark this wild bird; nor, indeed, would any one else have marked it much, it being no uncommon circumstance; only now almost the least heedful eye seemed to see some sort of cunning meaning in almost every sight.

"Your hat, your hat, sir!" suddenly cried the Sicilian seaman, who being posted at the mizen-mast-head, stood directly behind Ahab, though somewhat lower than his level, and with a deep gulf of air dividing them.

But already the sable wing was before the old man's eyes; the long hooked bill at his head: with a scream, the black hawk darted away with his prize.

An eagle flew thrice round Tarquin's[1] head, removing his cap to replace it, and thereupon Tanaquil, his wife, declared that Tarquin would be king of Rome. But only by the replacing of the cap was that omen accounted good. Ahab's hat was never restored; the wild hawk flew on and on with it; far in advance of the prow: and at last disappeared; while from the point of that disappearance, a minute black spot was dimly discerned, falling from that vast height into the sea.

Chapter 131

The Pequod meets the Delight

The intense Pequod sailed on; the rolling waves and days went by; the life-buoy-coffin still lightly swung; and another ship, most miserably mis-named the Delight, was descried. As she drew nigh, all eyes were fixed upon her broad beams, called shears, which, in some whaling-ships, cross the quarter-deck at the height of eight or nine feet; serving to carry the spare, unrigged, or disabled boats.

Upon the stranger's shears were beheld the shattered, white ribs, and some few splintered planks, of what had once been a whale-boat; but you now saw through this wreck, as plainly as you see through the peeled, half-unhinged, and bleaching skeleton of a horse.

"Hast seen the White Whale?"

"Look!" replied the hollow-cheeked captain from his taffrail; and with his trumpet he pointed to the wreck.

"Hast killed him?"

"The harpoon is not yet forged that will ever do that," answered the other, sadly glancing upon a rounded hammock on the deck, whose gathered sides some noiseless sailors were busy in sewing together.

"Not forged!" and snatching Perth's levelled iron from the crotch, Ahab held it out, exclaiming—"Look ye, Nantucketer; here in this hand I hold his death! Tempered in blood, and tempered by lightning are these barbs; and I swear to temper them triply in that hot place behind the fin, where the White Whale most feels his accursed life!"

1. Legendary last king of Rome (6th century B.C.E.).

"Then God keep thee, old man—see'st thou that"—pointing to the hammock—"I bury but one of five stout men, who were alive only yesterday; but were dead ere night. Only *that* one I bury; the rest were buried before they died; you sail upon their tomb." Then turning to his crew—"Are ye ready there? place the plank then on the rail, and lift the body; so, then—Oh! God"—advancing towards the hammock with uplifted hands—"may the resurrection and the life——"[1]

"Brace forward! Up helm!" cried Ahab like lightning to his men.

But the suddenly started Pequod was not quick enough to escape the sound of the splash that the corpse soon made as it struck the sea; not so quick, indeed, but that some of the flying bubbles might have sprinkled her hull with their ghostly baptism.

As Ahab now glided from the dejected Delight, the strange life-buoy hanging at the Pequod's stern came into conspicuous relief.

"Ha! yonder! look yonder, men!" cried a foreboding voice in her wake. "In vain, oh, ye strangers, ye fly our sad burial; ye but turn us your taffrail to show us your coffin!"

Chapter 132

The Symphony

It was a clear steel-blue day. The firmaments of air and sea were hardly separable in that all-pervading azure; only, the pensive air was transparently pure and soft, with a woman's look, and the robust and man-like sea heaved with long, strong, lingering swells, as Samson's chest in his sleep.[1]

Hither, and thither, on high, glided the snow-white wings of small, unspeckled birds; these were the gentle thoughts of the feminine air; but to and fro in the deeps, far down in the bottomless blue, rushed mighty leviathans, sword-fish, and sharks; and these were the strong, troubled, murderous thinkings of the masculine sea.

But though thus contrasting within, the contrast was only in shades and shadows without; those two seemed one; it was only the sex, as it were, that distinguished them.

Aloft, like a royal czar and king, the sun seemed giving this gentle air to this bold and rolling sea; even as bride to groom. And at the girdling line of the horizon, a soft and tremulous motion—most seen here at the equator—denoted the fond, throbbing trust, the loving alarms, with which the poor bride gave her bosom away.

Tied up and twisted; gnarled and knotted with wrinkles; haggardly firm and unyielding; his eyes glowing like coals, that still glow in the ashes of ruin; untottering Ahab stood forth in the clearness of the morn;

---

1. A phrase from the burial service in the Anglican Book of Common Prayer (from John 11.25).
1. In Judges 13 an angel tells Manoah's barren wife that she will conceive a son who will be a Nazarite, whose hair will never be cut, and who will resist the Philistine oppressors. Grown to manhood, Samson has the strength of a giant. In Judges 16 he loves the Philistine Delilah, who inveigles him into telling his secret, that his strength will go from him if his hair is cut. Overpowered after she has his hair shaved off, he is blinded by the Philistines. Melville imagines him breathing tranquilly, in all his strength.

lifting his splintered helmet of a brow to the fair girl's forehead of heaven.

Oh, immortal infancy, and innocency of the azure! Invisible winged creatures that frolic all round us! Sweet childhood of air and sky! how oblivious were ye of old Ahab's close-coiled woe! But so have I seen little Miriam and Martha, laughing-eyed elves, heedlessly gambol around their old sire; sporting with the circle of singed locks which grew on the marge of that burnt-out crater of his brain.

Slowly crossing the deck from the scuttle, Ahab leaned over the side, and watched how his shadow in the water sank and sank to his gaze, the more and the more that he strove to pierce the profundity. But the lovely aromas in that enchanted air did at last seem to dispel, for a moment, the cankerous thing in his soul. That glad, happy air, that winsome sky, did at last stroke and caress him; the step-mother world, so long cruel—forbidding—now threw affectionate arms round his stubborn neck, and did seem to joyously sob over him, as if over one, that however wilful and erring, she could yet find it in her heart to save and to bless. From beneath his slouched hat Ahab dropped a tear into the sea; nor did all the Pacific contain such wealth as that one wee drop.

Starbuck saw the old man; saw him, how he heavily leaned over the side; and he seemed to hear in his own true heart the measureless sobbing that stole out of the centre of the serenity around. Careful not to touch him, or be noticed by him, he yet drew near to him, and stood there.

Ahab turned.

"Starbuck!"

"Sir."

"Oh, Starbuck! it is a mild, mild wind, and a mild looking sky. On such a day—very much such a sweetness as this—I struck my first whale—a boy-harpooneer of eighteen! Forty—forty—forty years ago!—ago! Forty years of continual whaling! forty years of privation, and peril, and storm-time! forty years on the pitiless sea! for forty years has Ahab forsaken the peaceful land, for forty years to make war on the horrors of the deep! Aye and yes, Starbuck, out of those forty years I have not spent three ashore. When I think of this life I have led; the desolation of solitude it has been; the masoned, walled-town of a Captain's exclusiveness, which admits but small entrance to any sympathy from the green country without—oh, weariness! heaviness! Guinea-coast slavery[2] of solitary command!—when I think of all this; only half-suspected, not so keenly known to me before—and how for forty years I have fed upon dry salted fare—fit emblem of the dry nourishment of my soul!—when the poorest landsman has had fresh fruit to his daily hand, and broken the world's fresh bread, to my mouldy crusts—away, whole oceans away, from that young girl-wife I wedded past fifty, and sailed for Cape Horn the next day, leaving but one dent in my marriage pillow—wife? wife?—rather a widow with her husband alive! Aye, I widowed that poor girl when I married her, Starbuck; and then, the madness, the frenzy, the boiling blood and the smoking brow, with which, for a thousand lowerings old Ahab has furiously, foamingly chased his prey—more a demon than a man!—aye, aye! what a forty years' fool—fool—old fool, has old Ahab been!

2. As absolute as in the ancient country on the west African coast.

Why this strife of the chase? why weary, and palsy the arm at the oar, and the iron, and the lance? how the richer or better is Ahab now? Behold. Oh, Starbuck! is it not hard, that with this weary load I bear, one poor leg should have been snatched from under me? Here, brush this old hair aside; it blinds me, that I seem to weep. Locks so grey did never grow but from out some ashes! But do I look very old, so very, very old, Starbuck? I feel deadly faint, bowed, and humped, as though I were Adam, staggering beneath the piled centuries since Paradise. God! God! God!—crack my heart!—stave my brain!—mockery! mockery! bitter, biting mockery of grey hairs, have I lived enough joy to wear ye; and seem and feel thus intolerably old? Close! stand close to me, Starbuck; let me look into a human eye; it is better than to gaze into sea or sky; better than to gaze upon God. By the green land; by the bright hearth-stone! this is the magic glass, man; I see my wife and my child in thine eye. No, no; stay on board, on board!—lower not when I do; when branded Ahab gives chase to Moby Dick. That hazard shall not be thine. No, no! not with the far away home I see in that eye!"

"Oh, my Captain! my Captain! noble soul! grand old heart, after all! why should any one give chase to that hated fish! Away with me! let us fly these deadly waters! let us home! Wife and child, too, are Starbuck's—wife and child of his brotherly, sisterly, play-fellow youth; even as thine, sir, are the wife and child of thy loving, longing, paternal old age! Away! let us away!—this instant let me alter the course! How cheerily, how hilariously, O my Captain, would we bowl on our way to see old Nantucket again! I think, sir, they have some such mild blue days, even as this, in Nantucket."

"They have, they have. I have seen them—some summer days in the morning. About this time—yes, it is his noon nap now—the boy vivaciously wakes; sits up in bed; and his mother tells him of me, of cannibal old me; how I am abroad upon the deep, but will yet come back to dance him again."

"'Tis my Mary, my Mary herself! She promised that my boy, every morning, should be carried to the hill to catch the first glimpse of his father's sail! Yes, yes! no more! it is done! we head for Nantucket! Come, my Captain, study out the course, and let us away! See, see! the boy's face from the window! the boy's hand on the hill!"

But Ahab's glance was averted; like a blighted fruit tree he shook, and cast his last, cindered apple to the soil.

"What is it, what nameless, inscrutable, unearthly thing is it; what cozening, hidden lord and master, and cruel, remorseless emperor commands me; that against all natural lovings and longings, I so keep pushing, and crowding, and jamming myself on all the time; recklessly making me ready to do what in my own proper, natural heart, I durst not so much as dare? Is Ahab, Ahab?[3] Is it I, God, or who, that lifts this arm? But if the great sun move not of himself; but is as an errand-boy in heaven; nor one single star can revolve, but by some invisible power; how then can this one

3. This is the reading of the first American edition, which may be what Melville meant. However, he may have changed it on proofs to the English reading, "Is it Ahab, Ahab?"—a reading in which Ahab would be questioning the possibility that he is the one responsible, not some "cozening, hidden lord and master," and not God. In favor of the English reading is the sentence structure at the start of the paragraph: "What is it" and in the following sentence: "Is it I, God, or who, that lifts this arm." Any reading should take into account the possibility that Melville meant either what was in the American edition or what was in the English edition.

small heart beat; this one small brain think thoughts; unless God does that beating, does that thinking, does that living, and not I. By heaven, man, we are turned round and round in this world, like yonder windlass, and Fate is the handspike. And all the time, lo! that smiling sky, and this unsounded sea! Look! see yon Albicore! who put it into him to chase and fang that flying-fish? Where do murderers go, man! Who's to doom, when the judge himself is dragged to the bar? But it is a mild, mild wind, and a mild looking sky; and the air smells now, as if it blew from a far-away meadow; they have been making hay somewhere under the slopes of the Andes, Starbuck, and the mowers are sleeping among the new-mown hay. Sleeping? Aye, toil we how we may, we all sleep at last on the field. Sleep? Aye, and rust amid greenness; as last year's scythes flung down, and left in the half-cut swaths—Starbuck!"

But blanched to a corpse's hue with despair, the Mate had stolen away.

Ahab crossed the deck to gaze over on the other side; but started at two reflected, fixed eyes in the water there. Fedallah was motionlessly leaning over the same rail.

Chapter 133

The Chase—First Day

That night, in the mid-watch, when the old man—as his wont at intervals—stepped forth from the scuttle in which he leaned, and went to his pivot-hole, he suddenly thrust out his face fiercely, snuffing up the sea air as a sagacious ship's dog will, in drawing nigh to some barbarous isle. He declared that a whale must be near. Soon that peculiar odor, sometimes to a great distance given forth by the living sperm whale, was palpable to all the watch; nor was any mariner surprised when, after inspecting the compass, and then the dog-vane,[1] and then ascertaining the precise bearing of the odor as nearly as possible, Ahab rapidly ordered the ship's course to be slightly altered, and the sail to be shortened.

The acute policy dictating these movements was sufficiently vindicated at daybreak, by the sight of a long sleek on the sea directly and lengthwise ahead, smooth as oil, and resembling in the pleated watery wrinkles bordering it, the polished metallic-like marks of some swift tide-rip, at the mouth of a deep, rapid stream.

"Man the mast-heads! Call all hands!"

Thundering with the butts of three clubbed handspikes on the forecastle deck, Daggoo roused the sleepers with such judgment claps that they seemed to exhale from the scuttle, so instantaneously did they appear with their clothes in their hands.

"What d'ye see?" cried Ahab, flattening his face to the sky.

"Nothing, nothing, sir!" was the sound hailing down in reply.

"T'gallant sails!—stunsails! alow and aloft, and on both sides!"

All sail being set, he now cast loose the life-line, reserved for swaying him to the main royal-mast head; and in a few moments they were hoist-

1. Small tubular flag at the masthead, like a wind sock.

ing him thither, when, while but two thirds of the way aloft, and while
peering ahead through the horizontal vacancy between the main-top-sail
and top-gallant-sail, he raised a gull-like cry in the air, "There she
blows!—there she blows! A hump like a snow-hill! It is Moby Dick!"

Fired by the cry which seemed simultaneously taken up by the three
look-outs, the men on deck rushed to the rigging to behold the famous
whale they had so long been pursuing. Ahab had now gained his final
perch, some feet above the other look-outs, Tashtego standing just
beneath him on the cap of the top-gallant-mast, so that the Indian's head
was almost on a level with Ahab's heel. From this height the whale was
now seen some mile or so ahead, at every roll of the sea revealing his high
sparkling hump, and regularly jetting his silent spout into the air. To the
credulous mariners it seemed the same silent spout they had so long ago
beheld in the moonlit Atlantic and Indian Oceans.

"And did none of ye see it before?" cried Ahab, hailing the perched men
all around him.

"I saw him almost that same instant, sir, that Captain Ahab did, and I
cried out," said Tashtego.

"Not the same instant; not the same—no, the doubloon is mine, Fate
reserved the doubloon for me. *I* only; none of ye could have raised the
White Whale first. There she blows! there she blows!—there she blows!
There again!—there again!" he cried, in long-drawn, lingering, methodic
tones, attuned to the gradual prolongings of the whale's visible jets. "He's
going to sound! In stunsails! Down top-gallant-sails! Stand by three boats.
Mr. Starbuck, remember, stay on board, and keep the ship. Helm there!
Luff, luff a point! So; steady, man, steady! There go flukes! No, no; only
black water! All ready the boats there? Stand by, stand by! Lower me, Mr.
Starbuck; lower, lower,—quick, quicker!" and he slid through the air to
the deck.

"He is heading straight to leeward, sir," cried Stubb, "right away from
us; cannot have seen the ship yet."

"Be dumb, man! Stand by the braces! Hard down the helm!—brace up!
Shiver her!—shiver her! So; well that! Boats, boats!"

Soon all the boats but Starbuck's were dropped; all the boat-sails set—
all the paddles plying; with rippling swiftness, shooting to leeward; and
Ahab heading the onset. A pale, death-glimmer lit up Fedallah's sunken
eyes; a hideous motion gnawed his mouth.

Like noiseless nautilus shells, their light prows sped through the sea;
but only slowly they neared the foe. As they neared him, the ocean grew
still more smooth; seemed drawing a carpet over its waves; seemed a
noon-meadow, so serenely it spread. At length the breathless hunter came
so nigh his seemingly unsuspecting prey, that his entire dazzling hump
was distinctly visible, sliding along the sea as if an isolated thing, and continually set in a revolving ring of finest, fleecy, greenish foam. He saw the
vast, involved wrinkles of the slightly projecting head beyond. Before it,
far out on the soft Turkish-rugged waters, went the glistening white
shadow from his broad, milky forehead, a musical rippling playfully
accompanying the shade; and behind, the blue waters interchangeably
flowed over into the moving valley of his steady wake; and on either hand
bright bubbles arose and danced by his side. But these were broken again

by the light toes of hundreds of gay fowl softly feathering the sea, alternate with their fitful flight; and like to some flag-staff rising from the painted hull of an argosy, the tall but shattered pole of a recent lance projected from the white whale's back; and at intervals one of the cloud of soft-toed fowls hovering, and to and fro skimming like a canopy over the fish, silently perched and rocked on this pole, the long tail feathers streaming like pennons.

A gentle joyousness—a mighty mildness of repose in swiftness, invested the gliding whale. Not the white bull Jupiter swimming away with ravished Europa[2] clinging to his graceful horns; his lovely, leering eyes sideways intent upon the maid; with smooth bewitching fleetness, rippling straight for the nuptial bower in Crete; not Jove, not that great majesty Supreme! did surpass the glorified White Whale as he so divinely swam.

On each soft side—coincident with the parted swell, that but once laving him, then flowed so wide away—on each bright side, the whale shed off enticings. No wonder there had been some among the hunters who namelessly transported and allured by all this serenity, had ventured to assail it; but had fatally found that quietude but the vesture of tornadoes. Yet calm, enticing calm, oh, whale! thou glidest on, to all who for the first time eye thee, no matter how many in that same way thou may'st have bejuggled and destroyed before.

And thus, through the serene tranquillities of the tropical sea, among waves whose hand-clappings were suspended by exceeding rapture, Moby Dick moved on, still withholding from sight the full terrors of his submerged trunk, entirely hiding the wrenched hideousness of his jaw. But soon the fore part of him slowly rose from the water; for an instant his whole marbleized body formed a high arch, like Virginia's Natural Bridge, and warningly waving his bannered flukes in the air, the grand god revealed himself, sounded, and went out of sight. Hoveringly halting, and dipping on the wing, the white sea-fowls longingly lingered over the agitated pool that he left.

With oars apeak, and paddles down, the sheets of their sails adrift, the three boats now stilly floated, awaiting Moby Dick's reappearance.

"An hour," said Ahab, standing rooted in his boat's stern; and he gazed beyond the whale's place, towards the dim blue spaces and wide wooing vacancies to leeward. It was only an instant; for again his eyes seemed whirling round in his head as he swept the watery circle. The breeze now freshened; the sea began to swell.

"The birds!—the birds!" cried Tashtego.

In long Indian file, as when herons take wing, the white birds were now all flying towards Ahab's boat; and when within a few yards began fluttering over the water there, wheeling round and round, with joyous, expectant cries. Their vision was keener than man's; Ahab could discover no sign in the sea. But suddenly as he peered down and down into its depths, he profoundly saw a white living spot no bigger than a white weasel, with wonderful celerity uprising, and magnifying as it rose, till it turned, and then there were plainly revealed two long crooked rows of white, glistening teeth, floating up from the undiscoverable bottom. It was Moby Dick's

2. In Greek mythology, the princess whom Jupiter (in the form of a bull) carried away.

open mouth and scrolled jaw; his vast, shadowed bulk still half blending
with the blue of the sea. The glittering mouth yawned beneath the boat
like an open-doored marble tomb; and giving one sidelong sweep with his
steering oar, Ahab whirled the craft aside from this tremendous apparition. Then, calling upon Fedallah to change places with him, went forward to the bows, and seizing Perth's harpoon, commanded his crew to
grasp their oars and stand by to stern.

Now, by reason of this timely spinning round the boat upon its axis, its
bow, by anticipation, was made to face the whale's head while yet under
water. But as if perceiving this stratagem, Moby Dick, with that malicious
intelligence ascribed to him, sidelingly transplanted himself, as it were, in
an instant, shooting his pleated head lengthwise beneath the boat.

Through and through; through every plank and each rib, it thrilled for
an instant, the whale obliquely lying on his back, in the manner of a biting shark, slowly and feelingly taking its bows full within his mouth, so
that the long, narrow, scrolled lower jaw curled high up into the open air,
and one of the teeth caught in a row-lock. The bluish pearl-white of the
inside of the jaw was within six inches of Ahab's head, and reached higher
than that. In this attitude the White Whale now shook the slight cedar as
a mildly cruel cat her mouse. With unastonished eyes Fedallah gazed, and
crossed his arms; but the tiger-yellow crew were tumbling over each
other's heads to gain the uttermost stern.

And now, while both elastic gunwales were springing in and out, as the
whale dallied with the doomed craft in this devilish way; and from his
body being submerged beneath the boat, he could not be darted at from
the bows, for the bows were almost inside of him, as it were; and while
the other boats involuntarily paused, as before a quick crisis impossible to
withstand, then it was that monomaniac Ahab, furious with this tantalizing vicinity of his foe, which placed him all alive and helpless in the very
jaws he hated; frenzied with all this, he seized the long bone with his
naked hands, and wildly strove to wrench it from its gripe. As now he thus
vainly strove, the jaw slipped from him; the frail gunwales bent in, collapsed, and snapped, as both jaws, like an enormous shears, sliding further aft, bit the craft completely in twain, and locked themselves fast
again in the sea, midway between the two floating wrecks. These floated
aside, the broken ends drooping, the crew at the stern-wreck clinging to
the gunwales, and striving to hold fast to the oars to lash them across.

At that preluding moment, ere the boat was yet snapped, Ahab, the first
to perceive the whale's intent, by the crafty upraising of his head, a movement that loosed his hold for the time; at that moment his hand had made
one final effort to push the boat out of the bite. But only slipping further
into the whale's mouth, and tilting over sideways as it slipped, the boat
had shaken off his hold on the jaw; spilled him out of it, as he leaned to
the push; and so he fell flat-faced upon the sea.

Ripplingly withdrawing from his prey, Moby Dick now lay at a little distance, vertically thrusting his oblong white head up and down in the billows; and at the same time slowly revolving his whole spindled body; so
that when his vast wrinkled forehead rose—some twenty or more feet out
of the water—the now rising swells, with all their confluent waves, daz-
zlingly broke against it; vindictively tossing their shivered spray still higher

into the air.[3] So, in a gale, the but half baffled Channel billows only recoil from the base of the Eddystone, triumphantly to overleap its summit with their scud.

But soon resuming his horizontal attitude, Moby Dick swam swiftly round and round the wrecked crew; sideways churning the water in his vengeful wake, as if lashing himself up to still another and more deadly assault. The sight of the splintered boat seemed to madden him, as the blood of grapes and mulberries cast before Antiochus's elephants in the book of Maccabees.[4] Meanwhile Ahab half smothered in the foam of the whale's insolent tail, and too much of a cripple to swim,—though he could still keep afloat, even in the heart of such a whirlpool as that; help-less Ahab's head was seen, like a tossed bubble which the least chance shock might burst. From the boat's fragmentary stern, Fedallah incuri-ously and mildly eyed him; the clinging crew, at the other drifting end, could not succor him; more than enough was it for them to look to them-selves. For so revolvingly appalling was the White Whale's aspect, and so planetarily swift the ever-contracting circles he made, that he seemed hor-izontally swooping upon them. And though the other boats, unharmed, still hovered hard by; still they dared not pull into the eddy to strike, lest that should be the signal for the instant destruction of the jeopardized castaways, Ahab and all; nor in that case could they themselves hope to escape. With straining eyes, then, they remained on the outer edge of the direful zone, whose centre had now become the old man's head.

Meantime, from the beginning all this had been descried from the ship's mast heads; and squaring her yards, she had borne down upon the scene; and was now so nigh, that Ahab in the water hailed her;—"Sail on the"—but that moment a breaking sea dashed on him from Moby Dick, and whelmed him for the time. But struggling out of it again, and chanc-ing to rise on a towering crest, he shouted,—"Sail on the whale!—Drive him off!"

The Pequod's prow was pointed; and breaking up the charmed circle, she effectually parted the white whale from his victim. As he sullenly swam off, the boats flew to the rescue.

Dragged into Stubb's boat with blood-shot, blinded eyes, the white brine caking in his wrinkles; the long tension of Ahab's bodily strength did crack, and helplessly he yielded to his body's doom: for a time, lying all crushed in the bottom of Stubb's boat, like one trodden under foot of herds of elephants. Far inland, nameless wails came from him, as desolate sounds from out ravines.

But this intensity of his physical prostration did but so much the more abbreviate it. In an instant's compass, great hearts sometimes condense to one deep pang, the sum total of those shallow pains kindly diffused through feebler men's whole lives. And so, such hearts, though summary in each one suffering; still, if the gods decree it, in their life-time aggre-gate a whole age of woe, wholly made up of instantaneous intensities; for

---

3. This motion is peculiar to the sperm whale. It receives its designation (pitchpoling) from its being likened to that preliminary up-and-down poise of the whale-lance, in the exercise called pitch-poling, previously described. By this motion the whale must best and most comprehensively view whatever objects may be encircling him [Melville's note].

4. 1 Maccabees 6.34, in the Apocrypha: "And to the end they might provoke the elephants to fight, they shewed them the blood of grapes and mulberries."

even in their pointless centres, those noble natures contain the entire cir-
cumferences of inferior souls.

"The harpoon," said Ahab, half way rising, and draggingly leaning on
one bended arm—"is it safe?"

"Aye, sir, for it was not darted; this is it," said Stubb, showing it.

"Lay it before me;—any missing men?"

"One, two, three, four, five;—there were five oars, sir, and here are five
men."

"That's good.—Help me, man; I wish to stand. So, so, I see him! there!
there! going to leeward still; what a leaping spout!—Hands off from me!
The eternal sap runs up in Ahab's bones again! Set the sail; out oars; the
helm!"

It is often the case that when a boat is stove, its crew, being picked up
by another boat, help to work that second boat; and the chase is thus continued with what is called double-banked oars. It was thus now. But the
added power of the boat did not equal the added power of the whale, for
he seemed to have treble-banked his every fin; swimming with a velocity
which plainly showed, that if now, under these circumstances, pushed on,
the chase would prove an indefinitely prolonged, if not a hopeless one;
nor could any crew endure for so long a period, such an unintermitted,
intense straining at the oar; a thing barely tolerable only in some one brief
vicissitude. The ship itself, then, as it sometimes happens, offered the
most promising intermediate means of overtaking the chase. Accordingly,
the boats now made for her, and were soon swayed up to their cranes—
the two parts of the wrecked boat having been previously secured by her—
and then hoisting everything to her side, and stacking her canvas high up,
and sideways outstretching it with stun-sails, like the double-jointed
wings of an albatross; the Pequod bore down in the leeward wake of Moby
Dick. At the well known, methodic intervals, the whale's glittering spout
was regularly announced from the manned mast-heads; and when he
would be reported as just gone down, Ahab would take the time, and then
pacing the deck, binnacle-watch in hand, so soon as the last second of the
allotted hour expired, his voice was heard.—"Whose is the doubloon now?
D'ye see him?" and if the reply was, No, sir! straightway he commanded
them to lift him to his perch. In this way the day wore on; Ahab, now aloft
and motionless; anon, unrestingly pacing the planks.

As he was thus walking, uttering no sound, except to hail the men
aloft, or to bid them hoist a sail still higher, or to spread one to a still
greater breadth—thus to and fro pacing, beneath his slouched hat, at
every turn he passed his own wrecked boat, which had been dropped
upon the quarter-deck, and lay there reversed; broken bow to shattered
stern. At last he paused before it; and as in an already over-clouded sky
fresh troops of clouds will sometimes sail across, so over the old man's
face there now stole some such added gloom as this.

Stubb saw him pause; and perhaps intending, not vainly, though, to
evince his own unabated fortitude, and thus keep up a valiant place in his
Captain's mind, he advanced, and eyeing the wreck exclaimed—"The this-
tle the ass refused;[5] it pricked his mouth too keenly, sir; ha! ha!"

5. The proverb or fable Stubb alludes to is unlocated.

"What soulless thing is this that laughs before a wreck? Man, man! did I not know thee brave as fearless fire (and as mechanical) I could swear thou wert a poltroon. Groan nor laugh should be heard before a wreck."

"Aye, sir," said Starbuck drawing near, "'tis a solemn sight; an omen, and an ill one."

"Omen? omen?—the dictionary! If the gods think to speak outright to man, they will honorably speak outright; not shake their heads, and give an old wives' darkling hint.—Begone! Ye two are the opposite poles of one thing; Starbuck is Stubb reversed, and Stubb is Starbuck; and ye two are all mankind; and Ahab stands alone among the millions of the peopled earth, nor gods nor men his neighbors! Cold, cold—I shiver!—How now? Aloft there! D'ye see him? Sing out for every spout, though he spout ten times a second!"

The day was nearly done; only the hem of his golden robe was rustling. Soon, it was almost dark, but the look-out men still remained unset.

"Can't see the spout now, sir;—too dark"—cried a voice from the air.

"How heading when last seen?"

"As before, sir,—straight to leeward."

"Good! he will travel slower now 'tis night. Down royals and top-gallant stun-sails, Mr. Starbuck. We must not run over him before morning; he's making a passage now, and may heave-to a while. Helm there! keep her full before the wind!—Aloft! come down!—Mr. Stubb, send a fresh hand to the fore-mast head, and see it manned till morning."—Then advancing towards the doubloon in the main-mast—"Men, this gold is mine, for I earned it; but I shall let it abide here till the White Whale is dead; and then, whosoever of ye first raises him, upon the day he shall be killed, this gold is that man's; and if on that day I shall again raise him, then, ten times its sum shall be divided among all of ye! Away now!—the deck is thine, sir."

And so saying, he placed himself half way within the scuttle, and slouching his hat, stood there till dawn, except when at intervals rousing himself to see how the night wore on.

Chapter 134

The Chase—Second Day

At day-break, the three mast-heads were punctually manned afresh.

"D'ye see him?" cried Ahab, after allowing a little space for the light to spread.

"See nothing, sir."

"Turn up all hands and make sail! he travels faster than I thought for;—the top-gallant sails!—aye, they should have been kept on her all night. But no matter—'tis but resting for the rush."

Here be it said, that this pertinacious pursuit of one particular whale, continued through day into night, and through night into day, is a thing by no means unprecedented in the South sea fishery. For such is the wonderful skill, prescience of experience, and invincible confidence acquired by some great natural geniuses among the Nantucket commanders; that from the simple observation of a whale when last descried, they will, under certain given circumstances, pretty accurately foretell both the direction in which he will continue to swim for a time, while out of sight, as well as his probable rate of progression during that period. And, in these cases, somewhat as a pilot, when about losing sight of a coast, whose general trending he well knows, and which he desires shortly to return to again, but at some further point; like as this pilot stands by his compass, and takes the precise bearing of the cape at present visible, in order the more certainly to hit aright the remote, unseen headland, eventually to be visited: so does the fisherman, at his compass, with the whale; for after being chased, and diligently marked, through several hours of daylight, then, when night obscures the fish, the creature's future wake through the darkness is almost as established to the sagacious mind of the hunter, as the pilot's coast is to him. So that to this hunter's wondrous skill, the proverbial evanescence of a thing writ in water, a wake, is to all desired purposes well nigh as reliable as the steadfast land. And as the mighty iron Leviathan of the modern railway is so familiarly known in its every pace, that, with watches in their hands, men time his rate as doctors that of a baby's pulse; and lightly say of it, the up train or the down train will reach such or such a spot, at such or such an hour; even so, almost, there are occasions when these Nantucketers time that other Leviathan of the deep, according to the observed humor of his speed; and say to themselves, so many hours hence this whale will have gone two hundred miles, will have about reached this or that degree of latitude or longitude. But to render this acuteness at all successful in the end, the wind and the sea must be the whaleman's allies; for of what present avail to the becalmed or windbound mariner is the skill that assures him he is exactly ninety-three leagues and a quarter from his port? Inferable from these statements, are many collateral subtile matters touching the chase of whales.

The ship tore on; leaving such a furrow in the sea as when a cannon-ball, missent, becomes a plough-share and turns up the level field.

"By salt and hemp!" cried Stubb, "but this swift motion of the deck creeps up one's legs and tingles at the heart. This ship and I are two brave fellows!—Ha! ha! Some one take me up, and launch me, spine-wise, on the sea,—for by live-oaks! my spine's a keel. Ha, ha! we go the gait that leaves no dust behind!"

"There she blows—she blows!—she blows!—right ahead!" was now the mast-head cry.

"Aye, aye!" cried Stubb, "I knew it—ye can't escape—blow on and split your spout, O whale! the mad fiend himself is after ye! blow your trump—blister your lungs!—Ahab will dam off your blood, as a miller shuts his water-gate upon the stream!"

And Stubb did but speak out for well nigh all that crew. The frenzies of the chase had by this time worked them bubblingly up, like old wine worked anew. Whatever pale fears and forebodings some of them might have felt before; these were not only now kept out of sight through the growing awe of Ahab, but they were broken up, and on all sides routed, as timid prairie hares that scatter before the bounding bison. The hand of Fate had snatched all their souls; and by the stirring perils of the previous

day; the rack of the past night's suspense; the fixed, unfearing, blind, reckless way in which their wild craft went plunging towards its flying mark;
by all these things, their hearts were bowled along. The wind that made
great bellies of their sails, and rushed the vessel on by arms invisible as
irresistible; this seemed the symbol of that unseen agency which so
enslaved them to the race.

They were one man, not thirty. For as the one ship that held them all;
though it was put together of all contrasting things—oak, and maple, and
pine wood; iron, and pitch, and hemp—yet all these ran into each other
in the one concrete hull, which shot on its way, both balanced and
directed by the long central keel; even so, all the individualities of the
crew, this man's valor, that man's fear; guilt and guiltlessness, all varieties
were welded into oneness, and were all directed to that fatal goal which
Ahab their one lord and keel did point to.

The rigging lived. The mast-heads, like the tops of tall palms, were out-
spreadingly tufted with arms and legs. Clinging to a spar with one hand,
some reached forth the other with impatient wavings; others, shading
their eyes from the vivid sunlight, sat far out on the rocking yards; all the
spars in full bearing of mortals, ready and ripe for their fate. Ah! how they
still strove through that infinite blueness to seek out the thing that might
destroy them!

"Why sing ye not out for him, if ye see him?" cried Ahab, when, after
the lapse of some minutes since the first cry, no more had been heard.
"Sway me up, men; ye have been deceived; not Moby Dick casts one odd
jet that way, and then disappears."

It was even so; in their headlong eagerness, the men had mistaken some
other thing for the whale-spout, as the event itself soon proved; for hardly
had Ahab reached his perch; hardly was the rope belayed to its pin on deck,
when he struck the key-note to an orchestra, that made the air vibrate as
with the combined discharges of rifles. The triumphant halloo of thirty
buckskin lungs was heard, as—much nearer to the ship than the place of
the imaginary jet, less than a mile ahead—Moby Dick bodily burst into
view! For not by any calm and indolent spoutings; not by the peaceable gush
of that mystic fountain in his head, did the White Whale now reveal his
vicinity; but by the far more wondrous phenomenon of breaching. Rising
with his utmost velocity from the furthest depths, the Sperm Whale thus
booms his entire bulk into the pure element of air, and piling up a mountain of dazzling foam, shows his place to the distance of seven miles and
more. In those moments, the torn, enraged waves he shakes off, seem his
mane; in some cases, this breaching is his act of defiance.

"There she breaches! there she breaches!" was the cry, as in his immeasurable bravadoes the White Whale tossed himself salmon-like to Heaven.
So suddenly seen in the blue plain of the sea, and relieved against the still
bluer margin of the sky, the spray that he raised, for the moment, intolerably glittered and glared like a glacier; and stood there gradually fading
and fading away from its first sparkling intensity, to the dim mistiness of
an advancing shower in a vale.

"Aye, breach your last to the sun, Moby Dick!" cried Ahab, "thy hour
and thy harpoon are at hand!—Down! down all of ye, but one man at the
fore. The boats!—stand by!"

Unmindful of the tedious rope-ladders of the shrouds, the men, like shooting stars, slid to the deck, by the isolated backstays and halyards; while Ahab, less dartingly, but still rapidly was dropped from his perch.

"Lower away," he cried, so soon as he had reached his boat—a spare one, rigged the afternoon previous. "Mr. Starbuck, the ship is thine—keep away from the boats, but keep near them. Lower, all!"

As if to strike a quick terror into them, by this time being the first assailant himself, Moby Dick had turned, and was now coming for the three crews. Ahab's boat was central; and cheering his men, he told them he would take the whale head-and-head,—that is, pull straight up to his forehead,—a not uncommon thing; for when within a certain limit, such a course excludes the coming onset from the whale's sidelong vision. But ere that close limit was gained, and while yet all three boats were plain as the ship's three masts to his eye; the White Whale churning himself into furious speed, almost in an instant as it were, rushing among the boats with open jaws, and a lashing tail, offered appalling battle on every side; and heedless of the irons darted at him from every boat, seemed only intent on annihilating each separate plank of which those boats were made. But skilfully manœuvred, incessantly wheeling like trained chargers in the field; the boats for a while eluded him; though, at times, but by a plank's breadth; while all the time, Ahab's unearthly slogan tore every other cry but his to shreds.

But at last in his untraceable evolutions, the White Whale so crossed and recrossed, and in a thousand ways entangled the slack of the three lines now fast to him, that they foreshortened, and, of themselves, warped the devoted boats towards the planted irons in him; though now for a moment the whale drew aside a little, as if to rally for a more tremendous charge. Seizing that opportunity, Ahab first paid out more line: and then was rapidly hauling and jerking in upon it again—hoping that way to disencumber it of some snarls—when lo!—a sight more savage than the embattled teeth of sharks!

Caught and twisted—corkscrewed in the mazes of the line, loose harpoons and lances, with all their bristling barbs and points, came flashing and dripping up to the chocks in the bows of Ahab's boat. Only one thing could be done. Seizing the boat-knife, he critically reached within—through—and then, without—the rays of steel; dragged in the line beyond, passed it, inboard, to the bowsman, and then, twice sundering the rope near the chocks—dropped the intercepted fagot of steel into the sea; and was all fast again. That instant, the White Whale made a sudden rush among the remaining tangles of the other lines; by so doing, irresistibly dragged the more involved boats of Stubb and Flask towards his flukes; dashed them together like two rolling husks on a surf-beaten beach, and then, diving down into the sea, disappeared in a boiling maelstrom, in which, for a space, the odorous cedar chips of the wrecks danced round and round, like the grated nutmeg in a swiftly stirred bowl of punch.

While the two crews were yet circling in the waters, reaching out after the revolving line-tubs, oars, and other floating furniture, while aslope little Flask bobbed up and down like an empty vial, twitching his legs upwards to escape the dreaded jaws of sharks; and Stubb was lustily

singing out for some one to ladle him up; and while the old man's line—
now parting—admitted of his pulling into the creamy pool to rescue
whom he could;—in that wild simultaneousness of a thousand concreted
perils,—Ahab's yet unstricken boat seemed drawn up towards Heaven by
invisible wires,—as, arrow-like, shooting perpendicularly from the sea, the
White Whale dashed his broad forehead against its bottom, and sent it,
turning over and over, into the air; till it fell again—gunwale downwards—
and Ahab and his men struggled out from under it, like seals from a sea-
side cave.

The first uprising momentum of the whale—modifying its direction as he
struck the surface—involuntarily launched him along it, to a little distance
from the centre of the destruction he had made; and with his back to it, he
now lay for a moment slowly feeling with his flukes from side to side; and
whenever a stray oar, bit of plank, the least chip or crumb of the boats
touched his skin, his tail swiftly drew back, and came sideways smiting the
sea. But soon, as if satisfied that his work for that time was done, he pushed
his pleated forehead through the ocean, and trailing after him the intertan-
gled lines, continued his leeward way at a traveller's methodic pace.

As before, the attentive ship having descried the whole fight, again
came bearing down to the rescue, and dropping a boat, picked up the
floating mariners, tubs, oars, and whatever else could be caught at, and
safely landed them on her decks. Some sprained shoulders, wrists, and
ankles; livid contusions; wrenched harpoons and lances; inextricable intricacies of rope; shattered oars and planks; all these were there; but no fatal
or even serious ill seemed to have befallen any one. As with Fedallah the
day before, so Ahab was now found grimly clinging to his boat's broken
half, which afforded a comparatively easy float; nor did it so exhaust him
as the previous day's mishap.

But when he was helped to the deck, all eyes were fastened upon him;
as instead of standing by himself he still half-hung upon the shoulder of
Starbuck, who had thus far been the foremost to assist him. His ivory leg
had been snapped off, leaving but one short sharp splinter.

"Aye aye, Starbuck, 'tis sweet to lean sometimes, be the leaner who he
will; and would old Ahab had leaned oftener than he has."

"The ferrule has not stood, sir," said the carpenter, now coming up; "I
put good work into that leg."

"But no bones broken, sir, I hope," said Stubb with true concern.

"Aye! and all splintered to pieces, Stubb!—d'ye see it.—But even with a
broken bone, old Ahab is untouched; and I account no living bone of mine
one jot more me, than this dead one that's lost. Nor white whale, nor man,
nor fiend, can so much as graze old Ahab in his own proper and inaccessible being. Can any lead touch yonder floor, any mast scrape yonder
roof?—Aloft there! which way?"

"Dead to leeward, sir."

"Up helm, then; pile on the sail again, ship keepers! down the rest of
the spare boats and rig them—Mr. Starbuck away, and muster the boats'
crews."

"Let me first help thee towards the bulwarks, sir."

"Oh, oh, oh! how this splinter gores me now! Accursed fate! that the
unconquerable captain in the soul should have such a craven mate!"

"Sir?"

"My body, man, not thee. Give me something for a cane—there, that shivered lance will do. Muster the men. Surely I have not seen him yet. By heaven it cannot be!—missing?—quick! call them all."

The old man's hinted thought was true. Upon mustering the company, the Parsee was not there.

"The Parsee!" cried Stubb—"he must have been caught in——"

"The black vomit wrench thee!—run all of ye above, alow, cabin, fore-castle—find him—not gone—not gone!"

But quickly they returned to him with the tidings that the Parsee was nowhere to be found.

"Aye, sir," said Stubb—"caught among the tangles of your line—I thought I saw him dragging under."

"*My* line! *my* line? Gone?—gone? What means that little word?—What death-knell rings in it, that old Ahab shakes as if he were the belfry. The harpoon, too!—toss over the litter there,—d'ye see it?—the forged iron, men, the white whale's—no, no, no,—blistered fool! this hand did dart it!—'tis in the fish!—Aloft there! Keep him nailed—Quick!—all hands to the rigging of the boats—collect the oars—harpooneers! the irons, the irons!—hoist the royals higher—a pull on all the sheets!—helm there! steady, steady for your life! I'll ten times girdle the unmeasured globe; yea and dive straight through it, but I'll slay him yet!"

"Great God! but for one single instant show thyself," cried Starbuck; "never, never wilt thou capture him, old man—In Jesus' name no more of this, that's worse than devil's madness. Two days chased; twice stove to splinters; thy very leg once more snatched from under thee; thy evil shadow gone—all good angels mobbing thee with warnings:—what more wouldst thou have?—Shall we keep chasing this murderous fish till he swamps the last man? Shall we be dragged by him to the bottom of the sea? Shall we be towed by him to the infernal world? Oh, oh,—Impiety and blasphemy to hunt him more!"

"Starbuck, of late I've felt strangely moved to thee; ever since that hour we both saw—thou know'st what, in one another's eyes. But in this mat-ter of the whale, be the front of thy face to me as the palm of this hand—a lipless, unfeatured blank. Ahab is for ever Ahab, man. This whole act's immutably decreed. 'Twas rehearsed by thee and me a billion years before this ocean rolled. Fool! I am the Fates' lieutenant; I act under orders. Look thou, underling! that thou obeyest mine.—Stand round me, men. Ye see an old man cut down to the stump; leaning on a shivered lance; propped up on a lonely foot. 'Tis Ahab—his body's part; but Ahab's soul's a cen-tipede, that moves upon a hundred legs. I feel strained, half stranded, as ropes that tow dismasted frigates in a gale; and I may look so. But ere I break, ye'll hear me crack; and till ye hear *that*, know that Ahab's hawser tows his purpose yet. Believe ye, men, in the things called omens? Then laugh aloud, and cry encore! For ere they drown, drowning things will twice rise to the surface; then rise again, to sink for evermore. So with Moby Dick—two days he's floated—to-morrow will be the third. Aye, men, he'll rise once more,—but only to spout his last! D'ye feel brave, men, brave?"

"As fearless fire," cried Stubb.

"And as mechanical," muttered Ahab. Then as the men went forward, he muttered on:—"The things called omens! And yesterday I talked the same to Starbuck there, concerning my broken boat. Oh! how valiantly I seek to drive out of others' hearts what's clinched so fast in mine!—The Parsee—the Parsee!—gone, gone? and he was to go before:—but still was to be seen again ere I could perish—How's that?—There's a riddle now might baffle all the lawyers backed by the ghosts of the whole line of judges:—like a hawk's beak it pecks my brain. *I'll, I'll* solve it, though!"

When dusk descended, the whale was still in sight to leeward.

So once more the sail was shortened, and everything passed nearly as on the previous night; only, the sound of hammers, and the hum of the grind-stone was heard till nearly daylight, as the men toiled by lanterns in the complete and careful rigging of the spare boats and sharpening their fresh weapons for the morrow. Meantime, of the broken keel of Ahab's wrecked craft the carpenter made him another leg; while still as on the night before, slouched Ahab stood fixed within his scuttle; his hid, heliotrope glance anticipatingly gone backward on its dial; set due eastward for the earliest sun.

Chapter 135

The Chase—Third Day

The morning of the third day dawned fair and fresh, and once more the solitary night-man at the fore-mast-head was relieved by crowds of the daylight look-outs, who dotted every mast and almost every spar.

"D'ye see him?" cried Ahab; but the whale was not yet in sight.

"In his infallible wake, though; but follow that wake, that's all. Helm there; steady, as thou goest, and hast been going. What a lovely day again! were it a new-made world, and made for a summer-house to the angels, and this morning the first of its throwing open to them, a fairer day could not dawn upon that world. Here's food for thought, had Ahab time to think; but Ahab never thinks; he only feels, feels, feels; *that's* tingling enough for mortal man! to think's audacity. God only has that right and privilege. Thinking is, or ought to be, a coolness and a calmness; and our poor hearts throb, and our poor brains beat too much for that. And yet, I've sometimes thought my brain was very calm—frozen calm, this old skull cracks so, like a glass in which the contents turn to ice, and shiver it. And still this hair is growing now; this moment growing, and heat must breed it; but no, it's like that sort of common grass that will grow anywhere, between the earthy clefts of Greenland ice or in Vesuvius lava. How the wild winds blow it; they whip it about me as the torn shreds of split sails lash the tossed ship they cling to. A vile wind that has no doubt blown ere this through prison corridors and cells, and wards of hospitals, and ventilated them, and now comes blowing hither as innocent as fleeces. Out upon it!—it's tainted. Were I the wind, I'd blow no more on such a wicked, miserable world. I'd crawl somewhere to a cave, and slink there. And yet, 'tis a noble and heroic thing, the wind! who ever conquered it? In every fight it has the last and bitterest blow. Run tilting at it, and you but run through it. Ha! a coward wind that strikes stark naked men, but will not stand to receive a single blow. Even Ahab is a braver thing—a nobler thing than *that*. Would now the wind but had a body; but all the things that most exasperate and outrage mortal man, all these things are bodiless, but only bodiless as objects, not as agents. There's a most special, a most cunning, oh, a most malicious difference! And yet, I say again, and swear it now, that there's something all glorious and gracious in the wind. These warm Trade Winds, at least, that in the clear heavens blow straight on, in strong and steadfast, vigorous mildness; and veer not from their mark, however the baser currents of the sea may turn and tack, and mightiest Mississippies of the land swift and swerve about, uncertain where to go at last. And by the eternal Poles! these same Trades that so directly blow my good ship on; these Trades, or something like them—something so unchangeable, and full as strong, blow my keeled soul along! To it! Aloft there! What d'ye see?"

"Nothing, sir."

"Nothing! and noon at hand! The doubloon goes a-begging! See the sun! Aye, aye, it must be so. I've oversailed him. How, got the start? Aye, he's chasing *me* now; not I, *him*—that's bad; I might have known it, too. Fool! the lines—the harpoons he's towing. Aye, aye, I have run him by last night. About! about! Come down, all of ye, but the regular look outs! Man the braces!"

Steering as she had done, the wind had been somewhat on the Pequod's quarter, so that now being pointed in the reverse direction, the braced ship sailed hard upon the breeze as she rechurned the cream in her own white wake.

"Against the wind he now steers for the open jaw," murmured Starbuck to himself, as he coiled the new-hauled main-brace upon the rail. "God keep us, but already my bones feel damp within me, and from the inside wet my flesh. I misdoubt me that I disobey my God in obeying him!"

"Stand by to sway me up!" cried Ahab, advancing to the hempen basket. "We should meet him soon."

"Aye, aye, sir," and straightway Starbuck did Ahab's bidding, and once more Ahab swung on high.

A whole hour now passed; gold-beaten out to ages. Time itself now held long breaths with keen suspense. But at last, some three points off the weather bow, Ahab descried the spout again, and instantly from the three mast-heads three shrieks went up as if the tongues of fire had voiced it.

"Forehead to forehead I meet thee, this third time, Moby Dick! On deck there!—brace sharper up; crowd her into the wind's eye. He's too far off to lower yet, Mr. Starbuck. The sails shake! Stand over that helmsman with a top-maul! So, so; he travels fast, and I must down. But let me have one more good round look aloft here at the sea; there's time for that. An old, old sight, and yet somehow so young; aye, and not changed a wink since I first saw it, a boy, from the sand-hills of Nantucket! The same!—the same!—the same to Noah as to me. There's a soft shower to leeward. Such lovely leewardings! They must lead somewhere—to something else than common land, more palmy than the palms. Leeward! the white whale goes that way; look to windward, then; the better if the bitterer quarter. But good bye, good bye, old mast-head! What's this?—green? aye, tiny mosses in these warped cracks. No such green weather stains on Ahab's head! There's the difference now between man's old age and matter's. But aye, old mast, we both grow old together; sound in our hulls, though, are we not, my ship? Aye, minus a leg, that's all. By heaven this dead wood has the better of my live flesh every way. I can't compare with it; and I've known some ships made of dead trees outlast the lives of men made of the most vital stuff of vital fathers. What's that he said? he should still go before me, my pilot; and yet to be seen again? But where? Will I have eyes at the bottom of the sea, supposing I descend those endless stairs? and all night I've been sailing from him, wherever he did sink to. Aye, aye, like many more thou told'st direful truth as touching thyself, O Parsee; but, Ahab, there thy shot fell short. Good by, mast-head—keep a good eye upon the whale, the while I'm gone. We'll talk to-morrow, nay, to-night, when the white whale lies down there, tied by head and tail."

He gave the word; and still gazing round him, was steadily lowered through the cloven blue air to the deck.

In due time the boats were lowered; but as standing in his shallop's stern, Ahab just hovered upon the point of the descent, he waved to the mate,—who held one of the tackle-ropes on deck—and bade him pause.

"Starbuck!"

"Sir?"

"For the third time my soul's ship starts upon this voyage, Starbuck."

"Aye, sir, thou wilt have it so."

"Some ships sail from their ports, and ever afterwards are missing, Starbuck!"

"Truth, sir: saddest truth."

"Some men die at ebb tide; some at low water; some at the full of the flood;—and I feel now like a billow that's all one crested comb, Starbuck. I am old;—shake hands with me, man."

Their hands met; their eyes fastened; Starbuck's tears the glue.

"Oh, my captain, my captain!—noble heart—go not—go not!—see, it's a brave man that weeps; how great the agony of the persuasion then!"

"Lower away!"—cried Ahab, tossing the mate's arm from him. "Stand by the crew!"

In an instant the boat was pulling round close under the stern.

"The sharks! the sharks!" cried a voice from the low cabin-window there; "O master, my master, come back!"

But Ahab heard nothing; for his own voice was high-lifted then; and the boat leaped on.

Yet the voice spake true; for scarce had he pushed from the ship, when numbers of sharks, seemingly rising from out the dark waters beneath the hull, maliciously snapped at the blades of the oars, every time they dipped in the water; and in this way accompanied the boat with their bites. It is a thing not uncommonly happening to the whale-boats in those swarming seas; the sharks at times apparently following them in the same prescient way that vultures hover over the banners of marching regiments in the east. But these were the first sharks that had been observed by the Pequod since the White Whale had been first descried; and whether it was that Ahab's crew were all such tiger-yellow barbarians, and therefore their flesh more musky to the senses of the sharks—a matter sometimes well known to affect them,—however it was, they seemed to follow that one boat without molesting the others.

"Heart of wrought steel!" murmured Starbuck gazing over the side, and following with his eyes the receding boat—"canst thou yet ring boldly to that sight?—lowering thy keel among ravening sharks, and followed by them, open-mouthed to the chase; and this the critical third day?—For when three days flow together in one continuous intense pursuit; be sure the first is the morning, the second the noon, and the third the evening and the end of that thing—be that end what it may. Oh! my God! what is this that shoots through me, and leaves me so deadly calm, yet expectant,—fixed at the top of a shudder! Future things swim before me, as in empty outlines and skeletons; all the past is somehow grown dim. Mary, girl! thou fadest in pale glories behind me; boy! I seem to see but thy eyes grown wondrous blue. Strangest problems of life seem clearing; but clouds sweep between—Is my journey's end coming? My legs feel faint; like his who has footed it all day. Feel thy heart,—beats it yet?—Stir thyself, Starbuck!—stave it off—move, move! speak aloud!—Mast-head there! See ye my boy's hand on the hill?—Crazed;—aloft there!—keep thy keenest eye upon the boats:—mark well the whale!—Ho! again!—drive off that hawk! see! he pecks—he tears the vane"—pointing to the red flag flying at the main-truck—"Ha! he soars away with it!—Where's the old man now? sees't thou that sight, oh Ahab!—shudder, shudder!"

The boats had not gone very far, when by a signal from the mast-heads—a downward pointed arm, Ahab knew that the whale had sounded; but intending to be near him at the next rising, he held on his way a little sideways from the vessel; the becharmed crew maintaining the profoundest silence, as the head-beat waves hammered and hammered against the opposing bow.

"Drive, drive in your nails, oh ye waves! to their uttermost heads drive them in! ye but strike a thing without a lid; and no coffin and no hearse can be mine:—and hemp only can kill me! Ha! ha!"

Suddenly the waters around them slowly swelled in broad circles; then quickly upheaved, as if sideways sliding from a submerged berg of ice, swiftly rising to the surface. A low rumbling sound was heard; a subterraneous hum; and then all held their breaths; as bedraggled with trailing ropes, and harpoons, and lances, a vast form shot lengthwise, but obliquely from the sea. Shrouded in a thin drooping veil of mist, it hovered for a moment in the rainbowed air; and then fell swamping back into the deep. Crushed thirty feet upwards, the waters flashed for an instant like heaps of fountains, then brokenly sank in a shower of flakes, leaving the circling surface creamed like new milk round the marble trunk of the whale.

"Give way!" cried Ahab to the oarsmen, and the boats darted forward to the attack; but maddened by yesterday's fresh irons that corroded in him, Moby Dick seemed combinedly possessed by all the angels that fell from heaven. The wide tiers of welded tendons overspreading his broad white forehead, beneath the transparent skin, looked knitted together; as head on, he came churning his tail among the boats; and once more flailed them apart; spilling out the irons and lances from the two mates' boats, and dashing in one side of the upper part of their bows, but leaving Ahab's almost without a scar.

While Daggoo and Tashtego were stopping the strained planks; and as the whale swimming out from them, turned, and showed one entire flank as he shot by them again; at that moment a quick cry went up. Lashed round and round to the fish's back; pinioned in the turns upon turns in which, during the past night, the whale had reeled the involutions of the lines around him, the half torn body of the Parsee was seen; his sable raiment frayed to shreds; his distended eyes turned full upon old Ahab.

The harpoon dropped from his hand.

"Befooled, befooled!"—drawing in a long lean breath—"Aye, Parsee! I see thee again.—Aye, and thou goest before; and this, *this* then is the hearse that thou didst promise. But I hold thee to the last letter of thy word. Where is the second hearse? Away, mates, to the ship! those boats are useless now; repair them if ye can in time, and return to me; if not, Ahab is enough to die—Down, men! the first thing that but offers to jump from this boat I stand in, that thing I harpoon. Ye are not other men, but my arms and my legs; and so obey me.—Where's the whale? gone down again?"

But he looked too nigh the boat; for as if bent upon escaping with the corpse he bore, and as if the particular place of the last encounter had been but a stage in his leeward voyage, Moby Dick was now again steadily swimming forward; and had almost passed the ship,—which thus far had been sailing in the contrary direction to him, though for the present her headway had been stopped. He seemed swimming with his utmost velocity, and now only intent upon pursuing his own straight path in the sea.

"Oh! Ahab," cried Starbuck, "not too late is it, even now, the third day, to desist. See! Moby Dick seeks thee not. It is thou, thou, that madly seekest him!"

Setting sail to the rising wind, the lonely boat was swiftly impelled to leeward, by both oars and canvas. And at last when Ahab was sliding by the vessel, so near as plainly to distinguish Starbuck's face as he leaned over the rail, he hailed him to turn the vessel about, and follow him, not too swiftly, at a judicious interval. Glancing upwards, he saw Tashtego, Queequeg, and Daggoo, eagerly mounting to the three mast-heads; while the oarsmen were rocking in the two staved boats which had but just been hoisted to the side, and were busily at work in repairing them. One after the other, through the port-holes, as he sped, he also caught flying glimpses of Stubb and Flask, busying themselves on deck among bundles of new irons and lances. As he saw all this; as he heard the hammers in the broken boats; far other hammers seemed driving a nail into his heart. But he rallied. And now marking that the vane or flag was gone from the main-mast-head, he shouted to Tashtego, who had just gained that perch, to descend again for another flag, and a hammer and nails, and so nail it to the mast.

Whether fagged by the three days' running chase, and the resistance to his swimming in the knotted hamper he bore; or whether it was some latent deceitfulness and malice in him: whichever was true, the White Whale's way now began to abate, as it seemed, from the boat so rapidly nearing him once more; though indeed the whale's last start had not been

so long a one as before. And still as Ahab glided over the waves the unpitying sharks accompanied him; and so pertinaciously stuck to the boat; and
so continually bit at the plying oars, that the blades became jagged and
crunched, and left small splinters in the sea, at almost every dip.

"Heed them not! those teeth but give new rowlocks to your oars. Pull
on! 'tis the better rest, the shark's jaw than the yielding water."

"But at every bite, sir, the thin blades grow smaller and smaller!"

"They will last long enough! pull on!—But who can tell"—he muttered—"whether these sharks swim to feast on the whale or on Ahab?—
But pull on! Aye, all alive, now—we near him. The helm! take the helm;
let me pass,"—and so saying, two of the oarsmen helped him forward to
the bows of the still flying boat.

At length as the craft was cast to one side, and ran ranging along with
the White Whale's flank, he seemed strangely oblivious of its advance—
as the whale sometimes will—and Ahab was fairly within the smoky
mountain mist, which, thrown off from the whale's spout, curled round
his great, Monadnock[1] hump; he was even thus close to him; when, with
body arched back, and both arms lengthwise high-lifted to the poise, he
darted his fierce iron, and his far fiercer curse into the hated whale. As
both steel and curse sank to the socket, as if sucked into a morass, Moby
Dick sideways writhed; spasmodically rolled his nigh flank against the
bow, and, without staving a hole in it, so suddenly canted the boat over,
that had it not been for the elevated part of the gunwale to which he
then clung, Ahab would once more have been tossed into the sea. As it
was, three of the oarsmen—who foreknew not the precise instant of the
dart, and were therefore unprepared for its effects—these were flung
out; but so fell, that, in an instant two of them clutched the gunwale
again, and rising to its level on a combing wave, hurled themselves bodily inboard again; the third man helplessly dropping astern, but still
afloat and swimming.

Almost simultaneously, with a mighty volition of ungraduated, instantaneous swiftness, the White Whale darted through the weltering sea. But
when Ahab cried out to the steersman to take new turns with the line, and
hold it so; and commanded the crew to turn round on their seats, and tow
the boat up to the mark; the moment the treacherous line felt that double strain and tug, it snapped in the empty air!

"What breaks in me? Some sinew cracks!—'tis whole again; oars! oars!
Burst in upon him!"

Hearing the tremendous rush of the sea-crashing boat, the whale
wheeled round to present his blank forehead at bay; but in that evolution,
catching sight of the nearing black hull of the ship; seemingly seeing in it
the source of all his persecutions; bethinking it—it may be—a larger and
nobler foe; of a sudden, he bore down upon its advancing prow, smiting
his jaws amid fiery showers of foam.

Ahab staggered; his hand smote his forehead. "I grow blind; hands!
stretch out before me that I may yet grope my way. Is't night?"

"The whale! The ship!" cried the cringing oarsmen.

"Oars! oars! Slope downwards to thy depths, O sea, that ere it be for

1. Mountain in New Hampshire.

ever too late, Ahab may slide this last, last time upon his mark! I see: the ship! the ship! Dash on, my men! Will ye not save my ship?"

But as the oarsmen violently forced their boat through the sledge-hammering seas, the before whale-smitten bow-ends of two planks burst through, and in an instant almost, the temporarily disabled boat lay nearly level with the waves; its half-wading, splashing crew, trying hard to stop the gap and bale out the pouring water.

Meantime, for that one beholding instant, Tashtego's mast-head hammer remained suspended in his hand; and the red flag, half-wrapping him as with a plaid, then streamed itself straight out from him, as his own forward-flowing heart; while Starbuck and Stubb, standing upon the bowsprit beneath, caught sight of the down-coming monster just as soon as he.

"The whale, the whale! Up helm, up helm! Oh, all ye sweet powers of air, now hug me close! Let not Starbuck die, if die he must, in a woman's fainting fit. Up helm, I say—ye fools, the jaw! the jaw! Is this the end of all my bursting prayers? all my life-long fidelities? Oh, Ahab, Ahab, lo, thy work. Steady! helmsman, steady. Nay, nay! Up helm again! He turns to meet us! Oh, his unappeasable brow drives on towards one, whose duty tells him he cannot depart. My God, stand by me now!"

"Stand not by me, but stand under me, whoever you are that will now help Stubb; for Stubb, too, sticks here. I grin at thee, thou grinning whale! Who ever helped Stubb, or kept Stubb awake, but Stubb's own unwinking eye? And now poor Stubb goes to bed upon a mattrass that is all too soft; would it were stuffed with brushwood! I grin at thee, thou grinning whale! Look ye, sun, moon, and stars! I call ye assassins of as good a fellow as ever spouted up his ghost. For all that, I would yet ring glasses with ye, would ye but hand the cup! Oh, oh! oh, oh! thou grinning whale, but there 'll be plenty of gulping soon! Why fly ye not, O Ahab! For me, off shoes and jacket to it; let Stubb die in his drawers! A most mouldy and over salted death, though;—cherries! cherries! cherries! oh, Flask, for one red cherry ere we die!"

"Cherries? I only wish that we were where they grow. Oh, Stubb, I hope my poor mother's drawn my part-pay ere this; if not, few coppers will now come to her, for the voyage is up."

From the ship's bows, nearly all the seamen now hung inactive; hammers, bits of plank, lances, and harpoons, mechanically retained in their hands, just as they had darted from their various employments; all their enchanted eyes intent upon the whale, which from side to side strangely vibrating his predestinating head, sent a broad band of overspreading semi-circular foam before him as he rushed. Retribution, swift vengeance, eternal malice were in his whole aspect, and spite of all that mortal man could do, the solid white buttress of his forehead smote the ship's starboard bow, till men and timbers reeled. Some fell flat upon their faces. Like dislodged trucks,[2] the heads of the harpooneers aloft shook on their bull-like necks. Through the breach, they heard the waters pour, as mountain torrents down a flume.

---

2. Small wooden caps at the tops of mastheads.

"The ship! The hearse!—the second hearse!" cried Ahab from the boat; "its wood could only be American!"

Diving beneath the settling ship, the whale ran quivering along its keel; but turning under water, swiftly shot to the surface again, far off the other bow, but within a few yards of Ahab's boat, where, for a time, he lay quiescent.

"I turn my body from the sun. What ho, Tashtego! let me hear thy hammer. Oh! ye three unsurrendered spires of mine; thou uncracked keel; and only god-bullied hull; thou firm deck, and haughty helm, and Pole-pointed prow,—death-glorious ship! must ye then perish, and without me? Am I cut off from the last fond pride of meanest shipwrecked captains? Oh, lonely death on lonely life! Oh, now I feel my topmost greatness lies in my topmost grief. Ho, ho! from all your furthest bounds, pour ye now in, ye bold billows of my whole foregone life, and top this one piled comber of my death! Towards thee I roll, thou all-destroying but unconquering whale; to the last I grapple with thee; from hell's heart I stab at thee; for hate's sake I spit my last breath at thee. Sink all coffins and all hearses to one common pool! and since neither can be mine, let me then tow to pieces, while still chasing thee, though tied to thee, thou damned whale! *Thus,* I give up the spear!"

The harpoon was darted; the stricken whale flew forward; with igniting velocity the line ran through the groove;—ran foul. Ahab stooped to clear it; he did clear it; but the flying turn caught him round the neck, and voicelessly as Turkish mutes bowstring their victim, he was shot out of the boat, ere the crew knew he was gone. Next instant, the heavy eye-splice in the rope's final end flew out of the stark-empty tub, knocked down an oarsman, and smiting the sea, disappeared in its depths.

For an instant, the tranced boat's crew stood still; then turned. "The ship? Great God, where is the ship?" Soon they through dim, bewildering mediums saw her sidelong fading phantom, as in the gaseous Fata Morgana;[3] only the uppermost masts out of water; while fixed by infatuation, or fidelity, or fate, to their once lofty perches, the pagan harpooneers still maintained their sinking lookouts on the sea. And now, concentric circles seized the lone boat itself, and all its crew, and each floating oar, and every lance-pole, and spinning, animate and inanimate, all round and round in one vortex, carried the smallest chip of the Pequod out of sight.

But as the last whelmings intermixingly poured themselves over the sunken head of the Indian at the mainmast, leaving a few inches of the erect spar yet visible, together with long streaming yards of the flag, which calmly undulated, with ironical coincidings, over the destroying billows they almost touched;—at that instant, a red arm and a hammer hovered backwardly uplifted in the open air, in the act of nailing the flag faster and yet faster to the subsiding spar. A sky-hawk that tauntingly had followed the main-truck downwards from its natural home among the stars, pecking at the flag, and incommoding Tashtego there; this bird now chanced to intercept its broad fluttering wing between the hammer and the wood; and simultaneously feeling that etherial thrill, the submerged savage beneath, in his death-grasp, kept his hammer frozen there; and so the bird

---

3. Mirage, from the Italian for Morgan le Fay, sorceress sister of King Arthur in Celtic legends.

of heaven, with archangelic shrieks, and his imperial beak thrust upwards, and his whole captive form folded in the flag of Ahab, went down with his ship, which, like Satan, would not sink to hell till she had dragged a living part of heaven along with her, and helmeted herself with it.

Now small fowls flew screaming over the yet yawning gulf; a sullen white surf beat against its steep sides; then all collapsed, and the great shroud of the sea rolled on as it rolled five thousand years ago.[4]

Epilogue

"And I only am escaped alone to tell thee."
                                        Job.[1]

The drama's done. Why then here does any one step forth?—Because one did survive the wreck.

It so chanced, that after the Parsee's disappearance, I was he whom the Fates ordained to take the place of Ahab's bowsman, when that bowsman assumed the vacant post; the same, who, when on the last day the three men were tossed from out the rocking boat, was dropped astern. So, floating on the margin of the ensuing scene, and in full sight of it, when the half-spent suction of the sunk ship reached me, I was then, but slowly, drawn towards the closing vortex. When I reached it, it had subsided to a creamy pool. Round and round, then, and ever contracting towards the button-like black bubble at the axis of that slowly wheeling circle, like another Ixion I did revolve. Till, gaining that vital centre, the black bubble upward burst; and now, liberated by reason of its cunning spring, and, owing to its great buoyancy, rising with great force, the coffin life-buoy shot lengthwise from the sea, fell over, and floated by my side. Buoyed up by that coffin, for almost one whole day and night, I floated on a soft and dirge-like main. The unharming sharks, they glided by as if with padlocks on their mouths; the savage sea-hawks sailed with sheathed beaks. On the second day, a sail drew near, nearer, and picked me up at last. It was the devious-cruising Rachel, that in her retracing search after her missing children, only found another orphan.

FINIS

---

4. At the time of Noah's flood.
1. Job 1.14–19, the formula with which each of four messengers concludes his terrible news about the loss of Job's animals, his servants, and his children.

CONTEXTS

Melville's Reading and
Moby-Dick: An Overview
and a Bibliography†

First, this note traces Melville's whaling sources, both those he already knew in January 1850 (when he devoted many hours of a long voyage across the Atlantic to planning the book he would start to write once he arrived in New York City), and other books and articles on whaling that he encountered later. Second, it surveys some of the most important non-nautical books that influenced *Moby-Dick,* particularly the Bible and Shakespeare. Third, it lists all these works with full titles for ready reference by anyone using our footnotes to the text of *Moby-Dick.* The list includes a few documentary modern books (e.g., the one by Stuart Frank) along with those Melville read. This note is not exhaustive; not every known or suggested influence is listed, and new sources remain to be discovered.

Melville's reading of whaling stories may have dated from the time he was a young man living with his mother in Lansingburgh, just north of Albany, New York. Weeks before he sailed to Liverpool on his first voyage, the May 1839 issue of a popular New York magazine, the *Knickerbocker,* published J. N. Reynolds's "Mocha Dick: or the White Whale of the Pacific: A Leaf from a Manuscript Journal," an account that readers found enthralling—and memorable, for people alluded to it in print for years afterward. A reviewer of *Moby-Dick* late in 1851 was to recall that every "old 'Jack-tar'" knew the story of Mocha Dick; and in the early 1840s the young jack-tar Herman Melville found good chances to know it, or part of it, from print or from sailors' yarns and perhaps even then had chances to retell it. On May 27, 1839, the Albany *Argus* printed "Method of Taking the Whale" from the British surgeon Thomas Beale's *The Natural History of the Sperm Whale,* an excerpt that included the powerful passage about the death flurry of the immense creature, mad with his agonies. If Melville somehow missed that sample of Beale, he had another chance to read it after his return from his first voyage, because a paper just across the Hudson from Lansingburgh, the West Troy *Advocate,* devoted two columns to it on October 23, 1839 (six months after the *Advocate* had reprinted one of his own earliest publications, one of two pieces of fiction he called "Fragments from a Writing Desk").

Melville may have thought of writing about whaling even before he was twenty, because he was already a writer, with two "Fragments" printed in local papers in May 1839, the month Reynolds's article appeared and the month the excerpt from Beale was published in the Albany *Argus.* Early the next month, in June 1839, Melville considered shipping on a whaler in Sag Harbor, on the eastern tip of Long Island, before he signed on the merchant ship

---

† This is a discursive guide to Melville's source-books cited in the footnotes to the text of *Moby-Dick* of this NCE and an annotated ready-reference list of them. Hershel Parker adapted the discursive part from "The Breaching of Mocha Dick: January 1850," ch. 33 of his *Herman Melville: A Biography, 1819–1851.*

for a voyage to Liverpool; he and his older brother Gansevoort went so far as to calculate distances from Manhattan to Sag Harbor by two different routes. When he sailed on the whaler the *Acushnet* at the start of 1841, Melville would naturally have thought that he might write about whaling, if he survived the perilous voyage. Later in 1841 he was deeply stirred when he read Owen Chase's account of the sinking of the *Essex* by a vengeful whale (Chase was certain as to the vengefulness), in a copy of the book providentially loaned him by a young whaleman, a son of Chase himself, while in Pacific waters not far from the site of the disaster. Chase's narrative (and the circumstances of his first reading it) affected Melville's imagination powerfully, then and for many years later. (See an excerpt from Chase on p. 565 herein and Melville's notes in his copy of Chase on p. 571 herein.)

Whatever Melville's thoughts in 1841–43 (his whaling years) that he might write about whaling, drawing on his experiences and what others told him, it turned out that once he jumped ship in Nukuheva in the summer of 1842 and lived (however briefly) among the Typees, he had a different sort of story to tell. His tale of life among the cannibals proved irresistible to everyone he met, from fellow whalemen and sailors on a U.S. frigate to, a little later, the chief justice of the supreme court of the Commonwealth of Massachusetts and his daughter. Unquestionably, *Typee* (1846) had to be written first, and then to establish himself as something more than a one-book writer Melville had to produce its sequel, *Omoo* (1847), set a few months later, mainly on his second whale ship and on Tahiti. Melville's reading, in the library of the frigate the *United States* (1843–44) and in libraries ashore, continued to expose him to books on whaling he could test against his own experiences. During his work on his first books Melville acquired or became familiar with several of the works that were to become source books for *Moby-Dick*. For *Omoo* he used Charles Wilkes's *United States Exploring Expedition*, and he purchased his own copy in April 1847 for work on *Mardi*, so it was available for use in *Moby-Dick*. (See the repeated references to Wilkes in the section "Before *Moby-Dick*: International Controversy over Melville" on p. 465 herein)

Melville's third book, *Mardi* (1849), started off in a whale ship, and he may for a while have meant it to be his book about whaling. In 1847, during the early stages of his work on *Mardi*, he acquired a copy of Frederick Debell Bennett's *Whaling Voyage round the Globe*. He owned J. Ross Browne's *Etchings of a Whaling Cruise* from early in 1847, when he reviewed it for the *Literary World* (see "Reviews and Letters by Melville" on p. 511 herein). By early 1849, Melville knew at least one of two works by William Scoresby Jr. on whaling, the *Voyage to the Northern Whale Fishery*, because he made offhand mention of it in his review for Duyckinck's *Literary World* (April 28, 1849) of Cooper's *The Sea Lions*. These are only some of the whaling sources Melville had at hand by the end of the 1840s. He had, all in all, a good working library on whaling when he sailed for England in October 1849, arriving in time to read reviews of his fourth book, *Redburn*. His purpose was to sell his fifth book, *White-Jacket* (1850), a feat he accomplished, but only after such delays that he had to relinquish the hope of making a grand tour of Europe and possibly the Near East.

In January 1850, brooding in the Atlantic on his voyage home about what he might use to supplement or spark his memories of whaling, Melville would have thought of Reynolds and Chase above all other printed sources. We fixate on printed sources, but from the personal experiences of his shipmates on three whalers and their accumulations of stories from *their* previous voyages, Melville held in his memory hundreds of observations, anecdotes, and longer stories now quite irrecoverable. Merely from his own memory of Reynolds's article, Melville could plan, at sea, a book about the pursuit of a great white whale famous in the fishery by the name of Mocha Dick, or some similar name. Reynolds had vividly described the death of Mocha Dick, but Melville's white whale, rather than being killed, could sink a ship deliberately and revengefully, and then swim triumphantly away, like the consciously vengeful whale Chase described. And Chase offered Melville, ready made, a stupendous catastrophe, more awesome even than Reynolds's. As he planned a book on whaling, Melville knew he could get hold of Thomas Beale's book and any other scientific books of whaling he learned of. From printed sources already available to him, once he reached home, he knew he would lay hand on many set scenes, expected in whaling books. It was already conventional, for instance, to describe the chicanery by which villainous landsmen lured green youths to sign on a whaling voyage. Once launched, Melville could write his own vivid descriptions of captains, mates, harpooneers, and other members of a crew, perhaps even more vivid than Reynolds's splendid portrait of the first mate who killed the white whale. He would have known from the start that he could make something luridly moody from another essential scene that had been attempted before, a description of the try-works at night.

If Melville on the voyage home thought he knew of all the books he would need, he soon learned better, for Henry T. Cheever's *The Whale and His Captors* was waiting for him, just published at the end of 1849 by the Harpers. Finding himself in some ways scooped, Melville must have asked himself how the Harpers would respond to a new book on the same subject, but there was no stopping his creative process. Over the next year and a half Melville found still other whaling sources. In the course of things, once he began the book he was led to new sources, and friends began to call books to his attention and to send him choice little passages about whales that went into his "Extracts."

The whaling books he owned or had heard about would be essential, Melville knew, for he had been from the outset a writer who borrowed heavily from previous writers (perhaps even more than from oral storytellers he had known). Desiring to appear to be writing from his own experience, he often went to some trouble to disguise the nature and extent of the borrowing, and very early he developed a habit of making fun of some of his sources even as he failed to acknowledge them or misled readers as to the nature of his debts. Yet in his mind, Reynolds and Chase aside, the writings that meant most to Melville's ambitions as he planned his whaling book on shipboard (most of them lodged in his memory, a few newly purchased ones packed in his sea chest on the *Independence*) were primarily the sort of old books that he had surprised his editor friend Evert A. Duyckinck two years earlier by borrowing and commenting on with acuity unexpected in a sailor. Melville imposed his habitual way of using books even upon the classics, for he tended to take hold of them providentially, as when he discovered a large-print edition of Shakespeare early in 1849 just when he was ready to grapple with the plays and just when he had many days in Boston with not much else to do besides look in on his wife and newborn son, and read. (The son was Malcolm, a name in the Scottish "Melvill" family, but also, everyone knew, the young man who at the end of *Macbeth* is hailed as the king of Scotland.) The book he wrote in the year and a half after reaching home at the beginning of February 1850 would be pervasively influenced by Shakespeare's plays (where King Lear and other tragic heroes provided models for Ahab's rhetoric). It would also be pervasively influenced by the Bible (in particular the Book of Job, which provided an analogue for Ahab's quarrel with God, and the Book of Jonah, which provided an analogue for Ishmael's less defiant method of coming to terms with the universe). Melville had never stopped reading the Bible, usually in the King James Version, and the language of *Moby-Dick* is suffused with echoes of the long-familiar Bible and the freshly absorbed (or reabsorbed) Shakespeare. The Bible and Shakespeare shaped the language and psychology of *Moby-Dick* as decisively as J. N. Reynolds and Owen Chase shaped the plot.

Other non-nautical works (including classics of English literature, along with some European classics, in translation) may be listed in the order in which Melville encountered them, or re-encountered them, before beginning *Moby-Dick* (taking evidence of purchase or borrowing as a rough guide, and only that, to the sequence in which he read or reread them). The presiding genius of his brooding adolescence, Lord Byron, and Byron's self-portraits in the heroes of book-length poems like *Childe Harold's Pilgrimage* and *Manfred*, decisively influenced the characterization of Bulkington, so important, it seems, in Melville's early concept of his whaling book. Sir Walter Scott exerted a powerful influence over the imagination of all young readers in Melville's youth by his immensely popular poetry then by novels that transformed the scope and historical seriousness fiction might aim at; for Melville, who followed his own career as prose writer with a long second career as poet, Scott showed what being a complete literary man might be. Furthermore, Scott was blessedly Scottish, like the Melvills (the final "e" was added only in Melville's youth); Melville's father once called on his not distant cousin, the earl of Leven and Melvill. The subject of Scott's importance to Melville awaits the attention of a scholar equally knowledgeable in both writers; Melville's familiarity with Scott appears casually in *Moby-Dick* (ch. 72, "The Monkeyrope").

Beginning in 1847, Robert Burton's *Anatomy of Melancholy* served as Melville's sonorous textbook on morbid psychology. Early in 1848 he bought Montaigne's works, where he read the *Essays*, finding there a wordly wise skepticism that braced him against the superficial pieties demanded by his time. From his friend Duyckinck early in 1848 Melville borrowed Sir Thomas Browne's *Religio Medici*, then astonished the lender by calling Browne "a kind of 'crack'd Archangel.'" ("Was ever any thing of this sort said before by a sailor?" Duyckinck wrote his brother.) Melville absorbed the seductive prose rhythms that Browne had put to the service of a dumbfoundingly self-possessed idiosyncrasy; in London late in 1849 he bought the 1686 folio of Browne's works, where he read *Vulgar Errors*, alluded to in *Moby-Dick*. In mid 1848 he obtained a copy of Dante, where he found an anatomy of human sinfulness. Inspired by the accessibility of what he considered a large-type Shakespeare early in 1849, he sought out an edition of Milton by the same publisher in a similar format and soon was rereading *Paradise Lost* (from which he derived some of Ahab's qualities as Satanic opponent). A little later in 1849 he obtained Pierre Bayle's *An Historical and Critical Dictionary* in four folio volumes, rejoicing in the blandly ironic Enlightenment skepticism toward lives of historical and literary people and toward philosophical questions.

In London in December 1849 Melville bought and read Laurence Sterne's *Tristram Shandy*, reveling in its liberating gamesomeness toward the lofty task of bookmaking. A few days later he devoured Thomas De Quincey's *Confessions of an English Opium Eater* ("A wonderful thing, that book," he wrote in his journal). He found there a Malay whose Asiatic associations he soon infused into Fedallah and his boat's crew and found also an apparently inimitable prose style that to Melville was as natural as his own voice. In London late in 1849 he bought Christopher Marlowe's *Dramatic Works* and soon read at least *Doctor Faustus*. Well before he began *Moby-Dick* he knew Goethe's *Faust* (where, as in *Doctor Faustus*, he found analogues of demonic temptation and heroic obsession). In London he bought Goethe's *Auto-Biog-*

raphy, the account of a philosophical and artistic life that he had to hold up against Lord Byron's as he weighed his relationships to the two men who loomed as the great European writers of his era. In Thomas Hope's *Anastasius; or, Memoirs of a Greek*, which he bought twice on his European trip late in 1849 (the first copy seized by the English customs officers at Dover as obscene), he found hints for his character Ishmael's twists of mind and actions, not least a ceremonial marriage between men. In London he obtained Mary Shelley's *Frankenstein* (which may have influenced Ahab's prolonged revenge pursuit). In London he bought Coleridge's lectures on Shakespeare, finding in the one on *Hamlet* the definition of the Shakespearean hero that he worked into ch. 16, "The Ship."

In mid-1850 Melville borrowed Carlyle's *Sartor Resartus* and *Heroes and Hero-Worship*, finding a congenial rhetoric, an appealing sardonic verbal playfulness, a compelling depiction of the physical universe as emblematical, and an incisive analysis of Oliver Cromwell from which he took hints for his tyrannical captain. Before he finished *Moby-Dick*, he encountered in the London *Quarterly Review* for July 1823 an anonymous article (by Sir Francis Palgrave), "Superstition and Knowledge," which so impressed him that he made notes on it—rather oddly, in his Shakespeare, so that modern scholars long took it for granted that they were closely connected with Shakespeare in his mind. (See Geoffrey Sanborn, "The Name of the Devil" on p. 582 herein.) This article in the *Quarterly Review* clarified for Melville his own vulnerable position of a writer pursued by fanatical witch hunters and gave him the formula he quoted to Hawthorne about the book's baptism. Such a list of works, even cursorily annotated, has the virtue of emphasizing what should be kept most obvious—that in Melville's resolve "to give the world a book, which the world should hail with surprise and delight" (words already ironic, because of the failure of *Moby-Dick*, when he wrote them for *Pierre*, 1852), his wondrous book would itself be the original product of the assimilation of many other books.

Works that appear in our footnotes to *Moby-Dick* without full citations are listed here, in alphabetical order, works of high literature mixed higgledy-piggledy with nautical works (J. Ross Browne cheek by jowl with Sir Thomas Browne, in true Melvillean fashion) along with Melville's dictionaries and encyclopaedias (whenever possible, in the editions Melville used), and a few modern books such as Stuart Frank's *Herman Melville's Picture Gallery*, which contains reproductions of many of the works of art and artifacts mentioned in *Moby-Dick*. Full titles are used, not only because such titles are richly evocative to us, as they were to Melville, but also because they concisely provide specific information about their contents and the larger geographical and economic contexts.

Detailed information about Melville's books is in Merton M. Sealts Jr., *Melville's Reading: Revised and Enlarged Edition* (Columbia: University of South Carolina Press, 1988); one important whaling book, the Bennett, is listed by Sealts in "A Third Supplementary Note to *Melville's Reading* (1988)," *Melville Society Extracts*, 112 (March 1998), 12–14. (Steven Olsen-Smith, a contributor to "Analogues and Sources" [p. 585 herein] was charged by Sealts, who died in 2000, with keeping *Melville's Reading* updated.) Still more information is in Mary K. Bercaw, *Melville's Sources* (Evanston, IL: Northwestern University Press, 1987). Sealts lists only books that can be shown to have been in Melville's hands, books he owned or borrowed or is known to have seen. Bercaw, by contrast, lists not only books that Melville is known to have held but books that evidence in his writings shows that he *must* have held. Sealts does not list Amasa Delano's *Voyages*, the main source for *Benito Cereno*, because a copy cannot be tied to Melville by purchase or borrowing; Bercaw does list the book, for (as Sealts knew, of course) Melville plainly had a copy of it. Both Sealts and Bercaw are essential for study of Melville's sources.

Bayle, Pierre. *An Historical and Critical Dictionary.* Translated by Jacob Tonson, London, 1710.

Beale, Thomas. *The Natural History of the Sperm Whale to Which Is Added a Sketch of a South-Sea Whaling Voyage in Which the Author Was Personally Engaged.* London: Van Voorst, 1839.

Bennett, Frederick Debell. *Narrative of a Whaling Voyage round the Globe, from the Year 1833 to 1836. Comprising Sketches of Polynesia, California, the Indian Archipelago, etc., with an Account of Southern Whales, the Sperm Whale Fishery, and the Natural History of the Climates Visited.* London: Bentley, 1840.

Browne, J. Ross. *Etchings of a Whaling Cruise, with Notes of a Sojourn on the Island of Zanzibar. To Which Is Appended a Brief History of the Whale Fishery.* New York: Harper, 1846.

Browne, Sir Thomas. *Religio Medici* (A doctor's religion), 1642, 1643, and *Pseudodoxia Epidemica* (Vulgar errors), 1646. In *Works, Including His Life and Correspondence.* London: Pickering, 1835–36. Also in *The Works . . . With Alphabetical Tables.* London: Basset, 1686.

Bunyan, John. *The Pilgrim's Progress, from this World to that which is to come.* Edition unknown.

Burton, Robert *Anatomy of Melancholy; as It Proceeds from the Disposition and Habit, the Passion of Love, and the Influence of Religion.* London: Vernor & Hood, 1801.

Melville bought this book in the 1840s not realizing that it had once belonged to his father. He also owned the 1847 Wiley edition.

Byron, George Gordon Noel, 6th Baron. *Don Juan, Dramas, Miscellanies,* and *Tales.* London: Murray, 1837.

In July 1847, the month before her wedding, Elizabeth Shaw Melville was given this volume. Probably individual book-length poems (besides *Don Juan*) were in the house, perhaps the copy of *The Bride of Abydos* that Gansevoort Melville read in 1834, very likely *Manfred,* but the known *Poetical Works* from Melville's library is an edition published after *Moby-Dick.*

Byron, John. *The Narrative of the Honourable John Byron . . . Containing an Account of the Great Distresses Suffered by Himself and His Companions on the Coast of Patagonia, from the Year 1740, till Their Arrival in England, 1746. With a Description of St. Jago de Chili, and the Manners and Customs of the Inhabitants. Also a Relation of the Loss of the Wager, Man of War, One of Admiral Anson's Squadron.* London: Baker & Leigh, 1768.

Carlyle, Thomas. *Heroes and Hero-Worship.* Edition unknown.

———. *Sartor Resartus.* Edition unknown.

The Carlyle volumes were borrowed from Evert Duyckinck in 1850.

Cervantes Saavedra, Miguel de. *Don Quixote.* 1605, 1615. Edition unknown.

Chase, Owen. *Narrative of the Most Extraordinary and Distressing Shipwreck of the Whale-Ship Essex, of Nantucket; Which Was Attacked and Finally Destroyed by a Large Spermaceti-Whale in the Pacific Ocean; with an Account of the Unparalleled Sufferings of the Captain and Crew.* New York: Gilley, 1821.

Cheever, Henry T. *The Whale and His Captors; or, The Whaleman's Adventures, and the Whale's Biography, as Gathered on the Homeward Cruise of the "Commodore Preble."* New York: Harper, 1849.

Coleridge, Samuel Taylor. *Notes and Lectures upon Shakespeare and Some of the Old Poets and Dramatists; with Other Literary Remains.* London: William Pickering, 1849.

Colnett. *A Voyage to the South Atlantic and Round Cape Horn into the Pacific Ocean, for the Purpose of Extending the Spermaceti Whale Fisheries, and other Objects of Commerce, by ascertaining the Ports, Bays, Harbours, and Anchoring Births, in Certain Islands and Coasts in those Seas at which the Ships of the British Merchants might be Refitted.* London: W. Bennett, 1798.

Cook, Captain James A. *A Collection of Voyages round the World . . . Containing a Complete Historical Account of Captain Cook's Voyages.* London: A. Millar, W. Law, and R. Cater, 1790.

———. *A Voyage to the Pacific for Making Discoveries in the Northern Hemisphere (1776–1780).* London: Printed by H. Hughs for G. Nicol and T. Cadell, 1785.

Cooper, James Fenimore. *The Sea Lions; or, The Lost Sealers: a Tale of the Antarctic Ocean.* New York: Stringer & Townsend, 1849.

Craik, George Lillie. *The New Zealanders.* London: Charles Knight, 1830.

Cuvier, Frederick. *De l'historie naturelle des cetaces.* Paris, 1836.

Melville knew *Natural History of Whales* in some translation, perhaps only in excerpts.

Cuvier, Georges, Baron. *The Animal Kingdom. . . .* London: Whittaker, 1827–43.

Dampier, William. *A Collection of Voyages* (London: Knapton, 1729).

———. *A New Voyage Round the World, Describing Particularly, the Isthmus of America, Several Coasts and Islands in the West Indies . . . the South Sea Coasts of Chili, Peru, and Mexico . . . voyages and Descriptions.* London, 1697–1707.

Dante, Alighieri. *The Vision; or Hell, Purgatory, and Paradise.* Translated by Rev. Henry Francis Cary. London: Henry G. Bohn, 1847.

De Quincey, Thomas. *Confessions of an English Opium Eater.* London: Taylor & Hessey, 1822.

D'Wolf, John. *A Voyage to the North Pacific and a Journey Through Siberia More than Half a Century Ago.* Boston: Welch & Bigelow, 1861. Reprint Bristol, RI: Rulon-Miller Books, 1983.

Melville had heard many stories from D'Wolf, his uncle, before writing *Moby-Dick.*

Eckermann, Johann. *Conversations with Goethe in the Last Years of His Life*. Translated by M[argaret] Fuller. Boston: Hilliard, Gray, and Co., 1839.

Frank, Stuart M. *Herman Melville's Picture Gallery: Sources and Types of the "Pictorial" Chapters of "Moby-Dick."* Fairhaven, MA: Edward J. Lefkowicz, Inc., 1986.

Froissart, Jean. *Chronicles of England, France and Spain*. Translated by John Bourchier, Lord Berners. Edition unknown.

> Melville's surviving copy was published in 1854.

Gillies, Robert Pearce. *Tales of a Voyager to the Arctic Ocean*. London: Henry Colburn, 1826.

Goethe, Johann Wolfgang von. *The Auto-Biography of Goethe. Truth and Poetry: From My Own Life*. London, Bohn, 1848–49.

———. *Faust*. Edition unknown.

Goldsmith, Oliver. *Goldsmith's Natural History*. Philadelphia: Thomas Desilver, 1829.

———. *History of the Earth and Animated Nature*. London: J. Nourse, 1774.

Hakluyt, Richard. *The Principall Navigations, Voyages, Traffics, & Discoveries of the English Nation*. London, 1598. Edition unknown.

Hart, Joseph C. *Miriam Coffin; or, The Whale-Fishermen*. New York: Carvill; Philadelphia: Carey & Hart, 1834.

Harris, John. *Navigantium atque Itinerarium Bibliotheca; or, a Compleat Collection of Voyages and Travels*. London, 1705.

Hope, Thomas. *Anastasius; or, Memoirs of a Greek*. London: Murray, 1836.

Kitto, John, ed. *Cyclopædia of Biblical Literature*. New York; Mark H. Newman, 1845.

Krusenstern, Adam Ivan. *Voyage round the World, in the Years 1803–1806*. London: John Murray, 1813.

Langsdorff, George H. von. *Voyages and Travels in Various Parts of the World . . . 1803–1807*. London; Henry Colburn, 1813.

Macy, Obed. *The History of Nantucket; Being a Compendious Account of the First Settlement of the Island by the English, together with the Rise and Progress of the Whale Fishery. . . .* Boston: Hilliard, Gray, 1835.

Marlowe, Christopher. *The Tragical History of Doctor Faustus*. Edition unknown.

Martin, Kenneth R. *Whalemen's Paintings and Drawings: Selections from the Kendall Whaling Museum Collection*. Sharon, MA: The Kendall Whaling Museum, 1983.

Milton, John. *The Poetical Works of John Milton. With Notes, and A Life of the Author, by John Mitford*. 2 vols. Boston: Hilliard, Gray, 1836.

Olafsen, Eggert, and Bjarni Povelsen. *Travels in Iceland*. London: R. Phillips, 1805.

Olmsted, Francis Allyn. *Incidents of a Whaling Voyage. To Which Are Added Observations on the Scenery, Manners and Customs, and Missionary Stations of the Sandwich and Society Islands*. New York: D. Appleton, 1841.

[Palgrave, Sir Francis.] "Superstition and Knowledge." *London Quarterly Review*, July 1823, 440–475. Reprint. in *The Collected Historical Works of Sir Francis Palgrave*. Vol. 10. Edited by Sir R. H. Inglis Palgrave. Cambridge, UK: Cambridge University Press, 1922.

Parker, Hershel. *Herman Melville: A Biography, 1819–1851*. Baltimore: Johns Hopkins, 1996.

The Penny Cyclopædia of the Society for the Diffusion of Useful Knowledge. London: Charles Knight, 1833–43.

Plato. *Phaedon; or, A Dialogue on the Immortality of the Soul*. New York: William Gowan, 1833.

———. *Republic*. Edition unknown.

Povelsen. *See* Olafsen.

Rabelais, Françoise. *The Works*. London: Smith, Miller, 1844?.

Reynolds, J. N. "Mocha Dick: or the White Whale of the Pacific: A Leaf from a Manuscript Journal." (New York) *Knickerbocker*, 13 (May 1839).

Scoresby, William Jr. *An Account of the Arctic Regions, with a History and Description of the Northern Whale-Fishery*. Edinburgh: Constable, 1820.

———. *Journal of a Voyage to the Northern Whale Fishery; Including Researches and Discoveries on the Eastern Coast of West Greenland . . . in . . . 1822*. Edinburgh: Constable, 1823.

Shakespeare, William. *The Dramatic Works of William Shakespeare; with a Life of the Poet, and Notes, Original and Selected*. Boston: Hilliard, Gray, 1837.

Shelley, Mary Woollstonecraft Godwin. *Frankenstein; or, The Modern Prometheus*. London: Bentley, 1849.

Sibbald, Robert. *A History, Ancient and Modern, of the Sheriffdoms of Fife and Kinross*. Cupar-Fife, Scotland, 1803.

Sterne, Laurence. *The Life and Opinions of Tristram Shandy, Gent*. Edition unknown.

Vidocq, Françoise Eugene. *Memoirs of Vidocq, Principal Agent of the French Police until 1827, Written by Himself*. Edition unknown.

> Possibly, Philadelphia: Cary & Hart, 1834.

Wafer, Lionel. *A New Voyage and Description of the Isthmus of America, Giving an Account of the Author's Abode There*. London: James Knapton, 1699.

Wilkes, Charles. *United States Exploring Expedition. During the Years 1838 . . . 1842. Under the Command of Charles Wilkes, U. S. N*. Philadelphia: Sherman (or Lea & Blanchard), 1844–46.

Whaling and Whalecraft

Glossary of Nautical Terms

To preserve something of the tang of nautical idioms contemporary with Melville and to avoid introducing anachronistic definitions, we have drawn on nineteenth-century dictionaries of sea terms in compiling this glossary, mainly Richard Henry Dana's *The Seaman's Friend* (Boston, 1856, 8th Edition), W. H. Smyth's *Sailor's Word-Book* (London, 1867), and W. Clark Russell's *Sailor's Language* (London, 1883). We have not included every nautical term in *Moby-Dick* (notably those like "pitch-poling" and "waif pole" that Melville defines himself), and we have defined a few words *not* in *Moby-Dick*, because they occur in definitions of other words. Not all the meanings given here are exactly those carried by the terms in *Moby-Dick*: Melville uses some of these words, like "grapnels" or "slip the cable," metaphorically; and he sometimes invests the *Pequod* with unusual properties, such as a tiller made not of wood or metal but of bone.

abaft Toward the stern of a vessel; behind (Anything behind another thing is called *abaft* it. Russell).

abeam In a line at right angles to the vessel's length. Smyth.

aft Toward the hinder part of a ship (the stern).

a-lee the helm So place the helm that the rudder is brought on the weather side of the stern-post. Smyth.

alow A term sometimes but very rarely used for *below*, and then perhaps only for the sake of alliteration, as "She had studding-sails aloft and alow." Russell.

articles A ship's articles are the document in which are recorded the names and signatures of the crew, their wages, the food to be given, etc. Russell.

athwart Across.

athwartships Across the ship, or across anything; opposed to fore-and-aft.

avast An order to stop hauling or heaving, or to stop doing anything.

avast heaving The cry to arrest the capstan when any impediment occurs in heaving the cable, not infrequently when a hand, foot, or finger, is jammed;—stop! Smyth.

azimuth compass An instrument for finding the magnetic azimuth or amplitude of a heavenly object. Russell.

back (to back a sail) To brace its yard so that the wind may blow directly on the front of the sail, and thus retard the ship's course. Smyth.

backstay A rope to support a mast and leading down abaft it to the side of the vessel. Russell.

ballast Heavy material, as iron, lead, or stone, placed in the bottom of the hold, to keep a vessel from upsetting. Dana.

bank A seat.

batten down   The hatches [hatchways] are said to be *battened down* when they are covered up with gratings or hatches, and tarpaulins which are secured by battens [pieces of wood or iron] to prevent them from being washed away. Russell.

battering-ram   A large piece of timber, armed at each end with iron caps and fitted with ropes. It is used for removing the angular blocks when a docked ship is sitting on them. Russell.

before the mast   Living in the forecastle, serving as a "common sailor." Russell.

belay   To make a rope fast by taking a turn with it over a belaying-pin. Russell.

belaying pins   Iron, brass, or wooden bars tapered, placed in holes in rails, hoops, etc., to make the running gear [running ropes] fast to. Russell.

bells   The denoting of time on board ship [by striking a bell every half hour]. Eight bells signify noon or midnight, eight or four o'clock; half-past twelve, one bell; one o'clock, two bells; half-past one, three bells, and so on to eight bells. [To make eight bells a single bell is sounded eight times with a pause after each two strikes.] Russell.

bend   To attach. To *bend a sail* is to attach it to the yard. Russell.

binnacle   A stand or box of brass or wood in which a compass is placed. Russell.

binnacle lamp   A lamp to throw light upon the compass-card. From Smyth.

block   A piece of wood with sheaves, or wheels, in it, through which the running rigging passes, to add to the purchase. Dana.

bluff   A term applied to a ship's bows, and meaning full and square. Russell.

boat hook   A pole furnished with an iron hook and spike for shoving off or holding on to an object when in a boat. Russell.

boom   A long spar run out to extend or boom out the foot of a particular sail. A ship is said to come booming forwards when she comes with all the sail she can make. Smyth.

bow   The rounded part of a vessel, forward. Dana. [The *bows* of the ship are the sides at the stem, and for some way back.]

bowline   A rope leading forward from the leech [the vertical edge] of a square sail, to keep the leech well out when sailing close-hauled. Dana.

bowman (also bowsman)   The headmost rower in a boat. Russell.

bowsprit   A large spar projecting over the bows.

brace sharp up   To *brace up*, or *brace sharp up*, [is] to lay the yards more obliquely fore and aft, by easing off the weather-braces and hauling in the lee ones, which enables a ship to lie as close to the wind as possible. Smyth.

braces   The braces are ropes belonging to all the yards of a ship. Smyth. [Their function is to position the yards in the horizontal plane.]

breakers   Small barrels for containing water or other liquids. Also, those billows which break violently over reefs, rocks, or shallows, lying immediately at, or under, the surface of the sea. Smyth.

breaking out   The act of extricating casks or other objects from the hold-stowage. Smyth.

bring by the lee   To incline so rapidly to leeward that the lee-side is unexpectedly brought to windward, and by laying the sails all aback exposes her to the danger of oversetting. Smyth.

bulkhead   The bulkhead, afore, is the partition between the forecastle and gratings in the head. [Gratings are open wood-work of cross battens, forming the cover for the hatchways. and permitting light to enter the lower decks.] From Smyth.

bull's-eye A sort of block without a sheave, for a rope to reeve through. Also, a hemispherical piece of ground glass of great thickness, inserted into small openings in the decks and scuttle-hatches, for admission of light below. Smyth.

bulwarks The protection around a vessel's weather deck, consisting of solid planking fixed to stanchions. Russell.

burton A kind of tackle. From Dana.

capstan A barrel of wood or iron revolved by bars [used for lifting great weights]. Russell.

capstan-head The flat, circular top of the capstan, with square holes around its edge. From Smyth.

carlines (carlings) Pieces of timber about five inches square, lying fore and aft, along from one beam to another. On and athwart these the ledges rest, whereon the planks of the deck and other portions of carpentry are made fast. Smyth.

chocks Wooden supports for the bottom of a boat to rest on while not in use. From Russell.

chronometer A timepiece to indicate Greenwich mean time for the purpose of finding the longitude. Russell.

cleat (or cleet) A piece of wood used in different parts of a vessel to belay ropes to. Dana

clumsy-cleat A knee-brace in the bow of a whale-boat. Russell.

close-haul A vessel is close-hauled when she is sailing with her yards braced up so as to get as much as possible to windward; *full and by* is the same as close-hauled. From Dana.

close-reefed When all the reefs of the top-sails are taken in. From Smyth.

companion-way The staircase to the cabin. Smyth.

compass-card The circular card attached to the needles of a mariner's compass on which are marked 32 points of the compass and the 360 degrees of the circle.

copper-bottomed Said of a wooden ship whose bottom is sheathed with copper. Russell.

cross-trees Cross-pieces of timber on top of the trestletrees [fore-and-aft pieces on each side of a mast]. From Russell.

crowd To *crowd sail* is to set all sail. Russell.

crown That part of an anchor where the shank and arms meet. Russell.

cutting stages Platforms hung over the side for men to stand on while cutting in.

darbies Handcuffs.

dog-vane A small flag or streamer at the mast-head or at the side to indicate the direction of the wind. Russell.

double banked A boat is double banked when two oars, one opposite the other, are pulled by men seated on the same thwart. Dana.

douse To lower or slacken down suddenly; expressed of a sail in a squall of wind, an extended hawser, etc. Smyth.

drawing water The number of feet from the waterline to the lower-most part of the keel.

fiddle-head The head of a ship that has no figure, but is decorated with a scroll shaped like a fiddle. Russell.

fore The forward part of a vessel; opposed to aft.

forecastle deck The deck over the forecastle [the compartment where sailors live, in the bows of a ship]. From Russell.

fore-mast The lower mast nearest the bows of a ship. Russell.

fore-scuttle A hatchway by which the forecastle is entered.

furl To roll and bind a sail neatly on its respective yard or boom. Smyth.

gaff An instrument like a boat-hook used in the blubber-room of whalers; also, a spar used to extend the heads of fore-and-aft sails which are not set on stays. From Russell.

galliots A Dutch or Flemish vessel for cargoes, with very rounded ribs and flattish bottom, with a mizenmast stept far aft, carrying a square-mainsail and main-topsail. Smyth.

gangway A part of the vessel's side, nearly amidships, by which people enter and leave a ship. Russell.

give way! An order to men who are rowing to pull with more force. Russell.

grapnel A sort of small anchor for boats, having a ring at one end, and four palmed claws at the other. Smyth.

gunwale The gunwale [pronounced gun'l] of a boat is a piece of timber going round the upper sheer-strake as a binder for its top-work. Smyth. [The sheer-strake is the line of plank on a vessel's side, running fore-and-aft under the gunwale. Dana.]

halyards (often halliards) The ropes or tackles used to hoist or lower sail. From Smyth.

handspike A lever of wood used in heaving round a windlass [a large barrel, revolved by handles, on the forecastle, and used in getting up the anchor]. Russell.

hard a-lee "Hard a lee!" means hard over—put the rudder as far as it will go to windward. Russell.

hatches Openings in the deck for admission into the interior of a ship. Also, the open wood-work of cross battens and ledges forming cover for the hatchways.

hatchway A square or oblong opening in the middle of the deck of a ship, of which there are generally three—the fore, main, and after—affording passages up and down from one deck to another, and again descending into the hold. The hatches of a smaller kind are distinguished by the name of *scuttles*. Smyth.

hawser A large rope used for towing, etc. Russell.

head The fore end of a ship.

head-wind A breeze blowing from the direction of the ship's intended course. Smyth.

headway A vessel's direct passage through the water. Russell.

heave down To drag one side of a ship down with tackles affixed to the mast-heads, in order to repair an injury which is below the water line on the other side, From Smyth and Russell.

heave to To put a vessel in the position of *lying-to*, by adjusting her sails so as to counteract each other, and thereby check her way, or keep her perfectly still. In a gale, it implies to set merely enough sail to steady the ship. Smyth.

helm A term for all the steering arrangements of a ship. Russell.

helmsman Steersman.

hold The interior of a vessel, where the cargo is stored. Dana.

jib A large triangular sail, set on a stay, forward. Smyth.

jib-stay A stay is a rope that supports a mast by leading forward; a jib-stay is the stay on which the jib is set.

jury-mast A temporary mast to replace one that has been lost. Russell.

keel The lowest and principal timber of a vessel, running fore-and-aft its whole length, and supporting the whole frame. It is composed of several pieces, placed lengthwise, and scarfed and bolted together. Dana.

kelson (often keelson) An internal keel, laid upon the middle of the floor-timbers, immediately over the keel, and serving to bind all together by means of long bolts driven from without, and clinched on the upper side of the keelson. Smyth.

kentledge Pieces of iron for ballast, usually laid over the kelson-plates. From Russell and Smyth.

knight-heads Timbers next to the stem [the foremost piece uniting the bows of a ship], the ends of which come up through the deck and form a support for the bowsprit. From Russell and Smyth.

lanyards Ropes rove through dead-eyes (holes in wooden discs) for setting up rigging. Also, a rope made fast to anything to secure it, or as a handle. Dana.

larboard The left side of a vessel, looking forward. Same as port.

lead line A line attached to a leaden weight and used for ascertaining the depth of water. Russell.

league Three nautical miles, or 3041 fathoms. From Smyth.

lee (or leeward) The side opposite to that from which the wind is blowing. *Lee-shore* means the wind is blowing toward the shore, which is on the lee side of the ship. From Smyth.

lee-beam On the lee side of the ship, at right angles with the keel. Smyth.

lee way What a vessel loses by drifting to leeward in her course. Smyth.

lifts Ropes which reach from each mast-head to their respective yard-arms to steady and suspend the ends. Smyth.

line-of-battle ships Before the days of ironclads, ships of seventy-four guns and upwards. Russell.

log-line A line wound on a reel. At the end of the line is a piece of wood with a peg in it called a [log or] logship. On the logship being thrown overboard the velocity with which the vessel leaves it astern is measured by a sand glass which runs a certain number of seconds. From Russell.

loggerhead A sort of post fitted to a whaling-boat's bottom and rising about two feet above the level of the stern platform. Russell.

lubber An awkward unseamanlike fellow. Smyth.

lubber's hole An aperture in the tops so called because raw hands [being timid climbers] prefer to creep through it to going over the shroud. Russell.

luff To luff is to bring a ship closer to the wind. Russell. [A ship is close to the wind when her head is just so near the wind as to fill the sails without shaking them. From Smyth.]

lugger A small vessel with four-cornered cut sails, set fore-and-aft. Smyth.

main brace A purchase attached to the main-yard for trimming it to the wind. Smyth.

main-royal mast The mast above the main-topgallant mast. Russell.

main-yard The lowest yard on the main-mast. Russell.

make To make is to descry. From Russell.

marline A kind of small line, composed of two strands very little twisted. Smyth.

marlingspike An iron pin, sharpened at one end, and having a hole in the other for a lanyard. Dana.

mast-head The portion of the mast above the top of the rigging. From Russell.

midships The middle part of the vessel, either with regard to her length or breadth. Smyth.

muffled oars Oars are muffled by putting mats or canvass round their looms in the row-locks. (The loom is the part of the oar between the handle or grip and the blade.) From Dana.

mincing knives Knives for mincing the horse-pieces of blubber for the try-pots. From Russell.

mizen-mast The mizen (mizzen) mast is the aftermost mast of a ship. Smyth.

offing Distance from the shore. Russell.

orlop The lowest deck, consisting of a platform laid over the beams in the hold, whereon the cables [are] usually coiled. Smyth.

perch A pole stuck up on a shoal as a beacon; or a spar erected on or projected from a cliff whence to watch fish. Smyth.

pike A long, slender, round staff, armed at the end with iron. Smyth.

piled up A vessel is piled up when all sails are set.

plug-hole A hole in the bottom of a boat to let water drain out. Russell.

point of the compass The 32nd part of the circumference, or 11° 15′. Smyth.

poop The aftermost and highest part of a large ship's hull. Smyth.

port-hole An aperture in a ship's side to point a gun through. A window for a cabin. Russell.

post-captain A [Royal Navy] captain of three years' standing. Smyth.

preventer A rope used as an additional support for masts, booms, etc. Russell.

proas [prahu, Malay for boat] The larger war-vessels among the Malays, ranging from 55 to 156 feet in length and carrying 76 to 96 rowers, with about 40 to 60 fighting men. From Smyth.

prow The projecting front part of a ship; the bow.

purchase A mechanical power which increases the force applied. Dana.

quarter (on the quarter) 45° abaft the beam. Smyth.

quarter-boat A boat suspended on davits [curved iron bars affixed to a ship's sides] near the quarters [the after sides of a ship]. Russell.

quarter-deck The part of the upper deck which is abaft the main-mast. Smyth.

range Range alongside, to draw abreast. Russell.

razeed A ship is razeed when one entire deck is cut down. From Russell.

reef To diminish the expanse of a sail by knotting the reef points in it upon the yard, or at the foot. Russell. A certain portion of a sail comprehended between the head of a sail and any of the reef-bands. The intention of each reef is to reduce the sail in proportion to the increase of the wind. Reef is also a group or continuous chain of rocks, sufficiently near the surface of the water to occasion its breaking over them. Smyth.

riggers Men who fit the standing ["permanent"] and running ["temporary"] rigging, or dismantle them. From Smyth.

rigging Standing rigging consists of all those ropes which are fixed, such as shrouds, backstays, etc., running rigging of all those ropes which can be pulled upon, such as halliards, clew-lines, etc. Russell.

ring-bolt An iron bolt with an eye at one end, wherein is fitted a circular ring. Smyth.

round-house A cabin built on deck roofed by the poop. Russell.

rowlocks (rollocks) Places cut in the gunwale of a boat for the oar to rest in while pulling. Dana.

royal masthead The upper end of the topmost mast of a ship, unless skysail masts are carried.

royal yard The yard above the topgallant yard to which the royal sail is bent [to bend a sail is to attach it to a yard]. Russell.

run The hollow curving in a vessel's bottom that rises and narrows under the quarters. From Dana.

scud To drive before a gale, with no sail, or only enough to keep the vessel ahead of the wind. Also, low, thin clouds that fly swiftly before the wind. Dana.

scuppers The gutter of a ship's decks; the water-ways. Russell.

scuttle A small hole or port cut either in the deck or side of a ship. generally for ventilation. That in the deck is a small hatch-way. Smyth.

scuttle-butt   A cask on deck in which fresh water is kept. Russell.

seas   Waves (as in "three seas off").

seize   To seize is to make a thing fast, by securing it to a place; as to seize a flag in the rigging. Russell.

seizings   The seizings are lines with which anything is made fast.

sheave   The wheel inside a block which revolves with the rope that is hauled through it. Russell.

sheet home   To extend the sheets [the ropes fastened to one or both the lower corners of a sail] to the outer extremities of the yards. From Smyth.

shiver   To shiver a ship is to trim a ship's yards so that the wind strikes on the edges of the sails, making them flutter in the wind. The same effect may be intentionally produced by means of the helm. Smyth.

shorten sail   To reduce [take in some of, or reef some of] the sails that are set. From Smyth.

shrouds   A set of ropes reaching from the mast-heads to the vessel's sides, to support the masts. Dana.

sky-larking   Horse-play. Russell.

skysail   A small square sail set above a royal sail.

skysail-pole   A mast on which the sky-sail yard travels. It is a continuation of the royal mast. Russell.

slip the cable   To *slip*, is to let go the cable with a buoy on the end, and quit the position, from any sudden requirement, instead of weighing the anchor. Smyth.

soundings   To be off soundings is to be in water whose bottom cannot be reached by the [line and] lead. [Or, to be within soundings is to be in water shallow enough for the depth to be measured thus; hence, to know where the ship is.] From Russell.

spar   Any kind of mast, boom, etc. Russell.

sprung spar   A spar is *sprung* when the fibres of the wood are injured by straining. Russell.

spile   A small wooden pin. Smyth.

splice   To join two untwisted ends of rope together.

square yards   Literally, when the yards lie fair upon the masts exactly athwartships, but the term is also applied to very long yards. Russell.

stand by!   The order to be prepared to do something. From Smyth.

stand by the braces!   The order to take hold of the braces (preparatory to executing some further order). From Smyth.

starboard   The right-hand side of a vessel (as one faces toward the bow).

star-bolins   (or star-boleens) The old familiar term for the men of the starboard watch. Smyth.

stay   A supporting rope that leads forward from the upper end of the mast (the shrouds extend not forward but on each side). Russell.

stem-piece   The foremost timber fastening together the bows of a ship.

storm-trysail   A fore-and-aft sail, hoisted by a gaff, but having no boom at its foot, and used only in foul weather. Smyth.

strike   To strike is to lower anything.

strike down   To lower casks, etc., into the hold. Smyth.

stun' sails   Fine-weather sails set outside the squaresails. Smyth.

sway up   To apply a strain on a mast-rope in order to lift the spar upwards, so that the fid may be taken out, previous to lowering the mast. [A fid is a square bar of wood or iron, with a shoulder at one end, used to support the weight of the topmast when erected at the head of the lower mast.] Smyth.

tackle   (Pronounced *tay-cle*.) A purchase, formed by a rope rove through one or more blocks. Dana.

taffrail   The upper part of a ship's stern, a curved railing, the ends of which unite to the quarter-pieces. Smyth.

tell-tale   A compass hanging face downwards from the beams in the cabin, showing the position of the vessel's head. Smyth.

thole-pins   Pins in the gunwale of a boat serving to retain the oars in position when pulling. Smyth.

thwart   A rower's seat in an open boat—so called because the thwart lies athwart, or across, the boat.

tierce   A cask of beef. Russell.

tiller   A piece of timber or metal fitted upon the rudder-head fore-and-aft and used for steering. Russell.

timber heads   The heads of the timbers that rise above the decks and are used for belaying hawsers, large ropes, etc. Smyth.

top-blocks   Large single iron-bound blocks used for sending top-masts up or down. Russell.

topgallant-mast   The third mast above the deck; the uppermost before the days of royals and flying kites. Smyth.

top-gallant sails   The third sails above the decks. Smyth.

top-maul   A large hammer used by riggers. Russell.

top-sails   The second sails above the decks. Smyth.

transom   Timbers bolted to a ship's stern-post for receiving the ends of deck planks; a crossbeam attached to the stern-post and used as a seat.

tree-nails   Long cylindrical oak pins driven through the planks and timbers of a vessel to connect her various parts. Smyth.

trim dish   To adjust a vessel's posture properly. From Russell.

trysail   A fore-and-aft sail, set with a boom and gaff, and hoisted on a small mast abaft the lower mast, called a *trysail-mast*. Dana.

trucks   Circular [wooden] caps on the upper mastheads. Smyth.

turn to   To go to work. To fall to. Russell.

under weigh   A ship is *under weigh* when she has weighed [heaved up] her anchor; a ship *under way* is beginning to move under her canvas after her anchor is weighed. From Smyth.

waist   The deck between the main deck and the forecastle. Russell.

weather   The opposite of lee—the windward side of a ship. From Smyth.

weather-sheets   Those fast to the weather-clues of the sails. [Clues are the lower corners of a square sail.] From Smyth.

whip   A single rope rove through a single block to hoist in light articles. Smyth.

windlass   A large barrel, revolved by handles, on the forecastle, and used in getting up the anchor. Russell.

windlass-bitts   The bitts [perpendicular pieces of timber going through the deck] which support the ends or spindles of the windlass. Smyth.

work   A ship is said *to work* when she strains in a tempestuous sea, so as to loosen her joints. Smyth.

yard   A long cylindrical timber suspended upon the mast of a vessel to spread a sail. Smyth.

yaw   The motion of a vessel when she goes off from her course. Dana.

JOHN B. PUTNAM

Whaling and Whalecraft: A Pictorial Account

From its beginning, when Captain John Smith hunted whales along the New England coast under a crown permit in 1614, to its end, with the wreck of the bark *Wanderer* off Cuttyhunk in 1924, the American whale fishery was basically a struggle between men in wooden ships and boats against the world's largest mammals, inhabitants of an inhospitable ocean. The Cape Cod or Nantucket whaleman of the seventeenth century would have felt very much at home on the New Bedford barks of the early twentieth, for neither the sailing ship nor the craft of whaling had changed much during the intervening centuries.

There were, to be sure, modifications and refinements in ship design, whaleboat construction, and whaling weaponry, as the industry became increasingly standardized toward the end of the nineteenth century. In the 1840's, when Melville sailed in the *Acushnet*, American whaling was in its most striking period of transition: the Industrial Revolution made possible greater quantities of better harpoons, lances, whaleline, and the like; and the growing scarcity of skilled carpenters willing to go to sea made it necessary for whalers to carry better built boats, and more of them, against the inevitable destruction attendant upon the rigors of a whaling voyage. Accordingly, the following brief discussion of whaling and whalecraft will concentrate on whaling as Melville knew it and wrote of it; where possible, we shall refer to appropriate chapters in Moby-Dick for further detail.

The American whaleship, in the days when Ishmael embarked in the *Pequod*, was generally built especially for its task, but it was not uncom-

Elevation and Plan View of a Typical Whaleship

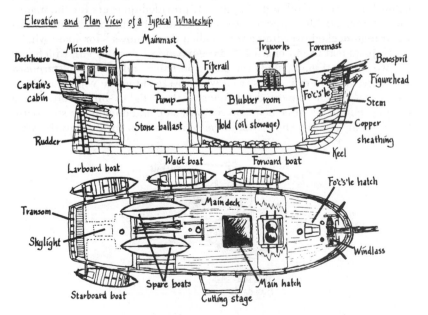

Whaling bark under sail

mon to find vessels of exceptionally sturdy construction that had been converted from merchantman to whaler. The whaler, owing to the heavy stresses she was subjected to in "cutting-in" a whale and to the long periods she would spend at sea without opportunity for overhaul, had to be especially heavy-timbered and stoutly built. Both modern and contemporary writers have tended to regard the whaler as lubberly in appearance and design (see Melville's comments in Chapter 16), but it was generally the longevity and durability of these sturdy vessels that caused them to compare so unfavorably with the more modern—but shorter-lived— men of war and merchantmen with which they shared the seas.

The whaler's cluttered superstructure and sparse spread of canvas also contributed to her awkward appearance. In order to allow more space below for barrels of oil, a deckhouse aft provided quarters for the mates, the harpooneers, the carpenter, the cooper, and the smith. Forward of this was a high decked-over framework, called the "gallows," for spare whaleboats. Just abaft the foremast stood the tryworks (Chapter 96), which had its own shelter. Finally, along the entire port side and aft on the starboard side were the towering davits from which were slung the whaleboats and the cranes which supported the keels of these lightly-built craft. There would generally be three boats on the port side and one on the starboard. Occasionally a large whaler would carry a fifth boat forward on the star-

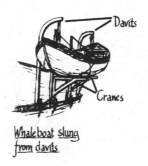

Davits

Cranes

Whaleboat slung from davits

board side, and very rarely another might be carried on "tail-feathers," or stern davits, across the transom.

A whaler seldom carried as much sail as a merchantman of equal tonnage, for a variety of reasons; first of all, it was necessary to keep the rig short and simple in order that it might be handled safely and quickly by the small force of shipkeepers—usually no more than six men—left aboard when the boats were away on the chase. Then too, sails were costly and subject to considerable wear during a three- or four-year voyage, and owners and officers alike were reluctant to spend hard-earned cash on the luxury of unnecessary canvas.

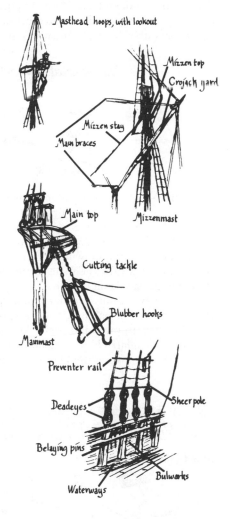

Finally, since there was no pressure on a whaler to get anywhere in a great hurry, only sufficient sail was carried to maintain steerageway and to run down to faraway boats after a long chase to leeward. On a passage to or from the whaling grounds, a whaler might carry royals or skysails to save time, but while cruising on the grounds and seeking whales, these upper sails were unbent and the spars unrigged, and the whaler would loaf along under top sails and topgallantsails.

Four features in particular were unique to the rigging of the whaler. The most conspicuous of these were the masthead hoops in which the lookouts stood during the daylight hours to watch for whales (see Chapter 35). Then there was the cutting-in tackle, consisting of four large double blocks assembled in two falls, and the attached blubber hooks. This assembly was suspended below the maintop, just forward of the main yard; it was used in stripping the blubber from a whale's carcass while cutting-in alongside. Less noticeable were the preventer pin rails, mounted in the standing rigging several feet above deck level. The running rigging (lines used in setting sails and squaring yards), usually secured to belaying pins inside the main bulwarks, was belayed to these preventer rails while cutting-in a whale to prevent its becoming fouled by the unwieldy blanket piece of blubber as it was hauled inboard by the cutting-in tackle. Finally, although most whal-

ing vessels were bark-rigged—with no square yards on the mizzen mast—
there was a short spar just below the mizzen top platform, called a crojack
(originally crossjack), to which were led the main braces, which on vessels other than whalers were led to the deck aft. This peculiarity, like the
preventer pin rails, was designed to keep the braces clear of the deck area
and superstructure.

The American whaleboat was perhaps the most nearly perfect sea-going
small craft ever developed. Combining the lightness and streamlining of
the Indian canoe, on which it was patterned, with the strength and durability of the wooden boat, it was unequalled in speed and seaworthiness.
Its lines have survived essentially intact in the whaleboats and motor
whaleboats used by the seamen of a nuclear age.

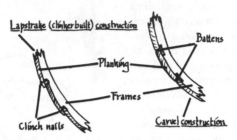

During Melville's years at sea, the whaleboat was undergoing a transition; although essentially unchanged in size and hull form, the whale-
boat of the second half of the nineteenth century differed from that of
the first in having a centerboard and in being carvel-built, as opposed
to clinker-built (see drawing). Minor changes included the substitution
of metal oarlocks for the older tholepins, and more sophisticated means
of stepping, or raising, the mast.

The boat was built of cedar planking on a temporary form, and light
steam-bent ribs of oak or ash were sprung in to give the hull transverse
strength. The thwarts and their "knees" added strength also. Since the
hull was still relatively limber, however, special supports called "cranes"
cradled the keel when the boat was slung from the davits, and the heavy

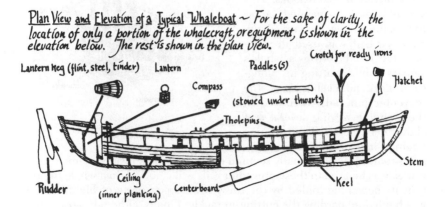

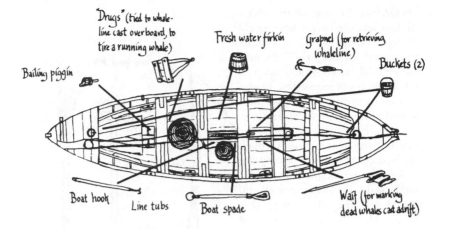

"Drugs" (tied to whale-line cast overboard, to tire a running whale)

Fresh water firkin

Grapnel (for retrieving whaleline)

Buckets (2)

Bailing piggin

Boat hook

Line tubs

Boat spade

Waif (for marking dead whales cast adrift)

line tubs were stowed on deck until the boat had been lowered away. Color schemes varied somewhat, but boats were typically painted white outside with black sheer strakes. Interiors were painted gray, blue, or buff. The oars were of unequal length, owing to the fact that the oarsmen sat at varying distances from their respective tholepins; the steering sweep or oar was longest of all, some twenty-two feet in length. It was used while rowing or being towed by a whale; under sail, the boatsteerer used a removable rudder.

In "going on the whale," as the approach was called, the boat was rowed or sailed to within a hundred yards or so of the quarry; the oars were then peaked—their handles thrust into peaking cleats fastened to the side of the boat opposite the tholepins; then the crew used paddles to close the distance to the whale, in order to avoid gallying or frightening him with the rumble of the oars against the tholepins.

In "getting fast," the harpooneer used a one- or two-flued iron (the better-known toggle iron was not yet in wide use in Melville's day), which he attempted to embed in the tough knot of muscles at the sperm whale's hump. The struck whale would at once run, breach, or sound, towing the boat along at a violent clip on a "Nantucket sleighride." Meanwhile, the boat-

Whaleboat under sail

Cross section of whaleboat amidships, showing oar in peaked position

steerer, usually one of the ship's
officers, and the harpooneer would
change places—not a simple
maneuver under the circumstances. All hands would keep as
low in the boats as possible to prevent its capsizing; the peaked oars
helped in this as well. Meanwhile,
the whaleline was sizzling the
length of the boat and out through
the bow chocks. For a description
of how the whaleline was stowed
and rigged refer to Chapter 60 and
the sketch (p. 451). Note that
while Melville mentions that
American boats carry only one line
tub, and English boats two, our
sketch shows two. This development took place during Melville's
time, and was owing partly to
the introduction of the centerboard and partly to greater ease in
handling.

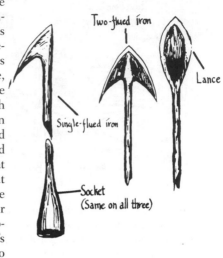

As the whale began to tire, the crew would laboriously haul in on the
line until abeam of the animal. The mate would now lance the exhausted
beast, repeatedly thrusting the sharp, long-shafted lance into the lungs
and churning it about. Here again, we must turn to Melville (Chapters 60
through 63) for the best possible description of the chase and kill. When
at last the whale had gone through his flurry and turned fin-out, he was
marked by a waif and set adrift, or towed to the ship for cutting-in.

The whale's carcass was now hauled alongside the starboard side of the
whaler and made fast with chains around the flukes. The cutting-stage was
lowered away, and the jaw cut loose and hoisted aboard for the extraction of
the ivory in the case of a sperm whale, or the baleen in the case of a right or
bowhead whale. The junk and case of the sperm whale were also cut loose
and raised on deck at this point. Melville's description of the cutting-in
(Chapter 67) is, once again, far better than any we can give here.

The trying-out was a hot, messy, malodorous process that could stretch
into days if a whaler made a number of kills from a single "pod," or group
of whales. The tryworks sat just abaft the foremast in a low square enclosure called the "goosepen." This wooden-sided trough was floored with
bricks checkerboard fashion to allow water to be poured in and to flow
freely beneath the firebox, in order to prevent the wooden deck beneath
from igniting. On this base was built a square structure of bricks and mortar, into which were set the trypots, twin round cauldrons of about 250
gallons capacity each. The whole business was covered either by a removable cover such as Melville describes in Chapter 66, or more often by a
structure similar to the gallows further aft.

One whaleman pitches "bible leaves" into the trypot as another ladles hot oil into the cooling tank. Barrels await cooled oil.

Whalemen man windlass, taking a strain on cutting tackle, which in turn hauls in blanket piece.

Smith sharpens spades and knives.

Fluke chains hold carcass.

The case of a small sperm whale has been cut from the head and hoisted aboard. A whaleman bails the spermaceti through a slit cut in the case.

Men on cutting stage strip blanket piece from carcass with cutting spades as mate stands by with boarding knife.

Blanket pieces are cut into "horse pieces," which in turn are sliced into "books," or "bible leaves."

When the tryworks were first lit off, firewood was used in the fireboxes. Thereafter, however, the scrap from the tried-out blubber was fished from the bubbling oil and pitched into the firebox to sustain the fires. The hot oil was ladled from the trypots with large long-handled dippers and poured into cooling tanks before being stored in barrels below. The greasy smoke from the tryworks blackened sails, rigging, topsides, and whalemen with a sticky black soot that was the hallmark of a successful whaler.

Melville's description of bailing the case (Chapter 78) gives an excellent idea of the hazards to be endured once the whale was killed and secure alongside. Whaling was always a business of long handles, sharp edges, and sudden deaths for the clumsy or unwary. The rolling of the ship, the slippery footing in blood and blubber, the frenzied tearing of sharks at the whale's carcass inches below the cutting stage, the perilous swoop of tons

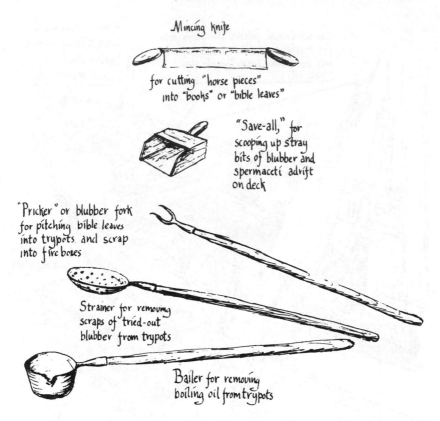

Mincing knife

for cutting "horse pieces"
into "books" or "bible leaves"

"Save-all," for
scooping up stray
bits of blubber and
spermaceti adrift
on deck

"Pricker" or blubber fork
for pitching bible leaves
into trypots and scrap
into fire boxes

Strainer for removing
scraps of tried-out
blubber from trypots

Bailer for removing
boiling oil from trypots

of blubber across the foredeck as the blanket-piece was severed—all combined to make the whale fishery amongst the most arduous and dangerous of livings.

Contemporary Engravings

"THERE SHE BLOWS!"
A fairly accurate rendition of the spreaders at the head of one of the top-masts of a squarerigger. It should be noted, however, that the lookouts on a whaler routinely stood their watches in hoops at the head of the topgallant mast—a full mast higher than shown here—where they could command a more far-reaching view.

STRUCK ON A BREACH.
This view gives an excellent idea of the shape and location of the sperm whale's lower jaw. A whale "breaches" when he leaps clear of the water. Normally, the boat-steerer (at left, in stern of boat) would be facing forward, toward the whale. Note the whaleboat at right, under sail.

LANCING.
In this picture, the boats' crews have hauled in on the whaleline until abreast of the exhausted prey, and the boatheaders are using the long-handled, barbless lances to complete the kill. See Chapter 61: "Stubb Kills a Whale."

BOAT DESTROYED BY A WHALE.
The flukes, spanning a dozen feet or more, could reduce a whaleboat to splinters with a single blow; the sort of mishap shown here was an all-too-frequent occurrence in the whale fishery. The boats shown here, incidentally, are atypical, in being manned by ten rather than six men, and in being square-sterned rather than double-ended.

IN THE WHALE'S JAW.
A peculiarity of the sperm whale is its habit of rolling over on its side or back to snap at a tormentor with its strong lower jaw. There are no teeth in the upper jaw, but rather sockets for the teeth of the lower jaw.

BAILING THE "CASE."
A shark's-eye view of the case, or upper portion of the head, of a sperm whale, held up on the whaleship's starboard by the cutting tackle. To the left of the whaleman in the picture is the case-bucket, which was used to remove the spermaceti through a small hole cut atop the case. The bucket was tapered toward both ends, barrel fashion, to prevent its becoming jammed inside the case.

"CUTTING-IN."
One of the cutting falls with its blubber hook taking in the blanket piece. Normally, the two planks shown here were connected by another at their outboard ends to form the cutting stage. Note the fluke chain leading from the bow of the ship; it was passed around the root of the flukes to allow the carcass to revolve as the blanket piece was stripped.

TRYING OUT.
A view of the tryworks from the foremast. This picture shows three try-pots, but the use of only two was virtually universal in the American fishery. The pitchfork-like implement held by the whaleman is a "pricker" or blubber-fork, used to put the blubber into the pots, and to fish out the tried-out scraps to feed the fires.

"THERE SHE BLOWS!"

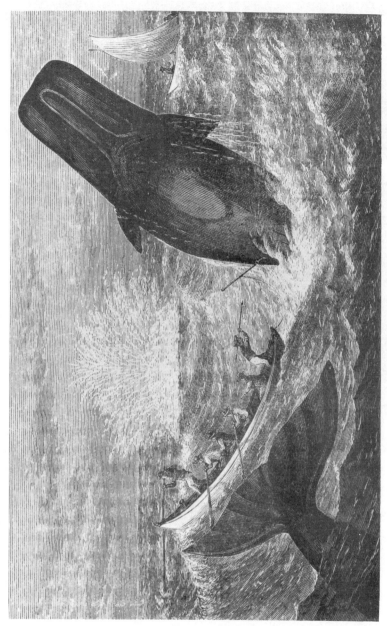

STRUCK ON A BREACH.

LANCING.

BOAT DESTROYED BY A WHALE.

IN A WHALE'S JAW.

BAILING THE "CASE."

"CUTTING-IN."

TRYING OUT.

The Original Queequeg

SELF-PORTRAIT OF THE FACE OF TUPAI CUPA, DRAWN WITHOUT A MIRROR. From George Lillie Craik, *The New Zealanders* (London: Charles Knight, 1830).

Before *Moby-Dick*:
International Controversy
over Melville

Herman Melville was the second son of a once-wealthy father who died early and left his widow and eight children impoverished at the start of the second term of Andrew Jackson; they were plunged into still more hopeless poverty in the Panic of 1837, at the start of the Van Buren administration. Put to work in a bank in Albany at age twelve, then put to work in his older brother Gansevoort's cap and fur store, Melville attended school for a few months during some of the next years. Raised as he was, he found no niche for himself when he tried to get work as a surveyor maintaining the Erie Canal, or when he taught for a pittance in several rural or village schools, or when he turned twenty in Liverpool as a sailor on a merchant ship. Yet in retrospect the rootless, restless, deprived young man had the extraordinary luck to be at the right place in historic times, or near enough to the right time so as to make a good story. Going west to the Mississippi frontier of Illinois in 1840 in the futile hope of making a living there, he witnessed in Detroit the media-whipped hysteria of the Log Cabin Campaign by which the Whigs would win the presidency for a decrepit veteran (though hardly a great hero) of the War of 1812, William Henry Harrison. (Politics had always used symbols, of course, and George Washington had literally been iconic, pictured on everything from tablecloths to statues, but he had created a country; the campaign of 1840 was a triumph of show over substance.) Later on the Upper Great Lakes and the Mississippi Melville saw American Indians of several tribes living (he could only assume) much as they had lived before the whites came. Chicago was a raw little town on Lake Michigan, only a few years old. However briefly, Melville saw the Mississippi Valley before white settlers had displaced the buffalo from the Great Plains, when Daniel Boone had been dead only twenty years and Davy Crockett only four.

Melville sailed from Fairhaven, Massachusetts, on a whaler in the first week of 1841, expecting (as young people do) matters to proceed normally at home—his Uncle Peter Gansevoort's friend Martin Van Buren to leave office in March and Harrison to be president when he returned, John Tyler to be vice president. His ship arrived in Nukuheva in 1842 when the Marquesan Islands "had just been taken possession of by Rear Admiral Du Petit Thouars, in the name of the invincible French nation" (*Typee*, ch. 2). Melville deserted there and became the "Modern Crusoe," as reviewers of *Typee* said in London in 1846, a civilized American who had lived with South Sea natives (cannibals, he hinted) and had returned to write about the feat. Later in 1842, on his second whaler, he arrived at Tahiti just in time to witness a still more cynical triumph of French colonialism, Du Petit Thouars's thuggish extension of "the protection of His Majesty Louis Phillippe" to the Society Islands. Melville wrote in the appendix to *Typee* that he had "arrived at Tahiti the very day that the iniquitous designs of the French were consummated by inducing the subordinate chiefs, during the absence of their queen, to ratify an artfully drawn treaty, by which she was virtually deposed. Both menaces and caresses were employed on this occasion, and the 32-pounders that peeped out of the portholes of the frigate were the principal arguments adduced to quiet the scruples of the more conscientious islanders."

In 1843 Melville arrived in Hawaii (still often called the Sandwich Islands) after it had been seized by the British under the cover of a "provisional cession" by King Kamehameha III. Melville had seen abuses by missionaries in Tahiti, but in Hawaii he saw American Protestant missionaries all but enslaving the native Hawaiians they had come to Christianize. He was on hand in Honolulu on July 28, 1843, when, after angry protests from the American president (Tyler, as Melville had learned sometime in 1841 or 1842), the Union Jack was hauled down and the flag of the Sandwich Islands hoisted, all accompanied by ceremonial cannoning from British warships.

Few Americans of his time knew better what colonialism and imperialism looked like, up close; and no other American writer of his time had Melville's intimate experience of life among "natives" of another race in their own world (in the interior of a Pacific Island), not yet deeply contaminated by contact with the occasional runaway sailor over the previous decades and not yet reached by missionaries. No other American writer of his time had Melville's intimate experience with living in close quarters (forecastles) for prolonged periods with as many men of different races and nationalities (and ages and levels of learning).

Away from U.S. "civilization," brooding under the southern constellations that he identified as making him receptive to new ideas, Melville developed a keen sense of cultural relativity that set him at odds with the pious conventionalities of his society. For him the Polynesians would never be savages waiting to be evangelized whatever the cost to their culture, their health, and their lives. The dominant American racial attitude toward all "uncivilized" (and unchristianized) races was that of the proper Bostonian Francis Parkman, who infused *The California and Oregon Trail* (1849) with disdain for the American Indians he encountered on the Great Plains (and who soon after the book was published married another proper Bostonian, a second cousin of Melville's). Even as late as the 1860s and 1870s prominent ministers of Melville's acquaintance could look forward coolly to the necessary extirpation of the Red Race as white settlement of the West went inevitably forward. (In 1876 Melville's eighteen-thousand-line centennial poem, *Clarel*, was all but ignored as newspapers filled their columns with reports that the Sioux under Sitting Bull and Crazy Horse had annihilated U.S. troops under George Custer at Little Big Horn, an Indian victory that signaled ultimate white triumph.)

When his U.S. Navy frigate the *United States* reached Boston in October 1844, Melville and others were kept aboard for days during which the fate of a slave on the ship was decided by the chief justice of the supreme court of Massachusetts, Lemuel Shaw, his father's old friend, the fiancé of his aunt Nancy Melvill who died before they could marry, and the man who in 1847 became his father-in-law. Shaw declared the man free because his owner, the purser, had deliberately taken him aboard the ship that had now anchored in a free state. Melville was in New York for the election of 1844, in time to hear his brother Gansevoort instruct a mass meeting of Democrats across the Hudson in Newark on the "history, geographical position, and undeveloped resources of Texas" and "the constitutionality and expediency of re-annexation," then enter "into a very ingenious and lucid argument for the purpose of demonstrating that the annexation of Texas would necessarily lead to the gradual extinction of slavery in the slave-holding States, and their consequent vastly increased prosperity." Gansevoort Melville had gained national fame as the man chosen to go to Tennessee that summer and assure westerners of the loyalty of the easterners to the Democratic nominee, James K. Polk, who had promised to annex Texas.

Through the mid-1840s many Americans, like Polk, were committed not only to annex Texas but to fight off any British attempt to seize more than what Americans decided was an acceptably minimal share of Oregon. While Melville was still stuck on the *United States* in the Boston Navy Yard in October 1844, Gansevoort had convinced an audience of Schenectady, New York, Democrats "that England was, as she ever has been, painfully alive to, and jealous of, the stately steppings of our young and growing Republic, and that she is insidiously attempting to check our territorial extension, and to increase her colonial possessions in America." As secretary of the American legation in London in late 1845 and early 1846 (until his sudden death), Gansevoort impetuously warned against British imperialism on the Pacific coast of North America. The American publisher George P. Putnam recalled decades later that Gansevoort had been an incendiary: "Replying to a formal toast, 'The President of the United States,' the Secretary electrified the diplomatic circle by a Tammany speech, winding up somewhat thus: 'I was one who helped to place Mr. Polk where he now is, and I know that he will not *dare* to recede from 54–40!' "—the southernmost latitude firebrands were prepared to concede to England.

In March 1846 Gansevoort Melville and three other Americans took a train from London to visit Cambridge University. In the library, Gansevoort walked up

> to an immense terrestrial globe suspended in the centre of one of the rooms, and placing his hand upon it, said, "Look here, gentlemen, and see if any American can carefully examine the map of our globe, and not feel a gratitude and just pride at seeing the geographical position our country holds upon its face. Here lies Asia and the whole East, with its immense wealth. There is the mouth of the Columbia River, almost as near Canton as London is to New York. Now here is a little speck called Europe, upon the Eastern shores of the Atlantic, and a smaller speck on its Western shore called New England, including New York city, which have ever held the trade of this immense region, at the expense of passing Cape Horn, or the Cape of Good Hope, the South Atlantic, Indian Ocean, ["] &c. &c. "Look here," said he, "and tell me if any American can give up, or barter away the valley of the Columbia, and not, Esau like, sell his birthright?"

[From an obituary notice in the New York *Journal of Commerce* as reprinted in the Albany *Argus*, June 4, 1846. (For Esau, see Genesis 25.27–34.)]

War against the mother country was a real possibility as Melville began his career with a book published first in London through the good offices of Gansevoort (and welcomed by the publisher in part because of its pro-British, anti-French sentiments). Putnam, who happened to be in London early in 1846, accepted *Typee* for Wiley & Putnam of New York on the advice of his most prized author, the most famous American writer of the last half century, now the outgoing minister to Spain, Washington Irving, who happened to arrive in London just then and who naturally visited his old haunt, the legation, where he had once held Gansevoort's job. In New York John Wiley, a devout Congregationalist (a sect closely allied with the Presbyterians, both missionary minded), rushed the book into print without reading it.

Melville's first two books, *Typee* and *Omoo*, became sensationally controversial, at first because *Typee* was thought to be a hoax, then because Melville had dared to criticize the American Protestant missionaries who functioned as informal agents of potential American colonialism, then because of the sexual stance Melville had taken in those books, where he described the open sexuality of sailors with South Sea island women but ambiguously and teasingly portrayed himself as possibly a shocked onlooker, possibly an active participant. Wiley quickly forced Melville to expurgate *Typee*, so that from mid-1846 only the so-called revised edition was sold in the United States, whereas Murray's unexpurgated edition went all over the British Empire in sets of his "Home and Colonial Library." Melville moved to Harper & Brothers with *Omoo*, the Methodists willing for a time to put profit over the cause of evangelicalism, for that book also attacked the behavior of missionaries.

Very oddly and unpredictably, Melville was the right man at the right time to become the first and for some years the only American literary sex symbol. This began with *Typee* (a happy dog, the *Times* of London called him), but reviewers of *Omoo* consolidated the public view of Melville as a man with a sexual history, to be envied or condemned by readers. Some readers—see the reviews by Horace Greeley (p. 486 herein) and G. W. Peck (p. 487 herein)— to their extreme discomfiture, found themselves simultaneously envying and condemning. In 1847 Melville and Elizabeth Shaw could not marry in church for fear his fans would crowd into it; in 1849 a woman holding *Omoo* as she read on shipboard would look over at him appraisingly; just after the publication of *Moby-Dick* a newspaper correspondent from Lenox, Massachusetts, described him as "one whose name often lingers now in terms of adulation upon many rosy lips." Because *Typee* and *Omoo* were his most popular books throughout his lifetime, many readers continued to see him as a literary sex symbol, even after the psychological novel *Pierre* (1852), widely declared to be insane, broke that image for reviewers. (To judge from the reviews and biographical record, Melville was a heterosexual sex symbol; two decades after his career began, he would have deduced from at least one correspondent, Charles W. Stoddard, that *Typee* and *Omoo* could be perceived as a guide to homosexual adventures in the South Seas.)

Melville began *Moby-Dick* in a New York City house with his mother and four sisters and his wife and son and his brother and *his* wife and daughter (and four live-in servants); then wrote in an isolated farmhouse outside Pittsfield, Massachusetts, with wife, son, mother and three or for a while all four sisters (for the last half year of the composition, his wife in her second pregnancy), and at least one servant. All the time he was composing *Moby-Dick* in such intensely domestic situations, he knew that he was, like Lord Byron but like no American before him, a writer whose appeal was partly based on sexual notoriety that he had teasingly created and exploited. He knew, that is, that just as any religious flippancy would be seized on, any sexual teasing he wrote into *Moby-Dick* would arouse intense responses merely because of the public perception of him as a sexual celebrity (whatever the reality of his sexual experiences in the South Seas or elsewhere).

Melville was not in the right place to witness the European revolutions of 1848, but when the news reached New York City he promptly altered the direction of his work in progress, *Mardi* (1849), so as to write the events into his manuscript, and two years later he got his own look at Paris after the latest revolution. One of the Harper brothers—the publishers of *Moby-Dick*— won the mayorship of New York City in 1849 as a Nativist, a member of the xenophobic party (precursor of the Know-Nothings) that opposed unlimited immigration, especially of the Irish. Protestants took doctrinal differences seriously (why else be a Congregationalist and not a Methodist, unless to save your soul?) and strove for clarity and triumph of belief, not for a tolerant ecumenicalism. In this climate, it was easy to enflame the citizenry with identity-politics, and in the ensuing violence of the 1830s and early 1840s a Catholic convent and a school were burned. Melville had seen immigrants up close when he returned from Liverpool in 1839 on a ship overfilled with steerage passengers, and in Chapter 58 of *Redburn* (1849) he wrote passionately: "Let us waive that agitated national topic, as to whether such multitudes of foreign poor should be landed on our American shores; let us waive it, with the one only thought, that if they can get here, they have God's right to come; though they bring all Ireland and her miseries with them. For the whole world is the patrimony of the whole world; there is no telling who does not own a stone in the Great Wall of China."

When he began *Moby-Dick*, Melville was a young man (only thirty) of remarkable experiences and deep if hit-or-miss learning, who had been an eyewitness to history. His wide-ranging historical and political allusions in *Moby-Dick* and his allusions to recent European and Latin American history are grounded both in his reading and his personal experiences in post-Revolutionary and Jacksonian America, then in the Pacific and the coast of South America in the early 1840s, and the United States and Europe in the later 1840s. When Melville began *Moby-Dick* what he saw in Europe, in the Pacific, in the Americas, what he gathered from his reading about Asia and Africa, was that much of the world was up for grabs, ripe for the taking. The Hawaiian Islands had been seized by the British (partly to prevent their being seized by the French) and might again be seized, by the British, the French, or the czar of Russia, who still owned Alaska and needed warmer ports. And who was to stop the United States from seizing Canada and Cuba? England might be the nation to reap the profits of forcibly opening up Japan to European trade, England might further challenge the Bostonians and New Yorkers as masters of the China trade. Mexico had been up for grabs in the mid-1840s, and at the end of "the Mexican War," two years before Melville started writing *Moby-Dick*, it had surrendered a gigantic stretch of southwestern territory to the United States, which then paid good Yankee dollars for another hunk: when would the conquest or purchases stop?

In 1850 much of the vastly expanded United States was up for grabs, vulnerable, even the plains territories of Kansas and possibly Nebraska, to the extension of slavery. The very existence of the young United States was more vulnerable than ever before during the year 1850, the first year Melville worked on *Moby-Dick*; he was writing obsessively in December when his Pittsfield, Massachusetts, neighbors rallied to support the Compromise of 1850, which committed the North to return fugitive slaves to their owners in the South to preserve the Union. American slaves in Virginia had revolted in Melville's adolescence: might slaves again rise against their masters out of desperation at another remedy, now that the South seemed to be supported by all the North except what responsible people, Democrats or Whigs alike, thought of as a lunatic fringe of abolitionists? Even the sanctity of marriage was endangered, many thought, by the presence of followers of the slain Joseph Smith anywhere on the vast continent. Characteristically, Melville identified with the outcasts; in a letter to his friend Evert A. Duyckinck written just as he began *Moby-Dick*, he said his unpopular *Mardi* (1849) had been "driven forth like a wild, mystic Mormon into shelterless exile." The whole of the United States was up for grabs from a foreign religious state, the Vatican, if you believed the rabid preachers and journalists who had been proclaiming for years in papers like the *American Protestant Vindicator* that Jesuits were prowling the United States in disguise (peddlers, blacksmiths, opticians, one never knew), ready for the signal to throw off their disguises and unite with all the Irish immigrants to seize the country for the pope. Among the American writers, Washington Irving was old, and the younger new poets and fiction writers seemed too tame: American literary greatness was also up for grabs, as Melville made clear in an essay he wrote while halfway through *Moby-Dick*, "Hawthorne and his Mosses." The time was right. It was no coincidence that Walt Whitman's magnificent *Leaves of Grass* followed *Moby-Dick* by less than four years. H.P.

GANSEVOORT MELVILLE

A Scene at the "Hermitage"[†]

* * * Why, here, if a gentleman offers his hand to a fashionable lady she receives it in a sort of minimy pinimy, don't touch me sort of an air, that may perhaps affect him unpleasantly; but these Tennessee girls take right hold as if they meant it, and in a way that is really delightful to a plain, backward, bashful man like myself. (Great laughter and cheers) And then the Tennesseans of the man sex have peculiaristics of manner which are decidedly interesting and characteristic. One of these peculiarities is, that they make a man talk such an unconscionable time. If a man gets up to speak, and they don't happen to like him, they soon shout out—"Hello, stranger, you've mistaken your vocation—slope!" (Roars of laughter.) And if he won't slope, they make him. (Renewed laughter) Tennessee is, indeed, the land of social democracy. I have seen men clad in linsey-woolsey garments, and with unshod feet, setting in Colonel Polk's[1] parlor, and at the table of Andrew Jackson. (Loud cheers) They are ever frank and free in expressing their opinion, be it pleasant to the hearer or the reverse. On one occasion, after I had addressed a large popular assemblage, a sturdy frontier's man, who was about six feet high, without a superfluous ounce of flesh upon his stalwart frame, one of your men who never turn their backs on either friend or foe, and who looked as if he could whip his weight in wild cats, (laughter) strode up to me and grasped my hand with an iron energy that * * * reminded me forcibly of a vice, and suddenly withdrawing his grasp, slapped me on the back with tremendous force, sung out—"Old horse—I love you!" (Roars of laughter, repeated again and again.) * * *

When Andrew Jackson dies, he will not drivel his path to the grave like a slobbering dotard, as the whig press falsely call him; but when HE dies—when the great soul within shall have utterly consumed its outer tenament of clay—why, then, a MAN will die! And our children, and children's children, will go up to that corner of the little garden at the Hermitage, where his wife now lies—and by whose side he will sleep in death—and that will forever be to us and our descendants, next to Mount

---

† New York *Herald*, November 5, 1844. An election-day report of Gansevoort Melville's speech in Newark at Washington Hall on November 2. The title is one of the synoptic headings the *Herald* placed before the speech. *The Hermitage:* Jackson's name for his beloved house outside Nashville. Gansevoort Melville had been the guest of Jackson there in August 1844.
1. James K. Polk (1795–1849) of Tennessee; president 1845–49.

Vernon,[2] the holiest and most sacred spot on American soil. . . . (Great manifestation of feeling amongst the audience).[3]

ANONYMOUS

[An American Sailor on the Missionaries][†]

* * * Had this work been put forward as the production of an English common sailor, we should have had some doubts of its authenticity, in the absence of distinct proof. But in the United States it is different. There social opinion does not invest any employment with caste discredit; and it seems customary with young men of respectability to serve as common seamen, either as a probationership to the navy or as a mode of seeing life. Cooper and Dana[1] are examples of this practice. The wide-spread system of popular education also bestows upon the American a greater familiarity with popular literature and a readier use of the pen than is usual with classes of the same apparent grade in England. Striking as the style of composition may sometimes seem in a *Residence in the Marquesas*, there is nothing in it beyond the effects of a vivacious mind, acquainted with popular books, and writing with the national fluency; or a reading sailor spinning a yarn; nothing to indicate the student or the scholar. Yet we should like to have had the story of the book; to have known the motives of the publication, and whether it is an American reprint or a conjoint appearance, or whether Mr. Murray has the sole right of publishing. There are certain sea freedoms, too, that might as well have been removed before issuing it for family reading. * * *

The "service" has had the effect of enlarging Mr. Melville's mind and making him less provincial in feeling than many of his countrymen. It has also given him some knowledge of the South Seas generally, which appears in the comparisons he incidentally introduces; and has impressed him with an indifferent opinion of (to say the least) the self-seeking and worldly spirit of the missionaries. Here is an example of them at the Sandwich Islands.[2]

2. The home of the revered first president, George Washington, near Washington, DC.

3. Melville's ambition as a writer was fired by the collision in his imagination of his older and better-educated brother's new fame and prestige and his own recent insignificance as a whaleman and an ordinary seaman. If a boy as poor as Jackson could be thundered higher than a throne, so, perhaps, could a boy as poor and uneducated as Melville himself.

† London *Spectator* 19 (February 28, 1846): 209–10.

1. Melville's predecessors as American sea-writers. James Fenimore Cooper (1789–1851), a foremast hand and a midshipman after being dismissed from Yale, started writing nautical novels with *The Pilot* (1823) and even after his fame as the creator of Leatherstocking wrote *The Red Rover* (1827) and other sea books. Richard Henry Dana Jr., who sailed for California after leaving Harvard because of eye troubles, became a lawyer and gained fame for *Two Years Before the Mast* (1840), before becoming a leading opponent of the Fugitive Slave Law. Friendly with Melville in 1847–50, united by their hostility to their mutual publisher, Harper & Brothers (who twisted the *Two Years* copyright out of Dana for a pittance), they went separate ways, perhaps because of Dana's fury at Melville's father-in-law, Judge Lemuel Shaw, for enforcing the Fugitive Slave Law in 1851 and 1854.

2. Here the *Spectator* quotes what it titles "The Missionary Equipage" from ch. 26, where Melville introduces a depiction of missionary outrages in Hawaii with this heightened rhetorical passage:

Let the savages be civilized, but civilize them with benefits, and not with evils; and let heathenism be destroyed, but not by destroying the heathen. The Anglo-Saxon hive have extir-

ANONYMOUS

[A Bewitching Work]†

Since the joyous moment when we first read Robinson Crusoe and believed it all, and wondered all the more because we believed, we have not met with so bewitching a work as this narrative of Herman Melville's, which forms the thirtieth and thirty-first parts of Mr. Murray's *Home and Colonial Library*. Like Robinson Crusoe, however, we cannot help suspecting that if there be really such a person as Herman Melville, he has either employed a Daniel Defoe to describe his adventures, or is himself both a Defoe and an Alexander Selkirk.[1]

The work professes to be written by an American common sailor, who, with one of his comrades, escaped from the *Dolly*,[2] a South Sea whaler (in consequence of the cruelty of the captain), when she touched at Nukuheva, the principal of that group of islands in the Pacific known by the name of the Marquesas—so called in honour of the Marquess de Mendoza, Viceroy of Peru, under whose auspices, in the year 1595, the navigator sailed who first visited them.

Nothing is said as to whether this work is a reprint from an American edition, or whether it has been transmitted to this country in manuscript for publication; while the tone of the article which appears in the appendix, warmly vindicating the conduct of Lord George Paulet in the affair of the Sandwich Islands, would almost justify the suspicion that the work is not written by an American at all.[3] When too, we consider the style of

---

> pated Paganism from the greater part of the North American continent; but with it they have likewise extirpated the greater portion of the Red race. Civilization is gradually sweeping from the earth the lingering vestiges of Paganism, and at the same time the shrinking forms of its unhappy worshippers.

He goes on:

> Among the islands of Polynesia, no sooner are the images overturned, the temples demolished, and the idolators converted into *nominal* Christians, than disease, vice, and premature death make their appearance. The depopulated land is then recruited from the rapacious hordes of enlightened individuals who settle themselves within its borders, and clamorously announce the progress of the Truth. Neat villas, trim gardens, shaven lawns, spires, and cupolas arise, while the poor savage soon finds himself an interloper in the country of his fathers, and that too on the very site of the hut where he was born.

Melville's outrage culminates in a depiction of the behavior of missionaries and their families in Hawaii:

> Not until I visited Honolulu was I aware of the fact that the small remnant of the natives had been civilized into draught horses, and evangelized into beasts of burden. But so it is. They have been literally broken into the traces, and are harnessed to the vehicles of their spiritual instructors like so many dumb brutes!

Melville gave one memorable sketch of a heavily built missionary's wife beating the men harnessed to her "go-cart," to make them pull her faster.

† London *John Bull*, March 7, 1846.
1. Defoe (1660–1731) wrote *Robinson Crusoe* (1719) based partly on an account of the experience of the Scottish seaman Alexander Selkirk (1676–1721), who lived alone on Juan Fernandez (1704–09) after being put ashore. At this time, American readers usually had access only to condensed and expurgated versions of *Robinson Crusoe* (as was the case also with Jonathan Swift's *Gulliver's Travels*, 1726).
2. Melville's fictional name for the *Acushnet*.
3. Melville's extremely partisan "appendix" to *Typee* contrasted the brutal French seizure of Tahiti with the British Lord George Paulet's benignant acceptance of the provisional cession of the Sandwich Islands early in 1843 and his restoration of power to the Hawaiian king a few months later. The villains in Hawaii were Dr. Gerritt Judd and his "junto of ignorant and designing Methodist elders in the councils of a half-civilized king, ruling with absolute sway over a nation

composition, so easy, so graceful, and so graphic, we own the difficulty we feel in believing that it is the production of a common sailor. It is "affectionately inscribed" to "Lemuel Shaw, Chief Justice of the Commonwealth of Massachusetts."[4] Be the author, however, whom and what he may, he has produced a narrative of singular interest, not merely as regards his own personal adventures, which are in the highest degree exciting and romantic, but as regards the remarkable people (the Typees) among whom he sojourned for some time, and whose manners and customs he delineates with so much power. More than three years, he informs us, have elapsed since the occurrence of the events he has described, and as the account of them, he says, when "spun as a yarn," not only relieved the weariness of many a night watch at sea, but excited the warmest sympathies of the author's "shipmates," he was "led to think that his story could scarcely fail to interest those who are less familiar than the sailor with a life of adventure." There are a few passages, here and there, obnoxious[5] to the same censure which was bestowed upon Dr. Hawkesworth for his account of Otaheite, in Cook's Voyages.[6]

[NATHANIEL HAWTHORNE]

[Melville's "Freedom of View" (not "Laxity of Principle")][†]

The present numbers of this excellent and popular series [Wiley & Putnam's *Library of American Books*] contain a very remarkable work, entitled *Typee, or a Peep at Polynesian Life*. It records the adventures of a young American who ran away from a whale ship at the Marquesas, and spent some months as the guest, or captive, of a native tribe, of which scarcely anything had been hitherto known to the civilized world.—The book is lightly but vigorously written; and we are acquainted with no work that gives a freer and more effective picture of barbarian life, in that unadul-

---

just poised between barbarism and civilization." Paulet had taken action partly because the Methodist junta, systematically keeping Catholic priests out of the Hawaiian islands, had dared to deport two who had arrived in a British ship. Lord Paulet was making a pre-emptive strike, for the junta had so outraged the French in the Pacific that they might have seized the islands first to make them safe for Catholicism: better the Anglican British than the Catholic French.

4. Lemuel Shaw (1781–1861), Barnstable-born, Harvard-educated lawyer, chief justice of the Commonwealth of Massachusetts (1830–60), whose only daughter, Elizabeth Knapp Shaw, married Herman Melville on August 4, 1847.

5. Liable.

6. John Hawkesworth (1715–1773) edited the journals of the British explorer Captain James Cook (1728–1779, killed by residents of Hawaii) and Philip Carteret (d. 1796; British admiral and explorer of the Pacific) for his *Account of the Voyages . . . in the Southern Hemisphere* (1773), where he portrayed the natives of Tahiti (or Otaheite) as innocently sensual.

† Salem (Massachusetts) *Advertiser*, March 25, 1846. Hawthorne's *Journal of an African Cruiser* (1845) preceded Melville's *Typee* in Wiley & Putnam's *Library of American Books*, and *Mosses from an Old Manse* soon followed it, so they, along with other writers, including Edgar Allan Poe, Caroline Kirkland, and Margaret Fuller, were often listed together in various volumes of the prestigious series and in advertisements for it.

Sophia Hawthorne was particularly taken with the voluptuous depiction of Fayaway in *Typee*, to the point of imagining her when she first looked on Melville's face in 1850; that is, she saw Melville, as many did, in terms of his presumed exotic and erotic experiences without considering the possibility that Fayaway might have been to some extent a fictional portrait. In 1850 Hawthorne read *Typee* again (probably in the expurgated "revised edition") as well as *Omoo*, *Mardi*, *Redburn*, and *White-Jacket*, when Evert A. Duyckinck sent them to him in Lenox, Massachusetts, in a package delivered by Melville himself, who was unwitting of its contents.

terated state of which there are now so few specimens remaining. The
gentleness of disposition that seems akin to the delicious climate, is
shown in contrast with traits of savage fierceness;—on one page, we read
of manners and modes of life that indicate a whole system of innocence
and peace; and on the next, we catch a glimpse of a smoked human head,
and the half-picked skeleton of what had been (in a culinary sense) a *well-
dressed* man. The author's descriptions of the native girls are voluptuously
colored, yet not more so than the exigencies of the subject appear to
require. He has that freedom of view—it would be too harsh to call it lax-
ity of principle—which renders him tolerant of codes of morals that may
be little in accordance with our own; a spirit proper enough to a young
and adventurous sailor, and which makes his book the more wholesome
to our staid landsmen.[1] The narrative is skillfully managed, and in a literary point of view, the execution of the work is worthy of the novelty and
interest of its subject.

ANONYMOUS

[A Unique Eyewitness][†]

One of the most delightful narratives of adventure ever published. This
book divulges the cant, humbug, and glaring inaccuracy of the nonsense
respecting Polynesia which has at intervals been palmed upon the English
public as the experience of trustworthy travellers. Swallowing, with all the
voracity of marvel-lovers, every absurd "yarn" spun by a jocular tar over
his grog in the forecastle, and noting them down as likely to sell excellently among the credulous readers at home, the majority of "writers of
travel" accumulate their information from hearsay, and retail such fallac-
ies with whatever additions may tend to heighten their attractiveness.
With very few exceptions indeed, these assertions hold good. Among the
mass of "Voyages and Travels" already printed an enormous library of fiction might be collected, and that fiction the most extravagant and improbable. The writer of this work, an American sailor, stands however totally
apart from those scribblers; he is the eyewitness of every circumstance he
relates; and, from having lived (during a captivity of four months) among

---

1. The English edition and the first American printing contained a description of the way the native
women swam out naked (holding a girdle of tappa above the water) to the whale ship and boarded
it, where the sailors greeted them. Such descriptions had been printed before, so the fact of sexual orgies was no news to seasoned readers. What was new was Melville's teasing tone, in lines
in ch. 2 soon to be expurgated from the American "revised edition": "What a sight for us bachelor sailors! how avoid so dire a temptation? For who could think of tumbling these artless creatures overboard, when they had swam miles to welcome us?" More upsetting to some readers was
Melville's having it both ways, apparently participating in the actions yet seeming to distance himself from the behavior of every other man in the crew:

> Our ship was now wholly given up to every species of riot and debauchery. Not the feeblest
> barrier was interposed between the unholy passions of the crew and their unlimited gratifica-
> tion. The grossest licentiousness and the most shameful inebriety prevailed, with occasional
> and but short-lived interruptions, through the whole period of her stay. Alas for the poor sav-
> ages when exposed to the influence of these polluting examples!

† London *Sun*, March 30, 1846.

the Typea inhabitants of Nukuheva Island, he had assuredly sufficient opportunities of becoming acquainted with the customs, disposition, social relations, and mode of life as visible among the so-called "savages" of the South Sea archipelago. From the first moment of his desertion from the whaler at Nukuheva harbour, to his escape from the Typea Valley; or, to speak plainer, from the first line in the first page to the last in the last, interest, information, and the most genial freshness of description, pervades the whole volume. It is all but visiting the Marquesas ourselves. Poee-Poee becomes a familiar dish, tappa is cinctured round your loins; you are sanctified by the Taboo, and clamber up the long shaft of the cocoa nut, while reading this singular production. Throughout it there are snatches of drollery that are occasionally irresistibly comic; drollery of observation; and sometimes reflections of the most unstrained and winning pathos. If alone as likely to correct the popular notion regarding the character of savages, this book will perform a high mission, and is deserving of every possible praise. The Typees, to whom the writer's remarks are especially referable, are a nation of Indians, totally ignorant of any intercourse with white men; Europeans have never ventured to anchor on their shores; civilization has never insinuated itself among their bamboo huts; they have the reputation of being the most sanguinary barbarians, and the most ruthless *cannibals* in the Marquesas. * * *

[MARGARET FULLER]

[A Challenge to the Sewing Societies][†]

"Typee" would seem, also, to be the record of imaginary adventures by some one who had visited those regions. But it is a very entertaining and pleasing narrative, and the Happy Valley[1] of the gentle cannibals compares very well with the best contrivances of the learned Dr. Johnson to produce similar impressions. Of the power of this writer to make pretty and spirited pictures as well as of his quick and arch manner generally, a happy specimen may be seen in the account of the savage climbing the cocoa-tree p. 273, vol. 2d. Many of the observations and narratives we suppose to be strictly correct. Is the account given of the result of the missionary enterprises in the Sandwich Islands of this number? We suppose so from what we have heard in other ways. With a view to ascertaining the truth, it would be well if the sewing societies, now engaged in providing funds for such enterprises, would read the particulars, they will find in this book beginning p. 249, vol. 2d, and make inquiries in consequence, before going on with their efforts. Generally, the sewing societies of the country villages will find this the very book they wish to have read while

---

† New York *Tribune*, April 4, 1846. Fuller was one of the very earliest American female journalists, thanks to her philosophical kinship with the erratic reformer Horace Greeley, founder and editor of the *Tribune*.
1. The lexicographer Samuel Johnson (1709–1784) wrote the popular mildly philosophical *History of Rasselas, Prince of Abyssinia* (1759), which depicts a moderately "Happy Valley," in Abyssinia, but discourages the hope of attaining great happiness anywhere.

assembled at their work. Othello's hair-breadth 'scapes[2] were nothing to those by this hero in the descent of the cataracts, and many a Desdemona might seriously incline her ear to the descriptions of the lovely Fay-a-way.

ANONYMOUS

[Happy Dog: Herman in the Typee Valley][†]

Mr. Murray's *Home and Colonial Library* does not furnish us with a more interesting book than this; hardly with a cleverer. It is full of the captivating matter upon which the general reader battens; and is endowed with freshness and originality to an extent that cannot fail to exhilarate the most enervated and *blasé* of circulating-library loungers. * * *

Mr. Melville, after all his troubles, is most agreeably surprised and sumptuously entertained. He is provided with provisions and attendants, a home is given to him, and the houris of whom he had dreamt on board the Dolly—but lovelier far than even his excited imagination had pictured them—hover around him, eager to enhance his bliss. Enviable Herman! A happier dog it is impossible to imagine than Herman in the Typee Valley. * * *

We have been somewhat prolix in the narration of this history; first, because the book of Mr. Melville is really a very clever production; and, secondly, because it is introduced to the English public as authentic, which we by no means think it to be. We have called Mr. Melville a common sailor; but he is a very uncommon sailor, even for America, whose mariners are better educated than our own. His reading has been extensive. In his own province, the voyages of Cook, Carteret, Byron, Kotzebue, and Vancouver are familiar to him; he can talk glibly of Count Bouffon and Baron Cuvier, and critically, when he likes, of Teniers.[1] His descriptions of scenery are lifelike and vigorous, His descriptions of scenery are lifelike and vigorous, sometimes masterly, and his style throughout is rather that of an educated literary man than of a poor outcast working seaman on board of a South Sea whaler. * * *

2. Readers of the adventurous parts of *Typee* were irresistibly reminded of the eloquent account by Shakespeare's Moor of how he won Desdemona's love through his stories of his "hair-breadth 'scapes" (*Othello* 1.3.136). Melville would have read these comparisons edgily, because, as the public could not know, he had won Elizabeth Shaw's love just that way.
† London *Times*, April 6, 1846.
1. David Teniers, realistic Flemish painter of low-life scenes, is either the father (1582–1649) or the son (1610–1690). John Hawkesworth edited the journals of Captain James Cook and Philip Carteret, *Account of the Voyages . . . in the Southern Hemisphere* (1773). John Byron (1723–1786), grandfather of Lord Byron, published a narrative of the shipwreck off Chile of the *Wager*, on which he was a midshipman, *The Narrative of the Honourable John Byron . . . Containing an Account of the Great Distresses Suffered by Himself and His Companions on the Coast of Patagonia, from the Year 1740, till Their Arrival in England, 1746. With a Description of St. Jago de Chili, and the Manners and Customs of the Inhabitants. Also a Relation of the Loss of the Wager, Man of War, One of Admiral Anson's Squadron* (London: Baker & Leigh, 1768). Melville purchased a copy in December 1849. Lord Byron's father was Captain John Byron, "Mad Jack" Byron. Otto von Kotzebue wrote *A New Voyage round the World . . . 1823–1826* (1823–1826) (London, 1830). George Vancouver, English navigator (1758–1798) left his name in the Pacific northwest. Georges Louis Leclerc, Count de Buffon (1707–1788), was a French naturalist as was Georges Leopold Dagobert, Baron Cuvier (1769–1832), called the founder of comparative anatomy (and brother of Frederick Cuvier, 1773–1838, also a naturalist).

The evidence against the authenticity of the book is more than sufficient to satisfy a court of justice. Our limits forbid us to prosecute it further. Of evidence against the smartness and talent of the production there is none. The author, be he American or Englishman, has written a charming little book, and, as it appears to us, with a laudable and Christian purpose. Let it be regarded as an apology for the Pagan; a plea for the South Sea Islanders, governments, and missionaries, who understand so little the sacred charge which God commits to them, when He places in their hands the children of His favoured sunny regions; may they learn from fiction a lesson which experience has hitherto failed to teach them—viz., that if it be needful for Christianity to approach the Heathen, it is equally necessary that it should approach him *reverently and tenderly*.

H[ENRY T.] C[HEEVER]

[A Prurient Book, That Preys on the Imagination][†]

If this be not sheer romance, (which there is reason to suspect,) it is the extremely exaggerated, but racily-written narrative of a forecastle-runaway from an American whale ship, who met the fortune those fish did in fable, that jumped out of the frying-pan into the fire. He had life among Marquesan cannibals to his liking; a plenty of what pleases the vicious appetite of a sailor, or of sensual human generally. He seems to have been pleased enough with his captors, but glad to get away uneaten. "Horrible and fearful (he says) as the custom of cannibalism is, still I assert that those who indulge in it are in other respects humane and virtuous!"

The book abounds in praises of the life of nature, *alias* savageism, and in slurs and flings against missionaries and civilization. When the author alludes to, or touches matters of fact at the Sandwich Islands, he shows the sheerest ignorance, and utter disregard of truth.

The work was made, not for America, but for a circle, and that not the highest, in London, where theatres, opera-dancers, and voluptuous prints have made such unblushing walks along the edge of modesty as are here delineated to be rather more admired than we hope they are yet among us. We are sorry that such a volume should have been allowed a place in the "Library of American Books." It can only have been without reading it beforehand, and from deference to the publisher on the other side.[1]

---

† H. C., New York *Evangelist*, April 9, 1846. C. Randall Cluff in a paper communicated to Hershel Parker in 2000 shows that the reviewer was Henry T. Cheever, later the author of *The Whale and His Captors* (1850), which Melville mentions in *Moby-Dick*. Cheever had been in Hawaii while Melville was there and was the brother of George Cheever, the Congregationalist minister of John Wiley's church in New York. Until the end of 1846 George Cheever was the editor of the *Evangelist*, a Presbyterian paper (a somewhat awkward conflict, though the doctrinal differences between the sects would have seemed minor in the eyes of members of other sects).

1. This review was an inside job, written for Wiley, who had in fact rushed the book into print without reading it, having relied on the opinion of his partner, George Palmer Putnam, who had accepted the book in London and had relayed it to Wiley with the enthusiastic recommendation of the great Washington Irving. The Cheevers knew very well that Wiley would be demanding expurgations, and, as Cluff suggests, since at least one of the Cheevers, Henry, had read the book, the brothers may have pointed out to Wiley the passages in the first edition that most needed to be deleted.

We have long noted it as true in criticism, that what makes a large class
of books bad, immoral, and consequently injurious, is not so much what
is plainly expressed, as what is left to be imagined by the reader. Apply this
rule to the work in hand, and while everybody will admit it is written with
an attractive vivacity, and (except where it palpably lies) with great good
humor, it cannot escape severe condemnation.

ANONYMOUS

[Melville's Moral Obtuseness]†

We were not disposed at first to say any thing against this volume. The
rather free and easy style in which it is written, and the sort of clever-
heartedness that seemed indicative of the author's disposition, made us
suppose that whatever errors of fact the book contained were probably
unintentional, and that its statements with some allowance might be
received. On reading farther, however, we entirely changed our views; for
it is difficult to believe that the author was not actuated, either by a perverse spirit of intentional misrepresentation, or that he is not utterly incapable, from moral obtuseness, of an accurate statement. If we were to
sum up the author's mind, gathered from his whole book, we should say
he was one who had first been fretted out of good humor by civilized life;
that he had then become a wanderer until he had forgotten his ill nature,
and also the advantages of civilization; that he had then chanced to be
thrown, for a while, on the Sandwich Islands, where he perhaps came into
uncomfortable collision with the civil authority, which engendered a special prejudice against those who were striving to civilize those islands; that
he had then been wandering two or three years longer in various parts of
the earth, till what he remembered of the Islands of the Pacific had
become a sort of confused mass in his own brain; after which he came to
this country, and sat down to write a book. These facts seem to be scattered along through the volume. This moral obtuseness appears, whenever there is an opportunity for exhibiting a correct spirit. No opportunity
slips by for giving a glowing description of savage life, and for launching
quips and small anathemas against civilization. For missionaries and missionary labor,—except in *general*,—he has a special abhorrence. The
cause of Missions is a good thing—except where it raises man from cannibalism to civilization. If he meets a native female Islander, she is a goddess;—if a missionary's wife, she is a blowzy looking, red-faced, fat
oppressor of the poor native—reducing him to the station of drudge. All
statements made by missionaries are, with slight exceptions, infinitely
exaggerated; and those whose money is asked for the blessed work of
sending men to elevate the character of the savage, had best be careful
that their money does not go into other channels. The vices of savages are
much overdrawn; and for the vices that do exist, their counterpart, or
what is worse, is found every where in Christian nations. Of truths of gen-

† New Haven *New Englander* 4 (July 1846): 449–50.

eral history he seems to know nothing. The fact of the depopulation of the Sandwich Islands, seems to him to be something new; and this is specially brought about by the efforts of missionaries and their hypocrisy. The fact that wherever civilization comes in contact with savage life, there the savage wastes away; or at least that this has been so, wherever the Saxon[1] stock comes into contact with it; he never thought of;—and now for the first time seeing the fact he gives his own crude explanation of it, and would have the world then receive his volume as a work of authority. Now justice to the cause of truth demands that we say, that whosoever shall read this book, and its statements touching the Islands of the Pacific, should ask themselves a moment as to the capability of a man to give an accurate statement of moral facts, when, according to his own showing, he has not been in a course of life calculated greatly to improve his moral eye sight. They should think who and what is writing, when such facts are recorded; and then, though they may not think the writer *intends* to misrepresent, they will at least be prepared to resist the false impressions, which a book with such statements is most certain to produce. The book is not without literary merit. It is a very companionable one. As a specimen of the lighter writing of the day, it is entitled to notice. But as to the writer's ability to treat on some of the matters of his volume, it would rank well with Joseph Smith's[2] competency to give an exegetical work on the book of Genesis, or Bishop Southgate's to pronounce on the authenticity of an ancient MS. among the Armenians of Turkey.[3]

ANONYMOUS

Typee: The Traducer of Missions[†]

An apotheosis of barbarism! A panegyric on cannibal delights! An apostrophe to the spirit of savage felicity! Such are the exclamations instinctively springing from our lips as we close a book entitled "Typee: a Residence in the Marquesas," lately published in Wiley & Putnam's interesting "Library of American Books." It is even so, reader! A work coming from the press of one of the first houses in this country, and published

1. Here, English, or British.
2. Upstate New York autodidact mystic (1805–1844), the translator and publisher of *The Book of Mormon*, a gift to him from the angel Moroni. Smith was killed by a mainly Protestant mob in Carthage, near the Mormon town of Nauvoo, Illinois, partly because he had recently sanctioned polygamy.
3. Horatio Southgate while a student at the Calvinist Andover had converted from the Congregationalist Church to the Episcopal Church and gone to Turkey as a missionary in 1836–38 and again in 1840–44. The April 1845 *New Englander* printed a long (twenty-eight page), virulent personal attack on the renegade Southgate ("Right Reverend Horatio Southgate, Missionary Bishop of the Protestant Episcopal Church of the United States, to the dominions and dependencies of the Sultan of Turkey") for allegedly trying to keep the "dissenting" Protestant missionaries (many of them trained at Andover!) away from their chance to evangelize the Armenians and other groups under Turkish rule. More than 200 years after dissenters had settled New England to escape the persecution of the Anglican Church, some American Protestants still could ferociously hate all things Anglican (or in its American form, Episcopalian). In *Typee* Melville had hurled himself into a fiery religious cauldron kept bubbling for centuries with ever-freshened Christian hatred.
† New York *Christian Parlor Magazine* 3 (July 1846): 74–83.

simultaneously by the same house in London, gemmed with enthusiastic descriptions of the innocent felicity of a savage tribe—tinselled with ornate pencillings of cannibal enjoyments—drawing frequent contrasts between the disadvantages and miseries of civilization, and the uninterrupted paradisiacal bliss of a tribe which has traced in ominous characters of blood on the outer battlements of its natural fortresses of rock and mountain that omnipotent and talismanic "*tabu*."

We do not purpose in our examination of this book to enter into an analysis of its contents, its literary execution, or its claims to fidelity in the general description it gives of the people among whom our author resided during a period of some four months. Such a "review" belongs properly to the acknowledged critical journals of the day, and would occupy far more space than we can appropriate to such a task. Nevertheless, we shall attempt to canvass some of its statements, wherein the cause of *missions* is assailed, with a pertinacity of misrepresentation and degree of *hatred*, which can only entitle the perpetrator to the just claim of traducer. We know what we are saying when we use these terms; we have read this book word by word; we have studied it carefully with reference to these very points, for to all that appertains to the missionary work we are sensitively alive; and were gladdened when we first saw it, with the prospect of learning something more from an impartial source concerning the practical operations of the missionary enterprise in that interesting region of the earth known as *Polynesia*. But we were soon disappointed; instead of a calm and unbiased view, we have on every occasion a tissue of misrepresentation, and detraction of the labors of the devoted men and women who have exiled themselves for the purpose of carrying the blessings of the gospel to some of the most degraded and benighted children of Adam—who have been debased from the spiritual "image and likeness" of their God to naked and roving savages; and who, in the wildness of their character and the helplessness of their social condition, are but little exalted above the "brutes that perish."

We do not look at the history of the missionary work from the merely enthusiastic or poetic point of view. We do not view the overthrow of the system of idolatry, the destruction of *Maraes*, the burning of idols, the cessation of infanticide, the extinction of the Arcoi, the abandonment of cannibalism, the termination of desolating wars, and the partial substitution of the arts of civilization and of peace—together with the construction of a written code of laws and the presentation of a written and printed language to the Polynesians, as a brilliant establishment of Christianity in the hearts of the people of those insulated tribes. These are but pulling down the outworks of the fortresses of idolatry and spiritual degradation, which have their foundations in the hearts and souls of the people. But these results are not the less brilliant because the soul, which has become inwrought in its inmost tissues with everything that is corrupt and degraded, has not been taken, as it were, by a Gabriel,[1] and in a moment, by a stupendous miracle of all-sanctifying grace, washed from its impurities and prepared for the fullest beamings of unsullied bliss: they are not the less splendid because the laborers have not been able to pour the

---

1. The archangel entrusted with making significant announcements.

broad beam of day upon every soul, and extirpate every vestige of barbarism and sin. No! the history of the world furnishes no parallel to the reformation in the South Seas, except under the preaching of the inspired apostles, when the enlightened and refined idolators of Rome and Greece forsook the temples of their gods, both known and unknown, and offered up the daily incense of praise from the altars of sanctified hearts, and sang round their wide domains the songs of a purer faith.

The results of the missionary enterprise are to be measured not by what is to be done, but by what has been achieved; and when a contrast is made between the present condition of the Polynesians, and that in which they were found by the early navigators, and even only thirty years ago, callous indeed must be the heart of that man who would not rejoice with every lover of the gospel, in the change which has been made in their political and social condition—deeply stained with depravity must he be who would not be gladdened by the improvement in their moral and spiritual aspects. Partial the change certainly is, and it could not, in the short space of one generation, be much more extensive under the circumstances, than we see it; but the work has been begun—the citadel has been thrown down, the altars destroyed, and the Christian religion acknowledged as infinitely superior to the ancient and bloody superstitions.

It would occupy too much space for us to present these contrasts now; we shall incidentally allude to them, and as we have future occasion shall endeavor to make known to the Christian public the past, the present, and the future of the missionary work. And here we revert to the task before us.

The book whose title we have given may be called a respectable publication. The author seems to possess a cultivated taste and a fair education, but a deficient reading, and to this latter cause we assign many of his errors of general fact, as well as gross misstatements concerning the missionaries. With a lively imagination and a good and often graceful description, together with a somewhat happy strain of narrative, he has written an attractive history of personal adventure and unwilling *abandon* among the happy and sequestered Typees. * * *

We have remarked that this is a respectable book, but yet we have doubted whether it were worth a notice. To give circulation to such statements as our author makes may seem unwise, but as extracts from it of the nature we condemn are obtaining a channel through the public journals, we have determined to do our part in the work of making him known to the public. Although ordinarily we should not have regarded it as being worth an extended notice, we think the mode of its publication and the rank it holds, deserve a passing remark. In the first place it is dedicated to Hon. LEMUEL SHAW, *Chief Justice of Massachusetts*; it is published by WILEY & PUTNAM, in *New York* and *London*; and it is permanently lettered XIII. and XIV. in their *Library of American Books*. These considerations serve, then, to give the book a respectability and an influence which it could not have without them, and without which we should probably have passed it by.

Before proceeding to our investigation of his statements concerning the missionaries, we remark of the book generally: 1. It is filled with the most palpable and absurd contradictions; 2. These contradictions are so carelessly put together as to occur in consecutive paragraphs; 3. It is throughout laudatory of the innocence and freedom from care of the barbarians of the South Seas, particularly the Marquesans; 4. It compares their condition with civilized society as being the more desirable of the two; 5. It either excuses and wilfully palliates the cannibalism and savage vices of the Polynesians, or is guilty of as great a crime in such a writer, that of ignorance of his subject; and, 6. It is redundant with bitter charges against the missionaries, piles obloquy upon their labor and its results, and broadly accuses them of being the cause of the vice, misery, destitution, and unhappiness of the Polynesians wherever they have penetrated. * * *

Some of our readers will perhaps be surprised at our review of "Typee: or Residence in the Marquesas." It is a matter of surprise to us that such a work could have obtained the name of LEMUEL SHAW, and such a press as that of WILEY & PUTNAM. The author manifests a palpable ignorance in regard to every question of interest, and redeems that feature by laying his tribute upon the altar of cannibal felicity and barbaric society. He looks at the savage life with a captivated eye, and seals his approbation with a constant phrenzy to be freed from this happy vale—being in almost daily fear of finding himself hashed in the most approved style of Typee epicurean rites, or tenderly roasted and served up in calabashes for "the regal and noble Mehevi" and his chiefs!

We have borne with the pretensions of this book as though it were a narrative of real events. It may be, and likely is, though somewhat highly colored. But whether true or false, the real or pseudonymic author deserves a pointed and severe rebuke for his flagrant outrages against civilization, and particularly the missionary work. The abuse he heaps upon the latter belongs to the vagabonds, fugitives, convicts, and deserters of every grade—and there let it rest. We have meditated nothing in a spirit of harshness or "bigotry." We have sought only to present the other side of the case to the public, with the hope of rendering at least a little service to the cause of truth; while we regret that a book possessed of such high merit in other respects, should have been made the vehicle of so many prejudiced misstatements concerning missions.

We purpose on some future occasion to take a view of the present state of the missionary work, and what is needed to make it more efficient and exceptionless than it is, and shall endeavor to give every side a fair hearing. We shall probably give Typee a glance among the authorities, as a specimen of that genus of writers whose poetry and poetic feelings lead them to admire only what is savage, and condemn, under assumed pretexts, the ripening fruit of the gospel of Christ. The author having anticipated and challenged investigation, will doubtless duly appreciate our pains-taking in comparing his statements with the contemporaneous reports of Capt. Wilkes[2] and other authorities.

---

2. The *Narrative of the United States Exploring Expedition* (1844) was the five-volume report of the 1838–42 American expedition to the Pacific and Antarctic under the command of Charles Wilkes, U.S.N. (1798–1877). The prose was pedestrian and highly biassed (e.g., in strong support of the Protestant missionary interests), but some of the engravings depicting remote places and peoples were remarkable. (Hawthorne had passed up a chance to go on the voyage as literary recorder.) The repeated references to Captain Charles Wilkes in the reviews in this section suggest just how important the Exploring Expedition was in expanding the American consciousness, comparable in attention getting to landing Americans on the moon, but with the difference that in the mid-1840s any American could foresee immediate commercial, political, and religious opportunities and hazards from the news Wilkes had brought home.

ANONYMOUS

[Melville and Missionary Fund-Raising—
A Review of *Omoo*]†

To those who have revelled and rioted on the first book it will be only necessary to say that here is more of the same sort. Instead of the primitive valley of stark paganism, and unsophisticated nature, the mongrel mixture of savagism and Christianity is here the subject. There is no lack of scenes, however, that are wholly Captain Cookish,[1] and painted in the liveliest colors.—The author seems not to be a prejudiced witness, yet in describing the results of the Missionary operations he pitches his tune a full octave below the Missionary Herald's—indeed, he tells some stories which would not have a very happy effect upon the contribution box at a "Monthly Concert." We intend to give a few extracts one of these days.

[THURLOW WEED?]

Who Reads an American Book?‡

It is but a few years since this question was sneeringly asked in English Reviews![1] But such questions are no longer asked. American Books, "that *are* Books," have not only readers but admirers in England.

Mr. Melville's "Omoo," which appeared simultaneously in London and New York, is thus spoken of in the London Spectator of April:—"Unlike most sequels, "Omoo" is equal to its predecessor. * * * The true characteristic of the book is its nautical pictures. The crew of the Julia were a mixture of all nations, but with a character in each. Among them was a New Zealander, who, rated harpooner, ranked as a gentleman in the South Sea whaling school. From Melville's account, this man required nothing but the help of a novel-grinder to be turned into the hero of a romance. He had all the gloom and mystery of a Byronic hero;[2] but the unsentimental sailors rather attributed to him Cannibal propensities than secret griefs. * * *

---

† Boston *Chronotype*, May 6, 1847.
1. Like that in the journals of Captain James Cook.
‡ Albany *Evening Journal*, May 12, 1847.
1. Magazines, especially the quarterlies (appearing in four issues a year). Americans never forgave Sydney Smith (1771–1845) for his scorn in the *Edinburgh Review* (1820): "In the four quarters of the globe, who reads an American book?" The British magazines (brilliantly written by the best critical minds in this golden age of essay writing) were often reprinted (in full or part) in the United States soon after publication, even in smaller cities like Albany. All any American printer needed was a single imported copy of a magazine, because, in the absence of an international copyright law, nothing had to be paid to a British publisher or author; and American printers had a ready market for any such cheap reprint in a young America dedicated to self-improvement and mutual advancement.
2. Like the melancholy hero of Lord Byron's poem *Childe Harold's Pilgrimage* (1812–18), a hero who travels across the Mediterranean region and central Europe, brooding aloud amid sublime classical ruins, in picturesque natural settings, or while visiting places filled for him with significances, such as battlefields, where he can display the range of his knowledge of and feeling for history. Such a figure, easy to parody, was enormously influential on Melville's generation, the way only Ernest Hemingway influenced other writers in the 20th century. Upon the publication of the first part of *Childe Harold's Pilgrimage*, Lord Byron wrote that he awoke to find himself famous; Melville quoted that passage, self-deprecatingly but tellingly, in a letter of July 24, 1846, seeing himself as Byronic.

The extracts we have given will indicate the character of the composition; which is clear, fresh, veracious and full of matter. Melville's descriptions not only convey distinctly what he means to convey; but they abound in subordinate, or incidental pictures respecting the whole of the life described."

ANONYMOUS

[Melville's Spite against Religion and Its Missionaries][†]

These lively sketches steal one's favor and approbation in spite of himself. They are so graphic and spirited, and narrate scenes of such strange and surpassing interest, that the reader is borne along through the checkered history, without stopping to inquire how much is true or false, or what reliance is to be placed on the author's most deliberate statements. But on arriving at the end and looking back, the conviction speedily arises that it is but little else than romance. Its only merit is what a well-told tale, founded on some Polynesian facts, would have. The author's mendacity is sometimes flagrantly visible, as well as his spite against religion and its missionaries.

[B.]

[Polynesian Cannibalism *vs.* American Slavery][‡]

"Typee" proved the most successful hit in book-making, since the publication of Stephen's first book of Travels.[1] An English critic said it was "Yankee all over."[2] By which he meant that it was entirely new, fresh, and devil-may-care; free from the dry, stale, and wearisome conventionalities of trained literature. It was a book of itself, not made up of pickings from other books, but from the personal observations and individualities of the author. This was enough to ensure it popularity; but, in addition to this, it opened to the reading world views of a new existence, more novel and startling than any of the revelations of Swedenborg,[3] in his "Heaven and

---

† New York *Evangelist,* May 27, 1847.
‡ New York *National Anti-Slavery Standard* 7 (May 27, 1847): 207.
1. The first book by John Lloyd Stephens (1805–1852) was *Incidents of Travel in Egypt, Arabia Petraea, and the Holy Land,* to which Melville alludes in *Redburn.* An even greater adventure resulted in his *Incidents of Travel in Central America, Chiapas and Yucatan* (1841), memorably illustrated by the English artist who accompanied him, Frederick Catherwood.
2. Modern scholars have not yet discovered this review. Parker's computer search of the known reviews (transcribed into his working copy of *The New Melville Log*) reveals nothing close to this phrase. Many 19th-century newspapers and magazines have been lost altogether or in part through natural attrition. Some British papers were destroyed in the Blitz in World War II, and many American papers were deliberately trashed after the mid-20th century as libraries discarded old papers to save space, sometimes wrongly thinking everything had been preserved in microfilm. (One great newspaper, the New York *Tribune,* is available nationally via Inter-Library Loan only in microfilm which lacks the "Supplements" in which important articles on Melville appear; these survive, at risk, in one hard copy at the New York Historical Society.) Some surviving papers have not yet been searched for references to Melville, so this reference may yet be discovered.
3. Emanuel Swedenborg (1688–1772), Swedish scientist and mystic, who influenced many later writers (e.g., William Blake and Ralph Waldo Emerson) by his descriptions of his frequent conversations with angels and his theory of God as divine man and man as God.

Hell." In truth, Typee resolved "the great problem of the age," and proved that happiness was not only possible without the aid of pastry cooks, lawyers, tailors, and clergymen, but that men could be happier without these excrescences of civilization than with them. It proved another important fact, the most important of all facts for Americans, that Slavery is not, as Charles J. Ingersoll told Mrs. Maury,[4] indigenous to the tropics, and, like mosquitoes, always most troublesome when the weather is hottest. It is true that the Typees eat their enemies, but then they do not eat them alive; they have the humanity to wait until their victims are dead before they begin to feast upon them. Here, we reverse the rule, and feed on each other while living. One dead enemy was sufficient to feast a whole tribe of Typees; but with us, a hundred slaves hardly suffice to furnish food for one Southern family. The Typee craunches the tendons and muscles of his dead enemy between his molars, but inflicts no pain upon him; but with us, the Calhouns, Clays, and Polks,[5] feed daily upon the sweat, the tears, the groans, the anguished hearts and despairing sighs, of living men and women; they do not eat the insensible flesh of their dead slaves, but they lacerate it when alive with whips, and cauterize it with hot branding-irons. We would advise our readers who are sick at heart, from reading the daily reports of the murders committed by our army in Mexico;[6] or of the inhuman cruelties of our slaveholders at the South; or of the daily outrages upon the rights of humanity practised by Christian judges and lawyers in our Halls of Justice, to turn for relief to the amiable savages of Typee, whose greatest cruelty consists in devouring the body of an enemy who has been killed in a hand-to-hand scuffle.

Omoo is a continuation of the author's adventures in the Pacific after he escaped from the valley of the Typees. It is written in the same free and jocular style as Typee, but it contains nothing so purely novel as some of the scenes recorded in that pleasant and bewitching volume. The sketches of sea-life and character, are very lively and accurate, and the insight which it gives of the state of society in the half-Christianized islands of the Pacific, entertaining and instructive. Mr. Melville has had the misfortune to encounter the same kind of doubters, who attempted to discredit the narratives of Bruce,[7] but we have found noth-

---

4. This may be the wife of the pioneer student of ocean currents, Lieutenant Matthew Fontaine Maury, whom Melville cites in a footnote in *Moby-Dick* as the author of *Explanations and Sailing Directions to Accompany the Wind and Current Charts* (Washington, 1851). Charles J. Ingersoll (1782–1862), congressman from Pennsylvania, wrote *Inchiquin, the Jesuit's Letters* (1810), purporting to be travel letters by a Jesuit whose approval of what he saw in the United States contrasted with the scorn displayed by most British visitors. The occasion of this exchange is not yet identified.
5. Southern Democrats and Whigs are lumped together here as supporters of slavery. John C. Calhoun (1782–1850), senator from South Carolina. Henry Clay (1777–1852), senator from Kentucky. James K. Polk (1795–1849) of Tennessee; president 1845–49.
6. The Mexican War (1846–48) gained the United States vast territories in the southwest, including California, but it was from the start condemned by some Whigs as an "Executive's War" started by President Polk over a trumped-up international incident, in violation of the Constitution, which gives Congress war-making powers. Even a few idealistic Democrats, like William Cullen Bryant, editor of the New York *Post*, opposed the war, fearing that slavery would be extended into any new lands that were gained. The Whigs, initially caught off guard by the popularity of the war, soon realized that they could win the next presidential election by running one or another of Polk's generals—Zachary Taylor, as it turned out, eating their idealistic cake while gaining the presidency.
7. James Bruce (1730–1794), author of *Travels to Discover the Source of the Nile* (1790), cruelly denounced (by Dr. Johnson and many others) as having faked his adventures, vindicated only long afterward, and in the 21st century celebrated for his reliability.

ing in his volumes that contradicts or transcends the many oral and written accounts we have received from travellers in that part of the world which he visited.

HORACE GREELEY

Up the Lakes, 8 June 1847 [The *Tone* Is Bad]†

Blest, since leaving New York, with a long-coveted opportunity to devote some hours to the deliberate perusal of a few lately issued works of remarkable character, I wish to speak of them in revisal or confirmation of what may have already been uttered. * * *

—"OMOO," by HERMAN MELVILLE, is replete alike with the merits and the faults of its forerunner, "Typee." All of us were mistaken who thought the fascination of "Typee" owing mainly to its subject, or rather to the novel and primitive state of human existence it described. "Omoo" dispels all such illusions and proves the author a born genius, with few superiors either as a narrator, a describer, or a humorist. Few living men could have invested such scenes, incidents and persons as figure in "Omoo" with anything like the charm they wear in Melville's graphic pages; the adventures narrated might have occurred to any one, as others equally exciting have done to thousands of voyagers in the South Seas; but who has ever before described any so well? "Typee" and "Omoo," doubtless in the main true narratives, are worthy to rank in interest with Robinson Crusoe and in vivacity with the best of Stephens's Travels.—Yet they are unmistakably defective if not positively diseased in moral tone, and will very fairly be condemned as dangerous reading for those of immature intellects and unsettled principles. Not that you can put your finger on a passage positively offensive; but the *tone* is bad, and incidents of the most objectionable character are depicted with a racy lightness which would once have been admired but will now be justly condemned. A *penchant* for bad liquors is everywhere boldly proclaimed, while a hankering after loose company not always of the masculine order, is but thinly disguised and perpetually protruding itself throughout the work. This is to be deplored not alone for the author's sake, nor even for that of the large class which it will deter from perusing his adventures. We regret it still more because it will prevent his lucid and apparently candid testimony with regard to the value, the effect and the defects of the Missionary labors among the South Sea

---

† Written by the editor, Horace Greeley, during his upstate vacation, and sent down for publication in his New York *Weekly Tribune* (June 26, 1847). Greeley was a Whig, but unreliable as a partisan because of his own Quixotic causes, one of which had been the mainly Democratic cause of "Repeal"—repeal of the union between England and Ireland and the re-establishment of a National Irish Parliament, which happened to be the cause that Gansevoort Melville, Herman's brother, had chosen as his ticket to a national reputation. Gansevoort, an honorary Bostonian by virtue of being a grandson of a hero of the Tea Party of December 1773, introduced Greeley to the Repeal audience at Boylston Hall on October 30, 1843, where they both spoke, Gansevoort much more eloquently than the editor. Greeley mocked Gansevoort's "gas and glory" rhetoric in the campaign of 1844, and he held a special ambivalent attitude toward the younger brother, Herman Melville, from the time he entered the New York literary scene.

Islanders from having its due weight with those most deeply interested. It is needless here to restate the hackneyed question as to the proper mode of effecting the desired renovation of savage, heathen tribes.— "Preach the Gospel to them," say the devout: "convert them to Christianity, and their Civilization follows of course."—"Nay," interposes another class: "you must civilize them, to some extent, before they can even comprehend Christianity, much less truly embrace and adhere to it."—The Truth obviously lies between these assertions, or rather, embraces them both. A Christianity which does not include Civilization, a Civilizing which does not involve Christianizing, will not answer. Above all, alike to their conversion and their civilization a change in their Social condition and habits—a change from idleness and inefficiency to regular and well directed industry—is absolutely essential.—Without this, the convert of to-day is constantly in danger of relapsing into avowed and inveterate heathenism. This is the moral of Mr. Melville's facts, as indeed of all other impartial testimonies on the subject. Reiterating my regret that he has chosen so to write that his statements will not have that weight with the friends of Missions which the interest of Truth requires, I bid adieu to "Omoo."

G[EORGE] W[ASHINGTON] P[ECK]

[Melville as Sexual Braggart][†]

* * * Omoo seemed so easy—the fancy so naturally loves to wander away to those fair islands whither the romance of nature has been gradually banished—that it appeared the lightest task that could be, to run off a few pages giving a common-place estimate of its merits, and selecting some of the most striking passages, after the approved custom of reviewers. * * *

Perhaps it is from this feeling that we have a difficulty in arranging our thoughts into order, and so beginning what we would say in the regular manner. In general, and at first, we can barely observe that we have read Omoo with interest, and yet with a perpetual recoil. We were ready to acknowledge that it was written with much power; that the style, though loose in sentences and paragraphs, was not without character, and the

---

† GWP, New York *American Whig Review* 6 (July 1847): 36–46. This review did Melville irreparable damage with many people, appearing as it did a few weeks before his marriage into a staunchly Whig family with staunchly Whig associates in Boston. Peck was an enemy driven by a weirdly perverse sexual jealousy, a hopeless alcoholic of good New England family, at this time exiled to New York City, where he lived in successively more squalid lodgings, ultimately in a cock loft under the eaves of a dilapidated house near Canal Street, nursing his venom for his final onslaught on Melville, an unforgettably vicious and unimaginably long review of *Pierre* in 1852. Shortly afterward, his last long-suffering friends, including Richard Henry Dana Jr., bundled him aboard a ship for Australia, hoping that once out of sight in the Antipodes he could be out of mind. Peck is a recurrent type in journalism, the malicious reviewer who retreats into suspended animation until his chosen victim publishes another book; it was Melville's bad luck that Peck fixated on him. Bound copies of this very popular political magazine, the title usually shortened as the *Whig Review*, the rival to the *United States Magazine and Democratic Review*, were around on library shelves to humiliate Melville all his life, decades after the Whig Party itself died.

pictures it presented vividly drawn; yet we were ready to say, in the words of the old epigram—

> "I do not like thee, Doctor Fell,"[1] &c.

The reckless spirit which betrays itself on every page of the book—the cool, sneering wit, and the perfect want of *heart* everywhere manifested in it, make it repel, almost as much as its voluptuous scenery-painting and its sketchy outlines of stories attract. It is curious to observe how much difficulty the newspapers have had in getting at these causes of dislike. They are evidently not pleased with the book; but—as most writers would, sitting down to write a hasty notice of it immediately after running it through—the daily critics find nothing worse to say respecting it than that they do not believe it. Generally, all over the country, in most of the newspapers which we have seen, (and our opportunities are quite as extensive as any one could desire,) this has been the burden of the short notices of the press, where intended to be at all critical. * * *

Alas, Omoo finds it easier to address himself to the pit of the world than to the boxes. His heart is hard, and he prefers painting himself to the public of his native land as a jolly, rollicking blade—a charming, rattling, graceless ne'er-do-well. He meets no man, in all his wanderings, whom he seems to care for—no woman whom he does not consider as merely an enchanting animal, fashioned for his pleasure. Taken upon his own showing, in two volumes, and what is he but what a plain New Englander would call a "*smart scamp?*"

The phrase is a hard one, but it is certainly well deserved. Here is a writer who spices his books with the most incredible accounts and dark hints of innumerable amours with the half-naked and half-civilized or savage damsels of Nukuheva and Tahiti—who gets up voluptuous pictures, and with cool, deliberate art breaks off always at the right point, so as without offending decency, he may stimulate curiosity and excite unchaste desire. Most incredible, we style these portions of his stories, for several reasons.

First: He makes it appear always, that he was unusually successful with these poor wild maidens, and that his love-making was particularly acceptable to them. Now, if this had been so, we fancy we should have heard less of it. A true manly mind cannot sit down and coin dramas, such as these he gives us, for either others' delectation or its own. It is nothing new to hear conceited men boast of their perfect irresistibleness with the sex. "Oh, it is the easiest thing in the world," we remember, one of these gentry used to say, *a la* Mantalini;[2] "a woman is naturally cunning, now only you keep cool and you'll soon see through her; a man must look out for *him*self, a woman for *her*self," &c. This very person, as we happened to know, through a confidential medical friend, could no more, at that very time, when his conversation was in this lofty strain, have wronged a woman, than Charteris[3] could have committed the crime for which he

---

1. Dr. John Fell (1625–1686), dean of Christ Church, Oxford, subject of the infamous epigram by the satirist Thomas Brown (1663–1704), an anglicization of an epigram by the Roman poet Martial.
2. A cockney fop in Dickens's *Nicholas Nickleby* (1838–39).
3. Sir Patrick Charteris, the provost of Perth, Sir Walter Scott's *The Fair Maid of Perth* (1828).

was hung. Since then, and confirmed by various other experience, we have always doubted when we hear a man, especially on a short acquaintance, and most especially in a book that goes to the public, pluming himself on his virility—letting it be no secret that he is a "very devil among the women." Once, at a refectory in ———, we were supping with a friend, when, the tables being full, there came a little, long-knecked [sic], falling-shouldered, pumpkin-faced young man, and took the end of ours. We exchanged a few words, and presently he dashed, without previous preparation, into a full confession of what he styled his "peculiar weakness," in which, if we were to believe him, he let out enough to show that he might have out-bidden the Satyrs, in Spencer, for the favors of Helena.[4] Our friend, who has command of visage, drew him on till he could not help smiling at his own lies. We made inquiry, and learned afterwards that he was a sheriff's clerk, or some such sort of thing, and that his name was Joseph.[5]

Now, with a thousand such instances sleeping in the memory of years, we have no sort of confidence in the man who paints himself the hero of voluptuous adventures. Suppose any one of us—you or I, gentle reader—had been through the scenes Omoo depicts, we might—yea, even the best of us—have done as badly as he represents himself to have done; cast away from home and country, drifting about on the rim of the world, surrounded by license, and brimfull of animal health, we should very probably have made sad deviations from the "path of rectitude," but should we have come home and *told of it*? On the contrary, we should have kept as dark about the matter as possible; and nothing but some overmastering passion or motive could ever have made us reveal it. Native manhood is as modest as maidenhood, and when a man glories in his licentiousness, it raises a strong presumption that he is effete either by nature or through decay.

And this remark leads to our *second* reason for doubting the credibility of these amours. Taking the evidence of imbecility afforded by the reason just given, in conjunction with all that Omoo would have us believe he did (for he does not speak out in plain words like old Capt. Robert Boyle[6] and it cannot be possible, without Sir Epicure Mammon's[7] wished-for elixir, that he could have the *physical ability* to play the gay deceiver at such a rate among those brawny islanders. This body of ours is very yielding it is true, and if a man resolutely sets his mind to imbrute himself he may go a great way; but a half year of such riotous life would have sufficed for one so proud of his exploits (if, indeed, this very display is not rather the result than one of the causes of a *blasé* condition—perhaps it is both).

Thirdly. We do not believe these stories, for the reason that those poor savage maids could not possibly have been such as Omoo describes them;

---

4. Peck is just the man to allude so intimately to one of the lesser-known (and quite pornographic) passages in Edmund Spenser's *Faerie Queene*, book 3, canto 10. Helena, the wife of Malbeccoes, treacherously elopes with Paridell, who soon abandons her to a herd of satyrs (goat-men) who satisfy her very well. The salacious canto is packaged, not very successfully, as a moral study of jealousy.
5. That is, a virtuous virgin, as Joseph presumably was when he fled from his master's wife's advances, only to have her denounce him for attempted rape (Genesis 39.7–20), so that he was imprisoned.
6. Captain Robert Boyle is not yet identified (not the great English chemist Robert Boyle, 1627–1691).
7. Sir Epicure Mammon is the sex-hound knight in Ben Jonson's *The Alchemist* (1610).

they are not half so attractive. We have seen the drawings of Catlin, the elaborate French engravings of the South American Indians, Humboldt, Deprez, also some of New Zealand and those of our Exploring Expedition,[8] and never yet saw we a portrait of a female half so attractive as the dumpiest Dutch butter-woman[9] that walks our markets. Time out of mind we have heard whaling-captains dilate on the Marquesan beauties, but we always reflected that they appeared under peculiar advantages to the eyes of rough men just from long, greasy cruises, being somewhat negligently clad and without any of the restraint of civilization. Omoo may titillate the appetites of many of his readers by describing how he swung in a basket for hours at Tahiti with "some particular friends of his," but he touches us not a jot. He is quite welcome to his "particular friends," they are not ours. The next stout boat-steerer that came along, with a rusty nail or a shred of an old bandanna handkerchief, would disturb, we fear, our domestic felicity—knock us out of the basket, and go to swinging himself. * * *

In fine we cannot help believing the missionary influence to be much more beneficial than this book represents it—perhaps it is true that the lower orders of the people are afraid of the missionaries; the missionaries may have found it necessary to keep them so. Perhaps the whole condition of the people of Tahiti is still very bad, yet we will not believe it to have been so bad as he makes it appear, (alas, the island is now in the hands of the French!) We have ample ground for discrediting his evidence, from his own admissions, from the spirit he everywhere manifests in giving his testimony, and from the unreasonableness of his statements. It is to preserve the poor barbarians as much as possible from such as he tells us he was that the missionaries remain exiled among them, and all that they ever did learn of good has been through those pious, or it may have sometimes been fanatical, instructors. However defective the teaching, however misguided the enthusiasm, that has aided this work of benevolence, we cannot but have some confidence in the sincere endeavors of honest men. Seen through the pages of Omoo, the missionaries affect us like some mysterious baleful *presence*, some invisible power that delights in exercising arbitrary sway over the poor natives, without any adequate motive—it cannot be so. Men do not change their natures by sailing a few thousand miles over the rotundity of this orb. The missionaries did not go there to harass and torture people, and it is not in the nature of things to suppose that the climate affects their brains and turns plain men and women into absolute fools. The contact of savage with civilized life, is always the worse for the former, and no nations have ever suffered more severely than the unfortunate Polynesians; it is a duty the

---

8. Charles Wilkes was head of the great U.S. Exploring Expedition (1838–42). George Catlin (1796–1872), artist, historically important for his unique records of American Indian life. Alexander, Baron von Humboldt (1769–1859), great naturalist, physical geographer, meteorologist, who explored South America and wrote about it in *Voyages au régions équinoxiales du Nouveau Continent, fait en 1799–1804* (Paris, 1807). *Deprez:* may be a misprint for Captain Guillermo Dupaix, whose drawings of the Mayan sites and hieroglyphics (including facsimiles of ancient paintings and hieroglyphics) were published in *Antiquities of Mexico* (London, 1830–48) by Edward King, Viscount Kingsborough.
9. This is the ethnic slur of a Yankee forced to work in what had been New Amsterdam. Many New York citizens were still entirely Dutch in lineage, although the language was dying out. (Melville's mother seems to have spoken Dutch at home, at least to some members of the older generations, but she did not speak it to her children.)

enlightened of the earth owe those whose bodies they have poisoned with
their fell diseases, to do all that can be done for their souls. Let us, therefore, have other subjects for satirical writing than missionary ill success.
* * *

W[ILLIAM] O. B[OURNE]

[Traducer of Loftier and Better Men]†

To the Editor of the Tribune:
  Your own protracted absence from home, and a more recent tour on my
part, have prevented me from offering you a few strictures on the last
work of Herman Melville—the last and least of that class of published
narratives which, while professing to present truth, are filled with the
most palpable errors, if not willful misrepresentations. * * *
  From a consideration of the whole subject I pronounce Mr. Melville's
book, so far as its pretended facts are concerned, a tissue of uninformed
misrepresentations, of prejudiced ignorance, and of hostility characteristic of one who loves South Sea adventure for South Sea abandonment
and "independence." His caricatures of the Missionaries, whether in the
pulpit or surrounded by a crowd of gaping natives—his contempt for the
constituted authorities and the consuls and officers—his insubordina-
tion—his skulking in the dark where he could not be seen by decent
men—his choice of low society—his frequent draughts of "Pisco" or other
liquors—his gentle associations with Tahitian and Marquesan damsels—
and the unsullied purity of his life and conversation, all entitle him to
rank as a man, where his absurdities and misstatements place him as a
writer—the shameless herald of his own wantonness, and the pertinacious traducer of loftier and better men. * * *

WILLIAM O. BOURNE

[Melville's Encouraging of "Rum and Romanism"]‡

  * * * The latest writer on Polynesia [Herman Melville], is the author
of the work named at the head of this article. This is the second narrative
from his pen, Omoo having been preceded by "Typee: a Residence in the
Marquesas." Of the author or his works we design not now to inform our
readers, further than they have reference to the practical operations of the
missionary enterprise in Polynesia. * * *
  The invasion of Tahiti by the French, and the Roman Priests, is made
the subject of running comment through several chapters. * * *

---

† W. O. B., New York *Tribune*, October 2, 1847.
‡ From William O. Bourne, "Missionary Operations in Polynesia," New Haven *New Englander* 6
(January 1848): 41–58.

The prominent principle which led to the rejection of the Romanists[1] is obvious to a thinking mind. The half-refined idolaters see in the image of the Virgin, the crucifix, the paintings, the wafer, and the beads, only the elements of a baptized idolatry. Much as we may deplore their intellectual incapacity to discriminate here, it does not modify or change the fact. That they are not alone to be condemned for this obliquity, is evident from the history of the world. * * *

It might be a matter of some interest to an enlightened statesman to inquire, to what extent French captains have the privilege of invading the rights of Americans abroad, of dishonoring the flag of the United States, and menacing the lives of those under its protection. * * * If the French government and its officers present themselves to the world as the agents in forcing rum and Romanism[2] on the less refined nations of the earth, it may not be unimportant to the American people to know how far their rights are to be invaded in the persons of their fellow citizens who exile themselves in the noblest of all human enterprises. * * *

ANONYMOUS

[The Total Failure of Protestant Missionaries][†]

When "Typee" first appeared about a year ago, there was not a little speculation afloat among the critics as to the author and the character of the book. While all agreed in awarding to the author, whoever he might be, the credit of uncommon merit as a writer, some were inclined to suspect the genuineness of the work, or, at least, the accuracy of the narrative. The adventures related were so startling, the descriptions of life in the happy valley of Typee were so glowing, and the style of the book was, withal so poetical and romantic, that some were half inclined to view the whole as a gorgeous fiction—a son of Robinson Crusoe—portraying an Eutopia[1] in Savagedom; while others, of a more sober temperament, professed to believe that the basis of the story might indeed be true, but that the details of the narrative were greatly exaggerated, or, at least, highly colored. To these last named critics it seemed almost to surpass belief, that a common mariner before the mast should have turned out so gifted a writer of his own adventures, and should have produced a narrative almost as smooth and as highly wrought as Irving's Astoria.[2]

Others again, professing to be more conversant with life in Polynesia, or to be personally acquainted with the author, could see nothing in the work

---

1. Roman Catholics (always derogatory).
2. Decades later, in 1884, the Republican nominee for president, James G. Blaine, lost the election partly because one of his Protestant supporters outraged Catholics (by that time a substantial voting bloc) when he called the Democrats "the Party of Rum, Romanism, and Rebellion."
† From "Protestantism in the Society Islands," Baltimore *United States Catholic Magazine and Monthly Review* 7 (January 1848), 1–10. The place of publication of this magazine was not coincidental: Maryland had been hospitable to Catholics from its founding.
1. From Sir Thomas More's *Utopia* (1516), meaning "Nowhere land," an imaginary work about the best form of government, modeled on early voyage literature.
2. Irving's *Astoria* (1836) was an account of John Jacob Astor's fur-trading empire very much from the perspective of Astor, known as the wealthiest man in the United States.

which was either impossible or improbable; and were therefore disposed to regard it as a veritable book of travels, worthy of fully as much credit as others of the same kind. Those who had read the Journal of the late Captain Porter,[3] published several years ago in this country, and replete with incidents fully as marvelous as those related by the author of Typee, could see nothing in the latter work at all incompatible with its genuineness and substantial accuracy; and these were even inclined to smile at the skepticism of those more dashing critics, who, without knowing any thing either of the author or of the extraordinary people among whom he was thrown in the South Seas, ventured to pronounce at once that the narrative was a fit sequel to Robinson Crusoe and Gulliver's Travels.[4]

When the work was republished in England, the general opinion of the English press was decidedly favorable to its genuineness and accuracy. Douglas Jerrold's paper, the London Sun, the London Examiner, the London Spectator, and the London Critic—not to mention several other English periodicals,—all professed to receive and vindicate the work as a genuine book of travels, entitled to credit so far as the substance of the narrative goes. We will be pardoned for inserting a few extracts from the literary notices furnished by the papers just named.

The London Examiner says:

> "The authority of the work did not seem very clear to us at first, but on closer examination we are not disposed to question it. A little coloring there may be here and there, but the result is a thorough impression of reality."

The London Spectator thus answers the objection of the London Times—that the book is too well written to have been the production of a common sailor:

> "Had this work been put forward as the production of an English common sailor, we should have had some doubts of its authenticity in the absence of distinct proof. But in the United States it is different. There social opinion does not invest any employment with discredit, and it seems customary with young men of respectability to serve as common seamen, either as a probationership to the navy or as a mode of seeing life. Cooper and Dana are examples of this practice."

The London Critic says:

> "The author is no common man. The picture drawn of Polynesian life and scenery is incomparably the most vivid and forcible that has ever been laid before the public . . . The coloring may be often overcharged, yet in the narrative generally there is a vraisemblance that cannot be feigned; for the minuteness and novelty of the details could only have been given by one who had before him nature as his model."

In a second notice, the same periodical adds:

---

3. Captain David Porter, *Journal of a Cruise Made to the Pacific Ocean* (1815). Melville had not read it when he started *Typee*, but he used it in some later-written sections.
4. See a notice of *Omoo* in a late number [May 8, 1847] of the *Literary World*, a periodical of great merit, published in New York [Author's note].

"We have said in our first notice of this book that there is a vraisemblance that never could be counterfeit, and have furthermore found evidence of the assertion in the book just quoted [John M. Coulter's *Adventures in the Pacific* (Dublin, 1845)]."

The New York Courier and Enquirer thus refers to these testimonies in its second notice of Typee:

"No doubt is entertained of the truth of this book by many persons here, whose intimacy with the author and general acquaintance with the subject peculiarly fit them to form an intelligent opinion on this point. And in England, as far as we can judge from the criticisms of the press, the general opinion appears to be favorable to its accuracy."

A further confirmation of the statements made in "Typee" is found in the publication, which some months ago went the rounds of the Eastern papers, to the effect, that Toby, the mysterious comrade of Mr. Melville, who had disappeared from the valley of Typee, is said to have reappeared and vouched for the truth of all the statements of the narrative so far as he himself was concerned in them. If this be the fact—and we see no reason for doubting it—it will go far to strengthen the conviction, which seems already pretty general among the best judges, that there is no valid reason for suspecting the truth of Mr. Melville's narrative of adventures in Polynesia and the South Seas. * * *

But there is one portion of his statements which is not so immediately connected with the narrative of his own personal adventures, which is of a much graver character, and which is therefore still more entitled to credence. We refer to his remarks and reasonings on the results of Protestant missionary enterprise in Polynesia. A Protestant himself, who takes no pains to conceal his prejudice against the Catholic church, it is not to be supposed that he had any motive for under-rating the effects produced by the labors of the Protestant missionaries on the morals and civilization of the South Sea Islanders; and it is not to be presumed that he was disposed either to misstate or to deal in exaggeration on this subject. During a sojourn of several months among the inhabitants of the various groups of islands scattered over the Pacific, in which he became acquainted with the doings of the missionaries and mingled with the islanders on terms of social intimacy, he had ample opportunities to judge accurately of the social condition and of the alleged Christian character and standing of the latter.

Though he tells many stern truths which must be painful to the liberal advocates of Protestant missionary enterprise in the United States, yet he sets down nought in malice; he deals not in denunciation or invective; he evidently writes more in sorrow than in anger; and he makes his statements rather with a view to direct public attention to the subject and to have the evils alleged by him corrected by the proper authority, than to quench or even to check missionary zeal among his Protestant brethren. This seems, in fact, to have been one of the principal objects he had in contemplation in publishing his adventures in the South Seas; and he tells us as much in the preface, to both Typee and Omoo.

Moreover, he takes special pains to confirm all his more important statements on this subject by the testimonies of other Protestant travellers of unimpeachable veracity and great weight of authority. What he tells us, then, under this head, may be fully and implicitly relied on as the truth. And we have no doubt that the popularity and general circulation of his two works will have a most beneficial influence on the opinion of the religious community in this country in regard to Protestant missions in the Pacific; and that his statement of stubborn facts which fell under his own observation, united with his graphic and life-like pictures of Polynesian manners and morals, will undeceive many well disposed persons who had permitted themselves to be misled and to be robbed of their money by the glowing statements and pious frauds of the missionaries.[5] A man who dares tell the truth under such circumstances, if not a hero, may well be set down as an honest man and a benefactor of his species. Let the truth be told, no matter who suffers by it,—seems to have been the motto of Mr. Melville; and in these days of boasted enlightenment and independence, but of real truckling and subserviency to popular prejudice or clamor, this is, at least, an unusual maxim for the guidance of any young writer who courts popularity. We are delighted to find that Mr. Melville has obtained popularity without seeming to court it; and we are disposed to award much honor to his fearless independence.

From the statements scattered through the two works of Mr. Melville, it appears that Protestant missionary effort in the Pacific has turned out a complete failure, if not an arrant imposition on the pious credulity of the public. Brother Jonathan[6] is equally as liberal, and almost as *good-natured*, as his respected sire; but we are deceived as to his real character, if he does not become "wide awake," when he has once discovered a gigantic scheme devised by certain reverend men for draining his pockets of their surplus cash under false pretenses.

The statements of our author, extracted from "Typee," in reference to the religious condition of the Sandwich Islanders, have been already spread before the American public in a recent publication.[7] We propose at present to furnish a rapid analysis of what he says in reference to the doings of the Protestant missionaries at Tahiti and the other islands of the Society group, and to the influence exerted by their teaching on the civilization of the inhabitants. We shall confine ourselves to his last work— Omoo. * * *

Such is then, from unquestionable evidence, the sad and deplorable condition to which the Tahitians have been reduced under the teaching of the Protestant missionaries. After having labored to bestow upon the natives the blessings of Christian civilization, for a period of nearly sixty years; after having expended millions of money for their conversion to Christianity; after having boasted a thousand times of their brilliant success "in evangelizing the heathen," and thereby succeeded in extorting immense amounts from the credulity of their confiding friends in Eng-

5. As stated in this magazine (vol. vi., November, p. 580, note,) the *second* edition of Typee does not contain those passages which are most unfavorable to the Protestant missions. Every body can understand that a book, which recorded such unpalatable truth, required to be *expurgated* in order to suit the *general* demand. The statements of Omoo show plainly that the *expunging* of Typee was not dictated by any zeal for the diffusion of the truth [Author's note].

6. Type name for an American, like John Bull for an Englishman.

7. General Evidences of Catholicity, &c. By M.J. Spalding, D.D. Appendix to Lecture III. See also U.S.C. Magazine, vol. vi, November, 1847 [Author's note].

land; the whole mission turns out to be, not only a complete and signal failure, but a disgrace and a burning shame to the Christian name. The Tahitians are now infinitely worse off,—physically and morally,—than they were before they saw the face of the godly missionaries. They have been mocked with the vision of civilization which they were destined never to realize. The missionaries have grown rich at the expense of their boasted converts. The latter have become the victims of the trust they reposed in the professions of the former. They were promised every thing, and, in the end, received nothing. Poverty, degradation, extinction—were their unfortunate lot and doom. They were left nothing else to hope for.

* * *

How are we to explain this singular phenomenon? Are we to say, that the missionaries were nothing but arrant hypocrites and impostors? We would not take upon ourselves the responsibility of making such a charge. We may even believe that most of them were upright and honest men, who sincerely wished to convert and civilize the natives. Many of them certainly labored with great apparent zeal and earnestness. Whence, then, their notorious failure? It can be explained only on the principle which all ecclesiastical history proclaims as true and certain,—that no sect, separated from Catholic unity, has ever succeeded, or can ever succeed, in converting and civilizing a single heathen nation. God does not bless the efforts of proud separatists; he gives his graces only to the meek and humble laborer in his own vineyard: and his divine Son has accordingly said, "he that gathereth not with me, scattereth."[8]

It is only the pure and immaculate spouse of Christ—the Catholic church—that can be the fruitful mother of *his* children. Protestantism, like all other human sects, is necessarily doomed to barrenness. "Unless God build the house, in vain do they labor who build it."[9] The failure of the Tahitian mission, is but an additional link in the long chain of reasoning which clearly establishes the falsity of Protestantism and the truth of Catholicity. View the subject in what light you will, this is the conclusion which every logical Christian mind must necessarily reach on the subject. The Protestant sects have always and every where signally failed in their missionary enterprises; therefore they cannot claim to have the blessing of God; therefore, they are not the heirs to the promises made by Christ to his first ministers in the commission which he gave them to teach all nations.

This is, we have not the slightest doubt, the principal cause of the total failure of Protestant missionary effort in the islands of the Pacific, and the world over. But there are other causes of a secondary nature, connected with the mode employed by the missionaries for operating on the minds of the natives. They relied entirely too much on mere worldly means; and too little on the assistance of God. They hoped to convert the natives to Christianity by distributing among them Bibles and tracts;—a means neither warranted by the Scriptures themselves, nor conformable to the teachings of reason and experience. They also placed too much confidence in those exciting exhibitions of fanaticism, generally known by the

8. Luke 11.23 (Douay Bible).
9. Psalm 127.1 (Douay Bible).

name of "revivals." These may carry away the multitude for the moment, but they usually produce no permanent results. When the excitement dies away, the converts made under its influence also usually fall off; and often become worse sinners than they were before. * * *

E. B. H.

Catholic and Protestant Missions[†]

Whatever may be thought of the character of Christians, and the success or failure of their efforts to carry forward their religion to the fulfilment of its predictions, there can be but one opinion of the magnitude of the work, or the vast amount of life and treasure devoted to its accomplishment. We are apt to mourn, if not to murmur, at the apathy of Christ's followers, their selfishness and sloth, their unfaithfulness to the Master and distance from the mark, the narrow limits of the kingdom and the exceeding slowness of its advance. And reason enough is there for sorrow and humiliation; imperfection, inconsistency, and wickedness enough is there within the kingdom itself, so called, within the very pale of the Church, in the hearts and lives of avowed disciples. Looking at the religion as it stands in its record and its Lord, looking at the commission given and the object proposed, the powers and means possessed, yet the little absolutely accomplished, the view is dark, the thought oppressive. We wonder not that those "of little faith" stumble, that those of no faith cavil, or that impatient believers look round for some new agencies, a new order of society, or a different administration of religion. It is easy, by fixing the mind on failure and evil alone, to work ourselves up to any degree of disappointment or despondency. But is this a Christian view? Is it reasonable, in consideration of our nature, the nature of the work, the providence of God, or the actual results already seen? Even if these results were far less distinct and beneficent than they are, though it be said that they are not yet tested and by many are disputed, we would still maintain that the efforts themselves, the zeal, the liberality, the self-sacrifice, the unwearied and constantly extended enterprise, in the grand work of converting the world to Christ, are evidence of strong faith, and must bring a blessing to their authors, if to no others.

Our attention is called to the subject now by the simultaneous appearance of many publications, Catholic and Protestant, touching every portion of the vast missionary field, and suggesting as well as answering many inquiries as to veritable facts and positive results. The works whose titles we have given make but a small part of those recently published of similar character. And not only works which treat directly and exclusively of missions, but books of travels, of scientific research, of general literature, biography, and fiction, have entered this province to a greater or less degree, and thrown light upon many of the most interesting points.

† E. B. H., "Catholic and Protestant Missions," Boston *Christian Examiner* 44 (May 1848): 417, 437–38.

Among these might be mentioned the five large volumes of the "United States Exploring Expedition," and the lighter productions of Melville, to both of which we shall have occasion to refer. It is rather singular that the last named works, "Typee" and "Omoo," whose character, as fact or fiction, has been a matter of question, are taken up by the Catholics as authority, and made the groundwork of a new attack upon Protestant missions. At the same time, the Catholics themselves are making new efforts, and sending out new publications and professions, with reference to the propagation of their faith in this country and abroad. Not attempting to go over the whole field, nor wishing to take sides in the controversy, we propose to give some idea of the facts of the case, as they stand in the publications themselves, and to refresh our own, possibly our readers', acquaintance with the extent and progress of the great missionary enterprise. * * *

But the Catholics bring other charges. They have always said that Protestant missions would be failures, because of the heresy that taints and enervates them. They now aver that they are failures, and that the very best of them are proved to be so by notorious facts, and even by Protestant confessions. These allegations they are making at this moment, and in this country, more confidently and busily, we think, than at any former period. And what is their authority for these statements, so startling and important to all, if true? Their chief authority, so far as we learn, is Mr. Melville, in the two books to which we referred at the beginning,— "Typee" and "Omoo." These works are favorably noticed and largely used in the "Catholic Magazine," whose title and official authority we have given in full. The numbers of that journal for November and January last contain remarkable specimens of assertion and exultation, in regard to the utter futility, if not iniquity, of all the South Sea missions; and Melville most, though not alone, is adduced as establishing the important fact. It is undeniable that Melville does favor this view of the matter. We have only glanced at his books, but have read enough, and find enough in these extracts before us, if fairly given, to be satisfied that he has made assertions which ought either to be admitted or refuted. For ourselves, we place little reliance on these assertions; first, because the real design of the books that contain them is a matter of dispute; next, because the author himself has dropped them from the second edition of "Typee"; then, because the assertions do not all agree; and lastly, because they are unsustained, and contradicted, by other writers and eyewitnesses. Indeed, we doubt if Mr. Melville himself is not surprised that any one should form an opinion, or change an opinion, on this great subject, from his books alone; especially when it is seen, that, as we just implied, all his assertions are not against the missions, but some of them strongly in favor. Similar accounts of intemperance and licentiousness witnessed in the islands are often given by missionaries themselves, as greatly to be deplored, but still not incompatible with solid good. The passages in which he not only declares the beneficial effect of missions, but ascribes some of their failures to "disorders growing out of the proceedings of the French," are not quoted in the "Catholic Magazine." We do fear a want of ingenuousness in these assailants. We have sought in vain to verify some of their allegations, and even direct quotations, by referring to the authorities given.

Some quotations are so torn from their connections as to prove nothing, and some are not easily found, though we cannot assert, and mean not to imply, that they are not to be found at all. But the mode of referring to them is unsatisfactory, and unwarrantable as the basis of such serious charges and sweeping conclusions. * * *

[WILLIAM GILMORE SIMMS?]

[Review of *Mardi*]†

Mr. Melville is well and favorably known as the writer of two very pleasant books of South Sea experience, in which the critic persuaded himself that he found as many proofs of the romancer, as of the historian. Mr. Melville alludes to this doubt and difficulty, and somewhat needlessly warns us that, in the present work, we are to expect nothing but fiction. His fiction takes the form of allegory rather than action or adventure. His book, in fact, is a fanciful voyage about the world in search of happiness. In this voyage the writer gives a satirical picture of most of the deeds and doings of the more prominent nations, under names which preserve the sound of the real word to the ear, while slightly disguising it to the eye. In this progress, which is a somewhat monotonous one, the author gives us many glowing rhapsodies, much epigrammatic thought, and many sweet and attractive fancies; but he spoils every thing to the Southern reader when he paints a loathsome picture of Mr. Calhoun,[1] in the character of a slave driver, drawing mixed blood and tears from the victim at every stroke of the whip. We make no farther comments.

ANONYMOUS

[Civilized Bodies, Barbarous Souls]‡

* * * The Highlander is crowded with poor Irish emigrants, for which the cupidity of the captain has provided no accommodation and to whom the villainy of the shipping agents has given no warning of the hardships in store for them at sea. * * * As might have been foreseen, pestilence soon made its appearance on board the Highlander. Five hundred human beings crowded in the hold of a vessel without ventilation, except at the hatches, without comfort, without cleanliness, without adequate food,

---

† Charleston, South Carolina, *Southern Quarterly Review* 16 (October 1849): 260–61.
1. *Mardi* was fiction, but contained an allegorical section interpolated during the "Red Year" 1848, partly on the new European revolutions, partly on the United States presidential campaign of that year. In ch. 162, "They Visit the Extreme South of Vivenza," Melville depicts the land of slavery, lorded over by "one Nulli," obviously John C. Calhoun, always ready to nullify a federal law not explicitly authorized by the Constitution or else passed by Congress and upheld by the Supreme Court. (Nullification was an extreme concept, but it was Calhoun's strategy for forestalling more extreme secessionists in his state and elsewhere in the South.)
‡ London *Observer*, October 7, 1849.

carry the seeds of fever infallibly about them. The ship became a floating pest house; and every day the tribute of mortality was paid to the stormy deep—six, seven, eight, nine and ten bodies of a morning, were thrown overboard. "We talk of the Turks," says the author, alluding to the neglect of the poorer classes of emigrants shown by the English and by American legislators. "We talk of the Turks and abhor the Cannibals, but may not some of *them* go to heaven before some of *us*? We may have civilized bodies, and yet barbarous souls. We are blind to the real sights of the world; deaf to its voice, and dead to its death. And not till we know that one grief outweighs ten thousand toys will we become what Christianity is striving to make us."[1]

* * *

ANONYMOUS

[The Improving Condition of "Live Cargo"][†]

* * * The details of the horrors aboard such a vessel as the Highlander, when returning to New York with a cargo of poor Irish emigrants, are peculiarly deserving of notice; we believe some amelioration has taken place, and that some care is now taken of these live cargoes of human beings, but still these emigrant vessels require to be closely watched.

ANONYMOUS

[A Magisterial Caution from "Maga"][‡]

* * * We are now in Liverpool. Much of what Redburn there sees, says, and does, will be more interesting to American than to English readers, although to many even of the latter there will be novelty in his minute account of sailor life ashore—of their boarding-houses, haunts, and habits; of the German emigrant ships, and the salt-droghers and Lascars, and of other matters seemingly commonplace, but in which his observant eye detects much that escapes ordinary gazers. We ourselves, to whom the aspect and ways of the great trading city of northern England are by no

---

1. It is fair to remark that the legislature of Great Britain has provided by the "Passengers' Act" of the last session, a most efficient and practical remedy against the evils here complained of [Author's note].
† London *Morning Post*, October 29, 1849.
‡ *Blackwood's Edinburgh Magazine* 66 (November 1849): 567–80. These short excerpts from a very long review ("long story about a short book," Melville wrote in his journal after reading it in London) capture the high seriousness, not to say pomposity, of "Maga" (the self-applied sobriquet, from "Magazine," as if it were the only one worth counting). Melville may have invented the harrowing scene in Launcelott's-Hey, or parts of it, but he had seen Liverpool from the bottom, as "Maga" had not. Ironically, at the same time in 1839 Evert A. Duyckinck, some of whose reviews are reprinted here, was seeing Liverpool from above, from the Adelphi, the best hotel, high up a hill overlooking the Mersey.

means unfamiliar, have derived some new lights from Redburn's account of what he there saw. Clergymen of the Church of England, we are informed, stand up on old casks, at quay corners, arrayed in full canonicals, and preach thus, *al fresco*, to sailors and loose women. Paupers are allowed to linger and perish unaided, almost in the public thoroughfare, within sight and knowledge of neighbours and police. * * *

Neither will he, we apprehend, gain much praise, that is worth having, for such exaggerated exhibitions of the horrible as that afforded in chapter VI. of his second volume. Passing through Lancelott's Hey, a narrow street of warehouses, Redburn heard "a feeble wail, which seemed to come out of the earth. * * * I advanced to an opening, which communicated downwards with deep tiers of cellars beneath a crumbling old warehouse; and there, some fifteen feet below the walk, crouching in nameless squalor, with her head bowed over, was the figure of what had been a woman. Her blue arms folded to her livid bosom two shrunken things like children, that leaned towards her, one on each side. At first I knew not whether they were dead or alive. They made no sign; they did not move or stir; but from the vault came that soul-sickening wail." We cannot quite realise the "opening" in question, but take it for granted to be some sufficiently dreary den, and are only puzzled to conjecture how, considering its depth, the woman and children got there. Redburn himself seems at a loss to account for it. This, however, his compassionate heart tarried not to inquire; but, perceiving the poor creatures were nearly dead with want, he hurried to procure them assistance. In an open space hard by, some squalid old women, the wretched *chiffonières*[1] of the docks, were gathering flakes of cotton in the dirt heaps. To these Redburn appealed. They knew of the beggar-woman and her brats, who had been three days in the pit or vault, with nothing to eat, but they would not meddle in the matter; and one hag, with an exaggerated morality that does not sound very probable, declared "Betsy Jennings desarved it, for she had never been married!" Turning to a more frequented street, Redburn met a policeman. "None of my business, Jack," was the reply to his application. "I don't belong to that street. But what business is it of yours? Are you not a Yankee?"

"Yes," said I; "but come, I will help you to remove that woman, if you say so."

"There now, Jack, go on board your ship, and stick to it, and leave these matters to the town."

Two more policemen were applied to with a like result. Appeals to the porter at an adjacent warehouse, to Handsome Mary the hostess, and Brandy Nan the cook at the Sailors' boardinghouse, were equally fruitless. Redburn took some bread and cheese from his dinner-room, and carried it to the sufferers, to whom he gave water to drink in his hat—descending with great difficulty into the vault, which was like a well. The two children ate, but the woman refused. And then Redburn found a dead infant amongst her rags, (he describes its appearance with harrowing minuteness,) and almost repented having brought food to the survivors, for it could but prolong their misery, without hope of perma-

---

1. Ragpickers.

nent relief. And on reflection, "I felt an almost irresistible impulse to do them the last mercy, of in some way putting an end to their horrible lives; and I should almost have done so, I think, had I not been deterred by thought of the law. For I well knew that the law, which would let them perish of themselves, without giving them one sup of water, would spend a thousand pounds, if necessary, in convicting him who should so much as offer to relieve them from their miserable existence." The whole chapter is in this agreeable style, and indeed we suppress the more revolting and exaggerated passages. Two days longer, Redburn informs us, the objects of his compassion linger in their foul retreat, and then the bread he throws to them remains untasted. They are dead, and a horrible stench arises from the opening. The next time he passes, the corpses have disappeared, and quicklime strews the ground. Within a few hours of their death the nuisance has been detected and removed, although for five days, according to Redburn, they had been allowed to die by inches, within a few yards of frequented streets, and with the full knowledge and acquiescence of sundry policemen. We need hardly waste a comment on the more than improbable, on the utterly absurd character, of this incident. It will be apparent to all readers. Mr Melville is, of course, at liberty to introduce fictitious adventure into what professes to be a narrative of real events; the thing is done every day, and doubtless he largely avails of the privilege. He has also a clear right to deal in the lugubrious, and even in the loathsome, if he thinks an occasional dash of tragedy will advantageously relieve the humorous features of his book. But here he is perverting truth, and leading into error the simple persons who put their faith in him. * * *

Part of the Highlander's cargo on home-voyage was five hundred emigrants, to accommodate whom the "between-decks" was fitted up with bunks, rapidly constructed of coarse planks, and having something the appearance of dog-kennels. The weather proved unfavourable, the voyage long, the provisions of many of the emigrants (who were chiefly Irish) ran short, and the consequences were disorder, suffering, and disease. Once more upon his own ground, and telling of things which he knows, and has doubtless seen, Mr Melville again rises in our estimation. His details of emigrant life on board are good; and so is his account of the sailors' shifts for tobacco, which runs short, and of Jackson's selfishness, and singular ascendancy over the crew. And also, very graphic indeed, is the picture of the steerage, when the malignant epidemic breaks out, and it becomes a lazar-house, frightful with filth and fever * * *

When this review of his last work meets the eye of Mr Herman Melville, which probably it will do, we would have him bear in mind that, if we have now dwelt upon his failings, it is in the hope of inducing him to amend them; and that we have already, on a former occasion, expended at least as much time and space on a laudation of his merits, and many undeniable good qualities, as a writer. It always gives us pleasure to speak favourably of a book by an American author, when we conscientiously can do so. First, because Americans, although cousins, are not *of the house;* although allied by blood, they are in some sort strangers; and it is an act of more graceful courtesy to laud a stranger than one of ourselves. Secondly, because we hope thereby to encourage Americans to the cultivation of literature—to induce some to write, who, having talent, have not hitherto revealed it; and to stimulate those who have already written to increased exertion and better things. For it were false modesty on our part to ignore the fact, that the words of Maga have much weight and many readers throughout the whole length and breadth of the Union—that her verdict is respectfully heard, not only in the city, but in the hamlet, and even in those remote back-woods where the law of Lynch prevails. And, thirdly, we gladly praise an American book because we praise none but good books, and we desire to see many such written in America, in the hope that she will at last awake to the advantages of an international copyright. For surely it is little creditable to a great country to see her men of genius and talent, her Irvings and Prescotts, and we will also say her Coopers and Melvilles, publishing their works in a foreign capital, as the sole means of obtaining that fair remuneration which, although it should never be the sole object, is yet the legitimate and honourable reward of the labourer in literature's paths.

ANONYMOUS

[The "Middle Passage" for the Irish][†]

* * * Occasional samples we have here of a quiet, subdued humour, but the mode of thought is serious, and even the incidents described are almost entirely cast in the same mould. Ashore—with slight variations—we have poverty, vice, and degradation: afloat, the horrors of an emigrant ship's voyage across the Atlantic are made to rival the awful scenes of the "middle passage"[1] in a slaver. Several chapters are devoted to Liverpool—not as it is generally described to, and often seen by, American tourists, but as the sailor-boy finds it when transferred from the forecastle of his ship to the loathsome haunts of his shipmates. Persons of very delicate nerves will recoil from some of the details here given of the destitution and degradation prevalent in that abode of merchant princes. * * *

ANONYMOUS

[Melville: Prejudiced, Incompetent, and Truthless][‡]

Falsehood is a thing of almost invincible courage; overthrow it to-day, and with freshened vigour it will return to the lists to-morrow. 'Omoo' illustrates this fact. We were under the illusion that the abettors of infidelity and the partisans of popery had been put to shame by the repeated refutation and exposure of their slanders against the 'Protestant Missions'

---

† The New York *Albion* 8 (November 24, 1849): 561. The *Albion* was a New York weekly edited by expatriate British for expatriate British, so its point of view was unique—a British sensibility displayed in New York City.
1. The route of slave ships between West Africa and the Caribbean and the United States.
‡ London *Eclectic Review* 28 (October 1850): 425–36.

in Polynesia; but Mr. Melville's production proves that shame is a virtue with which these gentry are totally unacquainted, and that they are resharpening their missiles for another onset.

In noticing Mr. Melville's book, our object is to show that his statements respecting the Protestant Mission in Tahiti are perversions of the truth—that he is guilty of deliberate and elaborate misrepresentation, and—admitting the accuracy of the account which he gives of *himself*, and taking his own showing with regard to the opportunities he had to form a correct opinion on the subject—that he is a prejudiced, incompetent, and truthless witness. This is our object; and we intend that Mr. Melville himself shall establish the chief counts in our indictment. The conclusion is obvious: if we thus sustain our charges against him on so serious and grave a topic, it, of course, follows that his South-Sea narratives—instead of being esteemed, as some of our leading contemporaries have pronounced them to be, faithful pictures of Polynesian life—should at once take their place beside the equally veracious pages of *Baron Munchausen*![1] In the preface to 'Omoo,' Mr. Melville says:—

> 'In every statement connected with missionary operations
> . . . are better qualified to do so.' [para. 5]

This paragraph plainly manifests that Mr. Melville was perfectly aware of the nature of the task in which he was engaged when he attacked the Polynesian 'missionary operations.' Whatever else he may be guilty of, none can accuse him of want of deliberation. He is not unconscious of the importance of his statements. He intimates that he has carefully weighed every word he has penned. The passage also marks his fear, lest, in the multitude of jocularities with which his book abounds, the reader should lose sight of the 'facts' to which he has 'scrupulously observed' the truth. He quietly insinuates that he is not the only one who has noted the same deplorable condition of things, and therefore he 'deems it advisable to quote previous voyagers' in support of what he has written. Finally, he reveals his *motive* for bringing the subject thus prominently before the public. Do not err, good reader! He is no emissary of the Propaganda, no *elève* of Father Roothan,[2] no 'good hater' of Protestantism, but, on the contrary—if we take his own word for it—he is an earnest lover of the truth; and, if he were not, nothing could lead him 'to touch on this subject at all!' Thus our author, with no common skill, throws the reader off his guard, and prepares him to receive, without doubt, what follows.

It is, however, worthy of notice, that he refrains from suggesting any remedy for the 'evils' he describes. He knew he could consistently recommend but one, and that would be the complete abandonment of our missions in the South Seas, and the entire withdrawal of all confidence and support from the London Missionary Society. This Mr. Melville does not

1. Munchausen was the putative author of a book of fantastic imaginary travel adventures, published in England in 1785 by a German, Rudolf Erich Gaspe.
2. Father Joannes Philippus Roothaan (1785–1853), a Dutch priest, was head of the Society of Jesus 1829–53. The reviewer means merely that Melville is not a Catholic, not a tool of the Jesuits, who were then less generally feared in England than in the United States, which was deluged with accounts of Jesuits plotting a takeover of the government, and where militant Protestants were determined to "keep" (or make) the United States a Protestant country. As Melville should have known, anything he wrote about Protestants and Catholics in *Moby-Dick* would be read in the United States in passionately partisan ways.

propose. But why does he not? The reason is as visible as light at noonday: it would uncover the cloven foot, and betray the real object for which 'Omoo' was written! He is evidently too deeply versed in the science of human nature not to feel confident that, in whatever quarter his assertions were credited, a single penny would never be obtained to aid South Sea, or any other, 'missionary operation;' and that there, likewise, the London Missionary Society would be denounced as an 'organized hypocrisy.'

So much for the Preface. Now for the 'facts' of which it is the herald.

We begin with Mr. *Melville's* account of the rise and establishment of Christianity in Tahiti; and if it does not prove to be 'a new thing' to most well-informed persons, we are strangely mistaken. The gospel, he tells us, overthrew idolatry neither by its enlightenment of the judgment, nor by its influence on the consciences of the natives. It obtained the mastery, not by the force of persuasion, but by the persuasion of force! Here is the narrative:—

> 'Every reader of "Cook's Voyages" must remember Otoo, who in that navigator's time was king of the peninsula of Tahiti. Subsequently, assisted by the muskets of the *Bounty's* men, he extended his rule over the entire island. This Otoo before his death has his name changed into Pomaree, which has ever since been the royal patronymic. He was succeeded by his son Pomaree II., the most famous prince in the annals of Tahiti. Though a sad debauchee and drunkard, and even charged with unnatural crimes' (mark the vile insinuation), '*he was a great friend of the missionaries*, and one of the very first of their proselytes. During the religious wars *into which he was hurried by his zeal for the new faith*, he was defeated and expelled from the island. After a short exile, he returned from Imeeo, with an army of eight hundred warriors, and in the battle of Naru routed the rebellious pagans with great slaughter, and re-established himself upon the throne. Thus,' exclaims Mr. Melville, '*by force of arms was Christianity finally triumphant in Tahiti.*'—P. 230.

We supposed that it became 'finally triumphant' through the influence of the 'law of the Spirit of Life in Christ Jesus.' 'Nothing more erroneous,' says Mr. Melville—'it was by the club-law of the drunken and debauched *friend of the missionaries*, Pomaree II.!' This is a fair specimen of our author's mode of dealing with the *Protestant* missions in the South Seas. It exhibits his historic fidelity and honesty of purpose. It is impossible to mistake the animus that dictated this passage—a passage that is justly entitled to take precedence in the annals of mendacity. * * *

In dealing with the evidence, we cannot be too careful in the investigation of the character and competency of the deponent. Knowing this, our readers may ask, who is Mr. Herman Melville? and what opportunities had he of forming a judgment on the 'missionary operations' in Tahiti? Before replying to those questions, we beg to premise it as our opinion, that whatever object Mr. Melville had in view when he sought to damage or ruin the character of the Protestant missionaries, we have no reason to suspect him of giving an unfair description of himself. Our information respecting him is solely derived from his own works—so he cannot take exception to our authority—and we are bound to admit the force of the supposition that *his own* account of himself is most likely to be the *best* that could possibly be given. But if so, the best is exceedingly *bad!*

In his Preface, he speaks of the advantageous position which he occupied as an observer of the 'operations' of the missionaries, and of the state of the native population. These are his words: '*As a roving sailor, the author spent about three months in various parts of the islands of Tahiti and Imeeo, and under circumstances most favourable for correct observations on the social condition of the natives.*' What the character of this 'roving sailor' is, and how he spent the 'three months' in Tahiti and 'Imeeo,' he shall himself inform us. We derive the following statements from the volume before us, and from another work by him entitled 'Typee; a Peep at Polynesian Life,' &c., of which 'Omoo' professes to be a continuation. * * *

Our task is done. We have permitted Mr. Melville to paint his own picture, and to describe his own practices. By doing so, we have fulfilled our promise, and have proved him to be a prejudiced, incompetent, and *truthless* witness. We have thus contributed our quota towards the formation of a correct estimate of his character; and we trust that our brethren of the press in North America—where he at present resides, and where his volumes have had an extensive circulation—will do justice to the Protestant missionaries and missions in Polynesia, by unmasking their maligner—MR. HERMAN MELVILLE.

ANONYMOUS

[Unfortunate Mr. Melville][†]

Mr. Melville's "Omoo" is reviewed with much severity in the October number of the London *Eclectic Review*, in an article entitled "Mr. Melville and the South Sea Missions." We think Mr. Melville has been very unfortunate in his hostility to the Protestant Missions in Polynesia. If we remember correctly a writer in *The Tribune*, immediately after the appearance of his book, by very ample and satisfactory evidence proved him to be altogether wrong in facts and opinions in this case.

[EVERT A. DUYCKINCK]

[A Defense against the "Anti-Popery Mania"][‡]

A "savage" attack is made by the last (London) *Eclectic Review* upon Mr. Herman Melville on the ground of a passage or two in his earliest books, "Typee" and "Omoo," touching the missionaries in the South Seas, the point of which is considerably broken by the reviewer, who, with the

† New York *International Miscellany* 1 (November 1850): 478.
‡ New York *Literary World* 198 (November 16, 1850): 393–94.

anti-popery mania in his head, evidently considers the author a *Jesuit in disguise*,[1] bent on the destruction of Protestantism in the Islands. He speaks of "a certain ecclesiastical chief, to whom, we believe, Mr. Melville looks up with the most devout reverence." This is the POPE! The stupidity into which a leading idea sometimes betrays a man was never more ludicrously illustrated. We have heard of Jesuits in dominoes, in all parts of the earth, in camps, courts, and colleges, but this is the first example we have met with of a Jesuit in masquerade on the high seas in a tarpaulin. A Father Confessor in a tar bucket! A further absurdity is the arraignment of Mr. Melville for various high crimes and misdemeanors against civilized society, the civilization of well-propertied England, that is, in the humorous wanderings of "Omoo"—as if a vagabond, *in a book,* in a barbarous tropical island, was to be measured by the same standard as a polite *flaneur*[2] on the Boulevards or Regent street. "Typee" and "Omoo," it does not seem to have penetrated the wool of this reviewer, are books of incident and adventure, and as such are considered by good judges, his own London *Times* at the head of them, as exceedingly well constructed and vastly entertaining in the reading thereof. What is said of the Missionaries is not a Parliamentary report on an Exeter Hall or Tabernacle commission, but simply a matter of personal observation of an outsider, set down with a statement of the observer's exact point of view—from which, and the general spirit of the book, no reader can be at a loss in taking the testimony for exactly what it is worth. We do not undertake to say that Mr. Melville has given the whole view of the case, or to enter upon his defence, but the modicum of fact which the English journal calls upon him to restate in another edition might, we think, have been presented with a little more courtesy, less billingsgate,[3] less pruriency, less nonsense on the part of the missionary reviewer.

[EVERT A. DUYCKINCK]

[*White-Jacket* and a Warning to Melville][†]

* * * Herman Melville tests all his characters by their manhood. His book is thoroughly American and democratic. There is no patronage in his exhibition of a sailor, any more than in his portraits of captains and commodores. He gives all fair play in an impartial spirit. There is no railing,

1. An ironic reference to a staple of extreme Protestant paranoia current in the *American Protestant Vindicator* and other publications: Jesuits pretending to be ordinary workmen would throw off their disguises at a signal from the pope and seize the country as a colony of the Vatican. The more Irish who were allowed into the United States during these years of the great famine, of course, the more Jesuits would be prowling and the more Catholics would respond to the signal to overthrow the government. The Dutch Duyckinck family in an earlier generation had moved up in religion from the Dutch Reformed Church (good enough for Melville's Gansevoort mother until she died in 1872) to the Episcopalian Church, where more of the Manhattan elite assembled. As an Episcopalian, Duyckinck looked skeptically both at the aims and accomplishments of missionary-minded Protestant sects abroad and at the anti-Catholic frenzy agitating the United States at home.
2. A dandy or an intellectual idler, from one who strolls the streets so as to be seen.
3. Coarse and abusive language such as one would hear at the fish market near Billingsgate, a gate in the old wall below London Bridge.
† New York *Literary World* 163 (March 16, 1850): 271–72.

no scolding; he never loses his temper when he hits hardest. A quaint, satirical, yet genial humor is his grand destructive weapon. It would be a most dangerous one (for what is there which cannot be shaken with ridicule?), were it not for the poetic element by which it is elevated. Let our author treasure this as his choicest possession, for without it his humor would soon degenerate into a sneer, than which there is nothing sadder, more fatal. In regarding, too, the spirit of things, may he not fall into the error of undervaluing their forms, lest he get into a bewildering, barren, and void scepticism![1]

ANONYMOUS

[A Jibe at "The Essential Dignity of Man"][†]

Two extracts from this book, that appeared lately in our columns, will have prepared readers for a work of rare merit; and a perusal of it entire will fully confirm that impression—at least on the minds of those who do not "hate the sea," and have not very dainty nerves. * * *

Flogging is anathematised in as plain and emphatic language as man can use, denounced as "religiously, morally, and immutably *wrong.*" Almost every occurrence on board the *Neversink* is painfully interwoven with allusions to the "gratings," past, present, or to come. And yet, in spite of this pervading effort to represent things as we fear they too often are, we cannot say that the perusal of White Jacket's narrative induces us to join him in his eloquent cry for the immediate abolition of flogging in the Navy, at all risks and every hazard. Page after page, our indignation has been aroused, and our sense of humanity and justice outraged—not by the fact that flogging is recognised by naval law, but by proofs that punishment is sometimes atrociously converted into torture, and that caprice, malice or ignorance on the part of irresponsible officers too often renders justice null and void. Curiously enough, though the comments of "Jack"[1] on naval discipline, and other matters pertaining to man-of-war life, are here set down with a remarkable air of truth, we remember no direct testimony that "Jack" himself considered flogging, *per se,* as the most intolerable of his grievances. In so able, so practical, and so large-minded an author as Herman Melville, we scarcely expected to find the "essential dignity of man" and "the spirit of our domestic institutions" lugged in on such a question as this. Is it consistent with the "essential dignity," that one man should sweep the floor of Congress, and another make laws upon it which his democratic countrymen must obey?[2] If the world were

---

1. Melville paid no attention to this mildly stated warning not to write irreverently. For the consequences, see Duyckinck's review of *Moby-Dick,* (p. 610 herein).
† New York *Albion,* March 30, 1850. The *Albion* was a New York weekly edited by expatriate British for expatriate British (see source note on p. 503 herein).
1. Type name for a sailor (also jack-tar).
2. This passage lies behind Melville's appeal in ch. 26 of *Moby-Dick* that the "great democratic God" justify him against "all mortal critics" (meaning the reviewers, the only critics who had written on him) if he (through his narrator Ishmael) were to weave tragic graces around "meanest mariners, and renegades and castaways." Melville nursed his resentments, as much as he strove to be stoical.

big enough, and each man had his desolate island to himself, Robinson Crusoe fashion, we might keep up this pleasant non-committal delusion, but in the "world in a man-of-war," or in the world out of it, this phantom may be left to the Transcendentalists, amongst whom our author is by far too good a fellow to be classed. Ere we leave this part of White Jacket's adventures and opinions, let us moreover acknowledge how candidly he admits, that in English ships of war there is less of tyranny than in his own. * * *

Reviews and Letters by Melville

TWO REVIEWS IN THE *LITERARY WORLD*

Etchings of a Whaling Cruise†

Etchings of a Whaling Cruise, with Notes of a Sojourn on the Island of Zanzibar. To which is appended, a Brief History of the Whale Fishery; its Past and Present Condition. *By J. Ross Browne. Illustrated with numerous Engravings on Steel and Wood. Harper & Brothers: 1846. 8vo.*

Sailors' Life and Sailors' Yarns. *By Captain Ringbolt. New York: C. S. Francis & Co. 1847. 12mo.*

From time immemorial many fine things have been said and sung of the sea. And the days have been, when sailors were considered veritable mermen; and the ocean itself, as the peculiar theatre of the romantic and wonderful. But of late years there have been revealed so many plain, matter-of-fact details connected with nautical life that at the present day the poetry of salt water is very much on the wane. The perusal of Dana's Two Years Before The Mast, for instance, somewhat impairs the relish with which we read Byron's spiritual address to the ocean. And when the noble poet raves about laying his hands upon the ocean's mane (in other words manipulating the crest of a wave) the most vivid image suggested is that of a valetudinarian bather at Rockaway,[1] spluttering and choaking in the surf, with his mouth full of brine.

Mr J. Ross Browne's narrative tends still further to impair the charm with which poesy and fiction have invested the sea. It is a book of unvarnished facts; and with some allowances for the general application of an individual example unquestionably presents a faithful picture of the life led by the 20 thousand seamen employed in the 700 whaling vessels which pursue their game under the American flag. Indeed, what Mr Dana has so admirably done in describing the vicissitudes of the merchant sailor's life, Mr Browne has very creditably achieved with respect to that of the hardy whaleman's. And the book which possesses this merit deserves much in the way of com-

† Printed in the *Literary World* (March 6, 1847). The manuscript of this two-in-one review is in the Duyckinck Collection in the New York Public Library. It is in Melville's own hand (except for the heading). By permission of Northwestern University Press this text is reprinted from the *Piazza Tales* volume of *The Writings of Herman Melville*, where full textual and other information is given on pp. 625–36.

1. A beach on the south shore of Long Island. *Two Years before the Mast*: this book (1840) by Richard Henry Dana Jr. anticipated Melville's books in telling his experience of shipboard life as a common sailor, not an officer. For Melville's reading of it, see p. 532 herein. In *Childe Harold's Pilgrimage* (1816) Lord Byron declaims, "Roll on, thou deep and dark blue ocean—roll!" and declares, "from a boy / I wanton'd with thy breakers / And trusted to thy billows far and near, / And laid my hand upon thy mane" (stanzas 179, 184).

mendation. The personal narrative interwoven with it, also, can not fail to enlist our sympathies for the adventurous author himself. The scenes presented are always graphicly and truthfully sketched, and hence fastidious objections may be made to some of them, on the score of their being too coarsly or harshly drawn. But we take it, that as true unreserved descriptions they are in no respect faulty—and doubtless the author never dreamed of softening down or withholding anything with a view of rendering his sketches the more attractive and pretty. The book is eminently a practical one; and written with the set purpose of accomplishing good by revealing the simple truth. When the brutal tyranny of the Captain of the "Styx" is painted without apology or palliation, it holds up the outrageous abuse to which seamen in our whaling marine are actually subjected, a matter which demands legislation. Mr Browne himself—it seems, was to some extent, the victim of the tyranny of which he complains, and, upon this ground, the personal bitterness in which he at times indulges may be deemed excusable, though it is rather out of place.

As the book professes to embrace a detailed account of all that is interesting in the business of whaling, and, essentially, possesses this merit, one or two curious errors into which the author has unaccountably fallen may, without captiousness, be pointed out.—We are told, for example, of a whale's *roaring* when wounded by the harpoon. We can imagine the veteran Coffins and Colemans and Maceys of old Nantucket elevating their brows at the bare announcement of such a thing. Now the creature in question is as dumb as a shad, or any other of the finny tribes. And no doubt, if Jonah himself could be summoned to the stand, he would cheerfully testify to his not having heard a single syllable, growl, grunt, or bellow engendered in the ventricle cells of the leviathan, during the irksome period of his incarceration therein.[2]

That in some encounters with the sperm whale a low indistinct sound *apparently* issues from the monster is true enough. But all Nantucket and New Bedford are divided as to the causes which produce the phenomenon. Many suppose, however, that it is produced—not by the creature itself—but by the peculiar motion in the water of the line which is attached to the harpoon. For, if upon being struck, the whale "sounds" (descends) as is usually the case, and remains below the surface for any length of time, the rope frequently becomes as stiff as the cord of a harp and the struggles of the animal keep it continually vibrating.

Considering the disenchanting nature of the revelations of sea life with which we are presented in Mr Browne's book we are inclined to believe that the shipping agents employed in our various cities by the merchants of New Bedford will have to present additional inducements to "enterprising and industrious young Americans of good moral character" in order to persuade them to embark in the fishery. In particular the benevolent old gentleman in Front Street (one of the shipping agents of whom our author discourseth) who so politely accosted Browne and his comrade, upon their entering his office for the purpose of seeking further information touching the rate of promotion in the whaling service—this

2. Melville has been proved wrong. See the fascinating section on whale songs in Roger Payne's *Among Whales* (New York: Scribner, 1995), 144–67. For Jonah in the whale, see Jonah 1–2 and *Moby-Dick*, ch. 9.

old gentleman, we say, must hereafter infuse into his address still more of the *suaviter in modo.*[3]

As unaffectedly described by Browne the scene alluded to is irresistably comic. The agent's business, be it understood, consists in decoying "green hands" to send on to the different whaling ports. A conspicuous placard without the office announces to the anxious world, that a few choice vacancies remain to be filled in certain crews of whalemen about to sail upon the most delightful voyages imaginable (only four years long)—To secure a place, of course, instant application should be made.

Our author and his friend attracted by the placard, hurry up a ladder to a dark loft above, where the old man lurks like a spider in the midst of his toils.—But a single glance at the gentlemanly dress and white hands of his visitors impresses the wily agent with the idea that notwithstanding their calling upon him, they may very possibly have heard disagreeable accounts of the nature of whaling. So, after making a bow, and offering a few legs of a chair, he proceeds to disabuse their minds of any unfavorable impressions.—Succeeding in this, he then becomes charmingly facetious and complimentary; assuring the youths that they need not be concerned because of their slender waists and silken muscles; for those who employed him were not so particular about weight as beauty. In short the captains of whaling vessels preferred handsome young fellows who dressed well and conversed genteelly—in short, those who would reflect credit upon the business of tarring down rigging and cutting up blubber. Delighted with the agreeable address of the old gentleman and with many pleasant anticipations of sea-life the visitors listen with increased attention. Whereupon the agent waxes eloquent, and enlarges upon his animating theme in the style parliamentary. "A whaler, gentlemen" he observes "is the home of the unfortunate—the asylum of the oppressed &c &c &c"

Duped Browne! Hapless H————— ! In the end, they enter into an engagement with the old gentleman, who subsequently sends them on to New Bedford consigned to a mercantile house there. From New Bedford the adventurers at length sail in a small whaling barque bound to the Indian ocean. While yet half dead with sea sickness the unfortunate H————— is sent by the brutal captain to the mast-head, to stand there his allotted two hours on the look out for whale-spouts. He receives a stroke of the sun, which, for a time, takes away his reason and endangers his life. He raves of home and friends, and poor Browne watching by his side, upbraids himself for having been concerned in bringing his companion to such a state.—Ere long the vessel touches at the Azores, where H————— being altogether unfit for duty is left to be sent home by the American consul.

He never recovered from the effects of his hardships; for in the sequel Browne relates that after reaching home himself, he visited his old friend in Ohio, and found him still liable to temporary prostrations directly referable to his sufferings at sea.

With a heavy heart our author after leaving the Azores weathers the

3. Ironic Latin phrase, meaning not just smoothness or suaveness but "slickness of manner." *Front Street:* in New York City, runs from the Battery north, a block from the East River. *Old gentleman:* the fatherly conman who gulls greenhorns into signing on whaleships.

Cape of Good Hope and enters upon the Indian ocean. The ship's company—composed mostly of ignorant, half-civilized Portuguese from the Western Islands—are incessantly quarrelling and fighting; the provisions are of the most wretched kind;—their success in the fishery is small; and to crown all, the captain himself is the very incarnation of all that is dastardly, mean, and heartless.

We can not follow Browne through all his adventures. Suffice it to say, that heartily disgusted with his situation he at length, with great difficulty, succeeds in leaving the vessel on the coast of Zanzibar. Here he tarries for some months, and his residence in this remote region (the Eastern coast of Africa, near Madagascar) enables him to make sundry curious observations upon men and things, of which the reader of his work has the benefit. From Zanzibar he ultimately sails for home in a merchant brig; and at last arrives in Boston thoroughly out of conceit of the ocean.

Give ear, now, all ye shore-disdaining, ocean-enamored youths, who labor under the lamentable delusion, that the sea—the "glorious sea" is always and in reality "the blue, the fresh, the ever free!"[4] Give ear to Mr J. Ross Browne, and hearken unto what that experienced young gentleman has to say about the manner in which Barry Cornwall has been humbugging the rising generation on this subject.—Alas! Hereafter we shall never look upon an unsophisticated stripling in flowing "duck" trowsers and a bright blue jacket, loitering away the interval which elapses before sailing on his maiden cruise, without mourning over the hard fate in store for him.—In a ship's forecastle, alas, he will find no Psyche glass[5] in which to survey his picturesque attire. And the business of making his toilet will be comprised in trying to keep as dry and comfortable as the utter absence of umbrellas, wet decks, and leaky forecastles will admit of.—We shudder at all realities of the career they will be entering upon. The long, dark, cold night-watches, which, month after month, they must battle out the best way they can,—the ship pitching and thumping against the bullying waves—every plank dripping—every jacket soaked—and the Captain not at all bland in issuing his order for the poor fellows to mount aloft in the icy sleet and howling tempest.—"Bless me, Captain, go way up there this excessively disagreeable night?"—"Aye up with you, you lubber—*bare*, I say, or look out for squalls"—a figurative expression, conveying a remote allusion to the hasty application of a sea-bludgeon to the head.

Then the whaling part of the business.—My young friends, just fancy yourselves, for the first time in an open boat (so slight that three men might walk off with it) some 12 or 15 miles from your ship and about a hundred times as far from the nearest land, giving chase to one of the oleaginous monsters. "Pull, Pull, you lubberly *hay-makers!*" cries the boat-header jumping up and down in the stern-sheets in a frenzy of professional excitement, while the gasping admirers of Captain Marryat[6] and

---

4. The first line of "The Sea" (1832) by British barrister and literary man Brian Waller Proctor (1787–1874), who used the pseudonym Barry Cornwall.
5. Large mirror in which one can see one's whole body.
6. Captain Frederick Marryat (1792–1848), British author of *Peter Simple* (1834) and other popular novels of sea adventure. In *Typee* ch. 4 Melville jokes that "long-haired, bare-necked youths, who, forced by the united influences of Captain Marryat and hard times, embark at Nantucket for a pleasure excursion to the Pacific, and whose anxious mothers provide them with bottled milk for the occasion, oftentimes return very respectable middle-aged gentlemen."

the sea, tug with might and main at the buckling oars—"Pull, Pull, I say; Break your lazy backs!" Presently the whale is within "darting distance" and you hear the roar of the waters in his wake.—How palpitating the hearts of the frightened oarsmen at this interesting juncture! My young friends, just turn round and snatch a look at that whale—. There he goes, surging through the brine, which ripples about his vast head as if it were the bow of a ship. Believe me, it's quite as terrible as going into battle to a raw recruit.

"Stand up and give it to him!" shrieks the boat-header at the steering-oar to the harpooneer in the bow. The latter drops his oar and snatches his "iron". It flies from his hands—and where are we then, my lovelies?— It's all a mist, a crash,—a horrible blending of sounds and sights, as the agonized whale lashes the water around him into suds and vapor—dashes the boat aside, and at last rushes, madly, through the water towing after him the half-filled craft which rocks from side to side while the disordered crew, clutch at the gunwale to avoid being tossed out. Meanwhile all sorts of horrific edged tools lances, harpoons and spades—are slipping about; and the imminent line itself—smoking round the logger-head and passing along the entire length of the boat—is almost death to handle, though it grazes your person.

But all this is nothing to what follows. As yet you have but simply *fastened* to the whale: he must be fought and killed. But let imagination supply the rest:—the monster staving the boat with a single sweep of his ponderous flukes;—taking its bows between his jaws (as is frequently the case) and playing with it, as a cat with a mouse. Sometimes he bites it in twain; sometimes crunches it into chips, and strews the sea with them.

—But we forbear. Enough has been said to convince the uninitiated what sort of a vocation whaling in truth is. If further information is desired, Mr Browne's book is purchasable in which they will find the whole matter described in all its interesting details.

After reading the "Etchings of a Whaling Cruise" a perusal of "Sailors' Life and Sailors' Yarns" is in one respect at least like hearing "the other side of the question". For, while Browne's is a "Voice from the Forecastle" Captain Ringbolt hails us from the quarter deck, the other end of the ship. Browne gives us a sailor's version of sailors' wrongs, and is not altogether free from prejudices acquired during his little experience on ship board; Captain Ringbolt almost denies that the sailor has any wrongs and more than insinuates that sea-captains are not only the best natured fellows in the world but that they have been sorely maligned. Indeed he explicitly charges Mr Dana and Mr Browne with having presented a decidedly one sided view of the matter. And he mournfully exclaims that the Captain of the Pilgrim—poor fellow!—died too soon to vindicate his character from unjust aspersions.

—Now as a class ship owners are seldom disposed partially to judge the captains in their employ. And yet we know of a verity that at least one of the owners of the Pilgrim,—an esteemed citizen of the good old town of Boston—will never venture to dispute that to the extent of his knowledge at least Mr Dana's captain was a most "strict and harsh disciplinarian", which words so applied by a ship owner,[7] mean that the man in question was nothing less than what Mr Dana describes him to have been.—But where is Browne's captain? He is alive and hearty we presume. Let him come forward then and show why he ought not to be regarded in the decidedly unfavorable light in which he is held up to us in the narrative we have noticed? Now for ought we know to the contrary this same Captain of the Styx—who was such a heartless domineering tyrant at sea—may be quite a different character ashore. In truth we think this very probable. For the god Janus[8] never had two more decidedly different faces than your sea captain. Ashore his Nautical Highness has nothing to ruffle him—friends grasp him by the hand and are overjoyed to see him after his long absence—he is invited out and relates his adventures pleasantly and everybody thinks what lucky dogs his sailors must have been to have sailed with such a capital fellow.

—But let poor Jack have a word to say—Why Sir, he will tell you that when they embarked His Nautical Highness left behind him all his "quips and cranks and wanton smiles".[9] Very far indeed is the Captain from cracking any of his jokes with his crew—that would be altogether too condescending. But then there is no reason why he should bestow a curse every time he gives an order—there is no reason why he should never say a word of kindness or sympathy to his men. True; in this respect all sea captains are not alike but still there is enough truth in both Mr Dana's and Mr Browne's statements to justify nearly to the full, the general conclusions to be drawn from what they have said on this subject.—

But Captain Ringbolt's book is very far from being a mere plea for the class to which he belongs.—What he has to say upon the matter is chiefly contained in one brief sketch under the head of Sailors' Rights and Sailors' Wrongs.—The rest of the book is made up of little stories of the sea, simply and pleasantly told and withall entertaining.

---

7. *Pilgrim:* the name of Dana's ship. The owner referred to is unidentified, but Melville at this time had social access to wealthy Bostonians through his father-in-law-to-be, the chief justice of the Commonwealth of Massachusetts.
8. The Roman god with faces on front and rear of his head.
9. An adaptation of lines 27–28 of Milton's "L'Allegro": "Quips, and Cranks, and wanton Wiles, / Nods, and Becks, and wreathed Smiles."

BY A VIRGINIAN SPENDING JULY IN VERMONT[1]

Hawthorne and His Mosses[†]

A papered chamber in a fine old farm-house—a mile from any other dwelling, and dipped to the eaves in foliage—surrounded by mountains, old woods, and Indian ponds,—this, surely, is the place to write of Hawthorne. Some charm is in this northern air, for love and duty seem both impelling to the task. A man of a deep and noble nature has seized me in this seclusion. His wild, witch voice rings through me; or, in softer cadences, I seem to hear it in the songs of the hill-side birds, that sing in the larch trees at my window.

Would that all excellent books were foundlings, without father or mother, that so it might be, we could glorify them, without including their ostensible authors. Nor would any true man take exception to this;—least of all, he who writes,—"When the Artist rises high enough to achieve the Beautiful, the symbol by which he makes it perceptible to mortal senses becomes of little value in his eyes, while his spirit possesses itself in the enjoyment of the reality."[2]

But more than this. I know not what would be the right name to put on the title-page of an excellent book, but this I feel, that the names of all fine authors are fictitious ones, far more so than that of Junius,[3]—simply standing, as they do, for the mystical, ever-eluding Spirit of all Beauty, which ubiquitously possesses men of genius. Purely imaginative as this fancy may appear, it nevertheless seems to receive some warranty from the fact, that on a personal interview no great author has ever come up to the idea of his reader. But that dust of which our bodies are composed, how can it fitly express the nobler intelligences among us? With reverence be it spoken, that not even in the case of one deemed more than man, not even in our Saviour, did his visible frame betoken anything of the august-

---

1. Melville's revisions in the manuscript show that he added this fictional pseudonymous Virginian, here and in all five later passages, after he had written most of the essay expressing his own fervent feelings, which he thus distanced from himself, advised by Evert Duyckinck, editor of the New York *Literary World* (hereafter *LW*), who had a hand in other revisions and who published it anonymously, August 17 and 24, 1850. Still other things told in the essay are not true, including that Melville wrote it before he met Hawthorne, that the book was given to him by a "Cousin Cherry," and that it was "verdantly bound" and had green Salem moss pressed to the flyleaf; see the NN *Piazza Tales* volume (652–90) for these and other contextual details. Melville had no chance to correct proofs and found "ugly errors" in the printed essay. The typesetters' names on the manuscript pages show their differing treatment of its spelling and punctuation and who made some of the many changes and misreadings.

† By permission of Northwestern University Press. This text is reprinted from the *Piazza Tales* volume of *The Writings of Herman Melville*, where complete textual information is reported. The manuscript, in the Duyckinck Collection of the New York Public Library, is a fair copy made by Melville's wife, Elizabeth Shaw Melville, from his hastily scrawled nonextant draft. Here many of the footnotes are from the Hayford-Parker 1967 NCE, later adapted for the NN edition and now readapted; others are adaptations from new footnotes in the NN edition; still others are new, added on the basis of Parker's work on his *Herman Melville: A Biography (1819–1851)* (1996). The most detailed narrative account of the composition of this essay and the aftermath is now Parker, ch. 36, "Hawthorne and His *Mosses*: 8 August–September 1850."

2. From the ending of "The Artist of the Beautiful." Melville adapted the wording of this and other quotations slightly.

3. Pseudonym of unidentified British author of famous political satires (1769–72), now thought to have been Sir Philip Francis.

ness of the nature within. Else, how could those Jewish eyewitnesses fail to see heaven in his glance.

It is curious, how a man may travel along a country road, and yet miss the grandest, or sweetest of prospects, by reason of an intervening hedge, so like all other hedges, as in no way to hint of the wide landscape beyond. So has it been with me concerning the enchanting landscape in the soul of this Hawthorne, this most excellent Man of Mosses. His "Old Manse" has been written now four years, but I never read it till a day or two since. I had seen it in the book-stores—heard of it often—even had it recommended to me by a tasteful friend, as a rare, quiet book, perhaps too deserving of popularity to be popular. But there are so many books called "excellent", and so much unpopular merit, that amid the thick stir of other things, the hint of my tasteful friend was disregarded; and for four years the Mosses on the old Manse never refreshed me with their perennial green. It may be, however, that all this while, the book, like wine,[4] was only improving in flavor and body. At any rate, it so chanced that this long procrastination eventuated in a happy result. At breakfast the other day, a mountain girl, a cousin of mine, who for the last two weeks has every morning helped me to strawberries and raspberries,—which, like the roses and pearls in the fairy-tale, seemed to fall into the saucer from those strawberry-beds her cheeks,—this delightful creature, this charming Cherry says to me—"I see you spend your mornings in the hay-mow; and yesterday I found there 'Dwight's Travels in New England"[5] Now I have something far better than that,—something more congenial to our summer on these hills. Take these raspberries, and then I will give you some moss."—"Moss!" said I.—"Yes, and you must take it to the barn with you, and good-bye to 'Dwight'".

With that she left me, and soon returned with a volume, verdantly bound, and garnished with a curious frontispiece in green,—nothing less, than a fragment of real moss cunningly pressed to a fly-leaf.—"Why this," said I spilling my raspberries, "this is the 'Mosses from an Old Manse'".[6] "Yes" said cousin Cherry "yes, it is that flowery Hawthorne."— "Hawthorne and Mosses" said I "no more: it is morning: it is July in the country: and I am off for the barn".

Stretched on that new mown clover, the hill-side breeze blowing over me through the wide barn door, and soothed by the hum of the bees in the meadows around, how magically stole over me this Mossy Man! and how amply, how bountifully, did he redeem that delicious promise to his guests in the Old Manse, of whom it is written[7]—"Others could give them

---

4. Misprinted in LW as "likewise."
5. Timothy Dwight's (1752–1817) Travels in New-England and New-York, 4 vols. (1821–22).
6. Melville's heavily marked copy of Hawthorne's Mosses from an Old Manse (1846), is now in the Melville Collection of the Houghton Library of Harvard University.
7. During the composition of Mardi (see Log, 276), Mrs. Melville in a letter to her stepmother apologized for perhaps having left out punctuation marks, explaining that as Herman's copyist she was in the habit of leaving all the punctuation for him to supply. This passage (4.2–4.8 in the manuscript) is clear proof that in 1850 she was still omitting punctuation. In Melville's hand, in different ink, are the following additions and changes: he added the comma after "clover"; he altered "with the hill side breeze blowing over me from the wide barn door" to "the hill-side breeze blowing over me thro' the wide barn door," (Melville's comma after "door"); he added a comma after "around"; he changed the M's in "mossy man" to capitals; he added an exclamation point after "Man" and commas after "amply" and "bountifully"; and he changed "old manse" to "Old Manse." Presumably the extraordinary absence of dozens of necessary periods and quotation marks in the first American edition of Mardi may be due to Melville's failure to add the punctuation, and certain unusual absences of commas in Moby-Dick may be due to the same cause.

pleasure, or amusement, or instruction—these could be picked up any-where—but it was for me to give them rest. Rest, in a life of trouble! What better could be done for weary and world-worn spirits? what better could be done for anybody, who came within our magic circle, than to throw the spell of a magic spirit over him?"—So all that day, half-buried in the new clover, I watched this Hawthorne's "Assyrian dawn, and Paphian sunset and moonrise, from the summit of our Eastern Hill."[8]

The soft ravishments of the man spun me round about in a web of dreams, and when the book was closed, when the spell was over, this wizard "dismissed me with but misty reminiscences, as if I had been dreaming of him".

What a mild[9] moonlight of contemplative humor bathes that Old Manse!—the rich and rare distilment of a spicy and slowly-oozing heart. No rollicking rudeness, no gross fun fed on fat dinners, and bred in the lees of wine,—but a humor so spiritually gentle, so high, so deep, and yet so richly relishable, that it were hardly inappropriate in an angel. It is the very religion of mirth; for nothing so human but it may be advanced to that. The orchard of the Old Manse seems the visible type of the fine mind that has described it. Those twisted, and contorted old trees, "that stretch out their crooked branches, and take such hold of the imagination, that we remember them as humorists, and odd-fellows." And then, as surrounded by these grotesque forms, and hushed in the noon-day repose of this Hawthorne's spell, how aptly might the still fall of his ruddy thoughts into your soul be symbolized by "the thump of a great apple, in the stillest afternoon, falling without a breath of wind, from the mere necessity of perfect ripeness"! For no less ripe than ruddy are the apples of the thoughts and fancies in this sweet Man of Mosses.

"Buds and Bird-voices"—What a delicious thing is that!—"Will the world ever be so decayed, that Spring may not renew its greenness?"—And the "Fire-Worship". Was ever the hearth so glorified into an altar before? The mere title of that piece is better than any common work in fifty folio volumes. How exquisite is this:—"Nor did it lessen the charm of his soft, familiar courtesy and helpfulness, that the mighty spirit, were opportunity offered him, would run riot through the peaceful house, wrap its inmates in his terrible embrace, and leave nothing of them save their whitened bones. This possibility of mad destruction only made his domes-

---

8. Both quotations in this paragraph and those in the next two paragraphs are from the book's introductory essay, "The Old Manse," which tells about the Hawthornes' happy early married years there in Concord (1842–46). The second quotation is from the description of its "little nook of a study" where Emerson, while living there, wrote "Nature" (1836) and, as he wrote in that book, "used to watch the Assyrian dawn and the Paphian sunset and moonrise, from the summit of our eastern hill." Hawthorne is paraphrasing Emerson, as Melville may not have realized.

9. Misprinted in LW as "wild," as misread by Mrs. Melville, and corrected in the NN edition. The correction is part of a curious history, for Parker in the 1970s in Los Angeles realized from the context that "wild" was wrong and Hayford later verified the surmise by recourse to the manuscript at the New York Public Library (NYPL). Recently, Parker at the NYPL Duyckinck Collection saw that in the description of the picnic on Monument Mountain on August 5, 1850, the day Melville and Hawthorne met, Evert A. Duyckinck's description of Hawthorne as looking "mildly" about, the reading in The Melville Log (1951), was wrong: "The rain did not do its worst and we scattered over the cliffs, Herman Melville to seat himself, the boldest of all, astride a projecting bow sprit of rock while little D' Holmes peeped about the cliffs and protested it affected him like ipecac. Hawthorne looked wildly about for the great Carbuncle" (an allusion to one of his own early stories). Hawthorne, in other words, was behaving with a humorous theatricality that Melville and others found charming.

tic kindness the more beautiful and touching. It was so sweet of him, being endowed with such power, to dwell, day after day, and one long, lonesome night after another, on the dusky hearth, only now and then betraying his wild nature, by thrusting his red tongue out of the chimney-top! True, he had done much mischief in the world, and was pretty certain to do more, but his warm heart atoned for all. He was kindly to the race of man."

But he has still other apples, not quite so ruddy, though full as ripe;—apples, that have been left to wither on the tree, after the pleasant autumn gathering is past. The sketch of "The Old Apple Dealer" is conceived in the subtlest spirit of sadness; he whose "subdued and nerveless boyhood prefigured his abortive prime, which, likewise, contained within itself the prophecy and image of his lean and torpid age". Such touches as are in this piece can not proceed from any common heart.[1] They argue such a depth of tenderness, such a boundless sympathy with all forms of being, such an omnipresent love, that we must needs say, that this Hawthorne is here almost alone in his generation,—at least, in the artistic manifestation of these things. Still more. Such touches as these,—and many, very many similar ones, all through his chapters—furnish clews, whereby we enter a little way into the intricate, profound heart where they originated. And we see, that suffering, some time or other and in some shape or other,—this only can enable any man to depict it in others. All over him, Hawthorne's melancholy rests like an Indian Summer, which though bathing a whole country in one softness, still reveals the distinctive hue of every towering hill, and each far-winding vale.

But it is the least part of genius that attracts admiration. Where Hawthorne is known, he seems to be deemed a pleasant writer, with a pleasant style,—a sequestered, harmless man, from whom any deep and weighty thing would hardly be anticipated:—a man who means no meanings. But there is no man, in whom humor and love, like mountain peaks, soar to such a rapt height, as to receive the irradiations of the upper skies;—there is no man in whom humor and love are developed in that high form called genius; no such man can exist without also possessing, as the indispensable complement of these, a great, deep intellect, which drops down into the universe like a plummet.[2] Or, love and humor are only the eyes, through which such an intellect views this world. The great

---

1. The first part of this sentence occurs in 6.22 of the manuscript. In the left margin is a small penciled X—erased, but still visible. An examination of the whole manuscript reveals that such marginal X's were Mrs. Melville's way of reminding herself that she was uncertain about what she had copied and that she would have to ask her husband for the correct reading. After she had checked with him, she would erase the X—but lightly enough so that most are still readily visible. Here she first copied "Such tones as are in this piece" and later inserted the correct word "*touches*," above "tones." Often enough in the manuscript inserted words are simply revisions by Melville, but frequently, as here, the reading Mrs. Melville first copied can never have been what Melville wrote.

2. At 7.21 in the manuscript Mrs. Melville copied "into the universe like a planet"; she later marked out "planet" and inserted the correct "plummet" above it. Here no X is visible in the margin, perhaps an indication that she had not questioned her reading. It is not clear why the correction is in her hand instead of Melville's: perhaps she simply caught the error herself later and corrected it, as she did at other points; perhaps she was reading her copy aloud to him to spare his eyes and making the changes herself; perhaps he was proofreading with her nearby to enter any corrections. Compare this passage to the one on the Catskill eagle at the end of ch. 96 of *Moby-Dick* (p. 328 herein).

beauty in such a mind is but the product of its strength. What, to all readers, can be more charming than the piece entitled "Monsieur du Miroir"; and to a reader at all capable of fully fathoming it, what, at the same time, can possess more mystical depth of meaning?—Yes, there he sits, and looks at me,—this "shape of mystery", this "identical Monsieur du Miroir".—"Methinks I should tremble now, were his wizard power of gliding through all impediments in search of me, to place him suddenly before my eyes".

How profound, nay appalling, is the moral evolved by the "Earth's Holocaust"; where—beginning with the hollow follies and affectations of the world,—all vanities and empty theories and forms, are, one after another, and by an admirably graduated, growing comprehensiveness, thrown into the allegorical fire, till, at length, nothing is left but the all-engendering heart of man; which remaining still unconsumed, the great conflagration is nought.

Of a piece with this, is the "Intelligence Office", a wondrous symbolizing of the secret workings in men's souls.[3] There are other sketches, still more charged with ponderous import.

"The Christmas Banquet", and "The Bosom Serpent" would be fine subjects for a curious and elaborate analysis, touching the conjectural parts of the mind that produced them. For spite of all the Indian-summer sunlight on[4] the hither side of Hawthorne's soul, the other side—like the dark half of the physical sphere—is shrouded in a blackness, ten times black. But this darkness but gives more effect to the ever-moving dawn, that forever advances through it, and circumnavigates his world.[5] Whether Hawthorne has simply availed himself of this mystical blackness as a means to the wondrous effects he makes it to produce in his lights and shades; or whether there really lurks in him, perhaps unknown to himself, a touch of Puritanic gloom,—this, I cannot altogether tell. Certain it is, however, that this great power of blackness in him derives its force from its appeals to that Calvinistic sense of Innate Depravity and Original Sin, from whose visitations, in some shape or other, no deeply thinking mind is always and wholly free. For, in certain moods, no man can weigh this world, without throwing in something, somehow like Original Sin, to strike the uneven balance. At all events, perhaps no writer has ever wielded this terrific thought with greater terror than this same harmless Hawthorne. Still more: this black conceit pervades him, through and through. You may be witched by his sunlight,—transported by the bright gildings in the skies he builds over

---

3. In the manuscript 8.14 reads "of secret workings in this world. There are" (in Mrs. Melville's hand); in Melville's hand "the" is inserted before "secret," and "this world" is altered to "men's souls." Mrs. Melville evidently did not suspect she had miscopied, for no X is visible in the margin.
4. In this sentence at 8.20 in the manuscript is a clear instance of Mrs. Melville's misreading Melville's "on" as "in." She copied the passage as "sunlight in the hither side of Hawthorne's soul"; and Melville mended the "in" to "on," which must have been the original reading.
5. At 8.25 in the manuscript Mrs. Melville left two blanks: "that forever   through it, and   "; then she put *two* X's in the margin. Later, presumably after consulting her husband, she added "advances" in the first space, and "circumnavigates" in the second. It is almost always easy to detect which words have been added later by the unusual spacing and the anomalous slanting of the added word. In *Moby-Dick* there are instances of Melville's adding words in the English edition that seem likely to have been in his manuscript, though they do not appear in the first American edition.

you;—but there is the blackness of darkness beyond; and even his bright gildings but fringe, and play upon the edges of thunder-clouds.—In one word, the world is mistaken in this Nathaniel Hawthorne. He himself must often have smiled at its absurd misconception of him. He is immeasurably deeper than the plummet of the mere critic. For it is not the brain[6] that can test such a man; it is only the heart. You cannot come to know greatness by inspecting it; there is no glimpse to be caught of it, except by intuition; you need not ring it, you but touch it, and you find it is gold.[7]

Now it is that blackness in Hawthorne, of which I have spoken, that so fixes and fascinates me. It may be, nevertheless, that it is too largely developed in him. Perhaps he does not give us a ray of his light for every shade of his dark. But however this may be, this blackness it is that furnishes the infinite obscure of his back-ground,—that back-ground, against which Shakespeare plays his grandest conceits, the things that have made for Shakespeare his loftiest, but most circumscribed renown, as the profoundest of thinkers. For by philosophers Shakespeare is not adored as the great man of tragedy and comedy.—"Off with his head! so much for Buckingham!" this sort of rant, interlined by another hand, brings down the house,[8]—those mistaken souls, who dream of Shakespeare as a mere man of Richard-the-Third humps, and Macbeth daggers. But it is those deep far-away things in him; those occasional flashings-forth of the intuitive Truth in him; those short, quick probings at the very axis of reality;—these are the things that make Shakespeare, Shakespeare. Through the mouths[9] of the dark characters of Hamlet, Timon, Lear, and Iago, he craftily says, or sometimes insinuates the things, which we feel to be so terrifically true, that it were all but madness for any good man, in his own proper character, to utter, or even hint of them. Tormented into desperation, Lear the frantic King tears off the mask, and speaks the sane madness[1] of vital truth, But, as I before said, it is the least part of genius that attracts admiration. And so, much of the blind, unbridled admiration that has been heaped upon Shakespeare, has been lavished upon the least part of him. And few of his endless commentators and critics seem to have remembered, or even perceived, that the immediate products of a great mind are not so great, as that undeveloped, (and sometimes undevel-

6. At 9.23 in the manuscript a word clearly baffled Mrs. Melville. She put an X in the margin, and left a blank, in which she later inserted the word "brain."
7. At 9.27 in the manuscript is a clear instance of Mrs. Melville's omitting words that Melville restored as he proofread her copy. She copied "you ring it you but touch it and you find"; he later inserted "need not" before "ring" and added a comma after both the first and the second "it."
8. A line added in 1700 by Colley Cibber (1671–1757) in adapting *Richard III*, to be spoken by the humpbacked king. The dagger with which Macbeth kills Duncan and the daggers of the sleeping grooms figure dramatically in *Macbeth* 2.1 and 2.2. At 10.12–13 in the manuscript Mrs. Melville copied "'Buckingham' this sort of rant introduced by some other hand bring down the house those." Melville crowded in an exclamation point between the word "Buckingham" and the double quotes, added a comma after "rant," inserted "interlined" in place of "introduced," marked out "some" and altered "other" to "another," added a comma after "hand," added (or traced over) the "s" in "brings," and added a comma and dash after "house" but no separating punctuation before "this."
9. At 10.21 in the manuscript Mrs. Melville copied "Through the issues of the dark characters"—an impossible reading. In Melville's hand "issues" is marked out and replaced with "mouths"; no X is visible in the margin.
1. Melville complained to Mrs. Hawthorne about "one provoking mistake" in the *LW* printing—"same madness" for "sane madness."

opable) yet dimly-discernable[2] greatness, to which these immediate products are but the infallible indices. In Shakespeare's tomb lies infinitely more than Shakspeare[3] ever wrote. And if I magnify Shakespeare, it is not so much for what he did do, as for what he did not do, or refrained from doing. For in this world of lies, Truth is forced to fly like a sacred white doe in the woodlands; and only by cunning glimpses will she reveal herself, as in Shakespeare and other masters of the great Art of Telling the Truth,—even though it be covertly, and by snatches.[4]

But if this view of the all-popular Shakespeare be seldom taken by his readers, and if very few who extol him, have ever read him deeply, or, perhaps, only have seen him on the tricky stage, (which alone made, and is still making him his mere mob renown)—if few men have time, or patience, or palate, for the spiritual truth as it is in that great genius;—it is, then, no matter of surprise that in a contemporaneous age, Nathaniel Hawthorne is a man, as yet, almost utterly mistaken among men. Here and there, in some quiet arm-chair in the noisy town, or some deep nook among the noiseless mountains, he may be appreciated for something of what he is. But unlike Shakespeare, who was forced to the contrary course by circumstances, Hawthorne (either from simple disinclination, or else from inaptitude) refrains from all the popularizing noise and show of broad farce, and blood-besmeared tragedy; content with the still, rich utterances of a great intellect in repose, and which sends few thoughts into circulation, except they be arterialized at his large warm lungs, and expanded in his honest heart.

Nor need you fix upon that blackness in him, if it suit you not. Nor, indeed, will all readers discern it, for it is, mostly, insinuated to those who may best understand it, and account for it; it is not obtruded upon every one alike.

Some may start to read of Shakespeare and Hawthorne on the same page. They may say, that if an illustration were needed, a lesser light might have sufficed to elucidate this Hawthorne, this small man of yesterday. But I am not, willingly, one of those, who, as touching Shakespeare at least, exemplify the maxim of Rochefoucault,[5] that "we exalt the reputation of some, in order to depress that of others";—who, to teach all noble-souled aspirants that there is no hope for them, pronounce Shakespeare absolutely unapproachable. But Shakespeare has been approached. There are minds that have gone as far as Shakespeare into the universe. And hardly a mortal man, who, at some time or other, has not felt as great

2. At 11.7 in the manuscript Mrs. Melville copied "divinely" then at once realized her error, marked out "divinely" and on the same line added "dimly-discerned" (which Melville later altered to "dimly-discernable"—a misspelling corrected in *LW*).
3. An acceptable variant spelling then, and Melville's own spelling here (and sometimes elsewhere), even though "Shakespeare" is Mrs. Melville's consistent spelling, which he let stand twice in this passage, all through the essay, and used himself four times in revising her fair copy. The NN editors do not emend such spellings (see "Spencer" at 252.7, 8 and "Marlow" at 252.37).
4. In *Herman Melville: A Biography* (1.756) Parker introduced the emendation of "sacred white doe" instead of "scared white doe" on the analogy of John Dryden's "milk-white Hind" in "The Hind and the Panther" (1687) and William Wordsworth's "White Doe of Rylstone" (1807) although Mrs. Melville wrote "scared." At 11.12 in the manuscript Mrs. Melville copied "Truth is found" and recorded her doubt with an X in the margin. Later she marked out "found" and inserted "forced." Melville himself, still later, added a comma after "herself" (line 11.15) and altered the impossible reading "other writers" to "other masters" (there is no X at this point to indicate Mrs. Melville was uncertain about what she copied). In 11.16 Melville altered "art" to "Art" and inserted a comma and dash after "Truth." In the next line he inserted a comma after "covertly," even though it had to be crowded in.
5. François de la Rochefoucauld (1613–1680), French moralist noted for his acerbic *Moral Reflections & Maxims* with their dim view of human nature.

thoughts in him as any you will find in Hamlet. We must not inferentially malign mankind for the sake of any one man, whoever he may be. This is too cheap a purchase of contentment for conscious mediocrity to make. Besides, this absolute and unconditional adoration of Shakespeare has grown to be a part of our Anglo Saxon superstitions. The Thirty Nine articles[6] are now Forty. Intolerance has come to exist in this matter. You must believe in Shakespeare's unapproachability, or quit the country. But what sort of a belief is this for an American, a man who is bound to carry republican progressiveness into Literature, as well as into Life? Believe me, my friends, that Shakespeares are this day being born on the banks of the Ohio.[7] And the day will come, when you shall say who reads a book by an Englishman that is a modern?[8] The great mistake seems to be, that even with those Americans who look forward to the coming of a great literary genius among us, they somehow fancy he will come in the costume of Queen Elizabeth's day,—be a writer of dramas founded upon old English history, or the tales of Boccaccio.[9] Whereas, great geniuses are parts of the times; they themselves are the times; and possess a correspondent coloring. It is of a piece with the Jews, who while their Shiloh[1] was meekly walking in their streets, were still praying for his magnificent coming; looking for him in a chariot, who was already among them on an ass. Nor must we forget, that, in his own life-time, Shakespeare was not Shakespeare, but only Master William Shakespeare of the shrewd, thriving, business firm of Condell, Shakespeare & Co., proprietors of the Globe Theatre in London; and by a courtly author, of the name of Greene,[2] was

6. Articles of faith issued in 1551 and 1553 by the Church of England, acceptance of which is obligatory for its clergy. The phrase came to refer to any such basic list of beliefs.
7. Melville, surely at Duyckinck's urging, toned this down to "that men not very much inferior to Shakespeare are being born on the banks of the Ohio." See Parker (1.757) for an analysis of the way Melville was characteristically twisting the words of his unnamed source, here Maurice Morgann, famous in late-18th-century London for his "Essay on the Dramatic Character of Sir John Falstaff," in which he celebrates the majesty of Shakespeare's language by saying that Shakespeare's words would resound in the Appalacian mountains and on "the banks of the Ohio," long after Shakespeare's critics and editors and Voltaire and the very French language had been forgotten. Melville knew as he wrote that a man capable of writing a mighty book in the tradition of Shakespeare had been born in the United States three decades earlier a stone's throw from a great bay and two rivers, the East and the Hudson.
8. A reversal of the contemptuous putdown of American works by the Scottish critic Sydney Smith (1771–1845) in the *Edinburgh Review* (January 1820): "In the four quarters of the globe, who reads an American book? Or goes to an American play? Or looks at an American picture or statue?" It was especially resented, and contested, by American writers from 1820 to 1860, who strove to create a great national literature, including Melville, who passionately advocates the cause in this essay in part by arguing for recognition of the greatness of Hawthorne's achievement in *Mosses from an Old Manse*. See also p. 483 herein.
9. Tales in the *Decameron* (1349–51) of Giovanni Boccaccio (1313–1375).
1. From Genesis 49.10, a messiah or expected great leader, most often applied to Jesus.
2. Melville's manuscript has "Chettle" here. The NN editors emend to "Greene" because it was not the publisher Henry Chettle but the playwright Robert Greene who, in *A Groatsworth of Wit* (1592) thus maligned the young Shakespeare. However, Melville's writing "Chettle" is not a simple error (see Parker 1.705, 739, 758). In Thomas Powell's *Living Authors of America* (1850) Melville had read in the chapter on Henry Wadsworth Longfellow a theory of literary influence: "Imitation has been charged on all poets, and we know that the indignation of Robert Green[e] was so soured by the appropriations of Shakspeare, that he denounced him 'as a jay strutting about in our feathers, and fancying himself as the only *Shakscene* of the country.' This charge is always more or less true of a young author, and it is in the very nature of things." Every poet, Powell had concluded, "commences with more or less of some predominant mind, the most assimilant to his own." Melville also knew John Payne Collier's edition of Shakespeare that contained a "Life," in which Paine enunciated the theory that Chettle was the author of *A Groatsworth of Wit*, a theory that Melville may have accepted and combined with Powell's ideas about originality and imitation. Like Powell, Melville is careless with the epithet in *Groatsworth*: "an upstart crow, beautified with our feathers."

hooted at, as an "upstart crow" beautified "with other birds' feathers". For, mark it well, imitation is often the first charge brought against real origi- nality. Why this is so, there is not space to set forth here. You must have plenty of sea-room to tell the Truth in; especially, when it seems to have an aspect of newness, as America did in 1492, though it was then just as old, and perhaps older than Asia, only those sagacious philosophers, the common sailors, had never seen it before; swearing it was all water and moonshine there.

Now, I do not say that Nathaniel of Salem is a greater than William of Avon, or as great. But the difference between the two men is by no means immeasurable. Not a very great deal more, and Nathaniel were verily William.

This, too, I mean, that if Shakespeare has not been equalled, he is sure to be surpassed, and surpassed by an American born now or yet to be born.[3] For it will never do for us who in most other things out-do as well as out-brag the world, it will not do for us to fold our hands and say, In the highest department advance there is none. Nor will it at all do to say, that the world is getting grey and grizzled now, and has lost that fresh charm which she wore of old, and by virtue of which the great poets of past times made themselves what we esteem them to be. Not so. The world is as young today, as when it was created; and this Vermont morn- ing dew is as wet to my feet, as Eden's dew to Adam's. Nor has Nature been all over ransacked by our progenitors, so that no new charms and mysteries remain for this latter generation to find. Far from it. The tril- lionth[4] part has not yet been said; and all that has been said, but multi- plies the avenues to what remains to be said. It is not so much paucity, as superabundance of material that seems to incapacitate modern authors.

Let America then prize and cherish her writers; yea, let her glorify them. They are not so many in number, as to exhaust her good-will. And while she has good kith and kin of her own, to take to her bosom, let her not lavish her embraces upon the household of an alien. For believe it or not England, after all, is, in many things, an alien to us. China has more bowels[5] of real love for us than she. But even were there no Hawthorne, no Emerson, no Whittier, no Irving, no Bryant, no Dana, no Cooper, no Willis (not the author of the "Dashes", but the author of the "Belfry Pigeon")[6]—were there none of these, and others of like calibre among us,

---

3. We follow the manuscript, not the *LW* text, because Duyckinck almost certainly was the one who toned the passage down to read "if Shakespeare has not been equalled, give the world time, and he is sure to be surpassed, in one hemisphere or the other."
4. At 15 1/2.28 in the manuscript is one of Mrs. Melville's more striking misreadings. A very faint X in the margin signals her doubt about "brilliant part"—and she has marked out "brilliant and inserted the correct "trillionth."
5. Melville corrected his wife's misreading "bonds."
6. Melville's first wording (in his wife's hand) was "no Hawthornes Emersons Whittiers Danas Coopers"; he revised and expanded that to "no Hawthorne no Emerson no Whittier, no Irving, no Bryant, no Dana no Cooper no Willis (not the author of the 'Dashes,' but the author of the 'Bel- frey Pigeon')." Melville's journalist friend Nathaniel Parker Willis (1806–1857) wrote *Dashes at Life with a Free Pencil* (1845) and the poem "The Belfry Pigeon" (1831), the latter a weakly sen- timental affair. Duyckinck might have let all the names stay if Melville had not politely included his friend Willis, with whom Duyckinck had been feuding ferociously (see Parker 1.713, 720, 723). As editor Duyckinck lined out the individual names and worded the passage in more gen- eral terms, so that it was long known in this form: "China has more bowels of real love for us than she. But even were there no strong literary individualities among us, as there are some dozen at least; nevertheless, let America first praise mediocrity even, in her own children."

nevertheless, let America first praise mediocrity even, in her own children, before she praises (for everywhere, merit demands acknowledgment from every one) the best excellence in the children of any other land. Let her own authors, I say, have the priority of appreciation. I was much pleased with a hot-headed Carolina cousin of mine, who once said,—"If there were no other American to stand by, in Literature,—why, then, I would stand by Pop Emmons[7] and his 'Fredoniad,' and till a better epic came along, swear it was not very far behind the Iliad." Take away the words, and in spirit he was sound.

Not that American genius needs patronage in order to expand. For that explosive sort of stuff will expand though screwed up in a vice, and burst it, though it were triple steel. It is for the nation's sake, and not for her authors' sake, that I would have America be heedful of the increasing greatness among her writers. For how great the shame, if other nations should be before her, in crowning her heroes of the pen. But this is almost the case now. American authors have received more just and discriminating praise (however loftily and ridiculously given, in certain cases) even from some Englishmen, than from their own countrymen. There are hardly five critics in America; and several of them are asleep. As for patronage, it is the American author who now patronizes his country, and not his country him. And if at times some among them appeal to the people for more recognition, it is not always with selfish motives, but patriotic ones.

It is true, that but few of them as yet have evinced that decided[8] originality which merits great praise. But that graceful writer,[9] who perhaps of all Americans has received the most plaudits from his own country for his productions,—that very popular and amiable writer, however good, and self-reliant in many things, perhaps owes his chief reputation to the self-acknowledged imitation of a foreign model, and to the studied avoidance of all topics but smooth ones. But it is better to fail in originality, than to

---

7. "Pop" Emmons is a result of Melville's confusion. As a child he was taken for walks on the Boston Common where a local orator, William (Pop) Emmons kept a concessionaire's stand at which he sold what the Portland, Maine *Daily Advertiser* on November 14, 1851, recalled as "a delectable beverage known in those days as 'egg pop,'" hence the soubriquet "Pop Emmons." In the stand Emmons also kept for sale copies of his patriotic orations, which he would willingly repeat. When Melville later saw the four-volume nationalistic epic poem about naval battles in the war of 1812 *The Fredoniad* he assumed it was by the man he remembered, but the poem was actually by Pop Emmons's brother Richard Emmons.

8. An X in the margin indicates Mrs. Melville's uncertainty. She left a space after "as yet have" and later filled it in with "evinced." It *appears* that "decided" was also added later, but it may not have been.

9. Washington Irving (1783–1859), often called the American Goldsmith, from the resemblance of his style to that of Oliver Goldsmith (1728–1774), on whom he wrote a highly derivative biography (1849). See Parker (1.769–71) for his newly discovered record of how angry Irving and his nephew Pierre Irving were when they read this passage in the *LW* and how long the words of the "Virginian" rankled in Pierre's memory. Irving had been Melville's fairy godfather in London in 1846, reading the proofs of *Typee* at Gansevoort Melville's request and recommending the book to George P. Putnam for publication in New York by Wiley & Putnam. Once the minister to England, Louis McLane, returned to London and told old friend Irving that he had been trying to get President Polk to remove Gansevoort from his office because of his partisan recklessness on the Oregon question, Irving withdrew his friendship from the Melvilles and through many years of literary correspondence is not known to have mentioned Herman Melville once. The world of New York publishing was small, and Duyckinck was an intimate of Irving's who may later have confided the authorship of this piece, if asked. The strangest part of this all is that Duyckinck let a slighting reference to Irving go into print in his *LW*; he may simply have been so excited about the adventure of meeting Hawthorne and exacting this fervid essay from Melville that, in his great haste to rush the thing into print, he just overlooked the slight.

succeed in imitation. He who has never failed somewhere, that man can not be great. Failure is the true test of greatness. And if it be said, that continual success is a proof that a man wisely knows his powers,—it is only to be added, that, in that case, he knows them to be small. Let us believe it, then, once for all, that there is no hope for us in these smooth pleasing writers that know their powers. Without malice, but to speak the plain fact, they but furnish an appendix to Goldsmith, and other English authors. And we want no American Goldsmiths; nay, we want no American Miltons. It were the vilest thing you could say of a true American author, that he were an American Tompkins.[1] Call him an American, and have done; for you can not say a nobler thing of him.—But it is not meant that all American writers should studiously cleave to nationality in their writings;[2] only this, no American writer should write like an Englishman, or a Frenchman; let him write like a man, for then he will be sure to write like an American. Let us away with this Bostonian[3] leaven of literary flunkeyism towards England. If either must play the flunkey in this thing, let England do it, not us. And the time is not far off when circumstances may force her to it.[4] While we are rapidly preparing for that political supremacy among the nations, which prophetically awaits us at the close of the present century; in a literary point of view, we are deplorably unprepared for it; and we seem studious to remain so. Hitherto, reasons might have existed why this should be; but no good reason exists now. And all that is requisite to amendment in this matter, is simply this: that, while freely[5] acknowledging all excellence, everywhere, we should refrain from unduly lauding foreign writers and, at the same time, duly recognize the meritorious writers that are our own;—those writers, who breathe that unshackled, democratic spirit of Christianity in all things, which now takes the practical lead in this world, though at the same time led by ourselves—us Americans. Let us boldly contemn all imitation, though it comes to us graceful and fragrant as the morning; and foster all originality, though, at first, it be crabbed and ugly as our own pine knots. And if any of our authors fail, or seem to fail, then, in the words of my enthusiastic Carolina cousin, let us clap him on the shoulder, and back him against all Europe for his second round. The truth is, that in our[6] point of view, this matter of a national literature has come to such a pass with us, that in some sense we must turn bullies, else the day is lost, or superiority so far beyond us, that we can hardly say it will ever be ours.

And now, my countrymen, as an excellent author, of your own flesh and

---

1. Melville substituted "Tompkins" for what he first wrote, "Milton." Melville means "any Tom, Dick, or Harry," an "American Anybody," judging from William Makepeace Thackeray's contemporary usage in an unpleasant comment about Charlotte Brontë, before her marriage, that she needed "some Tomkins or another to love her and be in love with."
2. At 17.7 in the manuscript Mrs. Melville copied "studiously cleave to nationality   in their," leaving a space about as long as that taken up by the word "writers" in the line above. There is an erased X in the margin, but the space is not filled in. Presumably the erased X means that she had thought that there might be another word in the manuscript; she *may* have left a much longer space and filled in "nationality", though that word does not appear to have been added at a later time.
3. Melville canceled this word, probably under Duyckinck's pressure, which was restored by the NN editors.
4. The NN editors restore this prophetic sentence, which Melville canceled, apparently under Duyckinck's influence.
5. Misprinted in *LW* as "fully."
6. Misprinted in *LW* as "one."

blood,—an unimitating, and, perhaps, in his way, an inimitable man—
whom better can I commend to you, in the first place, than Nathaniel
Hawthorne. He is one of the new, and far better generation of your writers. The smell of your beeches[7] and hemlocks is upon him; your own
broad praries are in his soul; and if you travel away inland into his deep
and noble nature, you will hear the far roar of his Niagara. Give not over
to future generations the glad duty of acknowledging him for what he is.
Take that joy to your self, in your own generation; and so shall he feel
those grateful impulses in him, that may possibly prompt him to the full
flower of some still greater achievement in your eyes. And by confessing
him, you thereby confess others; you brace the whole brotherhood. For
genius, all over the world, stands hand in hand, and one shock of recognition[8] runs the whole circle round.

In treating of Hawthorne, or rather of Hawthorne in his writings (for I
never saw the man;[9] and in the chances of a quiet plantation life, remote
from his haunts, perhaps never shall) in treating of his works, I say, I have
thus far omitted all mention of his "Twice Told Tales",[1] and "Scarlet Letter". Both are excellent; but full of such manifold, strange and diffusive
beauties, that time would all but fail me, to point the half of them out.
But there are things in those two books, which, had they been written in
England a century ago, Nathaniel Hawthorne had utterly displaced many
of the bright names we now revere on authority. But I am content to leave
Hawthorne to himself, and to the infallible finding of posterity; and however great may be the praise I have bestowed upon him, I feel, that in so
doing, I have more served and honored myself, than him. For, at bottom,
great excellence is praise enough to itself; but the feeling of a sincere and
appreciative love and admiration towards it, this is relieved by utterance;
and warm, honest praise ever leaves a pleasant flavor in the mouth; and it
is an honorable thing to confess to what is honorable in others.

But I cannot leave my subject yet. No man can read a fine author, and
relish him to his very bones, while he reads, without subsequently fancying to himself some ideal image of the man and his mind. And if you
rightly look for it, you will almost always find that the author himself has
somewhere furnished you with his own picture.—For poets (whether in
prose or verse), being painters of Nature, are like their brethren of the
pencil, the true portrait-painters, who, in the multitude of likenesses to be
sketched, do not invariably omit their own; and in all high instances, they
paint them without any vanity, though, at times, with a lurking something,
that would take several pages to properly define.

I submit it, then, to those best acquainted with the man personally,
whether the following is not Nathaniel Hawthorne;—and to himself,

7. Melville corrected his wife's misreading "birches" but did not catch the reverse misreading
"beech" canoes for "birch" canoes in Moby-Dick, ch. 54, emended by the NN editors.
8. This phrase is commonly misinterpreted to mean the shock a great reader feels at encountering
a great author. See the NN Moby-Dick (613 n. 14, 861–62).
9. In fact, Melville had met Hawthorne just before writing the essay. The NN "Historical Note"
(611–12) is now superseded by Parker's use of additional manuscript letters in the first volume
of his Herman Melville: A Biography, ch. 35, "Pittsfield and Hawthorne: June–7 August 1850,"
and ch. 36, "Hawthorne and His Mosses: 8 August–September 1850." These chapters confirm
Hayford's long-held theory that Melville met Hawthorne before writing the essay.
1. For Melville's reading of Twice-Told Tales (1837) see his letter to Duyckinck February 12, 1851.
(p. 535 herein).

whether something involved in it does not express the temper of his mind,—that lasting temper of all true, candid men—a seeker, not a finder yet:—

> "A man now entered, in neglected attire, with the aspect of a thinker, but somewhat too rough-hewn and brawny for a scholar. His face was full of sturdy vigor, with some finer and keener attribute beneath; though harsh at first, it was tempered with the glow of a large, warm heart, which had force enough to heat his powerful intellect through and through. He advanced to the Intelligencer, and looked at him with a glance of such stern sincerity, that perhaps few secrets were beyond its scope.
> "'I seek for Truth', said he."

• • •

Twenty four hours have elapsed since writing the foregoing. I have just returned from the hay mow, charged more and more with love and admiration of Hawthorne. For I have just been gleaning through the Mosses, picking up many things here and there that had previously escaped me. And I found that but to glean after this man, is better than to be in at the harvest of others. To be frank (though, perhaps, rather foolish) notwithstanding what I wrote yesterday of these Mosses, I had not then culled them all; but had, nevertheless, been sufficiently sensible of the subtle essence, in them, as to write as I did. To what infinite height of loving wonder and admiration I may yet be borne, when by repeatedly banquetting on these Mosses, I shall have thoroughly incorporated their whole stuff into my being,—that, I can not tell. But already I feel that this Hawthorne has dropped germinous seeds into my soul. He expands and deepens down, the more I contemplate him; and further, and further, shoots his strong New-England roots into the hot soil of my Southern soul.

By careful reference to the "Table of Contents", I now find, that I have gone through all the sketches; but that when I yesterday wrote, I had not all read two particular pieces, to which I now desire to call special attention,—"A Select Party", and "Young Goodman Brown". Here, be it said to all those whom this poor fugitive scrawl of mine may tempt to the perusal of the "Mosses," that they must on no account suffer themselves to be trifled with, disappointed, or deceived by the triviality of many of the titles to these Sketches. For in more than one instance, the title utterly belies the piece. It is as if rustic demijohns containing the very best and costliest of Falernian and Tokay, were labelled "Cider", "Perry," and "Elderberry wine". The truth seems to be, that like many other geniuses, this Man of Mosses takes great delight in hoodwinking the world,—at least, with respect to himself. Personally, I doubt not, that he rather prefers to be generally esteemed but a so-so sort of author; being willing to reserve the thorough and acute appreciation of what he is, to that party most qualified to judge—that is, to himself. Besides, at the bottom of their natures, men like Hawthorne, in many things, deem the plaudits of the public such strong presumptive evidence of mediocrity in the object of them, that it would in some degree render them doubtful of their own powers, did they hear much and vociferous braying concerning them in the public pastures. True, I have been braying myself (if you please to be witty enough, to have it so) but then I claim to be the first that has so brayed in this particular matter; and therefore, while pleading guilty to the charge still claim all the merit due to originality.

But with whatever motive, playful or profound, Nathaniel Hawthorne has chosen to entitle his pieces in the manner he has, it is certain, that some of them are directly calculated to deceive—egregiously deceive, the superficial skimmer of pages. To be downright and candid once more, let me cheerfully say, that two of these titles did dolefully dupe no less an eagle-eyed[2] reader than myself; and that, too, after I had been impressed with a sense of the great depth and breadth of this American man. "Who in the name of thunder" (as the country-people say in this neighborhood) "who in the name of thunder", would anticipate any marvel in a piece entitled "Young Goodman Brown"? You would of course suppose that it was a simple little tale, intended as a supplement to "Goody Two Shoes".[3] Whereas, it is deep as Dante; nor can you finish it, without addressing the author in his own words—"It is yours to penetrate, in every bosom, the deep mystery of sin". And with Young Goodman, too, in allegorical pursuit of his Puritan wife, you cry out in your anguish,—

> "'Faith!' shouted Goodman Brown, in a voice of agony and desperation; and the echoes of the forest mocked him, crying—'Faith! Faith!' as if bewildered wretches were seeking her all through the wilderness."

Now this same piece, entitled "Young Goodman Brown", is one of the two that I had not all read yesterday; and I allude to it now, because it is, in itself, such a strong positive illustration of that blackness in Hawthorne, which I had assumed from the mere occasional shadows of it, as revealed in several of the other sketches. But had I previously perused "Young Goodman Brown", I should have been at no pains to draw the conclusion, which I came to, at a time, when I was ignorant that the book contained one such direct and unqualified manifestation of it.

The other piece of the two referred to, is entitled "A Select Party", which, in my first simplicity upon originally taking hold of the book, I fancied must treat of some pumpkin-pie party in Old Salem, or some chowder party on Cape Cod. Whereas, by all the gods of Peedee![4] it is the sweetest and sublimest thing that has been written since Spencer[5] wrote. Nay, there is nothing in Spencer that surpasses[6] it, perhaps, nothing that equals it. And the test is this: read any canto in "The Faery Queen", and then read "A Select Party", and decide which pleases you the most,—that is, if you are qualified to judge. Do not be frightened at this; for when Spencer was alive, he was thought of very much as Hawthorne is now,— was generally accounted just such a "gentle" harmless man. It may be, that to common eyes, the sublimity of Hawthorne seems lost in his sweetness,—as perhaps in this same "Select Party" of his; for whom, he has

2. Misprinted in *LW* as "eager-eyed."
3. A nursery tale, attributed to Goldsmith.
4. Melville substituted "Peedee" for his original "Greece." Peedee is a river in the Carolinas.
5. A then accepted variant of Edmund Spenser (1552?–1599) whose allegorical *Faerie Queene* (1590, 1596) was favorite reading of both Hawthorne and Melville.
6. Melville crossed out "equals," wrote in "surpasses," and added the rest of the sentence.

builded so august a dome of sunset clouds, and served them on richer plate, than Belshazzar's when he banquetted his lords in Babylon.[7]

But my chief business now, is to point out a particular page in this piece, having reference to an honored guest, who under the name of "The Master Genius" but in the guise of "a young man of poor attire, with no insignia of rank or acknowledged eminence", is introduced to the Man of Fancy, who is the giver of the feast. Now the page having reference to this "Master Genius", so happily expresses much of what I yesterday wrote, touching the coming of the literary Shiloh of America, that I cannot but be charmed by the coincidence; especially, when it shows such a parity of ideas, at least in this one point, between a man like Hawthorne and a man like me.

And here, let me throw out another conceit of mine touching this American Shiloh, or "Master Genius", as Hawthorne calls him. May it not be, that this commanding mind has not been, is not, and never will be, individually developed in any one man? And would it, indeed, appear so unreasonable to suppose, that this great fullness and overflowing may be, or may be destined to be, shared by a plurality of men of genius? Surely, to take the very greatest example on record, Shakespeare cannot be regarded as in himself the concretion of all the genius of his time; nor as so immeasurably beyond Marlow,[8] Webster, Ford, Beaumont, Jonson, that those great men can be said to share none of his power? For one, I conceive that there were dramatists in Elizabeth's day, between whom and Shakespeare the distance was by no means great. Let anyone, hitherto little acquainted with those neglected old authors, for the first time read them thoroughly, or even read Charles Lamb's Specimens[9] of them, and he will be amazed at the wondrous ability of those Anaks of men, and shocked at this renewed example of the fact, that Fortune has more to do with fame than merit,—though, without merit, lasting fame there can be none.

Nevertheless, it would argue too illy of my country were this maxim to hold good concerning Nathaniel Hawthorne, a man, who already, in some few minds, has shed "such a light, as never illuminates the earth, save when a great heart burns as the household fire of a grand intellect."

The words are his,—in the "Select Party"; and they are a magnificent setting to a coincident sentiment of my own, but ramblingly expressed yesterday, in reference to himself. Gainsay it who will, as I now write, I am Posterity speaking by proxy—and after times will make it more than good, when I declare—that the American, who up to the present day, has evinced, in Literature, the largest brain with the largest heart, that man is Nathaniel Hawthorne. Moreover, that whatever Nathaniel Hawthorne may hereafter write, "The Mosses from an Old Manse" will be ultimately accounted his masterpiece. For there is a sure, though a secret sign in some works which prove the culmination of the powers (only the developable ones, however) that produced them. But I am by no means desirous of the glory of a prophet. I pray Heaven that Hawthorne may yet prove me an impostor in this prediction. Especially, as I somehow cling to

---

7. The "great feast" Belshazzar, king of Babylon (6th century B.C.E.), gave "to a thousand of his lords" (Daniel 5.1).
8. An accepted variant of Marlowe (252.37).
9. *Dramatic Poets Who Lived about the Time of Shakespeare* (1808), edited by the English essayist Charles Lamb (1775–1834).

the strange fancy, that, in all men, hiddenly reside certain wondrous, occult properties—as in some plants and minerals—which by some happy but very rare accident (as bronze was discovered by the melting of the iron and brass in the burning of Corinth)[1] may chance to be called forth here on earth; not entirely waiting for their better discovery in the more congenial, blessed atmosphere of heaven.

Once more—for it is hard to be finite upon an infinite subject, and all subjects are infinite. By some people, this entire scrawl of mine may be esteemed altogether unnecessary, inasmuch, "as years ago" (they may say) "we found out the rich and rare stuff in this Hawthorne, whom you now parade forth, as if only *yourself* were the discoverer of this Portuguese diamond[2] in our Literature".—But even granting all this; and adding to it, the assumption that the books of Hawthorne have sold by the five-thousand,—what does that signify?—They should be sold by the hundred-thousand; and read by the million; and admired by every one who is capable of admiration.

MELVILLE'S LETTERS AT THE TIME OF *MOBY-DICK*

These excerpts from Melville's letters during the composition of *Moby-Dick* are reprinted with permission of Northwestern University Press from Volume 14 of the Northwestern-Newberry *The Writings of Herman Melville,* the *Correspondence*, edited by Lynn Horth with the help of Parker, Tanselle, and especially Hayford. It is a complete revision, augmented, of *The Letters of Herman Melville* (1960), edited by Merrell R. Davis and William H. Gilman. Some of the footnotes here draw on those in the *Letters* and *Correspondence*. The anomalous spellings and punctuation are Melville's own or are those in the best available transcription of now-missing letters. One important letter formerly dated June 1?, 1851, is redated to early May 1851, on the basis of evidence in Parker's *Herman Melville: A Biography* (1.841–44).

To Richard H. Dana Jr.

NEW YORK May 1, 1850

I thank you very heartily for your friendly letter; and am more pleased than I can well tell, to think that any thing I have written about the sea has at all responded to your own impressions of it. Were I inclined to undue vanity, this one fact would be far more to me than acres & square miles of the superficial shallow praise of the publishing critics. And I am specially delighted at the thought, that those strange, congenial feelings, with which after my first voyage, I for the first time read "Two Years Before the Mast", and while so engaged was, as it were, tied & welded to you by a sort of Siamese link of affectionate sympathy— ——that these

1. Greek city plundered and burned by the Romans in 146 B.C.E.
2. A diamond cut according to an elaborate system—two rows of rhomboidal and three rows of triangular facets above and below the girdle (the widest part).

feelings should be reciprocated by you, in your turn, and be called out by any White Jackets or Redburns of mine—this is indeed delightful to me. In fact, My Dear Dana, did I not write these books of mine almost entirely for "lucre"—by the job, as a woodsawyer saws wood—I almost think, I should hereafter—in the case of a sea book—get my M.S.S. neatly & legibly copied by a scrivener—send you that one copy—& deem such a procedure the best publication. * * *

About the "whaling voyage"—I am half way in the work, & am very glad that your suggestion so jumps with mine.[1] It will be a strange sort of a book, tho', I fear; blubber is blubber you know; tho' you may get oil out of it, the poetry runs as hard as sap from a frozen maple tree;—& to cook the thing up, one must needs throw in a little fancy, which from the nature of the thing, must be ungainly as the gambols of the whales themselves. Yet I mean to give the truth of the thing, spite of this. * * *

To Richard Bentley

NEW YORK June 27, 1850

In the latter part of the coming autumn I shall have ready a new work;[2] and I write you now to propose its publication in England.

The book is a romance of adventure, founded upon certain wild legends in the Southern Sperm Whale Fisheries, and illustrated by the author's own personal experience, of two years & more, as a harpooneer.

Should you be inclined to undertake the book, I think that it will be worth to you £200.[3] Could you be positively put in possession of the copyright, it might be worth to you a larger sum—considering its great novelty; for I do not know that the subject treated of has ever been worked up by a romancer; or, indeed, by any writer, in any adequate manner. But as things are, I say £200, because that sum was given for "White-Jacket"; and it does not appear, as yet, that you have been interfeared with in your publication of that book; & therefore there seems reason to conclude, that, at £200, "White Jacket" must have been, in some degree, profitable to you.

In case of an arrangement, I shall, of course, put you in early & certain possession of the proof sheets, as in previous cases.

Being desirous of early arranging this matter in London,—so as to lose

---

1. Melville's first known reference to *Moby-Dick*, important for his estimate of his progress (he had been working on it almost three months, and the year before he had written two long books in a four-month stretch) and for his definition of the aesthetic challenge he was confronting (to present the reality of whaling and yet wring poetry from the unpromising material).
2. Although Melville expected to "have ready" by the autumn of 1850 the "romance of adventure" proposed in this letter, proofs of the American edition were not sent to Bentley until the next autumn—on September 10, 1851. Bentley published it with Melville's original title, *The Whale*, in October of 1851. The book made use of Melville's whaling experiences of "two years & more" (about twenty-six months) aboard three different whaleships—the *Acushnet*, the *Lucy Ann*, and the *Charles and Henry*—only on the last of which, for six months, was he possibly rated as a harpooneer (boatsteerer).
3. About one thousand dollars in 1850 money—enough to support a small family for half a year or more. It helps to envision what a few thousand dollars would buy. In 1850 Melville's Uncle Thomas's heirs sold the grand house and 250 acres south of Pittsfield (where the Melvilles spent the summer) to J. Rowland Morewood for sixty-five hundred dollars, the same price that Melville (or his father-in-law) paid for the contiguous Arrowhead, a rundown farmhouse with 160 acres.

no time, when the book has passed thro' the Harpers' press here—I beg, Mr Bentley, that you at once write me as to your views concerning it.

Circumstances make it indispensable, that if the book suits you at the sum above-named, that on the day of sale, you give your note for that sum—at four months say—to whomever I depute to ratify the arrangement with you. * * *

To Evert A. Duyckinck

ARROWHEAD December 13, 1850

Do you want to know how I pass my time?—I rise at eight—thereabouts—& go to my barn—say good-morning to the horse, & give him his breakfast. (It goes to my heart to give him a cold one, but it can't be helped) Then, pay a visit to my cow—cut up a pumpkin or two for her, & stand by to see her eat it—for it's a pleasant sight to see a cow move her jaws—she does it so mildly & with such a sanctity.——My own breakfast over, I go to my work-room & light my fire—then spread my M.S.S on the table—take one business squint at it, & fall to with a will. At 2½ P.M. I hear a preconcerted knock at my door, which (by request) continues till I rise & go to the door, which serves to wean me effectively from my writing, however interested I may be. My friends the horse & cow now demand their dinner—& I go & give it them. My own dinner over, I rig my sleigh & with my mother or sisters start off for the village—& if it be a Literary World[4] day, great is the satisfaction thereof.—My evenings I spend in a sort of mesmeric state in my room—not being able to read—only now & then skimming over some large-printed book.—Can you send me about fifty fast-writing youths, with an easy style & not averse to polishing their labors? If you can, I wish you would, because since I have been here I have planned about that number of future works & cant find enough time to think about them separately.—But I dont know but a book in a man's brain is better off than a book bound in calf—at any rate it is safer from criticism. And taking a book off the brain, is akin to the ticklish & dangerous business of taking an old painting off a panel—you have to scrape off the whole brain in order to get at it with due safety—& even then, the painting may not be worth the trouble.—— * * *

To Evert A. Duyckinck

ARROWHEAD February 12, 1851

"A dash of salt spray"![5]—where am I to get salt spray here in inland Pittsfield? I shall have to import it from foreign parts. All I now have to

---

4. That is, a day when the weekly *Literary World*, edited by Duyckinck and his brother George, would arrive from New York, usually on a Friday (if it was sent a day earlier than the date of the issue) or Saturday.
5. Duyckinck had asked Melville to contribute a nautical piece to *Holden's Dollar Magazine*, a monthly that he was now editing in addition to the weekly *Literary World*.

do with salt, is when I salt my horse & cow—not *salt them down*—I dont mean that (tho' indeed I have before now dined on "salt-horse") but when I give them their weekly salt, by way of seasoning all their week's meals in one prospective lump.

How shall a man go about refusing a man?[6]—Best be round-about, or plumb on the mark?——I can not write the thing you want. I am in the humor to lend a hand to a friend, if I can;—but I am not in the humor to write the kind of thing you need—and I am not in the humor to write for Holden's Magazine. If I were to go on to give you all my reasons—you would pronounce me a bore, so I will not do that. You must be content to beleive that I *have* reasons, or else I would not refuse so small a thing.— As for the Daguerreotype (I spell the word right from your sheet) that's what I can not send you, because I have none. And if I had, I would not send it for such a purpose, even to you.—Pshaw! you cry—& so cry I.— "This is intensified vanity, not true modesty or anything of that sort!"— Again, I say so too. But if it be so, how can I help it. The fact is, almost everybody is having his "mug" engraved nowadays; so that this test of distinction is getting to be reversed; and therefore, to see one's "mug" in a magazine, is presumptive evidence that he's a nobody. So being as vain a man as ever lived; & beleiving that my illustrious name is famous throughout the world—I respectfully decline being *oblivionated* by a Daguerretype (what a devel of an unspellable word!)

We are all queer customers, Mr Duyckinck, you, I, & every body else in the world. So if I here seem queer to you, be sure, I am not alone in my queerness, tho' it present itself at a different port, perhaps, from other people, since every one has his own distinct peculiarity. But I trust you take me aright. If you dont' I shall be sorry—that's all.

After a long procrastination, I drove down to see Mr Hawthorne a couple of weeks ago. I found him, of course, buried in snow; & the delightful scenery about him, all wrapped up & tucked away under a napkin, as it were. He was to have made me a day's visit, & I had promised myself much pleasure in getting him up in my snug room here, & discussing the Universe with a bottle of brandy & cigars. But he has not been able to come, owing to sickness in his family.—or else, he's up to the lips in the *Universe* again.

By the way, I have recently read his "Twice Told Tales"[7] (I had not read but a few of them before) I think they far exceed the "Mosses"—they are, I fancy, an earlier vintage from his vine. Some of those sketches are wonderfully subtle. Their deeper meanings are worthy of a Brahmin. Still there is something lacking—a good deal lacking—to the plump sphericity of the man. What is that?—He does'nt patronise the butcher—he needs roast-beef, done rare.—Nevertheless, for one, I regard Hawthorne (in his books) as evincing a quality of genius, immensely loftier, & more pro-

6. Duyckinck expected to include an engraving of Melville in an upcoming issue of *Holden's* as that month's literary personality. Melville's refusal seemed inexplicable to the editor, who enlisted Melville's formidable mother to try to make her son listen to reason. The upshot of Melville's refusal is that we have no reliable image of him until 1860, only a vague image in a painting made soon after the publication of *Typee*. Chapter 33 of *Moby-Dick* is the best explanation of Melville's seemingly perverse and ultimately suicidal attitude: he was one of God's true princes of the Empire, kept from the world's hustings.
7. Melville had borrowed *Twice-Told Tales* (1837) from Duyckinck in his busy (two-book) summer of 1849, and on January 22, 1851, received two inscribed copies from Hawthorne himself (first series, 1845, and vol. 2, second series, 1842). See Sealts, *Melville's Reading* (1988), nos. 258–60.

found, too, than any other American has shown hitherto in the printed form. Irving is a grasshopper to him—putting the *souls* of the two men together, I mean.[8]—But I must close. * * *

I am just on the point of starting a'foot for the village, and have glanced over the previous letter, before sealing.——I thought there seemed an unkindness in it—& that had I, under the circumstances, rec'd such a letter from you, in reply to such a letter as yours to me—I would deem it not well of you.—Still, I can't help it—and I may yet be of some better service to you than merely jotting a paragraph for Holden's. * * *

To Nathaniel Hawthorne

ARROWHEAD [April 16?], 1851

"The House of the Seven Gables: A Romance. By Nathaniel Hawthorne. One vol. 16mo, pp. 344."[9] The contents of this book do not belie its rich, clustering, romantic title. With great enjoyment we spent almost an hour in each separate gable. This book is like a fine old chamber, abundantly, but still judiciously, furnished with precisely that sort of furniture best fitted to furnish it. There are rich hangings, wherein are braided scenes from tragedies! There is old china with rare devices, set out on the carved buffet; there are long and indolent lounges to throw yourself upon; there is an admirable sideboard, plentifully stored with good viands; there is a smell as of old wine in the pantry; and finally, in one corner, there is a dark little black-letter volume in golden clasps, entitled "Hawthorne: A Problem." It has delighted us; it has piqued a reperusal; it has robbed us of a day, and made us a present of a whole year of thoughtfulness; it has bred great exhilaration and exultation with the remembrance that the architect of the Gables resides only six miles off, and not three thousand miles away, in England, say. We think the book, for pleasantness of running interest, surpasses the other works of the author. The curtains are more drawn; the sun comes in more; genialities peep out more. Were we to particularize what has most struck us in the deeper passages, we would point out the scene where Clifford, for a moment, would fain throw himself forth from the window to join the pro-

8. See the "Mosses" essay (p. 526 herein) for Melville's defying the dominant opinion that Irving was America's greatest writer. Long before this time Duyckinck may have learned of the distress the essay had caused Irving and his biographer-nephew Pierre.

9. On April 11, 1851, when Melville visited the Hawthornes at Lenox, Hawthorne gave him an inscribed copy of the newly published *The House of the Seven Gables*. In this letter Melville pretends to be reviewing it for an imaginary *Pittsfield Secret Review*. On May 7, Mrs. Hawthorne wrote her sister Elizabeth Peabody about the "review" and Melville's admiration for Hawthorne:

The fresh, sincere, glowing mind that utters it is in a state of "fluid consciousness," & to Mr Hawthorne speaks his innermost about GOD, the Devil & Life if so be he can get at the Truth—for he is a boy in opinion—having settled nothing yet—informe—ingens—& it would betray him to make public his confessions & efforts to grasp—because they would be considered perhaps impious, if one did not take in the whole scope of the case. Nothing pleases me better than to sit & hear this growing man dash his tumultuous waves of thought up against Mr Hawthorne's great, genial, comprehending silences—out of the profound of which a wonderful smile, or one powerful word sends back the foam & fury into a peaceful booming, calm—or perchance, not into a calm—but a murmuring expostulation—for there is never a "mush of concession" in him—Yet such a love & reverence & admiration for Mr Hawthorne as is really beautiful to witness.

cession; or the scene where the Judge is left seated in his ancestral chair. Clifford is full of an awful truth throughout. He is conceived in the finest, truest spirit. He is no caricature. He is Clifford. And here we would say that, did circumstances permit, we should like nothing better than to devote an elaborate and careful paper to the full consideration and analysis of the purport and significance of what so strongly characterizes all of this author's writings. There is a certain tragic phase of humanity which, in our opinion, was never more powerfully embodied than by Hawthorne. We mean the tragicalness of human thought in its own unbiassed, native, and profounder workings. We think that into no recorded mind has the intense feeling of the visable truth ever entered more deeply than into this man's. By visable truth, we mean the apprehension of the absolute condition of present things as they strike the eye of the man who fears them not, though they do their worst to him,—the man who, like Russia or the British Empire, declares himself a sovereign nature (in himself) amid the powers of heaven, hell, and earth. He may perish; but so long as he exists he insists upon treating with all Powers upon an equal basis. If any of those other Powers choose to withhold certain secrets, let them; that does not impair my sovereignty in myself; that does not make me tributary. And perhaps, after all, there is *no* secret. We incline to think that the Problem of the Universe is like the Freemason's mighty secret, so terrible to all children. It turns out, at last, to consist in a triangle, a mallet, and an apron,—nothing more! We incline to think that God cannot explain His own secrets, and that He would like a little information upon certain points Himself. We mortals astonish Him as much as He us. But it is this *Being* of the matter; there lies the knot with which we choke ourselves. As soon as you say *Me, a God, a Nature*, so soon you jump off from your stool and hang from the beam. Yes, that word is the hangman. Take God out of the dictionary, and you would have Him in the street.

There is the grand truth about Nathaniel Hawthorne. He says NO! in thunder; but the Devil himself cannot make him say *yes*. For all men who say *yes*, lie; and all men who say *no*,—why, they are in the happy condition of judicious, unincumbered travellers in Europe; they cross the frontiers into Eternity with nothing but a carpet-bag,—that is to say, the Ego. Whereas those *yes*-gentry, they travel with heaps of baggage, and, damn them! they will never get through the Custom House. What's the reason, Mr. Hawthorne, that in the last stages of metaphysics a fellow always falls to *swearing* so? I could rip an hour. You see, I began with a little criticism extracted for your benefit from the "Pittsfield Secret Review," and here I have landed in Africa.

Walk down one of these mornings and see me. No nonsense; come. Remember me to Mrs. Hawthorne and the children.

H. Melville.

P.S. The marriage of Phoebe with the daguerreotypist is a fine stroke, because of his turning out to be a *Maule*.[1] If you pass Hepzibah's cent-shop, buy me a Jim Crow (fresh) and send it to me by Ned Higgins.

---

1. In his reference to characters in *The House of the Seven Gables* Melville puns on the name of one of them (Maule) and the hammer-like tool (maul).

To Nathaniel Hawthorne

ARROWHEAD Early May 1851[2]

I should have been rumbling down to you in my pine-board chariot a long time ago, were it not that for some weeks past I have been more busy than you can well imagine,—out of doors,—building and patching and tinkering away in all directions. Besides, I had my crops to get in,— corn and potatoes (I hope to show you some famous ones by and by),— and many other things to attend to, all accumulating upon this one particular season. I work myself; and at night my bodily sensations are akin to those I have so often felt before, when a hired man, doing my day's work from sun to sun. But I mean to continue visiting you until you tell me that my visits are both supererogatory and superfluous. With no son of man do I stand upon any etiquette or ceremony, except the Christian ones of charity and honesty. I am told, my fellow-man, that there is an aristocracy of the brain. Some men have boldly advocated and asserted it. Schiller seems to have done so, though I don't know much about him.[3] At any rate, it is true that there have been those who, while earnest in behalf of political equality, still accept the intellectual estates. And I can well perceive, I think, how a man of superior mind can, by its intense cultivation, bring himself, as it were, into a certain spontaneous aristocracy of feeling,—exceedingly nice and fastidious,—similar to that which, in an English Howard,[4] conveys a torpedo-fish thrill at the slightest contact with a social plebeian. So, when you see or hear of my ruthless democracy on all sides, you may possibly feel a touch of a shrink, or something of that sort. It is but nature to be shy of a mortal who boldly declares that a thief in jail is as honorable a personage as Gen. George Washington. This is ludicrous. But Truth is the silliest thing under the sun. Try to get a living by the Truth—and go to the Soup Societies. Heavens! Let any clergyman try to preach the Truth from its very stronghold, the pulpit, and they would ride him out of his church on his own pulpit bannister. It can hardly be doubted that all Reformers are bottomed upon the truth, more or less; and to the world at large are not reformers almost universally laughing-stocks? Why so? Truth is ridiculous to men. Thus easily in my room here do I, conceited and garrulous, reverse the test of my Lord Shaftesbury.[5]

2. Redated from June 1?, 1851, by Parker (1.841–44). The complicated evidence turns on a previously unknown letter Melville's copyist-sister Augusta Melville wrote her brother Allan on May 16, 1850, a letter deposited at Arrowhead by Anna Morewood a few years before her death in the 1990s. She was the widow of Henry Gansevoort Morewood (much older than she) and the daughter-in-law of Allan's daughter Maria (Milie), born in February 1849.
3. Melville seems to have had in mind the quality pointed out in Menzel's criticism of Schiller as quoted by Longfellow in *The Poets and Poetry of Europe* (1845, 308):

   We turn now to the second secret of the beauty belonging to Schiller's ideal characters. This is their nobleness, —their honorableness. His heroes and heroines never discredit the pride and dignity which announce a loftier nature; and all their outward acts bear the stamp of magnanimity and inborn nobleness. Its perfect opposite is the vulgar character, and that conventional spirit which serves for a bridle and leading-strings to the vulgar nature.

4. Among English families, the Howards had long held first place, its head being the duke of Norfolk. See *Moby-Dick*, ch. 89.
5. Shaftesbury maintained that one test of truth was its power to survive ridicule. "Truth," he wrote in "An Essay on the Freedom of Wit and Humour,"

It seems an inconsistency to assert unconditional democracy in all things, and yet confess a dislike to all mankind—in the mass. But not so.—But it's an endless sermon,—no more of it. I began by saying that the reason I have not been to Lenox is this,—in the evening I feel completely done up, as the phrase is, and incapable of the long jolting to get to your house and back. In a week or so, I go to New York, to bury myself in a third-story room, and work and slave on my "Whale" while it is driving through the press. *That* is the only way I can finish it now,—I am so pulled hither and thither by circumstances. The calm, the coolness, the silent grass-growing mood in which a man *ought* always to compose,—that, I fear, can seldom be mine. Dollars damn me; and the malicious Devil is forever grinning in upon me, holding the door ajar. My dear Sir, a presentiment is on me,—I shall at last be worn out and perish, like an old nutmeg-grater, grated to pieces by the constant attrition of the wood, that is, the nutmeg. What I feel most moved to write, that is banned,—it will not pay. Yet, altogether, write the *other* way I cannot. So the product is a final hash, and all my books are botches. I'm rather sore, perhaps, in this letter; but see my hand!—four blisters on this palm, made by hoes and hammers within the last few days. It is a rainy morning; so I am indoors, and all work suspended. I feel cheerfully disposed, and therefore I write a little bluely. Would the Gin were here! If ever, my dear Hawthorne, in the eternal times that are to come, you and I shall sit down in Paradise, in some little shady corner by ourselves; and if we shall by any means be able to smuggle a basket of champagne there (I won't believe in a Temperance Heaven), and if we shall then cross our celestial legs in the celestial grass that is forever tropical, and strike our glasses and our heads together, till both musically ring in concert,—then, O my dear fellow-mortal, how shall we pleasantly discourse of all the things manifold which now so distress us,—when all the earth shall be but a reminiscence, yea, its final dissolution an antiquity. Then shall songs be composed as when wars are over; humorous, comic songs,—"Oh, when I lived in that queer little hole called the world," or, "Oh, when I toiled and sweated below," or, "Oh, when I knocked and was knocked in the fight"—yes, let us look forward to such things. Let us swear that, though now we sweat, yet it is because of the dry heat which is indispensable to the nourishment of the vine which is to bear the grapes that are to give us the champagne hereafter.

But I was talking about the "Whale." As the fishermen say, "he's in his flurry" when I left him some three weeks ago. I'm going to take him by his jaw, however, before long, and finish him up in some fashion or other.

'tis supposed, may bear *all* Lights: and *one* of those principal Lights or natural Mediums, by which Things are to be view'd, in order to a thorow Recognition, is *Ridicule* itself, or that Manner of Proof by which we discern whatever is liable to just Raillery in any Subject. So much, at least, is allow'd by All, who at any time appeal to this *Criterion*. The gravest Gentlemen, even in the gravest Subjects, are suppos'd to acknowledge this: and can have no Right, 'tis thought, to deny others Freedom of this Appeal; whilst they are free to censure like other Men, and in their gravest Arguments make no scruple to ask, *Is it not ridiculous? Characteristicks of Men, Manners, Opinions, Times* (1737, 6th ed., 1.161).

He cites too, the fact that Socrates' character and doctrines seemed only the more "solid and just" after they had "stood the Proof" of Aristophanes' ridicule (1.31). But whereas Shaftesbury is saying that you can know a thing is true if it survives ridicule, Melville is saying that you can know a thing is true because it is considered ridiculous. Melville is reversing Shaftesbury's test. Julian Hawthorne had printed "revere," not "reverse."

What's the use of elaborating what, in its very essence, is so short-lived as a modern book? Though I wrote the Gospels in this century, I should die in the gutter.—I talk all about myself, and this is selfishness and egotism. Granted. But how help it? I am writing to you; I know little about you, but something about myself. So I write about myself,—at least, to you. Don't trouble yourself, though, about writing; and don't trouble yourself about visiting; and when you *do* visit, don't trouble yourself about talking. I will do all the writing and visiting and talking myself.—By the way, in the last "Dollar Magazine" I read "The Unpardonable Sin."[6] He was a sad fellow, that Ethan Brand. I have no doubt you are by this time responsible for many a shake and tremor of the tribe of "general readers." It is a frightful poetical creed that the cultivation of the brain eats out the heart. But it's my *prose* opinion that in most cases, in those men who have fine brains and work them well, the heart extends down to hams. And though you smoke them with the fire of tribulation, yet, like veritable hams, the head only gives the richer and the better flavor. I stand for the heart. To the dogs with the head! I had rather be a fool with a heart, than Jupiter Olympus with his head. The reason the mass of men fear God, and *at bottom dislike* Him, is because they rather distrust His heart, and fancy Him all brain like a watch. (You perceive I employ a capital initial in the pronoun referring to the Diety; don't you think there is a slight dash of flunkeyism in that usage?) Another thing. I was in New York for four-and-twenty hours the other day, and saw a portrait of N. H. And I have seen and heard many flattering (in a publisher's point of view) allusions to the "Seven Gables." And I have seen "Tales," and "A New Volume" announced, by N. H.[7] So upon the whole, I say to myself, this N. H. is in the ascendant. My dear Sir, they begin to patronize. All Fame is patronage. Let me be infamous: there is no patronage in *that*. What "reputation" H. M. has is horrible. Think of it! To go down to posterity is bad enough, any way; but to go down as a "man who lived among the cannibals"! When I speak of posterity, in reference to myself, I only mean the babies who will probably be born in the moment immediately ensuing upon my giving up the ghost. I shall go down to some of them, in all likelihood. "Typee" will be given to them, perhaps, with their gingerbread. I have come to regard this matter of Fame as the most transparent of all vanities. I read Solomon more and more, and every time see deeper and deeper and unspeakable meanings in him. I did not think of Fame, a year ago, as I do now. My development has been all within a few years past. I am like one of those seeds taken out of the Egyptian Pyramids, which, after being three thousand years a seed and nothing but a seed, being planted in English soil, it developed itself, grew to greenness, and then fell to mould.[8] So I. Until I was twenty-five, I had no development at all. From my twenty-fifth year I date my life. Three weeks have scarcely passed, at any time between then and now, that

---

6. Hawthorne's story had been reprinted in *Holden's Dollar Magazine* for May 1851.
7. Melville may have seen any one of a number of Hawthorne portraits, possibly the 1850 one by Cephas Thompson (see *Correspondence*, 188–89). Announcements of Hawthorne's forthcoming books appeared in the *Literary World* and elsewhere during and after May 1851.
8. At about this time, the English novelist G. P. R. James carried on an experiment at Stockbridge south of Pittsfield of planting some Egyptian wheat seed taken from the inside of a mummy case. His son, Charles Leigh James described the planting, saw it come up, and observed that "it did not seed 'worth a continental.'" See S. M. Ellis, *The Solitary Horseman, or the Life and Adventures of G. P. R. James*, as cited in *American Notes and Queries* 7 (December 1947), 41.

I have not unfolded within myself. But I feel that I am now come to the inmost leaf of the bulb, and that shortly the flower must fall to the mould. It seems to me now that Solomon was the truest man who ever spoke,[9] and yet that he a little *managed* the truth with a view to popular conservatism; or else there have been many corruptions and interpolations of the text—In reading some of Goethe's sayings, so worshipped by his votaries, I came across this, "*Live in the all.*" That is to say, your separate identity is but a wretched one,—good; but get out of yourself, spread and expand yourself, and bring to yourself the tinglings of life that are felt in the flowers and the woods, that are felt in the planets Saturn and Venus, and the Fixed Stars. What nonsense! Here is a fellow with a raging toothache. "My dear boy," Goethe says to him, "you are sorely afflicted with that tooth; but you must *live in the all,* and then you will be happy!" As with all great genius, there is an immense deal of flummery in Goethe, and in proportion to my own contact with him, a monstrous deal of it in me.[1]

H. Melville

P.S. "Amen!" saith Hawthorne.

N.B. This "all" feeling, though, there is some truth in. You must often have felt it, lying on the grass on a warm summer's day. Your legs seem to send out shoots into the earth. Your hair feels like leaves upon your head. This is the *all* feeling. But what plays the mischief with the truth is that men will insist upon the universal application of a temporary feeling or opinion.

P.S. You must not fail to admire my discretion in paying the postage on this letter.

To Nathaniel Hawthorne

ARROWHEAD June 29, 1851

The clear air and open window invite me to write to you. For some time past I have been so busy with a thousand things that I have almost forgotten when I wrote you last, and whether I received an answer. This most

---

9. See *Moby-Dick* (ch. 96): "The truest of all men was the Man of Sorrows, and the truest of all books is Solomon's, and Ecclesiastes is the fine hammered steel of woe. 'All is vanity.' ALL. This wilful world hath not got hold of unchristian Solomon's wisdom yet."

1. Melville's exact source remains to be discovered. The idea is general in Goethe; the particular thought is doubtless a translation of a phrase in stanza four of "Generalbeichte":

> Willst du Absolution
> Deinen Treuen geben,
> Wollen wir nach deinem Wink
> Unablässlich streben,
> Uns von Halben zu entwohnen
> Und in Ganzen, Guten, Schönen
> Resolut zu leben.

Carlyle, in whom Melville was well read, translates it "To live . . . in the Whole."(Death of Goethe," *Critical and Miscellaneous Essays*, 1839, 3, 205), and John S. Dwight renders it "living" "In the Whole" (George Ripley, ed., *Specimens of Foreign Standard Literature*, Vol. 3, *Select Minor Poems from the German of Goethe and Schiller*, 1839, 48). One of Ripley's notes on Goethe may have helped give currency to the idea Melville was lampooning: "Total occupation of himself, heart and soul, in the subject nearest him,—living *in* it, and identifying himself with it for the time,— left no room for sick yearnings, made each little sphere a world, each moment an eternity. This is evidently what he meant by 'Living in the Whole,' by finding 'All in One, and One in All'" (365).

persuasive season has now for weeks recalled me from certain crotchetty and over doleful chimearas, the like of which men like you and me and some others, forming a chain of God's posts round the world, must be content to encounter now and then, and fight them the best way we can. But come they will,—for, in the boundless, trackless, but still glorious wild wilderness through which these outposts run, the Indians do sorely abound, as well as the insignificant but still stinging mosquitoes. Since you have been here, I have been building some shanties of houses (connected with the old one) and likewise some shanties of chapters and essays. I have been plowing and sowing and raising and painting and printing and praying,—and now begin to come out upon a less bustling time, and to enjoy the calm prospect of things from a fair piazza at the north of the old farm house here.

Not entirely yet, though, am I without something to be urgent with. The "Whale" is only half through the press; for, wearied with the long delay of the printers, and disgusted with the heat and dust of the babylonish brick-kiln of New York, I came back to the country to feel the grass—and end the book reclining on it, if I may.—I am sure you will pardon this speaking all about myself,—for if I *say* so much on that head, be sure all the rest of the world are thinking about themselves ten times as much. Let us speak, though we show all our faults and weaknesses,—for it is a sign of strength to be weak, to know it, and out with it,—not in set way and ostentatiously, though, but incidentally and without premeditation.—But I am falling into my old foible—preaching. I am busy, but shall not be very long. Come and spend a day here, if you can and want to; if not, stay in Lenox, and God give you long life. When I am quite free of my present engagements, I am going to treat myself to a ride and a visit to you. Have ready a bottle of brandy, because I always feel like drinking that heroic drink when we talk ontological heroics together. This is rather a crazy letter in some respects, I apprehend. If so, ascribe it to the intoxicating effects of the latter end of June operating upon a very susceptible and peradventure feeble temperament.

Shall I send you a fin of the *Whale* by way of a specimen mouthful? The tail is not yet cooked—though the hell-fire in which the whole book is broiled might not unreasonably have cooked it all ere this. This is the book's motto (the secret one),—Ego non baptiso te in nomine—but make out the rest yourself.[2]

---

2. Melville's diabolical baptismal formula at the end of this letter appears in fuller form in *Moby-Dick*, ch. 113, when Captain Ahab uses the blood of the pagan harpooneers to baptize the harpoon with which he plans to kill the white whale, declaring: "Ego non baptizo te in nomine patris, sed in nomine diaboli!" It also appears in more detail among the notes that Melville jotted in the back of the seventh volume of his set of Shakespeare. See p. 582 herein for Geoffrey Sanborn's discovery of Melville's source for the Latin formula, a magazine article on witch hunting; and see Parker (1.847) for an interpretation of Melville's notes as indicating that he saw some of his religious reviewers as witch hunters and identified himself with those persecuted and killed as witches.

To Richard Bentley

ARROWHEAD July 20, 1851

I promptly received your note of the 3ᵈ Inst: in reply to mine concerning the publication of my new book.

I accept your offer for the work;[3] but not without strong hope that before long, we shall be able to treat upon a firmer basis than now, & heretofore; & that with the more assurance you will be disposed to make overtures for American books. And here let me say to you,—since you are peculiarly interested in the matter—that in all reasonable probability no International Copyright will ever be obtained—in our time, at least—if you Englishmen wait at all for the first step to be taken in this country. Who have any motive in this country to bestir themselves in this thing? Only the authors.—Who are the authors?—A handful. And what influence have they to bring to bear upon any question whose settlement must necessarily assume a political form?—They can bring scarcely any influence whatever. This country & nearly all its affairs are governed by sturdy backwoodsmen—noble fellows enough, but not at all literary, & who care not a fig for any authors except those who write those most saleable of all books nowadays—ie—the newspapers, & magazines. And tho' the number of cultivated, catholic men, who may be supposed to feel an interest in a national literature, is large & every day growing larger; yet they are nothing in comparison with the overwhelming majority who care nothing about it. This country is at present engaged in furnishing material for future authors; not in encouraging its living ones.

Nevertheless, if this matter by any means comes to be made nationally conspicuous; and if you in England come out magnanimously, & protect a foreign author; then there is that sort of stuff in the people here, which will be sure to make them all eagerness in reciprocating. For, be assured, that my countrymen will never be outdone in generosity.—Therefore, if you desire an International Copyright—hoist your flag on your side of the water, & the signal will be answered; but look for no flag on this side till then.

I am now passing thro' the press, the closing sheets of my new work; so that I shall be able to forward it to you in the course of two or three weeks— perhaps a little longer. I shall forward it to you thro' the Office of the Legation. And upon your receipt of it, I suppose you will immediately proceed to printing; as, of course, publication will not take place here, till you have made yourself safe.—You say you will give me your notes at three & six months; I infer that this means from the time of receiving the book. * * *

To Nathaniel Hawthorne

ARROWHEAD July 22, 1851

This is not a letter, or even a note—but only a passing word said to you over your garden gate. I thank you for your easy-flowing long letter

---

3. Bentley had made a generous offer, £150.

(received yesterday) which flowed through me, and refreshed all my meadows, as the Housatonic—opposite me—does in reality. I am now busy with various things—not incessantly though; but enough to require my frequent tinkerings; and this is the height of the haying season, and my nag is dragging me home his winter's dinners all the time. And so, one way and another, I am not yet a disengaged man; but shall be, very soon. Meantime, the earliest good chance I get, I shall roll down to you.

My dear fellow-being, we—that is, you and I—must hit upon some little bit of vagabondism, before Autumn comes. Graylock—we must go and vagabondize there. But ere we start we must dig a deep hole and bury all the Blue Devils,[4] there to abide till the Last Day. * * *

To Sarah Huyler Morewood

ARROWHEAD September 12 [or 19?], 1851

* * * The "Hour & the Man" is exceedingly acceptable to me. "Zanoni" is a very fine book in very fine print—but I shall endeavor to surmount that difficulty. At present, however, the Fates have plunged me into certain silly thoughts and wayward speculations,[5] which will prevent me, for a time, from falling into the reveries of these books—for a fine book is a sort of revery to us—is it not?—So I shall regard them as my Paradise in store, & Mrs Morewood the goddess from whom it comes.

To Evert A. Duyckinck

ARROWHEAD November 7, 1851

Your letter received last night had a sort of stunning effect on me.[6] For some days past being engaged in the woods with axe, wedge, & beetle,[7] the Whale had almost completely slipped me for the time (& I was the merrier for it) when Crash! comes Moby Dick himself (as you justly say) & reminds me of what I have been about for part of the last year or two. It is really & truly a surprising coincidence—to say the least. I make no doubt it is Moby Dick himself, for there is no account of his capture after the sad fate of the Pequod about fourteen years ago.—Ye Gods! What a Commentator is this Ann Alexander whale. What he has to say is short & pithy & very much to the point. I wonder if my evil art has raised this monster.

The Behrings Straits Disaster, too, & the cording along the New Foundland coast of those scores & scores of fishermen, and the inland gales on

---

4. The blues, or hypos, such as Ishmael feels at the start of "Loomings."
5. The "silly thoughts and wayward speculations" concerned his next book, *Pierre*. Mrs. Morewood's gifts were Harriet Martineau's *The Hour and the Man* (1841) and Edward George Bulwer-Lytton's *Zanoni* (1842).
6. Duyckinck had sent Melville a clipping about the sinking of the *Ann Alexander* by a whale off Chile, a sensation especially in the largest whaling states of New York and Massachusetts. The news arrived in the United States in a copy of the Panama *Herald* of October 16, 1851 (see Parker 1. 877–78 and *Correspondence* 208).
7. A heavy hammering tool, like a maul.

the Lakes. Verily the pot boileth inside & out. And woe unto us, we but live in the days that have been. Yet even then they found time to be jolly. Why did'nt you send me that inestimable item of "Herman de Wardt" before?[8] Oh had I but had that pie to cut into! But that & many other fine things doubtless are omitted. All one can do is to pick up what chips he can buy round him. They have no Vatican[9] (as you have) in Pittsfield here.

* * *

To Nathaniel Hawthorne

ARROWHEAD November 17, 1851

Your letter[1] was handed me last night on the road going to Mr. More-wood's, and I read it there. Had I been at home, I would have sat down at once and answered it. In me divine magnanimities are spontaneous and instantaneous—catch them while you can. The world goes round, and the other side comes up. So now I can't write what I felt. But I felt pantheistic then—your heart beat in my ribs and mine in yours, and both in God's. A sense of unspeakable security is in me this moment, on account of your having understood the book. I have written a wicked book, and feel spotless as the lamb. Ineffable socialities are in me. I would sit down and dine with you and all the gods in old Rome's Pantheon. It is a strange feeling—no hopefulness is in it, no despair. Content—that is it; and irresponsibility; but without licentious inclination. I speak now of my profoundest sense of being, not of an incidental feeling.

Whence come you, Hawthorne? By what right do you drink from my flagon of life? And when I put it to my lips—lo, they are yours and not mine. I feel that the Godhead is broken up like the bread at the Supper, and that we are the pieces. Hence this infinite fraternity of feeling. Now, sympathizing with the paper, my angel turns over another page. You did

8. Duyckinck's second enclosure about "Herman [*possibly* Norman] de Wardt" is unidentified. Leyda conjectured an allusion to Wynkyn de Worde's *The Boke of Keruynge* (*Log* 1.431) a 1508 book on carving that includes a brief instruction about whalemeat, which would fit with Melville's comment that he wanted to "cut into" it (de Worde's book was not reprinted until 1867, however). Whatever the inestimable item was, it clearly contained some more of the sort of "random allusions to whales" Melville had been accumulating for his "Extracts" at the start of *Moby-Dick*.
9. Library. Duyckinck's great book collection went largely to the New York Public Library, where it was dispersed. His manuscript material, kept more nearly intact, has proved inexhaustible. As late as 1990 Parker found an unknown Melville letter in a folder of undated letters from unidentified correspondents, and long-printed texts of some documents still contain mistranscriptions.
1. The biographical context of this letter is outlined in *Correspondence* (210–11), and more fully detailed in ch. 1 of Parker's second volume. From evidence in a letter and in a newspaper article, we now know that Melville and Hawthorne had met twice that month, first on November 4 at the house in Lenox of the lawyer Charles Sedgwick, then at the Little Red Inn in Lenox, around November 14, when Melville gave Hawthorne the copy of *Moby-Dick*, which he read at once, despite the confusion of packing up for a move to the eastern part of the state, and wrote Melville about. Melville later destroyed Hawthorne's letter and the presentation copy of *Moby-Dick* was lost before or during the Hawthornes' long stay in England and Italy beginning in 1853. Parker's first volume concludes with the scene in which the two men sit all alone together through an early afternoon in the dining room at the Little Red Inn, where a writer in a newspaper said they were a source of great amusement to the Lenox gawkers, who thought the two reclusive celebrities had chosen this odd way of getting acquainted (it not being the custom for people living locally to dine at the hotel). Hawthorne knew the publication of *Moby-Dick* was imminent, but the dedication was an astounding surprise. The men had taken farewell of each other, the presentation copy of *Moby-Dick* before them, only two or three or four days before Melville received Hawthorne's praise-filled letter (see Parker 1. 879–83).

not care a penny for the book. But, now and then as you read, you understood the pervading thought that impelled the book—and that you praised. Was it not so? You were archangel enough to despise the imperfect body, and embrace the soul. Once you hugged the ugly Socrates because you saw the flame in the mouth, and heard the rushing of the demon,—the familiar,—and recognized the sound; for you have heard it in your own solitudes.

My dear Hawthorne, the atmospheric skepticisms steal into me now, and make me doubtful of my sanity in writing you thus. But, believe me, I am not mad, most noble Festus! But truth is ever incoherent, and when the big hearts strike together, the concussion is a little stunning. Farewell. Don't write a word about the book.[2] That would be robbing me of my miserly delight. I am heartily sorry I ever wrote anything about you—it was paltry. Lord, when shall we be done growing? As long as we have anything more to do, we have done nothing. So, now, let us add Moby Dick to our blessing, and step from that. Leviathan is not the biggest fish;—I have heard of Krakens.[3]

This is a long letter, but you are not at all bound to answer it. Possibly, if you do answer it, and direct it to Herman Melville, you will missend it— for the very fingers that now guide this pen are not precisely the same that just took it up and put it on this paper. Lord, when shall we be done changing? Ah! it's a long stage, and no inn in sight, and night coming, and the body cold. But with you for a passenger, I am content and can be happy. I shall leave the world, I fell, with more satisfaction for having come to know you. Knowing you persuades me more than the Bible of our immortality.

2. Hawthorne had offered to review *Moby-Dick*—just as Melville had written on *Mosses from an Old Manse* in the *Literary World*. Following Melville's directive, Hawthorne did not—although he wrote to Duyckinck on December 1, 1851: "What a book Melville has written! It gives me an idea of much greater power than his preceding ones. It hardly seemed to me that the review of it, in the *Literary World* [November 15 and 22], did justice to its best points" (*Letters, 1843–1853*, edited by Thomas Woodson, L. Neal Smith, and Norman Holmes Pearson, 1985, 508). *Festus:* Melville defends the "gibberish" (below) of his letter with his biblical reference to Festus: "And as he thus spake for himself, Festus said with a loud voice, Paul, thou art beside thyself; much learning doth make thee mad. But he said, I am not mad, most noble Festus; but speak forth the words of truth and soberness" (Acts 26.24–25).
3. A reference to *Pierre*, which he was envisioning as more profound than *Moby-Dick*. How Melville could have thought so has proved difficult for critics to understand, primarily because what he had in mind and on his writing desk at this time was not the book that was published in 1852. As Melville completed it at the end of December 1851, *Pierre* was the tragic story of the psychological awakening of a youthful idealist who makes the grotesque mistake of trying to put Christian principles into practice. In New York City, bolstered by hostile reviews and weak sales of *Moby-Dick*, the Harpers offered Melville an insulting and ruinous contract—twenty cents on the dollar after they had recouped their costs on the old basis of fifty cents on the dollar. Only then did Melville write into the manuscript a transparently autobiographical and ultimately suicidal account of his career. See Parker's introduction in the reconstruction of the "Kraken Edition" of *Pierre* (1995, xi–xlvi), notable for the illustrations by Maurice Sendak. The dust-jacket copy contains this hopeful passage: "*Moby-Dick* and the reconstructed *Pierre* are at last revealed as complexly interlinked companion studies of the moods of thought—the *Typee* and *Omoo* of depth psychology * * * Not offered as 'definitive' but as supplementary to the standard Northwestern-Newberry text, this edition of *Pierre* is a close approximation of what Melville in a letter to Hawthorne alluded to as his "kraken" book, grander than the book whose original title was *The Whale*, just as the legendary krakens were more awesome than sperm whales." See p. 720 herein.

　Melville bids Hawthorne farewell because the Hawthornes were all but gone: they took the train in Pittsfield on November 21 in a fierce snow storm, never to return to the Berkshires. Melville's "endless riband" postscript echoes his May 1, 1850, letter to Dana, in which he imagined writing only for him and spoke of feeling "welded" to him by a "Siamese link of affectionate sympathy." His intellectual, psychological, and aesthetic growth in a year and a half is measured by the two ideal readers he envisioned.

What a pity, that, for your plain, bluff letter, you should get such gibberish! Mention me to Mrs. Hawthorne and to the children, and so, good-
by to you, with my blessing.

Herman.

I can't stop yet. If the world was entirely made up of Magians, I'll tell
you what I should do. I should have a paper-mill established at one end
of the house, and so have an endless riband of foolscap rolling in upon my
desk; and upon that endless riband I should write a thousand—a million—billion thoughts, all under the form of a letter to you. The divine
magnet is in you, and my magnet responds. Which is the biggest? A foolish question—they are *One*.

H.

Don't think that by writing me a letter, you shall always be bored with
an immediate reply to it—and so keep both of us delving over a writing-
desk eternally. No such thing! I sha'n't always answer your letters, and you
may do just as you please.

To Sophia Peabody Hawthorne

NEW YORK CITY January 8, 1852

I have hunted up the finest Bath I could find, gilt-edged and stamped,
whereon to inscribe my humble acknowledgement of your highly flattering letter of the 29th Dec.[4] It really amazed me that you should find any
satisfaction in that book. It is true that some *men* have said they were
pleased with it, but you are the only *woman*—for as a general thing,
women have small taste for the sea. But, then, since you, with your spir-
itualizing nature, see more things than other people, and by the same
process, refine all you see, so that they are not the same things that other
people see, but things which while you think you but humbly discover
them, you do in fact create them for yourself—therefore, upon the whole,
I do not so much marvel at your expressions concerning Moby Dick. At
any rate, your allusion for example to the "Spirit Spout" first showed to
me that there was a subtle significance in that thing—but I did not, in
that case, *mean* it. I had some vague idea while writing it, that the whole
book was susceptible of an allegoric construction, & also that *parts* of it
were—but the speciality of many of the particular subordinate allegories,
were first revealed to me, after reading Mr Hawthorne's letter, which,

4. Sophia Hawthorne's letter was delayed by being forwarded to Melville from Pittsfield to New
York, where he had gone with the completed manuscript of *Pierre* in its short form, without the
sections on the hero as an author. Characteristically, Melville kept his distress out of his reply,
but he may already have begun making his interpolations into the manuscript, knowing if not
admitting that his career as a book writer might be over. Mrs. Hawthorne's admiration for
Melville was firmly grounded in the fact that at times he had spoken almost as glowingly about
her husband as she always did. Two letters newly acquired by Stanford University demonstrate
the profundity of Sophia Hawthorne's interest in Melville during 1852, months after she had read
Moby-Dick, both as a young admirer of her husband and as himself a man of incalculable qualities. For his part, Melville was rather too appreciative of Sophia as a literary-minded woman,
unlike his own wife; Melville's sister Augusta quoted him on the Hawthornes in a letter to their
sister Helen on January 24, 1851 (New York Public Library, Gansevoort-Lansing): "Herman says
that they are the loveliest family he ever met with, or anyone can possibly imagine."

without citing any particular examples, yet intimated the part-&-parcel allegoricalness of the whole.—But, My Dear Lady, I shall not again send you a bowl of salt water. The next chalice I shall commend, will be a rural bowl of milk. * * *[5]

Now, Madam, had you not said anything about Moby Dick, & had Mr Hawthorne been equally silent, then had I said perhaps, something to both of you about another Wonder-(-full) Book.[6] But as it is, I must be silent. How is it, that while all of us human beings are so entirely disembarrassed in censuring a person; that so soon as we would praise, then we begin to feel awkward? I never blush after denouncing a man: but I grow scarlet, after eulogizing him. And yet this is all wrong; and yet we can't help it; and so we see how true was that musical sentence of the poet when he sang—"We can't help ourselves"

For tho' we know what we ought to be; & what it would be very sweet & beautiful to be; yet we can't be it. That is most sad, too. Life is a long Dardenelles,[7] My Dear Madam, the shores whereof are bright with flowers, which we want to pluck, but the bank is too high; & so we float on & on, hoping to come to a landing-place at last—but swoop! we launch into the great sea! Yet the geographers say, even then we must not despair, because across the great sea, however desolate & vacant it may look, lie all Persia & the delicious lands roundabout Damascus.

So wishing you a pleasant voyage at last to that sweet & far countree— * * *

---

5. Melville knew that Sophia Hawthorne knew that the chalice commended in *Macbeth* (1.7.11) was a "poison'd" one; the rural bowl of milk was *Pierre*, a book set perhaps almost entirely in the country, before this week of January, when he began enlarging it with the Pierre-as-author sections—but it was first completed as a book of ambiguous psychological depths, not a tale of innocent rustics at work and play, as Melville was ironically implying.

6. On November 7, 1851, while still in Lenox, Hawthorne had sent a copy of his new *A Wonder Book for Boys and Girls* to Malcolm, the Melvilles' first child, then not quite three years old. In a section called "Bald Summit: After the Story," written in July 1851, Hawthorne had paid a neighborly compliment (which incidentally records what he thought the title of Melville's new book was to be): "On the hither side of Pittsfield sits Herman Melville, shaping out the gigantic conception of his 'White Whale,' while the gigantic shape of Graylock looms upon him from his study-window." The father was meant to preserve the book for the son, but meantime he was to enjoy the compliment to himself. Hawthorne had written this surprise for Melville into his new book while Melville was preparing his own surprise by dedicating his own new book to Hawthorne.

7. Dardanelles or Hellespont, strait connecting the Sea of Marmara and the Aegean Sea.

Analogues and Sources

RALPH WALDO EMERSON

[Journal Entry on a White Whale][†]

Boston, Feb. 19 [1834] A seaman in the coach told the story of an old sperm whale which he called a white whale which was known for many years by the whalemen as Old Tom & who rushed upon the boats which attacked him & crushed the boats to small chips in his jaws, the men generally escaping by jumping overboard & being picked up. A vessel was fitted out at New Bedford, he said, to take him. And he was finally taken somewhere off Payta head by the Winslow or the Essex.

J. N. REYNOLDS

Mocha Dick:

Or the white whale of the Pacific: A leaf from a manuscript journal.[‡]

We expected to find the island of Santa Maria still more remarkable for the luxuriance of its vegetation, than even the fertile soil of Mocha; and the disappointment arising from the unexpected shortness of our stay at the latter place, was in some degree relieved, by the prospect of our remaining for several days in safe anchorage at the former. Mocha lies upon the coast of Chili, in lat. 38° 28′ south, twenty leagues north of Mono del Bonifacio, and opposite the Imperial river, from which it bears w. s. w. During the last century, this island was inhabited by the Spaniards, but it is at present, and has been for some years, entirely deserted. Its climate is mild, with little perceptible difference of temperature between the summer and winter seasons. Frost is unknown on the lowlands, and snow is rarely seen, even on the summits of the loftiest mountains.

† From *The Journals and Miscellaneous Notebooks of Ralph Waldo Emerson*, Volume IV, edited by Alfred R. Ferguson (Cambridge, Mass.: Belknap Press of Harvard University Press, 1964), p. 265. Copyright © 1964 by the President and Fellows of Harvard University Press.
‡ From J. N. Reynolds, "Mocha Dick," the New York *Knickerbocker* 12 (May 1839): 377–92. This is the chief printed account before Melville's *Moby-Dick* of the great white whale of oral legend. For further discussions see Howard P. Vincent, *The Trying-Out of "Moby-Dick"* (1949), and Janez Stanonick, *"Moby-Dick": The Myth and the Symbol* (1962), in which scattered reports are brought together.

It was late in the afternoon, when we left the schooner; and while we bore up for the north, she stood away for the southern extremity of the island. As evening was gathering around us, we fell in with a vessel, which proved to be the same whose boats, a day or two before, we had seen in the act of taking a whale. Aside from the romantic and stirring associations it awakened, there are few objects in themselves more picturesque or beautiful, than a whaleship, seen from a distance of three or four miles, on a pleasant evening, in the midst of the great Pacific. As she moves gracefully over the water, rising and falling on the gentle undulations peculiar to this sea; her sails glowing in the quivering light of the fires that flash from below, and a thick volume of smoke ascending from the midst, and curling away in dark masses upon the wind; it requires little effort of the fancy, to imagine one's self gazing upon a floating volcano.

As we were both standing to the north, under easy sail, at nine o'clock at night we had joined company with the stranger. Soon after, we were boarded by his whale-boat, the officer in command of which bore us the compliments of the captain, together with a friendly invitation to partake the hospitalities of his cabin. Accepting, without hesitation, a courtesy so frankly tendered, we proceeded, in company with Captain Palmer, on board, attended by the mate of the Penguin, who was on his way to St. Mary's to repair his boat, which had some weeks before been materially injured in a storm.

We found the whaler a large, well-appointed ship, owned in New-York, and commanded by such a man as one might expect to find in charge of a vessel of this character; plain, unassuming, intelligent, and well-informed upon all the subjects relating to his peculiar calling. But what shall we say of his first mate, or how describe him? To attempt his portrait by a comparison, would be vain, for we have never looked upon his like; and a detailed description, however accurate, would but faintly shadow forth the *tout ensemble* of his extraordinary figure. He had probably numbered about thirty-five years. We arrived at this conclusion, however, rather from the untamed brightness of his flashing eye, than the general appearance of his features, on which torrid sun and polar storm had left at once the furrows of more advanced age, and a tint swarthy as that of the Indian. His height, which was a little beneath the common standard, appeared almost dwarfish, from the immense breadth of his overhanging shoulders; while the unnatural length of the loose, dangling arms which hung from them, and which, when at rest, had least the appearance of ease, imparted to his uncouth and muscular frame an air of grotesque awkwardness, which defies description. He made few pretensions as a sailor, and had never aspired to the command of a ship. But he would not have exchanged the sensations which stirred his blood, when steering down upon a school of whales, for the privilege of treading, as master, the deck of the noblest liner that ever traversed the Atlantic. According to the admeasurement of his philosophy, whaling was the most dignified and manly of all sublunary pursuits. Of this he felt perfectly satisfied, having been engaged in the noble vocation for upward of twenty years, during which period, if his own assertions were to be received as evidence, no man in the American spermaceti fleet had made so many captures, or met with such wild adventures, in the exercise of his perilous profession.

Indeed, so completely were all his propensities, thoughts, and feelings, identified with his occupation; so intimately did he seem acquainted with the habits and instincts of the objects of his pursuit, and so little conversant with the ordinary affairs of life; that one felt less inclined to class him in the genus *homo*, than as a sort of intermediate something between man and the cetaceous tribe.

Soon after the commencement of his nautical career, in order to prove that he was not afraid of a whale, a point which it is essential for the young whaleman to establish beyond question, he offered, upon a wager, to run his boat 'bows on' against the side of an 'old bull,' leap from the 'cuddy' to the back of the fish, sheet his lance home, and return on board in safety. This feat, daring as it may be considered, he undertook and accomplished; at least so it was chronicled in his log, and he was ready to bear witness, on oath, to the veracity of the record. But his conquest of the redoubtable MOCHA DICK, unquestionably formed the climax of his exploits.

Before we enter into the particulars of this triumph, which, through their valorous representative, conferred so much honor on the lancers of Nantucket, it may be proper to inform the reader who and what Mocha Dick was; and thus give him a posthumous introduction to one who was, in his day and generation, so emphatically among fish the 'Stout Gentleman' of his latitudes. The introductory portion of his history we shall give, in a condensed form, from the relation of the mate. Substantially, however, it will be even as he rendered it; and as his subsequent narrative, though not deficient in rude eloquence, was coarse in style and language, as well as unnecessarily diffuse, we shall assume the liberty of altering the expression; of adapting the phraseology to the occasion; and of presenting the whole matter in a shape more succinct and connected. In this arrangement, however, we shall leave our adventurer to tell his *own story*, although not always in his own words, and shall preserve the person of the original.

But to return to Mocha Dick—which, it may be observed, few were solicitous to do, who had once escaped from him. This renowned monster, who had come off victorious in a hundred fights with his pursuers, was an old bull whale, of prodigious size and strength. From the effect of age, or more probably from a freak of nature, as exhibited in the case of the Ethiopian Albino, a singular consequence had resulted—*he was white as wool!* Instead of projecting his spout obliquely forward, and puffing with a short, convulsive effort, accompanied by a snorting noise, as usual with his species, he flung the water from his nose in a lofty, perpendicular, expanded volume, at regular and somewhat distant intervals; its expulsion producing a continuous roar, like that of vapor struggling from the safety-valve of a powerful steam engine. Viewed from a distance, the practised eye of the sailor only could decide, that the moving mass, which constituted this enormous animal, was not a white cloud sailing along the horizon. On the spermaceti whale, barnacles are rarely discovered; but upon the head of this *lusus naturæ*, they had clustered, until it became absolutely rugged with the shells. In short, regard him as you would, he was a most extraordinary fish; or, in the vernacular of Nantucket, 'a genuine old sog,' of the first water.

Opinions differ as to the time of his discovery. It is settled, however, that previous to the year 1810, he had been seen and attacked near the island of Mocha. Numerous boats are known to have been shattered by his immense flukes, or ground to pieces in the crush of his powerful jaws; and, on one occasion, it is said that he came off victorious from a conflict with the crews of three English whalers, striking fiercely at the last of the retreating boats, at the moment it was rising from the water, in its hoist up to the ship's davits. It must not be supposed, howbeit, that through all this desperate warfare, our leviathan passed scathless. A back serried with irons, and from fifty to a hundred yards of line trailing in his wake, sufficiently attested, that though unconquered, he had not proved invulnerable. From the period of Dick's first appearance, his celebrity continued to increase, until his name seemed naturally to mingle with the salutations which whalemen were in the habit of exchanging, in their encounters upon the broad Pacific; the customary interrogatories almost always closing with, 'Any news from Mocha Dick?' Indeed, nearly every whaling captain who rounded Cape Horn, if he possessed any professional ambition, or valued himself on his skill in subduing the monarch of the seas, would lay his vessel along the coast, in the hope of having an opportunity to try the muscle of this doughty champion, who was never known to shun his assailants. It was remarked, nevertheless, that the old fellow seemed particularly careful as to the portion of his body which he exposed to the approach of the boat-steerer; generally presenting, by some well-timed manœuvre, his back to the harpooner; and dexterously evading every attempt to plant an iron under his fin, or a spade on his 'small'. Though naturally fierce, it was not customary with Dick, while unmolested, to betray a malicious disposition. On the contrary, he would sometimes pass quietly round a vessel, and occasionally swim lazily and harmlessly among the boats, when armed with full craft, for the destruction of his race. But this forbearance gained him little credit, for if no other cause of accusation remained to them, his foes would swear they saw a lurking deviltry in the long, careless sweep of his flukes. Be this as it may, nothing is more certain, than that all indifference vanished with the first prick of the harpoon; while cutting the line, and a hasty retreat to their vessel, were frequently the only means of escape from destruction, left to his discomfited assaulters.

Thus far the whaleman had proceeded in his story, and was about commencing the relation of his own individual encounters with its subject, when he was cut short by the mate of the Penguin, to whom allusion has already been made, and who had remained, up to this point, an excited and attentive listener. Thus he would have continued, doubtless, to the end of the chapter, notwithstanding his avowed contempt for every other occupation than sealing, had not an observation escaped the narrator, which tended to arouse his professional jealousy. The obnoxious expression we have forgotten. Probably it involved something of boasting or egotism; for no sooner was it uttered, than our sealer sprang from his seat, and planting himself in front of the unconscious author of the insult, exclaimed:

'*You!*—you whale-killing, blubber-hunting, light-gathering varmint!— *you* pretend to manage a boat better than a Stonington sealer! A Nantucket whaleman,' he continued, curling his lip with a smile of supreme disdain, 'presume to teach a Stonington sealer how to manage a boat! Let all the small craft of your South Sea fleet range among the rocks and breakers where I have been, and if the whales would not have a peaceful time of it, for the next few years, may I never strip another jacket, or book another skin! What's taking a whale? Why, I could reeve a line through one's blow-hole, make it fast to a thwart, and then beat his brains out with my seal-club!'

Having thus given play to the first ebullition of his choler, he proceeded with more calmness to institute a comparison between whaling and sealing. 'A whaler,' said he, 'never approaches land, save when he enters a port to seek fresh grub. Not so the sealer. *He* thinks that his best fortune, which leads him where the form of man has never before startled the game he's after; where a quick eye, steady nerve, and stout heart, are his only guide and defence, in difficulty and danger. Where the sea is roughest, the whirlpool wildest, and the surf roars and dashes madly among the jagged cliffs, there—I was going to say there *only*—are the peak-nosed, black-eyed rogues we hunt for, to be found, gambolling in the white foam, and there must the sealer follow them. Were I to give you an account of my adventures about the Falkland Isles; off the East Keys of Staten Land; through the South Shetlands; off the Cape, where we lived on salt pork and seal's flippers; and finally, the story of a season spent with a single boat's crew on Diego Ramirez,[1] you would not make such a fuss about your Mocha Dick. As to the straits of Magellen, Sir, they are as familiar to me, as Broadway to a New-York dandy; though *it* should strut along that fashionable promenade twelve dozen times a day.'

Our son of the sea would have gone on to particularize his 'hair-breadth 'scapes and moving accidents,' had we not interposed, and insisted that the remainder of the night should be devoted to the conclusion of Dick's history; at the same time assuring the 'knight of the club' that so soon as we met at Santa Maria, he should have an entire evening expressly set apart, on which he might glorify himself and his calling. To this he assented, with the qualification, that his compliance with the general wish, in thus yielding precedence to his rival, should not be construed into an admission, that Nantucket whalemen were the best boatmen in the world, or that sealing was not as honorable and as pretty a business for coining a penny, as the profession of 'blubber-hunting' ever was.

The whaler now resumed. 'I will not weary you,' said he, 'with the uninteresting particulars of a voyage to Cape Horn. Our vessel, as capital a ship as ever left the little island of Nantucket, was finely manned and commanded, as well as thoroughly provided with every requisite for the peculiar service in which she was engaged. I may here observe, for the information of such among you as are not familiar with these things, that soon after a whale-ship from the United States is fairly at sea, the men are summoned aft; then boats' crews are selected by the captain and first mate, and a shipkeeper, at the same time, is usually chosen. The place to be filled by this individual is an important one; and the person designated should be a careful and sagacious man. His duty is, more particularly, to

1. Diego Ramirez is a small island, lying s.w. from Cape Horn.

superintend the vessel while the boats are away, in chase of fish; and at these times, the cook and steward are perhaps his only crew. His station, on these occasions, is at the mast-head, except when he is wanted below, to assist in working the ship. While aloft, he is to look out for whales, and also to keep a strict and tireless eye upon the absentees, in order to render them immediate assistance, should emergency require it. Should the game rise to windward of their pursuers, and they be too distant to observe personal signs, he must run down the jib. If they rise to leeward, he should haul up the spanker; continuing the little black signal-flag at the mast, so long as they remain on the surface. When the 'school' turn flukes, and go down, the flag is to be struck, and again displayed when they are seen to ascend. When circumstances occur which require the return of the captain on board, the colors are to be hoisted at the mizzen peak. A ship-keeper must farther be sure that provisions are ready for the men, on their return from the chase, and that drink be amply furnished, in the form of a bucket of 'switchel.' 'No whale, no switchel,' is frequently the rule; but I am inclined to think that, whale or no whale, a little rum is not amiss, after a lusty pull.

'I have already said, that little of interest occurred, until after we had doubled Cape Horn. We were now standing in upon the coast of Chili, before a gentle breeze from the south, that bore us along almost imperceptibly. It was a quiet and beautiful evening, and the sea glanced and glistened in the level rays of the descending sun, with a surface of waving gold. The western sky was flooded with amber light, in the midst of which, like so many islands, floated immense clouds, of every conceivable brilliant dye; while far to the northeast, looming darkly against a paler heaven, rose the conical peak of Mocha. The men were busily employed in sharpening their harpoons, spades, and lances, for the expected fight. The look-out at the mast-head, with cheek on his shoulder, was dreaming of the 'dangers he had passed,' instead of keeping watch for those which were to come; while the captain paced the quarter-deck with long and hasty stride, scanning the ocean in every direction, with a keen, expectant eye. All at once, he stopped, fixed his gaze intently for an instant on some object to leeward, that seemed to attract it, and then, in no very conciliating tone, hailed the mast-head:

"Both ports shut?' he exclaimed, looking aloft, and pointing backward, where a long white bushy spout was rising, about a mile off the larboard bow, against the glowing horizon. 'Both ports shut? I say, you leaden-eyed lubber! Nice lazy son of a sea-cook *you* are, for a look-out! Come down, Sir!'

"There she blows!—sperm whale—old sog, sir;' said the man, in a deprecatory tone, as he descended from his nest in the air. It was at once seen that the creature was companionless; but as a lone whale is generally an old bull, and of unusual size and ferocity, more than ordinary sport was anticipated, while unquestionably more than ordinary honor was to be won from its successful issue.

'The second mate and I were ordered to make ready for pursuit; and now commenced a scene of emulation and excitement, of which the most vivid description would convey but an imperfect outline, unless you have been a spectator or an actor on a similar occasion. Line-tubs, water-kegs, and wafe-poles, were thrown hurriedly into the boats; the irons were placed in the racks, and the necessary evolutions of the ship gone through, with a quickness almost magical; and this too, amidst what to a landsman would have seemed inextricable confusion, with perfect regularity and precision; the commands of the officers being all but forestalled by the enthusiastic eagerness of the men. In a short time, we were as near the object of our chase, as it was considered prudent to approach.

"Back the main-top-s'll!' shouted the captain. 'There she blows! there she blows!—there she blows!'—cried the look-out, who had taken the place of his sleepy shipmate, raising the pitch of his voice with each announcement, until it amounted to a downright yell. 'Right ahead, Sir!—spout as long an 's thick as the mainyard!'

"Stand by to lower!' exclaimed the captain; 'all hands; cook, steward, cooper—every d—d one of ye, stand by to lower!'

'An instantaneous rush from all quarters of the vessel answered this appeal, and every man was at his station, almost before the last word had passed the lips of the skipper.

"Lower away!'—and in a moment the keels splashed in the water. 'Follow down the crews; jump in my boys; ship the crotch; line your oars; now pull, as if the d—l was in your wake!' were the successive orders, as the men slipped down the ship's side, took their places in the boats, and began to give way.

'The second mate had a little the advantage of me in starting. The stern of his boat grated against the bows of mine, at the instant I grasped my steering-oar, and gave the word to shove off. One sweep of my arm, and we sprang foaming in his track. Now came the tug of war. To become a first-rate oarsman, you must understand, requires a natural gift. My crew were not wanting in the proper qualification; every mother's son of them pulled as if he had been born with an oar in his hand; and as they stretched every sinew for the glory of darting the first iron it did my heart good to see the boys spring. At every stroke, the tough blades bent like willow wands, and quivered like tempered steel in the warm sunlight, as they sprang forward from the tension of the retreating wave. At the distance of half a mile, and directly before us, lay the object of our emulation and ambition, heaving his huge bulk in unwieldly gambols, as though totally unconscious of our approach.

"There he blows! An old bull, by Jupiter! Eighty barrels, boys, waiting to be towed alongside! Long and quick—shoot ahead! Now she feels it; waist-boat never could beat us; now she feels the touch!—now she walks through it! Again—*now!*' Such were the broken exclamations and adjurations with which I cheered my rowers to their toil, as, with renewed vigor, I plied my long steering-oar. In another moment, we were alongside our competitor. The shivering blades flashed forward and backward, like sparks of light. The waters boiled under our prow, and the trenched waves closed, hissing and whirling, in our wake, as we swept, I might almost say were *lifted*, onward in our arrowy course.

'We were coming down upon our fish, and could hear the roar of his spouting above the rush of the sea, when my boat began to take the lead.

"Now, my fine fellows,' I exclaimed, in triumph, 'now we'll show them our stern—only spring! Stand ready, harpooner, but do n't dart, till I give the word.'

"Carry me on, and his name's *Dennis!*'[2] cried the boat-steerer, in a confident tone. We were perhaps a hundred feet in advance of the waist-boat, and within fifty of the whale, about an inch of whose hump only was to be seen above the water, when, heaving slowly into view a pair of flukes some eighteen feet in width, he went down. The men lay on their oars. 'There he blows, again!' cried the tub-oarsman, as a lofty, perpendicular spout sprang into the air, a few furlongs away on the starboard side. Presuming from his previous movement, that the old fellow had been 'gallied' by other boats, and might probably be jealous of our purpose, I was about ordering the men to pull away as softly and silently as possible, when we received fearful intimation that he had no intention of balking our inclination, or even yielding us the honor of the first attack. Lashing the sea with his enormous tail, until he threw about him a cloud of surf and spray, he came down, at full speed, 'jaws on,' with the determination, apparently, of doing battle in earnest. As he drew near, with his long curved back looming occasionally above the surface of the billows, we perceived that it was *white as the surf around him*; and the men stared aghast at each other, as they uttered, in a suppressed tone, the terrible name of MOCHA DICK!

"Mocha Dick or the d—l,' said I, 'this boat never sheers off from any thing that wears the shape of a whale. Pull easy; just give her way enough to steer.' As the creature approached, he somewhat abated his frenzied speed, and, at the distance of a cable's length, changed his course to a sharp angle with our own.

"Here he comes!' I exclaimed. 'Stand up, harpooner! Do n't be hasty— do n't be flurried. Hold your iron higher—firmer. Now!' I shouted, as I brought our bows within a boat's length of the immense mass which was wallowing heavily by. '*Now!—give it to him solid!*'

'But the leviathan plunged on, unharmed. The young harpooner, though ordinarily as fearless as a lion, had imbibed a sort of superstitious dread of Mocha Dick, from the exaggerated stories of that prodigy, which he had heard from his comrades. He regarded him, as he had heard him described in many a tough yarn during the middle watch, rather as some ferocious fiend of the deep, than a regular-built, legitimate whale! Judge then of his trepidation, on beholding a creature, answering the wildest dreams of his fancy, and sufficiently formidable, without any superadded terrors, bearing down upon him with thrashing flukes and distended jaws! He stood erect, it cannot be denied. He planted his foot—he grasped the coil—he poised his weapon. But his knee shook, and his sinewy arm wavered. The shaft was hurled, but with unsteady aim. It just grazed the back of the monster, glanced off, and darted into the sea beyond. A second, still more abortive, fell short of the mark. The giant animal swept on for a few rods, and then, as if in contempt of our fruitless and childish attempt to injure him, flapped a storm of spray in our faces with his broad tail, and dashed far down into the depths of the ocean, leaving our little skiff among the waters where he sank, to spin and duck in the whirlpool.

'Never shall I forget the choking sensation of disappointment which came over me at that moment. My glance fell on the harpooner. 'Clumsy

2. A whale's name is "Dennis," when he spouts blood.

lubber!' I vociferated, in a voice hoarse with passion; '*you* a whaleman! You are only fit to spear eels! Cowardly spawn! Curse me, if you are not *afraid* of a whale!'

'The poor fellow, mortified at his failure, was slowly and thoughtfully hauling in his irons. No sooner had he heard me stigmatize him as 'afraid of a whale,' than he bounded upon his thwart, as if bitten by a serpent. He stood before me for a moment, with a glowing cheek and flashing eye; then, dropping the iron he had just drawn in, without uttering a word, he turned half round, and sprang head-foremost into the sea. The tub-oarsman, who was re-coiling the line in the after part of the boat, saw his design just in season to grasp him by the heel, as he made his spring. But he was not to be dragged on board again without a struggle. Having now become more calm, I endeavored to soothe his wounded pride with kind and flattering words; for I knew him to be a noble-hearted fellow, and was truly sorry that my hasty reproaches should have touched so fine a spirit so deeply.

'Night being now at hand, the captain's signal was set for our return to the vessel; and we were soon assembled on her deck, discussing the mischances of the day, and speculating on the prospect of better luck on the morrow.

'We were at breakfast next morning, when the watch at the foretop-gallant head sung out merrily, 'There she breaches!' In an instant every one was on his feet. 'Where away?' cried the skipper, rushing from the cabin, and upsetting in his course the steward, who was returning from the caboose with a replenished biggin of hot coffee. 'Not loud but deep' were the grumblings and groans of that functionary, as he rubbed his scalded shins, and danced about in agony; but had they been far louder, they would have been drowned in the tumult of vociferation which answered the announcement from the mast-head.

''Where away?' repeated the captain, as he gained the deck.

''Three points off the leeward bow.'

''How far?'

''About a league, Sir; heads same as we do. There she blows!' added the man, as he came slowly down the shouds, with his eyes fixed intently upon the spouting herd.

''Keep her off two points! Steady!—steady, as she goes!'

''Steady it is, Sir,' answered the helmsman.

''Weather braces, a small pull. Loose to'-gallant-s'ls! Bear a hand, my boys! Who knows but we may tickle their ribs at this rising?'

'The captain had gone aloft, and was giving these orders from the main-to'-gallant-cross-trees. 'There she top-tails! there she blows!' added he, as, after taking a long look at the sporting shoal, he glided down the back stay. 'Sperm whale, and a thundering big school of 'em!' was his reply to the rapid and eager inquiries of the men. 'See the lines in the boats,' he continued; 'get in the craft; swing the cranes!'

'By this time the fish had gone down, and every eye was strained to catch the first intimation of their reappearance.

''There she *spouts!*' screamed a young greenhorn in the main chains, 'close by; a mighty big whale, Sir!'

''We'll know that better at the trying out, my son,' said the third mate, drily.

"Back the main-top-s'l!' was now the command. The ship had little headway at the time, and in a few minutes we were as motionless as if lying at anchor.

"Lower away, all hands!'And in a twinkling, and together, the starboard, larboard, and waist-boats struck the water. Each officer leaped into his own; the crews arranged themselves at their respective stations; the boat-steerers began to adjust their 'craft;' and we left the ship's side in company; the captain, in laconic phrase, bidding us to 'get up and get fast,' as quickly as possible.

'Away we dashed, in the direction of our prey, who were frolicking, if such a term can be applied to their unwieldly motions, on the surface of the waves. Occasionally, a huge, shapeless body would flounce out of its proper element, and fall back with a heavy splash; the effort forming about as ludicrous a caricature of agility, as would the attempt of some over-fed alderman to execute the Highland fling.

'We were within a hundred rods of the herd, when, as if from a common impulse, or upon some preconcerted signal, they all suddenly disappeared. 'Follow me!' I shouted, waving my hand to the men in the other boats; 'I see their track under water; they swim fast, but we'll be among them when they rise. Lay back,' I continued, addressing myself to my own crew, 'back to the thwarts! Spring *hard!* We'll be in the thick of 'em when they come up; only *pull!'*

'And they did pull, manfully. After rowing for about a mile, I ordered them to 'lie.' The oars were peaked, and we rose to look out for the first 'noddle-head' that should break water. It was at this time a dead calm. Not a single cloud was passing over the deep blue of the heavens, to vary their boundless transparency, or shadow for a moment the gleaming ocean which they spanned. Within a short distance lay our noble ship, with her idle canvass hanging in drooping festoons from her yards; while she seemed resting on her inverted image, which, distinct and beautiful as its original, was glassed in the smooth expanse beneath. No sound disturbed the general silence, save our own heavy breathings, the low gurgle of the water against the side of the boat, or the noise of flapping wings, as the albatross wheeled sleepily along through the stagnant atmosphere. We had remained quiet for about five minutes, when some dark object was descried ahead, moving on the surface of the sea. It proved to be a small 'calf,' playing in the sunshine.

"Pull up and strike it,' said I to the third mate; 'it may bring up the old one—perhaps the whole school.'

'And so it did, with a vengeance! The sucker was transpierced, after a short pursuit; but hardly had it made its first agonized plunge, when an enormous cow-whale rose close beside her wounded offspring. Her first endeavor was to take it under her fin, in order to bear it away; and nothing could be more striking than the maternal tenderness she manifested in her exertions to accomplish this object. But the poor thing was dying, and while she vainly tried to induce it to accompany her, it rolled over, and floated dead at her side. Perceiving it to be beyond the reach of her caresses, she turned to wreak her vengeance on its slayers, and made directly for the boat, crashing her vast jaws the while, in a paroxysm of rage. Ordering his boat-steerer aft, the mate sprang forward, cut the line loose from the calf, and then snatched from the crotch the remaining iron, which he plunged with his gathered strength into the body of the mother, as the boat sheered off to avoid her onset. I saw that the work was well done, but had no time to mark the issue; for at that instant, a whale 'breached' at the distance of about a mile from us, on the starboard quarter. The glimpse I caught of the animal in his descent, convinced me that I once more beheld my old acquaintance, Mocha Dick. That falling mass was white as a snow-drift!

'One might have supposed the recognition mutual, for no sooner was his vast square head lifted from the sea, than he charged down upon us, scattering the billows into spray as he advanced, and leaving a wake of foam a rod in width, from the violent lashing of his flukes.

"He's making for the bloody water!' cried the men, as he cleft his way toward the very spot where the calf had been killed. 'Here, harpooner, steer the boat, and let me dart!' I exclaimed, as I leaped into the bows. 'May the '*Goneys*' eat me, if he dodge us *this* time, though he were Beelzebub himself! Pull for the red water!'

'As I spoke, the fury of the animal seemed suddenly to die away. He paused in his career, and lay passive on the waves, with his arching back thrown up like the ridge of a mountain. 'The old sog's lying to!' I cried, exultingly. 'Spring, boys! spring *now*, and we have him! All my clothes, tobacco, every thing I've got, shall be yours, only lay me 'longside that whale before another boat comes up! My *grimky!* what a hump! Only look at the irons in his back! No, do n't *look*—PULL! Now, boys, if you care about seeing your sweethearts and wives in old Nantuck!—if you love Yankee-land—if you love *me*—pull ahead, *wont* ye? Now then, to the thwarts! Lay back, my boys! I feel ye, my hearties! Give her the touch! Only five seas off! *Not* five seas off! One minute—*half* a minute more! Softly—no noise! Softly with your oars! That will do——'

'And as the words were uttered, I raised the harpoon above my head, took a rapid but no less certain aim, and sent it, hissing, deep into his thick white side!

"Stern all! for your lives!' I shouted; for at the instant the steel quivered in his body, the wounded leviathan plunged his head beneath the surface, and whirling around with great velocity, smote the sea violently, with fin and fluke, in a convulsion of rage and pain.

'Our little boat flew dancing back from the seething vortex around him, just in season to escape being overwhelmed or crushed. He now started to run. For a short time, the line rasped, smoking, through the chocks. A few turns round the loggerhead then secured it; and with oars a-peak, and bows tilted to the sea, we went leaping onward in the wake of the tethered monster. Vain were all his struggles to break from our hold. The strands were too strong, the barbed iron too deeply fleshed, to give way. So that whether he essayed to dive or breach, or dash madly forward, the frantic creature still felt that he was held in check. At one moment, in impotent rage, he reared his immense blunt head, covered with barnacles, high above the surge; while his jaws fell together with a crash that almost made me shiver; then the upper outline of his vast form was dimly seen, gliding amidst showers of sparkling spray; while streaks of crimson on the white surf that boiled in his track, told that the shaft had been driven home.

'By this time, the whole 'school' was about us; and spouts from a hundred spiracles, with a roar that almost deafened us, were raining on every side; while in the midst of a vast surface of chafing sea, might be seen the black shapes of the rampant herd, tossing and plunging, like a legion of maddened demons. The second and third mates were in the very centre of this appalling commotion.

'At length, Dick began to lessen his impetuous speed. 'Now, my boys,' cried I, 'haul me on; wet the line, you second oarsman, as it comes in. Haul away, ship-mates!—why the devil don't you haul? Leeward side—*leeward!* I tell you! Do n't you know how to approach a whale?'

'The boat brought fairly up upon his broadside as I spoke, and I gave him the lance just under the shoulder blade. At this moment, just as the boat's head was laid off; and I was straitening for a second lunge, my lance, which I had 'boned' in the first, a piercing cry from the boat-steerer drew my attention quickly aft, and I saw the waist-boat, or more properly a fragment of it, falling through the air, and underneath, the dusky forms of the struggling crew, grasping at the oars, or clinging to portions of the wreck; while a pair of flukes, descending in the midst of the confusion, fully accounted for the catastrophe. The boat had been struck and shattered by a whale!

''Good heaven!' I exclaimed, with impatience, and in a tone which I fear showed me rather mortified at the interruption, than touched with proper feeling for the sufferers; 'good heavens!—had n't they sense enough to keep out of the red water! And I must lose this glorious prize, through their infernal stupidity!' This was the first outbreak of my selfishness.

''But we must not see them drown, boys,' I added, upon the instant; 'cut the line!' The order had barely passed my lips, when I caught sight of the captain, who had seen the accident from the quarter-deck, bearing down with oar and sail to the rescue.

''Hold on!' I thundered, just as the knife's edge touched the line; 'for the glory of old Nantuck, hold on! The captain will pick them up, and Mocha Dick will be ours, after all!'

'This affair occurred in half the interval I have occupied in the relation. In the mean time, with the exception of a slight shudder, which once or twice shook his ponderous frame, Dick lay perfectly quiet upon the water. But suddenly, as though goaded into exertion by some fiercer pang, he started from his lethargy with apparently augmented power. Making a leap toward the boat, he darted perpendicularly downward, hurling the after oarsman, who was helmsman at the time, ten feet over the quarter, as he struck the long steering-oar in his descent. The unfortunate seaman fell, with his head forward, just upon the flukes of the whale, as he vanished, and was drawn down by suction of the closing waters, as if he had been a feather. After being carried to a great depth, as we inferred from the time he remained below the surface, he came up, panting and exhausted, and was dragged on board, amidst the hearty congratulations of his comrades.

'By this time two hundred fathoms of line had been carried spinning through the chocks, with an impetus that gave back in steam the water cast upon it. Still the gigantic creature bored his way downward, with undiminished speed. Coil after coil went over, and was swallowed up. There remained but three flakes in the tub!

"Cut!' I shouted; 'cut quick, or he'll take us down!' But as I spoke, the hissing line flew with trebled velocity through the smoking wood, jerking the knife he was in the act of applying to the heated strands out of the hand of the boat-steerer. The boat rose on end, and her bows were buried in an instant; a hurried ejaculation, at once shriek and prayer, rose to the lips of the bravest, when, unexpected mercy! the whizzing cord lost its tension, and our light bark, half filled with water, fell heavily back on her keel. A tear was in every eye, and I believe every heart bounded with gratitude, at this unlooked-for deliverance.

'Overpowered by his wounds, and exhausted by his exertions and the enormous pressure of the water above him, the immense creature was compelled to turn once more upward, for a fresh supply of air. And upward he came, indeed; shooting twenty feet of his gigantic length above the waves, by the impulse of his ascent. He was not disposed to be idle. Hardly had we succeeded in bailing out our swamping boat, when he again darted away, as it seemed to me with renewed energy. For a quarter of a mile, we parted the opposing waters as though they had offered no more resistance than air. Our game then abruptly brought to, and lay as if paralyzed, his massy frame quivering and twitching, as if under the influence of galvanism. I gave the word to haul on; and seizing a boat-spade, as we came near him, drove it twice into his small; no doubt partially disabling him by the vigor and certainty of the blows. Wheeling furiously around, he answered this salutation, by making a desperate dash at the boat's quarter. We were so near him, that to escape the shock of his onset, by any practicable manœuvre, was out of the question. But at the critical moment, when we expected to be crushed by the collision, his powers seemed to give way. The fatal lance had reached the seat of life. His strength failed him in mid career, and sinking quietly beneath our keel, grazing it as he wallowed along, he rose again a few rods from us, on the side opposite that where he went down.

"Lay around, my boys, and let us set on him!' I cried, for I saw his spirit was broken at last. But the lance and spade were needless now. The work was done. The dying animal was struggling in a whirlpool of bloody foam, and the ocean far around was tinted with crimson. 'Stern all!' I shouted, as he commenced running impetuously in a circle, beating the water alternately with his head and flukes, and smiting his teeth ferociously into their sockets, with a crashing sound, in the strong spasms of dissolution. 'Stern all! or we shall be stove!'

'As I gave the command, a stream of black, clotted gore rose in a thick spout above the expiring brute, and fell in a shower around, bedewing, or rather drenching us, with a spray of blood.

"There's the flag!' I exclaimed; 'there! thick as tar! Stern! every soul of ye! He's going in his flurry!' And the monster, under the convulsive influence of his final paroxysm, flung his huge tail into the air, and then, for the space of a minute, thrashed the waters on either side of him with quick and powerful blows; the sound of the concussions resembling that of the rapid discharge of artillery. He then turned slowly and heavily on his side, and lay a dead mass upon the sea through which he had so long ranged a conqueror.

"He's fin up at last!' I screamed, at the very top of my voice. 'Hurrah! hurrah! hurrah!' And snatching off my cap, I sent it spinning aloft, jumping at the same time from thwart to thwart, like a madman.

'We now drew alongside our floating spoil; and I seriously question if the brave commodore who first, and so nobly, broke the charm of British invincibility, by the capture of the Guerriere, felt a warmer rush of delight, as he beheld our national flag waving over the British ensign, in assurance of his victory, than I did, as I leaped upon the quarter deck of Dick's back, planted my wafe-pole in the midst, and saw the little canvass flag, that tells so important and satisfactory a tale to the whaleman, fluttering above my hard-earned prize.

'The captain and second mate, each of whom had been fortunate enough to kill his fish, soon after pulled up, and congratulated me on my capture. From them I learned the particulars of the third mate's disaster. He had fastened, and his fish was sounding, when another whale suddenly rose, almost directly beneath the boat, and with a single blow of his small, absolutely cut it in twain, flinging the bows, and those who occupied that portion of the frail fabric, far into the air. Rendered insensible, or immediately killed by the shock, two of the crew sank without a struggle, while a third, unable in his confusion to disengage himself from the flakes of the tow-line, with which he had become entangled, was, together with the fragment to which the warp was attached, borne down by the harpooned whale, and was seen no more! The rest, some of them severely bruised, were saved from drowning by the timely assistance of the captain.

'To get the harness on Dick, was the work of an instant; and as the ship, taking every advantage of a light breeze which had sprung up within the last hour, had stood after us, and was now but a few rods distant, we were soon under her stern. The other fish, both of which were heavy fellows, lay floating near; and the tackle being affixed to one of them without delay, all hands were soon busily engaged in cutting in. Mocha Dick was the longest whale I ever looked upon. He measured more than seventy feet from his noddle to the tips of his flukes; and yielded one hundred barrels of clear oil, with a proportionate quantity of 'head-matter.' It may emphatically be said, that 'the scars of his old wounds were near his new,' for not less than twenty harpoons did we draw from his back; the rusted mementos of many a desperate rencounter.'

The mate was silent. His yarn was reeled off. His story was told; and with far better tact than is exhibited by many a modern orator, he had the modesty and discretion to stop with its termination. In response, a glass of 'o-be-joyful' went merrily round; and this tribute having been paid to courtesy, the vanquisher of Mocha Dick was unanimously called upon for a song. Too sensible and too good-natured to wait for a second solicitation, when he had the power to oblige, he took a 'long pull' and a strong, at the grog as an appropriate overture to the occasion, and then, in a deep, sonorous tone, gave us the following professional ballad, accompanied by a superannuated hand-organ, which constituted the musical portion of the cabin furniture:

I.

'Do n't bother my head about catching of seals!
To me there's more glory in catching of eels;
Give me a tight ship, and under snug sail,
And I ask for no more, 'long side the sperm whale,

In the Indian Ocean,
Or Pacific Ocean,
No matter *what* ocean;
Pull ahead, yo heave O!

II.

'When our anchor's a-peak, sweethearts and wives
Yield a warm drop at parting, breathe a prayer for our lives;
With hearts full of promise, they kiss off the tear
From the eye that grows rarely dim—never with fear!
Then for the ocean, boys,
The billow's commotion, boys,
That's our devotion, boys,
Pull ahead, yo heave O!

III.

'Soon we hear the glad cry of 'Town O!'—there she blows!'
Slow as night, my brave fellows, to leeward she goes:
Hard up! square the yards! then steady, lads, so!
Cries the captain, 'My maiden lance soon shall she know!'
'Now we get near, boys,
In with the gear, boys,
Swing the cranes clear, boys;
Pull ahead, yo heave O!'

IV.

'Our boat's in the water, each man at his oar
Bends strong to the sea, while his bark bounds before,
As the fish of all sizes, still flouncing and blowing,
With fluke and broad fin, scorn the best of hard rowing:
'Hang to the oar, boys,
Another stroke more, boys;
Now line the oar, boys;
Pull ahead, yo heave O!'

V.

'Then rises long Tom, who never knew fear;
Cries the captain, 'Now nail her, my bold harpooner!'
He speeds home his lance, then exclaims, 'I am fast!'
While blood, in a torrent, leaps high as the mast:
'Starn! starn! hurry, hurry, boys!
She's gone in her flurry, boys,
She'll soon be in 'gurry,' boys!
Pull ahead, yo heave O!'

VI.

'Then give me a whaleman, wherever he be,
Who fears not a fish that can swim the salt sea;

Then give me a tight ship, and under snug sail,
And last lay me 'side of the noble sperm whale;
                    'In the Indian ocean,
                    Or Pacific ocean,
                    No matter *what* ocean;
                    Pull ahead, yo heave O!'

The song 'died away into an echo,' and we all confessed ourselves delighted with it—save and except the gallant knight of the seal-club. He indeed allowed the lay and the music to be well enough, considering the subject; but added: 'If you want to hear genuine, heart-stirring harmony, you must listen to a rookery of fur seal. For many an hour, on the rocks round Cape Horn, have I sat thus, listening to these gentry, as they clustered on the shelving cliffs above me; the surf beating at my feet, while——'

'Come, come, my old fellow!' exclaimed the captain, interrupting the loquacious sealer; 'you forget the evening you are to have at Santa Maria. It is three o'clock in the morning, and more.' Bidding farewell to our social and generous entertainers, we were soon safely on board our ship, when we immediately made all sail to the north.

To me, the evening had been one of singular enjoyment. Doubtless the particulars of the tale were in some degree highly colored, from the desire of the narrator to present his calling in a prominent light, and especially one that should eclipse the occupation of sealing. But making every allowance for what, after all, may be considered a natural embellishment, the facts presented may be regarded as a fair specimen of the adventures which constitute so great a portion of the romance of a whaler's life; a life which, viewing all the incidents that seem inevitably to grow out of the enterprise peculiar to it, can be said to have no parallel. Yet vast as the field is, occupied by this class of our resolute seamen, how little can we claim to know of the particulars of a whaleman's existence! That our whale ships leave port, and usually return, in the course of three years, with full cargoes, to swell the fund of national wealth, is nearly the sum of our knowledge concerning them. Could we comprehend, at a glance, the mighty surface of the Indian or Pacific seas, what a picture would open upon us of unparalleled industry and daring enterprise! What scenes of toil along the coast of Japan, up the straits of Mozambique, where the dangers of the storm, impending as they may be, are less regarded than the privations and sufferings attendant upon exclusion from all intercourse with the shore! Sail onward, and extend your view around New-Holland, to the coast of Guinea; to the eastern and western shores of Africa; to the Cape of Good Hope; and south, to the waters that lash the cliffs of Kergulan's Land, and you are ever upon the whaling-ground of the American seaman. Yet onward, to the vast expanse of the two Pacifics, with their countless summer isles, and your course is still over the common arena and highway of our whalers. The varied records of the commercial world can furnish no precedent, can present no comparison, to the intrepidity, skill, and fortitude, which seem the peculiar prerogatives of this branch of our marine. These characteristics are not the growth of forced exertion; they are incompatible with it. They are the natural result

of the ardor of a free people; of a spirit of fearless independence, generated by free institutions. Under such institutions alone, can the human
mind attain its fullest expansion, in the various departments of science,
and the multiform pursuits of busy life.

OWEN CHASE

[The *Essex* Wrecked by a Whale][†]

I have not been able to recur to the scenes which are now to become
the subject of description, although a considerable time has elapsed, without feeling a mingled emotion of horror and astonishment at the almost
incredible destiny that has preserved me and my surviving companions
from a terrible death. Frequently, in my reflections on the subject, even
after this lapse of time, I find myself shedding tears of gratitude for our
deliverance, and blessing God, by whose divine aid and protection we
were conducted through a series of unparalleled suffering and distress,
and restored to the bosoms of our families and friends. There is no knowing what a stretch of pain and misery the human mind is capable of contemplating, when it is wrought upon by the anxieties of preservation; nor
what pangs and weaknesses the body is able to endure, until they are visited upon it; and when at last deliverance comes; when the dream of hope
is realized, unspeakable gratitude takes possession of the soul, and tears
of joy choke the utterance. We require to be taught in the school of some
signal suffering, privation, and despair, the great lessons of constant
dependence upon an almighty forbearance and mercy. In the midst of the
wide ocean, at night, when the sight of the heavens was shut out, and the
dark tempest came upon us; then it was, that we felt ourselves ready to
exclaim, "Heaven have mercy upon us, for nought but that can save us
now." But I proceed to the recital.—On the 20th of November, (cruising
in latitude 0° 40′ S. longitude 119° 0′ W.) a shoal of whales was discovered off the lee-bow. The weather at this time was extremely fine and
clear, and it was about 8 o'clock in the morning, that the man at the mast-
head gave the usual cry of, "there she blows." The ship was immediately
put away, and we ran down in the direction for them. When we had got
within half a mile of the place where they were observed, all our boats
were lowered down, manned, and we started in pursuit of them. The ship,
in the mean time, was brought to the wind, and the main-top-sail hove
aback, to wait for us. I had the harpoon in the second boat; the captain
preceded me in the first. When I arrived at the spot where we calculated
they were, nothing was at first to be seen. We lay on our oars in anxious
expectation of discovering them come up somewhere near us. Presently
one rose, and spouted a short distance ahead of my boat; I made all speed

† From Owen Chase, *Narrative of the Most Extraordinary and Distressing Shipwreck of the Whale-
Ship Essex, of Nantucket; Which Was Attacked and Finally Destroyed by a Large Spermaceti-Whale
in the Pacific Ocean* . . . (1821), 23–41. The selection is all of ch. 2 and the beginning of ch.
3, which is given to show how, for dramatic effect, Melville made the *Pequod* sink much faster
than did the *Essex*. Melville's extended reference to the *Essex* disaster in *Moby-Dick* is in ch. 45.
His manuscript notes, inserted in his own copy of Chase's *Narrative*, are reprinted next.

towards it, came up with, and struck it; feeling the harpoon in him, he threw himself, in an agony, over towards the boat, (which at that time was up alongside of him,) and, giving a severe blow with his tail, struck the boat near the edge of the water, amidships, and stove a hole in her. I immediately took up the boat hatchet, and cut the line, to disengage the boat from the whale, which by this time was running off with great velocity. I succeeded in getting clear of him, with the loss of the harpoon and line; and finding the water to pour fast in the boat, I hastily stuffed three or four of our jackets in the hole, ordered one man to keep constantly bailing, and the rest to pull immediately for the ship; we succeeded in keeping the boat free, and shortly gained the ship. The captain and the second mate, in the other two boats, kept up the pursuit, and soon struck another whale. They being at this time a considerable distance to leeward, I went forward, braced around the mainyard, and put the ship off in a direction for them; the boat which had been stove was immediately hoisted in, and after examining the hole, I found that I could, by nailing a piece of canvass over it, get her ready to join in a fresh pursuit, sooner than by lowering down the other remaining boat which belonged to the ship. I accordingly turned her over upon the quarter, and was in the act of nailing on the canvass, when I observed a very large spermaceti whale, as well as I could judge, about eighty-five feet in length; he broke water about twenty rods off our weather-bow, and was lying quietly, with his head in a direction for the ship. He spouted two or three times, and then disappeared. In less than two or three seconds he came up again, about the length of the ship off, and made directly for us, at the rate of about three knots. The ship was then going with about the same velocity. His appearance and attitude gave us at first no alarm; but while I stood watching his movements, and observing him but a ship's length off, coming down for us with great celerity, I involuntarily ordered the boy at the helm to put it hard up; intending to sheer off and avoid him. The words were scarcely out of my mouth, before he came down upon us with full speed, and struck the ship with his head, just forward of the fore-chains; he gave us such an appalling and tremendous jar, as nearly threw us all on our faces. The ship brought up as suddenly and violently as if she had struck a rock, and trembled for a few seconds like a leaf. We looked at each other with perfect amazement, deprived almost of the power of speech. Many minutes elapsed before we were able to realize the dreadful accident; during which time he passed under the ship, grazing her keel as he went along, came up alongside of her to leeward, and lay on the top of the water, (apparently stunned with the violence of the blow,) for the space of a minute; he then suddenly started off, in a direction to leeward. After a few moments' reflection, and recovering, in some measure, from the sudden consternation that had seized us, I of course concluded that he had stove a hole in the ship, and that it would be necessary to set the pumps going. Accordingly they were rigged, but had not been in operation more than one minute, before I perceived the head of the ship to be gradually settling down in the water; I then ordered the signal to be set for the other boats, which, scarcely had I despatched, before I again discovered the whale, apparently in convulsions, on the top of the water, about one hundred rods to leeward. He was enveloped in the foam of the sea, that his continual and violent thrashing about in the water had created around him, and I could distinctly see him smite his jaws together, as if distracted with rage and fury. He remained a short time in this situation, and then started off with great velocity, across the bows of the ship, to windward. By this time the ship had settled down a considerable distance in the water, and I gave her up as lost. I however, ordered the pumps to be kept constantly going, and endeavoured to collect my thoughts for the occasion. I turned to the boats, two of which we then had with the ship, with an intention of clearing them away, and getting all things ready to embark in them, if there should be no other resource left; and while my attention was thus engaged for a moment, I was aroused with the cry of a man at the hatchway, "here he is—he is making for us again." I turned around, and saw him about one hundred rods directly ahead of us, coming down apparently with twice his ordinary speed, and to me at that moment, it appeared with tenfold fury and vengeance in his aspect. The surf flew in all directions about him, and his course towards us was marked by a white foam of a rod in width, which he made with the continual violent thrashing of his tail; his head was about half out of water, and in that way he came upon, and again struck the ship. I was in hopes when I descried him making for us, that by a dexterous movement of putting the ship away immediately, I should be able to cross the line of his approach, before he could get up to us, and thus avoid, what I knew, if he should strike us again, would prove our inevitable destruction. I bawled out to the helmsman, "hard up!" but she had not fallen off more than a point, before we took the second shock. I should judge the speed of the ship to have been at this time about three knots, and that of the whale about six. He struck her to windward, directly under the cathead, and completely stove in her bows. He passed under the ship again, went off to leeward, and we saw no more of him. Our situation at this juncture can be more readily imagined than described. The shock to our feelings was such, as I am sure none can have an adequate conception of, that were not there: the misfortune befel us at a moment when we least dreamt of any accident; and from the pleasing anticipations we had formed, of realizing the certain profits of our labour, we were dejected by a sudden, most mysterious, and overwhelming calamity. Not a moment, however, was to be lost in endeavouring to provide for the extremity to which it was now certain we were reduced. We were more than a thousand miles from the nearest land, and with nothing but a light open boat, as the resource of safety for myself and companions. I ordered the men to cease pumping, and every one to provide for himself; seizing a hatchet at the same time, I cut away the lashings of the spare boat, which lay bottom up across two spars directly over the quarter deck, and cried out to those near me, to take her as she came down. They did so accordingly, and bore her on their shoulders as far as the waist of the ship. The steward had in the mean time gone down into the cabin twice, and saved two quadrants, two practical navigators, and the captain's trunk and mine; all which were hastily thrown into the boat, as she lay on the deck, with the two compasses which I snatched from the binnacle. He attempted to descend again; but the water by this time had rushed in, and he returned without being able to effect his purpose. By the time we had got the boat to the waist, the ship had filled with water, and was going down on her beam-ends: we shoved our boat as quickly as possible from the plank-shear into the water, all hands jumping in her at the same time, and launched off clear of the ship. We were scarcely two boat's lengths distant from her, when she fell over to windward, and settled down in the water.

Amazement and despair now wholly took possession of us. We contemplated the frightful situation the ship lay in, and thought with horror upon the sudden and dreadful calamity that had overtaken us. We looked upon each other, as if to gather some consolatory sensation from an interchange of sentiments, but every countenance was marked with the paleness of despair. Not a word was spoken for several minutes by any of us; all appeared to be bound in a spell of stupid consternation; and from the time we were first attacked by the whale, to the period of the fall of the ship, and of our leaving her in the boat, more than ten minutes could not certainly have elapsed! God only knows in what way, or by what means, we were enabled to accomplish in that short time what we did; the cutting away and transporting the boat from where she was deposited would of itself, in ordinary circumstances, have consumed as much time as that, if the whole ship's crew had been employed in it. My companions had not saved a single article but what they had on their backs; but to me it was a source of infinite satisfaction, if any such could be gathered from the horrors of our gloomy situation, that we had been fortunate enough to have preserved our compasses, navigators, and quadrants. After the first shock of my feelings was over, I enthusiastically contemplated them as the probable instruments of our salvation; without them all would have been dark and hopeless. Gracious God! what a picture of distress and suffering now presented itself to my imagination. The crew of the ship were saved, consisting of twenty human souls. All that remained to conduct these twenty beings through the stormy terrors of the ocean, perhaps many thousand miles, were three open light boats. The prospect of obtaining any provisions or water from the ship, to subsist upon during the time, was at least now doubtful. How many long and watchful nights, thought I, are to be passed? How many tedious days of partial starvation are to be endured, before the least relief or mitigation of our sufferings can be reasonably anticipated. We lay at this time in our boat, about two ship's lengths off from the wreck, in perfect silence, calmly contemplating her situation, and absorbed in our own melancholy reflections, when the other boats were discovered rowing up to us. They had but shortly before discovered that some accident had befallen us, but of the nature of which they were entirely ignorant. The sudden and mysterious disappearance of the ship was first discovered by the boat-steerer in the captain's boat, and with a horror-struck countenance and voice, he suddenly exclaimed, "Oh, my God! where is the ship?" Their operations upon this were instantly suspended, and a general cry of horror and despair burst from the lips of every man, as their looks were directed for her, in vain, over every part of the ocean. They immediately made all haste towards us. The captain's boat was the first that reached us. He stopped about a boat's length off, but had no power to utter a single syllable: he was so completely overpowered with the spectacle before him, that he sat down in his boat, pale and speechless. I could scarcely recognise his countenance, he appeared to be so much altered, awed, and overcome, with the oppression of his feelings, and the dreadful reality that lay before him. He was in a short time however enabled to address the inquiry to me, "My God, Mr. Chase, what is the matter?" I answered, "We have been stove by a whale." I then briefly told him the story. After a few moments' reflection he observed, that we must cut away her masts, and endeavour to get something out of her to eat. Our thoughts were now all accordingly bent on endeavours to save from the wreck whatever we might possibly want, and for this purpose we rowed up and got on to her. Search was made for every means of gaining access to her hold; and for this purpose the lanyards were cut loose, and with our hatchets we commenced to cut away the masts, that she might right up again, and enable us to scuttle her decks. In doing which we were occupied about three quarters of an hour, owing to our having no axes, nor indeed any other instruments, but the small hatchets belonging to the boats. After her masts were gone she came up about two-thirds of the way upon an even keel. While we were employed about the masts the captain took his quadrant, shoved off from the ship, and got an observation. We found ourselves in latitude 0° 40′ S. longitude 119° W. We now commenced to cut a hole through the planks, directly above two large casks of bread, which most fortunately were between decks, in the waist of the ship, and which being in the upper side, when she upset, we had strong hopes was not wet. It turned out according to our wishes, and from these casks we obtained six hundred pounds of hard bread. Other parts of the deck were then scuttled, and we got without difficulty as much fresh water as we dared to take in the boats, so that each was supplied with about sixty-five gallons; we got also from one of the lockers a musket, a small canister of powder, a couple of files, two rasps, about two pounds of boat nails, and a few turtle. In the afternoon the wind came on to blow a strong breeze; and having obtained every thing that occurred to us could then be got out, we began to make arrangements for our safety during the night. A boat's line was made fast to the ship, and to the other end of it one of the boats was moored, at about fifty fathoms to leeward; another boat was then attached to the first one, about eight fathoms astern; and the third boat, the like distance astern of her. Night came on just as we had finished our operations; and such a night as it was to us! so full of feverish and distracting inquietude, that we were deprived entirely of rest. The wreck was constantly before my eyes. I could not, by any effort, chase away the horrors of the preceding day from my mind: they haunted me the live-long night. My companions—some of them were like sick women; they had no idea of the extent of their deplorable situation. One or two slept unconcernedly, while others wasted the night in unavailing murmurs. I now had full leisure to examine, with some degree of coolness, the dreadful circumstances of our disaster. The scenes of yesterday passed in such quick succession in my mind that it was not until after many hours of severe reflection that I was able to discard the idea of the catastrophe as a dream. Alas! it was one from which there was no awaking; it was too certainly true, that but yesterday we had existed as it were, and in one short moment had been cut off from all the hopes and prospects of the living! I have no language to paint out the horrors of our situation. To shed tears was indeed altogether unavailing, and withal unmanly; yet I was not able to deny myself the relief they served to afford me. After several hours of idle sorrow and repining I began to reflect upon the accident, and endeavoured to realize by what unaccountable destiny or design, (which I could not at first determine,) this sudden and most deadly attack had been made upon us: by an animal, too, never before suspected of premeditated violence, and proverbial for its insensibility and inoffensiveness. Every fact seemed to warrant me in concluding that it was any thing but chance which directed his operations; he made two several attacks upon the ship, at a short interval between them, both of which, according to their direction, were calculated to do us the most injury, by being made ahead, and thereby combining the speed of the two objects for the shock; to effect which, the exact manœuvres which he made were necessary. His aspect was most horrible, and such as indicated resentment and fury. He came directly from the shoal which we had just before entered, and in which we had struck three of his companions, as if fired with revenge for their sufferings. But to this it may be observed, that the mode of fighting which they always adopt is either with repeated strokes of their tails, or snapping of their jaws together; and that a case, precisely similar to this one, has never been heard of amongst the oldest and most experienced whalers. To this I would answer, that the structure and strength of the whale's head is admirably designed for this mode of attack; the most prominent part of which is almost as hard and as tough as iron; indeed, I can compare it to nothing else but the inside of a horse's hoof, upon which a lance or harpoon would not make the slightest impression. The eyes and ears are removed nearly one-third the length of the whole fish, from the front part of the head, and are not in the least degree endangered in this mode of attack. At all events, the whole circumstances taken together, all happening before my own eyes, and producing, at the time, impressions in my mind of decided, calculating mischief, on the part of the whale, (many of which impressions I cannot now recall,) induce me to be satisfied that I am correct in my opinion. It is certainly, in all its bearings, a hitherto unheard of circumstance, and constitutes, perhaps, the most extraordinary one in the annals of the fishery.

November 21st. The morning dawned upon our wretched company. The weather was fine, but the wind blew a strong breeze from the SE. and the sea was very rugged. Watches had been kept up during the night, in our respective boats, to see that none of the spars or other articles (which continued to float out of the wreck,) should be thrown by the surf against, and injure the boats. At sunrise, we began to think of doing something; what, we did not know: we cast loose our boats, and visited the wreck, to see if any thing more of consequence could be preserved, but every thing looked cheerless and desolate, and we made a long and vain search for any useful article; nothing could be found but a few turtle; of these we had enough already; or at least, as many as could be safely stowed in the boats, and we wandered around in every part of the ship in a sort of vacant idleness for the greater part of the morning. We were presently aroused to a perfect sense of our destitute and forlorn condition, by thoughts of the means which we had for our subsistence, the necessity of not wasting our time, and of endeavouring to seek some relief wherever God might direct us.

HERMAN MELVILLE

[Manuscript Notes on Owen Chase]†

[2]   *General Evidences*

This thing of the Essex is found (stupidly[1] abbreviated) in many compilations of nautical adventure made within the last 15 or 20 years.

The Englishman Bennett in his exact work ("Whaling Voyage round the
Globe") quotes the thing as an acknowledged fact.

Besides seamen, several landsman (Judge Shaw & others) acquainted
with Nantucket, have evinced to me their unquestioning faith in the
thing; having seen Captain Pollard himself, & being conversant with his
situation in Nantucket since the disaster[2]

[3]   *What I Know of Owen Chase &c*

When I was on board the ship Acushnet of Fairhaven, on the passage
to the Pacific cruising-grounds, among other matters of forecastle conversation at times was the story of the Essex. It was then that I first
became acquainted with her history and her truly astounding fate.

But what then served to specialise my interest at the time was the circumstance that the [4] Second mate of our ship, Mr Hall, an Englishman
& Londoner by berth [birth], had for two three-years voyages sailed with
Owen Chace (then in command of the whaleship "William Wirt" * (I think
it was) of Nantucket.) This Hall always spoke of Chace with much inter-

---

† While writing *Moby-Dick* Melville asked his father-in-law, Lemuel Shaw, chief justice of the Massachusetts Supreme Court, to help him locate a copy of the exceedingly rare *Narrative* by the Nantucket whaler Owen Chase (see p. 565 herein), knowing that Shaw was widely acquainted in
Nantucket, where he held court every summer. Thomas Macy searched for Shaw but found only a
copy lacking several pages; that volume Melville happily received around April 1851, too late to be
much if any direct help with *Moby-Dick*. Prizing the imperfect book, Melville soon had it bound
with blank leaves at the end and began making notes in it, and resumed doing so years later. The
volume is now in the Houghton Library of Harvard University and the notes are transcribed by permission, the 1967 Hayford-Parker text being slightly modified by insertions in square brackets to
record three or four later readings in the NN edition (1988). The NN edition prints a clear photo
facsimile of each page of Melville's notes and a line-by-line transcription of those notes, as well as
fuller information about the provenience of the book and the dating and accuracy of the notes.

    Melville's notes contain some obvious errors of fact: it is impossible that the whale hunter who
came aboard the *Acushnet* was Owen Chase, who was not at sea at the time; also, Chase's son
whom Melville met was not the son of the unfaithful wife, and Chase's divorce from her (Judge
Shaw presiding in the case) had occurred in 1840, before Melville sailed on the *Acushnet*. See
Parker, *Herman Melville* (1.194–99): "In all Melville's life he is not known to have so intricately
tangled up so much misapprehension and misinformation as he did about Owen Chase."
Melville's confusions about Chase (whose name he always misspelled Chace), the *Charles Carroll*, the *William Wirt*, and other matters signal not a lack of interest but rather a powerfully
heightened imaginative interest in American men who had survived by eating human flesh. During a decade of brooding over the wreck of the *Essex* Melville had come to associate survival by
cannibalism with the Greek myth in which Cronos swallows his children and had begun to make
personal application to his own father's eating of his eight children's inheritances before he died.
When he makes Ahab call himself "cannibal old me" (ch. 132) Melville had at least "some inkling
of why he had been so moved when he saw an American he thought had been a cannibal—even
when he identified the wrong man" (Parker, 199).

1. The NN edition prints "stupedly"; here we give Melville the benefit of the doubt and print "stupidly"; later we print some very clear misspellings ("mear," for instance) but follow them by the
correct word in square brackets. Some transcriptions are doubtful ("specialise"? "specialize"?),
but Melville's clear and regular misspelling "Chace" is followed throughout.

2. On July 8, 1852, when Melville accompanied Judge Shaw during his judicial duties in Nantucket.

est & sincere regard—but he did not seem to know any thing more about him or the Essex affair than any body else.

Somewhere about the latter part of A. D. 1841, in this same ship the Acushnet, we spoke the [5] "Wm Wirt*" of Nantucket, & Owen Chace was the Captain, & so it came to pass that I saw him. He was a large, powerful well-made man; rather tall; to all appearances something past forty-five or so; with a handsome face for a Yankee, & expressive of great uprightness & calm unostentatious courage. His whole appearance impressed me pleasurably. He was the most prepossessing-looking whale-hunter I think I ever saw.

——Being a mear [mere] foremast-hand I had no opportunity of conversing with Owen (tho' he was [6] on board our ship for two hours at a time) nor have I ever seen him since. But I should have before mentioned, that before seeing Chace's ship, we spoke another Nantucket craft & *gammed* with her. In the forecastle I made the acquaintance of a fine lad of sixteen or thereabouts, a son of Owen Chace. I questioned him concerning his father's adventure; and when I left his ship to return again the next morning (for the two vessels were to sail in company for a few days [7] he went to his chest & handed me a complete copy (same edition as this one) of the *Narrative*. This was the first printed account of it I had ever seen, & the only copy of Chace's Narrative (regular & authentic) except the present one. The reading of this wondrous story upon the landless sea, & close to the very latitude of the shipwreck had a surprising effect upon me. [*Pages 8–13 are blank.*]

[14]   *Authorship of the Book*

There seems no reason to suppose that Owen himself wrote the Narrative. It bears obvious tokens of having been written for him; but at the same time, its whole air plainly evinces that it was carefully & conscientiously written to Owen's dictation of the facts.—It is almost as good as tho' Owen wrote it himself.

[15]   *Another Narrative of the Adventure*

I have been told that Pollard the Captain, wrote, or caused to be wrote under his own name, his version of the story. I have seen extracts purporting to be from some such work. But I have never seen the work itself.—I should imagine Owen Chace to have been the fittest person to narrate the thing.

[16]   *Note*

Vide ante p.p. 4-5, M.S.

I was doubtful a little at the time of writing whether this ship was the W^m. Wirt. I am now certain that it was the *Charles Carroll* of which [17] Owen Chace was Captain for several voyages.

Since writing the foregoing I—somewhere about 1850–3—saw Capt. Pollard on the island of Nantucket, and exchanged some words with him. To the islanders he was a nobody—to me, the most [18] impressive man, tho' wholly unassuming, even humble—that I ever encountered. [*Pages 19–20 are missing.*]

[21]   *Sequel*

——I can not tell exactly how many more pages the complete narrative contains—but at any rate, very little more remains to be related.—The boat was picked up by the ship, & the poor fellows were landed in Chili & in time sailed for home. Owen Chace returned to his business of whaling, & in due time became a Captain, as related in the beginning.

Captain Pollard's boat (from which Chace's had become separated) was also after a miserable time, picked up by a ship, but not [22] until two of its crew had died delirious, & furnished food for the survivors.

The third boat, it does not appear, that it was ever heard of, after its sub-separation from Pollard's.

Pollard himself returned to Nantucket, & subsequently sailed on another whaling voyage to the Pacific, but he had not been in the Pacific long, when one night, his ship went ashore on unknown rocks, & was dashed to peaces. The crew, with Pollard, put off in their boats, & were soon picked up by [23] another whale-ship, with which, the day previous, they had sailed in company.—I got this from Hall, Second Mate of the *Acushnet*.—

Pollard, it seems, now took the hint, & after reaching home from this second shipwreck, vowed to abide ashore. He has ever since lived in Nantucket. Hall told me that he became a butcher there. I believe he is still living. [*Added in pencil and underlined three times:* A night-watchman.]

Concerning the three men left on the island;—they were taken off at last (in a sad state enough) by a ship, which [24] purposely touched there for them, being advised of them, by their shipmates who had been previously landed in Chili.

——All the sufferings of these miserable men of the Essex might, in all human probability, have been avoided, had they, immediately after leaving the wreck, steered straight for Tahiti, from which they were not very distant at the time, & *to* which, there was a fair Trade wind. But they dreaded cannibals, & strange to tell knew not that for more than 20 years, the English [25] missionaries had been resident in Tahiti; & that in the same year of their shipwreck—1820—it was entirely safe for the mariner to touch at Tahiti.[3]

——But they chose to stem a head wind, & make a passage of several thousand miles (an unavoidably roundabout one, too) in order to gain a civilised harbor on the coast of South America.

[26]   *Further Concerning Owen Chace*

The miserable pertinaciousness of misfortune which pursued Pollard the Captain, in his second disastrous & entire shipwreck, did likewise hunt[4] poor Owen, tho' somewhat more dilatory in over-taking him, the second time.

---

3. In this paragraph, the italicized "to" in "*to* which" and the word "their" in "their shipwreck" are NN readings. In the 1967 NCE "to" was in roman type and "their" was misread as "the."

For, while I was in the *Acushnet* we heard from some whale-ship that we spoke, that the Captain of the "*Charles* [27] *Carrol*"—that is Owen Chace—had recently received letters from home, informing him of the certain infidelity of his wife, the mother of several children, one of them being the lad of sixteen, whom I alluded to as giving me a copy of his father's narrative to read. We also heard that this receipt of this news had told most heavily upon Chace, & that he was a prey to the deepest gloom.

DAVID H. BATTENFELD

The Source for the Hymn in *Moby-Dick*†

In Herman Melville's *Moby-Dick*, before Father Mapple preaches his now famous sermon, he leads his congregation in a hymn which, as Yvor Winters remarks, "contains the essence of the sermon."[1] A critical edition of *Moby-Dick* notes:

> No original has been found for this hymn. Its aptness for Melville's artistic purposes and the imaginative freedom with which it was written (notably in the avoidance of the conventional rhyme in the fourth stanza) suggest that Melville himself was the author.[2]

Nevertheless, an original does exist. The source is the rhymed version of the first part of Psalm 18, as found in the psalms and hymns of the Reformed Protestant Dutch Church, the Church in which Melville was brought up.[3] Needing an appropriate hymn for his artistic purposes, Melville may have remembered this psalm from his youth, or he may simply have gone looking through the hymnal. In any case, the subtitle, "Deliverance from despair," surely caught his attention, for Jonah's plight is parallel to that of the psalmist. The Psalm, however, speaks only of a very generalized situation; Melville's problem therefore was to alter it to fit the specific reference to the story of Jonah. How well he succeeded may be best seen in a line-by-line comparison of the two versions.

Psalm 18. First Part. L.M.   Melville's version.
Deliverance from despair.

1 Thee will I love, O Lord, my
     strength,
My rock, my tower, my high
     defence:
They mighty arm shall be my
     trust:

---

4. Among the debatable readings, the word "hunt" (as in 1967 and 1988) might possibly be "haunt." We print "disastrous" from the 1988 text instead of the 1967 "disaster."
† From David H. Battenfeld, "The Source for the Hymn in *Moby-Dick*," *American Literature* 27.4 (November 1955): 393–96. Reprinted by permission of Duke University Press.
1. *In Defense of Reason* (Denver, 1947), p. 206.
2. Edited by Luther Mansfield and Howard Vincent (New York, 1952), p. 616.
3. *The Psalms and Hymns . . . of the Reformed Protestant Dutch Church in North America* (Philadelphia, 1854), pp. 34–35. This book was compiled by Dr. John H. Livingston in 1789, and was expanded in 1830 and 1846. The volume cited was approved by the General Synod in 1846.

For I have found salvation
  thence.

2 Death, and the terrors of the
   grave,
  Spread over me their dismal
    shade;
  While floods of high tempta-
    tions rose,
  And made my sinking soul
    afraid.

"The ribs and terrors in the
   whale,
  Arched over me a dismal
    gloom,
While all God's sun-lit waves
  rolled by,
  And left me deepening down
    to doom.

3 I saw the opening gates of hell,
  With endless pains and sor-
    rows there,
  Which none but they that
    feel, can tell;
  While I was hurried to des-
    pair.

"I saw the opening maw of hell,
  With endless pains and sor-
    rows there;
Which none but they that feel
  can tell—
  Oh, I was plunging to despair.

4 In my distress I call'd my God,
  When I could scarce believe
    him mine;
  He bow'd his ear to my com-
    plaints;
  Then did his grace appear
    divine.

"In black distress, I called my
   God,
  When I could scarce believe
    him mine,
He bowed his ear to my com-
  plaints—
  No more the whale did me
    confine.

5 With speed he flew to my
   relief,
  As on a cherub's wings he
    rode:
  Awful and bright as lightning
    shone
  The face of my deliv'rer, God.

"With speed he flew to my
   relief,
  As on a radiant dolphin
    borne;
Awful, yet bright, as lightning
  shone
  The face of my Deliverer God.

6 Temptations fled at his re-
   buke,
  Dispell'd by his almighty
    breath:
  He sent salvation from on
    high,
  And drew me from the depths
    of death.

7 Great were my fears, my foes
   were great,
  Much was their strengh, and
    more their rage,
  But Christ, my Lord, is con-
    qu'ror still,
  In all the wars that devils
    wage.

8 My song for ever shall record

"My song for ever shall record

That terrible, that joyful hour;	That terrible, that joyful hour;
And give the glory to the Lord,	I give the glory to my God,
Due to his mercy and his pow'r.	His all the mercy and the power."

Melville omits the first stanza of the Psalm. Since it sums up the theme, his narrative purpose is thereby enhanced, and he is able to fit his hymn to the Jonah story from the beginning. The second stanza is almost completely rewritten to state Jonah's situation, though both the meter and rhyme scheme are adhered to. The use of "ribs" makes natural the substitution of "arched" for "spread." The rest of the changes were probably suggested by the Book of Jonah: "For thou hadst cast me into the deep, in the midst of the seas; and the floods compassed me about: all thy billows and thy waves passed over me."[4] The rhyme change may be only for assonance and the alliteration in the last line,[5] but it should be observed that the Bible makes no mention of Jonah's fear, only of his state of despair. It is interesting that Melville rejects the natural word "floods" in the Psalm, even though it also appears in the Jonah story.

The change of "gates" to "maw" in stanza three of the Psalm is in keeping with the whale imagery, and the changes in the final line of the stanza heighten the emotional quality and substitute a more vividly specific image. Melville's substitution of "black" for "my" in the fourth stanza is also an improvement, and his revision of the final line is most skilful, enabling him as it does to keep the rhyme. Likewise, in the next stanza the change from the cherub to the dolphin is ingenious. "Borne" eliminates the partial rhyme of "rode" and "God," but manages to get another partial rhyme with "shone". The substitution of "yet" for "and" may be explained by the change in meaning of "awful" from the older "filling with awe" to the more modern "terrible," the sense that Melville usually gives it.

The sixth and seventh stanzas of the Psalm are rejected by Melville. They deal with "temptations" and "wars that devils wage," and as such are not apt for the Jonah story. Jonah is not subject to temptations, but rather suffering just punishment for his sin. In the final stanza, Melville changes "Lord" to "God," avoiding a rhyme, and revises the final line to get rid of the awkward initial trochaic foot.

We observe that Melville's changes and revisions are of two kinds. Substantially, they are to change the generalized theme of the Psalm to attain specific correspondence to the story of Jonah. The omission of three stanzas is fairly automatic, but the revisions within the stanzas used demonstrate a very real ability to keep within the framework of his source while substituting particularized relevant material. Also, a number of changes are purely stylistic, and in every case I believe they are an improvement on the original. Thus, this single example of poetic revision from a given source shows the same kind of imaginative re-creation as do those prose revisions that have been studied at length, in *Moby-Dick* and elsewhere,

---

4. Jonah: 2:3 (King James version).
5. It seems to me conclusive from the tense of the source that Melville's verb should be "left," as in the first English edition, rather than "lift," as most commonly reprinted.

and again raises the question whether sources as yet undiscovered exist for many other key Melville passages—possibly even Father Mapple's sermon itself.

HOWARD P. VINCENT

[Sources of "The Try-Works"][†]

"Looking into the red heat of the fire"

In "The Try-Works" (96), Melville takes up the most spectacular of all the operations in the sperm whale fishery: the trying-out of the blubber in the try-pots resting in a great brick oven built on the deck. Into these two great try-pots the crew tossed the chunks of blubber, the "bible-leaves" minced into thin slices by the "archbishoprick" in his strange cassock. Frederick Debell Bennett described the entire process succinctly in *A Whaling Voyage Round the Globe:*

> Previous to being boiled, or "tryed-out," the blubber is cleared from adhering flesh, and cut with spades into slips, or "horse-pieces," which, (after they had been "minced," or scored by a broad and thin knife, upon an elevated block of wood, termed the "horse,") are consigned to the boilers of the try-works. The "head" is first boiled, and its produce kept as distinct as possible from the "Body"; since the one is considered as Spermaceti, or "head-matter," and the other as Sperm-oil.
>
> It must be regarded as a curious circumstance, and as one highly essential to the economy of these ships, that the process of boiling the oil supplies also the fuel required for that purpose; the "scraps," or refuse from which the oil has been extracted, burning, when placed in the furnace, with a fierce and clear flame and intense heat, and being sufficient in quantity to render any other fuel unnecessary; the scraps remaining from one affair of oil being reserved to commence a second.
>
> In a dark night, the process of "trying out" in the open ocean presents a spectacle partaking much of the grand and terrific. The dense volumes of smoke that roll before the wind and over the side of the vessel, as she pursues her course through the water—the roaring of the flames, bursting in lofty columns from the works, and illuminating the ship and surrounding expanse of sea—and the uncouth garb and implements of the crew, assembled around the fires—produce a peculiarly imposing effect; though one that is not altogether to be reconciled with the ordinary character of marine scenery.

Bennett's description, especially in the last paragraph, probably contributed to Melville's account of the try-works; it is almost certain that Melville had read it. More important borrowing is to be found in comparing the words of *Moby-Dick* with J. Ross Browne's description in *Etch-*

---

† From Howard P. Vincent, *The Trying-Out of "Moby-Dick"* (Boston: Houghton Mifflin Company, 1949). Reprinted by permission of Kent State University Press.

ings of a Whaling Cruise. Writing with a fuller feeling for the picturesque qualities of the scene than had Bennett, Browne exploited the sensational possibilities of his material at greater length and with more imaginative sweep, the allusions to Salvator Rosa and Dante, for instance, adding considerably to the superiority of his version:

> A "trying-out" scene is the most stirring part of the whaling business, and certainly the most disagreeable. . . . We will now imagine the works in full operation at night. Dense clouds of lurid smoke are curling up to the tops, shrouding the rigging from the view. The oil is hissing in the try-pots. Half a dozen of the crew are sitting on the windlass, their rough, weather-beaten faces shining in the red glare of the fires, all clothed in greasy duck, and forming about as savage a looking group as ever was sketched by the pencil of Salvator Rosa. The cooper and one of the mates are raking up the fires with long bars of wood or iron. The decks, bulwarks, railing, try-works, and windlass are covered with oil, and slime of black-skin, glistening with the red glare from the try-works. Slowly and doggedly the vessel is pitching her way through the rough seas, looking as if enveloped in flames. . . .
>
> . . . A trying-out scene has something peculiarly wild and savage in it; a kind of indescribable uncouthness, which renders it difficult to describe with anything like accuracy. There is a murderous appearance about the blood-stained decks, and the huge masses of flesh and blubber lying here and there, and a ferocity in the looks of the men, heightened by the red, fierce glare of the fires, which inspire in the mind of the novice feelings of mingled disgust and awe. But one soon becomes accustomed to such scenes and regards them with the indifference of a veteran in the field of battle. I know of nothing to which this part of the whaling business can be more appropriately compared than to Dante's pictures of the infernal regions. It requires but little stretch of the imagination to suppose the smoke, the hissing boilers, the savage-looking crew, and the waves of flame that burst now and then from the flues of the furnace, part of the paraphernalia of a scene in the lower regions.

Browne's passage is excellent—compact and vivid, alive to surfaces and lights. To improve on it was a challenge to Melville's subtlest skill. How he met and surpassed Browne may be seen by studying this short sample from *Moby-Dick:*

> The hatch, removed from the top of the works, now afforded a wide hearth in front of them. Standing on this were the Tartarean shapes of the pagan harpooneers, always the whale-ship's stokers. With huge pronged poles they pitched hissing masses of blubber into the scalding pots, or stirred up the fires beneath, till the snaky flames darted, curling, out of the doors to catch them by the feet. The smoke rolled away in sullen heaps. To every pitch of the ship there was a pitch of the boiling oil, which seemed all eagerness to leap into their faces. Opposite the mouth of the works, on the further side of the wide wooden hearth, was the windlass. This served for a sea-sofa. Here lounged the watch, when not otherwise employed, looking into the red heat of the fire, till their eyes felt scorched in their heads. Their tawny features, now all

begrimed with smoke and sweat, their matted beards, and the contrasting barbaric brilliancy of their teeth, all these were strangely revealed in the capricious emblazonings of the works. As they narrated to each other their unholy adventures, their tales of terror told in words of mirth; as their uncivilized laughter forked upwards out of them, like the flames from the furnace; as to and fro, in their front, the harpooneers wildly gesticulated with their huge pronged forks and dippers; as the wind howled on, and the sea leaped, and the ship groaned and dived, and yet steadfastly shot her red hell further and further into the blackness of the sea and the night, and scornfully champed the white bone in her mouth, and viciously spat round her on all sides; then the rushing Pequod, freighted with savages, and laden with fire, and burning a corpse, and plunging into that blackness of darkness, seemed the material counterpart of her monomaniac commander's soul.

Stirred by his personal memories and by the graphic accounts in Browne and Bennett,[1] Melville has deepened his description by developing the Dantesque associations suggested in *Etchings*. Melville etches every detail with the sharpness, and the feeling for chiaroscuro, of a Rembrandt, and to the photographic fidelity of his words he adds a haunting suggestiveness Ryderesque in quality. What shows Melville's skill most completely, however, is the way in which he subordinates and unites his word-painting to the characterization of Ahab and to the emotional-philosophical currents of *Moby-Dick*. Interesting though it is in itself, the description is fused with the total structure of the novel. Here, certainly, is a single fact described not only for itself but also for its implications—a fact seen in its totality.

Although such an unforgettable bit of wit as the description of the smoke from the try-works, "It smells like the left-wing of the day of judgment," may possibly have been inspired by Browne's down-Easter who, choking with the fumes, swore: "if this warn't he-l on a small scale, he didn't know what to call it"; nevertheless, Melville's entire chapter reaches heights of meaning independent of, although extended from, fish documents. From the masterly exposition of the trying-out process Melville modulates back to his original theme, Selfhood, and to his original character, Ishmael.

Ishmael's vantage point from which he had seen the trying-out had been the tiller of the ship, apart but not far from the flaming try-pots. The physical separation suggests spiritual separation as well, which Melville subtly points up by having Ishmael describe the crew as capering fiend shapes much like flickering shapes moving about a great cauldron of evil. Watching the whalemen's sabbath, "that night, in particular, a strange

---

1. And, also, possibly by *Ribs and Trucks* (Boston, 1842): "but one thing, I pray thee forget not to honor with a parting glance—a night-scene around the 'try-works';—it is too like purgatory, to be neglected. Three ovens, amidships, surmounted by three huge cauldrons of oil; the oil boiling, the ovens lapping out tongues of flickering flame; the watch clustering and flitting and gibbering, in a light now lurid, now livid—some feeding the gaping furnaces with fuel, some couchant on the windlass, 'spinning yarns': one brandishing a mighty fork, another 'spairging about the brumstane c[l]ootie,' with a long, long ladle, and occasionally anointing the fire, till it makes the rigging and the sails and the weltering waters gleam again in its blaze; and each busy, smutty, diabolical-looking figure at hand flash into second daylight;—all, together, afford a spectacle 'beautiful as rare,' and leave nothing to be guessed at, would you fancy to yourself a 'situation' in the freehold of 'auld Nickie-Ben.' [*Brumstane clootie*: brimstone devil, "clootie" from "hoof," in Scottish dialect. *Nickie-Ben*: another name for the devil. Editors' note.]

(and ever since inexplicable) thing occurred to me." Ishmael fell into a doze.

> I was half conscious of putting my fingers to the lids and mechan-
> ically stretching them still further apart. But, spite of all this, I could
> see no compass before me to steer by; though it seemed but a minute
> since I had been watching the card, by the steady binnacle lamp illu-
> minating it. Nothing seemed before me but a jet gloom, now and
> then made ghastly by flashes of redness. Uppermost was the impres-
> sion, that whatever swift, rushing thing I stood on was not so much
> bound to any haven ahead as rushing from all havens astern. A stark,
> bewildered feeling, as of death, came over me. Convulsively my
> hands grasped the tiller, but with the crazy conceit that the tiller was,
> somehow, in some enchanted way, inverted. My God! what is the
> matter with me? thought I. Lo! in my brief sleep I had turned myself
> about, and was fronting the ship's stern, with my back to her prow
> and the compass. In an instant I faced back, just in time to prevent
> the vessel from flying up into the wind, and very probably capsizing
> her. How glad and how grateful the relief from this unnatural hallu-
> cination of the night, and the fatal contingency of being brought by
> the lee!

The episode is dramatic, arising naturally but suddenly out of the rich painting of the preceding paragraphs. We may never know whether Melville was transferring journalistic fact to his novel, but it is possible to suggest that the scene may have been built from one which he had already used. The narrow escape of the *Pequod* suggests a similar event in *White-Jacket*, in which the *Neversink* is saved just in the nick of time when "Mad Jack" mutinously countermands the previous orders of Captain Claret. In *White-Jacket* Melville uses the scene to point up his contrast between the efficiency of the subordinate as against the bungling stupidity of the superior. Melville adapted this scene from a little volume entitled *Scenes in "Old Ironsides."* Possibly the idea of the ship saved at the last minute by a reversal of controls, which we have here in *Moby-Dick*, was Melville's second adaptation of an episode which had already served him well.

But whatever the source of the narrative section of "The Try-Works," Melville's manipulation of the episode is of course uniquely his own. What is the secondary meaning of the event? Ishmael, remember, said that it was "inexplicable." May it not illustrate the folly of isolation from the social norm, the sinfulness of what Hawthorne has called the Unpardonable Sin, when man has "lost his hold of the magnetic chain of humanity"? Melville makes the point obliquely through symbolism:

> Look not too long in the face of the fire, O man! Never dream with
> thy hand on the helm! Turn not thy back to the compass; accept the
> first hint of the hitching tiller; believe not the artificial fire, when its
> redness makes all things look ghastly. To-morrow, in the natural sun,
> the skies will be bright; those who glared like devils in the forking
> flames, the morn will show in far other, at least gentler, relief; the
> glorious, golden, glad sun, the only true lamp—all others but liars!

Without the capacity to sense our relatedness to our fellows we cut ourselves off from the capacity for change, and starve or destroy ourselves.
One needs an awareness of one's separate identity but too complete a separation cuts us from human growth.

In the chapter on "The Mast-Head" Melville had satirized the neo-Pla-
tonic idealist, his identity lost in the infinite, dreamily unable to keep a
sharp eye for the physical and harsh facts (symbolized by the whales) and
therefore in imminent danger of plunging from the masthead into the
Descartian vortices of the sea. If Transcendentalism errs in too great an
insistence on unity and too little heeds multiety, it also errs in too great
an insistence on self-reliance. Too great an emphasis on self, he says
implicatively, may lead to self-destruction just as surely as too great a disregard for appearances had done. Ishmael looking at the whalemen, his
fellow crew members, pitchforking the blubber, saw them pictorially and
then metaphorically as devils from hell—but himself at the tiller as none.
(Such confidence in his own selfhood was almost suicide—and the
destruction of the crew.) These devils in the forking flames will show in
the next morning's sun as human beings like himself. Man—Ishmael—
may look into the fire to see the demonic shapes, but he must also recognize them as his own companions also.

The flame into which Ishmael stares resembles the lime-kiln fire into
which Ethan Brand, in Hawthorne's story of that title, had too long gazed
and by which he is destroyed. In both "Ethan Brand" and *Moby-Dick* the
fire symbolizes the demonic and irrational forces to which Freud gave the
name the "Id"; the bawdy, maenadic, and orgiastic foundations of the
human personality. Amiel describes his fear at facing these terrifying, subterranean forces: "I too have been reduced to nothingness, and I shudder
on the brink of the great abysses that yawn within my being, in the grip of a
longing for the unknown, weakened by a thirst for the infinite, humbled
before the ineffable." Ethan Brand and, momentarily, Ishmael were guilty,
in Hawthorne's words, of "the sin of an intellect that triumphed over the
sense of brotherhood with man and reverence for God, and sacrificed
everything to its own mighty claims!" Melville had already indicated his
awareness of the abysses of the human soul[2] when he wrote in *Mardi*: "To
scale great heights, we must come out of lowermost depths. The way to
heaven is through hell. We need fiery baptisms in the fiercest flames of our
own bosoms," a passage similar in insight to Milton's famous dictum:

> The mind is its own place and in itself
> Can make a heaven of hell, a hell of heaven.

Here, in "The Try-Works," Melville implies again the necessity of the fiery
baptism, for, as he says, "the sun hides not Virginia's Dismal Swamp, nor
Rome's accursed Campagna, nor wide Sahara, nor all the millions of miles
of deserts and griefs beneath the moon. . . . So, therefore, that mortal man
who hath more of joy than sorrow in him, that mortal man cannot be true—

---

2. Compare Nietzsche's Apothegm 146 from *Beyond Good and Evil:* "He who fights with monsters
   should be careful lest he thereby become a monster. And if thou gaze long into an abyss, the abyss
   will also gaze into thee." Some student might well study Melville's markings in his volumes of
   Nietzsche (written of course long after *Moby-Dick*) to see how Melville was impressed by the German writer and also to see how Melville had anticipated his thought.

not true, or undeveloped." The fire of the primitive Self must be recognized, but abandonment to it means spiritual death; Melville's warning is specific:

> Give not thyself up, then, to fire, lest it invert thee, deaden thee; as for the time it did me. There is a wisdom that is woe; but there is a woe that is madness. And there is a Catskill eagle in some souls that can alike dive down into the blackest gorges, and soar out of them again and become invisible in the sunny spaces. And even if he for ever flies within the gorge, that gorge is in the mountains; so that even in his lowest swoop the mountain eagle is still higher than other birds upon the plain, even though they soar.

"Art," Fauré wrote, "is therefore a game, as the philosophers have called it. It is a matter of dancing on the edge of the abyss, or hiding it with flowers." And so, implies Melville, is Life; it is a mean between unfettered Selfhood and regimented sociality. But looking into depths of the try-works Ishmael found what Gerard Manley Hopkins later discerned:

> . . . O the mind, mind has mountains; cliffs of fall
> Frightful, sheer, no-man-fathomed.

Into these blackest gorges of Life only Catskill eagles like Shakespeare and Melville dive to explore the depths of tragic horror, then soar to the heights of human—individual and social—experience, recorded for us in ambiguous symbol.

GEOFFREY SANBORN

The Name of the Devil: Melville's Other "Extracts" for *Moby-Dick*[†]

In the winter of 1933–34, Charles Olson became the first scholar to examine Herman Melville's seven-volume Shakespeare set, then in the possession of Melville's granddaughter, Frances Osborne. On the front of the last blank leaf of the seventh volume, he found the following notes in Melville's hand:

> It is better to laugh & not sin than to weep & be
> wicked.—Ten loads of coal to burn him.—
> Brought to the stake—warmed himself by the
> fire.
> Ego non baptizo te in nominee Patris et

---

† From Geoffrey Sanborn, "The Name of the Devil: Melville's Other 'Extracts' for *Moby-Dick*," *Nineteenth-Century Literature* 47.2 (September 1992): 212–35. Copyright © 1992 by the Regents of the University of California. Reprinted by permission. In his title Sanborn alludes to the conclusion of Melville's June 29, 1851, letter to Hawthorne (p. 542 herein): "Shall I send you a fin of the *Whale* by way of a specimen mouthful? The tail is not yet cooked—though the hell-fire in which the whole book is broiled might not unreasonably have cooked it all ere this. This is the book's motto (the secret one),—Ego non baptiso te in nomine—but make out the rest yourself." Sanborn discovered that that Melville encountered these Latin words in an article in the London *Quarterly Review* in an account of witch hunts during which priests had been convicted of baptising not in the name of the Father, the Son, and the Holy Ghost, but of the devil. Precisely what Melville meant about the motto of *Moby-Dick* is still debatable, but Sanborn's discovery helps fix the intellectual context. In his biography (1.847) Parker assumes that Melville identified himself with the victims of witch hunts.

Filii et Spiritus Sancti—sed in nomine
Diaboli.—Madness is undefinable—
It & right reasons extremes of one.
—Not the (black art) Goetic but Theurgic
  magic—
seeks converse with the Intelligence, Power, the
Angel.[1]

* * *

The notes beginning with the Satanic invocation, like Melville's letters to Hawthorne, have now become part of the extended body of *Moby-Dick*, a book whose long critical history has made the boundaries between text and context unusually thin. Though some critics have tried to guess where Melville might have picked up the Latin sentence and the technical terms for white and black magic, none have doubted that the notes are Melville's own invention, a terse but suggestive representation of his private thought. * * *

But Melville did not invent these notes. All but one of the sentences on this page of the Shakespeare volume were extracted from various parts of an essay called "Superstition and Knowledge" in the July 1823 issue of the *Quarterly Review*. The essay, whose anonymous author was Sir Francis Palgrave,[2] may have influenced Hawthorne's "The Birth-mark" as well as *Moby-Dick*, and strong traces of it continue to appear in Melville's later work. The rediscovery of Palgrave's essay obviously forces us to revise the critical history of these notes, which has depended so heavily on the assumption that they were a record of Melville's creative thought. Since Melville was not responsible for the substance of the notes, we must drastically scale down our sense of Shakespeare's influence on them, and thoroughly reevaluate the nature and extent of their relationship to *Moby-Dick*. I will begin my survey of this relationship by reporting the details of Melville's borrowings from Palgrave's essay, and then consider some corollary evidence that could help us determine both when and how it influenced his work.

The ostensible subjects of Palgrave's review are two books entitled *A Collection of rare and curious Tracts on Witchcraft, and the Second Sight, or an*

---

1. I use the transcription included in *Moby-Dick, or The Whale*, ed. Harrison Hayford, Hershel Parker, and G. Thomas Tanselle, vol. 6 of *The Writings of Herman Melville* (Evanston and Chicago: Northwestern Univ. Press and The Newberry Library, 1988), p. 970 (further quotations from *Moby-Dick* in the text are from this edition). These notes are on the page in the Shakespeare volume numbered [523] by the Northwestern-Newberry editors; on the reverse side of this leaf, page [524], Melville took up an entire page with additional notes. Because those notes are not associated with my findings, I do not discuss them here. For convenience's sake, when I refer to the "notes," I mean only the notes on page [523]. [In saying Charles Olson "found the following notes in Melville's hand" Sanborn politely avoids saying that Olson did not transcribe them precisely the way the NN editors were later able to do. Editors' note.]

2. The essay is reprinted in volume 10 of *The Collected Historical Works of Sir Francis Palgrave*, ed. Sir R. H. Inglis Palgrave (Cambridge: Cambridge Univ. Press, 1922), 245–83. Because "Superstition and Knowledge" was never reprinted in Melville's lifetime, Melville must have encountered the essay in the *Quarterly Review*. [Melville may have encountered the essay not in the original *Quarterly Review* but in a cheap American reprint of that magazine, for in the absence of international copyright American publishers, even in smaller cities, often reprinted important British magazines in full; and American magazines and newspapers could reprint any article from British magazines without paying the author or original publisher. Editors' note.]

original Essay on Witchcraft, and *The famous History of Friar Bacon, containing the wonderful Things that he did in his Life, also the Manner of his Death; with the Lives and Deaths of the two Conjurers, Bungay and Vandermast*. In accordance with the conventions of early-nineteenth-century quarterlies, however, Palgrave simply uses these books as an occasion for a discursive essay of his own, concerning the parallels between medieval superstition and modern forms of irrational belief, including the political idealism of the French Revolution and the scientific idealism of Lamarckian materialism. All of Melville's notes come from the first half of the essay, which explores the aberrant psychology of witches and witch hunters in relation to the "superstitions" of medieval Christianity and science.

The only sentence on the page of notes in the Shakespeare volume that does not derive from the *Quarterly Review* essay is the first one: "It is better to laugh & not sin than to weep & be wicked." All the rest are clearly drawn, more or less intact, from Palgrave. Early in the essay, as an example of how "the cruelty of the [witch trial] proceedings appears enhanced by the formality and precision with which they are narrated," Palgrave quotes from the bill presented by the Scottish town of Kirkaldy in 1633 to William Coke and Alison Dick, charging them three pounds, six shillings and eight pence to cover the cost of "*ten loads of coals to burn them*" (p. 444; emphasis added). Shortly thereafter Palgrave records the painful details of the "last execution of a Scottish witch," a grandmother executed at Dornock in 1722: "After being *brought out for execution*, the weather proving very severe, the poor old woman sat composedly before the pile, *warming herself by the fire* prepared to consume her" (p. 446; emphasis added). Melville's changes in Palgrave's wording, particularly his transformation of "them" to "him" and "herself" to "himself," suggest that he was reading the essay with an eye toward using its details in a story of his own.

The more influential borrowings begin at this point, and the space left on the page in the Shakespeare volume between "warmed himself by the fire" and "Ego non baptizo . . ." may indicate Melville's sudden excitement as he came across the Satanic baptismal formula. After observing that over six hundred women were executed in the German bishopric of Bamberg early in the seventeenth century, Palgrave declares that the accusations of their persecutors "bear the stamp of raving madness. Priests were convicted of baptising in the following form:—*Ego non baptizo te in nomine Patris et Filii et Spiritus Sancti—sed in nomine Diaboli*" (p. 447; emphasis added). Two pages later Palgrave more fully articulates his attribution of madness to the witch hunters:

> Without seeking to enter into the dread question of moral responsibility, we may in some degree extenuate, without excusing, the crimes of the persecutors, by ascribing them to virtual insanity. In considering the actions of the mind, it should never be forgotten, that its affections pass into each other like the tints of the rainbow: though we can easily distinguish them when they have assumed a decided colour, yet we can never determine where each hue begins. . . . *Madness is almost undefinable. Right reason and insanity are merely the extreme terms of a series of mental action, which need not be very long.* (p. 449; emphasis added)

Melville emphasizes the indefinability of madness by dropping the word "almost," and, apparently accidentally, transcribes "right reason" as "right reasons." More important, as I will discuss later, he calls madness and right reason "extremes of one," stressing the underlying identity of these "extremes" rather than the ambiguity of borderline cases.

Finally, Melville copies down details from Palgrave's discussion of the respectibility of magic in medieval Spain, where the colleges at Toledo, Salamanca, and Simancas "enjoyed a species of classical reputation" for their instruction in "unhallowed lore" (p. 452). Palgrave notes:

> The doctrine delivered at Simancas, however, was *not Goetic Magic*, or that which is vulgarly termed the *Black Art*, but the high and pure Theurgy which repels all converse with the evil demon.
>   *Theurgical magic*, the magic which *seeks its converse with the Power, the Intelligence, and the Angel*, might have been first diffused in Spain by the sectaries of the Gnostic doctrines, who appear to have found numerous adherents in that country during many centuries. (pp. 452–53; emphasis added)

Melville's reversal of the words "Power" and "Intelligence" may be significant, but it was more likely an error of hasty transcription, like his truncation of "Theurgical." Though he clearly abridges and revises Palgrave's wording in several places, there can be little doubt, on the basis of the overwhelming correlations between the essay and the notes, that Melville extracted all these passages directly from the pages of the *Quarterly Review*. * * *

STEVEN OLSEN-SMITH

[Melville's Poetic Use of Thomas Beale's *Natural History of the Sperm Whale*]†

Herman Melville acquired Thomas Beale's *Natural History of the Sperm Whale* on July 10, 1850, two months and nine days after having informed his friend Richard Henry Dana (in a letter of May 1) that he had a whaling narrative of his own "half way" written. In the same letter Melville had forewarned Dana that his "whaling voyage" would be "a strange sort of a book":

> [B]lubber is blubber you know; tho' you may get oil out of it, the poetry runs as hard as sap from a frozen maple tree;—& to cook the thing up, one must needs throw in a little fancy, which from the

† Excerpted and adapted from Steven Olsen-Smith, "Herman Melville's Erased Marginalia in Thomas Beale's *Natural History of the Sperm Whale*: Recovering a Source of Evidence for the Composition of *Moby-Dick*." Reprinted by permission of the author. The discoveries set forth in this publication were made possible through financial support from the William Reese Company of New Haven, Connecticut, through permission from the Houghton Library curatorial staff, and through the guidance of Dennis Marnon, Administrative Officer of the Houghton Library. The recovery of erased marginalia was facilitated in part by technical assistance arranged by Marnon and administered by Craigen Bowen, of the Fogg Art Museum, Harvard University.

> nature of the thing, must be ungainly as the gambols of the whales
> themselves. Yet I mean to give the truth of the thing, spite of this.

The declaration reveals that in composing his masterwork one of
Melville's major aesthetic struggles consisted in the creation of imaginative literature from known facts about sperm whales and about the whaling industry. In rising to the challenge Melville employed as major sources
at least five different factual studies of whales and whaling.[1] Two of these
books are known to survive in imperfect states: the sparsely marked first
volume of Melville's two-volume *Narrative of a Whaling Voyage*, by Frederick Debell Bennett (London: Richard Bentley, 1840), and Melville's
once heavily marked copy of Beale's *Natural History of the Sperm Whale*.
Although most of Melville's marginalia to Beale has unfortunately been
erased, newly recovered annotations in the volume furnish the closest evidence available to the lost manuscript of *Moby-Dick* and illuminate
Melville's efforts to obtain poetry from blubber.

A compelling example of Melville's poetic use of Beale's narrative occurs
with an annotation erased from Chapter 13 of *Natural History of the Sperm
Whale*. In describing the "Chase and Capture of the Sperm Whale," Beale
concludes his account of a protracted battle between a whale and whalemen with a provocative depiction of the animal's death-throes:

> As the life's blood gurgled thick through the nostril, the immense
> creature went into his "flurry" with excessive fury, the boats were
> speedily sterned off, while he beat the water in his dying convulsions
> with a force that appeared to shake the firm foundation of the
> ocean![2]

Melville scored the entire passage and penciled both a circle and an "X" in
the outside margin. He drew an "X" in the margin in order to reference his
annotation to Beale's description of the defeated whale, almost fully recov-
erable despite its erasure. After recording a corresponding "X" at the left
end of the bottom margin, Melville filled the bottom of the page by writing:

> As when the water issuing [—?—] off from a
> fountain [—?—] slowly lowers—so the
> dying spout of the whale.[3]

Although clearly prompted by it, the annotation is notably irrelevant to
Beale's observation. Melville likens the whale's dying spout to a diminish-
ing fountain, whereas Beale had written of the whale's violent convulsions
and had recorded nothing about the final act of spouting in his description of the whale's death. Rather than comment directly on Beale's passage (normally the point of an annotation), Melville responded in the
form of a poetic reflection uncorroborated by any information in Beale's

---

1. See Howard P. Vincent, *The Trying-out of Moby-Dick* (Boston: Houghton Mifflin, 1949), 128–35.
2. Thomas Beale, *Natural History of the Sperm Whale* (London: John Van Voorst, 1839), 182 (hereafter cited parenthetically).
3. *AC85.M4977.Zz839b. By permission of the Houghton Library, Harvard University. In all transcriptions words and characters printed outside of brackets represent readings of which I am fully
   confident. Erased phrases, words and portions of erased words that remain unrecovered appear
   within brackets as a question mark flanked by hyphens. When transcriptions can be hazarded on
   the basis of recovered individual characters, parts of characters (such as ascenders and descen-
   ders), and other forms of evidence, the conjectural reading appears italicized within brackets.

factual study. Purely fanciful in nature, the example underscores Melville's creative engagement with sources. Melville later worked the annotation into what became Chapter 81 of *Moby-Dick*, "The Pequod Meets the Virgin," where an old, blind, mutilated whale spouts its last breath after Flask delivers its death stroke.

In composing the episode Melville drew heavily from Beale. As Howard Vincent first recognized, the whale itself comes from chapter 2 of *Natural History of the Sperm Whale*, where Melville had used a circle to mark Beale's description of a blind whale once captured by the British whale-ship *Sarah and Elizabeth* (Beale 36; Vincent 268). On the page he anno-tated Melville also circled, checked, and underlined Beale's report that in the fight with the whale a "boat drew up over his flukes." From this van-tage point, Beale goes on, "the lance was darted" (182). In Melville's indebted account of the whale's death the *Pequod*'s boats "perilously drew over his swaying flukes, and the lances were darted into him" (Chapter 81, p. 282). Both appropriations exemplify Melville's unabashed plunder-ing of sources both for subject matter and for phrasing. But along with taking information and phraseology from Beale, Melville likewise lifted his annotation as the basis for a concluding simile. As Ishmael observes of the vanquished animal's final moments:

> It was most piteous, that last expiring spout. As when by unseen hands the water is gradually drawn off from some mighty fountain, and with half-stifled melancholy gurglings the spray-column lowers and lowers to the ground—so the last long dying spout of the whale. (282)

The published passage shows how elaborately Melville embellished his marginal conception while working it into his narrative. In portraying the fountain-image Melville added the poignant "half-stifled melancholy gur-glings" to his description of the declining spray-column (apparently the purport of the still-undeciphered erasures), and in the last half of his comparison he prefixed the alliterative "last long" to "dying spout of the whale." Melville thus transformed his roughly conceived analogy into a polished simile of Homeric proportions. But the evolution of the annota-tion is most memorable for how it reflects the thematic intentions that came to prevail as Melville's narrative progressed. In *Moby-Dick* the "fountain" becomes a "mighty fountain" brought down by "unseen hands," an apt metaphor for the ill-fated conflict of Ahab (Melville's "mighty pageant creature") with "intangible malignity" (282, 73, 156). Melville's elaboration of the annotation reveals how his "mighty theme" for the book—Ahab's mortal outrage—came to infuse even topical por-tions of his narrative derived from a factual source.

In fact themes of transgression and conflict emerge from within much of the recovered marginalia, such as Melville's response to Beale's expla-nation of "breaching" in his section on "Actions of the Sperm Whale" (Chapter 5 of *Natural History*). Endeavoring to account for the sperm whale's spectacular behavior of impelling itself above and beyond the ocean surface after charging upward from the depths, Beale theorizes that the "sperm whale often resorts to this action of breaching for the purpose of ridding itself of various animals which infest its skin, such as large 'sucking fish,' and other animals which resemble small crabs" (48). Actively seeking source material as the basis for dramatic incident as well as for authentic information, Melville declined Beale's hum-drum theory and instead responded with yet another poetic simile intended for his narrative in progress. He marked Beale's explanation with an "X" and, keying it to the bottom margin, provided his own explanation for the sperm whale's mysterious act of breaching:

> It may also [be that breaching is his] act of
> defiance, as a h[orse sha]king his mane,—
> [for] the waves then [—?—] the mane
> of the monster.

Melville's frequent use of horse-imagery in *Moby-Dick* helps to corroborate the conjectural reading even though he eliminated his reference to the horse when he finally worked his breaching annotation into the narrative. Moreover, the theory of breaching inspired by that comparison still made it eminently useful for the plot's final conflict.

There Melville's explanation of breaching concludes this passage from "The Chase—Second Day" (Chapter 134), where in luring the *Pequod* to its catastrophic fate Moby Dick reveals his belligerent presence to the incensed crew for the next to last time:

> The triumphant halloo of thirty buckskin lungs was heard, as—much nearer to the ship than the place of the imaginary jet, less than a mile ahead—Moby Dick bodily burst into view! For not by any calm and indolent spoutings; not by the peaceable gush of that mystic fountain in his head, did the White Whale now reveal his vicinity; but by the far more wondrous phenomenon of breaching. Rising with his utmost velocity from the furthest depths, the Sperm Whale thus booms his entire bulk into the pure element of air, and piling up a mountain of dazzling foam, shows his place to the distance of seven miles and more. In those moments, the torn, enraged waves he shakes off, seem his mane; in some cases, this breaching is his act of defiance. (415)

Here Melville's appropriation of source material displays his habitual fondness for excess, adding an extra mile ("and more") to Beale's assertion (immediately preceding the sentence Melville had annotated) that "the breach of a whale may be seen from the mast-head on a clear day at the distance of six miles" (48). The published passage also hints of the compositional procedure whereby an already existing annotation can influence and even give rise to separate material conceived by Melville in subsequent phases of writing. The logical progression of the narration (the white whale emerges *not* by calmness and indolence; *not* by peacefulness; *but* by . . . defiance) indicates that Melville composed the entire passage with his previously written annotation in mind. As with his poetic reflection on the "dying spout of the whale," the breaching passage illustrates Melville's instrumental use of annotations for climactic points in his narrative, such as for closure of individual episodes and of extended observations.

Yet another instance of closure in the published narrative derives from Melville's annotation to Beale on "Herding, and other Particulars, of the

Sperm Whale" (Chapter 6 of *Natural History*), where Beale observes that with "each herd or school of females are always from one to three large 'bulls'—the lords of the herd, or as they are called, the 'schoolmasters'" (51). Even if unfamiliar with Vincent's original research, readers of *Moby-Dick* will readily infer a connection between Beale's explanation and "Schools and Schoolmasters" (Chapter 88). In his copy of *Natural History* Melville underscored "'schoolmasters,'" and within the outer margin he recorded a circle along with his characteristic "X," again referencing the bottom of the page. There he alluded to "Vidocq in his 'Memoirs'"—so far the only recovered portion of an annotation clearly intended to note the irony of applying instructor-student metaphors to a herding instinct motivated by raw sexual energy. In *Moby-Dick* Melville's annotation formed the basis of a passage ending Ishmael's discussion of the dominant bull in "Schools and Schoolmasters":

> His title, schoolmaster, would very naturally seem derived from the name bestowed upon the harem itself ["school"], but some have surmised that the man who first thus entitled this sort of Ottoman whale, must have read the memoirs of Vidocq, and informed himself what sort of a country-schoolmaster that famous Frenchman was in his younger days, and what was the nature of those occult lessons he inculcated into some of his pupils. (307)

With an explanatory note intended for readers unfamiliar with *Memoires de Vidocq*, Harrison Hayford and Hershel Parker observe in this edition of *Moby-Dick* that the country-schoolmaster must be of the sort who seduces his female students.

Unmistakable in "Schools and Schoolmasters," the governing libidinal theme played no less prominent a role in Melville's creative response to Beale's chapter on herding, where in yet another annotation libido combines with the larger theme of conflict. In describing the developing behavior of young male sperm whales, Beale comments: "When about three-fourths grown, or sometimes only half, they separate from each other, and go singly in search of food" (54). Implying by way of mythical analogy that the motive for disbanding is more than just food, Melville responded to the passage with a classic example of violence motivated by sex. Whereas Beale maintains that the maturing young bulls break up to feed, Melville remarked:

> until they attain their [—?—] like old
> Ixion's [—?—] & his sins & punishment.

Chained to a wheel of fire as punishment for his attempt upon Hera, the mortal king Ixion of Greek myth here represents the reproductive instincts of the young bull sperm whales and their eventual conflicts with the older males. For when the younger males attain their sexual maturity, Melville implies, they invade the pods and attempt to wrest the females away from the established bulls who, like Zeus, retaliate in fury.

Although Melville probably recorded the annotation with the intent to work it into his narrative, in finally writing about the dispersal of young bull sperm whales he instead lifted the passage he had annotated. As is common in Melville's appropriations of this sort, phrasal parallels show that he likely had his source open in front of him while he wrote. Whereas Beale observes that when "three-fourths grown" the males "separate from each other, and go singly in search of food," Ishmael in "Schools and Schoolmasters" explains that the young bulls, "when about three fourths grown, break up, and separately go about in quest of settlements, that is, harems" (307). Instead of Zeus (frequently alluded to as Jove in *Moby-Dick*), Melville kept with the Turkish imagery evoked by "harems" and settled upon "the Bashaw" as title for a dominant bull guarding his females. The intruder-bull becomes "Lothario," the seducer from Sir William Davenant's *The Cruel Brother*, which Melville read in a folio volume he had recently purchased in London. But even though he chose not to make use of his annotation in *Moby-Dick*, the persistence of Melville's original response to Beale is clear. Nowhere in his chapter on herding does Beale comment upon the violent encounters of bulls spurred by reproductive impulses, yet Melville made it central to "Schools and Schoolmasters," retaining the revisionary point of his annotation by finally asserting in the appropriated passage that young bachelor groups disband not just for food but for copulation.

Presenting hints of aesthetic intentions abandoned in the course of composition, Melville's annotation on the dispersal of young bulls stands with other recovered annotations nowhere discernable in *Moby-Dick*. Yet the presence of Ixion in the margins of *Natural History of the Sperm Whale* remains intriguing for its connection to the concluding "Epilogue" of Melville's novel. There, after the white whale has stove the *Pequod*, and the vortex created by the sinking hulk has carried down every trace of ship and crew, Ishmael explains how he alone survived:

> [F]loating on the margin of the ensuing scene, and in full sight of it, when the half-spent suction of the sunk ship reached me, I was then, but slowly, drawn towards the closing vortex. When I reached it, it had subsided to a creamy pool. Round and round, then, and ever contracting towards the button-like black bubble at the axis of that slowly wheeling circle, like another Ixion I did revolve. (427)

Just as he had employed annotations for individual points of closure in *Moby-Dick*, Melville reserved his use of Ixion for the ultimate conclusion of his narrative, where Ishmael's resemblance to the classical transgressor emblematizes the cosmic punishment towards which Melville's epic narrative moves. The original appearance of Ixion in Beale's chapter on herding represents not an abandoned intention but one actually reoriented within separately conceived material.

Remarkably, with yet another annotation in *Natural History* Melville had already recorded the image of a vortex created by a sinking ship. Never erased, the annotation remains clearly perceptible on page 45 of Melville's source, where he applied an "X" alongside Beale's observation that when a whale is alarmed by hunters and descends before having achieved its allowance of oxygen, "he sinks without having assumed the perpendicular position." Also marking the passage with a circle, Melville commented that the spooked whale creates a "White and green vortex in the blue—as when a ship sinks." Although Melville marked the passage for potential use, in *Moby-Dick* he never employs Beale's explanation, nor does he ever make a point of linking the image of the whale's alarmed descent with the image of a sinking ship. But like the figure of Ixion the image of the vortex became paramount as Melville's narrative developed. The interconnected fates of the *Pequod* and of Ishmael affirm the lingering relevance of both annotations: in the margins of Beale two discrete, unrelated images brought together by Melville for stunning fruition in the conclusion of his narrative.

CRITICISM

Reviews of *Moby-Dick*

Authors listed in "Melville's Reading and *Moby-Dick*" (p. 431 herein), such as Burton, De Quincey, and Scoresby, and footnoted in the text of *Moby-Dick*, are not usually footnoted when they are mentioned in these reviews. This sampling includes the reviews in the London *Athenæum* and the *Spectator*, the two English reviews that were reprinted and quoted in the United States so as decisively to affect the American reception, where no one understood that the English edition lacked Melville's "Epilogue." A few of the extremely favorable English reviews are included to suggest the delight *The Whale* occasioned in some London readers; such praise, as far as we know, except that in *The Leader*, never reached Melville's eyes: he died without knowing that along with severe criticism in London the book had received extraordinary praise. Also included are British reviews recently discovered by Parker and reprinted here for the first time since 1851, among them the only Scottish review yet discovered.

ANONYMOUS

[A Credit to His Country]†

To convey an adequate idea of a book of such various merits as that which the author of "Typee" and "Omoo" has here placed before the reading public, is impossible in the scope of a review. High philosophy, liberal feeling, abstruse metaphysics popularly phrased, soaring speculation, a style as many-coloured as the theme, yet always good, and often admirable; fertile fancy, ingenious construction, playful learning, and an unusual power of enchaining the interest, and rising to the verge of the sublime, without overpassing that narrow boundary which plunges the ambitious penman into the ridiculous: all these are possessed by Herman Melville, and exemplified in these volumes.

In the first chapter, bearing the title of "Loomings," we are introduced to the author, who on its threshold desires us to call him Ishmael. The very name being significant of a propensity to wander, we are prepared for an adventurer's acquaintance.

We have said that the writer is philosophically playful, and we will back his opening chapter, descriptive of New York, with its disquisitions on men's motives, the sea, nay water in the abstract as well as the concrete, against the same amount of prose in any book of fiction for the last dozen years, with a couple of exceptions, which we shall keep to ourselves. * * *

† London *Morning Advertiser*, October 24, 1851.

The portraits of these men, which you can see must have been taken from the life, and that they are the types of a class, are exquisitely finished. The signing ship's articles, by our hero and Queequeg, with the latter's fast, or ramadan, and the reasoning thereon, to which that ceremony gives rise, will well repay perusal. Captain Ahab, who is the hero of the whaling voyage, the commander of the Pequod, and thereafter the soul of the romance, is now introduced.

We will not weaken the effect which must be produced upon every one fortunate enough to obtain this work, by such brief extracts as we could here give: suffice it to say, that the fierce monomaniac, Ahab, has long pursued in the vast southern ocean a white whale, of unparalleled ferocity, size, and cunning. Not only has this monster of the deep baffled him, but in his last voyage has added to the destruction of his boats and stores a fearful mutilation; no less than the tearing off with its fearful jaws of the old whaler-captain's leg. The deficient limb is characteristically supplied by a supplemental piece of fish ivory, whereon the fierce old whale-hunter supports himself, steadied, when on deck, by a couple of socket-holes made in the ship's floor on each side of the vessel, at convenient holding-distance from the shrouds of the mizenmast. As a sample of Herman Melville's learning, we may refer to the chapter headed "Cetology," in the second volume; and that we have not overrated his dramatic ability for producing a prose poem, read the chapter on the "whiteness of the whale," and the scene where Ahab nails the doubloon to the mast, as an earnest of the reward he will give to the seamen, who just "sights" "Moby Dick," the white whale, the object of his burning and unappeasable revenge. Then come whale adventures wild as dreams, and powerful in their cumulated horrors. Now we have a Carlylism of phrase, then a quaintness reminding us of Sir Thomas Brown[e], and anon a heap of curious out-of-the-way learning after the fashion of the Burton who "anatomised" "melancholy." Mingled with all this are bustle, adventure, battle and the breeze. In brief the interest never palls, although we are free to confess that in the latter scenes of Ahab's fierce madness we were fain to exclaim, "Somewhat too much of this!" * * *

Did space permit us we might be tempted to the injustice of giving more of the defence [of whalehunters]; as it is, we can only again refer the reader to the volumes, than which three more honourable to American literature, albeit issued in London, have not yet reflected credit on the country of Washington Irving, Fenimore Cooper, Dana, Sigourney, Bryant, Longfellow, and Prescott.[1]

1. William Hickling Prescott (1796–1859), historian, author of basic sources on Central and South America for many Americans, the History of the Conquest of Mexico (1843) and The Conquest of Peru (1847), both influenced by the epic narration of Sir Walter Scott's historical romances. Washington Irving (1783–1859). James Fenimore Cooper (1789–1851). Probably Richard Henry Dana Jr. (1815–1882), although his father, Richard Henry Dana Sr. (1787–1879) was known in England as a poet. Lydia Huntley Sigourney (1791–1865), Connecticut poet. William Cullen Bryant (1794–1878), poet, known in the United States as owner and editor of the New York Evening Post. Henry Wadsworth Longfellow (1807–1882), poet and Harvard professor of languages.

ANONYMOUS

[An Ill-Compounded Mixture]†

This is an ill-compounded mixture of romance and matter-of-fact. The idea of a connected and collected story has obviously visited and abandoned its writer again and again in the course of composition. The style of his tale is in places disfigured by mad (rather than bad) English; and its catastrophe is hastily, weakly, and obscurely managed.[1] The second title—"Moby Dick"—is the name given to a particular sperm whale, or white sea monster, more malignant and diabolical even than the sperm whale in general is known to be. This ocean fiend is invested with especial horrors for our ship's crew;—because, once upon a time, a conflict with him cost their Captain a limb. Captain Ahab had an ivory leg made,—took an oath of retribution,—grew crazy,—lashed himself up into a purpose of cruising in quest of his adversary,—and bound all who sailed with him to stand by him in his wrath. With this cheerful Captain, on such a wise and Christian voyage of discovery, went to sea Ishmael, the imaginary writer of this narrative.

Frantic though such an invention seems to be, it might possibly have been accepted as the motive and purpose of an *extravaganza* had its author been consistent with himself. Nay, in such a terrible cause—when Krakens and Typhoons and the wonders of Mid-Ocean, &c. &c. were the topics and toys to be arranged and manoeuvred—we might have stretched a point in admission of electrical verbs and adjectives as hoarse as the hurricane. There is a time for everything in imaginative literature;—and, according to its order, a place for rant as well as for reserve; but the rant must be good, honest, shameless rant, without flaw or misgiving. The voice of "the storm wind Euroclydon" must not be interrupted by the facts of Scoresby and the figures of Cocker.[2] Ravings and scraps of useful knowledge flung together salad-wise make a dish in which there may be much surprise, but in which there is little savour. The real secret of this patchiness in the present case is disclosed in Mr. Melville's appendix; which contains such an assortment of curious quotations as Southey might have wrought up into a whale-chapter for 'The Doctor,'—suggesting the idea that a substantial work on the subject may have been originally contemplated.[3] Either Mr. Melville's purpose must have changed, or his power must have fallen short. The result is, at all events, a most provoking book,—neither so utterly extravagant as to be entirely comfortable, nor so instructively complete as to take place among documents on the subject of the Great Fish, his capabilities, his home and his capture. Our author must be henceforth numbered in the company of the incorrigibles who occasionally tantalize us with indications of genius, while they con-

† London *Athenæum* 1252 (October 25, 1851): 1112–13.
1. This sentence, based on the absence of the "Epilogue," was quoted twice in the United States and alluded to at least two other times.
2. Edward Cocker (1631–1675), English arithmetician.
3. Melville had taken the idea of prefacing his book with extracts from *The Doctor* (1834–47), a loosely connected miscellany by Robert Southey (1774–1843), poet laureate for his last three decades. Melville's knowledge of Southey's prose and poetry has not been adequately explored.

stantly summon us to endure monstrosities, carelessnesses, and other such harassing manifestations of bad taste as daring or disordered ingenuity can devise.

The opening of this wild book contains some graphic descriptions of a dreariness such as we do not remember to have met with before in marine literature. Sick of shore, Ishmael, the narrator, resolves to go to sea in a whaler; and on his way to Nantucket with that object, he is detained at New Bedford. The following passage will give gentlemen who live at home—as the song says—a new idea of taking their ease in their inn.—

> "Having a night, a day * * * and they began capering about most obstreperously [sic]." [ch. 2, paras. 3–9, and ch. 3, paras. 1–21, condensed]

The dark-complexioned harpooner turned out to be a cannibal, one Queequeg,—as sweet-tempered a savage as if he had been a prize vegetarian. It seemed odd enough to find Miss Martineau[4] in her "Eastern Travel" professing that "she had never rested till she had mastered the religious idea involved in cannibalism,"—but Mr. Melville's impersonation of the virtues and humanities which are to light up and relieve his terrible story is yet odder as a selection. The Battas, who, as Sir Stamford Raffles[5] assures us, eat their progenitors when the latter are sixty years old, are henceforth not beyond the reach of *rehabilitation*:—nay, those most dismal of Gnomes, the aborigines who devour clay, may now expect their laureate and their apologist. To such lengths will a craving for effect carry a sane man!

We have little more to say in reprobation or in recommendation of this absurd book,—having detailed its leading incident. Mr. Melville has been on former occasions characterized by us as one who thoroughly understands the tone of sea superstition. There is a wild humorous poetry in some of his terrors which distinguishes him from the vulgar herd of fustian-weavers. For instance, his interchapter on "The Whiteness of the Whale" is full of ghostly suggestions for which a Maturin or a Monk Lewis would have been thankful. Mr. Melville has to thank himself only if his horrors and his heroics are flung aside by the general reader, as so much trash belonging to the worst school of Bedlam literature,—since he seems not so much unable to learn as disdainful of learning the craft of an artist.

---

4. Harriet Martineau (1802–1876), English author of *Eastern Life, Present and Past* (London: Edward Moxon, 1848).
5. Sir Stamford Raffles (1781–1826), governor of Java before the British returned it to the Dutch, published *The History of Java* (1817), just before becoming lieutenant governor of Sumatra. By the time of *Moby-Dick* the Battas of Sumatra had become notorious as cannibals who ate their enemies piece by piece, keeping them alive as long as possible, then decapitating them and making drinking vessels of their skulls, and decorating their huts with skulls and teeth of their victims. They were said to treat their wives and children as slaves and to sell them when the chance arose.

ANONYMOUS

A Singular Medley[†]

This sea novel is a singular medley of naval observation, magazine article writing, satiric reflection upon the conventionalisms of civilized life,
and rhapsody run mad. So far as the nautical parts are appropriate and
unmixed, the portraiture is truthful and interesting. Some of the satire,
especially in the early parts, is biting and reckless. The chapter-spinning
is various in character; now powerful from the vigorous and fertile fancy
of the author, now little more than empty though sounding phrases. The
rhapsody belongs to wordmongering where ideas are the staple; where it
takes the shape of narrative or dramatic fiction, it is phantasmal—an
attempted description of what is impossible in nature and without probability in art; it repels the reader instead of attracting him.

The elements of the story are a South Sea whaling voyage, narrated by
Ishmael, one of the crew of the ship Pequod, from Nantucket. Its "probable" portions consist of the usual sea matter in that branch of the industrial marine; embracing the preparations for departure, the voyage, the
chase and capture of whale, with the economy of cutting up, &c., and the
peculiar discipline of the service. This matter is expanded by a variety of
digressions on the nature and characteristics of the sperm whale, the history of the fishery, and similar things, in which a little knowledge is made
the excuse for a vast many words. The voyage is introduced by several
chapters in which life in American seaports is rather broadly depicted.

The "marvellous" injures the book by disjointing the narrative, as well
as by its inherent want of interest, at least as managed by Mr. Melville. In
the superstition of some whalers, (grounded upon the malicious foresight
which occasionally characterizes the attacks of the sperm fish upon the
boats sent to capture it,) there is a *white* whale which possesses supernatural power. To capture or even to hurt it is beyond the art of man; the
skill of the whaler is useless; the harpoon does not wound it; it exhibits a
contemptuous strategy in its attacks upon the boats of its pursuers; and
happy is the vessel where only loss of limb, or of a single life, attends its
chase. Ahab, the master of the Pequod—a mariner of long experience,
stern resolve, and indomitable courage, the high hero of romance, in
short, transferred to a whale-ship—has lost his leg in a contest with the
white whale. Instead of daunting Ahab, the loss exasperates him; and by
long brooding over it his reason becomes shaken. In this condition he
undertakes the voyage; making the chase of his fishy antagonist the sole
object of his thoughts, and, so far as he can without exciting overt insub-
ordination among his officers, the object of his proceedings.

Such a groundwork is hardly natural enough for a regular-built novel,
though it might form a tale, if properly managed. But Mr. Melville's mysteries provoke wonder at the author rather than terror at the creation; the
soliloquies and dialogues of Ahab, in which the author attempts delineat-

† London *Spectator* 24 (October 25, 1851): 1026–27. This review was reprinted in the New York
International Magazine (December 1851).

ing the wild imaginings of monomania, and exhibiting some profoundly speculative views of things in general, induce weariness or skipping; while the whole scheme mars, as we have said, the nautical continuity of story—greatly assisted by various chapters of a bookmaking kind.

Perhaps the earliest chapters are the best, although they contain little adventure. Their topics are fresher to English readers than the whale-chase, and they have more direct satire. One of the leading personages in the voyage is Queequeg, a South Sea Islander, that Ishmael falls in with at New Bedford, and with whom he forms a bosom friendship.

> "Queequeg was a native of Kokovoko * * * I'll die a Pagan." [ch. 12, paras. 1–4]

The strongest point of the book is its "characters." Ahab, indeed, is a melodramatic exaggeration, and Ishmael is little more than a mouthpiece; but the harpooners, the mates, and several of the seamen, are truthful portraitures of the sailor as modified by the whaling service. The persons ashore are equally good, though they are soon lost sight of. The two Quaker owners are the author's means for a hit at the religious hypocrisies. Captain Bildad, an old sea-dog, has got rid of everything pertaining to the meeting-house save an occasional "thou" and "thee." Captain Peleg, in American phrase "professes religion." The following extract exhibits the two men when Ishmael is shipped.

> "I began to think * * * to the fiery pit, Captain Peleg.'" [ch. 16, paras. 54–65]

It is a canon with some critics that nothing should be introduced into a novel which it is physically impossible for the writer to have known: thus, he must not describe the conversation of miners in a pit if they *all* perish. Mr. Melville hardly steers clear of this rule, and he continually violates another, by beginning in the autobiographical form and changing ad libitum into the narrative. His catastrophe overrides all rule: not only is Ahab, with his boat's-crew, destroyed in his last desperate attack upon the white whale, but the Pequod herself sinks with all on board into the depths of the illimitable ocean. Such is the go-ahead method.

ANONYMOUS

[People Who Delight in Mulligatawny]†

There are people who delight in mulligatawny. They love curry at its warmest point. Ginger cannot be too hot in the mouth for them. Such people, we should think, constitute the admirers of Herman Melville. He spices his narrative with uncommon courage, and works up a story amazingly. If you love heroics and horrors he is your man. Sit down with him on a winter's eve, and you'll find yourself calling for candles before the night sets in. If you desire your hair to stand on end in a natural Brutus,

† London *News of the World*, November 2, 1851.

or your teeth to chatter in unnatural discord, listen to what this man of strange lands and strange waters has to tell, and your wishes will be fulfilled. You will have a supper for a very long night's digestion. * * *

ANONYMOUS

[A Most Extraordinary Work]†

The Whale is a most extraordinary work. There is so much eccentricity in its style and in its construction, in the original conception and in the gradual development of its strange and improbable story, that we are at a loss to determine in what category of works of amusement to place it. It is certainly neither a novel nor a romance, although it is made to drag its weary length through three closely printed volumes, and is published by Bentley, who, *par excellence*, is the publisher of the novels of the fashionable world, for who ever heard of novel or romance without a heroine or a single love scene? The plot of the narrative is scarcely worthy of the name, as it hangs entirely on the inveterate pursuit by a monomaniac old Captain after a certain humpbacked whale, who in some previous voyage had bitten off one of his legs, and whose destruction he had bound himself and his crew by terrible oaths to accomplish, in revenge for the injury he had himself sustained. The tragical catastrophe, which innumerable signs, omens, and superstitious warnings are constantly predicting to the infatuated commander, is the wreck of the ship, and the loss of the whole crew in the frantic attack that is made upon the invincible white whale.

The story has merit, but it is a merit *sui generis*, and does not consist in the work either when viewed as a whole or with reference to the arrangement of its separate parts. The plot is meagre beyond comparison, as the whole of the incident might very conveniently have been comprised in half of one of these three interminable volumes. Nevertheless, in his descriptions of character, in his analysis of the motives of actions, and in the novelty of the details of a whaling expedition, the author has evinced not only a considerable knowledge of the human heart, combined with a thorough acquaintance with the subject he is handling, but a rare versatility of talent. The crew of the Pequod, the inharmonious name given to the whaler, is composed of mariners of all countries and all colours, from the civilised British sailor to the savage and cannibal harpooner of the South Sea Islands. In describing the idiosyncracies of all these different castes of men our author has evinced acuteness of observation and powers of discrimination, which would alone render his work a valuable addition to the literature of the day. The monomaniac Captain Ahab, whose whole soul, to the exclusion of every other idea, is bent upon the destruction of "Moby Dick," the nickname of the whale who robbed him of his leg, is a most eccentric conception, and is well contrasted with the character of his common-place mates, Starbuck, Stubb, and Flask. Queequeg, the cannibal harpooner, notwithstanding his man-eating propensities, is

† London *Britannia*, November 8, 1851.

made a most interesting hero amongst whale-slayers, and in the curious details of this heathen's worship of his idol, "Yojo," our author has shown that he has a fund of humour at command. Tashtego, the unmixed Indian, and Daggoo, the coal-black negro slave, are excellent types of their class, and by no means common-place characters. These original sketches constitute as we have said the principal merit of the work, but in the latter half of the third volume, the action of the story, which had halted considerably through the preceding chapters, assumes all at once an exciting interest, which is as gratifying as it is unexpected. The three days' chase of the destructive white whale, whose attempted capture had lured so many mariners to their destruction, are most graphically described. The following account of the approach of the boats on the first day, when after months of pursuit the watch on the forecastle had at last described the dreaded antagonist, is characteristic of the author's style:—

> Soon all the boats but Starbuck's were dropped * * * streaming like pennons. [ch. 133, paras. 15–16]

The concluding paragraph of the last chapter, in which the white whale, after spurning the small fry of boats from which harpoons are darted into it on all sides, shoots itself against the advancing prows of the vessel which it staves in, is at once so grand, so awful, and so harrowing, that we quote the paragraph:—

> The harpoon was darted; . . . as it rolled five thousand years ago. [ch. 135, paras. 59–62]

The first and second volumes are spun out with long descriptions of the various cetacious tribes, which do now, and have at different periods of time inhabited the ocean. The information these chapters convey may be important to naturalists or whalers, but will have little interest for the general reader. Bating a few Americanisms, which sometimes mar the perspicuity and the purity of the style, the language of the work is appropriate and impressive; and the stirring scenes with which the author concludes are abundant evidence of the power he possesses of making his narrative intensely interesting.

ANONYMOUS

[Fascination No Criticism Will Thwart]†

Want of originality has long been the just and standing reproach to American literature; the best of its writers were but second-hand Englishmen. Of late some have given evidence of originality; not *absolute* originality, but such genuine outcoming of the American intellect as can be safely called national. Edgar Poe, Nathaniel Hawthorne, Herman Melville are assuredly no British offshoots; nor is Emerson—the *German* American that he is! The observer of this commencement of an American liter-

† London *Leader* 2 (November 8, 1851): 1067–69.

ature, properly so called, will notice as significant that these writers have a wild and mystic love of the supersensual, peculiarly their own. To move a horror skilfully, with something of the earnest faith in the Unseen, and with weird imagery to shape these Phantasms so vividly that the most incredulous mind is hushed, absorbed—to do this no European pen has apparently any longer the power—to do this American literature is without a rival. What *romance* writer can be named with Hawthorne? Who knows the terrors of the seas like Herman Melville?

The Whale—Melville's last book—is a strange, wild, weird book, full of poetry and full of interest. To use a hackneyed phrase, it is indeed "refreshing" to quit the old, wornout pathways of romance, and feel the sea breezes playing through our hair, the salt spray dashing on our brows, as we do here. One tires terribly of ballrooms, dinners, and the incidents of town life! One never tires of Nature. And there is Nature here, though the daring imagery often grows riotously extravagant.

Then the ghostly terrors which Herman Melville so skilfully evokes, have a strange fascination. In vain Reason rebels. Imagination is absolute. Ordinary superstitions related by vulgar pens have lost their power over all but the credulous; but Imagination has a credulity of its own respondent to power. So it is with Melville's superstitions: we believe in them imaginatively. And here we will take the occasion to introduce the reader to a splendid passage from our greatest prose writer, descriptive of the superstitious nature of sailors—(you divine that we are to quote from De Quincey). He says they are all superstitious. "Partly, I suppose, from *looking out so much upon the wilderness of waves empty of human life*, for mighty solitudes are generally fear-haunted and fear-peopled; such, for instance, as the solitudes of forests where, in the absence of human forms and ordinary human sounds, are discerned forms more dusky and vague not referred by the eye to any known type, and sounds imperfectly intelligible. Now, the sea is often peopled amidst its ravings with what seem innumerable human voices, 'ancestral voices prophesying war';[1] often times laughter mixes from a distance (seeming to come also from distant times as well as distant places) with the uproar of waters; and, doubtless, shapes of fear or shapes of beauty not less awful are at times seen upon the waves by the diseased eye of the sailor. Finally, the interruption habitually of all ordinary avenues to information about the fate of their dearest relatives; the consequent agitation which must often possess those who are reëntering upon home waters; and the sudden burst, upon stepping ashore, of *heart-shaking news in long-accumulated arrears*—these are circumstances which dispose the mind to look out *for relief towards signs and omens as one way of breaking the shock by dim anticipations*."

This passage is a fit prelude to the thrilling pages of Melville's *Whale*. The book is not a romance, nor a treatise on Cetology. It is something of both: a strange, wild work with the tangled overgrowth and luxuriant vegetation of American forests, not the trim orderliness of an English park. Criticism may pick many holes in this work; but no criticism will thwart its fascination. As we mean you to read it and relish it, we shall give no

1. From "Kubla Khan" (1816) by S. T. Coleridge (1772–1834).

hint of the story: an extract or so by way of whet to the appetite is all you must expect. * * *

There is a chapter on the "Whiteness of the Whale" which should be read at midnight, alone, with nothing heard but the sounds of the wind moaning without, and the embers falling into the grate within. * * *

ANONYMOUS

[Not Worth the Money Asked for It]†

We have read nearly one half of this book, and are satisfied that the London Athenæum is right in calling it "an ill-compounded mixture of romance and matter-of-fact." It is a crazy sort of affair, stuffed with conceits and oddities of all kinds, put in artificially, deliberately and affectedly, by the side of strong, terse and brilliant passages of incident and description. The Athenæum's notice throughout seems to us a fair one, and we copy the greater portion for the sake of economy and good taste:

> "The style of his tale is in places disfigured by mad (rather than bad) English . . .¹ Our author must be henceforth numbered in the company of the incorrigibles who occasionally tantalize us with indications of genius, while they constantly summon us to endure monstrosities, carelessnesses, and other such harassing manifestations of bad taste as daring or disordered ingenuity can devise."

After giving an interesting and powerfully written extract, the Athenæum resumes:—

> "The dark-complexioned harpooner turned out to be a cannibal, one Queequeg . . . Mr Melville has to thank himself only if his horrors and his heroics are flung aside by the general reader, as so much trash belonging to the worst school of Bedlam literature—since he seems not so much unable to learn as disdainful of learning the craft of an artist."

The production under notice is now issued by the Harpers in a handsome bound volume for *one dollar and fifty cents*—no mean sum, in these days. It seems to us that our publishers have gone from one extreme to the other, and that instead of publishing good books in too cheap a form, they are issuing poor books, in far too costly apparel. "The Whale" is not worth the money asked for it, either as a literary work or as a mass of printed paper. Few people would read it more than once, and yet it is issued at the usual cost of a standard volume. Published at *twenty five cents*, it might do to buy, but at any higher price, we think it a poor speculation.

---

† Boston *Post*, November 20, 1851.
1. The *Post* here quoted all the *Athenæum* said about the ending; then the entire *Post* review was reprinted in the Boston *Statesman* on November 22, 1851.

"H."

[A Primitive Formation of Profanity and Indecency][†]

The name given to this burly volume reminds us of an observation of Burton in his Anatomy of Melancholy, where he says that it is a kind of policy in these days to prefix a fantastical title to a book which is to be sold, because as larks come down to a day-net, many readers will tarry and stand gazing like silly passengers[1] at an antic picture in a painter's shop, that will not look at a judicious piece. There are harlequin writers at this day as ready as in Burton's time to make themselves Merryandrews and Zanies, in order to raise the wind of curiosity about their literary wares.

In the volume before us there are some of the queerest specimens of ground and lofty tumblings in the literary line, to which the world has been lately treated. Up to the middle of the book the writer is half the time on his head, and the other half dancing a pirouette on one toe. By the time these *outré* gayeties are a little spent, the reader gets an inkling that Moly-Dick [sic] is a very famous and most deadly Monster, a Sperm Whale of an uncommon magnitude and malignity, having as many lives as a cat, and all of them immortal. After this the realities and the fabrications of whaling life are dashed into with a bold hand; and mixed with a great deal of myth and mystery, there are exciting descriptions, curious information, and strange adventures, which would have not a shade of probability, were not truth in whaling life often stranger than fiction.

The writer evinces the possession of powers that make us ashamed of him that he does not write something better and freer from blemishes. And yet we doubt if he could, for there is a primitive formation of profanity and indecency that is ever and anon shooting up through all the strata of his writings; and it is this which makes it impossible for a religious journal heartily to commend any of the works of this author which we have ever perused. Let his mind only turn on the poles of truth, and be fixed with the desire to do good rather than to tickle and amuse by the exposure of his foolish vagaries, and few could do more than the author of Moly-Dick [sic] to furnish instructive literary aliment for the Sons of the Sea.

The Judgment day will hold him liable for not turning his talents to better account, when, too, both authors and publishers of injurious books will be conjointly answerable for the influence of those books upon the wide circle of immortal minds on which they have written their mark. The book-maker and the book-publisher had better do their work with a view to the trial it must undergo at the bar of God.

---

† New York *Independent*, November 20, 1851.
1. Passersby.

ANONYMOUS

[Not Lacking Much of Being a Great Work]†

This mere announcement of the book's and the author's name will prepare you in a measure for what follows; for you know just as well as we do that Herman Melville is a practical and practised sea-novelist, and that what comes from his pen will be worth the reading. And so indeed is "Moby-Dick," and not lacking much of being a great work. How it falls short of this, we shall presently endeavour to show. Let us in the first place briefly describe it.

It treats then mainly of whales, whaling, whalers, and whaling-men— incidentally it touches on mythology, sharks, religion, South Sea islanders, philosophy, cannibalism and curiosity shops. The writer uses the first person in narrating his tale, without however any attempt at making himself its hero. He was (or says he was, which is the same thing) but a seaman on board the vessel whose voyage he relates, and a consequent eye-witness of the strange characters on board her. Foremost amongst these is the Captain, in the conception of whose part lies the most original thought of the whole book, stamping it decidedly as the production of a man of genius. This Captain, a Nantucketer, Ahab by name, has lost a leg; it was snapped off by Moby-Dick, in the course of a boat adventure with an individual sperm-whale of the most dangerous kind, whose peculiar appearance, and repeated escapes from harpooners, together with the amount of destruction done by him, had earned him a nick-name and made him a terror in the trade. The bodily and mental anguish endured by Capt. Ahab had, ere the commencement of our tale, converted him into a monomaniac, whose sole and absorbing object in life was revenge on Moby-Dick. The *Pequod* of Nantucket is outfitted under his command for a new voyage, the officers and crew shipping, as usual, in quest of oil and gain therefrom, whilst their commander is bent on circumnavigating the globe, in hopes of satiating his thirst for vengeance. At times the subordinates murmur at his palpable neglect of their interests; but his undaunted courage and authoritative air, and their own superstitious fears of him, prevail over every other consideration.

"Aye, Starbuck; aye, my hearties * * * go draw the great measure of grog." [ch. 36, paras. 32–34]

The idea of even a nautical Don Quixote chasing a particular fish from ocean to ocean, running down the line of the Equator, or rushing from Torrid to Temperate zones—this may seem intolerably absurd. But the author clearly shows the *possibility* of such a search being successful, which is more than sufficient motive.

---

† New York, *Albion* 10 (November 22, 1851): 561. The *Albion* was unique, a paper written in New York for British visitors or expatriates by a British staff (especially in these early years of its existence) (see pp. 103, 503, and 508 herein). This review provides the best hint of how the British reviewers might have responded to *Moby-Dick* if the text of the English edition had ended with Melville's "Epilogue," although comparisons are not truly valid, because the reviewer in the *Albion* was reading the uncensored American text, which retained, among other passages, the slights against royalty that had been cut from the English edition.

Now, to any one not fully acquainted * * * without prospect of a meeting. [ch. 44, paras. 4, 7]

A variety of interesting details proves the personal identity of whales; and the author, not without reason, thus apostrophises a set of Cetacean braves.

But not only did each of these famous whales * * * or Sylla to the classic scholar. [ch. 45, para. 5]

A deadly strife, then, between Capt. Ahab and Moby-Dick, is the vein of romance woven through the varied wanderings of the good ship *Pequod* and her crew, and to which the reader is brought back from matter-of-fact details of the fishery, from abstruse and sceptical and comical speculations on men and things, from hand-breadth escapes, and from thrilling adventures. The book opens with the writer's personal search for a berth on shipboard, at New Bedford and Nantucket, and closes with the total loss of the *Pequod* in the Pacific, the fated vessel being deliberately run into by Moby-Dick, just as the *Ann Alexander* was lately sunk in the same seas by a malicious sperm whale, as mentioned in our columns a few weeks since. It is a singular coincidence that Mr. Melville should have wound up with this catastrophe, and that its truthfulness should have met such sad and immediate confirmation. Be it further noted that "Moby-Dick" was published in London, before the fate of the *Ann Alexander* could have been known there.

Not only is there an immense amount of reliable information here before us; the *dramatis personæ*, mates, harpooneers, carpenters, and cooks, are all vivid sketches done in the author's best style. What they do, and how they look, is brought to one's perception with wondrous elaborateness of detail; and yet this minuteness does not spoil the broad outline of each. It is only when Mr. Melville puts words into the mouths of these living and moving beings, that his cunning fails him, and the illusion passes away. From the Captain to the Cabin-boy, not a soul amongst them talks pure seaman's lingo; and as this is a grave charge, we feel bound to substantiate it—not by an ill-natured selection of isolated bits, but by such samples as may be considered an average. We pass by Capt. Ahab for a few moments, and take his mates. Starbuck is the Chief; Ahab had nailed a sixteen-dollar gold doubloon to the main-mast as a prize for the first man that sighted Moby-Dick.

"No fairy fingers can have pressed the gold, * * * He goes below; let me read." [ch. 99, para. 8]

The soliloquy of Stubb, the second Mate—a bold, jolly tar as ever flung harpoon—at the moment when Moby-Dick rushes headlong on the *Pequod*, is ludicrous in the extreme.

"Stand not by me, but stand under me * * * Oh, Flask, for one red cherry ere we die!" [ch. 135, para. 53]

Flask, the third mate, happily for us says little; but the Carpenter thus mutters to himself over a new bone leg, that he is making for Capt. Ahab.

Oh! I don't wonder he looked so scornful at me! * * * as brewery-men go round collecting old beer barrels, to fill 'em up again. [ch. 108, last para.]

But there is no pleasure in making these extracts; still less would there be in quoting anything of the stuff and nonsense spouted forth by the crazy Captain; for so indeed must nine-tenths of his dialogue be considered, even though one bears in mind that it has been compounded in a maniac's brain from the queer mixture of New England conventicle phraseology with the devilish profanity too common on board South-Sea Whalers. The rarely-imagined character has been grievously spoiled, nay altogether ruined, by a vile overdaubing with a coat of book-learning and mysticism; there is no method in his madness; and we must needs pronounce the chief feature of the volume a perfect failure, and the work itself inartistic. There is nevertheless in it, as we have already hinted, abundant choice reading for those who can skip a page now and then, judiciously; and perhaps, when one's mind is made up to disregard the continuous interest, the separate portions may be better relished. We offer a sample or two of the best. There is for instance both truth and satire in the following peep into a particular mood of mind.

> There are certain queer times and occasions in this strange mixed affair we call life when a man takes this whole universe for a vast practical joke, though the wit thereof he but dimly discerns, and more than suspects that the joke is at nobody's expense but his own. * * * I now regarded the whole voyage of the *Pequod*, and the great White Whale its object. [ch. 49, para. 1]

It is to be hoped that this sketch of one of the owners of the *Pequod* was not drawn from the life at Nantucket.

> Now Bildad, I am sorry to say, * * * like the worn nap of his broad-brimmed hat. (ch. 16, para. 45]

We conclude with part of a clever chapter on the honour and glory of whaling.

> There are some enterprises * * * why not the prophet? [ch. 82, paras. 1–7]

Mr. Melville has crowded together in a few prefatory pages a large collection of brief and pithy extracts from authors innumerable, such as one might expect as headings for chapters. We do not like the innovation. It is having oil, mustard, vinegar, and pepper served up as a dish, in place of being scientifically administered sauce-wise.

[GEORGE RIPLEY]

[Melville's Whaliad, the Epic of Whaling]†

Everybody has heard of the tradition which is said to prevail among the old salts of Nantucket and New-Bedford, of a ferocious monster of a whale, who is proof against all the arts of harpoonery, and who occasion-

---

† [George Ripley], New York *Tribune*, November 22, 1851.

ally amuses himself with swallowing down a boat's crew without winking. The present volume is a "Whaliad," or the Epic of that veritable old leviathan, who "esteemeth iron as straw, and laughs at the spear, the dart, and the habergeon," no one being able to "fill his skin with a barbed iron, or his head with fish-hooks." Mr. Melville gives us not only the romance of his history, but a great mass of instruction on the character and habits of his whole race, with complete details of the wily stratagems of their pursuers.

The interest of the work pivots on a certain Captain Ahab, whose enmity to Moby-Dick, the name of the whale-demon, has been aggravated to monomania. In one rencounter with this terror of the seas, he suffers a signal defeat; loses a leg in the contest; gets a fire in his brain; returns home a man with one idea; feels that he has a mission; that he is predestined to defy his enemy to mortal strife; devotes himself to the fulfillment of his destiny; with the persistence and cunning of insanity gets possession of another vessel, ships a weird, supernatural crew of which Ishmael, the narrator of the story, is a prominent member; and after a "wild huntsman's chase" through unknown seas, is the only one who remains to tell the destruction of the ship and the doomed Captain Ahab by the victorious, indomitable Moby-Dick.

The narrative is constructed in Herman Melville's best manner. It combines the various features which form the chief attractions of his style, and is commendably free from the faults which we have before had occasion to specify in this powerful writer. The intensity of the plot is happily relieved by minute descriptions of the most homely processes of the whale fishery. We have occasional touches of the subtle mysticism, which is carried to such an inconvenient excess in Mardi, but it is here mixed up with so many tangible and odorous realities, that we always safely alight from the excursion through mid-air upon the solid deck of the whaler. We are recalled to this world by the fumes of "oil and blubber," and are made to think more of the contents of barrels than of allegories. The work is also full of episodes, descriptive of strange and original phases of character. One of them is given in the commencement of the volume, showing how "misery makes a man acquainted with strange bed-fellows." We must pass over this in which the writer relates his first introduction to Queequeg, a South Sea cannibal, who was his chum at a sailor boarding house in New-Bedford and afterward his bosom friend and most devoted confederate. We will make room for the characteristic chapter, which describes the ripening of their acquaintance into the honeymoon of friendship:

> Returning to the Spouter-Inn * * * and all the world. [ch. 10, paras. 1–9]

But we must go out to sea with Ishmael, if we would witness his most remarkable exploits. We are now, then, in the midst of things, and with good luck, may soon get a sight of Moby-Dick. Meantime, we may beguile our impatience with the description of a rope, on which Melville gives us a touch of his quaint moralizings.

> With reference to the whaling scene * * * not a harpoon, by your side. [ch. 60, paras, 1–10]

We are now ready to kill our first whale. Here is the transaction in full:

KILLING A WHALE.

If to Starbuck * * * eyeing the vast corpse he had made. [ch. 61, paras. 1–22]

At last, Moby-Dick, the object of such long vigilant, and infuriate search, is discovered. We can only give the report of

THE CHASE—FIRST DAY.

That night, in the mid-watch * * * as desolate sounds from out ravines. [ch. 133, paras. 1–32]

Here we will retire from the chase, which lasts three days, not having a fancy to be in at the death. We part with the adventurous philosophical Ishmael, truly thankful that the whale did not get his head, for which we are indebted for this wildly imaginative and truly thrilling story. We think it the best production which has yet come from that seething brain, and in spite of its lawless flights, which put all regular criticism at defiance, it gives us a higher opinion of the author's originality and power than even the favorite and fragrant first-fruits of his genius, the never-to-be-forgotten Typee.

[EVERT A. DUYCKINCK]

[A Friend Does His Christian Duty]†

A difficulty in the estimate of this, in common with one or two other of Mr. Melville's books, occurs from the double character under which they present themselves. In one light they are romantic fictions, in another statements of absolute fact. When to this is added that the romance is made a vehicle of opinion and satire through a more or less opaque allegorical veil, as particularly in the latter half of Mardi, and to some extent in this present volume, the critical difficulty is considerably thickened. It becomes quite impossible to submit such books to a distinct classification as fact, fiction, or essay. Something of a parallel may be found in Jean Paul's German tales,[1] with an admixture of Southey's Doctor. Under these combined influences of personal observation, actual fidelity to local truthfulness in description, a taste for reading and sentiment, a fondness for fanciful analogies, near and remote, a rash daring in speculation, reckless at times of taste and propriety, again refined and eloquent, this volume of Moby Dick may be pronounced a most remarkable sea-dish—an intellectual chowder of romance, philosophy, natural history, fine writing, good

---

† [Evert A. Duyckinck], New York *Literary World* 251 (November 22, 1851): 403–4. This was the second notice. The first, on November 15, was mainly concerned with the coincidental arrival of news that the whaleship *Ann Alexander* had been sunk in the Pacific by a whale. See "Hawthorne and His Mosses" (p. 517 herein) and "Letters by Melville" (pp. 534–36 and 544 herein) for a sense of Duyckinck's importance to Melville through this time. Hawthorne reproached Duyckinck for this review, saying bluntly that he thought the *Literary World* had hardly done justice to *Moby-Dick*.

1. Jean Paul Richter (1763–1825), German Romantic novelist.

feeling, bad sayings—but over which, in spite of all uncertainties, and in spite of the author himself, predominates his keen perceptive faculties, exhibited in vivid narration.

There are evidently two if not three books in Moby Dick rolled into one. Book No. I. we could describe as a thorough exhaustive account admirably given of the great Sperm Whale. The information is minute, brilliantly illustrated, as it should be—the whale himself so generously illuminating the midnight page on which his memoirs are written—has its level passages, its humorous touches, its quaint suggestion, its incident usually picturesque and occasionally sublime. All this is given in the most delightful manner in "The Whale." Book No. II is the romance of Captain Ahab, Queequeg, Tashtego, Pip & Co., who are more or less spiritual personages talking and acting differently from the general business run of the conversation on the decks of whalers. They are for the most part very serious people, and seem to be concerned a great deal about the problem of the universe. They are striking characters withal, of the romantic spiritual cast of the German drama; realities of some kinds at bottom, but veiled in all sorts of poetical incidents and expressions. As a bit of German melodrama, with Captain Ahab for the Faust of the quarter-deck, and Queequeg with the crew, for Walpurgis night[2] revellers in the forecastle, it has its strong points, though here the limits as to space and treatment of the stage would improve it. Moby Dick in this view becomes a sort of fishly moralist, a leviathan metaphysician, a folio Ductor Dubitantium, in fact, in the fresh water illustration of Mrs. Malaprop,[3] "an allegory on the banks of the Nile." After pursuing him in this melancholic company over a few hundred squares of latitude and longitude, we begin to have some faint idea of the association of whaling and lamentation, and why blubber is popularly synonymous with tears.

The intense Captain Ahab is too long drawn out; something more of *him* might, we think, be left to the reader's imagination. The value of this kind of writing can only be through the personal consciousness of the reader, what he brings to the book; and all this is sufficiently evoked by a dramatic trait or suggestion. If we had as much of Hamlet or Macbeth as Mr. Melville gives us of Ahab, we should be tired even of their sublime company. Yet Captain Ahab is a striking conception, firmly planted on the wild deck of the Pequod—a dark disturbed soul arraying itself with every ingenuity of material resources for a conflict at once natural and supernatural in his eye, with the most dangerous extant physical monster of the earth, embodying, in strongly drawn lines of mental association, the vaster moral evil of the world. The pursuit of the White Whale thus interweaves with the literal perils of the fishery—a problem of fate and destiny—to the tragic solution of which Ahab hurries on, amidst the wild stage scenery of the ocean. To this end the motley crew, the air, the sky, the sea, its inhabitants are idealized throughout. It is a noble and praiseworthy conception; and though our sympathies may not always accord with the train of

2. The night of the witches' celebration, known best from Goethe's *Faust*.
3. A character in Richard Brinsley Sheridan's *The Rivals* (1775) who blunders astonishingly in her use of words (named from the French *mal à propos*, "inappropriate"). *Ductor Dubitantium*: a work of casuistry like Jeremy Taylor's *Ductor Dubitantium, or the Rules of Conscience in all her General Measures, Serving as a great Instrument for the Determination of Cases of Conscience* (London, 1660).

thought, we would caution the reader against a light or hasty condemnation of this part of the work.

Book III., appropriating perhaps a fourth of the volume, is a vein of moralizing, half essay, half rhapsody, in which much refinement and subtlety, and no little poetical feeling, are mingled with quaint conceit and extravagant daring speculation. This is to be taken as in some sense dramatic; the narrator throughout among the personages of the Pequod being one Ishmael, whose wit may be allowed to be against everything on land, as his hand is against everything at sea. This piratical running down of creeds and opinions, the conceited indifferentism of Emerson, or the run-a-muck style of Carlyle is, we will not say dangerous in such cases, for there are various forces at work to meet more powerful onslaught, but it is out of place and uncomfortable. We do not like to see what, under any view, must be to the world the most sacred associations of life violated and defaced.

We call for fair play in this matter. Here is Ishmael, telling the story of this volume, going down on his knees with a cannibal to a piece of wood, in the second story fire-place of a New-Bedford tavern, in the spirit of amiable and transcendent charity, which may be all very well in its way; but why dislodge from heaven, with contumely, "long-pampered Gabriel, Michael and Raphael." Surely Ishmael, who is a scholar, might have spoken respectfully of the Archangel Gabriel, out of consideration, if not for the Bible (which might be asking too much of the school), at least for one John Milton, who wrote Paradise Lost.

Nor is it fair to inveigh against the terrors of priestcraft, which, skilful though it may be in making up its woes, at least seeks to provide a remedy for the evils of the world, and attribute the existence of conscience to "hereditary dyspepsias, nurtured by Ramadans"—and at the same time go about petrifying us with imaginary horrors, and all sorts of gloomy suggestions, all the world through. It is a curious fact that there are no more bilious people in the world, more completely filled with megrims and head shakings, than some of these very people who are constantly inveighing against the religious melancholy of priestcraft.

So much for the consistency of Ishmael—who, if it is the author's object to exhibit the painful contradictions of this self-dependent, self-torturing agency of a mind driven hither and thither as a flame in a whirlwind, is, in a degree, a successful embodiment of opinions, without securing from us, however, much admiration for the result.

With this we make an end of what we have been reluctantly compelled to object to this volume. With far greater pleasure, we acknowledge the acuteness of observation, the freshness of perception, with which the author brings home to us from the deep, "things unattempted yet in prose or rhyme,"[4] the weird influences of his ocean scenes, the salient imagination which connects them with the past and distant, the world of books and the life of experience—certain prevalent traits of manly sentiment. These are strong powers with which Mr. Melville wrestles in this book. It would be a great glory to subdue them to the highest uses of fiction. It is still a great honor, among the crowd of successful mediocrities which

4. John Milton, Paradise Lost, I.16.

throng our publishers' counters, and know nothing of divine impulses, to be in the company of these nobler spirits on any terms.

ANONYMOUS

[Too Much for Our Money][†]

Such a mass of information about the whale was probably never brought together in one book before, certainly never in a work of fiction. "Moby-Dick," as a medium of information, cannot be found fault with. As a work of fiction it is liable to the objection which presents itself to all Melville's writings since "Typee." Typee was just perfect. In the attempt to make the rest better, and improve upon perfection, we think he runs into the grave error of giving us altogether too much for our money. He spreads his subject out beyond all reasonable bounds; until the scene becomes altogether too long for the motive, and the finest writing will not prevent it from being tiresome. If any writer of the present day could play with his subject, after this fashion, with impunity, it would be Melville; for his style is a rare mixture of power and sweetness, and, indeed, under the influence of the least excitement becomes as truly poetry as if every line were measured for verse, and the fine madness of his soul poured out in lyric flow instead of straightened into prose. But, even his power of expression, and elegance of style, will not redeem a book from being prosy after the natural interest of its subject has been exhausted. More than five acts of the best tragedy would be too much for mere mortals to bear.

ANONYMOUS

[Information: The Only Redeeming Point][‡]

These volumes—tastefully done up in blue, white, and gold, with a huge sperm whale sprawling on the back of each volume—contain a strange mixture of smart observations, quaint philosophy, American vulgarisms, and grandiose writing. The author's object is to detail, in the form of a novel, the natural history of the sperm whale, and the leading incidents of a fishing voyage in the South Seas. The information thus afforded is the only redeeming point in the work, for assuredly both the story and the style are sufficiently absurd.

A vessel called "The Pequod" sails from Nantucket on a whaling cruise. She has scarcely left the harbour when the crew discover that they have a madman for their captain. The skipper, however, turns out to be mad only on one point, and his monomania consists in this. On a previous voyage a large whale had by a stroke of its tail, so injured Captain Ahab's leg

† New York *Parker's Journal* 1 (November 22, 1851): 586.
‡ Edinburgh *Evening Courant*, November 25, 1851. Reprinted here for the first time.

that the limb required to be amputated. The whale, it seems, was well known in the southern latitudes for its enormous size and extraordinary fierceness, and went by the name of "Moby Dick." The author assures us that some particular whales are known to the fishers, and have been pursued for years by various ships without success, like a marked stag that, season after season, sets all stalkers at defiance. Now, Captain Ahab had resolved to be revenged on Moby Dick. This was his sole, absorbing idea. The interests of his employers, the safety of his crew, and every other consideration gave way to this.

> "No love-lorn swain, in lady's bower,
> E'er panted for the appointed hour"

as did Captain Ahab to fall in with Moby Dick. We have a full account of this marvellous mariner, and the various incidents of the Pequod's cruise, but our faith in the narrative is somewhat shaken, when at last we find that, after years of persevering search, Captain Ahab does encounter Moby Dick, but, instead of realising his long-cherished projects of vengeance, he, his ship, and all the crew, are sent to the bottom of the ocean by a wisk of Moby's tail.

As a specimen of what is really interesting in the book, we may quote the following description of the "Try-works," or boiling apparatus, on board an American whaler, and fortunately the passage is wonderfully free from the slang phraseology or bombastic inflatedness of style, one or other of which too often disfigures Mr Melville's pages. * * *

ANONYMOUS

[A "Many-Sided" Book]†

Our friend Melville's books begin to accumulate. His literary family increases rapidly. He had already a happy and smiling progeny around him, but lo! at the appointed time another child of his brain, with the accustomed signs of the family, claims our attention and regard. We bid the book a hearty welcome. We assure the "happy father" that his "labors of love" are no "love's labor lost."

We confess an admiration for Mr. Melville's books, which, perhaps, spoils us for mere criticism. There are few writers, living or dead, who describe the sea and its adjuncts with such true art, such graphic power, and such powerfully resulting interest. "Typee," "Omoo," "Redburn," "Mardi," and "White Jacket," are equal to anything in the language. They are things of their own. They are results of the youthful experience on the ocean of a man who is at once philosopher, painter, and poet. This is not, perhaps, a very unusual mental combination, but it is not usual to find

† New York *Spirit of the Times* 21 (December 6, 1851): 494. The editor of this magazine was the remarkable William T. Porter, publisher of some extraordinary stories set in the American backwoods, now often denigrated as "southwestern humor" or "Big Bear literature." Porter, like Melville, did not make distinctions between hunting stories and literature. "Our friend Melville" may be a mere bon-vivant flourish, but Porter and Melville may well have been acquainted in the late 1840s.

such a combination "before the mast." So far Mr. Melville's early experiences, though perhaps none of the pleasantest to himself, are infinitely valuable to the world. We say *valuable* with a full knowledge of the terms used; and, not to enter into details, which will be fresh in the memory of most of Mr. Melville's readers, it is sufficient to say that the humanities of the world have been quickened by his works. Who can forget the missionary *exposé*, the practical good sense which pleads for "Poor Jack," or the unsparing but just severity of his delineations of naval abuses, and that crowning disgrace to our navy—flogging? Taken as matters of art these books are amongst the largest and the freshest contributions of original thought and observation which have been presented in many years. Take the majority of modern writers, and it will be admitted that however much they may elaborate and rearrange the stock of ideas pre-existent, there is little added to the "common fund." Philosophers bark at each other—poets sing stereotyped phrases—John Miltons re-appear in innumerable "Pollock's Courses of Time"—novelists and romances stick to the same overdone incidents, careless of the memories of defunct Scotts and Radcliffs, and it is only now and then when genius, by some lucky chance of youth, ploughs deeper into the soil of humanity and nature, that fresher experiences—perhaps at the cost of much individual pain and sorrow—are obtained; and the results are books, such as those of Herman Melville and Charles Dickens. Books which are living pictures, at once of the practical truth, and the ideal amendment: books which mark epochs in literature and art.

It is, however, not with Mr. Melville generally as a writer that we have now to deal, but with "Moby Dick, or the Whale," in particular; and at first let us not forget to say that in "taking titles" no man is more felicitous than our author. Sufficiently dreamy to excite one's curiosity, sufficiently explicit to indicate some main and peculiar feature. "Moby Dick" is perhaps a creation of the brain—"The Whale" a result of experience; and the whole title a fine polished result of both. A title may be a truth or a lie. It may be clap-trap, or true art. A bad book may have a good title, but you will seldom find a good book with an inappropriate name.

"Moby Dick, or the Whale," is all whale. Leviathian is here in full amplitude. Not one of your museum affairs, but the real, living whale, a bona-fide, warm-blooded creature, ransacking the waters from pole to pole. His enormous bulk, his terribly destructive energies, his habits, his food, are all before us. Nay, even his lighter moods are exhibited. We are permitted to see the whale as a lover, a husband, and the head of a family. So to speak, we are made guests at his fire-side; we set our mental legs beneath his mahogany, and become members of his interesting social circle. No book in the world brings together so much whale. We have his history, natural and social, living and dead. But Leviathan's natural history, though undoubtedly valuable to science, is but a part of the book. It is in the personal adventures of his captors, their toils, and, alas! not unfrequently their wounds and martyrdom, that our highest interest is excited. This mingling of human adventure with new, startling, and striking objects and pursuits, constitute one of the chief charms of Mr. Melville's books. His present work is a drama of intense interest. A whale, "Moby Dick"—a dim, gigantic, unconquerable, but terribly destructive being, is one of the persons of the drama. We admit a disposition to be critical on this character. We had doubts as to his admissibility as an actor into dramatic action, and so it would seem had our author, but his chapter, "The Affidavit," disarms us; all improbability or incongruity disappears, and "Moby Dick" becomes a living fact, simply doubtful at first, because he was so new an idea, one of those beings whose whole life, like the Palladius or the Sea-serpent, is a romance, and whose memoirs unvarnished are of themselves a fortune to the first analist or his publisher.

"Moby Dick, or the Whale," is a "many-sided" book. Mingled with much curious information respecting whales and whaling there is a fine vein of sermonizing, a good deal of keen satire, much humor, and that too of the finest order, and a story of peculiar interest. As a romance its characters are so new and unusual that we doubt not it will excite the ire of critics. It is not tame enough to pass this ordeal safely. Think of a monomaniac whaling captain, who, mutilated on a former voyage by a particular whale, well known for its peculiar bulk, shape, and color—seeks, at the risk of his life and the lives of his crew, to capture and slay this terror of the seas! It is on this idea that the romance hinges. The usual staple of novelists is entirely wanting. We have neither flinty-hearted fathers, designing villains, dark caverns, men in armor, nor anxious lovers. There is not in the book any individual, who, at a certain hour, *"might have been seen"* ascending hills or descending valleys, as is usual. The thing is entirely new, fresh, often startling, and highly dramatic, and with those even, who, oblivious of other fine matters, scattered with profusest hand, read for the sake of the story, must be exceedingly successful.

Our space will not permit us at present to justify our opinions by long quotations; but, at the risk of doing Mr. Melville injustice by curtailment, let us turn to the chapter headed "The Pequod meets the Rose Bud," p. 447, in which a whaling scene is described with infinite humor. * * *

Did our limits permit we would gladly extract the fine little episode, contained in the chapter called "The Castaway," as a favorable specimen of Mr. Melville's graphic powers of description. But we must conclude by strongly recommending "Moby Dick, or the Whale," to all who can appreciate a work of exceeding power, beauty, and genius.

[WILLIAM A. BUTLER]

[A Prose Epic on Whaling]†

* * * If we were disposed on the present occasion to follow the example * * * set us by our betters, we should forthwith proceed, taking "Moby Dick, or the Whale," as our text, to indite a discourse on cetology. Such, however, is not our intention. Nor do we propose, like a veritable devil's advocate, to haul Mr. Herman Melville over the coals for any offences committed against the code of Aristotle and Aristarchus:[1] we

---

† [William A. Butler], Washington *National Intelligencer*, December 16, 1851.
1. Greek critic (220?–150 B.C.E.). Aristotle (384–322 B.C.E.), Greek author of the *Poetics*, the foundation of European aesthetic theory.

have nothing to allege against his admission among the few writers of the present day who give evidence of some originality; but, while disposed to concede to Mr. Melville a palm of high praise for his literary excellencies, we must enter our decided protest against the querulous and cavilling innuendoes which he so much loves to discharge, like barbed and poisoned arrows, against objects that should be shielded from his irreverent wit. On this point we hope it is unnecessary to enlarge in terms of reprehension, further than to say that there are many passages in his last work, as indeed in most that Mr. Melville has written, which "dying he would wish to blot." Neither good taste nor good morals can approve the "forecastle scene," with its maudlin and ribald orgies, as contained in the 40th chapter of "Moby Dick." It has all that is disgusting in Goethe's "Witches' Kitchen," without its genius.[2] * * *

Moby-Dick, or the Whale, is the narrative of a whaling voyage; and, while we must beg permission to doubt its authenticity in all respects, we are free to confess that it presents a most striking and truthful portraiture of the whale and his perilous capture. We do not imagine that Mr. Melville claims for this his latest production the same historical credence which he asserted was due to "Typee" and "Omoo;" and we do not know how we can better express our conception of his general drift and style in the work under consideration than by entitling it a prose Epic on Whaling. In whatever light it may be viewed, no one can deny it to be the production of a man of genius. The descriptive powers of Mr. Melville are unrivalled, whether the scenes he paints reveal "old ocean into tempest toss'd," or are laid among the bright hillsides of some Pacific island, so warm and undulating that the printed page on which they are so graphically depicted seems almost to palpitate beneath the sun. Language in the hands of this master becomes like a magician's wand, evoking at will "thick-coming fancies," and peopling the "chambers of imagery" with hideous shapes of terror or winning forms of beauty and loveliness. Mr. Melville has a strange power to reach the sinuosities of a thought,[3] if we may so express ourselves; he touches with his lead and line depths of pathos that few can fathom, and by a single word can set a whole chime of sweet or wild emotions into a pealing concert. His delineation of character is actually Shakespearean—a quality which is even more prominently evinced in "Moby Dick" than in any of his antecedent efforts. Mr. Melville especially delights to limn the full-length portrait of a savage, and if he is a cannibal it is all the better; he seems fully convinced that the

2. Personal jealousy and anger lies behind this passage. Knowing Butler and his new bride were passing through Pittsfield on a train on August 9, 1850, Melville, with Butler's friend Evert Duyckinck, boarded the car and whisked them out, Melville then driving the bride away in a buggy to the Melvill house (now the Pittsfield Country Club) where he was staying, leaving Butler to follow with Duyckinck, drawn by a slower horse. As outlined in the headnote on p. 468 herein, with *Typee* Melville had become an international sex symbol, the first American writer to be so dubiously honored; for years people who met him saw him in the light of his presumed sexual experiences with the Fayaway of *Typee* or other native women. To have his bride swept from the car by a bearded sex symbol, a stranger to her although a literary lion, was excruciatingly humiliating to the young Butler, and still rankled late the next year. See Parker's *Herman Melville: A Biography (1819–1851)* (760–61), for an explanation of Melville's extraordinarily excited state, his having just an hour or two earlier finished writing "Hawthorne and His Mosses."
3. In his hostile, mocking review of Whitman's *Leaves of Grass* in the same paper on February 18, 1856, Butler recycled this striking phrase in describing his attempt to trail Whitman's "transcendental sinuosities of thought."

highest type of man is to be found in the forests or among the anthropophagi of the Fejee Islands. Brighter geniuses than even his have disported on this same fancy; for such was the youthful dream of Burke, and such was the crazy vision of Jean Jacques Ro[u]sseau.[4]

The humor of Mr. Melville is of that subdued yet unquenchable nature which spreads such a charm over the pages of Sterne. As illustrative of this quality in his style, we must refer our readers to the irresistibly comic passages scattered at irregular intervals through "Moby Dick;" and occasionally we find in this singular production the traces of that "wild imagining" which throws such a weird-like charm about the Ancient Mariner of Coleridge; and many of the scenes and objects in "Moby Dick" were suggested, we doubt not, by this ghastly rhyme. The argument of what we choose to consider as a sort of prose epic on whales, whalers, and whaling may be briefly stated as follows:

Ishmael, the pseudonymous appellative assumed by Mr. Melville in his present publication, becoming disgusted with the "tame and docile earth," resolves to get to sea in all possible haste, and for this purpose welcomes the whaling voyage as being best adapted to open to his gaze the floodgates of the oceanic wonder world; the wild conceits that swayed him were two—floating pictures in his soul of whales gliding through the waters in endless processions, and "midst them all one grand hooded phantom, like a snow hill in the air." This "grand hooded phantom," thus preternaturally impressed on his mental retina, proves to be *Moby Dick*, a great white whale, who had long been the terror of his "whaling grounds," noted for his invincible ferocity and for a peculiar snow-white wrinkled forehead, and a high pyramidical white hump on his back. It is not, however, his prodigious magnitude, nor his strange white hue, nor his deformed visage that so much invested the monster with unnatural terror, as the unexampled and intelligent malignity which he had repeatedly evinced when attacked by different whalers, so that no turbaned Turk; no hired Venetian or Malay, could smite his foes with more seeming malice. Ishmael embarks on board the whaling vessel "Pequod," whose captain, Ahab, had been previously bereft of a leg in an encounter with the terrible "Moby Dick;" a spirit of moody vindictiveness enters his soul, and he determines to be avenged upon the fell monster that had, with such intelligent and prepense maliciousness, rendered him a cripple for life; the white whale swam before him as the incarnation of all those wicked agencies which some deep men, according to Mr. Melville, feel eating in them, till they are left living on with half a heart and half a lung; in other words, Capt. Ahab became a monomaniac, with the chase and capture of Moby-Dick for his single idea; so that all his powers were thus concentrated and intensified with a thousand-fold more potency than he could have brought to bear on one reasonable object. The "Pequod" encounters Moby Dick, and in the deadly struggle which ensues the whole crew perish save the fortunate Ishmael. On such a slender thread hangs the whole of this ingenious romance, which for variety of incident and vigor of style can scarcely be exceeded.

---

4. Jean-Jacques Rousseau (1712–1778), Swiss-born French author of *Confessions* (1781–88), famous for advocating a return to primitive innocence, as Melville could be read as doing in *Typee*.

ANONYMOUS

[Pristine Powers and Old Extravagance]†

When the author of "Omoo" and "Typee" appeared, we were happy to hail a new and bright star in the firmament of letters. There was vast promise in these finely imagined fictions. Sea stories had been gradually waning in attraction. A vast number of respectable sailors, who never ought to have had their hands blacked in any fluid save tar, were discolouring them in ink. Cooper was not much imitated, but Marryat[1] had a shoal of clumsy followers, who believed that the public liked to read of the most ordinary naval manoeuvers told in technical language, and who imagined and let loose upon the world a swarm of *soi-disant* naval characters, who were either weak and conventional, or wildly extravagant and clumsily caricatured. Herman Melville was a man of different mettle; originality—thorough originality—was stamped upon every line he wrote. There never was a fresher author. He took up a new subject, and treated it in a new fashion. Round his readers he flung a new atmosphere, and round his fictions a new light. Herman Melville, in fact, gave the world a new sensation: springing triumphantly away from the old scenes of naval romances, abjuring the West Indies, and the English Channel, and the North Sea; recognising as classic ground neither the Common Hard nor Portsmouth Point—treating us to no exciting frigate battles—absolutely repudiating all notion of daring cuttings out of French luggers moored under batteries of tremendous power—never chasing slavers, and never being chased by pirates—inventing no mysterious corsairs, and launching no renowned privateers, Herman Melville flung himself entirely into a new naval hemisphere. The Pacific, with its eternally sunny skies and tranquil seas—the great ocean of the world—with its mysterious inhabitants—its whales, to which the whales of Greenland are babies, and its ships—worn, battered, warped, and faded ships, cruising for months and months, and years and years in that great illimitable flood—its glorious isles, too—ocean Edens—the very gardens of the south, coral girt and palm crowned, set in sparkling surf, smiled over by everlasting summer skies, and fanned by never-dying summer breezes—the birth-place of a happy, mirthful, Epicurean race, living in the balmy air and the tepid seas—pure and beautiful in their wildness, loving and kind, simple and truthful—such was the semi-fairy world into the gorgeous midst of which Herman Melville, like a potent and beneficent magician, hurled his readers. The power and the skill of the new literary enchanter were at once admitted. With a bursting imagination, and an intellect working with muscles which seemed not likely soon to tire, Herman Melville bid high for a high place among the spirits of the age. There never was an author more instinct with the flush of power and the pride of mental wealth. He dashed at his pages and overflowed them with the rushing fulness of his mind. A perception of the picturesque and of the beautiful—equally pow-

---

† London *Morning Chronicle*, December 20, 1851.
1. Frederick Marryat (1792–1848), British naval officer, author of *Peter Simple* (1834) and other popular sea fiction.

erful and equally intense—an imagination of singular force, and capable of calling up the wildest, most vivid, and most gorgeous conceptions, and a genuine, hearty, warm, and genial earnestness—in all he imagined, and in all he wrote—marked Herman Melville, not for a man of talent and a clever writer, but for a genius. And his style was just as thoroughly characteristic. Its strength, its living energy, its abounding vitality, were all his own. He seemed to write like a giant refreshed. He bounded on and on, as if irresistibly impelled by the blast of his own inspiration, and the general happiness of phrase, and the occasional flash of thought rendered in the most deliciously perfect words, were subsidiary proofs of the genuineness of the new powers which addressed the world.

But still, even in the best parts of the best books of the American sailor, there lurked an ominous presence which we hoped would disappear, but which, as we feared, has increased and multiplied. We could not shut our eyes to the fact that constantly before us we saw, like a plague spot, the tendency to rhapsody—the constant leaning towards wild and aimless extravagance, which has since, in so melancholy a degree, overflown, and, so to speak, drowned the human interest—the very possibility of human interest—in so great a portion of Herman Melville's works. First, indeed, there was but a little cloud the size of a man's hand.[2] Unhappily it has overspread the horizon, and the reader stumbles and wanders disconsolately in its gloom. It was in "Mardi" that the storm of extravagance burst fairly forth. The first volume was charming. What could be more poetic, yet life-like, than the picture of the sea-worn whaler, with her crew yearning again for a sight of a clod of dry green land—what finer than the canoe voyage—what more strangely thrilling, yet truth-like, than the falling in with the island schooner, with her grass ropes and cotton sails, drifting with two savages along the sea? So far Melville had held his fine imagination in curb. It had worked legitimately, and worked right well. It had proceeded by the eternal rules of art and the unchanging principles of the truthful and the symmetrical. But with the second volume the curb of judgment is removed. Common sense, which Herman Melville can depose or keep enthroned at will, was driven out by one *coup d'état*,[3] and the two last volumes are melancholy rhodomontade—half raving, half babble—animated only by the outlines of a dull cold allegory, which flits before the reader like a phantom with a veiled face, and a form which is but the foldings of vapour wreaths. You yearn for the world again—for sea and sky and timber—for human flesh, white or brown—for the solid wood of the ship and the coarse canvass of the sail—as did the whaler's crew for land and grass. What are these impalpable shadows to you? What care you for these misty phantoms of an indefinite cloud land? You want reality—you want truth—you want *vraisemblance*. Close the book—there are none in the last two volumes of "Mardi."

2. In 1 Kings 18.43, even though King Ahab is threatening to kill him, the prophet Elijah arranges a test of power, after which the prophets of Baal are slain. Elijah sends his servant to look toward the sea, but the servant returns having seen nothing. Elijah sends him "again seven times," and on the last time the man reports (in verse 44): "Behold, there ariseth a little cloud out of the sea, like a man's hand"—at which Elijah sends the servant with a message to Ahab, who hastens to his wife Jezebel with the news that her prophets are dead. She swears to kill Elijah by the next day.
3. A sudden overthrow of the government by force.

Next, if we remember rightly, came a three-volume series of sketches called "White Jacket." They depicted life on board an American frigate in the Pacific—the severe, and in many points brutal, discipline of a Transatlantic ship of war, elaborated with such daguerreotype exactitude and finish, so swarming with the finest and minutest details, and so studded with little points never to be imagined, that you are irresistibly impelled to the conclusion that, from the first word to the last, every syllable is literal, down-right truth. Here Herman Melville rushes into the other extreme from "Mardi." In one he painted visions, in the other he engraves still life. The first is all broad, vague dashes—the second all carefully finished lines. You look at one book, as it were, through a hazy telescope with many coloured glasses—at the other, through a carefully cleaned microscope, which shows you every infinitesimal blister of the tar in the ship's seams—every fibre in a topsail haul-yard, and every hair in a topman's whisker. And yet, every now and then, even in the midst of all this Dutch painting, comes a dash at the old fashion of raving. Every now and then a startling chapter lugs you from the forecastle, or the cock-pit, or the cable-tiers, or the very run, up into the highest, bluest Empyrean—you are snatched up from bilge-water to the nectar of the Gods—you are hurried from the consideration of maggots in biscuits, to that of the world beyond the stars or the world before the flood: in one chapter there is a horrifying account of the amputation of a man's leg—in the next you are told how the great mountain peaks of the Andes raised all their organ notes to peal forth hallelujahs on the morning when the world was born.

One other work by Herman Melville divides his wildly extravagant "Mardi" from the little less extravagant fiction before us. It is called, if we remember right, "My First Voyage," and is the literally and strongly told experiences of a sailor boy on his first trip from New York to Liverpool. The work smacks strongly of reality, but it is written in a lower, less buoyant, and less confident key than the earlier fictions. It seemed to us, also, as we read it, that some, at all events, of the virtue of the author had departed, and that he knew it. He walked feebly and groped. The inward sunshine was wanting, and the strong throb of the vigorous brain was neither so full nor so steady as before.

Here, however—in "The Whale"—comes Herman Melville, in all his pristine powers—in all his abounding vigour—in the full swing of his mental energy, with his imagination invoking as strange and wild and original themes as ever, with his fancy arraying them in the old bright and vivid hues, with that store of quaint and out-of-the-way information—we would rather call it reading than learning—which he ever and anon scatters around, in, frequently, unreasonable profusion, with the old mingled opulence and happiness of phrase, and alas! too, with the old extravagance, running a perfect muck throughout the three volumes, raving and rhapsodising in chapter after chapter—unchecked, as it would appear, by the very slightest remembrance of judgment or common sense, and occasionally soaring into such absolute clouds of phantasmal unreason, that we seriously and sorrowfully ask ourselves whether this can be anything other than sheer moonstruck lunacy.

Let us put it to our readers, for example, what they think of the following as the speech of a whaling captain to his crew:—

CAPTAIN AHAB.

"'Drink and pass!' * * * hunt Moby Dick to his death!'" [ch. 36, paras. 44–50]

But it may be replied that Captain Ahab is represented as being a mono-maniac. So be it: but the crew are not, and what is to be thought of such a conversation as the following amongst the hands of a whaler:—

FORECASTLE TALK.
"MATE'S VOICE FROM THE QUARTER-DECK"

"Eight bells there forward * * * showest thy black brow, Seeva!" [ch. 40, paras. 3–23]

And so on indefinitely.

But it is high time to inform our readers what they may expect to find in "The Whale." The author tells the story, as usual *in propria persona*. He determines to sail from the harbour of New Bedford on board a whaler, for a four years' cruise in the Pacific. In a sailors' tavern, roughly and pow-erfully drawn, he is put to sleep with a South Sea Island harpooner, a tatooed cannibal, and a Pagan who worships a wretched little black graven image called Gogo, and in whom Herman recognises a noble and heroic soul—insomuch, indeed, that with certain philosophic mental reserva-tions—he does not scruple to go on his knees to Gogo, set upright in the empty grate as a shrine, and join the orisons of his South Sea acquain-tance. As soon as this personage appears, the story assumes that night-mare unreality, and becomes overshadowed by that uncertain looming of imaginative recklessness, which is only here and there dispersed by the intensely-written whaling adventures, and the minute truth of the descriptions not only of the whales themselves, but of the utensils used for capturing them, and the process of cutting up the monsters and extracting the oil. Queequeg, the harpooneer, and Herman Melville embark on board the Pequod, an ancient whaler—a sort of mystic prophet of evil—a strange sepulchral voiced phantom-like man having several times warned them against the voyage in vain. All this, and in fact the entire book, except the portions we have mentioned, reads like a ghost story done with rare imaginative power and noble might of expression. The captain of the Pequod—Captain Ahab—is a mystery of mysteries. He looms out of a halo of terrors—scents prophecies, omens, and auguries. He is an ancient mariner—an ancient whaler—and there seems on him a doom and a curse. His destiny is linked to the destiny of a certain whale—a strange horrible whale—perfectly white—an albino whale, a monster famous since the South Sea fisheries began for his ferocity, his cunning, and his strength. This white whale's name is "Moby Dick." He is held to be hundreds, if not thousands, of years old. He has ploughed the oceans before a sail was set above them. He may have been, for all Captain Ahab knows, the very whale who swallowed Jonah. Well, this whale has Captain Ahab pursued voyage after voyage. This whale he has chased, we know not how many times round the earth; to kill this whale he has devoted all his means, all his energies, all his thoughts in this world, and, so far as we can make out, is supposed to have bartered all his prospects in the next.

Often has he encountered it, but Moby Dick bears a charmed life. There are scores and scores of rusted harpoons wedged deeply in his blubber. He trails miles of line behind him, until the hemp rots off and sinks in the brine. He has smashed boats by scores—drowned men by dozens. Every South Sea man knows the "white whale," and, taught by dread experience, gives him a wide berth. The sailors tell dreadful tales of him in the sleepy mid-watch. He is, in fact, a sort of ocean fiend—a tremendous *bogey* of the sea—an apparition which no one seeks but Captain Ahab, whose destiny is bound up in the doomed pursuit. So, then, the Pequod turns her battered bows to the Indian Ocean, and Captain Ahab commences his final hunt of Moby Dick * * *

ANONYMOUS

[A Most Agreeable and Exciting Work][†]

This is a most agreeable and exciting work, in three volumes, quaintly told, but full of life and anecdote. It purports to be the history of a whaling voyage, in which that good ship the "Pequod," Captain Ahab, of Nantucket, was engaged. The names which occur in the course of the following extracts are those of certain individuals comprising the whaler's crew. Perhaps there is no employment so dangerous or exciting as that of the whale fishery; and the graphic sketches of fierce combats with monsters of the deep, as given in the three volumes now before us, afford a good idea of the perils those engaged in its pursuit encounter. * * *

ANONYMOUS

[Mr. Melville Has Survived His Reputation][‡]

Mr. Melville is evidently trying to ascertain how far the public will consent to be imposed upon. He is gauging, at once, our gullibility and our patience. Having written one or two passable extravagancies, he has considered himself privileged to produce as many more as he pleases, increasingly exaggerated and increasingly dull. The field from which his first crops of literature were produced, has become greatly impoverished, and no amount of forcing seems likely to restore it to its pristine vigor. In bombast, in caricature, in rhetorical artifice—generally as clumsy as it is ineffectual—and in low attempts at humor, each one of his volumes has been an advance upon its predecessors, while, in all those qualities which make books readable, it has shown a decided retrogression from former efforts. Mr. Melville never writes naturally. His sentiment is forced, his wit is forced, and his enthusiasm is forced. And in his attempts to display to the

† London *Reynolds's Newspaper: A Weekly Journal of Politics, History, Literature, and General Intelligence*, December 21, 1851. Reprinted here for the first time.
‡ New York *United States Magazine and Democratic Review* 30 (January 1852): 93.

utmost extent his powers of "fine writing," he has succeeded, we think, beyond his most sanguine expectations.

The truth is, Mr. Melville has survived his reputation. If he had been contented with writing one or two books, he might have been famous, but his vanity has destroyed all his chances of immortality, or even of a good name with his own generation. For, in sober truth, Mr. Melville's vanity is immeasurable. He will either be first among the book-making tribe, or he will be nowhere. He will centre all attention upon himself, or he will abandon the field of literature at once. From this morbid self-esteem, coupled with a most unbounded love of notoriety, spring all Mr. Melville's efforts, all his rhetorical contortions, all his declamatory abuse of society, all his inflated sentiment, and all his insinuating licentiousness.

"Typee" was undoubtedly a very proper book for the parlor, and we have seen it in company with "Omoo," lying upon tables from which Byron was strictly prohibited, although we were unable to fathom those niceties of logic by which one was patronized, and the other proscribed. But these were Mr. Melville's triumphs. "Redburn" was a stupid failure, "Mardi" was hopelessly dull, "White Jacket" was worse than either; and, in fact, it was such a very bad book, that, until the appearance of "Moby Dick," we had set it down as the very ultimatum of weakness to which its author could attain. It seems, however, that we were mistaken.

We have no intention of quoting any passages just now from "Moby Dick." The London journals, we understand, "have bestowed upon the work many flattering notices,"[1] and we should be loth to combat such high authority. But if there are many of our readers who wish to find examples of bad rhetoric, involved syntax, stilted sentiment and incoherent English, we will take the liberty of recommending to them this precious volume of Mr. Melville's.

[WILLIAM GILMORE SIMMS?]

[Grounds for a Writ *de lunatico* against Melville][†]

In all those portions of this volume which relate directly to the whale, his appearance in the oceans which he inhabits; his habits, powers and peculiarities; his pursuit and capture; the interest of the reader will be kept alive, and his attention fully rewarded. We should judge, from what is before us, that Mr. Melville has as much personal knowledge of the whale as any man living, and is better able, than any man living, to display this knowledge in print. In all the scenes where the whale is the performer or the sufferer, the delineation and action are highly vivid and exciting. In all other respects, the book is sad stuff, dull and dreary, or ridiculous. Mr. Melville's Quakers are the wretchedest dolts and drivellers, and his Mad Captain, who pursues his personal revenges against

---

1. If this is an exact quotation, it has not been located; the words are not in the Higgins-Parker *Herman Melville: The Contemporary Reviews* and not in Parker's working version of *The New Melville Log*. Perhaps the Harpers had put out a brief advertisement not yet discovered.

† Charleston, South Carolina, *Southern Quarterly Review* 5 (January 1852): 262.

the fish who has taken off his leg, at the expense of ship, crew and own-ers, is a monstrous bore, whom Mr. Melville has no way helped, by enveloping him in a sort of mystery. His ravings, and the ravings of some of the tributary characters, and the ravings of Mr. Melville himself, meant for eloquent declamation, are such as would justify a writ *de lunatico* against all the parties.

Posthumous Praise and the Melville Revival: 1893–1927

ANONYMOUS

[A Marvellous Odyssey]†

It was not until this remarkable romance came out, over forty years ago, that Herman Melville, that strange compound of Dutch, English and Huguenot blood, merited the name of the American prose Victor Hugo. In fact it was after the publication of "Moby-Dick" that Hugo's really great romances of the sea and land came out; so that one might truthfully turn the tables and almost say that Victor Hugo was the French Melville. So striking, so suspicious is the resemblance between "Moby-Dick" and "Les Travailleurs de la Mer," that one is sorely tempted to the enticing accusation of a certain sort of plagiarism on the part of the Sage of Guernsey, of that general and diffusive kind which critics love to point out between Swift and Lucian, Goethe and Marlowe, Faust and Manfred, and Coleridge and Mme. de Staël. A gigantic devil-fish is one of the *dramatis personæ* of "Moby-Dick" as it is of "The Toilers of the Sea," and the fantastic learning, the episodic style, the wonderful picturings of the sea in all its beauty and terror, and the peculiar manipulation of imaginative effects in both books, emphasize the fact of their essential kinship. Hugo was familiar enough with English literature to command it completely, and it is far from incredible that he knew the works of Melville. Hawthorne paid the warmest tribute to Melville's surpassing imagination, and to him "Moby-Dick" was very appropriately dedicated.

Indeed there is no romance of Hawthorne's that surpasses this whaling-story in witching power, in grasp on the pulse, in almost supernatural strength of description, and in ability to quicken the blood. The undreamt poesy lying in the lives of Natucket whalers in the fifties has for once received epical treatment, and the result is a marvellous Odyssey of adventure in warm seas and in icy, in halcyon and in purgatorial latitudes, over such a range of sunlit or storm-smitten billows as could occur only in actual experience before the mast in search of real whales on the real deep. Hugo never travelled; and therefore his lovely poems of the sea or his "Hans d'Islande" are conceived from the shore—powerful but shadowy idealizations of things he had never really seen. His empty shells Melville fills full of the

† From the New York *Critic*, n.s. 19 (April 15, 1893): 232. No one has identified the author of this remarkable tribute occasioned by the publication of the United States Book Company edition of *Moby-Dick*, authorized by Melville's widow.

living breath, the roar, the music, the vibration of the living sea, Whit-manesque in its intensity and realism, the memories of one who had lived years in the troughs or on the mountain-crests of Homeric waves, and who therefore in his work simply transcribed ineffaceable impressions. Mohammedanism has been described as mere "paint"; even so Hugo's seas are painted seas as compared with the streaming or starlit or surging oceans of this real mariner. To depict the guillotining of Louis XVI, it is not neces-sary indeed to feel the actual flash of the axe itself across one's arteries, but a certain amount of actual knowledge is always welcome if not indispens-able in depicting the mighty phenomena of great voyages, great emotions or great deeds. This Hugo did not possess, and his phantom romances are mere husks, mere *larvæ* or *simulacra*, illumined by an unnatural interior light, like a jack o'lantern, as compared with the healthy, wholesome, rude but terrible realities of such books as "Moby-Dick."

In this story Melville is as fantastically poetical as Coleridge in the "Ancient Mariner," and yet, while we swim spellbound over the golden rhythms of Coleridge feeling at every stroke their beautiful improbability, everything in "Moby-Dick" might have happened. The woe-struck cap-tain, his eerie monomania, the half-devils of the crew, the relentless pur-suit of the ever-elusive vindictive white whale, the storms and calms that succeed each other like the ups and downs of a mighty hexameter, all the weird scenery of the pursuit in moonlight and in daylight, all are so won-derfully fresh in their treatment that they supersede all doubt and impress one as absolutely true to the life. Even the recondite information about whales and sea-fisheries sprinkled plentifully over the pages does not interfere seriously with the intended effect; they are the paraphernalia of the journey. The author's extraordinary vocabulary, its wonderful coinages and vivid turnings and twistings of worn-out words, are comparable only to Chapman's translations of Homer. The language fairly shrieks under the intensity of his treatment, and the reader is under an excitement which is hardly controllable. The only wonder is that Melville is so little known and so poorly appreciated.

ARCHIBALD MacMECHAN

The Best Sea Story Ever Written[†]

Anyone who undertakes to reverse some judgment in history or criticism, or to set the public right regarding some neglected man or work, becomes at once an object of suspicion. Nine times out of ten he is called a liter-ary snob for his pains, or a prig who presumes to teach his betters, or a "phrase-monger," or a "young Osric," or something equally soul-subduing.

† Reprinted from the Kingston, Ontario *Queen's Quarterly* 7 (October 1899): 120–30. Still a youngish man although already Munro Professor of English at Dalhousie University, MacMechan (1862–1933) wrote Melville on November 21, 1889, a letter remarkable for its extraordinary praise of *Moby-Dick*: "I have read and re-read 'Moby-Dick' with increasing pleasure on every perusal: and with this study, the conviction has grown up that the unique merits of that book have never received due recognition." It was also remarkable for MacMechan's offer to dedicate him-self to doing Melville justice:

Besides, the burden of proof lies heavy upon him. He preaches to a sleeping congregation. The good public has returned its verdict upon the case, and is slow to review the evidence in favour of the accused, or, having done so, to confess itself in the wrong. Still, difficult as the work of rehabilitation always is, there are cheering instances of its complete success; notably, the rescue of the Elizabethan dramatists by Lamb and Hazlitt and Leigh Hunt. Nor in such a matter is the will always free. As Heine says, ideas take possession of us and force us into the arena, there to fight for them. There is also the possibility of triumph to steel the raw recruit against all dangers. Though the world at large may not care, the judicious few may be glad of new light, and may feel satisfaction in seeing even tardy justice meted out to real merit. In my poor opinion much less than justice has been done to an American writer, whose achievement is so considerable that it is hard to account for the neglect into which he has fallen.

This writer is Herman Melville, who died in New York in the autumn of 1891, aged eighty-three [sic]. That his death excited little attention is in consonance with the popular apathy towards him and his work. The civil war marks a dividing line in his literary production as well as in his life. His best work belongs to the *ante-bellum* days, and is cut off in taste and sympathy from the distinctive literary fashions of the present time. To find how complete neglect is, one has only to put question to the most cultivated and patriotic Americans north or south, east or west, even professed specialists in the nativist literature, and it will be long before the Melville enthusiast meets either sympathy or understanding. The present writer made his first acquiantance with *Moby-Dick* in the dim, dusty Mechanics' Institute Library (opened once a week by the old doctor) of an obscure Canadian village, nearly twenty years ago; and since that time he has seen only one copy of the book exposed for sale, and met only one person (and that not an American) who had read it. Though Kingsley has a good word for Melville, the only place where real appreciation of him is to be found of recent years is in one of Mr. Clark Russell's dedications. There occurs the phrase which gives this paper its title. Whoever takes the trouble to read this unique and original book will concede that Mr. Russell knows whereof he affirms.

I find myself in a position which enables me to give myself to literature as a life-work. I am anxious to set the merits of your books before the public and to that end, I beg the honour of correspondence with you. * * * In the matter of style, apart from the matter altogether, I consider, your books, especially the earlier ones, the most thoroughly New World product in all American literature.

Melville replied politely, but cautiously, explaining that he had entered his eighth decade and had "latterly come into possession of unobstructed leisure," but only just as his vigor had begun noticeably to decline. What little vigor was left, Melville explained, he husbanded "for certain matters as yet incomplete, and which indeed may never be completed," among them, he did not specify, the *Billy Budd* manuscript, which was not quite completed at his death in 1891.

It had been assumed that by this belated publication of an article in a small Canadian periodical MacMechan had meant well but had not profoundly affected the course of the Melville Revival. Frederick J. Kennedy and Joyce Deveau Kennedy in "Archibald MacMechan and the Melville Revival," *Leviathan* 1 (October 1999): 5–37, show that MacMechan carried out the pledge he offered to Melville: he devoted his life to awakening appreciation of *Moby-Dick* in Canada, in the United States, and in England, tirelessly proselytizing friends at Johns Hopkins and Harvard and other universities, and getting his "The Best Sea Story Ever Written" reprinted and reprinted in ways that brought it to an ever-expanding audience. The Kennedy and Kennedy article is a superb piece of research into literary history and a much-deserved tribute to the accomplishments of a well-meaning and well-doing admirer of Melville.

Melville is a man of one book, and this fact accounts possibly for much of his unpopularity. The marked inferiority of his work after the war, as well as changes in literary fashion, would drag the rest down with it. Nor are his earliest works, embodying personal experience like *Redburn* and *White Jacket*, quite worthy of the pen which wrote *Moby Dick*. *Omoo* and *Typee* are little more than sketches, legitimately idealized, of his own adventures in the Marquesas. They are notable works in that they are the first to reveal to civilized people the charm of life in the islands of the Pacific, the charm which is so potent in *Vailima Letters* and *The Beach of Falesà*. Again, the boundless archipelagos of Oceanica furnish the scenes of *Mardi*, his curious political satire. This contains a prophecy of the war, and a fine example of obsolete oratory in the speech of the great chief Alanno from Hio-Hio. The prologue in a whale-ship and the voyage in an open boat are, perhaps, the most interesting parts. None of his books are without distinct and peculiar excellences, but nearly all have some fatal fault. Melville's seems a case of arrested literary development. The power and promise of power in his best work are almost unbounded; but he either did not care to follow them up or he had worked out all his rifts of ore. The last years of his life he spent as a recluse.

His life fitted him to write his one book. The representative of a good old Scottish name, his portrait shows distinctively Scottish traits. The head is the sort that goes naturally with a tall, powerful figure. The forehead is broad and square; the hair is abundant; the full beard masks the mouth and chin; the general aspect is of great but disciplined strength. The eyes are level and determined; they have speculation in them. Nor does his work belie his blood. It shows the natural bent of the Scot towards metaphysics; and this thoughtfulness is one pervading quality of Melville's books. In the second place, his family had been so long established in the country (his grandfather was a member of the "Boston tea-party") that he secured the benefits of education and inherited culture: and this enlightenment was indispensable in enabling him to perceive the literary "values" of the strange men, strange scenes and strange events amongst which he was thrown. And then, he had the love of adventure which drove him forth to gather his material at the ends of the earth. He made two voyages; first as a green hand of eighteen [*sic*] in one of the old clipper packets to Liverpool and back; and next, as a young man of twenty-three [*sic*], in a whaler. The latter was sufficiently adventurous. Wearying of sea-life, he deserted on one of the Marquesas Islands, and came near being killed and eaten by cannibal natives who kept him prisoner for four months. At last he escaped, and worked his way home on a U.S. man-o'-war. This adventure lasted four years and he went no more to sea.

After his marriage, he lived at Pittsfield for thirteen years, in close intimacy with Hawthorne, to whom he dedicated his chief work. My copy shows that it was written as early as 1851, but the title page is dated exactly twenty years later. It shows as its three chief elements this Scottish thoughtfulness, the love of literature and the love of adventure.

When Mr. Clark Russell singles out *Moby Dick* for such high praise as he bestows upon it, we think at once of other sea-stories,—his own, Marryat's, Smollett's perhaps, and such books as Dana's *Two Years before the Mast.* But the last is a plain record of fact; in Smollett's tales, sea-life is only part of one great round of adventure; in Mr. Russell's mercantile marine, there is generally the romantic interest of the way of a man with a maid; and in Marryat's the rise of a naval officer through various ranks plus a love-story or plenty of fun, fighting and prize-money. From all these advantages Melville not only cuts himself off, but seems to heap all sorts of obstacles in his self appointed path. Great are the prejudices to be overcome; but he triumphs over all. Whalers are commonly regarded as a sort of sea-scavengers. He convinces you that their business is poetic; and that they are finest fellows afloat. He dispenses with a love-story altogether; there is hardly a flutter of a petticoat from chapter first to last. The book is not a record of fact; but of fact idealized, which supplies the frame for a terrible duel to the death between a mad whaling-captain and a miraculous white sperm whale. It is not a love-story but a story of undying hate.

In no other tale is one so completely detached from the land, even from the very suggestion of land. Though Nantucket and New Bedford must be mentioned, only their nautical aspects are touched on; they are but the steps of the saddle-block from which the mariner vaults upon the back of his sea-horse. The strange ship "Pequod" is the theatre of all the strange adventures. For ever off soundings, she shows but as a central speck in a wide circle of blue or stormy sea; and yet a speck crammed full of human passions, the world itself in little. Comparison brings out only more strongly the unique character of the book. Whaling is the most peculiar business done by man upon the deep waters. A war-ship is but a mobile fort or battery; a merchantman is but a floating shop or warehouse: fishing is devoid of any but the ordinary perils of navigation; but sperm-whaling, according to Melville, is the most exciting and dangerous kind of big game hunting. One part of the author's triumph consists in having made the complicated operations of this strange pursuit perfectly familiar to the reader; and that not in any dull, pedantic fashion, but touched with the imagination, the humor, the fancy, the reflection of a poet. His intimate knowledge of his subject and his intense interest in it make the whaler's life in all its details not only comprehensible but fascinating.

A bare outline of the story, though it cannot suggest its peculiar charm, may arouse a desire to know more about it. The book takes its name from a monstrous, invincible, sperm whale of diabolical strength and malice. In an encounter with this leviathan, Ahab, the captain of a Nantucket whaler, has had his leg torn off. The long illness which ensues drives him mad; and his one thought upon recovery is vengeance upon the creature that has mutilated him. He gets command of the "Pequod," concealing his purpose with the cunning of insanity until the fitting moment comes: then he swears the whole crew into his fatal vendetta. From this point on, the mad captain bears down all opposition, imposes his own iron will upon the ship's company, and affects them with like heat, until they are as one keen weapon fitted to his hand and to his purpose. In spite of all difficulties, in spite of all signs and portents and warnings, human and divine, he drives on to certain destruction. Everything conduces to one end, a three day's battle with the monster, which staves and sinks the ship, like the ill-fated "Essex."

For a tale of such length, *Moby Dick* is undoubtedly well constructed. Possibly the "Town-Ho's Story," interesting as it is, somewhat checks the progress of the plot; but by the time the reader reaches this point, he is infected with the leisurely, trade-wind, whaling atmosphere, and has no desire to proceed faster than at the "Pequod's" own cruising rate. Possibly the book might be shortened by excision, but when one looks over the chapters it is hard to decide which to sacrifice. The interest begins with the quaint words of the opening sentence: "Call me Ishmael"; and never slackens for at least a hundred pages. Ishmael's reasons for going to sea, his sudden friendship with Queequeg, the Fijian harpooneer, Father Mapple's sermon on Jonah, in the seamen's bethel, Queequeg's rescue of the country bumpkin on the way to Nantucket, Queequeg's Ramadan, the description of the ship "Pequod" and her two owners, Elijah's warning, getting under way and dropping the pilot, make up an introduction of great variety and picturesqueness. The second part deals with all the particulars of the various operations in whaling from manning the mast-heads and lowering the boats to trying out the blubber and cleaning up the ship, when all the oil is barrelled. In this part Ahab, who has been invisible in the retirement of his cabin, comes on deck and in various scenes different sides of his vehement, iron-willed, yet pathetic nature, are made intelligible. Here also is much learning to be found, and here, if anywhere, the story dawdles. The last part deals with the fatal three days' chase, the death of Ahab, and the escape of the White Whale.

One striking peculiarity of the book is its Americanism—a word which needs definition. The theme and style are peculiar to this country. Nowhere but in America could such a theme have been treated in such a style. Whaling is peculiarly an American industry; and of all whale-men, the Nantucketers were the keenest, the most daring, and the most successful. Now, though there are still whalers to be found in the New Bedford slips, and interesting as it is to clamber about them and hear the unconscious confirmation of all Melville's details from the lips of some old harpooneer or boat-header, the industry is almost extinct. The discovery of petroleum did for it. Perhaps Melville went to sea for no other purpose than to construct the monument of whaling in this unique book. Not in his subject alone, but in his style is Melville distinctly American. It is large in idea, expansive; it has an Elizabethan force and freshness and swing, and is, perhaps, more rich in figures than any style but Emerson's. It has the picturesqueness of the new world, and, above all, a free-flowing humour, which is the distinct *cachet* of American literature. No one would contend that it is a perfect style; some mannerisms become tedious, like the constant moral turn, and the curiously coined adverbs placed before the verb. Occasionally there is more than a hint of bombast, as indeed might be expected; but, upon the whole, it is an extraordinary style, rich, clear, vivid, original. It shows reading and is full of thought and allusion; but its chief charm is its freedom from all scholastic rules and conventions. Melville is a Walt Whitman of prose.

Like Browning he has a dialect of his own. The poet of *The Ring and the Book* translates the different emotions and thoughts and possible words of pope, jurist, murderer, victim, into one level uniform Browningese; reduces them to a common denominator, in a way of speaking, and

Melville gives us not the actual words of American whalemen, but what they would say under the imagined conditions, translated into one consistent, though various Melvillesque manner of speech. The life he deals with belongs already to the legendary past, and he has us completely at his mercy. He is completely successful in creating his "atmosphere." Granted the conditions, the men and their words, emotions and actions, are all consistent. One powerful scene takes place on the quarter-deck of the "Pequod" one evening, when, all hands mustered aft, the Captain Ahab tells of the White Whale, and offers a doubloon to the first man who "raises" him:

> "'Captain Ahab,' said Tashtego, 'that White Whale must be the same that some call Moby Dick.'
>
>   *   *   *
>
> If man will strike, strike through the mask!'"
>
> (ch 36)

Then follows the wild ceremony of drinking round the capstan-head from the harpoon-sockets to confirm Ahab's curse. "Death to Moby Dick. God hunt us all, if we do not hunt Moby Dick to the death!" The intermezzo of the various sailors on the forecastle which follows until the squall strikes the ship is one of the most suggestive passages in all the literature of the sea. Under the influence of Ahab's can, the men are dancing on the forecastle. The old Manx sailor says:

> "I wonder whether those jolly lads bethink them of what they are dancing over. I'll dance over your grave, I will—that's the bitterest threat of your night-women, that beat head-winds round corners. O, Christ! to think of the green navies and the green-skulled crews."

Where every page, almost every paragraph, has its quaint or telling phrase, or thought, or suggested picture, it is hard to make a selection; and even the choicest morsels give you no idea of the richness of the feast. Melville's humour has been mentioned; it is a constant quality. Perhaps the statement of his determination after the adventure of the first lowering is as good an example as any:

> "Here, then, from three impartial witnesses, I had a deliberate statement of the case.
>
>   *   *   *
>
> 'Queequeg,' said I, 'come along and you shall be my lawyer, executor and legatee.'"
>
> (ch. 49)

The humour has the usual tinge of Northern melancholy, and sometimes a touch of Rabelais. The exhortations of Stubb to his boat's crew, on different occasions, or such chapters as "Queen Mab," "The Cassock," "Leg and Arm," "Stubb's Supper," are good examples of his peculiar style.

But, after all, his chief excellence is bringing to the landsman the very salt of the sea breeze, while to one who has long known the ocean, he is as one praising to the lover the chiefest beauties of the Beloved. The magic of the ship and the mystery of the sea are put into words that form pictures for the dullest eyes. The chapter, "The Spirit Spout," contains these two aquarelles of the moonlit sea and the speeding ship side by side:

"It was while gliding through these latter waters that one serene and moonlight night, when all the waves rolled by like scrolls of silver; and by their soft, suffusing seethings all things made what seemed a silvery silence, not a solitude; on such a silent night a silvery jet was seen far in advance of the white bubbles at the bow. Lit up by the moon it looked celestial; seemed some plumed and glittering god uprising from the sea.

* * *

Walking the deck, with quick, side-lunging strides, Ahab commanded the t'gallant sails and royals to be set, and every stunsail spread. The best man in the ship must take the helm. Then, with every mast-head manned, the piled-up craft rolled down before the wind. The strange, upheaving, lifting tendency of the taffrail breeze filling the hollows of so many sails made the buoyant, hovering deck to feel like air beneath the feet."

In the chapter called "The Needle," ship and sea and sky are blended in one unforgettable whole:

"Next morning the not-yet-subsided sea rolled in long, slow billows of mighty bulk, and striving in the "Pequod's" gurgling track, pushed her on like giants' palms outspread. The strong, unstaggering breeze abounded so, that sky and air seemed vast outbellying sails; the whole world boomed before the wind. Muffled in the full morning light, the invisible sun was only known by the spread intensity of his place; where his bayonet rays moved on in stacks. Emblazonings, as of crowned Babylonian kings and queens, reigned over everything. The sea was a crucible of molten gold, that bubblingly leaps with light and heat."

It would be hard to find five consecutive sentences anywhere containing such pictures and such vivid, pregnant, bold imagery: but this book is made up of such things.

The hero of the book is, after all, not Captain Ahab, but his triumphant antagonist, the mystic white monster of the sea, and it is only fitting that he should come for a moment at least into the saga. A complete scientific memoir of the Sperm Whale as known to man might be quarried from this book, for Melville has described the creature from his birth to his death, and even burial in the oil casks and the ocean. He has described him living, dead and anatomized. At least one such description is in place here. The appearance of the whale on the second day of the fatal chase is by "breaching," and nothing can be clearer than Melville's account of it:

"The triumphant halloo of thirty buckskin lungs was heard

* * *

to the dim mistiness of an advancing shower in a vale."

(ch. 134)

This book is at once the epic and the encyclopaedia of whaling. It is a monument to the honour of an extinct race of daring seamen; but it is a monument overgrown with the lichen of neglect. Those who will care to scrape away the moss may be few, but they will have their reward. To the class of gentleman-adventurer, to those who love both books and free life under the wide and open sky, it must always appeal. Melville takes rank with Borrow, and Jefferies, and Thoreau, and Sir Richard Burton; and his place in this brotherhood of notables is not the lowest. Those who feel the salt in their blood that draws them time and again out of the city to the wharves and the ships, almost without their knowledge or their will; those who feel the irresistible lure of the spring, away from the cramped and noisy town, up the long road to the peaceful companionship of the awaking earth and the untained sky; all those—and they are many—will find in Melville's great book an ever fresh and constant charm.

WILLIAM LIVINGSTON ALDEN

[Let Us Have a Melville Society][†]

Now that George Borrow[1] has been rediscovered, and there is a prospect that we shall have a Borrowian cult, will not somebody make an effort to revive the books of Herman Melville? They have been forgotten except by the few, just as were "Lavengro" and "The Romany Rye," but their day will surely come. Let us hasten it. Why should we not have a Melville society? We have Ibsen societies, and there is more true poetry in Melville's books than there is in all of Ibsen's plays. Besides the poetry, Melville's books are full of genuine realism, and not genuine power. We may grant all their defects, their occasional melodrama and pathos, and rank rubbish, which Mr. Melville sometimes shot into them, but for all that Herman Melville is far and away the most original genius that America has produced, and it is a National reproach that he should be so completely neglected.

Of course I know that many of the readers of *The Times Saturday Review* will not agree with me, but have they read Melville? Do they know the opening chapters of "Mardi"—I won't say a word in behalf of the rest of the book? Have they read "Moby Dick," that masterpiece of sea lore

† William Livingston Alden, "London Literary Letter," *The New York Times*, August 5, 1899. George Monteiro first discovered this document by Alden (1837–1908), a London correspondent for *The New York Times*, and published them (along with letters from others) in "'Far and Away the Most Original Genius That America Has Produced': Notations on the New York *Times* and Melville's Literary Reputation at the Turn of the Century," *Resources for American Literary Study* 5 (Spring 1975): 69–80. As Monteiro explained,

> An unwritten chapter in accounts of Herman Melville's literary reputation lies in the interest taken in his work by reviewers, columnists, and readers in the book supplement of the New York *Times* at the turn of the century. Notices of impending English editions, the publication of Frank T. Bullen's sea books, and the personal enthusiasm for Melville shown by the *Times*'s literary correspondent in London, all combined in the period from 1899 to 1905 to keep Melville's name before potential American readers.

> Oddly enough, the history of the Melville Revival, often dated to articles published in the centennial of his birth, 1919, or to the publication of Raymond Weaver's *Herman Melville: Mariner and Mystic* (1921), has not yet been written as one coherent and detailed story drawing together information from both American and British (which means worldwide) sources. See the notes to the essay by MacMechan (p. 628 herein) and to the Morley and Tomlinson selection (p. 637 herein). The fullest survey is Parker's in section 8 of the NN "Historical Note" (1988): 732–54.

1. Borrow (1803–1881) was often admired by British literary people who also admired Melville.

and sea poetry? Have they seen Jackson fall from the yard in "Redburn," and have they lounged with White Jacket in the frigate's maintop? Melville needs to be studied with care, just as does Walt Whitman. The reader must recognize the chaff and the wheat and refrain from making the mistake of assuming that because Whitman and Meville wrote pages of unmitigated rubbish they did not also write pages of which their country should be forever proud. By all means let us have a Melville society, which will devote organized effort to the task of securing for Melville the recognition which he deserves.

LOUIS BECKE

[The Strangest, Wildest, and Saddest Story][†]

Many years ago, when the present writer was supercargo of a small trading schooner, sailing from the beautiful port of Apia, in the Samoan group—those lovely clustering gems of the blue Pacific, whose names are now familiar and endeared to all English-speaking people through the memory of the man[1] who rests on the verdured slopes of Vailima Mountain,—there came on board our ship, one day, a sweet, dainty little English lady, whom we rough wandering island traders loved, and feared as well; for with all the gentleness that filled her woman's heart, she could, as we knew at times by our burning cheeks of shame, be very, but justly, bitter to us when we had done those things which we ought not to have done. And in Samoa, in those days, men did those things which they ought not to have done very frequently.

"I have brought you some books," she said to our grizzled old captain; "and among them are three volumes by an American writer—Herman Melville. It is called 'The Whale,' and it is the strangest, wildest, and saddest story I have ever read." * * *

The captain of our little schooner was the one well-educated man of our ship's company—a man with a very heavy hand and a very kindly Scotsman's heart. The mate and myself were not always in perfect accord with him, and often bitter words had passed between us; but "Moby Dick" brought us happily together again. For "the old man" had a deep, resonant voice, and he read the story to us from beginning to end. And although he would stop now and again, and enter into metaphysical matters, we forgave him, for we knew that he too, like us, was fascinated with the mad

---

† From the "Introduction" to *Moby-Dick* (London: G. P. Putnam's Sons, 1901), ix–xii. This evocative account, long known only in the form of a sentence quoted in a list of notable publications by Richard Bentley, appeared as an introduction to the 1901 reissue of 270 copies of the 1893 United States Book Company edition imported in 1900. In the 1970s Richard Colles Johnson obtained a copy of the introduction for Parker from the only known surviving copy of the 270, the one in the British Library. Someone may yet date the event more closely, but it seems to have been around 1872 that Becke (born 1855 in New South Wales) heard *The Whale* read aloud— from three volumes that might now be auctioned for well over a hundred thousand dollars.

1. Robert Louis Stevenson (1850–1894), Scottish author of *Kidnapped* (1886) and other immensely popular works, who went to the Pacific in 1888 hoping his tuberculosis would progress more slowly there. He took *Typee* and *Omoo* with him, as all literate British and American travelers did.

Captain Ahab and the brave mate Starbuck and the rest of the ill-fated crew of the "Pequod."

"A WAYFARER" [H. W. MASSINGHAM?]

[A Deposition from a New Reader][†]

It is clear that the wind of the spirit, when it once begins to blow through the English literary mind, possesses a surprising power of penetration. A few weeks ago it was pleased to aim a simultaneous blast in the direction of a book known to some generations of men as "Moby Dick." A member of the staff of THE NATION was thereupon moved in the ancient Hebrew fashion to buy and to read it. He then expressed himself on the subject, incoherently indeed, but with signs of emotion as intense and as pleasingly uncouth as Man Friday betrayed at the sight of his long-lost father. While struggling with his article, and wondering what the deuce it could mean, I received a letter from a famous literary man, marked on the outside "Urgent," and on the inner scroll of the MS. itself "A Rhapsody." It was about "Moby Dick." Having observed a third article on the same subject, of an equally febrile kind, I began to read "Moby Dick" myself. Having done so I hereby declare, being of sane intellect, that since letters began there never was such a book, and that the mind of man is not constructed so as to produce such another; that I put its author with Rabelais, Swift, Shakespeare, and other minor and disputable worthies; and that I advise any adventurer of the soul to go at once into the morose and prolonged retreat necessary for its deglutition. And having said this, I decline to say another word on the subject now and for evermore.

CHRISTOPHER MORLEY AND
H. M. TOMLINSON

[*Moby-Dick*: "The Immense Book of the Sea"][‡]

One we have mentioned several times before, who knows what he is talking about, writes to us from London. We hope he won't mind our quoting a portion of his letter, which was not intended for print:

† From the London *Nation*, January 22, 1921, p. 572. The Wayfarer, identified in *Doubloon* as John Middleton Murry, is more likely (as Kevin J. Hayes says in his 1994 *The Critical Response to Herman Melville's "Moby-Dick"*) the editor of the *Nation*, Massingham, whose familiarity with *Moby-Dick* is attested in the Morley and Tomlinson piece (below).

‡ From Christopher Morley, "The Bowling Green" [column], New York *Evening Post*, February 5, 1921. Henry Major Tomlinson (1873–1958), English novelist and journalist, as literary editor of the London *Nation* 1917–23 and afterward in the 1920s did as much as any Englishman to popularize Melville. Morley (1890–1957), American novelist, dramatist, editor, and journalist, helped keep Americans abreast of the burgeoning British praise of Melville. In the New York *Saturday Review of Literature* 2 (May 1, 1926): 755, he printed this passage of a letter from a London correspondent: "Melville, it is supposed, has been re-discovered recently. Actually, folk here rave hysterically about 'Moby Dick,' principally, and apparently lack the wit to know that 'Pierre' is one of the most important books in the world, profound beyond description in its metaphysic."

I've been reading again a writer I've never heard an American mention. Not once. I cannot recall that I've ever seen him referred to in a book on American letters. (You'll be surprised, perhaps alarmed, to hear that Concord, Mass., is a place of such august memories to me that perhaps it is best I should never visit it.)[1] But this writer—an American all right—puts it across *all* the sea writers I know. For that sort of work your side of the water not only holds the belt, but is going to keep the championship. The title *cannot* be contested. You have held the championship since 1851. Conrad, Masefield, Marryat[2]—not on your life! They're not in it. I regret to have to say it, but there it is. This very sea book (which I have not named to you) was, in my presence this week, admitted by Arnold Bennett, Augustine Birrell, Massingham, John Middleton Murry, and Swinnerton,[3] to be

---

Morley's insistence that Melville had "long been accepted as a classic" is not justified by the way Melville had been treated in literary histories and textbooks, but it suggests that Morley had learned from his journalist elders something of the separate flurries of attention paid to *Moby-Dick* in the two decades before the centennial of his birth, 1919, and that as a working journalist Morley may well have been aware of "a little Melville racket" here and there that Melville scholars have not yet discovered. Melville's reputation was on the point of a revival for decades before 1919–21, by which time it was an unmistakable fact. See the footnote to MacMechan (p. 628 herein) for the Kennedys' new discoveries.

1. For decades British admirers of American writers had made pilgrimages to Concord, the lifelong home of Thoreau, the longtime home of Emerson, and the home for extended periods of Hawthorne and Bronson Alcott (and his young daughter Louisa May Alcott). For decades, also, the Boston firm of Ticknor and Fields and its successors up through Houghton Mifflin had controlled American textbooks so as to canonize Boston-area men and to exclude anyone else, such as the New Yorkers Walt Whitman and Herman Melville.

2. Popular British sea writers, named out of chronological order. Polish-born Joseph Conrad (1857–1924), author of *Lord Jim* (1900). John Masefield (1878–1967), author of *Salt-Water Ballads* (1902), who read Melville very early, in, of all places, Yonkers, New York. Frederick Marryat (1792–1848), author of *Peter Simple* (1834), a book the young Melville knew. Masefield, who became poet laureate in 1930, persistently praised *Moby-Dick* early in the 20th century, before the Melville Revival, as in *The Mainsail Haul* (1905); Conrad protested too vehemently about not being influenced by *Moby-Dick* and Melville's other books; see the January 15, 1907, letter printed in *Moby-Dick as Doubloon* (122–23) on *The Whale* ("a rather strained rhapsody with whaling for a subject and not a single sincere line in the 3 vols of it").

3. A clutch of famous and successful British writers, with ties to the Bloomsbury group and the *Nation*. Arnold Bennett (1867–1931), author of *The Old Wives' Tale* (1908), in the 1928 *The Savour of Life: Essays in Gusto* showed himself a rare admirer of Melville's *Pierre*. Augustine Birrell (1850–1933) wrote "The Great White Whale: A Rhapsody," London *Athenæum*, no. 4735 (January 28, 1921), 99–100, as a notice of the new Oxford World's Classics edition with an introduction by Viola Meynell. Birrell's piece, reprinted in *Doubloon* (137–40) as one of the great stories about encountering Melville, includes this passage in which he explains that he was over thirty when he first heard Melville's name:

> I owed my introduction to "Omoo," "Typee" and "The Whale" to that exquisite judge of a good book, Sir Alfred Lyall, who was shocked at my ignorance, and most emphatically urged me to read "Omoo" and "Typee"; but, as ill luck would have it, he did not specially dwell upon "The Whale." To hear was, in those days, to obey, and a second-hand bookseller almost at once supplied me with these three books. Even then I was not out of the Wood of Ignorance, for though I was greatly taken with "Omoo" and "Typee" I was not so bewitched by them as to begin at once upon the three volumes of "The Whale"—which I allowed to remain for a whole decade unread. One happy day I took them down, and then and then only did Moby Dick swim into my ken. Oh, woeful waste! Is there, I wonder (looking all round me), another such book lying neglected in this very room? And yet now, when full of my wrongs, I have discovered that all this time I had intimate friends, and even relatives, not much addicted to holding their peace, who knew all about Ahab and Bildad and Peleg and Moby Dick, and yet never gave me a hint of their existence. What on earth were they talking about all these years! I cannot remember!

Henry William Massingham (1860–1924), was editor of the *Nation* 1907–23. John Middleton Murry (1889–1957), editor of the *Athenæum* 1919–21, is remembered as the husband of Katherine Mansfield and the friend of D. H. Lawrence (and lover of Frieda Lawrence), as well as an early publisher of Virginia Woolf and T. S. Eliot. Turbulent and erratic, he promoted Melville's reputation in occasional passionate outbursts rather than sustained appreciations. Frank Swinnerton (1884–1982) was a critic, novelist, and editor at Chatto and Windus; in the New York *Bookman* in May 1921, he threw a dash of cool water on the London enthusiasm for *Moby-Dick* (see "It Is Not Everybody's Book" in *Doubloon*, 140–41).

the—well, to be IT. There ain't nothing like it. There never will be again. What book is that? My stars, I'd belt some of you Americans over your really tremendous classic when you bring forward the English sea writers.

The way America has taken to Conrad, considers Masefield a classic, and has even bought up an edition of *Old Junk*, and another of *The Sea and the Jungle*,[4] makes writers on this side very grateful. But MOBY DICK . . . ah, the secret is out! That's the Immense book of the sea.

H. M. Tomlinson

But it does seem a little odd to us that Mr. Tomlinson has never seen *Moby Dick* mentioned in American journalism. Melville, like Dana, has so long been accepted as a classic over here that he is more or less taken as a matter of course (as a matter of college course too often, we fear) and too little mentioned. Yet we have never seen a year go by without a little Melville racket cropping up somewhere. In 1919, the year of his centennial, there was a big Melville hullabaloo over here. *Moby Dick* has lately been reissued in England (by the Oxford University Press, in its admirable *World's Classic* [sic] series) which has brought it to the eye of English reviewers. (It went into the blessed company of *Everyman's Library* in 1907.) We must confess, for our own part, that we never read it until 1919, when the Melville centennial came along. But all that Mr. Tomlinson says is true. No man of sense needs to read sixty pages of *Moby Dick* to know it is one of the world's great books. Its fertile mysticism, its extraordinary humor and melancholy ("All noble things are touched with that"), betray an author "with a globular brain and a ponderous heart."

The only reason we can give for Mr. Tomlinson's not having seen Melville praised in American print—and we would like to give it as politely and deferentially as possible—is, quite simply, that, like most English journalists, he probably does not read the American prints nearly as thoroughly as we do the British. Now, let us be honest. When we get back to the office we will send him an accurate list of the British journals which are subscribed to by the *Evening Post*. Will he, in turn, tell us how many American papers and magazines are taken in the office (his own) of the London *Nation*? We have always been amazed at the complete agnosticism of many British editors as to what is going on over here in a literary way. The favorite preoccupation of most intelligent American editors is more mutualism among the English-speaking peoples. In reply to which we are greeted by that recent novennial quaintness from Mr. Punch. Mr. Tomlinson, for whom we have such affectionate regard, will not misunderstand our gentle plea. We speak for the good of the house.

---

4. Tomlinson is alluding to two of his own books: *Old Junk* (1918) and *The Sea and the Jungle* (1912), an account of his voyage up the Amazon.

WILLIAM FAULKNER

[I Wish I Had Written That][†]

It is a difficult question. I can name offhand several books which I should like to have written, if only for the privilege of rewriting parts of them. But I dare say there are any number of angels in heaven today [particularly recent American arrivals] who look down upon the world and muse with a little regret on how much neater they would have done the job than the Lord, in the fine heat of His creative fury, did.

I think that the book which I put down with the unqualified thought "I wish I had written that" is Moby Dick. The Greek-like simplicity of it: a man of forceful character driven by his sombre nature and his bleak heritage, bent on his own destruction and dragging his immediate world down with him with a despotic and utter disregard of them as individuals; the fine point to which the various natures caught [and passive as though with a foreknowledge of unalterable doom] in the fatality of his blind course are swept—a sort of Golgotha of the heart become immutable as bronze in the sonority of its plunging ruin; all against the grave and tragic rhythm of the earth in its most timeless phase: the sea. And the symbol of their doom: a White Whale. There's a death for a man, now; none of your patient pasturage for little grazing beasts you can't even see with the naked eye. There's magic in the very word. A White Whale. White is a grand word, like a crash of massed trumpets; and leviathan himself has a kind of placid blundering majesty in his name. And then put them together!!! A death for Achilles, and the divine maidens of Patmos to mourn him, to harp white-handed sorrow on their golden hair.

And yet, when I remember Moll Flanders and all her teeming and rich fecundity like a market-place where all that had survived up to that time must bide and pass; or when I recall When We Were Very Young, I can wish without any effort at all that I had thought of that before Mr. Milne did.

---

† From the Chicago *Tribune* (July 16, 1927), p. 12, one of a series of letters under the general title "Confessions." Copyright 1927 Chicago Tribune Company. All rights reserved. Used with permission. For the column Fanny Butcher had asked William Faulkner what book he would like most to have written; this letter is his reply. Hans Bungert found the letter in the clippings made from "Confessions" by Herbert Kleist and printed it in *Studi Americani* 9 (1963): 371–75, but with the wrong date and the inadvertent omission of twelve words. The square brackets in the letter are from the *Tribune*.

A Handful of Critical Challenges

WALTER E. BEZANSON

Moby-Dick: Work of Art[†]

* * * Interest in *Moby-Dick* as direct narrative, as moral analogue, as modern source, and as spiritual autobiography has far outrun commentary on it as a work of art. A proper criticism of so complex a book will be a long time in the making and will need immense attention from many kinds of critics. In the meantime I am struck by the need just now for contributions toward a relatively impersonal criticism directed at the book itself. The surrounding areas—such as *Moby-Dick* and Melville, *Moby-Dick* and the times in which it was made—are significant just because the book is a work of art. To ask what the book means is to ask what it is about, and to ask what it is about is in turn to ask how art works in the case at hand.

My remarks are therefore in this direction. Beginning with a look at the materials out of which *Moby-Dick* is created, we shall explore the means of activation and some of the forms that contain and define them. The three roadmarks we shall follow are *matter, dynamic,* and *structure.*

I

By *matter* I mean here the subject (or subject matter) in the gross sense. *Moby-Dick* has as its gross subject not Indian fighting or railroad building but whaling.

Any book about mid-nineteenth-century American whaling must in some fashion or other deal with certain phenomena, artifacts, and processes. There they are, and they must be used or the book is not about whaling. A rough inventory of data would include at least the following areas:

NATURAL WORLD: *The seas and oceans,* covering three-fifths of the globe: on the surface—tides, currents, winds, and weather; under the surface—countless forms of life of extreme diversity. Marine animals of the order *Cetacea,* ranging from small dolphins and porpoises to whales, the largest form of life in earth history (up to 125 tons). The Sperm Whale (*Physeter Macrocephalus*): one of the larger varieties (up

† From Walter E. Bezanson, "*Moby-Dick*: Work of Art," in *Moby-Dick: Centennial Essays*, edited by Tyrus Hillway and Luther S. Mansfield (Dallas: Southern Methodist University Press, 1953). Reprinted by permission of the author. Bezanson's paper was read at Oberlin College on November 13, 1951, at exercises to commemorate the one-hundredth year of publication of *Moby-Dick*. The opening paragraph and half of the second are omitted here.

to 75–85 feet), wrapped in a fat blanket (blubber) like other whales but unique in carrying a pool of pure spermaceti oil (up to 500 gallons) in his great square head; protects himself with rows of ivory teeth and the slap of his tail (20 feet across), or dives to the sea bottom; known to attack great objects which threaten him.

HISTORICAL WORLD: *Man*, a prolific, social, land animal constantly in search of animal, mineral, and vegetable resources for survival and use. *Seventeenth century*: discovering the use of whale products especially the oil for lighting, man begins to bring to bear on the pursuit of whales the technologies developed in transportation and war. *Nineteenth century*: the United States, a newly created and powerfully expanding democracy in the early stages of capitalism, builds a whaling fleet of over seven hundred vessels and commits itself to a sea frontier that girdles the globe. New Bedford, Nantucket, and Sag Harbor become the world centers for the pursuit of sperm whales.

ARTIFACTS: *The whale-ship*: a wooden vessel, length about 105 feet, beam about 28 feet; three vertical masts (foremast, mainmast, mizzenmast), each with four horizontal yards (cross-pieces); rigged to the yards more than thirty separate sails, each named for identification. *Nautical equipment*: windlass, capstan, chocks, pins, block and tackle, pumps; lines for handling sails, anchors, cargo. *Navigation equipment*: chronometer, quadrant, compass, charts, log and line, wheel or tiller; for finding location and keeping on course. *Spaces*: below decks two levels of compartments, including forecastle bunkroom for the crew and cabins aft for the captain and mates; storage quarters for food, water, whaling gear, casks, shooks (staves and barrel heads); sail and chain lockers, blubber room, holds for the cargo. *Pursuit equipment*: whaleboats of cedar planking, length 25 feet; plank seats for five oarsmen, platforms bow and stern for harpooner and boatsteerer; five pair of oars, steering oar, harpoons, lances, waif poles (for signal flags), line tubs, assorted gear. *Processing equipment*: try-works (deck furnaces), kettles, forks, spades, mincing knives, etc.

TECHNIQUES: innumerable skills demanded by all artifacts, especially ship and boat handling, maintenance, attack, butchering.

SOCIAL ORGANIZATION: *In the background*: Yankee owners who furnish capital and artifacts for voyages, to whom the products of voyages are returnable for sale at a profit. *In the foreground*: a ship's company of about thirty-five men brought aboard under individual contracts giving each a percentage of the profits (lay) according to his skill with men or artifacts. *The hierarchy*, in descending order of authority: absentee owners; captain, three mates, three harpooners, boat crews, blacksmith, cooper, cook, cabin boy. *Politics*: manhandling.

OBJECT OF VOYAGE: in three or four years' time to sight, chase, kill, and process into oil as many whales as possible, returning to port safely with a profitable cargo.

These are the given elements of whaling as a major industry in nine-teenth-century America. They may be thought of as simply existing in nature and experience; we have been thinking of them independent of communication, though they are necessarily written down here. In art, however, communication is the heart of the matter; and the subject of whaling, it chances, offers good historical instances of some planes on which the communication problem may be conceived.

Looking back into nineteenth-century Anglo-American history, we find at least four different levels of communication of whaling. The first was that of the typical whaling logbook. A whaleman's log was a record kept for the owners by the mates or captain; it consisted of daily entries giving the ship's position, weather, landfalls, ships sighted or hailed, whales taken and their size (expressed in barrels of oil), crew desertions, injuries, deaths, etc. What any of this felt like or meant, except in terms of navigation and trade, was purposely excluded. The whaler's log was meant to be an abstraction of group experience in terms of pragmatic ends.

A second level was that of the standard histories. The aim here was the compilation of reliable data on the natural history of the whale (as part of the zoölogical record) or on the happenings in the fishery (as a contribution to economic history). Classic examples of the histories that had wide circulation in the second quarter of the nineteenth century include Thomas Beale's *Natural History of the Sperm Whale* (1835, 1839), Frederick Bennett's *A Whaling Voyage Round the Globe, from the Year 1833 to 1836* (1840), and William Scoresby's *An Account of the Arctic Regions with a History and Description of the Northern Whale Fishery* (1820). Empirical knowledge set the aims and limits for such books as these, too; their meaning and function were conditioned by the rise of the life sciences and of inductive historiography.

A third level of communication was the simple transcription of generalized personal experience. Americans who had never been whaling were interested to know something of the representative experiences of the seventeen thousand men engaged in the American fisheries in the 1840's. So came the reports of scenes and adventures, of duties and dangers, in books like J. Ross Browne's *Etchings of a Whaling Cruise* (1846) and the Reverend Henry Cheever's *The Whale and His Captors; or the Whaleman's Adventures and the Whale's Biography* . . . (1849). Such books were records of outward experience to whose general validity any ex-whaleman could testify. They were the journalism of the whaling industry, written by the Lowell Thomases and John Gunthers of the day (or perhaps one should say *Jonah* Gunthers, as no doubt he would have called his book *Inside the Whale*).

A generous distance beyond these logbooks, histories, and personal narratives lies the problem of fiction. When Melville was composing *Moby-Dick* in 1850 and 1851 he did not hesitate to make quite shameless use of all the books just named, as well as others, in the preparation of his own. Reading for facts and events, for recall and extension, he took on an enormous cargo of whaling matter. But facts are not fiction. In *Moby-Dick* the inert matter of whaling has been subjected to the purposes of art through a dynamic and a structure.

II

By the term "dynamic" I mean the action of forces on bodies at rest. The whaling matter in *Moby-Dick* is in no sense at rest, excepting as here or there occurs a failure in effect. For the most part the stuff and data of whaling are complexly subject to the action of a force which can be defined and illustrated. So too is the whole narrative base of the book, which is something far more than a record of what anyone aboard the *Pequod* would agree had happened. There is a dynamic operating on both matter and narrative which distinguishes *Moby-Dick* from logs, journals, and histories.

One of two forces, or their combination, is commonly assumed to provide the dynamic of *Moby-Dick*. The first, of course, is Captain Ahab, the dark protagonist, the maimed king of the quarter-deck whose monomania flows out through the ship until it drowns his men—mind and (finally) body. That he is the dominant "character" and the source of "action" seems obvious. The reader's image of him is a lasting one. Is Ahab the dynamic?

The alternative force, it is commonly assumed, is Moby Dick himself, that particular white "spouting fish with a horizontal tail" about whom legend and murmured lore have woven enchantments, so that he looms a massive phantom in the restless dreams of the *Pequod's* captain and crew. His name gives the novel its title. He is prime antagonist of the tale. Is Moby Dick the dynamic?

Both these interpretations have their uses, especially when taken together in a subject-predicate relation. But there is a third point of view from which neither Ahab nor the White Whale is the central dynamic, and I find it both compelling and rewarding, once recognized. This story, this fiction, is not so much about Ahab or the White Whale as it is about Ishmael, and I propose that it is he who is the real center of meaning and the defining force of the novel.

The point becomes clearer when one realizes that in *Moby-Dick* there are two Ishmaels, not one. The first Ishmael is the enfolding sensibility of the novel, the hand that writes the tale, the imagination through which all matters of the book pass. He is the narrator. But who then is the other Ishmael? The second Ishmael is not the narrator, not the informing presence, but is the young man of whom, among others, narrator Ishmael tells us in his story. He is simply one of the characters in the novel, though, to be sure a major one whose significance is possibly next to Ahab's. This is forecastle Ishmael or the younger Ishmael of "some years ago." There is no question here of dual personality or *alter ego*, such as really exists, for instance, in Poe's "William Wilson" or Conrad's "The Secret Sharer." Narrator Ishmael is merely young Ishmael grown older. He is the man who has already experienced all that we watch forecastle Ishmael going through as the story is told.

The distinction can be rendered visual by imagining, for a moment, a film version of the novel. As the screen lights up and the music drops to an obbligato we look on the face of narrator Ishmael (a most marvelous face, I should judge), and the magic intonation begins:

> Call me Ishmael. Some years ago—never mind how long pre-
> cisely—having little or no money in my purse, and nothing particular

to interest me on shore, I thought I would sail about a little and see the watery part of the world. It is a way I have of driving off the spleen, and regulating the circulation. Whenever I find myself . . .

And as the cadenced voice goes on, the face of the Ishmael who has a tale to tell fades out, the music takes up a brisk piping air, and whom should we see tripping along the cobbled streets of New Bedford, carpetbag in hand, but forecastle Ishmael. It is a cold winter's night, and this lonely young man is in search of lodgings. For very soon now he plans to go a-whaling.

Meanwhile we hear the voice, always the magic voice, not of the boy we watch with our eyes, but of one who long since went aboard the *Pequod*, was buried in the sea and resurrected from it. This voice recounts the coming adventures of young Ishmael as a story already fully experienced. Experienced, but not fully understood; for as he explicitly says: "It was the whiteness of the whale that above all things appalled me. But how can I hope to explain myself here; and yet, in some dim, random way, explain myself I must, else all these chapters might be naught." So we are reminded by shifts of tense from time to time that while forecastle Ishmael is busy hunting whales narrator Ishmael is sifting memory and imagination in search of the many meanings of the dark adventure he has experienced. So deeply are we under the spell of the narrator's voice that when at last the final incantation begins—" 'And I only am escaped alone to tell thee'. . . . The drama's done. . . ."—then at last, as forecastle Ishmael floats out of the *Pequod's* vortex, saved, we look again on the face of Ishmael narrator. And we realize that for many hours he has been sitting there and has never once moved, except at the lips; sitting in profound reverie, yet talking, trying to explain "in some dim, random way" what happened, for "explain myself I must."

The distinction between the function of the two Ishmaels is clear. Yet it would be a mistake to separate them too far in temperament. Certainly young Ishmael is no common sailor thoughtlessly enacting whatever the fates throw his way. He is a pondering young man of strong imagination and complex temperament; he will, as it were, become the narrator in due time. But right now he is aboard the *Pequod* doing his whaleman's work and trying to survive the spell of Ahab's power. The narrator, having survived, is at his desk trying to explain himself to himself and to whoever will listen. The primary use of the distinction is to bring the narrator forward as the essential sensibility in terms of which all characters and events of the fiction are conceived and evaluated. The story is his. What, then, are some of his primary commitments of mind and imagination as he shapes his story through one hundred and thirty-five chapters?

As a lover of laughter and hilarity, Ishmael delights in the incongruities. Of whales, for instance: whales spout steam because they think so much; they have no nose, but don't really need one—there are no violets in the sea; they are very healthy, and this is because they get so much exercise and are always out of doors, though rarely in the fresh air; and they like to breakfast on "sailor tarts, that is whaleboats full of mariners." Ishmael has too a deep belly laugh for the crudities and obscenities that mark the life of animal man, making much more than is proper of some talk about gentlemen harpooning ladies, relishing a Rabelaisian remark about "head winds" versus "winds from astern," and penning a memorable canonization of a rarely discussed part of the anatomy in "The Cassock." But as a purveyor of the "genial, desperado philosophy," his most characteristic humor is that of the hyena laugh: he begins his tale with a mock confession of suicidal impulses; he sends young Ishmael running to his bunk after his first encounter with a whale to make out his will; he reports that some sailors are so neat that they wouldn't think of drowning "without first washing their faces"; and he delights in Queequeg's solemn decision, when he seems mortally ill, whereby the good savage suddenly "recalled a little duty ashore, which he was leaving undone; and therefore . . . changed his mind about dying." Beneath Ishmael's mask of hypochondria is the healthy grimace of a man who stands braced to accept "the universal thump" and to call out: "Who ain't a slave?" To Ishmael "a good laugh is a mighty good thing, and rather too scarce a good thing; the more's the pity."

As narrator Ishmael betrays a passion for all faraway places and things, "Patagonian sights and sounds," imagined cities, fabled heroes, the sepulchers of kings. His rich imagination is stirred by all that is secret, mysterious, and undecipherable in the great riddles of mankind. He both cherishes and mocks the great systems of the philosophers, the operations of "chance, free will, and necessity," the great religions and heresies of the past. His fascination with ancient lore and wisdom runs from Adam to Zoroaster; to help him tell his tale he marshals the great mythic figures of past centuries and all black-letter commentaries thereon.

His temperament is complex. If one of its facets, that of the "Sub-Sub-Librarian," has an antiquarian glint, another glows with the love of action. Each cry from the masthead alerts him from dreamy speculations to the zest of the hunt. Every lowering away starts his blood pounding. He is a superb narrator of the frenzied strivings of the boat crew as they press in for the kill, chanting their terror and competence as they enter "the charmed, churned circle" of eternity. When the death-deed is done, when the whirl slowly widens, he takes up the song of dismemberment. For the weapons of the chase, the red tools of slaughter, the facts of procedure, he has an insatiable curiosity. Cutting in, trying out, stowing down—the whole butcher-slab routine of processing the dead whale he endows with ritual certainty, transforming dirty jobs into acts of ceremonial dignity. Ishmael's voice translates the laughter and wild deeds of the bloody crew into the ordered rites of primitive tribal priests.

Narrator Ishmael has an instinct for the morally and psychologically intricate. He presses close in after the intertwinings of good and evil, tracks down the baffling crisscross of events and ideas, ponders their ambiguities and inversions. He is keen for a paradox and quick to see polarities—so keen in fact that the whole experience seems a double vision of what is at once noble and vile, of all that is lovely and appalling. This two-fold sensitivity marks his probings into the life-images of those he has known—whether in his grandscale exposition of the "ungodly, godlike man, Captain Ahab" or in the compassionate recollection of little Pip, for a time lost overboard in the "heartless immensity" of the sea, and gone divinely mad from it. Whether noting that Queequeg's tomahawk-pipe "both brained his foes and soothed his soul" or contemplating "the inter-linked terrors and wonders of God," he turns the coin both ways. He makes it a crisis of the first order that young Ishmael, both a brooder and a good companion, was drawn with the rest of the crew by the dark mag-netic pull of the captain's monomania, wavering between allegiance to that uncommon king—Ahab—and to "the kingly commons"—the crew. Only the traumatic revulsion on the night of "The Try-Works" saved young Ishmael—"a strange (and ever since inexplicable) thing" which the narra-tor now explains symbolically: "Give not thyself up, then, to fire, lest it invert thee, deaden thee; as for the time it did me."

Above all one notes the narrator's inexhaustible sense of wonder. Won-der at the wide Pacific world, with its eternal undulations; wonder at the creatures of the deep; wonder at man—dreamer, doer, doubter. To him in retrospect the whale has become a mighty analogue of the world, of man, of God. He is in awe before the whale: its massive bulk, tiny eyes, great mouth, white teeth; its narrow throat and cavernous belly; the spout; the hump; the massed buttress of its domed head; the incomparable power and magic of its fanning, delicate tail. It is wonder that lies at the center of Ishmael's scale of articulation, and the gamut runs out either way toward fear and worship.

Enough of evocation. Every reader of *Moby-Dick* can and will want to enlarge and subtilize the multiple attributes of Ishmael. The prime expe-rience for the reader is the narrator's unfolding sensibility. With it we have an energy center acting outward on the inert matter of nature and expe-rience, releasing its possibilities for art. Whereas forecastle Ishmael drops in and out of the narrative with such abandon that at times a reader won-ders if he has fallen overboard, the Ishmael voice is there every moment from the genesis of the fiction in "Call me Ishmael" to the final revelation of the "Epilogue" when "The drama's done." It is the narrator who creates the microcosm and sets the terms of discourse.

But this Ishmael is only Melville under another name, is he not? My suggestion is that we resist any one-to-one equation of Melville and Ish-mael. Even the "Melville-Ishmael" phrase, which one encounters in criti-cal discussions, though presumably granting a distinction between auto-biography and fiction, would seem to be only a more insistent confusion of the point at stake unless the phrase is defined to mean either Melville or Ishmael, not both. For in the process of composition, even when the artist knowingly begins with his own experience, there are crucial inter-ventions between the act that was experience and the re-enactment that is art—intrusions of time, of intention, and especially of form, to name only a few. Which parts of Ishmael's experience and sensibility coincide with Melville's own physical and psychological history and in just what ways is a question which is initially only tangential to discussion of *Moby-Dick* as a completed work of art.

III

But what of structure? That there is a dynamic excitation in *Moby-Dick* sympathetic readers have not denied. Is the effect of Ishmael's energy, then, simply to fling the matter in all directions, bombarding the reader with the accelerated particles of his own high-speed imagination? Is Ishmael's search for "some dim, random way" to explain himself not merely a characterization of the complexity of his task but also a confession of his inadequacy to find form? The questions are crucial, for although readers will presumably go on reading *Moby-Dick* whichever way they are answered, the critical reader will not be encouraged to keep coming back unless he can "see" and "feel" the tension of controlling forces.

To an extraordinary extent Ishmael's revelation of sensibility is controlled by rhetoric. Throughout the tale linguistic versatility and subtle rhythmic patterns exploit sound and sense with high calculation. Almost at random one chooses a sentence: "And ever, as the white moon shows her affrighted face from the steep gullies in the blackness overhead, aghast Jonah sees the rearing bowsprit pointing high upward, but soon beat downward again towards the tormented deep." It is a successful if traditional piece of incantation with its rising and falling movements manipulated to bring a striking force on the qualitative word "aghast." Its mood is typically Gothic-romantic (pictorial equivalents would be certain passages from Poe or the sea-paintings of Ryder), but structurally its allegiance is to the spacious prose of the seventeenth century. Although the passage is from Father Mapple's sermon, it is in no way unrepresentative; there are scores of sentences throughout *Moby-Dick* of equal or greater rhetorical interest.

Of the narrative's several levels of rhetoric the simplest is a relatively straightforward *expository* style characteristic of many passages scattered through the cetological accounts. But it is significant that such passages are rarely sustained, and serve chiefly as transitions between more complex levels of expression. Thus a series of expository sentences in the central paragraph of the chapter on "Cutting In" comes to this point: "This done, a broad, semicircular line is cut round the hole, the hook is inserted, and the main body of the crew striking up a wild chorus, now commence heaving in one dense crowd at the windlass." Whether it cannot or will not, Ishmael's sensibility does not endure for long so bare a diction: "When instantly, the entire ship careens over on her side; every bolt in her starts like the nail-heads of an old house in frosty weather; she trembles, quivers, and nods her frighted mastheads to the sky." The tension is maintained through a following sentence, strict exposition returns in the next, and the paragraph concludes with an emotionally and grammatically complex sentence which begins with exposition, rises to a powerful image of whale flesh hoisted aloft where "the prodigious blood-dripping mass sways to and fro as if let down from the sky," and concludes with a jest about getting one's ears boxed unless he dodges the swing of the bloody mess. Even in the rhetorically duller chapters of exposition it is a rare paragraph over which heat lightning does not flicker.

A second level of rhetoric, the *poetic*, is well exemplified in Ahab's soliloquy after the great scene on the quarter-deck. As Matthiessen has shown, such a passage can easily be set as blank verse:

> I leave a white and turbid wake;
> Pale waters, paler cheeks, where'er I sail.
> The envious billows sidelong swell to whelm
> My track; let them; but first I pass.

Because the rhythms here play over an abstract metrical pattern, as in poetry, they are evenly controlled—too evenly perhaps for prose, and the tone seems "literary."

Quite different in effect is a third level of rhetoric, the *idiomatic*. Like the poetic it occurs rather rarely in a pure form, but we have an instance in Stubb's rousing exordium to his crew:

> "Pull, pull, my fine hearts-alive; pull, my children; pull, my little ones
> . . . Why don't you break your backbones, my boys? . . . Easy,
> easy; don't be in a hurry—don't be in a hurry. Why don't you snap
> your oars, you rascals? Bite something, you dogs! . . ."

Here the beat of oars takes the place of the metronomic meter and allows more freedom. The passage is a kind of rowing song and hence is exceptional; yet it is related in tone and rhythm to numerous pieces of dialogue and sailor talk, especially to the consistently excellent idiom of both Stubb and young Ishmael.

One might venture a fourth level of rhetoric, the *composite*, simply to assure the inclusion of the narrator's prose at its very best. The composite is a magnificent blending of the expository, the poetic, the idiomatic, and whatever other elements tend to escape these crude categories:

> The Nantucketer, he alone resides and riots on the sea; he alone,
> in Bible language, goes down to it in ships; to and fro ploughing it as
> his own special plantation. *There* is his home; *there* lies his business,
> which a Noah's flood would not interrupt, though it overwhelmed all
> the millions in China. He lives on the sea, as prairie cocks in the
> prairie; he hides among the waves, he climbs them as chamois
> hunters climb the Alps. For years he knows not the land; so that
> when he comes to it at last, it smells like another world, more
> strangely than the moon would to an Earthsman. With the landless
> gull, that at sunset folds her wings and is rocked to sleep between bil-
> lows; so at nightfall, the Nantucketer, out of sight of land, furls his
> sails, and lays him to his rest, while under his very pillow rush herds
> of walruses and whales.

The passage is a great one, blending high and low with a relaxed assurance; after shaking free from the literary constrictions of the opening lines, it comes grandly home. And how does it relate to event and character? Ishmael's memory of the arrival at Nantucket, a mere incident in the movement of the plot, is to Ishmael now an imaginative experience of high order; and this we must know if we are to know about Ishmael. The whole chapter, "Nantucket," is a prose poem in the barbaric jocular vein, and it is as valuable a part of the documentation of Ishmael's experience as are the great "scenes." It is less extraneous to the meaning of the book than are many of the more average passages about Captain Ahab. The same could be said for other great passages of rhetoric, such as the marvelous hymn to spiritual democracy midway in "Knights and Squires." The first level of structure in *Moby-Dick* is the interplay of pressure and control through extraordinarily high rhetorical effects.

Beneath the rhetoric, penetrating through it, and in a sense rising above it, is a play of symbolic forms which keeps the rhetoric from dropping into exercise or running off in pyrotechnics. The persistent tendency in *Moby-Dick* is for facts, events, and images to become symbols. Ahab makes the most outright pronouncement of the doctrine of correspondences on which such a tendency depends, and to which almost all characters in the book are committed: "O Nature, and O soul of man! how far beyond all utterance are your linked analogies! not the smallest atom stirs or lives on matter, but has its cunning duplicate in mind." No less sensitive to symbolic values than Ahab is the young Ishmael in the forecastle. It is he who unfolds moral analogues from the mat-making, from the monkey-rope, from squeezing the case. He resembles Ahab in his talent for taking situations "strongly and metaphysically."

So on down the roster of the crew, where symbols and superstitions blend. Can there be any doubt that it is above all the enfolding imagination of the narrator which sets and defines the symbolic mode that pervades the entire book? From the richly emblematic theme of "meditation and water" in the opening chapter, to the final bursting of the "black bubble" of the sea which releases young Ishmael, the narrator sets the symbolic as the primary mode of self-examination and communication. He is predisposed to see events, however incidental, as "the sign and symbol" of something larger. To Ishmael "some certain significance lurks in all things, else all things are little worth, and the round world itself but an empty cipher. . . ."

Most commonly the symbols begin with a generative object: a waif-pole, a coin, a compass needle, a right-whale's head. The symbolic events begin with a chance incident: the dropping of his speaking trumpet by the Captain of the *Goney* (the nameless future), finding ambergris in a blasted whale (unexpected sweetness at the core of corruption), the chasing of the *Pequod* by Malay pirates (the pursuer pursued). Both give the tale solidity, for the objects and events are objects and events before they become meanings. But all the symbols do not rise out of tangible referents. We have to take into account also the narrator's love for "a furious trope" which often far exceeds the simple metaphorical function of comparison; the thing to which analogy is made—a pyramid, an elephant, a Leyden jar, a bird, a mythic figure—may itself enter the circle of symbolic values through recurrent reference. Thus the imagery brings scope to the limited range of symbols available on board the *Pequod*. Whereas the object-symbols in a sense carry the "plot," elucidating the experience of young Ishmael, Ahab, the mates and crew (as well as serving the narrator), the image-symbols chiefly reveal the psyche of the narrator through images of procreation and animality, mechanization and monomania, enchantment and entombment.

Though simpler objects, events, or images may connote primarily some one thing, as a shark means rapacious evil, most symbols which Ishmael develops in his narration express a complex of meanings which cannot easily be reduced to paraphrase and are not finally stable in other than their own terms. So it is with the *Pequod* herself and the ships she passes, with the root metaphors of earth, air, fire, and water which proliferate so subtly; and so it is with the most dynamic word-image-symbol of the tale: "white" (or "whiteness"). Their meanings are not single but multiple: not precisely equatable but ambiguous; not more often reinforcing than contradictory. The symbolism in *Moby-Dick* is not static but is in motion; it is in process of creation for both narrator and reader. Value works back and forth: being extracted from objects, it descends into the consciousness; spiraling up from the consciousness, it envelops objects.

Symbolism is so marked a characteristic of the narrator's microcosm that it is possible to phrase Ahab's tragedy not only in moral, social, and psychological terms, but in "structural" terms as well. Clearly Ahab accepts the symbolic as a source of cognition and of ethics. It was a symbolic vision that brought him on his quest, as no one senses with stronger discomfort than Starbuck, who stands alone in his sturdy, limited world of facts and settled faith. Yet the tragedy of Ahab is not his great gift for symbolic perception, but his abandonment of it. Ahab increasingly reduces all pluralities to the singular. His unilateral reading of events and things becomes a narrow translation in the imperative mood. Unlike young Ishmael, who is his equal in sensitivity but his inferior in will and authority, Ahab walls off his receptiveness to the complexities of experience, replacing "could be" or "might be" with "must." His destruction follows when he substitutes an allegorical fixation for the world of symbolic potentialities.

Ishmael's predilection for keying his narrative in the symbolic mode suggests another aspect of structure. *Moby-Dick* lies close to the world of dreams. We find the narrator recalling at length a remembered dream of his childhood. Stubb attempts a long dream-analysis to Flask after he has been kicked by Ahab. It is not strange, then, that young Ishmael's moment of greatest crisis, the night of the try-works when he is at the helm, should be of a traumatic order. More subtly, numerous incidents of the narrative are bathed in a dream aura: the trancelike idyll of young Ishmael at the mast-head, the hallucinatory vision of the spirit spout, the incredible appearance on board of the devil himself accompanied by "five dusky phantoms," and many others. The narrator's whole effort to communicate the timeless, spaceless concept of "The Whiteness of the Whale" is an act of dream analysis. "Whether it was a reality or a dream, I never could entirely settle," says the narrator of his childhood dream; and so it was with much of what occurred aboard the *Pequod*. Ishmael's tale is to be listened to in terms of a tradition that runs from Revelation to *Finnegans Wake*. Dream sense is an important mood in *Moby-Dick*; and dream form, to the extent there is such a verbal form, is an incipient structural device of the book. At regular intervals the narrator, in his intense effort to explain himself, resorts to a brief passage in which there is a flashing concentration of symbols that hold for a moment and then disappear. It is a night device for rendering daytime experience, and in *Moby-Dick* it happens again and again.

Any rigorous definition of structure must lead us on to consider the nature and relation of the constituent parts. Since the tale is divided into "parts" by the narrator himself (135 chapters, plus prefatory materials and "Epilogue"), one cannot escape considering the extent to which individual chapters themselves are structural units. We shall have to pass over such chapters, probably the largest group, as are devoted to the movement of narrative or to character analysis; the form here falls in a general way within the customary patterns of novelistic structure. Two chapter forms, however, are sufficiently non-novelistic to invite comment, the first of these being the dramatic. The term "dramatic" is here used in a technical, not qualitative sense, and refers to such devices of the playwright's script as italicized stage directions, set speeches with the speaker named in capitals, straight soliloquies, and dialogue without commentary. More than a tenth of the chapters are in this sense dramatic, some ten having strictly dramatic form without narrative intrusion, and another half-dozen or so using some script devices along with the narrative. The most successful of the strict-form group is certainly "Midnight, Forecastle," a ballet-like scene which superbly objectifies the crew in drunken exaltation over the quest. But the two greatest are in the second group. "The Quarter-Deck," Ishmael's curtain-raising treatment of the quest theme, is a triumph of unified structure, conceived with extreme firmness and precision of detail. The powerful dramatic structure of the chapter—prologue, antiphonal choral address, formal individual debate, and group ceremonial—is a superb invention on free-traditional lines, unhampered by stage techniques yet profiting from them. The other great dramatic scene, a counterpart to "The Quarter-Deck" both thematically and structurally, is the massive Ahab-and-his-crew scene late in the book, "The Candles." The chapter is not so firmly conceived as its forerunner; and this, rather than its subject matter, is what brings it dangerously close to seeming overwrought and a bit out of hand. The key to the structure here lies in the narrator's word "tableau," a dramatic device of considerable currency in nineteenth-century America. As the primary symbols of fire and whiteness melt hotly into each other for the first time, we see a series of memorable tableaux lit by storm lightning and corposant flames between "intervals of profound darkness." The piece is a series of blinding kaleidoscopic flashes which reveal the alarmed mates, the primitives in their full demonic strength, Ahab in a fury of ritual power. The "enchanted" crew, which near this same quarter-deck had made its jubilant pledge, now hangs from the rigging "like a knot of numbed wasps"; and when Ahab brandishes his burning harpoon among them (an unstated completion of the image), "the mariners did run from him in a terror of dismay." The two chapters, "The Quarter-Deck" and "The Candles," are twin centers of gravity in ordering the structure of the Ahab theme. The two fields of force are possibility and necessity, and Ahab's shift is from initial ecstasy to final frenetic compulsiveness.

A second unusual element of chapter structure in *Moby-Dick* grows out of the sermon form. Most famously there is Father Mapple's sermon (chapter nine), a piece of sustained eloquence in the idiomatic-composite style. From his *text* in Jonah the old sailor-preacher moves at once to two *doctrines* (the Christian pattern of sin and repentance, and the hardness of obeying God); enters a highly imaginative narrative *explication* of the Biblical story; comes next to *applications* and *uses* (that the congregation shall take Jonah as "a model for repentance" and the preacher shall "preach the Truth to the face of Falsehood"); and concludes with an *exhortation* (the very subtly constructed incantation on the double-themed coda of Woe and Delight). Somewhat buried away in another chapter, "Stubb's Supper," is the shorter sermon in which Fleece, the Negro cook, one night preaches to the sharks in a seriocomic vein. As he peers over the *Pequod's* side with his lantern at the murderous feasting down below, Fleece addresses his "congregation" first as "Fellow-critters," then as "Belubed fellow-critters," and finally as "Cussed fellow-critters," the final imprecation sharpening Fleece's ominous doctrine that "all angel is not'ing more dan de shark well goberned." The structural pattern, especially in its repetitive address, is clearly derived from the folk tradition of the Negro sermon.

These are not the only two "sermons" in *Moby-Dick.* Although the free essay tradition from Montaigne to Hazlitt provides a more comfortable prototype for the more loosely ordered speculative chapters, most of these have a prophetic or protestant vein that pulls them over toward the sermon tradition. Again and again throughout the narrative a chapter comes to its climax in a final paragraph of moral exhortation (Mapple) or imprecation (Fleece). Nor should we forget that young Ishmael's crisp moral analogues (above) start with symbols and end as parables. It is especially interesting to note that some of the cetological chapters can be analyzed in terms of sermon structure. In "The Line," for instance, the narrator takes hemp for his text, makes a full-scale explication of its history and uses, gives admonitions on its subtleties and dangers, and concludes with a full-scale application of the doctrine that "All men live enveloped in whale-lines." In "The Blanket" the text is whale blubber; and preacher Ishmael comes inevitably to the doctrine of internal temperatures, raising it to a high exhortation (Mapple) and then cutting it down with three lines of wry counter-statement (Fleece). Nor is it hard to identify text, inferences, uses, doctrine, and admonition in the brief "sermon" the narrator preaches over the peeled white body of a whale in "The Funeral." The technique lies midway between the Protestant sermon of the nineteenth century and the tradition of the digressive-antiquarian essay.

Coming to the problem of the mutual relation of the chapters in *Moby-Dick,* we can observe several tendencies, of which *chapter sequences* is one. The simplest sequence is likely to be one of narrative progression, as in "The Chapel," "The Pulpit," and "The Sermon," or in the powerful concluding sequence on "The Chase": "First Day," "Second Day", "Third Day." Or we get chapter sequences of theme, as in the three chapters on whale paintings. Or again sequences of structural similarity: the five chapters beginning with "The Quarter-Deck" all use dramatic techniques, as do the four beginning with "The Candles." More typical than strict sequences, however, are the *chapter clusters* in which two or three (or five or six) chapters are linked by themes or root images, other chapters intervening. For example, chapters xlii, li, lii, and lix make a loose cluster that begins with "The Whiteness of the Whale" and carries through the white apparitions in "The Spirit-Spout," "The Albatross," and "Squid." Similarly, later in the narrative, fire imagery becomes dominant, breaking out in young Ishmael's fire-dream ("The Try-Works") and running intermittently until the holocaust of Ahab's defiance ("The Candles"). In addition to sequences and clusters there are also widely separated *balancing chapters,* either of opposites ("Loomings" and the "Epilogue") or of similars ("The Quarter-Deck" and "The Candles"); here the problem is infinitely complex, for the balancing units shift according to the standard of comparison: theme, event, root image, structure, and so forth. Two points can be made in tentative summary of this complex aspect of structure: there are definable relations between any given chapter and some other chapter or chapters; and these relations tend to be multiple and shifting. Like the symbols, the chapters are "in process."

Looking beyond chapter units and their interrelations we find the most obvious larger structural effect in the narrative line of the book, such as it is, which records the preparations for going on board, leaving port, encountering adventures, and meeting some final consequence. Along this simple linear form of The Voyage occur two sets of events: the whale killings and the ship meetings. The question is whether either of these event groups performs more for the structure than the simple functions of marking the passage of time and adding "interest." Of the whale pursuits and killings some ten or more are sufficiently rendered to become events. They begin when the narrative is already two-fifths told and end with the final lowerings for Moby Dick during which the killers are themselves killed. The first lowering and the three-day chase are thus events which enclose all the whaling action of the novel as well as what Howard Vincent has aptly called "the cetological center," and the main point I wish to make about the pursuits is that in each case a killing provokes either a chapter sequence or a chapter cluster of cetological lore growing out of the circumstances of the particular killing. The killings in themselves, except for the first and last, are not so much narrative events as structural occasions for ordering the whaling essays and sermons. Their minimized role is proof enough, if any were needed, that Ishmael's tale is not primarily a series of whaling adventures.

Much more significant structurally than the killings is the important series of ship meetings also occurring along the time line of the voyage. The nine gams of the *Pequod* are important in several ways, of which three might concern us here. First of all, even a glance at the numbers of the chapters in which the gams occur shows a clear pattern: the first two are close together; the central group are well spaced (separated by an average of twelve chapters with not very wide divergences); the last two are close together. The spatial pattern looks like this:

1 2   3   4   5   6   7   8 9

This somewhat mechanical pattern is a stiffening element in the structure of the book, a kind of counterforce, structurally, to the organic relationship of parts we have been observing. The gams are bones to the book's flesh. Secondly, their sequence is meaningful in terms of the Ahab theme. The line of Ahab's response from ship to ship is a psychograph of his monomania showing the rising curve of his passion and diagramming his moral hostility. The points on the graph mark off the furiously increasing distance between Ahab and the world of men. And thirdly, their individual meanings are a part of the Ishmael theme. Each ship is a scroll which the narrator unrolls and reads, like a prophet called to a king's court. They provide what Auden calls "types of the relation of human individuals and societies in the tragic mystery of existence," though his superbly incisive reading of each type is perhaps too narrowly theological and does scant justice to either the tone of the episodes (are not the *Jungfrau* and *Rosebud* accounts hilariously comic and ironic?) or their rich amplitude of meanings. The ships the *Pequod* passes may be taken as a group of metaphysical parables, a series of biblical analogues, a masque of the situations confronting man, a pageant of the humors within men, a parade of the nations, and so forth, *as well as* concrete and symbolic ways of thinking about the White Whale. Any single systematic treatment of all of the ships does violence to some of them. The gams are symbolic, not allegorical.

It is time in fact to admit that our explorations of structure suggest elaborate interrelations of the parts but do not lead to an overreaching formal pattern. For the reader predisposed to feel that "form" means "classical form," with a controlling geometric structure, *Moby-Dick* is and will remain an aesthetically unsatisfying experience. One needs only to compare it with *The Scarlet Letter*, published a year and a half earlier, to see how nonclassical it is. If this is the sort of standard by which one tries to judge *Moby-Dick*, he will end by dismissing it as one of the more notable miscarriages in the history of literary lying-in. But surely there is no one right form the novel must take—not the one used by Hawthorne, not even the form, one might wryly add, perfected by James. For Hawthorne the structural frame of reference was neoclassical; for Melville it was romantic.

To go from *The Scarlet Letter* to *Moby-Dick* is to move from the Newtonian world-as-machine to the Darwinian world-as-organism. In the older cosmology the key concepts had been law, balance, harmony, reason; in the newer, they became origin, process, development, growth. Concurrently biological images arose to take the place of the older mechanical analogies: growing plants and life forms now symbolized cosmic ultimates better than a watch or the slow-turning rods and gears of an eighteenth-century orrery. It is enough for our purposes to note that the man who gave scientific validity to the organic world view concluded the key chapter of his great book, *The Origin of Species*, with an extended image of "the great Tree of Life . . . with its ever branching and beautiful ramifications." It was a crucial simile that exploited not the tree but the tree's growth.

Of course the poets had been there first. Coleridge had long since made his famous definition of organic form in literature. The roots of his theory had traveled under the sea to the continent of Emerson, Thoreau, and Whitman (as Matthiessen brilliantly showed in *American Renaissance*), where they burst into native forms in the minds of a few men haunted simultaneously by the implications of the American wilderness, by the quest for spiritual reality, and by the search for new literary forms. *Moby-Dick* is like Emerson's *Essays* and *Poems*, like *Walden*, like *Leaves of Grass*, in its structural principles. In the literature of the nineteenth century it is the single most ambitious projection of the concept of organic form.

Recharting our explorations we can see now where we have been. The matter of *Moby-Dick* is the organic land-sea world where life forms move mysteriously among the elements. The dynamic of the book is the organic mind-world of Ishmael whose sensibility rhythmically agitates the flux of experience. The controlling structure of the book is an organic complex of rhetoric, symbols, and interfused units. There is no over-reaching formal pattern of literary art on which *Moby-Dick* is a variation. To compare it with the structure of the Elizabethan play, or the classical epic, or the modern novel is to set up useful analogies rather than congruous models. It is a free form that fuses as best it can innumerable devices from many literary traditions, including contemporary modes of native expression. In the last analysis, if one must have a prototype, here is an intensively heightened rendition of the logs, journals, and histories of the Anglo-American whaling tradition.

Organic form is not a particular form but a structural principle. In *Moby-Dick* this principle would seem to be a peculiar quality of making and unmaking itself as it goes. The method of the book is unceasingly genetic, conveying the effect of a restless series of morphic-amorphic movements. Ishmael's narrative is always in process and in all but the most literal sense remains unfinished. For the good reader the experience of *Moby-Dick* is a participation in the act of creation. Find a key word or metaphor, start to pick it as you would a wild flower, and you will find yourself ripping up the whole forest floor. Rhetoric grows into symbolism and symbolism into structure; then all falls away and begins over again.

Ishmael's way of explaining himself in the long run is not either "dim" or "random." He was committed to the organic method with all its possibilities and risks. As he says at the beginning of one chapter: "There are some enterprises in which a careful disorderliness is the true method." And at the beginning of another chapter we have an explicit image whose full force as a comment on method needs to be recognized: "Out of the trunk, the branches grow; out of them, the twigs. So, in productive subjects, grow the chapters."

IV

From our considerations of *Moby-Dick* a few simple, debatable propositions emerge. More accurately they are, I suppose, the assumptions which underlie what has been said. The first is that *nature*, ultimately, is chaos. Whatever order it has in the mind of God, its meaning is apparent to man only through some more or less systematic ordering of what seems to be there. The second is that *experience* is already one remove from nature; filtered through a sensibility, nature begins to show patterns qualified by the temperament and the culture of the observer. And the third is that *art*, which is twice removed from nature, is a major means for transforming experience into patterns that are meaningful and communicable. As in part it is the function of religion to shape experience for belief and conduct, and of science to organize nature for use and prediction, so it is the business of art to form man's experience of nature for communication. In art the way a thing is said is what is being said. To the maker the form is completion; to the receiver it is possibility. Art is an enabling act for mankind without which life may easily become meager, isolated; with it the mind can be cleared and the spirit refreshed; through it memory and desire are rewoven.

The great thing about fiction, which is simply the telling of a story in written words, is that it is fiction. That it is "made up" is not its weakness but, as with all art, its greatest strength. In the successful work of fiction certain kinds of possibilities, attitudes, people, acts, situations, necessities, for the first and last time exist. They exist only through form. So it is with *Moby-Dick*—Ishmael's vast symbolic prose-poem in a free organic form. From *olim erat* to *finis* is all the space and time there is.

HARRISON HAYFORD

"Loomings": Yarns and Figures in the Fabric[†]

A linked image cluster that recurs throughout Melville's works also figures centrally in the initial chapter of *Moby-Dick*. My aim in this essay is to demonstrate how some recurrent items ("images") and topics ("motifs") in "Loomings" carry a few basic strands of thought ("themes") in the book; how these elements relate to each other; and also how they relate to syntax, rhetoric, and such larger elements as the book's characters, plot, and thought. My analysis takes up elements as they occur locally in Chapter I and relates them to similar elements in other parts of the work. The immediate effect of my discussion is to illustrate the dense imaginative coherence of *Moby-Dick*. Its images, motifs, and themes are yarns closely woven into figures in its fabric, as the chapter title "Loomings" can be taken to imply.[1]

Somewhat arbitrarily, I focus my discussion on the element of character. Specifically, I focus on Ishmael and on the ways in which the elements I analyze show similarities and differences between him and Ahab. My critical strategy is to take the narrative, from its opening sentence "Call me Ishmael," as altogether the work of Ishmael, its ostensible narrator, and to interpret all its elements as coming from Ishmael and hence characterizing Ishmael, not Melville. In this way the dense imaginative coherence is transferred from the book and its author to the mind of Ishmael as its ground and cause. In this perspective, the action of the work takes place in the observing and participating mind of Ishmael. His mind "contains" the tragedy of Ahab as Ishmael confronted it some years ago in experience and now confronts it once again in the telling. Of course this approach is not new, for perhaps the chief discovery criticism has made in the interpretation of *Moby-Dick* in the past generation is to recognize the presence and centrality of Ishmael. Most earlier critics had overlooked him altogether because they were so taken by Ahab and the White

---

† Reprinted from *Artful Thunder: Versions of the Romantic Tradition in Honor of Howard P. Vincent*, ed. Robert J. DeMott and Sanford E. Marovitz (Kent, OH: Kent State University Press, 1975). Reprinted by permission of Kent State University Press.

1. On August 1, 1969, Herman Melville's 150th birthday was celebrated at Kent State University. Of course Howard P. Vincent was the organizer as he has indefatigably been, alone and with others, of so many such occasions, from the great Williamstown one in 1951, for the 100th birthday of *Moby-Dick*, to the Paris one of May 1974. It was at his instigation that I delivered a paper at Williamstown in 1951 titled "Melville's Prisoners," in which I set out a peculiar image cluster I had found in Melville's works. It was also at his instigation that I delivered a paper at Kent in 1969 titled "Birthdays of Herman Melville," of which a razeed version of the paper now offered was substantially the central section. (A tape recording preserves the whole ebullient session at which it was presented.) I hope Howard will think it an appropriate offering, because it was worked up for him in the first place, because it may remind him of that happy Kent occasion, and because (in spite of his efforts over the years of our long association) it is the only offshoot of my larger study, the long-in-process *Melville's Prisoners*, yet to reach print.

Whale.[2] A close corollary perception has been recognition of the thematic importance of the juxtaposition between Ishmael and Ahab. Both points are now usually taken for granted in interpretations of the book, however at odds readings may otherwise be. Neither point, though, entails taking the whole work as Ishmael's—a strategy I am adopting here provisionally and only for convenience.

One further bit of strategy needs a word. All along I refer to Ahab in the present tense. This is the way we usually discuss a fictional character, since we imagine him dramatically alive as we read, though the narrative is told in past tense and we may know the story ends with his death. In *Moby-Dick* Ishmael only occasionally makes any point of Ahab's being already dead and gone, and for my purposes no harm is done by my not doing so. On the other hand, since it is of more consequence that Ishmael is narrating in the present tense, I use tenses for him that distinguish between Ishmael at the time of the *Pequod's* voyage and Ishmael at the later time he is telling about it. What is involved in Ishmael-then vs. Ishmael-now is the quite unsettled interpretive problem of Ishmael's development in character and outlook.[3] It is not part of my purpose to deal with this problem here. Let me simply declare that in my reading he did not change and has not changed, from then to now, in his essential nature. Ishmael is forever Ishmael. Call him Ishmael.

I

In *Moby-Dick* Ishmael plays the role—a frequent one in Melville's writings—of sympathetic but perplexed observer. What he chiefly confronts and observes is the tragedy of Ahab in his revengeful attack upon the great White Whale. In this perspective the book's early chapters are preparation for Ahab. Before Ahab's appearance, Ishmael builds up in them the physical and conceptual worlds which make probable Ahab's character, his language, his thought, and his actions. In "Loomings" Ishmael starts on his narrative way as participant and observer. As he tells the story, his manner with words, his habitual ways of perceiving and dealing with situations, his preoccupations of thought, all reveal his character. Through these means the first chapter begins to establish the grounds both of Ishmael's sympathy with Ahab and of the differences between them that mark his dissociation from Ahab.

An initial similarity between Ishmael and Ahab is the way both of them turn every object, situation, and person they confront into a problem, one

---

2. I believe William Ellery Sedgwick, in *Herman Melville: The Tragedy of Mind* (Cambridge, Mass.: Harvard University Press, 1944), was the first critic to discuss Ishmael equally with Ahab. It was Howard Vincent who contributed as much as anyone else to this delineation of Ishmael's role, in *The Trying-Out of Moby-Dick* (1949). Others who have pursued this line of interpretation include Walter Bezanson, "*Moby-Dick*: Work of Art," Tyrus Hillway and Luther Mansfield, eds., *Moby-Dick Centennial Essays* (Dallas: Southern Methodist University Press, 1953), pp. 30–58; Merlin Bowen, *The Long Encounter* (Chicago: University of Chicago Press, 1960); Paul Brodtkorb, *Ishmael's White World* (New Haven: Yale University Press, 1965); and Edgar Dryden, *Melville's Thematics of Form* (Baltimore: Johns Hopkins Press, 1968). Most recently, the approach attributing all to Ishmael is systematically followed in Robert Zoellner's full length treatment of *Moby-Dick*, *The Salt-Sea Mastodon* (Berkeley: University of California Press, 1973), whose basic assumption is that "every word of *Moby-Dick*, including even the footnotes, comes from Ishmael rather than Melville" (p. xi).

3. For example, refer to Carl Strauch, "Ishmael: Time and Personality in *Moby-Dick*," *Studies in the Novel*, I (Winter 1969), 468–83.

which cannot be solved, a mystery whose lurking meaning cannot be followed to its ultimate elucidation. This habit of mind shapes the rhetorical form of the first chapter; and many later chapters also take the shape of their development from it. Chapters of exposition, especially, often treat their subjects as problematical and end up by declaring them inexplicable. But narrative chapters, too, are frequently constructed on a pattern of confrontation-exploration-nonsolution of a problem.

Simply in vocabulary items, apart from context, this propensity of Ishmael's is illustrated. In this very first chapter, for example, wonder and mystery are constantly being evoked, at the same time that inability to solve or to understand is being declared. One running series of words connotes wonder and mystery: *magic, enchanting, romantic, tranced, charm, mystical, marvelous, secretly, portentous and mysterious, marvels, wonderworld, hooded phantom.* Intertwined with these words runs another series denoting or evoking inability to solve or identify: *ungraspable, invisible, secretly, unaccountable, unimaginable, undeliverable.* The two series continue intertwined throughout the book, and as vocabulary items alone they imply not only a habit of Ishmael's perception but a major thematic proposition of the book: life—the cosmos and everything in it taken as a microcosm—confronts man as a compelling but insoluble mystery.

In the first chapter, Ishmael sets out to tell the story of this particular whaling voyage. But no further along than his third sentence, the narrative mode shades into exposition, as Ishmael begins explaining his reasons not only for having gone on this voyage but for his voyaging in general. And then, by the end of the first paragraph, the reasons themselves have come to require explanation; the problem has arisen of communicating some sense of his feelings toward the ocean, feelings which, though nearly universal, are not easy for him to convey in statements. Already the narrative has generated what I take to be a basic motif of the book: that of confronting an insoluble problem.

Why he went to sea has become, in the telling, a problem to Ishmael. Initially it is a problem in communicating just what it is that he felt and feels, but soon it becomes something of a problem to himself. For to Ishmael, as to Ahab, motives have lower and yet lower layers. While Ishmael is developing this problem of his motivation it splits into three successive questions: 1. Why does he go to sea? (paragraphs 1–6) 2. Why does he go as a common sailor? (paragraphs 7–11) 3. And why did he go that voyage on a whaler rather than on a merchant ship? (paragraphs 11–14).

As Ishmael deals with each of these three questions through the rest of the chapter, he shows further traits of mind and patterns of reaction which he shares with Ahab. But in his treatment of each question, and especially of the second, he also reveals traits which set him off from Ahab, and which, indeed, define a crucial distinction between them.

II

To answer his first question—why he goes to sea (initially why he went on this particular voyage)—Ishmael begins with two immediately assignable conditions, both of them negative and somewhat aimless rather than positive reasons: he had little money in his purse and nothing in particular to

interest him on shore. Then he adds his general motive for going to sea
not only on that voyage but at various times: he says it is a way he has of
driving off the spleen—driving off spells of melancholy—and a substitute
for his impulses toward violence against others or himself whenever he
feels depressed. But actually his motives on that and other such occasions, he realizes, reach deeper than these personal ones, specific or general; there is something universal in them. For nearly all men, he says,
share his feelings towards the ocean.

Next, to suggest that which he cannot analyze in what he declares is an
almost universal feeling towards the ocean, he leaps at once (paragraph
3) from declarative statements to a series of parallel analogies couched in
imperatives and interrogatives. He exhorts us to confront, and, if we can,
to explain the meaning of a series of analogical situations, stated in various images. The basic motif these situations exemplify is confrontation:
in each situation men are drawn toward water, gaze fixedly upon it, and
meditate its mystery. They come in crowds, "pacing straight for the water,
and seemingly bound for a dive." And "They must get just as nigh the
water as they possibly can without falling in." This motif of confronting a
mystery implies a consequent motif: that of self-destruction. For one may
come too close to the fascinating object, the water—may take a dive or fall
in. This implication becomes explicit in the climactic analogy of the
series: "Surely all this is not without meaning. And still deeper the meaning of that story of Narcissus, who because he could not grasp the tormenting, mild image he saw in the fountain, plunged into it and was
drowned." The water-gazing analogies coincide with the plot shape of
Moby-Dick: Ahab with the crew of the *Pequod* thrusts off from land into
the ocean, and in his effort to grasp a tormenting image, the White
Whale, plunges in and is drowned. "But," says Ishmael, here in the first
chapter commenting on the plunge of Narcissus, "that same image, we
ourselves see in all rivers and oceans. It is the image of the ungraspable
phantom of life; and this is the key to it all." This Narcissus analogy
indeed is the "key" to a thematic argument of the book: something in man,
now as throughout his history, forces him to confront the mystery of life,
to pursue that phantom; but it is "ungraspable"; and the man who goes
too far in the effort, who crowds too close upon the mystery, destroys himself. Such is Ahab's pursuit of Moby Dick, and such is his fate.

Ishmael, likewise, feels the attraction of the phantom. In the final
words of this chapter he declares that "one grand hooded phantom, like a
snow hill in the air" swayed him to his purpose of embarking on the whaling voyage. Similarly, the Spirit Spout is later a "phantom" luring the
Pequod and her crew on and on (Ch. 51). After Ahab had revealed his purpose on this voyage, Ishmael realized, at least dimly, what the end must
be. His shouts, he says, went up with the rest. "A wild, mystical, sympathetical feeling was in me; Ahab's quenchless feud seemed mine." But Ishmael "while yet all arush to encounter the whale, could see naught in that
brute but the deadliest ill" (Ch. 41). And again Ishmael comments, "But
in pursuit of those far mysteries we dream of, or in tormented chase of
that demon phantom that, some time or other, swims before all human
hearts; while chasing such over this round globe, they either lead us on in
barren mazes or midway leave us whelmed" (Ch. 52).

Later Ahab shows repeatedly that he too realizes what Ishmael indicates from the beginning; that the issue of such an aggressive quest can only be self-destruction. For a single example, when Captain Boomer, who has lost an arm to Moby Dick, warns Ahab that "He's best let alone; don't you think so, Captain?" Ahab replies, "He is. But he will still be hunted, for all that. What is best let alone, that accursed thing is not always what least allures. He's all a magnet!" (Ch. 100).

Yet this first chapter makes a decisive point about Ishmael. Despite the magnetic attraction he feels towards the mystery which lures one on to destruction, he is still not by nature disposed, like Ahab, to press up so close to it as to plunge in and drown. This difference, a decisive one, between Ishmael's nature and Ahab's is manifested in several ways in the first chapter. For one thing, it is evident in Ishmael's second reason for going to sea at all, since the voyage was—as his voyages still are—his conscious substitute for aggressive action, for expressing his frustrations destructively on others or himself, either by "deliberately stepping into the street, and methodically knocking people's hats off" or by following funerals (to the graveyard) or stabbing or shooting himself. To him, going to sea is not in itself aggressive; it is rather his "substitute for pistol and ball." Even at the outset, Ishmael half-consciously recognizes death may be the ultimate goal of his journey. Omens, icons, and monuments of death attend his progress on this voyage, as they do Ahab's, and cannot swerve him from his purpose to take ship.

III

The second question Ishmael raises is why he goes to sea as a common sailor. Although, unlike his first and third questions, this question presents no problem to Ishmael, his treatment of it leads again to definition of the same distinction between himself and Ahab. In this second section of the chapter (paragraphs 7–11) the difference comes out more fully, but so does an essential similarity. Ishmael feels as strongly as does Ahab a sense of personal dignity, heightened by pride, and he too is galled by the weight of indignities which superiors impose upon his body, mind, and spirit. But from the beginning, where he tells of his custom of going to sea as a "simple sailor" rather than as an officer, he announces his habitual acceptance of subordinate positions, indeed (as if he had a choice) his settled preference for them. At the same time, he displays his feeling that this subjection is one he shares with men in general, that his lot merges with the common lot of men, all of whom, he says, are slaves or victims in one way or another and should therefore help each other endure their common lot. Ahab's parallel perception of humanity's general suffering gives him no comfort and only exacerbates his sense of outrage.

The section is couched in motifs that are recurrent in *Moby-Dick*, of which the leading and dominant one is that of the inferior-superior relationship, involving the acceptance or rejection of imposed authority. Associated motifs include money; food; bodily impairment or injury; injustice or insult; antiquity; masonry and massive objects; personal dignity; and family. All are constituents of the image cluster I referred to earlier as recurring throughout Melville's works.

When Ishmael goes to sea, he explains, he never goes as a passenger, because to do so requires a purse. Nor does he go as an officer, for he abominates all honorable, respectable posts and responsibilities and will not identify himself with them. First, the motif of money which comes in the second sentence of the chapter ("having little or no money in my purse") appears again: "you must needs have a purse, and a purse is but a rag unless you have something in it"; then the money motif is dropped until it recurs at the end of the section in the image of "paying" (paragraph 10).

Next (still in paragraph 7) the motif of food develops, in the image of Ishmael's rejecting the possibility of shipping as cook. Though a cook is "a sort of officer on ship-board," with "considerable glory," Ishmael explains that "I never fancied broiling fowls;—though once broiled, judiciously buttered, and judgmatically salted and peppered, there is no one who will speak more respectfully, not to say reverentially, of a broiled fowl than I will." Here motifs of food, authority, and bodily impairment are linked as they often are in the book. In his joshing way, Ishmael seems merely to be saying he has never cared to cook fowls, though once they are properly cooked and seasoned he has a very good appetite for them. The motifs he employs, however, carry in undercurrent the more generalized theme that he does not take pleasure as superiors (here reductively made comic as "cooks") do, from subjecting the bodies of inferiors ("fowls") to radical physical impairment ("broiling")—though once the bodies so treated have by such official and legal process ("judiciously," "judgmatically") been dignified and transformed, he is respectful, almost reverential toward them, in a way inverting superior and inferior. In short, he does not care to be a superior to inflict the physical hurt, but once it has been, as it were, legally and duly done he accepts and respects the result. He is as willing as anyone to "swallow" and "stomach" it. In a jocose second sentence, Ishmael quickly recapitulates the same motifs: food (victimized bodies eaten), authority, reverence—but twines them now with two further motifs, of antiquity and of massive masonry, in a single compressed image: "It is out of the idolatrous dotings of the old Egyptians upon broiled ibis and roasted river horse, that you see the mummies of those creatures in their huge bake-houses the pyramids." The general effect of this analogy, as of those in the earlier paragraphs, is to universalize the personal attitude Ishmael has just stated by associating it with a parallel instance in antiquity, one which (in "mummies" and "pyramids") has preserved and monumentalized the situation through the ages.

The arc of feeling traversed in the two sentences about cooking and eating fowl becomes thematically characteristic in *Moby-Dick*. Ishmael repeatedly moves from opposing ("I abominate . . .") a physically threatening person, object, or situation that is somehow "superior," to reconciling himself with it ("no one will speak more respectfully . . ."). And the particular motifs that carry the theme restate it repeatedly in the book. The motifs of food and eating are often linked to the motif of a superior in situations which are treated in a humorous tone, and sometimes the superior is embodied as a comic figure in authority, or has an attendant comic figure. Such a situation occurs in the next chapters when Ishmael confronts the cannibal Queequeg (who might eat him!) and ends up smoking and eating with him and even "married" to him. Another occurs when Ishmael and Queequeg eat their chowders under the dominating eye of shrewish Mrs. Hussey, who is scolding a man as the eating scene begins and who takes away Queequeg's harpoon as it ends (Ch. 15). Another is the scene in which the mates silently eat at table with the domineering Ahab, to be followed by the savage harpooners attended by comic Dough-Boy (Ch. 34). And still another, the most fully developed, is that in which Stubb masticates his whale steak (cooked too much for his taste) while humorously baiting Old Fleece the comic black cook into delivering a sermon to a congregation of sharks who are also devouring a whale's body (Ch. 64. Cf. also Ch. 65 on "The Whale as a Dish").

Now very likely the reading I have just given seems somewhat far-fetched, particularly in its generalizing the specific imagery of broiling, salting, and peppering a fowl into a motif designated as "bodily impairment." And it would really be only a facile translation if that motif did not become a central theme in *Moby-Dick*. In Ishmael's outer and inner worlds, of whaling and of consciousness, a major theme is that living bodies, animal and human, are subjected to physical outrage, to all the possible range of injury, maiming, mangling, destruction—to the "horrible vulturism of earth." Victimizers act upon victimized bodies, superiors upon inferiors. The central instance is Ahab's dismemberment when his leg is reaped away by the White Whale's jaw; and the sustained context is the whaling world, in which bodies of men and animals are given to mutual injury and destruction in the normal course of existence, in the whole routine of chase, slaughter, and dismemberment—the hunter's and butcher's bloody work that is the whaleman's life and may be his death when the persecuted whale retaliates on his body.[4] In this destructive bodily collision of whaleman and whale the relationship of superior-inferior shifts, from one passage to another, in ways that depend as much on Ishmael's perspective and mood as on any facts of the immediate instance. He recognizes this world's general condition of mutual bodily victimization and identifies at different times either with superior or inferior, with biter or bitten. And often, as in the sentences just examined, his initial sympathy with the inferior, whose body is victimized, shifts, and he accepts the superior's victim as now transmuted into "food." The generalized motif of such a shift in feeling can be termed reconciliation.

Despite such strategies of reconciliation with the superior, however, Ishmael is habitually and characteristically on the side of the inferior. He feels victimized and his feeling of being put upon is carried by constant bodily images in the flow of his narration. He is unusually conscious of his own body, and in the course of the first chapter he names many of his bodily parts, functions, sensations, positions, and actions. Often he expresses his feelings in images of bodily discomfort or malfunction: "driving off the spleen, and regulating the circulation," "growing grim about the mouth," "a damp, drizzly November in my soul," "hazy about the eyes," "over conscious of my lungs"—these occur with some frequency.

---

4. Robert Lowell, in "The Quaker Graveyard in Nantucket," restated this theme accurately and magnificently.

Ishmael's signing on as a simple sailor, he admits, entails subjection to authority and an affront to his self-respect and family pride as well as the relinquishment of his own superior authority as a schoolmaster. "True, they rather order me about some. . . . And at first, this sort of thing is unpleasant enough. It touches one's sense of honor, particularly if you come of an old established family in the land. . . . And more than all, if just previous to putting your hand into the tar-pot, you have been lording it as a country schoolmaster, making the tallest boys stand in awe of you." Evidently Ishmael's sensitivity is rubbed raw on precisely the same point as Ahab's. Both resent the indignity of being ordered about, of being thumped and punched by superiors, particularly because each feels the pride of distinguished lineage and is accustomed to order tall fellows about and make them stand in awe. Ahab's sensitivity is exposed to the metaphysical thumping and punching of the gods, and the distinguished lineage he feels is not literal but the metaphysical dignity of the race of man, human dignity. Unlike Ahab, however, Ishmael has nonaggressive strategies for alleviating such indignities. Here, his first strategy is recourse to the folk wisdom of "grin and bear it," fortified by the book wisdom of Stoic philosophy; the transition from schoolmaster to sailor is a keen one requiring "a strong decoction of Seneca and the Stoics to enable you to grin and bear it." Furthermore, patience helps; for even this feeling of indignity "wears off in time."

Another jocular gambit of alleviation takes up the next paragraph (paragraph 9). Suppose some "old hunks of a sea-captain" does order Ishmael to sweep the decks (an indignity to an able seaman since this broom business is the prescriptive province of the boys, as we learn in Chapter 54)— what does this indignity amount to, weighed in the scales of the New Testament? Or does Ishmael's prompt obedience make the archangel Gabriel think less of him? And finally,

> Who ain't a slave? Tell me that. Well, then, however the old sea-captains may order me about—however they may thump and punch me about, I have the satisfaction of knowing that it is all right; that everybody else is one way or other served in much the same way— either in a physical or metaphysical point of view, that is; and so the universal thump is passed round, and all hands should rub each other's shoulder-blades and be content.[5]

In both the physical and metaphysical points of view, this recognition of universal slavery, this "thump," enrages Ahab past endurance and impels his physical attack upon the whale and his metaphysical attack upon whatever powers may stand behind the whale. But from the first, although Ishmael is as sensitive as Ahab to the indignity of physical subordination, he declares strategies, if not principles, of nonaggression: Stoic endurance, New Testament and democratic equality in suffering and slavery, fellow-feeling and mutual help—such are his remedies. Only too late does Ahab catch a glimpse through Pip, of something resembling Ishmael's insight into the emollient effect of shared suffering, of mankind full of sweet things of love and gratitude.

---

5. In *The Salt-Sea Mastodon* Robert Zoellner calls this "universal thump" concept a "central preoccupation of *Moby-Dick*" (p. 54).

Another of Ishmael's remedies, evident from the first paragraph and one which in the end may be the most important of all, is the saving practicality of his humor. From the beginning the tone of his voice has been varied and flexible. Its serious flow yields to rifts of humor which usually break the tension just when the topic has become most serious and its tone most magniloquent. In the first paragraph a swelling exaggeration of language and structure creates a suspicion that ultimately he will not take altogether solemnly his own feelings and motives which are real enough but overdramatized: "Whenever . . . ; whenever . . . ; whenever . . . ; and especially whenever . . . ; then. . . ." The suspicion is at once confirmed by the next sentence where the irreverent wording of the qualifying alliterative phrase "With a philosophical flourish" reduces Cato's classical suicide to mock heroism in contrast to Ishmael's own underplayed sensible substitute, "I quietly take to the ship." In this middle section of the chapter, directly after the peroration of the first section (the series of analogies ending with the high-keyed climactic image of Narcissus which is "the key to it all"), his tone relaxes into jocularity all through the four and a half paragraphs (7–11) just discussed. As Ishmael discourses, his fluid consciousness is marked by varying tones and never settles into the monotone of a single attitude. His range does not reach the heights or the depths of Ahab's noble monomania, though it at times approaches them; he is brought back to a habitable mid-region by his humorous sense of his own practical situation, which allows him to take "a strong decoction of Seneca and the Stoics" to help him "grin and bear it." This practical humorousness is a saving quality Ishmael shares with Stubb, the second mate, a quality that distinguishes them both from Ahab in the high seriousness of his tragic nobility.

By these strategies of attitude and tone, then, the tension of the chapter's middle section is relaxed and resolved. But in diminuendo Ishmael goes on to advance two further reasons for shipping as a sailor rather than as a passenger or officer. Both of these involve the motif of inferior-superior. In each of them he now argues in consciously sophistical rhetoric that the inferior is really the superior. His tone is jocular, but, as often, its jocularity barely veils his underlying hostility to anybody in a position of social and economic superiority. Passengers, as financially superior to sailors, are dealt with in the linked motifs of money-injustice. For passengers, so his resumed argument runs, must pay when they go to sea, whereas sailors are paid—and paying is the most uncomfortable infliction the two orchard-thieves, Adam and Eve, entailed upon their descendants. "But *being paid*,—what will compare with it?" Even here, however, Ishmael turns the thought against those above him: momentarily it is he, a poor sailor, not they, enjoying the felicity of being paid. But—so his thought runs on—to receive much pay leads to wealth, and wealth leads to destruction, for money is "the root of all earthly ills," and "on no account can a monied man enter heaven." And he moralizes, "How cheerfully we consign ourselves to perdition!"

In this last line of thought two motifs are twined: that of money (coupled with injustice) and that of self-destruction, in the image of consigning ourselves to perdition. The first paired motif, that of money-injustice, comes in for fuller development in the following chapter in Ishmael's lack

of money for a night's lodging and in the passage about Lazarus and
Dives. The second, that of self-destruction in the image of damnation or
going-to-hell, first appears as such here but will often recur. For the whole
voyage of the *Pequod* is, in fact, Ahab's wilful self-consignment to perdition. Of this fact we are reminded throughout the book, both directly and
indirectly, even to the final scene where the ship "sinks to hell."

Ishmael's last reason for shipping as a common sailor rather than in any
position of honor is a humorously specious one that again develops the
inferior-superior motif, reversing the positions. His reason is that the
Commodore on the quarter-deck aft gets the air he breathes only at second hand from the forecastle sailors. The schoolmaster's learnedly
indecorous joke, turning on the Pythagorean maxim to avoid eating beans,
covertly vents contempt on the officers. "In much the same way do the
commonalty lead their leaders in many other things, at the same time that
the leaders little suspect it." At the end of the section, thus, analogizing
from the sailors' station forward on the ship (of state) as she sails, Ishmael
transforms the sailor-followers into "leaders" and the officer-leaders aft
into "followers"—so the last shall be first and the first, last.

IV

At this point in the chapter (in the middle of paragraph 11), Ishmael by
the foregoing strategies has handled two of the three questions into which
he divides the problem of his going to sea. Now he takes up his final question: why did he go that voyage on a whale-ship? Why, having repeatedly
smelt the sea as a merchant sailor did he then go on a whaling voyage?
(Note that this is the only one of the three questions that refers solely to
the *Pequod's* voyage, not to the motivations for Ishmael's voyages in general.) With this question, too, Ishmael deals in the recurrent motifs. He
posits his motivation as a mystery. The dominant motif is that of the
supernatural, while linked to it is that of injustice (or wrong) in the form
of mystery-deception, or mystery-concealment. As Ahab characteristically
does, Ishmael generalizes this particular question back into the problem
of the universe—what he later calls "the universal problem of all things"
(Ch. 64).

Why he took it into his head to go this time on a whaling voyage is a
puzzle to Ishmael, one which is answerable only as part of the cosmic
mystery, and which he deals with in a series of linked images. In the first
witty image, Ishmael declares semi-seriously that he is secretly dogged
and unaccountably influenced by an "invisible police-officer of the Fates,"
who can better answer than anyone else. His going whaling was doubtless
his fate, or his predestined lot—in a second image "part of the grand programme of Providence that was drawn up a long time ago." For himself,
he cannot tell (continuing the second image and showing some of his customary irreverence for high authorities over him) why it was that "those
stage managers, the Fates," put him down for "this shabby part of a whaling voyage" when they assigned to others "magnificent parts in high
tragedies" and to still others parts in comedies and farces. Here there
lurks some irony on Ishmael's part, for on this whaling voyage high
tragedy is indeed to be enacted (as well as comedy and farce), though the

tragic role in it is to be Ahab's, not Ishmael's. But Ahab is a transfigured, transvaluated, common old whaleman exalted to the heights in a "democratic" tragedy. And Ahab, too, is convinced, as he cries to Starbuck, that his role was determined by the Fates: "This whole act's immutably decreed.—'Twas rehearsed by thee and me a billion years before this ocean rolled. . . . I am the Fates' lieutenant; I act under orders" (Ch. 134). Whatever motives of their own the Fates may have had in assigning Ishmael his part (Ishmael refrains from exploring that byway!), they cunningly presented to him, under various disguises, certain illusory motives as his own, into which he thinks he can now see a little way. Some of these motives, as he now recalls them in images of characteristic connotation, were: the curiosity "roused" in him by the "portentous and mysterious" monster, "the overwhelming idea of the great whale himself"; the "undeliverable, nameless perils" and "attending marvels" of the whale; the "torment" of his own "everlasting itch for things remote." These images associate the coming voyage with the motif of confrontation—the numinous fascination of the mysterious, here, as often, embodied in the massive and associated with the perilous (the danger of destruction from approaching it too close). Ishmael, like Ahab, like all men in their degree, feels this attraction. He feels, too, its frequently associated quality of forbiddenness. Paradoxically, to move toward the region where all these qualities coalesce is to respond actively to an attraction which is at the same time forbidden; he says (in active verbs), "I love to sail forbidden seas and land on barbarous coasts." But unlike Ahab, Ishmael by his characteristic strategy again dissolves into sociality the aggressive, implied motive of invasion. To his sociality of feeling the barbarous horrors themselves will turn out to be just fellow "inmates" of this prison world: "Not ignoring what is good, I am quick to perceive a horror, and could still be social with it—would they let me—since it is but well to be on friendly terms with all the inmates of the place one lodges in."

So far as Ishmael can see into his motives when he confronts them as a problem, the foregoing were his reasons. "By reason of these things, then, the whaling voyage was welcome." But there is a still lower layer—for he realizes that these felt motives only "cajoled" him into "the delusion that it was a choice resulting from my own unbiased freewill and discriminating judgment." The climactic and final image of the chapter reasserts Ishmael's conviction that his motives were somehow imposed upon him as a passive receiver: "The great floodgates of the wonder-world swung open, and in the wild conceits that swayed me to my purpose, two and two there floated into my inmost soul, endless processions of the whale, and, midmost of them all, one grand hooded phantom, like a snow hill in the air." By the syntax of this sentence Ishmael becomes the passive recipient of conceits that "float" into his "inmost soul" from some exterior source; he is "swayed" by them rather than being their active originator. This image of something "floating" into the mind is one more metaphor (perhaps for an experiential sensation, perhaps for a metaphysical concept) to explain the same process Ishmael alluded to above in the theatrical image as a cleverly deceitful casting operation of the stage-managing Fates: "the springs and motives which being cunningly presented to me under various disguises, induced me to set about performing the part I did."

Here, indeed, the imagery brings up one of the major themes of *Moby-Dick*. In most general terms the theme may be defined as the problem of free will, of responsibility for one's actions. Already in this chapter the theme has been broached in three different metaphors, or concepts. First it was introduced as discussed above, under the image of "magnetic virtue," the attraction of water. Then it appeared under the loosely equivalent image or concept of "the Fates" and "Providence," with supplementary allusion to an "invisible police-officer of the Fates," who is evidently a sort of special daemon or supervisory angel put into modern dress and so comically demeaned as a petty official who "dogs" one. Finally, it is restated here in terms of the sensation of a psychological process, of something "floating" into the consciousness from outside—a metaphor evidently derived from a conceptual system of "atmospheric influences" frequently invoked elsewhere in *Moby-Dick* (and at great length in *Pierre*, where the etiology of motivation is examined with great intensity). Of all three images—magnetic influences, Fates or Providence, and "atmospheric influences"—the common denominator is their postulation of exterior forces determining the action of the mind. The mind is essentially their passive instrument, and its subjective sense of "a choice resulting" from "unbiased freewill and discriminating judgment" is only a "delusion" cunningly contrived and made pleasant by invisible superior powers.

The syntax of many sentences in the chapter supports the tenor of these metaphors in the motif of active-passive, and it here bears out Ishmael's explicit declaration that he has no free will. Many passive verb constructions and dissociations of self occur. In the opening paragraph, for example, a kind of struggle goes on in Ishmael between what he feels happening independently in him ("I find myself growing grim about the mouth"; "it is a damp, drizzly November in my soul"; "I find myself involuntarily pausing"; "hypos get such an upper hand of me") and his assertive will opposing it ("a way I have of driving off the spleen"; "it requires a strong moral principle to prevent me"). In this sentence, the syntactical structure declares the control of Ishmael's active will in the struggle, for that assertion is placed in the main clause; but the declaration is only that he must get away to sea "as soon as I can," and "quietly take to the ship." The forces are still working upon him, even in his supposition that he "close" this evasion of the aggression and suicide towards which they are driving him; for in passively ("quietly") taking to ship, as in welcoming the whaling voyage, he is actually shipping on Ahab's aggressive mission, which leaves him in "abandonment" at the end (in the last words of his epilogue), "another orphan."

V

This discussion of "Loomings" has, I hope, illustrated what I called at its beginning the dense imaginative coherence of *Moby-Dick*, the close weaving of yarns in the figures of its fabric. I suppose readers have been at least as uneasily aware all along as I have of the limitations of some of my strategical assumptions, and especially do I sense the artificiality of my main working assumption that everything in the book is coming to us from its narrator Ishmael. When one should ascribe such elements as imagery, syntax, rhetoric, and their implications for thought and character in *Moby-Dick* to the fictional narrator Ishmael and when to his creator Melville is, I suspect, perhaps more a matter of critical strategy and relevance than of inherent propriety. If readers have noticed points in the discussion where taking such linguistic elements to characterize Ishmael seems unsually arbitrary, such points may indicate where it might have been better to assign them to Melville instead. Ultimately, this must somehow be done if sense is to be made of such recurrent images, motifs, and themes as I have been most concerned with displaying, especially since those which figure centrally in "Loomings" and the rest of *Moby-Dick*, where Ishmael is narrator, also permeate the whole of Melville's work from *Typee* to *Billy Budd*, where of course he is not. The total imaginative coherence of these works must have as its ground the mind of Melville, as author of them all.

PAUL BRODTKORB JR.

[Selfhood and Others][†]

* * * The fact of otherness may of course be accepted without being seen in a comic mode. The native harpooners, Fedallah, and the "tiger yellow" (ch. 48) Manillas of Ahab's boat crew are all kept far from the reader, yet seem disturbingly near by virtue of their portentousness. In their shifting, unresolved distance from us, they resemble those strange, natural animate objects of the sea that have the quality of the numinous which attracts and repels at once. The harpooners' strange, natural tattoos (Queequeg's legs, it will be recalled, are "marked as if a parcel of dark green frogs were running up the trunks of young palms") or markings ("Fedallah was calmly eyeing the right whale's head, and ever and anon glancing from the deep wrinkles there to the lines in his own hand" [ch. 73] indicate how much a part of this sort of nature they are; like Fedallah, they are creatures such "as civilized, domestic people in the temperate zone only see in their dreams" (ch. 50). There is a sense, of course, in which the entire crew of the Pequod, indeed even the reader, is "natural"—Ishmael asks, "who is not a cannibal?" (ch. 65) and admits "I myself am a savage" (ch. 57); Ahab calls himself "cannibal old me" (ch. 132)—but such naturalness merely suggests potentiality for savage behavior. In addition to it, men show degrees of sympathetic attunement to the rhythms and forces of nature, and it is those natives most attuned who strike us as most completely and mysteriously *other*.

They seem as self-sufficient as nature itself; they don't need us or our understanding for completion. Like Queequeg, men experienced by us in this mode are content with their own companionship and always equal to themselves (ch. 10). To us, they seem *unconscious* (ch. 13) because they act spontaneously, prereflectively, according to the natural demands of the

† From Paul Brodtkorb Jr., *Ishmael's White World: A Phenomenological Reading of "Moby-Dick"* (New Haven, CT: Yale University Press, 1965). Copyright 1965 by Yale University Press.

situation, of which they are instinctively and instantly aware (as when
Queequeg rescues a poor, civilized "bumpkin" while "all hands were in a
panic," unable to decide what to do, so that "nothing was done, and nothing seemed capable of being done" [ch. 13] until Queequeg, with spontaneous grace, acts). In harmony with natural processes, even part *of* them,
such men accept nature fully. They have not become estranged from
nature by thinking *about* it, as more civilized men have. They may worship
nature gods, like Queequeg's benign and familiar Yojo: "a rather good sort
of god, who perhaps meant well enough upon the whole, but in all cases
did not succeed in his benevolent designs" (ch. 16), a god so un-awe-
inspiring that he can be taken up by Queequeg "very unceremoniously,
and bagged . . . in his grego pocket as carelessly as if he were a sportsman bagging a dead woodcock" (ch. 3); or they may worship the more
powerful and ambiguous sun itself, as Fedallah does. In either case, they
feel their gods to be within the natural order, and they accept what the
god chooses to grant or deny. Ages ago, perhaps, "in the ghostly aboriginalness of earth's primal generations, when the memory of the first man
was a distinct recollection . . . all men his descendants, unknowing
whence he came, eyed each other as real phantoms, and asked of the sun
and the moon why they were created and to what end" (ch. 50); but they
have long since stopped asking such questions, because now, to their own
satisfaction at least, they *know*. Nature seems to speak to them directly
and clearly, as it does among civilized men only to the insane, like Elijah;
and therefore they seem able to prophesy, their prophecies ranging from
Queequeg's unspectacular greasing of his boat, "working in obedience to
some particular presentiment" (ch. 84) of a whale about to be sighted, to
Fedallah's precisely accurate foreknowledge that only hemp could kill
Ahab (ch. 117). Such men are not afraid of death; they face it as part of
nature: for Queequeg, it is no more than a trifle, to be accepted if it is
convenient and rejected if it is not (ch. 110), while Fedallah with "fatal-
istic despair" (ch. 118) persists in what seems to be his mission of betrayal
even though he knows it must end in his death. Because they are in tune
with processes of nature, men like this impress us as graceful. Their grace
is feline and savage, not feminine. Queequeg's gentleness coexistent with
his headhunting, and Fedallah's "subtilty" (ch. 48) are as close to female
qualities as any of the inhabitants of this masculine world get. Their natural grace allows them to seem part of the rhythms of nature, but it is also
a sign of their distance from us, and from the more awkward sailor savages of the Pequod. They are always outside of us; as Queequeg's hieroglyphics, and Queequeg himself, remain "unsolved to the last" (ch. 110),
so the white "hair-turbaned Fedallah remained a muffled mystery to the
last" (ch. 50). To such men, bits of animate nature, we can never come
very close at all.

We can get closer to men like Ishmael, who are less forbiddingly of a
piece, who show signs of occasional indecision, and seem rather like ourselves at times. Thus the last major way of encountering the other is also
embodied in a fictional technique that reflects a mode of perception. As
the book proceeds, the purely comic portraiture loses priority, and the
narrator begins to let us overhear private soliloquies, interior conversations less spoken than thought. The other seems much less of an external

object to us; it is almost as if we, together with Ishmael (who simply disappears at such points), *become* the other.

But we do so by virtue of a literary convention. And partly because the convention here is noticeably archaic (soliloquies are not "realistic" even in the nineteenth-century romance terms that Melville employs) it calls attention to itself as theatrical; we notice it as a convention—one that forcibly simplifies the complexities of private mental experience. When we "become" the other by means of a soliloquy, we are not in the presence of an unmediated encounter; instead, we remain within the consciousness of a storyteller who *imagines* the other. Thus we break out of solipsism into an intersubjective world by a technique which maintains the problematic boundaries of selfhood: overtly, the gap between self and other has been bridged, but covertly its eternal existence is acknowledged.

What is revealed of the other by this last method is therefore not inmost, essential selfhood. What is revealed is something like the little lower layer, a stylized, ordered substratum, the revelation of which makes us aware of Ishmael's awareness that an exterior role—Ahab, say, the inflexibly fixed captain bent on revenge—has interior components; and, most typically, that what comprises the interior is self-divided, in process, debating with itself even as it creates masks and roles to conceal its tenuous balances. Thus Starbuck's role of "staid, steadfast man, whose life for the most part was a telling pantomime of action" (ch. 26) is revealed in soliloquy to be capable of harboring a consciousness whose "miserable office" is "to obey, rebelling; and worse yet, to hate with touch of pity!" (ch. 38).

Sometimes Ishmael is willing to go beyond the mere presentation of self-division in order to find abstract, conventional terms for the components of this divided self:

> Starbuck's body and Starbuck's coerced will were Ahab's, so long as Ahab kept his magnet at Starbuck's brain; still he knew that for all this the chief mate, in his soul, abhorred his captain's quest, and could he, would joyfully disintegrate himself from it, or even frustrate it.
>
> [ch. 46]

Spirit or soul ("the eternal, living principle" [ch. 44] in a man) is here at war with mind or will (the "life-spot" [ch. 44] of a man where the spirit resides "leagued with" the mind), which in turn controls body, the outer vessel of the self—these three elements, which may operate together harmoniously as well as discordantly, constitute one schema of total identity for Ishmael.

Of the inwardly discordant characters, Ahab, who outwardly "did long dissemble" (ch. 41), is of course the major example. When Ishmael analyzes him, he uses terms similar to those he uses to explain Starbuck. An important occasion for analysis is provided by Ahab's behavior during his frequent nightmares, when "a wild cry would be heard through the ship; and with glaring eyes Ahab would burst from his state room" (ch. 44). Outwardly the "unappeasedly steadfast hunter of the white whale," inwardly Ahab is torn apart, so that at night this Ahab that had gone to his hammock, was not the agent that so caused him to burst from it in horror again. The latter was the eternal, living principle or soul in him; and in sleep, being for the time dissociated from the characterizing mind, which at other times employed it for its outer vehicle or agent, it spontaneously sought escape from the scorching contiguity of the frantic thing, of which, for the time, it was no longer an integral. But as the mind does not exist unless leagued with the soul, therefore it must have been that, in Ahab's case, yielding up all his thoughts and fancies to his one supreme purpose, that purpose, by its own sheer inveteracy of will, forced itself against gods and devils into a kind of self-assumed, independent being of its own. Nay, could grimly live and burn, while the common vitality to which it was conjoined, fled horror-stricken from the unbidden and unfathered birth. Therefore, the tormented spirit that glared out of bodily eyes, when what seemed Ahab rushed from his room, was for the time but a vacated thing, a formless somnambulistic being, a ray of living light, to be sure, but without an object to color, and therefore a blankness in itself. God help thee, old man, thy thoughts have created a creature in thee; and he whose intense thinking thus makes him a Prometheus; a vulture feeds upon that heart for ever; that vulture the very creature he creates.

[ch. 44]

The conceptual gist of this difficult passage would seem to be that, when asleep, Ahab's soul, temporarily dissociated from what has insanely used it, rebels. Yet the judiciously analytic Ishmael faced with Ahab's psychic profundities does not simplify his analysis to any such "gist." The passage is full of complex abstractions, qualifications, extensions, synonyms with subtle distinctions implied between them, and second thoughts. Ishmael's first hypothesis is that soul, the eternal, living principle, is dissociated in sleep from Ahab's dominant mind, a mind which in the daytime uses soul for its "outer vehicle or agent." But here Ishmael corrects himself: since mind does not exist apart from soul even in sleep, the first analysis must be wrong. Ishmael tries again: Ahab's mind has created a purpose which at first reflexively characterizes that mind, then itself grows into a discrete entity of monstrous proportions (a vulture feeding upon the heart of its Prometheus-creator) from which flees the "common vitality"—soul plus mind[1]—now animating Ahab's body. The second try, however, is not wholly successful either: it leaves Ahab's "independent purpose" spatially unaccounted for (perhaps a literal-minded quibble, yet the passage does have the air of analytic interpretation as well as of poetry) and it blurs the relation between "common vitality" and "tormented spirit"—presumably one of identity, but we can't be sure—because unstated distinctions seem to be implied. In short, there are loose ends to the precision of Ishmael's analysis; he makes too many abstract synonyms. Indeed, the whole passage, in addition to being susceptible of that kind of exegetical attention it has often received, also shows Ishmael unable to create and revise sufficiently quickly enough static abstractions to keep up with the shifting

---

1. "Common vitality" I construe to mean in context that vitality or animating principle which is both soul and mind ("the mind does not exist unless leagued with the soul") rather than a vague ordinary vitality which would be out of keeping with Ishmael's labored attempt at precision here.

complexity that is his experience of Ahab. The initially statue-like Ahab of the quarter-deck, "shaped in an unalterable mould, like Cellini's cast Perseus" (ch. 28), his bone leg steadied in an auger hole as if he were a component part of the ship, has here become fragmented almost into incoherence.

Part of what this suggests is that "becoming" the other—becoming, for example, Ahab—by means of soliloquy is more of a deception than my first account of it suggested, for it seems we have become the other only to be able to explain him less convincingly than when he appeared to us as a distanced, animate object, wholly exterior, but at the same time possibly more favorable to the categorial manipulations of the mind—more accessible to thinking about *because* we experienced him as an object. The Ahab of the soliloquies and Ishmael's analyses exists in the duration of time, changing from moment to moment in his secret proportions, and in this moment of nightmare has become "a blankness in itself," a formula which, perversely, seems more adequately descriptive of him even when he is awake than "crazy Ahab" does. The latter is touched with hypocrisy: it pretends to explain Ahab by labeling him, but the label is simply the name that we give to others with whom we can make little or no contact, and therefore can have no real sense of; while the former at least focuses unequivocally on the mystery of Ahab's being. Ahab is a blankness, a whiteness (Ishmael is aware that "blank" means "white" in his usage of it in chapter 42), with all the ambiguity of that color; but he is also a strange kind of emptiness, a lack, and perhaps a lack in Ishmael's and our rationalizing understanding of him as well as a lack in himself. But how, from our point of view, can a blankness be understood; a being so tormented, so at war with himself; so often at interior variance with his exterior, however much the latter signals the division within; a man, as Ishmael admits near the end (and the sense of which admission has been repeated throughout like a refrain), "every revelation" of whose "deeper part" partakes "more of significant darkness than of explanatory light" (ch. 106)?

The way in which Ishmael tends to understand Ahab is suggested by the phrase "without an object to color." Because these words occur soon after the scientific theory that earthly colors are not inherent in substances, but are illusions bestowed upon substances by the whiteness of light which itself contains all other colors, what is meant by the phrase is something like this: the mysterious self of Ahab, the mind-soul, is a "ray of living light" which requires for its normal daytime existence an "object to color." Like light, the self contains all possibilities of color, but color other than white can be selectively drawn out of the self's blankness only by its having an object—that is, a goal. The self is here conceived of as a kind of closed circuit between itself and some purpose within itself that can give it normal human character. Since to the Starbuckian triad mind-soul-body must be added object or purpose, and since it is in fact Ahab's willful purpose that characterizes him in his inflexible moods when he is "for ever Ahab," it is Ahab's purpose which is the focus of most of Ishmael's major analyses of him. If Ahab differs from the common run of men chiefly in his sheer *quantity*, in his "greatly superior natural force, with a globular brain and a ponderous heart," all of which adds up to "one in a whole nation's census—a mighty pageant creature, formed for noble tragedies" (ch. 16); if, as Peleg says, "There's a good deal more of him" (ch. 16); or, as Elijah says, "*He's* got enough . . . [soul] to make up for all deficiencies of that sort in other chaps" (ch. 19); then all these quantitative differences come together and achieve definition in the strength of his characterizing purpose. When he is the self-divided Ahab, his purpose momentarily waning, he more obviously "has his humanities" (ch. 16); he seems more anonymous, more an ordinary fellow creature; it is easier, then, to feel that "all of us are Ahabs" (ch. 123)—but even then, the force of his self-divisions is greater than most men ever experience, and this force points right back to the singular purpose that sets him apart from all men: as Ishmael says, the "symptoms" of his nightmare ambivalence are "but the plainest tokens of . . . [the] intensity" of "his own resolve" (ch. 44).

HARRISON HAYFORD

Unnecessary Duplicates: A Key to the Writing of *Moby-Dick*[†]

The lock contains no key. Hearing him foolishly fumbling there, the Captain laughs lowly to himself. Chap. 9.

I

Melville introduces the *Pequod's* carpenter by remarking that if you seat yourself 'sultanically' among the moons of Saturn 'high abstracted man alone' seems 'a wonder, a grandeur, and a woe' but that from the same viewpoint 'mankind in mass' for the most part seem 'a mob of unnecessary duplicates' (ch. 107). Something of the same sort can be said about two such ways of looking at *Moby-Dick*. From an integrative critical viewpoint the book gives a unified impression of wonder, grandeur, and tragic woe. But on close scrutiny many of its compositional elements seem, in ordinary fictional terms, to be 'a mob of unnecessary duplicates'. You could call both views 'sultanically' elevated, since each is way outside any view mundane readers are likely to take of the book. In this essay I am going, arbitrarily enough, to disregard the integrative view and take the second way of looking at it. First I'll point out the curious pattern of duplicates I see in it, and then I'll go on to use this pattern as evidence for a major hypothesis I'll offer about Melville's shifting intentions for some of the central characters in *Moby-Dick* as it developed through several phases during the year and a half he was writing it. I believe these duplicates give us a new key, to add to the several we already have, to fumble with (let's hope not altogether foolishly) as we keep trying to open some of the interlocked complications of the book's genesis, to which there is no master key we know of.

† From *New Perspectives on Melville*, ed. Faith Pullen (Edinburgh: Edinburgh University Press, 1978), 128–61. The cover of the Edinburgh University Press offprint bore the notice "for Leon Howard," Hayford's old friend and the author of *Herman Melville: A Biography* (1951); born in 1903, Howard died in 1982.

Duplicates begin at once. It takes not one but two chapters to do the narrative job of getting Ishmael started out to see the watery part of the world on his first whaling voyage. Chapter 1 loses narrative headway after its third sentence, so that chapter 2 must duplicate its job and start him again, as he stuffs a shirt or two in his bag and sets out for a whaling port, New Bedford. But at once there's another duplicate; he tells us he won't sail from that first port but from a second, Nantucket. Moreover, since at New Bedford he misses the Nantucket boat and it's Saturday night he must spend not one but two nights and the intervening Sunday there, getting no closer to a whaleship. The job of the rest of chapter 2 is to deal with his problem of finding an inn. Presumably the inn, like the whole chapter, serves the book's larger fictional purpose of illustrating the whaleman's world as a tyro encounters it; but presenting two whaling ports entails presenting two inns—duplicates breed duplicates. Why need we be shown the whaleman's shore life via *two* inns, one at New Bedford run by an officious humorous landlord, and a second at Nantucket run by an officious humourless landlady? Seeking a suitable inn, Ishmael passes up a couple of 'too expensive and jolly' ones and blunders into and out of a Negro church before he manages to select the Spouter-Inn.

The first of the two problems in the Spouter-Inn (ch. 3) is for Ishmael to find a sleeping-place there. And he finds duplicates, not one place but two, and goes to bed twice, first on a cold narrow bench alone, then in a warm prodigious bed with a harpooneer bedfellow. Why both?

The chapter's second problem is the larger narrative job of introducing an experienced whaleman to become tyro Ishmael's comrade and probably also his mentor in 'this business of whaling'. But the chapter proceeds to introduce not one but two such characters, first Bulkington, then Queequeg—duplicates. Bulkington enters the inn with the *Grampus* crew, just landed from a three years' whaling voyage; he is a 'huge favorite' with the crew and evidently an experienced whaleman. Ishmael describes Bulkington, he says, because he'll be a shipmate—only to explain in an immediate parenthesis and metaphor that he won't: 'This man interested me at once; and since the sea-gods had ordained that he should soon become my shipmate (though but a sleeping-partner one, so far as this narrative is concerned), I will here venture upon a little description of him.' After a portentous description of Bulkington in romantic-heroic terms he is said to slip away unobserved, and we are told 'I saw no more of him till he became my comrade on the sea'. The word 'comrade' applied to Bulkington here is a noteworthy one; it postulates a special personal relationship transcending that of a mere 'shipmate', and later in the book Ishmael applies the word in the singular to only one man, not to Bulkington but to Queequeg (chs 13, 18, 72). At once Bulkington slips away, is missing from the following shore chapters, is seen once more as the ship puts out to sea, and then is altogether absent from the book. Thus he sets a pattern of 'hiding out' that is to be duplicated by several characters who are themselves duplicates. But, oddly, the bulk of chapter 3 is then given over to the spun-out practical-joke introduction of a duplicate comrade.

This duplicate is a second experienced whaleman, a harpooneer, who is missing (a second 'hide out') until near the chapter's end; there, after 'sec-

ond thoughts' on the part of both landlord and Ishmael, he's accepted as
the tyro's literal 'sleeping-partner' that Saturday night. And in the course
of Sunday evening, after Ishmael sallies out twice, first for a morning
sightseeing stroll then to visit the Whaleman's Chapel and hear Father
Mapple's sermon, Queequeg further becomes Ishmael's 'bosom-friend'
and is a second time his sleeping-partner. He resolves to accompany Ishmael on his whaling voyage and share his every hap. Ishmael tells us, "To
all this I joyously assented; for besides the affection I now felt for Queequeg, he was an experienced harpooneer, and as such, could not fail to be
of great usefulness to one, who, like me, was wholly ignorant of the mysteries of whaling . . .' (chs 4–12).

Monday morning, in chapter 13, Ishmael sets off with Queequeg—'my
comrade' as he twice calls him—for Nantucket, to the second whaling
port, second inn, second dominating keeper, and even two chowders. The
next problem, in chapter 16, is for them to choose a ship and sign aboard.
Ishmael had 'not a little relied upon Queequeg's sagacity to point out the
whaler best fitted' for their voyage, and certainly Queequeg's novelistic
job, as experienced-whaleman mentor, should be to 'be of great usefulness'. Nevertheless, he declares he can't do so, reassigns the job to his little god Yojo, and 'hides out' a second time. Consequently, since he does-
n't accompany Ishmael to the docks, not one but two signing-aboard
scenes must be presented, first one for Ishmael then another for Queequeg; that is, duplicate chapters (16, 18) must be devoted to business that
might have been economically accomplished in a single one.

So tyro Ishmael goes alone and himself decides on the *Pequod*—or
duplicates Yojo's pre-decision. In chapter 16, 'The Ship', in which he does
so, duplications continue. First, there are duplications with respect to the
ship herself. For some of the *Pequod*'s attractive peculiarities are specified
here in particulars that are later to be negated by discrepant duplicate
specifications. Here, for example, she's said to have 'unpanelled, open
bulwarks' all round; but later, off the Cape of Good Hope, the crew seek
shelter from the heavy seas 'along the bulwarks in the waist', which must,
therefore, be panelled ones (ch. 51), Here, again (as in chapters 96, 123)
she's said to sport instead of a turnstile wheel 'a tiller . . . curiously
carved from the long narrow lower jaw of her hereditary foe'; but twice
later she's given a wheel with spokes (chs 61, 118).

Besides these minor duplications in the ship's details, there are at once
major duplicates among characters associated with her, notably in her
having not one but three 'captains'. For as Ishmael first goes aboard the
Pequod, who's in charge? Not, as might be expected, just one agent,
owner, or captain to sign him on, but two—both retired Quaker captains
who are also the two chief owners, Peleg and Bildad. And—though it's old
Captain Peleg who has served for years on the Indian-named ship, who
sits in a 'wigwam' of whalebone on her deck, and who has, we're told,
done the curious whalebone carving work that dresses her in 'barbaric'
apparel—it turns out to be not Peleg but still a third duplicate old Quaker
captain, Ahab, who is to be her actual captain in command on the upcoming voyage and who (not Peleg) possesses the most striking piece of whalebone carving, a 'barbaric white leg' which 'had at sea been fashioned from
the polished bone of the sperm whale's jaw' (ch. 28). But this third dupli-

cate captain is not to be seen until days after the ship sails; he's said to be sick (like Bulkington and Queequeg he 'hides out'), and so his appearance will require a later separate chapter (ch. 28). The two old Quaker captains who do appear in chapter 16, Peleg and Bildad, so overlap in fictional uses that they may seem to be duplicates as indistinguishable as Rosenkranz and Guildenstern, though they are given individualizing peculiarities. Peleg is a profane 'blusterer' while Bildad is a quiet, pious canter who solemnly declares his fear that impenitent Peleg's leaky conscience will sink him 'foundering down to the fiery pit'. Peleg angrily rejects Bildad's prophecy, rephrasing it in plain English: 'Fiery pit! fiery pit! ye insult me, man; past all natural bearing, ye insult me. It's an all-fired outrage to tell any human creature that he's bound to hell'. But, as it turns out, it is not the first captain, Peleg, with his mild everyday profanities, but the third captain, Ahab, with his outraged sense of the insults and indignities heaped upon the human creature, and with his major blasphemies, who is the one indeed 'bound to hell' and who drives the *Pequod* and all her crew (save one) to 'sink to hell' (ch. 135).

And very soon further duplications of characters follow, centering upon the role of prophet of Ahab's fate. Bildad's prophecy here in chapter 16 makes him the first of seven duplicate prophets, all of whom take up in their various direct or indirect ways the burden of Christian Bildad's initial prediction of a profane captain's hell-bound career (though not Peleg's, it turns out, but Ahab's). After Bildad, these prophets are, in order, three who are introduced ashore—'the old squaw, Tistig, at Gay-head' (ch. 16); an old sailor, Elijah (chs 19, 21); the Parsee Fedallah (who's hiding out in chapter 21); and two more who are introduced at sea, upon Ahab's first appearance, in chapter 28: 'Tashtego's senior, an old Gay-Head Indian among the crew', and 'a grey Manxman . . ., an old sepulchral man'. To these six prophets closely associated with Ahab on shore or ship can be added a seventh encountered on another ship, the crazy Shaker Gabriel, who also warns Ahab to 'beware of the blasphemer's end!' and prophesies, 'thou art soon going that way' (ch. 71).

Among these prophets along Ahab's hell-bound route the most curiously conspicuous duplicates are three Gay-Head Indians (the book uses the place name in several forms as quoted here). The first, the old squaw Tistig, is followed in prophetic role by the old Gay-Head Indian crewman, 'Tashtego's senior', and both of these Gay-Headers know circumstances of Ahab's birth and speak portentously about his career. The old crewman appears only once, and two of the three items of Ahab's history he gives out are later contradicted by discrepant duplicate information: 'Aye, he was dismasted off Japan,' he volunteers, 'but like his dismasted craft, he shipped another mast without coming home for it. He has a quiver of 'em'—whereas later it's established that it was on the equator (and not off Japan) that Moby Dick took off Ahab's leg (ch. 130), and also shown that Ahab has no quiver of extras but must order a new one to be made by the carpenter when his original one is wrenched (chs. 106, 108). This old Indian crewman, 'Tashtego's senior', never reappears, but his prophetic role is duplicated by Tashtego, 'an unmixed Indian from Gay Head' (ch. 27) who is prominent as one of the *Pequod*'s three pagan harpooneers. 'To look at the tawny brawn of his lithe snaky limbs, you would almost have credited the superstitions of some of the earlier Puritans, and half believed this wild Indian to be a son of the Prince of the Powers of the Air' (ch. 27). It is Tashtego, this third Gay-Head Indian, who at the masthead sights and sings out for the *Pequod*'s first whale and in doing so is described as like a prophet or seer:

> High aloft in the cross-trees was that mad Gay-Header, Tashtego . . . . As he stood hovering over you half suspended in air, so wildly and eagerly peering towards the horizon, you would have thought him some prophet or seer beholding the shadows of Fate, and by those wild cries announcing their coming. (ch. 47)

Months later, when Moby Dick is sighted for the first time, it is Tashtego again at the masthead who 'saw him at almost the same instant that Captain Ahab did' and cried out—just missing award of the doubloon (ch. 133). And on the final day, in the moments of Ahab's fated end when the unanimous prophecy of all these duplicate prophets is fulfilled, it is for some reason the red Indian Tashtego who at Ahab's command is nailing Ahab's red flag of no-surrender to the mast of the fated *Pequod* during the moments when she must 'sink to hell' (ch. 135).

As for the other two prophets introduced ashore before the ship sails, Elijah, though 'crazy', is a true prophet, an 'old sailor chap' who has sailed under Ahab and calls him 'Old Thunder'; he reveals to Ishmael and Queequeg some hints of Ahab's character and history, and warns them of the soul-peril of shipping on the *Pequod*—'that ship'—with him. Elijah also hints the existence of Ahab's false prophet-companion, Fedallah, the Parsee of vague East Indian or else devilish origin, whom Ahab smuggles aboard along with his oriental four-man duplicate boat-crew, to 'hide out' below until the first lowering (ch. 48). Why all these seven duplicate prophets?

At long last chapter 22 gets the *Pequod* hauled out from the Nantucket wharf. The twenty-one shore chapters have already taken up about a fifth of the book—surely a disproportionate share—before the whaling voyage begins, before Ishmael sees anything of the watery part of the world, before the book's tragic protagonist appears, and before its plot and Ahab's mighty antagonist are revealed. There have been two narrative starts, two whaling ports, two inns (and two chowders), two innkeepers, two beds and goings-to-bed, two comrades (one dismissed already), two signings-aboard, two Quaker captain-owners and a third Quaker captain-in-command, four (of an eventual seven) prophets, four hide-outs, and an extra boat-crew. No wonder it has taken so much space, with so much duplication already! Did Melville think the book itself had to be stocked with duplicates just as the *Pequod* had to be provided with 'spare boats, spare spars, and spare lines and harpoons, and spare everythings, almost, but a spare Captain and duplicate ship'? (ch. 20).

Nor does this space-demanding pattern of duplicates cease when the ship has left the wharf. As the *Pequod* is worked out of Nantucket harbour into the open sea, not just one pilot but two are aboard. What need two? Again it is those two old Quaker owner-captains (the ship's commanding Quaker captain, Ahab, still hides out in his cabin); both of them are 'going it with a high hand on the quarter-deck, just as if they were to be joint-commanders at sea, as well as to all appearances in port'. Captain Peleg's first order is one that Captain Ahab significantly duplicates fourteen chapters later, to open the 'Quarter-Deck' scene (ch. 36). Peleg's is an order that by usage a captain would give his mate soon after such a ship got under way—'Call all hands, then. Muster 'em aft here. . . .' This order customarily initiated one or two routines neither of which follows Peleg's order here. On an actual voyage the crew thus mustered aft might be harangued by the captain, who would lay down the purpose of the voyage, the crew's duties, and his own policies; and the mates would choose up men for their watches. (For accounts see Melville's own *Redburn*, or R. H. Dana's *Two Years Before the Mast*, J. N. Reynolds' 'Mocha Dick', and J. Ross Browne's *Etchings of a Whaling Cruise*—works Melville knew and used in writing *Moby-Dick*.) In *Moby-Dick*, however, the all-hands sequence does not get played out normally but is curiously split in two after the duplicate orders in chapters 22 and 36. Profane Captain Peleg (standing in here for Captain Ahab) begins it with his first order to the mate, 'Well, call all hands, then. Muster 'em aft here—blast 'em!' But Peleg, it turns out, doesn't want them all aft for either of the usual routines just mentioned; no, what he wants done there by the 'sons of bachelors' is only to have his whalebone tent struck—scarcely a duty requiring all hands. Apparently something went askew in Peleg's—or Melville's—orders. (Peleg's next order, however, is a proper one, actually requiring all hands, though for duty forward not aft: 'Man the capstan! Blood and thunder!—jump!' This is the order to raise the anchor, an order, indeed, that normally came *before* the order to muster, lest the crew might sober up and desert before the ship got under way.) On the *Pequod*, Captain Ahab's duplicate muster order comes after the ship has been at sea for many days, with the mates and crew doing their regular duties, though, as was just pointed out, no account of choosing up watches (indeed nothing in detail about deck or forecastle life at all) has been given before Captain Ahab, at last out of hiding, appears above hatches (ch. 28). When Ahab 'impulsively' orders the mate to send everybody aft, Starbuck is said to be 'astonished at an order seldom or never given on ship-board except in some extraordinary case' (chs 46, 36). True enough, at *that* stage of a voyage. But what then ensues on the quarterdeck is, in form, one part of the long-overdue normal follow-up of Peleg's order days ago—the captain's harangue to the crew about the voyage's purpose and his own policies—though in *content*, as Starbuck sees and the narrator tells us, Ahab's 'prime but private purpose', is a mad usurpation of any proper purpose and policy. In sum, Melville has his duplicate captains give duplicate muster orders; Peleg's is too early (in harbour) and is not followed by either customary routine; while Ahab's is fourteen chapters too late (at sea) and is followed by a customary but subverted routine. It's as if Ahab took up right where Peleg left off.

And this duplication of orders is not the only or most significant duplication that occurs in the Christmas-day departure chapter. While profane Peleg rips and swears astern at the crew 'in the most frightful manner', Ishmael pauses in his efforts at the capstan forward to think of the perils he and Queequeg are running 'in starting on the voyage with such a devil for a pilot'—though even a tyro whaleman should realize that a *pilot*, soon to go ashore, could offer them no peril on the voyage itself. Then Ishmael feels a 'sudden sharp poke in my rear' and is horrified to see Captain Peleg 'withdrawing his leg' from 'my immediate vicinity'. And he remarks, 'That was my first kick'. Yes, but it's not the first we've heard of Peleg's leg, or the last we'll hear of a kick from a captain. There's in fact some confused duplication of legs and kicks on the *Pequod*. Already in the first signing-aboard scene (ch. 16) Peleg has for some reason called Ishmael's special attention to his leg though apparently it's just a normal leg, Ahab's being the only remarkable one, of whalebone: 'Dost see that leg?—I'll take that leg away from thy stern, if ever thou talkest of the marchant service to me again.' So sure enough, though for another offence, here at up-anchor time Peleg does kick Ishmael with 'that leg'. It's Ishmael's 'first kick', as he says; and, though this expression implies more kicks, it's also his last kick and indeed anybody's last actual kick of the voyage, apart from those Peleg gives in 'using his leg very freely' as the anchor is being raised. Yet, more kicks and kicking soon do follow, but only in a reported dream, including a dream-kick from a captain with a more noteworthy leg than Peleg's. The recipient this time is not Ishmael (a common sailor) but Stubb (an officer—who sounds like a duplicate of the Ishmael of chapter 1) in his 'Queen Mab' dream of his own kicking a pyramid, of being invited to kick a merman's marlinspike-bristling rump, and of having been kicked by Ahab's ivory leg, and in his wide-awake rationalizing of his wisdom in not kicking back (ch. 31). Duplicate legs-and-kicking galore!

In the course of chapter 22 the *Pequod* at last gains an offing in the wintry Atlantic, and the duplicate pilot-captains (the swearing-kicking fearsome Quaker 'devil' Peleg with 'that leg' and the pious Quaker prophet Bildad) both say their reluctant farewells to the ship and both drop into the pilot boat to go ashore, leaving the third and still hidden-out duplicate Quaker captain, the soon-to-be-revealed Satanic Ahab, in command for the voyage.

The *Pequod* is at sea. But the book's duplicative treatment of three central and closely related novelistic jobs still confronts us with questions we might suppose Melville should have settled by this point. These are questions as to its narrator and narrative point-of-view, its protagonist or hero, and the over-all shape of its narrative line—its action or plot. For each of these questions, however, we have already been offered, or are about to be given, several duplicate answers. Nor do duplications of other kinds cease in the sea chapters. I'll leave readers the pleasure of compiling their own lists. Some duplicates are not obvious but no one will overlook the series of deaths and averted near-deaths (I think of it as the 'man-overboard' pattern); or the closely related series of rescues and redeemings by Queequeg already begun ashore; or the series of ship-meetings, sometimes miscalled gams; or the *Pequod*'s final three-day trio of encounters with tragic-hero Ahab's great antagonist; or the duplicate names of that antagonist, the 'White Whale' some call 'Moby Dick'; or the book's own successive duplicate titles, *The Whale* and *Moby-Dick*. But the ones I have just listed in the shore-narrative—taken with the sea-narrative matters they implicate—already give me more duplicates than I can deal with in this essay. As a key, they give me enough, as I try to account for them, to give rise to my major hypothesis about a part of the genetic history of some of the book's characters.

II

Among the duplicate characters, Bulkington and Queequeg are the best pair to begin with, because it's so obvious which of them came first, and because our seeing the compositional ways Melville handled this pair leads us on, by a somewhat devious path, to see the ways he handled the other major duplicate characters, and thus to my major hypothesis. My line of reasoning about the composition stages is simple enough, but since it has to work backwards from what's in the printed book to earlier inferred stages, it will be easier to follow if I list the stages here by numbers and use them all along in my discussion. I provisionally distinguish three stages through which Melville's shore-narrative must have gone—I mean just with respect to this pair of alternate comrades, not to its whole writing history. Stage 1 included neither Bulkington nor Queequeg; Stage 2 added Bulkington; Stage 3 dismissed Bulkington and added Queequeg, ending up as the version printed. All three probably included substages.[1]

In the finished book, Bulkington, unlike any of the other duplicate characters, sticks out as vestigial because in the two early passages that he enters (chs 3, 23) he is assigned the dual roles of comrade and truth-seeker, but is not developed later in either role; indeed, in both passages Melville explicitly dismisses him from appearing in any role at all in the ensuing narrative. The explanation of this anomalous assignment-dismissal procedure must be that two compositional stages are involved in the passages as they stand, that at the earlier (Stage 2) Melville intended him to play these roles but then at the later (Stage 3) changed his intention and revised the passages to dismiss him from both roles, yet for some reason did not discard him, or the passages, altogether.

Not only is Bulkington vestigial, he is one of our duplicates—in chapter 3 he and Queequeg pair in the one-man role of narrator's comrade. Again, the explanation must be that two composition stages are involved. Bulkington must have been either Melville's earlier or his later intended choice for the comrade role; and it is easy to see that he was earlier (Stage 2) than Queequeg, since it was he whom Melville (Stage 3) dismissed and Queequeg whom he kept and developed in this and other chapters.

So far I've distinguished Stages 2 and 3 and in a moment I'll distinguish the still earlier Stage 1, at which Melville had not yet got around to assigning the narrator any companion at all. First, however, I want to look more closely at Stage 2, to see what Melville did and didn't have in his shore-narrative about these two characters at that time. We have just seen that in it Bulkington, not Queequeg, was to be the narrator's comrade; so Bulkington was there, but we must infer that Queequeg wasn't. Bulkington was there, presumably, in only the same two passages he occupies in chapters 3 and 23 of the book—meaning those passages as they stood

---

1. Hayford's hypothesizing is delightfully complicated and clarified by Geoffrey Sanborn's recent discovery (reported in the footnotes herein to *Moby-Dick*) that Queequeg was based on a real man, Tupai Cupa, whose story was told by George Lillie Craik in *The New Zealanders* (1830). Now any speculation about Bulkington and Queequeg must deal with the possibility that (after the creation of Bulkington?) Melville encountered the Craik book and became enchanted with the characterization of Tupai Cupa, seeing in it the chance of playing variations on the theme of noble cannibals vs. ignoble Christians and of inculcating charming lessons in cultural relativity [Editors' note].

before Melville made the later (Stage 3) revisions by which he dismissed him, from one of them by the curious 'sleeping-partner' parenthesis, and from the other by the two-and-a-half new or recast paragraphs in which he managed both to bury and to praise him.

Well then, at Stage 2, as in the book, Bulkington entered the shore-narrative in the four-paragraph episode in which the narrator reports his coming into the Spouter-Inn with the *Grampus* crew, describes him (because he later became a shipmate), and says he slipped out pursued by the crew and wasn't seen again by the narrator 'till he became my comrade on the sea'. That last clause tells us Bulkington left the shore-narrative then and there and played no further part in it; and I see no good reason to suppose he ever did so. But what about Bulkington at sea? Had Melville already written—or did he later write—any passages for him there? I mean, aside from his standing at the helm (in Stage 2, as now) when the *Pequod* thrust off. Of course he now doesn't appear in the sea-narrative, and so far I can identify only one passage I think Melville wrote for him in it. But I can see further passages Melville *may* have written for him; and I have my major hypothesis to offer in due course about Melville's intentions, when I take up what I believe he did at Stage 3 with the two roles he had assigned at Stage 2 to Bulkington as comrade and as truth-seeker.

Let me regress from Stage 2 for a moment to distinguish Stage 1, the earliest narrative stage I infer from the duplicates I am considering here. In Stage 1, I infer that Melville had in hand a first-person shore-narrative in which Bulkington played no part at all. In it, Melville had evidently not yet assigned his narrator a comrade for the voyage (and possibly not yet the name Ishmael). Since Queequeg, as we've seen, wasn't yet present in Stage 2, he can't have been in this earlier stage either. Bulkington's absence at Stage 1 is inferred from the two compositional procedures by which, in the four-paragraph *Grampus*-crew episode, Melville simultaneously introduced him into and got him right off the Spouter-Inn scene. Clearly, Melville (at Stage 2) inserted that episode into an already-written sequence (first procedure). It is detachable, unintegrated with anything that precedes or follows, a patch designed to introduce Bulkington as the narrator's prospective comrade (though the dramatic whaling-life vignette that encapsules him yields a surplus illustrative value). At the same time, the transparent purpose served by Melville's ending it with Bulkington's disappearance and the narrator's statement (second procedure) that 'I saw no more of him till he became my comrade on the sea' (i.e. with what I've called Bulkington's 'hiding out') was to spare Melville the necessity of incorporating Bulkington more thoroughly into his existing shore-narrative (of Stage 1). Furthermore, that second compositional procedure seems to me to explain the pattern of 'hide outs' by duplicate characters to which I have called attention: of Bulkington, Queequeg, Ahab, and Fedallah with his boat-crew. Each of them, I am saying, was occasioned by Melville's procedure of inserting the character at an early point (or points) into an already-written narrative, and by his then sparing himself the revisional work of writing the character into further passages of that existing narrative by instead supplying some rationalization for the character's not appearing in it but in effect 'hiding out'. Sometimes, however,

Melville chose (notably in the case of Queequeg) to write and insert entirely *new passages* about the character. I believe some of the book's most awkward anomalies were induced and some of its best passages inspired in just these ways.

Now I return to the matter of Queequeg's absence from Stage 2 and of what its lean narrative was like then without him; after that I'll go on to the meatier matter of just how much more was involved when Melville was introducing and developing him at Stage 3.

As readers of *Moby-Dick* we may not care much that the vestigial Bulkington was no more important in the Stage 2 shore scenes than he is now; but as readers we do care a great deal about Queequeg, so long known to us in his central, even indispensable, role that we assume Melville must have conceived him as the narrator's comrade from the time he first set pen to paper to write the book. So it's startling to realize, following my line of reasoning, that at Stage 2 Queequeg can't have played any part at all in the shore-narrative. The reason he can't have done so is that his *only* shore role even now is the integral one of narrator's comrade—the role which at that stage Melville had assigned to Bulkington. Well, what can that Stage 2 narrative have been like without him? Can it have stood in anything like its printed form without the extended passages in which Queequeg is so important? Surprisingly, it can, though much abridged. For the most part we can excise him simply by bracketing whatever involves him. (That is to say, conversely, during Stage 3 Melville inserted whatever now involves him, with very little *rewriting*, though a fair amount of new writing, including several new chapters.) And to me at least, the excision of Queequeg from the shore-chapters seems to demonstrate that the curious pattern of duplicates did result, as I'm suggesting, from separate composition stages. For with that excision many of the duplicates in these chapters disappear: the two comrades, two sleeping places (and 'second thoughts'), two signing-aboard scenes—each of these pairs shrinks to a single member. Not only do these duplications disappear, but, of course, so do the wonderful Queequeg matters that swell the number of shore-narrative passages so disproportionately before the narrator finally gets to sea.

Let's follow the book's shore chapters in detail to see what was and wasn't there at Stage 2, judging simply by what's left after excision of the Queequeg (Stage 3) materials. In the Stage 2 Spouter-Inn passage (now in chapter 3) Melville solved each of its two narrative problems—of a sleeping-place and a comrade—only once, not twice (by duplicates) as at Stage 3. When the narrator asked Peter Coffin for a room the landlord simply told him there was 'not a bed unoccupied'. The narrator responded, 'I'll try the bench here'. And after a supper in an adjoining room cold as Iceland, and the landlord's futile attempt to plane the bench smooth, he spent a drafty night on it, in the winter cold that afflicts him throughout the shore and early sea chapters. So much for the sleeping problem. At Stage 2 Melville handled the second problem more simply. He supplied a comrade by inserting the four-paragraph irruption of the *Grampus* crew with the momentary glimpse it gave the narrator of Bulkington, his comrade-to-be, who slipped away leaving him companionless for the rest of the shore-narrative, to reappear at the *Pequod's* helm in a scene presumably written at Stage 2.

What our excision of Queequeg reveals as not yet present at Stage 2 is of course—besides Queequeg himself—what's now the warm comic heart of the Spouter-Inn chapter, the whole business set off by the landlord's 'second thoughts' practical joke of offering tyro Ishmael half of a har-pooneer's blanket. That is, Ishmael's own series of 'second thoughts'—first reluctantly agreeing, then changing his mind and trying the bench, then changing his mind again and consenting to share the harpooneer's bed, then his strange meeting and sensible acceptance of the cannibal, followed by his warm night's sleep. All this, it would seem, was Melville's brilliant comic elaboration by which he wrote the 'hidden-out' Queequeg into the bare Stage 2 narrative he had written earlier for his cold and alienated narrator.

Next morning, at Stage 2, the companionless narrator woke up, break-fasted alone, and strolled alone to see the New Bedford street sights; per-haps he sallied out again to the Chapel alone, as the sky 'changed from clear, sunny cold, to driving sleet and mist', to hear Father Mapple's ser-mon alone, like the other solitary worshippers. (But more likely the dupli-cate sally, the Chapel and sermon episode, was inserted at Stage 3.) The only important Stage 3 Queequeg matter that this sequence (now in chap-ters 4–9) lacked was the whole of chapter 4, where Ishmael wakes up caught in the 'comical predicament' of his sleeping-partner's 'bridegroom clasp', and Queequeg dresses first in his own outlandish way. Elsewhere Melville brought Queequeg into the sequence with only slight revisions and minor insertions: in the first three paragraphs and the last one of chapter 5; in the discrepant reference to him in the first sentence of chap-ter 6; and in the three adjacent sentences in chapter 7 that briefly and rather implausibly bring the pagan (who's 'given up' on Christians) into the Chapel.

In the remaining shore-narrative at Stage 2, the narrator sailed to Nan-tucket alone, stayed and ate alone at Mrs Hussey's, signed aboard the *Pequod* alone (as he now does). He encountered Elijah alone. And he sailed alone. A possibility I cannot pursue here is suggested by some of the duplicates I have pointed out: the two whaling ports, two inns, two innkeepers. Perhaps at a very early stage the narrator went to and sailed from only one port, New Bedford. Bulkington's appearing there then pop-ping up on a Nantucket ship might suggest this. But it's an intricate prob-lem. Can the ship—or its earlier duplicate—with all or any of its duplicate captains have at first been from New Bedford? Similarly, can the dupli-cate prophet Elijah (whose Biblical name, at least, seems dependent on Ahab) have been generated somewhere in the process that induced Ahab's series of prophets? As I have remarked, there were probably substages within the three stages I have needed to distinguish here, perhaps other major stages as well.

As from earlier chapters, Queequeg can be readily excised from the pre-sent chapters 10–21. Since he is undetachably central to chapters 10, 11, 12, where his bosom-friendship with Ishmael develops, these chapters belong to Stage 3. The same is true of much of chapter 13, 'Wheelbar-row', with Queequeg's anecdote in comparative anthropology and his res-cue of the bumpkin, though its paragraphs 5, 6, and part of 7 may have been part of the Stage 1 narrative. Chapter 14, 'Nantucket', has no reference to Queequeg (nor does it have the narrative mode or dramatized first-person narrator after its first sentence, and in this, like its twin chapter 6 on New Bedford, it anticipates the imminent fictional truancy of the companions). Queequeg is easily removed from chapter 15, 'Chowder', by bracketing a few phrases and sentences, changing the first-person plural pronouns to singular, and cutting out the byplay with Mrs Hussey about his harpoon. The sequence of chapters 16–18 shows Melville engaging in a compositional procedure we've already observed. I think he already had written at Stage 1 the scene of the narrator's signing aboard the *Pequod*. Rather than revise it to include Queequeg, what he did, I think, was to write a new passage (the first two and a half paragraphs of chapter 16) in which he provided reasons why Queequeg could not 'be of great usefulness' and choose their ship as he should do in his role of experienced-whaleman mentor: Queequeg assigns Yojo that job and also 'hides out' (a second time) for his 24-hour Ramadan. This procedure kept him out of chapter 16, where Melville might have managed to have him too sign aboard; and it motivated the two fine new comic chapters 17–18, about Queequeg's Ramadan and signing-aboard. From chapters 19–22, Queequeg is again easily removed by cutting out or changing the few words here and there by which Melville (at Stage 3) established his presence. The thematic common denominator of Melville's additions occasioned by his introduction of Queequeg is the contrast of savage and civilized, pagan and Christian; their cumulative effect is an eclectic enrichment of the religious dimensions of the book's world.

So much for the lean narrative of Stage 2 and the startling but negative matter of Queequeg's absence from it. Now I'll move further into the positive matter of just how much more was involved for his central characters while Melville was introducing Queequeg into Bulkington's vacated place as Ishmael's comrade at Stage 3. Above, I called this a 'meatier' matter; and so it was, because it was part of a larger process in which Melville was doing far more than fleshing out the then lean shore-narrative by importing an exotic new comrade and the newly-written passages about him which were not present at Stage 2, when even Bulkington was barely there.

III

The larger process in which Melville was engaged at this point was a multiple reassignment of roles among four of his central characters. I even dare surmise this was the decisive turning-point in their genetic development, and in the definition of the narrator himself. What I've called the major hypothesis of this essay is my formulation of the several interconnected reassignments involved. I'll state the hypothesis now, in two different perspectives, in advance of my presentation of the specific compositional evidence by which I'll later support it. Because up to here I've approached the hypothesis piecemeal, through Melville's treatment of Bulkington and Queequeg, I'll state it first in that perspective.

At Stage 3 of his shore-narrative Melville decided to dismiss Bulkington from his dual role of comrade and of truth-seeker, and from any active role in the narrative. He reassigned Bulkington's comrade role to Queequeg, as we've just seen. And he also, I now add, made two further closely-related reassignments which involved two more characters. He reassigned Bulkington's truth-seeker role to a newly-invented character (who was even more startlingly absent—in the book 'hiding out'—up to this point)—Ahab. He simultaneously reassigned to Ahab the sea-role of captain of the *Pequod*, taking that commanding role away from the captain who had first held it—Peleg—and reducing Peleg thus to his present shore role as her 'captain' without command, retired chief-mate, and duplicate part-owner and pilot. The narrator, too, was redefined in the reassignment of his comrades.

Now I'll restate the hypothesis from a second perspective (with recognizable reference to the pattern of duplicates I have summarized but still without detailed compositional evidence). The hypothesis is this. Four central characters of *Moby-Dick* were involved, at this crucial stage of the book's development, in a multiple reassignment of roles, which also redefined a fifth, the narrator. (By a 'role' I mean intentions Melville had projected for a character, some of which were actually written but some were still only in his mind, though signalled in what he had written.) In the process of reassignment, each of the four became in certain ways a duplicate; but while two of them gained and consequently became major characters, two of them lost and became to a degree vestigial—'unnecessary duplicates'.

The two gainers were Queequeg and Ahab—and, coincidentally, Ishmael himself. Queequeg, up to this point, had not been brought into the shore-narrative; but in its continuation in the already-written sea-narrative he by then was one of the three harpooneers, and was (then as now) usually named and presented there not singly but linked with the other two, though in several passages he already played a separate role and was sometimes individually characterized. Queequeg received from Bulkington at Stage 3 of the shore-narrative the role of Ishmael's comrade; but Melville made him a quite different comrade from what Bulkington would have been, by not assigning him as well the alienated, aggressive component implicit in Bulkington's romantic, truth-seeking role. Instead, Queequeg embodied a reconciling principle. While he brought over with him from the sea-narrative the aggressive filed teeth of a cannibal and the harpoon of a whaleman, he brought also a noble savage's 'calm self-collectedness of simplicity', a tranquil piety, and a capacity for bosom-friendship. His tomahawk-pipe shows the union in him of war and peace. Whereas Bulkington, that unresting voyager (in 'the deep shadows' of whose eyes 'floated some reminiscences that did not seem to give him much joy'), as a comrade would have engaged and heightened Ishmael's own alienated and aggressive tendencies (even while ennobling them), Queequeg caused him to feel 'a melting in me'. 'No more my splintered heart and maddened hand were turned against the wolfish world. This soothing savage had redeemed it' (ch. 10). Queequeg's pagan warmth softened and assuaged the aggressive disaffection from cold Christendom that had driven Ishmael, as a 'substitute for pistol and ball', to take to the ship in midwinter—and did so even before he had found and signed aboard the vindictive *Pequod*! Thus Melville's substitution of Queequeg for Bulkington as the narrator's comrade signalized, or perhaps even precipitated, a reorientation in Ishmael's psychology. And this reorientation was explicitly defined and delimited by Melville's elaboration of the new shore-narrative episodes, told by Ishmael in his own individualized first-person, that dramatize the terms of their likewise individualized bosom-friendship. So Ishmael, too, as an emergently defined fictional character, was a gainer from the reassignment of comrades. At least he gained in the shore segment of the narrative, where Melville elaborated his relationship with Queequeg; however, in the already-written episodes of its sea segment that bring Queequeg and the narrator together Melville did not fully carry through the elaboration of their relationship.

The second (not to count Ishmael), and of course even greater, gainer by the reassignments was Ahab. Up to this decisive point Ahab had simply not existed at all as a character in either the shore or the sea segment of Melville's earlier narrative, but only in large fractions of the potential roles Melville had so far assigned to two other characters, Bulkington and Peleg. (You could say that these fractions of Bulkington and Peleg went into the initial making of Ahab.) From Bulkington, Ahab received the projected role of heroic truth-seeker, with its Gothic and Romantic penumbra of 'noble' traits and its inherent alienated, aggressive component. Possibly he was also given by revision some passages Melville had already written for Bulkington. Just possibly, too, Ahab's quest of the White Whale was to have been Bulkington's—I am not yet sure. From Peleg, on the other hand, Ahab received (purged of original comic overtones) the role of ungodly Quaker commanding captain of the whalebone-apparelled, Indian-named, vindictive *Pequod*; along with the whalebone leg (and whalebone stool?); probably the attendant old Gay-Head devil-associated Indian prophet who gets so duplicated as the narrative goes on; and (if it had indeed been Peleg's not Bulkington's) the hell-bound, devil-involved, vindictive quest of the particular whale who had taken off his fleshly leg, very likely the White Whale some call Moby Dick. So Ahab was, as Peleg aptly said, 'something like me—only there's a good deal more of him'.

The two losers by Melville's reassignments were Bulkington and Peleg. Bulkington's loss was in fact fatal: while in a spiritual sense you could say he 'became' the god-like Ahab in his apotheosis, in the quite literal sense he became only the vestigial description and eulogy which make clear Melville's original intention for his character before reassigning both his roles. One role, as Ishmael's comrade, went to Queequeg (but, as I've said, without its aggressive component). If, as seems likely, Bulkington was also projected to be a harpooneer, perhaps that role too was quite early transferred to Queequeg in the sea-narrative, where some significant passages suggest he was not originally conceived as one. The second loser was Peleg; he is quasi-vestigial, if not unnecessary, because Melville gave his original role as *Pequod*'s sea-commander to Ahab along with his whalebone appurtenances. Peleg lost to Ahab his whalebone leg (probably his fleshly one was lost, like the *Pequod*'s masts, 'off Japan', just as the no doubt well-informed old Gay-Head Indian said). And so he lost by transfer to Ahab the self-pitying epithet 'a poor pegging lubber'. Also, probably, along with 'that leg' and epithet Peleg lost one letter from his original name (I dare say it): Pegleg—too homely and comic a sailor soubriquet to

reassign to the lofty and tragic new captain, to whom Melville gave a Biblical name that 'the old squaw Tistig, at Gay-head', said 'would somehow
prove prophetic' (ch. 16). But even so Peleg as a duplicate retains vestiges
of all these; he is still 'Captain' Peleg, in half-command of the *Pequod* in
dock and in getting her to sea and ordering all hands about. It is still he
who did the whalebone carving-work for the ship; who was aboard her
(though as mate under Ahab, not captain himself) in that dismasting
typhoon off Japan; who has 'that leg' (now of restored flesh—possibly his
only gain!) with which he threatens and delivers kicks; and who, despite
now having both good legs, does his mildly comic 'roaring' (and perhaps
'hobbling'), 'clattering' about the decks, and profane swearing (including
the epithet 'thunder'); and who still has his prophet, Bildad, to tell him
he's hell-bound, and also his Indian-named ship *Pequod* and his 'wigwam'
as links to Indians, and is himself still a 'devil'.

There, in duplicate summary, is my major hypothesis. Now I pick up my
line of reasoning upon the compositional evidence that suggested and
supports it, with Bulkington's quietus. Melville carried out his Stage 3
decision to remove Bulkington from both of his roles simply by inserting
into the already-written sentence that makes him the narrator's 'shipmate'
(at Stage 2) the contradictory parenthesis '(though but a sleeping-partner
one, so far as this narrative is concerned)'. Did the metaphor suggest the
literal 'sleeping-partner' sequence that introduced his replacement? He
also at this time revised the first sea episode, where Bulkington appears
at the *Pequod*'s helm, and with a eulogy but no epitaph made that 'six-inch
chapter' his 'stoneless grave'. (And thereby too he made Bulkington the
first of the duplicate 'man-overboard' casualties who mark the wake of
Melville's compositional voyage.) Just why Melville kept these two vestiges
of Bulkington rather than discard him altogether one can only guess, and
I have now no guess to offer, beyond the humdrum one that Melville, like
lesser writers, found it hard to throw away good words he had written.

Bulkington is disposed of in chapter 23, and Ishmael opens chapter 24
saying, 'Queequeg and I are now fairly embarked in this business of whaling'. But no sooner is this said than—in the very same sentence—two
abrupt and linked shifts occur: in narrative voice and in presentation
of the Ishmael-Queequeg relationship. Not only does the voice of tyro
Ishmael give way to the (duplicate) voice of a veteran and sometimes
omniscient whaleman who is only putatively the same tyro Ishmael grown
older (several duplicate voices can be distinguished within that unsingle
voice, among them Herman Melville's own). Suddenly, also, the narrative
mode gives way to the argumentative and expository, and the presentation
no longer focuses closely on the experiences of tyro Ishmael and his
harpooneer-mentor and comrade Queequeg. From now on the tyro voice
is heard only intermittently, in sporadic episodes; and few episodes show
the pair engaged in either comradeship or pupil-teacher relationships.
Even in those episodes where both Ishmael and Queequeg are included
by name or inference they are usually not brought together in any personal interchange—they just don't seem to be aware of each other. Surely,
this abrupt double shift, of narrative voice and of presentational focus,
between the shore and sea segments of the book is fictionally the most
curious oddity among many in *Moby-Dick*. What is the explanation?

On the face of it, one might guess that Melville lost either his interest in the comradeship or his technical control of the materials. Another explanation is more circumstantially genetic. The few scholars who have theorized about the book's genesis have thought, as I do, that it is possible to distinguish various parts of the book as written earlier or later in the course of its composition, that its pages were not necessarily written, by any means, in the order in which they now stand. Whatever their more specific theories may be, however, these scholars have all thought that the shore-narrative, with the Ishmael-Queequeg comradeship, belongs to the earliest distinguishable writing stage. Nobody has seen a means of distinguishing stages within its development as regards Ishmael and Queequeg, as I have just done, though they have seen that anticipatory references to Ahab were inserted. Nor has anybody tried to explain the abrupt double shift between the two parts of the book by hypothesizing that some of the veteran-narrator passages and Ishmael-Queequeg passages in the sea segment were written before not after the relevant tyro-narrator passages in the shore segment, as I am now doing.

But the fact is that the truancy both of the tyro-narrator and of the close comrades (hard on the heels of Bulkington's disappearance) can most plausibly be explained this way. As for Queequeg, the infrequency and spareness of his involvement with Ishmael in the sea chapters means not that Melville lost interest in developing their comradeship, but that, by and large, those passages as they touch on the pair had already been written, before not after, those relevant passages in the shore chapters which include Queequeg and develop their comradeship in detail. Melville certainly made some appropriate revisions and numerous brief insertions in the earlier-written sea-narrative but did not carry through into it the detailed elaboration by which, as I have argued, he had incorporated Queequeg into the shore-narrative. What Melville lost, I venture, was not interest but 'Time, Strength, Cash, and Patience'—maybe heart, too—for continuing the job: near the end of it, in June 1851, he wrote Hawthorne, 'What's the use of elaborating what, in its very essence, is so short-lived as a modern book?'

When Melville imported cannibal Queequeg at Stage 3 into the shore segment of his narrative, he did not invent him at that point as a new character. For Queequeg, as I shall now argue, already had a place in the sea segment of the narrative, from an earlier stage, though not as the narrator's comrade. Examination of compositional details in three scenes involving Ishmael and Queequeg strongly supports this conclusion. The first is representative, the other two central to my argument.

The scene I've taken as 'representative', the mat-making passage in chapter 47, is the first in which Ishmael and Queequeg are brought together since just before the ship sailed, twenty-six chapters back, in chapter 21, where Ishmael expostulated with Queequeg for sitting on a sleeping rigger's 'face'. In the intervening chapters, Queequeg is 'there' in these ways: he is mentioned only once, misnamed by Peleg, in the departure scene, chapter 22; he and Ishmael are named together in the first sentence of chapter 24, and Queequeg is named once in a later paragraph but isn't there; Queequeg's selection as Starbuck's harpooneer is reported in two brief sentences of chapter 27; he's discrepantly grouped with the other barbaric har-

pooneers, but not named, in chapter 28; he's named, and shown eating in
the officers' cabin with the two other savage harpooneers in chapter 34, but
Ishmael isn't there, unless by implication he, 'like any mere sailor', can see
him through the cabin skylight; he's named casually once in chapter 35
when Ishmael says that he might 'have a chat with Queequeg, or any one
else off duty'; he's one of the three harpooneers in Ahab's quarter-deck ritual in chapter 36, where Ishmael is only inferentially present; he's missing
from the forecastle midnight roysterings (ch. 40), though the stage directions call for 'Harpooneers'; and he next is named in Ishmael's company in
the mat-making passage. This chapter sequence just summarized illustrates Melville's technique of introducing Queequeg's name, without really
building him into scenes, and they seem more likely to have been written
before than after the shore Ishmael-Queequeg scenes—otherwise there's
no reason Melville shouldn't more often have engaged Ishmael and Queequeg in them somehow. And so it goes through the rest of the book. I must
ask readers to check for themselves exactly how, in compositional terms,
Melville established Queequeg's existence, presence, actions, and only
occasionally his involvement with Ishmael.

   In the mat-making passage, Ishmael is acting as 'the attendant or page'
of Queequeg in weaving a sword-mat for 'our boat'. Perhaps this fits the
forecast tyro-mentor relationship well enough, though nothing is said of
Queequeg's teaching, or Ishmael's learning, anything—they are just doing
it, which suggests that Melville hadn't yet thought of their special mentor-
pupil relation when he wrote it. Moreover, no personal interaction of any
sort is worded; on the contrary, 'each silent sailor' acts on his own, Queequeg 'idly looking off upon the water', Ishmael weaving his own analogical thoughts. Queequeg is not personalized by so much as one word; in
fact only his name, given four times, and his usual epithet the 'savage'
(shared with the two other pagan harpooneers) attach him to the passage.
Another shipmate—say Bulkington—would do as well, which is to say the
passage can have been reassigned to Queequeg by changing these few
words from an earlier named or unnamed incumbent. I keep pointing out
how inorganically present Queequeg is all along, first to call attention
to Melville's relative lack of concern about him, in his special comrade-
mentor relation to Ishmael; second, to show the possibility that at a quite
early stage Melville wrote many such passages without any particular or
individualized characters in mind, and only later assigned names and did
more or less 'elaborating'. In the process he may have reassigned roles. I
entertain seriously the possibility that earlier Bulkington indeed occupied
some of Queequeg's present name slots, so to speak, and was a harpooneer, and I am considering the possibility that some of Ahab's may
have been reassigned from Bulkington. I am calling this mat-making passage 'representative' because what is true of its handling of Queequeg simply by name, with no individual detail, turns out, upon examination, to be
characteristic of many passages that stick in our minds as presenting the
two in a comradely relationship, which in fact nothing in the passage
really establishes. Again, I must ask readers to check for themselves.

   Two further Queequeg passages, however, are crucial to my argument
from compositional detail. On inspection significant details of their wording show pretty conclusively that Melville wrote them before not after he

wrote the shore-narrative chapters in which he developed their bosom-friendship.

The monkey-rope episode (ch. 72) is one of those frequent passages where Melville dramatizes his initially present-tense exposition of a whaling routine by attaching it to a particular occasion and to named characters of the *Pequod*'s voyage. Here, as often, the expository mode and purpose come foremost, and the named characters play their part in the scene primarily by virtue of their shipboard station and only secondarily in ways calling on their individual traits (so that Melville might easily have assigned the name of another character of the same station). Here, Queequeg, 'whose duty it was, as harponeer', was overboard upon the whale's back; Ishmael, 'being the savage's bowsman, that is, the person who pulled the bow-oar in his boat', had the duty of safeguarding his movements by means of the monkey-rope which was attached to both of them. The scene specifies no particular qualities of Queequeg. He is the 'savage' and repeatedly 'poor' Queequeg, like 'poor' Tashtego in the scene of his falling into the whale's head (ch. 78). His special relationship to Ishmael is specified by epithets at two points: the first reference is 'my particular friend Queequeg whose duty it was, as harpooneer . . .'; the second is 'my dear comrade and twin-brother, thought I'. A third reference is Ishmael's comment on Queequeg's Highland costume, a shirt and socks, ' . . . in which to my eyes, at least, he appeared to uncommon advantage . . .'. In the light of what follows, I argue that Melville later inserted 'my particular friend' and 'my dear comrade', perhaps as well the third reference quoted, and added the comic dramatic scene with Stubb at the end. The third reference does not necessarily presuppose the bosom-friendship, however, and may have been original in the passage. Nothing else in that scene of the chapter is written in a way that presumes or requires the pair to be comrades already. Indeed, the central monkey-rope metaphor, and the way Melville has Ishmael apply it, makes that prior-established bosom-friendship highly unlikely. Furthermore it suggests the likelihood that it was his writing of this scene and this metaphor that opened to Melville the possibility of making the pair bosom-friends in the shore sequence when he removed Bulkington from the comrade role. As Ishmael states his perilous monkey-rope attachment to Queequeg, he develops it into a metaphor: 'So that for better or for worse, we two, for the time, were wedded'. To me it is not conceivable that Melville could write 'for the time, we were wedded'—especially the phrase *'for the time'*—if he had already written the shore chapters in which he dramatized the bosom-friendship of Queequeg and Ishmael, starting off with Queequeg's declaration, 'Henceforth we were married'. 'Henceforth', not 'for the time'. Could Melville have forgotten he'd written—if in fact he had—the paragraph in which Ishmael and Queequeg are compared to 'man and wife', ending with the sentence, 'Thus, then, in our hearts' honeymoon, lay I and Queequeg—a cosy, loving pair'? (ch. 10). And the comic anticipatory marital imagery of chapter 4? And Ishmael's declaration, 'From that hour I clove to Queequeg like a barnacle'? (ch. 13). Nor is that all that's askew in this monkey-rope passage. It goes on from the 'wedded' metaphor to, 'So, then, an elongated Siamese ligature united us. Queequeg was my own inseparable twin brother', and twice repeats the twin figure. If this figure in itself is not incongruous enough with the 'wedded' image, surely its re-insistence that the mere monkey-rope was what tied the pair together, at this late point—weeks, and chapters, after their New Bedford union—thickens the unlikelihood that Melville had already provided that union. No, I must conclude, Melville had not yet written those earlier passages or yet conceived the bosom-friendship they establish.

My third Queequeg scene, on Queequeg in his coffin (ch. 110), is the most telling in its compositional betrayals. Most glaringly, though his bosom-friend is dying, Ishmael is not placed bodily on the scene at all, or even represented as having witnessed it. The focus is not once that of a first-person participating narrator. The pair's special relationship is signalled at only two points, one of eight words early in the chapter, one of a single word near its end. The first is in the single-sentence second paragraph that effects a transition between the expository first and third paragraphs about the process of breaking out leaky casks and Queequeg's catching a fever while performing his routine duties on them in the hold as a harpooneer. (The chapter thus has the same compositional structure, and I think genetic pattern, as 'The Monkey-Rope'.) The sentence reads: 'Now, at this time it was that my poor pagan companion, and fast bosom-friend, Queequeg, was seized with a fever, which brought him nigh to his endless end.' The double epithet and the pronoun 'my' that tie Queequeg to Ishmael here were patently inserted. The epithets' content is contradicted by the whole chapter's detached (though sentimental) omniscient presentation of the death scene. At the second point that ties the (elsewhere) 'cosy, loving pair' the tie is effected in the next-to-last paragraph, when the crisis has passed, by the single word 'my' in 'So, in good time my Queequeg gained strength'—again a patently inserted word. The sentence could do better without it, because 'my' makes an even more abrupt and gratuitous break in point-of-view than the first 'my' above. The absence of Ishmael from the side of his 'fast bosom-friend' is made still more glaring by further compositional details. We are told, 'Not a man of the crew but gave him up'. (Not even 'We all. . . .') Including Ishmael? Did *he* have feelings about it? Why not say so? Then Queequeg has some dying wishes. He wants someone to get him a coffin made. Does he call his 'fast bosom-friend'? No: 'He called one to him . . ., and taking his hand', made his first request—made it of some indefinite 'one'! And the request was transmitted not even by this indefinite 'one' but simply 'was made known aft' in agentless passive voice. When Queequeg is satisfied with his coffin, he tells an indefinite 'one', again, his second dying request—not Ishmael, who should be the only 'one' to rummage his bag on such an errand; no, he 'told one to go to his bag and bring out his little god, Yojo'. Throughout the chapter Queequeg is repeatedly called 'poor' Queequeg, 'savage', 'pagan', 'waning savage', etc., with no word of a more intimate feeling than pity and awe. Even a barnacle would feel more affection and cleave closer! The point of view shifts about (but is never first-person) from that of a disembodied third-person observer into several sentences of close focus on Queequeg's eyes and facial expression observed by a disembodied 'you' (four times), who 'sat by his side', and who fuses into an omniscient sententious authorial 'us' ('let us say'), and declares selfconsciously that 'only an author from the dead' could adequately tell Queequeg's expression. Well, Melville's handling of point-of-view is often wayward enough; but he could scarcely have handled it this way in Queequeg's dying scene had he already written the foregoing shore scenes that bound them as bosom-friends.

A further glaring inconsistency throughout chapter 110 directs me to a new area of genetic questions and possibilities, one which I've hinted in my hypothesis but which I can't do more than outline. It concerns Queequeg as harpooneer and the whole unexplored topic of the role of harpooneers in the book. As noted, Queequeg is a harpooneer in the chapter's third paragraph. In its middle he gets assistance (in a series of passive constructions, not from Ishmael) in stocking his coffin-canoe with his needs for his eternal voyage, including the iron part of his harpoon; and also at its end, 'poising a harpoon', he said he was fit for a fight. So he's a harpooneer at three spots. But the glaring discrepancy is that Melville has gone out of his way in 'The Specksynder' (ch. 33) to establish the social status of the harpooneer, entailing where he is quartered: 'The grand political maxim of the sea demands, that he should nominally live apart from the men before the mast, and be in some way distinguished as their professional superior; though always, by them, familiarly regarded as their social equal.' A grand distinction, he goes on, 'drawn between officer and man at sea, is this—the first lives aft, the last forward', and in most American whalers 'the harpooneers are lodged in the after part of the ship' and so 'take their meals in the captain's cabin, and sleep in a place indirectly communicating with it'. Why then, does Melville—who has properly shown him and the two other pagan harpooneers eating in the captain's cabin, in chapter 34—show the dying Queequeg, throughout chapter 110, quartered *forward, in the crew's forecastle*? The carpenter is twice said to go 'forward' to the forecastle about his coffin, and Starbuck looked 'down the scuttle' at Queequeg in his coffin. Oddly, it is one of the book's very few forecastle scenes, and dying in it is a harpooneer who belongs aft. (He's also—contrary to whaleship usage— in a hammock; but so are several others, including Ahab and Stubb.) Did Queequeg, at the time Melville wrote his dying scene (at least that layer of it) *belong* in the forecastle, because he was then a common sailor, not yet a harpooneer? This is only the first of many questions the book's compositional details arouse about its harpooneers. Why are there a number of misassignments of harpooneers to the wrong mates' boats? Did Melville nod, or are they vestigial? Why do so many chapters focus on the harpooneer and harpoon? Why did Melville describe his work in progress to his English publisher in late June 1850, as 'illustrated by the author's own personal experience, of two years & more, as a harpooneer'? (As to his own career it was a gross exaggeration; but perhaps this book was to be set up as if that were true.) Such questions suggest a genetic phase of *Moby-Dick* when Melville was projecting a book that would focus both its narrative line and its whaling activities on the harpooneers. And even, it could be, on a harpooneer hero—on Bulkington, whom he intended to be Ishmael's comrade at sea, before he substituted the harpooneer Queequeg. In the opening three paragraphs of 'The Specksynder' (ch. 33), Melville carefully established the harpooneer class of officers as intermediary between crewmen and officers; the harpooneer is in a sense both and thus provides a social bridge between them. Fictionally, in these three paragraphs Melville was preparing the way for some narrative situation that was to follow. But nothing does follow from it. The chapter in its fourth paragraph drops the har-pooneers altogether and with a shaky transition via the topic of officer-crew relations is soon discussing Ahab's relations with his crew, in highly exalted terms. Some ill-spliced genetic seam divides the chapter into two ill-matched parts. The Specksynder-harpooneer is displaced by the captain: perhaps Bulkington by Ahab? Its first part is the one passage (to which I referred some pages above) that I can now identify as one I think Melville wrote for Bulkington. My suspicion is that these opening paragraphs were setting up Bulkington, Ishmael's comrade-to-be, for a role which involved his harpooneer status between officers and men. If so, several inferences follow. If Bulkington as harpooneer was to be the book's heroic figure, Ish-mael as his comrade would have been personally close to the action and the main actor, whereas now he has no plausible close access to Ahab—one reason for the book's curious hiatus in point-of-view, and for the veteran-narrator's (putatively Ishmael's) reporting various matters he could know nothing about. As I've said, I think that Bulkington, in Melville's mind, out-grew his station, 'becoming', in his heroic role, Ahab. For if Bulkington was a heroic harpooneer, at what was his harpoon, in more than a routine whaleman's way, to be pointed? At the White Whale some call Moby Dick? Was that whale among the 'reminiscences that did not seem to give him much joy'? (ch. 3).

But here two trains of my present speculations collide. For my hypoth-esis, as summarized, points also to Captain Peleg as the duplicate who may have yielded to Ahab in that hell-bound devil-guided quest.

In conclusion, two of Captain Peleg's shore chapters require brief examination to show the compositional signs they betray—apart from what's on the face of matters I've already catalogued—for my notion that as a duplicate Peleg is the vestige of the *Pequod*'s original commanding captain, a large fraction of whom Melville reassigned to Ahab. I need not discuss the first, 'The Ship', (ch. 16) in detail. I think my summary of its duplicates reveals the pattern that suggests Captain Ahab was grafted into the chapter. (Other scholars, using other keys, are in consensus.) I sug-gest only that readers try the experiment of bracketing out all that refers to Ahab and then looking at the literal words left, to see their changed sig-nificance when taken to apply to Peleg: for example, Bildad's first answer to Ishmael's inquiry whether he's captain of the *Pequod*; and the way 'that leg' of Peleg's may have been whalebone; and how his remarks and 'hearty grief' originally could refer to his *own* (not Ahab's) loss of a leg to 'the monstrousest parmacetty that ever chipped a boat'; and so on.

With the hypothesis that Peleg was originally captain, and Ahab nonexis-tent, readers should continue the bracketing experiment with 'Merry Christmas' (ch. 22). To me its compositional oddities seem enough proof in themselves that at some earlier composition stage Peleg actually sailed on this voyage as the ship's captain. Ishmael would more justifiably fear 'such a devil' as *captain* than as 'pilot' (for Melville a one-word substitution there). Ahab's later supplanting Peleg would have called for only simple revisions in this earlier already-written episode. Ahab's 'hiding out' (as earlier and later)—now an effective device of suspense rationalized by his moody sick-ness—would be genetically explained by his then non-existence. The four brief direct references to him are local and dissect out neatly. The one indirect reference to Ahab (as an old shipmate of Bildad) would originally in fact have applied even better to Peleg ('in which an old shipmate sailed as captain; a man almost as old as he'), for nowhere else is it said that Bildad and Ahab were old shipmates—whereas Bildad and Peleg are so described in chapters 16 and 22. Peleg's part in the chapter is just what it would be, except for his farewells and leaving the ship at the end. The few revisional words tying Peleg to the stay-at-home role would be simple to insert ('with Peleg'; 'the two pilots'; etc.). Bracketing out the two words 'both dropt' from the passage where both Peleg and Bildad now go over into the pilot boat, leaves the context a perfect statement, as is the whole scene, of Bildad's being the only one who's to go ashore, while Peleg is to go with the ship. Most conclusively, the paragraph about the two captains' reactions at leaving-time is so written that it would make more sense (cutting out references to Peleg's going) if Bildad alone, not Peleg as well, were leaving. The first sentence joins them, but at once moves back, awkwardly, to Bildad alone and develops only his (not Peleg's) feelings: 'It was curious . . . how Peleg and Bildad were affected at this juncture, especially Captain Bildad'. Bildad acts for all the world as if he's giving Peleg a *goodbye* handshake and taking a last (for three years) long look at him by holding up the lantern: '. . . poor old Bildad lingered long; . . . convulsively grasped stout Peleg by the hand, and holding up a lantern, for a moment stood gazing heroically in his face. . . .' Why does he do that, if they are not separating? 'As for Peleg himself' [why 'himself'?], his less emotional behaviour fits that of the person going the voyage though 'there was a tear twinkling in his eye when the lantern came too near'. Apart from the easily adjustable farewells to the mates the rest of Peleg's words and actions fit perfectly the situation of his urging Bildad to stop talking and leave them: '"Come, come, Captain Bildad; stop palavering,—away!" and with that, Peleg hurried him over the side and [both dropt] into the boat'.

Remaining questions are large, my answers uncertain. As to Queequeg's place in the harpooneer mixups, I can only suspect that in his earliest appearances in Melville's sea-narrative he was not yet a harpooneer. Similar discrepancies suggest that Tashtego too may not have originally been a harpooneer. (For example, in the first paragraph of 'The Town-Ho's Story'—chapter 54—he's sleeping forward with the crew.) At some stage, perhaps, Melville conceived the schematic trio of pagan harpooneers and promoted Queequeg and Tashtego, already existing crewmen, into these roles. If so, perhaps it was from Bulkington that Queequeg took over his (you'd think inseparable) harpoon, along with the comrade role? Wasn't Tashtego, the wild Indian harpooneer, generated (by adding the possessive and the word 'senior' to the name 'Tashtego' in his epithet 'Tashtego's senior'?) from the 'old Gay-Head Indian' prophet, who thus became vestigial in his one appearance while the thus-created Tashtego took over his name and Indian-devil role as Ahab's (Peleg's?) original accompanying prophet and his original series of masthead prophetic assignments, a role to be duplicated by all those other prophets, notably Fedallah? More conjectures than I can now resolve.

Finally, if Peleg was to sail as the *Pequod*'s captain, what of Ahab? Simple: he didn't yet exist; he was invented later. Then conversely, with the invention of Ahab what was Melville to do with the original captain?

Drown him? (Perhaps; I mean, he could have worked him into the remarkable 'man overboard' series of duplicate deaths and near deaths that, like the so-called 'gams', punctuate the voyage.) Melville's actual solution was to demote and retire him. This solution had the advantage of not requiring Melville to throw away but only to adapt the lively chapters built around him and Bildad. Did the newly created 'grand, ungodly, god-like man', Captain Ahab—who had still further developments to undergo—take up his vengeful quest of the White Whale from this quasi-comic old Quaker 'devil' Captain Peleg, along with his ship—or from the truth-seeking Bulkington? I cannot now tell. And that is only the most pressing of my unanswered questions and loose ends.

IV

Maybe scholarly prudence should have kept me from offering with such apparent confidence this sketch of what I think was a crucial phase in the writing of *Moby-Dick*. Still, I am confident that the unnecessary duplicates do give us a new key to Melville's work on the book. I'm not committed to my hypothesis in detail, and likely enough before it is printed will have reformulated it in some ways. Its essentials, I think, don't conflict with those of the more comprehensive theories already offered by Leon Howard, George Stewart, Howard P. Vincent, James Barbour, and others, who have used different keys, and I believe it can be synthesized with theirs to improve our understanding. All of us must go on with our fumbling—with any combination of keys we can find—at what I've called the interlocked complications of the book's genesis.

Melville wrote a great book. In writing it he worked hard at the job, and during the year and a half his work went on he said so in various ways, both in his letters and in the book itself. Often he identified his writer's job with those of many common workmen, from cooks to ditchers. He introduced his carpenter with remarks I quoted at the beginning. As the carpenter, having made Ahab a duplicate ivory leg, is commanded in chapter 126 to rework the unnecessary coffin he made for Queequeg into its duplicate, the life-buoy that saves Ishmael, and grumbles over his job, isn't Melville describing and grumbling over his own reworking of *Moby-Dick*?

> Are all my pains to go for nothing with that coffin? And now I'm ordered to make a life-buoy of it. It's like turning an old coat; going to bring the flesh on the other side now. I don't like this cobbling sort of business—I don't like it at all; it's undignified; it's not my place. Let tinkers' brats do tinkerings; we are their betters. I like to take in hand none but clean, virgin, fair-and-square mathematical jobs, something that regularly begins at the beginning, and is at the middle when midway, and comes to an end at the conclusion; not a cobbler's job, that's at an end in the middle, and at the beginning at the end.[2]

2. *Note of acknowledgement*: Leon Howard, to whom this essay is offered in professional homage and affectionate friendship, initiated nearly forty years ago our scholarly study of the genesis of *Moby-Dick*, and he has done more than anyone else over the years to advance our understanding of it. George Stewart, Howard P. Vincent, and James Barbour, among others, have made distinguished contributions. In this undocumented essay, none of their works needed to be cited specifically, but I wrote it with their approaches, theories, and discoveries in mind and could not have developed the hypothesis I sketch here without them. I gratefully acknowledge my conscious and unconscious debts to them. Since my approach in the essay happens to be through close exami-

CAMILLE PAGLIA

[*Moby-Dick* as Sexual Protest]†

Moby-Dick rejects male sexual destiny, which Romanticism portrays as servitude to female power. Melville declares: I shall revive the chthonian but in masculine form. The novel subtly hermaphroditizes the great whale without genuinely diluting his masculinity. Moby-Dick steals his "uncommon magnitude" from mother nature. Like *Pym*, the book honors a subterranean or submarine deity, a mute, amoral counterconception to talkative, lawgiving Jehovah. The whale inhabits the primeval realm, from which he makes capricious epiphanies.

The novel's nonfiction sections, surveying the whale and its species, have two purposes. *Moby-Dick* aspires to epistemology, organizing the known, if only to dramatize what cannot be known. Melville plumbs and dissects his whale, measuring and naming each part. But his epic catalogs are *feignings of inclusiveness*. They give every name to the great whale but one: mother. The novel's cognitive data are fragments shored against male ruin. Again and again, Melville elevates the masculine principle above the feminine, driving back and limiting female power. This book, which takes the whiteness or blankness of nonmeaning as its premiere symbol and which is the first novel to acknowledge "the heartless voids and immensities of the universe," should logically take a depersonalized view of nature. But Melville's treatment of nature is amazingly inconsistent, full of the swerves of sexual anxiety.

Moby-Dick is a lavish portrait of rapacious Sadean nature, "the universal cannibalism of the sea" and the "horrible vulturism of earth." Melville rejects Christian and Wordsworthian tenderness: "We are all killers, on land and on sea." "Butchers we are" of "sharkish" will. Like Baudelaire, he challenges the hypocrite reader: "Go to the meat-market of a Saturday night and see the crowds of live bipeds staring up at the long rows of dead quadrupeds. . . . Cannibals? who is not a cannibal?" Humanism and liberalism are daytime masks. Night releases our animal appetites. One of the novel's supreme moments is its archetypal vision of the great squid:

---

nation of compositional peculiarities in the book, with little recourse to outside evidence, the approach used up to now chiefly by George Stewart, I am most immediately indebted to his work. My assumptions about Melville's compositional procedures draw confidence from my own close textual study of *Moby-Dick*, with Hershel Parker and G. Thomas Tanselle, and especially, with Merton M. Sealts, Jr, of his semi-final draft manuscript of *Billy Budd, Sailor*, where similar procedures are demonstrable. [Hayford's section 5 of the "Historical Note" in the Northwestern-Newberry *Moby-Dick* (648–59, documented partly in "Sources," 756–62), traces the history of scholarly speculation about the genesis of *Moby-Dick* referred to here and discusses as well the dissertation written under Leon Howard by James Barbour at the University of California at Los Angeles and Barbour's "The Composition of *Moby-Dick*," *American Literature* 47 (November 1975), 343–60. In *Writing the American Classics*, ed. James Barbour and Tom Quirk (Chapel Hill: University of North Carolina Press, 1990), Barbour's "'All My Books Are Botches': Melville's Struggle with *The Whale*" (25–52) distills his arguments and prints helpful graphics (such as a chart of chapters in *Moby-Dick* that can be dated more or less closely). However, Barbour's argument depends at points on biographical assumptions now known to be wrong, as when, following Leon Howard, he puts Melville in Boston, with immediate access to libraries, in December 1850. Editors' note.]

† From Camille Paglia, *Sexual Personae: Art and Decadence from Nefertiti to Emily Dickinson* (New Haven, CT: Yale University Press, 1990). Copyright 1990 by Yale University Press. We eschew footnotes, Paglia's and ours, in this freewheeling essay that has the rare virtue of seeing *Moby-Dick* in European (as well as American) perspective.

A vast pulpy mass, furlongs in length and breadth, of a glancing cream-color, lay floating on the water, innumerable long arms radiating from its centre, and curling and twisting like a nest of anacondas, as if blindly to clutch at any hapless object within reach. No perceptible face or front did it have; no conceivable token of either sensation or instinct; but undulated there on the billows, an unearthly, formless, chance-like apparition of life.

This is the snaky Medusa-head of nature, swampy and inert, a Burne-Jones thicket at sea. The squid is faceless, but is it sexless? We will see this "pulpy mass" again in Melville's story *The Paradise of Bachelors and The Tartarus of Maids*, where it represents woman's nonstop fertility.

The squid is what Melville will not let his whale become. It is the female grossness of matter, a sticky, viscous web. He later revises the squid into the magnificent loom of vegetable nature, humming in its lush South Seas "bower." Bowers, as bequeathed by Spenser through Milton to the Romantics, are the secret cells of female power. Melville does not simply drop the bower's traditional gender for a scientific inspection of nature's machinery, which would be understandable. He strenuously personalizes and resexualizes his bower in the opposite direction. The loom is run by a "weaver-god" called "he." This god is surprisingly like the Christian deity whom *Moby-Dick* is otherwise eager to belittle and defame. Melville cannot bear to leave his loom gender-neutral, despite its appropriateness to his coldly stringent cosmology. Why? He feels too strongly *the presence of female power* in his Romantic spectacle of seething greenery. The ultimate weaver of world mythology is woman, and the loom is her body. Here Melville follows Blake in refusing to concede female control over procreation.

I suspect the heart of *Moby-Dick* was generated by Melville's ambivalent reaction to Hawthorne's female-centered work. Running through the novel's bulky midsection is a chain of improvised sexual images reflecting, I theorize, a process of association from Melville's dream life. The weaver-god chapter is a sexual cancellation of an earlier chapter, "The Grand Armada," where a whaleboat is drawn into the eye of a whale herd moving in concentric circles. The boat rests in the "enchanted calm" of an "exceedingly transparent" lake. Far below float pregnant and nursing whales. At first disturbance, everything vanishes. The episode has been compared to the *Paradiso*, where rings of angels form a mystic rose of light. So this is Melville's chthonian substitute for the Christian sublime. But there are no ambivalences in Dante's vision. Midchapter, Melville compares the stillness to the "mute calm" amid "the tornadoed Atlantic of my being." Man's inner life is female, in the Romantic way. *Billy Budd* calls the heart "sometimes the feminine in man," like a "piteous woman" appealing to a judge for mercy. But at this unearthly moment in *Moby-Dick*, Melville's axiom is too calculated and sententious. As with Coleridge glossing his *Mariner*, the fearful and impersonal are rationalized and weakened. The first Grand Armada threatened America's motherland, ruled by a queen. Who or what is menaced by Melville's armada?

That the whaleboat is "becalmed" in the maternal lake should alert us. Everything else in *Moby-Dick* champions the driven and stormy over the quiet and sheltered, that "lee shore" with which Melville identifies the "treacherous, slavish" complacencies of society and religion. D. H. Lawrence says Melville's sea voyages were flights from "HOME and MOTHER": "The two things that were his damnation." The becalmed whale-boat is in a fallen, not a redeemed state. Masculine movement and action are paralyzed by straying too near a magnetic omphalos-spot. This contemplative bliss is experienced by men who have turned to stone. Through the glassy uterine waters, mother and child are seen united and in repose, but achingly across space and time, for their peaceful uncomplexity of relation belongs to infancy. Man can regain this paradise state only by shrinking to a captive minnow, a genie in a female bottle.

"The Grand Armada" is a spectacle of uncanny luminosity with hidden dangers. Melville adds a strange footnote, an afterthought betraying his ambivalences. He says of the breasts of female whales: "When by chance these precious parts in a nursing whale are cut by the hunter's lance, the mother's pouring milk and blood rivallingly discolor the sea for rods. The milk is very sweet and rich; it has been tasted by man; it might do well with strawberries." Welcome to one of Huysmans' grotesque banquets, Coleridge's milk of paradise served bloody rare. Melville sensualizes the blood and water of Christ's spear wound. Milk and blood aggressively compete with each other and with the stained sea. Mother and hunter are enemies. Archetypally, the hunter cuts her to escape from her. The attraction and repulsion and the sequence of images are Decadent. The vivid strawberries, which follow rather than more humanely precede the spilled blood, are fleshy mammaries or red corpuscles forcing the bittersweet brew of milk and blood into the reader's mouth. * * *

The chapters following "The Grand Armada" withdraw step by step from its already qualified vision of female origins. On the next page, we are asked to admire the vast size of the male whale, an "Ottoman" among smaller, "delicate," self-sacrificing "concubines." Twenty pages later comes the first mention of the male weaver, when a castaway loses his wits and sees "God's foot upon the treadle of the loom." Next page, the narrator Ishmael and his shipmates knead tubs of spermaceti: "Squeeze! squeeze! squeeze!" The men clasp hands in the goo and exchange sentimental looks. "Would that I could keep squeezing that sperm for ever! . . . In visions of the night, I saw long rows of angels in paradise, each with his hands in a jar of spermaceti." This is Melville's real heaven, an all-male platoon, each with his hand in someone else's pocket. The circle jerk is another Romantic uroboros. Melville's spermy male hands are a joyous dream-substitution for Hawthorne's "bloody hand" of female nature. Turn another page, and we are in *Moby-Dick*'s most totemic chapter, which focuses on the whale's penis, a "grandissimus" so heavy it takes three men to carry it. This "very strange, enigmatical object" or "unaccountable cone" is the "idol" of a male nature cult. Melville is practicing representational gigantism, the style I found in Michelangelo and Blake and defined as a defense against female power. To mince blubber, a sailor dons the whale's tough penis skin like a priest's cassock. This chapter is funny, but for the wrong reasons. Ithyphallos/ichthyphallos: Greek comedy's erections turn sodden and lugubrious in Melville. The whale has become a cartoon kingpin.

Thus by a series of linked passages, in which the female is minimized in size and temper and the male maximized in member and function, Melville in less than fifty pages inverts the maternal dominion of "The Grand Armada" into male control of the loom of vegetable nature. Mythologically, there never has been a purely masculine vegetation deity. Melville demotes the female to a lower order of being. I called *Moby-Dick*'s nature Sadean, but it is really Coleridgean. The great squid, for example, is a version of *The Ancient Mariner*'s undulating sea snakes. Melville wants Coleridge's nature without Coleridge's vampire queen, the Nightmare Life-in-Death. Hence he exaggerates his whale into the male "Titanism of power." He indulgently dwells on the whale's massive penis to give masculinity integrity and visibility in the female sea of dissolution that is "Queen Nature." He names Michelangelo as a fellow admirer of the "robustness" and "brawniness" of true divinity, which "the soft, curled, hermaphroditical Italian pictures" fail to show. Whenever he gives his whale some feminine trait, Melville immediately cancels it by a masculine afterthought—of violence or rape. Masculinity struggles for dominance throughout *Moby-Dick*. The great whale's "mighty mildness" is a homoerotic tenderness, part of the longing for comradeship that Melville shares with Whitman, Lawrence, and Forster.

Moby-Dick begins with a ritual of male bonding. Ishmael and Queequeg are tied by "matrimonial" language and bedroom embraces. The first chapters record the assembly and knitting together of men before they launch out onto nature's turbulent bosom. Even the ship is an androgyne, with "bearded" bows. The "ship's navel" is a gold doubloon, the badge of men not born of women or of men who have struck out their female origins. The first mate laments he must "sail with such a heathen crew that have small touch of human mothers in them." Woman enters *Moby-Dick* only as displaced chthonian force. Her sexual allure is never acknowledged, except in bawdy banter among three foreign sailors on watch. Woman's allure is diverted into "the pagan harpooneers," delegates of the races. Each bears some hermaphroditic sign: Tashtego and Fedallah have long hair; Daggoo wears gold ear hoops; Queequeg's body is adorned with tattoos that burn with "Satanic blue flames." Melville's Byronic harpooneers tower with imaginative authority. "Tawny features" set off by the "barbaric brilliancy" of their teeth, they are a lustrous coalescence of the ugly and the beautiful. The harpooneers are daemonic archangels, tanned by hellfire. I view their multiracialism as a sexual transposition. As Romantic sexual personae, silent, solitary, and proudly self-complete, they have stolen their dark glittering glamour from repressed woman.

Masculinity's quest for dominance in *Moby-Dick* is struggling against a major Romantic principle, impairment of the masculine. The novel ingeniously evades this rule by half-surrender. Its climax is the most devastating reversal of male will in Romanticism, as the ship, smashed by the whale, sinks in the infernal "vortex" of Poe's maelstrom. But only *human* masculinity suffers this crushing subordination, the penalty for its hubris of assertion. Its chastiser is not female nature but a brute male dominator, perfect in unintelligible force. The tax laid upon masculinity in *Moby-Dick* is evident in the burden of sexual symbolism borne by Captain Ahab, the Romantic outlaw. He stands upon the "dead stump" of an amputated leg, a sexual injury consistent with his one-night-stand marriage. His artificial leg nearly pierces his groin, leaving an incurable wound: he is thigh-torn Adonis, severed from mother nature by his "unsurrenderable wilfulness." A missing limb lingers as a "pricking" phantom memory. Therefore the harpoon Ahab darts at Moby-Dick is a phallic mental projection, born of frustrated desire. During his wildest speech, the harpoon lies "firmly lashed in its conspicuous crotch," a disturbingly suggestive phrase.

The scar running down Ahab's face and body is "a birth-mark," the mark of Cain. Ahab seems "made of solid bronze, . . . like Cellini's cast Perseus," that western paradigm. Bronze is the Apollonian strategy of a man hardening himself against nature. Ahab's scar is his birthmark because he has no navel. It is from his golden body that the ship's doubloon has been struck. He hails the pagan lightning as his divine sire and, like Athena, claims to know no mother. He usurps motherhood into his own overbearing will: "The queenly personality lives in me, and feels her royal rights." It is Actium, and transsexualized Ahab is Cleopatra defeated at sea.

Ahab commandeers ship and crew in his lust for unconditional freedom. But like liberal Romanticism itself, the worshipper of autonomy is under internal and external compulsion. Ahab is driven by a "hidden lord and master, and cruel, remorseless emperor": "I act under orders." Melville declares: "All men live enveloped in whale-lines. All are born with halters round their necks." This umbilical halter, the harpoon line that will strangle Ahab, is Aeschylus' "harness of Necessity." It is Clytemnestra's net, the femme fatale of nature symbolized in the writhing great squid. Earlier, Melville speaks of "that immaculate manliness we feel within ourselves" that remains "intact" through all disaster. The innermost self is a *virgo intacta* ravished by life's physical indignities. Immaculate manliness belongs to those untouched by the humiliating "bloody hand" of Hawthorne's female nature, which thrusts us into the world. Whipsawed between paradoxes, Melville forces his own sexual resolution on his Romantic materials. In *Moby-Dick*, his attempt to suppress the indebtedness of male to female has produced a stunning sadomasochistic spectacle of male subdued to male.

For perfect consistency, the great whale should be sexually neuter, its "appalling" whiteness an obliteration of person, gender, and meaning. But acrid, Late Romantic family romance intrudes upon a High Romantic epic of raw Dionysian energy. Why is *Moby-Dick* staggeringly greater than anything else Melville wrote? The novel's operatic gigantism comes from its force of *sexual protest*. Its storminess is a reaction against the paralyzing bliss of female stasis, glimpsed in "The Grand Armada." Man searching for the secrets of nature is like "an Ohio honey-hunter, who seeking honey in the crotch of a hollow tree, found such exceeding store of it, that leaning too far over, it sucked him in, so that he died embalmed." On the same page, Queequeg plays "obstetrics" in rescuing Tashtego from a sinking whale's head. The head is the prison of male intellect, says Melville, immediately revising his hollow tree into "Plato's honey head," in which so many have perished. But this head is another of Melville's inflated male members, a hoaxing subterfuge. The real honeyed crotch in which we all drown is the womb-tomb of mother nature.

JOHN WENKE

Ahab and "the Larger, Darker, Deeper Part"[†]

When Ishmael asks Captain Peleg the seemingly simple question— "Who is Captain Ahab?"—Melville presents the nexus between Ishmael as tyro actor and process narrator. In depicting the scene, Ishmael juxtaposes his past ignorance with what he now knows. While the tyro listens to Peleg's fascinating tale of Ahab's dismemberment, the narrator supplies two kinds of information: the testimony of a knowing, presumably authoritative source (Peleg); and the testimony of a presumably authoritative witness turned narrator (Ishmael). As Peleg tells his tale, the narrating voice interpolates a broad range of personal and cultural aspects that evoke, without limiting, the prodigious, if not fabulous, dimensions of Ahab's being. Ishmael seeks to dramatize not only the tyro's induction into Ahab's mystery but the degree to which the mystery itself poses a problem of aesthetic representation.

Well before "[r]eality outran apprehension" and Ahab stands on the *Pequod's* deck, Ishmael wrestles with the complexities of Ahab's language, origin, and identity (108). For example, "the stately dramatic thee and thou of the Quaker idiom" license Ishmael's attempt to compose a language commensurate with Ahab's stature (73). Along with "receiving all nature's sweet or savage impressions fresh from her own virgin, voluntary, and confiding breast," Ahab comes "to learn a bold and nervous lofty language." Counterpointing the tyro's ignorance is Ishmael's highly rhetorical portrait of Ahab as a unique man of tragic proportions: his "greatly superior natural force . . . [his] globular brain and . . . ponderous heart" complement his tendency "to think untraditionally and independently" (73). As process narrator, Ishmael admits to straying beyond the tyro's incremental experience: "But, as yet we have not to do with such an one, but with quite another" (74). It falls to Peleg to continue sketching Ahab's hyperbolic nature: "He's a grand, ungodly, god-like man . . . Ahab's above the common; Ahab's been in colleges, as well as 'mong the cannibals; been used to deeper wonders than the waves; fixed his fiery lance in mightier, stranger foes than whales. . . . he's Ahab, boy. . . . stricken, blasted, if he be, Ahab has his humanities" (78–79, Melville's emphasis).

With these disjunctive narrative modes, Ishmael is not flaunting convention so much as dramatizing how Ahab was a mysterious actor and is now a fictionalized character. During the voyage, Ahab remains distant and unapproachable. As a sailor, Ishmael never directly engages Ahab. In fact as far as Ahab is concerned, Ishmael is just another contemptible integer in "a mob of unnecessary duplicates" (356). After the *Pequod's* wreck, Ahab's actions and the related story remain as vestigial fragments amorphously retained within the sole survivor's memory. During the voyage, Ishmael was a marginal participant; now that he "only am escaped alone to tell thee" (427), he exists as a procreant voice. In telling the tale

† Reprinted from John Wenke, *Melville's Muse: Literary Creation and the Forms of Philosophical Fiction* (Kent, OH: Kent State University Press, 1995). Reprinted by permission of Kent State University Press.

and in casting the fragments in terms of incidents and exposition, Ishmael constructs the arena within which he not only explains himself but addresses the problem of Ahab's "hidden self" (157), whose perplexities can only be rendered as an inspired product of Ishmael's imagination. Here he translates his memories into words:

> But Ahab, my Captain, still moves before me in all his Nantucket grimness and shagginess; and in this episode touching Emperors and Kings, I must not conceal that I have only to do with a poor old whale-hunter like him; and, therefore, all outward majestical trappings and housings are denied me. Oh, Ahab! what shall be grand in thee, it must needs be plucked at from the skies, and dived for in the deep, and featured in the unbodied air! (127)

Similarly, in "The Ship" Ishmael authorizes himself through peremptory declamation: "For all men tragically great are made so through a certain morbidness. Be sure of this, O young ambition, all mortal greatness is but disease" (74). Such assertions reflect an ethos of self-assured interpretive power, and in fact Ishmael is fond of making grand syntheses. His pronouncements, however, must be recognized as hypothetical statements—propositions to be tested within the subsequent narrative. His apparently authoritative assertions coexist with contending attitudes on a continuum extending from utter ignorance, to informed speculation, to qualified knowledge. His story, therefore, conflates provisional and determinate formulations. Ishmael's life-experience authorizes his tale, but what issues from the narrative cannot be dissociated from his invention.

As seen in the Peleg episode, Ishmael's primary technique for exploiting narrative license is his use of the essayistic excursion. Ishmael's present-tense representations of Ahab tend to constitute inquiries into his "larger, darker, deeper part" (157). It is one thing to view Ahab as a monomaniac; it is quite another to examine his unidirectional madness in relation to the great complexity of his character. Taking pains to delineate the ontology of Ahab's madness, Ishmael does not find it "probable that this monomania . . . took its instant rise at the precise time of his bodily dismemberment" (156). Instead, Ahab was steeped in rage and sorrow; then "his torn body and gashed soul bled into one another; and so interfusing, made him mad" (156). Physical and spiritual domains converge to transform the captain. Though able to affect a "firm, collected front," Ahab still "in his hidden self, raved on." The nature of this "hidden self" looms among Ishmael's most vexing hermeneutical problems, for as Ishmael realizes, what he fathoms must be little more than a frustrating prelude to what cannot be fathomed. In the end, analytical activity inevitably leads to the exhaustion of analysis. To comprehend the implications of Ahab's "deepeningly contracted" madness—especially how his "great natural intellect" accelerates rather than diminishes his potency—would be a considerable achievement. But as Ishmael admits, it merely brings him to the threshold of a more daunting problem: "Ahab's larger, darker, deeper part remains unhinted" (157).

Ishmael satisfactorily contends with surface behavior, but the "root" of Ahab's "awful essence" is buried beneath multiple layers. By constructing images of excavation, Ishmael delves into the depths of Ahab's being. Ishmael's striking architectural image of the Hotel de Cluny inducts his "nobler, sadder" readers to the netherworld—the lowest layers—of personal and collective identity:

> Winding far down from within the very heart of this spiked Hotel de Cluny where we here stand—however grand and wonderful, now quit it;—and take your way, ye nobler, sadder souls, to those vast Roman halls of Thermes; where far beneath the fantastic towers of man's upper earth, his root of grandeur, his whole awful essence sits in bearded state; an antique buried beneath antiquities, and throned on torsoes! (157)

Ishmael describes Ahab's innermost recesses as a ruined effigy, a costumed figure, an image that encompasses individual and ancestral identities. In this "proud, sad king," Ishmael conflates time, paternity, the unconscious, and the mystery of origin. In plunging into such depths, he recognizes a "family likeness" (157), another allusion to Narcissus. Here the self is not reflected in Nature's pool but in a "grim sire," the inscrutable patriarch of time, a figure who will never yield "the old State-secret." Ahab's innermost self must remain closed. No inquirer can appropriate the secret of another's being; nor can one transcend the chronological fact of one's own exile from a putatively primal, unifying self. To mine buried depths is to find a shattered icon left by mocking gods: "So with a broken throne, the great gods mock that captive king; so like a Caryatid, he patient sits, upholding on his frozen brow the piled entablatures of ages" (157).

Ishmael's extended figure depicts the inevitable failure of one's quest for a fully explicable truth. It is "vain to popularize profundities," Ishmael exclaims, "and all truth is profound" (157). At the self's deepest layers, Ishmael discovers an insuperable ignorance of the unconscious self. The buried king personifies this ontological paradigm: it fuses personal and mythic contexts; it applies to self and other; it offers an approach to the rich lode buried as the unconscious; and it conceals what the ultimate "State-secret" might be (157). Characteristically, Ishmael's excursions exhaust what he thinks he can know in the act of defining—or suggesting—what he cannot. Neither motive nor being, thanks to the "subterranean miner that works in us all," are ultimately explicable: "[A]ll this to explain, would be to dive deeper than Ishmael can go" (158).

In the absence of full understanding, Ishmael fashions a dialectical model that dramatizes the elemental war racking Ahab. After pouring over maps to track the White Whale's migratory patterns, Ahab succumbs to "a weariness and faintness of pondering" (169). His "insufferable anguish" afflicts him in sleep:

> [A]nd when, as was sometimes the case, these spiritual throes in him heaved his being up from its base, and a chasm seemed opening in him, from which forked flames and lightnings shot up, and accursed fiends beckoned him to leap down among them; when this hell in himself yawned beneath him, a wild cry would be heard through the ship; and with glaring eyes Ahab would burst from his state room, as though escaping from a bed that was on fire. (169)

This lurid description reflects the intensity of Ahab's self-consumption. To enlarge his portrait Ishmael depicts Ahab's schizophrenia as a fierce dialectic. Describing two contending selves, Ishmael speaks of "the scheming, unappeasedly steadfast hunter" that struggles with

> the agent that so caused him to burst from [his bed] in horror again. The latter was the eternal, living principle or soul in him; and in sleep, being for the time dissociated from the characterizing mind, which at other times employed it for its outer vehicle or agent, it spontaneously sought escape from the scorching contiguity of the frantic thing, of which, for the time, it was no longer an integral. (169–70)

Within Ahab, where two beings vie for sovereignty, the "living principle" is no match for the "characterizing mind." His essential self falls hostage to the "frantic thing." The "characterizing mind" had an "unbidden and unfathered birth"—that is, it has no connection to organic human nature and instead possesses a "self-assumed, independent being of its own." Ahab's "intense thinking thus makes him a Prometheus; a vulture feeds upon that heart for ever; that vulture the very creature he creates" (170).

Ishmael also uses representational characters to reflect aspects of Ahab's ontology. On the *Pequod*, Fedallah and Pip embody projections of Ahab's innermost being—Fedallah as the demonic aspect of Ahab's "characterizing mind" and Pip as the mad, maimed, indigent sign and justification of Ahab's purpose. At one point, Fedallah and Ahab inhabit the same shadow: "And Ahab chanced so to stand, that the Parsee occupied his shadow; while, if the Parsee's shadow was there at all it seemed only to blend with, and lengthen Ahab's" (261). Later, Ishmael makes explicit their reciprocity: "At times, for longest hours, without a single hail, they stood far parted in the starlight; Ahab in his scuttle, the Parsee by the mainmast; but still fixedly gazing upon each other; as if in the Parsee Ahab saw his forethrown shadow, in Ahab the Parsee his abandoned substance" (401). Toward the conclusion of "The Symphony," after rejecting Starbuck's pleas to end the hunt, Ahab turns from his "human eye" and looks over the rail into the water (406). Here Ahab gazes into another version of Narcissus's pool and "started at two reflected, fixed eyes in the water there. Fedallah was motionlessly leaning over the same rail" (407). By accentuating how Ahab and Fedallah mirror one another, Ishmael completes the shadow/substance trope.

Ahab's affiliation with Pip, unlike Fedallah, might easily be seen as an expression of Ahab's "humanities," his capacity, as it were, for love and affection. But it must be recognized that their relationship is so marginal that it also reflects Ahab's alienation from society. Pip's experience as castaway fits him to be Ahab's counterpart. After his soul is "carried down alive to wondrous depths," Pip watches the "unwarped primal world" and witnesses "God's foot upon the treadle of the loom" (321–22). From Ahab's perspective, Pip's apparent madness, then, is really a case of perceptual transcendence. He sees through the masks of material causes to the origins of experience, to the activity of the "weaver God" working on the Loom of Time. Ahab sees Pip as "holiness" (391), a conduit of "most wondrous philosophies" (396). While Pip does indeed touch Ahab's "inmost centre" (392), their bond accentuates Ahab's isolation and cosmic rage. Pip impels Ahab more forcefully in his attempted usurpation of the god-realm. He rages at the "creative libertines" who did "beget this luckless child, and have abandoned him."

The gods reflect a final projection of Ahab's ontology. For Ahab, it is an ontological axiom that he participates in the grandeur of divine being. But unlike Fedallah and Pip, the gods are absent figures. They achieve presence only in the fevered tropes of Ahab's self-reflexive rhetoric. Indeed, Ahab remakes the gods in his own image. Through the "unfathered birth" of his "characterizing mind," Ahab locates himself on an equal plain with the immortals. Ahab's "heart-woes" imbue him with "archangelical grandeur," an asocial quality that he also projects on the gods (355). Ahab's "high mortal miseries" stamp him not only with the constricting burdens of the Fall, but with the very signature of the gods themselves. According to Ishmael, Ahab's excessive suffering becomes contorted into a self-proclaimed genealogical connection that goes all the way back to the primal nonexistence of time: "To trail the genealogies of these high mortal miseries, carries us at last among the sourceless primogenitures of the gods. . . . the gods themselves are not for ever glad. The ineffaceable, sad birth-mark in the brow of man, is but the stamp of sorrow in the signers." Ishmael imagines Ahab as reconstructing divine being through the hyperbolic range of his wrenched emotions. Ahab's affiliation with Fedallah, Pip, and the gods reflect his attempts to reject his "humanities"—his actual ontological condition—in favor of a self-ordained myth of Promethean vent.

Ahab's "characterizing mind"—the monomaniacal schemer hunting Moby Dick—shapes the terms of his self-dramatization, including the self-definitions manifest in his speech. Unlike Ishmael, with his expansive, flexible voice and sensibility, Ahab articulates a philosophical rhetoric of narrow definition. His speech and actions usually generate from unwavering principles. In believing that all evils "were visibly personified, and made practically assailable in Moby Dick" (156), Ahab reduces interpretation to a series of redactions and action to a linear, obsessive pursuit of resolution. The primary expression of this closed rhetorical system appears in "The Quarter-Deck," when Ahab engages in a manipulative philosophical dialogue. Through a series of questions and answers, Ahab inflames the crew, extracting their oaths of vengeance. Starbuck, however, resists. Recognizing that the first mate is impervious to his emotional appeals and therefore "requirest a little lower layer" (140), Ahab describes his intense desire for revenge and also explains his metaphysical justification.

Ahab is an inverted Platonist. Like any Platonist, Ahab sees the material world as a sign of invisible forms. Unlike a Platonist, he believes that malice animates the "pasteboard masks" of matter (140). Thus Ahab's pursuit of the White Whale is designed to defeat the "unknown but still reasoning thing" that expresses its nature from behind "the unreasoning mask." Ahab's fixed theory of reality is diametrically opposed to Ishmael's multiple formulations. Ahab declares:

> All visible objects, man, are but as pasteboard masks. But in each event—in the living act, the undoubted deed—there, some unknown but still reasoning thing puts forth the mouldings of its features from

behind the unreasoning mask. If man will strike, strike through the mask! How can the prisoner reach outside except by thrusting through the wall? To me, the white whale is that wall, shoved near to me. Sometimes I think there's naught beyond. But 'tis enough. He tasks me; he heaps me; I see in him outrageous strength, with an inscrutable malice sinewing it. That inscrutable thing is chiefly what I hate; and be the white whale agent, or be the white whale principal, I will wreak that hate upon him. (140)

This metaphysical construct justifies his Promethean self-image: "Talk not to me of blasphemy, man; I'd strike the sun if it insulted me. . . . Who's over me? Truth hath no confines." Ahab thus decrees his dispensation from contingency.

While Ahab's self-fashioned deific identity is the most self-empowering dimension of his tortured being, the validity of this god-self is assailed by his intermittent recognition of his "humanities." The perceptual gap between god-self and mortal self usually appears as a consequence of the crippling limitations of his body and, less frequently, of his experience of fellowship. His physical infirmities exacerbate his case against the gods, even while manifestly undermining his assertions of cosmic status. Continually, Ahab makes qualifications that dissociate his "proper and inaccessible being" from the maimed evidence of his corporeality (417).

The conflict between Ahab's god-self and his indigent self emerges not only in Ahab's various dialogues but also in his soliloquies and irruptive declamations. In the latter part of the "Sunset" chapter, for instance, Ahab soliloquizes on how the fixations of his will express an absolutistic purpose: "What I've dared, I've willed; and what I've willed, I'll do! . . . Naught's an obstacle, naught's an angle to the iron way!" (143). In the early part of this chapter, in "The Pipe," and "The Sphynx," Ahab speaks in soliloquy and offers his most indigent self-dramatization. At such times he reveals a rich, though repressed, sense of human affection and communal interdependence. In his address to the severed whale's head and his apostrophe to the dying whale, Ahab contends with inscrutable mysteries of creation. In both instances, he mourns the loss of sailors:

> Oh, thou dark Hindoo half of nature, who of drowned bones hast builded thy separate throne somewhere in the heart of these unverdured seas; thou art an infidel, thou queen, and too truly speakest to me in the wide-slaughtering Typhoon, and the hushed burial of its after calm . . . All thy unnamable imminglings float beneath me here; I am buoyed by breaths of once living things, exhaled as air, but water now. (376)

In these scenes, Ahab appears as a reflective, inquiring, pondering man momentarily loosed from the hell of his "characterizing mind." Eschewing the solipsism that is indigenous to the god-self, Ahab federates with the mothers of drowned sailors and feels empathy enlarged by grief (249).

Like his dialogues and his soliloquies, Ahab's declamations usually reflect his tendency toward self-dramatization and express the dialectic between his god-self and his corporeal self. After his whalebone leg is crushed, Ahab cries, "But even with a broken bone, old Ahab is untouched. . . . Nor white whale, nor man, nor fiend, can so much as graze old Ahab in his own proper and inaccessible being" (417). Despite the vicissitudes of experience, Ahab claims that his essential self remains inviolate. Here Ahab accepts as a given the ideal properties of his being. The anguish of his spirit derives from his rhetorical assessment of the disparity between the "unconquerable captain in the soul" and the pitiable evidence offered by his "craven mate. . . . [my] body" (417). Ahab laments the humiliation heaped on him by the phenomenal world. Ahab rejects any notion that Ishmael's "universal thump" (21) should be passed to him, and he curses social interdependence. His assertions of absolute existence, however, appear to be psychologically compensatory, as when he constructs ontological self-portraits that replace his maimed flesh with a transcendent soul: "Ye see an old man cut down to the stump; leaning on a shivered lance; propped up on a lonely foot. 'Tis Ahab—his body's part; but Ahab's soul's a centipede, that moves upon a hundred legs" (418).

Rhetorically, his declamations are addressed to no one in particular and thereby reinforce his self-willed isolation. At one point, disgusted with having to deal with the carpenter, Ahab apostrophizes, "Oh, Life! Here I am, proud as a Greek god, and yet standing debtor to this blockhead for a bone to stand on! Cursed be that mortal inter-indebtedness which will not do away with ledgers. I would be free as air; and I'm down in the whole world's books" (360). In one respect, Ahab's indigent aspect, which he narrowly and mistakenly associates with his body rather than his emotions, makes his quest self-defeating. To be in voice inevitably is to be in body; he can never be like the wind, bodiless as an object but not as an agent (420). In another respect Ahab's insistence on his soul's incorruptible essence establishes the point to which he proceeds. To vindicate this self-image, Ahab must perform his great action. He must, in body, fulfill the soul's mandate. To slay Moby Dick would be to eradicate "all evil," thus altering the fundamental terms of human existence by imposing the dictates of his own soul on the malign forces that control the phenomenal domain.

Ahab's preeminent declamatory speech occurs in "The Candles." With the "corpusants" (381) flaring atop the masts, Ahab articulates his sense of theology ("right worship is defiance"), cosmology and ontology ("In the midst of the personified impersonal, a personality stands here"), and genealogy ("But thou are but my fiery father; my sweet mother, I know not") (382, 383). While depicting himself as orphaned, Ahab nevertheless claims a knowable origin by naming his father. In doing so, Ahab becomes superior to the "unbegun" deific principle: "I know that of me, which thou knowest not of thyself. . . . Oh, thou foundling fire . . . thou too hast thy incommunicable riddle, thy unparticipated grief. Here again, with haughty agony, I read my sire" (383). Rejecting a biological patriarchy for a cosmic one, Ahab thus diverts filial obligation into defiant, hateful imperatives.

If in "The Candles" Ahab asserts his cosmic identity, then in "The Symphony" he questions his most basic knowledge of the self. In this remarkable chapter, Ahab's dialogue with Starbuck (with its attending communalism) gives way to soliloquy (with its attending solipsism). Ishmael dramatizes Ahab's shift from the human interdependence imaged by Starbuck to the stark alienation expressed by Fedallah's diabolical gaze. When Ahab wonders, "Is Ahab, Ahab," he is considering the question of agency. Already he has rejected Starbuck's overtures to return home. Now he revolves the chill implications of why he—or some extrinsic force—drives himself so. Though the question is now moot, he continues to examine the schizoid split between the "inscrutable, unearthly" demands of the god-self and the "natural lovings and longings" (406) associated with his "humanities" (79). Now, however, Ahab does not depict himself as equal to the gods. He perceives the gods not (as they hitherto have been) as immanent beings but as mechanical forces outside the self. He questions, in effect, the stability of his identity, the very efficacy of his hitherto deified volition: "Is Ahab, Ahab? Is it I, God, or who that lifts this arm?"[1] He rejects absolute freedom in favor of a mechanistic analogy: "By heaven, man, we are turned round and round in this world, like yonder windlass, and Fate is the handspike" (407). The province of Fate absolves Ahab from having to think seriously of Starbuck's tempting scenario. Instead, he translates his self-generated constructs into a predetermined force that controls human agency. Ahab's most unsettling moment of ontological uncertainty culminates in his most rigid act of self-definition. Paradoxically, Ahab's rhetorical repudiation of self-propelled agency derives from his own volition. Ahab translates, as it were, his own desires into a script of cosmic determinism in which Fate inevitably manifests his most encompassing (and self-restricting) fiction. As Ahab earlier says, "For with little external to constrain us, the innermost necessities in our being, these still drive us on" (141).

Ishmael's celebration of a shared human condition and Ahab's attempt to dissociate himself from such federation comprise *Moby-Dick*'s informing ontological drama. Both characters pursue elemental questions of being, agency, and teleology; they attempt to understand one's essential identity as reflected in the passage from origin to ending. Ishmael presents his ontological concerns by focusing on rhetoric and behavior. To him, being achieves expression through language and action. It may seem that Melville polarizes the voices of Ishmael and Ahab, as he does with *Mardi*'s genialist and solipsistic voices. Crucially, though, Ahab's "humanities" complicate his pursuit of self-deification, his desire to stand on equal terms with the gods. Significantly, the voices and identities of Ishmael and Ahab are not polarized. There are times when Ishmael speaks in the voice of Ahab and Ahab in the voice of Ishmael. Ishmael's admission, "Ahab's quenchless feud seemed mine," points to an underlying affinity between them (152). Indeed, in identifying the demonic quest as an integral element of collective human experience, Ishmael describes the "demon phantom that, some time or other, swims before all human hearts" (196). This cosmic lure, though promising transcendence, leads to frustration or destruction: "while chasing such over this round globe, they either lead us on in barren mazes or midway leave us whelmed." The philosophical quester either embarks on the

1. For an illuminating discussion of the suggested reading, "Is it Ahab, Ahab?" see *Moby-Dick* (Northwestern-Newberry), 903.

endless search of Babbalanja or Bulkington or achieves the "utter wreck" (*Mardi* 557) of Taji or Ahab.

Ishmael's access to Ahab's inner life depends on his capacity to use imagination and extend himself into another psyche. When Ishmael claims, for example, "There is a wisdom that is woe; but there is a woe that is madness," he is suggesting that a continuum might well carry one from wisdom to woe to madness; in fact, the three states manifest degrees of a single complex (328). Whereas Pip's passage to madness is a one-way transit, Ishmael and Ahab seem able to move in either direction, though each reflects a primary emphasis: Ishmael's wisdom that is woe, and Ahab's wisdom that is woe becoming madness. In "The Try-Works," Ishmael's admission that he gave himself up to "fire" reflects his felt affinity with Ahab's absolutism (328). On occasion, Ishmael even has aspirations to cosmic status. At the conclusion of Chapter 57 he conflates the figures of Perseus destroying the whale and Prometheus assaulting the heavens, thereby casting himself in terms of titanic action. This hyperbolic act of self-fashioning echoes Taji's rhetoric in "Dreams": "With a frigate's anchors for my bridle-bitts and fasces of harpoons for spurs, would I could mount that whale [the constellation Cetus] and leap the topmost skies, to see whether the fabled heavens with all their countless tents really lie encamped beyond my mortal sight!" (223).[2] Similarly, Ahab at times expresses the inquisitive qualities of Ishmael's voice. When confronted with the possibility that the coffin life buoy might symbolize an "immortality-preserver," Ahab propounds a series of open-ended questions: "Here now's the very dreaded symbol of grim death, by a mere hap, made the expressive sign of the help and hope of most endangered life. A life-buoy of a coffin! Does it go further? Can it be that in some spiritual sense the coffin is, after all, but an immortality-preserver! I'll think of that" (396). Ahab's speculation comes to a curt ending: "But no. So far gone am I in the dark side of earth, that its other side, the theoretic bright one, seems but uncertain twilight to me." Ishmaelean speculation gives way to the rhetoric of narrow definition. By aligning himself with darkness, Ahab negates the potentially curative engagement with multiple values and perspectives.

The rhetorical and ontological symbiosis of Ishmael and Ahab has its culminating, and most teasing, manifestation in the important textual crux in "The Gilder." The chapter's long speech beginning "Oh, grassy glades! oh, ever vernal endless landscapes in the soul" might belong either to Ishmael or Ahab (373). Prior to the 1989 Northwestern-Newberry edition of *Moby-Dick*, Melvillian scholars treated this address as Ishmael's. In no edition prior to Northwestern-Newberry do quotation marks bracket the long paragraph, though this reading was considered but rejected in the 1967 Norton Critical Edition (494). In "Discussions of Adopted Readings," the Northwestern-Newberry editors contend, "The structure of the chapter conclusively shows that the paragraph should be spoken by Ahab, for the chapter moves from Ishmael's definition of the effect of 'times of dreamy quietude' (491.13) in the Pacific upon a rover like himself, to the

---

2. For Merton M. Sealts's discussion of this passage and its implications regarding philosophical skepticism see his "Melville and the Platonic Tradition" in *Pursuing Melville 1940–1980* (Madison: University of Wisconsin Press, 1982), 278–336.

effect of such scenes upon Ahab, upon Starbuck, and finally upon Stubb" (901). "The Gilder" chapter dramatizes an unfolding scenic tableau structurally parallel to the speeches in "The Doubloon." The Northwestern-Newberry editors suggest that Melville had not "visualized the scene" fully, but it is also possible that either Melville accidentally left out the quotation marks, in which case the speech reflects Ahab's "temporary" refuge (373), or Melville intended the speech to be Ishmael's response to the fact that "such soothing scenes" had only a temporary effect on Ahab. The speech sounds like Ishmael, especially with the images of the Loom of Time: "But the mingled, mingling threads of life are woven by warp and woof: calms crossed by storms, a storm for every calm." Ishmael also seems to be evoked through the depiction of life as repetitive process: "There is no steady unretracing progress in this life; we do not advance through fixed gradations, and at the last one pause. . . . But once gone through, we trace the round again; and are infants, boys, and men, and Ifs eternally." But whereas the content of the speech favors Ishmael, the dramatic context favors Ahab. The chapter unfolds as a series of speeches with the longest one seeming to belong to Ahab, the narrative's most dramatically resonant actor.

The crux of the speech emphasizes a conflation of rhetorical and ontological aspects evident elsewhere in the text. Certainly, the speech addresses the ontological mystery of both Ishmael and Ahab, if not the human collective. The speaker offers a probing meditation on psychological flux and how lost origin predetermines the inscrutability of one's ending. In wondering about the "final harbor, whence we unmoor no more," the speaker images the soul as an orphan, a foundling in search of what only another world can supply: "Where is the foundling's father hidden? Our souls are like those orphans whose unwedded mothers die in bearing them: the secret of our paternity lies in their grave, and we must there to learn it" (373). Whether Ishmael or Ahab (or, given the possibility that Ishmael elides into Ahab in the compositional moment, both characters at once), the speaker here ponders the mystery of human dispossession, linking the mind's wavering motion with the complexities of lost origin, uncertain identity, and teleological suspension. Paternity inscribes one's place in time and society. Without this patriarchy, one is limited to the implications of a name—an Ishmael or an Ahab—and the unfolding tendency of one's being as expressed through language and behavior. The prospective ending, in its potential for revelation, looms as an unreadable future. Significantly, the soul—the absolute and unknowable essence—remains outside the time-space of genealogy and constitutes a word-sign of teasing, alluring nondefinition.

Biographical Cross-Light

HERSHEL PARKER

Damned by Dollars: *Moby-Dick* and the Price of Genius†

One of Melville's younger granddaughters told her children that the price of genius was too high for a family to pay. My topic is the price of genius, the price of beauty—what it cost Melville and his family for him to give us *Moby Dick*.

In early May 1851, when he had finished almost all of *Moby-Dick* except the concluding chapters and late insertions, Melville wrote Hawthorne about "the silent grass-growing mood in which a man *ought* always to compose," a mood that could seldom be his: "Dollars damn me; and the malicious Devil is forever grinning in upon me, holding the door ajar." Critics have tended to take these words as a playful commentary on the strains of authorship: the printer's devil, the boy who runs with copy from author to compositor, is always there, peering in, needing more pages to carry to the print shop; the harassed author never has enough time quite to perfect his prose before surrendering it to the printer.

Melville went on to say that because dollars damned him, because he was so rushed, "the product is a final hash," and all his books were botches. We have not taken Melville's own judgment seriously, partly because for a long time, after the Melville revival in the decade after 1919, the centenary of his birth, we have seen him as a great writer and *Moby-Dick* as a great book, not a botch. *Moby-Dick* was seldom taught in colleges before 1950. Indeed, there were very few professors of American Literature until a few years after the War, when for the first time American Literature programs or departments became common. Before that, in the 1920s and 1930s, most teachers who loved *Moby-Dick* had to wait twenty or thirty years to teach it, as the late American scholar Robert Spiller told me ruefully. The wide teaching of *Moby-Dick* in colleges coincided with the triumph of a theory of literature, the New Criticism, which dictated a method of classroom teaching appropriate to a period when new colleges were being founded to accommodate the returning GIs, colleges that of necessity had to start their libraries from scratch, competing

† Previously unpublished; here printed with permission of the author, this piece was delivered at the Old Dartmouth Historical Society New Bedford Whaling Museum at Johnny Cake Hill (across from the Seamen's Bethel) as the Samuel D. Rusitzky Lecture on June 26, 1997. An extremely condensed account of the grim effects of *Moby-Dick* on Melville's subsequent career, it draws on the last eight chapters of Parker's *Herman Melville: A Biography*, vol. 1, and on research reported throughout vol. 2. For an account of a previously unknown book by Melville, see Hershel Parker, "Herman Melville's *The Isle of the Cross*: A Survey and a Chronology," *American Literature* 62 (March 1990): 1–16.

with many other new colleges doing the same thing. Old books and news-paper files were hard to get, useful manuscript collections all but unob-tainable. It was a good thing that the new teachers of *Moby-Dick* were committed, by their theory, to ignore biographical evidence as irrelevant to criticism, and were committed to seeing any poem or novel as a perfect work of art, not as a botch. It made the life of a teacher simple. Even works which any commonsensical reader would regard as utterly un-uni-fied—such as Melville's *Pierre*—could be celebrated cleverly by articles entitled "The Unity of *Pierre*." Far more intensely did critics celebrate the unity of *Moby-Dick*. They did so, decade after decade, by resolutely ignor-ing Melville's own words, and by ignoring some obvious anomalies in the text such as the momentous introduction and sudden removal of Bulk-ington. Of course, *Moby-Dick* was a masterpiece, not a botch. Of course, dollars had not damned Melville: within three decades after his death, he had ascended into the highest literary realms, compared not to J. Ross Browne the American whaler but to Sir Thomas Browne, the Restoration physician and moralist, compared not to William Scoresby the whaling authority but to William Shakespeare. This literary approach which ignored biographical facts is still dominant in the study of American Lit-erature, however disguised over the last decades as phenomenology, as structuralism, as deconstructionism, as the New Historicism. Here I use forbidden evidence, biographical evidence, in looking at Melville's gamble that he could write a great book which would be immensely popular, and at the human consequences of that gamble.

Melville's career began with the popular semi-autobiographical *Typee* (London: John Murray; New York: Wiley & Putnam, 1846), an account of his brief stay with natives in the Marquesas, and was consolidated by *Omoo* (London: John Murray; New York, Harper & Brothers, 1847), a semi-autobiographical account of his experiences on his second whale ship and in the islands of Tahiti and Eimeo. During most of this time, he was living with his mother and four sisters in a rented house in Lansing-burgh, New York, now part of Troy, across the river from Albany. With his attacks on the missionaries in his first book, he aligned the religious right against him, and for the rest of his active career he was hounded by what we would see as right wing Christians. He may not have bought any source books for *Typee*, but once he found he could run up a tab at the Wiley & Putnam and then at the Harpers bookstore, he began buying books that he needed if he were to write books, eating up his profits in advance. On the strength of the popularity of *Omoo* Elizabeth Shaw and her father Lemuel Shaw, the chief justice of the Massachusetts Supreme Court, decided that their eleven-month engagement could be followed, in August 1847, by marriage.

Herman Melville did not have enough money to get married. His father-in-law set him up in New York City, advancing him $2,000, a thou-sand of which went as down payment on a twenty-one year indenture of lease on a house on Fourth Avenue priced at $6,000. That left a thousand dollars of Shaw's money for Melville to use in moving himself, his bride, his mother, and his four sisters from Lansingburgh to Manhattan, setting up housekeeping there, and living on until it ran out. His lawyer brother Allan and his own bride, Sophia, from a wealthy Bond Street family, moved in at the same time, and by 1850 there were four live-in servants. Allan may have contributed to payments listed in the indenture as "rent," or may have made mortgage payments, and may have contributed to household expenses in other ways. We do not know the details, but there were mortgage payments to make on the $5,000 as well as the "rent," whatever that was. Now, no one has done a good job with equivalents, even the U.S. government with its inflation charts, which would suggest that $2,000 in 1847 would equal $50-some thousand. But in terms of comparable New York City property values, $2,000 in 1847 would buy something roughly like $2,000,000 now: you have to multiply not by twenty-five or thirty but by a thousand. Everyone acknowledges that a million dollars is not what it used to be, and $2,000 now certainly isn't anything like what it used to be. This was very serious money—two or three years' income for an average urban family, perhaps.

Melville had made a start on his third book, *Mardi*, before his marriage, and after the marriage and the move to New York he admitted that he was eating up his profits by buying books and began systematically borrowing books instead, whenever he could restrain himself, but he gave himself permission to take more than a year and a half in writing that book, the first in which he dared to be ambitious of literary greatness. The Melvilles' first child, Malcolm, was born early in 1849, shortly before *Mardi* (London: Richard Bentley; New York, Harper, 1849), was published and attacked—having already lost Melville his first English publisher, who read it and rejected it. Melville abandoned his hopes to turn at once to another ambitious book and wrote a book designed to be popular, *Redburn* (London, Bentley; New York, Harper, 1849), and then immediately wrote another one, *White-Jacket* (again Bentley and the Harpers, 1850). Hurt by a new London ruling that held that Americans could not obtain copyright in Great Britain, Melville managed to sell *White-Jacket* in England only because he went there and charmed Bentley into taking a chance on it, although several other publishers had rejected it outright. Melville did not get enough from Bentley for *White-Jacket* for him to fulfill his most intense desire. His heart was set on a Wanderjahr, a footloose exploration of Italy, the Holy Land—the grand tour, made utterly responsible, for a thirty-year-old husband and father, by the fact that he would be gathering material for new books. On the especially long voyage home, in January 1850, frustrated, ambivalent, aspiring, he began planning a book that would be popular as well as ambitious—a book about whaling.

He worked hard on it. After three months of work, he described it to the younger Richard Henry Dana as half done—not unrealistic, because the previous summer he had written *Redburn* in two months then had written *White-Jacket* in the next two months. His first break, a short one, seems to have been an excursion to West Point. He was at the point at which he needed some basic books about whales as well as books about whaling, and he had to wait for an important one: Putnam had to order Thomas Beale's *Natural History of the Sperm Whale* (1839) from England. By the time it arrived, on July 10, 1850, Melville needed more of a vacation. Melville's visit to the old Melvill house south of Pittsfield in 1850 began *merely* as a vacation, although he had the manuscript there, and for at least a few days in the second half of August he worked on it there, at his late uncle's farm, which his aunt and cousins had just sold, although they would retain possession for some months. They had sold the great old house, in need of repairs—moldering, but a mansion—and the land (250 acres) for $6,500. Melville had not known it was for sale. Once he found that he had just missed the chance to buy the farm (one of his cousins in 1848 had called the farm his "first love"), he was filled with an absolutely unreasonable jealousy. Once he had made friends with Nathaniel Hawthorne, who for several months had been living outside nearby Lenox, he knew that if he were to do justice to his book he had to live in Berkshires, starting immediately. Melville's behavior makes some sense if you calculate the power of the Berkshires in his memory, when he had visited his uncle Thomas Melvill, when he had worked the farm one summer, then had boarded there during his rural schoolteaching. His behavior makes some emotional sense if you take account of his disillusion with the endless petty sniping of the New York literati, and his fascination with the possibility of finishing his book with Mount Greylock in view to the north and his new friend Nathaniel Hawthorne a few miles away to the south. If he remained in Manhattan, he could not make the book as good as it could be. Besides, he had been amazingly responsible several months before: he had cut short his stay in London just as he was meeting marvelous literary men and artists, and he had sacrificed the year-long Grand Tour that would have proved of such high economic benefit to his family, in the long run. Now the most important thing in his life was that he make the whole book as great as he thought the part he had written was.

Melville was not being rational, but he was persuasive. His father-in-law, who had already advanced him $2,000 in 1847, advanced him $3,000 more toward the purchase of Dr. John Brewster's farm adjoining the old Melvill property. For a total of $6,500—exactly the price of the Melvill farm—he bought a much smaller farm (160 acres) and a decrepit old farmhouse—a house that had never been grand, as his uncle's had been and would be again. This might seem barely rational of Shaw. But for his money Shaw got the assurance that as long as he paid his annual September visit to hold court in Lenox he could see his daughter and her family in Pittsfield, and during the rest of the year she would be only a direct ride away on the new railroad, right across Massachusetts.

In mid-September 1850 Melville probably turned over to Brewster the $3,000 that Shaw had just advanced him. He arranged at the same time that Brewster would hold a mortgage of $1,500 on the property. That leaves a discrepancy of $2,000. The best I can figure it, Brewster agreed, verbally, to wait a while for the $2,000, say a month or two, until the indenture of lease on the highly desirable Fourth Avenue house could be sold at a tidy profit and Melville could turn over $2,000 of the proceeds to him. When Melville returned to New York, T. D. Stewart (a friend from Lansingburgh) offered to loan him whatever he needed to tide him over, but Melville refused: he would not need the loan. In October 1850 Melville and his wife along with his mother and three of his sisters moved to the farm, which he promptly named Arrowhead, leaving his brother Allan and *his* wife and two children, one a new baby, at Fourth Avenue, along with one Melville sister, but preparing to move out within a few weeks; perhaps Allan had already purchased his new house on Thirty-First Street. By Christmas the Fourth Avenue house was empty, but unsold. In January 1851 Allan talked about buying it himself, because he and his wife were unhappy being so far out of town (Thirty-First Street was remote from everything), but that proved to be just talk. Meantime, Melville had not gotten settled in a writing room until well into November, and then he had to be dispossessed for the family Thanksgiving (including the aunt and cousins) to be held there, because there was no room on the first floor big enough for the tables. His wife was not there— she had taken the baby and fled the chaos to have a real Thanksgiving (which you could have only in Boston), and did not return until New Year's Day 1851. The older sister also fled, hurt as she left by Herman's irritation at having to drive her to the station during his writing hours, and his mother and two remaining sisters spent December in frustration, imprisoned: he would not trust them to drive the horse and he hated taking time off from writing to drive them where they wanted to go and wait for them. In January, he was so desperate for concentrated writing time that he suddenly let them test-drive Charlie and thereafter trusted them to go where they wanted.

The discomforts and inadequacies of the farmhouse became more apparent all the time, and by the end of February 1851, it was clear that the cooking facilities were too primitive for the cook (they must have had a cook already, as they always did), the outdoor well was inconvenient, they needed an inside kitchen pump, the parlor walls were soiled, some of the upholstered furniture looked worse after the move, certain rooms needed painting, and the barn in particular required painting. In the dead of winter, Melville hired men to start the renovations—maybe before the first of March. The first order of business was utterly impractical—digging foundations in the still-frozen ground, and not just for a kitchen and a wood house but also for a narrow piazza on the cold north side of the house, a piazza too small for a whole family to use. It would be Herman's vantage point for viewing Greylock from the first floor, just below his small window for viewing it in his writing room before starting his day's task.

In March the lease on the house in town was sold, the buyer paying $7,000, of which $5,000 went to the mortgage, which had remained at that figure. That left $2,000 for Melville, minus any rents or other fees that he may have owed. If he were behind in payments on the mortgage, then that amount would have come out of the $2,000. In any case, as he admitted five years later, the sum received had fallen "short of the amount expected to have been realized." Instead of having $2,000 to turn over to Dr. Brewster, six months late, perhaps with no interest being charged on it, he had somewhat less than $2,000, and he had workmen to pay as well as Dr. Brewster. He would need more money, just to pay Dr. Brewster the remainder of the purchase money, not counting the $1,500 mortgage. In March Melville began thinking of taking Mr. Stewart up on his generous offer to help a friend in need, but as a last resort. First, on April 25, Melville wrote to Fletcher Harper asking for an advance on his whaling manuscript. A clerk at the Harpers brought Melville's account up to date on April 29, and on April 30 the Harpers sent their refusal, citing their "extensive and expensive addition" to their plant and pointing out that Melville was already in debt to them for "nearly seven hundred dollars." At once, on May 1, Melville borrowed $2,050 from Stewart, for five years, at 9 percent interest. Some of the money, maybe a good deal of it, went to make up the $2,000 Melville had to pay Dr. Brewster, some of it went for the workmen at Arrowhead, some of it Melville earmarked to pay a compositor in New York City, for in his anger at the Harpers he decided to pay for the setting and plating of the book himself in the hope of selling the plates to another publisher for a better deal than the Harpers would give him. In early May, not later, as we had thought, Melville carried the bulk of the manuscript to town and left it with Robert Craighead, the man who had stereotyped *Typee* for Wiley & Putnam. *Moby-Dick* had to be a great financial success, and there was some hope that it would be. Richard Bentley, Melville's British publisher, gave him £150 ($703), after being discounted for early payment. Melville had the cash to make the $90 annual mortgage payment to Dr. Brewster in September and to pay Stewart his semi-annual interest of $92.50 on November 1, 1851, a week after his second child, Stanwix, was born, and two weeks before the publication of the Harper *Moby-Dick*.

Long before he saw a set of the three-volume English edition, *The Whale*, Melville saw two British reviews that were printed, reprinted, and widely quoted in the United States. Normally, many British reviews had been reprinted in this country. This time, for crucial weeks, the only two known in the United States were the extremely hostile ones published in London on the same day, October 25, in the London *Spectator* and the *Athenæum*. They were hostile largely because there was no epilogue in the English edition to explain just how Ishmael survived. Most likely, Bentley had told his compositors to put all the etymology and extracts, all that distracting junk, in the back of the third volume, and in the process of shifting things around the single sheet (half a page of type) had gotten lost. To many British reviewers, Melville seemed guilty of violating the basic contract between writer and reader: if you create a first person narrator, you make sure he or she lives to tell the story. The loss of the epilogue was bad luck, for it tainted the whole British reception. The fact that only the *Spectator* and *Athenæum* reviews were reprinted in the United States was worse than bad luck—it was disastrously bad, for as it happened neither of these reviewers specified just what was wrong with the ending each of them was condemning. No American, picking up the new book just in time to read these two London reviews and the early American reviews (many influenced by these London ones), could possibly figure out that Melville may have been guilty of many literary sins, but not of botching the ending. No one had a chance to say, "Aren't these Brits odd? They are saying Ishmael does not survive, but right here in my copy Ishmael is rescued by the *Rachel*."

In England Richard Bentley lost money on the three-volume *The Whale* (Melville's earlier title), but some of the reviews were full of extravagant praise, despite the baffling ending. On October 24, 1851, the London *Morning Advertiser* concluded a long review: the three volumes reflected more credit on America, were "more honourable to American literature" than any other works they could name. On October 25 *John Bull* called it the most extraordinary of Melville's books: "Who would have looked for philosophy in whales, or for poetry in blubber? Yet few books which professedly deal in metaphysics, or claim the parentage of the muses, contain as much true philosophy and as much genuine poetry as the tale of the *Pequod*'s whaling expedition." The *Leader* on November 8 said that *The Whale* was "a strange, wild, weird book, full of poetry and full of interest." The *Morning Post* on November 14 said that "despite its occasional extravagancies, it is a book of extraordinary merit, and one which will do great things for the literary reputation of the author." The *Weekly News and Chronicle* on November 29 echoed the *Leader:* it was "a wild, weird book, full of strange power and irresistible fascination for those who love to read of the wonders of the deep." Melville saw a handful of some of the short quotations from a few reviews besides the *Spectator* and *Athenæum*, including *John Bull* and the *Leader*, but he never, in all the rest of his life, ever had any idea that despite the loss of the epilogue many British reviewers had showered honor on him as a great prose stylist.

In the United States Melville's friend Evert Duyckinck reviewed the book promptly in two successive weeks in the New York *Literary World*—an influential, tone-setting paper. The first installment was devoted to the great coincidence of the publication of the book at the time the news was arriving of the sinking of the *Ann Alexander* by a whale off Chile. In the second, November 22, Duyckinck complained about the irreverence toward religion, the "piratical running down of creeds and opinions." He had warned Melville politely in his review of *White-Jacket* early in 1850 that he would not countenance irreverance. There was strong praise from some reviewers in the United States, but it did not last long, and it was submerged by the ferocious religious reviews, such as the one in the New York *Independent* on November 20: "The Judgment day will hold him liable for not turning his talents to better account, when, too, both authors and publishers of injurious books will be conjointly answerable for the influence of those books upon the wide circle of immortal minds on which they have written their mark. The book-maker and the book-publisher had better do their work with a view to the trial it must undergo at the bar of God." The religious press would have leapt on Melville anyhow, but Duyckinck lent intellectual and literary respectability to such attacks.

In the first two weeks after publication the Harpers sold 1,535 copies of *Moby-Dick*, but in the next two months or so only 471 more were sold, and sales after that dwindled rapidly. Meanwhile, Melville was writing a new book, a psychological novel based on what he had learned about his own mind in the last years. My best guess is that in late May 1849 Melville had decided to write *Redburn* as a book he could write expeditiously. The subject was easy. His nineteen-year-old brother, Tom, was just sailing out of Manhattan for China, the age he had sailed from Manhattan to Liverpool, and going on board Tom's ship triggered memories of ten years earlier. Melville was psychologically naive still in planning a fast and easy expedition into his childhood. He had done a reckless thing, to use his later words: he had dipped an angle into the well of childhood, gone fishing in his own memory, where who knew what monstrous creatures might be brought up. The intense psychological unfolding began in the aftermath of having written *Redburn* and allowed Melville to write *Moby-Dick* and *Pierre*—or the first version of *Pierre*.

What happened to *Pierre* I have told in the HarperCollins Kraken Edition (1995), illustrated by Maurice Sendak. Briefly, Melville took the manuscript to New York about the first day of 1852, just as some extremely hostile religious reviews of *Moby-Dick* were appearing. The Harpers read the manuscript and offered him an impossible contract: not the usual fifty cents on the dollar after costs but twenty cents on the dollar after costs. *Moby-Dick* was not going to be as popular as *Typee,* not even as popular as *Redburn,* sales figures showed. What was he to do? What was he to do? What he did, after a few days, was reckless to the point of being suicidal. He began enlarging the manuscript with pages about Pierre as a juvenile author (a wholly new turn in an already completed manuscript), then with pages about Pierre's immaturely attempting a great book. In some of these pages he maligned Pierre's publishers. The Harpers kept their contract to publish *Pierre* at ruinous terms to Melville, but by the next summer, after the ferocious reviews of *Pierre* began to appear, they quietly began letting literary people know that they thought Melville was crazy—"a little crazy," to be exact—not too crazy to keep people from buying *Redburn* and *White-Jacket. Pierre* lost Melville his English publisher, who figured if he continued to sell copies of the books he had in print he would eventually lose only £350 ($1,650) or thereabouts, by publishing Melville, somewhat short of $50,000 in present purchasing power. Bentley would have printed it, expurgated (as he had silently expurgated *The Whale,* without consulting Melville at all), if Melville had taken his generous offer to publish it without an advance and to divide with Melville any profits he made. During most of 1851 Melville had felt little guilt about his secretly borrowing $2,050 from Stewart: after all, the whaling book was so good that it had to succeed, and he could pay Stewart back before his wife and father-in-law found out about it. After January 1852, when he knew the Harper contract was disastrous, he may have hoped against hope for three or four months that all would work out, that Bentley would like *Pierre* and offer a handsome advance, or even that against all odds *Pierre* might sell so well in the United States that he would make money—even at twenty cents for every dollar the Harpers took in (after paying their expenses) rather than fifty cents. Melville may have denied in January 1852 and denied again in April and May 1852 that his career was over, no matter how he tried to stave off the actual death gasps.

When *Pierre* was published in the summer of 1852 it was savaged as no significant American book had ever been savaged. "Herman Melville Crazy," read one headline. That fall Melville tried to interest Hawthorne in writing a story he had heard that summer about a woman living on the coast of Massachusetts who had nursed a shipwrecked sailor and married him, only to have him desert her. From mid-December 1852 or so, Melville wrote the story himself, finishing it on or around May 22, 1853, the day his first daughter, Elizabeth, was born. The fate of *Moby-Dick* and *Pierre,* and his new labors on the book about the abandoned woman, *The Isle of the Cross,* had taken their toll on his health. As a sailor, Melville had been an athlete, a gymnast, and still showed off for the passengers on his voyage to

England late in 1849. As late as the summer of 1851 he was ostentatiously climbing trees. That vigor disappeared. In a memorandum made after his death Melville's widow recalled: "We all felt anxious about the strain on his health in Spring of 1853"—perhaps as early as April, when his mother was so concerned that she wrote her brother Peter Gansevoort hoping he could persuade his political friends to gain Herman a foreign consulship from the new president, Hawthorne's college friend Franklin Pierce:

> The constant in-door confinement with little intermission to which Hermans occupation as author compels him, does not agree with him. This constant working of the brain, & excitement of the imagination, is wearing Herman out.

The year before, on May 1, 1852, Melville had defaulted on the semiannual interest payment of $92.50 that he owed his friend Stewart, and he had defaulted on it that November. His mother's letter was written a week before he defaulted for the third time on his interest payments to Stewart. Elizabeth Shaw Melville may have recalled this period in early spring as the time when the family was most concerned about Melville, but the worst came at the end of spring, in June, when he carried *The Isle of the Cross* to New York City only to have the Harpers refuse to publish it, just at the time when it was quite clear that he had no hope of gaining a foreign consulship.

Melville was thoroughly beaten, but bravely he started writing short stories within weeks or even days of returning home with the manuscript of *The Isle of the Cross,* which he retained for some months, at least, and probably some years, before presumably destroying it. When a single letter of his has sold for much more than $100,000, the value of that manuscript, if it emerged today, might rival that of the most expensive paintings in the world. But in September 1853, with the manuscript in his possession still, Melville defaulted on the payment of $90 due to Dr. Brewster; the money went for preparations for the wedding of his sister Kate to John C. Hoadley. Several weeks later, he defaulted, as he did every six months, on the interest he owed Stewart.

Melville wrote to the Harpers late in November 1853 that he had "in hand, and pretty well on towards completion," a book, "partly of nautical adventure"; then he qualified himself: "or rather, chiefly, of Tortoise Hunting Adventure." At that time he promised it for "some time in the coming January," and asked for and received the advance—a dollar for each of the three hundred estimated pages. He had specified that he was expecting "the old basis—half profits"—not the ruinous terms he had accepted for *Pierre.* Now he paid Dr. Brewster the $90 he should have paid in September. This slight relief was followed by catastrophe. On December 10, 1853, much of the Harper stock of printed books and sheets was destroyed by fire, and the brothers charged Melville all over again for costs before giving him royalties on his books—in effect, hanging on to the next $1,000 or so he earned, although they had already charged expenses against him before paying him any royalties. They charged him twice for their expenses.

If in mid-December Melville thought that after their disaster the Harpers could not possibly publish any book right away, then the straightforward thing would have been to write them and ask in so many words if they would be able to publish the book they had just given him the advance for. If they had said they could not be back in business for six months, he could not have returned their advance because he had already spent much or most of it ($90 of it to Dr. Brewster), but he could have asked their permission to try to place the tortoise manuscript elsewhere and to turn over to them $300 if he got that sum from another source or, more reasonably, turn over to them $300 worth of articles for their magazine. What he did was not quite as culpable as it looks to us, perhaps, but at some point here he made an expedient, emotional decision that does not look wholly defensible. He decided to get more money from another publisher for the tortoise story—or at least for *part* of the tortoise material—or at least material also dealing with tortoises. On February 6, 1854, Melville wrote G. P. Putnam: "Herewith I send you 75. pages adapted for a magazine. Should they suit your's, please write me how much in present cash you will give for them." The batch of pages seems to be what was published in the March issue of *Putnam's* as the first four sketches of *The Encantadas*, including Sketch Two, "Two Sides to a Tortoise."

In mid-February 1854 Melville endured a "Horrid week" of pain in his eyes, his brother Allan Melville wrote to Augusta Melville on March 1. Melville had been crowding Augusta with pages to copy for him, overworking himself, and suffering from public shame brought on him by *Pierre*, private shame at having been late with a payment to Brewster, and shame at his continually defaulting on the interest he owed Stewart, compounded by shame at doing something with the tortoise material that looks less than honorable, no matter that the Harpers were themselves behaving abominably. No wonder he was sick.

In the next two years Melville wrote a full-length book, *Israel Potter*; several stories; and "Benito Cereno," long enough to be serialized in three installments at the end of 1855. Early that year, with "Benito Cereno" far along, if not quite finished, he collapsed. In her memoir his widow recorded: "In Feb 1855 he had his first attack of severe rheumatism in his back—so that he was helpless." How long he was helpless is not clear. The timing of the attack suggests the possibility of couvade, because his wife gave birth to her fourth child, Frances, on March 2, 1855. This pregnancy proceeded in pace with the monthly installments of *Israel Potter*, the last of which appeared in March, before book publication. Melville knew that his sister Kate Hoadley was also pregnant (she bore her daughter on May 30, 1855). In "Tartarus of Maids" Melville made the narrator say: "But what made the thing I saw so specially terrible to me was the metallic necessity, the unbudging fatality which governed it." The unbudging fatality of the gestation process was a reminder to him, during each of the last two of his wife's pregnancies, of the passing of months, including the Mays and Novembers in which he missed interest payments to Stewart and the September so far in which he had missed one payment to Brewster (paid three months late). (He missed the September 1855 payment, too.) The day of reckoning was approaching remorselessly—May 1, 1856—and he was progressively less able to avert the disaster. Malcolm's life had begun in triumph; Stanwix's life had begun in distress—with Lizzie's horribly painful breast infection and a doctor-enforced early weaning of the baby, while Melville was reading reviews of *Moby-Dick* and writing *Pierre.* Melville's daughters' lives began when his state was even more miserable. After Bessie's birth Melville had failed to get *The Isle of the Cross* into print and had failed to obtain a consulship; before Frances's birth he had become helpless from rheumatism.

According to his widow, Melville's first attack of severe rheumatism in February 1855 was followed in June by an attack of sciatica, which lasted through August, according to some comments made in September 1855. Nevertheless, later that year he began a satire on American optimism, *The Confidence-Man,* and continued to work on it during the early months of 1856; during all this time, apparently, T. D. Stewart was threatening to seize the farm, the only collateral there could be for his loan. The trouble is that the farm was mortgaged to Dr. Brewster. In April 1856, just before the entire loan of $2,050 and back interest (and probably interest on the interest) became due, after living with the literally crippling secret of his debt since the first of May 1851, Melville had to confess his plight to Judge Shaw and throw himself on Shaw's mercy. For once, luck favored Melville, and he managed to sell off half the farm swiftly, gaining enough money to repay Stewart. Shaw, loving and magnanimous, recognized how ill Herman was and advanced him more money for a trip abroad. Melville had completed *The Confidence-Man,* which on its publication in 1857 earned him not a penny, so he was out for the paper and ink on which he wrote it, and the paper and ink with which his sister Augusta copied it, and Augusta had copied it for nothing. At least she could see it in print, unlike *The Isle of the Cross,* which she had also copied.

After his return from his journey to the Holy Land and Europe in 1856–57, the next word on Melville's health is in 1858, in his widow's memoir: "A severe attack of what he called crick in the back laid him up at his mothers in Gansevoort in March 1858—and he never regained his former vigor & strength." The next year on November 21, 1859, his neighbor Sarah Morewood wrote to a friend: "Herman Melville is not well—do not call him moody, he is ill." The back pain recurred: Melville's mother at Christmas 1867 described Herman as then being able to go out: "his trouble was a 'Kink in his back.'" In 1882 he had what his wife described as "one of the attacks of "crick in the back.""

In the late 1850s Melville may not have put enough food on the table. At least one year, his father-in-law sent money for winter provisions. Melville earned a little money from lecturing for three seasons, late 1857 to early 1860. In early 1860 he completed a book of poems that two publishers rejected and that was never published, though some of the poems may survive. In 1861 Judge Shaw died and Elizabeth Melville inherited enough money to support her and her four children and husband for a few years. Melville's old debt to the Harpers was finally erased by sales in 1865, and he published a poorly received book of Civil War poems, *Battle-Pieces,* in the summer of 1866, but he did not have regular earnings until late in 1866, when he took a $4-a-day job as a custom officer in New York City, a job he held nineteen years. We know now that there was a terrible marital crisis in early 1867 and that Elizabeth was advised to leave her husband. That fall the Melville's oldest child, Malcolm, shot himself to death at age eighteen. Melville's life contracted even more tightly after 1869, when he began secretly working on a new poem that grew to 18,000 lines. He paid to have *Clarel* printed in 1876, using money his uncle Peter Gansevoort had left for that purpose; it was contemptuously reviewed, and in 1879 the publisher made him authorize the destruction of the remaining bound copies and sheets, which were in their way at the office.

In the next decades after its publication *Moby-Dick* was seldom mentioned in print. Melville's friend Henry T. Tuckerman (a real friend, I have found) praised it in 1863 as having "the rare fault of redundant power." In 1884, in a piece Melville saw, the English sea-novelist W. Clark Russell said the sailors' talk in the forecastle scene in *Moby-Dick* "might truly be thought to have come down to us from some giant mind of the Shakespearean era." Even before Melville's death in September 1891, and abundantly thereafter, Elizabeth Shaw knew that her husband was being recognized as one of the greatest American writers, and she proudly guarded his reputation as best she could. In this endeavor her older daughter, Bessie, born on or about the day *The Isle of the Cross* was completed, assisted. Mrs. Melville died in 1906, Bessie in 1908—late enough to have met with a would-be biographer, Frank Jewett Mather, whose plans fell through because Houghton Mifflin would not advance him $500 for the project. In the centennial of Melville's birth and in the next few years, first in England and then in the United States, Melville was at last saluted as belonging with Shakespeare and other great writers of the world.

None of this extraordinary fame impressed Melville's surviving daughter, Frances. Until she died in 1938 she blamed him for her sister Bessie's arthritis (caused by insufficient food, she thought), blamed him for her brother Malcolm's suicide in 1867, blamed him for innumerable acts, such as rousting her and her older sister out of bed at least one night to help him proofread *Clarel* in 1876, blamed him for her brother Stanwix's wasted life and early death (in 1886). She alone remembered that her father's in-laws (always excepting Judge Shaw) had believed every newspaper and magazine assertion that Melville was insane; she alone remembered that for some time in the 1860s her mother also had thought him insane, on the basis of his behavior, presumably, as well as on the full authority of many unimpeachable writers in the press; and she alone knew the circumstances of her mother's thinking of trying to separate from her father in the spring of 1867, only to decide that her Christian duty was to stay with him. Frances Melville Thomas told her oldest daughter that she did not know "H.M." in the new light of world fame: her resentments were so strong that his new reputation was a disparagement of her own memories and her own feelings. Two of her daughters were old enough to remember Melville well and to have known Mrs. Melville intimately, as young women, so they were able to correct Frances's views by their own memories, but the two younger daughters, born near the time of Melville's death, remembered Mrs. Melville less clearly and were more dependent on Frances for information about their grandfather. At least one of them absorbed Frances's lesson that the price of genius was too high for any family to pay. Now, in the 21st century, the surviving great-grandchildren and the great-great-grandchildren (themselves middle-aged) feel they are entitled to whatever simple or complex pleasures they can find in being descended from Herman Melville. For them, the high price of genius has at last been paid, perhaps in full.

Selected Bibliography

• indicates items included or excerpted in this Norton Critical Edition.

This highly selective bibliography focuses on the most reliable documentary guides to the study of Melville, especially *Moby-Dick*. It also lists historical, scientific, and polemical books on whaling, and books on Melville and art that are of interest to almost any student or general reader. It does not attempt to list the many dozens of critical books on *Moby-Dick*, all of which are easy to access via card catalogs and on-line catalogs. There have been so many hundreds of articles on *Moby-Dick* that we simply refer the curious to *American Literary Scholarship: An Annual* (Duke University Press), which, true to its subtitle, every year starting in 1963 has devoted a chapter to new publications on Melville.

• Bercaw, Mary K. *Melville's Sources.* Evanston: Northwestern University Press, 1987.

Indispensable.

• Bezanson, Walter E. *"Moby-Dick:* Work of Art." In *Moby-Dick: Centennial Essays.* Edited by Tyrus Hillway and Luther S. Mansfield. Dallas: Southern Methodist University Press, 1953.
• Brodtkorb, Paul, Jr. *Ishmael's White World: A Phenomenological Reading of "Moby-Dick."* New Haven, CT: Yale University Press, 1965.

Bryant, John, ed. *A Companion to Melville Studies.* Westport, CT: Greenwood, 1986.

A collection by some two dozen contributors. Among the pieces largely on *Moby-Dick* are M. Thomas Inge's description of fascinating oddities in "Melville in Popular Culture" (illustrated) and a magnificent essay, G. Thomas Tanselle's "Melville and the World of Books."

Busch, Briton Cooper. *Whaling Will Never Do for Me: The American Whaleman in the Nineteenth Century.* Lexington: University Press of Kentucky, 1994.

The lavish citations in footnotes and the bibliography make this an indispensable research tool.

Cluff, Randall. "'Thou Man of the *Evangelist*': Henry Cheever's Review of *Typee." Leviathan* 3 (March 2001): 61–72.

Coffler, Gail H. *Melville's Classical Allusions: A Comprehensive Index and Glossary.* Westport, CT: Greenwood, 1985.

Frank, Stuart M. *Herman Melville's Picture Gallery: Sources and Types of the "Pictorial" Chapters of "Moby-Dick."* Fairhaven, MA: Edward J. Lefkowicz, Inc., 1986.

Hayes, Kevin J. *The Critical Response to Herman Melville's "Moby-Dick."* Westport, CT: Greenwood, 1994.

• Hayford, Harrison. "'Loomings': Yarns and Figures in the Fabric." In *Artful Thunder: Versions of the Romantic Tradition in Honor of Howard P. Vincent.* Edited by Robert J. Demott and Sanford E. Marovitz. Kent, OH: Kent State University Press, 1975.

• ———. "Unnecessary Duplicates: A Key to The Writing of *Moby-Dick.*" In *New Perspectives on Melville.* Edited by Faith Pullen. Edinburgh: Edinburgh University Press, 1978.

Heffernan, Thomas Farel. *Stove by a Whale: Owen Chase and the "Essex."* Hanover, NH: Wesleyan University Press and University Press of New England, 1990.

Higgins, Brian. *Herman Melville: An Annotated Bibliography.* Volume 1: *1846–1930.* Boston: G. K. Hall, 1979.

———. *Herman Melville: A Reference Guide, 1931–1960.* Boston: G. K. Hall, 1987.

The publisher changed the title, but this is vol. 2 of Higgins's annotated bibliography of criticism on Melville.

———, and Hershel Parker. *Herman Melville: The Contemporary Reviews.* New York: Cambridge University Press, 1995.

Irey, Eugene F. *A Concordance to Herman Melville's "Moby-Dick."* 2 vols. New York: Garland, 1982.

Kennedy, Frederick J., and Joyce Deveau Kennedy. "Archibald MacMechan and the Melville Revival." *Leviathan* 1 (October 1999): 5–37.

Kier, Kathleen E. *A Melville Encyclopedia: The Novels.* Troy, NY: Whitston, 1990.

Kruse, Joachim. *Illustrationen zu Melvilles Moby-Dick.* Schleswig: Schleswig-Holsteinisches Landesmuseum, 1976.

Samples illustrations in editions of *Moby-Dick* (including some of Rockwell Kent's great images) and documentary photographs, movie stills, comic strips, etc. A rich resource.

Leyda, Jay. *The Melville Log: A Documentary Life of Herman Melville: 1819–1891.* 2 vols. New York: Harcourt Brace, 1951. Reprinted in 2 vols. with a supplement. New York: Gordian Press, 1969.

Since 1986 Hershel Parker has been expanding *The New Melville Log,* incorporating into it the "Augusta Papers" (mainly at the New York Public Library) and many hundreds of other documents; it is to be published in several volumes, one at a time, with the editorial assistance of Steven Olsen-Smith.

Martin, Kenneth R. *Whalemen's Paintings and Drawings: Selections from the Kendall Whaling Museum Collection.* Sharon, MA: Kendall Whaling Museum, 1983.

Melville, Herman. *Moby-Dick.* Edited by Luther S. Mansfield and Howard P. Vincent. New York: Hendricks House, 1952.

Textual and biographical passages are wholly superseded, but most of the "Explanatory Notes" are still valuable (and have been drawn on for this NCE).

———. *The Writings of Herman Melville.* Edited by Harrison Hayford, Hershel Parker, and G. Thomas Tanselle. Northwestern University Press and the Newberry Library, 1968–.

Thirteen volumes are in print as of 2001. Vol. 6, *Moby-Dick* (1988), is indispensable for advanced study of the book. Melville's *Correspondence* is Vol. 14.

Miller, Pamela A. *And the Whale Is Ours: Creative Writing of American Whalemen.* Boston: David R. Godine, and Sharon, MA: Kendall Whaling Museum, 1979.

Morris, David B. *Earth Warrior: Overboard with Paul Watson and His Sea Shepherd Conservation Society.* Golden, CO: Fulcrum, 1995.

• Paglia, Camille. *Sexual Personae: Art and Decadence from Nefertiti to Emily Dickinson.* New Haven, CT: Yale University Press, 1990.

Parker, Hershel. "Herman Melville." In *American National Biography.* Vol. 15. New York: Oxford University Press, 1998, pp. 277–83.

The most reliable "nutshell" account of Melville's life.

———. *Herman Melville: A Biography, 1819–1851.* Baltimore: Johns Hopkins University Press, 1996.

Indispensable for chs. 33–40 on the composition and publication of *Moby-Dick* (688–883). Supersedes previous biographical accounts. Vol. 2, 1851–1891, describes the reception of *Moby-Dick* (chs. 1, 2, and 4) and of *The Whale* (ch. 5).

———, and Harrison Hayford. *"Moby-Dick" as Doubloon: Essays and Extracts (1851–1970).* New York: W. W. Norton, 1970.

A large and diverse sampling of criticism, including all the then-known contemporary reviews.

———, and Brian Higgins. *Critical Essays on Herman Melville's "Moby-Dick."* New York: G. K. Hall, 1992.

The fullest collection of criticism, particularly on the Melville Revival.

Payne, Roger. *Among Whales.* New York: Scribner, 1995.

The classic study, from the marine biologist who discovered that whales sing.

Philbrick, Nathaniel. *In the Heart of the Sea: The Tragedy of the Whaleship "Essex."* New York: Viking, 2000.

A popular retelling, with new evidence.

Sanborn, Geoffrey. *The Sign of the Cannibal: Melville and the Making of a Postcolonial Reader.* Durham, NC: Duke University Press, 1998.

Schultz, Elizabeth A. *Unpainted to the Last: "Moby-Dick" and Twentieth-Century American Art.* Lawrence: University of Kansas Press, 1995.

A lavish art book and history.

Sealts, Merton M., Jr., *Melville's Reading: Revised and Enlarged Edition.* Columbia : University of South Carolina Press, 1988.

Indispensable; see p. 435 herein.

Tanselle, G. Thomas. *A Checklist of Editions of "Moby-Dick": 1851–1976.* Evanston, IL, and Chicago: Northwestern University Press and the Newberry Library, 1976.

An elegant booklet enhanced by Rockwell Kent illustrations and photographs of editions of *Moby-Dick.*

• Vincent, Howard. *The Trying Out of "Moby-Dick."* Boston: Houghton Mifflin, 1949.

Wallace, Robert K. *Melville & Turner: Spheres of Love and Fright.* Athens: University of Georgia Press, 1992.

Watson, Paul. *Ocean Warrior: My Battle to End the Illegal Slaughter on the High Seas.* Foreword by Farley Mowat. Toronto: Key Porter Books, 1994.

• Wenke, John. *Melville's Muse: Literary Creation and the Forms of Philosophical Fiction.* Kent, OH: Kent State University Press, 1995.

Wojnar, Mark. "A Possible Source for the name 'Fedallah.'"

In this manuscript note supplied to the editors, Wojnar cites the essay on Daniel Defoe in Sir Walter Scott's *Miscellaneous Prose Works* (1827). Defoe is said to have entered the minds of his characters as readily and fully as King Fadlallah's soul transmigrated from one body to another.